BENSON and HEDGES

Cricket Year

BENSON** and **HEDGES

Cricket Year

Seventeenth Edition

September 1997 to September 1998

Editor **David Lemmon**

Foreword by **Mike Procter**

BLOOMSBURY

First published in 1998 by
Bloomsbury Publishing Plc
38 Soho Square
London W1V 5DF

A copy of the CIP entry for this book is available from the British Library

ISBN 07475 3459 4

10 9 8 7 6 5 4 3 2 1

Designed by Carroll Associates
Typeset by Book Creation Services, London

Printed by Bath Press, Great Britain

Contents

Editor's note

The aim of *Benson and Hedges Cricket Year* is to give the cricket enthusiast an opportunity to read through the events in the world of cricket in the twelve months preceding the end of the England season in mid-September 1998. So much international cricket is being played that it becomes increasingly difficult to draw lines of demarcation. Before the last ball in the Britannic County Championship was bowled, the one-day tournament between India and Pakistan in Canada had already started.

The structure of the book, as in the past, offers a three-dimensional look at twelve months of cricket – narrative, photographs and statistics. This year's foreword is written by the great South African all-rounder Mike Procter, who recalls happy times in the Benson and Hedges Cup.

The symbol * indicates captain or not out according to the context, while † denotes wicket-keeper.

Once more I would like to give thanks to several people whose kindness and co-operation makes my job so much easier – Les Hatton, expert on the AXA League; Gamini Senadhira of Sri Lanka; Anthony Lalley, a wonderfully consistent and full correspondent from Australia; Ian Smith in New Zealand; Charlie Wat in Australia; Andrew Samson, a mine of information on South Africa; Qamar Ahmed; Victor Isaacs; Phil Bailey; Jo King; Ed Lewis; Brian Murgatroyd of the ECB; and others, like county secretaries, who are unstinting in their assistance and never too busy to answer queries.

Above all, I should like to record my appreciation of all that my dear friend Brian Croudy does for me in a variety of ways. He is tireless in tracking down faults and vagaries, and he covers the whole breadth of world cricket.

My thanks, too, are due to Melanie Porte of Book Creation Services for her patience and good humour in dealing with me and putting the whole book together. Without her expertise it would not be published as quickly as it is.

I continue to be thankful to the game of cricket for the good friends it has brought me and the good people that I have met.

David Lemmon

Comment

by David Lemmon

In spite of the weather, there was much to be enjoyed in 1998. There was victory for England over South Africa in wonderfully dramatic circumstances, and there was the glorious cricket played by Sri Lanka at The Oval. There was, sadly, the last Benson and Hedges Cup, and there was the thrilling fight for the County Championship, which went to the last game of the season, but these joys should not obscure the problems that remain and which we must address.

The policy of starting matches on a Wednesday has meant that fewer people are able to watch county cricket, the life blood of the game. Far too often did we note that when men and women were free from work and able to attend a match, Saturday, there was no match for them to see. Many games were over in three days or offered very little action on the Saturday. If people cannot see a game, they will lose interest in it.

There is, too, the question of cost. It is becoming increasingly more expensive to have a family day out at an international match, and we are in danger of making the game inaccessible to a generation of young people. Television and radio coverage is splendid, but the appeal of cricket is its humanity, its sociability. There is no synthetic substitute for those qualities however virtual the reality. Those who have been entrusted with guiding and administering the game have an awesome responsibility. They must continue to establish a sound economic structure, but they must never lose sight of the people whose presence at matches is essential if the game is to stay alive. The county member may now contribute only a small fraction of the income that cricket needs, but he remains of vital importance, because without him the game will die, and his wishes and desires must be heard.

The game is moving forward. Floodlit cricket has been a success at Edgbaston, Old Trafford, Headingley, Bristol, The Oval and Hove. Restructured in administration and revitalised on the field under Chris Adams's leadership, Sussex have given an example of an approach that can rekindle enthusiasm within a county. Yorkshire's youth policy is bringing to the fore an exciting crop of

bowlers – Silverwood, Hutchison, Hoggard, Hamilton and Sidebottom. Derbyshire overcame recent traumas to reach the NatWest Final, give a more spirited display in the championship and provide a stable platform for some good young players like Spendlove and Dean. Gloucestershire showed what a team working as a happy unit can achieve.

Cricket is alive and is progressing, but it must never lose contact with its roots. If it does, it will wither and die.

David Lemmon

Sponsor's Message

This has been a sad year for us at Benson and Hedges for, as I am sure you will all be aware, 1998 was the last year of the Benson and Hedges Cup. However, the end of the competition gave us the opportunity to re-live many great cricketing moments from the last 27 years. Who could forget the thrilling end to the 1989 Benson and Hedges Cup Final when Eddie Hemmings hit John Lever for four off the last ball to win the Cup for Nottinghamshire; or Aravinda de Silva's magical innings for Kent in the 1995 Cup Final; or the exploits of Viv Richards, Joel Garner and Ian Botham when Somerset dominated the competition in 1981 and 1982. These are but a few of the fine memories and I hope that you too have enjoyed the cricket provided by the Benson and Hedges Cup.

We are delighted that one of the 'stars' of the Benson and Hedges Cup, Mike Procter, has written the foreword for the book this year. Mike produced a match-winning performance for Gloucestershire in their 1977 semi-final when he took Hampshire's first four wickets in five balls, including a hat-trick, to finish with 6 for 13. We thank him for his observations on the competition, on the recent Cornhill Test series against his native South Africa, and on English cricket in general. It is always interesting to read the views of those not directly involved with cricket in this country and his observations obviously hold great weight with his knowledge of domestic cricket as a player with Gloucestershire and a coach at Northamptonshire, as well as his international experience from his time as South African coach and now as a selector.

However, while we have spent a year reminiscing, we have also had a year of cricket to consider. David Lemmon has once again had the unenviable job of ensuring that every first-class match played throughout the world is recorded in the Benson and Hedges Cricket Year and as usual he has done this superbly, ensuring that we can produce a complete record of the year from September 1997 to September 1998 within weeks of the English cricket season ending. We thank him for all his hard work.

We are delighted that, while the Benson and Hedges Cup may no longer be taking place, this seventeenth edition of the Benson and Hedges Cricket Year will not be the last and we look forward to bringing you the eighteenth edition next year.

Jim Elkins
Special Events Director
Benson and Hedges

Foreword

by Mike Procter

I left England at the end of the 1998 season with mixed feelings as I made my way home to Durban. The first was a sense of disappointment that the South African team, which I had helped to pick, had fallen short of their ambition to win all three of the prizes that were up for grabs.

But the second sprang from the affection I have always had for English cricket and its traditions since my 14 years with Gloucestershire and coaching spell at Northampton – a sense of pleasure that they are back on the rails again after a decade on the branch lines.

I still think England could do with a genuine out-and-out fast bowler to spearhead their attack if they are to achieve consistent success against the top sides. If you look at the history of Test cricket you will see that from time to time a spinner like Shane Warne will win you Test matches. But year in and year out it's the quick fellas who bring home the bacon – and if you have a pair of them, so much the better. Add an exciting, larger than life star like, dare I say it, Ian Botham, and the crowds will come rolling in.

The counties should never have thrown out Lord MacLaurin's report *Raising the Standard* as quickly as they did. To me, and to other cricketers and ex-cricketers I have spoken to, their actions were amazing and it seems the power in English cricket is invested in the wrong hands.

But, having said that, the summer of 1998 showed the doubters had the wrong end of the stick in one vital respect – out on the field English cricket is still alive and well, even if some of those counties who rejected Lord MacLaurin's hard work are making it difficult. They should remember that if you don't have a winning national side, there wouldn't be any county cricket anyway. That is where the money and the sponsorship come from, so that total emphasis must be on the England team.

Mike Procter.

As a South African I don't want to be seen telling England what to do, but I am certain that at home, and in Australia, all cricket sponsorship would dry up if the national team had the sort of record England have had over the past dozen years or so. Yet England seem to get away with it. But don't despair – in the summer of 1998 I saw hope.

And for that, a lot of the credit must go to Alec Stewart. He did a good job as captain and, above all else, he brought the best out of the players in an exciting Test series, which, though marred by some of the umpiring, was always close and competitive. The England team have always played with great spirit. I have never doubted them in that respect – English cricketers have always been competitive. Now Alec is injecting into them that little bit extra that makes the difference between winning and losing over a period of time.

One of the reasons England have not done so well of late is the way they can come to accept defeat if they play too much. Now I'm not blaming the players for this, but in England you can accept defeat so much easier than they do in South Africa or Australia because you play so much cricket that you are bound to lose more games. If you play for a top side in South Africa, and you are also playing in a successful Test team, the amount of games you are going to lose over a given period of, say two or three years, is minimal compared to being in England, where, if you play more games in a season, then you are bound to lose more. In South Africa or Australia it would take five seasons to lose as many games as an English side can lose in one season. Yet there is nobody to blame, apart from the fact that you are playing such a lot of cricket and you know that if you fail you will soon have another chance – and another chance, and another chance.

Which makes it even more amazing to me as an outsider looking at the plain facts that the counties took Lord MacLaurin's plan, which was intended to help the five-

Mike Procter bowling against Hampshire, Benson and Hedges Cup, 1977.

day game, and came up with some sort of scheme in which the top eight sides in the Championship can end up playing in a one-day tournament.

For the life of me I cannot believe that is the way to help the England team to perform better at Test level. It is amazing to me, absolutely amazing. There is room for one day cricket, as the Benson and Hedges competition has proved over the last quarter of a century – though not as a breeding ground for success at Test level.

In fact, I shall be sorry to see the Benson and Hedges Cup go. It was always a great competition and all the players enjoyed it because of the group system and the fact that we could look forward to playing a Lord's final at the height of summer in early July. The Benson and Hedges Cup always got the season off to a good start and it will be badly missed by everyone in the game.

International Rankings

For many years, we have offered a simple system of establishing an order of merit in Test and one-day international cricket. Two points are given for a win and one for a draw. Points gained are divided by points possible to arrive at a percentage. It is interesting to note that while the number of limited-over internationals played proliferates year by year, the number of Test matches played shows only a slight increase.

In the period covered by this book, there were 48 Test matches as opposed to 43 in 1996–97 while the number of one-day internationals rose from 113 to 122. While the number of Test matches being played remains more or less the same, there is a regular increase of nine or ten a year in limited-over games. There is a danger that domestic cricket will be choked to death if this increase continues unabated.

David Lemmon

Test Rankings

	P	W	L	D	Pts won	Pts poss	%
Pakistan	11	5	2	4	14	22	63.63
Australia	9	4	2	3	11	18	61.11
Sri Lanka	13	5	3	5	15	26	57.69
India	8	2	1	5	9	16	56.25
South Africa	16	5	4	7	17	32	53.12
New Zealand	10	3	4	3	9	20	45.00
West Indies	9	3	4	2	8	18	44.44
England	12	3	5	4	10	24	41.66
Zimbabwe	8	–	5	3	3	16	18.75

Limited-Over International Rankings

	P	W	L	T	Pts won	Pts poss	%
South Africa	27	21	6		42	54	77.77
Sri Lanka	27	16	10	1	33	54	61.11
Australia	25	14	11		28	50	56.00
India	42	22	17	3	47	84	55.95
West Indies	12	6	6		12	24	50.00
England	15	7	8		14	30	46.66
New Zealand	28	10	15	3	23	56	41.07
Pakistan	28	11	17		22	56	39.28
Zimbabwe	23	8	24	1	17	46	36.95
Kenya	11	4	7		8	22	36.36
Bangladesh	10	1	9		2	20	10.00

Benson and Hedges Cricket Year World XI 1998

The World XI becomes harder to choose. There have been exciting and consistent performers, but there have been others who have flattered to deceive, and bowlers have been more to the fore than batsmen. Well as he did against England, Ambrose fared badly in Pakistan, and it was thought that his Test career might end there. Wasim Akram had wonderful moments and led Lancashire with great dash, but he flitted in and out of international cricket, mostly at the whim of selectors. Pollock was not quite the player in England that he had been in Pakistan and South Africa, and the Pakistani batsmen, of whom Inzamam-ul-Haq was the most consistent, took it in turns to thrive. Mohammad Wasim and Azhar Mahmood are surely destined for future greatness. Hussain played some memorable innings, but there were several failures, and Azharuddin's brilliance cannot quite edge out the resilience of Stewart.

Sanath Jayasuriya (Sri Lanka)
Jayasuriya began the twelve-month period with a triple Test match hundred and ended it with a memorable double century in the Test match against England at The Oval. He adapts to all forms of cricket and is among the most exciting batsmen in world cricket.

Above: Sanath Jayasuriya (Sri Lanka)
(Mike Hewitt / Allsport)

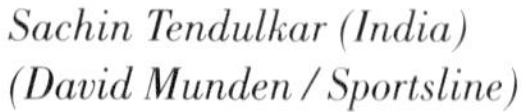

Sachin Tendulkar (India)
(David Munden / Sportsline)

Below: Aravinda de Silva (Sri Lanka)
(Mike Hewitt / Allsport)

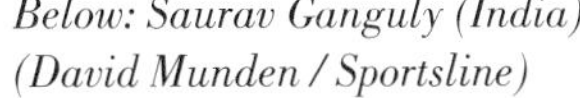

Above: Alec Stewart (England)
(Graham Chadwick / Allsport)

Above: Steve Waugh (Australia)
(Mike Hewitt / Allsport)

Below: Saurav Ganguly (India)
(David Munden / Sportsline)

Below: Ian Healy (Australia)
(Mike Hewitt / Allsport)

Shane Warne (Australia)
(Mike Hewitt / Allsport)

Allan Donald (South Africa)
(Mike Hewitt / Allsport)

Sachin Tendulkar (India)
Tendulkar was deprived of the captaincy of India because it was thought his form was being affected by the responsibility. He was averaging above 60, but since relinquishing the captaincy he has thrived consistently. He scores fluently and briskly. He has command of every shot. To watch, he is the major delight in world cricket.

Aravinda de Silva (Sri Lanka)
De Silva ranks alongside Tendulkar as the most entertaining batsman in world cricket. He now has 17 Test centuries to his credit, and he bats with a style and urgency that is a constant reminder of the golden age. Like Tendulkar and Jayasuriya, he is at home in all forms of cricket.

Alec Stewart (England)
Stewart does not rank with Tendulkar or de Silva but he has a determination, an unwillingness to be beaten, which is a most valuable quality. In spite of the burden of captaincy and keeping wicket, he scored heavily in 1998, and he fought some wonderful rearguard battles. His innings in the Old Trafford Test was a monument to his character and approach to the game, and had he not been needlessly run out at The Oval, England might well have saved the day against Sri Lanka.

Saurav Ganguly (India)
Outstanding in both Test and limited-over international cricket in 1997–98. His batting, often as partner to Tendulkar, has gained in consistency without losing its panache, and he can now be considered a genuine all-rounder.

Steve Waugh (Australia)
One of the most reliable and consistent players in world cricket. His resolve has been at the heart of much of the

Angus Fraser (England)
(Mike Hewitt / Allsport)

Muttiah Muralitharan (Sri Lanka)
(Mike Hewitt / Allsport)

Australian success. Captain of the one-day side, Waugh is a shrewd, knowledgeable leader, and it is hard to conceive of an Australian side without him.

Ian Healy (Australia)
Healy remains supreme among world wicket-keepers, and the Australian selectors faced a barrage of criticism when they omitted him from their one-day side. He is now firmly established as one of the great wicket-keepers of the post war period.

Shane Warne (Australia)
Continues to perplex and bemuse in spite of operations and rumours of career-ending injury. He was the architect of Australia's victories over New Zealand and South Africa, and only in India, where he was again troubled by injury, did he fail to find his best form. He remains the most feared bowler in world cricket.

Allan Donald (South Africa)
Donald could also lay claim to the description of most feared bowler. He recovered from injury in Pakistan to excel in South Africa and in England. He combines pace, intelligence and endeavour. He ranks with the great fast bowlers of Test history.

Angus Fraser (England)
Fraser was discarded a couple of years ago but, having been recalled, he dominated the series against West Indies and South Africa. He relies on accuracy, late movement and an unquenchable spirit. He served England nobly in 1998.

Muttiah Muralitharan (Sri Lanka)
Muralitharan must now be considered as the equal of Shane Warne as the leading spin bowler in world cricket. His magnificent 16-wicket haul at The Oval was simply the climax of an outstanding year during which he took 68 Test wickets at 18.50 runs each.

West Indies

Rarely has West Indian cricket started a year in such a state of disarray and conflict as it began 1998. The Test side had suffered total humiliation in Pakistan, losing all three Tests and only once forcing the home side to bat twice. Even then, this was for a meagre target which was reached in five overs. The side's eclipse in Pakistan was followed by failure in Sharjah, with the result that Walsh was relieved of the captaincy and Lara appointed in his stead.

Robert Croft appeals for a wicket in the match Guyana v. England in Georgetown.

The England Tour
President's Cup
First-Class Averages

Lara's own form and commitment had been severely criticised in Pakistan, and Walsh meditated for some time before agreeing to make himself available for the Test series.

There was little comfort on the domestic front. After a season of return matches in what was the Red Stripe Cup, the first-class competition reverted to its less satisfactory one-round format. This reversion was brought about by a lack of sponsorship. The West Indies Cricket Board agreed that Red Stripe should transfer its sponsorship to the limited-over tournament at an increased fee, but the Board was then unable to find a backer for the interterritorial competition that had started as the Shell Shield in 1966 and which now found itself sponsorless for the first time. It was to be known simply as the President's Cup.

The new Red Stripe Bowl embraced Bermuda and Canada as well as the six West Indian territories with first-class status and was played in October, 1997, so that all the leading players were available. Guyana and Leeward Islands qualified for the final. Arthurton and Sylvester Joseph added 118 for Leewards after two wickets had fallen for 14. Keith Arthurton went on to reach 100 off 154 balls with two sixes and seven fours, and his side made 245. Guyana needed someone to play a big innings, but Sarwan was top-scorer with 42, and they finished on 215 for nine. So Leewards were first winners of the Red Stripe Bowl, which, to the sponsors' delight, was televised in the United States. Coloured clothing was introduced in the competition, and Arthurton, Man of the Match in the final, was named Most Valuable Player, a much needed accolade after his traumas in the World Cup. Kenny Benjamin was the leading wicket-taker, but the tournament brought no new stars to the fore.

There was apprehension in the Caribbean, for, in January, Atherton and his men arrived. 'Thus comes the English with full power upon us.'

The England Tour

The England party arrived early, but rain frustrated attempts at practice. There were, too, frustrations for Darren Gough, who was forced to withdraw from the party because he was in need of medical treatment. His place was taken by his Yorkshire colleague Chris Silverwood who had originally been chosen for the 'A' side. Neither Cork nor Malcolm had been selected, so the England pace attack looked as if it had been deprived of much of its menace. Ashley Cowan, the young Essex bowler, was a choice for the future, a man of promise rather than of proven performance. Headley and Caddick remained enigmatic figures of uncertain and inconsistent quality, and the recall of Angus Fraser to the colours had surprised many. It was generally accepted that Fraser was Atherton's choice, for, above all, the Middlesex bowler was a man who could be relied upon.

16, 17 and 18 January 1998
at Jarrett Park, Montego Bay
England XI 286 for 8 dec. (G.P. Thorpe 89)
Jamaica 125 (D.W. Headley 5 for 32, A.R. Caddick 4 for 24) and 96 (D.W. Headley 4 for 14, P.C.R. Tufnell 4 for 33)
England XI won by an innings and 65 runs

After frustrations over practice, England's tour of West Indies finally got under way on a pitch of doubtful quality. Montego Bay had not staged an international match for 12 years, and the venue had little to commend it.

Atherton won the toss, and England batted first against a Jamaican side that was not at full strength. The day was cut short by rain and bad light, and the tourists finished on 179 for five. Adam Hollioake made a resolute 40, and Thorpe batted into the second day. He and Russell shared a sixth wicket stand of 80, a partnership that was gritty and determined, and Atherton declared as soon as Thorpe was caught at extra cover. Headley and Caddick tore into the Jamaican batting, relishing the help given by the pitch. Headley had both openers caught behind without scoring, and Caddick wrecked the middle order. The home side finished the day on 108 for eight. Headley took the last two wickets on the third morning, and Jamaica followed on. In their second innings, they lasted only 37.1 overs. Tufnell bowled with admirable control, and the game was over in three days.

22, 23, 24 and 25 January, 1998
at Chedwin Park, Kingston, Jamaica
England XI 400 for 8 dec. (N. Hussain 159, G.P. Thorpe 81) and 181 for 4
West Indies 'A' 434 (R.I.C. Holder 183, L.R. Williams 67 not out, K.F. Semple 54, A.R.C. Fraser 5 for 99, P.C.R. Tufnell 4 for 107)
Match drawn

England played only two matches before the first Test, which meant that four members of the party did not get a game in the early part of the tour and had no opportunity to press their claims for selection. West Indies 'A' side, led by Roland Holder, provided strong opposition, and pace men King and McLean, who had been with the 'A' side in South Africa, soon benefited from Holder's decision to ask England to bat when he won the toss. Inside 11 overs, the visitors lost Atherton, Stewart and Crawley, and only 30 runs had been scored. The position might have been worse had Hussain been caught when he was four, but the England vice-captain survived and went on to bat in a regal manner, reaching his first century in the Caribbean. In 63 overs of positive application, he and Thorpe added 184. Thorpe's form at the start of the tour was most encouraging, and with Hussain showing his dominance, England had much about which to be pleased . Hussain batted into the second day, and his innings lasted for seven hours 20

minutes. He and Adam Hollioake, a controversial choice for many, put on 110 for the fifth wicket, and Atherton declared as soon as 400 was posted. Fraser bowled with accuracy and economy, and he captured the wickets of both openers. Semple and Holder added 95, and the home side closed on 156 for three. There was misfortune for England when Adam Hollioake damaged his right shoulder in diving to stop a ball. With Ramprakash unwell, Hollioake was likely to be included in the eleven for the first Test.

The game died on the last two days. Holder emphasised his claims for a place in the West Indian Test side when he made the highest score of his career, and he achieved much in that his team were 186 for five on the Saturday morning before he and all-rounder Laurie Williams steered them to a 34-run lead. West Indies 'A' batted into the last day, and all that remained for England was batting practice of which nobody really took adequate advantage, save the in-form Thorpe.

First Test Match

West Indies *v.* England

The signs were not good from the start. There was concern as to the state of the Test pitches in the Caribbean from the moment the England party arrived, although it must be said the gravest doubts were expressed about playing in Guyana, where political tension was high. The wicket at Jamaica's Sabina Park had been relaid, but its appearance gave no one in the England squad any confidence.

Adam Hollioake was decreed fit to play, but since Russell was unwell, Stewart took on the wicket-keeping gloves. Mark Butcher also was brought in. This was hard on Ramprakash, a far better player in every respect and now fit, but neither he nor Butcher had played in the two matches that began the tour. West Indies brought back Jimmy Adams and gave a debut to Nixon McLean as the fourth pace bowler. Spin did not seem to form a major role in their deliberations. Atherton won the toss, and England batted.

The England captain clipped the first ball from Walsh off his toes for two, but there the joy ended. The ball began to leap and shoot. Deliveries rose head high from a length. Atherton tried to avoid a ball from Walsh but was caught at gully. Butcher went first ball, a searing lifter being touched high to third slip. Hussain was caught low at second slip. In between these mishaps, the physiotherapist Wayne Morton was on and off the field as batsmen were struck about the

Mark Butcher tries to avoid a delivery from Courtney Walsh, but is caught at slip first ball. A few overs later, the first Test match was abandoned.
(David Munden / Sportsline)

First Test Match – West Indies *v.* England

Jamaica 29 January 1998 at Sabina Park, Kingston

England

	First Innings	
M.A. Atherton*	c Campbell, b Walsh	2
A.J. Stewart †	not out	9
M.A. Butcher	c S.C. Williams, b Walsh	0
N. Hussain	c Hooper, b Ambrose	1
G.P. Thorpe	not out	0
J.P. Crawley		
A.J. Hollioake		
A.R. Caddick		
D.W. Headley		
A.R.C. Fraser		
P.C.R. Tufnell		
	b 4, nb 1	5
		17 (for 3 wickets)

	O	M	R	W
Walsh	5.1	1	10	2
Ambrose	5	3	3	1

Fall of Wickets
1–4, 2–4, 3–9

West Indies

S.C. Williams
S.L. Campbell
B.C. Lara*
S. Chanderpaul
C.L. Hooper
J.C. Adams
D. Williams †
N.A.M. McLean
I.R. Bishop
C.E.L. Ambrose
C.A. Walsh

Umpires: S.A. Bucknor & S. Venkataraghavan

Match Abandoned

arms and body. Stewart was hit three times, Hussain on the right hand and on each arm. In all, Morton was on the field six times in 56 minutes, which was the full extent of playing time in the match.

At the instigation of umpire Venkataraghavan, captains and authority met in the middle of the pitch and, after deliberation, took the only wise course. The match was abandoned because the pitch was dangerous and unfit for cricket. It had lasted 10.1 overs.

This was another sad day for West Indian cricket, and a most embarrassing occasion. An enquiry was set up and hasty rescheduling done. The match against Trinidad and Tobago was reduced to two days and an extra Test arranged for Port-of-Spain. The series had yet to begin, but the scores at Sabina Park remained in the record book.

1 and 2 February 1998

at Guaracara Park, Pointe-a-Pierre, Trinidad

England XI 351 (R.C. Russell 77, A.J. Stewart 73, N. Hussain 66, M.A. Atherton 61, D. Ramnarine 5 for 72, A. Samaroo 4 for 91)

Trinidad & Tobago 274 (P.V. Simmons 78 not out, L.A. Roberts 60)

Match drawn

With an extra Test being arranged for Port of Spain, England's game against Trinidad was reduced to two days and a draw was inevitable. Fielding almost a full Test side, England enjoyed batting practice, but leg-spinner Dinanath Ramnarine also West Indian bowled impressively.

Second Test Match

West Indies v. England

Both sides made one change from the sides that had been selected for the first Test. Fit again, Russell returned to the England XI and Butcher stood down. Crawley was moved to number three. West Indies had Kenny Benjamin as a replacement for Bishop. Atherton won the toss, and England batted.

There was a solid start against Walsh and Ambrose, but the introduction of McLean provided both Atherton and Stewart with unexpected problems, and Atherton succumbed when he edged Ambrose to first slip. England reached lunch at 70 for one. They then enjoyed some fortune. Stewart was missed at slip by both Lara and Hooper while Crawley could have been caught down the leg side off Benjamin, who bowled with pace and variety. Having reached 50 with seven fours, Stewart went back to Benjamin and was leg before. Crawley batted two and a half hours for his 17 before being caught at third slip, and Thorpe was out on the stroke of tea when he attempted to cut a ball from Hooper. It was a poor shot. Immediately after tea, Hollioake was run out in controversial fashion. The batsman was well short of his line, but wicket-keeper Williams dislodged a

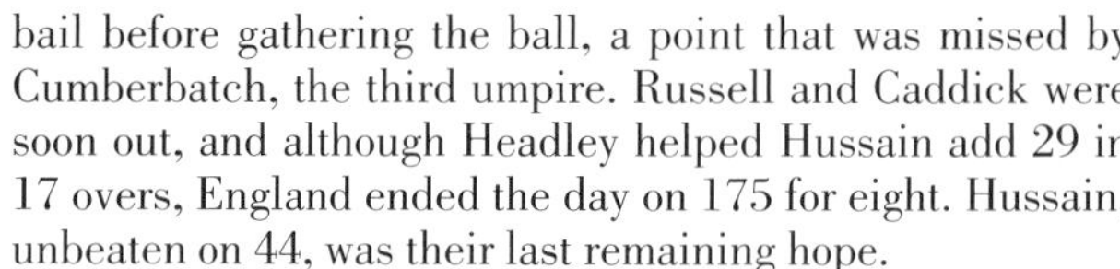

bail before gathering the ball, a point that was missed by Cumberbatch, the third umpire. Russell and Caddick were soon out, and although Headley helped Hussain add 29 in 17 overs, England ended the day on 175 for eight. Hussain, unbeaten on 44, was their last remaining hope.

If the first day belonged to West Indies, the second was emphatically in favour of England. At the start, Hussain batted magnificently. He displayed intelligence in all that he did, farming the bowling and choosing his shots judiciously. Fraser gave him splendid assistance for 98 minutes in all as they added an invaluable 92. Tufnell went first ball, and Hussain was unbeaten for 61 which had come off 202 balls. He had batted for five and a quarter hours and shown all the resilience that England so desperately needed.

Fraser's heroics did not end with his batting. Neither Campbell nor Stuart Williams found life easy, and Campbell was caught behind off a vicious ball from Headley that kept low. Stuart Williams was taken at extra cover. Fraser, coming on as first change, immediately found a challenging length. Hooper was bowled behind his legs to leave West Indies 48 for three, but Lara moved on to the attack as he and Chanderpaul added 78. Caddick, economic at first, was now expensive, but Fraser accounted for both batsmen. Chanderpaul, having become becalmed, was taken at first slip, while Lara skied to leg. Adams was leg before offering no shot, and West Indies closed on 177 for seven. Fraser had five for 47 to his credit.

The Middlesex pace bowler captured the remaining three wickets on the third morning to give him figures of eight for 53, the best figures ever recorded by an English bowler against West Indies. Fraser himself had established the previous record, eight for 75, four years earlier. Atherton and Stewart had the luxury of beginning England's second innings with their side 23 runs to the good. They built well on this advantage by scoring 91 for the first wicket, and West Indies began to look sluggish. McLean

Jimmy Adams is caught by Thorpe off Fraser, who bowled magnificently to take eight for 53 in the second Test. (Clive Mason / Allsport)

roused them when he dismissed Stewart, who batted impressively, and Crawley in one spell, but Hussain and Thorpe battled hard on a pitch that made run-scoring a laborious task. Hussain was caught and bowled on the seventh ball of an over, and England closed at 219 for four, a lead of 242 and a commanding position.

On the fourth morning, Ambrose took five for 16 in a devastating eight-over spell. The big fast bowler had limped out of the Pakistan series, his Test career seemingly at an end, his thrust and pace blunted; now he reasserted himself as one of cricket's most feared opponents. Walsh, too, had disproved the belief that he was a spent force, accounting for Thorpe during a withering over in which he bowled round the wicket at a fast pace and had the batsman in constant trouble. In spite of the efforts of these giants, West Indies were left with the uneviable task of trying to score 282 to win on a pitch that favoured bowlers more than it aided batsmen.

Headley and Caddick were short and wayward in the opening overs, but Campbell was out in the third over of the innings, caught at second slip. That wicket fell to Headley, but once again it was Fraser who gave England the advantage. He caused uncertainty in the mind of Lara, and the West Indies' captain was caught behind off a thick edge. Chanderpaul spooned a catch to Thorpe, and Stuart Williams, who had taken several blows on the body, went before him, caught at short-leg. Adams edged to second slip, and West Indies were 124 for five with Hooper the only recognised batsman remaining. By the close, he and David

West Indies on their way to victory in the second Test. Carl Hooper plays the ball through the off side during his innings of 94 not out. (Lawrence Griffiths / Allsport)

Second Test Match – West Indies v. England

5, 6, 7, 8 and 9 February 1998 at Queen's Park Oval, Port-of-Spain, Trinidad

England

	First Innings		Second Innings	
M.A. Atherton *	c Lara, b Ambrose	11	b Walsh	31
A.J. Stewart	lbw, b Benjamin	50	c Hooper, b McLean	73
J.P. Crawley	c S.C. Williams, b Ambrose	17	lbw, b McLean	22
N. Hussain	not out	61	c and b Walsh	23
G.P. Thorpe	c D. Williams, b Hooper	8	c Lara, b Walsh	39
A.J. Hollioake	run out	2	c Lara, b Ambrose	12
R.C. Russell †	c S.C. Williams, b McLean	0	lbw, b Ambrose	8
A.R. Caddick	lbw, b Walsh	8	c D. Williams, b Ambrose	0
D.W. Headley	c D. Williams, b Ambrose	11	not out	8
A.R.C. Fraser	c D. Williams, b Benjamin	17	c Hooper, b Ambrose	4
P.C.R. Tufnell	c Lara, b Benjamin	0	c D. Williams, b Ambrose	6
	b 6, lb 10, nb 13	29	b 5, lb 15, w 1, nb 11	32
		214		258

	O	M	R	W	O	M	R	W
Walsh	27	7	55	1	29	5	67	3
Ambrose	26	16	23	3	19.5	3	52	5
McLean	19	7	28	1	12	1	46	2
Benjamin	24	5	68	3	15	3	40	–
Hooper	9	3	14	1	19	8	33	–
Adams	3	–	8	–				
Chanderpaul	1	–	2	–				

Fall of Wickets
1–26, 2–87, 3–105, 4–114, 5–124, 6–126, 7–143, 8–172, 9–214
1–91, 2–143, 3–148, 4–202, 5–228, 6–238, 7–239, 8–239, 9–246

West Indies

	First Innings		Second Innings	
S.L. Campbell	c Russell, b Headley	1	c Stewart, b Headley	10
S.C. Williams	c Atherton, b Fraser	19	c Crawley, b Fraser	62
B.C. Lara *	c Atherton, b Fraser	55	c Russell, b Fraser	17
C.L. Hooper	b Fraser	1	not out	94
S. Chanderpaul	c Thorpe, b Fraser	34	c Thorpe, b Tufnell	0
J.C. Adams	lbw, b Fraser	1	c Stewart, b Fraser	2
D. Williams †	lbw, b Tufnell	16	c Thorpe, b Headley	65
C.E.L. Ambrose	c and b Fraser	31	c Russell, b Headley	1
K.C.G. Benjamin	b Fraser	0	not out	6
N.A.M. McLean	c Caddick, b Fraser	2		
C.A. Walsh	not out	0		
	b 12, lb 5, nb 14	31	b 10, lb 8, nb 7	25
		191	(for 7 wickets)	282

	O	M	R	W	O	M	R	W
Headley	22	6	47	1	16	2	68	3
Caddick	14	4	41	–	16	2	58	–
Fraser	16.1	2	53	8	27	8	57	3
Tufnell	21	8	33	1	34.2	6	69	1
Hollioake	5	–	12	–				

Fall of Wickets
1–16, 2–42, 3–48, 4–126, 5–134, 6–135, 7–167, 8–177, 9–190
1–10, 2–68, 3–120, 4–121, 5–124, 6–253, 7–259

Umpires: S.A. Bucknor & S. Venkataraghavan

West Indies won by 3wickets

Williams had taken the score to 181, with the wicket-keeper having scored 36 of the runs added.

Williams was the surprise. In all, he batted for 217 minutes, faced 172 balls and hit seven fours in scoring 65 out of a sixth wicket partnership of 129 with Hooper that took West Indies in sight of an improbable victory. Hooper was majestic. He is the most elegant of players who has too often been profligate with his talent, but now he seized the day and won the game for his side. Headley dismissed Williams and Ambrose in quick succession, but Hooper remained calm, and he and Kenny Benjamin steered West Indies to victory in early afternoon. Hooper, Man of the Match, batted for more than five and three quarter hours, faced 203 deliveries and hit 10 fours. England could only rue missed opportunities and some wasteful new ball bowling by Caddick and Headley. West Indies had played their 'Get Out of Jail' card and won the game.

Third Test Match

West Indies *v.* England

Butcher for Hollioake was the only change that either side made as the third Test followed four days after the exciting conclusion of the second. England must have considered other changes. Caddick, in particular, had bowled loosely in the first encounter at Queen's Park Oval, and Russell's wicket-keeping had been well below par. But, in truth England had few options. Atherton again won the toss, but this time he asked West Indies to bat first on a pitch that looked as if it would encourage the seamers. However, England captured only one wicket in the morning session, that of Stuart Williams who was caught at slip. Further doubts were cast on Atherton's decision when Caddick's first over after lunch produced 19 runs.

It was Angus Fraser who changed the course of the innings. He sent back Campbell, Hooper and Lara for seven runs in the space of 36 balls. Campbell was taken at first slip, Hooper was spectacularly caught in mid-air by Mark Butcher at cover and Lara under-edged a pull to the keeper. Chanderpaul and Adams battled doggedly for 113 minutes in an attempt to steady the innings, but once Adams was caught at short extra-cover off a firm drive, the frailty of West Indies' lower order was cruelly exposed. David Williams was yorked first ball, while Ambrose and Benjamin went third and second ball respectively. Chanderpaul was ninth out, having batted for two hours 40 minutes and having hit one boundary. Fraser captured his fifth wicket when he had McLean caught in the deep. West Indies were all out for a meagre 159, the last nine wickets having gone down for 66 runs, and England purred with contentment. The satisfaction turned to apprehension when Ambrose's breakback trapped Atherton leg before. The tall fast bowler was too quick for Crawley's defensive prod, and Stewart should have been out when he edged Walsh to slip where the usually reliable Lara missed a straightforward chance. England closed uneasily on 22 for two.

Bad light had brought the players off with four balls of an Ambrose over remaining, and the bowler needed just four balls to dispose of Headley on the second morning. This was the beginning of England's troubles. Hussain was dreadfully unlucky to be given out caught behind to leave England 27 for four, though the following partnership between Stewart and Thorpe proved to be the best of the innings. It was worth 44 in nine overs, and it was brought to an end somewhat surprisingly by Hooper, who had been brought on with 25 minutes of the pre-lunch session remaining. Stewart edged to the keeper, and Thorpe was out in the same manner when he tried to cut a ball that was too close to him. It was a repetition of the stroke that had cost him his wicket in the second Test. Butcher was only playing because Hollioake had a back injury and Ramprakash was suffering from a severe cold, but he fared as well as anyone for two hours until giving Adams a simple return catch shortly before tea. Two overs later, Caddick was rightly sent back by Russell but could not beat Lara's throw to the bowler. After the break, Ambrose quickly ended the innings, and England trailed by 14 runs – a bitter disappointment.

Caddick offered a selection of half-volleys when West Indies began their second innings, 16 runs coming in the first two overs. Atherton's body language was a clear expression of his feelings, but he was far happier when he clung onto a fierce square-cut from Stuart Williams in Caddick's fourth over. Campbell was content to defend resolutely, but he was leg before to a ball from Fraser that kept low, and West Indies were 71 for two at the close.

With Lara unbeaten on 30, West Indies began the third day in good heart, but they soon lost night-watchman Benjamin to Fraser, who brought England right back into contention when he had Lara leg before on the back foot. Hooper suffered a battering at the hands of Headley before becoming his Kent colleague's first victim of the match, and it was left to Chanderpaul and Adams to resurrect the innings with a stand of 54. Their good work was undone by

England's outstanding bowler of the series, Angus Fraser, traps Sherwin Campbell leg before for 13 to give his side hope of victory in the third Test.
(Lawrence Griffiths / Allsport)

All too familiar a sight. Atherton is dismissed by Ambrose, lbw for two in the third Test.
(Lawrence Griffiths / Allsport)

Headley, who took the wickets of Chanderpaul, David Williams and Ambrose in a seven-ball burst while conceding just one run. England had brought West Indies to the brink of total collapse, but for an hour either side of tea McLean offered Adams sensible support and 30 precious runs were added. Adams was last out, his 53 coming from 161 balls and containing six fours. England needed 225 to win, a stiff task on an unpredictable pitch, and Stewart and Atherton survived 25 difficult overs to score 52.

There was a blend of frustration and anxiety on the fourth day, which was interrupted by rain and finished in fading light after an extension beyond the normal playing time. Stewart and Atherton were not separated until a quarter of an hour after lunch, when the England captain was caught off his gloves. Crawley dithered and was run out by Benjamin's throw to the keeper, and Stewart, having batted boldly for five hours, was caught behind off Walsh's away-swinger. Hussain had wretched luck. He had batted sensibly and confidently for an hour when he received a horrible grounder that hit him on the boot in front of off stump. England were 168 for four and it was left to Thorpe and Butcher to add 19 more hard-earned runs before the close.

Fourteen runs into the last day, with much still to do, Thorpe was caught behind off Ambrose. This left great responsibility on Butcher as the last recognised batsman. He and Russell added 12, vital in the context of the match, before the Gloucestershire man was caught at slip. Caddick was caught behind next ball, and English nerves jangled. Headley's nerves withstood the test, and lunch came with England seven runs short of levelling the series. Walsh began the first over after the interval and broke in his delivery stride to warn Headley for backing up too far. Headley later responded by on-driving Walsh for three, while Butcher was desperately close to being leg before to the next ball. The end, as so often, was anticlimactic.

Third Test Match – West Indies *v.* England

13, 14, 15, 16 and 17 February 1998 at Queen's Park Oval, Port-of-Spain, Trinidad

West Indies

	First Innings		Second Innings	
S.L. Campbell	**c** Thorpe, **b** Fraser	**28**	lbw, **b** Fraser	**13**
S.C. Williams	**c** Thorpe, **b** Caddick	**24**	**c** Atherton, **b** Caddick	**23**
B.C. Lara *	**c** Russell, **b** Fraser	**42**	lbw, **b** Fraser	**47**
C.L. Hooper	**c** Butcher, **b** Fraser	**1**	(5) lbw, **b** Headley	**5**
S. Chanderpaul	lbw, **b** Fraser	**28**	(6) **c** Russell, **b** Headley	**39**
J.C. Adams	**c** Atherton, **b** Caddick	**11**	(7) **c** Atherton, **b** Fraser	**53**
D. Williams †	**b** Caddick	**0**	(8) lbw, **b** Headley	**0**
C.E.L. Ambrose	**b** Caddick	**4**	(9) **b** Headley	**0**
K.C.G. Benjamin	lbw, **b** Caddick	**0**	(4) **c** Russell, **b** Fraser	**1**
N.A.M. McLean	**c** Headley, **b** Fraser	**11**	**c** Stewart, **b** Caddick	**2**
C.A. Walsh	not out	**5**	not out	**1**
	nb **5**	**5**	lb **16**, nb **10**	**26**
		159		**210**

	O	M	R	W	O	M	R	W
Headley	14	–	40	**–**	26	3	77	**4**
Caddick	22	7	67	**5**	19	6	64	**2**
Fraser	20.4	8	40	**5**	25.3	11	40	**4**
Tufnell	9	5	11	**–**	15	6	13	**–**
Butcher	2	1	1	**–**				

Fall of Wickets
1–**36**, 2–**93**, 3–**95**, 4–**100**, 5–**132**, 6–**132**, 7–**140**, 8–**140**, 9–**150**
1–**27**, 2–**66**, 3–**82**, 4–**92**, 5–**102**, 6–**158**, 7–**159**, 8–**159**, 9–**189**

England

	First Innings		Second Innings	
A. Atherton *	lbw, **b** Ambrose	**2**	**c** D. Williams, **b** Walsh	**49**
A.J. Stewart	**c** D. Williams, **b** Hooper	**44**	**c** D. Williams, **b** Walsh	**83**
J.P. Crawley	**b** Ambrose	**1**	run out	**5**
D.W. Headley	**b** Ambrose	**1**	(9) not out	**7**
N. Hussain	**c** D. Williams, **b** Walsh	**0**	(4) lbw, **b** Hooper	**5**
G.P. Thorpe	**c** D. Williams, **b** Hooper	**32**	(5) **c** D. Williams, **b** Ambrose	**19**
M.A. Butcher	**c** and **b** Adams	**28**	(6) not out	**24**
R.C. Russell †	not out	**20**	(7) **c** Hooper, **b** Ambrose	**4**
A.R. Caddick	run out	**0**	(8) **c** D. Williams, **b** Ambrose	**0**
A.R.C. Fraser	**c** and **b** Ambrose	**5**		
P.C.R. Tufnell	lbw, **b** Ambrose	**0**		
	b **1**, lb **4**, nb **7**	**12**	b **2**, lb **15**, nb **12**	**29**
		145	(for 7 wickets)	**225**

	O	M	R	W	O	M	R	W
Walsh	17	4	35	**1**	38	11	69	**2**
Ambrose	15.4	5	25	**5**	33	6	62	**3**
McLean	9	2	23	**–**	4	–	17	**–**
Benjamin	13	3	34	**–**	11	3	24	**–**
Hooper	15	3	23	**2**	16	3	31	**1**
Adams	2	2	–	**1**	6	3	5	**–**

Fall of Wickets
1–**5**, 2–**15**, 3–**22**, 4–**27**, 5–**71**, 6–**101**, 7–**134**, 8–**135**, 9–**145**
1–**129**, 2–**145**, 3–**152**, 4–**168**, 5–**201**, 6–**213**, 7–**213**

Umpires: E. Nicholls & D.B. Hair

England won by 3 wickets

Headley scrambled a single, Ambrose bowled a no-ball and then sent a delivery wide down the leg side for the winning bye. Anticlimax it may have been, but England had levelled the series with a most courageous effort that was founded on Angus Fraser's fine bowling, for which he rightly took the individual award.

21, 22 and 23 February 1998

at Everest Cricket Club, Georgetown, Guyana

Guyana 184 (V. Nagamootoo 55, R.D.B. Croft 6 for 50) and 131 (P.C.R. Tufnell 5 for 42, R.D.B. Croft 5 for 51)

England XI 239 (M.R. Ramprakash 77, N.C. McGarrell 7 for 71) and 33 for 3

Match drawn

England narrowly failed to beat Guyana on a pitch that encouraged spin. They needed to make 77 from the last 14 overs, and 12 runs came off the first over, but, at 33 for three after 10 overs, they called off the chase. The match was a total success for Mark Ramprakash and Robert Croft, both of whom were selected for the fourth Test. Ramprakash, one felt, should have been chosen ahead of Butcher and Crawley earlier in the tour. The decision to play one spinner had restricted Croft's opportunities, but he seized his chance against Guyana with 11 for 101 in the match. There was also some fine bowling from Guyana's left-arm spinner Neil McGarrell, and only Ramprakash played him with confidence.

Fourth Test Match

West Indies v. England

West Indies made two changes from the side beaten in Trinidad, Bishop and Ramnarine replacing McLean and Kenny Benjamin. The uncharacteristically dry conditions had played some part in West Indies decision to give leg-spinner Ramnarine his first Test cap. Crawley and Caddick were the players to make room for Ramprakash and Croft in the England side. Lara won the toss for the first time in the series, and West Indies batted.

Neither Campbell nor Stuart Williams had impressed in the previous Tests, and they did nothing to enhance their reputations at Bourda. Stuart Williams drove Fraser through the covers for four and got a top edge off Headley that went for six before he edged Fraser low to first slip. Campbell laboured for 70 minutes and then gloved Headley to the wicket-keeper. England were now to pay dearly for dropped catches. Chanderpaul, an uneasy starter, was badly dropped by Stewart at slip off the bowling of Fraser. The batsman had only nine at the time, and 45 runs on he was again reprieved by Stewart. Lara needed no such fortune. He drove Croft high and far for six, and he pulled a long-hop from Headley over mid-wicket for another six. He was the dominant partner in a stand worth 159, and it seemed that he must reach a glorious hundred

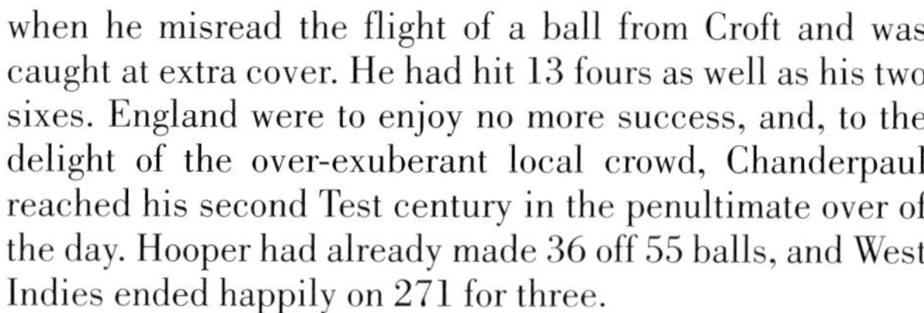

when he misread the flight of a ball from Croft and was caught at extra cover. He had hit 13 fours as well as his two sixes. England were to enjoy no more success, and, to the delight of the over-exuberant local crowd, Chanderpaul reached his second Test century in the penultimate over of the day. Hooper had already made 36 off 55 balls, and West Indies ended happily on 271 for three.

The second day began encouragingly for England but ended in disaster. Tufnell and Croft were mainly instrumental in capturing West Indies' last seven wickets for 57 runs, and Chanderpaul and Hooper were both cut down when they had given indication that they could run riot. Facing a total that was not as great as had been anticipated, England needed a good start. It was not to be. Ambrose again quickly accounted for Atherton. The England skipper was rooted to his crease indecisively, and Ambrose found the edge of his bat for Lara to hold the catch at first slip. More alarms followed. Butcher was trapped leg before by Bishop, and Stewart was out four runs later when, caught in two minds, he edged to the wicket-keeper. Hussain's wretched luck continued when he received a cruel leg before decision, the ball striking him high when he himself was off the ground. Thorpe became Ramnarine's first Test victim when he mistakenly tried to sweep, and Russell almost immediately became the leg-spinner's

Chanderpaul celebrates reaching his century in the fourth Test, which West Indies went on to win by 242 runs.
(Lawrence Griffiths / Allsport)

second victim. Croft stayed with Ramprakash, 13, until the close when England were 87 for six.

England staged a wonderful fightback on the third day. It began with Ramprakash and Croft, who extended their seventh wicket partnership until it was worth 64, at which point Croft was caught at slip off Hooper. Headley was out fourth ball when he pushed at Hooper and was caught behind, and Fraser presented Ramnarine with his third wicket of the innings. Like Thorpe, he swept unwisely and, running from slip, Lara took the catch at short fine-leg. This left England at 140 for nine, with Ramprakash on 39. At lunch, he was still there, and the score was 150. Ramprakash's fifty came immediately after the interval. When Ambrose finally accounted for Tufnell, Ramprakash had batted with courage and determination for 221 minutes and hit seven fours off the 180 balls he had faced. The promise so long in evidence was being fulfilled.

England trailed by 182 runs, an enormous deficit, but Stuart Williams was soon caught at second slip, and Campbell turned Fraser into the hands of short-leg. Next ball, Chanderpaul took a silly run to Hussain, an outstanding fielder, at cover and paid the price. Seven runs later, England sipped their tea in a happier frame of mind than they had done 24 hours earlier. After the break, things got even better. Lara had been twice dropped, but now he was caught bat and pad. Hooper received a leg before decision as dubious as Hussain's, and Ramprakash claimed his first Test wicket when he had Williams caught at square-leg. Adams and Ambrose were both leg before

Courtney Walsh displays the plate presented to him to mark his 100th Test match.
(Lawrence Griffiths /Allsport)

offering no stroke at deliveries from Croft, and Walsh was caught behind at the death: four wickets, three of them to Croft, had fallen for four runs. West Indies ended the day at 127 for nine.

A swift end to the West Indian innings was anticipated on the fourth morning, after which England

Fourth Test Match – West Indies *v.* England

27, 28 February, 1 and 2 March 1998 at Bourda, Georgetown, Guyana

West Indies

	First Innings		Second Innings	
S.L. Campbell	c Russell, b Headley	10	c Ramprakash, b Fraser	17
S.C. Williams	c Thorpe, b Fraser	13	c Stewart, b Headley	0
B.C. Lara *	c Thorpe, b Croft	93	c Butcher, b Tufnell	30
S. Chanderpaul	c Thorpe, b Fraser	118	run out	0
C.L. Hooper	c Hussain, b Headley	43	lbw, b Headley	34
J.C. Adams	lbw, b Tufnell	28	lbw, b Croft	18
D. Williams †	c Croft, b Headley	0	c Tufnell, b Ramprakash	15
I.R. Bishop	c Butcher, b Croft	14	not out	44
C.E.L. Ambrose	c Headley, b Tufnell	0	lbw, b Croft	2
C.A. Walsh	not out	3	c Russell, b Croft	0
D. Ramnarine	c Russell, b Croft	0	c Russell, b Headley	19
	B 4, lb 14, nb 12	30	B 1, lb 11, nb 6	18
		352		197

	O	M	R	W	O	M	R	W
Headley	31	7	90	3	13	5	37	3
Fraser	33	8	77	2	11	2	24	1
Butcher	3	–	15	–				
Croft	36.1	9	89	3	22	9	50	3
Tufnell	25	10	63	2	24	5	72	1
Ramprakash	2	1	2	1				

Fall of Wickets
1–16, 2–38, 3–197, 4–295, 5–316, 6–320, 7–347, 8–349, 9–352
1–4, 2–32, 3–32, 4–75, 5–93, 6–123, 7–123, 8–127, 9–127

England

	First Innings		Second Innings	
M.A. Atherton *	c Lara, b Ambrose	0	lbw, b Ambrose	1
A.J. Stewart	c D. Williams, b Walsh	20	lbw, b Walsh	12
M.A. Butcher	lbw, b Bishop	11	lbw, b Hooper	17
N. Hussain	lbw, b Walsh	11	c Adams, b Walsh	0
G.P. Thorpe	c D. Williams, b Ramnarine	10	c Ramnarine, b Ambrose	3
M.R. Ramprakash	not out	64	c D. Williams, b Walsh	34
R.C. Russell †	lbw, b Ramnarine	0	c Lara, b Ambrose	17
R.D.B. Croft	c Lara, b Hooper	26	c D. Williams, b Hooper	14
D.W. Headley	c D. Williams, b Hooper	0	c Chanderpaul, b Ambrose	9
A.R.C. Fraser	c Lara, b Ramnarine	0	c Walsh, b Hooper	2
P.C.R. Tufnell	c Bishop, b Ambrose	2	not out	0
	B 10, lb 2, nb 14	26	B 9, lb 2, w 1, nb 16	28
		170		137

	O	M	R	W	O	M	R	W
Walsh	27	7	47	2	15	4	25	3
Ambrose	12.1	5	21	2	14.1	3	38	4
Ramnarine	17	8	26	3	11	5	23	–
Bishop	13	4	34	1	3	1	4	–
Adams	3	2	1	–	1	–	5	–
Hooper	15	5	29	2	18	8	31	3

Fall of Wickets
1–1, 2–37, 3–41, 4–65, 5–73, 6–75, 7–139, 8–139, 9–140
1–6, 2–22, 3–28, 4–28, 5–58, 6–90, 7–118, 8–125, 9–135

Umpires: S.A. Bucknor & D.B. Hair

West Indies won by 242 runs

would be able to chase a target that, though very difficult, would be within their capabilities. Unfortunately, the swift end did not materialise. Ramnarine was missed four times, twice before he had scored, and he and Bishop, who struck the ball cleanly, added a record 70 as they defied the England attack for 110 minutes. England were left with the task of coring 380 to win, or, realistically, surviving for five sessions.

England had performed shoddily, and now their batting matched their out-cricket. Atherton and Stewart were both leg before, and Hussain, caught in mid-stroke, was taken at short-leg second ball. Thorpe was very well caught at backward short-leg, and when Butcher fell to Hooper England were 58 for five, all hope gone.

Ramprakash showed much of the good form he had shown in the first innings before being caught behind off a splendid delivery from Walsh. Croft and Russell, (whose wicket-keeping had again been sub-standard) held out for an hour before Croft was deceived by Hooper's arm ball. A refreshed Ambrose then had Russell magnificently caught at first slip by Lara, who held the ball right-handed as he fell. Fraser hit Hooper high to deep mid-wicket, and Headley was taken at fourth slip. England had been bowled out in just under four and a quarter hours. It was an abject display of batting.

West Indies had gained a big advantage from winning the toss, but they had used that advantage well with some fine batting on the first day. Lara and Chanderpaul, Man of the Match, had taken control of the game during their partnership of 159, and, in spite of a sloppy second innings batting display, West Indies had never really lost control. Ramprakash and Croft apart, England earned no plaudits. The selection of two spinners was a controversial decision, but England will continue to carry an unbalanced look until they find a genuine all-rounder of quality.

7, 8 and 9 March 1998

at Kensington Oval, Bridgetown, Barbados

Barbados 472 for 6 dec. (R.I.C. Holder 158, P.A. Wallace 68, R.L. Hoyte 64, F.L. Reifer 60) and 51 for 1

England XI 382 (M.A. Butcher 79, G.P. Thorpe 58, A.J. Stewart 52, T. Rollock 4 for 56)

Match drawn

In their last first-class match before the fifth and sixth Tests, England were kept in the field for nine hours as Roland Holder played his second large innings against the tourists and assured himself of a recall to the West Indian side. He and Reifer added 133 for the fourth wicket, and he shared a fifth wicket stand of 144 with wicket-keeper Hoyte. Hussain led the England side in the absence of Atherton and saw his side bat solidly. Stewart and Butcher scored 117 for the first wicket, but most batsmen were troubled by the leg-spin of Terry Rollock. When Barbados batted a second time, Ashley Cowan had Sherwin Campbell caught behind. It was his only wicket of the tour.

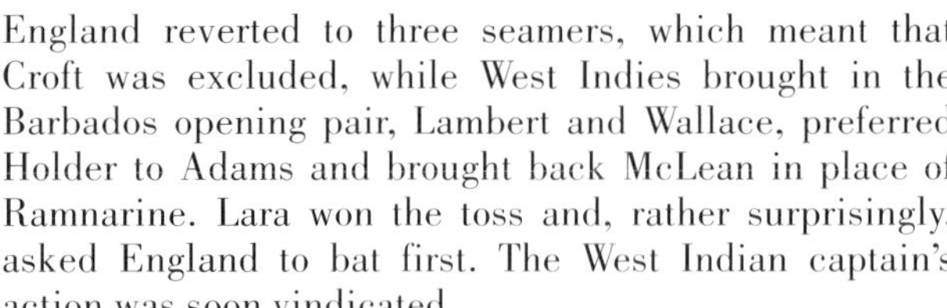

Fifth Test Match

West Indies *v.* England

England reverted to three seamers, which meant that Croft was excluded, while West Indies brought in the Barbados opening pair, Lambert and Wallace, preferred Holder to Adams and brought back McLean in place of Ramnarine. Lara won the toss and, rather surprisingly, asked England to bat first. The West Indian captain's action was soon vindicated.

Stewart had hit two fours and made 12 off as many balls in 19 minutes when he flicked at Walsh and was caught behind. One run later, Atherton attempted to hook the same bowler and arrowed the ball straight to Ambrose at long-leg. Hussain was next to go. Taking his eyes off a short delivery from McLean, he dangled his bat and diverted the ball obligingly to slip. Ambrose had bowled an economic first spell; now he was recalled and claimed the wicket of Butcher, caught low down at second slip. Lunch arrived with England 55 for four. Things could have been worse, for Ramprakash should have been caught and bowled by Ambrose.

Thorpe did not reappear after lunch: he was nursing a back injury. Russell partnered Ramprakash and batted refreshingly for 98 minutes while 76 runs were scored. He fell to Hooper, but Thorpe was now fit to return, and he and Ramprakash revived England's spirits as they moved the score to 229 for five by the close. Thorpe had time to complete his fifty, and Ramprakash, his coming of age now proven, was unbeaten on 80 after 283 minutes at the crease.

At lunch on the second day, Ramprakash and Thorpe were still together, and Ramprakash had reached his maiden Test century. He was ecstatic. The hundred had been seven years in coming, and Ramprakash had suffered many trials and tribulations on the way, but his goal could not have been reached at a more appropriate or difficult time. When he arrived at the wicket, England were 53 for four; when he gave McLean a return catch 529 minutes later, England were 382 for seven. He had faced 387 balls and hit 20 fours, and he had displayed elegance, character and determination. He and Thorpe added 205, a record for England against West Indies. Thorpe played an admirable innings, facing 268 balls and hitting eight fours. His was the only wicket to fall in the afternoon session. He edged Hooper to slip, and the amount of turn that Hooper achieved and the manner in which he troubled the batsmen suggested that Lara had too long neglected his off-spin.

Ramprakash was out in the second over after tea, but Headley had already given good support. England reached a healthy 403. Hooper confirmed Lara's previous negligence by taking the last three wickets and finishing with five for 80.

The quality of the pitch was emphasised when Lambert and Wallace, the new opening pair, raced to 82 in 95 minutes, runs coming at more than four an over, before

Centurion heroes of the fifth Test, Graham Thorpe and Mark Ramprakash. They shared a record partnership of 205. *(Clive Mason / Allsport)*

Wallace fell to Headley. Night-watchman Bishop added two more runs before the close.

The third day belonged to England. Tufnell bowled throughout the morning session and quickly disposed of Bishop, who was caught behind pushing forward. Lambert, whose one previous Test appearance had been at The Oval seven years earlier, was haunted by the fact that his impetuosity against Tufnell then had cost him dearly. Now, at the age of 36, he was determined not to make the same mistake again and to lengthen his Test career. In two hours before lunch, he scored 12. In contrast, Lara was eager to attack, but he became complacent against Headley and drove lazily into the hands of cover. In the afternoon, after four and a half hours at the crease, Lambert edged Caddick to Russell, who had been guilty of a serious miss when he dropped Chanderpaul off Tufnell. The England wicket-keeper had a very bad series, and his decline brings the team a problem that must be solved quickly and efficiently.

Ramprakash turned the ball appreciably; he bowled Holder having already had him dropped twice by Butcher. After tea, England enjoyed some fortune through a ludicrous piece of umpiring. Chanderpaul had batted well, and he was negotiating the second new ball sensibly when he drove at a full toss from Fraser and edged it into the ground whence it bounced into the hands of Stewart at slip. Incredibly and shamefully, there was an appeal, and incredibly and shamefully umpire Nicholls raised his finger. Williams drove Caddick to cover, and, on the same score, a becalmed Hooper was leg before to Fraser.

Fifth Test Match – West Indies *v.* England

12, 13, 14, 15 and 16 March 1998 at Kensington Oval, Bridgetown, Barbados

England

	First Innings		Second Innings	
M.A. Atherton *	c Ambrose, b Walsh	11	c D. Williams, b Bishop	64
A.J. Stewart	c D. Williams, b Walsh	12	c Lara, b Bishop	48
M.A. Butcher	c Hooper, b Ambrose	19	c Lambert, b Ambrose	26
N. Hussain	c Lara, b McLean	5	not out	46
G.P. Thorpe	c Lara, b Hooper	103	not out	36
M.R. Ramprakash	c and b McLean	154		
R.C. Russell †	c Wallace, b Hooper	32		
D.W. Headley	c Holder, b Hooper	31		
A.R. Caddick	c Chanderpaul, b Hooper	3		
A.R.C. Fraser	c Walsh, b Fraser	3		
P.C.R. Tufnell	not out	1		
	lb 10, w 2, nb 17	29	b 1, lb 6, nb 6	13
		403	(for 3 wickets, dec.)	233

	O	M	R	W	O	M	R	W
Walsh	34	8	84	2	12	1	40	–
Ambrose	31	6	62	1	12	4	48	1
McLean	27	5	73	2	7	–	16	–
Hooper	37.5	7	80	5	21	5	58	–
Bishop	20	1	74	–	14	1	51	2
Chanderpaul	4	–	20	–	5	3	13	–

Fall of Wickets
1–**23**, 2–**24**, 3–**33**, 4–**53**, 5–**131**, 6–**336**, 7–**382**, 8–**392**, 9–**402**
1–**101**, 2–**128**, 3–**173**

West Indies

	First Innings		Second Innings	
C.B. Lambert	c Russell, b Caddick	55	c Headley, b Fraser	29
P.A. Wallace	lbw, b Headley	45	lbw, b Caddick	61
I.R. Bishop	c Russell, b Tufnell	4		
B.C. Lara *	c Butcher, b Headley	31	(3) not out	13
S. Chanderpaul	c Stewart, b Fraser	45	(4) not out	3
R.I.C. Holder	b Ramprakash	10		
C.L. Hooper	lbw, b Fraser	9		
D. Williams †	c Ramprakash, b Caddick	2		
N.A.M. McLean	not out	7		
C.E.L. Ambrose	st Russell, b Tufnell	26		
C.A. Walsh	c and b Headley	6		
	b 13, lb 2, nb 7	22	b 1, lb 4, nb 1	6
		262	(for 2 wickets)	112

	O	M	R	W	O	M	R	W
Headley	17.3	1	64	3	2	-	14	
Fraser	22	5	80	2	11	3	33	1
Caddick	17	8	28	2	6	1	19	1
Tufnell	33	15	43	2	16.3	4	38	
Ramprakash	18	7	32	1	2	1	3	–

Fall of Wickets
1–**82**, 2–**91**, 3–**134**, 4–**164**, 5–**190**, 6–**214**, 7–**221**, 8–**221**, 9–**255**
1–**72**, 2–**108**

Umpires: E.G. Nicholls & C.J. Mitchley *Thorpe retired hurt at 55 for 4 and returned at 131 for 5 (first innings)* **Match drawn**

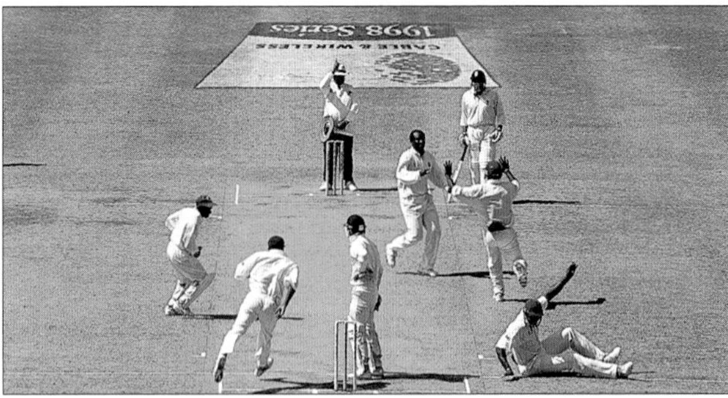

Jack Russell is caught by Wallace off Hooper for 32. The West Indian all-rounder took five for 80 in England's first innings in the fifth Test.
(David Munden / Sportsline)

Ambrose swung lustily until he was stumped off Tufnell, and West Indies subsided for 262. England increased their lead by two runs in two overs and were very much on top.

Atherton and Stewart produced their first century opening stand of the series on the fourth day, notching up 101 before Stewart edged to slip after 147 minutes. Atherton's innings ended 27 runs later when he was caught behind off Bishop. He had made 64, his first fifty in 17 Test innings. Butcher was the third man out, but Hussain and Thorpe batted so positively that Atherton was able to declare and leave West Indies 90 minutes and a day in which to score 375 to win. For two days, England had been in charge, but on that fourth evening Lambert and Wallace launched a violent attack on the England bowling and scored 71 in 19 overs. Their approach set up an intriguing final day, but, sadly, rain brought an anticlimax. Play did not start until 1 pm, and there were two interruptions. In all, only 18.2 overs were bowled, during which England captured the wickets of both openers. England's only consolation was that Ramprakash was named Man of the Match.

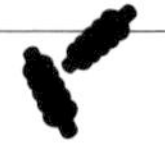

Sixth Test Match

West Indies *v.* England

There had been great disappointment in the England camp when rain destroyed their hopes of victory in the Barbados Test, but, in truth, an English win was by no means assured. The chance of winning the series had gone, though an unchanged side was optimistic of winning in Antigua and levelling the rubber. West Indies made three changes. Ramnarine was recalled in place of McLean, and Rose replaced Bishop whose bowling had lost much of its pace, menace and variety. There was also a change of wicket-keeper. David Williams, hero of the second Test, had barely scored a run since and was replaced by Junior Murray (it seemed that West Indian wicket-keepers were part of a merry-go-round). Only 93 minutes play was possible on the first day, and, having been put into bat, England lost Atherton and Butcher as they scored 35 runs in 21.3 overs. Atherton was caught in the gully, while Butcher was caught at third slip on a pitch that seemed spiteful. It should be stated, however, that both wickets, were lost to poor shots against good bowling.

The idea that the pitch was in any way to blame for England's failings was eradicated on the second day. Night-watchman Headley soon provided Lara with another slip catch, and Stewart's patient innings came to an end when he tried to attack Rose and was bowled between bat and pad. Thorpe was leg before to Ramnarine, whose emergence during the series was a positive gain for West Indies, and England were 66 for five. The hundred was passed without further loss, and Hussain, who batted most sensibly for two and a half hours with Ramprakash appeared to be reviving England. Then came disaster. Hussain erred when he top-edged a sweep and Holder dived forward to take a fine catch at short fine-leg. Russell was out second ball, and, in the next over, Ramprakash was caught at cover. Three wickets had fallen for two runs, and there was no way back for England. Ramnarine captured the wicket of Caddick to finish with the heartening figures of four for 29. In 27 overs before the close, Wallace and Lambert put the England attack to the sword and scored 126 without being parted. They were greatly aided by some dreadfully wasteful new-ball bowling.

England's batting was put into complete perspective on the third day when West Indies advanced their score to 451 for five. Wallace, having batted for 182 minutes and faced 135 balls, looked set for a spectacular maiden Test century until he played on to Headley. He had hit a six and 11 fours. He was followed by Lara, who seized the opportunity to give one of his dazzling displays of virtuosity, hitting a six and 12 fours in his 94-ball innings. Appropriately, he was out to a superb catch by

The end of a spectacular opening partnership of 167: Philo Wallace is bowled by Dean Headley in the sixth Test.
(David Munden / Sportsline)

Clayton Lambert – a maiden Test hundred.
(Clive Mason / Allsport)

Stewart at mid-wicket who dived to hold on to a savage pull off a wretched long-hop by Caddick, who continued for the most part in wasteful vein. Lambert reached his maiden Test century before being out in the last over before tea. He batted 364 minutes, faced 232 balls and hit a six and 10 fours. He had given the innings the foundation that is expected of an opening batsman, and he had fully justified his recall to the Test side. Chanderpaul went cheaply, but Hooper and Holder continued the slaughter. In 141 minutes, they added 127 before Holder fell in the last over of the day. Hooper was on 85, and West Indies led by 324 runs.

Carl Hooper completed his ninth Test century on the fourth morning. Like several of the West Indian batsmen, he had benefited from dropped catches, but he had batted sublimely towards the close, and his 108 came off only 150 balls with 17 fours. There was a lively cameo from Ambrose, and Lara declared when the score reached 500.

England survived for 69 minutes without loss. But while Stewart took the attack to the enemy, Atherton again became Ambrose's victim, pinned leg before in no-man's land. Butcher was out for his second duck of the match, and England, 49 for two, faced a fight to save the game. Stewart finally deserted the positive approach and prodded forward at Hooper as fielders crowded the bat: Wallace took the catch at silly point. Hussain was looking very good and reached 54 by the end of the day. With Thorpe keeping him company, England were 173 for three and had every hope of avoiding defeat.

That hope was increased when morning rain and the subsequent mopping up process reduced the final day's play to 60 overs plus, if required, the extra hour. Hussain was technically and temperamentally assured, and he reached his sixth Test century. It was his first hundred against West Indies and was an innings of outstanding quality in every respect. Thorpe, too, batted well, but it was primarily his folly that brought the fourth wicket partnership of 168 to an end. He pushed the ball to mid-wicket, ran, hesitated when he saw

Sixth Test Match – West Indies *v.* England

20, 21, 22, 23 and 24 March 1998 at Recreation Ground, St John's, Antigua

England

	First Innings		Second Innings	
M.A. Atherton *	c Ramnarine, **b** Ambrose	**15**	lbw, **b** Ambrose	**13**
A.J. Stewart	**b** Rose	**22**	**c** Wallace, **b** Hooper	**79**
M.A. Butcher	**c** Lara, **b** Ambrose	**0**	**c** Murray, **b** Ambrose	**0**
D.W. Headley	**c** Lara, **b** Ambrose	**1**	(8) **c** Murray, **b** Ramnarine	**1**
N. Hussain	**c** Holder, **b** Ramnarine	**37**	(4) run out	**106**
G.P. Thorpe	lbw, **b** Ramnarine	**5**	(5) not out	**84**
M.R. Ramprakash	**c** Chanderpaul, **b** Walsh	**14**	(6) **b** Ramnarine	**0**
R.C. Russell †	**c** Lambert, **b** Ramnarine	**0**	(7) lbw, **b** Walsh	**9**
A.R. Caddick	**c** Walsh, **b** Ramnarine	**8**	**c** Murray, **b** Walsh	**0**
A.R.C. Fraser	**b** Walsh	**9**	**c** Chanderpaul, **b** Walsh	**4**
P.C.R. Tufnell	not out	**2**	**c** Lambert, **b** Walsh	**0**
	b **1**, lb **2**, nb **11**	**14**	b **6**, lb **4**, w **1**, nb **14**	**25**
		127		**321**

	O	M	R	W	O	M	R	W
Walsh	25.5	8	52	**2**	31.2	7	80	**4**
Ambrose	17	6	28	**3**	20	5	66	**2**
Ramnarine	17	5	29	**4**	46	19	70	**2**
Hooper	1	1	0	**–**	39	18	56	**1**
Rose	9	4	14	**1**	11	2	39	**–**
Lambert	1	–	1	**–**				

Fall of Wickets

1–**27**, 2–**27**, 3–**38**, 4–**57**, 5–**66**, 6–**105**, 7–**105**, 8–**105**, 9–**117**
1–**45**, 2–**49**, 3–**127**, 4–**295**, 5–**300**, 6–**312**, 7–**313**, 8–**316**, 9–**320**

West Indies

	First Innings	
C.B. Lambert	**c** Thorpe, **b** Ramprakash	**104**
P.A. Wallace	**b** Headley	**92**
B.C. Lara *	**c** Stewart, **b** Caddick	**89**
S. Chanderpaul	lbw, **b** Fraser	**5**
C.L. Hooper	not out	**108**
R.I.C. Holder	**c** and **b** Caddick	**45**
J.R. Murray †	**c** Hussain, **b** Headley	**4**
F.A. Rose	lbw, **b** Caddick	**2**
C.E.L. Ambrose	not out	**19**
C.A. Walsh		
D. Ramnarine		
	lb **14**, nb **18**	**32**
	(for 7 wickets, dec.)	**500**

	O	M	R	W
Caddick	26	3	111	**3**
Fraser	21	3	88	**1**
Headley	30	4	109	**2**
Tufnell	35	6	97	**–**
Ramprakash	19	–	81	**1**

Fall of Wickets

1–**167**, 2–**300**, 3–**317**, 4–**324**, 5–**451**, 6–**458**, 7–**465**

Umpires: S.A. Bucknor & C.J. Mitchley

West Indies won by an innings and 52 runs

Test Match Averages – West Indies v. England

West Indies Batting

	M	Inns	NOs	Runs	HS	Av	100s	50s
P.A. Wallace	2	3	–	198	92	66.00	2	
C.B. Lambert	2	3	–	188	104	62.66	1	1
B.C. Lara	6	9	1	417	93	52.12	3	
C.L. Hooper	6	8	2	295	108*	49.16	1	1
S. Chanderpaul	6	9	1	272	118	34.00	1	
I.R. Bishop	3	3	1	62	44*	31.00		
S.C. Williams	4	6	–	141	62	23.50		1
J.C. Adams	4	6	–	113	53	18.83		1
D. Williams	5	7	–	98	65	14.00		1
S.L. Campbell	4	6	–	79	28	13.16		
C.E.L. Ambrose	6	8	1	83	31	11.85		
C.A. Walsh	6	6	4	15	6	7.50		
N.A.M. McLean	4	4	1	22	11	7.33		
K.C.G. Benjamin	2	4	1	7	6*	2.33		

Played in two Tests: D. Ramnarine 0 & 19; R.I.C. Holder 10 & 45
Played in one Test: J.R. Murray 4; F.A. Rose 2

Bowling

	Overs	Mds.	Runs	Wks.	Average	Best	5/inn
C.E.L. Ambrose	205.5	62	428	30	14.26	5/25	2
D. Ramnarine	91	37	148	9	16.44	4/29	
J.C. Adams	15	7	19	1	19.00	1/0	
C.L. Hooper	190.5	61	355	15	23.66	5/80	1
C.A. Walsh	261.2	63	564	22	25.63	4/80	
N.A.M. McLean	78	15	203	5	40.60	2/46	
F.A. Rose	20	6	53	1	53.00	1/14	
I.R. Bishop	50	7	163	3	54.33	2/51	
K.C.G. Benjamin	63	14	166	3	55.33	3/68	
S. Chanderpaul	10	3	35	–	–		

Bowled in one innings: C.B. Lambert 1–0–1–0

Fielding Figures

19 – D. Williams; 13 – B.C. Lara; 5 – C.L. Hooper; 4 – S. Chanderpaul and C.A. Walsh; 3 – S.C. Williams, C.B. Lambert and J.R. Murray; 2 – J.C. Adams, C.E.L. Ambrose, D. Ramnarine, P.A. Wallace and R.I.C. Holder ; 1 – S.L. Campbell, N.A.M. McLean and I.R. Bishop

England Batting

	M.	Inns	NOs	Runs	H.S.	Av	100s	50s
M.R. Ramprakash	3	5	1	266	154	66.50	1	1
A.J. Stewart	6	11	1	452	83	45.20	4	0
G.P. Thorpe	6	11	3	339	103	42.37	1	1
N. Hussain	6	11	2	295	106	32.77	1	1
M.A. Atherton	6	11	–	199	64	18.09	1	0
M.A. Butcher	5	9	1	125	28	15.62		
R.C. Russell	5	9	1	90	32	11.25		
J.P. Crawley	3	4	–	45	22	11.25		
D.W. Headley	6	9	2	69	31	9.87		
A.R.C. Fraser	6	8	–	44	17	5.50		
A.R. Caddick	5	7	–	19	8	2.71		
P.C.R. Tufnell	6	8	3	11	6	2.20		

Played in two Tests: A.J. Hollioake 2 & 12
Played in one Test: R.D.B. Croft 26 & 14

Bowling

	Overs	Mds	Runs	Wks	Av	Best	10/m	5/inn
A.R.C. Fraser	187.2	50	492	27	18.22	8/53	1	
R.D.B. Croft	58.1	18	139	6	23.16	3/50		
D.W. Headley	171.3	28	546	19	28.73	4/77		
A.R. Caddick	120	31	388	13	29.84	5/67	1	
M.R. Ramprakash	41	9	118	3	39.33	1/2		
P.C.R. Tufnell	212.5	68	439	7	62.71	2/43		
M.A. Butcher	5	1	16	–	–			

Bowled in one innings: A.J. Hollioake 5–0–12–0

Fielding Figures

13 – R.C. Russell (ct 12 / st 1); 9 – G.P. Thorpe; 6 – A.J. Stewart; 5 – M.A. Atherton; 4 – M.A. Butcher and D.W. Headley; 2 – N. Hussain, A.R. Caddick and M.R. Ramprakash; 1 – J.P. Crawley, A.R.C. Fraser, P.C.R. Tufnell and R.D.B. Croft

Disaster for England. Hussain's fine innings comes to an end when he is run out for 106. Collapse and defeat followed.
(David Munden / Sportsline)

Hooper swoop, ran on and left Hussain beleaguered. It was a sad end to a very fine innings which had lasted for 378 invaluable minutes. Hussain hit 14 fours and faced 318 balls.

This was the breakthrough that West Indies needed, but they could not have expected the floodgates to have opened in so dramatic a manner. Ramprakash misjudged the line and was bowled by Ramnarine. Russell survived the spinners, but the return of Walsh saw him palpably leg before on the back foot, and when Headley was well caught behind off Ramnarine, England had lost four wickets for 18 runs and 17 overs still remained.

Thorpe has several qualities, but farming the bowling is not one of them, as he showed against Australia at Trent Bridge the previous summer. Caddick held out for half an hour before edging Walsh to Murray, and Fraser and Tufnell lasted three and four balls respectively. Both fell to Walsh who thereby moved to within one wicket of Malcolm Marshall's West Indian record of 376. The series had begun with Walsh contemplating retirement and Ambrose allegedly a spent force. If a week is a long time in politics, three months must be a lifetime in cricket.

The defeat had come so swiftly after Hussain's defiant century that England were left in a state of shock and dejection. Atherton's response was to resign from the captaincy that he had held since 1993. There was no obvious heir apparent. Vice-captain Nasser Hussain was not included in the party for the one-day games, which the selectors must now have regretted. Adam Hollioake, a player short of Test class, was in charge for the rest of the tour – a tour that had promised so much and that was now in danger of falling apart.

One-Day Series

It had originally been decided that Atherton would lead England in the limited-over series as well as the Test matches, but his sudden resignation at the end of the sixth Test meant that Adam Hollioake would now take over and that the side would virtually revert to the one which had been so successful in Sharjah. As he was no longer captain, Atherton immediately found his place in the England side in jeopardy. His recent form hardly suggested that he would be an automatic selection, and an obscene gesture at a batsman in the fifth Test seemed to indicate that had wilted under the pressures of international cricket. He was one of several players who seemed physically and mentally drained by the traumas of the Test series, and men like Hick, Knight, Ealham and Ben Hollioake, who had not suffered those traumas, now arrived fresh and eager.

Atherton found no place in the eleven that played against the Vice Chancellor's XI in Bridgetown nor in the side that took the field for the first international. Knight and Stewart were the openers in both matches. Stewart and Adam Hollioake put on 157 in 26 overs for England's fourth wicket against the Vice Chancellor's XI, whose innings was opened by Gordon Greenidge and Desmond Haynes. They offered a taste of vintage cricket in a stand of 108, but their colleagues, one of whom was Jeff Dujon, failed to capitalise on their effort. There was a two-hour lunch break as a stand was renamed in honour of Haynes and Greenidge.

27 March 1998
at Kensington Oval, Bridgetown, Barbados
England XI 289 for 7 (A.J. Stewart 108, A.J. Hollioake 76)
University of West Indies Vice Chancellor's XI 207 (D.L. Haynes 71)
England XI won on faster scoring rate

If there had been complaints that pitches for the first four Tests had been of a poor standard, none could dispute that the track provided for the first one-day international was a batsman's paradise. Put in to bat, England began with a record first-wicket stand against West Indies, Knight and Stewart putting on 165. Stewart made 74 off 85 balls before being bowled by Walsh, and Knight and Hick then added 62. Both men were out in the 43rd over, but Fleming and Ealham, in particular, plundered well at the close. The oustanding contribution to England's 293 came from Nick Knight, who reached his third century in one-day

First One-Day International – West Indies v. England

29 March 1998 at Kensington Oval, Bridgetown, Barbados

England

N.V. Knight	run out	**122**
A.J. Stewart †	**b** Walsh	**74**
G.A. Hick	**b** Lewis	**29**
G.P. Thorpe	**b** Simmons	**4**
A.J. Hollioake *	not out	**18**
M.A. Ealham	**b** Simmons	**20**
M.V. Fleming	not out	**22**
B.C. Hollioake		
D.R. Brown		
R.D.B. Croft		
D.W. Headley		
	lb **4**	**4**
	50 overs (for 5 wickets)	**293**

	O	M	R	W
Rose	6	–	31	**–**
Walsh	10	–	57	**1**
Ambrose	8	–	42	**–**
Hooper	10	–	46	**–**
Lewis	8	–	55	**1**
Simmons	8	–	58	**2**

Fall of Wickets
1–**165**, 2–**227**, 3–**228**, 4–**249**, 5–**271**

West Indies

C.B. Lambert	**c** Stewart, **b** Headley	**11**
P.A. Wallace	**c** Hick, **b** Brown	**13**
B.C. Lara *	run out	**110**
C.L. Hooper	**c** Headley, **b** Fleming	**45**
S. Chanderpaul	**c** Knight, **b** Croft	**8**
P.V. Simmons	**b** A.J. Hollioake	**18**
J.R. Murray †	**c** Stewart, **b** Headley	**7**
R.N. Lewis	**st** Stewart, **b** Ealham	**27**
F.A. Rose	**c** A.J. Hollioake, **b** Fleming	**24**
C.E.L. Ambrose	not out	**3**
C.A. Walsh	**b** Ealham	**0**
	lb **7**, w **1**, nb **3**	**11**
	46.5 overs	**277**

	O	M	R	W
Brown	5	1	32	**1**
Headley	10	–	63	**2**
Ealham	7.5	–	37	**2**
Fleming	7	–	54	**2**
Croft	10	–	37	**1**
A.J. Hollioake	7	1	47	**1**

Fall of Wickets
1–**25**, 2–**27**, 3–**115**, 4–**145**, 5–**187**, 6–**219**, 7–**222**, 8–**266**, 9–**274**

Umpires: E.G. Nichols & B. Morgan *Man of the Match*: N.V. Knight

England won by 16 runs

Alec Stewart, a consistent battler throughout the series is caught by Wallace off Hooper for 79.
(David Munden / Sportsline)

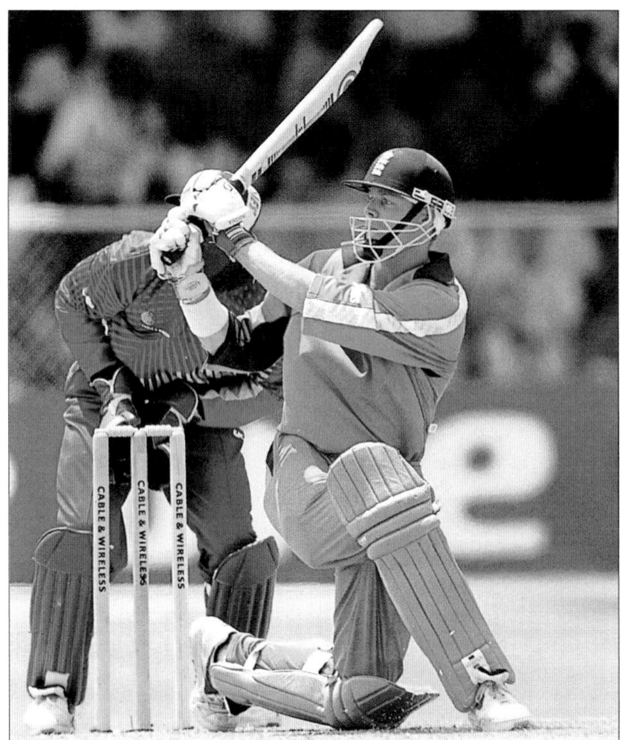

Nick Knight began the one-day series in spectacular fashion. He made 122 in the first match and 90 in the second.
(Clive Mason / Allsport)

internationals. He hit hard and often, and his 122 came off 130 balls and included 13 sixes and four fours. West Indies went off at a terrific gallop, and they scored 111 from the first 15 overs. At the same stage, England had made 78, but England had not lost a wicket, whereas West Indies had lost both openers. Lara was in total command, but once he had lost Hooper, who made 45 off 34 deliveries, he received little help. It seemed that he would win the game single-handed as he raced to his 12th one-day international hundred aided only by the limping Junior Murray, who was batting with a runner following a thigh muscle injury sustained while keeping wicket. With the score on 219, Lara was run out by a throw from deep mid-wicket. He had scored 110 off 106 balls and hit three sixes and 15 fours. There is no more glorious sight in cricket when he is in this form. England breathed a sigh of relief when he was out, but West Indies needed only 75 from 15 overs. Murray was soon out, but Lewis and Rose batted most sensibly in adding 44. The required run-rate was down to close on four an over, and there was no cause to be impetuous. Crucially, though Lewis was well stumped by Stewart off Ealham. There was then insufficient batting strength remaining for West Indies to take the victory that Lara had made possible.

Overnight rain left the pitch for the second match damp at the outset, and it was no surprise when Lara asked England to bat first. Thorpe, nursing an injury, had returned home and the England side contained only five players who were part of the Test squad. Nick Knight, who was not, again batted impressively and took the individual award for the second time. He was aggressive in approach and dominated the early stages of the game when the pitch was at its most doubtful. He made 90 off 107 balls while all about him fell, and his foundation enabled Ealham, Brown and Fleming, in particular, to wallop 96 from the last ten overs. England's 266 was a good score in the conditions, but West Indies went off at a furious rate and were 106 for three after 15 overs. The three men to have departed were Wallace, caught low at mid-off; Lambert, superbly run out by Knight; and, vitally for England, Lara, caught at cover after hitting 24 off 19 balls. Stuart Williams and Carl Hooper had little pressure on them as they added 132 to take the score to 211 by the 39th over; but both fell in successive overs, and when Simmons, the last recognised batsman, was leg before and Lewis run out, West Indies suddenly found themselves 226 for seven. In the 45th over, Rose was caught off Fleming, a valuable cricketer in this version of the game, and England scented victory. Ambrose and Jacobs, who had replaced the injured Junior Murray, had other ideas. Jacobs drove a six and Ambrose sliced a four, but Ambrose was out on the first ball of the last over with two still needed for victory. Walsh pushed his second ball for a single to level the score, and, with one ball remaining, Jacobs scampered the winning single. The series was now level.

In the first game in St Vincent, Adam Hollioake won the toss and decided to bat first. West Indies chose an unfamiliar attack. Walsh had asked to be excused the rest of the series as he prepared for his season with Gloucestershire, and the bowling was done mainly by leg-spinner Rawl Lewis, off-spinner Carl Hooper, slow off-cutter Phil Simmons and slow left-arm spinner Keith Arthurton. If it appeared that the West Indies offered a motley crew of bowlers, those bowlers proved to be far too good for England on a sluggish pitch. Knight again went off in positive mood, but his success in the one-day game cannot disguise grave technical deficiencies which will ever hinder his progress at Test level. He was caught off Ambrose who then retired to graze in the outfield. Ben

Second One-Day International West Indies v. England

1 April 1998 at Kensington Oval, Bridgetown, Barbados

England

N.V. Knight	lbw, **b** Simmons	**90**
A.J. Stewart †	**c** Lara, **b** Walsh	**3**
B.C. Hollioake	**c** and **b** Rose	**16**
G.A. Hick	**b** Lewis	**0**
M.R. Ramprakash	**c** Ambrose, **b** Lewis	**29**
A.J. Hollioake *	run out	**11**
M.A. Ealham	**c** Ambrose, **b** Simmons	**45**
D.R. Brown	**b** Simmons	**21**
M.V. Fleming	**c** S.C. Williams, **b** Ambrose	**28**
R.D.B. Croft	not out	**11**
D.W. Headley	**b** Ambrose	**0**
	lb **2**, w **9**, nb **1**	**12**
	50 overs	**266**

	O	M	R	W
Ambrose	10	–	44	**2**
Walsh	10	1	51	**1**
Rose	8	–	50	**1**
Lewis	10	–	40	**2**
Simmons	8	–	46	**3**
Hooper	4	–	33	**–**

Fall of Wickets
1–**21**, 2–**71**, 3–**72**, 4–**131**, 5–**154**, 6–**158**, 7–**206**, 8–**238**, 9–**257**

West Indies

C.B. Lambert	run out	**25**
P.A. Wallace	**c** A.J. Hollioake, **b** Brown	**22**
B.C. Lara *	**c** Ramprakash, **b** Headley	**24**
S.C. Williams	**c** Fleming, **b** A.J. Hollioake	**68**
C.L. Hooper	**c** Croft, **b** Fleming	**66**
P.V. Simmons	lbw, **b** Fleming	**5**
R.D. Jacobs †	not out	**28**
R.N. Lewis	run out	**4**
F.A. Rose	**c** A.J. Hollioake, **b** Fleming	**3**
C.E.L. Ambrose	**c** and **b** A.J. Hollioake	**14**
C.A. Walsh	not out	**1**
	lb **4**, w **1**, nb **2**	**7**
	49.5 overs (for 9 wickets)	**267**

	O	M	R	W
Brown	8	1	36	1
Headley	7	–	68	1
Croft	10	–	46	–
Ealham	8	–	29	–
Fleming	9	–	41	3
A.J. Hollioake	7.5	–	43	2

Fall of Wickets
1–**41**, 2–**54**, 3–**79**, 4–**211**, 5–**211**, 6–**221**, 7–**226**, 8–**236**, 9–**265**

Umpires: E.G. Nicholls & B. Morgan *Man of the Match*: N.V. Knight

West Indies won by 1 wicket

Third One-Day International – West Indies v. England

4 April 1998 at Arnos Vale, Kingstown, St Vincent

England

N.V. Knight	**c** Wallace, **b** Ambrose	**15**
A.J. Stewart †	**c** Arthurton, **b** Simmons	**33**
B.C. Hollioake	**c** Wallace, **b** Simmons	**35**
G.A. Hick	**c** S.C. Williams, **b** Arthurton	**45**
M.R. Ramprakash	**b** Hooper	**1**
A.J. Hollioake *	**b** Lewis	**31**
M.A. Ealham	**st** Jacobs, **b** Lewis	**23**
M.V. Fleming	**c** S.C. Williams, **b** Arthurton	**7**
D.R. Brown	not out	**2**
R.D.B. Croft	not out	**1**
A.R.C. Fraser		
	lb **7**, w **6**, nb **3**	**16**
	50 overs (for 8 wickets)	**209**

	O	M	R	W
Ambrose	5	–	12	**1**
McLean	7	–	33	**–**
Lewis	10	–	51	**2**
Simmons	10	–	45	**2**
Hooper	10	2	30	**1**
Arthurton	8	–	31	**2**

Fall of Wickets
1–**26**, 2–**84**, 3–**90**, 4–**91**, 5–**166**, 6–**184**, 7–**195**, 8–**208**

West Indies

C.B. Lambert	**c** Stewart, **b** Fraser	**22**
P.A. Wallace	**b** Fleming	**33**
B.C. Lara *	**c** A.J. Hollioake, **b** Ealham	**21**
C.L. Hooper	run out	**50**
C. Williams	**c** Knight, **b** Croft	**4**
K.L.T. Arthurton	not out	**35**
P.V. Simmons	not out	**23**
R.D. Jacobs †		
R.N. Lewis		
N.A.M. McLean		
C.E.L. Ambrose		
	b **1**, lb **16**, w **7**, nb **1**	**25**
	48.1 overs (for 5 wickets)	**213**

	O	M	R	W
Brown	5	–	32	**–**
Fraser	10	2	35	**1**
Ealham	7.1	–	41	**1**
Croft	10	3	18	**1**
Fleming	9	–	30	**1**
A.J. Hollioake	5	–	27	**–**
Hick	2	–	13	**–**

Fall of Wickets
1–**33**, 2–**71**, 3–**112**, 4–**125**, 5–**173**

Umpires: S.A. Bucknor & B. Doctrove *Man of the Match*: C.L. Hooper

West Indies won by 5 wickets

Fourth One-Day International West Indies v. England

5 April 1998 at Arnos Vale, Kingstown, St Vincent

England

N.V. Knight	c Jacobs, b Dillon	3
A.J. Stewart	c Lara, b McLean	1
B.C. Hollioake	c Jacobs, b McLean	2
G.A. Hick	b McLean	22
A.J. Hollioake *	c Hooper, b Dillon	23
R.C. Russell †	b Dillon	21
M.A. Ealham	st Jacobs, b Hooper	17
D.R. Brown	c Jacobs, b Lewis	19
M.V. Fleming	b Simmons	7
R.D.B. Croft	c Jacobs, b Simmons	12
A.R.C. Fraser	not out	12
	lb 2, w 8	10
	48.5 overs	149

	O	M	R	W
McLean	10	1	44	3
Dillon	10	–	32	3
Hooper	10	1	24	1
Simmons	9.5	–	26	2
Lewis	9	1	21	1

Fall of Wickets
1–**7**, 2–**9**, 3–**17**, 4–**33**, 5–**79**, 6–**83**, 7–**115**, 8–**120**, 9–**126**

West Indies

C.B. Lambert	c Ealham, b Croft	52
P.A. Wallace	b Fraser	4
S.C. Williams	c Knight, b Ealham	19
P.V. Simmons	lbw, b Croft	1
B.C. Lara *	b A.J. Hollioake	51
C.L. Hooper	c Fraser, b Fleming	15
R.D. Jacobs †	not out	0
K.L.T. Arthurton	not out	3
R.N. Lewis		
N.A.M. McLean		
M.V. Dillon		
	lb 2, w 1, nb 2	5
	37.4 overs (for 6 wickets)	150

	O	M	R	W
Fraser	6	–	27	1
Brown	4	–	20	–
Croft	9	2	41	2
B.C. Hollioake	4	–	18	–
Ealham	4	–	19	1
Fleming	5.4	1	11	1
A.J. Hollioake	5	–	12	1

Fall of Wickets
1–**18**, 2–**66**, 3–**67**, 4–**104**, 5–**137**, 6–**145**

Umpires: S.A. Bucknor & W. Doctrove *Man of the Match*: B.C. Lara

West Indies won by 4 wickets

Fifth One-Day International West Indies v. England

8 April 1998 at Queen's Park Oval, Port of Spain, Trinidad

West Indies

C.B. Lambert	c Stewart, b B.C. Hollioake	119
P.A. Wallace	run out	0
S.C. Williams	c Stewart, b B.C. Hollioake	27
B.C. Lara *	b Brown	93
C.L. Hooper	not out	35
L.R. Williams	lbw, b Brown	1
R.D. Jacobs †	not out	5
S. Chanderpaul		
C.M. Tuckett		
N.C. McGarrell		
M.V. Dillon		
	B 4, lb 15, w 3	22
	50 overs (for 5 wickets)	302

	O	M	R	W
Fraser	10	3	28	–
Brown	8	–	49	2
B.C. Hollioake	10	–	43	2
Croft	8	1	33	–
Ealham	5	1	41	–
Fleming	7	–	56	–
A.J. Hollioake	2	–	33	–

Fall of Wickets
1–**13**, 2–**67**, 3–**252**, 4–**266**, 5–**270**

England

N.V. Knight	run out	65
A.J. Stewart †	c Hooper, b Tuckett	12
B.C. Hollioake	run out	2
G.A. Hick	c Chanderpaul, b Tuckett	1
M.R. Ramprakash	c McGarrell, b Hooper	51
A.J. Hollioake *	b McGarrell	2
M.A. Ealham	c L.R. Williams, b Chanderpaul	26
D.R. Brown	st Jacobs, b Hooper	13
M.V. Fleming	c L.R. Williams, b S.C. Williams	10
R.D.B. Croft	not out	13
A.R.C. Fraser	run out	30
	lb 6, w 13, nb 1	20
	45.5 overs	245

	O	M	R	W
Dillon	5.5	–	41	–
Tuckett	8	–	41	2
L.R. Williams	8	–	32	–
McGarrell	10	–	46	1
Chanderpaul	5	–	23	1
S.C. Williams	4	–	30	1
Hooper	2	–	6	2
Lambert	2	–	8	–
Lara	1	–	12	–

Fall of Wickets
1–**41**, 2–**60**, 3–**71**, 4–**109**, 5–**115**, 6–**161**, 7–**186**, 8–**196**, 9–**201**

Umpires: E.G. Nicholls & Z. Macuum *Man of the Match*: C.B. Lambert

West Indies won by 57 runs

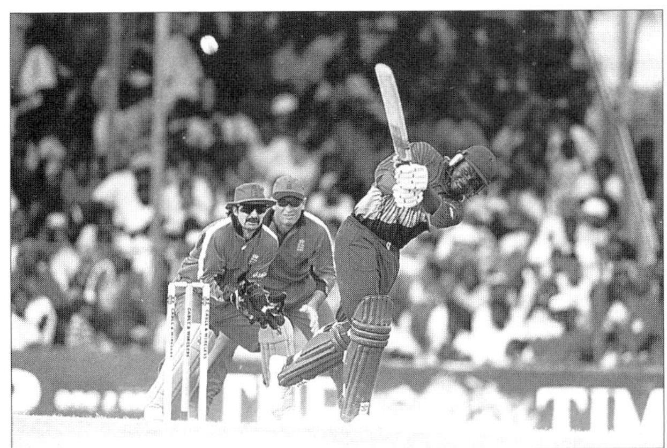

Brian Lara led West Indies with dash in both the Test and one-day series. He ended victorious in both.
Clive Mason / Allsport)

Hollioake hit 35 off 43 balls, but if his star shines brightly, it also shines briefly. After 15 overs, England had managed only 62 for the loss of Knight; by the time they reached the 24th over, they were 91 for four. Hick and Adam Hollioake were unable to blend recovery with urgency, which meant that the hitters, Fleming, Ealham and Brown, had little time in which to raise the tempo of the innings and England had to settle for a meagre 209.

Lambert blazed away at the start of the West Indian innings, and Lara kept up the momentum. Wallace was more circumspect, and Williams was becalmed, but Hooper was in majestic control until responding to a ludicrous call from Arthurton and being run out by Knight. No doubt loathe to return to the dressing room, Arthurton stayed to the end with Simmons, and victory came with 11 balls to spare.

The England one-day bubble was most comprehensively burst in the second game in St Vincent. They left out Ramprakash and brought in the left-handed Russell who kept wicket in place of Stewart. Adam Hollioake won the toss and again elected to bat first – but with even more disastrous results than on the previous day. Confronted by neither Ambrose nor Walsh, England found Dillon and McLean just as difficult. Stewart and Ben Hollioake both lasted four balls, and when Knight was caught behind off Dillon, England were 17 for three. Hick made 22 off 23 balls before being bowled by McLean, and, after 15 overs, England were a paltry 60 for four. Adam Hollioake and Russell added 46 for the fifth wicket without ever looking threatening; Dillon returned to have the first caught at mid-wicket and bowl the second behind his legs. There were brief flourishes from the one-day all-rounders, but the cause had long been lost. The England innings ended with seven balls unused and only 149 on the board.

Wallace went early, but West Indies had time and wickets to spare. Lambert hit 52 off 62 balls, and with three wickets down for 67, Lara arrived to hit seven fours in his 51 off 64 balls. He and Stuart Williams added 37 in four overs. The rest was easy, and victory came with 12.2 overs to spare. With the victory came an unassailable lead in the series. Lara took the individual award, but wicket-keeper Jacobs, with five dismissals, deserved more than a passing mention.

It was widely reported that Atherton had expressed a desire to play in the final game, the intention being to give more stability to the top order batting. But while he was not chosen, Ramprakash seemed a sensible replacement to Russell. There had been doubts about Lara's fitness, but he appeared, won the toss, and West Indies batted. They included the newcomers McGarrell, the left-arm spinner, and Tuckett, an all-rounder. England had a stroke of fortune early on. Lambert had made a flying start, but Wallace had not got off the mark when Lambert drove hard at a ball from Brown, which the bowler diverted onto the stumps with the non-striking batsman out of his ground. Stuart Williams was soon scoring freely. He hit Brown for three fours in one over, and when Ben Hollioake was introduced he hit him for a towering six. The younger Hollioake took revenge when he had Williams spectacularly caught by Stewart, one-handedly diving to his right. That marked the end of England's glee. In the next 31 overs, Lambert and Lara, the two left-handers, added 185, a West Indian record against England. Lambert, a towel guarding his neck against the scorching sun as if he were in the French Foreign Legion, continued to celebrate his recall to the West Indies side with another blistering innings. He hit two sixes and 17 fours in his 124-ball innings and savaged the bowling joyously. His running between the wickets with Lara was exemplary, and England fell apart under the cascade of strokes and the intelligence and energy of the running. Lambert was badly dropped on the boundary by Ramprakash. Adam Hollioake was hit for 19 in his first over and 14 in his second. Cricketing pyrotechnics lit up the Queen's Park Oval. Lambert was caught behind at 252, but the crowd bayed for Lara's century – only for the local hero to disappoint when he was deceived by Brown's slower ball after he had made 93 off 105 balls. He had hit ten fours in another display of regal splendour. Hooper continued the onslaught, and England faced a target of 303, which all sane followers knew was beyond them.

For some unfathomable reason, Stewart was declared not out when he was clearly run out in the first over. He did not last much longer. Ben Hollioake was run out fifth ball by McGarrell, who also ran out Knight and Fraser. The other newcomer, Tuckett, had Hick caught after a groping start, and Knight was fourth out having made his 65 off 67 balls. Ramprakash took up the challenge, but Adam Hollioake was as bemused by McGarrell as he had been by Warne. He was bowled fifth ball, and he looks neither a captain nor an international cricketer – and certainly not a combination of both. Ealham, Brown and Fleming batted with their usual flourish, and Ramprakash's 51 came off 67 balls, but the cause had long been lost.

So West Indies took the one-day series by four to one to complete the Caribbean double. They had redeemed themselves after the debacle in Pakistan, but problems had been deferred rather than answered. Lambert and Wallace had risen to the occasion splendidly, but no young batsman of talent had appeared to challenge the established players. The side was beginning to look more balanced, and Ramnarine had been a positive gain in the Test series. Walsh and Ambrose, Man of the Series, had performed nobly, but could for how much longer?

England were a side less united than we were asked to believe, and one tired of the extravagant claims and praise of Messrs Lloyd and Bennett. It would be more productive to face the truth with humility. The selection of two Englands was not a success, particularly when there is a priority search for a captain, an opening batsman and a wicket-keeper. Tactically, too, one was left confused. Was it sound to use Tufnell primarily as a defensive bowler? Is Fraser's accuracy and determination to be wasted by the profligacy of Caddick and Headley? In fairness, the loss of Gough and Cork through injury must have undermined selection, but what role did Cowan and Silverwood play on the tour? How could Adam Hollioake be selected ahead of Ramprakash? He bowls little in first-class cricket, and he is certainly not one of the six best batsmen in England. Messrs Graveney, Gooch and Gatting have much to ponder.

Considered to be the quickest of the West Indian pace bowlers, Nixon McLean was one player to show an advance during the domestic season. (Lawrence Griffiths / Allsport)

President's Cup

Without a sponsor, West Indies' first-class competition reverted to the formula of each territory meeting the other just once rather than on the home and away basis. The 15 matches were spread over a period of four months with few games being scheduled during the England tour. Those with the 'A' team in South Africa and with the under-19 side in the Youth World Cup were unavailable for the opening matches. The abandonment of the first Test affected the President's Cup itinerary and extended the season by a week.

9, 10, 11 and 12 January 1998

at Sabina Park, Kingston, Jamaica

Barbados 135 (C.A. Walsh 6 for 46, K.H. Powell 4 for 43) and 291 for 9 dec. (R.I.C. Holder 87, F.A. Rose 5 for 67, C.A. Walsh 4 for 56)

Jamaica 222 (P.I.C. Thompson 4 for 48, W.E. Reid 4 for 72) and 110 for 4

Match drawn

Jamaica 8 pts, Barbados 4 pts

at Webster Park, Anguilla

Guyana 186 (C.L. Hooper 63) and 166 for 1 (K.F. Semple 81, N.A. de Groot 54 not out)

Leeward Islands 339 for 6 dec. (S.C. Williams 63, K.L.T. Arthurton 63, J. Mitchum 57, C.M. Tuckett 54, R.D. Jacobs 50 not out, M.V. Nagamootoo 5 for 103)

Match drawn

Leeward Islands 8 pts, Guyana 4 pts

The first round of matches was hit by the weather and no play was possible on the third day in Anguilla. Reigning champions Barbados were put into bat on the relaid Sabina Park wicket and fell foul of Courtney Walsh and seamer Kirk Powell, who had done well in pre-season club tournaments. Jamaica lost their first three wickets for 15 but recovered to take first innings points. Walsh finished with match figures of 10 for 102 and took the individual award.

Guyana, too, suffered on being put in and would have been in deeper trouble but for skipper Carl Hooper's 63. Leewards batted with admirable consistency, and there was a pleasing return to form for Keith Arthurton.

15, 16, 17 and 18 January 1998

at Guaracara Park, Pointe-a-Pierre, Trinidad

Windward Islands 234 (I.R. Bishop 4 for 90) and 143 (R.B. Richardson 62 not out, I.R. Bishop 5 for 32)

Trinidad and Tobago 196 (A. Balliram 62, R.A.M. Smith 55, R.A. Marshall 4 for 46) and 182 for 4 (R.A.M. Smith 52 not out, B.C. Lara 52)

Trinidad and Tobago won by 6 wickets

Trinidad and Tobago 16 pts, Windward Islands 5 pts

16, 17, 18 and 19 January 1998
at Kensington Oval, Bridgetown, Barbados
Leeward Islands 224 (R.D. Jacobs 56, K.L.T. Arthurton 50, W.E. Reid 4 for 49) and 191 (D.R.E. Joseph 68, C.M. Tuckett 64, W.E. Reid 5 for 48)
Barbados 278 (F.L. Reifer 102, R.L. Hoyte 76 not out, K.C.G. Benjamin 4 for 71) and 139 for 2
Barbados won by 8 wickets
Barbados 16 pts, Leeward Islands 0 pts

The match at Guaracara Park marked the return to regional cricket of former Test captain Richie Richardson. He had last played, for Leeward Islands, in 1995. He failed to score in the first innings but made a battling unbeaten 62 in the second. Windwards led on the first innings when the left-arm spin of Roy Marshall brought about a Trinidad mid-innings collapse, five wickets going down for 12 runs. However, Bishop, fighting to retain his Test place, routed Windwards when they batted again, and Trinidad won early on the fourth day.

Barbados made a remarkable recovery to beat Leewards. Facing a total of 224, they were reduced to 44 for five by Ambrose and Kenny Benjamin. At 111 for six, they were still in trouble, but Floyd Reifer and Ricky Hoyte added 92. Reifer, a Test batsman against Sri Lanka in June the previous year, had suffered a dreadful tour with the 'A' side in South Africa, averaging under 11 in first-class matches, but he displayed great resolve in scoring 102. In their second innings, Leewards crashed to 33 for six before David Joseph and Carl Tuckett added 105. The stand could not avert defeat, and Barbados won before lunch on the last day. Man of the Match was veteran left-arm spinner Winston Reid, who took nine for 97.

Ridley Jacobs impressed for Leeward Islands with both his batting and wicket-keeping. He won a place in the West Indian side for the one-day internationals, in which he performed admirably.
(Clive Mason / Allsport)

22, 23, 24 and 25 January 1998
at Queen's Park Oval, Port of Spain, Trinidad
Trinidad and Tobago 125 (K.C.G. Benjamin 6 for 39) and 87 (C.M. Tuckett 4 for 17)
Leeward Islands 175 (K.L.T. Arthurton 72, I.R. Bishop 4 for 45, M.V. Dillon 4 for 51) and 38 for 0
Leeward Islands won by 10 wickets
Leeward Islands 16 pts, Trinidad and Tobago 0 pts

at Windsor Park, Roseau, Dominica
Windward Islands 211 (B.M. Watt 86 not out) and 152 (B.S. Murphy 7 for 48)
Jamaica 192 (T.O. Powell 54, V. Dumas 4 for 36) and 176 for 0 (C. Wright 95 not out, R.G. Samuels 72 not out)
Jamaica won by 10 wickets
Jamaica 16 pts, Windward Islands 5 pts

at Kensington Oval, Bridgetown, Barbados
Guyana 435 (S. Chanderpaul 115, C.B. Lambert 108, C.L. Hooper 61, W.E. Reid 5 for 100) and 99 for 4
Barbados 269 (H.R. Waldron 80, M.V. Nagamootoo 4 for 99) and 259 (P.A. Wallace 129, C.L. Hooper 4 for 61, N.C. McGarrell 4 for 66)
Guyana won by 6 wickets
Guyana 16 pts, Barbados 0 pts

The match at Port of Spain was over in two days with the visitors winning by ten wickets. Bishop and Kenny Benjamin both enhanced their chances of winning places in the Test side. Benjamin had eight for 57 in the match, but the outstanding performance came from born-again Keith Arthurton who played an outstanding innings of 72 in the most difficult of circumstances. He was given fine support by wicket-keeper Ridley Jacobs, like Arthurton a left-hander, whose 31 was the second highest score in a match dominated by bowlers.

Walsh and Rose reduced Windwards to 18 for four, but the innings gained substance from Watt's unbeaten 86. He and Dumas put on 91 for the eighth wicket. Jamaica struggled in reply and trailed by 19 on the first innings, but the game underwent a remarkable transformation. Tall leg-spinner Brian Murphy produced the best bowling performance of his career, taking seven for 48 in 20.5 overs, and Jamaica faced a target of 172. Carl Wright, who had been reserve for the West Indies under-19 side, playing his second first-class match, hit 95, and he and Robert Samuels scored 176 in 60.2 overs to win the match in three days.

Clayton Lambert launched a fierce attack on the Barbados bowling as Guyana reached 291 for four on the opening day in Bridgetown. Chanderpaul became the second centurion on the Friday, and the leg-breaks of Mahendra Nagamootoo were mainly responsible for Barbados suffering the indignity of having to follow on. Skipper Philo Wallace played a fine innings and batted into the final day in an attempt to save his side, but he received little support and Guyana took maximum points.

19, 20, 21 and 22 February 1998
at Chedwin Park, St Catherine, Jamaica
Trinidad and Tobago 288 (D. Ganga 68, S. Ragoonath 61, P.V. Simmons 51 not out) and 274 for 4 (R.A.M. Smith 108 not out, S. Ragoonath 74)
Jamaica 455 for 7 dec. (J.C. Adams 203 not out, L.V. Garrick 73)
Match drawn
Jamaica 8 pts, Trinidad and Tobago 4 pts

20, 21, 22 and 23 February 1998
at Tanteen Recreation Ground, Grenada
Windward Islands 319 (C.A. Davis 54, N.A.M. McLean 52, O.D. Gibson 4 for 80) and 270 (J.R. Murray 86, O.D. Gibson 4 for 76, W.E. Reid 4 for 92)
Barbados 435 for 8 dec. (A.F.G. Griffith 186, P.A. Wallace 87) and 155 for 3 (P.A. Wallace 79 not out)
Barbados won by 7 wickets
Barbados 16 pts, Windward Islands 0 pts

In his eighth season with Trinidad, Richard Smith hit his maiden first-class century. It was instrumental in saving his side from defeat against Jamaica for whom Jimmy Adams hit an unbeaten 203. Coupled with his good form for the 'A' side in South Africa, this innings enabled Adams to regain his place in the Test side.

The Tanteen Recreation Ground provided one of the few good pitches of the season, and batsmen seized their opportunity. Windwards' strength was in the tail, the last three wickets realising 153 runs. In contrast, Barbados began positively with Wallace and Griffith adding 118 for the second wicket. Adrian Griffith went on to make 186, a vitally important innings. The tall left-hander had toured Australia with the West Indian side in 1996–97, but he had a miserable time with the bat. His poor form continued into domestic cricket in 1997, so much so that he lost his place in the Barbados side. His early form in the President's Cup had suggested no return of confidence, and his 186 came as a relief to all. It also set up a victory for Barbados who, with one game remaining, led Jamaica by four points. Jamaica had two matches to play.

A spinner of quality in the West Indian Test team? Dinanath Ramnarine bowled well for Trinidad and played a significant part in West Indies winning the two Tests in which he appeared.
(David Munden / Sportsline)

5, 6, 7 and 8 March 1998
at Webster Park, Anguilla
Windward Islands 151 (K.C.G. Benjamin 4 for 39) and 118
Leeward Islands 257 (D.R.E. Joseph 65, K.L.T. Arthurton 54, A. Adams 53, R.N. Lewis 4 for 66, N.A.M. McLean 4 for 67) and 8 for 0
Leeward Islands won by 10 wickets
Leeward Islands 16 pts, Windward Islands 0 pts

at Enmore Recreation Ground, Guyana
Guyana 450 for 8 dec. (S. Chanderpaul 111, C.B. Lambert

106, C.L. Hooper 104) and 64 for 1
Trinidad & Tobago 211 (S. Ragoonath, N.C. McGarrell 5 for 61) and 282 (S. Ragoonath 98, P.V. Simmons 52, N.C. McGarrell 5 for 53)
Guyana won by 21 runs
Guyana 16 pts, Trinidad Tobago 0 pts

The match in Webster Park was over in two days. Bowlers were always on top, and a third wicket stand of 81 between Adams and Arthurton followed by a good knock from Dawnley Joseph gave Leewards enough substance in their batting to take a commanding first innings advantage. They never relinquished their hold on the game.

Astute captaincy by Carl Hooper played a big part in Guyana's victory over Trinidad after a limited first day. Lambert and de Groot scored 139 for Guyana's first wicket, with Lambert again in whirlwind mood, but it was a fifth wicket stand of 187 between Chanderpaul and Hooper which took the game out of Trinidad's reach. McGarrell, one of the season's outstanding successes, and Nagamootoo bowled the visitors out for 211, but Harper did not enforce the follow on. Guyana batted for 13 overs, and Harper then declared, leaving his bowlers just over a day in which to win the match. A fourth wicket stand of 101 between Ragoonath and skipper Simmons took Trinidad to 221, but their last seven wickets went down for 62 runs. McGarrell finished with match figures of 10 for 114.

11, 12, 13 and 14 April 1998

at Guaracara Park, Pointe-a-Pierre, Trinidad
Barbados 285 (S.L. Campbell 65) and 254 (P.A. Wallace 61, D. Ramnarine 5 for 57)
Trinidad & Tobago 332 (D. Ganga 138, R.M. Smith 50, V.C. Drakes 5 for 78) and 208 for 9 (H.R. Bryan 5 for 51)
Trinidad & Tobago won by 1 wicket
Trinidad & Tobago 16 pts, Barbados 0 pts

at Bourda, Guyana
Jamaica 148 and 318 for 4 dec. (J.C. Adams 108 not out, T.O. Powell 100 not out, W.W. Hinds 55)
Guyana 114 (B.S. Murphy 5 for 45) and 335 for 6 (S. Chanderpaul 89, C.B. Lambert 64, C.L. Hooper 62, N.A. de Groot 52, L.R. Williams 5 for 105)
Match drawn
Jamaica 8 pts, Guyana 4 pts

Trinidad gained the narrowest of victories over Barbados. Ganga's century had given them first innings advantage after three wickets had fallen for 33, and the task of scoring 208 in more than a day seemed an easy one. When the ninth wicket fell they were still two short of their target, but last man Ramnarine scored the necessary runs. The defeat ended Barbados's hopes of winning the cup.

Three and three quarter hours were lost on the opening day in Bourda because of a damp pitch. Leg-spinner Brian Murphy emphasised a successful season when he bowled Jamaica to a first innings lead, and Jimmy Adams and Tony Powell then shared an unbroken fifth wicket partnership of 202. Adams's declaration left Guyana a target of 353 at nearly five runs an over. They made a valiant challenge but fell 18 short of their target.

17, 18, 19 and 20 April 1998

at Arnos Vale, St Vincent
Windward Islands 202 (B.M. Watt 72, J.R. Murray 54) and 54 (N.C. McGarrell 4 for 15)
Guyana 307 (S. Chanderpaul 125, V. Dumas 4 for 41)
Guyana won by an innings and 51 runs
Guyana 16 pts, Windward Islands 0 pts

at Grove Park, Nevis
Jamaica 142 (W.K.L. Quinn 5 for 38) and 323 (J.C. Adams 112, G.A. Breese 62, K.C.G. Benjamin 4 for 88)
Leeward Islands 306 (K.L.T. Arthurton 93, R.D. Jacobs 76, D.R.E. Joseph 51, G.R. Breese 5 for 82) and 160 for 1 (S.C. Williams 108 not out)
Leeward Islands won by 9 wickets
Leeward Islands 16 pts, Jamaica 0 pts

Victories for both Guyana and Leeward Islands meant that they would finish level on points and share the championship with Leewards claiming the advantage as they had led Guyana on the first innings in their opening fixture. McGarrell completed a fine season as he played the major part in bowling Windwards out for 54, the lowest score of the season, in their second innings. Windwards' weakness was emphasised in that play did not begin until after lunch on the second day, and there was no play on the third. Skipper Stuart Williams took the individual honours for Leewards with a sparkling century in 43 overs against Jamaica. He dominated an opening stand of 157 with Adams.

President's Cup Final Table

	P	W	L	D	Pts
Leeward Islands	5	3	1	1	56
Guyana	5	3	–	2	56
Jamaica	5	1	1	3	40
Barbados	5	2	2	1	36
Trinidad & Tobago	5	2	2	1	36
Windward Islands	5	–	5	–	10

First-Class Averages

Batting

	M	Inns	NOs	Runs	HS	Av	100s	50s
M.R Ramprakash	5	8	2	389	154	64.83	1	2
R.I.C. Holder	8	12	2	584	183	58.40	2	1
C.L Hooper	10	14	3	620	108*	56.36	2	4
K.L.T Arthurton	5	6	–	332	93	55.33		5
G.P. Thorpe	9	15	4	603	103	54.81	1	4
P.A. Wallace	8	15	2	710	129	54.61	1	6
T.O. Powell	5	8	1	351	100*	50.14	1	2
C.B. Lambert	8	14	2	589	108	49.08	3	2
J.C. Adams	9	14	2	589	203*	49.08	3	1
S. Canderpaul	12	18	1	803	125	47.23	4	1
R.L. Hoyte	5	6	1	233	76*	46.60		2
R.D. Jacobs	5	6	1	230	76	46.00		3
A. Adams	2	4	1	133	53	44.33		1
D. Ganga	3	6	–	264	138	44.00	1	1
B.C. Lara	9	14	1	536	93	41.23		4
F.L. Reifer	5	7	1	244	102	40.66	1	1
R.A.M. Smith	5	10	2	318	108*	39.75	1	3
A.J. Stewart	9	15	1	538	83	38.42		5
N. Hussain	10	17	3	529	159	37.78	2	1
O.D. Gibson	3	4	1	106	45	35.33		
S. Ragoonath	5	10	–	346	98	34.60		4
D.R.E. Joseph	5	6	–	196	68	32.66		3
A.F.G. Griffith	6	12	1	358	186	32.54	1	
J.R. Murray	6	11	1	325	86	32.50		2
B.S. Murphy	6	8	3	162	54*	32.40		1
S.C. Willians	8	13	2	352	108*	32.00	1	2
H.R. Waldron	2	4	–	128	80	32.00		1
T.O. Rollock	4	6	1	160	40	32.00		
C.M. Tuckett	5	6	1	153	64	30.60		2
A.J. Hollioake	6	6	–	182	48	30.33		
N.A. de Groot	6	11	1	292	54*	29.20		2
C.O. Browne	2	4	–	114	35	28.50		
R.B. Richardson	8	1	1	198	62*	28.28		1
P.V. Simmons	5	10	1	254	52	28.22		2
K.F. Semple	6	10	1	250	81	27.77		2
B.M. Watt	5	10	1	238	86*	26.44		2
L.R. Williams	5	7	2	129	67*	25.80		1
C.Wright	5	9	1	201	95*	25.12		1
A. Balliram	4	7	–	171	62	24.42		1
V. Nagamootoo	5	7	1	140	55	23.33		1
S.L.campbell	10	18	1	391	65	23.00		1
L.A. Harrigan	4	7	2	112	28	22.40		
T.M. Dowlin	4	7	2	105	48	21.00		
M.A. Butcher	7	12	1	227	79	20.63		1
M.A. Atherton	9	16	–	312	64	19.50		1
A.N. Coley	6	8	1	135	37	19.28		
L.V. Garrick	5	8	–	154	73	19.25		1
N.A.M. McLean	9	13	2	205	52	18.63		1
C.A. Davis	5	10	2	148	54	18.50		1
I.R. Bishop	8	11	3	138	44*	17.25		
R.G. Samuels	5	9	1	135	72*	16.87		1
W.W. Hinds	5	8	–	133	55	16.62		1
G.R. Breese	5	8	–	128	42	16.00		
R.C. Russell	9	15	3	187	32*	15.58		
R.N. Lewis	5	3	–	139	46	15.44		
R.A. Marshall	5	10	–	154	42	15.40		
J.P. Crawley	6	8	–	121	41	15.12		
D. Williams	9	15	2	181	65	13.92		1
V. Dumas	4	8	–	101	31	12.62		
C.E.L. Ambrose	9	11	2	113	31	12.55		

(Qualification – 100 runs, average 10.00)

Bowling

	Overs	Mds	Runs	Wks	Best	Av	10/m	5/inn
N.C. McGarrell	302.4	113	505	34	7/71	14.85	1	4
C.E.L. Ambrose	273.5	80	597	38	5/25	15.71		2
W.K.L. Quinn	100.2	18	289	16	5/38	18.06		1
A.R.C. Fraser	232.2	60	617	32	8/53	19.28	1	3
C.M. Tuckett	68.1	20	193	10	4/17	19.30		
R.D.B. Croft	157.4	48	354	18	6/50	19.66	1	2
K.C.G. Benjamin	205.2	44	586	29	6/390	20.20		1
D.W. Headley	200.2	37	592	28	5/32	21.14		1
W.E Reid	340	135	664	31	5/48	21.41		2
D. Ramnarine	249.3	73	548	25	5/57	21.92		1
C.A. Walsh	364.4	89	817	36	6/46	22.69	1	1
R.D. King	103.2	30	303	13	3/45	23.30		
C.L. Hooper	280.5	80	540	23	5/80	23.47		1
O.D. Gibson	99.4	16	325	13	4/76	25.00		
F.A. Rose	117.3	25	344	13	5/67	26.46		1
B.S. Murphy	221.1	50	597	21	7/48	28.42		2
A.R Caddick	212	47	690	23	5/67	30.00		1
M.V. Nagamootoo	237.4	50	662	22	5/103	30.09		1
C.E.L. Stuart	128.2	25	401	13	3/51	30.84		
P.I.C. Thompson	130	26	444	14	4/48	31.71		
P.C.R. Tufnell	333.5	99	706	22	5/42	32.09		1
L.R. Williams	169	41	481	14	5/105	34.35		1
I.R. Bishop	194.5	23	656	19	5/32	34.52		1
M.V. Dillon	124.3	22	443	12	4/51	36.91		
N.A.M. McLean	226.3	40	657	17	4/67	38.64		
R.A. Marshall	153.2	33	410	10	4/46	41.00		
R.N. Lewis	134.3	26	415	10	4/66	41.50		

(Qualification – 10 wickets)
(for convenience, the averages of members of the Emgland party are included in the above)

Leading Fielders

27 – D. Williams; 25 – R.C. Russell (ct 23 / st 2); 21 – R.D. Jacobs (ct 20 / st 1); 18 – B.C. Lara; 15 – R.L. Hoyte (ct 13 / st 2); 14 – A.N. Coley (ct 13 / st 1); 12 – M.V. Nagamootoo(ct 11 / st 1); 10 – J.R. Murray (ct 8 / st 2), M.A. Atherton, S. Chanderpaul and A.J. Stewart; 9 – S.L. Campbell, C.L. Hooper, C.B. Lambert, C. Wright and G.P. Thorpe; 8 – A.F.G. Griffith and C.A. Walsh

Kenya

The victory over West Indies in the World Cup and success in the ICC Trophy, where Kenya were ranked second only to Bangladesh among the Associate Member countries, has excited wide interest in cricket throughout the African nation. Building upon the popularity of the quadrangular tournament of 1996–97, the Kenyan Cricket Association arranged a more ambitious programme for 1997–98.

Andy Flower, Zimbabwe wicket-keeper batsman, who was Man of the Triangular Series.
(Andrew Cornaga / Sportsline)

New Zealand Tour
Triangular Tournament – Kenya, Zimbabwe and Bangladesh
England 'A' Tour

Prior to their trip to Zimbabwe, the New Zealand side visited Kenya and engaged in two one-day internationals and a three-day game. None of these matches was recognised as having official or first-class status.

The games against the New Zealanders were followed by a triangular tournament involving the host nation, Zimbabwe and Bangladesh, and the England 'A' side were scheduled to play in Kenya in January.

New Zealand Tour

New Zealand proved a little too strong for a Kenyan side that, for various reasons, was deprived of the services of three of its leading players – skipper Maurice Odumbe, Dipak Chudasama and Sandip Gupta. Steve Tikolo gave a brilliant display in the three-day game, reaching 125 off 92 balls and hitting three sixes and 20 fours. He was the first Kenyan to score a century against a Test-playing nation. Fleming's declaration sportingly asked Kenya to make 275 in 255 minutes, but the task proved beyond the home side once Tikolo had been dismissed for 44. The limited-over matches saw New Zealand very much on top. In the first match, Cairns played an innings of 153, which included 13 sixes, and his last 105 runs came off 29 deliveries. The last five overs of the New Zealand innings produced 94 runs. Kenya responded bravely and Kennedy Otieno hit his side's first century in a one-day representative match. Spearman, Cairns and Vettori were rested from the second match, which New Zealand won by seven wickets with 11.4 overs to spare.

4, 5 and 6 September 1997
at Nairobi Gymkhana, Nairobi
New Zealand 280 for 6 dec. (C.M. Spearman 103, S.P. Fleming 61 not out) and 244 for 4 (M.J. Horne 64, C.L. Cairns 63, B.A. Pocock 63)
Kenya 250 (S.Tikolo 125) and 207 for 5 (A. Jadhar 62, P.J. Wiseman 4 for 64)
Match drawn

8 September 1997
at Nairobi Gymkhana, Nairobi
New Zealand 363 for 6 (C.L. Cairns 153, C.M. Spearman 70, S.P. Fleming 63)
Kenya 246 for 8 (K. Otieno 105)
New Zealand won by 117 runs

11 September 1997
at Agha Khan Club, Nairobi
Kenya 206 for 8 (A.Vadher 75 not out)
New Zealand 210 for 3 (B.A. Pocock 83 not out)
New Zealand won by 7 wickets

Zimbabwe won a major tournament for the first time when they triumphed over Kenya and Bangladesh in the President's Cup in Nairobi. They were led to victory by Alistair Campbell. (Sportsline)

Triangular Tournament

Kenya, Zimbabwe and Bangladesh

The President's Cup followed the expected pattern and Zimbabwe met the host nation in the final. Bangladesh, who had defeated Kenya in the ICC Trophy Final, continued the disappointing form they had shown since that success. They were shattered in the first match in the tournament when Kennedy Otieno and Dipak Chudasama hit Kenya's first centuries in an official limited-over international and established a world record with an opening stand of 225 (the previous record of 212 was held by Boon and Marsh for Australia against India in 1986–87). Kenya made their highest score in a one-day international after being put in to bat, and slow left-arm spinner Asif Karim completed a fine day for the home side when he returned his best bowling figures in a one-day international.

Leg-spinner Huckle made his one-day international debut for Zimbabwe against Bangladesh in the second match, but it was the openers who again dominated the game. The Flower brothers began with a partnership of 161, and a target of 306 was well beyond the capabilities of the Bangladesh batsmen.

Zimbabwe revealed their strength in the third match, which was interrupted by rain. Kenya batted well to score

250 in their 50 overs. Zimbabwe were 206 for four after 43.1 overs when rain meant their target was revised to 242 off 47 overs. Undeterred, Campbell and Wishart hit 38 runs off 20 deliveries to win the match.

Bangladesh were completely overwhelmed by Zimbabwe when the teams met for a second time. Bryan Strang took six for 20 in his ten-over quota. This win confirmed that Zimbabwe would be in the final, and when Kenya crushed Bangladesh the following day they, too, were confirmed as finalists. The sixth match, between Kenya and Zimbabwe, now had no relevance, but it produced another world record as Thomas Odoyo and Tony Suji shared a stand of 119 for Kenya's seventh wicket. Zimbabwe still won with ease, but Kenya had the consolation of two world records in the competition, evidence of the great advances that cricket was making in the country.

Rain disturbed both finals and there were revised targets. The Flower brothers put on 154 for the first wicket in the first match, and Kenya, chasing a revised target of 255 in 40 overs, could manage only 172 for seven. In the second final, Grant Flower and Gavin Rennie added 150 for the second wicket. Kenya were in dreadful trouble at 71 for seven before Hitesh Modi and Asif Karim saved blushes with a century stand. Andy Flower was named Man of the Series, but Kennedy Otieno, with 356 runs and an average of 71.20, also earned much deserved praise.

Kennedy Otieno, Kenyan opening batsman, hit 144 against Bangladesh and shared a record opening partnership of 225 with Dipak Chudasama. Kennedy Otieno's 144 was the highest ever made by a Kenyan in a one-day international, and he and Chudasama made the first centuries recorded for Kenya in an official one-day international.
(Graham Chadwick / Allsport)

Match One – Kenya v. Bangladesh

10 October 1997 at Nairobi Gymkhana Club

Kenya

D. Chudasama	c and b Hasibul Hussain	122
K. Otieno †	b Hasibul Hussain	144
S. Tikolo *	b Mohammad Rafique	32
M. Odumbe	not out	15
T. Odoyo	not out	18
Asif Karim		
A. Vadher		
H.S. Modi		
Mohammad Sheikh		
Rajab Ali		
T. Suji		
	b 1, lb 3, w 12	16
	50 overs (for 3 wickets)	347

	O	M	R	W
Saiful Islam	6.3	–	35	–
Hasibul Hussain	10	1	68	2
Athar Ali	4	–	29	–
Sheikh Salahuddin	10	–	80	–
Mohammad Rafique	10	–	71	1
Minhajul Arfeen	4	–	24	–
Akram Khan	3.3	–	22	–
Aminul Islam	2	–	14	–

Fall of Wickets
1–**225**, 2–**309**, 3–**316**

Bangladesh

Athar Ali	c and b Asif Karim	61
Shahriar Hussain	b Rajab Al	14
Jahangir Aslam	b Asif Karim	3
Aminul Islam	c Tikolo, b Asif Karim	1
Akram Khan *	lbw, b Asif Karim	37
Minhajul Arfeen	b Asif Karim	16
Mohammad Rafique	c and b Tikolo	19
Khalid Masud †	b Tikolo	1
Hasibul Hussain	c Otieno, b Mohammad Sheikh	21
Sheikh Salahuddin	not out	4
Saiful Islam	absent hurt	–
	b 4, lb 7, w 7, nb 2	20
	43.4 overs	197

	O	M	R	W
Suji	5	–	35	–
Rajab Ali	7	1	20	1
Asif Karim	10	2	33	5
Odumbe	7	–	37	–
Tikolo	6	–	31	2
Mohammad Sheikh	4.4	1	12	1
Modi	1	1	0	–
Odoyo	3	–	18	–

Fall of Wickets
1–**55**, 2–**90**, 3–**100**, 4–**123**, 5–**129**, 6–**163**, 7–**166**, 8–**176**, 9–**197**

Umpires: Salim Badar & R.E. Koertzen *Man of the Match*: K. Otieno

Kenya won by 150 runs

Match Two – Zimbabwe v. Bangladesh

11 October 1997 at Nairobi Gymkhana Club

Zimbabwe

G.W. Flower	c and b Aminul Islam	79
A. Flower †	c Akram Khan, b Aminul Islam	81
C.N. Evans	c Khalid Masud, b Aminul Islam	0
G.J. Whittall	not out	79
A.D.R. Campbell *	b Mohammad Rafique	29
G.J. Rennie	not out	17
C.B. Wishart		
P.A. Strang		
A.G. Huckle		
A.R. Whittall		
E. Matambanadzo		
	b 4, lb 4, w 8, nb 4	20
	50 overs (for 4 wickets)	305

	O	M	R	W
Hasibul Hussain	9	–	60	–
Shafiuddin	9	–	50	–
Mafizur Rahman	2	–	19	–
Athar Ali	6	–	38	–
Minhajul Arfeen	4	–	25	–
Mohammad Rafique	10	–	48	1
Aminul Islam	10	–	57	3

Fall of Wickets
1–161, 2–161, 3–188, 4–265

Bangladesh

Athar Ali	run out	32
Shahriar Hussain	c Evans, b Matambanadzo	10
Hasibul Bashar	c A.R. Whittall, b G.W. Flower	70
Aminul Islam	c Campbell, b Evans	16
Akram Khan *	c Rennie, b G.W. Flower	59
Minhajul Arfeen	run out	16
Mohammad Rafique	c G.J. Whittall, b A.R. Whittall	1
Khalid Masud †	c Evans, b P.A. Strang	6
Mafizur Rahman	run out	16
Hasibul Hussain	c G.W. Flower, b P.A. Strang	4
Shafiuddin	not out	0
	b 1, lb 5, w 15, nb 6	27
	47.1 overs	257

	O	M	R	W
Matamnandanzo	5	–	24	1
G.J. Whittall	5	–	38	–
P.A. Strang	9.1	1	32	2
A.R. Whittall	10	–	62	1
Evans	5	–	30	1
Huckle	6	–	35	–
G.W. Flower	7	–	30	2

Fall of Wickets
1–35, 2–72, 3–96, 4–183, 5–221, 6–224, 7–231, 8–242, 9–257

Umpires: M.J. Kitchen & R.E. Koertzen *Man of the Match*: G.W. Flower

Zimbabwe won by 48 runs

Match Three – Kenya v. Zimbabwe

12 October 1997 at Nairobi Gymkhana Club

Kenya

D. Chudasama	b G.J. Whittall	31
K. Otieno †	c Evans, b A.R. Whittall	87
S. Tikolo *	c Evans, b P.A. Strang	17
M. Odumbe	c B.C. Strang, b G.W. Flower	23
H. Modi	c Wishart, b B.C. Strang	31
T. Odoyo	b P.A. Strang	4
Asif Karim	run out	10
Mohammad Sheikh	c A.R. Whittall, b P.A. Strang	4
A. Vadher	not out	13
M. Owiti	not out	2
Rajab Ali		
	b 1, lb 12, w 12, nb 2	27
	50 overs for 8 wickets	249

	O	M	R	W
B.C. Strang	9	–	35	1
A.R. Whittall	10	–	44	1
G.J. Whittall	4	1	13	1
P.A. Strang	10	1	38	3
Evans	5	–	38	–
G.W. Flower	7	–	40	1
Huckle	5	–	28	–

Fall of Wickets
1–51, 2–95, 3–149, 4–197, 5–216, 6–216, 7–224, 8–242

Zimbabwe

G.W. Flower	c Modi, b Owiti	7
A. Flower †	c Otieno, b Odumbe	72
G.J. Rennie	run out	1
G.J. Whittall	c Mohammad Sheikh, b Odoyo	83
A.D.R. Campbell *	not out	47
C.B. Wishart	not out	18
C.N. Evans		
P.A. Strang		
A.G. Huckle		
A.R. Whittall		
B.C. Strang		
	b 3, lb 6, w 3, nb 4	16
	46.3 overs (for 4 wickets)	244

	O	M	R	W
Owiti	8	2	28	1
Rajab Ali	4	–	22	–
Odoyo	10	–	51	1
Asif Karim	7	–	41	–
Odumbe	8.3	1	39	1
Tikolo	5	–	34	–
Mohammad Sheikh	4	–	20	–

Fall of Wickets
1–12, 2–30, 3–162, 4–180

Umpires: M.J. Kitchen & Salim Badar *Man of the Match*: G.J. Whittall

Zimbabwe won on faster scoring rate

Match Four – Zimbabwe v. Bangladesh

14 October 1997 at Agha Khan Club, Nairobi

Zimbabwe

G.W. Flower	**c** Khalid Masud, **b** Shafiuddin	**15**
A. Flower †	**c** Shahriar, **b** Sheikh Salahuddin	**70**
C.N. Evans	**c** Khalid Masud, **b** Shafiuddin	**1**
G.J. Whittall	lbw, **b** Mohammad Rafique	**52**
A.D.R. Campbell *	**b** Hasibul Hussain	**40**
G.J. Rennie	**c** Khalid, **b** Mohammad Rafique	**15**
C.B. Wishart	**c** Khalid, **b** Hasibul Hussain	**30**
P.A. Strang	**b** Shafiuddin	**33**
B.C. Strang	run out	**3**
A.G. Huckle	run out	**1**
M. Mbangwa	not out	**0**
	lb **9**, w **9**, nb **6**	**24**
	50 overs	**284**

	O	M	R	W
Hasibul Hussain	10	1	63	**2**
Shafiuddin	10	1	42	**3**
Athar Ali	3	–	19	**–**
Akram Khan	3	–	23	**–**
Sheikh Salahuddin	8	–	37	**1**
Mohammad Rafique	10	–	65	**2**
Habibul Bashar	6	–	26	**–**

Fall of Wickets
1–**37**, 2–**55**, 3–**150**, 4–**160**, 5–**186**, 6–**237**, 7–**257**, 8–**275**, 9–**284**

Bangladesh

Athar Ali	**b** B.C. Strang	**9**
Shahriar Hussain	**c** P.A. Strang, **b** B.C. Strang	**0**
Habibul Bashar	**c** A. Flower, **b** B.C. Strang	**2**
Minhajul Arfeen	**c** A. Flower, **b** P.A. Strang	**18**
Jahangir Alam	lbw, **b** B.C. Strang	**1**
Akram Khan *	**c** Wishart, **b** B.C. Strang	**11**
Khalid Masud †	lbw, **b** B.C. Strang	**0**
Mohammad Rafique	lbw, **b** Huckle	**2**
Sheikh Salahuddin	not out	**6**
Hasibul Hussain	**c** Rennie, **b** Huckle	**16**
Shafiuddin	**b** P.A. Strang	**11**
	b **4**, lb **4**, w **6**, nb **2**	**16**
	33.3 overs	**92**

	O	M	R	W
B.C. Strang	10	2	20	**6**
Mbangwa	7	–	15	**–**
P.A. Strang	9.3	1	22	**2**
Huckle	7	–	27	**2**

Fall of Wickets
1–**3**, 2–**14**, 3–**20**, 4–**22**, 5–**38**, 6–**38**, 7–**53**, 8–**57**, 9–**77**

Umpires: R.E. Koertzen & Salim Badar *Man of the Match*: B.C. Strang

Zimbabwe won by 192 runs

Match Five – Kenya v. Bangladesh

15 October 1997 at Agha Khan Club, Nairobi

Bangladesh

Athar Ali	**c** Otieno, **b** Owiti	**0**
Mohammad Rafique	**c** Modi, **b** Owiti	**1**
Habibul Bashar	**b** Suji	**4**
Shahriar Hussain	**c** Tikolo, **b** Odoyo	**16**
Akram Khan *	**c** Odoyo, **b** Owiti	**7**
Minhajul Arfeen	**c** Odoyo, **b** Owiti	**5**
Khalid Masud †	**c** Vadher, **b** Asif Karim	**12**
Mafizur Rahman	**c** Mohammad Sheikh, **b** Asif	**16**
Sheikh Salahuddin	hit wkt., **b** Mohammad Sheikh	**12**
Hasibul Hussain	**c** Vadher, **b** Odumbe	**8**
Shafiuddin	not out	**0**
	lb **2**, w **10**, nb **7**	**19**
	41.2 overs	**100**

	O	M	R	W
Owiti	10	1	24	**4**
Suji	6	–	19	**1**
Odoyo	9	2	15	**1**
Asif Karim	9	1	21	**2**
Odumbe	5.2	1	16	**1**
Mohammad Sheikh	2	–	3	**1**

Fall of Wickets
1–**1**, 2–**9**, 3–**10**, 4–**28**, 5–**40**, 6–**51**, 7–**63**, 8–**88**, 9–**100**

Kenya

D. Chudasama	**c** Shahriar, **b** Hasibul Hussain	**4**
K. Otieno †	not out	**42**
S. Tikolo	**b** Hasibul Hussain	**0**
A. Vadher	not out	**42**
H.S. Modi		
M. Odumbe		
T. Odoyo		
Asif Karim *		
Mohammad Sheikh		
M. Owiti		
T. Suji		
	lb **2**, w **8**, nb **4**	**14**
	17 overs (for 2 wickets)	**102**

	O	M	R	W
Hasibul Hussain	6	–	54	**2**
Safiuddin	4	–	18	**–**
Mohammad Rafique	4	–	15	**–**
Sheikh Salahuddin	2	–	12	**–**
Mafizur Rahman	1	–	1	**–**

Fall of Wickets
1–**11**, 2–**11**

Umpires: M.J. Kitchen & Salim Badar *Man of the Match*: M. Owiti

Kenya won by 8 wickets

Match Six – Kenya v. Zimbabwe

16 October 1997 at Agha Khan Club, Nairobi

Kenya

D. Chudasama	c A. Flower, b Mbangwa	5
K. Otieno †	c Rennie, b Mbangwa	34
S. Tikolo	c Evans, b B.C. Strang	6
A. Vadher	c A. Flower, b G.J. Whittall	9
M. Odumbe	c G.J. Whittall, b Evans	2
H.S. Modi	lbw, b G.J. Whittall	1
T. Odoyo	c Rennie, b B.C. Strang	41
T. Suji	c and b G.J. Whittall	67
Asif Karim *	c A. Flower, b A.R. Whittall	5
M. Owiti	not out	9
Mohammad Sheikh	not out	5
	b 4, lb 3, w 10, nb 6	23
	50 overs (for 9 wickets)	207

	O	M	R	W
B.C. Strang	10	1	48	2
Mbangwa	8	3	24	2
G.J. Whittall	10	1	43	3
Evans	2	1	3	1
P.A. Strang	8	1	18	–
A.R. Whittall	8	–	41	1
G.W. Flower	4	–	23	–

Fall of Wickets
1–**22**, 2–**35**, 3–**64**, 4–**64**, 5–**68**, 6–**68**, 7–**187**, 8–**188**, 9–**200**

Zimbabwe

G.W. Flower	lbw, b Mohammad Sheikh	71
A. Flower †	c sub (J. Anagara), b Tikolo	66
G.J. Rennie	c Odoyo, b Asif Karim	27
G.J. Whittall	not out	20
A.D.R. Campbell *	not out	5
C.N. Evans		
C.B. Wishart		
P.A. Strang		
B.C. Strang		
A.R. Whittall		
M. Mbangwa		
	b 7, lb 5, w 5, nb 4	21
	41.2 overs (for 3 wickets)	210

	O	M	R	W
Owiti	5	–	22	–
Suji	2	–	9	–
Odoyo	6	–	38	–
Asif Karim	10	–	39	1
Odumbe	4	–	19	–
Tikolo	4.2	–	29	1
Mohammad Sheikh	10	–	42	1

Fall of Wickets
1–**124**, 2–**170**, 3–**200**

Umpires: M.J. Kitchen & Salim Badar *Man of the Match:* A. Flower

Zimbabwe won by 7 wickets

President's Cup First Final – Kenya v. Zimbabwe

18 October 1997 at Nairobi Gymkhana Ground

Zimbabwe

G.W. Flower	b Tikolo	69
A. Flower †	st Otieno, b Mohammad Sheikh	79
G.J. Rennie	c Vadher, b Tikolo	13
G.J. Whittall	c Owiti, b Tikolo	17
A.D.R. Campbell *	c Owiti, b Odumbe	51
C.B. Wishart	c Owiti, b Odumbe	18
C.N. Evans	b Odoyo	9
P.A. Strang	not out	10
B.C. Strang	b Odoyo	3
A.R. Whittall	not out	2
A.G. Huckle		
	lb 4, w 3, nb 3	10
	50 overs (for 8 wickets)	281

	O	M	R	W
Owiti	8	–	36	–
Odumbe	6	–	48	2
Suji	7	–	32	–
Asif Karim	3	–	22	–
Odoyo	6	–	44	2
Tikolo	10	–	41	3
Mohammad Sheikh	10	–	54	1

Fall of Wickets
1–**154**, 2–**154**, 3–**179**, 4–**193**, 5–**246**, 6–**262**, 7–**268**, 8–**279**

Kenya

D. Chudasama	b B.C. Strang	2
K. Otieno †	b G.J. Whittall	34
S. Tikolo	run out	28
M. Odumbe	c A.R. Whittall, b G.W. Flower	67
A. Vadher	b P.A. Strang	5
H.S. Modi	st A. Flower, b G.J. Whittall	6
T. Odoyo	c A. Flower, b G.W. Flower	18
T. Suji	not out	3
M. Owiti	not out	0
Asif Karim *		
Mohammad Sheikh		
	b 1, lb 3, w 2, nb 3	9
	40 overs (for 7 wickets)	172

	O	M	R	W
B.C. Strang	8	2	35	1
A.R. Whittall	7	1	22	–
P.A. Strang	8	–	29	1
Huckle	5	1	18	–
Evans	2	–	18	–
G.W. Flower	2	–	6	2
G.J. Whittall	8	–	40	2

Fall of Wickets
1–**3**, 2–**57**, 3–**83**, 4–**104**, 5–**127**, 6–**165**, 7–**172**

Umpires: M.J. Kitchen & R.E. Koertzen *Man of the Match:* G.W. Flower

Zimbabwe won on faster scoring rate

President's Cup Second Final – Kenya v. Zimbabwe

19 October 1997 at Nairobi Gymkhana Ground

Zimbabwe

G.W. Flower	run out	**78**
A. Flower †	**c** Otieno, **b** Suji	**7**
G.J. Rennie	lbw, **b** Mohammad Sheikh	**76**
G.J. Whittall	run out	**3**
A.D.R. Campbell *	**c** Otieno, **b** Odoyo	**28**
C.B. Wishart	**st** Otieno, **b** Odumbe	**7**
C.N. Evans	not out	**48**
P.A. Strang	not out	**3**
B.C. Strang		
A.R. Whittall		
A.G. Huckle		
	b **3**, lb **12**, w **4**, nb **3**	**22**
	49 overs (for 6 wickets)	**272**

	O	M	R	**W**
Suji	8	–	40	**1**
Anagara	6	–	34	**–**
Odoyo	4	–	47	**1**
Asif Karim	6	–	29	**–**
Tikolo	10	–	38	**–**
Mohammad Sheikh	9	–	43	**1**
Odumbe	6	–	26	**1**

Fall of Wickets
1–**18**, 2–**168**, 3–**175**, 4–**178**, 5–**241**

Kenya

D. Chudasama	**b** A.R. Whittall	**6**
K. Otieno †	**b** A.R. Whittall	**15**
S. Tikolo	**b** A.R. Whittall	**23**
M. Odumbe	**c** sub, **b** P.A. Strang	**14**
H.S. Modi	**c** B.C. Strang, **b** G.W. Flower	**57**
A. Vadher	**c** Campbell, **b** P.A. Strang	**0**
T. Odoyo	**c** sub, **b** P.A. Strang	**3**
T. Suji	run out	**2**
Asif Karim *	run out	**53**
Mohammad Sheikh	lbw, **b** G.W. Flower	**1**
J. Anagara	not out	**3**
	lb **7**, w **6**	**13**
	46.1 overs	**190**

	O	M	R	**W**
B.C. Strang	6	–	25	**–**
A.R. Whittall	10	2	23	**3**
G.W. Flower	9.1	–	44	**2**
Huckle	6	–	38	**–**
G.J. Whittall	5	–	16	**–**
P.A. Strang	10	2	37	**3**

Fall of Wickets
1–**21**, 2–**29**, 3–**62**, 4–**62**, 5–**66**, 7–**71**, 8–**171**, 9–**175**

Umpires: R.E. Koertzen & Salim Badar *Man of the Match*: A.R. Whittall *Man of the Series*: A. Flower **Zimbabwe won on faster scoring rate**

England 'A' Tour

England 'A' arrived in Kenya early in the New Year for the first leg of a tour that would also take them to Sri Lanka. Managed by Graham Gooch and coached by Mike Gatting, the party was a young one, with only skipper Nick Knight, vice-captain Steve James, and all-rounder Mark Ealham above 28. James, like Glamorgan team-mate Cosker, the Leicestershire pair Maddy and Ormond, and the Yorkshire pace bowler Hutchison, had earned his place with outstanding performances in the County Championship while Flintoff and Ben Hollioake had graduated from the Under-19 side. For the younger Hollioake, with one Test cap, perhaps prematurely, to his credit, the tour was crucial. His performances would be closely monitored to see if he really was of international class.

Shah of Middlesex and Powell of Essex were to join the party after the Under-19 World Cup. Off-spinner Powell was one of two great surprises in the selection. His first-class experience was limited in the extreme. An even greater surprise was the inclusion of Chris Read, a wicket-keeper from Gloucestershire, who was virtually third choice for his county behind Russell and Williams. He may have potential, but his selection seemed very hard on cricketers like Nixon and Rollins, who are young and proven.

3 January 1998
at Agha Khan Club, Nairobi
England 'A' 271 for 9 (A. Flintoff 104, S. Tikolo 4 for 42)
Kenya 73
England 'A' won by 152 runs

4 January 1998
at Nairobi Gymkhana, Nairobi
Kenya 177 for 7 (S. Tikolo 61, T. Odoyo 50)
England 'A' 147 for 3 (N.V. Knight 71 not out, A. Flintoff 53)
No result

The tour began with two 50-over matches. England completely outplayed Kenya in the first game after Thomas Odoyo had produced a good, brisk spell of bowling in which he sent back Maddy, Hollioake and Ealham. Flintoff took over and reached his century off 89 balls. The young Lancastrian hit five sixes and 24 fours. Kenya collapsed against Hollioake, Giles and Ealham, and only Tikolo, 24, and Asif Karim, 19, reached double figures. The last nine wickets fell for 29 runs.

Rain reduced the second match to 35 overs and ended the England innings when they were 147 for three in 30.3 overs. The groundstaff accidentally spilled water on the playing surface, and there could be no resumption.

The match was originally awarded to England, but the Kenyan Cricket Association protested, and 'no result' was declared.

6, 7 and 8 January 1998
at Ruaraka, Nairobi
England 'A' 402 for 4 dec. (D.L. Maddy 202, N.V. Knight 96)
Kenya 154 for 8 (R. Shah 57)
Match drawn

10 January 1998
at Ruaraka, Nairobi
Kenya v. England 'A'
Match abandoned

England 'A''s brief tour of Kenya came to a soggy end. Few three-day matches have been played in Kenya, and the game at Ruaraka was to have been the highlight of the tour. Knight and Maddy added 187 for the second wicket, and England closed the first day on 278 for two. Maddy went on to make the first double century of his career, and he made few mistakes in an innings that included four sixes and 24 fours. In bowling and fielding, Kenya wilted dreadfully, losing heart and discipline. In all aspects of the game, Tikolo remains a shining exception. He made 43 and shared a fourth wicket stand of 48 with Shah, but it was obvious that the gap between the two sides was enormous. Rain brought an early end to the match, and no play was possible on the last day.

The venue of the one-day game was twice changed, but the rain persisted, and the match was abandoned. So ended Kenya's latest attempt to enrich their cricketing experience. There is far to go before the country attains Test standard, but if enthusiasm and endeavour count for anything, that goal could be reached one day.

Lancashire's Andrew Flintoff earned high praise for his adventurous batting for England 'A' in Kenya.
(Graham Chadwick / Allsport)

Darren Maddy made his first double century in first-class cricket for England 'A' in Kenya, and the Leicester player was the outstanding success of the tour both in Kenya and Sri Lanka.
(Graham Chadwick / Allsport)

Canada

The first known reference to cricket in Canada concerned a game played in Montreal in 1785. In 1844, Canada met the United States of America in it's first international cricket match. Fifteen years later, George Parr brought an England touring team to Canada, and in 1870 a rather weak Canadian side toured England. In 1997, Canada's performance in Malaysia won it a place in the ICC rankings. For cricket fans in Canada, however, Toronto's hosting of the Sahara Cup between India and Pakistan is the high spot of the season.

Saurav Ganguly established a world record by winning the Man of the Match award in four consecutive one-day internationals in the Sahara Cup in Toronto. His prowess as a batsman was well-known, but he surprised many with his accurate medium-pace bowling. He returned figures of five for 16 in ten overs to bring India victory in the third match of the series.
(George Herringshaw / ASP)

If Canada has not been able to maintain a high profile in international cricket, enthusiasm for the game appears to be increasing, and the nation was placed seventh among associate members in the ICC's rankings following the Trophy matches in Malaysia in 1997. This ranking puts Canada in the first division for the next ICC Trophy.

More significantly, perhaps, Toronto appears to have become the annual venue for a one-day international series between India and Pakistan for the Sahara Cup. This 'friendship' series was first played at the Toronto Cricket, Skating and Curling Club in September, 1996, and exactly a year later, the two sides met again at the same venue with the weather marginally kinder than it had been for the first Sahara Cup, which Pakistan won by three matches to two. India was to gain ample revenge in 1997.

India introduced two new players to international cricket, Harvinder Singh, a medium pace bowler from the Punjab, and D.S. Mohanty, another medium pace bowler, from Orissa. Harvinder Singh ran into trouble on his debut, being warned about his future conduct by referee Hendricks when he celebrated in an over-exuberant manner on claiming his first wicket in international cricket, that of Shahid Afridi.

A lively and promising new recruit to the Indian attack, Harvinder Singh.
(Ben Radford / Allsport)

Mohammad Akram, Pakistan pace bowler
(David Munden / Sportsline)

Pakistan bowled their overs so slowly that they were deducted one over when they went in search of a target of 209. The Indian innings owed much to a fourth wicket stand of 91 between Azharuddin and Jadeja, but, with Saqlain taking five wickets, Rameez Raja could not have been disappointed with his decision to ask India to bat first when he won the toss. Unpredictable as ever, Pakistan lost both openers for five, and, in spite of Salim Malik's brave knock, they never looked likely to reach their target. Mohanty began his international career in splendid style, taking a wicket with his fifth delivery, and Azharuddin equalled Gavaskar's record with four catches. The individual award went to Jadeja, who hit four sixes and a four to give the Indian innings a necessary impetus.

India won the second match with considerable ease, and Pakistan suffered more woe. Heckled by a spectator with a megaphone, Inzamam-ul-Haq charged into the crowd brandishing his bat. That the spectator was being abusive is undeniable, but Inzamam's reaction was inexcusable, and

Match One India v. Pakistan

13 September 1997 at Toronto Cricket, Skating and Curling Club

India

S.R. Tendulkar *	c Mohammad Akram, b Azhar	17
S.C. Ganguly	c Shahid, b Mohammad Akram	17
R.S. Dravid	c Ijaz Ahmed, b Shahid Afridi	23
M. Azharuddin	st Moin Khan, b Saqlain	52
A.D. Jadeja	c Mohammad Akram, b Saqlain	49
R.R. Singh	b Saqlain Mushtaq	16
S.S. Karim †	b Aqib Javed	3
R.K. Chauhan	b Aqib Javed	0
A. Kuruvilla	c Saeed Anwar, b Saqlain Mushtaq	1
Harvinder Singh	c Aqib Javed, b Saqlain Mushtaq	1
D.S. Mohanty	not out	0
	b 1, lb 3, w 22, nb 3	29
	50 overs	208

	O	M	R	W
Aqib Javed	10	3	39	2
Mohammad Akram	9	1	41	1
Azhar Mahmood	10	1	28	1
Saqlain Mushtaq	10	–	45	5
Shahid Afridi	10	–	43	1
Salim Malik	1	–	8	–

Fall of Wickets
1–**52**, 2–**52**, 3–**85**, 4–**176**, 5–**199**, 6–**202**, 7–**203**, 8–**207**, 9–**208**

Pakistan

Saeed Anwar	b Mohanty	2
Rameez Raja *	c Azharuddin, b Kuruvilla	1
Ijaz Ahmed	c Azharuddin, b Gnguly	24
Inzamam-ul-Haq	c Jadeja, b Kuruvilla	13
Shahid Afridi	c Azharuddin, b Harvinder	13
Salim Malik	c Chauhan, b Harvinder	64
Moin Khan †	c R.R. Singh, b Ganguly	0
Azhar Mahmood	c Azharuddin, b Harvinder	9
Saqlain Mushtaq	run out	29
Aqib Javed	run out	2
Mohammad Akram	not out	0
	b 1, lb 4, w 21, nb 5	31
	44.2 overs	188

	O	M	R	W
Kuruvilla	8	2	27	2
Mohanty	7	–	22	1
R.R. Singh	10	1	35	–
Harvinder Singh	8.2	–	44	3
Ganguly	7	–	27	2
Tendulkar	2	–	13	–
Chauhan	2	–	15	–

Fall of Wickets
1–**4**, 2–**5**, 3–**52**, 4–**57**, 5–**82**, 6–**84**, 7–**107**, 8–**171**, 9–**188**

Umpires: R.E. Koertzen & S.A. Bucknor *Man of the Match*: A.D. Jadeja

India won by 20 runs

Match Two – India v. Pakistan

14 September 1997 at Toronto Cricket, Skating and Curling Club

Pakistan

Saeed Anwar	c Harvinder Singh, b Mohanty	12
Shahid Afridi	b Mohanty	0
Rameez Raja *	c Mohanty, b R.R. Singh	8
Ijaz Ahmed	c Azharuddin, b Mohanty	4
Inzamam-ul-Haq	c Karim, b R.R. Singh	10
Salim Malik	c and b Ganguly	36
Moin Khan †	run out	1
Saqlain Mushtaq	c Karim, b Kuruvilla	21
Azhar Mahmood	c Azharuddin, b Ganguly	8
Aqib Javed	c Azharuddin, b Kuruvilla	0
Kabir Khan	not out	1
	lb 4, w 6, nb 5	15
	45.2 overs	116

	O	M	R	W
Kuruvilla	10	–	29	2
Mohanty	7	1	15	3
Harvinder Singh	8.2	–	19	–
R.R. Singh	6	2	22	2
Ganguly	9	2	16	2
Kulkarni	5	–	11	–

Fall of Wickets
1–**7**, 2–**17**, 3–**26**, 4–**41**, 5–**50**, 6–**66**, 7–**91**, 8–**115**, 9–**115**

India

S.C. Ganguly	c Inzamam-ul-Haq, b Saqlain	32
S.S. Karim †	b Azhar Mahmood	9
R.S. Dravid	run out	14
S.R. Tendulkar *	not out	25
M. Azharuddin	not out	21
A.D. Jadeja		
R.R. Singh		
N.M. Kulkarni		
A. Kuruvilla		
Harvinder Singh		
D.S. Mohanty		
	b 1, lb 2, w 6, nb 7	16
	34.4 overs (for 3 wickets)	117

	O	M	R	W
Aqib Javed	10	2	46	–
Kabir Khan	0.3	–	0	–
Azhar Mahmood	9.3	1	28	1
Ijaz Ahmed	5	–	11	–
Saqlain Mushtaq	8	2	24	1
Shahid Afridi	1	–	3	–
Saeed Anwar	0.4	–	2	–

Fall of Wickets
1–**34**, 2–**63**, 3–**69**

Umpires: S.A. Bucknor & S.G. Randell *Man of the Match*: S.C. Ganguly

India won by 7 wickets

Match Three – India v. Pakistan

18 September 1997 at Toronto Cricket, Skating and Curling Club

India

Batsman	Dismissal	Runs
S.C. Ganguly	c Ijaz, b Azhar Mahmood	2
S.S. Karim †	c Moin Khan, b Aqib Javed	2
R.S. Dravid	c Saeed Anwar, b Salim Malik	25
S.R. Tendulkar *	c Moin, b Mohammad Akram	0
M. Azharuddin	c Azhar Mahmood, b Saqlain	67
A.D. Jadeja	c Moin, b Mohammad Akram	20
R.R. Singh	not out	32
A. Kuruvilla	not out	1
N.M. Kulkarni		
Harvinder Singh		
D.S. Mohanty		
	b 1, lb 12, w 19, nb 1	33
	40 overs (for 6 wickets)	182

	O	M	R	W
Aqib Javed	10	4	17	1
Azhar Mahmood	9	–	30	1
Saqlain Mushtaq	10	–	48	1
Mohammad Akram	10	–	28	2
Shahid Afridi	5	–	20	–
Salim Malik	6	1	26	1

Fall of Wickets
1–12, 2–12, 3–23, 4–89, 5–153, 6–164

Pakistan

Batsman	Dismissal	Runs
Saeed Anwar	c Dravid, b Mohanty	22
Shahid Afridi	c Tendulkar, b Kuruvilla	44
Rameez Raja *	c Ganguly, b Harvinder Singh	11
Ijaz Ahmed	c sub, b Ganguly	13
Salim Malik	c Tendulkar, b Ganguly	6
Hasan Raza	c Karim, b Ganguly	0
Moin Khan †	c Jadeja, b Ganguly	7
Saqlain Mushtaq	c Mohanty, b Kuruvilla	11
Azhar Mahmood	c Karim, b Mohanty	6
Aqib Javed	c Kuruvilla, b Ganguly	11
Mohammad Akram	not out	2
	lb 6, w 4, nb 5	15
	36.5 overs	148

	O	M	R	W
Kuruvilla	8.5	1	26	2
Mohanty	8	–	43	2
Harvinder Singh	5	–	41	1
R.R. Singh	5	1	16	–
Ganguly	10	3	16	5

Fall of Wickets
1–52, 2–79, 3–87, 4–103, 5–103, 6–116, 7–118, 8–126, 9–141

Umpires: S.A. Bucknor & S.G. Randell *Man of the Match*: S.C. Ganguly

India won by 34 runs

Match Four – India v. Pakistan

20 September 1997 at Toronto Cricket, Skating and Curling Club

Pakistan

Batsman	Dismissal	Runs
Saeed Anwar	b Kuruvilla	30
Shahid Afridi	c Karim, b Mohanty	2
Rameez Raja *	c Karim, b Ganguly	20
Ijaz Ahmed	c Jadeja, b Harvinder Singh	15
Salim Malik	c R.R. Singh, b Ganguly	17
Moin Khan †	c Tendulkar, b Harvinder Singh	23
Azhar Mahmood	not out	33
Saqlain Mushtaq	not out	0
Aqib Javed		
Shahid Nazir		
Mohammad Akram		
	lb 8, w 10, nb 1	19
	28 overs (for 6 wickets)	159

	O	M	R	W
Kuruvilla	6	–	29	1
Mohanty	5	–	35	1
Harvinder Singh	5	–	25	2
R.R. Singh	6	–	33	–
Ganguly	6	2	29	2

Fall of Wickets
1–31, 2–46, 3–72, 4–95, 5–107, 6–155

India

Batsman	Dismissal	Runs
S.R. Tendulkar *	c Moin Khan, b Shahid Nazir	6
S.C. Ganguly	not out	75
R.R. Singh	c Mohammad Akram, b Shahid	16
M. Azharuddin	c Ijaz Ahmed, b Shahid Nazir	7
A.D. Jadeja	not out	37
R.S. Dravid		
V.G. Kambli		
S.S. Karim †		
A. Kuruvilla		
D.S. Mohanty		
Harvinder Singh		
	b 1, lb 5, w 13, nb 2	21
	25.3 overs (for 3 wickets)	162

	O	M	R	W
Aqib Javed	4.3	–	35	–
Shahid Nazir	6	–	38	3
Mohammad Akram	5	–	27	–
Azhar Mahmood	5	–	25	–
Saqlain Mushtaq	5	–	31	–

Fall of Wickets
1–8, 2–41, 3–54

Umpires: S.A. Bucknor & R.E. Koertzen *Man of the Match*: S.C. Ganguly

India won by 7 wickets

he was banned for two matches. The whole incident caused the game to be held up for forty minutes.

The initial attempt to play the third match was ruined by rain, and the game had to be restarted the following day. Run-getting was not easy, but Azharuddin hit four fours in his 67, which occupied 110 balls. Pakistan began well enough, with Shahid Afridi hitting six fours as he made 44 off 38 balls. But total collapse followed as Saurav Ganguly wrought havoc on the middle order with the best bowling performance of his international career. Although two matches remained to be played, India had clinched the series.

Rain caused the fourth game to be reduced to 28 overs, and India were penalised two overs because of their slow over-rate. It had no influence on the outcome as India continued their winning streak. Winning the toss, Tendulkar asked Pakistan to bat first, and his bowlers responded admirably to the challenge. India had some concern when three wickets fell for 54, but Ganguly came to the rescue with 75 off as many deliveries. His innings included a six and eight fours, and it was instrumental in taking India to their fourth consecutive victory over

The first of a long line of captains of Pakistan during the year, Rameez Raja. Defeat in the Sahara Cup ended his reign and his international career.
(David Munden / Sportsline)

Match Five – India *v.* Pakistan

21 September 1997 at Toronto Cricket, Skating and Curling Club

India

S.R. Tendulkar *	lbw, **b** Azhar Mahmood	**51**
S.C. Ganguly	**c** Azhar Mahmood, **b** Saqlain Mushtaq	**96**
V.G. Kambli	**c** Saqlain Mushtaq, **b** Azhar Mahmood	**1**
M. Azharuddin	run out	**50**
A.D. Jadeja	not out	**23**
R.R. Singh	**c and b** Aqib Javed	**9**
R.S. Dravid	not out	**3**
S.S. Karim †		
A. Kuruvilla		
D.S. Mohanty		
Harvinder Singh		
	lb **5**, w **8**, nb **4**	**17**
	50 overs (for 5 wickets)	**250**

	O	M	R	W
Aqib Javed	10	3	40	**1**
Shahid Nazir	10	–	66	**–**
Azhar Mahmood	10	1	27	**2**
Saqlain Mushtaq	10	1	51	**1**
Shahid Afridi	9	–	48	**–**
Salim Malik	1	–	13	**–**

Fall of Wickets
1–**98**, 2–**102**, 3–**206**, 4–**214**, 5–**237**

Pakistan

Shahid Afridi	**c** Tendulkar, **b** Ganguly	**39**
Ijaz Ahmed	**c** Tendulkar, **b** Harvinder Singh	**60**
Salim Malik	**c** Karim, **b** Harvinder Singh	**8**
Rameez Raja *	**b** Ganguly	**0**
Inzamam-ul-Haq	not out	**71**
Hasan Raza	**c** Karim, **b** Mohanty	**41**
Moin Khan †	not out	**3**
Azhar Mahmood		
Saqlain Mushtaq		
Shahid Nazir		
Aqib Javed		
	b **2**, lb **9**, w **14**, nb **4**	**29**
	41.5 overs (for 5 wickets)	**251**

	O	M	R	W
Kuruvilla	9.5	–	80	**–**
Mohanty	9	1	66	**1**
Harvinder Singh	8	–	33	**2**
R.R. Singh	4	–	15	**–**
Ganguly	9	1	33	**2**
Jadeja	2	–	13	**–**

Fall of Wickets
1–**109**, 2–**109**, 3–**111**, 4–**127**, 5–**240**

Umpires: S.A. Bucknor & S.G. Randell *Man of the Match*: S.C. Ganguly

Pakistan won by 5 wickets

Pakistan – the first time they had achieved such a feat against their traditional rivals.

Pakistan gained some consolation by winning the final match, but again the main honours went to Saurav Ganguly. He shared an opening stand of 98 with Tendulkar and a third wicket stand of 104 with Azharuddin, and in the process he completed a thousand runs in limited-overs international cricket. Yet another slow over-rate cost Pakistan two overs from their quota, but Shahid Afridi, with two sixes and five fours, and Ijaz Ahmed, with two sixes and nine fours, set them on the path to victory with an opening stand of 109. Returning after suspension, Inzamam-ul-Haq hit 71 off 86 balls to complete the success.

Saurav Ganguly was the obvious choice as Man of the Series, and the Indians could be well pleased with the form shown by newcomers Harvinder Singh Sodhi and Mohanty, the first Orissa player to represent his country. They performed so well that Srinath and Venkatesh Prasad were hardly missed. In contrast, Pakistan must have regretted the absence of Wasim Akram, Waqar Younis, Mushtaq Ahmed and the controversial Aamir Sohail.

One liability about playing in Canada is the excessive amount of swing obtained by the pace bowlers. The ball moved so extravagantly that it brought an abundance of wides with balls pitching outside off stump often scuttling down the leg side.

Bangladesh

Bangladesh, ICC Champions and qualifiers for the World Cup, did not have the happiest of times in 1997–98. They struggled in Kenya and New Zealand, and their own limited-overs tournament, staged to celebrate their fifty years of independence, became more concerned with the cricketing affairs of India and Pakistan. Tendulkar was deposed as captain of India and replaced by Azharuddin while Chauhan, his bowling action again suspect, was once more sent into isolation.

Restored to the Indian captaincy, Mohammad Azharuddin celebrated with personal and team success in Bangladesh's Jubilee Independence Cup. (David Munden / Sportsline)

Triumphant in a Test series against West Indies, Wasim Akram resigned as captain of Pakistan. Rumours and accusations surrounded him, and he was not chosen for the Pakistan side in Bangladesh – mainly, it was said, on the grounds of fitness. Waqar Younis and Shoaib Akhtar were two other notable absentees, though Rashid Latif, omitted so often, was reinstated as wicket-keeper and captain. Pakistan cricket is ever submerged in mystery and politics.

It was no surprise that Bangladesh were eliminated from the competition within the first three days. They chose to bat first against India and soon found themselves 22 for four. Aminul Islam and Khalid Mahmud, one of three newcomers in the Bangladesh side, then added 109, and Animul Islam was to remain unbeaten on 69, which included seven fours and came off 96 balls. The game had started late because of mist and was reduced to 48 overs, but Robin Singh finished the innings with a ball to spare. Srinath bowled exceptionally well, taking five wickets in ten economical overs. India lost Sidhu, run out before a run was scored, and Ganguly at 14. This brought together Tendulkar and Azharuddin, deposed captain and reinstated captain. They put on 121 as Azharuddin celebrated his return to the captaincy with 84 off 120 balls. He hit seven fours. Tendulkar's 54 came off 76 balls. There was a mild tremor when they were out, but victory came with ten balls to spare.

More significantly, India beat Pakistan the following day in a match reduced to 37 overs by early morning mist. Tendulkar and Azharuddin shared another century stand, and Azharuddin hit a century off 111 balls with seven fours. Pakistan began uneasily and were never quite in touch in spite of Inzamam-ul-Haq's 77 off 69 balls. He hit three sixes

A surprise selection as captain of Pakistan in Bangladesh, Rashid Latif did not enjoy the best of tournaments with his wicket-keeping being far below his former standard.
(Nigel French / ASP)

Aqib Javed restored as Pakistan's main strike bowler.
(Nigel French / ASP)

and seven fours. Pakistan gave a debut to pace bowler Fazl-e-Akbar, but he bowled only two overs, conceded 19 runs and did not play again in the competition.

As expected, Pakistan duly qualified to meet India in the final when they demolished the hosts in the third match in the tournament. Bangladesh laboured against some tight bowling, and in Saeed Anwar's 73 off 69 balls he hit 13 fours.

The first final was a personal triumph for Sachin Tendulkar. He took three wickets to bring about a decline in the Pakistan middle order, and he shared an opening stand of 159 with Saurav Ganguly to help India to a resounding victory. Tendulkar's 95 came off 78 balls and included five sixes and six fours. Mist caused this game to be reduced to 46 overs.

The second final was the first match not to be affected by morning mist, and for once the Indian batting failed with only Azharuddin, 66 off 88 balls, showing his true form. Sparked by Saaed Anwar and Shahid Afridi, Pakistan raced to victory.

Match One – Bangladesh v. India

10 January 1998 at National Stadium, Dhaka

Bangladesh

Shahriar Hussain	c Tendulkar, b Srinath	1
Javed Omar	lbw, b Mohanty	4
Sanwar Hussain	c Tendulkar, b Srinath	9
Aminul Islam	not out	69
Akram Khan *	c and b Mohanty	2
Khalid Mahmud	run out	46
Mohammad Rafique	b Srinath	20
Khalid Masud †	c Srinath, b Mohanty	9
Hasibul Hussain	b Srinath	3
Saifuddin Ahmed	b Srinath	0
Sharif-ul-Haq	c and b R.R. Singh	10
	b 1, lb 8, w 6, nb 2	17
	47.5 overs	190

	O	M	R	W
Srinath	10	4	22	5
Mohanty	10	1	30	3
Bahutule	8	–	51	–
Ganguly	5	1	13	–
Kanitkar	7	1	27	–
R.R. Singh	5.5	–	23	1
Tendulkar	2	–	15	–

Fall of Wickets
1–**4**, 2–**16**, 3–**19**, 4–**22**, 5–**131**, 6–**158**, 7–**171**, 8–**179**, 9–**179**

India

S.C. Ganguly	c Khalid Masud, b Saifuddin	11
N.S. Sidhu	run out	0
M. Azharuddin *	c Akram Khan, b Saifuddin	84
S.R. Tendulkar	c and b Mohammad Rafique	54
A.D. Jadeja	b Hasibul Hussain	10
R.R. Singh	run out	8
H.H. Kanitkar	not out	13
S.V. Bahutule	not out	0
N.R. Mongia †		
J. Srinath		
D.S. Mohanty		
	b 1, w 8, nb 2	11
	46.2 overs (for 6 wickets)	191

	O	M	R	W
Hasibul Hussain	9.2	2	37	1
Saifuddin Ahmed	10	1	40	2
Khalid Mahmud	9	1	38	–
Mohammad Rafique	10	–	42	1
Sharif-ul-Haq	3	–	21	–
Aminul Islam	5	1	12	–

Fall of Wickets
1–**0**, 2–**14**, 3–**135**, 4–**162**, 5–**167**, 6–**190**

Umpires: D.B. Cowie & R.B. Tiffin *Man of the Match:* J. Srinath

India won by 4 wickets

Match Two – Pakistan v. India

11 January 1998 at National Stadium, Dhaka

India

S.C. Ganguly	c Inzamam-ul-Haq, b Aqib	13
S.R. Tendulkar	st Rashid Latif, b Saqlain	67
M. Azharuddin *	c Azhar, b Saqlain	100
N.S. Sidhu	c and b Azhar Mahmood	36
A.D. Jadeja	c Manzoor Akhtar, b Saqlain	6
R.R. Singh	c Saeed Anwar, b Aqib Javed	1
S.V. Bahutule	c Shahid Afridi, b Saqlain	1
N.R. Mongia †	not out	1
J. Srinath	not out	0
D.S. Mohanty		
Harvinder Singh		
	lb 10, w 6, nb 4	20
	37 overs (for 7 wickets)	245

	O	M	R	W
Aqib Javed	6	–	34	2
Fazl-e-Akbar	2	–	19	–
Azhar Mahmood	7	–	65	1
Saqlain Mushtaq	8	–	41	4
Shahid Afridi	8	–	38	–
Aamir Sohail	1	–	9	–
Manzoor Akhtar	5	–	29	–

Fall of Wickets
1–**14**, 2–**126**, 3–**215**, 4–**236**, 5–**239**, 6–**243**, 7–**243**

Pakistan

Shahid Afridi	c Tendulkar, b Mohanty	5
Ijaz Ahmed	b Harvinder Singh	18
Aamir Sohail	c Tendulkar, b Srinath	19
Saeed Anwar	c and b Harvinder Singh	13
Inzamam-ul-Haq	c and b Tendulkar	77
Manzoor Akhtar	run out	39
Azhar Mahmood	c Tendulkar, b Harvinder Singh	16
Rashid Latif * †	not out	14
Saqlain Mushtaq	b Srinath	11
Fazl-e-Akbar	run out	7
Aqib Javed		
	lb 4, w 3, nb 1	8
	37 overs (for 9 wickets)	227

	O	M	R	W
Srinath	8	–	40	2
Mohanty	3	–	31	1
Harvinder Singh	8	–	47	3
R.R. Singh	6	–	20	–
Bahutule	7	–	53	–
Ganguly	1	–	8	–
Tendulkar	4	–	24	1

Fall of Wickets
1–**5**, 2–**44**, 3–**44**, 4–**62**, 5–**147**, 6–**185**, 7–**197**, 8–**214**, 9–**227**

Umpires: D.B. Cowie & R.E. Koertzen *Man of the Match*: M. Azharuddin

India won by 18 runs

Match Three – Bangladesh v. Pakistan

12 January 1998 at National Stadium, Dhaka

Bangladesh

Javed Omar	b Mushtaq Ahmed	17
Habibul Bashar	c sub, b Mushtaq Ahmed	15
Sanwar Hussain	st Rashid, b Mushtaq Ahmed	13
Aminul Islam	run out	6
Akram Khan *	c Rashid, b Shahid Afridi	7
Khalid Mahmud	c Rashid, b Shahid Afridi	19
Mohammad Rafique	b Saqlain Mushtaq	29
Khalid Masud †	c and b Saqlain Mushtaq	3
Hasibul Hussain	b Aqib Javed	7
Saifuddin Ahmed	not out	6
Zakir Hussain	lbw, b Aqib Javed	0
	lb 7, w 4, nb 1	12
	39.3 overs	134

	O	M	R	W
Aqib Javed	7.3	1	27	2
Azhar Mahmood	8	1	22	–
Saqlain Mushtaq	8	–	33	3
Mushtaq Ahmed	8	–	20	2
Shahid Afridi	8	1	25	2

Fall of Wickets
1–33, 2–38, 3–52, 4–59, 5–76, 6–100, 7–116, 8–126, 9–134

Pakistan

Shahid Afridi	c Sanwar Hussain, b Saifuddin	11
Saeed Anwar	not out	73
Aamir Sohail	not out	37
Ijaz Ahmed		
Inzamam-ul-Haq		
Manzoor Akhtar		
Azhar Mahmood		
Rashid Latif * †		
Saqlain Mushtaq		
Mushtaq Ahmed		
Aqib Javed		
	b 1, lb 1, w 12, nb 1	15
	24.2 overs (for one wicket)	136

	O	M	R	W
Habibul Bashar	6	–	26	–
Saifuddin Ahmed	6	–	42	1
Zakir Hussain	4	–	18	–
Khalid Mahmud	2	–	19	–
Mohammad Rafique	5	1	18	–
Aminul Islam	1.2	–	11	–

Fall of Wickets
1–136

Umpires: D.B. Cowie & R.B.Tiffin *Man of the Match*: Saqlain Mushtaq

Pakistan won by 9 wickets

Silver Jubilee Independence Cup First Final – Pakistan v. India

14 January 1998 at National Stadium, Dhaka

Pakistan

Saeed Anwar	c Ganguly, b Bahutule	38
Shahid Afridi	c Ganguly, b Harvinder Singh	29
Aamir Sohail	c Mongia, b Mohanty	10
Ijaz Ahmed	st Mongia, b Tendulkar	34
Inzamam-ul-Haq	c Harvinder Singh, b Tendulkar	33
Azhar Mahmood	b Srinath	30
Manzoor Akhtar	st Mongia, b Tendulkar	9
Rashid Latif * †	c Azharuddin, b Srinath	1
Saqlain Mushtaq	not out	7
Mushtaq Ahmed	not out	10
Aqib Javed		
	lb 4, w 7	11
	46 overs (for 8 wickets)	212

	O	M	R	W
Srinath	9	1	40	2
Mohanty	9	–	46	1
Harvinder Singh	5	–	20	1
Bahutule	7	–	31	1
R.R. Singh	9	–	26	–
Tendulkar	7	–	45	3

Fall of Wickets
1–45, 2–73, 3–95, 4–142, 5–155, 6–172, 7–173, 8–197

India

S.C. Ganguly	lbw, b Mushtaq Ahmed	68
S.R. Tendulkar	b Shahid Afridi	95
M. Azharuddin *	not out	30
A.D. Jadeja	not out	11
N.S. Sidhu		
R.R. Singh		
S.V. Bahutule		
N.R. Mongia †		
J. Srinath		
D.S. Mohanty		
Harvinder Singh		
	lb 2, w 6, nb 1	9
	37.1 overs (for 2 wickets)	213

	O	M	R	W
Aqib Javed	4	1	24	–
Azhar Mahmood	4	–	26	–
Saqlain Mushtaq	10	–	53	–
Mushtaq Ahmed	9	–	48	1
Shahid Afridi	9	–	49	1
Manzoor Akhtar	1.1	–	11	–

Fall of Wickets
1–159, 2–182

Umpires: D.B. Cowie & R.B.Tiffin *Man of the Match*: S.R.Tendulkar

India won by 8 wickets

Silver Jubilee Independence Cup Second Final – Pakistan v. India

16 January 1998 at National Stadium, Dhaka

India

Batsman	Dismissal	Runs
S.C. Ganguly	**c** and **b** Mohammad Hussain	**26**
S.R. Tendulkar	**b** Azhar Mahmood	**1**
M. Azharuddin *	**c** Saeed, **b** Mohammad Hussain	**66**
N.S. Sidhu	**c** Azhar Mahmood, **b** Mohammad	**6**
A.D. Jadeja	**c** and **b** Aqib Javed	**34**
R.R. Singh	**c** Shahid Afridi, **b** Mohammad	**5**
N.R. Mongia †	**c** Aamir Sohail, **b** Saqlain	**10**
S.V. Bahutule	**st** Rashid Latif, **b** Saqlain	**11**
J. Srinath	**b** Aqib Javed	**12**
Harvinder Singh	not out	**3**
D.S. Mohanty	**c** Ijaz Ahmed, **b** Saqlain	**4**
	lb **3**, w **5**, nb **3**	**11**
	49.5 overs	**189**

	O	M	R	W
Aqib Javed	10	–	49	**2**
Azhar Mahmood	7	1	28	**1**
Saqlain Mushtaq	9.5	–	36	**3**
Mohammad Hussain	10	1	33	**4**
Shahid Afridi	10	2	21	**–**
Manzoor Akhtar	3	–	19	**–**

Fall of Wickets
1–**5**, 2–**82**, 3–**96**, 4–**116**, 5–**124**, 6–**151**, 7–**167**, 8–**182**, 9–**184**

Pakistan

Batsman	Dismissal	Runs
Saeed Anwar	**c** Ganguly, **b** Harvinder Singh	**51**
Shahid Afridi	**c** Bahutule, **b** Srinath	**21**
Aamir Sohail	**c** Azharuddin, **b** R.R. Singh	**36**
Ijaz Ahmed	not out	**40**
Inzamam-ul-Haq	**c** Sidhu, **b** R.R. Singh	**40**
Mohammad Hussain	not out	**0**
Rashid Latif * †		
Azhar Mahmood		
Manzoor Akhtar		
Saqlain Mushtaq		
Aqib Javed		
	lb **2**, w **1**, nb **2**	**5**
	31.3 overs (for 4 wickets)	**193**

	O	M	R	W
Srinath	7	1	38	**1**
Mohanty	2	–	26	**–**
Harvinder Singh	5	–	33	**1**
Bahutule	5	–	53	**–**
R.R. Singh	9	3	24	**2**
Tendulkar	3.3	–	17	**–**

Fall of Wickets
1–**31**, 2–**105**, 3–**123**, 4–**189**

Umpires: D.B. Cowie & R.E. Koertzen *Man of the Match*: Mohammad Hussain

Pakistan won by 6 wickets

Silver Jubilee Independence Cup Third Final – Pakistan v. India

18 January 1998 at National Stadium, Dhaka

Pakistan

Batsman	Dismissal	Runs
Saeed Anwar	**c** Azharuddin, **b** Harvinder	**140**
Shahid Afridi	**c** R.R. Singh, **b** Harvinder	**18**
Aamir Sohail	**c** Mongia, **b** Harvinder	**14**
Ijaz Ahmed	**c** Sidhu, **b** Srinath	**117**
Azhar Mahmood	**c** Azharuddin, **b** Tendulkar	**10**
Mohammad Hussain	not out	**2**
Inzamam-ul-Haq		
Manzoor Akhtar		
Rashid Latif * †		
Saqlain Mushtaq		
Aqib Javed		
	lb **7**, w **6**	**13**
	48 overs (for 5 wickets)	**314**

	O	M	R	W
Srinath	10	–	61	**1**
Harvinder Singh	10	–	74	**3**
R.R. Singh	8	–	47	**–**
Ganguly	2	–	5	**–**
Kanitkar	6	–	33	**–**
Tendulkar	7	–	49	**1**
Sanghvi	5	–	38	**–**

Fall of Wickets
1–**30**, 2–**66**, 3–**296**, 4–**301**, 5–**314**

India

Batsman	Dismissal	Runs
S.C. Ganguly	**b** Aqib Javed	**124**
S.R. Tendulkar	**c** Azhar Mahmood, **b** Shahid	**41**
R.R. Singh	**c** Aqib Javed, **b** Mohammad	**82**
M. Azharuddin *	**c** Aamir Sohail, **b** Saqlain	**4**
A.D. Jadeja	**b** Saqlain	**8**
N.S. Sidhu	lbw, **b** Saqlain	**5**
H.H. Kanitkar	not out	**11**
N.R. Mongia †	run out	**9**
J. Srinath	not out	**5**
R.L. Sanghvi		
Harvinder Singh		
	b **1**, lb **11**, w **13**, nb **2**	**27**
	47.5 overs (for 7 wickets)	**316**

	O	M	R	W
Aqib Javed	9.2	–	63	**1**
Azhar Mahmood	8	–	55	**–**
Shahid Afridi	6.4	–	56	**1**
Saqlain Mushtaq	9.5	–	66	**3**
Mohammad Hussain	10	–	40	**1**
Manzoor Akhtar	4	–	24	**–**

Fall of Wickets
1–**71**, 2–**250**, 3–**268**, 4–**274**, 5–**281**, 6–**296**, 7–**306**

Umpires: R.E. Koertzen & R.B. Tiffin *Man of the Match*: S.C. Ganguly

India won by 3 wickets

Slow left-arm bowler Rahul Sanghvi made his international debut in the deciding match. This provided some of the best cricket of the competition. Saeed Anwar and Ijaz Ahmed appeared to have won the game for Pakistan when they shared a third wicket stand of 230. Saed hit two sixes and 14 fours as he pounded 140 off 132 deliveries, while Ijaz hit a six and eight fours in a 112-ball innings. India were faced with a target of 315, a total no side batting second had ever reached to win a one-day international. Tendulkar and Ganguly gave them an ideal start with a stand of 71 in 8.2 overs. Tendulkar's 41 came off only 26 deliveries. Saurav Ganguly and Robin Singh maintained the momentum when they added 179 for the second wicket. Robin Singh hit two sixes and four fours and faced 83 balls, and when Ganguly's glorious innings was brought to an end by Aqib Javed he had hit a six and 11 fours and faced 138 balls. Most importantly, Ganguly had shown his side that victory was possible. Wickets tumbled against Saqlain as the batsmen scurried for runs, and when Mongia was run out off the last ball of the penultimate over, nine runs were still needed. Kanitkar and Srinath took six runs off the first four balls of the final over, while the left-handed Kanitkar, playing only his second innings in a one-day international, and in fading light, hit the fifth ball for four to secure a famous victory.

Azharuddin's reinstatement as captain had brought India the Independence Cup, and his predecessor, Sachin Tendulkar, had so refound his form as to be named Man of the Series.

Australia

Australia remained supreme in world cricket at the beginning of the 1997–98 season. They had retained the Ashes with much more ease than the score-line suggested, and so great were their resources that they could ignore the talents of such accomplished cricketers as Law and Lehmann. Nothing was to emphasise the depth and quality of their squad better than the ease with which they found replacements for Jason Gillespie, who had played such a vital part in the triumph over England.

Geoff Allott traps Paul Reiffel leg before for 77 in the first Test between Australia and New Zealand. Reiffel's late order batting success was a feature of the series and played a significant part in Australia's triumph.
(Stephen Laffer / Sportsline)

Gillespie was to miss most of the Australian season because of injury, but there was strong cover for him in the Test side.

The challenge in 1997–98 came from New Zealand and South Africa, who would both be engaged in three-Test series and would provide the opposition in the limited-over World Series. Having beaten Pakistan in Pakistan, South Africa presented the more serious challenge to Australian supremacy.

The season began on a rather sour note with the Board of Control and the players at odds over financial matters. The confrontation was a grave one, and there was threat of strike action, but an agreement was reached.

New Zealand Tour

New Zealand arrived in Australia via Kenya and Zimbabwe where they had been a little fortunate to share the Test and one-day series. The side, led by the twenty-four year old Stephen Fleming, was young and short of experience but, under the tutelage of Rixon, the former Australian wicket-keeper, was enthusiastic and eager to learn.

22, 23, 24 and 25 October 1997
at Cazaly Football Park, Cairns
New Zealanders 196 (B.A. Pocock 63, S.P. Fleming 57, A.J. Bichel 5 for 31) and 248 (B.A. Young 67, S.P. Fleming 62)
Queensland 571 for 9 dec. (M.L. Love 201 retired hurt, J.P. Maher 114, M.L. Hayden 73, A.C. Dale 55, D.L. Vettori 4 for 155)
Queensland won by an innings and 127 runs

The New Zealanders had an unhappy start to their tour, being totally outplayed by Queensland after Law had won the toss and asked them to bat first. A third wicket stand of 103 between Pocock and Fleming was followed by the loss of the last eight wickets for 69 runs. Hayden and Love began Queensland's reply with an opening stand of 129, and Martin Love went on to reach the first double century of his career. He hit three sixes and 27 fours and faced 281 balls. He and Maher shared an unbroken second wicket stand of 285, a record for any state against the New Zealanders. Love retired hurt at 414 for one. Trailing by 375 on the first innings, the tourists were 190 for four on the Friday but collapsed on the Saturday morning.

26 October 1997
at Cazaly Football Park, Cairns
Queensland 252 for 8 (A. Symonds 75, J.P. Maher 72)
New Zealanders 125 (P.W. Jackson 5 for 22)
Queensland won by 127 runs

New Zealand experienced their second defeat of the week-end when they were crushed in the fifty-over game. They were destroyed by the left-arm spin of Paul Jackson and bowled out in 36.1 overs. Earlier, Andrew Symonds hit 75 off 59 balls.

29 October 1997
at Coffs Harbour
New South Wales 156 (C.J. Richards 66)
New Zealanders 65 for 3
Match abandoned

31 October, 1, 2 and 3 November 1997
at Sports Ground, Newcastle
New South Wales 469 for 6 dec. (M.G. Bevan 143, M.J. Slater 137, G.R.J. Matthews 71 not
New Zealanders 214 (C.D. McMillan 62) and 160 (S.H. Cook 4 for 61)
New South Wales won by an innings and 95 runs

New Zealand's depression before the first Test was compounded when they suffered a second innings defeat at the hands of a state side. Slater and Bevan, both rejected by the Australian selectors, hit centuries for New South Wales, while Stuart MacGill performed the first hat-trick for the state since 1984–85 when he sent back Parore, Doull and O'Connor in the first innings.

First Test Match

Australia *v.* New Zealand

New Zealand gave a Test debut to Craig McMillan and named Horne as twelfth man, while Australia relied on those who had done so well in England and had Bichel, fit again, as twelfth man. Fleming won the toss and asked Australia to bat first.

It proved a good decision, for the home side were soon in trouble. Doull and Cairns bowled admirably without effective support. Cairns, coming on as first change, bowled at his very best, further evidence that he is responding well to the coaching of Rixon. In the morning session, he sent back Elliott, Blewett and the Waugh twins as Australia slumped to 52 for four, but the rest of the day belonged to Australia. Taylor and Ponting laid the foundations of a recovery with a stand of 56, but, not for the first time, it was Ian Healy who brought salvation, joining his captain in a partnership worth 117. Taylor was out 45 minutes before the close of play, having hit 112 off 258 deliveries. His innings included 10 fours and demonstrated that the selectors were right to keep faith with him. He had saved his side on a pitch that favoured the bowlers with its early dampness. Healy, twice dropped at slip, batted in his usual positive manner, and he and Reiffel took the score to 269 by the close.

New Zealand skipper Stephen Fleming falls leg before to Kasprowicz for 91. (Stephen Laffer / Sportsline)

Healy added only six to his overnight score on the second morning before chopping a ball from Doull into his stumps, but Reiffel moved boldly on to the attack. He and Warne added 55 in 53 minutes, and Reiffel struck ten fours as he plundered his way to his highest score in Test cricket. By the time he edged an extravagant drive to the wicket-keeper, he had made 77 off 113 balls.

The New Zealand innings began straight after lunch, and they quickly lost Young who edged a rising ball to slip. When Astle and Pocock got in a muddle, Ponting neatly ran out the former from backward point. A rout looked probable, but Pocock is a patient and determined batsman, and Fleming has gained authority and maturity since taking over the captaincy. They halted the decline with a stand of 98 that was broken only minutes before the close when Pocock was taken at slip off Warne.

The recovery continued unabated on the third morning. Nightwatchman Vettori offered useful resistance for nearly an hour, and Fleming was as purposeful as ever. He was within nine runs of a second Test hundred and had batted for just under four and three-quarter hours when he fell leg before to Kasprowicz. Fleming hit 13 fours. McMillan had shown excellent temperament on his debut and was never afraid to hit the ball. He and Cairns shared a lively partnership of 69, and he had struck eight fours before hitting Warne straight for six to bring up his fifty. The leg-spinner exacted immediate revenge, trapping McMillan leg before with a quicker ball. Parore fell to a sharply turned leg-break that edged low to Taylor's left, and Harris was bowled out of the rough. Cairns was bowled by McGrath after making 64 off 132 balls, and New Zealand were still very much in the match. When Taylor drove rashly at Cairns and was caught in the gully to leave Australia on 25 for one at the close, the visitors could claim that the day belonged to them.

Elliott added only four to his overnight score before falling to Vettori, who also captured the wicket of Mark Waugh as Australia slipped to 105 for four. But Vettori's success, welcome as it was, gave warning to New Zealand that they were likely to face problems against Warne in the last innings. Steve Waugh helped Blewett to add 58, and it was Blewett who gave the Australian innings the substance

First Test Match – Australia v. New Zealand

7, 8, 9, 10 and 11 November 1997 at Woolloongabba, Brisbane

Australia

	First Innings		Second Innings	
M.A. Taylor *	c Young, b Doul	112	(2) c Astle, b Cairns	16
M.T.G. Elliott	c Young, b Cairns	18	(1) c Fleming, b Vettori	11
G.S. Blewett	c Vettori, b Cairns	7	(4) c Fleming, b Cairns	91
M.E. Waugh	c Vettori, b Cairns	3	(5) c Fleming, b Vettori	17
S.R. Waugh	lbw, b Cairns	2	(6) c Parore, b Cairns	23
R.T. Ponting	c Pocock, b Doull	26	(7) not out	73
I.A. Healy †	b Doull	68	(3) c Fleming, b Allott	25
P.R. Reiffel	c Parore, b Allott	77	not out	28
S.K. Warne	c Fleming, b Vettori	21		
M.S. Kasprowicz	not out	13		
G.D. McGrath	c Fleming, b Doull	6		
	b 4, lb 9, w 1, nb 6	20	b 1, lb 4, nb 5	10
		373	(for 6 wickets, dec.)	294

	O	M	R	W	O	M	R	W
Doull	30	6	70	4	19	5	44	–
Allott	31	3	117	1	19.5	4	60	1
Cairns	24	5	90	4	16	4	54	3
Vettori	21	5	46	1	36	13	87	2
Astle	11	2	20	–	1	–	14	–
Harris	4	1	17	–	9	–	30	–

Fall of Wickets
1–**27**, 2–**46**, 3–**50**, 4–**52**, 5–**108**, 6–**225**, 7–**294**, 8–**349**, 9–**359**
1–**24**, 2–**36**, 3–**72**, 4–**105**, 5–**163**, 6–**217**

New Zealand

	First Innings		Second Innings	
B.A. Young	c Taylor, b Kasprowicz	1	(2) lbw, b McGrath	45
B.A. Pocock	c Taylor, b Warne	57	(1) c Taylor, b Reiffel	3
N.J. Astle	run out	12	c Blewett, b McGrath	14
S.P. Fleming *	lbw, b Kasprowicz	91	c Healy, b McGrath	0
D.L. Vettori	c S.R. Waugh, b Blewett	14	(9) c Taylor, b Warne	0
C.D. McMillan	lbw, b Warne	54	(5) lbw, b McGrath	0
C.L. Cairns	b McGrath	64	(6) b Reiffel	21
A.C. Parore †	c Taylor, b Warne	12	(7) not out	39
C.Z. Harris	b Warne	13	(8) b Warne	0
S.B. Doull	not out	2	c Healy, b McGrath	2
G.I. Allott	c Elliott, b McGrath	4	lbw, b Warne	0
	b 4, lb 4, nb 17	25	lb 2, nb 6	8
		349		132

	O	M	R	W	O	M	R	W
McGrath	32.2	6	96	2	17	6	32	5
Kasprowicz	24	6	57	2	8	1	17	–
Warne	42	13	106	4	25	6	54	3
Reiffel	21	6	53	–	12	4	27	2
M.E. Waugh	7	2	18	–				
Blewett	6	2	11	1				

Fall of Wickets
1–**2**, 2–**36**, 3–**134**, 4–**173**, 5–**210**, 6–**279**, 7–**317**, 8–**343**, 9–**343**
1–**4**, 2–**55**, 3–**68**, 4–**68**, 5–**69**, 6–**112**, 7–**115**, 8–**117**, 9–**126**

Umpires: S.G. Randell & V.K. Ramaswamy

Australia won by 186 runs

it needed with 91 off 203 balls in 262 minutes. It was Ponting, however, who seized the initiative. Instructed to attack, he hit 73 off 85 balls with two sixes and seven fours. Reiffel played another dashing knock, and Taylor was able to declare and set New Zealand a formidable target of 319 in a maximum of 93 overs.

With four to their credit, New Zealand began the last day and lost Pocock, caught at slip, to the first ball. A spell of four wickets in 22 balls by McGrath sent them reeling to 69 for five at lunch, and although Cairns and Parore offered brief resistance, Australia were not to be denied. Five wickets, three of them to Warne, fell for 20 runs, and Australia's only concern was that a groin injury might keep McGrath out of the second Test.

14, 15, 16 and 17 November 1997
at Optus Oval, Melbourne
New Zealanders 82 (D.W. Fleming 4 for 18, D.J. Saker 4 for 27) and 173 (D.J. Saker 6 for 39)
Victoria 173 (G.I. Allott 5 for 47) and 83 for 5 (D.L. Vettori 4 for 13)
Victoria won by 5 wickets

New Zealand's misery continued when they were dismissed in 50 overs for their lowest score in Australia this century. No play was possible on the first day because of rain, but by the end of the second, Victoria were 49 runs ahead with three wickets standing. The tourists showed better form in their second innings, but then lost six wickets for 30 runs in the final session of the third day.

Second Test Match

Australia v. New Zealand

New Zealand made one change from the side beaten in the first Test, O'Connor replacing Harris, while Australia brought in Simon Cook for the injured McGrath. Cook had begun his first-class career with Victoria before moving to New South Wales in 1995 and is recognised as a bowler of genuine pace.

Fleming won the toss and chose to bat in good conditions. Sadly, his batsmen generally floundered against some fine bowling and outstanding catching. Steve Waugh dived to his left to get rid of Young with only 12 runs on the board, and Healy made a breath-taking one-handed catch low down to dismiss Pocock and give Cook his first Test wicket. Blewett took two catches, the second, which accounted for Parore, being taken at short-leg off a full-blooded hit.This left New Zealand on 87 for five, and it was now up to McMillan and Cairns to attempt to repair the damage. McMillan had been impressive on his introduction to Test cricket, and again he revealed a sound temperament. He and Cairns added 74 in quick time before Taylor held McMillan at slip. Cairns fell when Mark Waugh took a stunning catch at mid-wicket. The fielder leapt to his right and held the ball in mid-air, one-handed. The Australian catching was, in itself, a potent attacking force. The final session after tea, the end of the New Zealand innings and the first 13 overs of the Australian innings, was historic in that it was played under floodlights. A new ICC ruling allows lights to be used when available if this makes it possible for play to continue when natural light fades. Australia ended the day on 32 for the loss of Taylor.

New Zealand could be quite pleased with their progress on the second day as Blewett and Elliott were back in the pavilion to leave Australia 71 for three after a delayed start due to rain. At this point, the Waugh twins came together. They began uncertainly, but they still scored briskly, putting on 50 in 43 minutes. Mark Waugh ended a period of drought with some glorious attacking shots, hitting Vettori for a six that was to become part of Test history. The batsman came down the pitch to the left-arm spinner and drove the ball back over the bowler's head. The ball landed on the roof of the five-tier Lillee-Marsh Stand some 130 yards from the crease. It was, in the opinion of many experienced cricketers, the biggest six that they had seen. The ball, 56 overs old, could not be retrieved. Apart from this six, Mark Waugh hit 12 fours as he made 86 off 149 balls. He and his brother put on 153 at a run a minute. Mark was caught behind shortly before the close, which came with Australia having established a lead of 18 runs with six wickets remaining.

Steve Waugh was unbeaten for 79 at the end of the second day, and he seemed to be moving relentlessly towards another Test century when he was beaten by an in-swinger from the tall, left-arm pace bowler, Shayne O'Connor. Steve Waugh had faced 161 balls and hit ten fours. Ponting's patience proved short, and he edged Cairns to slip: New Zealand had captured two vital wickets within the first hour of the third day. They were to have little joy thereafter. Healy's prowess is well known. He has no equal in the world as a wicket-keeper, and Australia are to be envied in having him as a late middle-order batsman. He became the highest-scoring wicket-keeper in Australian Test history, and with Reiffel displaying his new-found confident aggression with the bat, 116 runs came in 108 minutes. Reiffel was caught at slip, which allowed Warne to show his hitting powers. He made 35 off 24 balls and hit four fours and a six, which landed in the 17th row of the stand. He and Healy were out in quick succession, and Australia ultimately led by 244 runs.

New Zealand had not been at their best, and Fleming erred in the manipulation of his bowlers. On top of this, Pocock had a broken toe and McMillan a broken thumb so their batting was undermined both physically and psychologically. Pocock was immediately caught at short-leg; but Parore and Young appeared to be taking their side to calmer waters until Parore's judgement was at fault, and Young was run out by Elliott. Night-watchman Vettori was caught at slip after 18 minutes of stout defence, and, closing on 69 for three, New Zealand faced defeat inside four days.

Pace bowler Simon Cook had an outstanding Test debut for Australia in the second Test against New Zealand in Perth. He had match figures of seven for 75, but he was not called upon again during the season.
(Stephen Laffer / Sportsline)

So it transpired. The game was over half an hour into the afternoon. Warne soon accounted for Fleming, and Parore was out at 102. Debutant Cook then produced a devastating spell which saw him take five for 20 in 32 balls. His final figures of five for 39 were his best in first-class cricket, and they helped take Australia to their eighth series win in succession. New Zealand under-achieved yet again, but this was an outstanding Australian performance, and it was accomplished against the background of tense discussions and bitter dispute between the players and the Australian Board. The players agreed to continue discussions and to lift their threat of strike action over pay and conditions.

Third Test Match

Australia *v.* New Zealand

With the series won, Australia, who fielded an unchanged side, concentrated their attention on making a clean sweep in the rubber, while New Zealand looked only for some glimmer of respectability. The visitors made two changes, Horne replacing the injured Pocock, and Twose coming in for Allott, who had been in poor form. Taylor won the toss for the first time in the series and chose to bat, but, after 15 overs, with the score on 39, rain ended play for the day.

Australia advanced to 273 for five on the second day and once again totally dominated their opponents. Elliott and Blewett shared a second wicket stand of 197 in under

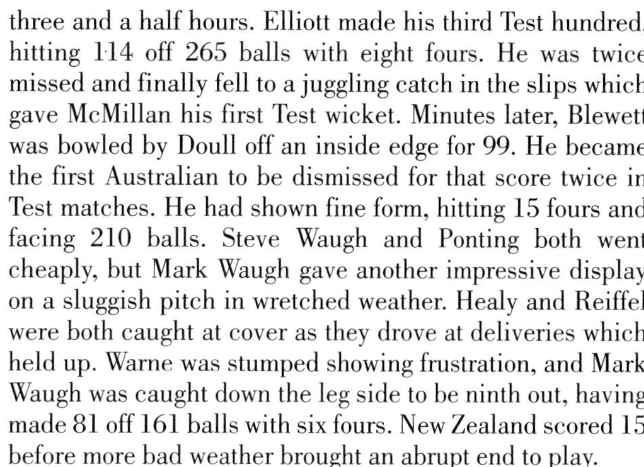

three and a half hours. Elliott made his third Test hundred, hitting 114 off 265 balls with eight fours. He was twice missed and finally fell to a juggling catch in the slips which gave McMillan his first Test wicket. Minutes later, Blewett was bowled by Doull off an inside edge for 99. He became the first Australian to be dismissed for that score twice in Test matches. He had shown fine form, hitting 15 fours and facing 210 balls. Steve Waugh and Ponting both went cheaply, but Mark Waugh gave another impressive display on a sluggish pitch in wretched weather. Healy and Reiffel were both caught at cover as they drove at deliveries which held up. Warne was stumped showing frustration, and Mark Waugh was caught down the leg side to be ninth out, having made 81 off 161 balls with six fours. New Zealand scored 15 before more bad weather brought an abrupt end to play.

The fourth day was probably New Zealand's best of the series. Matthew Horne and Bryan Young scored 60 for the first wicket, and Horne and Parore put on 132 for the second. Horne, sixth out at 229, went on to reach a maiden Test century. He hit two sixes and nine fours and faced 259 balls in a most commendable innings, but his side lost their way as Steve Waugh took three cheap wickets. They slipped from 192 for one to 229 for six, losing Fleming first ball. Astle and Cairns batted positively to restore the innings, and Fleming made a bold declaration, conceding Australia a first innings lead of 149 in an attempt to breathe life into a match which the weather had all but killed. Australia increased their lead by 14 runs before the close.

Taylor elected to continue the Australian innings until lunch on the last day. He and Blewett shared a second wicket stand of 92 in 83 minutes, and his declaration left New Zealand a target of 288 in what proved to be 61 overs. To their credit, the visitors made a bold attempt to reach their target, treating the game as if it were a fifty-over affair. Nathan Astle blasted 40 off 37 balls, and Horne hit 31 off 27 balls as the fifty came up after five overs. The partnership was broken by Reiffel, and Warne then began to work his magic against batsmen committed to attack. Three wickets fell for two runs as Fleming was out for his second 'duck' of the match. Still McMillan, Parore and Twose

A maiden Test century for Matt Horne, 133 for New Zealand against Australia at Hobart. Here he pulls Reiffel to the boundary, but the bowler was to gain revenge by dismissing him in both innings.
(Stephen Laffer / Sportsline)

maintained an aggressive approach, but, again, three wickets fell in quick succession as New Zealand went from 218 for six to 222 for nine. This left the last pair, Doull and O'Connor, 38 minutes, 10.4 overs, to survive if they were to save the match. Doull was dropped by Cook off Warne, who also had a vociferous appeal for a bat-pad catch against O'Connor rejected on his last ball of the day. So New Zealand achieved a brave draw, but it could not hide the fact that they had been totally outplayed in all three Tests and that they had been found wanting on several fronts.

With his twelfth five-wicket haul in Test cricket, Shane Warne had brought his total number of wickets in the series to 19, a record for a rubber between Australia and New Zealand. The Man of the Series award, however, went to Mark Taylor for his run-scoring, his catching and his leadership. On the same day, it was announced that the captaincy for the one-day series was to go to Steve Waugh, so presumably Taylor's career in limited-over internationals was at an end.

New Zealand called up Gavin Larsen for the one-day matches. They were certainly in need of reinforcements.

13 December 1997
at Woolloongabba, Brisbane
New Zealanders 266 for 5 (M.J. Horne 102, S.P. Fleming 95 not out)
Queensland 266 for 6 (M.L. Love 76)
Match tied

4 January 1998
at Adelaide Oval
South Australia 237 for 5 (D.A. Fitzgerald 72, B.A. Johnson 53)
New Zealanders 230 (B.A. Young 53, P. Wilson 4 for 43)
South Australia won by 7 runs

6 January 1998
at Mount Gambier
New Zealanders 316 for 5 (C.M. Spearman 111)
Australian Country XI 152 (A. Jones 70, C.D. McMillan 4 for 22)
New Zealanders won by 164 runs

12 January 1998
at MCG, Melbourne
New Zealanders 242 (S.P. Fleming 58, M.S. Kasprowicz 4 for 21)
Australia 'A' 221 (J.L. Langer 76, S.B. O'Connor 4 for 39)
New Zealanders won by 21 runs

Following the Test series, the New Zealanders played a number of fifty-over games in order to keep in trim for the World Series. The match against Queensland caused some controversy as umpire Parker signalled four when a hit from Geoff Foley quite obviously had cleared the boundary for six, which would have given Queensland victory. Recalled to the squad, Craig Spearman hit 111 off 130 balls against the Country XI.

Second Test Match – Australia v. New Zealand

20, 21, 22 and 23 November 1997 at WACCA Ground, Perth

New Zealand

	First Innings		Second Innings	
B.A. Young	c S.R. Waugh, b Kasprowicz	9	(2) run out	23
B.A. Pocock	c Healy, b Cook	15	(1) c Blewett, b Kasprowicz	1
A.C.Parore †	c Blewett, b Reiffel	30	lbw, b Kasprowicz	63
S.P. Fleming *	c Blewett, b Warne	10	(5) c Blewett, b Warne	4
N.J. Astle	c Healy, b Reiffel	12	(6) lbw, b Cook	19
C.D. McMillan	c Taylor, b Kasprowicz	54	(7) lbw, b Cook	23
C.L. Cairns	c M.E. Waugh, b Warne	52	(8) b Cook	7
D.L. Vettori	not out	14	(4) c Taylor, b Warne	1
S.B. Doull	c Taylor, b Warne	8	c S.R. Waugh, b Cook	17
S.B. O'Connor	c S.R. Waugh, b Cook	7	c Taylor, b Cook	7
G.I. Allott	b Warne	0	not out	2
	lb 3, nb 3	6	lb 2, nb 5	7
		217		174

	O	M	R	W	O	M	R	W
Kasprowicz	20	9	40	2	16	5	43	2
Reiffel	20	6	46	2	12	4	26	–
Cook	10	5	36	2	10.2	3	39	5
Warne	22.4	3	83	4	26	4	64	2
Blewett	2	1	9	–				

Fall of Wickets
1–12, 2–31, 3–51, 4–72, 5–87, 6–161, 7–187, 8–197, 9–214
1–2, 2–53, 3–55, 4–84, 5–102, 6–137, 7–145, 8–160, 9–174

Australia

	First Innings	
M.A. Taylor *	lbw, b O'Connor	2
M.T.G. Elliott	c O'Connor, b Cairns	42
G.S. Blewett	c Astle, b O'Connor	14
M.E. Waugh	c Parore, b Doull	86
S.R. Waugh	b O'Connor	96
I.A. Healy †	c Fleming, b Cairns	85
R.T. Ponting	c Fleming, b Cairns	16
P.R. Reiffel	c Fleming, b Cairns	54
S.K. Warne	c O'Connor, b Vettori	36
M.S. Kasprowicz	run out	9
S.H. Cook	not out	3
	b 6, lb 5, nb 7	18
		461

	O	M	R	W
Doull	21	3	78	1
O'Connor	31.4	7	109	3
Cairns	28	9	95	4
Vettori	29	7	84	1
Allott	22	3	84	–

Fall of Wickets
1–3, 2–53, 3–71, 4–224, 5–262, 6–287, 7–403, 8–449, 9–450

Umpires: D.B. Hair & G. Sharp

Australia won by an innings and 70 runs

Third Test Match – Australia v. New Zealand

27, 28, 29 and 30 November, 1 December 1997 at Bellerive Oval, Hobart

Australia

	First Innings		Second Innings	
M.T.G. Elliott	c Young, b McMillan	**114**		
M.A. Taylor *	b O'Connor	**18**	(1) not out	**66**
G.S. Blewett	b Doull	**99**	b Vettori	**56**
M.E. Waugh	c Parore, b O'Connor	**81**	(2) lbw, b O'Connor	**9**
S.R. Waugh	c McMillan, b Doull	**7**	not out	**2**
R.T. Ponting	c Parore, b Cairns	**4**		
I.A. Healy †	c Young, b O'Connor	**16**		
P.R. Reiffel	c Young, b Doull	**19**		
S.K. Warne	st Parore, b Vettori	**14**		
M.S. Kasprowicz	c Doull, b Cairns	**20**		
S.H. Cook	not out	**0**		
	lb **6**, w **1**, nb **1**	**8**	b **4**, lb **1**	**5**
		400	(for 2 wickets, dec.)	**138**

	O	M	R	W	O	M	R	W
Doull	33	11	87	**3**	8	1	28	–
O'Connor	34	8	101	**3**	9	2	32	**1**
Cairns	35.1	13	86	**2**				
Astle	12	5	32	–	7	–	25	–
McMillan	15	4	43	**1**				
Vettori	12	1	45	**1**	14	1	48	**1**

Fall of Wickets
1–**41**, 2–**238**, 3–**238**, 4–**246**, 5–**266**, 6–**291**, 7–**326**, 8–**353**, 9–**400**
1–**14**, 2–**106**

New Zealand

	First Innings		Second Innings	
B.A. Young	b Reiffel	**31**	(6) c Ponting, b Warne	**10**
M.J. Horne	c Elliott, b Reiffel	**133**	(1) lbw, b Reiffel	**31**
A.C. Parore †	lbw, b S.R. Waugh	**44**	(7) c Elliott, b Warne	**41**
S.P. Fleming *	c Healy, b S.R. Waugh	**0**	(4) st Healy, b Warne	**0**
R.G. Twose	lbw, b Warne	**2**	(8) run out	**29**
C.D. McMillan	lbw, b S.R. Waugh	**2**	(5) c Taylor, b Warne	**41**
N.J. Astle	not out	**22**	(2) c Ponting, b Reiffel	**40**
C.L. Cairns	not out	**10**	(3) st Healy, b Warne	**18**
D.L. Vettori	c Healy, b S.R. Waugh	**3**		
S.B. Doull	not out		S.B. O'Connor	not out
	b **1**, lb **2**, nb **4**	**7**	b **2**, lb **7**	**9**
	(for 6 wickets, dec.)	**251**	(for 9 wickets)	**223**

	O	M	R	W	O	M	R	W
Kasprowicz	13	1	43	–	3	–	33	–
Reiffel	14	8	27	**2**	14	2	47	**2**
Warne	27	4	81	**1**	28	6	88	**5**
Cook	13	2	50	–	4	–	17	–
M.E. Waugh	8	2	17	–	6	1	19	–
Blewett	5	1	10	–				
S.R. Waugh	9	2	20	**3**	6	4	10	**1**
Elliott	1	1	0	–				

Fall of Wickets
1–**60**, 2–**192**, 3–**192**, 4–**195**, 5–**198**, 6–**229**
1–**72**, 2–**93**, 3–**93**, 4–**95**, 5–**137**, 6–**152**, 7–**218**, 8–**221**, 9–**222**

Umpires: S.J. Davis & R.B. Tiffin

Match drawn

Test Match Averages – Australia v. New Zealand

Australia Batting

	M	Inns	NOs	Runs	HS	Av	100s	50s
P.R. Reiffel	3	4	1	178	77	59.33	2	
M.A. Taylor *	3	5	1	214	112	53.50	1	
G.S. Blewett	3	5	–	267	99	53.40	3	
I.A. Healy †	3	4	–	194	85	48.50	2	
M.T.G. Elliott	3	4	–	185	114	46.25	1	
R.T. Ponting	3	4	1	119	73	39.66	1	
M.E. Waugh	3	5	–	196	86	39.20	2	
S.R. Waugh	3	5	1	129	96	32.25	1	
S.K. Warne	3	3	–	71	36	23.66		
M.S. Kasprowicz	3	3	1	42	20	21.00		

played in two Tests – S.H. Cook 3 (capt) & 0 (capt)
played in one Test – G.D. McGrath 6

Bowling

	Overs	Mds	Runs	Wks	Average	Best	5/inn
S.R. Waugh	15	6	30		47.50	3/20	
G.D. McGrath	49.2	12	128	7	18.28	5/32	1
S.H. Cook	37.2	10	142	7	20.28	5/39	1
S.K. Warne	170.4	36	476	19	25.05	5/88	1
P.R. Reiffel	93	30	226	8	28.25	2/27	
G.S. Blewett	13	4	30	1	30.00	1/11	
M.S. Kasprowicz	84	27	233	6	38.83	2/40	
M.E. Waugh	21	5	54	–	–		

bowled in one innings – M.T.G. Elliott 1–1–0–0

Fielding Figures

10 – M.A. Taylor; 8 – I.A. Healy (ct 6 / st 2); 5 – G.S. Blewett; 4 – S.R. Waugh; 3 – M.T.G. Elliott; 2 – R.T. Ponting; 1 –M.E. Waugh

New Zealand Batting

	M	Inns	NOs	Runs	HS	Av	100s	50s
A.C Parore *	3	6	1	229	63	45.80	1	
C.L. Cairns	3	6	1	172	64	34.40	2	
C.D. McMillan	3	6	–	174	54	29.00	2	
N.J. Astle	3	6	1	119	40	23.80		
B.A. Young	3	6	–	119	45	19.83		
B.A. Pocock	2	4	–	76	57	19.00	1	
S.P. Fleming †	3	6	–	105	91	17.50	1	
S.B. Doull	3	5	2	30	17	10.00		
D.L. Vettori	3	5	1	32	14	8.00		
S.B. O'Connor	2	3	1	14	7	7.00		
G.I. Allott	2	4	1	6	4	2.00		

played in one Test: C.Z. Harris 13 & 0; M.J. Horne 133 & 31; R.G. Twose 2 & 29

Bowling

	Overs	Mds	Runs	Wks	Average	Best
C.L. Cairns	103.1	31	325	13	25.00	4/90
S.B. O'Connor	74.4	17	242	7	34.57	3/101
S.B. Doull	111	26	307	8	38.37	4/70
D.L. Vettori	112	27	310	6	51.66	2/87
G.I. Allott	72.5	10	261	2	130.50	1/60
C.Z. Harris	13	1	47	–	–	
N.J. Astle	31	7	91	–	–	

bowled in one innings – C.D. McMillan 15–3–43–1

Fielding Figures

9 – S.P. Fleming; 6 – A.C. Parore (ct 5 / st 1); 5 – B.A. Young; 2 – N.J. Astle, D.L. Vettori and S.B. O'Connor; 1 – B.A. Pocock, C.D. McMillan and S.B. Doull

South African Tour

Fresh from their success in Pakistan, South Africa arrived in Australia at the end of November, 1997, to play a three-Test series and to participate in the triangular one-day tournament. With injuries to fast bowlers Schultz and de Villiers, South Africa included the black, twenty years-old pace bowler Makkaya Ntini, in their party.

25 November 1997

at Lilac Hill, Perth

South Africans 282 for 5 (D.J. Cullinan 101 not out, J.H. Kallis 64)
ACB Chairman's XI 251 for 7 (M.E. Hussey 62, T.M. Moody 58 not out)
South Africans won by 31 runs

The South Africans gained a comfortable win in their opening match of the tour, a 50-over game against a side that included eight Western Australians augmented by the veterans Dennis Lillee, Graeme Pollock and Barry Richards.

27, 28, 29 and 30 November 1997

at WACA Ground, Perth

South Africans 468 (G. Kirsten 201, S.M. Pollock 100, P.L. Symcox 54, J. Stewart 4 for 121) and 167 for 3 dec. (A.M. Bacher 69 not out, W.J. Cronje 59 not out)
Western Australia 347 for 8 dec. (J.L Langer 60 not out, M.E. Hussey 59, D.R. Martyn 54, S.M. Katich 54, A.A. Donald 4 for 70) and 147 for 2 (M.E. Hussey 74 not out, D.R. Martyn 51)
Match drawn

Gary Kirsten hit 201 off 356 balls to give the tourists much satisfaction in their first first-class match of the tour. He and Shaun Pollock put on 171 for the sixth wicket with Pollock making 100 off 121 deliveries. Symcox gave further evidence of his batting powers with two sixes and six fours in his 44-ball innings. Western Australia's contribution came along more sedate lines, and a draw was inevitable.

2 December 1997

at Manuka Oval, Canberra

South Africans 268 for 6 (J.H. Kallis 50 not out)
Prime Minister's XI 257 for 7 (M.E. Hussey 91, M.J. Slater 70)
South Africans won by 11 runs

A narrow victory for the South Africans confirmed their good form. The Prime Minister's XI were given a splendid start by Hussey and Slater who put on 144, and they had reached 206 before their second wicket fell, but the later batsmen lost their way.

13, 14, 15 and 16 December 1997

at Formby Recreation Ground, Devonport

Tasmania 535 for 5 dec. (S. Young 145, D.J. Marsh 129 not out, J. Cox 73, D.F. Hills 68) and 147 for 7 dec.
South Africans 402 for 8 dec. (W.J. Cronje 165, A.A. Donald 55 not out, M.V. Boucher 55, M.W. Ridgway 4 for 105) and 94 for 2 (J.H. Kallis 51 not out)
Match drawn

Hills and Cox scored 134 for Tasmania's first wicket, and Young and Marsh added 151 for the fifth. Marsh reached a maiden first-class century, his 129 coming off 135 balls. The South Africans were in some trouble until Cronje's mighty innings which included three sixes and 14 fours.

19, 20, 21 and 22 December 1997

at Woolloongabba, Brisbane

South Africans 458 for 9 dec. (W.J. Cronje 107 not out, G. Kirsten 79, P.L. Symcox 55 not out, D.J. Richardson 55, H.H. Gibbs 54) and 220 for 7 dec. (D.J. Cullinan 83)
Australia 'A' 330 (J.L. Langer 89, M.J. Slater 80, D.S. Lehmann 66, L. Klusener 5 for 84, S.M. Pollock 4 for 68) and 122 for 1 (M.J. Slater 64 not out)
Match drawn

Greg Blewett is stumped by Dave Richardson off the bowling of Symcox. Richardson became South Africa's most successful wicket-keeper in the Test cricket when he surpassed John Waite's record of 144 victims during the first Test.
(Ben Radford / Allsport)

Cronje's second century in successive innings gave substance to the South Africans on the eve of the first Test. There was also some encouraging bowling by Pollock and Klusener against an Australian side that included six men with Test experience.

First Test Match

Australia *v.* South Africa

One of the most encouraging aspects of the first Test from the Australian point of view was that 73,812 people watched the first day's play, the highest attendance at the Melbourne Cricket Ground for 22 years. Australia named Bichel as twelfth man and fielded the expected eleven. Taylor won the toss and chose to bat, but he and his colleagues struggled painfully through the first two sessions, reaching tea at 92 for four. The post-tea period was in complete contrast to what had happened earlier in the day. Steve Waugh had batted with necessary caution when his side was in trouble, but once he and Ponting had established a platform they played some exquisite shots. They hit 114 runs in the final session, and the 129 by which they had increased the score since coming together had taken only 150 minutes. Steve Waugh was dropped at point just before the close, but nothing should detract from a fine achievement. South African wicket-keeper Richardson claimed three of the first four victims and passed John Waite's record of 144 dismissals.

Unbeaten on 87 overnight, Steve Waugh looked set for a century, but once more he fell in the nineties, caught by a juggling first slip as he attempted to drive off the back foot. Healy, warmly received, bustled busily for just under half an hour, and Reiffel again proved a most accomplished number eight batsman. He and Ponting had added 52 when Ponting fell to an off-break from Symcox that turned massively and to which the batsman offered no shot. Ponting had batted for 269 minutes, faced 208 balls and hit 14 fours in his second Test century which had come on his debut against South Africa. He is a wonderfully exciting player.

The visitors were soon in trouble. Bacher offered no shot to a ball from Kasprowicz that flicked the glove on its way to Healy. Kallis, too, was caught by the keeper. He dabbed at an off-cutter from McGrath, returning to first-class cricket after missing a month through injury, and South Africa were 62 for two. When Cullinan was run out by Ponting, they were 75 for three, and worse was to follow: Cronje failed to negotiate a leg-break and was out second ball. McMillan was happy to stay with Kirsten until the close. Of the 94 runs on the board, Kirsten had scored 61.

Kirsten and McMillan stayed together until twenty minutes before lunch on the third day, at which point Kirsten tried to cut an off-break from Mark Waugh and was caught behind. The left-handed opener had defied Australia for seven minutes under five and a half hours, a matter of some 82 overs. Warne, who bowled splendidly, trapped

Another victim for Symcox when Ponting is bowled for 105, his first Test century in Australia.
(David Munden / Sportsline)

Pollock with a delivery that turned less than others, and Richardson became Mark Waugh's second victim. McMillan, who batted for 227 minutes, was eighth out, and Klusener fell without addition. When Symcox was bowled by Kasprowicz, Australia claimed a first innings lead of 123 on a pitch that was offering generous help to the spinners and that was showing signs of disintegration.

A magnificent opening spell from Allan Donald, which brought him three wickets in ten overs either side of tea, brought South Africa back into the game. Pollock sent back Steve Waugh with a ball that raised a cloud of dust as it lifted from a full length and touched the glove on its way to the wicket-keeper. Australia closed on 67 for four, a lead of 190 and very much favourites to win.

On the fourth day, Donald became South Africa's leading wicket-taker in Test cricket as he produced another inspired spell of bowling. When he dismissed Warne, Australia were 146 for eight; but Reiffel's golden summer of batting continued, and Kasprowicz and McGrath helped him to add 111 for the last two wickets and to put the game out of South Africa's reach. Reiffel hit six fours as he made 79 off 115 balls, and he then claimed his 100th Test wicket when he bowled Kirsten with only two runs on the board.

First Test Match – Australia v. South Africa

26, 27, 28, 29 and 30 December 1997 at MCG, Melbourne

Australia

	First Innings		Second Innings	
M.T.G. Elliott	c Richardson, b Klusener	6	(2) lbw, b Donald	1
M.A. Taylor *	c Kirsten, b McMillan	20	(1) c Cullinan, b Symcox	59
G.S. Blewett	st Richardson, b Symcox	26	c McMillan, b Donald	6
M.E. Waugh	c Richardson, b Donald	0	b Donald	1
S.R. Waugh	c Cullinan, b Donald	96	c Richardson, b Pollock	17
R.T. Ponting	b Symcox	105	c and b Pollock	32
I.A. Healy †	b Donald	16	b Donald	4
P.R. Reiffel	b Symcox	27	not out	79
S.K. Warne	c and b Pollock	1	c Symcox, b Donald	10
M.S. Kasprowicz	c Bacher, b Symcox	0	c Kirsten, b Donald	19
G.D. McGrath	not out	0	c McMillan, b Pollock	18
	b 1, lb 6, nb 5	12	b 4, lb 3, nb 4	11
		309		257

	O	M	R	W	O	M	R	W
Donald	29	6	74	3	27	8	59	6
Pollock	28	6	76	1	21.2	5	56	3
Klusener	19	3	48	1	9	2	28	–
McMillan	10	3	19	1	2	–	6	–
Symcox	27.2	4	69	4	35	9	90	1
Kallis	4	2	5	–				
Cronje	4	2	11	–	2	–	11	–

Fall of Wickets
1–18, 2–42, 3–44, 4–77, 5–222, 6–250, 7–302, 8–309, 9–309
1–4, 2–10, 3–12, 4–44, 5–106, 6–128, 7–128, 8–146, 9–208

South Africa

	First Innings		Second Innings	
A.M. Bacher	c Healy, b Kasprowicz	3	(2) c Taylor, b Warne	39
G. Kirsten	c Healy, b M.E. Waugh	83	(1) b Reiffel	0
J.H. Kallis	c Healy, b McGrath	15	b Reiffel	101
D.J. Cullinan	run out	5	b Warne	0
W.J. Cronje *	c Blewett, b Warne	0	c Taylor, b S.R. Waugh	70
B.M. McMillan	c Healy, b Kasprowicz	48	c Taylor, b Warne	16
S.M. Pollock	lbw, b Warne	7	not out	15
D.J. Richardson †	lbw, b M.E. Waugh	1	lbw, b McGrath	11
L. Klusener	lbw, b Warne	11	not out	6
P.L. Symcox	b Kasprowicz	4		
A.A. Donald	not out	0		
	lb 2, w 1, nb 6	9	b 5, lb 4, nb 6	15
		186	(for 7 wickets)	273

	O	M	R	W	O	M	R	W
McGrath	17	9	20	1	28	11	57	1
Reiffel	14	5	32	–	18	8	24	2
Kasprowicz	13.5	3	28	3	14	1	45	–
Warne	42	15	64	3	44	11	97	3
M.E. Waugh	18	8	28	2	10	–	25	–
S.R. Waugh	2	–	12	–	7	2	12	1
Blewett	1	–	4	–				

Fall of Wickets
1–28, 2–62, 3–75, 4–76, 5–138, 6–155, 7–158, 8–182, 9–182
1–2, 2–88, 3–89, 4–211, 5–229, 6–241, 7–260

Umpires: S.A. Bucknor & S.G. Randell

Match drawn

Bacher and Kallis stood firm to take the score to 79 in 30 overs by the close.

Bacher added only five to his score before being brilliantly caught by Taylor at slip off Warne. The Australian captain took the ball left-handed low to the ground. Warne then bowled Cullinan for 0, and it seemed that the leg-spinner would run through the South African side. Kallis had other ideas. With skipper Cronje, he added 123 in 170 minutes, and when he was fifth out he had made 101 off 279 balls in 357 minutes and had helped save his side from defeat. It was his first Test century, and he had indicated the faith shown in his ability. But there was still work to be done: McMillan had to bat for 84 minutes, while Pollock had to curb his natural instincts to remain unbeaten for 101 minutes, to draw the match.

Second Test Match

Australia v. South Africa

Australia brought in Bevan for Kasprowicz, intending to use the emerging all-rounder's left-arm spin more than his batting, while South Africa reinforced their spin department by bringing in Adams for Klusener. They also replaced the

Jacques Kallis in action during his match-saving innings of 101 in Melbourne.
(Ben Radford / Allsport)

struggling Cullinan with Gibbs. Cronje won the toss and elected to bat. Play began half an hour late due to over-watering of a pitch close to the match strip.

Kirsten's was the only wicket to fall in the pre-lunch session. He was deceived by McGrath's movement off the pitch and edged to first slip. The introduction of Blewett into the attack half an hour after the interval brought immediate dividends, Bacher falling to his second delivery. Three balls later, Kallis was run out by a splendid piece of fielding from Ponting at short mid-wicket. Kallis, the non-striker, hesitated, and Ponting's throw broke the stumps with the batsman a yard short of his ground. Gibbs and Cronje then added 97 before Gibbs slashed at a wide-ish delivery from Bevan and was caught behind. Gibbs had completed his first half-century in Test cricket. The introduction of Bevan's left-arm spin was to prove as profitable as the advent of Blewett, for, two overs later, McMillan pulled a full toss into the hands of mid-on. South Africa ended the day on 197 for five, with Cronje having made 56 in an innings that had occupied almost four hours and which had tested the patience of the crowd.

The tenor of the game changed on the second morning when five boundaries came in the first five overs. The stand between Cronje and Pollock was worth 54 when Pollock edged Warne to first slip. This was a warning sign for South Africa, and the warning grew louder when Richardson was bowled by a ball that turned prodigiously. Warne changed

Shane Warne bowls Cullinan for 0. Cullinan had an unhappy series against the great leg-spinner.
(Ben Radford / Allsport)

Second Test Match – Australia *v.* South Africa

3, 4 and 5 January 1998 at SCG, Sydney

South Africa

	First Innings		Second Innings	
A.M. Bacher	lbw, **b** Blewet	**39**	(2) **c** Ponting, **b** Reiffel	**2**
G. Kirsten	**c** Taylor, **b** McGrath	**11**	(1) lbw, **b** McGrath	**0**
J.H. Kallis	run out	**16**	**b** Warne	**45**
W.J. Cronje *	**c** Taylor, **b** Warne	**88**	**c** Ponting, **b** Warn	**5**
H.H. Gibbs	**c** Healy, **b** Bevan	**54**	**c** Blewett, **b** Warne	**1**
B.M. McMillan	**c** Elliott, **b** Bevan	**6**	**b** Warne	**11**
S.M. Pollock	**c** Taylor, **b** Warne	**18**	**c** Taylor, **b** Warne	**4**
D.J. Richardson †	**b** Warne	**6**	**c** and **b** Warne	**0**
P.L. Symcox	**c** Healy, **b** Warne	**29**	**b** Reiffel	**38**
A.A. Donald	not out	**4**	**c** Healy, **b** Reiffel	**2**
P.R. Adams	**c** S.R. Waugh, **b** Warne	**0**	not out	**1**
	b **4**, lb **4**, w **1**, nb **7**	**16**	b **2**, lb **1**, nb **1**	**4**
		287		**113**

	O	M	R	W	O	M	R	W
McGrath	20	6	51	**1**	5	2	8	**1**
Reiffel	24	7	48	**–**	12	3	14	**3**
Warne	32.1	8	75	**5**	21	9	34	**6**
Bevan	23	5	56	**2**	3	–	18	**–**
Blewett	13	5	30	**1**	2	1	1	**–**
S.R. Waugh	8	4	10	**–**				
M.E. Waugh	3	1	5	**–**	10	2	35	**–**
Elliott	1	–	4	**–**				

Fall of Wickets
1–**25**, 2–**70**, 3–**70**, 4–**167**, 5–**174**, 6–**228**, 7–**236**, 8–**276**, 9–**287**
1–**1**, 2–**3**, 3–**21**, 4–**27**, 5–**41**, 6–**55**, 7–**55**, 8–**96**, 9–**112**

Australia

	First Innings	
M.T.G. Elliott	**c** McMillan, **b** Symcox	**32**
M.A. Taylor *	**c** Richardson, **b** Pollock	**11**
G.S. Blewett	**b** McMillan	**28**
M.E. Waugh	lbw, **b** Pollock	**100**
S.R. Waugh	**b** Donald	**85**
R.T. Ponting	**c** and **b** Adams	**62**
M.G. Bevan	**c** McMillan, **b** Symcox	**12**
I.A. Healey †	not out	**46**
P.R. Reiffel	**b** Donald	**0**
S.K. Warne	lbw, **b** Pollock	**12**
G.D. McGrath	**c** Richardson, **b** Donald	**14**
	b **1**, lb **12**, nb **6**	**19**
		421

	O	M	R	W
Donald	30.4	5	81	**3**
Pollock	33	8	71	**3**
Symcox	39	11	103	**2**
Adams	38	9	66	**1**
McMillan	18	5	55	**1**
Kallis	8	1	30	**–**
Cronje	1	–	2	**–**

Fall of Wickets
1–**35**, 2–**59**, 3–**103**, 4–**219**, 5–**317**, 6–**337**, 7–**354**, 8–**357**, 9–**385**

Umpires: D.B. Hair & P. Willey

Australia won by an innings and 21 runs

ends and had Cronje taken at slip when the batsman drove at a leg-break. Cronje had batted for 335 minutes and faced 261 deliveries; Warne had become the second most successful bowler in Australian Test history. Only Lillee, with 355 wickets, now stands ahead of him. The leg-spinner celebrated by taking the last two wickets, so ending a spell that had brought him five for 29 in 10.1 overs.

Australia began confidently, but Taylor unwisely cut at Pollock, and Elliott sliced Symcox to slip. Blewett and Mark Waugh seemed in total command until Blewett edged a wide ball into his stumps; but the dismissal only brought in Steve Waugh, who was playing in his 100th Test match and was about to celebrate the event with his twin brother. By the end of the day, they had taken the score to 174, and, ominously for South Africa, Mark Waugh was on 78.

He duly completed his twelfth Test hundred on the third morning, before falling to Pollock. Mark Waugh had batted for 211 minutes, faced 186 balls and hit a six and 12 fours. His stand with his brother had realised 116 and had given Australia a grip on the match. Ponting now helped confirm the advantage as he and Steve Waugh added 98. The stand was broken when Donald, who bowled magnificently on an unresponsive pitch in great heat, beat Steve Waugh with a fine delivery some 40 minutes before tea. The South African spinners lacked variety, and Cronje's tactics were too prone to veer towards the defensive. Ponting's enterprising and elegant innings came to an end when a leading edge provided Adams with a return catch, Healy bustled away as ever, and Australia closed at 392 for nine, a lead of 105, which was probably not quite as much as they might have anticipated.

In 10.4 overs on the fourth morning, it was extended by 29 runs, and South Africa faced a hard struggle if they were to save the game. They were aided by rain, which kept the players off the field for three hours after lunch. But by then they were already 85 for seven and sinking fast. Reiffel and McGrath gave Australia a wonderful start when they removed both openers with only three runs on the board.

Another victim for Ian Healy. Gibbs is caught off Bevan for 54. (Ben Radford / Allsport)

Shane Warne bowls Kallis for 45 to claim his 300th Test wicket. (Ben Radford /Allsport)

Warne completed what the pace bowlers had started, capturing five wickets while only 34 runs were scored. There was assistance for him in the pitch, and he was virtually unplayable. He is the supreme master of his art. Frustrated by the rain and by Kallis's technique of kicking away the leg-break that pitched outside leg stump, Warne deceived the batsman with a top-spinner that went between bat and pad and ended Kallis's 155-minute innings. It was Warne's 300th Test wicket. He was playing his 63rd Test, and, among spinners, only Lance Gibbs, with 309 wickets in 79 Tests, lies ahead of him.

Reiffel claimed the last two wickets, and Australia won by an innings inside four days. Warne, Man of the Match, had taken five wickets in a Test innings for the 14th time, and it was the fourth occasion on which he had taken ten or more wickets in a match. His figures for this Sydney Test were 11 for 109 in 53.1 overs.

---

13 January 1998
at Bowral
South Africans 288 (H.H. Gibbs 131, A.M. Bacher 57)
Bradman XI 133 (P.R. Adams 4 for 28)
South Africans won by 155 runs

Gibbs and Bacher put on 122 for the first wicket. Gibbs hit five sixes and 12 fours in his 131, which came off only 127 balls.

Third Test Match

Australia *v.* South Africa

Rhodes and Klusener for Adams and the injured Donald were the only changes in the South African line-up, while injuries to McGrath and Reiffel forced changes in the Australian side. Bichel and Kasprowicz were the replacements, and leg-spinner Stuart MacGill was awarded his first Test cap with Bevan standing down. Cronje again won the toss, and South Africa batted. There were no early sensations. Neither Bichel nor Kasprowicz passed the bat with any regularity, and Warne seemed out of sorts. Bacher and Kirsten batted for over three hours to score 140 before Bacher, losing patience, hung his bat out at a ball from Bichel and was well caught at second slip. Kirsten drove ambitiously and gave Warne a more straightforward catch. Kallis swept unwisely and became MacGill's first Test victim. Three wickets had fallen for 20 runs, and the initiative had been surrendered.

Cronje and Gibbs repaired the damage with a stand of 109. This was broken in the penultimate over of the day, when Gibbs drove at Blewett and was spectacularly caught by Healy, the world's best wicket-keeper, who was playing his 100th Test match. Cronje was content to make the last over a maiden.

With only three added to his overnight score, Cronje was deceived by a flipper from Warne, who also had Richardson taken at slip. Rhodes had hooked Kasprowicz into the hands of fine-leg, and South Africa were 305 for seven. The Australian attack disappointed, and McMillan and Pollock bravely took advantage of some loose bowling. They added 69, of which Pollock made 40 off 67 balls. The onslaught did not slacken. Klusener hit 38 off 59 balls before falling to a long hop, and Symcox, no doubt aggrieved at finding himself at number eleven after his recent exploits with the bat, raced to fifty in under half an hour. He dominated a last wicket stand of 75, but McMillan, who was unbeaten for 80 after 30 overs, an innings that included a six and 12 fours, had provided the composure that had allowed the last three wickets to realise 212 runs. Australia found themselves facing a formidable 517, and they soon lost Taylor, caught at third slip. They ended the day on 71 with the pitch still offering friendship to batsmen.

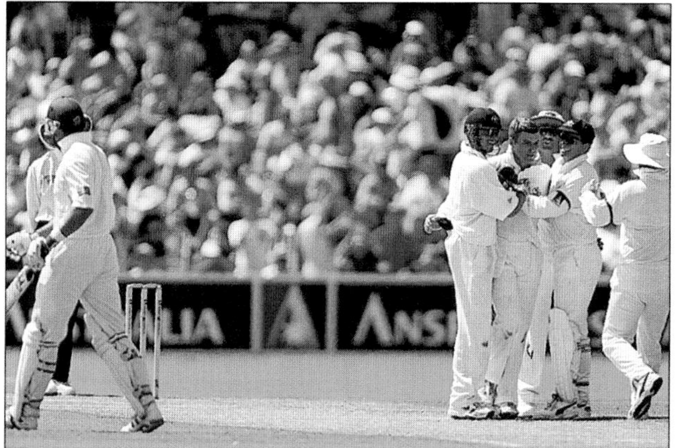

Stuart MacGill takes his first Test wicket when Kallis is leg before for 15 in Adelaide.
(Ben Radford / Allsport)

Controversial saviour – Mark Waugh, 115 not out.
(Ben Radford /Allsport)

Blewett ignored that friendship, falling to the fourth ball of the third day, but Taylor and Mark Waugh reasserted the dominance of the bat as they added 126 for the third wicket. Pollock broke the stand when he had Mark Waugh caught at cover, and he soon had the other Waugh caught behind. Ponting showed no sign of the form he had shown for most of the summer and was bowled by Klusener. When Pollock trapped Healy into giving a simple return catch and dismissed Bichel and Warne with successive deliveries, Australia faced the prospect of being forced to follow on.

Pollock had given a masterly display of pace bowling in intense heat, but Taylor, enjoying some fortune, had countered him with the bat. He and Kasprowicz saved the follow-on, and, although Kasprowicz fell to Kallis, Taylor remained until the end, unbeaten on 157 after nearly eight hours at the crease. Australia were 327 for nine.

Taylor duly became the 11th Australian, and the first for twelve years, to carry his bat through a complete Test innings. He batted for just over eight and a half hours and rescued his side from a difficult situation. It was hard to recall that his place in the Australian eleven had been in jeopardy only months earlier.

Gary Kirsten lofts a ball from Bichel to the boundary on the way to his unbeaten 108 in the third Test.
(Stephen Laffer / Sportsline)

South Africa led by 167 runs on the first innings, and their only hope of victory was to score quickly so that their attack had as much time as possible in which to bowl out the Australians. Bacher and Kirsten gave them an excellent start, scoring 80 before Bacher skied a ball from Warne. Kirsten kept up the momentum, and at tea South Africa were 144 for two, a lead of 311. There were thoughts that Cronje might declare, but he decided to bat on and wickets tumbled. He lobbed Kasprowicz to mid-on, and MacGill produced a good spell that brought him three wickets for 11 runs. His Test debut was impressive, as his five wickets indicate. If he lacks the variety of Warne, he turns the ball sufficiently to trouble most batsmen. Rhodes joined Kirsten in a brief, brisk partnership, and Cronje declared just before five. Kirsten remained unbeaten on 108, his sixth Test century. It was an innings of quality, fitted to the needs of the occasion and giving his side every chance of success.

That success looked most probable when Elliott, in the middle of a wretched spell, was caught behind, and Taylor was bowled by a short delivery that kept low. Blewett, nine, and Mark Waugh, 11, saw Australia to an uneasy close of 32 for two.

South Africa did not win because they did not hold their catches. They missed five chances in the first innings, and they put down ten in the second. Crucially, they dropped Mark Waugh on the Monday evening when he had one run to his credit. Pollock bowled outstandingly well in

Third Test Match – Australia *v.* South Africa

30, 31 January, 1, 2 and 3 February 1998 at Adelaide Oval, Adelaide

South Africa

	First Innings		Second Innings	
A.M. Bacher	c Warne, b Bichel	64	(2) c MacGill, b Warne	41
G. Kirsten	c Warne, b Kasprowicz	77	(1) not out	108
J.H. Kallis	lbw, b MacGill	15	b Kasprowicz	15
W.J. Cronje *	b Warne	73	c Warne, b Kasprowicz	5
H.H. Gibbs	c Healy, b Blewett	37	(7) st Healy, b MacGill	2
D.J. Richardson †	c Taylor, b Warne	15		
J.N. Rhodes	c Bichel, b Kasprowicz	6	(8) not out	19
B.M. McMillan	not out	87		
S.M. Pollock	c Blewett, b Kasprowicz	40		
L. Klusener	c Warne, b MacGill	38	(5) b MacGill	0
P.L. Symcox	lbw, b S.R. Waugh	54	(6) st Healy, b MacGill	2
	lb 8, w 2, nb 1	11	nb 1	1
		517	(for 6 wickets, dec.)	193

	O	M	R	W	O	M	R	W
Kasprowicz	39	7	125	3	18	5	55	2
Bichel	35	10	103	1	14	2	51	–
Warne	33	6	95	2	15	2	52	1
MacGill	29	7	112	2	7	1	22	3
M.E. Waugh	6	1	21	–				
Blewett	14	5	26	1				
S.R. Waugh	10	3	27	1	4	1	13	–

Fall of Wickets
1–140, 2–148, 3–160, 4–269, 5–275, 6–286, 7–305, 8–374, 9–442
1–80, 2–133, 3–155, 4–155, 5–157, 6–165

Australia

	First Innings		Second Innings	
M.A. Taylor *	not out	169	(2) b Klusener	6
M.T.G. Elliott	c Kallis, b Pollock	8	(1) c Richardson, b Pollock	4
G.S. Blewett	c Bacher, b Pollock	31	b Pollock	16
M.E. Waugh	c Gibbs, b Pollock	63	not out	115
S.R. Waugh	c Richardson, b Pollock	6	c Richardson, b Klusener	34
R.T. Ponting	b Klusener	26	c Symcox, b Klusener	23
I.A. Healy †	c and b Pollock	1	c Richardson, b Kallis	10
A.J. Bichel	c Symcox, b Pollock	0	lbw, b Klusener	7
S.K. Warne	c Richardson, b Pollock	0	not out	4
M.S. Kasprowicz	c Symcox, b Kallis	17		
S.C.G. MacGill	b Symcox	10		
	b 2, lb 12, nb 5	19	b 2, nb 6	8
		350	(for 7 wickets)	227

	O	M	R	W	O	M	R	W
Pollock	41	11	87	7	30.4	12	61	2
McMillan	23	5	60	–	13	2	33	–
Kallis	18	5	45	1	16	10	20	1
Klusener	27	6	104	1	30	10	67	4
Symcox	13.5	3	40	1	18	2	42	–
Cronje	1	–	2	–				

Fall of Wickets
1–15, 2–71, 3–197, 4–207, 5–263, 6–273, 7–279, 8–279, 9–317
1–6, 2–17, 3–54, 4–112, 5–185, 6–202, 7–215

Umpires: D.B. Cowie & S.G. Randell

Match drawn

stamina-sapping hot weather, but the wickets of Blewett in the first session and Steve Waugh in the second were all that the South Africans had to show for their efforts before tea. Ponting and Healy were out in the final session of the day, and Pollock was called up for a last supreme effort for the seventh of the last 15 overs. A short ball hit Mark Waugh, 107 magnificently defiant runs to his credit, on the forearm and lobbed to Symcox in the gully. The fielder appealed histrionically for a catch, and the appeal was rightly rejected. Meanwhile, Waugh, momentarily disturbed by the delivery, swished his bat at the stumps and dislodged a bail. The South Africans appealed again, and Randell, the square-leg umpire, turned to the third umpire (Davis) for a ruling. It was hard to see how such an action was covered by the terms of reference set down concerning the use of the television monitor. Davis debated at length before signalling that Waugh was not out. The South Africans remonstrated, and it was later revealed that, after play had ended, Cronje threw a stump through the door of the umpires' room, an action for which he apologised. His frustration was compounded by the fact that Waugh was dropped again on the last ball of the over, and was to remain unbeaten on 115 after six and a half hours at the crease to give Australia their ninth Test series victory in succession. For Pollock, the hero, the Man of the Match award was small consolation.

World Series

Australia, South Africa and New Zealand

The triangular one-day international tournament was compressed into two periods. The first six matches were played between the fourth and 17th of December, 1997, and the remaining six qualifying games between the ninth and 21st of January, 1998, with the finals scheduled between the 23rd and the 27th.

Australia adopted a new policy, naming Steve Waugh as captain for the one-day competition from which Taylor was omitted. Most surprisingly, Ian Healy was also omitted from the limited-over squad. Gilchrist was named as wicket-keeper. The new policy was not successful in the opening match, in which Australia were soundly beaten by South Africa. The Man of the Match was Pat Symcox, who at the age of 37 was in one of the best periods of his career. South Africa began badly, but Gary Kirsten laid the foundation of a solid innings on a difficult pitch. Cullinan, too, worked hard for his 33, and Donald and Symcox made vital contributions in a last wicket stand of 40. Symcox then went on to return his best bowling figures in a one-day international, four for 28, and his victims included the Waugh twins. Cronje was even able to rest his main bowlers

Test Match Averages – Australia v. South Africa

Australia Batting

	M	Inns	NOs	Runs	HS	Av	100s	50s
M.E. Waugh	3	5	1	279	115*	69.75	2	1
M.A. Taylor	3	5	1	265	169*	66.25	1	1
P.R. Reiffel	2	3	1	106	79*	53.00		1
R.T. Ponting	3	5	–	248	105	49.60	1	1
S.R. Waugh	3	5	–	238	96	47.60	2	
G.S. Blewett	3	5	–	107	31	21.40		
I.A. Healy	3	5	1	77	46*	19.25		
G.D. McGrath	2	3	1	32	18	16.00		
M.S. Kasprowicz	2	3	–	36	19	12.00		
M.T.G. Elliott	3	5	–	51	32	10.20		
S.K. Warne	3	5	1	27	12	6.75		

played in one match – M.G. Bevan 12; A.J. Bichel 0 & 7; S.C.G. MacGill 10

Bowling

	Overs	Mds	Runs	Wks	Average	Best	10/m	5/inn
S.K. Warne	187.1	51	417	20	20.85	6/34	1	2
P.R. Reiffel	68	23	118	5	23.60	3/14		
S.C.G. MacGill	36	8	134	5	26.80	3/22		
G.S. Blewett	30	11	61	2	30.50	1/26		
M.S. Kasprowicz	84.5	16	253	8	31.62	3/28		
G.D. McGrath	70	28	136	4	34.00	1/8		
M.G. Bevan	26	5	74	2	37.00	2/56		
S.R. Waugh	31	10	74	2	37.00	1/12		
M.E. Waugh	47	12	114	2	57.00	2/28		
A.J. Bichel	49	12	154	1	154.00	1/103		

bowled in one innings – M.T.G. Elliott 1–0–4–0

Fielding Figures

10 – I.A. Healy (ct 8 / st 2); 8 – M.A. Taylor; 5 – S.K. Warne; 3 – G.S. Blewett; 2 – R.T. Ponting; 1 –M.T.G. Elliott, S.R. Waugh, A.J. Bichel and S.C.G. MacGill

South Africa Batting

	M	Inns	NOs	Runs	HS	Av	100s	50s
G. Kirsten	3	6	1	279	108*	55.80	1	2
B.M. McMillan	3	5	1	168	87*	42.00	1	
W.J. Cronje	3	6	–	241	88	40.16	3	
J.H. Kallis	3	6	–	207	101	34.50	1	
A.M. Bacher	3	6	–	188	64	31.33	1	
P.L. Symcox	3	5	–	127	54	25.40	1	
H.H. Gibbs	2	4	–	94	54	23.50	1	
S.M. Pollock	3	5	1	84	40	21.00		
L. Klusener	2	4	1	55	38	18.33		
D.J. Richardson	35	–	33	15		6.60		
A.A. Donald	2	3	2	6	4*	6.00		

played in one match – D.J. Cullinan 5 & 0; P.R. Adams 0 & 1 (capt); J.N. Rhodes 6 & 19 (capt)

Bowling

	Overs	Mds	Runs	Wks	Average	Best	10/m	5/inn
A.A. Donald	86.4	19	214	12	17.83	6/59	1	
S.M. Pollock	154	42	351	16	21.93	7/87	1	
L. Klusener	85	21	247	7	35.28	4/67		
P.L. Symcox	133.1	29	344	8	43.00	4/69		
J.H. Kallis	46	18	100	2	50.00	1/20		
B.M. McMillan	66	15	173	2	86.50	1/19		
W.J. Cronje	8	2	26	–	–			

bowled in one innings – P.R. Adams 38–9–66–1

Fielding Figures

11 – D.J. Richardson (ct 10 / st 1); 4 – B.M. McMillan and P.L. Symcox; 3 – S.M. Pollock; 2 – G. Kirsten, A.M. Bacher and D.J. Cullinan; 1 – J.H. Kallis, H.H. Gibbs and P.R. Adams

Australia's one day all rounder, Ian Harvey of Victoria.
(Stephen Laffer / Sportsline)

and pressed Cullinan into action. He responded with two wickets as Australia were bowled out in 38 overs.

The second match saw the form book totally upset as New Zealand gained a convincing win over South Africa. New Zealand recovered from the loss of both openers for six and were much indebted to McMillan and Harris, who added 124 for the sixth wicket. McMillan, a growing force in New Zealand cricket, took the individual award, but he was admirably supported by an attack that was relentlessly accurate.

The following day, Australia beat New Zealand to give each side one win after the first round of matches. New Zealand batted well after winning the toss. Horne and Astle gave them a fine start, taking 32 off McGrath's first four overs, and there were useful contributions from Fleming, McMillan and Twose. Australia began with equal assertion, Mark Waugh and di Venuto scoring 156 for the first wicket. Mark Waugh reached his 11th hundred in one-day international cricket. His 104 was a typically spectacular affair, coming off 113 deliveries. With only one wicket down and 59 runs required in more than 13 overs, Australia were cruising to victory. The dismissal of Mark Waugh heralded a collapse. Five wickets fell for 57 runs, and Australia scraped home with just two balls to spare.

In Melbourne, Australia performed badly when chasing a moderate target of 171, set by South Africa. The home side, who had surprisingly recalled Tom Moody, fielded magnificently. Four South African batsmen were run out as they attempted to break free against an accurate attack that was weakened by the absence of McGrath. Again, Mark Waugh gave Australia a good start, and, in conjunction with Bevan, he took the score to 79 for three. He was out when he cut at a ball from Symcox and edged to point, and from then on Australia were in decline with only Gilchrist offering serious resistance. Lance Klusener finished with five wickets for 24 runs.

South Africa extended their lead at the top of the qualifying table when they beat New Zealand by the narrowest of margins in Hobart. Klusener was again the hero. Batting at number three, he, in collaboration with Gibbs and Symcox, maintained a run-rate of four an over. With the score on 71, Symcox was caught and bowled, and Cronje and Klusener were run out in quick succession. In spite of Kallis's effort, the South African innings never regained momentum. Klusener dismissed both New Zealand openers, Horne and Astle, in his first over. Cairns responded by hitting five fours, but he swung once too often at Klusener and was bowled. It was the eighth-wicket pair of Harris and Vettori who gave New Zealand a real hint of victory, but when the last ball arrived, bowled by Klusener, six runs were needed. Harris could succeed only in edging a delivery of full length for four.

The last of the pre-Christmas batch of matches saw Australia overwhelm New Zealand in Melbourne. New Zealand never recovered from being plunged to 45 for six, although Chris Harris battled nobly at the end of the innings. Australia lost di Venuto and the Waugh twins for 22 runs, but Ponting and Bevan added 95, and victory was achieved with more than 11 overs to spare.

Chris Cairns of New Zealand, an all-round force in one-day cricket.
(Stephen Laffer / Sportsline)

A new recruit to the Australian ranks, pace bowler Paul Wilson of South Australia.
(Stephen Laffer / Sportsline)

The restart of the competition provided another thrilling encounter between South Africa and New Zealand. Kirsten and Klusener gave South Africa a fine start with an opening partnership of 100, and the later batsmen never allowed the tempo to drop. Facing a daunting target of 301, New Zealand slipped to 97 for five and looked well beaten, but first Cairns, and then Parore and Nash, brought them back into the game. A ninth wicket stand between Nash and Vettori had realised 32 when the last ball arrived with three needed for victory. Nash hit hard and high to the outfield where Klusener took a fine running catch on the deep mid-wicket boundary to give South Africa the match. Klusener was enjoying a spectacular series.

South Africa triumphed at the Gabba again two days later, beating Australia by five wickets with 15 balls to spare and so qualifying for the finals. The Australian batting promised more than it achieved, and South Africa were again well served by Gary Kirsten, who took the individual award for his 89, which gave his side's innings the substance it needed. Kallis and Cronje also did well, and South Africa had few alarms.

The ninth match was interrupted by rain and reduced to 48 overs. Australia were without the Waugh twins and were led by Shane Warne. Australia were 36 for three before Ponting and Lehmann put on 132 in 25 overs. New Zealand failed to mount a challenge and were bowled out in 33.1 overs.

New Zealand suffered another crushing defeat at the hands of South Africa, for whom Jacques Kallis hit a maiden one-day international century. The match was notable for the fact that Makhaya Ntini became the first black cricketer to represent South Africa. The twenty-year old pace bowler, a product of the township development programme, celebrated his debut with the wickets of Fleming and Parore and bowled impressively.

South Africa's win over New Zealand ensured Australia of a place in the final, but the Australians themselves had generally performed well below expectations, and they were beaten in their last two matches. Steve Waugh was out first ball to Donald, who wrecked their innings in Perth, and, in spite of Ponting's century, they were beaten by New Zealand in Melbourne. New Zealand had not had the best of luck in the tournament, twice losing narrowly to South Africa, but skipper Stephen Fleming saw that they ended on a high note with a brilliant hundred, which brought victory in the final over.

Final Table

	P	W	L	Pts
South Africa	8	7	1	14
Australia	8	3	5	6
New Zealand	8	2	6	4

The Finals

Australia v. South Africa

Predictably, South Africa took first blood in the finals. Cullinan, so often vulnerable against Warne, was promoted to open and coped admirably, sharing an opening stand of 55 with Kirsten who was again in top form. Both openers fell to spinners, Cullinan being stumped in Warne's first over. Lehmann also proved effective, and South Africa were restricted to 241, a total that looked well within the reach of Australia. Several chances went begging as Steve Waugh

South African skipper Hansie Cronje employs the reverse sweep.
(Ben Radford / Allsport)

A century in the second final for Australia's Adam Gilchrist – a controversial celebration.
(Stephen Laffer / Sportsline)

and Bevan added 101 in 25 overs, but Donald produced a shattering spell that saw the home side lose their last five wickets for 17 runs.

Australia levelled the series with victory in Sydney on Australia Day. South Africa made a wretched start when Cullinan clouted a Mark Waugh full toss to mid-on, and Kallis, Kirsten and Klusener all fell to poor shots. Cronje and Rhodes finally gave the South African innings some purpose with a partnership of 134, but this was to be Australia's day. Promoted to open, Adam Gilchrist at last gave some indication as to why he had been chosen ahead of Healy. He hit 100 off 104 balls to take his side close to victory, which came with 53 balls to spare.

Severely and justifiably criticised for selection and performance, Australia came good at the last to win the World Series. South Africa were greatly handicapped by the absence of the injured Donald, but Australia played well and deserved their victory. The substance of the Australian innings came from Steve Waugh, 71 off 88 balls, his highest score in the season's competition, and Ricky Ponting whose 76 off 96 balls was his fourth score above fifty in nine matches in the tournament. The pair put on 102 for the fourth wicket. South Africa started badly when Man of the Series Gary Kirsten was run out. Bacher was caught behind and one run later, Kallis trod on his stumps. Thereafter, in spite of a brief flourish from Klusener, which made the final result seem closer than, in fact, it was, South Africa faded. Not for the first time they had fallen at the last, crucial hurdle.

With regard to Australia's team of one-day specialists, the jury has yet to make its decision. The dynamism and exceptional ability behind the stumps of Ian Healy might well have brought better results in the qualifying matches. The Australian selectors would be unwise to ignore him when they come to choose their World Cup squad.

Match One – Australia v. South Africa

4 December 1997 at SCG, Sydney

South Africa

G. Kirsten	**c** McGrath, **b** M.E. Waugh	**44**
J.H. Kallis	**c** Harvey, **b** McGrath	**8**
L. Klusener	**b** McGrath	**3**
D.J. Cullinan	run out	**33**
W.J. Cronje *	**c** and **b** Bichel	**21**
J.N. Rhodes	**b** Harvey	**12**
S.M. Pollock	run out	**6**
B.M. McMillan	**c** Warne, **b** Bichel	**19**
D.J. Richardson †	lbw, **b** Bichel	**0**
P.L. Symcox	not out	**27**
A.A. Donald	**c** Gilchrist, **b** McGrath	**11**
	lb **11**, w **1**, nb **4**	**16**
	50 overs	**200**

	O	M	R	W
McGrath	10	1	40	**3**
Reiffel	8	3	25	**–**
Bichel	9	–	46	**3**
Warne	10	–	33	**–**
M.E. Waugh	3	–	12	**1**
Harvey	10	1	33	**1**

Fall of Wickets
1–**28**, 2–**37**, 3–**96**, 4–**98**, 5–**113**, 6–**124**, 7–**153**, 8–**153**, 9–**160**

Australia

M.J. di Venuto	**c** Rhodes, **b** Pollock	**1**
M.E. Waugh	**b** Symcox	**45**
G.S. Blewett	**c** Rhodes, **b** Donald	**15**
S.R. Waugh *	lbw, **b** Symcox	**1**
M.G. Bevan	**st** Richardson, **b** Symcox	**16**
A.C. Gilchrist †	**c** and **b** Cullinan	**4**
I.J. Harvey	**c** Kallis, **b** Symcox	**4**
P.R. Reiffel	**c** Kirsten, **b** Klusener	**17**
S.K. Warne	lbw, **b** Cullinan	**17**
A.J. Bichel	run out	**3**
G.D. McGrath	not out	**0**
	b **5**, lb **1**, w **3**, nb **1**	**10**
	38 overs	**133**

	O	M	R	W
Pollock	6	1	12	**1**
Klusener	7	–	34	**1**
Cronje	2	–	9	**–**
Donald	5	–	13	**1**
Symcox	10	1	28	**4**
Cullinan	8	–	31	**2**

Fall of Wickets
1–**6**, 2–**61**, 3–**64**, 4–**71**, 5–**78**, 6–**89**, 7–**92**, 8–**122**, 9–**133**

Umpires: D.J. Harper & S.G. Randell *Man of the Match*: P.L. Symcox

South Africa won by 67 runs

Match Two – South Africa v. New Zealand

6 December 1997 at Adelaide Oval, Adelaide

New Zealand

Batsman	How out	Runs
M.J. Horne	c Rhodes, b Pollock	4
N.J. Astle	run out	0
C.L. Cairns	c Richardson, b Donald	55
S.P. Fleming *	c Richardson, b Pollock	10
C.D. McMillan	c Symcox, b Pollock	86
R.G. Twose	lbw, b Donald	1
C.Z. Harris	not out	52
A.C. Parore †	not out	2
G.R. Larsen		
D.L. Vettori		
S.B. O'Connor		
	b 1, lb 8, w 5	14
	50 overs (for 6 wickets)	224

	O	M	R	W
Pollock	10	2	36	3
Klusener	9	–	56	–
Cronje	10	–	57	–
Donald	10	3	17	2
Symcox	4	–	20	–
McMillan	7	1	29	–

Fall of Wickets
1–**6**, 2–**6**, 3–**58**, 4–**89**, 5–**93**, 6–**217**

South Africa

Batsman	How out	Runs
G. Kirsten	st Parore, b Astle	35
J.H. Kallis	c Astle, b O'Connor	14
L. Klusener	c Horne, b O'Connor	25
D.J. Cullinan	b Larsen	13
W.J. Cronje *	c Parore, b Cairns	11
J.N. Rhodes	lbw, b Larsen	3
S.M. Pollock	c Horne, b McMillan	37
B.M. McMillan	b Astle	3
P.L. Symcox	c and b Harris	9
D.J. Richardson †	not out	21
A.A. Donald	b Cairns	4
	lb 1, nb 1	2
	47.5 overs	177

	O	M	R	W
O'Connor	7	1	36	2
Cairns	9.5	1	29	2
Larsen	10	–	31	2
Harris	10	–	32	1
Astle	9	–	31	2
McMillan	2	–	17	1

Fall of Wickets
1–**23**, 2–**52**, 3–**85**, 4–**91**, 5–**94**, 6–**113**, 7–**126**, 8–**141**, 9–**161**

Umpires: R.A. Emerson & S.J. Davis *Man of the Match*: C.D. McMillan

New Zealand won by 47 runs

Match Three – Australia v. New Zealand

7 December 1997 at Adelaide Oval, Adelaide

New Zealand

Batsman	How out	Runs
M.J. Horne	lbw, b Warne	31
N.J. Astle	c Warne, b Bichel	66
S.P. Fleming *	c Harvey, b Bichel	61
C.D. McMillan	c Harvey, b Warne	43
C.L. Cairns	c Gilchrist, b McGrath	0
A.C. Parore †	b Harvey	9
R.G. Twose	c Bevan, b Warne	26
C.Z. Harris	not out	9
G.R. Larsen	not out	0
D.L. Vettori		
S.B. O'Connor		
	b 4, w 9, nb 2	15
	50 overs (for 7 wickets)	260

	O	M	R	W
McGrath	10	1	53	1
Dale	6	–	41	–
Warne	10	–	48	3
Harvey	10	–	39	1
M.E. Waugh	4	–	23	–
Bichel	10	1	52	2

Fall of Wickets
1–**77**, 2–**148**, 3–**186**, 4–**190**, 5–**220**, 6–**227**, 7–**259**

Australia

Batsman	How out	Runs
M.E. Waugh	c Parore, b Harris	104
M.J. di Venuto	st Parore, b Vettori	77
A.C. Gilchrist †	run out	29
G.S. Blewett	b Larsen	0
I.J. Harvey	c Parore, b Astle	3
S.R. Waugh *	lbw, b Larsen	7
M.G. Bevan	not out	25
S.K. Warne	b Larsen	5
A.J. Bichel	not out	4
A.C. Dale		
G.D. McGrath		
	lb 5, w 3, nb 1	9
	49.4 overs (for 7 wickets)	263

	O	M	R	W
O'Connor	4	1	23	–
Cairns	8	-	54	–
Harris	10	2	34	1
Astle	6	1	35	1
Larsen	9.4	–	56	3
Vettori	9	–	47	1
McMillan	3	–	9	–

Fall of Wickets
1–**156**, 2–**202**, 3–**209**, 4–**221**, 5–**221**, 6–**249**, 7–**259**

Umpires: D.B. Hair & T.A. Prue *Man of the Match*: M.E. Waugh

Australia won by 3 wickets

Match Four – Australia v. South Africa

9 December 1997 at MCG, Melbourne

South Africa

G. Kirsten	c Warne, b Reiffel	0
H.H. Gibbs	run out	15
L. Klusener	c Gilchrist, b Moody	17
W.J. Cronje *	run out	2
J.H. Kallis	st Gilchrist, b M.E. Waugh	27
J.N. Rhodes	run out	42
S.M. Pollock	c Moody, b M.E. Waugh	18
B.M. McMillan	run out	13
D.J. Richardson †	not out	18
P.L. Symcox	not out	4
A.A. Donald		
	lb 5, w 8, nb 1	14
	50 overs (for 8 wickets)	170

	O	M	R	W
Reiffel	10	1	18	1
Bichel	5	–	26	–
Moody	8	3	10	1
Harvey	7	–	36	–
Warne	10	–	36	–
M.E. Waugh	10	–	39	2

Fall of Wickets
1–**1**, 2–**36**, 3–**40**, 4–**44**, 5–**105**, 6–**125**, 7–**140**, 8–**161**

Australia

M.J. di Venuto	c Pollock, b Klusener	6
M.E. Waugh	c Pollock, b Symcox	45
S.R. Waugh *	c Richardson, b Klusener	0
R.T. Ponting	c Kirsten, b Klusener	15
M.G. Bevan	c Rhodes, b McMillan	19
A.C. Gilchrist †	not out	29
T.M. Moody	lbw, b Symcox	0
I.J. Harvey	lbw, b McMillan	1
P.R. Reiffel	run out	1
S.K. Warne	c Gibbs, b Klusener	5
A.J. Bichel	c McMillan, b Klusener	0
	lb 3, nb 1	4
	39.1 overs	125

	O	M	R	W
Pollock	8	1	25	–
Klusener	7.1	–	24	5
Donald	6	–	26	–
McMillan	8	–	29	2
Symcox	10	2	18	2

Fall of Wickets
1–**11**, 2–**12**, 3–**38**, 4–**79**, 5–**97**, 6–**97**, 7–**100**, 8–**104**, 9–**123**

Umpires: D.J. Harper & P.D. Parker *Man of the Match*: L. Klusener

South Africa won by 45 runs

Match Five – South Africa v. New Zealand

11 December 1997 at Bellerive Oval, Hobart

South Africa

G. Kirsten	b O'Connor	6
H.H. Gibbs	c Vettori, b O'Connor	12
L. Klusener	run out	37
P.L. Symcox	c and b Harris	15
W.J. Cronje *	run out	0
J.H. Kallis	c and b Harris	45
J.N. Rhodes	b Vettori	14
S.M. Pollock	c Larsen, b Cairns	31
B.M. McMillan	b Cairns	1
D.J. Richardson †	not out	9
A.A. Donald		
	w 4	4
	50 overs (for 9 wickets)	174

	O	M	R	W
O'Connor	7	–	42	2
Cairns	10	2	26	2
Harris	10	–	36	2
Larsen	8	1	23	–
Vettori	6	1	17	1
Astle	9	–	30	–

Fall of Wickets
1–**14**, 2–**41**, 3–**71**, 4–**72**, 5–**73**, 6–**99**, 7–**153**, 8–**155**, 9–**174**

New Zealand

M.J. Horne	lbw, b Klusener	3
N.J. Astle	c McMillan, b Klusener	1
C.L. Cairns	b Klusener	29
S.P. Fleming *	c Pollock, b Symcox	32
C.D. McMillan	c Kirsten, b Symcox	18
R.G. Twose	c Kirsten, b Pollock	11
A.C. Parore †	run out	6
C.Z. Harris	not out	37
D.L. Vettori	not out	25
G.R. Larsen		
S.B. O'Connor		
	lb 8, w 3	11
	50 overs (for 7 wickets)	173

	O	M	R	W
Pollock	10	2	24	1
Klusener	10	–	46	3
Donald	10	2	32	–
McMillan	10	1	28	–
Symcox	10	1	35	2

Fall of Wickets
1–**5**, 2–**6**, 3–**45**, 4–**83**, 5–**89**, 6–**97**, 7–**111**

Umpires: A.J. McQuillan & S.G. Randell *Man of the Match*: L. Klusener

South Africa won by 1 run

Match Six – Australia v. New Zealand

17 December 1997 at MCG, Melbourne

New Zealand

M.J. Horne	c Gilchrist, b Dale	3
N.J. Astle	c Gilchrist, b Dale	20
C.L. Cairns	b Wilson	0
S.P. Fleming *	c Bevan, b Wilson	6
C.D. McMillan	c Harvey, b Warne	9
R.G. Twose	run out	0
A.C. Parore †	c Gilchrist, b Wilson	5
C.Z. Harris	not out	62
D.L. Vettori	c Warne, b Bevan	14
G.R. Larsen	c S.R. Waugh, b Bevan	0
S.B. O'Connor	run out	8
	lb 4, w 5, nb 5	14
	49.3 overs	141

	O	M	R	W
Wilson	10	–	39	3
Dale	10	2	22	2
Warne	10	2	25	1
Bevan	10	–	26	2
Bichel	9	–	17	–
Harvey	0.3	–	8	–

Fall of Wickets
1–5, 2–9, 3–19, 4–45, 5–45, 6–45, 7–75, 8–108, 9–108

Australia

M.J. di Venuto	c Astle, b Cairns	7
M.E. Waugh	c Parore, b Cairns	9
R.T. Ponting	not out	60
S.R. Waugh *	c Parore, b Cairns	0
M.G. Bevan	c Astle, b Cairns	42
A.C. Gilchrist †	not out	11
I.J. Harvey		
S.K. Warne		
A.C. Dale		
A.J. Bichel		
P. Wilson		
	lb 4, w 8, nb 1	13
	38.5 overs (for 4 wickets)	142

	O	M	R	W
O'Connor	10	–	43	–
Cairns	10	3	40	4
Vettori	9	1	32	–
Harris	9.5	1	23	–

Fall of Wickets
1–17, 2–22, 3–22, 4–117

Umpires: R.A. Emerson & D.B. Hair *Man of the Match*: M.G. Bevan

Australia won by 6 wickets

Match Seven – South Africa v. New Zealand

9 January 1998 at Woolloongabba, Brisbane

South Africa

G. Kirsten	c Nash, b Harris	103
L. Klusener	b Nash	50
J.H. Kallis	c Parore, b Vettori	31
W.J. Cronje *	c Harris, b C.D. McMillan	55
H.H. Gibbs	lbw, b Harris	2
J.N. Rhodes	c Nash, b C.D. McMillan	23
S.M. Pollock	not out	14
P.L. Symcox	not out	12
B.M. McMillan		
D.J. Richardson †		
A.A. Donald		
	lb 5, w 5	10
	50 overs (for 6 wickets)	300

	O	M	R	W
O'Connor	6	–	50	–
Cairns	7	–	37	–
Nash	10	1	52	1
Harris	10	–	41	2
Vettori	7	–	46	1
Astle	5	–	42	–
C.D. McMillan	5	–	27	2

Fall of Wickets
1–100, 2–167, 3–231, 4–241, 5–269, 6–277

New Zealand

C.M. Spearman	c Symcox, b Pollock	11
N.J. Astle	c Richardson, b Donald	29
M.J. Horne	c B.M. McMillan, b Kallis	42
S.P. Fleming *	c Richardson, b Donald	2
C.D. McMillan	c Richardson, b Donald	4
C.Z. Harris	c B.M. McMillan, b Kallis	10
C.L. Cairns	run out	64
A.C. Parore †	c Symcox, b Donald	67
D.J. Nash	c Klusener, b Pollock	38
D.L. Vettori	not out	11
S.B. O'Connor		
	b 3, lb 11, w 4, nb 2	20
	50 overs (for 9 wickets)	298

	O	M	R	W
Pollock	10	1	58	2
Klusener	10	–	55	–
Donald	10	1	43	4
B.M. McMillan	8	–	52	–
Kallis	8	1	49	2
Symcox	4	–	27	–

Fall of Wickets
1–24, 2–84, 3–88, 4–94, 5–97, 6–124, 7–197, 8–266, 9–298

Umpires: S.J. Davis & A.J. McQuillan *Man of the Match*: G. Kirsten

South Africa won by 2 runs

Match Eight – Australia v. South Africa

11 January 1998 at Woolloongabba, Brisbane

Australia		
M.E. Waugh	c Richardson, b Donald	37
S.G. Law	c Richardson, b Donald	27
R.T. Ponting	c and b Symcox	31
D.S. Lehmann	c Rhodes, b Kallis	34
S.R. Waugh *	c Symcox, b Kallis	4
M.G. Bevan	not out	45
A.C. Gilchrist †	c Donald, b Pollock	21
P.R. Reiffel	c Rhodes, b Donald	5
S.K. Warne	run out	8
A.J. Bichel	not out	9
P. Wilson		
	lb 6, w 6, nb 2	14
	50 overs (for 8 wickets)	235

	O	M	R	W
Pollock	8	1	32	1
Klusener	9	–	65	–
McMillan	6	–	25	–
Donald	10	–	37	3
Symcox	10	–	38	1
Kallis	7	–	32	2

Fall of Wickets
1–**68**, 2–**75**, 3–**131**, 4–**140**, 5–**140**, 6–**192**, 7–**203**, 8–**217**

South Africa		
G. Kirsten	c Warne, b S.R. Waugh	89
L. Klusener	c Bevan, b Wilson	15
P.L. Symcox	run out	6
J.H. Kallis	lbw, b Wilson	47
W.J. Cronje *	not out	59
H.H. Gibbs	b Bichel	2
J.N. Rhodes	not out	14
B.M. McMillan		
S.M. Pollock		
D.J. Richardson †		
A.A. Donald		
	lb 3, w 1	4
	47.3 overs (for 5 wickets)	236

	O	M	R	W
Wilson	10	1	50	2
Reiffel	8	1	39	–
Warne	10	–	47	–
Bichel	10	–	47	1
Bevan	2.3	–	25	–
S.R. Waugh	4	–	14	1
M.E. Waugh	3	–	11	–

Fall of Wickets
1–**41**, 2–**72**, 3–**151**, 4–**189**, 5–**192**

Umpires: D.J. Harper & P.D. Parker *Man of the Match*: G. Kirsten

South Africa won by 5 wickets

Match Nine – Australia v. New Zealand

14 January 1998 at SCG, Sydney

Australia		
J.P. Maher	c Vettori, b O'Connor	8
S.G. Law	c Parore, b Cairns	12
I.J. Harvey	c Nash, b O'Connor	11
R.T. Ponting	b McMillan	84
D.S. Lehmann	c Young, b McMillan	52
M.G. Bevan	c and b Harris	25
A.C. Gilchrist †	c McMillan, b O'Connor	28
T.M. Moody	c and b Harris	0
P.R. Reiffel	c Fleming, b O'Connor	17
S.K. Warne *	not out	0
P. Wilson	run out	0
	lb 7, w 5, nb 1	13
	47.5 overs	250

	O	M	R	W
O'Connor	9.5	–	51	4
Cairns	7	–	29	1
Nash	10	–	56	–
Harris	10	–	42	2
Vettori	6	–	35	–
McMillan	5	–	30	2

Fall of Wickets
1–**18**, 2–**22**, 3–**36**, 4–**168**, 5–**190**, 6–**217**, 7–**217**, 8–**250**, 9–**250**

New Zealand		
C.M. Spearman	run out	6
B.A. Young	b Moody	22
M.J. Horne	c Gilchrist, b Wilson	14
S.P. Fleming *	c Bevan, b Harvey	28
C.D. McMillan	run out	10
C.L. Cairns	c Warne, b Harvey	5
C.Z. Harris	run out	8
A.C. Parore †	c Ponting, b Harvey	0
D.J. Nash	b Warne	5
D.L. Vettori	c Bevan, b Warne	4
S.B. O'Connor	not out	0
	lb 4, w 9, nb 4	17
	33.1 overs	119

	O	M	R	W
Wilson	8	–	29	1
Reiffel	6	–	28	–
Moody	6	1	22	1
Harvey	7	1	17	3
Warne	6.1	–	19	2

Fall of Wickets
1–**11**, 2–**51**, 3–**53**, 4–**78**, 5–**86**, 6–**99**, 7–**101**, 8–**109**, 9–**118**

Umpires: P.D. Parker & S.J. Davis *Man of the Match*: R.T. Ponting

Australia won by 131 runs

Match Ten – South Africa v. New Zealand

16 January 1998 at WACA Ground, Perth

South Africa		
G. Kirsten	run out	44
L. Klusener	c Vettori, b O'Connor	4
J.H. Kallis	c Nash, b C.D. McMillan	111
D.J. Cullinan	c Harris, b Cairns	26
H.H. Gibbs	c and b Harris	8
W.J. Cronje *	c O'Connor, b Cairns	6
J.N. Rhodes	c O'Connor, b Astle	2
S.M. Pollock	not out	22
P.L. Symcox	not out	5
M.V. Boucher †		
M. Ntini		
	lb 2, w 3	5
	50 overs (for 7 wickets)	233

	O	M	R	W
O'Connor	6	–	27	1
Cairns	10	1	50	2
Nash	8	–	41	–
Harris	10	–	39	1
Astle	9	–	39	1
Vettori	4	–	22	–
C.D. McMillan	3	–	13	1

Fall of Wickets
1–**7**, 2–**98**, 3–**171**, 4–**194**, 5–**199**, 6–**203**, 7–**211**

New Zealand		
B.A. Young	c Ntini, b Symcox	34
C.M. Spearman	c Rhodes, b Pollock	13
S.P. Fleming *	c Boucher, b Ntini	26
C.D. McMillan	c Gibbs, b Symcox	11
N.J. Astle	c Cullinan, b Pollock	18
C.L. Cairns	c Gibbs, b Pollock	17
C.Z. Harris	lbw, b Kallis	4
A.C. Parore †	c Boucher, b Ntini	8
D.J. Nash	c Gibbs, b Kallis	15
D.L. Vettori	run out	4
S.B. O'Connor	not out	2
	lb 3, w 10, nb 1	14
	45.1 overs	166

	O	M	R	W
Pollock	10	–	28	3
Klusener	8	1	41	–
Symcox	8	–	37	2
Ntini	10	–	31	2
Kallis	9.1	1	26	2

Fall of Wickets
1–**30**, 2–**60**, 3–**86**, 4–**89**, 5–**124**, 6–**127**, 7–**138**, 8–**144**, 9–**151**

Umpires: R.A. Emerson & A.J. McQuillan *Man of the Match*: J.H. Kallis

South Africa won by 67 runs

Match Eleven – Australia v. South Africa

18 January 1998 at WACA Ground, Perth

Australia		
S.G. Law	c Richardson, b Pollock	1
J.P. Maher	c Cronje, b Klusener	13
R.T. Ponting	c Kallis, b Symcox	16
D.S. Lehmann	c Rhodes, b Donald	10
S.R. Waugh *	c Richardson, b Donald	0
M.G. Bevan	c Cullinan, b McMillan	26
A.C. Gilchrist †	c Donald, b Symcox	6
I.J. Harvey	run out	43
B.E. Young	c Richardson, b Donald	5
A.J. Bichel	not out	27
P. Wilson	b Donald	0
	lb 6, w 8, nb 4	18
	48.2 overs	165

	O	M	R	W
Pollock	10	1	35	1
Symcox	10	1	33	2
Donald	9.2	–	29	4
Klusener	9	1	27	1
McMillan	8	3	27	1
Kallis	2	–	8	–

Fall of Wickets
1–**3**, 2–**27**, 3–**46**, 4–**46**, 5–**54**, 6–**70**, 7–**93**, 8–**108**, 9–**165**

South Africa		
G. Kirsten	run out	44
L. Klusener	c Law, b Wilson	11
J.H. Kallis	c Wilson, b Bichel	38
D.J. Cullinan	not out	35
W.J. Cronje *	not out	39
J.N. Rhodes		
S.M. Pollock		
P.L. Symcox		
B.M. McMillan		
D.J. Richardson †		
A.A. Donald		
	nb 3	3
	28.2 overs (for 3 wickets)	170

	O	M	R	W
Wilson	9.2	2	41	1
Bichel	8	–	55	1
Harvey	4	–	25	–
Young	7	–	49	–

Fall of Wickets
1–**34**, 2–**80**, 3–**100**

Umpires: D.B. Hair & T.A. Prue *Man of the Match*: A.A. Donald

South Africa won by 7 wickets

Match Twelve – Australia v. New Zealand

21 January 1998 at MCG, Melbourne

Australia

T.M. Moody	c O'Connor, b Harris	19
M.E. Waugh	c Nash, b Vettori	31
R.T. Ponting	c O'Connor, b Cairns	100
D.S. Lehmann	run out	46
S.R. Waugh *	not out	45
I.J. Harvey	not out	4
M.G. Bevan		
A.C. Gilchrist †		
P.R. Reiffel		
S.K. Warne		
P. Wilson		
	w 6	6
	50 overs (for 4 wickets)	251

	O	M	R	W
O'Connor	4	–	23	–
Cairns	10	2	46	1
Vettori	10	–	41	1
Harris	10	–	50	1
Astle	7	–	35	–
Nash	3	–	24	–
McMillan	6	–	32	–

Fall of Wickets
1–**51**, 2–**65**, 3–**153**, 4–**246**

New Zealand

C.M. Spearman	c Gilchrist, b Wilson	10
N.J. Astle	c sub (S.G. Law), b Wilson	13
B.A. Young	c M.E. Waugh, b Moody	8
S.P. Fleming *	not out	116
A.C. Parore †	c and b Moody	46
C.D. McMillan	lbw, b Warne	26
C.L. Cairns	c sub (S.G. Law), b Wilson	4
C.Z. Harris	not out	13
D.J. Nash		
D.L. Vettori		
S.B. O'Connor		
	b 1, lb 7, w 9	17
	49.1 overs (for 6 wickets)	253

	O	M	R	W
Wilson	10	1	39	3
Reiffel	8	1	31	–
Moody	10	1	52	2
Harvey	8	–	42	–
Warne	8.1	–	50	1
Bevan	5	–	33	–

Fall of Wickets
1–**25**, 2–**26**, 3–**42**, 4–**178**, 5–**219**, 6–**226**

Umpires: S.G. Randell & T.A. Prue *Man of the Match*: S.P. Fleming

New Zealand won by 4 wickets

First Final – Australia v. South Africa

23 January 1998 at MCG, Melbourne

South Africa

D.J. Cullinan	st Gilchrist, b Warne	26
G. Kirsten	st Gilchrist, b M.E. Waugh	70
L. Klusener	c Bevan, b Moody	0
J.H. Kallis	c Gilchrist, b Wilson	33
W.J. Cronje *	c Bevan, b Lehmann	29
J.N. Rhodes	c Gilchrist, b Lehmann	21
S.M. Pollock	c Bevan, b Warne	36
P.L. Symcox	b M.E. Waugh	10
B.M. McMillan	lbw, b Warne	2
D.J. Richardson †	not out	11
A.A. Donald		
	w 2, nb 1	3
	50 overs (for 9 wickets)	241

	O	M	R	W
Wilson	9	–	52	1
Reiffel	3	–	18	–
Warne	10	1	52	3
Moody	5	–	24	1
Harvey	9	–	39	–
M.E. Waugh	10	–	45	2
Lehmann	4	–	11	2

Fall of Wickets
1–**55**, 2–**62**, 3–**126**, 4–**137**, 5–**178**, 6–**186**, 7–**203**, 8–**210**, 9–**241**

Australia

M.E. Waugh	run out	3
A.C. Gilchrist †	c Symcox, b Pollock	20
R.T. Ponting	c Richardson, b Donald	33
D.S. Lehmann	run out	31
S.R. Waugh *	c Richardson, b McMillan	53
M.G. Bevan	run out	57
T.M. Moody	run out	15
I.J. Harvey	b Donald	7
P.R. Reiffel	c Richardson, b Donald	1
S.K. Warne	b Pollock	0
P. Wilson	not out	1
	lb 6, w 5, nb 3	14
	49.5 overs	235

	O	M	R	W
Pollock	9.5	1	39	2
Klusener	7	–	36	–
Symcox	10	1	56	–
Donald	10	–	36	3
McMillan	9	1	39	1
Kallis	4	–	23	–

Fall of Wickets
1–**15**, 2–**37**, 3–**94**, 4–**105**, 5–**206**, 6–**221**, 7–**231**, 8–**233**, 9–**234**

Umpires: S.G. Randell & D.B. Hair *Man of the Match*: A.A. Donald

South Africa won by 6 runs

Second Final – Australia v. South Africa

26 January 1998 at SCG, Sydney

South Africa

D.J. Cullinan	c Warne, b M.E. Waugh	3
G. Kirsten	c Gilchrist, b Wilson	14
L. Klusener	c Harvey, b Reiffel	31
J.H. Kallis	c Ponting, b Reiffel	10
W.J. Cronje *	c Bevan, b Warne	73
J.N. Rhodes	not out	82
S.M. Pollock	lbw, b Reiffel	3
P.L. Symcox	not out	5
B.M. McMillan		
D.J. Richardson †		
A.A. Donald		
	lb 4, w 3	7
	50 overs (for 6 wickets)	228

	O	M	R	W
Wilson	10	–	39	1
M.E. Waugh	5	–	17	1
Reiffel	10	1	32	3
Moody	8	–	28	–
Warne	10	–	52	1
Harvey	4	–	27	–
Lehmann	3	–	29	–

Fall of Wickets
1–**7**, 2–**35**, 3–**55**, 4–**64**, 5–**198**, 6–**211**

Australia

A.C. Gilchrist †	b McMillan	100
M.E. Waugh	b Klusener	25
R.T. Ponting	lbw, b Klusener	47
I.J. Harvey	not out	27
D.S. Lehmann	not out	17
S.R. Waugh *		
M.G. Bevan		
T.M. Moody		
P.R. Reiffel		
S.K. Warne		
P. Wilson		
	b 4, lb 2, w 5, nb 2	13
	41.5 overs (for 3 wickets)	229

	O	M	R	W
Pollock	8	–	39	–
Klusener	10	–	57	2
Donald	3	–	17	–
Symcox	9	–	39	–
McMillan	8	–	45	1
Cullinan	2	–	17	–
Cronje	1.5	–	9	–

Fall of Wickets
1–**51**, 2–**177**, 3–**184**

Umpires: D.B. Hair & S.G. Randell *Man of the Match*: A.C. Gilchrist

Australia won by 7 wickets

Third Final – Australia v. South Africa

27 January 1998 at SCG, Sydney

Australia

M.E. Waugh	b Klusener	21
A.C. Gilchrist †	b McMillan	6
R.T. Ponting	st Richardson, b Adams	76
D.S. Lehmann	c Rhodes, b Symcox	10
S.R. Waugh *	run out	71
M.G. Bevan	not out	36
T.M. Moody	c Bacher, b McMillan	0
I.J. Harvey	c Bacher, b McMillan	1
P.R. Reiffel	not out	11
S.K. Warne		
P. Wilson		
	lb 4, w 10, nb 1	15
	50 overs (for 7 wickets)	247

	O	M	R	W
Pollock	10	1	33	–
McMillan	10	–	47	3
Kallis	3	–	23	–
Klusener	10	–	59	1
Symcox	10	–	35	1
Adams	7	–	46	1

Fall of Wickets
1–**11**, 2–**58**, 3–**79**, 4–**181**, 5–**210**, 6–**210**, 7–**212**

South Africa

G. Kirsten	run out	3
A.M. Bacher	c Gilchrist, b Reiffel	45
J.H. Kallis	hit wkt, b Reiffel	14
W.J. Cronje *	st Gilchrist, b Warne	5
J.N. Rhodes	c and b M.E. Waugh	29
S.M. Pollock	st Gilchrist, b Bevan	28
L. Klusener	c S.R. Waugh, b Moody	46
P.L. Symcox	run out	22
B.M. McMillan	run out	15
D.J. Richardson †	c Ponting, b Reiffel	1
P.R. Adams	not out	15
	b 3, lb 6, w 1	10
	48.1 overs	233

	O	M	R	W
Wilson	10	1	55	–
M.E. Waugh	6	–	31	1
Reiffel	9	–	40	3
Moody	9	1	26	1
Warne	9.1	–	43	1
Bevan	5	–	29	1

Fall of Wickets
1–**25**, 2–**63**, 3–**64**, 4–**72**, 5–**122**, 6–**139**, 7–**191**, 8–**202**, 9–**202**

Umpires: D.B. Hair & S.J. Davis *Man of the Match*: R.T. Ponting *Man of the World Series*: G. Kirsten

Australia won by 14 runs

Transvaal Tour

As a prelude to their season in South Africa, Transvaal made a brief tour of Australia, but none of the matches in which they were engaged were accorded first-class status.

14, 15 and 16 September 1997
at Lilac Hill, Perth
Transvaal 163 (D.N. Crookes 61) and 224 for 6 dec. (K.R. Rutherford 103)
Western Australian Invitation XI 125 (D.N. Crookes 5 for 27, C.E. Eksteen 5 for 48) and 263 for 4 (M.G. Dighton 114, M.E. Hussey 63)
Western Australian Invitation XI won by 6 wickets

17 September 1997
at James Oval, Perth
Western Australia 276 for 7 (M.E. Hussey 101)
Transvaal (D.N. Crookes 53)
Western Australia won by 34 runs

20 September 1997
at Drummoyne Oval, Sydney
Transvaal 295 for 7 (D.N. Crookes 157 not out, N. Pothas 55)
New South Wales 202 for 6 (R. Chee Quee 92, J. Bray 66)
Transvaal won on faster run rate

26 September 1997
at Salter Oval, Bundaberg
Transvaal 261 for 6 (H.A. Manack 75, N.D. McKenzie 58)
Queensland Academy of Sport 222 for 3 (C. Perren 110 not out)
Queensland Academy of Sport won on faster scoring rate

27 September 1997
at Salter Oval, Bundaberg
Transvaal 195 for 9 (K.R. Rutherford 61)
Queensland 196 for 6 (L. Kahler 79 not out)
Queensland won by 4 wickets

28 September 1997
at Maryborough
Queensland 219 for 8 (S.A. Prestwidge 99)
Transvaal 208 (H.A. Manack 66)
Queensland won by 11 runs

29 September 1997
at Maryborough
Queensland 263 for 3 (J.P. Maher 151 not out)
Transvaal 150 (S.G. Koening 50)
Queensland won by 113 runs

Transvaal enjoyed few successes on their tour and lost all four matches in Queensland. The outstanding player was Derek Crookes, the all-rounder, but he did not appear in the matches in Queensland. The three-day game at Lilac Hill was played under the Mercantile Mutual Cup format, whereby twelve players are chosen but only eleven bat and field.

Sheffield Shield

15, 16, 17 and 18 October 1997
at Adelaide Oval, Adelaide
Tasmania 301 (M.J. di Venuto 68, S. Young 58, P. Wilson 4 for 53) and 396 for 5 dec. (R.T. Ponting 121, M.J. di Venuto 94, D.C. Boon 73 not out)
South Australia 381 (D.S. Lehmann 138, J.D. Siddons 91, C.R. Miller 6 for 77) and 207 for 6 (M.P. Faull 71)
Match drawn
South Australia 2 pts, Tasmania 0 pts

at Woolloongabba, Brisbane
New South Wales 464 (M.G. Bevan 153, M.A. Taylor 124, P.A. Emery 50, M.S. Kasprowicz 4 for 129) and 191 for 3 (M.E. Waugh 69 not out, M.A. Taylor 55)
Queensland 650 for 5 dec. (M.L. Hayden 181, M.L. Love 129, S.G. Law 107 retired hurt, G.I. Foley 70 not out, A. Symonds 63)
Match drawn
Queensland 2 pts, New South Wales 0 pts

Australia's premier competition began with Test players available for their states and sides at full strength. A fourth wicket stand of 123 between Lehmann and Siddons gave South Australia the edge over Tasmania. Lehmann's 138 came off only 156 balls and included 20 fours. Thanks to a third wicket stand of 176 between di Venuto and Ponting, Boon was able to set South Australia a target of 317 in 75 overs, a task which never seemed within the home state's reach. Adcock, a batsman for South Australia, and Wright, a pace bowler for Tasmania, made their debuts in the match.

There were five centurions in the high-scoring game in Brisbane. Ian Healy asked New South Wales to bat first when he won the toss, but his plans were upset by his Test colleagues Bevan and Taylor, who shared a third wicket stand of 200. Hayden and Love responded with an opening partnership of 286 in 274 minutes, a record for Queensland against New South Wales at the 'Gabba. Stuart Law reached 107 off 138 balls before being forced to retire injured when

Laurie Harper scored prolifically and patiently for Victoria at the start of the Sheffield Shield campaign.
(Stephen Laffer / Sportsline)

he was struck on the forearm by a ball from McGrath, who delivered a flurry of bouncers. Queensland batted into the fourth day so that a draw was inevitable.

22, 23, 24 and 25 October 1997
at North Sydney Oval, North Sydney
Victoria 509 for 6 dec. (M.T.G. Elliott 187, L.D. Harper 160, G.B. Gardiner 50 not out) and 279 for 8 dec. (I.J. Harvey 109, G.B. Gardiner 56)
New South Wales 407 for 4 dec. (S.R. Waugh 202 not out, S. Lee 81 not out, M.E. Waugh 72) and 225 for 3 (M.J. Slater 85, S.R. Waugh 60 not out, M.A. Taylor 50)
Match drawn
Victoria 2 pts, New South Wales 0 pts

23, 24, 25 and 26 October 1997
at WACA Ground, Perth
Western Australia 477 for 5 dec. (A.C. Gilchrist 203 not out, T.M. Moody 101)
South Australia 142 (T.M. Moody 5 for 20) and 258 (G.S. Blewett 76, J.D. Siddons 69, B.P. Julian 6 for 45)
Western Australia won by an innings and 77 runs
Western Australia 6 pts, South Australia 0 pts

A third wicket stand of 303 between Elliott and Harper, a record for Victoria against New South Wales, took the visitors to a commanding position in the game at North Sydney. Laurie Harper followed his maiden century in the final match of the 1996–97 season with 160 off 280 balls. His innings included a six and 22 fours. Elliott's 187 included two sixes and 25 fours and occupied 332 balls. New South Wales's first innings was dominated by a brilliant double century from Steve Waugh. He hit 29 fours and shared century stands with twin brother Mark and with Lee whose 81 included three sixes and seven fours. Taylor conceded first innings advantage when he declared 102 runs in arrears. Harvey made a sparkling century as Victoria struck out for quick runs, and Warne's declaration left New South Wales more than two sessions in which to score 382 to win, a target which assured a draw and which left the mighty New South Wales pointless after two matches.

Western Australia became the season's first winners when they crushed South Australia in Perth, clinching victory within an hour on the fourth day. The home state were 136 when Gilchrist joined Moody. The pair added 273, a fifth wicket record for Western Australia against South Australia. Gilchrist hit two sixes and 25 fours as he raced to 203 off 293 balls. It was his first double century and the innings did much to influence selectors in naming him in the World Series side. Skipper Moody followed the 57th century of his career with five wickets, three of them coming in the space of five balls. Following-on, South Australia fared only marginally better. Blewett, Lehmann and Siddons battled bravely, but the last five wickets went down for seven runs. The visitors gave a debut to medium-pace bowler Pickering.

31 October, 1, 2 and 3 November 1997
at Bellerive Oval, Hobart
Tasmania 366 for 5 dec. (R.T. Ponting 129 not out, M.J. di Venuto 87, S. Young 51) and 101 for 5 dec. (J. Angel 4 for 45)
Western Australia 101 for 3 dec. (J. Angel 52) and 367 for 4 (M.E. Hussey 108, D.R. Martyn 101, T.M. Moody 73 not out)
Western Australia won by 6 wickets
Western Australia 6 pts, Tasmania 2 pts

at MCG, Melbourne
Queensland 231 (M.L. Hayden 53, J.P. Maher 50, I.J. Harvey 4 for 27) and 313 for 9 dec (J.P. Maher 77, M.L. Hayden 76)
Victoria 318 for 9 dec. (D.M. Jones 151 not out, P.R. Reiffel 60) and 30 for 1
Match drawn
Victoria 2 pts, Queensland 0 pts

No play was possible on the first two days in Hobart where Boon and Moody did all that they could to keep the game alive. Ponting and di Venuto combined energy and grace in contrasting, vigorous innings. Ponting hit the 20th hundred of his career, and his unbeaten 129 came off 192 balls with a six and 12 fours. Western Australia hit 101 in 96 minutes, and Boon ultimately asked the visitors to make 367 at approximately five runs an over. Hussey provided the base with 108 off 153 balls, and Martyn batted gloriously to reach 101 off 103 deliveries with a six and nine fours. Moody and Gilchrist completed a brilliant victory with an unfinished stand of 87 in 58 minutes.

Rain restricted play on the first day in Melbourne where Queensland, without the injured Law, chose to bat first. They had an uneasy time against the ever-improving Harvey but struck back when they captured the first six Victorian wickets for 124. Dean Jones then found an able partner in Paul Reiffel, and the pair added 121 to give Victoria first innings points. Jones's 53rd first-class century was the slowest ever recorded at the MCG. It took him 406 minutes, and, in all, he was at the crease for 510 minutes and faced 393 balls. During the course of his innings he passed Sir Donald Bradman's aggregate to become the fourth highest run-scorer in the history of the Sheffield Shield. Consistent batting ensured that Queensland avoided any chance of defeat, and the match ended tamely. Keeper Darren Berry had nine dismissals in the match, seven catches and two stumpings, a record for Victoria against Queensland. The last of his victims, Bichel, gave him 300 dismissals in Shield cricket.

14, 15, 16 and 17 November 1997

at Newcastle

Queensland 187 (M.L. Love 74, D.A. Freedman 6 for 43) and 172 (S.C.G. MacGill 5 for 54, D.A. Freedman 4 for 55)

New South Wales 325 (M.A. Taylor 73, M.G. Bevan 61 not out, S.R. Waugh 53, M.J. Slater 50, A.C. Dale 4 for 69) and 35 for 1

New South Wales won by 9 wickets

New South Wales 6 pts, Queensland 0 pts

Sheffield Shield Cricketer of the Year – Dene Hills of Tasmania. (Stephen Laffer / Sportsline)

Three centuries in the season for New South Wales opening batsman Rodney Davison. (Stephen Laffer / Sportsline)

at Adelaide Oval, Adelaide

South Australia 452 for 9 dec. (J.D. Siddons 84, D.S. Webber 70 not out, D.A. Fitzgerald 62, D.S. Lehmann 54, G.S. Blewett 53) and 190 for 6 (D.A. Fitzgerald 85)

Western Australia 593 (J.L. Langer 235, M.E. Hussey 134, T.M. Moody 78, D.R. Martyn 51, P.E. McIntyre 5 for 175, B.E. Young 4 for 128)

Match drawn

Western Australia 2 pts, South Australia 0 pts

New South Wales gained their first win of the season when they beat Queensland inside three days in Newcastle. Healy chose to bat first, but the Queensland line-up, again without Law, looked very frail. They twice succumbed to the combined spin of Freedman, slow left-arm, and MacGill, a leg-break bowler threatening to emulate Shane Warne. Freedman had match figures of 10 for 98, and MacGill had seven for 100. New South Wales batted consistently with Taylor patiently showing a complete return to form.

Runs flowed at Adelaide Oval, where Western Australia batted into the fourth day. There were five century stands in the match, the highest being the second wicket partnership of 223 between Hussey and Langer. Langer made 235 off 359 balls with three sixes and 18 fours.

20, 21, 22 and 23 November 1997
at SCG, Sydney
New South Wales 138 (B.P. Julian 7 for 39) and 477 for 5 dec. (M.G. Bevan 132, R.J. Davison 113, K.J. Roberts 78 not out, P.A. Emery 51 not out)
Western Australia 361 (R.J. Campbell 177, D.R. Martyn 90, A.M. Stuart 7 for 76) and 194 (R.J. Campbell 51, S.C.G. MacGill 5 for 87)
New South Wales won by 60 runs
New South Wales 6 pts, Western Australia 2 pts

In a match of remarkable turns of fortune, New South Wales beat Western Australia on the last afternoon and moved to a challenging position in the table. Emery, leading New South Wales in the absence of Taylor and the Waugh twins, who were on Test duty, won the toss and chose to bat. The home side were all out in four and a quarter hours as Brendon Julian produced the best bowling performance of his career. The last six wickets went down for 31 runs. Western Australia seemed to have a total grip on the game when Campbell and Martyn added 204 for 1 the third wicket. Campbell made his second and higher century, and his 177 came off 255 balls with two sixes and 20 fours. Stuart emulated Julian with a career-best bowling performance as the last eight Western Australian wickets fell for 58 runs. Davison, in his first game of the season, and Bevan, eager to reclaim his Test place, established a New South Wales third wicket record against Western Australia when they added 218 in 276 minutes in the second innings. Roberts and Emery batted pugnaciously, and Emery was able to set the visitors a target of 255 in two sessions. Campbell raced to 51 out of 59 off 41 balls before becoming MacGill's first victim, and Hussey and Gilchrist put on 71 for the fourth wicket, but the last seven wickets mustered only 41 runs as MacGill and Freedman bowled New South Wales to a spectacular victory.

27, 28, 29 and 30 November 1997
at Optus Oval, Carlton
South Australia 452 (D.A. Fitzgerald 81, D.S. Webber 69, B.E. Young 66, J.D. Siddons 60)
Victoria 285 (D.M. Jones 58, L.D. Harper 57, P. Wilson 4 for 72) amd 393 for 4 (L.D. Harper 207 not out, G.B. Gardiner 133 not out)
Match drawn
South Australia 2 pts, Victoria 0 pts

at Woolloongabba, Brisbane
Tasmania 307 (D.J. Marsh 82 not out, S.A. Muller 5 for 73) and 179 (R.J. Tucker 77, J.H. Dawes 4 for 27, S.A. Muller 4 for 55)
Queensland 237 (J.P. Maher 71) and 252 for 4 (M.L. Hayden 117, S.G. Law 56 not out)
Queensland won by 6 wickets
Queensland 6 pts, Tasmania 2 pts

A blistering finish to the season for Western Australia's all-rounder Brendon Julian.
(David Munden / Sportsline)

The match at Optus Oval produced several records. Foremost among them was that set by Jamie Siddons, who overtook David Hookes's aggregate of 9,364 to become the leading run-scorer in the history of the Sheffield Shield. South Australia batted consistently, and the bowling of Wilson, George and Young made certain that Victoria would have to follow on. They were 77 for four in their second innings when Gardiner joined Harper. The pair shared an unbroken partnership of 316, a record for Victoria's fifth wicket in the Shield. Gardiner reached a maiden first-class hundred while Harper's innings was the highest of his career and the highest score made in a first-class game at Optus Oval. It was a patient affair. His 207 came off 389 balls and occupied 463 minutes. He hit 11 fours.

With Healy on Test duty, Law returned to lead Queensland to their first victory of the season. In spite of the efforts of Muller and debutant medium-pacer Dawes, Tasmania reached 307 mainly due to a seventh wicket stand of 121 between Atkinson and Marsh. Tasmania's debutant medium-pacer, Targett, began his career with a no-ball and had Hayden caught behind with his sixth delivery. He captured two more wickets and played a major part in Tasmania claiming a first innings lead of 70. Muller, Dawes and Dale bowled Queensland back into contention, and the home side faced a reasonable target of 250. Hayden's 30th first-class hundred set up the victory, and Law confirmed it with much aplomb, hitting 56 off 51 balls before lunch on the fourth day.

5, 6, 7 and 8 December 1997

at WACA Ground, Perth

Western Australia 404 for 9 dec. (T.M. Moody 160, J.L. Langer 76) and 314 for 9 dec. (J.L. Langer 113, R.J. Campbell 61, D.R. Martyn 50, P.J. Hutchinson 4 for 34)
Tasmania 360 for 8 dec. (D.C. Boon 146, S. Young 81, D.F. Hills 61) and 173 (J. Angel 4 for 47)
Western Australia won by 185 runs
Western Australia 6 pts, Tasmania 0 pts

Western Australia completed the 'double' over Tasmania although the visitors pressed hard for the first two and a half days. Western Australian skipper Tom Moody continued his highly successful season with a forceful innings that lasted for more than five hours. He completed 8,000 runs in the Sheffield Shield and took his 100th catch in the competition. Playing his 300th first-class match, David Boon reached the 64th century of his career. He declared 44 runs in arrears, but Campbell and Langer thwarted Tasmania's aims with some violent hitting. Campbell made 61 off 69 balls, and Langer scored 113 off 155 deliveries. Moody declared on the fourth morning, and Angel and Garnaut became the main instruments in Western Australia sealing victory.

Ryan Campbell hit a thrilling century in the Sheffield Shield final to set up Western Australia's victory over Tasmania. It was compensation for the 'pair' he had suffered the previous season. (Stephen Laffer / Sportsline)

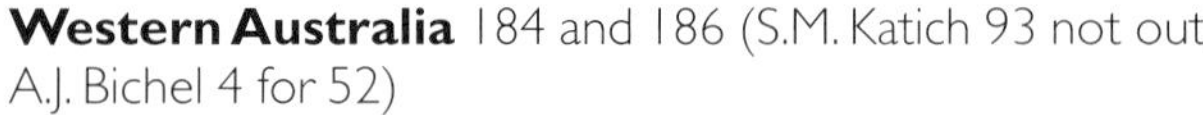

19, 20, 21 and 22 December 1997

at WACA Ground, Perth

Western Australia 184 and 186 (S.M. Katich 93 not out, A.J. Bichel 4 for 52)
Queensland 341 (A. Symonds 88, G.I. Foley 82, J. Angel 4 for 85) and 33 for 2
Queensland won by 8 wickets
Queensland 6 pts, Western Australia 0 pts

at Bellerive Oval, Hobart

Victoria 180 for 9 dec. (C.R. Miller 4 for 67) and 348 (L.P. Harper 152, I.J. Harvey 83)
Tasmania 130 (D.J. Saker 4 for 42) and 401 for 3 (D.F. Hills 205, J. Cox 95, M.J. di Venuto 53)
Tasmania won by 7 wickets
Tasmania 6 pts, Victoria 2 pts

at Adelaide Oval, Adelaide

South Australia 366 (D.S. Webber 145, D.A. Fitzgerald 57, S.H. Cook 4 for 86) and 168 (G.R. Robertson 5 for 37)
New South Wales 519 (S. Lee 183 not out, R.J. Davison 137, M.A. Taylor 50) and 16 for 0
New South Wales won by 10 wickets
New South Wales 6 pts, South Australia 0 pts

Queensland gained their second win in successive matches when they comprehensively accounted for Western Australia in three days at the WACA Ground. Kasprowicz bowled well in both innings, finishing with match figures of six for 78 from 35 overs. Bichel and Muller were also in good form. Katich batted valiantly for the highest score of his career but had little support. The substance in the Queensland batting came from a fifth wicket stand of 133 between Symonds and Foley.

Tasmania earned their first win of the season with an outstanding performance against Victoria who had established a first innings lead of 30. This was increased emphatically when Harper hit his third century in four matches. He and Harvey put on 184 for the fifth wicket, and Tasmania were set the daunting task of scoring 399 to win the match. By the Sunday evening, Hills and Cox had 179 to their credit, and they were not separated until their stand was worth 297, a record for Tasmania. Dene Hills went on to make 205 off 270 deliveries with 32 fours and so became the first Tasmanian batsman to score more than one double century. The islanders won with ease, an astonishing achievement.

New South Wales won their third match in succession and moved to within two points of Western Australia at the top of the table. Queensland were in third place, four points adrift of New South Wales, but Western Australia had played one game more than either of their main challengers. Cook reduced South Australia to 138 for five before Webber and Nielsen doubled the score. Webber hit a six and 18 fours in the fourth hundred of his career. South Australia welcomed back Gillespie, but he left the field with leg cramps on the third day and did not return during the New South Wales innings. The left-handed Robert Davison hit his second hundred of the season and the highest score of his career, and Shane Lee, once of Somerset, blasted an unbeaten 183 off 206 balls. He hit three sixes and 20 fours. Off-spinner Gavin Robertson destroyed South Australia when they batted a second time, and New South Wales won early on the fourth day.

7, 8, 9 and 10 January 1998
at MCG, Melbourne
New South Wales 532 for 9 dec. (R.J. Davison 169, M.J. Slater 137, C.J. Richards 67, B.J. Hodge 4 for 92) and 188 for 4 dec. (R.J. Davison 60)
Victoria 387 (D.S. Berry 166 not out, S.H. Cook 4 for 60) and 281 for 9 (D.M. Jones 57, S.A.J. Craig 52, S.C.G. MacGill 6 for 99)
Match drawn
New South Wales 2 pts, Victoria 0 pts

Davison's highest first-class score and an opening partnership of 219 with Slater was followed by a second wicket stand of 117 with Richards. These gave substance to New South Wales's huge score against Victoria, for whom off-break bowler Brad Hodge returned career best figures. By the end of the second day, Victoria looked destined for defeat at 149 for six, but Darren Berry played a masterly innings, making an unbeaten 166 off 335 balls. The last four wickets realised 269 runs and the follow-on was saved. Emery's declaration set Victoria a target of 334 in 65 overs. He entrusted the bowling almost exclusively to the spinners and MacGill, and they nearly brought New South Wales victory. But Inness, making his debut, held out for the last 17 minutes with Williams to save the day for Victoria. In the first innings, Innes had shared a last wicket stand of 118 with Berry, a record for Victoria against New South Wales.

15, 16, 17 and 18 January 1998
at Bellerive Oval, Hobart
South Australia 264 (J.D. Siddons 105, C.R. Miller 6 for 64) and 154 (C.R. Miller 6 for 55)
Tasmania 569 for 6 dec. (D.F. Hills 265, S. Young 105, J. Cox 73)
Tasmania won by an innings and 151 runs
Tasmania 6 pts, South Australia 0 pts

Dene Hills's second double century of the season, and the highest of his 14 three-figure scores, helped Tasmania to a resounding victory over South Australia. Put in to bat, the visitors lost their first three wickets for 76 runs, but Jamie Siddons's three-hour century took them to 264 by the end of the day. The second day belonged to Tasmania. Hills and Cox scored 150 for the first wicket, and, in a partnership that spread into the third day, Hills and Young put on 243

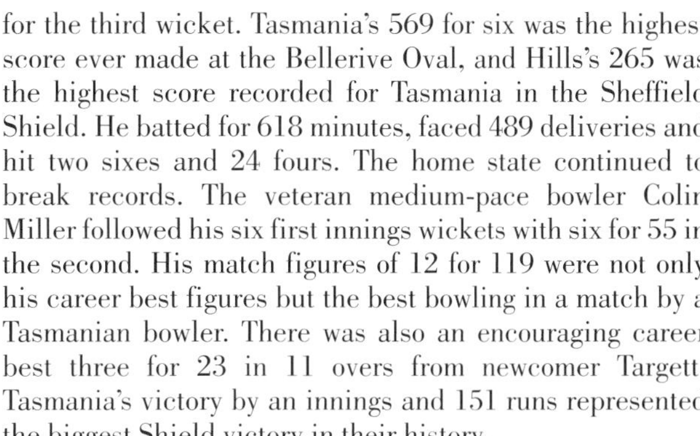
for the third wicket. Tasmania's 569 for six was the highest score ever made at the Bellerive Oval, and Hills's 265 was the highest score recorded for Tasmania in the Sheffield Shield. He batted for 618 minutes, faced 489 deliveries and hit two sixes and 24 fours. The home state continued to break records. The veteran medium-pace bowler Colin Miller followed his six first innings wickets with six for 55 in the second. His match figures of 12 for 119 were not only his career best figures but the best bowling in a match by a Tasmanian bowler. There was also an encouraging career best three for 23 in 11 overs from newcomer Targett. Tasmania's victory by an innings and 151 runs represented the biggest Shield victory in their history.

23, 24, 25 and 26 January 1998
at Woolloongabba, Brisbane
Queensland 408 (A.J. Bichel 110, A. Symonds 100, I.A. Healy 50, D.W. Fleming 5 for 68, M.W.H. Inness 4 for 80)
Victoria 170 (A.J. Bichel 4 for 33, M.S. Kasprowicz 4 for 45) and 98 (A.C. Dale 5 for 19, M.S. Kasprowicz 4 for 22)
Queensland won by an innings and 140 runs
Queensland 6 pts, Victoria 0 pts

Queensland beat Victoria in just over two days. Berry asked the home side to bat when he won the toss and he saw his bowlers reduce them to 81 for four. At this point, Symonds began to hit hard and often. He added 66 with Foley and 68 with Healy before being stumped off Hodge. His second Shield hundred had come off 120 balls and included 19 fours. Greater fireworks were to come as Andrew Bichel, dropped from the Australian one-day side, hit 110 off as many deliveries. The first century of his career contained 20 fours and 107 of his runs came in the final session. Queensland ended the day on 405 for nine, and the only consolation for Victoria was Inness's four for 80 in his second match. They lost 15 wickets on the second day, and, starting the third day on 88 for five, they quickly lost their remaining wickets.

3, 4, 5 and 6 February 1998
at MCG, Melbourne
Victoria 391 for 9 dec. (L.D. Harper 118, D.M. Jones 116, S.A.J. Craig 71 not out) and 247 for 9 dec. (D.M. Jones 70, B.J. Hodge 57)
Western Australia 327 for 7 dec. (B.P. Julian 121 not out, S.M. Katich 90) and 229 (J.M. Davison 5 for 84)
Victoria won by 82 runs
Victoria 6 pts, Western Australia 0 pts

4, 5, 6 and 7 February 1998
at SCG, Sydney
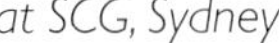
Tasmania 202 (D.C. Boon 61 not out, S.C.G. MacGill 6 for 64, D.A. Freedman 4 for 65) and 347 (R.J. Tucker 99, D.C. Boon 64, D.J. Marsh 50, D.A. Freedman 7 for 106)
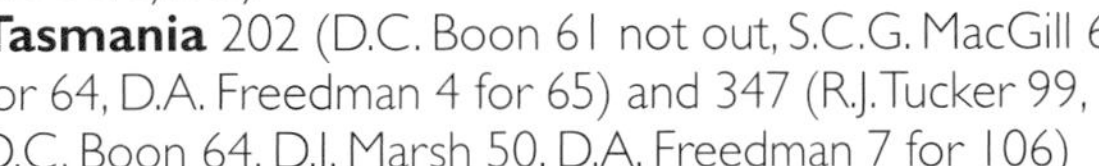

New South Wales 200 (M.A.Taylor 66, D.J. Marsh 7 for 57) and 269 (M.J. Slater 89, C.J. Richards 57, M.W. Ridgway 6 for 50)
Tasmania won by 80 runs
Tasmania 6 pts, New South Wales 0 pts

at Woolloongabba, Brisbane
Queensland 236 (M.L. Hayden 59, B.E.Young 5 for 64) and 154 (B.N.Wigney 5 for 37)
South Australia 218 (J.H. Dawes 4 for 46) and 173 for 6
South Australia won by 4 wickets
South Australia 6 pts, Queensland 2 pts

A fourth wicket stand of 139 between Harper and Jones provided the backbone to the Victorian innings and helped them to a strong position against Western Australia. The visitors were 174 for six when Brendon Julian came to the crease. He dominated the closing stages of the innings, hitting a six and 15 fours in his first Shield century, which was the highest score of his career. He was captaining Western Australia and declared 64 runs in arrears in an attempt to keep the game alive. Berry's declaration left the visitors a target of 312 runs at more than four an over. They were never in the hunt although Julian, 38 off 22 balls, took 22 off one over from Craig.

Daniel Marsh bowled Tasmania to a narrow first innings lead and ultimately to victory when he took seven for 57, a career best performance, against New South Wales, 4-7 February 1998. (Stephen Laffer / Sportsline)

Tasmania's magnificent form continued with a fine victory over New South Wales. Boon decided to bat when he won the toss, but he alone kept Tasmania's first innings alive with an unbeaten 61 off 125 balls. He hit 10 fours and was the only batsman to show confidence against the leg-breaks of MacGill, whose six for 64 was a career best, and the left-arm 'chinamen' of Freedman. Dismissed for 202, Tasmania fought back splendidly. Taylor, batting at number seven, and Emery put on 86 for the seventh wicket, but New South Wales lost their last four wickets for 17 runs, and Tasmania snatched first innings points. Their hero was Daniel Marsh, another specialist in 'chinamen', who took five wickets in an innings for the first time in his career and returned the best figures for a Tasmanian bowler in a Shield match against New South Wales. Freedman collected the best match bowling figures of his career, 11 for 171, but a fifth wicket stand of 129 between Boon and Tucker put Tasmania in control. Tucker's 99 included 13 fours. Needing 350 to win, New South Wales were given a good foundation by Slater and Richards, who scored 136 for the second wicket. Ridgway and Miller bowled with commendable determination, however, and New South Wales collapsed, losing their last five wickets for 24 runs.

Queensland were quickly earning a reputation for inconsistency. In spite of Young's first five-wicket haul, they led South Australia on the first innings but collapsed against Wigney and Harrity in their second innings and lost in three days. Queensland were without Healy, Dale, Law and Bichel and were led by Hayden.

10, 11, 12 and 13 February 1998
at Adelaide Oval, Adelaide
Victoria 442 for 4 dec. (M.T.G. Elliott 122, B.J. Hodge 116 not out, D.M. Jones 82, Arnberger 74) and 178 for 6 (D.M. Jones 53 not out, J.L. Arnberger 53, B.E.Young 4 for 62)
South Australia 205 (G.S. Blewett 111, D.W. Fleming 6 for 35) and 414 (T.J. Nielsen 115, G.S. Blewett 97, D.W. Fleming 4 for 72)
Victoria won by 6 wickets
Victoria 6 pts, South Australia 0 pts

11, 12, 13 and 14 February 1998
at Bellerive Oval, Hobart
Queensland 175 (B.N. Creevey 52, M.W. Ridgway 4 for 44) and 318 (A. Symonds 141, C.R. Miller 4 for 89)
Tasmania 292 (D.F. Hills 72, D.C. Boon 52, R.J. Tucker 52, B.N. Creevey 5 for 51) and 204 for 0 (D.F. Hills 121 not out, J. Cox 71 not out)
Tasmania won by 10 wickets
Tasmania 6 pts, Queensland 0 pts

14, 15, 16 and 17 February 1998
at WACA Ground, Perth

Western Australia 470 for 7 dec. (D.R. Martyn 141 not out, M.E. Hussey 120, R.J. Campbell 66)
New South Wales 150 (M.A. Taylor 61) and 183
Western Australia won by an innings and 137 runs
Western Australia 6 pts, New South Wales 0 pts

Victoria's challenging form had arrived too late in the season, but they claimed a second Shield victory by beating South Australia in a hard-fought contest. Elliott and Arnberger, who made his highest first-class score, shared an opening stand of 167, and Jones and Hodge put on 146 for the fourth. Berry declared before lunch on the second day, and, by the close, South Australia were 18 for one in their second innings. Fleming was their principal destroyer, but Blewett, captaining South Australia in the absence of the injured Siddons, batted splendidly. Only two other players reached double figures. Blewett was leg before to Saker just three runs short of his second century of the match, but Nielsen continued the fight. He and Minagall, 43, put on 74 for the eighth wicket, and he and Wigney added 103 for the ninth. Nielsen was last out, having equalled his career best score. Fleming finished with the best match figures of his career, 10 for 107, but Nielsen's rearguard action meant that Victoria had to score briskly to win. Arnberger set the pattern with nine fours as he made 53 off 83 balls, and Dean Jones and Harper completed the job.

Tasmania took another step towards the Sheffield Shield final with a crushing win over Queensland. Boon put Queensland in to bat, and Ridgway and Miller reduced them to 114 for eight. Creevey's highest score brought some relief, and he followed this with his second five wicket haul in the Shield, but Tasmania took a first innings lead of 117. When Queensland batted a second time they lost two wickets for 25 and Hayden retired hurt. Symonds came to the rescue with his third Shield century. His 141 included a six and 21 fours and was his highest score for the state. He gained consistent support, and Tasmania faced a last day target of 201. In 214 minutes, the runs were scored by openers Hills and Cox. Hills reached the 15th hundred of his career and hit 19 fours. To add to Queensland's woes, Foley was called for throwing by umpire Emerson.

MacGill took his 50th wicket of the season, but New South Wales were totally overwhelmed by Western Australia, who were moving relentlessly towards the Shield final. Campbell began with a flourish, and Hussey and Langer then added 153. Martyn dominated a sixth wicket stand of 111 in 90 minutes with Lavender, and, in all, Martyn made 141 off 168 balls with three sixes and 18 fours. Taylor, batting at number four, reached 1,000 runs for the season, but New South Wales were beaten in three days. They rushed to defeat, three of their batsmen being run out in the second innings.

5, 6, 7 and 8 March 1998
at Bellerive Oval, Hobart
New South Wales 332 (C.J. Richards 164, M.G. Bevan 58, C.R. Miller 5 for 88) and 226 (M.G. Bevan 65, C.R. Miller 6 for 75)
Tasmania 468 for 9 dec. (J. Cox 126, D.J. Marsh 70, S. Young 50, D.A. Freedman 5 for 77) and 94 for 1
Tasmania won by 9 wickets
Tasmania 6 pts, New South Wales 0 pts

at Adelaide Oval, Adelaide
Queensland 268 (A. Symonds 163, P.E. McIntyre 4 for 83) and 349 for 7 dec. (M.L. Hayden 101, A. Symonds 100 not out, A.J. Bichel 66, B.E. Young 5 for 69)
South Australia 302 (J.D. Siddons 63, C.J. Davies 55, A.J. Bichel 4 for 66) and 241 for 7 (J.D. Siddons 117, A.J. Bichel 4 for 44)
Match drawn
South Australia 2 pts, Queensland 0 pts

at WACA Ground, Perth
Western Australia 196 (A.C. Gilchrist 109, M.W.H. Inness 4 for 42, D.J. Saker 4 for 56) and 388 for 8 dec. (J.L. Langer 101, R.J. Campbell 100, T.M. Moody 64 not out)
Victoria 157 (M.P. Atkinson 4 for 36) and 315 (B.J. Hodge 95, M.P. Atkinson 4 for 60, S.R. Cary 4 for 96)
Western Australia won by 112 runs
Western Australia 6 pts, Victoria 0 pts

Tasmania and Western Australia assured themselves of places in the Sheffield Shield final with outright wins in the penultimate round of matches. Tasmania, in wonderful

Colin Miller of Tasmania, a record 70 wickets in the season.
(Stephen Laffer / Sportsline)

form, withstood a maiden first-class century by Richards to take a commanding first innings lead. Cox hit a patient 126 which gave the innings backbone, but there were substantial contributions throughout the order. Colin Miller, 34 years old, continued his gold summer with match figures of 10 for 163, which brought him to 59 first-class wickets for the season. Hills moved past a thousand runs for the season when he hit 43 in the second innings as his side won comfortably.

Andrew Symonds, still short of his 23rd birthday, hit 163 off 202 balls with three sixes and 19 fours in Queensland's first innings in Adelaide. It was his highest score for the state, bettering the 141 he had made a fortnight earlier. He made 100 runs between lunch and tea on the first day and followed this with another century in the second innings. Siddons hit the 33rd century of his career when South Australia went in search of a target of 316. Ultimately, they were happy to draw.

Western Australia were 35 for five when Gilchrist joined Moody. The pair added 53, and Gilchrist went on to record the seventh hundred of his career. From that point on, the home state dominated. Hussey and Campbell scored 99 for the first wicket when they batted a second time, and Campbell and Langer added 81 for the second wicket. Campbell made 100 off 110 balls with 20 boundaries while Langer took 185 balls for his 101. Victoria died bravely, but there was no stopping Western Australia.

12, 13, 14 and 15 March 1998

at Woolloongabba, Brisbane

Queensland 197 (M.L. Love 62) and 313 (M.L. Hayden 124, W.A. Seccombe 54 not out, A.J. Bichel 50, D.R. Martyn 4 for 46)

Western Australia 405 for 8 dec. (B.P. Julian 94, S.M. Katich 80, J.L. Langer 67, M.E. Hussey 61, D.R. Martyn 60, A.J. Bichel 4 for 104) and 106 for 5

Western Australia won by 5 wickets

Western Australia 6 pts, Queensland 0 pts

at Newcastle

South Australia 352 (D.A. Fitzgerald 65, J.M. Vaughan 61, M.P. Faull 58, J.D. Siddons 54) and 258 for 7 dec. (M.P. Faull 103, B.E. Young 64)

New South Wales 284 (B.E. McNamara 68 not out, C.J. Richards 61, P.E. McIntyre 4 for 92) and 63 for 1

Match drawn

South Australia 2 pts, New South Wales 0 pts

at MCG, Melbourne

Tasmania 373 for 9 dec. (D.F. Hills 128, S. Young 81, M.J. di Venuto 61, D.C. Boon 50, D.W. Fleming 4 for 59) and 200 (M.J. di Venuto 82, D.J. Saker 4 for 44, J.M. Davison 4 for 94)

Victoria 317 for 6 dec. (D.M. Jones 100 not out, D.J. Saker 50 not out) and 136 (C.R. Miller 7 for 49)

Tasmania won by 120 runs

Tasmania 6 pts, Victoria 0 pts

Justin Langer reached a thousand runs for the season and Damien Martyn's very occasional off-breaks brought him by far the best bowling figures of his career as Western Australia disposed of Queensland and gained their sixth outright win of the season.

Martin Faull made his first century in the match at Newcastle, but the game had little else to commend it. Siddons set an improbable target of 327 in 68 overs, but relief came when the final session was rained off.

Tasmania confirmed the best campaign in their Shield history with an emphatic win over Victoria. Dene Hills, Shield Player of the Year, notched another century, but the major honours went to Colin Miller, whose second innings figures of seven for 49 were the best of his career. When he trapped Craig leg before he beat Fleetwood-Smith's record of 60 wickets in a season which had stood since 1934–35. With the final still to come, Miller, discarded by both Victoria and South Australia, had 64 wickets to his credit.

Sheffield Shield Final Table

	P	W	L	D	Pts
Western Australia	10	6	3	1	40
Tasmania	10	6	3	1	40
Queensland	10	3	4	3	22
New South Wales	10	3	3	4	20
Victoria	10	2	4	4	18
South Australia	10	1	4	5	14

Western Australia topped the table and claimed home advantage in the final because their quotient was 1.324 to Tasmania's 1.271

Sheffield Shield Final

Western Australia *v.* Tasmania

David Boon won the toss and chose to bat, but, by the end of the first day, Tasmania's hopes of winning the Shield were vanishing. They had begun well enough with Hills and Cox scoring 80 for the first wicket, but following the departure of di Venuto at 136, wickets tumbled at regular intervals, and they closed on 244 for eight. If Tasmania were to be denied the silverware, they continued to break records. Following the achievements of Hills and Miller, Jamie Cox became the first man to carry his bat through the innings in a Shield final and the first Tasmanian to do it in any Shield match. He batted for six hours, faced 267 deliveries and hit 15 fours. His was a momentous achievement.

Western Australia were soon in total command. Hussey and Campbell scored 155 in 151 minutes for the first wicket. Ryan Campbell was responsible for 99 of the 155 runs, and his 104 came off 134 balls with a six and 16 fours, a sharp contrast to his 'pair' in the 1997 final. Martyn also scored briskly, and the day ended when night-watchman Angel was out to leave Western Australia 323 for five. The match was played in a fiercely competitive manner, and at one period there were angry exchanges between batsmen and fielders.

The third day saw Western Australia produce some fireworks. Tom Moody reached the 59th hundred of his career, his fourth in Shield finals, but the explosion came in the afternoon session when he was in partnership with Brendon Julian. Their stand was worth 136, and Moody made 28 of them. At lunch, Julian was five not out. He was dismissed on the stroke of tea for 124. The 119 runs he scored in the session established a Shield final record as did his century off 76 balls in 102 minutes. In all, he faced 105 balls and hit four sixes and 16 fours in what was the highest score of his career. A disheartened Tasmania finished the day on 92 for three. The loss of both Hills and Cox was a grievous blow.

Michael di Venuto remained firm. He had scored 59 on the third evening, and he carried the fight into the fourth day. He completed the eighth century of his career – four of them have been against Western Australia – and he was seventh out, having made 189 out of 329. He faced 273 balls and hit 30 fours, and he bravely delayed the inevitable, but Western Australia needed only 63 to win. The extra half hour was claimed on the fourth day, but only 11 minutes were needed. Moody pushed Targett for a single, and Western Australia had won with a day to spare. It was the 14th time they had won the Sheffield Shield. For Tasmania, still in search of their first Shield triumph, it was a disappointment, but they had enjoyed a memorable season.

Mercantile Mutual Cup

5 October 1997
at North Sydney Oval
New South Wales 319 for 7 (M.E. Waugh 76, S.R. Waugh 72, M.G. Bevan 56)
South Australia 282 (J.D. Siddons 58)
New South Wales (2 pts) won by 37 runs

Australia's limited-over competition increased to seven teams in 1997–98 with the inclusion of Canberra Comets from the Australian Capital Territories. In the opening match, the Waugh twins shared a third wicket stand of 141 for victorious New South Wales.

12 October 1997
at Woolloongabba, Bisbane
Queensland 230
New South Wales 232 for 9 (M.A. Taylor 70, M.G. Bevan 65 not out)
New South Wales (2 pts) won by 1 wicket

Sheffield Shield Final – Western Australia *v.* Tasmania

20, 21, 22 and 23 March 1998 at WACA Ground, Perth

Tasmania

	First Innings		Second Innings	
D.F. Hills	lbw, **b** Moody	**49**	**b** M.P. Atkinson	**17**
J. Cox	not out	**115**	**c** Gilchrist, **b** Angel	**0**
M.J. di Venuto	**c** Langer, **b** Angel	**34**	**c** Campbell, **b** M.P. Atkinson	**189**
S. Young	**c** Moody, **b** Angel	**13**	lbw, **b** Julian	**7**
D.C. Boon *	**c** Gilchrist, **b** M.P. Atkinson	**7**	**c** Julian, **b** Moody	**39**
R.J. Tucker	**c** Gilchrist, **b** M.P. Atkinson	**0**	**c** Julian, **b** M.P. Atkinson	**6**
D.J. Marsh	**c** Langer, **b** Julian	**13**	**c** Moody, **b** M.P. Atkinson	**12**
M.N. Atkinson †	**c** Campbell, **b** Julian	**7**	**c** Gilchrist, **b** M.P. Atkinson	**39**
B.S. Targett	**c** Moody, **b** Julian	**7**	**c** Gilchrist, **b** Angel	**0**
M.W. Ridgway	**c** Gilchrist, **b** Julian	**6**	lbw, **b** Julian	**5**
C.R. Miller	**c** and **b** Angel	**11**	not out	**9**
	lb **7**, nb **16**	**23**	lb **5**, w **2**, nb **18**	**25**
		285		**348**

	O	M	R	W	O	M	R	W
Angel	24.2	4	62	**3**	23	3	74	**2**
Julian	28	6	89	**4**	18.4	–	83	**2**
Moody	21	1	80	**1**	24	7	68	**1**
M.P. Atkinson	15	5	47	**2**	25	5	92	**5**
Oldroyd	9	2	26	**–**				

Fall of Wickets
1–**80**, 2–**136**, 3–**174**, 4–**193**, 5–**195**, 6–**216**, 7–**230**, 8–**242**, 9–**266**
1–**2**, 2–**42**, 3–**92**, 4–**198**, 5–**200**, 6–**245**, 7–**329**, 8–**330**, 9–**338**

Western Australia

	First Innings		Second Innings	
M.E. Hussey	**c** Hills, **b** Miller	**44**	not out	**39**
R.J. Campbell	**c** Tucker, **b** Young	**104**	**c** di Venuto, **b** Ridgway	**4**
J.L. Langer	lbw, **b** Targett	**19**	**c** M.N. Atkinson, **b** Ridhway	**12**
D.R. Martyn	lbw, **b** Ridgway	**83**	**c** M.N. Atkinson, **b** Targett	**7**
T.M. Moody *	**c** Marsh, **b** Targett	**125**	not out	**1**
J. Angel	**c** M.N. Atkinson, **b** Ridgway	**1**		
S.M. Katich	**c** Ridgway, **b** Targett	**22**		
A.C. Gilchrist †	**c** Miller, **b** Targett	**8**		
B.P. Julian	lbw, **b** Miller1	**24**		
M.P. Atkinson	not out	**9**		
B.J. Oldroyd	**b** Miller	**2**		
	b **4**, lb **15**, w **1**, nb **10**	**30**		
		571	(for 3 wickets)	**63**

	O	M	R	W	O	M	R	W
Ridgway	29	7	107	**2**	8	1	45	**2**
Miller	47.3	12	145	**3**	5	–	13	**–**
Young	25	7	92	**1**				
Targett	39	6	143	**4**	2.1	1	5	**1**
Marsh	11	4	50	**–**				
Tucker	4	–	15	**–**				

Fall of Wickets
1–**155**, 2–**163**, 3–**229**, 4–**311**, 5–**323**, 6–**376**, 7–**397**, 8–**533**, 9–**563**
1–**7**, 2–**31**, 3–**46**

Umpires: D.B. Hair & D.J. Harper

Western Australia won by 7 wickets

New South Wales made it two wins in two matches with a thrilling win over Queensland who were 162 for eight before Prestwidge and Kasprowicz added 62. Taylor gave New South Wales a good start, and when he fell to Prestwidge Bevan took over. Eight men were out for 219, and when Stuart was run out three runs were needed for victory. Bevan hit the next delivery for four to win the game with four balls remaining.

19 October 1997
at Adelaide Oval, Adelaide
South Australia 278 for 7 (J.D. Siddons 57, N.T. Adcock 57, G.S. Blewett 56)
Tasmania 209 (J. Cox 75, R.J. Tucker 68)
South Australia (2 pts) won by 69 runs

Medium-pace bowler Paul Wilson claimed three early wickets to leave Tasmania staggering at 48 for four. Cox and Tucker put on 55 for the sixth wicket, but Tasmania could never fully recover from the early blows.

26 October 1997
at North Sydney Oval
New South Wales 275 for 9 (M.J. Slater 68, M.G. Bevan 62 not out, M.E. Waugh 57)
Victoria 238 (D.S. Berry 64 not out, B.J. Hodge 53)
New South Wales (2 pts) won by 37 runs

Camberra Comets' wicket-keeper batsman Brad Haddin, 'the best new talent in the competition'.
(Stephen Laffer / Sportsline)

The Camberra Comets enter the Mercantile Mutual Cup. They pose with South Australia before the inaugural match at the Manuka Oval.
(Stephen Laffer / Sportsline)

Three wins in three matches virtually assured New South Wales of a place in the semi-finals. Bevan hit his third half-century in as many innings, but Berry took the individual award for his brave attempt to rouse his side from the low of 48 for five.

2 November 1997
at Manuka Oval, Canberra
South Australia 237 (G.S. Blewett 97, N.T. Adcock 51)
Canberra Comets 226
South Australia (2 pts) won by 11 runs

Canberra were given no chance of success against South Australia, but their team of Mike Veletta, Merv Hughes and nine little known players surprised all. They bowled the state side out in 49 overs and were in the hunt until the last over of their innings when Merv Hughes lost his middle stump to the third ball.

16 November 1997
at Bellerive Oval, Hobart
Canberra Comets 213 for 8 (P.J. Solway 56, M.G. Farrell 4 for 51)
Tasmania 214 for 6 (J. Cox 99)
Tasmania (2 pts) won by 4 wickets

Tasmania won with 7.4 overs to spare, but there was a bizarre finish when the home state lost three wickets, including that of Man of the Match Cox, with the score on 210.

23 November 1997
at Queen Elizabeth Oval, Bendigo
Canberra Comets 250 (B.J. Haddin 89, P.S. Solway 73)
Victoria 235 (D.M. Jones 64, B.J. Hodge 61)
Canberra Comets (2 pts) won by 15 runs

Canberra were 28 for three before Haddin and Solway added 174. A total of 250 was beyond Victoria, and a crowd of 3658 applauded Canberra's first victory.

5 December 1997
at Woolloongabba, Brisbane
Victoria 200 for 9 (S.A. Muller 5 for 43)
Queensland 202 for 3 (M.L. Hayden 59)
Queensland (2 pts) won by 7 wickets

Scott Muller became the first bowler in the season's competition to take five wickets in an innings. He was playing under the new ruling that allows a side to name 12 players, one of whom bowls but does not bat.

12 December 1997
at WACA Ground, Perth
Western Australia 285 for 5 (R.J. Campbell 72, T.M. Moody 71 not out, A.C. Gilchrist 59)

South Australia 149 (G.S. Blewett 61, K.M. Harvey 4 for 35)
Western Australia (2 pts) won by 136 runs

Western Australia made an emphatic entrance into the competition when they trounced South Australia. Campbell and Martyn sored 93 for the second wicket, and Gilchrist and Moody 126 for the fifth.

14 December 1997
at Manuka Oval, Canberra
Canberra Comets 192
New South Wales 192 for 5
New South Wales (2 pts) won on faster scoring rate

New South Wales entered the new year with maximum points. A 20-minute break reduced their target to 191 in 28 overs in Canberra.

2 January 1998
at WACA Ground, Perth
Western Australia 278 for 6 (J.L. Langer 86, D.R. Martyn 78)
Canberra Comets 126 (M.R.J. Veletta 50, K.M. Harvey 4 for 8)
Western Australia (2 pts) won by 152 runs

Langer and Martyn put on 149 for Western Australia's third wicket to set up a crushing victory over Canberra, whose task was made more difficult when they were deducted two overs for their slow over-rate.

4 January 1998
at MCG, Melbourne
Victoria 239 for 8 (D.M. Jones 91 not out, B.J. Hodge 58)
Tasmania 242 for 4 (M.J. di Venuto 60, R.J. Tucker 51, D.F. Hills 50)
Tasmania (2 pts) won by 6 wickets

Michael di Venuto's 60 off 54 balls in an opening partnership of 111 with Dene Hills set up Tasmania's second win of the season. Dean Jones gave backbone to Victoria's innings, but Tasmania won with 17 balls to spare.

10 January 1998
at Adelaide Oval, Adelaide
Queensland 260 for 8 (J.P. Maher 126, J.N. Gillespie 4 for 61)
South Australia 249 (D.A. Fitzgerald 61, J.D. Siddons 52)
Queensland (2 pts) won by 11 runs

Jimmy Maher scored the first century of the 1997–98 competition as Queensland gained a narrow victory over

South Australia. Maher's runs came off 129 balls, and he hit three sixes and 13 fours. Attempting to return to full fitness, Jason Gillespie took four wickets, but his 10 overs cost 61 runs.

17 January 1998
at Woolloongabba, Brisbane
Queensland 209 for 9 (S.A. Prestwidge 53)
Western Australia 210 for 9 (D.R. Martyn 93)
Western Australia (2 pts) won by 1 wicket

Chasing a target of 210, Western Australia were 96 for six, having lost four wickets for 15 runs. They were rescued by Damien Martyn, who hit 93 off 121 balls. He was out with the scores level, and it was number 11 Stewart who hit Muller for the winning run.

23 January 1998
at WACA Ground, Perth
New South Wales 283 for 3 (S. Lee 99 not out, M.J. Slater 63, M.A. Taylor 51)
Western Australia 185 (J.L. Langer 96, S.C.G. MacGill 4 for 32)
New South Wales (2 pts) won by 98 runs

An opening partnership of 122 in 24 overs between Taylor and Slater gave an excellent base to New South Wales's innings. Shane Lee, Man of the Match, followed with a blistering unbeaten 99. Langer played a lone hand for Western Australia who surrendered their unbeaten record. New South Wales, five wins in five matches, were assured of topping the table.

31 January 1998
at Bellerive Oval, Hobart
Western Australia 310 for 6 (D.R. Martyn 140, R.J. Campbell 55)
Tasmania 91 (K.M. Harvey 4 for 23)
Western Australia (2 pts) won by 219 runs

at Manuka Oval, Canberra
Queensland 275 for 7 (J.P. Maher 70)
Canberra Comets 227 (B.J. Haddin 52)
Queensland (2 pts) won by 48 runs

Western Australia made the highest team score of the season, while Damien Martyn continued the form which had won him a recall to the national squad with the season's biggest score, 140. Tasmania wilted before the huge total and surrendered meekly. Pace bowler Kade Harvey had another four-wicket haul.

With Jimmy Maher again in good form, Queensland cruised to victory over Canberra who could be well pleased with their first season in the competition.

7 February 1998
at MCG, Melbourne
Victoria 223 for 5 (S.A.J. Craig 60, D.M. Jones 57)
Western Australia 188 for 1 (D.R. Martyn 99 not out, J.L. Langer 83 not out)
Victoria (2 pts) won on faster scoring rate

8 February 1998
at SCG, Sydney
Tasmania 187 (R.J. Tucker 66, S.R. Clark 4 for 26)
New South Wales 191 for 3 (K.J. Geyer 92 not out)
New South Wales (2 pts) won by 7 wickets

Victoria gained their first victory of the season in the most fortunate of circumstances. Needing 224 to win, Western Australia were 36 runs short of their target with 6.4 overs remaining and nine wickets standing when it began to rain. Calculations gave the game to Victoria by 0.13 of a run. With Martyn unbeaten on 99 and Langer, 83, both in outstanding form, Western Australia had the right to feel aggrieved.

Man of the Match in the Mercantile Mutual Cup Final – Queensland's Scott Prestwidge.
(Stephen Laffer / Sportsline)

Kevin Geyer made his mark for New South Wales with an unbeaten 92 in 42.2 overs. He helped New South Wales to complete their sixth win of the season.

14 February 1998
at Adelaide Oval, Adelaide
South Australia 307 for 7 (D.A. Fitzgerald 92, G.S. Blewett 83)
Victoria 166 (M.A. Harrity 5 for 42)
South Australia (2 pts) won by 141 runs

15 February 1998
at Bellerive Oval, Hobart
Queensland 233 (J.H. Maher 68, C.T. Perren 52)
Tasmania 221 (R.J. Tucker 75, J. Cox 52)
Queensland (2 pts) won by 12 runs

The last two matches in the qualifying league saw South Australia and Queensland confirm their places in the semi-final.

Brad Haddin of Canberra won the award for the best new talent in the competition. The 20-year old wicket-keeper/batsman hit 205 runs, average 34.17, and his fifty off 36 balls against Queensland was the second fastest of the season. Player of the Series award went to Damien Martyn who scored 494 runs, average 98.80, a feat which earned him $5,000.

Mercantile Mutual Cup Final Table

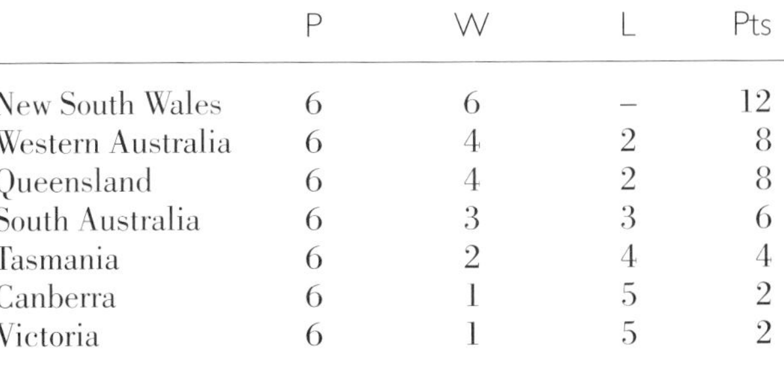

	P	W	L	Pts
New South Wales	6	6	–	12
Western Australia	6	4	2	8
Queensland	6	4	2	8
South Australia	6	3	3	6
Tasmania	6	2	4	4
Canberra	6	1	5	2
Victoria	6	1	5	2

Semi-Finals

21 February 1998
at WACA Ground, Perth
Western Australia 283 for 6 (T.M. Moody 63 not out, J.L. Langer 51, D.R. Martyn 50)
Queensland 284 for 7 (M.L. Love 75, J.P. Maher 56)
Queensland won by 3 wickets

22 February 1998
at SCG, Sydney
New South Wales 212 for 8 (M.G. Bevan 74)
South Australia 143
New South Wales won by 69 runs

Queensland, deducted one over because of their slow rate, equalled the second biggest winning score by a side batting second in Australian domestic limited-over cricket. They won in the 47th over. New South Wales won much more comfortably.

Final

1 March 1998
at SCG, Sydney
New South Wales 166
Queensland 167 for 8
Queensland won by 2 wickets

On a dry pitch which favoured the bowlers, Queensland won the one-day trophy for the sixth time. Searching for 167 to win, they began badly, but the late middle order of Prestwidge, who was Man of the Match, Seccombe and Bichel steered them to victory after seven wickets had fallen for 104 by the 35th over. Bichel and Prestwidge added 55, with Bichel, 30, hitting Bevan for a vital six. Thompson returned to have Bichel caught before Prestwidge hit two boundaries to win the match. He finished unbeaten on 42.

First-Class Averages

Batting

	M	Inns	NOs	Runs	HS	Av	100s	50s
G.R.J. Matthews	3	2	1	106	71*	106.00	1	2
T.M. Moody	8	13	4	702	160	78.00	3	3
M.G. Bevan	9	14	4	738	153	73.80	3	3
R.T. Ponting	9	15	4	697	129*	63.36	3	2
J.L. Langer	12	20	3	1075	235	63.23	3	4
D.F. Hills	12	23	1	1220	265	55.45	4	3
S.R. Waugh	10	17	4	720	202*	55.38	1	5
P.R. Reiffel	7	10	3	379	79*	54.14	4	
M.A. Taylor	13	21	2	1021	169*	53.73	3	8
D.M. Jones	11	21	4	896	151*	52.70	3	5
R.J. Davison	7	14	2	630	169	52.50	3	1
J.D. Siddons	9	17	1	838	117	52.37	2	6
L.D. Harper	11	21	2	992	207*	52.21	4	1
M.J. Slater	9	17	1	831	137	51.93	2	5
B.P. Julian	9	10	2	401	124	50.12	2	1
M.E. Waugh	11	17	2	747	115*	49.80	2	5
M.J. di Venuto	10	18	1	845	189	49.70	1	6
D.S. Lehmann	5	8	–	395	138	49.37	1	2
M.L. Hayden	11	19	–	934	181	49.15	4	4
M.E. Hussey	12	21	2	915	134	48.15	3	3
A.C. Gilchrist	9	12	3	429	203*	47.66	2	
A. Symonds	11	18	1	809	163	47.58	4	2
M.L. Love	10	17	2	713	201*	47.53	2	2
D.S. Webber	6	11	2	411	145	45.66	1	2
D.C. Boon	12	18	2	707	146	44.18	1	5
S. Lee	11	17	4	574	183*	44.15	1	1
J. Cox	12	23	3	860	126	43.00	2	4
D.R. Martyn	12	20	1	813	141*	42.78	2	7
S.M. Katich	7	13	2	462	93*	42.00	4	
G.S. Blewett	13	24	–	969	111	40.37	1	6
S. Young	12	21	2	751	145	39.52	2	5
R.J. Campbell	11	19	–	726	177	38.21	3	3
B.J. Hodge	7	14	1	494	116*	38.00	1	2
D.J. Marsh	12	20	5	566	129*	37.73	1	3
K.J. Roberts	3	6	2	143	78*	35.75	1	
G.B. Gardiner	6	11	2	321	133*	35.66	1	2
S.G. Law	6	9	2	249	107*	35.57	1	1
C.J. Richards	8	14	–	490	164	35.00	1	3
P.A. Emery	10	12	4	264	51*	33.00	2	
D.A. Fitzgerald	10	19	–	613	85	32.26	5	
M.P. Atkinson	6	7	3	127	35	31.75		
I.A. Healy	13	19	3	507	85	31.68	3	
R.J. Tucker	9	14	1	411	99	31.61	3	
M.P. Faull	5	9	–	282	103	31.33	1	2
M.T.G. Elliott	15	27	–	838	187	31.03	3	
I.J. Harvey	6	11	1	310	109	31.00	1	1
J.L. Arnberger	4	8	–	245	74	30.62	2	
J.C. Scuderi	3	5	1	122	43	30.50		
J.P. Maher	11	19	–	575	114	30.26	1	3
B.E. Young	9	16	4	358	66	29.83	2	
A.J. Bichel	8	13	1	341	110	28.41	1	2
S.A.J. Craig	6	12	3	251	71*	28.33	2	
G.I. Foley	11	18	2	441	82	27.56	2	
W.A. Seccombe	4	7	1	165	54*	27.50	1	
D.S. Berry	11	19	3	440	166*	27.50	1	
M.N. Atkinson	12	17	5	323	47	26.91		
D.J. Saker	10	14	6	207	50*	25.87	1	
C.J. Davies	3	6	–	151	55	25.16	1	
G.B. Hogg	6	8	2	146	37	24.33		
T.J. Nielsen	10	19	2	412	115	24.23	1	
K.J. Geyer	3	5	–	106	41	21.20		
R.M. Baker	5	9	–	185	46	20.55		
B.A. Johnson	6	11	–	212	39	19.27		
P.W. Jackson	10	14	5	154	41	17.11		
A.M. Stuart	9	9	3	101	28*	16.83		

Batting

	M	Inns	NOs	Runs	HS	Av	100s	50s
A.C. Dale	7	8	–	123	55	15.37	1	
M.P. Mott	5	9	1	122	44	15.25		
D.W. Fleming	8	11	3	116	45*	14.50		
S.K. Warne	9	12	2	138	36	13.80		
C.R. Miller	12	14	5	104	38	11.55		
G.R. Vimpani	6	12	1	125	30	11.36		
M.S. Kasprowicz	13	17	4	144	20	11.07		

(qualification – 100 runs, average 10.00)

Bowling

	Overs	Mds	Runs	Wks	Best	Av	10/m	5/inn
S.A. Muller	66	17	226	13	5/73	17.38	1	
D.W. Fleming	326.5	98	705	39	6/35	18.07	1	2
M.P. Atkinson	158	34	493	24	5/92	20.54	1	
J. Angel	304.1	78	800	36	4/45	22.22		
D.A. Freedman	339	89	915	38	7/106	24.07	2	3
J.H. Dawes	158.2	35	485	20	4/27	24.25		
A.J. Bichel	269	62	758	31	5/31	24.45	1	
M.S. Kasprowicz	432.4	113	1157	47	4/22	24.61		
A.C. Dale	244.1	74	571	23	5/19	24.82	1	
C.R. Miller	649.2	172	1749	70	7/49	24.98	2	5
B.P. Julian	324.3	74	988	39	7/39	25.33	2	
S.H. Cook	249.2	62	756	29	5/39	26.06	1	
D.J. Saker	382.1	99	1044	38	6/39	27.47	1	1
M.W.H. Inness	186	47	548	19	4/42	28.84		
S.C.G. MacGill	444.3	104	1443	50	6/64	28.86	4	
S.K. Warne	498.5	115	1381	47	6/34	29.38	1	3
B.N. Wigney	117.2	24	362	12	5/37	30.16	1	
T.M. Moody	256.4	73	665	22	5/20	30.22	1	
M.W. Ridgway	309.3	83	1005	33	6/50	30.45	1	
A. Symonds	109.4	28	320	10	2/22	32.00		
P.R. Reiffel	236.2	75	521	16	3/14	32.56		
B.S. Targett	262.1	68	791	23	4/143	34.39		
D.J. Marsh	317.2	89	906	26	7/57	34.84	1	
S.R. Cary	151.1	43	390	11	4/96	35.45		
I.J. Harvey	135.2	30	426	12	4/27	35.50		
G.D. McGrath	187.2	55	466	13	5/32	35.84	1	
M.A. Harrity	227.4	46	696	18	3/48	38.66		
P. Wilson	197.1	54	507	13	4/53	39.00		
B.E. Young	457.1	98	1329	34	5/64	39.08	2	
P.E. McIntyre	195.5	37	690	17	5/175	40.58	1	
J. Stewart	222.2	45	733	18	4/121	40.72		
M.S. Garnaut	179.4	51	601	14	3/31	42.92		
J.M. Davison	210.2	56	679	15	5/84	45.26	1	
P.W. Jackson	341	112	753	16	3/89	47.06		
S. Lee	175	28	614	13	3/26	47.23		
S. Young	299.4	85	884	18	3/69	49.11		
A.M. Stuart	226.4	52	791	16	7/76	49.43	1	

(qualification –10 wickets)

Leading Fielders

49 – A.C. Gilchrist; 45 – D.S. Berry (ct 39 / st 6); 41 – I.A. Healy (ct 37 / st 4); 38 – M.N. Atkinson (ct 36 / st 2); 33 – P.A. Emery (ct 24 / st 9); 26 – M.A. Taylor; 25 – T.J. Nielsen (ct 22 / st 3); 24 – R.J. Campbell; 20 – M.T.G. Elliott; 16 – G.I. Foley and D.F. Hills; 15 – W.A. Seccombe and L.P. Harper; 14 – G.S. Blewett; 13 – M.L. Love; 12 – M.L. Hayden; 11– J.P. Maher, D.J. Marsh, D.R. Martyn and S. Young,Y,

Sharjah

The lucrative tournaments in Sharjah have mainly been the preserve of the Asian nations. It was in 1983–84 that the United Arab Emirates first staged a limited-over competition between Test-playing countries. The Sharjah Trophy, which was competed for in December 1997, was the 22nd tournament to be played in the thirteen years since that inaugural festival.

Sharjah Cricket Association Stadium. (Graham Chadwick / Allsport)

Sharjah Trophy
Coca Cola Triangular Tournament

Pakistan won nine of the first 21 competitions in Sharjah, with India and West Indies taking four each, and, more recently, Sri Lanka taking two. Australia have won once, as have England, who visited Sharjah twice, in 1984–85 and two years later when they won the Sharjah Trophy. They returned in 1997 with a side chosen specifically for its expertise in one-day cricket.

The England side was led by Adam Hollioake, the Surrey captain, whose credentials as an international cricketer were very much under scrutiny. Arguably, England could not have returned to Sharjah at a more propitious time. The three teams with whom they would compete were beset by problems. West Indies came straight from Pakistan where they had suffered the greatest of indignities in losing all three Tests. There were rumours that their squad was rent by internal dispute, and they were a pale carbon copy of a once formidable side. Pakistan, heartened by their victories over West Indies, remained the model of inconsistency, while India were in a state of uncertainty. Tendulkar's form had fluctuated since he had succeeded Azharuddin as captain, and, in spite of the return of Srinath after nine months absence through injury, the bowling still presented problems.

India were England's opponents in the opening match of the tournament. Tendulkar chose to field first when he won the toss, and the Surrey pair, Alistair Brown and Stewart, gave England a brisk start. They had taken the score to 42 in the eighth over before Brown lofted Kuruvilla to mid-on. Knight, perhaps chastened that he was to lead the 'A' side to Kenya instead of being with the main party in the Caribbean, gave Stewart solid support in a stand of 89, and Hick, although never suggesting his best, made 32 off 42 balls. Like Knight, he hit a six and two fours. Hick and Stewart added 78, taking the score past 200. However, Hick's dismissal heralded a sensational collapse, the last eight wickets going down in ten overs for 41 runs. Stewart was out to the first ball of the 41st over when he pushed a ball from Kumble into the hands of cover. He had batted majestically for his highest score in a one-day international, facing 111 balls and hitting a six and nine fours. It was a truly splendid innings, but thereafter no one could pick up the momentum, and England's innings ended on a note of disappointment.

Moin Khan stumps Carl Hooper off the bowling of Saqlain Mushtaq, but West Indies beat Pakistan with ease in the second match in the Sharjah Cup.
(David Munden / Sportsline)

Chauhan is bowled by Fleming in the opening match of the four-nations tournament, and England are close to victory. Fleming, the Kent all-rounder, took four wickets on his international debut.
(David Munden / Sportsline)

England's disappointment seemed even greater as India had a whirlwind start. Karim was dropped by Stewart off Headley, but the lapse was not too costly as Headley got his man taken at extra cover in the 12th over. When Ealham bowled Ganguly in the next over and then quickly accounted for Sidhu, the game swung positively in England's favour. With Azharuddin failing for once, there appeared to be nothing that could stop England – unless it was Tendulkar. The Indian captain found a worthy ally in Jadeja, and, in 20

Warwickshire's Dougie Brown, a most capable one-day cricketer. (David Munden / Sportsline)

overs, they put on 108. Jadeja was caught at mid-wicket, but Tendulkar, unbeaten on 63, was at his brilliant best. He was driving hard and cutting purposefully, and 69 runs from the last ten overs seemed well within his capabilities if he were given competent support. Robin Singh hit 12 off 14 balls and helped the score to pass 200. Knight ran out Kumble at 221 – a good example of England's fine ground fielding. Tendulkar remained. He had hit two sixes and four fours before moving down the pitch to receive his 87th ball. He was deceived by Fleming and stumped. Five runs later, Srinath was bowled by Headley, and Fleming, making his international debut and bowling with intelligence and composure, finished the match and gave England a fine victory when he bowled Chauhan.

The following day, West Indies ended their losing run and gained some consolation for what they had endured in Pakistan by beating their tormentors by 43 runs. West Indies chose to bat first when they won the toss and were given a rousing start by Stuart Williams and Philo Wallace, who put on 81 in 16 overs. Lara then joined Williams in a stand worth 79, and Lara found his best form in scoring 88 off 80 balls with three sixes and seven fours. He was out in the 46th over, but he had helped West Indies to a challenging 275.

Pakistan began as if they would race to victory. Shahid Afridi hit four sixes and six fours in making 67 off 56 balls before he was run out by Lara, who also caught Saeed Anwar. At 124 for two in the 22nd over, Pakistan had seemed to be cruising to their target, but Walsh bowled with great economy to thwart the middle order, and the West Indian fielding became sharper. Pakistan's batting lost urgency, and West Indies won with surprising ease.

England virtually assured themselves of a place in the final when they beat West Indies in the third match in the competition. Walsh chose to bat first when he won the toss but West Indies began disastrously. Dougie Brown's first ball knocked back Wallace's off stump, his second passed the outside edge of Lara's bat, and his third had the left-hander leg before when he shuffled back onto his stumps. Stuart Williams and Carl Hooper were faced with the task of repairing the innings when they had been expecting to press for quick runs. They added 50 before Williams chipped Headley to mid-wicket, but, after 15 overs, West Indies were 57 for three and struggling. That they made a moderately reasonable score was due entirely to Hooper, who batted with a blend of intelligence and elegance. He hit six fours and faced 135 balls for his unbeaten century. Phil Simmons made 29 off 46 balls as 66 were added for the fifth wicket, but a total of 197 was hardly likely to tax England too much.

Walsh had Alistair Brown caught at square-leg in his third over, and Knight, lucky to survive an appeal for caught behind before he had scored, was spectacularly caught by

Alec Stewart runs out Saqlain Mushtaq and England have beaten Pakistan to gain a place in the final. Skipper Adam Hollioake joins in the appeal. (David Munden / Sportsline)

David Williams stumps Adam Hollioake off the bowling of Carl Hooper for 16 to leave England on 154 for five in the final against West Indies, but Thorpe Fleming keep their nerve and England win the Sharjah Cup.
(David Munden / Sportsline)

wicket-keeper Williams down the leg side five overs later. Stewart fell to Rose, but Hick and Thorpe took the score to 100 in the 24th over when Hick was brilliantly run out by Chanderpaul. Hollioake hooked rashly to deep square leg, but Ealham gave Thorpe sensible support, and although the Surrey player was caught behind off Hooper, an England victory was never in doubt.

India's interest in the tournament ended when they lost to the old enemy Pakistan before a capacity crowd, a contrast to the meagre attendance for the England–West Indies match. Winning the toss, Tendulkar elected to bat first, and his side was in a strong position at 143 in the 31st over before the second wicket fell. Sidhu was in particularly rampant form and Ganguly batted with great charm and purpose for 44 overs, but Tendulkar erred in delaying his and Azharuddin's entry into the fray. Even so, India remained on top and reduced Pakistan to 144 for five in 32 overs, the spinners dominant. Again Tendulkar's judgement had to be questioned when he replaced his spinners with medium-pacers, and Saeed Anwar and Moin Khan took advantage of this tactical error. Saeed moved to his 14th century in one-day international cricket (seven of them have been scored in Sharjah) and Moin Khan made the winning runs with 16 balls to spare.

Pakistan's dream of reaching the final evaporated the next day when they lost to England in a close encounter. Batting first, England were given an excellent start by Stewart and Ally Brown, but Manzoor Akhtar's wrist spin brought havoc to the middle order, while Saqlain Mushtaq thwarted the efforts of the later batsmen so that a total of 215 was bitterly disappointing. Pakistan lost both openers very cheaply, but Saeed Anwar continued his brilliant form of the previous day and raced to 54 off 66 balls. Ijaz Ahmed, too, was at his best, hitting two sixes and three fours, and Pakistan were roaring to victory. The loss of both at 99 appeared to make little difference, for Akhtar Sarfraz and Manzoor Akhtar batted responsibly, and when Matthew Fleming joined the attack 65 were needed from 13 overs with five wickets standing. Fleming immediately accounted for Moin Khan, and Wasim Akram perished when he was superbly caught by Dougie Brown on the leg-side boundary. The turning point came when Manzoor, who had batted so sensibly, had a rush of blood and embarked on a suicide run, only to fall victim to Knight's throw. With two overs remaining, Pakistan needed 18, and Azhar Mahmood hit Hollioake for two and four before skying a slower delivery, which Stewart ran from behind the stumps to catch in the region of mid-wicket. Next ball, Saqlain pushed forward and wandered into dreamland so that Stewart was able to collect and flick back onto the wicket to complete the run out.

West Indies confirmed themselves as England's opponents in the final by beating India in the last of the qualifying matches. Put in to bat, West Indies were well served by Stuart Williams, who batted throughout the 50 overs for his first century in a limited-over international. He and Hooper added 71 for the third wicket. The Indian spinners were particularly effective, and so, too, were Hooper, Chanderpaul and Lewis for West Indies. Ganguly and Sidhu gave India a fine start, and Dravid maintained the momentum. Disasters began for India when Ganguly went down the pitch to Lewis and missed. Worse followed as Tendulkar and Azharuddin were both run out by Lewis from square-leg, and the rest of the Indian batsmen missed when they attempted to hit it out. For them, a miserable tournament was over.

Final Table

	P	W	L	Pts
England	3	3	–	6
West Indies	3	2	1	4
Pakistan	3	1	2	2
India	3	–	3	–

Final

England *v.* West Indies

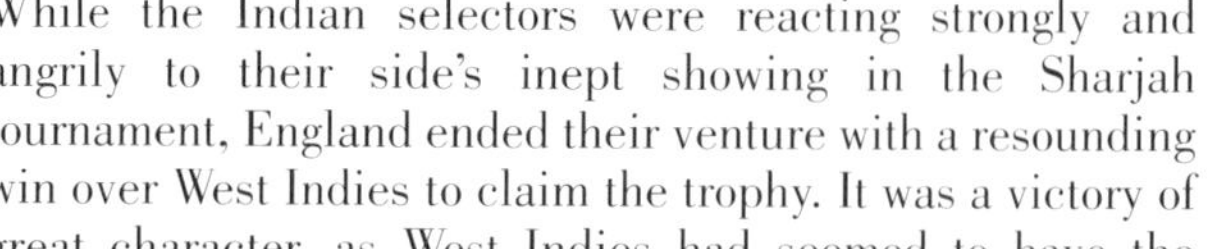

While the Indian selectors were reacting strongly and angrily to their side's inept showing in the Sharjah tournament, England ended their venture with a resounding win over West Indies to claim the trophy. It was a victory of great character, as West Indies had seemed to have the advantage for much of the game. Choosing to bat first, they

The most coveted wicket in the world. Tendulkar is stumped by Stewart off Fleming for 91. Tendulkar returned to Sharjah a few months later to destroy Australia in the Coca Cola Cup.
(David Munden / Sportsline)

were given a splendid start by Stuart Williams and Shivnarine Chanderpaul, who made 97 in 22 overs before Williams was caught at long-on. The bonus for England came in the next over when Lara over-balanced in facing Ealham and was stumped. Chanderpaul made 76 off 109 balls and repaired damage in a stand of 63 with Hooper, while Simmons hit robustly towards the close. Fleming bowled with intelligence and economy, and he ran out Chanderpaul with a diving stop and accurate throw from a prone position, a magnificent piece of fielding which symbolised much of England's out-cricket. In spite of this, England faced a target that was higher than any had managed in the qualifying matches.

The chances of England winning seemed remote when Alistair Brown was caught at cover in the fourth over. Knight and Stewart put on 75 for the second wicket, but they and Hick fell in quick succession to leave England on 107 for four in the 25th over. Thorpe and Adam Hollioake added 45 in 12 overs, and England were falling behind the asking rate. When Ealham heaved and missed in the 41st over England required 71 from nine overs with only four wickets standing. Thorpe and Fleming responded mightily. In seven overs, they scored 70 runs, an outstanding achievement, until Fleming was run out in a state of over-excitement. Dougie Brown touched the first ball he received to the third man boundary to win the match. Thorpe was left unbeaten for 66, made off 74 balls with five fours, and England were left with the trophy, an unbeaten record and a reputation much enhanced.

Match One – England *v.* India

11 December 1997 at Sharjah C.A. Stadium

England

A.D. Brown	c Ganguly, **b** Kuruvilla	**18**
A.J. Stewart †	c Azharuddin, **b** Kumble	**116**
N.V. Knight	c Kumble, **b** Chauhan	**42**
G.A. Hick	**b** Kuruvilla	**32**
A.J. Hollioake *	**b** Kuruvilla	**4**
M.A. Ealham	run out	**9**
G.P. Thorpe	run out	**3**
M.V. Fleming	c Karim, **b** Srinath	**9**
D.R. Brown	c Tendulkar, **b** Srinath	**6**
R.D.B. Croft	c Kuruvilla, **b** Srinath	**5**
D.W. Headley	not out	**1**
	lb **4**, w **1**	**5**
	49.5 overs	**250**

	O	M	R	W
Srinath	8.5	–	37	**3**
Kuruvilla	10	–	50	**3**
Kumble	10	–	53	**1**
R.R. Singh	6	–	34	**–**
Ganguly	2	–	14	**–**
Chauhan	9	–	34	**1**
Tendulkar	4	–	24	**–**

Fall of Wickets
1–**42**, 2–**131**, 3–**209**, 4–**211**, 5–**215**, 6–**218**, 7–**232**, 8–**237**, 9–**248**

India

S.S. Karim †	c Croft, **b** Headley	**29**
S.C. Ganguly	**b** Ealham	**29**
N.S. Sidhu	c Hollioake, **b** Ealham	**3**
S.R. Tendulkar *	st Stewart, **b** Fleming	**91**
M. Azharuddin	c Headley, **b** Hollioake	**3**
A.D. Jadeja	c Thorpe, **b** Fleming	**50**
R.R. Singh	lbw, **b** Fleming	**12**
A.R. Kumble	run out	**2**
R.K. Chauhan	**b** Fleming	**12**
J. Srinath	**b** Headley	**3**
A. Kuruvilla	not out	**1**
	lb **3**, w **3**, nb **2**	**8**
	49.3 overs	**243**

	O	M	R	W
D.R. Brown	7	–	44	**–**
Headley	9	–	38	**2**
Ealham	10	–	43	**2**
Hollioake	9	1	38	**1**
Croft	5	–	32	**–**
Fleming	9.3	–	45	**4**

Fall of Wickets
1–**60**, 2–**64**, 3–**65**, 4–**74**, 5–**182**, 6–**207**, 7–**221**, 8–**232**, 9–**237**

Umpires: S.A. Bucknor & K.T. Francis *Man of the Match*: A.J. Stewart

England won by 7 runs

Match Two – Pakistan v. West Indies

12 December 1997 at Sharjah C.A. Stadium

West Indies

P.A. Wallace	c Inzamam, b Saqlain	32
S.C. Williams	c Wasim, b Shahid Afridi	77
B.C. Lara	c Azhar Mahmood, b Wasim	88
C.L. Hooper	st Moin, b Saqlain Mushtaq	17
P.V. Simmons	c Aamir Sohail, b Saqlain	22
S. Chanderpaul	not out	16
F.A. Rose	b Wasim Akram	2
D. Williams †	c and b Wasim Akram	0
R.N. Lewis	not ou	1
M.V. Dillon		
C.A. Walsh *		
	b 1, lb 6, w 12, nb 1	20
	50 overs (for 7 wickets)	275

	O	M	R	W
Wasim Akram	10	–	62	3
Waqar Younis	10	–	53	–
Saqlain Mushtaq	10	–	35	3
Azhar Mahmood	10	–	61	–
Shahid Afridi	10	–	57	1

Fall of Wickets
1–**81**, 2–**160**, 3–**217**, 4–**243**, 5–**266**, 6–**271**, 7–**271**

Pakistan

Aamir Sohail	c Lewis, b Rose	17
Shahid Afridi	run out	67
Saeed Anwar	c Lara, b Dillon	22
Ijaz Ahmed	c Hooper, b Lewis	12
Inzamam-ul-Haq	run out	33
Akhtar Sarfraz	lbw, b Simmons	25
Wasim Akram *	c Chanderpaul, b Walsh	22
Moin Khan †	run out	8
Azhar Mahmood	c Simmons, b Walsh	4
Saqlain Mushtaq	not out	2
Waqar Younis	c Wallace, b Hooper	1
	lb 8, w 7, nb 4	19
	46 overs	232

	O	M	R	W
Walsh	8	–	14	2
Rose	6	–	47	1
Dillon	8	–	45	1
Hooper	9	–	56	1
Lewis	8	1	31	1
Simmons	7	–	31	1

Fall of Wickets
1–**24**, 2–**91**, 3–**124**, 4–**135**, 5–**178**, 6–**204**, 7–**222**, 8–**229**, 9–**230**

Umpires: C.J. Mitchley & B.C. Cooray *Man of the Match*: B.C. Lara

West Indies won by 43 runs

Match Three – England v. West Indies

13 December 1997 at Sharjah C.A. Stadium

West Indies

P.A. Wallace	b D.R. Brown	0
S.C. Williams	c Thorpe, b Headley	22
B.C. Lara	lbw, b D.R. Brown	0
C.L. Hooper	not out	100
S. Chanderpaul	lbw, b Ealham	16
P.V. Simmons	c Croft, b Hollioake	29
D. Williams †	run out	4
R.N. Lewis	b Fleming	13
F.A. Rose	not out	11
M.V. Dillon		
C.A. Walsh *		
	nb 2	2
	50 overs (for 7 wickets)	197

	O	M	R	W
D.R. Brown	7	1	28	2
Headley	7	1	24	1
Ealham	10	1	28	1
Croft	10	–	40	–
Hollioake	8	–	41	1
Fleming	8	1	36	1

Fall of Wickets
1–**0**, 2–**0**, 3–**50**, 4–**77**, 5–**143**, 6–**151**, 7–**181**

England

A.D. Brown	c Lewis, b Walsh	10
A.J. Stewart †	c Walsh, b Rose	23
N.V. Knight	c D. Williams, b Dillon	10
G.A. Hick	run out	28
G.P. Thorpe	c D. Williams, b Hooper	57
A.J. Hollioake *	c Chanderpaul, b Dillon	9
M.A. Ealham	not out	28
D.R. Brown	not out	16
M.V. Fleming		
R.D.B. Croft		
D.W. Headley		
	lb 7, w 4, nb 6	17
	45.5 overs (for 6 wickets)	198

	O	M	R	W
Walsh	9.5	1	51	1
Rose	10	–	38	1
Dillon	10	–	38	2
Lewis	6	–	34	–
Simmons	2	–	8	–
Hooper	8	1	22	1

Fall of Wickets
1–**21**, 2–**45**, 3–**53**, 4–**100**, 5–**123**, 6–**173**

Umpires: B.C. Cooray & K.T. Francis *Man of the Match*: C.L. Hooper

England won by 4 wickets

Match Four – India v. Pakistan

14 December 1997 at Sharjah C.A. Stadium

India

S.S. Karim †	run out	**18**
S.C. Ganguly	**b** Wasim Akram	**90**
N.S. Sidhu	run out	**54**
R.R. Singh	**c** Moin, **b** Azhar Mahmood	**0**
S.R. Tendulkar *	**c** Inzamam, **b** Manzoor Akhtar	**3**
M. Azharuddin	**c** Wasim, **b** Saqlain Mushtaq	**39**
A.D. Jadeja	**b** Saqlain Mushtaq	**6**
A.R. Kumble	not out	**11**
R.K. Chauhan		
J. Srinath		
A. Kuruvilla		
	lb **11**, w **4**, nb **3**	**18**
	50 overs (for 7 wickets)	**239**

	O	M	R	W
Wasim Akram	10	1	34	**1**
Aqib Javed	10	–	49	**–**
Azhar Mahmood	10	–	40	**1**
Saqlain Mushtaq	10	–	55	**2**
Manzoor Akhtar	10	–	50	**1**

Fall of Wickets
1–**31**, 2–**143**, 3–**143**, 4–**147**, 5–**200**, 6–**224**, 7–**239**

Pakistan

Saeed Anwar	**c** Karim, **b** Srinath	**104**
Shahid Afridi	**c** and **b** Chauhan	**19**
Ijaz Ahmed	lbw, **b** Kumble	**16**
Akhtar Sarfraz	**c** Azharuddin, **b** Chauhan	**7**
Manzoor Akhtar	lbw, **b** Kumble	**5**
Inzamam-ul-Haq	**c** Karim, **b** Ganguly	**19**
Moin Khan †	not out	**49**
Wasim Akram *	not out	**9**
Azhar Mahmood		
Saqlain Mushtaq		
Aqib Javed		
	lb **8**, w **6**, nb **1**	**15**
	47.2 overs (for 6 wickets)	**243**

	O	M	R	W
Srinath	10	–	43	**1**
Kuruvilla	8	1	43	**–**
Chauhan	9.2	–	47	**2**
Kumble	10	1	44	**2**
Ganguly	7	–	39	**1**
R.R. Singh	3	–	19	**–**

Fall of Wickets
1–**48**, 2–**79**, 3–**93**, 4–**102**, 5–**144**, 6–**226**

Umpires: S.A. Bucknor & C.J. Mitchley *Man of the Match*: Saeed Anwar

Pakistan won by 4 wickets

Match Five – England v. Pakistan

15 December 1997 at Sharjah C.A. Stadium

England

A.D. Brown	**c** Moin, **b** Saqlain Mushtaq	**41**
A.J. Stewart †	**b** Manzoor Akhtar	**47**
N.V. Knight	**b** Manzoor Akhtar	**18**
G.A. Hick	**b** Manzoor Akhtar	**40**
G.P. Thorpe	run out	**3**
A.J. Hollioake *	**c** Shahid Afridi, **b** Manzoor	**17**
M.A. Ealham	**c** and **b** Saqlain Mushtaq	**6**
D.R. Brown	not out	**18**
M.V. Fleming	**c** and **b** Saqlain Mushtaq	**0**
R.D.B. Croft	**c** Ijaz Ahmed, **b** Saqlain	**6**
D.W. Headley	not out	**6**
	b **1**, lb **4**, w **7**, nb **1**	**13**
	50 overs (for 9 wickets)	**215**

	O	M	R	W
Wasim Akram	6	1	34	**–**
Azhar Mahmood	7	1	31	**–**
Saqlain Mushtaq	10	1	26	**4**
Mushtaq Ahmed	10	–	43	**–**
Manzoor Akhtar	10	–	50	**4**
Shahid Afridi	7	–	26	**–**

Fall of Wickets
1–**71**, 2–**108**, 3–**121**, 4–**126**, 5–**168**, 6–**180**, 7–**185**, 8–**185**, 9–**203**

Pakistan

Aamir Sohail	**b** Headley	**1**
Shahid Afridi	**b** D.R. Brown	**0**
Saeed Anwar	**b** Croft	**54**
Ijaz Ahmed	**c** Croft, **b** Ealham	**41**
Akhtar Sarfraz	**b** Croft	**20**
Manzoor Akhtar	run out	**44**
Moin Khan †	**c** Knight, **b** Fleming	**10**
Wasim Akram *	**c** D.R. Brown, **b** Hollioake	**4**
Azhar Mahmood	**c** Stewart, **b** Hollioake	**12**
Saqlain Mushtaq	run out	**9**
Mushtaq Ahmed	not out	**0**
	lb **5**, w **5**, nb **2**	**12**
	49 overs	**207**

	O	M	R	W
D.R. Brown	5	–	29	**1**
Headley	8	–	33	**1**
Ealham	10	1	39	**1**
Croft	10	1	39	**2**
Hollioake	10	–	35	**2**
Fleming	6	–	27	**1**

Fall of Wickets
1–**1**, 2–**5**, 3–**99**, 4–**99**, 5–**134**, 6–**152**, 7–**177**, 8–**185**, 9–**207**

Umpires: K.T. Francis & S.A. Bucknor *Man of the Match*: Manzoor Akhtar

England won by 8 runs

Match Six – West Indies v. India

16 December 1997 at Sharjah C.A. Stadium

West Indies

P.A. Wallace	c Ganguly, b Srinath	8
S.C. Williams	not out	105
B.C. Lara	c Kumble, b Chauhan	23
C.L. Hooper	c Azharuddin, b Ganguly	38
S. Chanderpaul	c Jadeja, b Chauhan	16
P.V. Simmons	b Kumble	16
F.A. Rose	b Srinath	14
R.N. Lewis	not out	1
D. Williams †		
M.V. Dillon		
C.A. Walsh *		
	lb 5, nb 3	8
	50 overs (for 6 wickets)	229

	O	M	R	W
Srinath	9	1	48	2
Venkatesh Prasad	10	1	39	–
Kumble	10	–	52	1
Chauhan	10	1	30	2
Ganguly	7	–	38	1
Tendulkar	4	–	17	–

Fall of Wickets
1–26, 2–63, 3–134, 4–164, 5–202, 6–227

India

S.C. Ganguly	st D. Williams, b Hooper	70
N.S. Sidhu	c Wallace, b Lewis	25
R.S. Dravid	b Hooper	31
S.R. Tendulkar *	run out	1
M. Azharuddin	run out	4
A.D. Jadeja	b Hooper	8
S.S. Karim †	b Chanderpaul	26
A.R. Kumble	c and b Chanderpaul	6
J. Srinath	b Chanderpaul	4
R.K. Chauhan	not out	0
Venkatesh Prasad	b Hooper	1
	b 1, lb 5, w 4, nb 2	12
	42.2 overs	188

	O	M	R	W
Walsh	7	1	24	–
Rose	6	–	35	–
Dillon	6	–	30	–
Lewis	10	–	38	1
Hooper	8.2	–	37	4
Chanderpaul	5	–	18	3

Fall of Wickets
1–87, 2–126, 3–127, 4–136, 5–140, 6–162, 7–177, 8–187, 9–187

Umpires: C.J. Mitchley & B.C. Cooray *Man of the Match*: S.C. Williams

West Indies won by 41 runs

Sharjah Champions Trophy Final – England v. West Indies

19 December 1997 at Sharjah C.A. Stadium

West Indies

S.C. Williams	c A.D. Brown, b Croft	55
S. Chanderpaul	run out	76
B.C. Lara	st Stewart, b Ealham	2
C.L. Hooper	b Fleming	34
P.V. Simmons	not out	39
R.I.C. Holder	lbw, b Fleming	0
R.N. Lewis	b Fleming	16
F.A. Rose	run out	0
D. Williams †	not out	9
M.V. Dillon		
C.A. Walsh *		
	lb 3, w 1	4
	50 overs (for 7 wickets)	235

	O	M	R	W
D.R. Brown	5	–	35	–
Headley	7	–	39	–
Ealham	10	1	26	1
Hollioake	10	–	50	–
Croft	10	–	40	1
Fleming	8	–	42	3

Fall of Wickets
1–97, 2–101, 3–164, 4–174, 5–174, 6–200, 7–200

England

A.D. Brown	c Chanderpaul, b Rose	1
A.J. Stewart †	b Hooper	51
N.V. Knight	run out	24
G.A. Hick	c Hooper, b Lewis	9
G.P. Thorpe	not out	66
A.J. Hollioake *	st D. Williams, b Hooper	16
M.A. Ealham	b Walsh	4
M.V. Fleming	run out	33
D.R. Brown	not out	4
R.D.B. Croft		
D.W. Headley		
	b 1, lb 16, w 5, nb 9	31
	48.1 overs (for 7 wickets)	239

	O	M	R	W
Walsh	9.1	1	39	1
Rose	10	–	36	1
Dillon	6	–	36	–
Simmons	4	–	25	–
Lewis	9	–	51	1
Hooper	10	–	35	2

Fall of Wickets
1–14, 2–89, 3–107, 4–107, 5–152, 6–165, 7–235

Umpires: K.T. Francis & C.J. Mitchley *Man of the Match*: G.P. Thorpe *Man of the Tournament*: C.L. Hooper

England won by 3 wickets

Coca Cola Triangular Tournament

In April, Australia, New Zealand and India came together in a triangular tournament. Shane Warne had been doubtful for the series because of an injured shoulder, but he decided to play and delay the necessary surgery until later, a decision which did not seem totally wise.

In the opening match, India were given a good start by Tendulkar and Ganguly, who had enjoyed an outstanding year in one-day internationals. The openers put on 76, and Ganguly and Azharuddin followed this with a stand of 72. Nash brought about an amazing middle order collapse, and six wickets went down for 29 runs so that New Zealand faced a target that was not as daunting as they might have expected. They were soon in trouble, however, against the ever improving Agarkar and Venkatesh Prasad. At 85 for four, they looked doomed, but Fleming found an able partner in McMillan, and the score was doubled. Agarkar returned to dismiss them both, and five wickets fell for 20 runs before a spirited last wicket stand made the result look closer than it was.

Venkatesh Prasad re-found his form and was a most consistent bowler for India in the triangular tournament. He captured wickets in every match.
(Stu Foster / Allsport)

Bowler of the Triangular Tournament – Australia's Damien Fleming.
(Stuart Milligan / Sportsline)

New Zealand suffered a second defeat when Australia beat them by six wickets with 13.1 overs to spare. New Zealand's troubles began when Nathan Astle was run out by Ponting's direct hit on the stumps in the fourth over. Fleming again tried to rally his side, and he and Harris added 51 for the sixth wicket, but a miserable total of 159 was never likely to trouble the Australians. When Australia batted, Mark Waugh was an early casualty, but Gilchrist made 57 off 89 balls with three fours and a six, and Ponting two sixes and four fours. The pair shared a stand of 90, and Australia cruised to vistory. More significantly, Australia beat India the following day. Choosing to bat first, Australia showed consistency in reaching 264, and India were soon struggling when they lost Ganguly and Azharuddin cheaply. Tendulkar hit 80 off 72 balls, but Steve Waugh brought about a collapse when he captured four wickets, three of them in two overs, and the last four wickets went down for 14 runs.

There was another setback for India when New Zealand beat them in the return match. They committed cricket suicide early in their innings when Tendulkar, Azharuddin and Jadeja, three major batsmen, were all run out. Ganguly hit 31 off 36 balls, and Mongia 22 off 25, but Laxman, in spite of hitting a four, could find no rhythm, and the innings fell apart. New Zealand did not find the task of scoring 182 an easy one. Horne and Astle went cheaply. Fleming batted with purpose, and McMillan played the necessary anchor role. He hit a six and a four and faced 122 balls for his 59, and he steadied the innings when that was what was needed. Victory came with an over to spare.

New Zealand's joy was short-lived. The next day, they scored heavily against Australia but were were well beaten. Astle hit a six and six fours in his 125-ball 78, and Cairns made 56 off 50 balls with a six and five fours. Australia were consistent and emphatic. Tom Moody made 63 off 74 balls, and Michael Bevan hit 57 off 64 balls. Mark Waugh finished the match with a flourish, hitting 34 off 28 balls with a six and two fours.

A sandstorm interrupted the final match in the qualifying competition, and India's target was reduced to 276 from 46 overs. More importantly, they needed to score 237 to win a place in the final ahead of New Zealand on run rate. They failed to achieve the first target, but they reached the second and earned the right to meet Australia for the trophy. Bevan played a magnificent innings, 101 off 103 balls with nine fours, while Mark Waugh hit two sixes and seven fours in making 81 off 99 balls. Tendulkar responded with an innings of total magnificence, dominating all bowlers as he hit a majestic 142. Only Mongia, who hit a six and four fours, gave real support. Even so, India achieved their object by reaching the final.

Final

Australia *v.* India

Azharuddin won the toss and asked Australia to bat first. His action seemed totally justified when Mark Waugh was caught behind for seven, and Ponting edged Venkatesh Prasad to Mongia one run later. Moody became the third batsman to be caught by the wicket-keeper, and when Gilchrist, who made 45 off 60 balls, offered Mongia his fourth catch of the innings Australia were 85 for four. Bevan fought to get the innings in a positive mood, but Laxman's return to bowler Kumble left him short of his ground, and Australia were 121 for five. Now came the stand that turned the game in Australia's favour. Steve Waugh hit 70 off 71 balls, and Darren Lehmann made 70 off 59 balls as 103 were added. Australia closed on 272 for nine, a score which only they had bettered, in the previous match.

It suddenly seemed the smallest of scores when Sachin Tendulkar went to the crease. He routed the

Match One – India v. New Zealand

17 April 1998 at Sharjah C.A. Stadium

India

S.R. Tendulkar	**c** Doull, **b** Harris	**40**
S.C. Ganguly	**b** Nash	**105**
M. Azharuddin *	run out	**31**
N.S. Sidhu	lbw, **b** McMillan	**4**
A.D. Jadeja	**c** Horne, **b** Nash	**17**
H.H. Kanitkar	**c** Doull, **b** Nash	**1**
A.B. Agarkar	**b** Cairns	**9**
N.R. Mongia †	**c** Howell, **b** Nash	**0**
A.R. Kumble	not out	**3**
Venkatesh Prasad	run out	**5**
Harbhajan Singh	not out	**0**
	lb **2**, w **2**, nb **1**	**5**
	50 overs (for 9 wickets)	**220**

	O	M	R	W
Doull	6	1	25	**–**
Cairns	10	–	47	**1**
Nash	10	1	38	**4**
Harris	10	–	45	**1**
Priest	5	–	29	**–**
McMillan	9	–	34	**1**

Fall of Wickets
1–**76**, 2–**148**, 3–**157**, 4–**190**, 5–**195**, 6–**211**, 7–**212**, 8–**212**, 9–**219**

New Zealand

L.G. Howell	**c** Mongia, **b** Agarkar	**0**
N.J. Astle	**c** Mongia, **b** Venkatesh Prasad	**24**
C.L. Cairns	**b** Venkatesh Prasad	**4**
S.P. Fleming *	**c** Kumble, **b** Agarkar	**75**
M.J. Horne	**st** Mongia, **b** Harbhajan Singh	**16**
C.D. McMillan	lbw, **b** Agarkar	**49**
C.Z. Harris	**c** Mongia, **b** Kumble	**4**
A.C. Parore †	not out	**9**
D.J. Nash	**b** Agarkar	**2**
M.W. Priest	**c** Jadeja, **b** Kumble	**0**
S.B. Doull	**b** Kumble	**10**
	lb **5**, w **6**, nb **1**	**12**
	47.5 overs	**205**

	O	M	R	W
Agarkar	10	2	35	**4**
Venkatesh Prasad	8	–	48	**2**
Kumble	9.5	–	39	**3**
Harbhajan Singh	10	–	32	**1**
Ganguly	1	–	4	**–**
Kanitkar	7	–	29	**–**
Tendulkar	2	–	13	**–**

Fall of Wickets
1–**0**, 2–**24**, 3–**33**, 4–**85**, 5–**170**, 6–**184**, 7–**186**, 8–**189**, 9–**190**

Umpires: S.A. Bucknor & Javed Akhtar *Man of the Match*: A.B. Agarkar

India won by 15 runs

Match Two – Australia v. New Zealand
18 April 1998 at Sharjah C.A. Stadium

New Zealand

Batsman	Dismissal	Runs
L.G. Howell	lbw, **b** Fleming	13
N.J. Astle	run out	7
C.L. Cairns	**c** and **b** Moody	19
S.P. Fleming *	**b** Robertson	59
M.J. Horne	**c** Moody, **b** Warne	14
C.D. McMillan	**c** Lehmann, **b** Warne	1
C.Z. Harris	**c** Lehmann, **b** M.E. Waugh	26
A.C. Parore †	**b** Fleming	5
D.J. Nash	not out	2
M.W. Priest	**c** Gilchrist, **b** Fleming	2
S.B. O'Connor	lbw, **b** Fleming	0
	lb **7**, w **4**	11
	48.4 overs	159

Bowler	O	M	R	W
Fleming	9.4	1	28	4
Kasprowicz	6	–	24	–
Moody	5	–	16	1
Warne	10	1	28	2
Robertson	10	–	30	1
M.E. Waugh	8	–	26	1

Fall of Wickets
1–**20**, 2–**28**, 3–**61**, 4–**90**, 5–**92**, 6–**143**, 7–**153**, 8–**155**, 9–**159**

Australia

Batsman	Dismissal	Runs
A.C. Gilchrist †	**c** Astle, **b** Harris	57
M.E. Waugh	**c** Fleming, **b** O'Connor	11
R.T. Ponting	**c** Horne, **b** Harris	52
M.G. Bevan	not out	15
S.R. Waugh *	lbw, **b** McMillan	3
D.S. Lehmann	not out	11
T.M. Moody		
S.K. Warne		
G.R. Robertson		
M.S. Kasprowicz		
D.W. Fleming		
	lb **6**, w **3**, nb **2**	11
	36.5 overs (for 4 wickets)	160

Bowler	O	M	R	W
O'Connor	5	–	31	1
Cairns	5	–	24	–
Nash	4	1	15	–
Harris	10	2	31	2
Priest	9.5	1	42	–
McMillan	3	–	11	1

Fall of Wickets
1–**35**, 2–**125**, 3–**131**, 4–**134**

Umpires: Javed Akhtar & I.D. Robinson *Man of the Match*: D.W. Fleming

Australia won by 6 wickets

Match Three – Australia v. India
19 April 1998 at Sharjah C.A. Stadium

Australia

Batsman	Dismissal	Runs
M.E. Waugh	run out	16
A.C. Gilchrist †	**c** Kanitkar, **b** Harbhajan	25
R.T. Ponting	**c** Kumble, **b** Kanitkar	48
T.M. Moody	**c** Azharuddin, **b** Harbhajan	39
M.G. Bevan	**c** Jadeja, **b** Kumble	58
S.R. Waugh *	**b** Harvinder Singh	8
D.S. Lehmann	**b** Harbhajan Singh	12
D.R. Martyn	run out	30
S.K. Warne	**c** Harbhajan, **b** Venkatesh	19
M.S. Kasprowicz	not out	0
D.W. Fleming		
	lb **2**, w **7**	9
	50 overs (for 9 wickets)	264

Bowler	O	M	R	W
Venkatesh Prasad	8	–	41	1
Harvinder Singh	8	–	50	1
Harbhajan Singh	10	–	41	3
Kumble	10	–	57	1
Kanitkar	10	–	52	1
Tendulkar	4	–	21	–

Fall of Wickets
1–**33**, 2–**46**, 3–**110**, 4–**156**, 5–**173**, 6–**196**, 7–**227**, 8–**259**, 9–**264**

India

Batsman	Dismissal	Runs
S.C. Ganguly	**b** Kasprowicz	8
S.R. Tendulkar	**c** Gilchrist, **b** Fleming	80
M. Azharuddin*	**c** Gilchrist, **b** Fleming	9
N.S. Sidhu	**c** Lehmann, **b** Moody	11
A.D. Jadeja	**st** Gilchrist, **b** Warne	14
H.H. Kanitkar	lbw, **b** S.R. Waugh	35
N.R. Mongia †	**c** Ponting, **b** Kasprowicz	19
A.R. Kumble	not out	14
Harvinder Singh	**c** M.E. Waugh, **b** S.R. Waugh	1
Venkatesh Prasad	**c** M.E. Waugh, **b** S.R. Waugh	2
Harbhajan Singh	**b** S.R. Waugh	4
	lb **6**, w **3**	9
	44 overs	206

Bowler	O	M	R	W
Fleming	8	–	35	2
Kasprowicz	8	–	40	2
Moody	10	–	40	1
Warne	8	1	37	1
S.R. Waugh	9	–	40	4
Bevan	1	–	8	–

Fall of Wickets
1–**15**, 2–**48**, 3–**63**, 4–**94**, 5–**161**, 6–**161**, 7–**192**, 8–**196**, 9–**198**

Umpires: S.A. Bucknor & I.D. Robinson *Man of the Match*: S.R. Tendulkar

Australia won by 58 runs

Match Four – India v. New Zealand

20 April 1998 at Sharjah C.A. Stadium

India

S.R. Tendulkar	run out	38
S.C. Ganguly	c Fleming, b Cairns	31
M. Azharuddin *	run out	11
A.D. Jadeja	run out	11
V.V.S. Laxman	c O'Connor, b Priest	23
N.R. Mongia †	c McMillan, b Cairns	22
H.H. Kanitkar	b Priest	13
A.R. Kumble	b Astle	10
Harvinder Singh	b Cairns	0
Venkatesh Prasad	c Wiseman, b Astle	8
Harbhajan Singh	not out	3
	lb 3, w 8	11
	49.3 overs	181

	O	M	R	W
Doull	5	–	20	–
O'Connor	4	–	29	–
McMillan	6	–	25	–
Cairns	10	1	26	3
Harris	10	2	24	–
Priest	10	1	44	2
Astle	4.3	–	10	2

Fall of Wickets
1–**60**, 2–**82**, 3–**85**, 4–**100**, 5–**131**, 6–**153**, 7–**161**, 8–**162**, 9–**172**

New Zealand

M.J. Horne	c Azharuddin, b Harvinder	4
N.J. Astle	c Mongia, b Venkatesh	14
S.P. Fleming *	b Kumble	33
C.D. McMillan	c Mongia, b Tendulkar	59
C.L. Cairns	c Laxman, b Venkatesh	19
A.C. Parore †	c Harvinder Singh, b Kumble	27
C.Z. Harris	not out	9
M.W. Priest	not out	2
S.B. Doull		
P.J. Wiseman		
S.B. O'Connor		
	lb 8, w 5, nb 3	16
	49 overs (for 6 wickets)	183

	O	M	R	W
Venkatesh Prasad	10	–	34	2
Harvinder Singh	5	–	25	1
Kumble	10	–	26	2
Harbhajan Singh	10	1	30	–
Kanitkar	2	–	12	–
Tendulkar	7	–	28	1
Ganguly	5	–	20	–

Fall of Wickets
1–**18**, 2–**22**, 3–**82**, 4–**116**, 5–**165**, 6–**168**

Umpires: S.A. Bucknor & Javed Akhtar *Man of the Match*: C.D. McMillan

New Zealand won by 4 wickets

Match Five – Australia v. New Zealand

21 April 1998 at Sharjah C.A. Stadium

New Zealand

L.G. Howell	b Harvey	2
N.J. Astle	c and b Harvey	78
S.P. Fleming *	c and b Dale	20
C.D. McMillan	run out	43
C.L. Cairns	st Gilchrist, b Warne	56
A.C. Parore †	not out	22
C.Z. Harris	not out	26
D.J. Nash		
S.B. Doull		
M.W. Priest		
P.J. Wiseman		
	lb 5, w 6, nb 1	12
	50 overs (for 5 wickets)	259

	O	M	R	W
Dale	10	1	30	1
Harvey	10	–	59	2
Robertson	10	–	41	–
Warne	10	–	56	1
Moody	4	–	21	–
Lehmann	2	–	9	–
S.R. Waugh	4	–	38	–

Fall of Wickets
1–**9**, 2–**53**, 3–**138**, 4–**179**, 5–**229**

Australia

D.S. Lehmann	b McMillan	26
D.R. Martyn	c Harris, b Doull	16
S.R. Waugh *	lbw, b Wiseman	32
T.M. Moody	c Doull, b Nash	63
M.G. Bevan	c Parore, b Nash	57
M.E. Waugh	not out	34
A.C. Gilchrist †	not out	11
I.J. Harvey		
S.K. Warne		
G.R. Robertson		
A.C. Dale		
	b 2, lb 14, w 6	22
	47.5 overs (for 5 wickets)	261

	O	M	R	W
Doull	10	–	48	1
Cairns	8.5	–	52	–
Nash	9	1	39	2
McMillan	3	–	14	1
Priest	6	–	25	–
Wiseman	6	–	31	1
Astle	1	–	8	–
Harris	4	–	28	–

Fall of Wickets
1–**39**, 2–**59**, 3–**115**, 4–**185**, 5–**228**

Umpires: I.D. Robinson & Javed Akhtar *Man of the Match*: T.M. Moody

Australia won by 5 wickets

Match Six – Australia v. India
22 April 1998 at Sharjah C.A. Stadium

Australia

A.C. Gilchrist †	c Mongia, b Harvinder	11
M.E. Waugh	c Ganguly, b Tendulkar	81
R.T. Ponting	st Mongia, b Harbhajan	31
D.R. Martyn	b Kumble	1
M.G. Bevan	not out	101
S.R. Waugh *	run out	10
D.S. Lehmann	b Venkatesh Prasad	26
T.M. Moody	c Azharuudin, Venkatesh	5
S.K. Warne	not out	7
M.S. Kasprowicz		
D.W. Fleming		
	lb 4, w 6, nb 1	11
	50 overs (for 7 wickets)	284

	O	M	R	W
Venkatesh Prasad	8	–	41	2
Harvinder Singh	7	–	44	1
Harbhajan Singh	8	–	63	1
Kumble	10	–	41	1
Kanitkar	6	–	33	–
Tendulkar	5	–	27	1
Ganguly	2	–	15	–
Laxman	4	–	16	–

Fall of Wickets
1–**17**, 2–**84**, 3–**87**, 4–**177**, 5–**197**, 6–**250**, 7–**271**

India

S.C. Ganguly	lbw, b Fleming	17
S.R. Tendulkar	c Gilchrist, b Fleming	142
N.R. Mongia †	c M.E. Waugh, b Moody	35
M. Azharuddin *	b Moody	14
A.D. Jadeja	st Gilchrist, b S.R. Waugh	1
V.V.S. Laxman	not out	23
H.H. Kanitkar	not out	5
A.R. Kumble		
Harvinder Singh		
Venkatesh Prasad		
Harbhajan Singh		
	lb 6, w 3, nb 4	13
	46 overs (for 5 wickets)	250

	O	M	R	W
Fleming	10	–	47	2
Kasprowicz	9	–	55	–
Warne	9	–	38	–
Moody	9	–	39	2
S.R. Waugh	9	–	65	1

Fall of Wickets
1–**38**, 2–**107**, 3–**135**, 4–**138**, 5–**242**

Umpires: I.D. Robinson & S.A. Bucknor *Man of the Match*: S.R. Tendulkar

Australia won on faster scoring rate

Final – Australia v. India
24 April 1998 at Sharjah C.A. Stadium

Australia

M.E. Waugh	c Mongia, b Agarkar	7
A.C. Gilchrist †	c Mongia, b Kanitkar	45
R.T. Ponting	c Mongia, b Venkatesh Prasad	1
T.M. Moody	c Mongia, b Agarkar	1
M.G. Bevan	run out	45
S.R. Waugh *	c Agarkar, b Kanitkar	70
D.S. Lehmann	c Sanghvi, b Kumble	70
D.R. Martyn	run out	16
S.K. Warne	not out	6
M.S. Kasprowicz	c Kanitkar, b Venkatesh Prasad	0
D.W. Fleming	not out	1
	b 4, lb 3, w 2, nb 1	10
	50 overs (for 9 wickets)	272

	O	M	R	W
Venkatesh Prasad	10	1	32	2
Agarkar	8	1	61	2
Kumble	10	1	46	1
Kanitkar	10	–	58	2
Sanghvi	10	–	45	–
Laxman	1	–	11	–
Tendulkar	1	–	12	–

Fall of Wickets
1–**18**, 2–**19**, 3–**26**, 4–**85**, 5–**121**, 6–**224**, 7–**255**, 8–**263**, 9–**264**

India

S.C. Ganguly	c Moody, b Fleming	23
S.R. Tendulkar	lbw, b Kasprowicz	134
N.R. Mongia †	c Gilchrist, b Fleming	28
M. Azharuddin *	c Gilchrist, b Kasprowicz	58
A.D. Jadeja	not out	11
H.H. Kanitkar	not out	6
V.V.S. Laxman		
A.B . Agarkar		
A.R. Kumble		
Venkatesh Prasad		
R. Sanghvi		
	b 1, lb 7, w 5, nb 2	15
	48.3 overs (for 4 wickets)	275

	O	M	R	W
Fleming	10	1	47	2
Kasprowicz	10	–	48	2
Warne	10	–	61	–
Moody	9.3	–	63	–
M.E. Waugh	3	–	20	–
S.R. Waugh	6	–	28	–

Fall of Wickets
1–**39**, 2–**128**, 3–**248**, 4–**261**

Umpires: Javed Akhtar & S.A. Bucknor *Man of the Match*: S.R. Tendulkar

India won by 6 wickets

Australian attack. Warne was hammered to all parts of the ground, and Moody was punished with equal severity. Tendulkar hit three sixes and 12 fours before falling leg before to Kasprowicz for 124, which had come off 131 balls. He and Azharuddin added 120 for the third wicket, and India won the Coca Cola Cup with nine balls to spare. Victory came when Kanitkar hit the second ball he received, from Moody, for four.

Tendulkar was named Man of the Match and Man of the Series. He also won the prize for the fastest 50 of the tournament, 44 balls, and for hitting most sixes, nine. Damien Fleming was named Best Bowler of the Tournament, and Ricky Ponting Best Fielder. Australia had little consolation in winning every match but the one that mattered.

New Zealand's rising star – Craig McMillan. He was outstanding in the Triangular Tournment and won the Man of the Match award when New Zealand beat India, the eventual winners of the competition.
(Ben Radford / Allsport)

New Zealand

In 1997–98, New Zealand pursued the busiest cricket programme in their history. The Academy side went to South Africa, while the national side went to Kenya and Zimbabwe before going to Australia for a three-Test series and participation in the World Series alongside South Africa and the host nation. New Zealand struggled to earn a draw in Zimbabwe and were generally outplayed in Australia.

Lee Germon led Canterbury to triumph in the Shell Trophy and then announced his retirement from first-class cricket. He will be much missed.
(David Munden / Sportsline)

However, the tours in Africa and Australia were not without positive gains, notably in the emergence of McMillan and O'Connor as cricketers of international quality.

At home, New Zealand invited Bangladesh to compete in the Conference one-day and first-class competitions where they would be opposed to Northern, a combination of Auckland and Northern Districts, Southern (Central Districts and Otago) and Central (Canterbury and Wellington). This was to be followed by the Shell Cup and the Shell Trophy, a one-day series against Australia and Tests and one-day series against Zimbabwe. The side would then set off for a tournament in Sharjah and Test series and one-day internationals in Sri Lanka.

In the final of the Conference one-day competition, Northern beat Central by 80 runs although neither side lasted their full 50 overs. Roger Twose scored the only century of the tournament, 105 not out for Central against Bangladesh. He recorded the best bowling figures, 4 for 18, in the same match.

Shell Cup

The Shell Cup began on Boxing Day and finished on 24 January when Northern Districts beat Canterbury in the final at Hamilton. The Man of the Match was Northern Districts' medium-pacer Alex Tait, who took four wickets, three of them caught behind, in the 29th over to send Canterbury from 117 for five to 117 for nine.

Each team played eight matches before the complex semi-final stage. There were some outstanding individual performances. Chris Nevin, the Wellington wicket-keeper, hit 149 off 115 balls in the opening match against Central Districts, and there were centuries for Wells, Spearman, Oram, Richardson, Doody, Stead, Howell and Graeme Hick, who made 107 for Auckland against Otago. Bell and Douglas both hit two centuries. Douglas's hundreds came in successive matches for Central Districts, but in the second Bell made an unbeaten 121 off 124 balls to win the game for Wellington. Gary Stead and Llorne Howell made 100 and 134 not out respectively for Canterbury against Otago at Centennial Park, Oamani, and added 221 in 148 minutes for the fourth wicket. This is the highest stand ever recorded in the competition.

Two bowlers, Blake of Central Districts and Maxwell, the former Sheffield Shield player, of Canterbury took five wickets in an innings. Wellington had expected to have DeFreitas in their side as overseas player, but he returned home injured and was replaced by Warwickshire's Graeme Welch. Welch began the competition well, and, in the match against Central Districts in New Plymouth, he sent back Milnes and Oram in his opening over to leave the home side on one for two wickets. He then conceded 83 runs without taking another wicket, the third most expensive bowling analysis in the history of the competition.

Conference

17, 18 and 19 November 1997
at Victoria Park, Wanganui
Central 103 (W.A. Wisneski 4 for 37) and 211 (M.S. Sinclair 50)
Southern 159 (M.H. Richardson 67, E.J. Hoffer 5 for 65) and 159 for 9 (C.J.M. Furlong 4 for 66)
Southern won by 1 wicket
Southern 6 pts, Central 0 pts

at Westpac Trust Park, Hamilton
Northern 408 (M.D. Bailey 148, D.J. Nash 75, M.N. Hart 65, M.E. Parlane 58, Hasibul Hussain 6 for 143)
Bangladesh 125 (M.N. Hart 4 for 30) and 132 (Akram Khan 52, K.J. Walmsley 5 for 23, M.J. Haslam 5 for 25)
Northern won by an innings and 151 runs
Northern 6 pts, Bangladesh 0 pts

In the opening round of the competition, Southern won a thrilling match against Central. The game was dominated by bowlers, and when Southern's last man Sewell joined Wisneski four runs were needed to win. Sewell scored a single, and, with the scores level, Wisneski hit Furlong for four to win the match. Wisneski had an outstanding game. He had match figures of seven for 86 and scored 26 and 25 not out.

Bangladesh found themselves totally outclassed by Northern, who had century stands for the fifth and sixth wickets. There was welcome success for fast bowler Kerry Walmsley, seven for 50 in the match.

24, 25 and 26 November 1997
at Basin Reserve, Wellington
Bangladesh 120 and 174 (M.R. Jefferson 5 for 42, C.J.M. Furlong 4 for 95)
Central 311 (M.S. Sinclair 95, M.J. Greatbatch 63, R.G. Hart 57)
Central won by an innings and 17 runs
Central 6 pts 1 Bangladesh 0 pts

at Hagley Oval, Christchurch
Northern 235 (M.N. Hart 50, P.J. Wiseman 4 for 36) and 150 (M.N. Hart 66, D.G. Sewell 5 for 38)
Southern 109 (M.J. Haslam 4 for 11) and 190 (M.H. Richardson 51)
Northern won by 86 runs
Northern 6 pts, Southern 0 pts

The inclusion of Bangladesh in the Conference was part of New Zealand's policy of trying to help the development of cricket in the southern hemisphere. However, the visitors, qualifiers for the World Cup, were totally out of their depth and were beaten inside two days by Central.

Northern gained their second victory in a match in which the ball again dominated the bat. Northern were 26 for

six in their second innings before Matthew Hart, aided by Nevin and Walmsley, effected a recovery. Walmsley's unbeaten 39, which included a six and three fours, was the first time in his 12-match first-class career that he had exceeded 14.

1, 2, 3 and 4 December 1997
at Eden Park, Auckland
Northern 351 (D.J. Nash 107, M.E. Parlane 64, G.R. Jonas 5 for 102) and 108 for 4
Central 206 for 8 dec. (R.G. Hart 52 not out, M.W. Douglas 51, A.R. Tait 4 for 57)
Match drawn
Northern 2 pts, Central 0 pts

at Carisbrook, Dunedin
Bangladesh 286 for 9 dec. (Al Sahariar Rokon 102, Sanwar Hussain 54, P.J. Wiseman 4 for 101) and 244 (Javed Omar 89)
Southern 366 for 6 dec. (C.D. Cumming 103, G.R. Stead 96) and 165 for 3 (D.J. Murray 58)
Southern won by 7 wickels
Southern 6pts, Bangladesh 0 pts

The match in Auckland was badly affected by the weather, but first innings points were all that Northern needed for a place in the final. Skipper Dion Nash, concentrating on batting rather than bowling, hit the first century of his career.

Bangladesh performed with greater confidence against Southern, with Al Sahariar and Khalid Mahmud putting on 100 for the sixth wicket in the first innings. However, the home side won with ease to qualify for the final. Northern, had 14 points, Southern 12, Central 6, and Bangladesh 0.

Final

14, 15, 16 and 17 December 1997
at Eden Park, Auckland
Northern 504 (M.D. Bailey 121, B.A. Pocock 108, M.N. Hart 69, G.E. Bradbum 62, J.B. Chandler 59, P.J. Wiseman 4 for 118)
Southern 354 (D.J. Murray 110, A.J. Gale 57) and 76 for 3
Match drawn

Northern took the trophy on account of their first innings lead. Pocock and Bailey shared a second wicket stand of 132, and there was heavy scoring throughout the order. They batted into the second day, but rain on the third really prevented any chance of an outright win for Northern, although Southern were forced to follow on.

9, 10 and 11 December 1997
at Lincoln Green, Christchurch
Bangladesh 130 (D.G. Sewell 5 for 34) and 203 (Mehrab

Hussain 81, M.D.J. Walker 4 for 36, D.G. Sewell 4 for 47)
New Zealand Academy XI 448 for 7 dec. (M.E. Parlane 190, C.B. Gaffaney 112, H.D. Barton 53)
New Zealand Academy won by an innings and 115 runs

Bangladesh played one first-class game outside the Conference when they were heavily beaten by New Zealand's young guns. Left-arm pace bowler David Sewell enhanced his claim for a Test place with match figures of nine for 81. Matthew Walker's medium pace brought him by far the best bowling figures of his career. The highlight of the Academy innings was an opening stand of 213 between Gaffaney and Parlane. Parlane's 190 was the highest score of his career. He hit six sixes and 22 fours.

One-Day International Series

New Zealand v. Australia

The four-match series began on something of a sour note as Steve Waugh, the Australian captain, had made it publicly clear that he thought the eight-day tour was not welcomed by his team, who would have been resting ahead of the trip to India. The Australians had again chosen what they considered to be their specialist one-day side, omitting men of the calibre of Healy and Taylor. Warne withdrew on grounds of fitness, and neither McGrath nor Gillespie was available.

Stephen Fleming decided to take first use of an excellent Lancaster Park pitch when he won the toss, and his decision appeared correct as New Zealand moved to 104

Dion Nash returned to cricket after a long injury, regained his place in the New Zealand side and hit the first first-class century of his career.
(Ben Radford / Allsport)

for the loss of Astle. Howell reached his first one-day international fifty off 62 balls, but he was out next ball as he attempted to sweep off-spinner Gavin Robertson, who had been recalled to the Australian side after a four-year absence. Robertson bowled with immaculate control as he and Steve Waugh held the New Zealand batsmen in a vice-like grip. Harris and Nash broke free in a stand of 66 with the latter's 39 coming off the same number of deliveries. In spite of this stand, New Zealand's total was some fifty runs short of what might have been expected, and Gilchrist, who had finished the World Series in good style, and Mark Waugh soon put it into perspective with an opening stand of 146 in 26 overs. The rest was easy as Australia won with 11.4 overs to spare. Gilchrist swung his bat at everything and hit five sixes and 10 fours in his 117-ball innings as the New Zealand bowling and fielding disintegrated.

At Basin Reserve, Australia chose to bat first. They lost Gilchrist second ball, caught in the gully, but the Australian batsmen were soon blazing away. Mark Waugh and Ponting laid a foundation with 45 in 35 minutes, and Lehmann ran fast and often to score 62 off 66 balls. Mark Waugh was typically majestic, hitting seven fours as he made 85 off 112 balls, and Bevan and Steve Waugh provided the late impetus. Bevan made 39 at a run a ball, and Steve Waugh hit a six and three fours in his 47 off 40 balls. The Australian total of 297 was the highest made in a one-day intemational at the Basin Reserve. New Zealand soon lost Howell, but Astle and Cairns added 81. Astle was stumped off a wide and collapse followed with Fleming and Parore falling to silly run outs. Cairns, Harris and Nash all offered some defiance, but the Australian fielding put New Zealand to shame, and they fully deserved their two-nil lead in the series.

Winning the toss at Napier, Steve Waugh again elected to bat first, but the pitch was slower than expected. Australia began well enough, but they were slowed by a fine spell from Vettori – 12 overs passed without a boundary – and then devastated by Chris Cairns, who took five for 3 in 19 balls. His final figures of five for 42 were his best in a one-day international. There was New Zealand despair when Howell and Parore were out with just five scored, but Astle and Fleming scored 116 before the former was run out by Ponting's direct throw. Fleming now found another good partner in McMillan, and they scored the runs necessary to take New Zealand to victory. McMillan's 53 came off 59 balls, and Man of the Match Fleming reached his third century in limited-over internationals, 111 off 137 balls.

Having suffered much at the hands of Australia in recent months, New Zealand were elated by their success in Napier, which had given them the opportunity to draw the series. Both sides made changes for the final match. Australia brought in Dale for Moody while New Zealand included Mark Priest, a slow left-arm bowler, in place of the injured Vettori. Priest was playing his 12th one-day international, but it was his first in New Zealand. Going against what had happened in the first three matches, Steve Waugh chose to field when he won the toss.

Simon Doull enjoyed a fine season at international level. He took four wickets and played a major part in New Zealand's victory over Australia in the fourth one-day international.
(David Munden / Sportsline)

The pitch was slow and had a low bounce, but Howell and Astle gave New Zealand a rollicking start with 46 in eight overs. Robertson then bowled a fine spell in which he dismissed three front line batsmen and crippled the scoring-rate. New Zealand slumped to 134 for six, but Harris and Nash lifted the innings with a partnership worth 89, which was only ended when Harris, 55 off 57 balls, was run out on the last ball of the innings. Gilchrist and Mark Waugh scored 26 in four overs at the start of the Australian innings before Mark Waugh was leg before to Doull, who then bowled Ponting. This gave him two for 16 in six overs. Australia never truly recovered. Priest and Harris frustrated the Australians in their attempt to maintain the necessary run-rate and wickets fell regularly. At 88 for three, Steve Waugh collided with Nash, the bowler, in an incident that caused some debate, and was forced to retire hurt. He returned at 147 for six but could do nothing to halt the slide. New Zealand achieved a notable victory, just as they had done at McLean Park, through outstanding team work. Australia limped away a little chastened.

First One-Day International – New Zealand v. Australia

8 February 1998 at Lancaster Park, Christchurch

New Zealand

L.G. Howell	**b** Robertson	**50**
N.J. Astle	**b** Moody	**23**
A.C. Parore †	**c** Bevan, **b** Robertson	**29**
S.P. Fleming *	**c** and **b** Robertson	**2**
C.D. McMillan	run out	**4**
C.L. Cairns	**c** Dale, **b** S.R. Waugh	**16**
C.Z. Harris	**c** Law, **b** Moody	**38**
D.J. Nash	not out	**39**
S.B. Doull	not out	**0**
D.L. Vettori		
S.B. O'Connor		
	lb **7**, w **4**	**11**
	50 overs (for 7 wickets)	**212**

	O	M	R	W
Wilson	7	1	39	–
Dale	8	–	34	–
Moody	8	2	36	**2**
Robertson	10	–	32	**3**
S.R. Waugh	10	1	24	**1**
M.E. Waugh	3	–	19	–
Law	4	1	21	–

Fall of Wickets
1–**40**, 2–**104**, 3–**109**, 4–**109**, 5–**119**, 6–**136**, 7–**202**

Australia

A.C. Gilchrist †	**c** Cairns, **b** McMillan	**118**
M.E. Waugh	**c** Nash, **b** Vettori	**65**
T.M. Moody	**b** MacMillan	**17**
R.T. Ponting	not out	**10**
D.S. Lehmann	not out	**0**
S.R. Waugh *		
M.G. Bevan		
S.G. Law		
G.R. Robertson		
A.C. Dale		
P. Wilson		
	b **2**, lb **1**, w **1**, nb **1**	**5**
	38.2 overs	**215**

	O	M	R	W
O'Connor	4	–	31	–
Doull	4	–	25	–
Cairns	4	–	16	–
Harris	8	–	43	–
Vettori	10	–	44	**1**
Astle	2	–	15	–
McMillan	6.2	–	38	**2**

Fall of Wickets
1–**146**, 2–**173**, 3–**208**

Umpires: D.B. Cowie & D.M. Quested *Man of the Match*: A.C. Gilchrist

Australia won by 7 wickets

Second One-Day International – New Zealand v. Australia

10 February 1998 at Basin Reserve, Wellington

Australia

M.E. Waugh	**c** Howell, **b** Astle	**85**
A.C. Gilchrist †	**c** McMillan, **b** O'Connor	**0**
R.T. Ponting	**c** Fleming, **b** Nash	**26**
D.S. Lehmann	**c** Vettori, **b** O'Connor	**62**
M.G. Bevan	run out	**39**
S.R. Waugh *	**c** Fleming, **b** O'Connor	**47**
S.G. Law	not out	**13**
T.M. Moody	not out	**12**
A.J. Bichel		
G.R. Robertson		
A.C. Dale		
	lb **5**, w **3**, nb **5**	**13**
	50 overs (for 6 wickets)	**297**

	O	M	R	W
O'Connor	9	–	55	**3**
Cairns	9	–	55	–
Nash	10	–	52	**1**
Doull	4	1	16	–
Harris	6	–	31	–
Vettori	7	–	–	**49**
Astle	5	–	34	**1**

Fall of Wickets
1–**1**, 2–**46**, 3–**168**, 4–**191**, 5–**265**, 6–**277**

New Zealand

L.G. Howell	**c** Lehmann, **b** Dale	**1**
N.J. Astle	**st** Gilchrist, **b** Robertson	**37**
C.L. Cairns	lbw, **b** S.R. Waugh	**67**
S.P. Fleming *	run out	**3**
A.C. Parore †	run out	**0**
C.D. McMillan	**c** Robertson, **b** Bevan	**25**
C.Z. Harris	**b** Bevan	**45**
D.J. Nash	**c** Gilchrist, **b** Bevan	**23**
D.L. Vettori	**c** M.E. Waugh, **b** S.R. Waugh	**4**
S.B. Doull	not out	**9**
S.B. O'Connor	run out	**4**
	b **4**, lb **2**, w **7**	**13**
	47.3 overs	**231**

	O	M	R	W
Bichel	6	–	28	–
Dale	5	1	23	**1**
Robertson	9	–	40	**1**
Moody	8	1	34	–
Bevan	10	1	54	**3**
S.R. Waugh	9.3	–	46	**2**

Fall of Wickets
1–**1**, 2–**82**, 3–**86**, 4–**89**, 5–**132**, 6–**142**, 7–**193**, 8–**209**, 9–**219**

Umpires: D.M. Quested & E.A. Watkin *Man of the Match*: M.E. Waugh

Australia won by 66 runs

Third One-Day International – New Zealand v. Australia

12 February 1998 at McLean Park, Napier

Australia

Batsman	Dismissal	Runs
A.C. Gilchrist †	c Cairns, b Nash	40
M.E. Waugh	c Parore, b Vettori	42
R.T. Ponting	c Fleming, b Harris	30
D.S. Lehmann	c Parore, b Cairns	44
T.M. Moody	b Vettori	3
S.R. Waugh *	c Parore, b Cairns	42
M.G. Bevan	run out	10
S.G. Law	c Nash, b Cairns	1
A.J. Bichel	c Fleming, b Cairns	0
G.R. Robertson	not out	11
P. Wilson	c Fleming, b Cairns	2
	lb 6, w 4, nb 1	11
	48.4 overs	236

	O	M	R	W
O'Connor	5	–	20	–
Cairns	7.4	–	42	5
Doull	7	–	28	–
Nash	6	–	37	1
Vettori	10	–	35	2
Astle	3	–	16	–
Harris	10	–	52	1

Fall of Wickets
1–60, 2–98, 3–136, 4–141, 5–209, 6–210, 7–214, 8–215, 9–226

New Zealand

Batsman	Dismissal	Runs
L.G. Howell	c Gilchrist, b Wilson	4
N.J. Astle	run out	55
A.C. Parore †	b Bichel	0
S.P. Fleming *	not out	111
C.D. McMillan	not out	53
C.L. Cairns		
C.Z. Harris		
D.J. Nash		
D.L. Vettori		
S.B. Doull		
S.B. O'Connor		
	b 1, lb 6, w 3, nb 7	17
	48.2 overs (for 3 wickets)	240

	O	M	R	W
Wilson	6.2	–	42	1
Bichel	10	–	42	1
Moody	10	–	39	–
Robertson	10	1	38	–
S.R. Waugh	10	–	56	–
Law	2	–	16	–

Fall of Wickets
1–4, 2–5, 3–121

Umpires: B.F. Bowden & E.A. Watkin *Man of the Match*: S.P. Fleming

New Zealand won by 7 wickets

Four One-Day International – New Zealand v. Australia

14 February 1998 at Eden Park, Auckland

New Zealand

Batsman	Dismissal	Runs
L.G. Howell	lbw, b Robertson	51
N.J. Astle	c Robertson, b Bichel	20
A.C. Parore †	c Ponting, b Robertson	32
S.P. Fleming *	c Gilchrist, b Robertson	13
C.D. McMillan	b Lehmann	13
C.L. Cairns	c S.R. Waugh, b Bevan	2
C.Z. Harris	run out	55
D.J. Nash	not out	31
M.W. Priest		
S.B. Doull		
S.B. O'Connor		
	w 5, nb 1	6
	50 overs (for 7 wickets)	223

	O	M	R	W
Wilson	4	–	25	–
Dale	6	–	33	–
Bichel	7	–	33	–
Robertson	10	–	29	3
M.E. Waugh	2	–	11	–
Bevan	10	–	37	1
Lehmann	9	–	37	1
Law	2	–	18	–

Fall of Wickets
1–46, 2–85, 3–107, 4–120, 5–132, 6–134, 7–223

Australia

Batsman	Dismissal	Runs
A.C. Gilchrist †	c Parore, b Nash	42
M.E. Waugh	lbw, b Doull	4
R.T. Ponting	b Doull	10
D.S. Lehmann	c Astle, b Priest	26
S.R. Waugh *	c sub (S.J. Peterson), b Priest	23
S.G. Law	c Fleming, b McMillan	7
M.G. Bevan	c Nash, b Doull	37
A.J. Bichel	c Cairns, b Harris	21
G.R. Robertson	c Nash, b Doull	7
A.C. Dale	c Nash, b Cairns	6
P. Wilson	not out	1
	lb 4, w 4, nb 1	9
	49.1 overs	193

	O	M	R	W
O'Connor	2	–	21	–
Cairns	9.1	–	32	1
Doull	8	1	25	4
Nash	5	–	23	1
Priest	10	–	31	2
Harris	10	–	33	1
McMillan	3	–	14	1
Astle	2	–	10	–

Fall of Wickets
1–26, 2–48, 3–60, 4–105, 5–107, 6–147, 7–176, 8–183, 9–190

Umpires: R.S. Dunne & B.F. Bowden *Man of the Match*: C.Z. Harris

New Zealand won by 30 runs

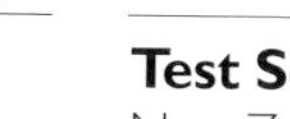

Zimbabwe Tour

Zimbabwe arrived in New Zealand to play five one-day internationals and two Tests. Two of the limited-over games were to be played before the Tests, the remainder after. Zimbabwe were also to play first-class matches outside the Tests.

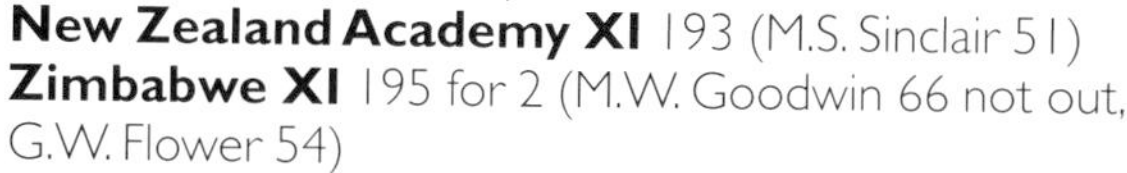

3 February 1998
at Owen Delany Park, Taupo
New Zealand Academy XI 193 (M.S. Sinclair 51)
Zimbabwe XI 195 for 2 (M.W. Goodwin 66 not out, G.W. Flower 54)
Zimbabwe XI won by 8 wickets

As a warm up for the one-day internationals, the tourists met the New Zealand Academy in a 50-over game and won convincingly. The Academy were bowled out in 48.3 overs, and Zimbabwe won with 13.1 overs to spare. Goodwin's unbeaten 66 came off 58 balls with four sixes and five fours.

8, 9, 10 and 11 February 1998
at Carisbrook, Dunedin
Zimbabwe XI 67 (A.R. Tait 5 for 16, C.J. Drum 4 for 18) and 195 (M.W. Goodwin 78, C.J. Drum 5 for 65)
New Zealand 'A' 271 for 8 dec. (C.M. Spearman 76, R.G. Twose 69, M.D. Bell 50, M. Mbangwa 4 for 49)
New Zealand 'A' won by an innings and 9 runs

In preparation for the Test matches, Zimbabwe played two first-class games. The first of them, against New Zealand 'A' proved a total embarrassment as they were dismissed for one of the lowest scores recorded by a touring side. They were all out in 36.2 overs for 67. Bell and Spearman scored 125 for the home side's second wicket after Young had gone early. Medium-pacer Chris Drum, 23 years old, had match figures of nine for 83.

13, 14, 15 and 16 February 1998
at Aorangi Park, Timaru
Canterbury 100 (P.A. Strang 4 for 20) and 266 (C.D. Cummings 86, H. James 50)
Zimbabwe XI 422 for 8 (A.D.R. Campbell 196, P.A. Strang 93, G.W. Flower 64)
Zimbabwe XI won by an innings and 56 runs

On the eve of the first Test, Zimbabwe gained a much needed boost to their confidence when they beat a weakened Canterbury side by an innings. They had two heroes, skipper Alistair Campbell who batted nearly six and a half hours for the highest score of his career, 196, and Paul Strang who had match figures of seven for 58 in 49 overs and hit 93 in a seventh wicket stand of 261 with his captain.

Test Series
New Zealand *v.* Zimbabwe

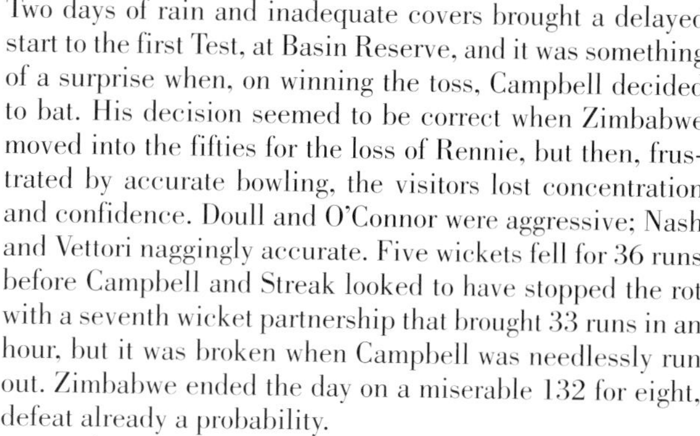

Two days of rain and inadequate covers brought a delayed start to the first Test, at Basin Reserve, and it was something of a surprise when, on winning the toss, Campbell decided to bat. His decision seemed to be correct when Zimbabwe moved into the fifties for the loss of Rennie, but then, frustrated by accurate bowling, the visitors lost concentration and confidence. Doull and O'Connor were aggressive; Nash and Vettori naggingly accurate. Five wickets fell for 36 runs before Campbell and Streak looked to have stopped the rot with a seventh wicket partnership that brought 33 runs in an hour, but it was broken when Campbell was needlessly run out. Zimbabwe ended the day on a miserable 132 for eight, defeat already a probability.

That probability came closer to actuality on the second day. Streak and Huckle offered resistance for the first hour, but O'Connor dismissed them both to finish with the best figures in an attack that maintained discipline and purpose throughout. New Zealand imme-diately lost Bryan Young, caught at second slip, but Horne and Parore laid the foundation of a big total with a second wicket stand of 103. Both were out before the close, but the home country's batting had a determined look, and Astle and Fleming took the score to 106 by the end of the day. Progress had not been spectacular; it had been determined and professional in pursuit of a significant first innings lead and ultimate victory.

Fleming was deceived by Huckle's googly and caught low down at slip at the start of the third day. Two more wickets fell before lunch, Astle being well caught by wicket-keeper Andy Flower and Cairns being run out on the last ball before the interval in an attempt to give McMillan his 50. The 21-year old did not need such wasteful help. He dominated the afternoon session as he and Nash shared a stand of 112. There were no nervous 90s for the young man. He went from 90 to his maiden Test century in five deliveries, and the hundred was reached when he hit Andy Whittall over long-on for six. He hit three more sixes and 18 fours in his 139, which came off 209 balls in 263 minutes. He led New Zealand to a first innings lead of 231, and by the end of the day, Zimbabwe were in desperate trouble having lost both openers with only 27 scored.

If Zimbabwe could survive the fourth day's play, there was hope that they could save the match, for rain was forecast for the Monday. It was not to be. Night-watchman Andy Whittall was run out by Man of the Match McMillan, and Cairns and Vettori ate out the heart of the middle order. Murray Goodwin battled for nearly three and three-quarter hours in an attempt to stave off defeat, and after Cairns had knocked Strang's off stump out of the ground second ball, Campbell and Streak came together in a brave stand. They had added 94 when Campbell had a rush of blood and hooked Cairns straight to Horne. The last two wickets followed immediately, and New Zealand claimed the extra

Matthew Horne hit 157 in the second Test against Zimbabwe at Auckland and shared a record fourth wicket partnership of 243 with . . .
(Ben Radford / Allsport)

half-hour. They needed only 23 balls to score the 20 runs they required. On the Monday, it rained, and Zimbabwe could only rue their profligacy.

Zimbabwe were unchanged for the second Test while New Zealand recalled Priest to Test cricket in place of O'Connor. For Zimbabwe, the second Test followed the pattern of the first but with greater humiliation. They chose to bat when they won the toss and lost Gavin Rennie, caught behind in the opening over off the bowling of Simon Doull, whose ability to swing the ball both ways was a constant source of embarrassment to the Zimbabwe batsmen. In his fifth over, Doull had Grant Flower caught behind. A half-hour break for rain followed, after which three batsmen were caught in the slips while two runs were scored. Doull claimed two of these wickets. A seventh wicket stand of 59 between Andy Flower and Paul Strang was the best Zimbabwe could offer, and the last three wickets fell to Cairns for two runs. The visitors struck back by dismissing Young and Parore cheaply before Horne and Fleming took the score to 69 by stumps on the first day.

Fleming was out on the second morning without addition to the score, which brought Astle in to join Horne. They proceeded to add a record 243 for the fourth wicket. They launched a brutal attack on the Zimbabwe bowling, which was, for the most part, negative and lacklustre. The field-placings were defensive and the fielding in general disintegrated with catches readily spilled. Matthew Horne batted for 396 minutes and faced 260 balls for his 157, his second Test century. He hit four sixes and 19 fours. Astle, who had been having a lean time, hit 16 fours in his 192-ball innings. Late in the day, McMillan smashed the ball to all parts of the ground as New Zealand ended on 441 for nine. When Campbell pulled his field back to allow McMillan the single, the batsman blocked four deliveries. When a fielder was brought in he pulled the ball over mid-wicket for his third six and then took a single off the last ball of the over. He was caught behind off Paul Strang, who had been kept out of the attack for far too long, but by then he had hit 11 fours as well as his sixes and made 88 off 83 balls.

Zimbabwe's second innings began badly on the third morning with Gavin Rennie taken at slip for his second 0 of the match, and Goodwin fell to an astonishing left-handed diving catch in the gully by McMillan. After lunch, wickets fell at regular intervals. Andy Flower gave real resistance with an elegant 83 in 169 minutes before falling to the second new ball. Paul Strang, less orthodox, hit an unbeaten 67 off 72 balls. Andy Whittall was the eighth man out on the stroke of what should have been the close of play, and Fleming claimed the extra half hour. Huckle and Strang scored 43 in that time before Doull dismissed Huckle and Mbangwa with the third and fourth balls of the last over of the day.

Horne was named Man of the Match. Doull, eight for 85, must have run him close. New Zealand had totally out classed Zimbabwe in both matches, and their spirits were much uplifted. The trials and tribulations of Australia seemed well in the past, and players like McMillan, Horne, Doull and O'Connor had given a good account of themselves. Zimbabwe had contributed greatly to their own downfall. Campbell had not had a good series as skipper, and the outlook was not promising.

3 February 1998
at Owen Delany Park, Taupo
New Zealand Academy 193 (M.S. Sinclair 51)
Zimbabwe XI 195 for 2 (M.W. Goodwin 66 not out, G.W. Flower 54)
Zimbabwe XI won by 8 wickets

In a warm-up 50-over match before the one-day series, Zimbabwe had an encouraging victory, winning with 13.1 overs to spare. Goodwin's 66 came off 58 balls. He hit four sixes and five fours.

. . . Nathan Astle, who made 114. (Ben Radford / Allsport)

First Test Match – New Zealand v. Zimbabwe

19, 20, 21 and 22 February 1998 at Basin Reserve, Wellington

Zimbabwe

	First Innings		Second Innings	
G.J. Rennie	**b** Doull	**13**	lbw, **b** Doull	**15**
G.W. Flower	**b** Nash	**38**	**c** and **b** Vettori	**4**
M.W. Goodwin	lbw, **b** Vettori	**8**	(4) **c** Fleming, **b** Cairns	**72**
G.J. Whittall	**c** Parore, **b** O'Connor	**6**	(5) **c** Astle, **b** Nash	**22**
A. Flower †	**c** Parore, **b** O'Connor	**2**	(6) **c** O'Connor, **b** Vettori	**6**
A.D.R. Campbell *	run out	**37**	(7) **c** Horne, **b** Cairns	**56**
P.A. Strang	**c** Young, **b** Doull	**1**	(8) **b** Cairns	**0**
H.H. Streak	lbw, **b** O'Connor	**39**	(9) not out	**43**
A.R. Whittall	**c** Parore, **b** Cairns	**1**	(3) run out	**12**
A.G. Huckle	**c** Parore, **b** O'Connor	**19**	lbw, **b** Vettori	**0**
M. Mbangwa	not out	**0**	lbw, **b** Cairns	**0**
	lb **10**, nb **6**	**16**	b **6**, lb **14**	**20**
		180		**250**

	O	M	R	W	O	M	R	W
Cairns	16	2	50	**1**	24.3	4	56	**4**
O'Connor	18.3	7	52	**4**	14	3	39	**–**
Doull	17	8	18	**2**	13	1	47	**1**
Nash	14	7	11	**1**	9	6	10	**1**
Vettori	20	10	39	**1**	41	18	73	**3**
McMillan	5	1	5	**–**	5	1	5	**–**

Fall of Wickets
1–**30**, 2–**53**, 3–**64**, 4–**70**, 5–**78**, 6–**89**, 7–**122**, 8–**131**, 9–**171**,
1–**18**, 2–**20**, 3–**65**, 4–**110**, 5–**125**, 6–**155**, 7–**155**, 8–**249**, 9–**249**

New Zealand

	First Innings		Second Innings	
B.A. Young	**c** P.A. Strang, **b** Streak	**0**	(2) not out	**10**
M.J. Horne	**c** A. Flower, **b** Mbangwa	**44**	(1) not out	**9**
A.C. Parore †	**c** A. Flower, **b** Huckle	**78**		
S.P. Fleming *	**c** Campbell, **b** Huckle	**36**		
N.J. Astle	**c** A. Flower, **b** Streak	**42**		
C.D. McMillan	**c** A.R. Whittall, **b** Huckle	**139**		
C.L. Cairns	run out	**0**		
D.J. Nash	**b** P.A. Strang	**41**		
D.L. Vettori	**b** P.A. Strang	**16**		
S.B. Doull	**c** Goodwin, **b** P.A. Strang	**8**		
S.B. O'Connor	not out	**2**		
	b **1**, lb **4**	**5**	lb **1**	**1**
		141	for no wicket	**20**

	O	M	R	W	O	M	R	W
W. Streak	22	6	74	**2**	2	–	13	**–**
Mbangwa	17	4	42	**1**				
P.A. Strang	49.3	13	126	**3**				
G.J. Whittall	5	2	12	**–**				
A.R. Whittall	12	–	50	**–**				
Huckle	40	10	102	**3**	1.3	–	6	**–**

Fall of Wickets
1–**0**, 2–**103**, 3–**144**, 4–**179**, 5–**240**, 6–**254**, 7–**362**, 8–**388**, 9–**397**

Umpires: R.S. Dunne & S.G. Randell

New Zealand won by 10 wickets

Second Test Match – New Zealand v. Zimbabwe

26, 27 and 28 February 1998 at Eden Park, Auckland

Zimbabwe

	First Innings		Second Innings	
G.J. Rennie	**c** Parore, **b** Doull	**0**	(2) **c** Fleming, **b** Cairns	**0**
G.W. Flower	**c** Parore, **b** Doull	**13**	(1) **c** Young, **b** Nash	**32**
M.W. Goodwin	**c** Young, **b** Doull	**28**	**c** McMillan, **b** Nash	**14**
A.D.R. Campbell *	**c** Astle, **b** Doull	**11**	**c** Horne, **b** Vettori	**22**
A. Flower	**c** McMillan, **b** Nash	**65**	**c** Parore, **b** Cairns	**83**
G.J. Whittall	**c** Young, **b** Nash	**1**	lbw, **b** Doull	**10**
H.H. Streak	**c** Fleming, **b** Nash	**12**	lbw, **b** Cairns	**24**
P.A. Strang	not out	**30**	not out	**67**
A.R. Whittall	lbw, **b** Cairns	**4**	**c** Parore, **b** Doull	**3**
A.G. Huckle	lbw, **b** Cairns	**0**	**b** Doull	**13**
M. Mbangwa	not out	**0**	**c** Fleming, **b** Doull	**0**
	b **1**, lb **3**, nb **2**	**6**	b **1**, lb **6**, nb **2**	**9**
		170		**277**

	O	M	R	W	O	M	R	W
W. Doull	20	6	35	**4**	19.4	5	50	**4**
Cairns	16.5	4	56	**3**	29	9	81	**3**
Nash	18	4	41	**3**	10	5	13	**2**
Vettori	2	–	15	**–**	20	5	60	**1**
Astle	5	1	15	**–**				
Priest	1	–	4	**–**	14	–	51	**–**
McMillan	2	–	15	**–**				

Fall of Wickets
1–**1**, 2–**32**, 3–**53**, 4–**54**, 5–**55**, 6–**98**, 7–**157**, 8–**168**, 9–**170**,
1–**4**, 2–**29**, 3–**71**, 4–**71**, 5–**90**, 6–**156**, 7–**227**, 8–**234**, 9–**277**

New Zealand

	First Innings	
B.A. Young	**b** Streak	**1**
M.J. Horne	**c** G.J. Whittall, **b** Mbangwa	**157**
A.C. Parore †	**c** A. Flower, **b** Mbangwa	**10**
S.P. Fleming *	**c** Huckle, **b** Mbangwa	**19**
N.J. Astle	**c** G.W. Flower, **b** Streak	**114**
C.D. McMillan	**c** A. Flower, **b** P.A. Strang	**88**
C.L. Cairns	**c** P.A. Strang, **b** Streak	**22**
D.J. Nash	lbw, **b** P.A. Strang	**1**
M.W. Priest	**c** G.J. Rennie, **b** P.A. Strang	**16**
D.L. Vettori	**c** Campbell, **b** P.A. Strang	**0**
S.B. Doull	not out	**6**
	b **8**, lb **17**, nb **1**	**26**
		460

	O	M	R	W
Streak	31	7	105	**3**
Mbangwa	27	10	78	**3**
G.J. Whittall	14	3	68	**–**
P.A. Strang	18.1	–	54	**4**
A.R. Whittall	11	1	37	**–**
Huckle	13	1	66	**–**
Goodwin	6	1	27	**–**

Fall of Wickets
1–**2**, 2–**40**, 3–**69**, 4–**312**, 5–**322**, 6–**382**, 7–**405**, 8–**431**, 9–**433**

Umpires: D.B. Cowie & S.G. Randell

New Zealand won by an innings and 13 runs

First One-Day International – New Zealand v. Zimbabwe

4 February 1998 at WestpacTrust Park, Hamilton

New Zealand

L.G. Howell	c and b P.A. Strang	24
N.J. Astle	c G.W. Flower, b P.A. Strang	49
A.C. Parore †	c Goodwin, b P.A. Strang	14
S.P. Fleming *	c J.A. Rennie, b A.R. Whittall	26
C.D. McMillan	b A.R. Whittall	16
C.L. Cairns	c Goodwin, b Mbangwa	43
C.Z. Harris	not out	52
D.J. Nash	c Wishart, b Streak	8
S.B. Doull	not out	0
D.L. Vettori		
S.B. O'Connor		
	lb 9, w 7	16
	50 overs (for 7 wickets)	248

	O	M	R	W
Streak	10	–	42	1
Mbangwa	9	1	63	1
J.A. Rennie	9	–	45	–
P.A. Strang	10	–	40	3
A.R. Whittall	10	–	39	2
G.W. Flower	2	–	10	–

Fall of Wickets
1–**73**, 2–**91**, 3–**107**, 4–**144**, 5–**144**, 6–**219**, 7–**240**

Zimbabwe

G.W. Flower	c and b Harris	32
C.B. Wishart	c Astle, b Vettori	37
M.W. Goodwin	c Astle, b Vettori	7
A. Flower †	st Parore, b Vettori	60
G.J. Whittall	c and b Harris	12
A.D.R. Campbell *	run out	22
P.A. Strang	c Vettori, b Nash	5
H.H. Streak	not out	16
J.A. Rennie	run out	0
A.R. Whittall	b Vettori	0
M. Mbangwa	c Cairns, b O'Connor	3
	lb 8, w 4, nb 2	14
	48.2 overs	208

	O	M	R	W
O'Connor	10	–	34	1
Cairns	4	1	10	–
Doull	5	–	21	–
Nash	7	–	24	1
Harris	10	–	47	2
Vettori	10	–	49	4
Astle	4	–	15	–

Fall of Wickets
1–**75**, 2–**75**, 3–**90**, 4–**113**, 5–**170**, 6–**182**, 7–**189**, 8–**190**, 9–**191**

Umpires: R.S. Dunne & C.E. King *Man of the Match*: C.Z. Harris

New Zealand won by 40 runs

Second One-Day International – New Zealand v. Zimbabwe

6 February 1998 at Basin Reserve, Wellington

Zimbabwe

G.W. Flower	c and b Doull	11
C.B. Wishart	c Astle, b O'Connor	0
M.W. Goodwin	c Fleming, b O'Connor	3
A. Flower †	c McMillan, b Cairns	0
A.D.R. Campbell *	c Harris, b O'Connor	23
G.J. Whittall	c and b Harris	31
D.P. Viljoen	c Parore, b Doull	36
P.A. Strang	b Nash	8
H.H. Streak	c Parore, b O'Connor	10
J.A. Rennie	b O'Connor	5
A.R. Whittall	not out	1
	lb 4, w 5, nb 1	10
	49 overs	138

	O	M	R	W
O'Connor	10	–	39	5
Cairns	7	2	10	1
Nash	7	1	14	1
Doull	10	1	26	2
Astle	5	1	16	–
Harris	10	2	29	1

Fall of Wickets
1–**1**, 2–**6**, 3–**7**, 4–**23**, 5–**48**, 6–**114**, 7–**114**, 8–**131**, 9–**133**

New Zealand

L.G. Howell	c Wishart, b Streak	7
N.J. Astle	run out	67
A.C. Parore †	not out	36
S.P. Fleming *	not out	17
C.D. McMillan		
C.L. Cairns		
C.Z. Harris		
D.J. Nash		
D.L. Vettori		
S.B. Doull		
S.B. O'Connor		
	b 2, lb 4, w 5, nb 1	12
	28.2 overs (for 2 wickets)	139

	O	M	R	W
Streak	7	–	20	1
J.A. Rennie	5	–	27	–
P.A. Strang	6	–	30	–
G.J. Whittall	5.2	1	16	–
A.R. Whittall	5	–	40	–

Fall of Wickets
1–**18**, 2–**121**

Umpires: C.E. King & E.A. Watkin *Man of the Match*: S.B. O'Connor

New Zealand won by 8 wickets

Daniel Vettori produced an outstanding all-round performance in the final one-day international match against Zimbabwe and earned the individual award. He also had the first five-wicket haul of his career for Northern Districts in the Shell Trophy.
(Ben Radford / Allsport)

One-Day International Series

New Zealand v. Zimbabwe

The one-day series straddled the two Test matches. Llorne Howell, the 25-year old opener from Canterbury, made his debut in the first match and shared an opening partnership of 73 with Astle, but New Zealand slipped to 144 for five, and it was Cairns and Harris who gave the innings its necessary thrust. They added 75 for the sixth wicket at more than a run a minute, and Zimbabwe were suddenly faced with a daunting target. Grant Flower and Wishart gave them a good start, and Andy Flower hit 60 off 66 balls. He received little support as New Zealand bowled tightly. Vettori returned his best figures in a one-day international as Zimbabwe fell apart.

The second match was best described by Zimbabwe coach Dave Houghton: 'We had an absolute shocker.' Put in to bat, the tourists lost three wickets for seven runs. Guy Whittall and Viljoen added 66 for the sixth wicket, but there was no significant recovery. O'Connor finished with his best figures in a one-day international, and Harris claimed his 100th wicket in limited-over internationals when he caught and bowled Guy Whittall. Astle and Parore hit 103 in an hour for New Zealand's second wicket, and victory came with 21.4 overs to spare.

The series restarted after the Tests, and Zimbabwe did well to win after being so outplayed in the major encounters. Again they were put in to bat and lost Grant Flower third ball. They were revived by Goodwin, who hit 58 off 77 balls. Guy Whittall also did well, making 50 off 63 balls towards the end of the innings. Howell and Astle gave New Zealand a splendid start with 125 in 84 minutes. Howell's 68 came off 71 balls and included a six and 12 fours. The middle order faded badly, and the last over arrived with New Zealand needing 10 to win. Streak had Parore caught off the first ball of the over, which left O'Connor and Vettori with the responsibility of scoring the runs. Vettori needed to hit a four off the last ball but could manage only two.

New Zealand clinched the series at McLean Park. Zimbabwe won the toss and batted. The batting was sluggish, and they collapsed to 153 for eight. The revival came from Paul Strang and John Rennie, who added 54 in 34 minutes. Strang made 31 off 36 balls, while Rennie's 23 came off 28 balls. Their efforts mattered little. Howell and Astle gave New Zealand another glorious start with a partnership of 147. Howell was caught off Viljoen after making 66 off 86 balls, but Astle finished the job in conjunction with Fleming, and his 104 came off 139 deliveries with three sixes and three fours.

The fifth game was of purely academic interest, but it produced a tense finish. Fleming chose to bat when he won the toss, and Howell had a rare failure, falling in the second over. Astle was again in prime form with 62 off 84 balls, but the innings stumbled, and it was left to Chris Harris to restore order with an unbeaten 52 off 82 balls. The fireworks came from Nash, 28 off 37 balls, and Vettori, 21 off 13 balls with a six and two fours. Zimbabwe batted steadily, but they were always a little behind the required run rate and lost wickets regularly. They were totally undermined by an accurate spell from Vettori, and the last over arrived with eight needed. Four were scored and Strang was run out so that Andy Whittall needed to hit Chris Cairns's last ball to the boundary. He lobbed a catch to McMillan, who dropped it, but the batsman could run only one. A blow for New Zealand was the loss of Dion Nash, who dislocated a shoulder while fielding.

A pace bowler of considerable talent, Shayne O'Connor established himself at international level and took five wickets in the second one-day international against Zimbabwe when he was named Man of the Match.
(Ben Radford / Allsport)

Third One-Day International – New Zealand v. Zimbabwe

4 March 1998 at Lancaster Park, Christchurch

Zimbabwe

G.W. Flower	**b** O'Connor	**0**
C.B. Wishart †	**b** Vettori	**28**
M.W. Goodwin	**b** Harris	**58**
A.D.R. Campbell *	run out	**38**
A. Flower	run out	**28**
G.J. Whittall	**c** Horne, **b** Doull	**50**
P.A. Strang	not out	**16**
D.P. Viljoen	**b** O'Connor	**4**
H.H. Streak	not out	**2**
J.A. Rennie		
A.R. Whittall		
	lb **3**, w **1**	**4**
	50 overs (for 7 wickets)	**228**

	O	M	R	W
O'Connor	7	1	31	**2**
Cairns	3	–	23	**–**
Vettori	10	–	36	**1**
Doull	5	1	19	**1**
McMillan	6	–	30	**–**
Harris	10	–	47	**1**
Astle	9	–	39	**–**

Fall of Wickets
1–**0**, 2–**38**, 3–**116**, 4–**127**, 5–**197**, 6–**211**, 7–**221**

New Zealand

L.G. Howell	**c** sub (H.K. Olonga), **b** P.A. Strang	**68**
N.J. Astle	**c** Campbell, **b** Viljoen	**69**
S.P. Fleming *	**b** A.R. Whittall	**4**
M.J. Horne	run out	**2**
C.D. McMillan	**c** A. Flower, **b** G.W. Flower	**15**
C.L. Cairns	**b** Viljoen	**1**
C.Z. Harris	**c** G.J. Whittall, **b** P.A. Strang	**22**
A.C. Parore †	**c** P.A. Strang, **b** Streak	**25**
S.B. Doull	**st** A. Flower, **b** P.A. Strang	**0**
D.L. Vettori	not out	**7**
S.B. O'Connor	not out	**1**
	lb **1**, w **12**	**13**
	50 overs (for 9 wickets)	**227**

	O	M	R	W
Streak	9	–	57	**1**
J.A. Rennie	4	–	23	**–**
A.R. Whittall	9	–	45	**1**
P.A. Strang	10	–	44	**3**
G.W. Flower	6	–	19	**1**
Goodwin	2	–	7	**–**
Viljoen	10	–	31	**2**

Fall of Wickets
1–**125**, 2–**137**, 3–**139**, 4–**159**, 5–**165**, 6–**168**, 7–**218**, 8–**219**, 9–**219**

Umpires: B.F. Bowden & C.E. King *Man of the Match*: M.W. Goodwin

Zimbabwe won by one run

Fourth One-Day International – New Zealand v. Zimbabwe

6 March 1998 at McLean Park, Napier

Zimbabwe

G.W. Flower	run out	**11**
C.B. Wishart	**c** Astle, **b** Harris	**41**
M.W. Goodwin	**c** Vettori, **b** Cairns	**1**
A.D.R. Campbell *	**c** Astle, **b** O'Connor	**18**
A. Flower †	**c** Parore, **b** Nash	**30**
G.J. Whittall	**b** Nash	**18**
D.P. Viljoen	**c** Fleming, **b** Nash	**7**
H.H. Streak	**c** and **b** Harris	**9**
P.A. Strang	not out	**31**
J.A. Rennie	not out	**23**
A.R. Whittall		
	lb **7**, w **9**, nb **2**	**18**
	50 overs (for 8 wickets)	**207**

	O	M	R	W
O'Connor	10	1	53	**1**
Cairns	10	1	39	**1**
Nash	10	2	29	**3**
Vettori	10	–	49	**–**
Harris	10	–	30	**2**

Fall of Wickets
1–**15**, 2–**25**, 3–**56**, 4–**107**, 5–**122**, 6–**134**, 7–**145**, 8–**153**

New Zealand

L.G. Howell	**c** Wishart, **b** Viljoen	**66**
N.J. Astle	not out	**104**
S.P. Fleming *	not out	**33**
M.J. Horne		
C.D. McMillan		
C.L. Cairns		
C.Z. Harris		
A.C. Parore †		
D.J. Nash		
D.L. Vettori		
S.B. O'Connor		
	lb **3**, w **5**	**8**
	45.4 overs (for one wicket)	**211**

	O	M	R	W
Streak	6	1	23	**–**
J.A. Rennie	7	–	35	**–**
A.R. Whittall	10	–	43	**–**
P.A. Strang	7	–	38	**–**
Viljoen	6	–	30	**1**
G.W. Flower	8	–	30	**–**
Goodwin	1.4	–	9	**–**

Fall of Wicket
1–**147**

Umpires: D.B. Cowie & R.A.L. Hill *Man of the Match*: N.J. Astle

New Zealand won by 9 wickets

Fifth One-Day International – New Zealand v. Zimbabwe

8 March 1998 at Eden Park, Auckland New Zealand

New Zealand

L.G. Howell	c P.A. Strang, b J.A. Rennie	1
N.J. Astle	c G.J. Whittall, b G.W. Flower	62
S.P. Fleming *	b A.R. Whittall	27
M.J. Horne	c J.A. Rennie, b P.A. Strang	11
C.D. McMillan	c Wishart, b P.A. Strang	3
C.L. Cairns	b A.R. Whittall	0
C.Z. Harris	not out	54
A.C. Parore †	c A. Flower, b Viljoen	7
D.J. Nash	c J.A. Rennie, b P.A. Strang	28
D.L. Vettori	c A. Flower, b Streak	21
S.B. Doull	not out	5
	lb 4, w 8	12
	50 overs (for 9 wickets)	231

	O	M	R	W
Streak	5	–	38	1
J.A. Rennie	5	–	45	1
P.A. Strang	10	1	44	3
Viljoen	10	–	35	1
A.R. Whittall	10	1	24	2
G.W. Flower	10	–	41	1

Fall of Wickets
1–3, 2–75, 3–88, 4–96, 5–96, 6–121, 7–135, 8–181, 9–213

Zimbabwe

G.W. Flower	c Fleming, b McMillan	55
C.B. Wishart	b Cairns	6
M.W. Goodwin	b Harris	27
A. Flower †	b Vettori	27
A.D.R. Campbell *	c Astle, b Vettori	30
G.J. Whittall	c Horne, b Doull	29
D.P. Viljoen	b Vettori	14
H.H. Streak	b Cairns	2
P.A. Strang	run out	23
J.A. Rennie	not out	2
A.R. Whittall	not out	1
	b 4, lb 6, w 2, nb 1	13
	50 overs (for 9 wickets)	229

	O	M	R	W
Doull	7	1	54	1
Cairns	10	–	43	2
Nash	7	–	26	–
Vettori	10	1	29	3
Harris	9	–	42	1
McMillan	7	–	25	1

Fall of Wickets
1–19, 2–76, 3–106, 4–143, 5–162, 6–180, 7–190, 8–224, 9–228

Umpires: D.B. Cowie & D.M. Quested *Man of the Match*: D.L. Vettori

New Zealand won by 2 runs

Shell Trophy

New Zealand's premier first-class competition was somewhat suffocated by the very full international programme, but the leading players were available to appear in several matches for their associations before doing battle with Australia and Zimbabwe and taking off for Sharjah and Sri Lanka. The Shell Trophy was limited to each side meeting the other in one four-day game, with the two top teams in the qualifying league competing in the final. The Trophy matches were completed in just under two months.

28, 29, 30 and 31 January 1998

at Basin Reserve, Wellington
Otago 231 for 9 dec. (M.J. Horne 90, M.P. Maynard 84, H.T. Davis 4 for 47) and 157 for 5 dec. (H.T. Davis 4 for 38)
Wellington 128 (P.J.B. Chandler 53, P.J. Wiseman 6 for 53) and 102 (S.B. O'Connor 6 for 31)
Otago won by 158 runs
Otago 6 pts, Wellington 0 pts

at Eden Park, Auckland
Canterbury 232 (S.P. Fleming 89, L.K. Germon 60) and 275 (S.P. Fleming 76, C.Z. Harris 61, B.J. Walker 8 for 107)
Auckland 176 (R.D. Burson 6 for 35) and 159 (A.C. Parore 63, M.W. Priest 4 for 70)
Canterbury won by 172 runs
Canterbury 6 pts, Auckland 0 pts

at Queen Elizabeth Park, Masterton
Northern Districts 403 (D.J. Nash 125, A.R. Tait 77, M.D. Bailey 55, G.E. Bradburn 50, C.E. Bulfin 5 for 99)
Central Districts 197 (M.S. Sinclair 55) and 142 (M.J. Greatbatch 53, D.L. Vettori 5 for 28)
Northern Districts won by an innings and 64 runs
Northern Districts 6 pts, Central Districts 0 pts

The first round of matches saw three crushing victories for the away sides. No play was possible on the second day in Wellington, so Lawson declared Otago's innings at the overnight score. Horne and Glamorgan's Matthew Maynard had shared a fourth wicket partnership of 128 after three wickets had gone for 14. Paul Wiseman, pressing for a place in the Test side, routed the home side on the third day, and another Test candidate, the left-arm pace bowler Shayne O'Connor, played a major part in Otago's victory on the last afternoon when Wellington lost their first seven wickets for 58 runs.

Canterbury were 7 for three and 67 for six before being rescued by the former and present New Zealand captains, Germon and Fleming, who added 112. Newcomer Burson made a fine impression with bat and ball, and, in spite of the young spinner Walker returning the best bowling figures of the season, Canterbury went on to win with ease. The match was over in three days.

So, too, was the match at Masterton. Dion Nash's return to cricket had witnessed an advance in batting. He hit a maiden first-class hundred in the Conference and followed it with his first century in the Shell Trophy. He and Alex Tait, who made a career-best 77, added 136 for Northern Districts's seventh wicket. Central offered little in return. Vettori had match figures of eight for 91.

2, 3 and 4 February 1998

Wellington 544 (S.R. Mather 170, M.R. Jefferson 114, T.A. Boyer 79, W.A. Wisneski 4 for 91)
Canterbury 183 and 257 (B.J.K. Doody 77, R.M. Frew 58)
Wellington won by an innings and 104 runs
Wellington 6 pts, Canterbury 0 pts

Stephen Mather hit the second and higher century of his career, and Mark Jefferson passed 50 in a first-class match for the first time as Wellington beat a Canterbury side whose leading players were on international duty in three days. Jefferson's 114 came off 135 balls and included 16 fours. He came in at number nine and made his runs out of 153 scored while he was at the wicket, a remarkable 74.5 per cent.

14, 15, 16 and 17 February 1998

at Westpac Trust Park, Hamilton
Auckland 249 (I.S. Billcliff 94) and 117
Northern Districts 167 and 202 for 7 (M.N. Hart 55, K.P. Walmsley 6 for 49)
Northern Districts won by 3 wickets
Northern Districts 6 pts, Auckland 2 pts

at Carisbrook, Dunedin
Central Districts 135 (M.W. Douglas 75) and 287 (M.S. Sinclair 81, C.M. Spearman 64)
Otago 108 (M.J. Mason 4 for 22, L.J. Hamilton 4 for 37) and 317 for 7 (M.H. Richardson 162 not out, M.J. Mason 4 for 87)
Otago won by 3 wickets
Otago 6 pts, Central Districts 2 pts

Northern Districts and Otago both claimed their second victories of the season, and both had trailed on the first innings. Auckland lost to Northern in spite of heroic efforts from Kerry Walmsley, who returned the best bowling figures of his career. In Dunedin, the hero was the left-hander Mark Richardson, who batted for 512 minutes, faced 402 balls and hit 21 fours in his unbeaten 162. It was the highest score of his career, and it took Otago to an outstanding victory over Central Districts. The match was completed in three days.

22, 23, 24 and 25 February 1998

at Queen's Park, Invercargill
Otago 123 and 189
Canterbury 211 (L.G. Howell 64, R.J. Kennedy 6 for 61) and 107 for 3
Canterbury won by 7 wickets
Canterbury 6 pts, Otago 0 pts

at Westpac Trust Park, Hamilton
Northern Districts 424 for 9 dec. (M.E. Parlane 121, M.D. Bailey 91, R.G. Petrie 4 for 79)
Wellington 131 (T.A. Boyer 75, A.R. Tait 4 for 42) and 186 for 4 (M.D. Bell 56)
Match drawn
Northern Districts 2 pts, Wellington 0 pts

at Pukekura Park, New Plymouth
Central Districts 321 for 8 dec. (M.S. Sinclair 93, M.D.J. Walker 86, C.M. Spearman 72, A.C. Barnes 4 for 60) and 22 for 1 dec.
Auckland 0 for 0 dec. and 279 (R.A. Jones 98, H.D. Barton 57, D.C. Blake 5 for 63)
Central Districts won by 64 runs
Central Districts 6 pts, Auckland 0 pts

Canterbury thoroughly trounced the previously unbeaten Otago in spite of losing most of the second day to rain. Put in to bat, Otago were routed by a varied attack in which Mark Hastings's medium pace brought him three for 12 in 12 overs. Llorne Howell made 64 off 53 balls, with two sixes and nine fours, as Canterbury moved into the lead. They did not let their advantage slip, in spite of being deprived of the services of Priest on the last day when he was called into the New Zealand squad. He was replaced by Pawson.

In Hamilton, rain on the last two days deprived Northern Districts of victory over Wellington. Mike Parlane hit three sixes and 12 fours in his 265-ball innings. There was no play possible on the second or third days at New Plymouth. Matthew Walker and Craig Spearman scored 141 for Central's first wicket, and Matthew Sinclair followed with 93 off 188 balls. He hit 15 fours. Greatbatch declared at the first day score, and Pocock declared after two balls. Richard Jones batted bravely in an attempt to bring Auckland victory, but he was run out for 98 after sharing a fourth wicket stand of 140 with Barton.

10, 11, 12 and 13 March 1998

at Eden Park, Auckland
Auckland 115 (P.J. Wiseman 4 for 16) and 299 (R.A. Jones 62, A.R. Adams 58, P.J. Wiseman 5 for 108)
Otago 425 (M.J. Horne 241)
Otago won by an innings and 11 runs
Otago 6 pts, Auckland 0 pts

at Dudley Park, Rangiora
Canterbury 375 (S.P. Fleming 95, C.D. McMillan 94, A.R. Tait 5 for 118)
Northern Districts 213 (M.N. Hart 82, C.L. Cairns 6 for 55) and 160 (C.L. Cairns 4 for 25)

Canterbury won by an innings and 2 runs
Canterbury 6 pts, Northern Districts 0 pts

at Basin Reserve, Wellington
Central Districts 460 for 4 dec. (C.M. Spearman 144, M.J. Greatbatch 139 not out, G.P. Sulzberger 67 not out) and 0 for 0 dec.
Wellington 143 for 0 dec. (M.D. Bell 71 retired hurt, R.G. Twose 60 not out) and 318 for 3 (R.G. Twose 109, M.D. Bell 98)
Wellington won by 7 wickets
Wellington 6 pts, Central Districts 2 pts

Otago beat Auckland inside three days and were level on points with Canterbury at the top of the table. Matt Horne continued his wonderful run with the first double century of his career. He hit a six and 30 fours and batted for five minutes under eight hours. He faced 371 deliveries. He was rivalled as Man of the Match by Paul Wiseman, the 27-year old off-break bowler, who had match figures of nine for 124.

No play was possible on the second day in Dudley Park, where Test colleagues Fleming and McMillan both missed centuries after playing exciting innings. Fleming's 95 came off 106 balls and included 17 fours, while McMillan hit five sixes amd 10 fours in his 127-ball 94. A third member of the New Zealand side, Chris Cairns, also had an outstanding game. He had match figures of ten for 80.

There was more big hitting at Basin Reserve, where Spearman hit two sixes and 20 fours and Greatbatch was more subdued. There was no play on the second day, and Central forfeited the second innings, leaving Wellington the final day in which to score 318 to win. An opening stand of 179 in 203 minutes between Twose and Bell made the task a simple one.

15, 16, 17 and 18 March 1998

at Westpac Trust Park, Hamilton
Otago 213 (C.B. Gaffaney 65, A.R. Tait 6 for 73) and 162 (D.L. Vettori 5 for 22)
Northern Districts 372 (M.D. Bailey 180 not out, S.B. O'Connor 5 for 122) and 6 for 1
Northern Districts won by 9 wickets
Northern Districts 6 pts, Otago 0 pts

at Fitzherbert Park, Palmerston North
Central Districts 213 (C.S. Martin 5 for 44) and 185 (G.S. Milnes 107)
Canterbury 279 (M.W. Priest 78, D.C. Blake 4 for 76) and 120 for 1 (G.D. Cumming 57 not out)
Canterbury won by 9 wickets
Canterbury 6 pts, Central Districts 0 pts

at Eden Park, Auckland
Wellington 501 for 3 dec. (M.D. Bell 216, J.D. Wells 115, R.G. Twose 87) and 144 for 2 dec. (M.D. Bell 67)
Auckland 305 for 2 dec. (B.A. Pocock 114 not out, A.C. Parore 111 not out, L. Vincent 51) and 300 (A.C. Parore 87, R.G. Twose 4 for 24)
Wellington won by 40 runs
Wellington 6 pts, Auckland 0 pts

Otago fell at the last fence. Put in to bat on a rain-restricted first day, they began well enough, but, on the second morning, they lost their last seven wickets for 51 runs. Mark Bailey held the Northern innings together. He was at the crease in the third over and batted for 406 minutes to remain unbeaten for the highest score of his career. He faced 392 balls and hit a six and 20 fours. His 180 not out was his third century of the season, as many as he had scored in his seven previous seasons in first-class cricket. When Otago batted a second time they fell to the left-arm spin of Daniel Vettori, whose five for 22 represented the best figures of his brief, mercurial career. The win put Northern Districts in the final.

Canterbury confirmed their place in the final with a win over Central Districts who, perhaps unwisely, chose to bat first when they won the toss on a first day truncated by rain. On the second morning, they lost five wickets for 22 runs before effecting a late recovery. Canterbury's recovery was more dramatic. They were 59 for six before climbing to 189 for eight, but it was a ninth wicket stand of 86 at a run a minute between Priest and Wisneski that gave them a hold on the match. Milnes, playing in only his second match, scored a maiden hundred, but Canterbury were not to be denied.

Auckland suffered their fifth defeat in as many matches, and the paucity of their bowling was again in evidence. Twose and Bell began Wellington's first innings with a stand of 153 in 145 minutes. Bell and Wells then added 287 for the second wicket, so beating the previous record of 252, which had stood for 79 years. Matthew Bell's 216 came off 376 and included 31 fours. It was, in fact, a maiden first-class hundred for the 21-year old. It was the second time in a week that a double century had been scored against the Auckland attack. Jason Wells, seven years Bell's senior, made the highest score of his career. Auckland responded vigously with Pocock and Parore sharing an unbroken third wicket partnership of 203 in 129 minutes. Parore's 111 came off 92 balls and included eight sixes and 10 fours. Auckland were left the final day in which to score 341 to win, but, in spite of another fine knock from Parore, they fell short of their target, losing their last seven wickets for 68 runs.

Shell Trophy Final Table

	P	W	L	D	Pts
Canterbury	5	4	1	–	24
Northern Districts	5	3	1	1	20
Wellington	5	3	1	1	18
Otago	5	3	2	–	18
Central Districts	5	1	4	–	10
Auckland	5	–	5	–	2

(Top two teams qualify for the final)

Shell Trophy Final

22, 23 and 24 March 1998
at Dudley Park, Rangiora
Canterbury 524 (W.A. Wisneski 89 not out, L.K. Germon 80, N.J. Astle 79, C.D. Cumming 58, C.D. McMillan 54, S.B. Doull 4 for 106)
Northern Districts 218 (M.D. Bailey 65, C.L. Cairns 4 for 39) and 250 (G.E. Bradburn 86 not out, M.W. Priest 4 for 24)
Canterbury won by an innings and 56 runs

Canterbury confirmed their status as the leading side in New Zealand by winning the Shell Trophy in resounding style. Germon won the toss and saw his side enjoy a fast pitch and an encouraging outfield to race to 364 for nine, at which point, the captain himself was joined by Wisneski. By the end of the day, they had taken the score to 432, and by the time Germon was caught of Bradburn, their partnership was worth 160. The runs had come in 149 minutes, and the stand was the second largest for the tenth wicket in New Zealand first-class cricket. Warren Wisneski's 89 not out came off 138 balls and included a six and 12 fours. It was the highest score ever made by a number 11 in New Zealand and was the fifth and highest of Wisneski's first-class fifties.

When Northern Districts batted their top order was demolished by Chris Cairns, and by the end of the second day, they were following on. The game, scheduled for four days, was over in three with Priest celebrating his renaissance season with four wickets. At the end of the match, Lee Germon announced that he was retiring from first-class cricket. He will be much missed. He has been an outstanding provincial captain, and his leadership of New Zealand in 12 Tests and 37 one-day internationals played a major part in helping the national side to restructure after a lean period. It was sad that his own form at international level never quite reached the heights that had been anticipated.

First-Class Averages

Batting

	M	Inns	NOs	Runs	HS	Av	100s	50s
J.D. Wells	5	7	5	259	115	129.50	1	
T.A. Boyer	4	4	1	211	79	70.33	2	
A.C. Parore	4	6	1	349	111*	69.80	1	3
M.J. Horne	6	10	1	625	241	69.44	2	1
S.P. Fleming	6	8	1	407	95	58.14	3	
C.D. McMillan	6	7	–	380	139	54.28	1	3
M.D. Bailey	11	16	1	786	180*	52.40	3	3
M.D. Bell	14	14	1	661	216	50.84	1	5
D.J. Nash	7	8	–	385	125	48.12	2	1
B.A. Pocock	5	9	2	327	114*	46.71	2	
N.J. Astle	5	6	–	272	114	45.33	1	1
S.R. Mather	5	8	1	298	170	42.57	1	
M.S. Sinclair	9	14	1	529	95	40.69	5	
R.G. Twose	7	12	2	405	109	40.50	1	3
M.N. Hart	10	14	–	553	82	39.50	6	
C.D. Cumming	10	17	2	580	103	38.66	1	3
M.H. Richardson	9	17	4	494	162*	38.00	1	2
M.J. Greatbatch	8	12	1	411	139*	37.36	1	2
M.E. Parlane	10	14	–	494	190	35.28	2	2
L.K. Germon	6	8	–	281	80	35.12	2	
C.M. Spearman	9	14	–	484	144	34.57	1	3
G.R. Stead	7	8	–	264	96	34.25	1	
S.B. Styris	4	6	1	167	47	33.40		
G.E. Bradburn	7	10	1	296	86*	32.88	3	
G.S. Milnes	2	4	–	124	107	31.00	1	
G.J. Hopkins	5	7	1	184	47	30.66		
R.G. Petrie	5	8	4	122	32*	30.50		
P.J.B. Chandler	8	10	2	243	59	30.37	2	
I.S. Billcliff	5	8	–	241	94	30.12	1	
M.P. Maynard	4	7	–	204	84	29.14	1	
M.W. Douglas	5	7	–	196	75	28.00	2	
L. Vincent	2	4	–	110	51	27.50	1	
W.A. Wisneski	10	14	3	298	89*	27.09	1	
A.R. Tait	8	11	2	240	77	26.66	1	
C.Z. Harris	4	5	–	133	61	26.60	1	
A.J. Gale	3	5	–	126	57	25.20	1	
R.M. Frew	2	4	–	100	58	25.00	1	
M.R. Jefferson	7	6	–	144	114	24.00	1	
C.B. Gaffaney	10	18	–	432	112	24.00	1	1
J.A.H. Marshall	4	7	1	143	39	23.83		
L.G. Howell	8	14	1	300	64	23.07	1	
B.J. Walker	6	9	2	195	44	22.14		
D.J. Murray	9	17	1	352	110	22.00	1	1
J.M. Allan	3	5	–	110	36	22.00		
R.A. Jones	8	14	–	301	98	21.50	2	
M.D.J. Walker	6	10	1	190	86	21.11	1	
G.P. Sulzberger	5	8	2	119	67*	19.83	1	
M.W. Priest	8	10	1	178	78	19.77	1	
R.G. Hart	10	14	3	216	57	19.63	2	
H.D. Barton	5	7	–	133	57	19.00	2	
R.A. Lawson	7	13	–	237	38	18.23		

Batting

	M	Inns	NOs	Runs	HS	Av	100s	50s
C.J.M. Furlong	7	10	2	142	49*	17.75		
B.J.K. Doddy	3	6	–	106	77	17.66	1	
D.L. Vettori	6	8	2	103	39	17.16		
M.G. Croy	6	8	1	103	47	14.71		
P.J. Wiseman	10	15	5	120	25	12.00		
A.C. Barnes	9	14	–	160	45	11.42		
C.E. Bulfin	7	10	1	101	37	11.22		

(Qualification – 100 runs, average 10.00)

Bowling

	Overs	Mds	Runs	Wks	Best	Av	10/m	5/inn
R.G. Twose	87.2	30	171	11	4/24	15.54		
C.L. Cairns	167.4	49	425	25	6/55	17.00	1	1
S.B. O'Connor	120.4	32	362	21	6/31	17.23	2	
A.R. Tait	229.2	69	675	38	6/73	17.76	3	
B.J. Walker	109.3	19	373	20	8/107	18.65	1	
P.J. Wiseman	351.1	100	836	44	6/53	19.00	2	
K.P. Walmsley	168.4	36	464	24	6/49	19.33	2	
S.B. Doull	154.4	43	394	20	4/35	19.70		
R.J. Kennedy	131.4	31	380	19	6/61	20.00	1	
C.J. Drum	208.1	62	551	27	5/65	20.40	1	
M.J. Haslam	205.1	69	433	21	5/25	20.61	1	
W.A. Wisneski	353	104	865	41	4/37	21.09		
M.J. Mason	130.3	34	344	16	4/22	21.50		
C.E. Bulfin	167.4	43	471	21	5/99	22.42	1	
D.G. Sewell	287.5	67	838	36	5/34	23.27	2	
M.N. Hart	197.1	61	448	19	4/30	23.57		
S.J. Hotter	97	24	286	12	5/65	23.83	1	
D.L. Vettori	186.3	59	509	20	5/22	25.45	2	
G.E. Bradburn	93.2	30	256	10	3/20	25.60		
D.R. Tuffey	157	42	420	16	3/37	26.25		
D.J. Nash	133	46	271	10	3/41	27.10		
C.S. Martin	150.2	45	395	14	5/44	28.21	1	
M.W. Priest	279	65	716	25	4/24	28.64		
G.R. Jonas	179.4	44	506	17	5/102	29.76	1	
M.R. Jefferson	218.4	57	585	19	5/42	30.78	1	
A.C. Barnes	133	22	416	13	4/60	32.00		
H.T. Davis	151.1	29	619	19	4/38	32.57		
C.J.M. Furlong	237	64	689	15	4/66	45.93		

(Qualification – 10 wickets)

Leading Fielders

35 – R.G. Hart; 22 – L.K. Germon; 15 – M.G. Croy (ct 14 / st 1); 14 – M.D. Bailey and W.A. Wisneski; 13 – A.C. Parore (ct 12 / st 1), M.A. Sigley (ct 12 / st 1) and B.A. Young; 12 – C.B. Gaffaney; 9 – P.J.B. Chandler, M.N. Hart and B.J. Lyon

Zimbabwe

Following their excellent showing against England the previous season, Zimbabwe looked forward confidently to visits from both New Zealand and Pakistan and to their own tours to Kenya, Sri Lanka and New Zealand. Because of the early arrival of the New Zealanders, the Logan Cup, Zimbabwe's domestic competition, began in August with the third and final match scheduled after the conclusion of the one-day series.

Mpumelelo Mbangwa gave pace an accuracy to the Zimbabwe attack.
(Andrew Cornaga / Sportsline)

Zimbabwe were encouraged by the fact that Dave Houghton relinquished his coaching post at Worcestershire to accept the position of national coach to his native country. There was further good news for the world's youngest Test nation when it was learned that Murray Goodwin, who had enjoyed considerable success as a member of Western Australia's Sheffield Shield side after emigrating to Australia as a teenager in 1986, was returning to Zimbabwe and would be available for the Test side. He would undoubtedly be a fine addition to the batting strength. Another to return to the fold was leg-spinner Adam Huckle, who had been operating in South Africa.

Logan Cup

28, 29 and 30 August 1997
at Harare South Country Club
Mashonaland 'A' 181 (G.J. Rennie 101) and 158 (G.J. Rennie 50, G.W. Flower 5 for 37)
Mashonaland 485 for 8 dec. (A. Flower 201, C.B. Wishart 144)
Mashonaland won by an innings and 146 runs

A splendid century by Rennie was the feature of the opening day. He reached his hundred off 183 balls in 216 minutes and hit 13 fours. The innings did much to win him a place in the Test side. His efforts proved of little value, as the 'A' side were overwhelmed by the senior's, for whom Andy Flower hit a maiden first-class double century and shared a third wicket stand of 295 with Wishart. Andy Flower's 201 came off 281 balls and included 26 fours. Brother Grant returned the best bowling figures of his career, five for 37, seven for 79 in the match.

4 and 5 September 1997
at Old Hararians Sports Club
Mashonaland 307 (A. Flower 116, G.W. Flower 89)
Matabeleland 129 (H.H. Streak 61 not out, B.C. Strang 5 for 49) and 142
Mashonaland won by an innings and 36 runs

Mashonaland won the Logan Cup when they gained their second innings victory, beating Matabeleland inside two days. Andy Flower made his second three-figured innings in succession, sharing a third wicket partnership of 161 with brother Grant.

23, 24 and 25 October 1997
at Bulawayo Athletic Club
Mashonaland 'A' 312 (M.W. Goodwin 78, T.L. Penney 76, J.A. Rennie 9 for 76) and 279 for 5 dec. (M.W. Goodwin 78)
Matabeleland 300 for 7 dec. (H.H. Streak 81, J.R. Craig 76) and 217 for 9 (J.A. Rennie 64, G.J. Whittall 61)
Match drawn

Murray Goodwin played his first first-class match in Zimbabwe in this final game in the Logan Cup. The encounter had little meaning as Mashonaland had already claimed the trophy, but Goodwin heartened selectors by scoring 78 in each innings. His second innings' knock was a spectacular affair, occupying only 46 balls and containing four sixes and nine fours. Mashonaland 'A' were led by Warwickshire's Trevor Penney, and Zimbabwe always nurse the dream that he and Hick could one day return to the fold. The outstanding feature of the match was the bowling of medium-pacer John Rennie on the opening day. He returned career best figures of nine for 76, the best analysis recorded since independence. Set to score 292 in 52 overs to win, Matabeleland just fell short in an exciting finish. Their captain, Heath Streak, did not bowl in the match because of an injury to his side.

New Zealand Tour

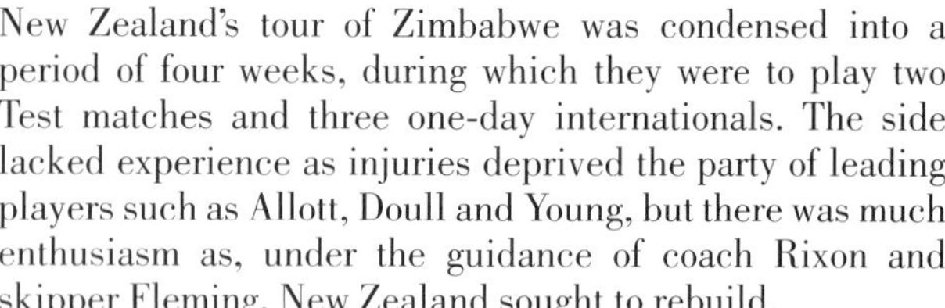

New Zealand's tour of Zimbabwe was condensed into a period of four weeks, during which they were to play two Test matches and three one-day internationals. The side lacked experience as injuries deprived the party of leading players such as Allott, Doull and Young, but there was much enthusiasm as, under the guidance of coach Rixon and skipper Fleming, New Zealand sought to rebuild.

12 September 1997
at Harare South Country Club
Zimbabwe Country Districts 190 for 6 (G.J. Rennie 74)
New Zealanders 194 for 8 (A.G. Huckle 4 for 38)
New Zealanders won by 2 wickets

The New Zealanders opened their tour with a fifty-over match against a strong Country Districts XI. Gavin Rennie and Bruk-Jackson batted well for the home side, while the tourists were somewhat perplexed by the leg-spin of Adam Huckle. They won with 7.2 overs to spare, but their eighth wicket went down at 151, and it was left to Cairns and Davis to see them home.

13, 14 and 15 September 1997
at Alexandra Sports Club, Harare
New Zealanders 174 (B.C. Strang 4 for 45) and 336 for 5 (M.J. Horne 181)
Mashonaland 351 (C.N. Evans 63, D.L. Houghton 59, G.W. Flower 55)
Match drawn

The home side could claim the advantage in the one first-class match in which the New Zealanders were engaged outside the Test series. The visitors fared badly on the opening day, losing their first five wickets for 43 runs. They succumbed to hostile pace bowling by Bryan Strang and Everton Matambanadzo. The last two wickets realised 74 runs to effect some sort of respectability. In contrast, Mashonaland batted consistently and took the lead with only three wickets down. The New Zealanders lost Pocock before the end of the second day, but Matthew showed great application on the final day, facing 303 deliveries and hitting 24 fours.

Test Series

Zimbabwe *v.* New Zealand

Zimbabwe introduced two players to Test cricket, Gavin Rennie and Adam Huckle, for the first encounter in Harare. New Zealand gave a first Test cap to left-arm medium-pace bowler Shayne O'Connor. In bringing Gavin Rennie into their side, Zimbabwe uniquely fielded three pairs of brothers, the Rennies, the Flowers and the Strangs. Fleming won the toss and asked Zimbabwe to bat first.

Gavin Rennie showed a positive approach on his debut. An hour was lost to rain at the start and overcast conditions did not make batting easy. Grant Flower took 40 minutes to open his score, but he and Rennie gave their side a solid beginning. Andy Flower went cheaply, but brother Grant proved immovable and was unbeaten on 85 at the close, with Zimbabwe 205 for four.

Grant Flower proved himself to be a Test batsman of high quality in 1997–1998. He scored a century in each innings of the first Test against New Zealand and carried his bat through the first innings of the first Test against Pakistan for 156.
(Sportsline)

New Zealand took a grip on the game on the second morning when they quickly accounted for Grant Flower, Houghton and Streak to reduce Zimbabwe to 244 for seven. The New Zealand position would have been stronger had Spearman not dropped Paul Strang in the gully. As it was, Paul Strang hit 42 and shared an eighth wicket stand of 51 in an hour with John Rennie. The last three wickets went down in 17 balls just after lunch. When Fleming caught John Rennie at slip he equalled the Test record with five catches in an innings, and Chris Cairns finished with five for 50, his fourth five-wicket haul in Test cricket.

Spearman was dropped at short-leg off the first ball of the innings, and he and Pocock appeared untroubled until Pocock was run out going for an unwise third run. Spearman fell next ball, caught at second slip, and Horne, having hooked one six, was caught at fine-leg attempting another. New Zealand ended the day on 91 for three.

Bryan Strang, left-arm fast medium, bowled well for Zimbabwe and had Astle caught behind early on the third morning. Cairns might also have gone quickly when he appeared to edge Streak to Gavin Rennie at short-leg, but the third umpire (G.R. Evans), newly empowered to deal with such matters, ruled not out. Adam Parore stood firm after the departure of Fleming, but the combined leg-spin of Huckle and Paul Strang was too much for the tail, and the last four wickets went down for 18 runs to give Zimbabwe a precious advantage of 91. Gavin Rennie and Grant Flower soon consolidated that advantage by taking the score to 115 by the close without being separated.

The pair took their opening stand to 156, a Zimbabwe record, on the fourth morning before Gavin Rennie fell to fellow debutant O'Connor. Both could draw satisfaction from their performances on their first appearances in Test cricket. Grant Flower went on to become the first Zimbabwe batsman to score a century in each innings of a Test. He hit three sixes, one of which took him to his century, and 12 fours in his 151, which came off 239 balls. In the course of his innings, he became Zimbabwe's leading run-scorer in Test cricket, the first to pass 1500 runs. The New Zealand over-rate was slow, responding to the size of the target that they were destined to face, and Campbell's declaration shortly after tea set that target at 403 in 128 overs. The odds were very much in favour of a Zimbabwe victory, shortening further when, following an opening stand of 63, two wickets fell quickly, and New Zealand began the last day on 64 for two.

Pocock and Fleming offered stern resistance on the last morning, and it was 80 minutes into the day before Fleming was leg before to Bryan Strang. Three balls later, Astle, so vital a part of the New Zealand side, edged Bryan Strang to gully, and when Pocock was out in the first over after lunch, New Zealand were 122 for five and looked doomed. Cairns and Parore then came together in a stand worth 78. Parore chose to attack, hitting 10 fours in his

A maiden first-class century in the Logan Cup earned Gavin Rennie a Test debut against New Zealand.
(Sportsline)

innings of 51, which came off 53 balls. He was finally out to Huckle, who marred his Test debut by being fined and receiving a suspended one-match ban. Huckle had displayed intimidatory attitudes to an umpire and had gesticulated at the batsman. His skipper, Campbell, was cautioned, and Parore was more than fortunate to escape censure.

Cairns' commitment to the New Zealand cause has not always seemed to be total, but he settled to curb his aggressive tendencies and to bat in a manner that saved his side from defeat when all had seemed lost. In all, he was at the crease for four hours 20 minutes and faced 238 balls. He hit Huckle for six and also hit seven fours. He offered one chance, edging to first slip when he was on 46. Houghton appeared to be unsighted, and the ball slipped through his hands. Cairns was given brave support by the later order. Harris held out for 82 balls, the precocious Vettori for 48, and, perhaps most courageous of all, O'Connor lasted 31 balls for his one not out. It was O'Connor who had to face Paul Strang's final over, and he survived to thwart Zimbabwe and draw the match.

Zimbabwe made one change for the second Test match, Everton Matambanadzo replacing John Rennie, while New Zealand brought in another debutant, young left-arm fast medium-pacer David Sewell, for Heath Davis. Campbell won the toss, and Zimbabwe batted. Gavin Rennie and Grant Flower again gave them a fine start, and by the end of the day, they were a very healthy 283 for four, Guy Whittall 66, Houghton four.

The second day belonged entirely to Guy Whittall. When the innings ended after tea he was unbeaten for 203, the first double century of his career, and he had batted for eight and a quarter hours. He hit two sixes and 22 fours and faced 360 balls. He owed a debt of gratitude to Everton Matambanadzo, who held out for 43 balls to give Whittall the chance to reach his double hundred.

Beginning the third day on 23 without loss, New Zealand entered an uncertain period against the leg-spin duet of Huckle and Paul Strang, who were gaining some assistance from the pitch. When Parore was caught off Huckle, six men were out for 162, and New Zealand were still 100 short of avoiding the follow-on. If New Zealand lack real class at Test level, they certainly do not lack for character and courage, and none has served them better in recent years than Nathan Astle, a cricketer of ability and the utmost determination. He hit two sixes and 13 fours in a forthright innings that brought his side back from the brink of defeat. He and Harris added 97 before Huckle dismissed Astle to achieve the break-through. Harris then found a

Guy Whittall, an unbeaten 203 for Zimbabwe in the second Test against New Zealand.
(Sportsline)

Adam Huckle took 11 wickets on his second appearance in Test cricket, Zimbabwe v. *New Zealand in Bulawayo. (Sportsline)*

most surprising partner in Vettori, who had been impressive as a young slow left-arm bowler and was now a revelation as a batsman. They added 112, and it was Vettori who was the more assertive. He batted for two-and-a-quarter hours and hit 14 fours in what was his highest first-class score. Had he scored ten runs more, he would have become New Zealand's youngest ever century maker. His stand with Harris virtually ensured that New Zealand would not lose. Vettori finally fell to Huckle, who finished with six worthy wickets to his credit, an outstanding performance in what was his second Test match.

Zimbabwe led by 58 on the first innings, and they increased their lead by another 152 for the loss of three wickets by the end of the fourth day, Grant Flower having played another entertaining innings. The home side went for quick runs on the final morning, and Campbell's declaration was challenging and adventurous, very unusual in Test cricket. He asked New Zealand to make 286 in 68 overs. By tea, aided by some unchar-acteristically sloppy fielding that saw four chances and a run out missed, New Zealand were 139 for three. Fleming, who batted with style and panache, was run out by Paul Strang, and the New Zealand challenge began to crumble. When Vettori was run out by Houghton the chase ended, and New Zealand earned the draw in a match and series in which they were generally struggling to survive. Huckle took five wickets in the second innings to give him match figures of 11 for 255, so making him the first Zimbabwe bowler to take ten or more wickets in a Test. Guy Whittall was named Man of the Match, and Grant Flower added the series award to the individual award he had won in the first Test, but for Zimbabwe there was more than a little disappointment.

One-Day International Series

Zimbabwe *v.* New Zealand

Like the Test series, the limited-over series was drawn. The main excitement was in the first encounter. Zimbabwe had seemed to be in sight of a most comfortable victory. They had made a commendable 233 in their fifty overs, a score which owed much to a third wicket stand of 77 between Grant Flower and Campbell, and they had then reduced New Zealand to 178 for eight.The improved batting powers of Vettori were again in evidence as he joined Harris in a stand worth 41. The wily Larsen came together with Harris, and the pair added 55, bringing the scores level. Larsen was run out on the last ball of the match as he went for what would have been the winning run. New Zealand's hero was Chris Harris, whose unbeaten 77 came off 103 balls. He took 92 balls to reach his fifty and had come to the wicket with his side on 100 for six.

The second match was a strange affair. Electing to bat when they won the toss, New Zealand found run-getting difficult. Astle and Horne had put on 55 for the second wicket when an appeal for run out against Horne went to the third umpire. Technical faults with the television replay caused a delay of five minutes before the verdict went against Horne. The man who thwarted New Zealand was Paul Strang, who conceded only 13 runs in his ten-over spell and bowled the dangerous Astle. Chasing a modest target, Zimbabwe were 42 for three, but Gavin Rennie and Campbell added 123 to put their side in sight of victory. Campbell hit three sixes and four fours and faced 116 balls while Gavin Rennie faced 125 balls and hit five fours. Rennie's was the first of four wickets to fall for 15 runs, but Campbell stood firm to see his side to a three-wicket victory. Gavin Rennie and Campbell were the only two batsmen to reach double figures.

The final match saw Zimbabwe field their three pairs of brothers plus the Whittall cousins, but New Zealand were comfortable winners. Cairns was promoted to open the innings and provided the necessary urgency with 71 off 78 balls. He hit a six and nine fours while McMillan hit five sixes in his 59-ball innings. Fleming, too, batted well, but he was fortunate to escape being given out before he had scored when he seemed clearly to have edged the ball to the wicket-keeper. The Flower brothers gave Zimbabwe a good start with 63 off 59 balls, but the middle order offered little, and New Zealand won with ease to level the series.

First Test Match – Zimbabwe v. New Zealand

18, 19, 20, 21 and 22 September 1997 at Harare Sports Club, Harare

Zimbabwe

	First Innings		Second Innings	
G.J. Rennie	**c** Fleming, **b** Cairns	**23**	**c** Harris, **b** O'Connor	**57**
G.W. Flower	**c** Parore, **b** Cairns	**104**	**c** Fleming, **b** O'Connor	**151**
A. Flower †	**c** Spearman, **b** Cairns	**8**	**c** Parore, **b** O'Connor	**20**
G.J. Whittall	**c** Fleming, **b** O'Connor	**33**	run out	**4**
A.D.R. Campbell *	**c** Pocock, **b** Astle	**18**	**c** Fleming, **b** Davis	**21**
D.L. Houghton	lbw, **b** Davis	**23**	**c** Davis, **b** Astle	**1**
P.A. Strang	**c** Fleming, **b** Davis	**42**	**c** Horne, **b** Davis	**17**
H.H. Streak	**c** Fleming, **b** Cairns	**0**	run out	**0**
J.A. Rennie	**c** Fleming, **b** Davis	**22**	**c** and **b** Astle	**16**
B.C. Strang	lbw, **b** Cairns	**1**	not out	**4**
A.G. Huckle	not out	**0**		
	b **1**, lb **5**, w **4**, nb **14**	**24**	lb **12**, nb **8**	**20**
		298	(for 9 wickets, dec.)	**311**

	O	M	R	W	O	M	R	W
O'Connor	26	1	104	**1**	26	3	73	**3**
Davis	20	1	57	**3**	13	2	45	**2**
Cairns	28.1	9	50	**5**	9	–	44	**–**
Astle	23	12	40	**1**	25.5	2	86	**2**
Vettori	4	–	14	**–**	13	2	40	**–**
Harris	13	5	27	**–**	5	3	11	**–**

Fall of Wickets
1–**47**, 2–**57**, 3–**117**, 4–**144**, 5–**214**, 6–**244**, 7–**244**, 8–**295**, 9–**298**
1–**156**, 2–**218**, 3–**230**, 4–**263**, 5–**264**, 6–**290**, 7–**290**, 8–**290**, 9–**311**

New Zealand

	First Innings		Second Innings	
C.M. Spearman	**c** Campbell, **b** B.C. Strang	**23**	(2) **c** A. Flower, **b** Huckle	**33**
B.A. Pocock	run out	**21**	(1) lbw, **b** Streak	**52**
M.J. Horne	**c** G.J. Whittall, **b** Streak	**24**	**c** A. Flower, **b** P.A. Strang	**0**
S.P. Fleming *	**c** A. Flower, **b** B.C. Strang	**52**	lbw, **b** B.C. Strang	**27**
N.J. Astle	**c** A. Flower, **b** B.C. Strang	**7**	**c** G.W. Flower, **b** B.C. Strang	**0**
C.L. Cairns	run out	**12**	not out	**7**[illegible]
A.C. Parore †	not out	**42**	lbw, **b** Huckle	**5**[illegible]
C.Z. Harris	lbw, **b** Huckle	**16**	lbw, **b** Streak	**4**[illegible]
D.L. Vettori	**c** J.A. Rennie, **b** P.A. Strang	**2**	**c** G.J. Rennie, **b** Huckle	**13**
S.B. O'Connor	**c** Houghton, **b** P.A. Strang	**2**	not out	[illegible]
H.T. Davis	**c** G.J. Rennie, **b** Huckle	**1**		
	b **4**, lb **1**	**5**	b **6**, lb **6**, w **1**, nb **2**	**15**
		207	(for 8 wickets)	**304**

	O	M	R	W	O	M	R	W
Streak	21	2	63	**1**	21	3	52	**2**
J.A. Rennie	8	1	32	**–**	3	1	5	**–**
B.C. Strang	19	–	29	**3**	26	10	56	**2**
P.A. Strang	15	2	31	**2**	42	17	76	**1**
G.J. Whittall	5	–	15	**–**	5	1	19	**–**
Huckle	14	3	32	**2**	31	9	84	**3**

Fall of Wickets
1–**44**, 2–**44**, 3–**89**, 4–**96**, 5–**135**, 6–**146**, 7–**189**, 8–**198**, 9–**204**
1–**63**, 2–**64**, 3–**16**, 4–**116**, 5–**122**, 6–**200**, 7–**266**, 8–**296**

Umpires: B.C. Cooray & I.D. Robinson

Match drawn

Second Test Match – Zimbabwe v. New Zealand

25, 26, 27, 28 and 29 September 1997 at Queen's Club, Bulawayo

Zimbabwe

	First Innings		Second Innings	
G.J. Rennie	**c** Harris, **b** O'Connor	**57**	lbw, **b** Astle	**24**
G.W. Flower	**c** Fleming, **b** Vettori	**83**	run out	**49**
A. Flower †	**c** Harris, **b** Vettori	**39**	**c** and **b** Harris	**7**
G.J. Whittall	not out	**203**	run out	**45**
A.D.R. Campbell *	**c** Astle, **b** O'Connor	**7**	not out	**59**
D.L. Houghton	**b** Cairns	**32**	**c** Harris, **b** Vettori	**13**
P.A. Strang	**c** Harris, **b** Vettori	**5**	lbw, **b** Vettori	**2**
H.H. Streak	lbw, **b** Cairns	**17**	run out	**1**
B.C. Strang	**c** Fleming, **b** Cairns	**0**	**b** Cairns	**10**
A.G. Huckle	**c** Parore, **b** Vettori	**0**	not out	**0**
E. Matambanadzo	**c** Fleming, **b** O'Connor	**4**		
	lb **10**, w **2**, nb **2**	**14**	b **2**, lb **7**, w **3**, nb **5**	**17**
		461	(for 8 wickets, dec.)	**227**

	O	M	R	W	O	M	R	W
Sewell	19	3	81	**–**	4	–	8	**–**
O'Connor	27	9	80	**3**	5	–	35	**–**
Cairns	36	10	97	**3**	11	1	49	**1**
Vettori	58	11	165	**4**	18	3	69	**2**
Harris	14	6	13	**–**	17	4	41	**1**
Astle	7	2	15	**–**	9	6	16	**1**

Fall of Wickets
1–**144**, 2–**148**, 3–**218**, 4–**244**, 5–**322**, 6–**343**, 7–**416**, 8–**420**, 9–**421**
1–**75**, 2–**80**, 3–**91**, 4–**172**, 5–**202**, 6–**204**, 7–**205**, 8–**219**

New Zealand

	First Innings		Second Innings	
C.M. Spearman	**c** Huckle, **b** P.A. Strang	**47**	(2) **c** Campbell, **b** Huckle	**27**
B.A. Pocock	lbw, **b** P.A. Strang	**27**	(1) **c** P.A. Strang, **b** Huckle	**62**
M.J. Horne	lbw, **b** P.A. Strang	**55**	**c** Campbell, **b** Huckle	**29**
S.P. Fleming *	**c** P.A. Strang, **b** Huckle	**27**	run out	**75**
N.J. Astle	**c** sub (A.R. Whittall), **b** Huckle	**96**	**c** G.W. Flower, **b** P.A. Strang	**21**
C.L. Cairns	**c** G.J. Rennie, **b** Huckle	**0**	**c** Houghton, **b** Huckle	**8**
A.C. Parore †	**c** G.W. Flower, **b** Huckle	**17**	**c** G.J. Whittall, **b** Huckle	**21**
C.Z. Harris	**b** Huckle	**71**	not out	**14**
D.L. Vettori	**c** B.C. Strang, **b** Huckle	**90**	run out	**7**
S.B. O'Connor	run out	**7**	not out	**0**
D.G. Sewell	not out	**1**		
	b **1**, lb **9**, nb **5**	**15**	b **5**, lb **4**, nb **2**	**11**
		403	(for 8 wickets)	**275**

	O	M	R	W	O	M	R	W
Streak	15	5	26	**–**				
Matambanadzo	15	4	52	**–**	2	–	14	**–**
P.A. Strang	47	19	110	**3**	23	1	81	**1**
Huckle	40.4	10	109	**6**	32	2	146	**5**
B.C. Strang	26	12	50	**–**	8	4	15	**–**
G.J. Whittall	6	1	14	**–**				
G.W. Flower	10	2	19	**–**	3	1	10	**–**
Campbell	2	–	13	**–**				

Fall of Wickets
1–**60**, 2–**76**, 3–**92**, 4–**130**, 5–**130**, 6–**162**, 7–**259**, 8–**371**, 9–**389**
1–**41**, 2–**89**, 3–**138**, 4–**207**, 5–**221**, 6–**240**, 7–**260**, 8–**275**

Umpires: R.B. Tiffin & S. Venkataraghavan

Match drawn

First One-Day International – Zimbabwe v. New Zealand

1 October 1997 at Queen's Club, Bulawayo

Zimbabwe

G.J. Rennie	**c** Fleming, **b** O'Connor	**6**
G.W. Flower	**c** Larsen, **b** Vettori	**66**
A.D.R. Campbell *	**c** Parore, **b** O'Connor	**5**
A. Flower †	**b** Larsen	**35**
G.J. Whittall	**c** Spearman, **b** Larsen	**24**
D.L. Houghton	**c** sub, **b** Astle	**40**
C.N. Evans	run out	**21**
P.A. Strang	not out	**17**
E.A. Brandes	**b** Cairns	**1**
J.A. Rennie	not out	**16**
A.R. Whittall		
	lb **1**, nb **1**	**2**
	50 overs (for 8 wickets)	**233**

	O	M	R	W
O'Connor	8	1	28	**2**
Cairns	10	–	59	**1**
Larsen	10	–	42	**2**
Harris	10	–	40	**–**
Vettori	6	–	42	**1**
Astle	6	–	21	**1**

Fall of Wickets
1–**14**, 2–**24**, 3–**101**, 4–**136**, 5–**139**, 6–**175**, 7–**204**, 8–**206**

New Zealand

C.M. Spearman	**c** A. Flower, **b** J.A. Rennie	**5**
N.J. Astle	**c** Campbell, **b** J.A. Rennie	**5**
M.J. Horne	run out	**55**
S.P. Fleming *	**c** A. Flower, **b** G.J. Whittall	**19**
C.L. Cairns	**c** Brandes, **b** Evans	**26**
C.D. McMillan	run out	**2**
A.C. Parore †	**b** P.A. Strang	**1**
C.Z. Harris	not out	**77**
D.L. Vettori	run out	**18**
G.R. Larsen	run out	**17**
S.B. O'Connor		
	lb **6**, w **2**	**8**
	50 overs (for 9 wickets)	**233**

	O	M	R	W
Brandes	7	–	42	**–**
J.A. Rennie	10	–	47	**2**
G.J. Whittall	2	–	25	**1**
P.A. Strang	10	–	26	**1**
Evans	8	–	39	**1**
A.R. Whittall	10	–	36	**–**
G.W. Flower	3	–	12	**–**

Fall of Wickets
1–**7**, 2–**14**, 3–**49**, 4–**85**, 5–**90**, 6–**100**, 7–**137**, 8–**178**, 9–**233**

Umpires: Q.D. Goosen & R.B. Tiffin *Man of the Match*: C.Z. Harris

Match tied

Second One-Day International – Zimbabwe v. New Zealand

4 October 1997 at Harare Sports Club, Harare

New Zealand

C.M. Spearman	**c** Campbell, **b** J.A. Rennie	**1**
N.J. Astle	**b** P.A. Strang	**36**
M.J. Horne	run out	**22**
S.P. Fleming *	**c** G.J. Rennie, **b** Evans	**5**
C.L. Cairns	**c** J.A. Rennie, **b** Evans	**16**
C.D. McMillan	**st** A. Flower, **b** A.R. Whittall	**38**
A.C. Parore †	**c** A. Flower, **b** J.A. Rennie	**15**
C.Z. Harris	not out	**29**
D.L. Vettori	not out	**3**
G.R. Larsen		
S.B. O'Connor		
	lb **6**, w **13**, nb **1**	**20**
	50 overs (for 7 wickets)	**185**

	O	M	R	W
Brandes	6	–	28	**–**
J.A. Rennie	9	1	48	**2**
G.J. Whittall	5	–	37	**–**
P.A. Strang	10	1	13	**1**
Evans	10	1	27	**2**
A.R. Whittall	10	1	26	**1**

Fall of Wickets
1–**6**, 2–**61**, 3–**74**, 4–**74**, 5–**116**, 6–**143**, 7–**160**

Zimbabwe

G.J. Rennie	lbw, **b** Astle	**72**
G.W. Flower	**c** Cairns, **b** Larsen	**4**
A. Flower †	**c** McMillan, **b** O'Connor	**5**
G.J. Whittall	**c** O'Connor, **b** Harris	**7**
A.D.R. Campbell *	not out	**77**
D.L. Houghton	**c** Vettori, **b** McMillan	**4**
C.N. Evans	**c** O'Connor, **b** Astle	**1**
P.A. Strang	**c** and **b** McMillan	**2**
E.A. Brandes	not out	**4**
J.A. Rennie		
A.R. Whittall		
	b **1**, lb **3**, w **6**, nb **2**	**12**
	48.2 overs (for 7 wickets)	**188**

	O	M	R	W
O'Connor	8	–	40	**1**
Larsen	10	–	32	**1**
Cairns	7	1	25	**–**
Harris	6	1	20	**1**
Astle	9.2	–	28	**2**
Vettori	4	–	22	**–**
McMillan	4	–	17	**2**

Fall of Wickets
1–**12**, 2–**28**, 3–**42**, 4–**165**, 5–**170**, 6–**174**, 7–**180**

Umpires: I.D. Robinson & Q.D. Goosen *Man of the Match*: P.A. Strang

Zimbabwe won by 3 wickets

Third One-Day International – Zimbabwe v. New Zealand

5 October 1997 at Harare Sports Club, Harare

New Zealand

Batsman	How out	Runs
N.J. Astle	**c** and **b** J.A. Rennie	**33**
C.L. Cairns	**c** G.J. Whittall, **b** A.R. Whittall	**71**
S.P. Fleming *	**c** A.R. Whittall, **b** Evans	**62**
M.J. Horne	**c** and **b** G.W. Flower	**13**
C.D. McMillan	**c** A.R. Whittall, **b** B.C. Strang	**66**
C.Z. Harris	not out	**18**
C.M. Spearman	**c** Campbell, **b** B.C. Strang	**0**
A.C. Parore †	**b** B.C. Strang	**14**
D.L. Vettori	not out	**7**
G.R. Larsen		
S.B. O'Connor		
	lb **4**, w **6**	**10**
	50 overs (for 7 wickets)	**294**

	O	M	R	W
J.A. Rennie	10	–	54	**1**
B.C. Strang	10	–	66	**3**
P.A. Strang	10	–	58	**–**
Evans	6	–	40	**1**
A.R. Whittall	9	–	48	**1**
G.W. Flower	5	–	24	**1**

Fall of Wickets
1–**58**, 2–**147**, 3–**164**, 4–**214**, 5–**263**, 6–**264**, 7–**287**

Zimbabwe

Batsman	How out	Runs
G.W. Flower	**c** Astle, **b** Cairns	**24**
A. Flower †	run out	**44**
G.J. Whittall	**b** Astle	**49**
A.D.R. Campbell *	run out	**2**
P.A. Strang	**c** Spearman, **b** Vettori	**27**
D.L. Houghton	run out	**1**
C.N. Evans	**c** Larsen, **b** Vettori	**5**
G.J. Rennie	**c** Vettori, **b** Larsen	**17**
J.A. Rennie	run out	**6**
B.C. Strang	**c** and **b** Vettori	**15**
A.R. Whittall	not out	**14**
	lb **5**, w **2**	**7**
	44.1 overs	**211**

	O	M	R	W
O'Connor	3	–	22	**–**
Larsen	7	–	42	**1**
Cairns	7	1	26	**1**
Harris	10	–	41	**–**
Astle	6	–	22	**1**
Vettori	7.1	–	41	**3**
McMillan	4	–	12	**–**

Fall of Wickets
1–**63**, 2–**92**, 3–**116**, 4–**125**, 5–**126**, 6–**140**, 7–**166**, 8–**176**, 9–**188**

Umpires: I.D. Robinson & R.B. Tiffin *Man of the Match*: C.L. Cairns *Man of the Series*: C.Z. Harris

New Zealand won by 83 runs

Man of the one-day international series between Zimbabwe and New Zealand – Chris Harris, the New Zealand all-rounder. (Ben Radford / Allsport)

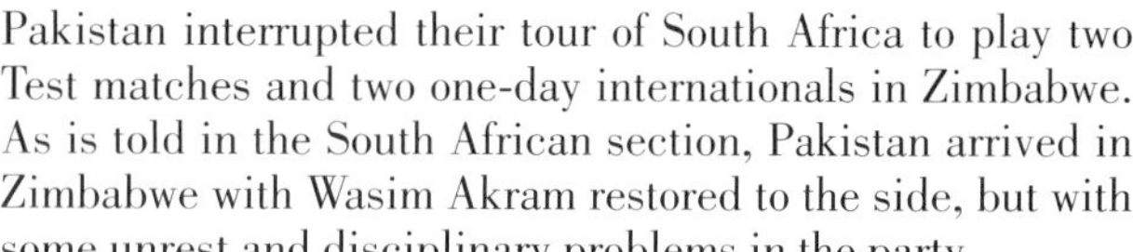

Pakistan Tour

Pakistan interrupted their tour of South Africa to play two Test matches and two one-day internationals in Zimbabwe. As is told in the South African section, Pakistan arrived in Zimbabwe with Wasim Akram restored to the side, but with some unrest and disciplinary problems in the party.

Test Matches

Like all countries, Zimbabwe are becoming difficult to beat in their own country, and they gave a good account of themselves in the first Test against Pakistan. They introduced two players to Test cricket, Trevor Madondo, a right-handed batsman who can keep wicket, and Dirk Viljoen, a left-handed opening batsman and slow left-arm bowler, who had appeared in one-day internatioanls.

Campbell won the toss, and Zimbabwe batted. They began disastrously, losing Viljoen and Goodwin for 'ducks' and having Campbell caught behind for 15 so that three wickets were down for 38. Waqar Younis was at his fastest and best, and Grant Flower showed his class and determination in negotiating this difficult period. His brother Andy joined him in a stand worth 77, but the real substance of the innings came in Grant Flower's partnership of 109 for the seventh wicket with Heath Streak. Andy Whittall helped take the score past 300, and, after their nightmare start, Zimbabwe could be well pleased with a total of 321.

The hero of Zimbabwe was Grant Flower, who became the second batsman from his country to carry his bat through a completed Test innings. He was at the crease for 512 minutes and faced 329 balls. He offered only one chance, when he was on 145, and displayed the utmost discipline and application. Pakistan were handicapped by the absence of both Wasim Akram and Mushtaq Ahmed because of illness, but nothing should detract from the quality of Grant Flower's innings. The Pakistan attack was always testing, with Shoaib Akhtar bowling very quickly and Azhar Mahmood ever a threat. For Waqar, there was another five-wicket haul.

The batting conditions were easier when Pakistan began their innings, but, although several batsmen promised much, only young Yousuf Youhana showed durability, reaching a maiden Test fifty on his second appearance at this level. Guy Whittall bowled his medium pace well, and the Zimbabwe attack, backed by keen fielding, was disciplined. The home side took a valuable first innings lead of 65.

It seemed that Pakistan had regained the advantage when they captured the first four wickets in Zimbabwe's second innings for 25 runs, but then came a record stand of 277 in 68 overs between Murray Goodwin and Andy Flower. This was the highest partnership for any Zimbabwe wicket. Goodwin, playing in his first Test in Zimbabwe, made 166 off 204 balls and proved himself to be a fine player of both pace and spin. His return to his native country has provided a tremendous boost to Zimbabwe cricket. Andy Flower reached 100 off 217 balls, and Campbell immediately declared. Pakistan were left a target of 368 in four sessions.

They began uncertainly and were reduced to 80 for four shortly after lunch on the final day, but Campbell lacks belief in himself and in his side. He failed to pressurise the opposition, and Yousuf Youhana and Moin Khan added 110. They were both dismissed, but still Campbell remained negative and even called the game off with 7.3 overs remaining, which astonished Pakistan.

For the second Test, Zimbabwe brought in Gavin Rennie for Viljoen, Huckle for the injured Paul Strang, and Bryan Strang for Andy Whittall. Pakistan welcomed back Wasim Akram and Mushtaq Ahmed and left out Shoaib Akhtar and Saqlain Mushtaq, while Mohammad Wasim came in for the injured Ijaz Ahmed. Once again Campbell won the toss; once again Zimbabwe batted first.

The pitch was slow, and batting was not easy, but Zimbabwe began sensibly and solidly and were 141 for two shortly before tea. From this point, they crashed to 153 for seven as five wickets went down in as many overs. Goodwin lost patience against Mushtaq and was out to a poor shot, and poor Madondo, the fourth black cricketer to play for Zimbabwe, was needlessly run out by Yousuf Youhana without facing a shot. Revival came from Guy Whittall and

Pakistan's victory in the second Test match owed much to an outstanding innings of 192, the highest of his career, from Mohammad Wasim.
(Stephen Laffer / Sportsline)

Bryan Strang, who put on 110 in 28 overs. The younger Strang reached a maiden Test fifty off 78 balls and clouted Mushtaq for six. Once they were separated, the innings quickly folded.

The Pakistan batsmen were tempted and frustrated by the Zimbabwe seamers and sold their wickets cheaply, all save Mohammad Wasim. Still short of his 21st birthday, the right-hander showed magnificent temperament in reaching his second, and higher, Test century. His innings rightly earned him the individual award and made possible a Pakistan victory. Zimbabwe erred badly in the field. Vital catches were dropped, and Pakistan, having seemed certain to trail on the first innings, took a lead of 77. Mohammad Wasim and Mushtaq Ahmed added 147 in 49 overs for the ninth wicket, and both batsmen were put down off straightforward chances. Mohammad Wasim's 192 was the highest score of his career, and he batted for 560 minutes.

Zimbabwe had thrown the game away, and their plight became worse when they were reduced to 38 for three in their second innings. It was Goodwin and Andy Flower who again showed admirable class and temperament as they added 95 in 42 overs at a time when Waqar, Wasim and Azhar Mahmood threatened to run through the side. Goodwin made his second fifty of the match, but he was out to the second new ball, caught at slip off a widish delivery, and although Streak struck some lusty blows, Zimbabwe were out for 268, and Pakistan needed 192 for victory.

This did not seem a difficult task, and they began the last day on 58 for one. Mohammad Wasim was immediately run out by Mbangwa, and Inzamam-ul-Haq charged wildly at Huckle and was stumped. Pakistan were vulnerable, but Zimbabwe bowled too many bad balls, and Campbell's tactics left much to be desired. He virtually ignored

Mbangwa and Bryan Strang and put all his trust in Huckle, who could find no consistent length. Pakistan made matters more difficult for themselves than they should have been, but Yousuf Youhana made 52 off 102 balls before being seventh out with just six needed. Zimbabwe disappointed, but the margin of victory was really greater than three wickets suggests. One thing is most evident, and that is that Pakistan can boast a wealth of young talent. If it is harnessed properly and the politics of cricket in Pakistan can be stabilised, they would be supreme among Test nations.

One-Day International Series

Zimbabwe v. Pakistan

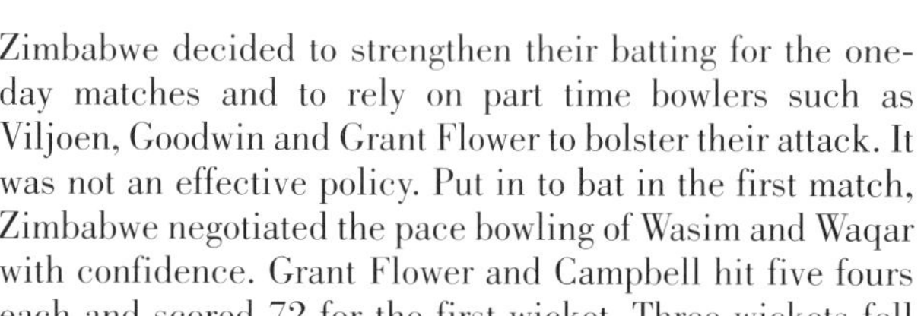

Zimbabwe decided to strengthen their batting for the one-day matches and to rely on part time bowlers such as Viljoen, Goodwin and Grant Flower to bolster their attack. It was not an effective policy. Put in to bat in the first match, Zimbabwe negotiated the pace bowling of Wasim and Waqar with confidence. Grant Flower and Campbell hit five fours each and scored 72 for the first wicket. Three wickets fell cheaply, but Guy Whittall, 42 off 49 balls, and Heath Streak, promoted to number six, 48 off 57 balls, put verve into the middle order, and Zimbabwe's 236 was a challenging score. Streak and Guy Whittall compounded their good work with the bat with early wickets, and Zimbabwe seemed to have seized the advantage. Aamir Sohail lived dangerously. He went for his shots from the start of the innings, hitting a six and eight fours in his 77 off 104 balls. Andy Whittall had a bad day, and the part-time bowlers were inadequate compensation. Yousuf Youhana made an unbeaten 59 off 62 balls, and Shahid Afridi provided the necessary acceleration with 30 off 20 balls, an innings that included two sixes and a four. Pakistan won with 14 balls to spare.

The second match again saw Zimbabwe put in to bat, and they performed commendably. Grant Flower dominated an opening stand of 64 with Campbell, and his 81 came off 103 balls. Goodwin, too, was in positive mood, and Guy Whittall was able to plunder a wilting attack and make 53 off 42 balls with a six and six fours. Pakistan faced a daunting target of 273, and they were given a perfect start by Saeed Anwar and Shahid Afridi, who made 57 with some audacious stroke play. Three quick wickets gave Zimbabwe some heart, but the young pairing of Mohammad Wasim and Yousuf Youhana took command with a well judged partnership of 144. When they were gone Mohammad Hussain came in to finish the match with a flourish, 31 off 20 balls with two sixes and a four, and Pakistan won with 20 balls to spare.

So ended Zimbabwe's season. It had promised much, but it had ended in disappointment and frustration.

First Test Match – Zimbabwe v. Pakistan

14, 15, 16, 17 and 18 March 1998 at Queen's Club, Bulawayo

Zimbabwe

	First Innings		Second Innings	
G.W. Flower	not out	**156**	lbw, **b** Waqar Younis	**6**
D.P. Viljoen	**c** Rashid Latif, **b** Waqar	**0**	lbw, **b** Shoaib Akhtar	**0**
M.W. Goodwin	**c** Rashid Latif, **b** Waqar	**0**	(4) not out	**166**
A.D.R. Campbell *	**c** Rashid Latif, **b** Azhar	**15**	(5) **c** Ijaz Ahmed, **b** Waqar	**5**
A. Flower †	**c** Latif, **b** Shoaib Akhtar	**44**	(6) not out	**100**
G.J. Whittall	lbw, **b** Waqar Younis	**1**		
T.N. Madondo	**c** Inzamam, **b** Waqar Younis	**14**		
H.H. Streak	**c** Ijaz, **b** Azhar Mahmood	**53**		
P.A. Strang	**c** Inzamam, **b** Shoaib Akhtar	**2**		
A.R. Whittall	**c** Rashid Latif,**b** Azhar	**17**	(3) **c** Yousuf Youhana, **b** Shoaib	**6**
M. Mbangwa	**c** Rashid Latif, **b** Waqar	**0**		
	b **3**, lb **13**, w **2**, nb **1**	**19**	lb **14**, w **1**, nb **4**	**19**
		321	(for 4 wickets, dec.)	**302**

	O	M	R	W	O	M	R	W
Waqar Younis	28.2	4	106	**5**	11	5	18	**2**
Azhar Mahmood	36	18	56	**3**	24	1	102	**–**
Shoaib Akhtar	27	6	83	**2**	23.2	5	67	**2**
Saqlain Mushtaq	20	1	60	**–**	14.3	–	63	**–**
Saeed Anwar	1	1	0	**–**	4	–	19	**–**
Ali Naqvi	2	–	11	**–**				
Inzamam-ul-Haq	1.3	–	8	**–**				

Fall of Wickets
1–**9**, 2–**15**, 3–**38**, 4–**115**, 5–**123**, 6–**159**, 7–**268**, 8–**272**, 9–**321**
1–**0**, 2–**15**, 3–**19**, 4–**25**

Pakistan

	First Innings		Second Innings	
Saeed Anwar	**c** A. Flower, **b** G.J. Whittall	**33**	**c** Goodwin, **b** P.A. Strang	**37**
Ali Naqvi	**c** Campbell, **b** Mbangwa	**27**	**c** Goodwin, **b** Mbangwa	**13**
Ijaz Ahmed	**c** A. Flower, **b** Mbangwa	**23**	(7) not out	**15**
Inzamam-ul-Haq	**c** and **b** P.A. Strang	**24**	**c** A. Flower, **b** Streak	**12**
Yousuf Youhana	**b** G.J. Whittall	**60**	**c** Viljoen, **b** Streak	**64**
Moin Khan	**c** A.R. Whittall, **b** G.J. Whittall	**12**	**c** Goodwin, **b** Viljoen	**97**
Azhar Mahmood	lbw, **b** P.A. Strang	**0**		
Rashid Latif * †	lbw, **b** Streak	**31**	not out	**0**
Saqlain Mushtaq	lbw, **b** P.A. Strang	**34**	(3) **c** A. Flower, **b** Streak	**8**
Waqar Younis	**c** P.A. Strang, **b** G.J. Whittall	**0**		
Shoaib Akhtar	not out	**7**		
	lb **5**	**5**	b **6**, lb **6**	**12**
		256	(for 6 wickets)	**258**

	O	M	R	W	O	M	R	W
Streak	24	5	74	**1**	18	6	42	**3**
Mbangwa	23	15	25	**2**	22	13	29	**1**
A.R. Whittall	7	1	29	**–**	8	3	28	**–**
G.J. Whittall	27	9	63	**4**	18	5	61	**–**
P.A. Strang	26.1	8	54	**3**	26.3	5	68	**1**
G.W. Flower	1	–	3	**–**				
Goodwin	1	–	3	**–**	2	–	3	**–**
Viljoen	4	–	15	**1**				

Fall of Wickets
1–**58**, 2–**80**, 3–**99**, 4–**118**, 5–**143**, 6–**144**, 7–**205**, 8–**230**, 9–**230**
1–**28**, 2–**54**, 3–**70**, 4–**80**, 5–**190**, 6–**258**

Umpires: I.D. Robinson & D.R. Shepherd

Match drawn

Second Test Match – Zimbabwe v. Pakistan

21, 22, 23, 24 and 25 March 1998 at Harare Sports Club, Harare

Zimbabwe

	First Innings		Second Innings	
G.W. Flower	c Rashid Latif, **b** Azhar	**39**	lbw, **b** Wasim Akram	**6**
G.J. Rennie	c Rashid Latif, **b** Azhar	**13**	c Yousuf Youhana, **b** Waqar	**0**
M.W. Goodwin	c Inzamam, **b** Mushtaq Ahmed	**53**	c Inzamam, **b** Waqar Younis	**81**
A.D.R. Campbell *	c Yousuf, **b** Mushtaq Ahmed	**23**	lbw, **b** Azhar Mahmood	**14**
A. Flower †	lbw, **b** Waqar Younis	**1**	c Inzamam, **b** Mushtaq Ahmed	**49**
G.J. Whittall	c Inzamam, **b** Wasim Akram	**62**	c Rashid Latif, **b** Azhar	**15**
T.N. Madondo	run out	**0**	c Rashid Latif, **b** Azhar	**2**
H.H. Streak	c Mohammad Wasim, **b** Waqar	**6**	not out	**37**
B.C. Strang	c and **b** Waqar Younis	**53**	c Yousuf Youhana, **b** Mushtaq	**21**
A.G. Huckle	**b** Waqar Younis	**0**	**b** Wasim Akram	**0**
M. Mbangwa	not out	**2**	lbw, **b** Wasim Akram	**3**
	b **6**, lb **14**, w **1**, nb **4**	**25**	b **13**, lb **15**, nb **12**	**40**
		277		**268**

	O	M	R	W	O	M	R	W
Wasim Akram	20.5	6	67	**1**	33	8	70	**3**
Waqar Younis	20	7	47	**4**	25	3	60	**2**
Mushtaq Ahmed	20	2	74	**2**	37	6	84	**2**
Azhar Mahmood	22	6	69	**2**	16	7	26	**3**

Fall of Wickets
1–**47**, 2–**75**, 3–**141**, 4–**142**, 5–**143**, 6–**144**, 7–**153**, 8–**263**, 9–**263**
1–**7**, 2–**9**, 3–**38**, 4–**133**, 5–**166**, 6–**175**, 7–**205**, 8–**255**, 9–**255**

Pakistan

	First Innings		Second Innings	
Saeed Anwar	lbw, **b** G.J. Whittall	**15**	c sub (A.R. Whittall), **b** G.J. Whittall	**65**
Ali Naqvi	c A. Flower, **b** G.J. Whittall	**13**	(7) c A. Flower, **b** Huckle	**8**
Mohammad Wasim	c Mbangwa, **b** G.J. Whittall	**192**	run out	**8**
Inzamam-ul-Haq	c and **b** B.C. Strang	**13**	st A. Flower, **b** Huckle	**10**
Yousuf Youhana	c A. Flower, **b** Mbangwa	**9**	c Goodwin, **b** G.J.Whittall	**52**
Moin Khan	**b** B.C. Strang	**12**	c Campbell, **b** Streak	**21**
Azhar Mahmood	c G.J. Whittall, **b** Mbangwa	**20**	(2) c Campbell, **b** Streak	**9**
Wasim Akram	c G.J. Rennie, **b** Mbangwa	**0**	not out	**12**
Rashid Latif * †	c sub (A.R. Whittall), **b** B.C. Strang	**4**	not out	**1**
Mushtaq Ahmed	c Campbell, **b** Streak	**57**		
Waqar Younis	not out	**8**		
	lb **8**, w **1**, nb **2**	**11**	b **2**, lb **3**, nb **1**	**6**
		354	(for 7 wickets)	**192**

	O	M	R	W	O	M	R	W
Streak	33	8	83	**1**	13	5	40	**2**
Mbangwa	32	12	56	**3**	2	–	11	**–**
B.C. Strang	28	10	65	**3**	5	–	20	**–**
G.J. Whittall	32.5	4	78	**3**	15	4	35	**2**
Huckle	21	8	55	**–**	18.5	1	81	**2**
Goodwin	2	–	9	**–**				

Fall of Wickets
1–**31**, 2–**46**, 3–**61**, 4–**88**, 5–**119**, 6–**169**, 7–**169**, 8–**187**, 9–**334**
1–**14**, 2–**59**, 3–**77**, 4–**105**, 5–**138**, 6–**162**, 7–**186**

Umpires S.G. Randell & R.B. Tiffin

Pakistan won by 3 wickets

First One-Day International – Zimbabwe v. Pakistan

28 March 1998 at Harare Sports Club, Harare

Zimbabwe

G.W. Flower	c Latif, **b** Azhar Mahmood	**32**
A.D.R. Campbell *	c and **b** Azhar Mahmood	**36**
M.W. Goodwin	**b** Shahid Afridi	**35**
A. Flower †	c Rashid, **b** Shoaib Akhtar	**5**
G.J. Whittall	c Ijaz Ahmed, **b** Shahid Afridi	**42**
H.H. Streak	not out	**48**
C.N. Evans	c Rashid Latif, **b** Aamir Sohail	**5**
P.A. Strang	not out	**15**
D.P. Viljoen		
A.R. Whittall		
M. Mbangwa		
	lb **6**, w **9**, nb **3**	**18**
	50 overs (for 6 wickets)	**236**

	O	M	R	W
Wasim Alkram	10	–	52	**–**
Waqar Younis	8	–	55	**–**
Azhar Mahmood	9	1	34	**2**
Shoaib Akhtar	5	–	10	**1**
Shahid Afridi	10	1	45	**2**
Aamir Sohail	8	–	34	**1**

Fall of Wickets
1–**72**, 2–**80**, 3–**95**, 4–**154**, 5–**171**, 6–**187**

Pakistan

Aamir Sohail	c Campbell, **b** Evans	**77**
Inzamam-ul-Haq	c Mbangwa, **b** Streak	**0**
Mohammad Wasim	c A.R. Whittall, **b** G.J. Whittall	**3**
Ijaz Ahmed	c G.W. Flower, **b** Evans	**43**
Yousuf Youhana	not out	**59**
Shahid Afridi	c Evans, **b** Goodwin	**30**
Azhar Mahmood	c Evans, **b** G.J. Whittall	**13**
Wasim Akram	not out	**2**
Rashid Latif * †		
Shoaib Akhtar		
Waqar Younis		
	b **2**, lb **1**, w **7**	**10**
	47.4 overs (for 6 wickets)	**237**

	O	M	R	W
Streak	10	–	48	**1**
Mbangwa	10	1	34	**–**
G.J. Whittall	9.4	1	35	**2**
A.R. Whittall	4	–	27	**–**
Evans	9	–	50	**2**
G.W. Flower	2	–	15	**–**
Goodwin	1	–	13	**1**
Viljoen	2	–	12	**–**

Fall of Wickets
1–**15**, 2–**27**, 3–**121**, 4–**137**, 5–**198**, 6–**225**

Umpires: K.C. Barbour & I.D. Robinson *Man of the Match*: Aamir Sohail

Pakistan won by 4 wickets

Second One-Day International – Zimbabwe v. Pakistan

29 March 1998 at Harare Sports Club, Harare

Zimbabwe

G.W. Flower	st Latif, b Mohammad Hussain	81
A.D.R. Campbell *	st Latif, b Mohammad Hussain	12
M.W. Goodwin	run out	47
A. Flower †	b Waqar Younis	21
G.J. Whittall	not out	53
H.H. Streak	not out	26
C.B. Wishart		
C.N. Evans		
P.A. Strang		
A.G. Huckle		
M. Mbangwa		
	b 1, lb 13, w 18	32
	50 overs (for 4 wickets)	272

	O	M	R	W
Wasim Akram	10	–	51	–
Waqar Younis	10	1	39	1
Azhar Mahmood	10	1	45	–
Shahid Afridi	10	–	63	–
Mohammad Hussain	10	–	60	2

Fall of Wickets
1–**64**, 2–**149**, 3–**177**, 4–**183**

Pakistan

Saeed Anwar	c Streak, b G.J. Whittall	25
Shahid Afridi	c A. Flower, b Streak	32
Mohammad Wasim	c P.A. Strang, b G.W. Flower	76
Ijaz Ahmed	lbw, b G.J. Whittall	4
Yousuf Youhana	b Streak	66
Moin Khan	lbw, b Goodwin	10
Azhar Mahmood	not out	14
Mohammad Hussain	not out	31
Rashid Latif * †		
Wasim Akram		
Waqar Younis		
	lb 7, w 9, nb 2	18
	46.4 overs (for 6 wickets)	276

	O	M	R	W
Streak	8	–	36	2
Mbangwa	10	–	72	–
G.J. Whittall	8	–	41	2
Huckle	10	–	45	–
Evans	5.4	–	35	–
G.W. Flower	3	–	25	1
Goodwin	2	–	15	1

Fall of Wickets
1–**57**, 2–**60**, 3–**65**, 4–**209**, 5–**225**, 6–**227**

Umpires G.R. Evans & R.B. Tiffin *Man of the Match*: Mohammad Wasim

Pakistan won by 4 wickets

First-Class Averages

Batting

	M	Inns	NOs	Runs	HS	Av	100s	50s
M.W. Goddwin	3	6	1	456	166*	91.20	1	4
G.W. Flower	7	11	1	742	156*	74.20	3	3
C.B. Wishart	3	3	–	195	144	65.00	1	
A. Flower	6	10	1	585	201	65.00	3	
G.J. Whittall	6	11	1	496	203*	49.60	1	2
G.J. Rennie	5	9	–	358	101	39.77	1	3
H.H. Streak	6	11	2	322	81	35.77	3	
D.L. Houghton	3	5	–	128	59	25.60	1	
T.G. Bartlett	2	4	–	102	40	25.50		
J.A. Rennie	3	6	–	124	64	20.66	1	
A.D.R. Campbell	7	11	1	192	59*	19.20	1	

Played in one match – T.L. Penney 76 & 44
(Qualification – 100 runs, average 10.00)

Bowling

	Overs	Mds	Runs	Wks	Best	Av	10/m	5/inn
J.A. Rennie	69.3	17	189	12	9/76	15.75	1	
B.C. Strang	171	68	356	19	5/49	18.73	1	
G.W. Flower	114.2	35	223	11	5/37	20.27	1	
A.G. Huckle	208.3	46	689	22	6/109	31.31	1	2
P.A. Strang	180.1	52	421	11	3/54	38.27		
H.H. Streak	160	36	440	11	3/42	40.00		

(Qualification – 10 wickets)

Leading Fielders

19 – A. Flower (ct 17 / st 2); 13 – A.D.R. Campbell; 9 – G.W. Flower; 5 – G.J. Whittall and M.W. Goodwin; 4 – C.N. Evans, G.J. Rennie and P.A. Strang

South Africa

South Africa set out in 1997–98 to prove themselves the best in the world. Their mission began favourably with victory in Pakistan, but this was soon followed by frustration and disappointment in Australia, where they lost narrowly in the Test series and, not for the first time, fell at the last hurdle in the one-day tournament. Defeat in the final of the World Series was hard to accept, for the side had swept all before them in the qualifying matches.

Mark Boucher succeeded Dave Richardson as South Africa's wicket-keeper. He shared in a world record ninth wicket partnership, and his 45 dismissals in all first-class cricket left him far ahead of his rivals. *(David Munden / Sportsline)*

The season in South Africa began with a visit from the New Zealand Academy party, and, on their return to the Republic, the national side were to play Test series against Pakistan and Sri Lanka, plus the inevitable one-day competition, before setting out for England and a five-Test series.

The batting relied heavily on the consistency of Gary Kirsten, but Kallis had begun to show signs of realising his full potential and providing South Africa with the middle order batsman of class that they needed so desperately. The pace bowling, with Pollock having matured into a player of world class, presented no problems, but, in spite of the efforts of the veteran Symcox, the spin department remained below par.

South African cricket is essentially solid, dependable and consistent. It is conservative in outlook, but, eventually, greatness will only come to those who dare.

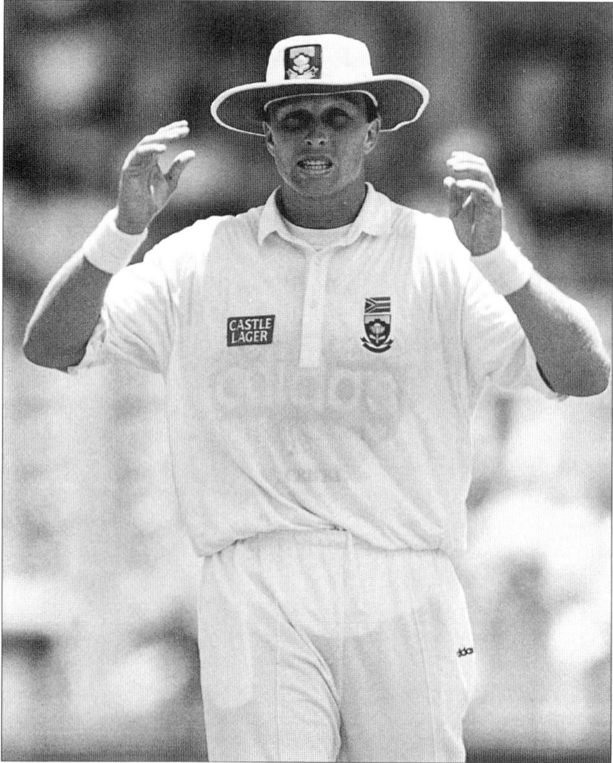

The best bowling performance of the season, 8 for 36, by veteran Brett Schultz, Western Province versus West Indies 'A' side. In spite of his outstanding performance, Schultz finished on the losing side. (David Munden / Sportsline)

New Zealand Academy Tour

The New Zealand Academy side arrived in South Africa to play three first-class and three one-day matches against the host country's Academy side. The New Zealand party was a strong one, and included several cricketers who had established themselves or were about to establish themselves in the Test side, notably O'Connor, McMillan and Vettori.

One-Day Series

14 August 1997
at Hoy Park, Durban
South African Academy 254 for 8 (M. Strydom 103)
New Zealand Academy 258 for 4 (C.D. McMillan 106 not out)
New Zealand Academy won by 6 wickets

21 August 1997
at Centurion Park, Centurion
South African Academy 193 for 8
New Zealand Academy 166
South African Academy won by 27 runs

27 August 1997
at Stan Friedman Oval, Khosa, Krugersdorp
New Zealand Academy 247 for 7 (M.D. Bell 79)
South African Academy 248 for 7 (M. Strydom 72, N. Boje 51, R. Maron 50)
South African Academy won by 3 wickets

South Africa took the one-day series by two matches to one. New Zealand won the opening game with three balls to spare. Morne Strydom hit 103 off 96 deliveries for the home side, but Craig McMillan responded with five sixes and five fours as he made an unbeaten 106 off 99 deliveries. He and Matthew Sinclair shared an unbroken partnership of 101 in 69 minutes.

Runs were harder to come by in Centurion, where New Zealand collapsed to 65 for six before Andrew Penn prevented total embarrassment with an innings of 48. The series was won in Krugersdorp, where consistent application saw South Africa to victory with an over to spare. The fireworks were provided by the left-handed Nico Boje, who hit 51 off 39 balls just when acceleration was needed.

First-Class Series

15, 16, 17 and 18 August 1997
at Chatsworth Stadium, Chatsworth, Durban
South African Academy 327 (G. Morgan 87, M. Strydom 73, T. Odoyo 55) and 211 for 7 dec. (M.L. Bruyns 88)
New Zealand Academy 275 (C.D. McMillan 63, L.G. Howell 52) and 191 for 5 (C.D. McMillan 62)
Match drawn

22, 23, 24 and 25 August 1997
at Centurion Park, Centurion
New Zealand Academy 242 (A.J. Penn 70) and 291 for 9 dec. (M.D. Bell 76, L.G. Howell 67)
South African Academy 201 (A.J. Hall 59, D.G. Sewell 6 for 40) and 185 (N. Boje 105 not out, D.L. Vettori 5 for 45)
New Zealand Academy won by 47 runs

28, 29, 30 and 31 August 1997
at Stan Friedman Oval, Khosa, Krugersdorp
South African Academy 324 (J.M. Henderson 135, N. Boje 54, S.B. O'Connor 4 for 56) and 190 for 6 dec. (A.J. Hall 62 not out)
New Zealand Academy 256 (M.S. Sinclair 59, E.O. Moleon 5 for 62) and 261 for 4 (M.D. Bell 105 not out, M.E. Parlane 58, C.D. McMillan 57)
New Zealand Academy won by 6 wickets

New Zealand showed their strength in the 'Test' series, winning the last two matches and displaying a tactical and technical experience their opponents did not possess. In the first game, South Africa were 89 for four before Morne Strydom, impressive in all encounters, and Grant Morgan added 115. New Zealand promised more than they achieved and eventually were set a target of 343 at more than five runs an over. They settled for a draw.

As in the one-day game, the pitch at Centurion Park was not conducive to run-scoring. Put in to bat, New Zealand were bowled out for 242 in just under 91 overs on the first day. They would have been in great trouble had not Penn and Morland put on 80 for the eighth wicket. South Africa descended to 96 for six and that they reached 200 was due mainly to Hall. New Zealand showed consistent professional application in their second innings, and Howell's declaration left South Africa more than a day in which to score 333 to win. Penn and Sewell made early strikes, and three wickets fell for 12 runs. On the final day, Boje played an heroic innings. He batted for 201 minutes, faced 158 balls and hit three sixes and eight fours in his unbeaten 105. He and Hall added 89 for the fifth wicket before three wickets fell for seven runs. Thereafter, South Africa were always fighting a losing battle.

Transvaal's left-hander Jimmy Henderson made the highest score of his career, hitting 23 fours to help South Africa to an encouraging 324 in the final match. Again, New Zealand batted consistently, and, trailing in the series, South Africa declared at the end of the third day. Parlane and Bell gave New Zealand a fine start with 96 at a run a minute, and Bell and McMillan added 79 for the fourth wicket. Twenty-year old Matthew Bell reached the first first-class century of his career. He hit two sixes and ten fours and faced 191 balls for his unbeaten 105. New Zealand could draw much comfort from the tour. There was batting of class from McMillan, and O'Connor and Sewell, like Vettori, gave evidence that they were bowlers of Test quality.

West Indies 'A' Tour

The West Indian Test side were humiliated in Pakistan, and the 'A' team fared little better in South Africa. Led by Jimmy Adams, until quite recently ranked as the world's leading batsman, West Indies 'A' included some half-dozen players with international experience, but they struggled against their South African counterparts. The home side may have lacked experience at the highest level, but they were competitive and professional. The lack of batting strength in West Indian cricket was cruelly exposed with only Adams (49.60) and all-rounder Laurie Williams (35.30) averaging above 33 in the first-class matches on the two-month tour.

11 November 1997
at Wollowmoore Park, Benoni
West Indies 'A' 237 for 4
Easterns 196 for 6 (W.R. Radford 67 not out)
West Indies 'A' won by 41 runs

14, 15, 16 and 17 November 1997
at Wanderers, Johannesburg
Gauteng 372 for 7 dec. (N. Pothas 138, N.D. McKenzie 85, S.G. Koening 69) and 141 for 8 dec.
West Indies 'A' 250 (L.V. Garrick 82, R.P. Snell 5 for 56) and 58 for 2
Match drawn

The tourists began with a win in the 50-over game in Benoni. They batted consistently, while Easterns relied heavily on the all-round abilities of Wayne Radford, but he could find no support after losing Norris, third man out, at 117.

Gauteng gave a hint of things to come in the four-day match at the Wanderers. They were 18 for three when Nic Pothas joined Sven Koenig. The pair added 105, and Pothas, a strong contender for a Test place, went on to reach the third century of his career. Garrick gave West Indies 'A' a sound start, but the middle order fell apart against Snell.

19 November 1997
at Soweto
Gauteng Invitation XI 152
West Indies 'A' 154 for 4
West Indies 'A' won by 6 wickets

21, 22, 23 and 24 November 1997
at Centurion Park, Centurion
West Indies 'A' 293 (J.C. Adams 123 not out, R.G. Samuels 55, P.S. de Villiers 7 for 80) and 202 (R.G. Samuels 57, D. Townsend 5 for 68)
Northern Gauteng 175 (R.D. King 5 for 63) and 253 (P.J.R. Steyn 105, P.T. Collins 4 for 58)
West Indies 'A' won by 67 runs

26 November 1997
at Boland Park, Paarl
Boland 202 for 6 (C. Grainger 81)
West Indies 'A' 196 for 8
Boland won by 6 runs

West Indies 'A' gained their first first-class victory of the tour when they beat Northern Gauteng at Centurion Park. Jimmy Adams led from the front with an unbeaten 123 of the last 212 runs of the first innings as de Villiers destroyed the rest of the visitors' batting with the best bowling performance of his career. He was to finish with match figures of ten for 111. Reon King bowled impressively for the West Indians, who took a first innings lead of 118 and eventually won comfortably in spite of a brave century from opening bat and wicket-keeper Philippus Steyn. Left-arm pace bowler Pedro Collins captured the wicket of Steyn and three others in a lively display.

28, 29, 30 November and 1 December 1997
at Newlands, Cape Town
West Indies 'A' 290 (L.R. Williams 110, J.C. Adams 52, M. George 4 for 79) and 174 (J.C. Adams 51, B.N. Schultz 8 for 36)
Western Province 199 (P. Kirsten 63, O.D. Gibson 4 for 36) and 242 (H.D. Ackerman 72, H. Pangarker 53, O.D. Gibson 5 for 85)
West Indies 'A' won by 23 runs

12, 13 and 14 December 1997
at St George's Park, Port Elizabeth
West Indies 'A' 299 (R.L. Hoyte 72, W.W. Hinds 63, A. Badenhorst 4 for 69) and 192 for 6 dec. (S. Ragoonath 76)
Eastern Province 140 (K.C. Wessels 52, N.A.M. McLean 6 for 28) and 51 for 3
Match drawn

West Indies 'A' fared better against the provincial sides than they were to do in the international series. At Newlands, all-rounder Laurie Williams played what manager Roger Harper described as 'the innings of the tour'. He hit a six and 14 fours and faced 144 balls after the first five wickets had gone for 72. The experienced Ottis Gibson and Dinanath Ramnarine, whose leg-breaks brought him 19 first-class wickets on the tour, bowled West Indies to a first innings lead of 91, but Brett Schultz brought Western Province back into the game with the best bowling figures of his career. In search of 266 to win, the home side were 176 for three before Gibson and Ramnarine again took control to give West Indies victory.

The match at St George's Park was played in between the first and second 'Tests'. The West Indian lower order rescued their side after the first four men had been dismissed for 40, and Nixon McLean, for whom the trip was

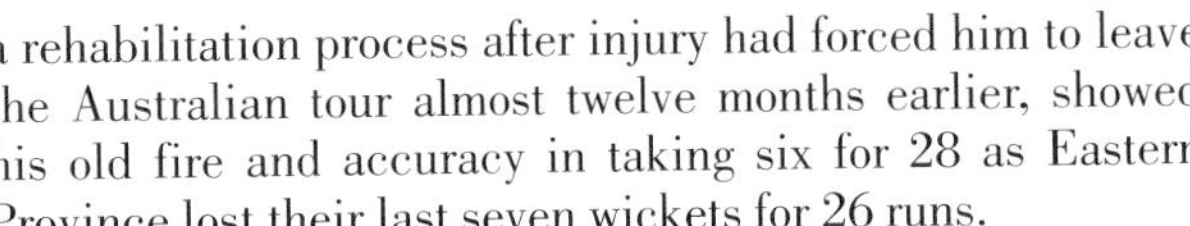

a rehabilitation process after injury had forced him to leave the Australian tour almost twelve months earlier, showed his old fire and accuracy in taking six for 28 as Eastern Province lost their last seven wickets for 26 runs.

International Series

4, 5, 6 and 7 December 1997
at Springbok Park, Bloemfontein
West Indies 'A' 187 (R.G. Samuels 76) and 314 (J.C. Adams 129, F.L. Reifer 62)
South Africa 'A' 306 (H.D. Ackerman 85, G.F.J. Liebenberg 84) and 199 for 4 (H.D. Ackerman 53 not out, D.M. Benkenstein 52)
South Africa 'A' won by 6 wickets

19, 20, 21 and 22 December 1997
at Buffalo Park, East London
South Africa 'A' 474 for 8 dec. (N. Pothas 120 not out, N.C. Johnson 89, A.G. Prince 71, D.M. Benkenstein 70, P.J. Botha 60, O.D. Gibson 4 for 104)
West Indies 'A' 280 (W.W. Hinds 115, S. Ragoonath 77, M. Hayward 6 for 51) and 166 (J.C. Adams 63, D.N. Crookes 6 for 50)
South Africa 'A' won by an innings and 28 runs

A fast bowler for the future, Mornantau Hayward. He had considerable success for the South African 'A' side in the series against West Indies. (David Munden / Sportsline)

26, 27, 28 and 29 December 1997
at Newlands, Cape Town
South Africa 'A' 129 and 301 (H.D. Ackerman 69, D.M. Benkenstein 66, G.F.J. Liebenberg 53, P.T. Collins 4 for 61, N.A.M. McLean 4 for 77)
West Indies 'A' 164 and 247 (L.R. Williams 84)
South Africa 'A' won by 19 runs

In the 'Test' series, West Indies 'A' suffered the same fate as their seniors in Pakistan – they were beaten by three matches to nil – a complete humiliation. South Africa fielded sides that were a mixture of youth and experience. They had genuine pace in Nantie Hayward, Roger Telemachus and Brett Schultz, and they offered contrasting spin in the off-breaks of Derek Crookes and the slow left-arm of Clive Eksteen, both of whom had toured with the senior side and had tasted international competition. Led by the 23-year old Dale Benkenstein, South Africa were consistent in batting, resolute in purpose and, with wicket-keeper Pothas a centurion at number eight in the second match, strong in depth. In contrast, West Indies lacked cohesion, were prone to injury, and, inevitably, had a lone spinner, Ramnarine.

Adams chose to bat first when he won the toss in Bloemfontein and saw his side overwhelmed. Samuels scored 76 out of 102 before being fourth out. Liebenberg and Ackerman, who was to gain Test honours later in the season, put on 166 for South Africa's third wicket, and there was a sting in the tail. Jimmy Adams hit his second century of the tour, and Reifer, of whom much had been expected, made his solitary fifty, but the last four wickets went down for 11 runs, and the South Africans were rarely troubled.

In East London, Johnson and Prince put on 121 for South Africa's second wicket, and Botha and Pothas 141 for the seventh. Nantie Hayward returned the best bowling figures of his career, and the one consolation for West Indies was a second wicket stand of 141 between Ragoonath and Hinds. Hinds had been picked for the tour after just one first-class match for Jamaica, and his century revealed the advance he had made and won praise from manager Roger Harper.

The third match showed the real power and character of the South African side. They chose to bat first when they won the toss and were bowled out for 129. West Indies lost nine wickets in passing that total, and only McLean's brave hitting at the last gave them a first innings advantage of 35. Resolutely and consistently, the hosts moved to 301 by the third day with Ackerman and Benkenstein, 233 runs, average 46.60 in the series, providing the substance in a fourth wicket stand of 129. At 84 for five, West Indies faced an embarrassing defeat, but Williams and Hoyte, who kept wicket well but generally disappointed with the bat, added 116. It restored dignity, but it could not stop South Africa achieving total triumph in the series.

Limited-Over Series

South Africa's domination of the 50-over series was as convincing as had been their domination of the 'Test' series. In the first match, Rindel began the South African innings with a partnership of 201. The left-handed Mike Rindel, playing his first game against the tourists, made 106 off 116 balls with a six and 11 fours, while Gerhard Liebenberg, later to win a place in the Test side, scored 89 from 111 balls with two sixes and eight fours. Facing a total of 291, West Indies 'A' collapsed to a humiliating 71 all out in 23.2 overs. Only Hoyte, 28, and Gibson, 10, reached double figures.

Two days later, Telemachus reduced the West Indians to 36 for four, and it needed skipper Adams, 42, and Nigel Francis, 45, to steer them to a more respectable 191. It proved totally inadequate as, having lost Rindel for 0, South Africa 'A' won with nine wickets and 31 balls to spare. Liebenberg and Johnson shared an unbroken partnership of 182. The match in Johannesburg was ruined by rain. Wavel Hinds produced West Indies 'A's one significant innings of

All-rounder Neil Johnson spent a year with Leicestershire and returned to South Africa to win a place in the 'A' side against West Indies.
(David Munden / Sportsline)

the series, hitting 80 off 91 balls. Gibson made 38 off 26 balls, but the game was reduced to 32 overs. South Africa 'A' were 108 for seven off 19 overs when the rain returned, and the match was abandoned.

2 January 1998
at Kingsmead, Durban
South Africa 'A' 291 for 6 (M.J.R. Rindel 106, G.F.J. Liebenberg 89)
West Indies 'A' 71
South Africa 'A' won by 220 runs

4 January 1998
at St George's Park, Port Elizabeth
West Indies 'A' 191
South Africa 'A' 192 for 1 (N.C. Johnson 90 not out, G.F.J. Liebenberg 79 not out)
South Africa 'A' won by 9 wickets

7 January 1998
at Wanderers, Johannesburg
West Indies 'A' 187 for 7 (W.W. Hinds 80)
South Africa 'A' 108 for 7
Match abandoned

Pat Symcox, the third number ten batsman to score a Test hundred. He made 108 in the first Test against Pakistan and shared a match-saving partnership of 195 for the ninth wicket, a world Test record. (David Munden / Sportsline)

Pakistan Tour

One thing that must be said about Pakistan cricket is that it is never dull, never without incident. When the party to tour South Africa was announced, commentators on the game were either bewildered or angered. Rashid Latif had been retained as captain, although his performances in Bangladesh as captain and wicket-keeper had been well below par, and Wasim Akram, one of the world's great all-rounders and a highly successful captain who had led Pakistan to total triumph over West Indies, was not among the chosen. No reasons were offered, but Rashid was quoted as saying that the national side was in the process of being rebuilt. There were others who indicated that the administrators were attempting to 'clean up' the game in Pakistan and that Wasim had treated the selectors in a cavalier fashion after the victories in the series against West Indies. Whatever the reasons, the Pakistan side bore a strange look.

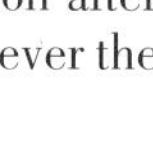

29 January 1998
at Randjesfontein
Pakistanis 299 for 4 (Inzamam-ul-Haq 107, Mohammad Wasim 73)
NFO XI 239 for 6 (D.M. Benkenstein 94, R.P. Snell 74)
Match drawn

30, 31 January, 1 and 2 February 1998
at Kimberley Country Club
Pakistanis 418 for 8 dec. (Saaed Anwar 117, Rashid Latif 98, Azhar Mahmood 59, Inzamam-ul-Haq 57) and 216 for 9 dec. (Aamir Sohail 61, G.J. Kruis 4 for 41)
Griqualand West 218 (P.H. Barnard 101, Mushtaq Ahmed 6 for 63) and 109 (Mushtaq Ahmed 5 for 18)
Pakistanis won by 307 runs

South Africa were still engaged in Test cricket in Australia when Pakistan began their tour of the Republic. They had a happy start, scoring heavily against Griqualand West, who then fell prey to Mushtaq Ahmed's leg-spin. His match figures of 11 for 81 boded well for the Test series. Pieter Barnard was the only batsman to cope with Mushtaq.

6, 7 and 8 February 1998
at Buffalo Park, East London
Pakistanis 232 for 9 dec. (Yousuf Youhana 77, Moin Khan 56) and 124 (D. Taljard 6 for 49)
Border 244 (W. Wiblin 82, M.V. Boucher 80, Azhar Mahmood 4 for 66) and 113 for 5
Border won by 5 wickets

Pakistan suffered a double blow on the eve of the first Test match. They were well beaten by Border, for whom medium pacer Dion Taljard, 28 years old, returned the best bowling figures of his brief career. In harness with Makhaya Ntini, the first black cricketer to represent South Africa, he routed the tourists in the second innings.

More seriously, Mohammad Akram and Saqlain Mushtaq were attacked and robbed when they were crossing the road outside their hotel and needed medical treatment. Saqlain needed to wear a neck brace, and Mohammad Akram sustained cuts and injuries to his right hand. In view of these circumstances, allied to the fact that Rashid Latif, Waqar Younis and Shoaib Akhtar were also injured, the start of the Test match was put back for 24 hours. In the event, only Rashid Latif and Mohammad Akram were not considered for selection on grounds of fitness, and Aamir Sohail led Pakistan.

The media coverage of the attack on Saqlain and Mohammad Akram did not please the Pakistan management or players, and, briefly, the tour was under threat; but eventually disagreement subsided.

Test Series

South Africa *v.* Pakistan

The postponement of the first Test for one day could not save it from being ruined by rain. It was fated from the outset with neither captain fit to play. Rashid Latif had a neck injury, and Aamir Sohail led Pakistan, while Gary Kirsten captained South Africa for the first time in the absence of Cronje, who was recovering from a cartilage operation. Hudson was recalled but batted in the middle order. With David Richardson having retired at the end of the tour of Australia, Mark Boucher took over as South Africa's wicket-keeper.

Aamir Sohail won the toss and asked South Africa to bat, a decision that seemed strange to most observers as the Wanderers' pitch was true and lacking spite. Nevertheless, Aamir's action was vindicated when Waqar Younis immediately accounted for Kirsten with a lifting delivery. Pakistan success continued, and they were in total control as, with Waqar and Mushtaq Ahmed doing most of the damage, they reduced their hosts to 166 for eight. Not for the first time, they failed to press home their advantage. Four straightforward catches were put down, and the fielding was generally sloppy. Aamir himself dropped Boucher when he was on two, and, by the close of play, the young wicket-keeper had reached 50 while Symcox was on 77, and South Africa were 296 for eight. Pakistan's frustrations were apparent when pace bowler Shoaib Akhtar, who was carrying an injury, clashed with Symcox, a disagreement that led later to intervention by the match referee John Reid.

The blend of age and youth continued their dominance on the second morning, taking their stand to a ninth wicket world Test record of 195. The partnership ended when Symcox, two months short of his 38th birthday, slogged Saqlain Mushtaq to mid-on. By then, he had become only the third number ten batsman to score a century in a Test match. His pugnacious innings lasted 151 deliveries and included 15 fours. Boucher was out shortly afterwards. His watchful innings lasted 265 minutes and included a six and nine fours.

Pakistan began as badly as South Africa had done when Boucher continued his joyful match by taking a low catch to account for Aamir Sohail off the bowling of Pollock. Next ball, Donald had Saeed Anwar taken at first slip. Mohammad Wasim and Ijaz Ahmed counter-attacked by adding 72 off 88 balls before the former was caught behind off a ball that lifted off a length. Inzamam-ul-Haq was soon bowled, and then came rain and lightning to cut 31 overs from the day and leave Pakistan on 106 for four. Before play was suspended, Pakistan had batted under floodlights, but the floodlights had done little to improve the poor light conditions.

Pakistan lost a fifth wicket early on the third morning, and Azhar Mahmood entered with his side in crisis. He had made a century against South Africa in Rawalpindi four months earlier, and now, in Johannesburg, he gave further indication that he is an all-rounder of real quality. He was to celebrate his 23rd birthday during the second Test match, but the real celebrations came at the Wanderers with an outstanding century. He and Moin Khan put on 107, and Azhar went on to reach a career best 132 before being last out. His century came in four hours, and he took his side from the dangers of having to follow on to within 35 of South Africa's score. When he was out gloom descended and play ended.

No play was possible on the fourth day, and only 10.2 overs on the fifth. Azhar Mahmood and Pat Symcox shared the Man of the Match award in a Test studded with gems, slow over-rates, a world record, mystery, police enquiry, confrontation and rain.

Having proved his fitness, Cronje returned to lead South Africa in the second Test. He replaced Cullinan, while Hylton Ackerman made his Test debut at the expense of Gibbs. In spite of his heroic deeds in Johannesburg, Symcox was relegated to twelfth man as South Africa decided upon an all pace attack and brought in Fanie de Villiers. With Inzamam unfit, Pakistan gave a first Test cap to Yousuf Youhana. Fazl-e-Akbar was the third Test debutant, replacing Saqlain Mushtaq. In an attempt to draw the crowds, live television coverage of the match was banned in the Durban area.

Cronje won the toss and asked Pakistan to bat. His decision seemed totally correct as his pace attack ripped through the visitors' top order. Pakistan slipped to 89 for five before Azhar Mahmood arrived to play another innings of the very highest quality. Even so, wickets continued to fall, and the score stood at 153 for eight when Shoaib Akhtar joined Azhar. Shoaib defended stoutly, but he owed a tremendous amount to Azhar, who nursed him through difficult periods and saw that Shoaib faced as little of the bowling as possible. To a ninth wicket partnership worth 90, Shoaib contributed six, but he gave Azhar brave support. When Azhar was finally bowled by Donald he

Azhar Mahmood hit centuries of the highest quality for Pakistan in the first and second Test matches.
(Dave Pinegar / ASP)

had scored 132 off 163 balls and his innings included 24 fours. Of the last 106 runs scored by Pakistan, he made 96, and he completed his third century in seven Test innings against South Africa. His second fifty came off 47 balls in 42 minutes with some scintillating drives, cuts and hooks. Here is an outstanding talent. His contribution to Pakistan's success continued when he took a catch in the gully to dismiss Kirsten and leave South Africa on 23 for one at the close.

The home side had a hard struggle on the second morning when only 42 runs were scored in the pre-lunch session. Fazl-e-Akbar captured his first Test wicket, having Bacher caught behind off an inside edge. Ackerman, understandably cautious on his Test debut, batted with intelligence and technical efficiency against the pace of Waqar and the spin of Mushtaq Ahmed, and it was Kallis who fell first victim in the afternoon. Troubled by an injured knee, Shoaib Akhtar did not bowl in the morning session, but, called into the attack after lunch, he immediately generated considerable pace and, in his fourth over, bowled Kallis, who had added 83 with Ackerman. With his next ball, Shoaib had Hudson leg before. Mushtaq was troubling all batsmen, and he accounted for both Cronje and Ackerman, whose impressive innings of 57 occupied three-and-a-half hours. Shoaib's dominance over the bat continued. He knocked back Boucher's middle stump with a yorker and beat both Klusener and de Villiers with his pace. Five wickets in 12 overs was no more than he deserved for hostile and accurate fast bowling. He had bowled Pakistan to an unexpected first innings lead of 28. It would have been more but for another fine innings from Pollock, firmly established as an international all-rounder. In spite of the use of lights, play ended four overs early because of the gloom. Saeed Anwar and Aamir Sohail had scored 11.

Events off the field continued to make the news. Having appeared before a parliamentary committee and been cleared of match-fixing allegations, Wasim Akram was told to fly to South Africa to bolster a squad weakened by injuries. His recall did not please all the selectors, and it became public knowledge that there was discord. Meanwhile, back at the Test, Aamir Sohail and Saeed Anwar completed the first century opening stand against South Africa since that country's return to Test cricket. They had seemingly put Pakistan in an impregnable position, and Saeed Anwar went on to complete his fifth Test hundred off 179 balls, with 16 fours.

That South Africa bounced back into the game was due entirely to Shaun Pollock. He had saved his side from rout with his unbeaten 70; now he brought about a collapse as Pakistan lost seven wickets for 61 runs.

Pollock had Yousuf caught behind off a ball that rose sharply. A break for bad light followed, but when play restarted the red-haired all-rounder trapped both Saeed and Moin leg before, had Azhar caught behind and had Waqar taken at mid-on. These four wickets had come in five overs at a personal cost of seven runs. Pakistan ended the day on 222 for eight, and, thanks to Pollock, the game was in the balance.

The last two wickets fell quickly the next morning, and Pollock finished with six for 50. He has matured into one of the world's top all-rounders. The ban on live television coverage appeared to have worked, for 15,000 people arrived to see the fourth day's play. When their side went in search of a target of 255 they soon suffered disappointment as Fazl-e-Akbar had Bacher leg before for 0. But it was spin rather than pace that proved to be South Africa's undoing. Mushtaq Ahmed was at his mesmerising best. He took six wickets, totally outwitting the batsmen, as South Africa plunged to 133 for eight. It seemed that Pakistan would win in four days, but an unlikely partnership developed between the old and the new: de Villers, 33 years old and playing in his penultimate Test, and Boucher, 21 and at the start of his international career. In the last hour of the day, they added 53. Boucher was correct and technically superior to the earlier batsmen in the way in which he dealt with Mushtaq. Fanie de Villiers was less disciplined and prone to use the reverse sweep, but he was effective. With bad weather forecast, it seemed that the pair might even save the game.

It was not to be. Having completed his second fifty in Test cricket, Boucher was bowled by Waqar Younis, who had taken the second new ball, and, in his next over, Waqar had the injured Donald leg before. In truth, Pakistan were more superior than their 29-run margin of victory would suggest. There were outstanding performances from Azhar Mahmood, Shoaib Akhtar, Saeed Anwar and Mushtaq Ahmed, whose match figures of nine for 149 earned him the individual award. There is such talent in this Pakistan side, most of it youthful, and one remains in despair that this talent is never consistently harnessed.

Wasim Akram, still a figure of controversy, arrived in South Africa and was selected for the final Test, replacing Fazl-e-Akbar. Inzamam-ul-Haq returned at the expense of Yousuf Youhana, and Rashid Latif declared himself fit and came in for Mohammad Wasim, with Moin Khan being retained as a specialist batsman. This hardly seemed the best way of utilising available resources. South Africa, having learned from their experiences in Durban, brought in spinner Adams in place of Klusener. Rashid surprised many by deciding to field when he won the toss, but events seemed to justify his move.

There appeared to be a lack of confidence in South Africa's top order. Bacher and Kallis fell without offering a shot to deliveries from Waqar Younis, and the pace man bowled Ackerman between bat and pad. Waqar claimed his fourth victim with the last ball before lunch, Kirsten edging the delivery into his stumps. South Africa were 81 for four, and Rashid Latif had been vindicated.

Mushtaq Ahmed threatened to weave his spell when he had Hudson caught, bat and pad, at silly point, but the demons in the pitch, if there had been any, were vanishing, and Cronje and Pollock added 78. Wasim had not looked at his best, but he broke the stand when he had Pollock taken at second slip. Boucher emulated his captain by hitting Mushtaq high for six, and he gave more evidence of his class in helping Cronje to put on 57. It was Cronje who became Waqar's fifth victim, and South Africa closed on 262 for seven.

Rain prevented any play on the Saturday, and although de Villiers was soon out on the Sunday morning, giving Waqar 250 wickets in 51 Tests, Boucher completed another useful fifty and steered South Africa to 293. This was not a formidable total, but it proved too big for Pakistan. It would be fair to say that the conditions aided swing bowling and that the pitch was now more favourable to pace, but some of Pakistan's batting was deplorable and only a last wicket stand of 22 saved them from the indignity of having to follow on. Donald was supreme and broke the back of the innings when he produced a burst that brought him four for 5 in 13 deliveries. His victims were Saeed, Ijaz (first ball), Aamir and Inzamam-ul-Haq. The Pakistan innings was in ruins. At this point, Fanie de Villiers took over. He had announced that this would be his

First Test Match – South Africa v. Pakistan

14, 15, 16, 17 and 18 February 1998 at Wanderers, Johannesburg

South Africa

	First Innings		Second Innings	
A.M. Bacher	lbw, **b** Waqar Younis	46	(2) not out	20
G. Kirsten *	**c** Azhar Mahmood, **b** Waqar	3	(1) not out	20
J.H. Kallis	**c** Mohammad Wasim, **b** Shoaib	15		
D.J. Cullinan	**b** Waqar Younis	16		
A.C. Hudson	**b** Mushtaq Ahmed	33		
H.H. Gibbs	lbw, **b** Mushtaq Ahmed	4		
S.M. Pollock	**c** Mushtaq, **b** Azhar Mahmood	21		
M.V. Boucher †	**c** Mohammad Wasim, **b** Saqlain	78		
L. Klusener	**b** Mushtaq Ahmed	6		
P.L. Symcox	**c** Shoaib, **b** Saqlain Mushtaq	108		
A.A. Donald	not out	0		
	b **2**, lb **21**, w **4**, nb **7**	34	b **2**, lb **2**	4
		364	(for no wicket)	44

	O	M	R	W	O	M	R	W
Waqar Younis	23	4	80	3	5.2	1	18	–
Shoaib Akhtar	21	2	84	1	5	–	22	–
Azhar Mahmood	20	1	52	1				
Mushtaq Ahmed	27	5	66	3				
Saqlain Mushtaq	12.2	–	47	2				
Aamir Sohail	1	–	12	–				

Fall of Wickets
1–**14**, 2–**56**, 3–**86**, 4–**91**, 5–**96**, 6–**149**, 7–**157**, 8–**166**, 9–**361**

Pakistan

	First Innings	
Saeed Anwar	**c** Cullinan, **b** Donald	2
Aamir Sohail *	**c** Boucher, **b** Pollock	12
Ijaz Ahmed	**c** Pollock, **b** Donald	34
Mohammad Wasim	**c** Boucher, **b** Klusener	44
Inzamam-ul-Haq	**b** Klusener	0
Moin Khan †	**c** Gibbs, **b** Klusener	46
Azhar Mahmood	**c** Donald, **b** Pollock	136
Saqlain Mushtaq	**c** Boucher, **b** Kallis	2
Mushtaq Ahmed	**c** Kirsten, **b** Kallis	10
Waqar Younis	**c** Hudson, **b** Klusener	10
Shoaib Akhtar	not out	4
	b **12**, lb **6**, w **3**, nb **8**	29
		329

	O	M	R	W
Donald	23	4	89	2
Pollock	24.1	10	55	2
Klusener	24	6	93	4
Kallis	18	7	58	2
Symcox	5	–	16	–

Fall of Wickets
1–**15**, 2–**15**, 3–**87**, 4–**91**, 5–**112**, 6–**219**, 7–**230**, 8–**255**, 9–**296**

Umpires: C.J. Mitchley & P. Willey

Match drawn

Second Test Match – South Africa v. Pakistan

26, 27, 28 February, 1 and 2 March 1998 at Kingsmead, Durban

Pakistan

	First Innings		Second Innings	
Saeed Anwar	lbw, **b** Donald	**43**	lbw, **b** Pollock	**118**
Aamir Sohail *	**c** Boucher, **b** Pollock	**17**	**c** Boucher, **b** Donald	**36**
Ijaz Ahmed	**c** de Villiers, **b** Pollock	**2**	**b** de Villiers	**24**
Mohammad Wasim	**c** Kallis, **b** Donald	**12**	run out	**5**
Yousuf Youhana	**c** Boucher, **b** Donald	**5**	**c** Boucher, **b** Pollock	**1**
Moin Khan †	**c** Donald, **b** de Villiers	**25**	lbw, **b** Pollock	**5**
Azhar Mahmood	**b** Donald	**132**	**c** Boucher, **b** Pollock	**1**
Mushtaq Ahmed	**c** Kallis, **b** Klusener	**2**	run out	**20**
Waqar Younis	**c** Hudson, **b** Donald	**6**	**c** Klusener, **b** Pollock	**0**
Shoaib Akhtar	**c** Boucher, **b** Klusener	**6**	not out	**1**
Fazl-e-Akbar	not out	**0**	**c** Klusener, **b** Pollock	**0**
	b **2**, lb **1**, w **2**, nb **4**	**9**	lb **7**, w **2**, nb **6**	**15**
		259		**226**

	O.	M.	R.	W	O	M	R	W
Donald	19.2	4	79	**5**	10	3	20	**1**
de Villiers	18	5	55	**1**	16	1	51	**1**
Pollock	18	3	55	**2**	22.3	6	50	**6**
Klusener	18	3	67	**2**	9	1	32	**–**
Cronje	5	–	20	**–**				
Kallis	17	1	46	**–**				

Fall of Wickets
1–**35**, 2–**37**, 3–**70**, 4–**82**, 5–**89**, 6–**127**, 7–**142**, 8–**153**, 9–**233**
1–**101**, 2–**159**, 3–**164**, 4–**182**, 5–**198**, 6–**203**, 7–**212**, 8–**220**, 9–**226**

South Africa

	First Innings		Second Innings	
A.M. Bacher	**c** Moin Khan, **b** Fazl-e-Akbar	**17**	(2) lbw, **b** Fazl-e-Akbar	**0**
G. Kirsten	**c** Azhar Mahmood, **b** Fazl-e-Akbar	**0**	(1) **c** sub (Rashid Latif) **b** Mushtaq Ahmed	**25**
J.H. Kallis	**b** Shoaib Akhtar	**43**	**c** Moin, **b** Mushtaq Ahmed	**22**
H.D. Ackerman	**c** Mohammad Wasim, **b** Mushtaq	**57**	lbw, **b** Mushtaq Ahmed	**11**
A.C. Hudson	lbw, **b** Shoaib Akhtar	**0**	**c** Fazl-e-Akbar, **b** Mushtaq	**8**
W.J. Cronje *	lbw, **b** Mushtaq Ahmed	**3**	**c** Moin Khan, **b** Waqar Younis	**11**
S.M. Pollock	not out	**70**	**st** Moin, **b** Mushtaq Ahmed	**30**
M.V. Boucher †	**b** Shoaib Akhtar	**2**	**b** Waqar Younis	**52**
L. Klusener	**b** Shoaib Akhtar	**6**	lbw, **b** Mushtaq Ahmed	**2**
P.S. de Villiers	**b** Shoaib Akhtar	**7**	not out	**46**
A.A. Donald	lbw, **b** Mushtaq Ahmed	**11**	lbw, **b** Waqar Younis	**0**
	b **4**, lb **2**, w **3**, nb **6**	**15**	lb **15**, nb **3**	**18**
		231		**225**

	O	M	R	W	O	M	R	W
Waqar Younis	19	3	63	**–**	17.2	1	60	**3**
Fazl-e-Akbar	8	2	16	**2**	5	2	16	**1**
Shoaib Akhtar	12	1	43	**5**	11	–	20	**–**
Mushtaq Ahmed	32	9	71	**3**	37	13	78	**6**
Azhar Mahmood	17	6	28	**–**	11	4	12	**–**
Aamir Sohail	2	–	4	**–**	7	1	24	**–**

Fall of Wickets
1–**4**, 2–**32**, 3–**115**, 4–**115**, 5–**120**, 6–**139**, 7–**154**, 8–**166**, 9–**178**
1–**2**, 2–**42**, 3–**49**, 4–**76**, 5–**79**, 6–**110**, 7–**120**, 8–**133**, 9–**219**

Umpires: D.L. Orchard & M.J. Kitchen

Pakistan won by 29 runs

Third Test Match – South Africa v. Pakistan

6, 7, 8, 9 and 10 March 1998 at St George's Park, Port Elizabeth

South Africa

	First Innings		Second Innings	
A.M. Bacher	lbw, **b** Waqar Younis	**3**	(2) **c** Rashid Latif, **b** Waqar	**11**
G. Kirsten	**b** Waqar Younis	**38**	(1) **c** Rashid Latif, **b** Azhar	**44**
J.H. Kallis	**b** Waqar Younis	**10**	**c** Rashid Latif, **b** Azhar	**69**
H.D. Ackerman	**b** Waqar Younis	**11**	**c** Inzamam-ul-Haq, **b** Azhar	**42**
A.C. Hudson	**c** Moin, **b** Mushtaq Ahmed	**42**	**b** Waqar Younis	**4**
W.J. Cronje *	lbw, **b** Waqar Younis	**85**	not out	**7**
S.M. Pollock	**c** Azhar, **b** Wasim Akram	**38**	**b** Waqar Younis	**7**
M.V. Boucher †	**c** Rashid, **b** Wasim Akram	**52**	**b** Waqar Younis	**4**
P.S. de Villiers	**c** Azhar Mahmood, **b** Waqar	**1**		
A.A. Donald	lbw, **b** Wasim Akram	**1**		
P.R. Adams	not out	**2**		
	lb **3**, nb **7**	**10**	b **1**, lb **6**, w **1**, nb **10**	**18**
		293	(for 7 wickets, dec.)	**206**

	O	M	R	W	O	M	R	W
Wasim Akram	26	8	70	**3**	16	3	37	**–**
Waqar Younis	23	6	78	**6**	17.4	4	55	**4**
Azhar Mahmood	21	7	47	**–**	15	1	49	**3**
Shoaib Akhtar	13	5	30	**–**	16	1	58	**–**
Mushtaq Ahmed	16	1	65	**1**				
Aamir Sohail	1	1	0	**–**				

Fall of Wickets
1–**3**, 2–**13**, 3–**36**, 4–**81**, 5–**122**, 6–**200**, 7–**257**, 8–**263**, 9–**269**
1–**17**, 2–**92**, 3–**170**, 4–**185**, 5–**197**, 6–**198**, 7–**206**

Pakistan

	First Innings		Second Innings	
Saeed Anwar	**c** Boucher, **b** Donald	**18**	**c** Kallis, **b** Donald	**55**
Aamir Sohail	**c** Hudson, **b** Donald	**3**	(7) lbw, **b** Adams	**7**
Ijaz Ahmed	**c** Boucher, **b** Donald	**0**	(2) lbw, **b** de Villiers	**15**
Inzamam-ul-Haq	**c** Boucher, **b** Donald	**6**	(3) **st** Boucher, **b** Aadms	**4**
Moin Khan	**c** Boucher, **b** de Villiers	**17**	(4) lbw, **b** Donald	**1**
Azhar Mahmood	**c** Adams, **b** de Villiers	**17**	**c** Kirsten, **b** Donald	**41**
Wasim Akram	not out	**30**	(5) **c** Boucher, **b** Pollock	**5**
Rashid Latif * †	lbw, **b** de Villiers	**0**	**c** Kallis, **b** Adams	**0**
Waqar Younis	**c** Kirsten, **b** de Villiers	**7**	**c** Boucher, **b** Donald	**3**
Shoaib Akhtar	**c** Boucher, **b** de Villiers	**0**	not out	**2**
Mushtaq Ahmed	**c** Boucher, **b** de Villiers	**5**	**b** de Villiers	**1**
	lb **3**	**3**		**0**
		106		134

	O	M	R	W	O	M	R	W
Donald	13	3	47	**4**	15	4	27	**4**
Pollock	16	5	33	**–**	17	2	46	**1**
de Villiers	11.5	5	23	**6**	12.5	3	25	**2**
Adams	16	8	36	**3**				

Fall of Wickets
1–**21**, 2–**21**, 3–**26**, 4–**29**, 5–**61**, 6–**61**, 7–**62**, 8–**84**, 9–**84**
1–**36**, 2–**67**, 3–**70**, 4–**75**, 5–**81**, 6–**93**, 7–**98**, 8–**120**, 9–**133**

Umpires: R.E. Koertzen & R.S. Dunne

South Africa won by 259 runs

Test Match Averages – South Africa v. Pakistan

South Africa Batting

	M	Inns	NOs	Runs	HS	Av	100s	50s
S.M. Pollock	3	5	1	166	70*	41.50	1	
M.V. Boucher	3	5	–	188	78	37.60	3	
W.J. Cronje	2	4	1	106	85	35.33	1	
J.H. Kallis	3	5	–	159	69	31.80	1	
H.D. Ackerman	2	4	–	121	57	30.25	1	
P.S. de Villiers	2	3	1	54	46*	27.00		
G. Kirsten	3	6	1	130	44	26.00		
A.M. Bacher	3	6	1	97	46	19.40		
A.C. Hudson	3	5	–	87	42	17.40		
L. Klusener	2	3	–	14	6	4.66		
A.A. Donald	3	4	–	12	11	3.00		

Played in one Test: D.J. Cullinan 16; H.H. Gibbs 4; P.L. Symcox 108; P.R. Adams 2*

Pakistan Batting

	M	Inns	NOs	Runs	HS	Av	100s	50s
Azhar Mahmood	3	5	–	327	136	65.40	2	
Saeed Anwar	3	5	–	236	118	47.20	1	1
Mohammad Wasim	2	3	–	61	44	20.33		
Moin Khan	3	5	–	94	46	18.80		
Aamir Sohail	3	5	–	75	36	15.00		
Ijaz Ahmed	3	5	–	75	34	15.00		
Mushtaq Ahmed	3	5	–	38	20	7.60		
Shoaib Akhtar	3	5	3	13	6	6.50		
Waqar Younis	3	5	–	26	10	5.20		
Inzamam-ul-Haq	2	3	–	10	6	3.33		

Played in one Test: Saqlain Mushtaq 2; Yousuf Youhana 5 & 1; Fazl-e-Akbar 0* & 0; Rashid Latif 0 & 0; Wasim Akram 30* & 5

South Africa Bowling

	Overs	Mds	Runs	Wks	Av	Best	5/inns
P.S. de Villiers	58.4	14	154	10	15.40	6/23	1
A.A. Donald	80.2	18	262	16	16.37	5/79	1
S.M. Pollock	97.4	26	239	11	21.72	6/50	1
L. Klusener	51	10	192	6	32.00	4/93	
J.H. Kallis	35	8	104	2	52.00	2/58	

Bowled in one innings: P.R. Adams 16–8–36–3; P.L. Symcox 5–0–16–0; W.J. Cronje 5–1–20–0

Pakistan Bowling

	Overs	Mds	Runs	Wks	Av	Best	10/m	5/inn
Fazl-e-Akbar	13	4	32	3	10.66	2/16		
Mushtaq Ahmed	112	28	280	13	21.53	6/78		1
Waqar Younis	105.2	19	354	16	22.12	6/78	1	1
Wasim Akram	42	11	107	3	35.66	3/70		
Shoaib Akhtar	78	9	257	6	42.83	5/43	1	
Azhar Mahmood	84	19	188	4	47.00	3/49		
Aamir Sohail	5	1	40	0	–			

Bowled in one innings: Saqlain Mushtaq 12.2 – 0 – 47 – 2

Fielding Figures

18 – M.V. Boucher (ct 17 / st 1); 4 – J.H. Kallis; 3 – G. Kirsten and A.C. Hudson; 2 – L. Klusener and A.A. Donald; 1 – D.J. Cullinan, H.H. Gibbs, S.M. Pollock, P.S. de Villiers and P.R. Adams

Fielding Figures

5 – Moin Khan (ct 4 / st 1); 4 – Azhar Mahmood and Rashid Latif (plus one as sub); 3 – Mohammad Wasim; 1 – Mushtaq Ahmed, Shoaib Akhtar, Fazl-e-Akbar and Inzamam-ul-Haq

last Test, and he celebrated the occasion by producing the best Test bowling figures of his career. He bowled South Africa to a first innings lead of 187, which must have astonished them, and, by the close, the lead had been increased by another 94 runs and only Bacher and Kirsten had been lost.

Waqar Younis took three wickets in the afternoon session of the fourth day to bring him match figures of 10 for 133. Six of his victims were clean bowled. He is a truly great bowler, and he deserved better support from his batsmen colleagues. In spite of Waqar's performance, South Africa never relaxed their grip on the game. Kallis and Ackerman had added 78 for the third wicket, and Cronje's declaration left Pakistan a target of 394. It soon became apparent that this was well beyond their reach.

Aamir Sohail had dropped down the order because of injury, and Ijaz Ahmed opened with Saeed Anwar. Ijaz fell to de Villiers, and the flood gates opened. Inzamam-ul-Haq scratched about for nearly an hour before being stumped off Adams, who also dismissed Aamir Sohail and Rashid Latif before the close, which came with Pakistan on 120 for seven. Rashid's miserable return had been compounded when he was out for a 'pair'.

The game lasted only 25 minutes on the fifth morning. Waqar was caught behind off Donald, and the catch gave Boucher his ninth dismissal of the match to equal the South African Test record for a wicket-keeper. Boucher, a cricketer of immense potential, took the individual award. Azhar Mahmood, one of the few to show appropriate discipline and correct technique, mishooked, and Fanie de Villiers brought the match and his Test career to an end when he bowled Mushtaq Ahmed.

South Africa had won well, but the side is undergoing much change, and there is a strong movement calling for the inclusion of more black players. Pakistan, it seems, are ever destined to frustrate. There is so much talent, so many lost opportunities, far too many political wranglings and unhealthy accusations. Azhar Mahmood had been named Man of the Series, but this was little consolation for a Pakistan side for whom troubles grew by the hour. Rashid had been appointed captain in an attempt to improve discipline and present the side in a more favourable light, but his own performances had left much to be desired, and, as the party set out for Zimbabwe, there was more disturbing news. Shoaib Akhtar and Fazl-e-Akbar, two of the younger players, were sent back to Pakistan in disgrace for breaches of discipline. It was alleged that they had been caught drinking long after the curfew hour imposed by Rashid and the management. Shoaib, in particular, is an outstanding talent and had played a major part in Pakistan's victory in the second Test. It was suggested that the two youngsters were not the only ones guilty of breaches of discipline and that senior members of the party had transgressed but that Rashid had been loathe to confront them. It was the saddest of ends to a series that had promised so much.

21, 22 and 23 February 1998
at Springbok Park, Bloemfontein
Free State 334 for 7 dec. (W.J. Cronje 150 not out) and 21 for 3
Pakistanis 441 (Inzamam-ul-Haq 119, Azhar Mahmood 111, Yousuf Youhana 54, J.F. Venter 4 for 106)
Match drawn

In between the first and second Test matches, the Pakistanis met Free State, who batted first on a good pitch. South Africa had cause to be content, for Hansie Cronje proved himself fit again after his cartilage operation with an unbeaten 150. The tourists still had the edge as Azhar Mahmood again battted most impressively, and, with Inzamam-ul-Haq, took his side to a first innings lead.

Fanie de Villiers ended his Test career in style. He had match figures of eight for 48 and completed South Africa's victory when he bowled Mushtaq Ahmed.
(David Munden / Sportsline)

Sri Lanka Tour

Sri Lanka came to South Africa to play two Test matches and to participate in the limited-over triangular tournament with Pakistan and the host nation. As preparation for the Test series, they met Gauteng and Boland in first-class matches. They failed to win either match.

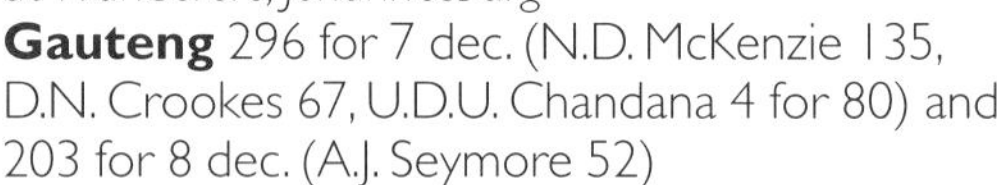

7, 8 and 9 March 1998
at Wanderers, Johannesburg
Gauteng 296 for 7 dec. (N.D. McKenzie 135, D.N. Crookes 67, U.D.U. Chandana 4 for 80) and 203 for 8 dec. (A.J. Seymore 52)
Sri Lankans 243 for 8 dec. (H.P. Tillekeratne 66 not out, R.S. Mahanama 52) and 138
Gauteng won by 118 runs

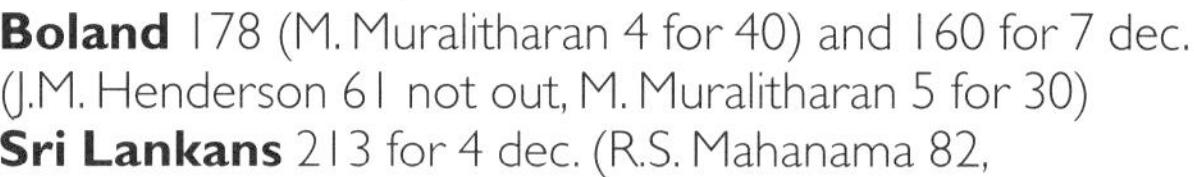

14, 15 and 16 March 1998
at Boland Bank Park, Paarl
Boland 178 (M. Muralitharan 4 for 40) and 160 for 7 dec. (J.M. Henderson 61 not out, M. Muralitharan 5 for 30)
Sri Lankans 213 for 4 dec. (R.S. Mahanama 82, H.P. Tillekeratne 52 not out) and 48 for 5
Match drawn

The closing stages of each match proved to be the unhappiest time for the tourists. McKenzie hit 19 fours and four sixes as Gauteng scored at four runs an over on the opening in Johannesburg. Sri Lanka declared 53 runs in arrears and had Gauteng in some trouble at 56 for five. Pothas and Snell brought about a recovery, and Eksteen set the visitors a target of 257. They lost their way completely, subsiding to 67 for six and losing three wickets for three runs at one period. Kaluwitharana offered defiance with nine fours in his 41 off 42 balls, but the recovery had come too late.

The bowling of off-spinner Muralitharan was the feature of the match at Paarl, where he returned match figures of nine for 70 and confirmed that he would pose the biggest threat to South Africa in the Test encounters. Sri Lanka's batting form was less encouraging, as, for the second time, Mahanama and Tillekeratne were the only players to show confidence. Set a target of 126 in 18 overs, Sri Lanka floundered to 11 for five before Aravinda de Silva joined Tillekaratne in restoring sanity.

Test Series
South Africa *v.* Sri Lanka

South Africa included Makhaya Ntini in their side for the first Test against Sri Lanka. A fast bowler, he became the first black cricketer to appear in the republic's Test side.

South Africa also brought back Cullinan, who had had an unhappy time in Australia, and they still seemed to be in search of a settled batting order. Sri Lanka's eleven presented no surprises. Cronje won the toss, and South Africa batted.

Bacher was soon caught at slip, and the introduction of Muralitharan into the attack posed problems for all batsmen. His action remains jerky, but he turns the ball viciously, and he soon deceived Ackerman. Cullinan may have trouble with leg-break bowling, but he finds off-spin less demanding. He dominated a stand of 95 with the patient Kirsten, and he and Cronje, ever positive, added 96 for the fourth wicket. Kallis went cheaply, and Cullinan, having lost patience, was out soon after. He was bowled by Wickremasinghe for 113. His runs came off 160 balls, and he hit a six and 13 fours. Pollock and Boucher took South Africa to 298 for six by the close.

They had put on 95 when Boucher was run out by Mahanama. The young wicket-keeper is a very promising batsman. He is temperamentally sound, and his concentration is admirable. He was at the crease for five minutes over two hours. Pollock was last out, having made 92, his highest Test score. He faced 135 balls and hit a six and eight fours. His best bowling and batting performances in Test cricket had come within weeks of each other.

Sri Lanka lost two early wickets, one of them being Jayasuriya, upon whom much depends, but Aravinda de Silva joined Atapattu in a partnership that realised 129 in 117 minutes. One has exhausted superlatives in describing de Silva. He hit 13 fours and faced 99 balls in making 77 before becoming Ntini's first Test victim. Atapattu was the patient anchor man. He batted three-and-a-quarter hours for his 60, and it is interesting to remember that he was once jettisoned by the Sri Lankan selectors because of his impetuosity. Sri Lanka closed on 212 for five, Atapattu and Ranatunga having fallen to successive deliveries from Adams.

Kaluwitharana was quickly out on the third morning, but the tail showed spirit, and Sri Lanka trailed South Africa by 112 runs on the first innings. When Vaas removed both openers for 18 the visitors had clawed their way back into the game, but Cullinan, again, and Kallis frustrated them in a stand of 116. Both were out before the end of the day, but South Africa had reached a commanding position by that time, 155 for four, a lead of 267.

Muralitharan and Jayasuriya monopolised the bowling on the fourth day, and runs were hard to come by against the accurate off-spin/left-arm combination. Cronje selected his shots carefully, defending solidly but ever eager to punish the loose ball. The spinners finished with four wickets each, but Sri Lanka faced a target of 377, a daunting task. They ended the day with 120 on the board and three men out, but two of those men were Jayasuriya and de Silva, the two on whom any hopes of an improbable victory would have rested.

The score moved to 171 before Atapattu's innings was brought to an end. He had batted for 243 minutes and faced 199 balls. Ranatunga was out four runs later, but Sri Lanka

Centuries for South Africa in both Tests against Sri Lanka by Daryll Cullinan.
(David Munden / Sportsline)

continued to fight. Any lingering hopes of victory vanished when Tillekeratne, Vaas and Kaluwitharana were out as only five runs were scored, Vaas being caught behind first ball. Wickremasinghe hit a maiden Test fifty, 51 off 44 balls, and was last out, being Ntini's second Test victim. Pollock was named Man of the Match.

South Africa made one change for the second Test, Liebenberg replacing Bacher, while Zoysa came in for the injured Vaas in the Sri Lankan side. Ranatunga won the toss, and Sri Lanka batted first. Jayasuriya played one of his whirlwind innings, 51 off 77 balls, but Sri Lanka lost three wickets for 68 runs in spite of South Africa losing Pollock with a groin strain. Mahanama and Ranatunga took the score to 165 before bad light ended play early.

Mahanama fell to Cronje on the second morning, but Tillekeratne batted defiantly and steered his side to a commendable 303. Donald had sustained an ankle injury, but he captured three wickets in the post-lunch session and blighted what threatened to be an even greater recovery from the low point of 68 of three. If Sri Lanka had been satisfied to reach 300, they were even more satisfied when

First Test Match – South Africa v. Sri Lanka

19, 20, 21, 22 and 23 March 1998 at Newlands, Cape Town

South Africa

	First Innings		Second Innings	
A.M. Bacher	c Mahanama, b Wickremasinghe	6	(2) c Kaulwitharana, b Vaas	0
G. Kirsten	lbw, b Vaas	62	(1) c Mahanama, b Vaas	15
H.D. Ackerman	c and b Muralitharan	23	(7) lbw, b Muralitharan	8
D.J. Cullinan	b Wickremasinghe	113	c Tillekeratne, b Muralitharan	68
W.J. Cronje *	c Mahanama, b Vaas	49	c Muralitharan, b Jayasuriya	74
J.H. Kallis	c Ranatunga, b Muralitharan	3	(3) st Kaluwitharana, b Jayasuriya	49
S.M. Pollock	lbw, b Wickremasinghe	92	(8) st Kaluwitharana, b Jayasuriya	6
M.V. Boucher †	run out	33	(6) c Jayasuriya, b Muralitharan	10
A.A. Donald	b Muralitharan	12	c Pushpakumara, b Jayasuriya	18
P.R. Adams	st Kaluwitharana, b Muralitharan	2	c Kaluwitharana, b Muralitharan	3
M. Ntini	not out	3	not out	0
	lb 8, nb 12	20	b 4, lb 3, w 1, nb 5	13
		418		264

	O	M	R	W	O	M	R	W
Vaas	21	2	75	2	11	3	41	2
Pushpakumara	20	3	81	–	8	–	24	–
Wickremasinghe	28.4	7	75	3	8	1	24	–
Muralitharan	45	8	135	4	41	10	108	4
Jayasuriya	6	1	29	–	33	7	53	4
P.A. de Silva	4	–	15	–	1	1	0	–
Atapattu	1	–	7	–				

Fall of Wickets
1–**20**, 2–**60**, 3–**155**, 4–**251**, 5–**260**, 6–**272**, 7–**367**, 8–**402**, 9–**414**
1–**5**, 2–**18**, 3–**134**, 4–**146**, 5–**166**, 6–**188**, 7–**219**, 8–**256**, 9–**260**

Sri Lanka

	First Innings		Second Innings	
S.T. Jayasuriya	c Boucher, b Donald	17	lbw, b Donald	0
M.A. Arapattu	c Cullinan, b Adams	60	cand b Adams	71
R.S. Mahanama	c Boucher, b Donald	9	c Kallis, b Pollock	11
P.A. de Silva	c Boucher, b Ntini	77	c Kallis, b Adams	37
A. Ranatunga*	c Ackerman, b Adams	20	c Kirsten, b Kallis	43
H.P. Tillekeratne	c Boucher, b Pollock	22	lbw, b Donald	13
R.S. Kaluwitharana †	lbw, b Pollock	13	b Pollock	45
W.P.U.J.C. Vaas	c Boucher, b Pollock	30	c Boucher, b Donald	0
G.P. Wickremasinghe	c sub (Klusener), b Pollock	11	b Ntini	51
M. Muralitharan	not out	15	run out	10
K.R. Pushpakumara	c Boucher, b Donald	4	not out	9
	b 8, lb 7, w 1, nb 12	28	b 5, lb 3, nb 8	16
		306		306

	O	M	R	W	O	M	R	W
Donald	21.3	7	66	3	20	4	64	3
Pollock	26	5	83	4	23	3	77	2
Ntini	10	1	57	1	5.3	–	17	1
Kallis	7	1	23	–	15	5	45	1
Adams	20	2	62	2	27	3	90	2
Cronje	5	3	5	–				

Fall of Wickets
1–**20**, 2–**36**, 3–**165**, 4–**194**, 5–**195**, 6–**219**, 7–**241**, 8–**270**, 9–**300**
1–**3**, 2–**27**, 3–**98**, 4–**171**, 5–**175**, 6–**234**, 7–**234**, 8–**239**, 9–**287**

Umpires: R.S. Dune & D.L. Orchard

South Africa won by 70 runs

Second Test Match South Africa v. Sri Lanka

27, 28, 29 and 30 March 1998 at Centurion Park, Centurion

Sri Lanka

	First Innings		Second Innings	
S.T. Jayasuriya	c Boucher, b Ntinia	51	b Donald	16
M.S. Atapattu	run out	12	c Boucher, b Donald	7
R.S. Mahanama	c Kallis, b Cronje	50	lbw, b Donald	0
P.A. de Silva	c Adams, b Ntini	1	run out	41
A. Ranatunga *	lbw, b Donald	73	c Boucher, b Cronje	0
H.P. Tillekeratne	c Kirsten, b Cronje	55	c sub (Crookes), b Cronje	0
R.S. Kaluwitharana †	c Boucher, b Donald	9	run out	0
G.P. Wickremasinghe	c Adams, b Donald	10	b Adams	21
D.N.T. Zoysa	lbw, b Kallis	0	c Boucher, b Donald	14
M. Muralitharan	c Boucher, b Cronje	11	c Kirsten, b Donald	15
K.R. Pushpakumara	not out	0	not out	0
	b 6, lb 14, w 3, nb 8	31	lb 5, nb 3	8
		303		122

	O	M	R	W	O	M	R	W
Donald	33	10	73	3	13.3	2	54	5
Pollock	7.1	3	9	–				
Kallis	19	7	42	1	7	3	12	–
Adams	22	6	77	–	7	1	25	1
Ntini	22.5	7	61	2	6	2	13	–
Cronje	14.3	3	21	3	8	3	13	2

Fall of Wickets
1–**53**, 2–**66**, 3–**68**, 4–**186**, 5–**228**, 6–**240**, 7–**254**, 8–**255**, 9–**290**
1–**19**, 2–**19**, 3–**40**, 4–**40**, 5–**42**, 6–**42**, 7–**85**, 8–**98**, 9–**118**

South Africa

	First Innings		Second Innings	
G.F.J. Liebenberg	lbw, b Pushpakumara	0	(2) lbw, b Muralitharan	45
G. Kirsten	b Muralitharan	13	(1) not out	75
H.D. Ackerman	b Zoysa	7	b Muralitharan	2
D.J. Cullinan	c Wickremasinghe, b Jayasuriya	103	lbw, b Muralitharan	0
W.J. Cronje *	st Kaluwitharana, b Muralitharan	10	c de Silva, b Jayasuriya	82
J.H. Kallis	c Kaluwitharana, b Wickremasinghe	12	not out	0
S.M. Pollock	b Muralitharan	1		
M.V. Boucher †	c Jayasuriya, b Muralitharan	13		
A.A. Donald	b Muralitharan	6		
P.R. Adams	c and b Jayasuriya	12		
M. Ntini	not out	2		
	b 1, lb 6, w 6, nb 8	21	b 8, lb 3, nb 11	22
		200	for 4 wickets	226

	O	M	R	W	O	M	R	W
Pushpakumara	16	2	55	1	7	2	27	–
Zoysa	12	2	29	1	2	–	11	–
Wickremasinghe	15	2	36	1	6	1	7	–
Muralitharan	30	8	63	5	23.5	4	94	3
Jayasuriya	5	2	10	2	19	6	62	1
P.A. de Silva	5	1	14	–				

Fall of Wickets
1–**0**, 2–**11**, 3–**75**, 4–**103**, 5–**122**, 6–**137**, 7–**170**, 8–**182**, 9–**186**
1–**89**, 2–**99**, 3–**99**, 4–**215**

Umpires: Javed Akhtar & R.E. Koertzen

South Africa won by 6 wickets

they captured the first three South African wickets for 75 before the close of play.

Of those 75 runs, Cullinan made 42, and he continued to thwart Sri Lanka on the third day. He reached his second century in successive Tests. He hit 13 fours, faced 185 balls and was eighth out, having batted for 307 minutes. None of his colleagues made 20. They succumbed to Muralitharan, who again turned the ball sharply to claim his 12th five-wicket haul in Test cricket. He bowled his side to a first innings lead of 103 and Sri Lanka looked set for victory, but they suffered a dreadful reverse in their second innings. Before the close of play on the third day, for no obvious reason, they lost seven wickets for 93 runs. Two of the batsmen were run out, the second being de Silva, who had hit a six and six fours and had doubled the score with Wickremasinghe before attempting a suicidal run.

Donald brought the innings to a swift close on the fourth morning, and South Africa needed 226 to win. Donald finished with five for 54 and now had more than 200 Test wickets to his credit.

Liebenberg and Kirsten gave South Africa a good start, scoring 89 in two hours before Muralitharan broke through, trapping Liebenberg leg before. The off-spinner quickly accounted for Ackerman and, vitally, Cullinan, and South Africa were 99 for three. Cronje responded to what could have been a crisis in a most positive manner. He took 11 off one over from Muralitharan and raced to his fifty off 31 balls, the second fastest in Test history. He had made 29 off 27 balls when he hit Muralitharan for a four, which was followed by three sixes. Sri Lanka missed chances, and when Cronje was finally caught he had made 82 off 63 balls with six sixes and eight fours. More significantly, he had taken South Africa to within 11 runs of victory.

Sri Lanka could only rue what might have been, and should have been. Donald was named Man of the Match, and Cullinan had most certainly booked himself a place on the tour of England. For South Africa, the opening partnership remained something of a problem.

11 March 1998
at Gert van Rensburg Stadium, Fochville
Sri Lankans 295 for 8 (R.P. Arnold 113, A. Ranatunga 80)
North West 202 (M.J. Lavine 51, P.A. de Silva 5 for 44)
Sri Lankans won by 93 runs

The Sri Lankans played a 50-over match before the Test series as a warm-up for the triangular tournament. Arnold, who did not figure in the Tests, hit 113 off 124 balls and added 165 with Ranatunga after three wickets had fallen for 35 runs. Aravinda de Silva produced one of his best bowling performances.

Triangular Tournament – Standard Bank International Series

South Africa, Pakistan and Sri Lanka

A capacity crowd at Kingsmead welcomed the start of the one-day series and saw a highly entertaining game. South Africa gave one-day international debuts to Elworthy, once of Lancashire, and Telemachus, both of them fast medium pace bowlers. Cronje won the toss and chose to bat first. Kirsten was out third ball, and Cullinan and Rindel were both back in the pavilion before the score reached 50. Cronje made 34 off 46 balls before being run out by Waqar, but this brought together Kallis and Rhodes, who established a South African fifth wicket record for limited-over internationals, adding 183 without being parted. Kallis made 109 off 114 balls and hit eight fours, and Rhodes, who passed 3,000 runs in one-day internationals, scored 94 off 95 balls with eight fours and two sixes.

Debutants Elworthy and Telemachus played a major part in helping South Africa to reduce Pakistan to 75 for seven, but the visitors' tail responded vigorously. Wasim Akram hit 34 off 27 balls, and Abdul Razzaq and Waqar Younis 72 for the last wicket. Abdul Razzaq's unbeaten 46 is the highest score made by a number ten in a one-day international.

South Africa took a giant step towards the final when they had a convincing win over Sri Lanka in the second match of the series. Kirsten and Rindel gave them a sound foundation, but once more it was Jonty Rhodes who brought the innings to life with 43 off 51 balls. His running between the wickets was exemplary. Crookes also sparkled with 26 off as many balls.

Roger Telemachus made his debut for South Africa in the Standard Bank International series and twice won the Man of the Match award.
(Davd Munden / Sportsline)

A dynamic contributor in every department of the game to South Africa's limited-over side, Lance Klusener.
(Nigel French / ASP)

Jayasuriya batted with considerable panache, making 68 off 83 balls, but he had little support, and Sri Lanka were never in contention. Playing in his second international, Telemachus captured four wickets and the individual award.

Sri Lanka suffered another defeat two days later. They batted splendidly: Jayasuriya and Kaluwitharana put on 107 for the first wicket, and Aravinda de Silva and Ranatunga added 142 for the third wicket. Aravinda de Silva's innings was quite remarkable in that he hit one six and one four yet made 62 off 79 balls. Ranatunga's 86 came off 82 balls and included five fours.

Pakistan were deducted an over as punishment for their slow over-rate, but they won with six balls to spare. Ijaz Ahmed and Inzamam-ul-Haq shared a thunderous third wicket stand of 80. Ijaz hit four sixes and three fours in his 55-ball innings, and Inzamam's unbeaten 116 came off 110 deliveries and included four sixes and four fours. He was ably supported as Pakistan romped to victory.

There was a second win for Pakistan over Sri Lanka in Paarl in spite of a middle order collapse that saw three wickets fall for one run. Saeed Anwar and Ijaz Ahmed had scored 80 for the second wicket to give the innings a good foundation, but it was the late order that gave Pakistan the initiative with some bold hitting. Wasim and Waqar destroyed Sri Lanka's top order, and there was to be no recovery.

The later order again gave Pakistan's innings some impetus in the match against South Africa in East London. Wasim Akram and Mohammad Hussain made 52 for the eighth wicket in the last six overs. Cronje had stifled the earlier batsmen with an excellent spell of bowling, and he rallied his side when it was his turn to bat. Rindel made 64 off 85 balls and was fourth out at 122. Pollock and Cronje then added 89. The South African skipper hit four sixes and three fours and faced 53 deliveries. Pollock was seventh out, but South Africa needed just nine to win by then, and victory came with 22 balls to spare.

The host nation had swept all before them in the competition while Sri Lanka were without a victory until the two teams met at St George's Park. Sri Lanka bowled well and fielded well, and South Africa were dismissed for 231 with one ball of their quota unused. Their total still seemed enough to win the match when Sri Lanka were reduced to 17 for three. Atapattu and Ranatunga had other ideas, and the pair added 108 for the fourth wicket before Atapattu was bowled by Kallis. Mahanama joined his skipper, and the last 107 runs required for victory came in 85 minutes. Ranatunga, who passed 4,500 runs in one-day international cricket, hit a six and nine fours and faced 119 balls for his unbeaten 93.

Ranatunga and Atapattu were again in form as Sri Lanka trounced Pakistan to keep alive their hopes of reaching the final. On this occasion, Ranatunga and Atapattu put on 138 for the fourth wicket, and Waqar Younis proved very expensive for the second time in the series. Facing a target of 289, Pakistan lost early wickets to Vaas and then succumbed to the off-spin of Muralitharan.

For the second time in three days, Pakistan surrendered weakly, losing their last four wickets for 10 runs and being bowled out in 41.5 overs by South Africa at Centurion Park. The home side lost Rindel in the opening over, but thereafter they had an easy path to victory.

The last of the qualifying matches arrived with the question as to who would meet South Africa in the final still unanswered. The question was soon resolved when Sri Lanka gave a dreadful batting performance and were all out for 105 in 36 overs. A small target gave South Africa few problems, and they were winners after 26.3 overs. Sri Lanka finished level on points with Pakistan who qualified for the final by virtue of having beaten Sri Lanka in two of the three encounters between the two sides.

Standard Bank International Series Qualifying Table

	P	W	L	Pts
South Africa	6	5	1	10
Pakistan	6	2	4	4
Sri Lanka	6	2	4	4

Match One – South Africa v. Pakistan

3 April 1998 at Kingsmead, Durban

South Africa

G. Kirsten	c Mohammad Wasim, b Wasim Akram	0
M.J.R. Rindel	c Moin Khan, b Waqar Younis	17
D.J. Cullinan	c Mohammad Wasim, b Wasim Akram	16
W.J. Cronje *	run out	34
J.H. Kallis	not out	109
J.N. Rhodes	not out	94
M.V. Boucher †		
L. Klusener		
P.L. Symcox		
S. Elworthy		
R. Telemachus		
	b **4**, lb **2**, w **2**, nb **2**	10
	50 overs (for 4 wickets)	280

	O	M	R	W
Wasim Akram	10	–	39	2
Waqar Younis	10	–	73	1
Azhar Mahmood	10	–	59	–
Abdul Razzaq	5.2	–	15	–
Shahid Afridi	9.4	–	52	–
Aamir Sohail	5	–	36	–

Fall of Wickets
1–**1**, 2–**26**, 3–**48**, 4–**97**

Pakistan

Saeed Anwar	lbw, b Elworthy	0
Shahid Afridi	c Cullinan, b Elworthy	19
Aamir Sohail *	b Telemachus	8
Mohammad Wasim	c and b Cronje	9
Ijaz Ahmed	c Cronje, b Klusener	5
Yousuf Youhana	run out	15
Moin Khan †	b Klusener	45
Azhar Mahmood	c Kallis, b Klusener	1
Wasim Akram	b Symcox	27
Abdul Razzaq	not out	46
Waqar Younis	b Telemachus	33
	b **2**, lb **6**, w **5**, nb **7**	20
	47.4 overs	228

	O	M	R	W
Elworthy	8	–	25	2
Telemachus	8.4	–	40	2
Cronje	9	–	31	1
Klusener	10	2	31	3
Kallis	5	–	50	–
Symcox	7	–	43	1

Fall of Wickets
1–**1**, 2–**18**, 3–**37**, 4–**45**, 5–**63**, 6–**72**, 7–**75**, 8–**128**, 9–**156**

Umpires: W.A. Diedricks & D.L. Orchard *Man of the Match*: J.H. Kallis

South Africa won by 52 runs

Match Two – South Africa v. Sri Lanka

5 April 1998 at Wanderers, Johannesburg

South Africa

M.J.R. Rindel	st Kaluwitharana, b Muralitharan	59
G. Kirsten	b P.A. de Sillva	29
L. Klusener	b P.A. de Silva	26
D.J. Cullinan	b Chandana	24
W.J. Cronje *	c P.A. de Silva, b Chandana	22
J.H. Kallis	c Vaas, b Chandana	5
J.N. Rhodes	not out	43
D.N. Crookes	c Wickremasinghe, b Dharmasena	26
M.V. Boucher †	b Jayasuriya	6
S. Elworthy	not out	14
R. Telemachus		
	lb **11**, w **1**	12
	50 overs (for 8 wickets)	266

	O	M	R	W
Vaas	7	–	33	–
Wickremasinghe	6	–	32	–
Dharmasena	6	–	37	1
P.A. de Silva	6	–	26	2
Muralitharan	10	–	39	1
Chandana	10	1	48	3
Jayasuriya	5	–	40	1

Fall of Wickets
1–**67**, 2–**117**, 3–**121**, 4–**160**, 5–**169**, 6–**172**, 7–**218**, 8–**243**

Sri Lanka

S.T. Jayasuriya	c Crookes, b Cronje	68
M.S. Atapattu	c Rhodes, b Telemachus	4
R.S. Mahanama	c Kirsten, b Elworthy	11
P.A. de Silva	c Rindel, b Cronje	28
R.S. Kaluwitharana †	c Boucher, b Telemachus	19
A. Ranatunga *	c Boucher, b Crookes	0
H.D.P.K. Dharmasena	c Rindel, b Crookes	21
U.D.U. Chandana	c Klusener, b Elworthy	26
W.P.U.J.C. Vaas	b Telemachus	8
G.P. Wickremasinghe	b Telemachus	0
M. Muralitharan	not out	13
	b **3**, lb **3**, w **3**, nb **2**	11
	46.3 overs	209

	O	M	R	W
Elworthy	8.3	1	34	2
Telemachus	10	–	43	4
Cronje	9	–	43	2
Klusener	9	–	46	–
Crookes	10	1	37	2

Fall of Wickets
1–**12**, 2–**51**, 3–**116**, 4–**127**, 5–**127**, 6–**151**, 7–**169**, 8–**182**, 9–**182**

Umpires: S.B. Lambson & C.J. Mitchley *Man of the Match*: R. Telemachus

South Africa won by 57 runs

Match Three – Pakistan v. Sri Lanka

7 April 1998 at Kimberley Country Club, Kimberley

Sri Lanka

S.T. Jayasuriya	c Rashid, b Abdul Razzaq	57
R.S. Kaluwitharana †	run out	54
P.A. de Silva	b Wasim Akram	62
A. Ranatunga*	c Azhar Mahmood, b Wasim Akram	86
R.S. Mahanama	b Wasim Akram	10
U.D.U. Chandana	run out	1
D.P.M. Jayawardene	run out	6
H.D.P.K. Dharmasena	not out	1
W.P.U.J.C. Vaas		
M. Muralitharan		
K.R. Pushpakumara		
	lb 2, w 15, nb 1	18
	50 overs (for 7 wickets)	295

	O	M	R	W
Wasim Akram	10	1	53	3
Waqar Younis	10	1	68	–
Abdul Razzaq	8	–	51	1
Azhar Mahmood	9	–	60	–
Mohammad Hussain	10	–	40	–
Ijaz Ahmed	3	–	21	–

Fall of Wickets
1–107, 2–128, 3–270, 4–287, 5–287, 6–291, 7–295

Pakistan

Saeed Anwar	c Mahanama, b Pushpakumara	17
Abdul Razzaq	c and b Pushpakumara	15
Ijaz Ahmed	c Pushpakumara	59
Inzamam-ul-Haq	not out	116
Moin Khan	c Vaas, b Dharmasena	34
Mohammad Hussain	b Vaas	20
Azhar Mahmood	c Pushpakumara, b Muralitharan	2
Wasim Akram	not out	19
Yousuf Youhana		
Rashid Latif * †		
Waqar Younis		
	b 1, lb 11, w 5, nb 1	18
	48 overs (for 6 wickets)	300

	O	M	R	W
Vaas	10	–	58	1
Pushpakumara	8	–	56	2
P.A. de Silva	1	–	11	–
Dharmasena	10	–	35	2
Muralitharan	10	–	61	1
Chandana	6	–	42	–
Jayasuriya	3	–	25	–

Fall of Wickets
1–31, 2–46, 3–126, 4–212, 5–160, 6–269

Umpires: D.F. Becker & R.E. Koertzen *Man of the Match*: Inzamam-ul-Haq

Pakistan won by 4 wickets

Match Four – Pakistan v. Sri Lanka

9 April 1998 at Boland Bank Park, Paarl

Pakistan

Saeed Anwar	c Jayasuriya, b Muralitharan	53
Shahid Afridi	c Dharmasena, b K.S.C. de Silva	17
Ijaz Ahmed	run out	65
Inzamam-ul-Haq	c Kaluwitharana, b Muralitharan	9
Yousuf Youhana	st Kaluwitharana, b Muralitharan	0
Azhar Mahmood	c Mahanama, b Chandana	0
Rashid Latif* †	c K.S.C. de Silva, b P.A. de Silva	36
Wasim Akram	c and b P.A. de Silva	22
Abdul Razzaq	c Jayawardene, b P.A. de Silva	22
Mohammad Hussain	c Mahanama, b P.A. de Silva	10
Waqar Younis	not out	2
	lb 4, w 6, nb 3	13
	48.5 overs	249

	O	M	R	W
Pushpakumara	8	–	46	–
K.S.C. de Silva	6	–	41	1
Dharmasena	10	–	49	–
Muralitharan	10	–	29	3
Chandana	4	–	19	1
Jayasuriya	3	–	16	–
P.A. de Silva	7.5	–	45	4

Fall of Wickets
1–31, 2–111, 3–141, 4–141, 5–142, 6–164, 7–214, 8–214, 9–240

Sri Lanka

S.T. Jayasuriya	lbw, b Waqar Younis	8
R.S. Kaluwitharana †	c Rashid, b Wasim Akram	18
R.S. Mahanama	lbw, b Wasim Akram	7
P.A. de Silva	b Abdul Razzaq	31
A. Ranatunga *	lbw, b Waqar Younis	2
D.P.M. Jayawardene	run out	11
H.D.P.K. Dharmasena	c Yousuf Youhana, b Mohammad Hussain	17
U.D.U. Chandana	c Rashid Latif, b Wasim	23
M. Muralitharan	c Shahid Afridi, b Azhar Mahmood	0
K.R. Pushpakumara	b Azhar Mahmood	0
K.S.C. de Silva	not out	0
	lb 6, w 15, nb 1	22
	34.2 overs	139

	O	M	R	W
Wasim Akram	7.2	1	24	3
Waqar Younis	7	–	41	2
Azhar Mahmood	10	1	27	2
Abdul Razzaq	5	–	16	1
Mohammad Hussain	5	–	25	1

Fall of Wickets
1–19, 2–39, 3–46, 4–54, 5–91, 6–93, 7–128, 8–132, 9–132

Umpires: W.A. Diedricks & C.J. Mitchley *Man of the Match*: Wasim Akram

Pakistan won by 110 runs

Match Five – South Africa v. Pakistan

11 April 1998 at Buffalo Park, East London

Pakistan

Saeed Anwar	c Gibbs, b Cronje	28
Azhar Mahmood	c Cronje, b Pollock	14
Ijaz Ahmed	c Boucher, b Cronje	0
Inzamam-ul-Haq	lbw, b Klusener	52
Yousuf Youhana	c Kallis, b Crookes	39
Wasim Akram	run out	57
Moin Khan	b Elworthy	9
Rashid Latif * †	run out	3
Mohammad Hussain	not out	26
Abdul Razzaq		
Waqar Younis		
	lb 7, w 13, nb 2	22
	50 overs (for 8 wickets)	250

	O	M	R	W
Pollock	10	–	47	1
Elworthy	9	–	70	1
Cronje	10	2	17	2
Klusener	10	–	50	1
Crookes	9	–	43	1
Kallis	2	–	16	–

Fall of Wickets
1–**37**, 2–**41**, 3–**56**, 4–**142**, 5–**162**, 6–**189**, 7–**198**, 8–**250**

South Africa

M.J.R. Rindel	b Abdul Razzaq	64
J.H. Kallis	b Wasim Akram	6
H.H. Gibbs	c Mohammad Hussain, b Waqar Younis	5
D.J. Cullinan	b Waqar Younis	11
S.M. Pollock	c Inzamam-ul-Haq, b Azhar Mahmood	66
W.J. Cronje *	b Azhar Mahmood	52
J.N. Rhodes	c Rashid, b Azhar Mahmood	10
D.N. Crookes	not out	3
L. Klusener	not out	5
M.V. Boucher †		
S. Elworthy		
	lb 9, w 17, nb 6	32
	46.2 overs (for 7 wickets)	254

	O	M	R	W
Wasim Akram	10	1	40	1
Waqar Younis	10	1	47	2
Azhar Mahmood	10	–	50	3
Abdul Razzaq	6.2	–	33	1
Ijaz Ahmed	4	–	35	–
Mohammad Hussain	6	–	40	–

Fall of Wickets
1–**11**, 2–**34**, 3–**83**, 4–**122**, 5–**211**, 6–**230**, 7–**242**

Umpires: S.B. Lambson & D.L. Orchard *Man of the Match*: W.J. Cronje

South Africa won by 3 wickets

Match Six – South Africa v. Sri Lanka

13 April 1998 at St George's Park, Port Elizabeth

South Africa

M.J.R. Rindel	b Vaas	35
G. Kirsten	c Atapattu, b Muralitharan	46
P.L. Symcox	c Muralitharan, b Dharmasena	13
H.H. Gibbs	c Muralitharan, b Jayasuriya	33
W.J. Cronje*	c Ranatunga, b Muralitharan	0
J.N. Rhodes	st Kaluwitharana, b Muralitharan	36
S.M. Pollock	c P.A. de Silva, b Chandana	22
J.H. Kallis	lbw, b Jayasuriya	1
M.V. Boucher †	lbw, b Vaas	14
L. Klusener	c Atapattu, b Vaas	18
R. Telemachus	not out	1
	b 1, lb 9, w 2	12
	49.5 overs	231

	O	M	R	W
Vaas	7.5	–	33	3
Wickremasinghe	6	–	28	–
Dharmasena	10	–	37	1
Muralitharan	10	1	47	3
Chandana	9	–	42	1
Jayasuriya	7	–	34	2

Fall of Wickets
1–**78**, 2–**94**, 3–**104**, 4–**104**, 5–**150**, 6–**186**, 7–**189**, 8–**201**, 9–**230**

Sri Lanka

S.T. Jayasuriya	c Cronje, b Telemachus	7
R.S. Kaluwitharana †	lbw, b Telemachus	4
M.S. Atapattu	b Kallis	63
P.A. de Silva	b Pollock	1
A. Ranatunga *	not out	93
R.S. Mahanama	not out	46
H.D.P.K. Dharmasena		
U.D.U. Chandana		
W.P.U.J.C. Vaas		
M. Muralitharan		
G.P. Wickremasinghe		
	lb 9, w 7, nb 2	18
	46.4 overs (for 4 wickets)	232

	O	M	R	W
Pollock	8	–	29	1
Telemachus	7	1	37	2
Klusener	8	–	47	–
Cronje	7.4	–	36	–
Kallis	7	–	30	1
Symcox	9	–	44	–

Fall of Wickets
1–**8**, 2–**15**, 3–**17**, 4–**125**

Umpires: D.F. Becker & R.E. Koertzen *Man of the Match*: A. Ranatunga

Sri Lanka won by 6 wickets

Match Seven – Pakistan v. Sri Lanka

15 April 1998 at Willowmoore Park, Benoni

Sri Lanka

S.T. Jayasuriya	**b** Azhar Mahmood	**30**
R.S. Kaluwitharana †	**c** Mushtaq Ahmed, **b** Wasim	**33**
M.S. Atapattu	**b** Wasim Akram	**94**
P.A. de Silva	**b** Abdul Razzaq	**2**
A. Ranatunga *	**b** Wasim Akram	**78**
G.P. Wickremasinghe	**c** Waqar Younis, **b** Wasim	**0**
R.S. Mahanama	run out	**2**
D.P.M. Jayawardene	**c** Rashid Latif, **b** Waqar	**0**
H.D.P.K. Dharmasena	**c** Shahid Afridi, **b** Waqar	**20**
W.P.U.J.C. Vaas	run out	**4**
M. Muralitharan	not out	**1**
	lb **12**, w **12**	**24**
	49.4 overs	**288**

	O	M	R	W
Wasim Akram	9.4	1	43	**4**
Waqar Younis	10	–	86	**2**
Abdul Razzaq	9	1	50	**1**
Azhar Mahmood	10	–	33	**1**
Mushtaq Ahmed	9	–	46	**–**
Shahid Afridi	2	–	18	**–**

Fall of Wickets
1–**56**, 2–**91**, 3–**94**, 4–**232**, 5–**232**, 6–**238**, 7–**238**, 8–**281**, 9–**286**

Pakistan

Saeed Anwar	**b** Muralitharan	**59**
Shahid Afridi	run out	**6**
Ijaz Ahmed	**c** Kaluwitharana, **b** Vaas	**8**
Abdul Razzaq	**b** Vaas	**0**
Inzamam-ul-Haq	**c** Kaluwitharana, **b** Wickremasinghe	**3**
Yousuf Youhana	run out	**29**
Azhar Mahmood	**c** Dharmasena, **b** Muralitharan	**13**
Wasim Akram	**st** Kaluwitharana, **b** Muralitharan	**13**
Rashid Latif* †	**b** Muralitharan	**6**
Waqar Younis	**c** Vaas, **b** Muralitharan	**17**
Mushtaq Ahmed	not out	**1**
	lb **12**, w **6**	**18**
	39.2 overs	**173**

	O	M	R	W
Vaas	7	–	33	**2**
Wickremasinghe	7	1	23	**1**
Jayawardene	3	–	17	**–**
Dharmasena	8	–	30	**–**
Muralitharan	9.2	–	23	**5**
Jayasuriya	5	–	35	**–**

Fall of Wickets
1–**11**, 2–**32**, 3–**33**, 4–**44**, 5–**108**, 6–**126**, 7–**142**, 8–**151**, 9–**156**

Umpires: S.B. Lambson & C.J. Mitchley *Man of the Match*: M.S. Atapattu

Sri Lanka won by 115 runs

Match Eight – South Africa v. Pakistan

17 April 1998 at Centurion Park, Centurion

Pakistan

Saeed Anwar	**c** Rhodes, **b** Klusener	**3**
Azhar Mahmood	**c** Cullinan, **b** Klusener	**20**
Mohammad Wasim	**c** Crookes, **b** Donald	**18**
Ijaz Ahmed	**b** Elworthy	**2**
Inzamam-ul-Haq	run out	**33**
Moin Khan	**c** Cronje, **b** Elworthy	**25**
Wasim Akram	**b** Rindel	**12**
Mohammad Hussain	run out	**14**
Rashid Latif* †	not out	**6**
Abdul Razzaq	**b** Elworthy	**0**
Mushtaq Ahmed	run out	**0**
	b **2**, lb **4**, w **5**, nb **1**	**12**
	41.5 overs	**145**

	O	M	R	W
Elworthy	9	1	28	**3**
Klusener	7.5	–	27	**2**
Cronje	6	–	18	**–**
Donald	8	–	22	**1**
Rindel	7	–	23	**1**
Crookes	4	–	21	**–**

Fall of Wickets
1–**10**, 2–**25**, 3–**31**, 4–**57**, 5–**95**, 6–**114**, 7–**135**, 8–**142**, 9–**142**

South Africa

M.J.R. Rindel	**c** Rashid Latif, **b** Wasim	**0**
G. Kirsten	**b** Azhar Mahmood	**35**
J.H. Kallis	not out	**79**
D.J. Cullinan	**c** Azhar Mahmood, **b** Mohammad Hussain	**14**
W.J. Cronje *	not out	**7**
J.N. Rhodes		
D.N. Crookes		
M.V. Boucher †		
L. Klusener		
S. Elworthy		
A.A. Donald		
	b **4**, lb **5**, w **2**, nb **3**	**14**
	35.3 overs (for 3 wickets)	**149**

	O	M	R	W
Wasim Akram	8	–	26	**1**
Mohammad Hussain	10	1	51	**1**
Azhar Mahmood	5	1	19	**1**
Mushtaq Ahmed	10	–	31	**–**
Abdul Razzaq	2.3	–	13	**–**

Fall of Wickets
1–**1**, 2–**65**, 3–**116**

Umpires: W.A. Diedricks & R.E. Koertzen *Man of the Match*: J.H. Kallis

South Africa won by 7 wickets

Match Nine – South Africa v. Sri Lanka

19 April 1998 at Springbok Park, Bloemfontein

Sri Lanka

Batsman	Dismissal	Runs
S.T. Jayasuriya	c Gibbs, b Telemachus	7
R.S. Kaluwitharana †	c Kirsten, b Telemachus	11
M.S. Atapattu	b Pollock	4
P.A. de Silva	c Boucher, b Pollock	0
A. Ranatunga*	c Boucher, b Donald	13
R.S. Mahanama	c Boucher, b Cronje	22
H.D.P.K. Dharmasena	c Kallis, b Pollock	14
U.D.U. Chandana	c Kirsten, b Kallis	5
W.P.U.J.C. Vaas	not out	10
G.P. Wickremasinghe	c Cronje, b Kallis	0
M. Muralitharan	c Pollock, b Symcox	0
	lb 8, w 10, nb 1	19
	36 overs	105

	O	M	R	W
Pollock	8	2	21	3
Telemachus	8	1	23	2
Donald	6	–	12	1
Cronje	6	1	23	1
Kallis	6	1	16	2
Symcox	2	–	2	1

Fall of Wickets
1–**14**, 2–**23**, 3–**23**, 4–**26**, 5–**50**, 6–**71**, 7–**93**, 8–**95**, 9–**104**

South Africa

Batsman	Dismissal	Runs
G. Kirsten	b Wickremasinghe	0
H.H. Gibbs	c Kaluwitharana, b Wickremasinghe	10
J.H. Kallis	c Atapattu, b Muralitharan	39
D.J. Cullinan	c and b Dharmasena	18
M.V. Boucher †	run out	5
J.N. Rhodes	not out	23
S.M. Pollock	not out	2
W.J. Cronje *		
P.L. Symcox		
R. Telemachus		
A.A. Donald		
	lb 2, w 6, nb 1	9
	26.3 overs (for 5 wickets)	106

	O	M	R	W
Vaas	5	–	30	–
Wickremasinghe	8	2	22	2
Muralitharan	8.3	1	34	1
Dharmasena	5	–	18	1

Fall of Wickets
1–**7**, 2–**24**, 3–**74**, 4–**80**, 5–**91**

Umpires: D.F. Becker & D.L. Orchard *Man of the Match*: R. Telemachus

South Africa won by 5 wickets

Standard Bank International Series Final – South Africa v. Pakistan

23 April 1998 at Newlands, Cape Town

Pakistan

Batsman	Dismissal	Runs
Saeed Anwar	c Boucher, b Klusener	30
Mohammad Wasim	run out	8
Ijaz Ahmed	c Kirsten, b Telemachus	0
Inzamam-ul-Haq	c Boucher, b Cronje	21
Moin Khan	c Rindel, b Klusener	19
Wasim Akram	run out	2
Azhar Mahmood	b Klusener	0
Rashid Latif * †	c Rhodes, b Klusener	3
Abdul Razzaq	c Kallis, b Klusener	6
Waqar Younis	c Kallis, b Telemachus	15
Mushtaq Ahmed	not out	0
	lb 1, w 8, nb 1	10
	37.1 overs	114

	O	M	R	W
Pollock	8	1	13	–
Telemachus	10	1	31	2
Donald	6	1	27	–
Klusener	7.1	1	25	5
Cronje	6	1	17	1

Fall of Wickets
1–**26**, 2–**27**, 3–**54**, 4–**84**, 5–**87**, 6–**87**, 7–**90**, 8–**93**, 9–**113**

South Africa

Batsman	Dismissal	Runs
M.J.R. Rindel	c Rashid Latif, b Wasim	20
G. Kirsten	not out	52
J.H. Kallis	not out	28
D.J. Cullinan		
W.J. Cronje *		
J.N. Rhodes		
S.M. Pollock		
L. Klusener		
M.V. Boucher †		
R. Telemachus		
A.A. Donald		
	lb 4, w 6, b 5	15
	27.4 overs (for one wicket)	115

	O	M	R	W
Wasim Akram	10	1	29	1
Waqar Younis	9	1	32	–
Azhar Mahmood	4	–	17	–
Abdul Razzaq	2	–	17	–
Mushtaq Ahmed	2.4	–	16	–

Fall of Wickets
1–**54**

Umpires: R.E. Koertzen & C.J. Mitchley *Man of the Match*: L. Klusener

South Africa won by 9 wickets

Still a powerful force in South Africa cricket, Kepler Wessels scored 899 runs, average 81.72, during the season. He hit four centuries. (David Munden / Sportsline)

Standard Bank International Final

South Africa *v.* Pakistan

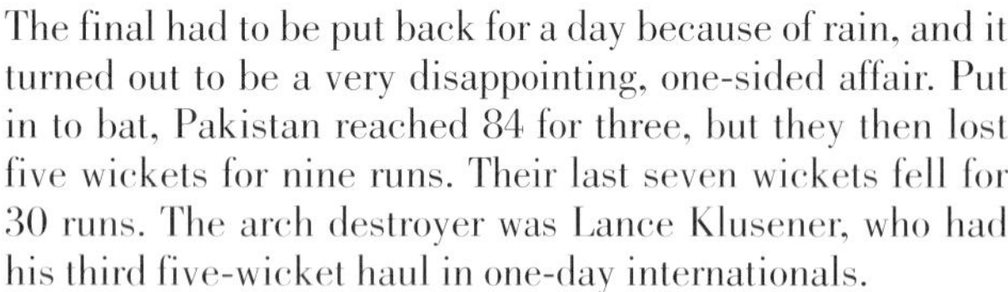

The final had to be put back for a day because of rain, and it turned out to be a very disappointing, one-sided affair. Put in to bat, Pakistan reached 84 for three, but they then lost five wickets for nine runs. Their last seven wickets fell for 30 runs. The arch destroyer was Lance Klusener, who had his third five-wicket haul in one-day internationals.

Confronted by a target of 115, South Africa had the easiest of tasks. There was no need to hurry. Rashid Latif used Wasim and Waqar to the full in an effort to bring about a collapse, but Rindel and Kirsten scored 54 for the first wicket, and Kirsten and Kallis finished the job so that victory came with 22.2 overs to spare.

Arjuna Ranatunga, with 272 runs, was the leading run-scorer in the series, although Jonty Rhodes hit 206 in five innings and was only dismissed twice. Wasim Akram took 15 wickets in seven matches, and Muttiah Muralitharan had 14 in six games. Interestingly, the three most economical bowlers in the competition were all South African – Donald, Pollock and Cronje.

Supersport Series

14, 15, 16 and 17 November 1997
at Boland Bank Park, Paarl
Boland 85 (V.C. Drakes 4 for 17) and 145 (P.J. Botha 6 for 32)
Border 221 (S.C. Pope 57 not out, C.W. Henderson 4 for 47) and 13 for 0
Border won by 10 wickets
Border 16 pts, Boland 4 pts

at Kimberley Country Club, Kimberley
Easter Province 307 (C.C. Bradfield 103, A.V. Birrell 57, H.R. Bryan 4 for 82) and 270 for 5 dec. (K.C. Wessels 122 not out)
Griqualand West 226 (M.I. Gidley 103, E.A.E. Baptiste 4 for 37) and 197 (M.W. Pringle 4 for 75)
Eastern Province won by 154 runs
Eastern Province 18 pts, Griqualand West 6 pts

at Kingsmead, Durban
Northerns 209 (M.J.R. Rindel 62, Zahir Shah 4 for 56) and 196 (Zahir Shah 5 for 67)
Natal 412 (N.C. Johnson 100, A.C. Hudson 74, E.L.R. Stewart 60, S.M. Pollock 54, G.J. Smith 4 for 99)
Natal won by an inninngs and 5 runs
Natal 18 pts, Northerns 5 pts

at Newlands, Cape Town
Free State 387 (J.F. Venter 86, L.J. Wilkinson 81, N. Boje 76, G.F.J. Liebenberg 72, C.R. Matthews 4 for 71) and 61 for 4
Western Province 193 (J.H. Kallis 52) and 253 (H.D. Ackerman 82)
Free State won by 6 wickets
Free State 17 pts, Western Province 3 pts

The first round of matches in the Supersport Series, the most recent name for what once was the Currie Cup, produced four outright results. Indeed, the match in Paarl was over in two days. Boland chose to bat when they won the toss but were all out in under 34 overs. Nineteen wickets fell on the first day, but, vitally, Pope and Ntini added 46 for Border's last wicket. The individual award went to Vasbert Drakes, Border's West Indian all-rounder, who had match figures of six for 40 and reduced Boland to 5 for three in their first innings.

Eastern Province won shortly after lunch on the fourth day in Kimberley. Carl Bradfield hit the first century of the season in the competition. It was the second hundred of his career and he hit 12 fours. Former Leicestershire left-hander Martyn Gidley responded with a century for Griqualand West, but the quickest hundred of the match came from Kepler Wessels, 40 years old, who made an unbeaten 122 off 168 balls with a six and 15 fours. It was the 63rd century of his career, earned him the individual award and set up his side's victory.

Natal beat Northerns by an innings inside three days. Another former Leicestershire player Neil Johnson hit 100 off 147 balls, but Shaun Pollock, 54 off 60 balls and five for 41 in the match, took the individual award.

Western Province were forced to follow on by Free State, who batted solidly and consistently into the second day. No play was possible on the third day, and Westerns' last four wickets proved obdurate. Eventually, Free State needed to score at nearly six an over to win. They lost two wickets for 3 runs, and were 28 for four when Venter joined Wilkinson. The pair scored 33 in 24 minutes to win the match.

21, 22, 23 and 24 November 1997
at Buffalo Park, East London
Border 341 (B.M. White 83, S.C. Pope 61, P.C. Strydom 51) and 265 for 7 dec. (P.C. Strydom 106, S.C. Pope 83)
Natal 350 (A.C. Hudson 125, D.M. Benkenstein 102)
Match drawn
Natal 6 pts, Border 4 pts

at St George's Park, Port Elizabeth
Eastern Province 293 (M. Hayward 55 not out, L. Masikazana 50, H.S. Williams 4 for 65) and 232 for 6 dec. (K.C. Wessels 130 not out)
Boland 274 (K.C. Jackson 81, C. Grainger 68) and 157 for 6
Match drawn
Eastern Province 6 pts, Boland 6 pts

at Newlands, Cape Town
Western Province 267 for 7 (P. Kirsten 91 not out)
v. **Gauteng**
Match drawn
Western Province 3 pts, Gauteng 3 pts

at Springbok Park, Bloemfontein
Free State 237 (H.C. Bakkes 62, H.R. Bryan 6 for 71) and 227 (H.R. Bryan 4 for 49)
Griqualand West 362 (P.H. Barnard 146, L. Bosman 96, H.C. Bakkes 5 for 70) and 106 for 2
Griqualand West won by 8 wickets
Griqualand West 17 pts, Free State 3 pts

A stand of 205 between Hudson and Benkenstein after three wickets had gone for 32 was the feature of Natal's innings against Border, who were 25 for four in their second innings. Skipper Strydom was joined by Pope, and the pair added 229 to save the game.

For Eastern Province, Masikazana and Hayward put on 108 for the last wicket, so breaking a record for the association that had stood since 1920–21. Both players hit maiden first-class fifties. Wessels hit his second century in successive matches, but Boland batted doggedly throughout the last day to earn a draw. Only 20 overs were possible on the first day at Newlands, and there were 79 overs bowled on the second. The last two days were blank.

Griqualand West pulled off the surprise of the season when they beat Free State in Bloemfontein. Facing a total of 237, Griqualand West were 80 for four. Bosman, making his debut, then joined Barnard and the pair added 243, so establishing a new fifth wicket record for the association. Bryan, 10 for 120 in the match, and Strydom kept Free State in check in the second innings, and Griqualand West won a famous victory early on the fourth day.

27, 28, 29 and 30 November 1997
at Kimberley Country Club, Kimberley
Border 278 (V.C. Drakes 98, G.A. Roe 4 for 35) and 192 (P.C. Strydom 68)
Griqualand West 257 (L. Bosman 77) and 162 (I.L. Howell 4 for 35)
Border won by 51 runs
Border 17 pts, Griqualand West 5 pts

28, 29, 30 November and 1 December 1997
at Wanderers, Johannesburg
Gauteng 89 (C.F. Craven 5 for 26) and 183 (C.F. Craven 4 for 24)
Free State 205 (S. Jacobs 5 for 55) and 70 for 3
Free State won by 7 wickets
Free State 16 pts, Gauteng 4 pts

at Centurion Park, Centurion
Boland 100 (M.J.R. Rindel 4 for 17, P.S. de Villiers 4 for 35) and 84 (P.S. de Villiers 5 for 30)
Northerns 213 (S. Elworthy 89, C. Langveldt 4 for 70)
Northerns won by an innings and 29 runs
Northerns 16 pts, Boland 4 pts

at Kingsmead, Durban
Eastern Province 238 for 6 dec. (K.C. Wessels 65, E.A.E. Baptiste 53 not out)
Natal 33 for 2
Match drawn
Natal 0 pts, Eastern Province 0 pts

Vasbert Drakes hit 98 off 127 balls with five sixes and 10 fours to boost Border's innings against Griqualand West, for whom Bosman again batted well. The home side's last three wickets realised 157 runs, but they still trailed by 21 runs on the first innings. Needing 214 to win, Griqualand West reached 142 for five before the last five wickets went down for 20 runs.

Gauteng looked far distant from the great Transvaal side under Clive Rice when they were routed by Free State in the rain-affected match at Wanderers. Christian Craven, who had only once taken five wickets in a match, took nine for 50 with his medium pace.

Boland suffered their second two-day defeat of the season. The first day saw 14 wickets fall with Rindel and de Villiers destroying Boland, whose last six wickets fell for 20 runs. Northerns (Northern Transvaal) lost six wickets in taking the lead, but Elworthy hit four sixes and 10 fours to take them to a lead of 113. Boland collapsed for a second time.

No play was possible on the first three days in Durban, so the game was played under single innings rules with no bonus points available.

12, 13, 14 and 15 December 1997
at Centurion Park, Centurion
Northerns 328 (G. Dros 96, M.J.R. Rindel 88 not out, P.J.R. Steyn 58, M. van Jaarsveld 53, G.J. Kruis 7 for 58) and 89 for 1
Griqualand West 104 (S. Elworthy 5 for 2, P.S. de Villiers 4 for 49) and 310 (M.I. Gidley 134, W. Bossenger 54, P.H. Barnard 53, S. Elworthy 5 for 82, P.S. de Villiers 4 for 105)
Northerns won by 9 wickets
Northerns 17 pts, Griqualand West 2 pts

at Wanderers, Johannesburg
Gauteng 361 (K.R. Rutherford 143, N. Pothas 76, V.C. Drakes 5 for 75) and 253 for 5 dec. (D.N. Crookes 106 not out)
Border 216 (P.C. Strydom 82, C.E. Eksteen 4 for 36) and 235 (B.C. Fourie 57, B.M. White 51, C.E. Eksteen 4 for 85)
Gauteng won by 163 runs
Gauteng 18 pts, Border 5 pts

at Boland Park, Paarl
Boland 165 (B.N. Schultz 4 for 42, A.C. Dawson 4 for 42) and 265 (K.M. Curran 67, A.C. Dawson 4 for 51)
Western Province 121 (R. Telemachus 4 for 36) and 242 (L.D. Ferreira 69, R. Telemachus 5 for 52)
Boland won by 67 runs
Boland 15 pts, Western Province 4 pts

at Springbok Park, Bloemfontein
Natal 106 (C.F. Craven 4 for 27, C.J. Vorster 4 for 34) and 127 (C.F. Craven 5 for 25, H.C. Bakkes 4 for 33)
Free State 269 (N. Boje 55, J. Beukes 52, J.F. Venter 50, C.M. Gilder 4 for 70)
Free State won by an innings and 36 runs
Free State 17 pts, Natal 4 pts

Northerns won a convincing victory over Griqualand West, for whom Gidley, leading the side, hit his second century of the season. The hero of the game was Steve Elworthy, who took ten wickets in a match for the second time in his career. He and de Villiers reduced Griquas to one for four in their first innings.

Gauteng gained their first victory and Border suffered their first defeat of the season. Former New Zealand skipper Rutherford made 143 off 193 balls with a six and 21 fours. Crookes hit a brisk century in the second innings. It was the eighth of his career.

Boland gained their first win of the season when they beat Western Province by 67 runs. It was Western's second

Andrew Hudson dropped down the order and recorded his first double century in first-class cricket, but his recall to the Test side did not meet with the success that had been anticipated.
(David Munden / Sportsline)

defeat in three matches. Kevan Curran took the individual award, but fast medium pace bowler Roger Telemachus had match figures of nine for 88.

An innings victory over Natal consolidated Free State's place at the top of the table. Natal were 30 for six in their first innings and were chasing the game ever after. Craven had another excellent match with the ball.

16, 17, 18 and 19 January 1998
at St George's Park, Port Elizabeth
Eastern Province 401 for 5 dec. (D.J. Callaghan 111 not out, L.J. Koen 104, K.C. Wessels 79, E.A.E. Baptiste 51 not out) and 259 for 6 dec. (J. Kemp 81 not out, E.A.E. Baptiste 53, C.E. Eksteen 4 for 97)
Gauteng 307 (D.N. Crookes 90, M.W. Pringle 7 for 78) and 236 (M.R. Benfield 59, M. Hayward 4 for 49)
Eastern Province won by 117 runs
Eastern Province 18 pts, Gauteng 6 pts

at Buffalo Park, East London
Border 375 (W. Wiblin 177, S.C. Pope 100, A.C. Dawson 5 for 80) and 270 for 8 dec. (W. Wiblin 119 not out, B.T. Player 4 for 96)

Western Province 395 (H.D. Ackerman 114, F. Davids 61) and 106 for 3 (L.D. Ferreira 56 not out)
Match drawn
Border 6 pts, Western Province 5 pts

at Kimberley Country Club, Kimberley
Griqualand West 184 (W. Bossenger 63, C.V. English 60, K.M. Curran 4 for 17) and 147 (L. Bosman 69 not out, C.W. Henderson 4 for 39)
Boland 166 and 169 for 4 (K.C. Jackson 53 not out, E.J. Ferreira 50)
Boland won by 4 wickets
Boland 15 pts, Griqualand West 5 pts

at Springbok Park, Bloemfontein
Free State 380 (C.F. Craven 105, N. Boje 104 not out, G.F.J. Liebenberg 79) and 218 for 5 dec. (H.H. Dippenaar 100 not out, L.J. Wilkinson 89)
Northerns 298 (M. van Jaarsveld 82, N. Boje 5 for 84) and 103 (N. Boje 6 for 34)
Free State won by 197 runs
Free State 17 pts, Northerns 6 pts

Centuries by Koen and Callaghan set up Eastern Province's victory over Gauteng, who were bowled out on the last day.

Border were 58 for four against Western Province before Wiblin and Pope added 253, a record partnership for the fifth wicket. Wayne Wiblin, a month short of his 19th birthday, made the highest score of his career, 177, and followed it with an unbeaten century in the second innings. Hylton Ackerman steered Western Province to a first innings lead, and, eventually, the match was drawn.

Boland gained their second win in successive matches when they beat Griqualand West in Kimberley. Choosing to bat first, Griqualand West slumped to 44 for five. Bossenger and English put on 101, and the home side went on to take a first innings lead. Batting a second time, they again began badly, and only Bosman, who batted four-and-a-half hours, held them together. Boland faced a difficult target on a crumbling pitch, but Jackson stayed at the crease for ten minutes under four hours to give them victory before lunch on the last day.

Free State made it four wins in five matches and took a firm grip on the league. Craven and Boje scored centuries. It was the second and higher hundred for Nicky Boje, who then took ten or more wickets in a match for the first time with his left-arm spin. On the last afternoon, he bowled Free State to victory and returned the best figures of his career, six for 34.

It was a season of best performances. Spinner Zahir Shah had begun his first-class career by taking nine wickets for Natal in the first match of the series, but he played in only two more matches, capturing just one more wicket. Gideon Kruis's medium pace had brought him career-best bowling figures for Griqualand West against Northerns, but he still finished on the losing side. He was overshadowed in the match by Steve Elworthy, who took 10 for 87, including a first innings haul of five for 2 in 8.2 overs, six of which were maidens.

23, 24, 25 and 26 January 1998
at Kingsmead, Durban
Natal 500 for 5 dec. (D.J. Watson 145, M.L. Bruyns 135, A.C. Hudson 119 not out, E.L.R. Stewart 51) and 25 for 3
Western Province 205 (G.M. Gilder 4 for 54, C.R. Tatton 4 for 60) and 319 (H.D. Ackerman 131, R.B. MacQueen 5 for 125)
Natal won by 7 wickets
Natal 18 pts, Western Province 2 pts

at Wanderers, Johannesburg
Northerns 235 (D.J.J. de Vos 64, G.J. Smith 51 not out, E.W. Kidwell 7 for 58) and 277 for 7 dec. (M. van Jaarsveld 134, D.J.J. de Vos 54, C.E. Eksteen 4 for 63)
Gauteng 202 for 7 dec. (K.R. Rutherford 78 not out) and 74 (P.S. de Villiers 4 for 11)
Northerns won by 236 runs
Northerns 15 pts, Gauteng 6 pts

An opening partnership of 194 between Bruyns and Watson set Natal on the path to victory over Western Province, for whom Ackerman continued to score heavily. Western were still without a win, and this was their third defeat in five matches. Hudson's refound form in the middle order was to win him a recall to the South African side.

Gauteng suffered another humiliation. They began well enough with fast bowler Errol Kidwell bowling out Northerns on the first day. Davis and Smith scored 94 for Northerns' last wicket. Rain restricted play on the second day, and Rutherford declared on the third day as soon as Gauteng had claimed a second batting point. Northerns scored briskly after losing two wickets for 0, and Davis's declaration left Gauteng a target of 311. Koenig and Benfield opened with a stand of 12, and six wickets fell at that total. A ninth wicket stand of 29 was the best that Gauteng could offer.

30, 31 January, 1 and 2 February 1998
at St George's Park, Port Elizabeth
Border 220 and 144 (E.A.E. Baptiste 4 for 28, G.T. Love 4 for 56)
Eastern Province 514 for 5 dec. (K.C. Wessels 179 not out, D.J. Callaghan 132, M.W. Rushmere 65)
Eastern Province won by an innings and 150 runs
Eastern Province 17 pts, Border 3 pts

at Boland Bank Park, Paarl
Gauteng 235 (A.J. Seymore 96, R. Telemachus 5 for 43) and 166 (M.R. Benfield 73)
Boland 228 (K.C. Jackson 79, C.E. Eksteen 6 for 56) and 174 for 1 (K.C. Jackson 102 not out, J.M. Henderson 51 not out)
Boland won by 9 wickets
Boland 16 pts, Gauteng 6 pts

Eastern Province renewed their challenge for the title with a crushing victory over Border. Wessels and Callaghan established a fourth wicket record for Eastern Province with a partnership of 289. Border began batting on the third day 294 behind on the first innings, and on the last morning they lost five wickets for 23 runs before the last two wickets gave a hint of respectability in adding 45.

Gauteng suffered their third defeat in succession and Boland claimed their third victory on the trot. The game at Paarl was over in three days. Ken Jackson was again Boland's hero. He hit a magnificent century in the second innings, 102 off 134 balls with nine fours. His runs came out of an unbroken stand of 153 for the second wicket with Jim Henderson.

6, 7, 8 and 9 February 1998
at Kingsmead, Durban
Natal 434 (A.C. Hudson 206, D.J. Watson 62, K.A. Forde 61, E.W. Kidwell 6 for 115) and 220 (A.C. Hudson 79, M.L. Bruyns 58, C.E. Eksteen 6 for 54)
Gauteng 333 (K.R. Rutherford 125, D.J. Cullinan 103, S.M. Adam 5 for 57) and 100 for 3
Match drawn
Natal 9 pts, Gauteng 6 pts

at Springbok Park, Bloemfontein
Boland 184 and 158 (K.C. Jackson 65, J.F. Venter 4 for 26)
Free State 471 (H.C. Bakkes 101, C.F. Craven 100, M.N. van Wyk 86, N. Boje 50)
Free State won by an innings and 129 runs
Free State 19 pts, Boland 4 pts

at Newlands, Cape Town
Western Province 145 (J. Kemp 4 for 12) and 427 for 8 dec. (H.H. Gibbs 152, H.D. Ackerman 100, B.T. Player 53 not out)
Eastern Province 204 and 245 (L.J. Koen 52, P.R. Adams 6 for 90)
Western Province won by 123 runs
Western Province 14 pts, Eastern Province 6 pts

Andrew Hudson hit the first double century of his career, confirming that dropping down to number four in the order had revitalised his form. Gauteng responded to Natal's 434 with centuries from Cullinan and Rutherford, who added 191 for the fourth wicket. The last day was curtailed by rain.

Free State beat Boland in three days. It was their fifth win of the season and virtually assured them of the championship. The highlight of their victory was an eighth wicket record stand of 191 between Bakkes and van Wyk, both of whom hit the highest scores of their careers. Bakkes's maiden century came off 141 balls with a six and 11 fours. He was batting at number nine.

Eastern Province's hopes of catching Free State were shattered when they lost to Western Province, previously without a win to their credit, after leading on the first innings. Gibbs and Ackerman put on 184 for Western Province's third wicket in the second innings.

13, 14, 15 and 16 February 1998
at Newlands, Cape Town
Griqualand West 239 (W. Bossenger 85, M.F. George 6 for 61) and 216 (M.I. Gidley 88, P.R. Adams 7 for 69)
Western Province 500 for 6 dec. (H.D. Ackerman 174, E.O. Simons 157 not out, A.G. Prince 60)
Western Province won by an innings and 45 runs
Western Province 16 pts, Griqualand West 3 pts

Western Province won their second match in succession and virtually condemned Griqualand West to the wooden spoon. Simons hit a career-best unbeaten 157 and shared a fifth wicket stand of 194 with the prolific Ackerman, while Paul Adams returned the best bowling figures of his career in Griqualand West's second innings.

20, 21, 22 and 23 February 1998
at Boland Bank Park, Paarl
Boland 177 and 253 (S.J. Palframan 71, N.C. Johnson 4 for 64)
Natal 190 and 242 for 4 (M.L. Bruyns 107, J.N. Rhodes 69 not out)
Natal won by 6 wickets
Natal 15 pts, Boland 5 pts

at Centurion Park, Centurion
Eastern Province 169 (D.J. Callaghan 58, G.J. Smith 4 for 48, P.S. de Villiers 4 for 63) and 431 for 4 dec. (L.J. Koen 174 not out, M.W. Rushmere 124)
Northerns 233 (D.J.J. de Vos 60) and 219 (S. Abrahams 4 for 101)
Eastern Province won by 148 runs
Eastern Province 15 pts, Northerns 6 pts

Bruyns hit the fourth century of his career and took the individual award as Natal beat Boland in early afternoon on the fourth day. Jonty Rhodes hit a sparkling unbeaten 69 off 75 balls with 14 fours.

Eastern Province recovered from a first innings deficit of 64 to gain a resounding win over Northerns. Rushmere and Koen hit centuries. Koen's unbeaten 174 came off 189 balls with two sixes and 28 fours, and Northerns fell on the last afternoon. No play had been possible on the first day.

26, 27, 28 February and 1 March 1998
at St George's Park, Port Elizabeth
Eastern Province 382 (K.C. Wessels 133, M.W. Rushmere 55, S. Abrahams 50) and 36 for 0
Free State 250 for 5 dec. (G.F.J. Liebenberg 68)

Match drawn
Eastern Province 5 pts, Free State 5 pts

at Buffalo Park, East London
Northerns 326 (D.Taljard 5 for 54)
Border 199 for 8 (S.C. Pope 70, V.C. Drakes 59)
Match drawn
Northerns 6 pts, Border 4 pts

Disappointingly, rain ruined the eagerly awaited contest between Free State and Eastern Province. There were only 11 overs possible on the third day and less than 33 on the fourth. Free State were confirmed as champions, and Wessels hit his fourth century of the competition to finish top of the Supersport Series Batting Averages. In East London, no play was possible after the second day.

6, 7, 8 and 9 March 1998
at Kimberley Country Club, Kimberley
Natal 379 (D.M. Benkenstein 96, N.C. Johnson 54, A.G. Botha 52, G.A. Roe 4 for 98) and 239 for 4 dec. (E.L.R. Stewart 61, J.N. Rhodes 60 not out)
Griqualand West 425 (W. Bossenger 124 not out, H.R. Bryan 71, M.I. Gidley 55) and 165 for 5 (J.M. Arthur 58, C.R. Tatton 4 for 62)
Match drawn
Griqualand West 5 pts, Natal 5 pts

Griqualand West wicket-keeper Wendell Bossenger hit a patient maiden first-class century in the drawn match with Natal, for whom Jonty Rhodes played another bubbling innings.

13, 14, 15 and 16 March 1998
at Buffalo Park, East London
Border 120 and 264 (V.C. Drakes 53, J.F. Venter 5 for 123)
Free State 459 (M.N. van Wyk 121, H.C. Bakkes 74, J.F. Venter 70)
Free State won by an innings and 75 runs
Free State 18 pts, Border 2 pts

at Wanderers, Johannesburg
Gauteng 431 (D.J. Cullinan 172, N.D. McKenzie 84)
Griqualand West 207 (M.I. Gidley 93, K. Ingram 4 for 43) and 128 (E.W. Kidwell 4 for 52)
Gauteng won by an innings and 96 runs
Gauteng 19 pts, Griqualand West 4 pts

at Centurion Park, Centurion
Northerns 483 (P.J.R. Steyn 141, M. van Jaarsveld 139) and 120 for 5
Western Province 153 (G.J. Smith 6 for 35) and 581 for 7 dec. (H.D. Ackerman 202 not out, J.H. Kallis 111, B.M. McMillan 64, H.H. Gibbs 63)
Match drawn
Northerns 8 pts, Western Province 3 pts

Clive Eksteen – left-arm spinner – the only bowler in the South African season to take 50 wickets.
(David Munden / Sportsline)

Free State ended the season with their sixth victory in eight matches to win the Supersport Series by a margin of 27 points from Eastern Province.

Gauteng finished their campaign with a welcome victory. Cullinan played a splendid innings, hitting three sixes and 15 fours. There was consolation for Gauteng in that they won the Standard Bank Cup, the 50-over competition.

The match at Centurion was drawn, but Hylton Ackerman created a record. He hit the first double century of his career and brought his total number of runs for the season to 1,373, so beating Barry Richards's aggregate of 1,285 in a South African season, which had stood as a record for 24 years.

Supersport Series Final Table

	P	W	L	D	Pts
Free State	8	6	1	1	112
Eastern Province	8	4	1	3	85
Northerns	8	3	3	2	79
Natal	8	3	1	4	75
Boland	8	3	4	1	69
Gauteng	8	2	3	2	68
Border	8	2	3	3	57
Western Province	8	2	3	3	50
Griqualand West	8	1	6	1	47

Record-breaker Hylton Ackerman scored 1,373 runs in the season, surpassing Barry Richards's previous record which had stood for 24 years. Ackerman's outstanding feat failed to win him a place in the party to tour Englad.
(Stuart Franklin / ASP)

UCB Bowl Division One

30, 31 October and 1 November 1997
at Newlands, Cape Town
Natal 'B' 324 (U.H. Goedeke 124, K.D. Donaldson 50, R. Munnik 4 for 63) and 212 (A.M. Amia 57, D.M. Koch 4 for 35)
Western Province 'B' 296 for 2 dec. (H. Pangarkar 128 not out, R. Maron 65, J. de Nobregar 64) and 241 for 6
Western Province 'B' won by 4 wickets
Western Province 'B' 18 pts, Natal 'B' 6 pts

The Bowl competition is divided into two divisions, and only the first division has first-class status. Even this is not an ideal situation as three of the six teams that make up the division are second elevens of Supersport teams. In the opening match, Goedeke hit 124 off 142 balls and Pangarkar, who ended the previous season well, made 128 off 134 balls with nine sixes and 10 fours.

13, 14 and 15 November 1997
at Centurion Park, Centurion
Northerns 'B' 322 for 9 dec. (P. de Bruyn 103, J. Rudolph 56) and 217 for 9 dec. (D.J. Smith 59, J. Rudolph 55, M.F. George 4 for 39)
Western Province 'B' 245 (R. Maron 59, R.T. Coetzee 7 for 74) and 181 for 6 (N. Adams 81 not out)
Match drawn
Northerns 'B' 8 pts, Western Province 'B' 6 pts

In spite of Adams's 81 off 110 balls, the match was drawn.

21, 22 and 23 November 1997
at Northwood Crusaders Club, Durban
North West 166 (A.G. Lawson 57) and 270 for 7 dec. (L.P. Vorster 89 not out, M.J. Lavine 86)
Natal 'B' 228 for 8 (C.B. Sugden 89)
Match drawn
Natal 'B' 6 pts, North West 5 pts

Natal 'B' led by 62 on the first innings when they had faced 100 overs, at which point, under the rules of the competition, the innings is closed.

27, 28 and 29 November 1997
at St George's Park, Port Elizabeth
Eastern Province 'B' 429 for 8 dec. (G.C. Victor 138, A.G. Prince 116, D. Moffat 105)
Natal 'B' 276 (A.G. Botha 94, K.A. Forde 66, A.L. Hobson 5 for 103, A. Badenhorst 4 for 53) and 127 (S. Abrahams 4 for 33)
Eastern Province 'B' won by an innings and 26 runs
Eastern Province 'B' 20 pts, Natal 'B' 6 pts

Moffat, making his debut, hit a century and shared a second wicket stand of 226 with another centurion, Prince. The chief honours, however, went to skipper Gavin Victor, who reached the sixth century of his career. His 138 came off 94 balls and included 15 fours and seven sixes. His side made their runs in 96.4 overs.

11, 12 and 13 December 1997
at Belville CC, Belville
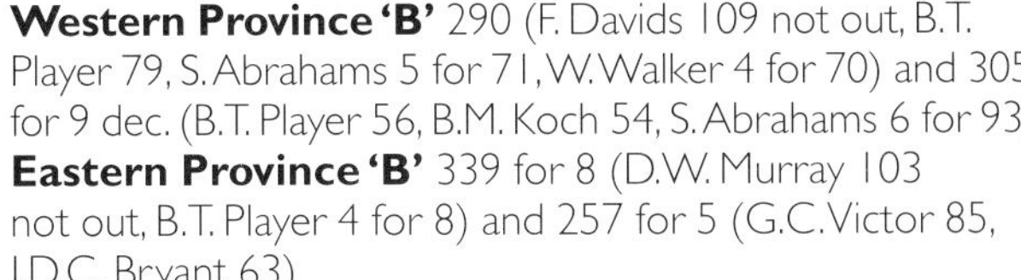
Western Province 'B' 290 (F. Davids 109 not out, B.T. Player 79, S. Abrahams 5 for 71, W. Walker 4 for 70) and 305 for 9 dec. (B.T. Player 56, B.M. Koch 54, S. Abrahams 6 for 93)
Eastern Province 'B' 339 for 8 (D.W. Murray 103 not out, B.T. Player 4 for 8) and 257 for 5 (G.C. Victor 85, J.D.C. Bryant 63)
Eastern Province 'B' won by 5 wickets
Eastern Province 'B' 18 pts, Western Province 'B' 7 pts

12, 13 and 14 December 1997
at Gert van Rensburg Stadium, Fochville
Easterns 236 (M.J. Mitchley 75) and 248 (G.W. Myburgh 50, L.C.R. Jordaan 6 for 67)
North West 361 for 9 (A.G. Lawson 110, G.M. Hewitt 96) and 124 for 2 (M.C. Venter 50 not out)
North West won by 8 wickets
North West 18 pts, Easterns 5 pts

Bradley Player returned remarkable analysis in the first innings of the match at Belville Cricket Club. He took four Eastern Province wickets for eight runs in 15 overs, eight of which were maidens, but he was not called upon to bowl in the second innings.

Lawson and Hewitt put on 176 for North West's second wicket, and the second innings hero was skipper Venter, who hit 50 off 30 balls when his side were racing against time.

16, 17 and 18 January 1998
at Willowmoore Park, Benoni
Eastern Province 'B' 160 (G.C. Victor 54, A. Nel 4 for 41) and 231 (A. Nel 5 for 74)
Easterns 166 (A. Badenhorst 5 for 48) and 175 for 9 (C.R. Norris 83, Q. Ferreira 4 for 17)
Match drawn
Easterns 6 pts, Eastern Province 'B' 6 pts

Needing 226 to win, Easterns lost both openers for one run. Norris and Myburgh added 105, but a collapse followed, and it was left to the last pair, Nel and Andrew Pollock, to save the game.

6, 7 and 8 February 1998
at St George's Park, Port Elizabeth
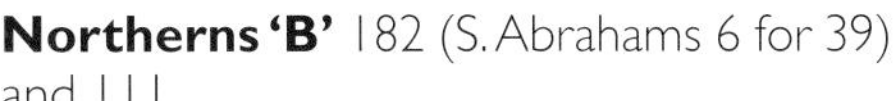
Northerns 'B' 182 (S. Abrahams 6 for 39) and 111
Eastern Province 'B' 164 (J.D.C. Bryant 65, M.G. Beamish 56, D.H. Townsend 5 for 26, P. de Bruyn 5 for 36) and 97 (P. Joubert 4 for 27, D.H. Townsend 4 for 43)
Northerns 'B' won by 32 runs
Northerns 'B' 16 pts, Eastern Province 'B' 6 pts

at Willowmoore Park, Benoni
Western Province 'B' 308 (H. Pangarkar 55, M. van Oist 54, C. Kruger 4 for 50) and 244 for 8 dec. (M. Crosoer 64, J. Uys 5 for 87)
Easterns 303 (J.S. Lerm 112, C.R. Norris 53) and 226
Western Province 'B' won by 23 runs
Western Province 'B' 17 pts, Easterns 8 pts

Eastern Province twice collapsed dramatically against Northerns. In the first innings, their last seven wickets went down for 27 runs.

Lerm hit a maiden first-class century for Easterns, hitting 15 fours in his innings of more than five-and-a-quarter hours, but he finished on the losing side.

20, 21 and 22 February 1998
at University of Port Elizabeth Oval, Port Elizabeth
Eastern Province 'B' 280 (J.D.C. Bryant 104, L.C.R. Jordaan 5 for 69) and 266 for 4 dec. (G.V. Grace 112 not out, G.C. Victor 65)
North West 259 for 6 (S. Nicolson 79, A.G. Lawson 78, J. September 4 for 30) and 178 for 4 (M.J. Lavine 60)
Match drawn
North West 7 pts, Eastern Province 'B' 6 pts

at L.C. de Villiers Oval, University of Pretoria, Pretoria
Easterns 112 (P. de Bruyn 4 for 31) and 255 (G. White 66, G.W. Myburgh 50, R.E. Bryson 5 for 63)
Northerns 'B' 351 for 9 dec. (J.G. Myburgh 203, D. Jordaan 60, C. Kruger 4 for 74, C.R. Norris 4 for 75) and 17 for 0
Northerns 'B' won by 10 wickets
Northerns 'B' 19 pts, Easterns 4 pts

Graham Grace hit a maiden first-class century and enlivened a rather tedious game in Port Elizabeth. His unbeaten 112 came off 141 balls and included 11 fours and four sixes.

Northerns won in Pretoria and were much indebted to Johan Myburgh. He became the youngest South African to score a first-class double century. He was 17 years, 122 days at the time, some eighteen months younger than the previous record holder Graeme Pollock. Johan Myburgh faced 264 balls and hit a six and 26 fours.

27, 28 February and 1 March 1998
at Centurion Park, Centurion
Northerns 'B' 256 (D. Jordaan 80, A.G. Botha 8 for 53) and 147 (A.G. Botha 4 for 42)
Natal 'B' 200 (A.G. Botha 64) and 205 for 9
Natal 'B' won by 1 wicket
Natal 'B' 17 pts, Northerns 'B' 8 pts

Natal won a thrilling match with their last pair, Storey and Bosch, adding 20 runs to clinch the narrowest of victories. Anthony Botha, slow left-arm, returned the best bowling figures of his career for innings and match. He was a month past his 22nd birthday.

5, 6 and 7 March 1998
at Fanie du Toit Stadium, Potchefstroom
Western Province 'B' 284 (R. Maron 75, R. Munnik 57, D.J. Pryke 5 for 38) and 151 (H. Pangarkar 78, D.J. Pryke 6 for 43)
North West 373 for 9 (A. Jacobs 112, H.M. de Vos 101, D.G. Payne 4 for 93) and 64 for 1
North West won by 9 wickets
North West 19 pts, Western Province 'B' 6 pts

6, 7 and 8 March 1998
at Kingsmead, Durban
Easterns 142 (M.J. Mitchley 63, J.E. Bastow 6 for 37) and 196 for 6 (M.J. Mitchley 79)
Natal 'B' 310 for 7 dec. (A. Mall 85, G.S. Katz 77, K.D. Donaldson 54)
Match drawn
Natal 'B' 8 pts, Easterns 0 pts

North West took a big step towards winning the Bowl with a fine victory over Western Province. They were 93 for three before Jacobs and de Vos added 109. Both made centuries. Jacobs hit furiously to score 112 off 125 balls with three sixes and 14 fours. Natal had the better of the rain-affected game in Durban.

13, 14 and 15 March 1998
at Gert van Rensburg Stadium, Fochville
Northerns 'B' 291 (D. Jordaan 107, J.G. Myburgh 60) and 64 (M.J. Lavine 4 for 31)
North West 338 (L.P. Vorster 115, S. Nicolson 58, C.T. English 51, J. Rudolph 5 for 98) and 20 for 0
North West won by 10 wickets
North West 18 pts, Northerns 'B' 6 pts

North West duly won the Bowl with a resounding victory over Northerns, their closest rivals. They were aided by a century from Vorster, who has appeared for Worcestershire, and by an astonishing second innings collapse by their opponents.

UCB Bowl Final Table

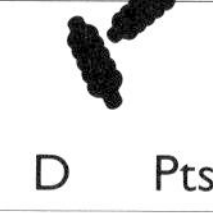

	P	W	L	D	Pts
North West	5	3	–	2	67
Northerns 'B'	5	2	2	1	57
Western Province 'B'	5	2	2	1	54
Eastern Province 'B'	5	2	1	2	51
Natal 'B'	5	1	2	2	42
Easterns	5	–	3	2	23

Western Province 'B' lost 4 points for a sub-standard pitch. Eastern Province 'B' 1, Easterns 3, and Natal 'B' 1 were deducted points for slow over-rates.

First-Class Averages

Batting

	M	Inns	NOs	Runs	HS	Av	100s	50s
L.P. Vorster	4	6	3	350	115	116.66	1	1
K.C. Wessels	9	15	4	899	179*	81.72	4	3
D.J. Cullinan	6	10	1	663	172	73.66	4	1
W.J. Cronje	6	10	2	511	150*	63.87	1	3
J.N. Rhodes	3	5	2	185	69*	61.66	2	
A. Jacobs	2	2	–	115	112	58.00	1	
N. Boje	11	16	4	683	105*	56.91	2	4
G.C. Victor	5	9	–	501	138	55.66	1	3
A.C. Hudson	10	16	2	779	206	55.64	3	2
J.G. Myburgh	5	10	2	427	203	53.37	1	1
A.G. Lawson	5	10	3	371	110	53.00	1	2
H.D. Ackerman	16	29	2	1373	202*	50.85	5	6
M. van Jaarsveld	9	16	2	709	139*	50.64	2	2
E.A.E. Baptiste	6	8	4	196	53	49.00	2	
K.R. Rutherford	8	13	2	532	143	48.36	2	1
H.M. de Vos	2	4	1	144	101	48.00	1	
W. Wiblin	9	17	2	688	177	45.86	2	1
M.N. van Wyk	7	11	3	366	121	45.75	1	1
G.S. Katz	2	3	–	136	77	45.33	1	
J.D.C. Bryant	4	7	1	261	104*	43.50	1	2
D.J. Callaghan	9	15	2	548	132	42.15	2	1
A.G. Prince	7	11	–	447	116	40.63	1	2
M.J.R. Rindel	5	7	1	240	88*	40.00	2	
H.C. Bakkes	8	9	1	319	101	39.87	1	2
S.M. Pollock	6	9	1	319	92	39.87	3	
J. Kemp	7	10	3	274	81*	39.14	2	
M.J. Lavine	5	7	–	273	86	39.00	2	
H.H. Gibbs	4	7	–	268	152	38.28	1	1
A.V. Birrell	2	4	1	113	57	37.66	1	
L.J. Koen	9	15	1	519	174*	37.07	2	1
C.B. Sugden	3	3	–	110	89	36.66	1	
M.I. Gidley	9	18	–	658	134	36.55	2	3
K.C. Jackson	9	18	2	579	102*	36.18	1	4
P.C. Strydom	9	16	1	541	106	36.06	1	3
M.C. Venter	3	4	1	108	50*	36.00	1	
C.R. Matthews	3	5	2	108	41*	36.00		
L.J. Wilkinson	9	14	3	396	89	36.00	2	
C.F. Craven	6	8	–	286	105	35.75	2	
P.J.R. Steyn	9	16	1	536	141	35.73	2	1
J.M. Henderson	6	12	2	355	135	35.50	1	2
U.H. Goedeke	3	5	–	177	124	35.40	1	
N.C. Johnson	10	14	2	421	100	35.08	1	2
S.C. Pope	9	16	2	487	100	34.78	1	4
E.O. Simons	7	11	1	346	157*	34.60	1	
M.L. Bruyns	10	16	–	551	135	34.43	2	2
M.J. Mitchley	5	10	–	334	79	33.40	3	
G. Kirsten	6	12	2	334	75*	33.40	2	
C.C. Bradfield	8	15	2	434	103	33.38	1	
S. Nicolson	4	8	1	233	79	33.40	2	
S. Hofmeyr	4	8	1	232	41	33.14		
G. Dros	8	13	1	396	96	33.00	1	
N. Adams	3	5	1	131	81*	32.75	1	
J.H. Kallis	7	13	1	393	111	32.75	1	2
J.F. Venter	9	13	2	358	86	32.54	3	
P. Kirsten	9	15	1	454	91*	32.42	2	
A.J. Hall	4	7	1	193	62*	32.16	2	
D.M. Benkenstein	11	17	–	544	102	32.00	1	4
A.J. Seymoore	4	7	–	221	96	31.57	2	
W. Bossenger	9	17	1	501	124*	31.31	1	3
J.B. Commins	3	5	–	156	44	31.20		
N. Pothas	13	20	3	528	138	31.05	2	1
M.T. Solomons	5	9	3	185	59*	30.83	1	
R.P. Snell	5	8	2	185	44	30.83		
J.S. Lerm	3	6	–	184	112	30.66	1	
M.V. Boucher	8	13	–	393	80	30.23	4	
M.W. Rushmere	9	14	–	422	124	30.14	1	2
N.D. McKenzie	9	15	–	450	135	30.00	1	2
D.J. Watson	9	14	–	418	145	29.85	1	1
D.N. Crookes	11	17	2	445	106*	29.66	1	2
P.H. Barnard	9	18	1	502	146	29.52	2	1
H. Pangarkar	9	17	1	469	128*	29.31	1	3
M. Crosoer	2	4	–	117	64	29.25	1	
E.L.R. Stewart	8	12	2	289	61	28.90	3	
D.J.J. de Vos	9	15	1	403	64	28.78	3	
P. de Bruyn	7	13	2	316	103	28.72	1	1
C.R. Norris	5	10	–	285	83	28.50	2	
V.C. Drakes	6	14	1	366	98	28.15	3	
B.M. McMillan	2	4	–	112	64	28.00	1	
A.G. Botha	7	11	–	306	94	27.81	3	

Batting

	M	Inns	NOs	Runs	HS	Av	100s	50s
D.J. Smith	6	10	1	248	59	27.55	1	
G.F.J. Liebenberg	13	21	–	575	84	27.38	5	
M. Hayward	12	10	4	162	55*	27.00	1	
L. Bosman	8	14	1	350	96	26.92	3	
G.W. Myburgh	5	10	–	266	50	26.60	2	
D.M. Koch	4	7	1	159	54	26.50	1	
B.C. Fourie	2	4	–	106	57	26.50	1	
K.A. Forde	6	10	2	208	66	26.00	2	
W.R. Wingfield	5	8	–	207	41	25.87		
A. Mall	3	5	–	129	85	25.80	1	
M.W. Pringle	8	6	2	103	30	25.75		
A. Paleker	2	4	–	101	46	25.25		
R. Maron	9	17	–	429	75	25.23	3	
B.T. Player	9	16	2	353	79	25.21	3	
G.V. Grace	5	9	1	199	112*	24.87	1	
B.M. White	8	16	1	369	83	24.60	2	
H.H. Dippenhaar	9	14	1	313	100*	24.07	1	
K.D. Donaldson	4	6	–	142	54	23.66	2	
D.W. Murray	4	7	1	140	103*	23.33	1	
M.G. Beamish	5	9	–	206	56	22.88	1	
D. Jordaan	10	19	1	410	107	22.71	1	2
J. Rudolph	4	8	1	159	56	22.71	2	
L.D. Ferreira	9	16	1	335	69	22.33	2	
K.M. Curran	8	15	1	308	67	22.00	1	
J. de Nobrega	6	11	1	218	64	21.80	1	
D. Moffat	5	9	–	196	105	21.77	1	
N. Martin	3	6	–	130	46	21.66		
C.V. English	5	10	1	193	60	21.44	1	
R.F. Pienaar	3	5	–	107	56	21.44	1	
S. Abrahams	6	9	1	170	50	21.25	1	
G.M. Hewitt	4	7	–	148	96	21.14	1	
Q. Ferreira	5	7	1	126	38	21.00		
H.R. Bryan	7	13	1	251	71	20.91	1	
G. White	5	10	–	206	66	20.60	1	
S. Elworthy	8	12	–	246	89	20.50	1	
J.M. Arthur	8	16	–	309	58	19.31	1	
A.P. Kuiper	9	17	1	302	36	18.87		
C.W. Henderson	8	14	5	159	33*	17.66		
Z. de Bruyn	4	8	–	139	45	17.37		
C. Grainger	9	17	–	295	68	17.35	1	
P.S. de Villiers	7	10	2	137	46*	17.12		
R. Munnik	5	9	–	151	57	16.77	1	
R. Telemachus	8	13	4	151	30	16.77		
M.J.G. Davis	9	15	3	201	42	16.75		
S.J. Palframan	9	16	–	264	71	16.50	1	
M. Strydom	11	21	1	330	73	16.50	1	
S.G. Koenig	6	10	–	164	69	16.40	1	
J. Uys	5	10	1	144	48	16.00		
C.E. Eksteen	13	17	4	194	33	14.92		
R.B. MacQueen	8	8	1	104	26	14.85		
A.M. Bacher	6	11	1	145	46	14.50		
P.J. Botha	12	20	–	289	60	14.45	1	
C.C. van der Merwe	4	7	–	100	34	14.28		
G.J. Kruis	9	16	1	211	34*	14.06		
G. Morgan	11	19	2	230	87	13.52	1	
E.J. Ferreira	8	16	–	204	50	12.75	1	
A.M. Amla	5	8	–	101	57	12.62	1	
A.C. Dawson	8	12	3	109	27	12.11		
W.M. Dry	7	13	1	135	30	11.25		

P.L. Symcox played in one match – 108
(Qualification – 100 runs, average 10.00)

Bowling

	Overs	Mds	Runs	Wkts	Best	Av	10/m	5/inn
C.F. Craven	71	26	165	21	5/25	7.85	2	
K.M. Curran	118.1	42	210	16	4/17	13.12		
P.S. de Villiers	240.1	59	708	47	7/80	15.06	1	3
B.N. Schultz	107.1	30	290	19	8/36	15.26	1	
D.J. Pryke	133.1	33	314	20	6/43	15.70	1	2
S. Abrahams	226.3	59	533	33	6/39	16.15	1	3
S.M. Adam	120.3	30	273	15	5/57	18.20	1	
E.A.E. Baptiste	189.2	66	346	19	4/28	18.21		
A. Badenhorst	150.2	37	429	23	5/48	18.65	1	
D.J. Callaghan	159.5	55	305	16	3/19	19.06		
J. Rudolph	95	23	267	14	5/987	19.07	1	

First-Class Averages (continued)

Bowling

	Overs	Mds	Runs	Wkts	Best	Av	10/m	5/inn
R. Telemachus	220	45	676	34	5/43	19.88	2	
Q. Ferreira	129.2	35	320	16	4/17	20.00		
H.C. Bakkes	202.2	46	484	24	5/70	20.16	1	
S.M. Pollock	181.5	49	449	22	6/50	20.40	1	
J.E. Bastow	83.4	21	254	12	6/37	21.16	1	
R.P. Snell	82.2	20	255	12	5/56	21.25	1	
G.M. Gilder	193.1	42	538	25	4/54	21.52		
C.E. Eksteen	511	167	1145	51	6/54	22.45	2	
L.C.R. Jordaan	190.3	60	427	19	6/67	22.47	2	
D.H. Townsend	152.4	38	434	19	5/26	22.84	2	
M.W. Pringle	309.4	74	801	35	7/78	22.88	1	1
A. Nel	138.4	21	417	18	5/74	23.16	1	
A.G. Botha	226	44	605	26	8/53	23.26	1	1
C.R. Tatton	233.2	68	493	21	4/60	23.47		
V.C. Drakes	240.1	64	592	25	5/75	23.68	1	
C.J. Vorster	115.5	27	357	15	4/34	23.80		
P.J. Botha	324.5	79	788	33	6/32	23.87	1	
E.W. Kidwell	189	24	742	31	7/58	23.93	2	
S. Jacobs	143.4	44	312	13	5/55	24.00	1	
D. Talyard	243.4	69	700	29	6/49	24.13	2	
M.J. Lavine	122.2	27	365	15	4/31	24.33		
H.S. Williams	232.4	66	489	20	4/65	24.45		
G.A. Roe	312.3	83	663	27	4/35	24.55		
M. Hayward	374.4	68	1156	47	6/51	24.59	1	
P. de Bruyn	162.3	41	472	19	5/36	24.84	1	
C. Kruger	67	8	249	10	4/50	24.90		
T. Bosch	120	37	275	11	3/28	25.00		
J.F. Venter	245.5	65	731	29	5/123	25.20	1	
D.G. Payne	97	27	328	13	4/93	25.23		
A.C. Dawson	273.2	82	686	27	5/80	25.40	1	
N. Boje	440.5	146	913	35	6/34	26.08	1	2
G.J. Smith	246.3	51	788	30	6/35	26.26	1	
R.E. Bryson	114	25	423	16	5/63	26.35	1	
C.W. Henderson	355.4	124	749	28	4/39	26.75		
R. Munnik	126.3	18	456	17	4/63	26.82		

Bowling

	Overs	Mds	Runs	Wkts	Best	Av	10/m	5/inn
G.J. Terbrugge	190.5	48	513	19	3/36	27.00		
P.R. Adams	299.5	72	836	30	7/69	27.86	2	
P. Joubert	181	48	449	16	4/27	28.06		
G.J. Kruis	297.4	64	900	32	7/58	28.12	1	
M.F. George	260.4	46	901	32	6/61	28.15	1	
Zahir Shah	86.5	18	289	10	5/67	28.90	1	
N.C. Johnson	191	46	468	16	4/64	29.25		
H.R. Bryan	223	37	683	23	6/71	29.69	1	1
E.O. Simons	158	56	301	10	3/39	30.10		
S.A. Cilliers	164	20	588	19	3/10	30.94		
S. Elworthy	265	65	776	25	5/2	31.04	1	2
D.M. Koch	104	21	315	10	4/35	31.50		
M. Ntini	142.2	28	528	16	3/45	33.00		
E.O. Moleon	116.4	25	410	12	5/62	34.16	1	
B.T. Player	269.2	63	696	20	4/8	34.80		
K. Ingram	102	12	373	10	4/43	37.30		
P.A.N. Emslie	169.2	32	453	12	3/55	37.75		
G.T. Love	169.4	47	448	11	4/56	40.72		
D.N. Crookes	249.5	48	656	16	6/50	41.00	1	
A.J. Swanepoel	225	57	554	13	3/23	42.61		
A.L. Hobson	158	21	531	12	5/103	44.25	1	
R.B. MacQueen	309.3	66	870	17	5/125	51.17	1	
M. Strydom	220.4	46	716	11	4/33	65.09		

(Qualification – 10 wickets)

Leading Fielders

45 – M.V. Boucher (ct 42 / st 3); 35 – W. Bossenger; 30 – N. Pothas (ct 27 / st 3); 25 – K.A. Forde (ct 23 / st 2) and S.J. Palframan (ct 24 / st 1); 24 – P. Kirsten (ct 23 / st 1); 21 – G. Morgan 19 – L. Masikazana; 18 – D.J. Smith (ct 15 / st 3); 17 – L.J. Wilkinson and M.T. Solomons (ct 14 / st 3); 16 – G.F.J. Liebenberg; 14 – EL.R. Stewart (ct 11 / st 3), M.L. Bruyns (ct 13 / st 1) and D. Jordaan; 13 – G. White and H.D. Ackerman; 12 – N.C. Johnson, S.C. Pope (ct 10 / st 2), B.M. White and H.H. Dippenaar (ct 11 / st 1)

India

An air of uncertainty pervaded Indian cricket at the start of the 1997–98 campaign. There was concern that, since his elevation to the captaincy, Tendulkar, who, when he plays well, is probably the best batsman in the world, had failed to produce his top form. There were still moments of glory and prolific scoring from Tendulkar, but, seemingly, the responsibility of leading the national side weighed heavily upon him.

Test centuries against Sri Lanka And Australia, 1,256 runs, average 114 in the season and totally dominant in the limited-over game, Sachin Tendulkar has a record in world cricket that is unapproached by any other batsman. Here he crashes another ball to the boundary during his unbeaten 155 against Australia. Ian Healy is the wicket-keeper. (Ben Radford / Allsport)

Sri Lankan Tour
Australian Tour
Triangular Series
Irani Trophy
Duleep Trophy
Ranji Trophy
Triangular Tournament
First-Class Averages

There were, too, worries about bowling resources in the continued absence through injury of Srinath, in the doubts as to Chauhan's action, and in the failure of both Kumble and Venkatesh Prasad to find consistency. The frustration of the Indian selectors was apparent when they publicly voiced their opinion that some of the players were undisciplined in approach and were not giving their best. One wonders if this is not a product of the imbalance in India's international programme. The high-scoring Test series in Sri Lanka was to be followed by a Sri Lankan visit to India and by a home Test series against Australia, but the staple diet of Indian cricket has become the one-day international, and the limited-over matches which accompanied the visits by Sri Lanka and Australia were to be augmented by India competing in one-day tournaments in Canada, Pakistan, Sharjah and Bangladesh.

Sri Lankan Tour

14, 15 and 16 November 1997
at Barabati, Cuttack
Indian Board President's XI 294 (W.V.S. Laxman 112, W. Jaffer 79, K.J. Silva 5 for 55) and 10 for 1
Sri Lankans 198 (H.P. Tillekeratne 77, R.L. Sanghvi 4 for 44)
Match drawn

In their one warm-up match before the Test series, the Sri Lankans were deprived of some practice by bad weather.

Test Series

India v. Sri Lanka

India welcomed back Srinath after his long absence through injury, and he was soon pressed into action as Tendulkar elected to field when he won the toss. It brought no reward, as Jayasuriya and Atapattu began the series with a stand of 98. The pair were not separated until after lunch. Jayasuriya has learned from experience and has matured into a fine Test cricketer. His 53 occupied almost two-and-a-half hours, and he nursed his partner, a batsman of talent still to prove himself at the highest level, through the difficult early stages. Atapattu grew in strength as his innings progressed, and he and Mahanama added 104 for the second wicket. Atapattu had hit 14 fours and had batted for just under six hours for his maiden Test century before falling to the second new ball. Aravinda de Silva played on to Kuruvilla, who had surprisingly been preferred to the recently named International Cricketer of the Year Venkatesh Prasad. This give India some consolation, but Sri Lanka closed on an assured 280 for four.

The second day belonged to India. Srinath celebrated his return to Test cricket with some impressive pace bowling, and Abey Kuruvilla, too, bowled well. During one

Abey Kuruvilla justified the selector's faith in him by taking six wickets in the first Test against Sri Lanka.
(David Munden / Sportsline)

period, four wickets fell for 12 runs, and only the defiance of Dharmasena took the visitors to 369. Sidhu and Mongia took India to 91 by the close, but runs came at less than two an over, and a draw loomed.

Such a result seemed an inevitability on the third day, when India advanced their score by 202 runs in the 90 overs available. The day was marred by an altercation between the Sri Lankan captain Ranatunga and the Indian umpire Venkataraghavan after two appeals for bat and pad catches against Sidhu had been rejected. Sidhu went on to score 131 off 372 balls in his eight-hour innings. The crawl – even Tendulkar took 93 balls to score 23 – seemed to reflect the attitude new coach Gaekwad had exuded when he played Test cricket. Former coach Madan Lal had paid the price for non-success and been sacked before the series.

India began the fourth day at 293 for four, and, belatedly, their batting began to show some urgency. This was due mainly to Saurav Ganguly, who played some delightfully elegant shots as he moved to his fourth Test century in 15 matches. His second fifty took only 51 deliveries, and his fine innings enabled Tendulkar to declare an hour after tea with a lead of 146. Ganguly and Kuruvilla, who hit three sixes, lifted Indian spirits; and spirits were lifted further when Srinath, bowling at a lively pace, sent back Jayasuriya and Mahanama to leave Sri Lanka in some trouble on 61 for two at the close.

Their troubles deepened when Atapattu and Ranatunga both fell to Kuruvilla in the first 45 minutes of the final day, and, on the stroke of lunch, Tillekeratne, who had never looked happy in this match, edged Chauhan to slip. This brought Sri Lanka to 106 for five, still 40 runs in arrears with only Aravinda de Silva remaining of their front-line batsmen. 'Only' is not a word that should be used in relation to de Silva. Among contemporary batsmen he reigns supreme. He curbed his natural aggression to bat for his side's safety, and he remained at the crease for six-and-a-half hours. For 144 minutes, Dharmasena stayed with him while 103 runs were scored, and Sri Lanka moved closer to avoiding defeat. The light began to fail, and the batsmen were offered the opportunity to go off. De Silva was on 98, but, without hesitation, he tucked his bat under his arm and walked to the pavilion. Thankfully, the cloud lifted and he was able to return to complete the century he so richly deserved. It was the 15th of his Test career, and his seventh in his last seven Tests. Team before self has ever been his motto, and this gracious man rightly took the individual award.

For the second Test match, Sri Lanka made two changes, Pushpakumara and Jayantha Silva replacing Dharmasena and Sajeeva de Silva. India brought in Kulkarni for Mohanty, a spinner for a pace bowler. It mattered little, for the game was totally ruined by rain. Only 41 overs were possible on the first day, when India, showing more urgency than they had done in the first Test, made 133 for one. Sidhu was in magnificent form, using his feet to the spinners and driving excitingly. He hit Muralitharan for one towering six and finished the day on 64, with the elegantly delicate Dravid on 47.

India continued to bat fluently on the second day and only Tendulkar failed, although he opened his scoring with a huge six. Sidhu could not refind his touch and left early, but Dravid again batted delightfully. He seemed certain to reach a century, but he played a poor shot, hooking to square-leg and was out for 92. It was the third time that he had been out in the nineties in his young Test career. Azharrudin produced some magnificent wristy on-side shots, and Ganguly and Kumble were soon pillaging runs to take India to 401 for five by the close.

Only two hours' play was possible on the third day, and India were bowled out for 485. Ganguly and Kumble were not separated until their partnership was worth 159. Kumble was in top form and was surprised to be given run out after being sent back and diving for safety. The third umpire ruled that although his bat was well over the line, it was in the air. Ganguly was positive and serene in all he did, but, on 99, he played at a wide ball from Pushpakumara and edged to second slip. Shortly after, the rains came, and that was the end of the match.

For the third Test, India brought back Venkatesh Prasad for Kulkarni, while Sri Lanka brought back Dharmasena for Muralitharan and included Pramodaya Wickremasinghe at the expense of Jayantha Silva. Wickremasinghe had immediate success, bowling Mongia in his first over after Ranatunga had won the toss and asked India to bat. Sidhu, too, was out before lunch. Having hit Dharmasena for three fours in one over, he tried to repeat his onslaught in the next and was caught at deep mid-on. The afternoon brought Sri Lanka no success as Dravid and Ganguly took 100 runs off 33 overs. Eventually, their stand was worth 160 and was ended when Dravid was taken at slip, once again getting agonisingly close but missing out on his century. India closed on 247 for three, with Ganguly 92 and Tendulkar on eight.

By the end of the second day, India were immune from defeat. Ganguly quickly completed his century with two boundaries, and he was not dismissed until the first over after tea, by which time he had scored 173, his highest Test score, and hit 25 fours and two sixes. He and Tendulkar established an Indian fourth wicket record with a stand of 256. On the first evening, Tendulkar had batted with the utmost caution, now he played with all the grace and power of the great batsman that he is. He moved from 87 to 99 with successive sixes before pushing the next ball to leg to reach his 14th Test century. He passed 4,000 Test runs and was finally beaten by Pushpakumara, who once more bowled at a lively pace. Tendulkar has been a dominant force in world cricket for such a long time that it is hard to believe that he did not celebrate his 25th birthday until April 1998. Ganguly is nine months his senior; Dravid seven months his junior. India can boast a wealth of young batting talent.

In a desperate dash for quick runs, India lost their last seven wickets while 41 were added. Jayasuriya began Sri Lanka's innings with a flourish, but he received bad blows on the helmet and on the arm and was caught off Kumble just before the close. A highly satisfactory day for India ended with Sri Lanka 66 for one.

Dharmasena again proved himself an invaluable night-watchman as he and Atapattu batted through the morning session of the third day. Their partnership was worth 115 when Dharmasena was caught at mid-wicket in trying to be too adventurous against Chauhan. Marvan Atapattu remained firm and was at the crease for six-and-a-half hours before being taken at silly point. He was the fourth batsman in the series to be out in the nineties. Ranatunga fell to a ball that, ominously, turned sharply, but Sri Lanka ended the day at 286 for five, only 27 runs short of avoiding the follow-on.

The follow-on was avoided without fuss, but the Sri Lankan innings disappointed. It was not helped by the fact that Lanka de Silva was forced to retire hurt when he was hit in the mouth by a delivery from Srinath. The ball crashed through the grille of his helmet, and he lost three teeth.

India scored at a brisk pace when they batted a second time, and Dravid played another innings of great charm and purpose. Dharmasena finished with his second five-wicket haul in Test cricket, and Sri Lanka were left a day and four overs in which to make 333 to win.

They began the last day with six runs on the board, and it was apparent from the manner in which Jayasuriya and Atapattu batted that they believed that it was possible to reach their target. They made 52 runs in the first hour before Atapattu swept at Chauhan and was caught at square-leg. Jayasuriya drove lavishly at Kumble and was caught at cover, and Sri Lanka lunched at 87 for two.

Their hopes of victory ended when Aravinda de Silva was out at 106. He hooked a bouncer from Srinath but discovered that Chauhan had run back from square-leg and was perfectly positioned to take the catch. Mahanama was adjudged leg before shortly before tea, and three wickets fell after the break. Tillekeratne was standing firm, but the Indian spinners were threatening to win the match when rain began to fall, and the match was called off with 12 overs unbowled.

So the two sides drew their fifth encounter in succession. Match referee Bobby Simpson named Saurav Ganguly Man of the Match and Man of the Series.

One-Day International Series

India *v.* Sri Lanka

On the Indian sub-continent, there is an insatiable appetite for the one-day game. Following the Test series against Sri Lanka, India took off for Sharjah and the Champions' Trophy. They did not fare well, losing all three matches and failing to qualify for the final. The selectors reacted angrily and axed several players when the side returned to India for the one-day series against Sri Lanka. Kumble, Venkatesh Prasad, Dravid and Karim, who had kept well in Sharjah, were among those to be dropped, while others were warned as to future form and attitude. Tendulkar's hold on the captaincy remained tenuous.

Sairaj Bahutule, a left-handed bat and leg-break bowler from Bombay, was the only newcomer in the first match of the series at Guwahati, but, in all, India made six changes from the team that had played in Sharjah. Mist delayed the start, and the match was reduced to 45 overs. Tendulkar won the toss and asked Sri Lanka to bat first. Mohanty soon accounted for Jayasuriya, Atapattu and Aravinda de Silva, and Sri Lanka were struggling at 30 for three. Mahanama batted with composure, and he and Ranatunga added 62, but as the later batsmen were forced to press for quick runs they fell to the accurate medium pace of Robin Singh. A talented all-rounder, Robin Singh has been neglected over the years and even his inclusion and promotion in Sharjah caused debate. His five for 22 represented his best performance in international cricket.

Two overs were deducted from the Indian innings because of their slow over-rate, and they soon lost Ganguly and Jadeja, but Sidhu batted firmly and Tendulkar was in all his glory with 82 off 86 balls. He and Azharuddin shared an unbroken stand of 79 to take their side to victory.

The second match, in Indore on Christmas Day, was an embarrassment for Indian cricket. India gave a debut to Hrishikesh Kanitkar, a left-handed batsman and occasional off-break bowler from Maharashtra. He had no chance to show his prowess, for when the match was only three overs old and Sri Lanka were 17 for one, it was abandoned. Mahanama was hit on the fingers by a ball from Srinath that lifted sharply from a length, and a group of officials, led by

First Test Match – India v. Sri Lanka

19, 20, 21, 22 and 23 November 1997 at Punjab C.A. Stadium, Mohali

Sri Lanka

	First Innings		Second Innings	
S.T. Jayasuriya	c Chauhan, b Srinath	53	c Mongia, b Srinath	17
M.S. Atapattu	lbw, b Srinath	108	c Chauhan, b Kuruvilla	31
R.S. Mahanama	lbw, b Kumble	42	lbw, b Srintah	11
P.A. de Silva	b Kuruvilla	33	not out	110
A. Ranatunga *	c Chauhan, b Srinath	30	c Dravid, b Kuruvilla	3
H.P. Tillekeratne	c Dravid, b Kumble	14	c Tendulkar, b Chauhan	9
S.K.L. de Silva †	b Kuruvilla	5	(8) not out	11
H.D.P.K. Dharmasena	not out	37	(7) b Srinath	25
W.P.U.J.C. Vaas	b Kuruvilla	2		
M. Muralitharan	c Srinath, b Kuruvilla	10		
S.C. de Silva	b Srinath	6		
	b 4, lb 13, nb 12	29	b 13, lb 9, nb 12	34
		369	(for 6 wickets)	251

	O	M	R	W	O	M	R	W
Srinath	27.2	4	92	4	22	3	75	3
Kuruvilla	27	7	88	4	15.1	4	29	2
Mohanty	19	1	57	–	16	4	32	–
Kumble	34	9	81	2	19	5	66	–
Ganguly	2	2	0	–	2	2	0	–
Chauhan	16	2	34	–	18	11	23	1
Azharuddin	1	–	4	–				

Fall of Wickets
1–98, 2–202, 3–254, 4–254, 5–301, 6–307, 7–307, 8–313, 9–333
1–22, 2–40, 3–67, 4–82, 5–106, 6–209

India

	First Innings	
N.R. Mongia †	b Muralitharan	57
N.S. Sidhu	run out	131
R.S. Dravid	c Ranatunga, b Jayasuriya	34
S.R. Tendulkar *	c Dharmasena, b Jayasuriya	23
M. Azharuddin	lbw, b Vaas	53
S.C. Ganguly	c Tillekeratne, b Vaas	109
A.R. Kumble	c Dharmasena, b Muralitharan	22
J. Srinath	c Mahanama, b S.C. de Silva	6
R.K. Chauhan	c Dharmasena, b Muralitharan	2
A. Kuruvilla	not out	35
D.S. Mohanty		
	b 19, lb 10, w 6, n 8	43
	(for 9 wickets, dec.)	515

	O	M	R	W
Vaas	36.5	11	107	2
S.C. de Silva	28	5	81	1
Dharmasena	34	11	65	–
Muralitharan	75	30	174	3
Jayasuriya	30	9	59	2
Ranatunga	3	3	0	–

Fall of Wickets
1–120, 2–214, 3–259, 4–274, 5–353, 6–400, 7–419, 8–426, 9–515

Umpires: S.A. Bucknor & S. Venkataraghavan

Match drawn

Second Test Match – India v. Sri Lanka

26, 27, 28, 29 and 30 November 1997 at Vidarbha C.A. Ground, Nagpur

India

	First Innings	
N.R. Mongia †	c Muralitharan, b Pushpakumara	11
N.S. Sidhu	c Atapattu, b Vaas	79
R.S. Dravid	c Atapattu, b Vaas	92
S.R. Tendulkar *	b Pushpakumara	15
M. Azharuddin	lbw, b Pushpakumara	62
S.C. Ganguly	c Tillekeratne, b Pushpakumara	99
A.R. Kumble	run out	78
J. Srinath	lbw, b Jayasuriya	11
R.K. Chauhan	c Vaas, b Jayasuriya	1
A. Kuruvilla	lbw, b Pushpakumara	0
N.M. Kulkarni	not out	1
	b 8, lb 13, w 3, nb 12	36
		485

	O	M	R	W
Vaas	31	3	80	2
Pushpakumara	32	3	122	5
Silva	28	6	81	–
Muralitharan	46	9	137	–
Ranatunga	1	–	8	–
Jayasuriya	16	4	32	2
Atapattu	1	–	4	–

Fall of Wickets
1–15, 2–152, 3–182, 4–272, 5–303, 6–462, 7–476, 8–484, 9–484

Sri Lanka

S.T. Jayasuriya
M.S. Atapattu
R.S. Mahanama
P.A. de Silva
A. Ranatunga *
H.P. Tillekeratne
S.K.L. de Silva †
W.P.U.J.C. Vaas
M. Muralitharan
K.J. Silva
K.R. Pushpakumara

Umpires: C.J. Mitchley & V.K. Ramaswamy

Match drawn

Third Test Match – India v. Sri Lanka

3, 4, 5, 6 and 7 December 1997 at Wankhede Stadium, Mumbai

India

	First Innings		Second Innings	
N.R. Mongia †	b Wickremasinghe	1	(6) not out	9
N.S. Sidhu	c Mahanama, b Dharmasena	35	c Pushpakumara, b Jayasuriya	43
R.S. Dravid	c Mahanama, b Ranatunga	93	c P.A. de Silva, b Dharmasena	85
S.C. Ganguly	c S.K.L. de Silva, b Dharmasena	173	(1) c Tillekeratne, b Wickremasinghe	11
S.R. Tendulkar *	b Pushpakumara	148	(4) c P.A. de Silva, b Jayasuriya	13
M. Azharuddin	lbw, b Pushpakumara	0	(5) c P.A. de Silva, b Dharmasena	4
A.R. Kumble	b Pushpakumara	6	c Mahanama, b Dharmasena	1
R.K. Chauhan	lbw, b Dharmasena	4	(9) run out	0
A. Kuruvilla	c Pushpakumara, b Wickremasinghe	6	(10) c P.A. de Silva, b Dharmasena	0
J. Srinath	not out	15	(8) c sub (Jayawardene), b Dharmasena	5
Venkatesh Prasad	run out	3		
	b 3, lb 15, w 4, nb 6	28	b 3, lb 6, nb 1	10
		512	(for 9 wickets, dec.)	181

	O	M	R	W	O	M	R	W
Vaas	26	4	86	–	5	1	19	–
Wickremasinghe	31.1	10	76	2	5	–	20	1
Pushpakumara	28	5	108	3	5	–	28	–
Dharmasena	48	12	144	3	12.4	–	57	5
Ranatunga	17	7	35	1				
Jayasuriya	12	2	45	–	15	1	48	2

Fall of Wickets
1–1, 2–55, 3–215, 4–471, 5–475, 6–476, 7–481, 8–487, 9–502
1–15, 2–103, 3–136, 4–149 5–173, 6–175, 7–181, 8–181, 9–181

Sri Lanka

	First Innings		Second Innings	
S.T. Jayasuriya	c Azharuddin, b Kumble	50	c Tendulkar, b Kumble	37
M.S. Atapattu	c sub (Jadeja), b Chauhan	98	c Kumble, b Chauhan	31
H.D.P.K. Dharmasena	c Kumble, b Chauhan	40	(6) c Azharuddin, b Kumble	8
R.S. Mahanama	c Kumble, b Venkatesh Prasad	20	(3) lbw, b Chauhan	35
P.A. de Silva	c Mongia, b Chauhan	66	(4) c Chauhan, b Srinath	18
A. Ranatunga *	c Azharuddin, b Chauhan	1	(5) b Chauhan	12
H.P. Tillekeratne	lbw, b Kuruvilla	25	not out	18
S.K.L. de Silva †	retired hurt	20	c Venkatesh Prasad, b Kumble	0
W.P.U.J.C. Vaas	c sub (Kulkarni), b Kuruvilla	4	not out	0
G.P. Wickremasinghe	b Srinath	2		
K.R. Pushpakumara	not out	0		
	b 7, lb 12, w 4, nb 12	35	lb 2, nb 5	7
		361	(for 7 wickets)	166

	O	M	R	W	O	M	R	W
Srinath	28.2	4	107	1	15	5	25	1
Venkatesh Prasad	18	6	30	1	8	3	23	–
Kuruvilla	19	2	62	2	3	2	1	–
Kumble	41	19	76	1	28	13	56	3
Chauhan	34	13	48	4	26	9	59	3
Ganguly	3	–	19	–				
Tendulkar	2	2	0	–				

Fall of Wickets
1–65, 2–180, 2–219, 4–259, 5–269, 6–312, 7–351, 8–359, 9–361
1–58, 2–73, 3–106, 4–133, 5–146, 6–160, 7–166

Umpires: S.A. Bucknor & A.V. Jayaprakash

Match drawn

Test Match Averages – India v. Sri Lanka

India Batting

	M	Inns	NOs	Runs	HS	Av	100s	50s
S.C. Ganguly	3	4	–	392	173	98.00	2	1
R.S. Dravid	3	4	–	304	93	76.00	2	
N.S. Sidhu	3	4	–	288	131	72.00	1	1
S.R. Tendulkar	3	4	–	199	148	49.75	1	
M. Azharuddin	3	4	–	119	62	29.75	2	
A.R. Kumble	3	4	–	107	78	26.75	1	
N.R. Mongia	3	4	1	78	57	26.00	1	
A. Kuruvilla	3	4	1	41	35*	13.66		
J. Srinath	3	4	1	37	15*	12.33		
R.K. Chauhan	3	4	–	7	4	1.75		

Played in one Test: N.M. Kulkarni 1*; Venkatesh Prasad 3; D.S. Mohanty did not bat

Sri Lanka Batting

	M	Inns	NOs	Runs	HS	Av	100s	50s
P.A. de Silva	3	4	1	227	110*	75.66	1	1
M.S. Atapattu	3	4	–	268	108	67.00	1	1
S.T. Jayasuriya	3	4	–	157	53	39.25	2	
H.D.P.K. Dharmasena	3	4	1	110	37*	36.66		
R.S. Mahanama	3	4	–	108	42	27.00		
H.P. Tillekeratne	3	4	1	66	25	22.00		
S.K.L. de Silva	3	4	2	36	20*	18.00		
A. Ranatunga	3	4	–	46	30	11.50		
W.P.U.J.C. Vaas	3	3	1	6	4	2.00		

Played in two Tests: M. Muralitharan 10; K.R. Pushpakumara 0*
Played in one Test: G.P. Wickremasinghe 2; K.J. Silva did not bat

India Bowling

	Overs	Mds	Runs	Wks	Av	Best	5/inn
R.K. Chauhan	94	35	164	8	20.50	4/48	
A. Kuruvilla	64.1	15	180	8	22.50	4/88	
J. Srinath	92.4	16	299	9	33.22	4/92	
A.R. Kumble	122	46	279	6	46.50	3/56	
Venkatesh Prasad	26	9	53	1	53.00	1/30	
S.C. Ganguly	7	4	19	–	–		

Bowled in one innings: S.R. Tendulkar 2–2–0–0; M. Azharuddin 1–0–4–0

Sri Lanka Bowling

	Overs	Mds	Runs	Wks	Average	Best	5/inn
S.T. Jayasuriya	73	16	184	6	30.66	2/32	
G.P. Wickremasinghe	36.1	10	96	3	32.00	2/76	
K.R. Pushpakumara	65	8	258	8	32.25	5/122	1
H.D.P.K. Dharmasena	94.4	23	266	8	33.25	5/57	1
A. Ranatunga	21	10	43	1	43.00	1/35	
W.P.U.J.C. Vaas	98.5	19	292	4	73.00	2/80	
M. Muralitharan	121	39	311	3	103.66	3/174	

Bowled in one innings: S.C. de Silva 28–5–81–1; K.J. Silva 28–6–81–0; M.S. Atapattu 1–0–4–0

Fielding Figures

4 – R.K. Chauhan; 3 – M. Azharuddin and A.R. Kumble; 2 – S.R. Tendulkar, R.S. Dravid and N.R. Mongia; 1 – J. Srinath, Venkatesh Prasad, sub (A.D. Jadeja) and sub (N.M. Kulkarni)

Fielding Figures

4 – P.A. de Silva and R.S. Mahanama; 3 – H.D.P.K. Dharmasena and H.P. Tillekeratne
2 – M.S. Atapattu and K.R. Pushpakumara; 1 – A. Ranatunga, S.K.L. de Silva, W.U.P.J.C. Vaas, M. Muralitharan and sub (R.S. Jayawardene)

First One-Day International – India v. Sri Lanka

22 December 1997 at Nehru Stadium, Guwahati

Sri Lanka

S.T. Jayasuriya	c Jadeja, b Mohanty	1
M.S. Atapattu	c Mongia, b Mohanty	8
R.S. Mahanama	c Jadeja, b R.R. Singh	68
P.A. de Silva	c Chauhan, b Mohanty	4
A. Ranatunga *	c R.R. Singh, b Ganguly	27
R.S. Kaluwitharana †	c Bahutule, b R.R. Singh	23
H.D.P.K. Dharmasena	c Bahutule, b R.R. Singh	9
U.U. Chandana	lbw, b R.R. Singh	4
W.P.U.J.C. Vaas	not out	7
M. Muralitharan	b R.R. Singh	1
S.C. de Silva	not out	3
	lb 9, w 6, nb 2	17
	45 overs (for 9 wickets)	172

	O	M	R	W
Srinath	9	4	16	–
Mohanty	9	1	31	3
Chauhan	7	–	30	–
Ganguly	6	–	31	1
R.R. Singh	5	–	22	5
Bahutule	9	–	33	–

Fall of Wickets
1–**5**, 2–**22**, 3–**30**, 4–**92**, 5–**133**, 6–**152**, 7–**156**, 8–**161**, 9–**167**

India

S.C. Ganguly	b Vaas	12
A.D. Jadeja	run out	7
N.S. Sidhu	c Atapattu, b Muralitharan	36
S.R. Tendulkar *	not out	82
M. Azharuddin	not out	28
S.V. Bahutule		
J. Srinath		
R.R. Singh		
N.R. Mongia †		
R.K. Chauhan		
D.S. Mohanty		
	lb 1, w 6, nb 1	8
	37.5 overs (for 3 wickets)	173

	O	M	R	W
Vaas	7	1	19	1
S.C. de Silva	7.5	–	31	–
Dharmasena	5	–	24	–
Jayasuriya	8	–	29	–
Muralitharan	7	–	49	1
Chandana	3	–	20	–

Fall of Wickets
1–**16**, 2–**26**, 3–**94**

Umpires: K.S. Gridharan & K. Murali *Man of the Match*: R.R. Singh

India won by 7 wickets

Second One-Day international – India v. Sri Lanka

25 December 1997 at Nehru Stadium, Indore

Sri Lanka

S.T. Jayasuriya	not out	**6**
R.S. Kaluwitharana †	**b** Srinath	**0**
R.S. Mahanama	not out	**5**
P.A. de Silva		
A. Ranatunga *		
H.P. Tillekeratne		
U.U. Chandana		
H.D.P.K. Dharmasena		
W.P.U.J.C. Vaas		
M. Muralitharan		
S.C. de Silva		
	b **4**, w **1**, nb **1**	**6**
	3 overs (for one wicket)	**17**

	O	M	R	W
Srinath	2	–	6	**1**
Chauhan	1	–	7	**–**

Fall of Wickets
1–**1**

India

A.D. Jadeja
S.C. Ganguly
N.S. Sidhu
S.R. Tendulkar *
M. Azharuddin
S.V. Bahutule
H.H. Kanitkar
N.R. Mongia †
R.R. Singh
J. Srinath
R.K. Chauhan

Umpires: S. Porel & N.D. Sharma

Match abandoned

Third One-Day International – India v. Sri Lanka

28 December 1997 at Arlem Ground, Margao

India

A.D. Jadeja	**c** Muralitharan, **b** Jayasuriya	**53**
S.C. Ganguly	**c** Tillekeratne, **b** Muralitharan	**61**
S.R. Tendulkar *	**c** S.C. de Silva, **b** Muralitharan	**6**
M. Azharuddin	**c** and **b** Muralitharan	**24**
N.S. Sidhu	run out	**17**
R.R. Singh	not out	**19**
N.R. Mongia †	**c** Muralitharan, **b** S.C. de Silva	**14**
S.V. Bahutule	not out	**0**
J. Srinath		
R.K. Chauhan		
D.S. Mohanty		
	lb **13**, w **20**, nb **1**	**34**
	50 overs (for 6 wickets)	**228**

	O	M	R	W
Vaas	9	–	28	**–**
S.C. de Silva	8	–	30	**1**
Dharmasena	10	–	38	**–**
Muralitharan	10	2	53	**3**
Jayasuriya	10	–	52	**1**
P.A. de Silva	3	–	14	**–**

Fall of Wickets
1–**131**, 2–**134**, 3–**152**, 4–**181**, 5–**190**, 6–**223**

Sri Lanka

S.T. Jayasuriya	**c** R.R. Singh, **b** Mohanty	**17**
M.S. Atapattu	**c** Azharuddin, **b** Mohanty	**14**
R.S. Mahanama	**b** Bahutule	**46**
P.A. de Silva	not out	**82**
A. Ranatunga *	**c** Jadeja, **b** Srinath	**20**
R.S. Kaluwitharana †	**b** Mohanty	**30**
H.D.P.K. Dharmasena	not out	**5**
H.P. Tillekeratne		
W.P.U.J.C. Vaas		
M. Muralitharan		
S.C. de Silva		
	lb **1**, w **13**, nb **1**	**15**
	48.2 overs (for 5 wickets)	**229**

	O	M	R	W
Mohanty	10	–	58	**3**
Srinath	10	1	26	**1**
Bahutule	10	–	46	**1**
Chauhan	9	–	37	**–**
Ganguly	3	–	25	**–**
R.R. Singh	5.2	1	29	**–**
Tendulkar	1	–	7	**–**

Fall of Wickets
1–**19**, 2–**51**, 3–**112**, 4–**164**, 5–**220**

Umpires: R.C. Sharma & K. Harihavan *Man of the Match*: P.A. de Silva

Sri Lanka won by 5 wickets

match referee Justice Ahmed Ibrahim of Zimbabwe, gathered on the pitch. After a discussion lasting some 40 minutes, they, in agreement with the captains, decided to abandon the match because the pitch was substandard and dangerous. There were suggestions that the groundsman, wishing to aid the home side, had been over-zealous and had produced a mud heap where the ball was breaking through the surface from the first delivery. In order to placate the crowd, an exhibition game was played.

Winning the toss in the third match, Tendulkar chose to bat. Jadeja and Ganguly scored 131 for the first wicket, but the stand occupied 31.2 overs and the later batsmen failed as they tried to force the pace. Facing a moderate target of 229, Sri Lanka began with a flourish as Jayasuriya hit four boundaries in Mohanty's first over, but the bowler exacted his revenge in his next over. Mohanty also accounted for Atapattu, but Aravinda de Silva gave his customary majestic display. His unbeaten 82 came off 90 balls, and Sri Lanka won with 10 balls to spare.

So ended a bad year for India, a year in which they had failed to win any of their 13 Tests and in which their solitary success in a one-day series had been against an injury-weakened Pakistan side in Canada. It was inevitable that drastic measures would be taken, and Tendulkar was relieved of the captaincy for the Silver Jubilee Independence Cup in Bangladesh. He was succeeded by Mohammad Azharuddin, the man he had replaced a year earlier.

Azharuddin faced no easy task, for, after the visit to Bangladesh, came the Australians, still supreme among Test-playing nations.

Man of the Match in the first one-day international against Sri Lanka, Rabindra 'Robin' Singh of Tamil Nadu. His five for 22 in five overs set up India's victory.
(David Munden / Sportsline)

Australian Tour

Australia's busy international schedule took them from New Zealand to India where they were to play a three-Test series and a one-day international tournament that would also involve Zimbabwe. The Australian selectors had dropped Elliott, so successful in England, and recalled Slater, while neither McGrath nor Gillespie was available for selection because of injury. India, refreshed by their triumph in Bangladesh, confirmed Azharuddin as captain against the Australians.

24, 25 and 26 February 1998
at Brabourne Stadium, Mumbai
Australians 305 for 8 dec. (M.J. Slater 98, R.T. Ponting 53) and 135 (G.S. Blewett 50, N.M. Kulkarni 5 for 23)
Mumbai 410 for 6 dec. (S.R. Tendulkar 204 not out, A. Pagnis 50) and 31 for 0
Mumbai won by 10 wickets

The Australians had an ominous start to their tour. A second wicket stand of 107 between Slater and Ponting gave encouragement on the opening day against Mumbai, but thereafter it was downhill all the way. Sachin Tendulkar, relieved of the cares of the Indian captaincy, dominated the Mumbai innings in making the highest score of his career. He savaged Warne, Australia's main hope for the series, and the leg-spinner finished with figures of 0 for 111 in 16 overs. In contrast, left-spinner Kulkarni routed the tourists when they batted a second time, and the home side won with considerable ease.

1, 2 and 3 March 1998
at Visakhapatnam
Indian Board President's XI 329 for 4 dec. (H.H. Kanitkar 102 not out, V.V.S. Laxman 65, V. Pratap 59 not out, S. Ramesh 58)
Australians 567 for 8 (M.J. Slater 207, R.T. Ponting 155, G.S. Blewett 57, M.E. Waugh 52)
Match drawn

In their last game before the first Test match, the Australians found batting form. The hosts were 155 for four before Kanitkar and Pratap came together in an unbeaten stand worth 174.

The President's XI's innings occupied 124.5 overs, and the Australians raced past the same score in half the number of overs. Slater and Blewett made 168 for the first wicket, and Slater and Ponting 206 for the second. Slater batted superbly, making 207 off 236 balls with six sixes and 22 fours. The only problem for Australia was that Steve Waugh had a gastric complaint and took no part in the final day's play.

Test Series

India v. Australia

In the first Test, India gave a debut to Harvinder Singh, the pace bowler who had done so well in limited-over internationals. Australia gave a first Test cap to the New South Wales off-spinner Gavin Robertson, who had also appeared in one-day internationals. Azharuddin won the toss, and India batted first on a docile pitch. Reiffel, in particular, and Kasprowicz presented few problems, and Warne and Robertson were soon brought into the attack in tandem. Sidhu immediately attacked Robertson, hitting him for six and four, and Taylor was forced to use Reiffel and Kasprowicz to contain one end while Warne threatened from the other. The opening stand was worth 122 when Mongia was cut behind as he attempted to square cut. In the next three overs, two more wickets fell. Sidhu had consistently gone down the pitch to smother Warne's spin, but he suddenly found himself stranded when he played a firm defensive shot to Mark Waugh at silly point, who threw down the stumps. Tendulkar drove the first delivery he received from Warne for four, but he edged the fifth and was brilliantly taken at slip by Taylor. Azharuddin had just begun to look majestic, when he, too, became a Warne victim, and when Robertson trapped Ganguly leg before, Australia had clawed back the advantage India had gained in winning the toss. Dravid, 42, and Kumble, 19, took the hosts to 232 for five by the close.

India collapsed on the second morning, losing their last five wickets for 10 runs. Their destroyers were the spin pair Warne and Robertson, who each finished with four wickets, outstanding achievements in the sapping heat. Srinath became the 51st victim of the Taylor/Warne combination, a world record that is certain to last for many years. The Indian innings had been held together by Dravid, who batted for more than four-and-a-quarter hours for his 52 and faced 169 balls.

Javagal Srinath returned to Test cricket against Sri Lanka after a worrying period of injury. He took 17 wickets in the series against Sri Lanka and Australia. He bowls Slater for 13, and India go on to win the first Test against Australia in Chennai.
(Ben Radford / Allsport)

Steve Waugh is caught by Dravid off the bowling of Venkatapathy Raju who had match figures of six for 85 in India's victory.
(Ben Radford / Allsport)

India soon made inroads into the Australian batting. Slater was caught bat and pad off Kumble, and, having survived uneasily for 103 minutes and faced 73 balls, Taylor became Harvinder Singh's first Test victim when he edged to the keeper. Steve Waugh, Ponting and Blewett were brushed aside, and only Mark Waugh's responsible innings saved Australia from a rout. He had batted for three hours and passed 5,000 Test runs before being caught at silly point off a well-flighted delivery from Venkatapathy Raju. Kumble claimed his third wicket of the day, and, in spite of Healy's positive riposte, Australia closed on a trembling 193 for seven.

Healy began the third day with 31 to his credit, and he soon lost Warne, who added only four to his overnight score. However the pitch, on which the ball had reared and turned so much on the second day that wicket-keeper Mongia wore a helmet, seemed to have lost its demons. Robertson and Healy, who has no superior in Test cricket as a fighter, added 96 for the ninth wicket and took Australia into an unexpected lead. Healy faced 194 balls and hit six fours before sweeping at Venkatapathy Raju and top-edging to Ganguly, while Robertson lasted 198 minutes for his first Test innings and looked solid and accomplished. There was a valuable flourish for the last wicket, and Australia were all out 20 minutes before tea with a lead of 71. In spite of losing Mongia, India quickly wiped off the arrears and ended the day on 100 for one.

The fourth day belonged to India in general and to Sachin Tendulkar in particular. Sidhu had launched an attack on Warne the previous evening, and the Indian batsmen continued their positive approach. Having hit 10 fours and a six, Sidhu was caught off Robertson, but there was no respite for the Australians. Tendulkar was in glorious form and put Warne to the sword. The leg-spinner conceded 79 runs from 22 overs during the day as he captured the wicket of Dravid. Azharuddin joined Tendulkar in a stand that realised 113 in two hours. When Azharuddin was out Ganguly maintained the momentum with 30 off 36 balls. It was Tendulkar, though, who dominated the day, with his unbeaten

Saurav Ganguly traps Robertson leg before in the second Test, in Calcutta. Ganguly had an outstanding year in international cricket. (Shaun Botterill / Allsport)

155 off 191 balls. He hit four sixes and 14 fours, and Australia were powerless in their attempts to constrain him.

Azharuddin's declaration left Australia a target of 348, and they had a day and 15 overs in which to get the runs. By the close of play on the fourth day, their chances of victory had vanished. Slater was bowled by Srinath, and, with his first ball, Kumble dismissed Blewett. With his tenth, the last ball of the day, he had Taylor caught, and Australia were 31 for three.

India duly completed a 179-run victory on the last day. The ball was again rearing and spitting, and Kumble, Chauhan and Venkatapathy Raju eagerly exploited the vagaries of the pitch. Mark Waugh was caught bat and pad 45 minutes into play, although the batsman clearly indicated that he thought umpire Venkataraghavan's decision was wrong. It was the English umpire Sharp, however, who drew most of the criticism. He had become most unpopular with the New Zealanders 12 months earlier; now he upset the Australians with some dubious decisions. Controversy or not, India were deserving winners. Their batting was thrilling; their bowling intelligent. Australia's main resistance came in an eighth wicket stand of 57 in 52 minutes between Healy, inevitably, and Warne, but Chauhan dismissed Warne and Robertson with successive deliveries. Kasprowicz denied the hat-trick and hit a boundary before becoming Kumble's eighth victim of the match.

For the second Test match, India made one change, opening batsman Laxman, prolific in the Ranji Trophy, replacing pace bowler Harvinder Singh. Australia had an enforced change, Paul Wilson coming in for his first Test cap in place of Reiffel. Taylor won the toss and chose to bat. Australia began disastrously. With the fifth and sixth balls of his opening over, Srinath had Slater caught at short-leg and bowled Blewett. Mark Waugh was third to go, and, after 10 overs of misery, Taylor touched a delivery from Ganguly, a highly successful makeshift new-ball bowler, to the wicket-keeper. The position could have been even worse had Ponting not been dropped by Mongia, but, having escaped, the Tasmanian stayed with Steve Waugh for 149 minutes while 112 were added. The elder of the Waugh twins batted with total composure even though he was forced to rely upon a runner in the later stages of his innings. Indeed, it was Blewett, the runner, who was left well short of his ground by Dravid's throw to Kumble when he attempted an insane single. There was further resistance for the ninth wicket between Robertson and Kasprowicz, who added 54, but Australia's 233 was a miserable effort.

On the second day, India took complete control of the match. From 90 overs, they plundered 369 runs for the loss of three wickets. Steve Waugh's groin injury kept him off the field, and Paul Wilson strained stomach muscles and was restricted to 12 overs. Neither of these Australian mishaps detracts from the quality of the Indian batting, which excited and delighted a crowd of 75,000. Laxman and Sidhu scored 95 before lunch, and 133 runs came in the afternoon session, which saw Sidhu leg before to Mark Waugh. The opening partnership was worth 191 in 204 minutes. Laxman left soon after Sidhu, but not before he had proved himself with 16 fours in his 161-ball innings. The slaughter continued with Tendulkar hitting two sixes and 12 fours as he made 79 off 86 balls. He and Dravid put on 140 in 109 minutes, and Dravid finished the day with 76 to his credit.

There was no respite for Australia on the third day. India lost Dravid before lunch as 94 runs were scored, but Ganguly joined Azharuddin in a fifth wicket stand worth 158. The stand was broken just before tea when Ganguly was caught at silly point, but nothing could disturb Azharuddin. Having been reinstated as captain, he had recaptured the affection of the public and had reasserted his position as one of the top batsmen in world cricket. He hit three sixes and 18 fours and faced 246 balls. One of his sixes, off Mark Waugh, took him to his century. When he declared, his side had a lead of 400 and Warne had 0 for 147 from 42 overs, the worst mauling he had endured since his first Test in 1991. To add to Australia's woe, Srinath bowled Slater before the close and they ended at 38 for one.

That Australia lasted until just before tea on the fourth day was in itself surprising. They had been hammered for a record score at Eden Gardens, and they had

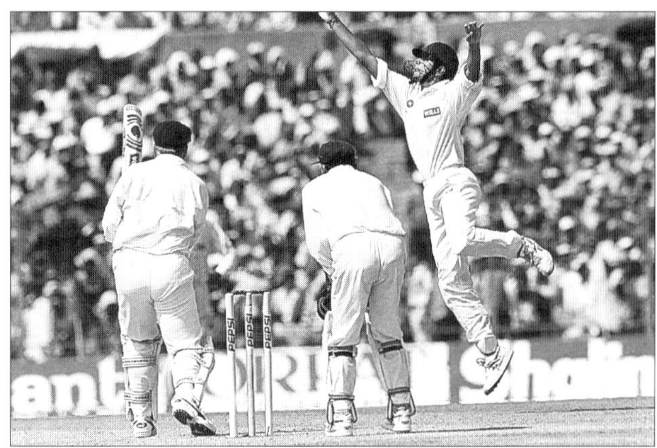

Laxman leaps to field a shot from Healy in the second Test. (Shaun Botterill / Allsport)

conceded more runs than any Australian side since Bradman's team went for 903 at The Oval in 1938. Their run of nine Test rubber victories in succession had been brought to a dramatic end. Blewett was soon leg before, Mark Waugh was taken at short-leg, and Ponting swept to square-leg. Taylor was run out from short-leg, and the only real resistance came from the injured Steve Waugh and the ever reliable Healy. Kumble picked up five wickets, but Srinath took the individual award for that opening burst which had set the pattern of the match. Australia were humiliated, and a crowd of a quarter of a million over the four days had revelled in it.

With the series decided, India allowed Srinath, who had a strained side, to rest and brought back Harvinder Singh. They gave a Test debut to 17-year old off-spinner Harbhajan Singh and Chauhan stood down. Injuries robbed Australia of Steve Waugh and Wilson, and Lehmann and Dale took their places. India won the toss and batted. Laxman went early, caught at slip off Kasprowicz, and, in two overs soon after lunch, Warne bowled both Sidhu and Dravid. Sidhu had again batted impressively in making his fourth score above 50 in his fourth innings of the series. Azharuddin joined Tendulkar, and the pair put on 139 at a run a minute. Azharuddin was caught behind off Lehmann, but Tendulkar played another dominant innings and reached his fifth century in his past eight Tests. India closed on 290 for four, Tendulkar 117.

In all, Tendulkar hit three sixes and 29 fours before becoming a victim of Dale and over-confidence. His 177 had come off 207 balls, and his genius continued to illuminate the series. He was seventh out, and Harvinder Singh followed next ball, but Kumble cajoled 34 from the last two wickets. In response, Slater gave Australia a blistering start. He was reprieved by Harbhajan Singh, who missed a return catch, but the fledgling off-spinner, with eight first-class matches to his credit, bowled Blewett with his tenth ball in Test cricket. Slater was caught behind at 143, but he had played a spectacular innings, 91 off 117 balls with two sixes and 15 fours. Mark Waugh and Lehmann took the score to 209 at the close without any further alarms.

The fourth wicket partnership was worth 106 when Lehmann gave Harbhajan Singh his second Test wicket. The off-spinner is young and inexperienced, but he has great potential. Kumble took five of the last six wickets, and Azharuddin claimed his 100th Test catch, but the man of the moment was Mark Waugh who made his highest Test score. A frustratingly profligate batsman of infinite ability, Mark Waugh, has had an inconsistent two years, but he blossomed again, hitting four sixes and 13 fours in his 267-ball innings to keep Australia's hopes alive. Eager to press for runs, India were denied by Warne, who sent back both openers, and with Robertson accounting for Dravid, India were 99 for three at the end of the third day.

In the fourth over of the fourth day, Kasprowicz held a one-handed return catch to dismiss Tendulkar and spark an Indian collapse. The last seven wickets went down for 58 runs, and pace bowler Kasprowicz, using the wearing pitch intelligently, captured five of the wickets. Australia were left needing 194 to win.

Harbhajan Singh is leg before to give Kasprowicz five wickets in the second innings of the final Test. Harbhajan Singh, a 17-year old off-spinner, was making his Test debut.
(Shaun Botterill / Allsport)

They were given the perfect start by Slater and Taylor, who scored 91 in 108 minutes. Blewett went cheaply, but Mark Waugh and Taylor hit off the required runs and gave their side some consolation for defeat in the series. Kasprowicz was named Man of the Match, and, not surprisingly, Tendulkar was Man of the Series. Australia looked tired and worn after constant international cricket, and they have not been helped by a selection policy which divided the captaincy, created a 'one-day team' and did much to undermine the Test side. England selectors should take note. The Indian batting is brilliant and the morale and application of the side has been restored. If only they had stronger support bowling.

13, 14 and 15 March 1998
at Keenan Stadium, Jamshedpur
India 'A' 216 for 9 dec. (S.C.G. MacGill 4 for 67) and 241 for 2 (A.R. Khurasiya 117 not out, J.J. Martin 52 not out)
Australians 391 (S.R. Waugh 107, D.S. Lehmann 76, M.A. Taylor 57, G.S. Blewett 57)
Match drawn

The tourists played one first-class match in between the first and second Tests. They were encouraged by the bowling of MacGill, and there were century stands between Blewett and Steve Waugh, and Steve Waugh and Lehmann. On the debit side, Dale was taken ill, and Reiffel was ruled unfit through injury. Khurasiya and Martin shared an unbroken third wicket stand of 153 for India 'A'.

First Test Match – India v. Australia

6, 7, 8, 9 and 10 March 1998 at Chidambaram Stadium, Chepauk, Chennai (Madras)

India

	First Innings		Second Innings	
N.R. Mongia †	c Healy, b Kasprowicz	58	lbw, b Blewett	18
N.S. Sidhu	run out	62	c Ponting, b Roberston	64
R.S. Dravid	c Robertson, b Warne	52	c Healy, b Warne	56
S.R. Tendulkar	c Taylor, b Warne	4	not out	155
M. Azharuddin *	c Reiffel, b Warne	26	c S.R. Waugh, b M.E. Waugh	64
S.C. Ganguly	lbw, b Robertson	3	not out	30
A.R. Kumble	c S.R. Waugh, b Robertson	30		
J. Srinath	c Taylor, b Warne	1		
R.K. Chauhan	c Healy, b Robertson	3		
Harvinder Singh	not out	0		
Venkatapathy Raju	b Robertson	0		
	b 8, lb 6, nb 4	18	b 18, lb 6, nb 7	31
		257	(for 4 wickets, dec.)	418

	O	M	R	W	O	M	R	W
Kasprowicz	21	8	44	1	14	6	42	–
Reiffel	15	4	27	–	9	1	32	–
Warne	35	11	85	4	30	7	122	1
Robertson	28.2	4	72	4	27	4	92	1
M.E. Waugh	1	–	4	–	9	–	44	1
S.R. Waugh	4	1	11	–	8	–	27	–
Blewett	10	2	35	1				

Fall of Wickets
1–**22**, 2–**126**, 3–**130**, 4–**186**, 5–**195**, 6–**247**, 7–**248**, 8–**253**, 9–**257**
1–**43**, 2–**115**, 3–**228**, 4–**355**

Australia

	First Innings		Second Innings	
M.A. Taylor *	c Mongia, b Harvinder Singh	12	(2) c Srinath, b Kumble	13
M.J. Slater	c Dravid, b Kumble	11	(1) b Srinath	13
M.E. Waugh	c Ganguly, b Raju	66	(5) c Dravid, b Kumble	18
S.R. Waugh	b Kumble	12	(6) c Dravid, b Raju	27
R.T. Ponting	c Mongia, b Raju	18	(7) lbw, b Venkatapathy Raju	2
G.S. Blewett	lbw, b Chauhan	9	(3) c Dravid, b Kumble	5
I.A. Healy †	c Ganguly, b Raju	90	(8) not out	32
P.R. Reiffel	c Dravid, b Kumble	15	(4) c Azharuddin, b Raju	8
S.K. Warne	c Tendulkar, b Kumble	17	c Kumble, b Chauhan	35
G.R. Robertson	c Mongia, b Srinath	57	b Chauhan	0
M.S. Kasprowicz	not out	11	c Srinath, b Kumble	4
	b 1, lb 6, nb 3	10	b 4, lb 3, nb 4	11
		328		168

	O	M	R	W	O	M	R	W
Srinath	17.3	3	46	1	6	4	9	1
Harvinder Singh	11	4	28	1	2	–	9	–
Kumble	45	10	103	4	22.5	7	46	4
Chauhan	25	3	90	1	22	7	66	2
Venkatapathy Raju	32	8	54	3	15	4	31	3

Fall of Wickets
1–**16**, 2–**44**, 3–**57**, 4–**95**, 5–**119**, 6–**137**, 7–**173**, 8–**201**, 9–**297**
1–**18**, 2–**30**, 3–**31**, 4–**54**, 5–**79**, 6–**91**, 7–**96**, 8–**153**, 9–**153**

Umpires: S. Venkataraghavan & G. Sharp

India won by 179 runs

Second Test Match – India v. Australia

18, 19, 20 and 21 March 1998 at Eden Gardens, Calcutta

Australia

	First Innings		Second Innings	
M.J. Slater	c Dravid, b Srinath	0	(2) b Srinath	5
M.A. Taylor *	c Mongia, b Ganguly	3	(1) run out	45
G.S. Blewett	b Srinath	0	lbw, b Srinath	25
M.E. Waugh	lbw, b Srinath	10	c Laxman, b Kumble	0
S.R. Waugh	run out	80	(7) lbw, b Kumble	33
R.T. Ponting	b Kumble	60	(5) c Srinath, b Kumble	9
I.A. Healy †	c Laxman, b Kumble	1	(6) lbw, b Srinath	38
S.K. Warne	c Azharuddin, b Kumble	11	c and b Kumble	9
G.R. Robertson	lbw, b Ganguly	29	c Azharuddin, b Kumble	0
M.S. Kasprowicz	c Azharuddin, b Ganguly	25	c Raju, b Chauhan	10
P. Wilson	not out	0	not out	0
	lb 2, nb 12	14	b 1, lb 3, nb 3	7
		233		181

	O	M	R	W	O	M	R	W
Srinath	17	–	80	3	19	6	44	3
Ganguly	13.4	5	28	3	4	–	9	–
Kumble	28	11	44	3	31	10	62	5
Tendulkar	2	–	6	–				
Chauhan	11	2	30	–	18.3	4	42	1
Venkatapathy Raju	17	2	42	–	16	7	20	–
Laxman	1	–	1	–				

Fall of Wickets
1–**1**, 2–**1**, 3–**15**, 4–**29**, 5–**141**, 6–**151**, 7–**168**, 8–**178**, 9–**232**
1–**7**, 2–**55**, 3–**56**, 4–**81**, 5–**91**, 6–**133**, 7–**158**, 8–**158**, 9–**181**

India

	First Innings	
V.V.S. Laxman	c Healy, b Robertson	95
N.S. Sidhu	lbw, b M.E. Waugh	97
R.S. Dravid	c and b Blewett	86
S.R. Tendulkar	c Blewett, b Kasprowicz	79
M. Azharuddin *	not out	163
S.C. Ganguly	c sub (Lehmann), b Robertson	65
N.R. Mongia †	not out	30
A.R. Kumble		
J. Srinath		
R.K. Chauhan		
Venkatapathy Raju		
	b 2, lb 7, nb 9	18
	(for 5 wickets, dec.)	633

	O	M	R	W
Kasprowicz	34	6	122	1
Wilson	12	2	50	–
Blewett	20	3	65	1
Warne	42	4	147	–
Robertson	33	2	163	2
M.E. Waugh	18	1	77	1

Fall of Wickets
1–**191**, 2–**207**, 3–**347**, 4–**400**, 5–**558**

Umpires: K. Parthasarathy & B.C. Cooray

India won by an innings and 219 runs

Third Test Match – India *v.* Australia

25, 26, 27 and 28 March 1998 at M. Chinnaswamy Stadium, Bangalore

India

	First Innings		Second Innings	
V.V.S. Laxman	c Taylor, b Kasprowicz	6	c Ponting, b Warne	15
N.S. Sidhu	b Warne	74	c Lehmann, b Warne	44
R.S. Dravid	b Warne	23	c Healy, b Robertson	6
S.R. Tendulkar	b Dale	177	c and b Kasprowicz	31
M. Azharuddin *	c Healy, b Lehmann	40	b Kasprowicz	18
S.C. Ganguly	lbw, b Dale	17	b Robertson	16
N.R. Mongia †	c Ponting, b Warne	18	not out	12
A.R. Kumble	c M.E. Waugh, b Robertson	39	lbw, b Robertson	9
Harvinder Singh	lbw, b Dale	0	lbw, b Kasprowicz	0
Venkatapathy Raju	c Lehmann, b Robertson	5	b Kasprowicz	2
Harbhajan Singh	not out	4	lbw, b Kasprowicz	0
	b 6, lb 6, nb 9	21	b 5, lb 5, nb 6	16
		424		169

	O	M	R	W	O	M	R	W
Kasprowicz	29	4	76	1	18	5	28	5
Dale	23	6	71	3	5	1	21	–
Warne	35	9	106	3	25	6	80	2
Blewett	14	3	50	–	1	–	2	–
Robertson	11.2	1	58	2	12	2	28	3
M.E. Waugh	4	–	24	–				
Lehmann	7	1	27	1				

Fall of Wickets
1–**24**, 2–**109**, 3–**110**, 4–**249**, 5–**294**, 6–**353**, 7–**390**, 8–**390**, 9–**415**
1–**50**, 2–**61**, 3–**92**, 4–**111**, 5–**127**, 6–**144**, 7–**158**, 8–**158**, 9–**163**

Australia

	First Innings		Second Innings	
M.J. Slater	c Mongia, b Harvinder Singh	91	(2) c Azharuddin, b Tendulkar	42
M.A. Taylor *	c Mongia, b Kumble	14	(1) not out	102
G.S. Blewett	b Harbhajan Singh	4	lbw, b Kumble	5
M.E. Waugh	not out	153	not out	33
D.S. Lehmann	c Laxman, b Harbhajan Singh	52		
R.T. Ponting	c Tendulkar, b Kumble	16		
I.A. Healy †	c Mongia, b Kumble	4		
S.K. Warne	c Harbhajan Singh, b Raju	33		
G.R. Robertson	c Azharuddin, b Kumble	4		
M.S. Kasprowicz	lbw, b Kumble	4		
A.C. Dale	c Laxman, b Kumble	5		
	b 12, lb 5, nb 3	20	b 8, lb 5	13
		400	(for 2 wickets)	195

	O	M	R	W	O	M	R	W
Harvinder Singh	7	–	44	1	3	–	17	–
Ganguly	2	–	10	–				
Kumble	41.3	8	98	6	22.4	5	63	1
Venkatapathy Raju	37	7	118	1	15	4	37	–
Harbhajan Singh	23	1	112	2	6	1	24	–
Laxman	1	–	1	–				
Tendulkar11.2	1	41	1					

Fall of Wickets
1–**68**, 2–**77**, 3–**143**, 4–**249**, 5–**274**, 6–**286**, 7–**350**, 8–**378**, 9–**394**
1–**91**, 2–**114**

Umpires: V.K. Ramaswamy & D.R. Shepherd

Australia won by 8 wickets

Test Match Averages – India *v.* Australia

India Batting

	M	Inns	NOs	Runs	HS	Av	100s	50s
S.R. Tendulkar	3	5	1	446	155*	111.50	2	1
M. Azharuddin	3	5	1	311	163*	77.75	1	1
N.S. Sidhu	3	5	–	341	97	68.20	4	
N.R. Mongia	3	5	2	136	58	45.33	1	
R.S. Dravid	3	5	–	223	86	44.60	3	
V.V.S. Laxman	2	3	–	116	95	38.66	1	
S.C. Ganguly	3	5	1	131	65	32.75	1	
A.R. Kumble	3	3	–	78	39	26.00		
Venkatapathy Raju	3	3	–	7	5	2.33		
Harvinder Singh	2	3	1	0	0*	0.00		

Played in two Tests: J. Srinath 1; R.K. Chauhan 3
Played in one Test: Harbhajan Singh 4* & 0

Australia Batting

	M	Inns	NOs	Runs	HS	Av	100s	50s
M.E. Waugh	3	6	2	280	153*	70.00	1	1
I.A. Healey	3	5	1	165	90	41.25	1	
S.R. Waugh	2	4	–	152	80	38.00	1	
M.A. Taylor	3	6	1	189	102*	37.80	1	
M.J. Slater	3	6	–	162	91	27.00	1	
R.T. Ponting	3	5	–	105	60	21.00	1	
S.K. Warne	3	5	–	105	35	21.00		
G.R. Robertson	3	5	–	90	57	18.00	1	
M.S. Kasprowicz	3	5	1	54	25	13.50		
G.S. Blewett	3	6	–	48	25	8.00		

Played in one Test: P.R. Reiffel 15 & 8;P. Wilson 0* & 0*; D.S. Lehmann 52; A.C. Dale 5

India Bowling

	Overs	Mds	Runs	Wks	Av	Best	5/inn
S.C. Ganguly	19.4	5	47	3	15.66	3/28	
A.R. Kumble	191	51	416	23	18.08	6/98	2
J. Srinath	59.3	13	179	8	22.37	3/44	
Venkatapathy Raju	132	32	302	7	43.14	3/31	
S.R. Tendulkar	13.2	1	47	1	47.00	1/41	
Harvinder Singh	23	4	98	2	49.00	1/28	
R.K. Chauhan	76.3	16	228	4	57.00	2/62	
Harbhajan Singh	29	2	136	2	68.00	2/112	
V.V.S. Laxman	2	–	2	–	–		

Australia Bowling

	Overs	Mds	Runs	Wks	Average	Best	5/inn
A.C. Dale	28	7	92	3	30.66	3/71	
G.R. Robertson	111.4	13	413	12	34.41	4/72	
M.S. Kasprowicz	116	29	312	8	39.00	5/28	1
S.K. Warne	167	37	540	10	54.00	4/85	
M.E. Waugh	32	1	149	2	74.50	1/44	
G.S. Blewett	45	8	152	2	76.00	1/35	
S.R. Waugh	12	1	38	–	–		
P. Wilson	12	2	50	–	–		
P.R. Reiffel	24	5	59	–	–		

Bowled in one innings: D.S. Lehmann 7–1–27–1

Fielding Figures

7 – N.R. Mongia; 6 – M. Azharuddin and R.S. Dravid; 4 – V.V.S. Laxman; 3 – J. Srinath
2 – S.R. Tendulkar, A.R. Kumble and S.C. Ganguly; 1 – Venkatapathy Raju and Harbhajan Singh

Fielding Figures

6 – I.A. Healey; 3 – M.A. Taylor and R.T. Ponting; 2 – S.R. Waugh, G.S. Blewett and D.S. Lehmann (plus one as sub); 1 – M.E. Waugh, P.R. Reiffel, G.R. Robertson and M.S. Kasprowicz

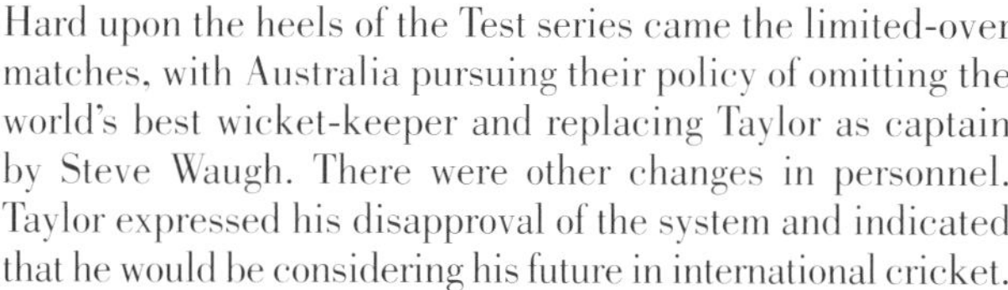

Triangular Series

India, Australia and Zimbabwe

Hard upon the heels of the Test series came the limited-over matches, with Australia pursuing their policy of omitting the world's best wicket-keeper and replacing Taylor as captain by Steve Waugh. There were other changes in personnel. Taylor expressed his disapproval of the system and indicated that he would be considering his future in international cricket.

India displayed another new bowler in Agarkar for the opening match, in which they maintained their form with an emphatic victory over Australia. The occasion was significant in that Mohammad Azharuddin, the Indian captain, appeared in his 274th one-day international, so surpassing Allan Border's record. He played a major part in India's revival after both openers had fallen with only 19 scored. He and Jadeja, considered to be a one-day expert rather than a Test player, put on 104 for the fourth wicket, and Jadeja dominated a fifth wicket stand of 121 with Kanitkar. Facing a daunting target, Australia were given a bright start by Gilchrist and Mark Waugh, but, on a pitch that made batting easy, Tendulkar produced a remarkable bowling performance and turned the game completely in India's favour.

Zimbabwe put up a brave fight against Australia in the second match but lost by 13 runs. Australia chose to bat when they won the toss and scored consistently, but they were kept in check by some good fielding, and a target of 253 was not beyond Zimbabwe's reach. Skipper Alistair Campbell opened with Grant Flower, who scored briskly before falling to Shane Warne. Goodwin then joined Campbell to add 91 for the second wicket, but the middle order succumbed to Fleming, Dale and Moody. Campbell battled on without support and was last out, bowled by Moody, for a magnificent 105.

The host nation assured themselves of a place in the final when they beat Zimbabwe by 12 runs, but they had to fight hard after a disastrous start in which Tendulkar and Azharuddin were dismissed with only 17 scored. India were rallied by Ganguly who, returning to the side, made 82 and shared vital stands with Kambli and Jadeja, who was again most impressive. Grant Flower and Alistair Campbell gave Zimbabwe a wonderful start with a partnership of 121, and Evans and Andy Flower kept them on course for victory. But the later batsmen lost their way, and India were relieved to gain a narrow win.

Indian dominance continued with an emphatic win over Australia in Kanpur. Facing a target of 223, India were put in total command by Ganguly and Tendulkar, who scored 175 for the first wicket, Tendulkar making exactly 100. Four wickets fell for 37 runs, but victory came with more than five overs remaining. In celebration, Azharuddin was reappointed captain for the Sharjah tournament later in the month and the competition in Bangladesh later in the year.

The fifth match in the series produced some sensational cricket. Put in to bat on a damp pitch, India were reduced to 26 for three. At this point, Jadeja joined Azharuddin, and the pair added 275 without being separated, a record fourth wicket partnership for a one-day international. Azharuddin's 153 came off 149 balls, while Jadeja hit his second century of the competition to bring his aggregate to 306 in four innings without being dismissed. Grant Flower made a defiant 102 in response, but Zimbabwe were always fighting a losing battle.

Australia duly claimed their place in the final alongside India, but once more Zimbabwe were spirited in defeat. A second wicket stand of 219 between Mark Waugh and Ricky Ponting gave substance to the Australian score, with Ponting making his highest one-day international score. If Zimbabwe lack strength in bowling, they did not lack character in batting. Grant Flower and Goodwin put on 96 for the second wicket; the Flower brothers 121 for the third. Sadly, collapse followed, and seven wickets went down for 41 runs.

On the eve of the final, Azharuddin warned his team against complacency. They had swept all before them in the preliminary matches and were firm favourites to take the trophy. When Azharuddin won the toss and chose to bat they had the opportunity to build a big total. The early loss of Tendulkar was a blow, and it heralded a period in which Australia bowled tightly and fielded tigerishly. Azharuddin and Sidhu added 70 for the third wicket, but no batsman played the innings of substance that was needed. Jadeja, the Man of the Series, was top scorer with 48, but India were restricted to a meagre 227. Australia immediately lost Gilchrist, and four wickets fell for 111. Bevan joined Steve Waugh in a stand worth 99, which took Australia to the brink of victory. Waugh hit three sixes before being bowled by Kumble, and Jadeja took a spectacular leaping catch to dismiss Moody, but Bevan took his side to their target with eight balls to spare.

Vinod Kambli played in the limited-over series against Australia, Zimbabwe and New Zealand but could not hold a place in the Indian Test side in spite of averaging 111.25 in the first-class season. (Stu Forster / Allsport)

Match One – India v. Australia

1 April, 1998 at Cochin

India

Batsman	Dismissal	Runs
N.S. Sidhu	c Gilchrist, b Kasprowicz	1
S.R. Tendulkar	c Ponting, b Kasprowicz	8
M. Azharuddin *	c M.E. Waugh, b Kasprowicz	82
V.G. Kambli	lbw, b Fleming	33
A.D. Jadeja	not out	105
H.H. Kanitkar	lbw, b Martyn	57
N.R. Mongia †	not out	2
A.B. Agarkar		
A.R. Kumble		
J. Srinath		
D.S. Mohanty		
	lb 11, w 8, nb 2	21
	50 overs (for 5 wickets)	309

	O	M	R	W
Fleming	10	–	61	1
Kasprowicz	8.2	2	50	3
Moody	10	–	60	–
Warne	10	–	42	–
Bevan	5	–	34	–
Martyn	3.4	–	30	1
M.E. Waugh	3	–	21	–

Fall of Wickets
1–11, 2–19, 3–80, 4–184, 5–305

Australia

Batsman	Dismissal	Runs
M.E. Waugh	c Agarkar, b Srinath	28
A.C. Gilchrist †	c Azharuddin, b Agarkar	61
R.T. Ponting	c Azharuddin, b Kanitkar	12
M.G. Bevan	c Mongia, b Tendulkar	65
S.R. Waugh *	c and b Tendulkar	26
D.S. Lehmann	lbw, b Tendulkar	8
T.M. Moody	c Mongia, b Tendulkar	23
D.R. Martyn	c Srinath, b Tendulkar	2
S.K. Warne	c Kanitkar, b Kumble	0
D.W. Fleming	c Kumble, b Srinath	5
M.S. Kasprowicz	not out	6
	b 4, lb 12, w 9, nb 7	32
	45.5 overs	268

	O	M	R	W
Srinath	7.5	1	41	2
Mohanty	5	–	51	–
Agarkar	5	–	31	1
Kumble	10	–	51	1
Kanitkar	8	–	46	1
Tendulkar	10	2	32	5

Fall of Wickets
1–101, 2–105, 3–142, 4–202, 5–222, 6–239, 7–253, 8–254, 9–259

Umpires: S.K. Bansal & A.V. Jayaprakash *Man of the Match*: S.R. Tendulkar

India won by 41 runs

Match Two – Australia v. Zimbabwe

3 April 1998 at Sardar Patel Stadium, Motera, Ahmedabad

Australia

Batsman	Dismissal	Runs
A.C. Gilchrist †	lbw, b Streak	12
M.E. Waugh	lbw, b A.R. Whittall	37
R.T. Ponting	run out	53
M.G. Bevan	c Streak, b Evans	65
S.R. Waugh *	b G.J. Whittall	49
D.S. Lehmann	b Streak	6
T.M. Moody	run out	2
S.K. Warne	not out	11
G.R. Robertson	not out	5
D.W. Fleming		
A.C. Dale		
	b 1, lb 3, w 8	12
	50 overs (for 7 wickets)	252

	O	M	R	W
Streak	10	–	48	2
G.J. Whittall	10	–	57	1
Huckle	10	–	47	–
A.R. Whittall	10	1	44	1
Viljoen	4	–	26	–
Evans	6	–	26	1

Fall of Wickets
1–19, 2–87, 3–142, 4–212, 5–233, 6–235, 7–238

Zimbabwe

Batsman	Dismissal	Runs
G.W. Flower	c Bevan, b Warne	35
A.D.R. Campbell *	b Moody	103
M.W. Goodwin	b Warne	55
A. Flower †	lbw, b Fleming	1
G.J. Whittall	c Gilchrist, b Fleming	0
H.H. Streak	b Fleming	5
C.B. Wishart	b Dale	11
C.N. Evans	c Gilchrist, b Moody	5
D.P. Viljoen	c Gilchrist, b Moody	0
A.R. Whittall	c Warne, b Dale	6
A.G. Huckle	not out	1
	b 4, lb 4, w 6, nb 3	17
	49.5 overs	239

	O	M	R	W
Fleming	10	–	30	3
Dale	8	–	50	2
Warne	10	–	46	2
Moody	9.5	1	39	3
M.E. Waugh	5	–	24	–
Robertson	5	–	28	–
Bevan	2	–	14	–

Fall of Wickets
1–52, 2–143, 3–149, 4–149, 5–163, 6–181, 7–192, 8–192, 9–210

Umpires: B.A. Jamula & R. Desraj *Man of the Match*: A.D.R. Campbell

Australia won by 13 runs

Match Three – India v. Zimbabwe

5 April 1998 at IPCL Ground, Baroda

India

S.C. Ganguly	**c** Wishart, **b** G.J. Whittall	**82**
S.R. Tendulkar	run out	**5**
M. Azharuddin *	**c** Campbell, **b** Streak	**0**
V.G. Kambli	run out	**39**
A.D. Jadeja	not out	**79**
H.H. Kanitkar	lbw, **b** Streak	**35**
N.R. Mongia †	not out	**4**
A.B. Agarkar		
A.R. Kumble		
Venkatesh Prasad		
R.L. Sanghvi		
	lb **13**, w **14**, nb **3**	**30**
	50 overs (for 5 wickets)	**274**

	O	M	R	W
Streak	10	1	42	**2**
Mbangwa	8	–	28	**–**
G.J. Whittall	9	–	70	**1**
A.R. Whittall	7	–	38	**–**
Evans	10	–	50	**–**
Huckle	6	–	33	**–**

Fall of Wickets
1–**17**, 2–**17**, 3–**95**, 4–**168**, 5–**246**

Zimbabwe

G.W. Flower	**c** Jadeja, **b** Tendulkar	**57**
A.D.R. Campbell *	**st** Mongia, **b** Kanitkar	**60**
M.W. Goodwin	**c** and **b** Kanitkar	**11**
C.N. Evans	**st** Mongia, **b** Sanghvi	**46**
A. Flower †	**c** Azharuddin, **b** Kumble	**25**
G.J. Whittall	**c** and **b** Sanghvi	**9**
H.H. Streak	not out	**17**
C.B. Wishart	**c** and **b** Sanghvi	**4**
A.R. Whittall	**b** Agarkar	**8**
M. Mbangwa	run out	**2**
A.G. Huckle	run out	**0**
	b **5**, lb **9**, w **5**, nb **4**	**23**
	(48.3 overs)	**262**

	O	M	R	W
Venkatesh Prasad	8	–	43	**–**
Agarkar	8.3	–	59	**1**
Ganguly	3	–	17	**–**
Kumble	9	–	27	**1**
Kanitkar	7	–	37	**2**
Sanghvi	8	–	29	**3**
Tendulkar	5	–	36	**1**

Fall of Wickets
1–**121**, 2–**136**, 3–**148**, 4–**212**, 5–**224**, 6–**226**, 7–**232**, 8–**246**, 9–**260**

Umpires: J. Singh & G.A. Pratap Kumar *Man of the Match*: S.C. Ganguly

India won by 12 runs

Match Four – India v. Australia

7 April 1998 at Green Park, Kanpur

Australia

M.E. Waugh	**c** Mongia, **b** Venkatesh Prasad	**6**
A.C. Gilchrist †	**c** Azharuddin, **b** Agarkar	**11**
R.T. Ponting	**c** Kanitkar, **b** Agarkar	**84**
M.G. Bevan	**b** Kanitkar	**16**
D.S. Lehmann	**b** Sanghvi	**18**
S.R. Waugh *	**st** Mongia, **b** Kanitkar	**0**
T.M. Moody	**b**Agarkar	**44**
S.K. Warne	**c** Mongia, **b** Kumble	**2**
G.R. Robertson	lbw, **b** Agarkar	**15**
M.S. Kasprowicz	not out	**2**
D.W. Fleming	not out	**3**
	lb **11**, w **7**, nb **3**	**21**
	50 overs (for 9 wickets)	**222**

	O	M	R	W
Venkatesh Prasad	6	–	33	**1**
Agarkar	10	–	46	**4**
Kanitkar	10	1	33	**2**
Sanghvi	10	1	38	**1**
Tendulkar	4	–	19	**–**
Kumble	10	–	42	**1**

Fall of Wickets
1–**12**, 2–**35**, 3–**71**, 4–**106**, 5–**108**, 6–**185**, 7–**190**, 8–**216**, 9–**218**

India

S.C. Ganguly	**c** Gilchrist, **b** Kasprowicz	**72**
S.R. Tendulkar	**c** sub (Martyn), **b** Warne	**100**
M. Azharuddin *	**c** and **b** Kasprowicz	**3**
V.G. Kambli	**b** Bevan	**17**
A.D. Jadeja	not out	**6**
H.H. Kanitkar	not out	**7**
N.R. Mongia †		
A.R. Kumble		
A.B. Agarkar		
Venkatesh Prasad		
R.L. Sanghvi		
	lb **3**, w **12**, nb **3**	**18**
	44.3 overs (for 4 wickets)	**223**

	O	M	R	W
Fleming	9	–	42	**–**
Kasprowicz	10	1	39	**2**
Robertson	7.3	–	34	**–**
Moody	3	–	26	**–**
Lehmann	4	1	28	**–**
Warne	9	–	43	**1**
Bevan	2	–	8	**1**

Fall of Wickets
1–**175**, 2–**183**, 3–**197**, 4–**212**

Umpires: C.R. Sathe & M.R. Singh *Man of the Match*: S.R. Tendulkar

India won by 6 wickets

Match Five – India v. Zimbabwe

9 April 1998 at Barbatti Stadium, Cuttack

India

S.C. Ganguly	**c** A. Flower, **b** Streak	**13**
S.R. Tendulkar	**c** A. Flower, **b** Mbangwa	**1**
V.V.S. Laxman	lbw, **b** Mbangwa	**0**
M. Azharuddin *	not out	**153**
A.D. Jadeja	not out	**116**
H.H. Kanitkar		
N.R. Mongia †		
A.B. Agarkar		
Venkatesh Prasad		
D.S. Mohanty		
R.L. Sanghvi		
	lb **2**, w **14**, nb **2**	**18**
	50 overs (for 3 wickets)	**301**

	O	M	R	W
Streak	10	–	56	**1**
Mbangwa	9	–	47	**2**
G.J. Whittall	8	–	68	**–**
Brent	5	–	26	**–**
Huckle	8	1	42	**–**
Evans	6	–	39	**–**
G.W. Flower	4	–	21	**–**

Fall of Wickets
1–**8**, 2–**8**, 3–**26**

Zimbabwe

G.W. Flower	**c** and **b** Sanghvi	**102**
A.D.R. Campbell *	**c** Azharuddin, **b** Venkatesh	**11**
M.W. Goodwin	**c** Kanitkar, **b** Agarkar	**47**
A. Flower †	**b** Agarkar	**3**
G.J. Whittall	run out	**13**
H.H. Streak	**b** Ganguly	**30**
P.A. Strang	run out	**8**
C.N. Evans	**b** Ganguly	**4**
G.B. Brent	**b** Kanitkar	**24**
M. Mbangwa	**c** Venkatesh Prasad, **b** Kanitkar	**8**
A.G. Huckle	not out	**0**
	lb **6**, w **9**, nb **4**	**19**
	48.4 overs	**269**

	O	M	R	W
Venkatesh Prasad	7	–	40	**1**
Mohanty	10	–	54	**–**
Agarkar	8	–	45	**2**
Ganguly	8	–	34	**2**
Sanghvi	7	–	44	**1**
Kanitkar	6.4	–	26	**2**
Tendulkar	2	–	20	**–**

Fall of Wickets
1–**23**, 2–**92**, 3–**104**, 4–**121**, 5–**188**, 6–**204**, 7–**211**, 8–**255**, 9–**269**

Umpires: R. Nagarajan & N. Menon *Man of the Match*: M. Azharuddin

India won by 32 runs

Match Six – Australia v. Zimbabwe

11 April 1998 at Ferozeshah Kotla Ground, Delhi

Australia

A.C. Gilchrist †	**c** A. Flower, **b** Mbangwa	**1**
M.E. Waugh	**b** Streak	**87**
R.T. Ponting	**c** Mbangwa, **b** G.J. Whittall	**145**
M.G. Bevan	not out	**33**
D.R. Martyn	not out	**8**
S.R. Waugh *		
D.S. Lehmann		
S.K. Warne		
G.R. Robertson		
M.S. Kasprowicz		
D.W. Fleming		
	lb **6**, w **13**, nb **1**	**20**
	50 overs (for 3 wickets)	**294**

	O	M	R	W
Mbangwa	10	–	58	**1**
Streak	10	–	64	**1**
G.J. Whittall	5	–	52	**1**
Huckle	8	–	45	**–**
A.R. Whittall	10	–	31	**–**
Evans	5	–	29	**–**
Goodwin	2	–	9	**–**

Fall of Wickets
1–**2**, 2–**221**, 3–**268**

Zimbabwe

G.W. Flower	**b** Warne	**89**
A.D.R. Campbell *	**c** S.R. Waugh, **b** Kasprowicz	**1**
M.W. Goodwin	**c** Kasprowicz, **b** S.R. Waugh	**46**
A. Flower †	run out	**73**
C.N. Evans	run out	**6**
H.H. Streak	not out	**27**
G.J. Whittall	**c** Warne, **b** Lehmann	**7**
P.A. Strang	lbw, **b** Fleming	**2**
A.R. Whittall	**b** Fleming	**0**
M. Mbangwa	**b** Kasprowicz	**0**
A.G. Huckle	not out	**5**
	lb **10**, w **7**, nb **5**	**22**
	50 overs (for 9 wickets)	**278**

	O	M	R	W
Kasprowicz	10	1	47	**2**
Fleming	10	1	39	**2**
Warne	10	–	54	**1**
S.R. Waugh	10	–	55	**1**
Robertson	4	–	31	**–**
Bevan	3	–	19	**–**
Lehmann	1	–	8	**1**
Martyn	2		15	**–**

Fall of Wickets
1–**2**, 2–**98**, 3–**219**, 4–**226**, 5–**227**, 6–**246**, 7–**256**, 8–**256**, 9–**260**

Man of the Match: R.T. Ponting

Australia won by 16 runs

Final – India v. Australia

14 April 1998 at Ferozeshah Kotla Ground, Delhi

India

S.C. Ganguly	**c** Gilchrist, **b** Moody	**29**
S.R. Tendulkar	**c** Gilchrist, **b** Fleming	**15**
M. Azharuddin *	**c** Bevan, **b** S.R. Waugh	**44**
N.S. Sidhu	**c** Fleming, **b** S.R. Waugh	**38**
A.D. Jadeja	**c** and **b** Kasprowicz	**48**
H.H. Kanitkar	**b** Fleming	**19**
A.B. Agarkar	**c** S.R. Waugh, **b** Warne	**4**
N.R. Mongia †	**c** Bevan, **b** Fleming	**14**
A.R. Kumble	not out	**1**
Venkatesh Prasad	**b** Kasprowicz	**1**
R.L. Sanghvi	run out	**0**
	b **2**, lb **5**, w **6**, nb **1**	**14**
	49.3 overs	**227**

	O	M	R	W
Fleming	10	1	47	**3**
Kasprowicz	9.3	–	43	**2**
Moody	10	–	40	**1**
Warne	10	–	35	**1**
S.R. Waugh	7	–	42	**2**
Lehmann	3	–	13	**–**

Fall of Wickets
1–**37**, 2–**58**, 3–**128**, 4–**144**, 5–**177**, 6–**185**, 7–**218**, 8–**225**, 9–**227**

Australia

M.E. Waugh	**b** Kumble	**20**
A.C. Gilchrist †	**c** Tendulkar, **b** Agarkar	**1**
R.T. Ponting	**st** Mongia, **b** Sanghvi	**41**
M.G. Bevan	not out	**75**
S.K. Warne	**b** Venkatesh Prasad	**14**
S.R. Waugh *	**b** Kumble	**57**
T.M. Moody	**c** Jadeja, **b** Agarkar	**4**
D.S. Lehmann	not out	**6**
D.R. Martyn		
M.S. Kasprowicz		
D.W. Fleming		
	lb **6**, w **5**, nb **2**	**13**
	48.4 overs (for 6 wickets)	**231**

	O	M	R	W
Venkatesh Prasad	7	–	43	**1**
Agarkar	10	1	53	**2**
Kumble	9.4	2	36	**2**
Kanitkar	7	–	35	**–**
Sanghvi	10	–	45	**1**
Tendulkar	5	–	13	**–**

Fall of Wickets
1–**6**, 2–**56**, 3–**84**, 4–**111**, 5–**210**, 6–**219**

Umpires: V. Chopra & V.K. Ramaswamy *Man of the Match:* S.R. Waugh

Australia won by 4 wickets

Irani Trophy

1, 2, 3, 4 and 5 October 1997
at Wankhede Stadium, Mumbai
Mumbai 473 (J.V. Paranjpe 113, A.A. Muzumdar 97, Wasim Jaffer 83, S.V. Bahutule 71, A.R. Kumble 4 for 140) and 93 (A.R. Kumble 7 for 33)
Rest of India 279 (N.R. Mongia 78 not out, G.K. Khoda 59, S. Sharath 59, S.V. Bahutule 5 for 97) and 233 (A.R. Kapoor 50, S.V. Bahutule 8 for 71)
Mumbai won by 54 runs

Mumbai won the Irani Trophy for the 15th time, beating the Rest of India by 54 runs in a game that produced two outstanding performances by leg-break bowlers. On the opening day, left-hander Jatin Paranjpe and Wasim Jaffer put on 140 for the second wicket, and Paranjpe made his first century in the annual fixture. Muzumdar, still trying to catch the eye of the selectors, batted serenely and hit 10 fours before being caught at slip off Kumble. Rest of India were in considerable trouble at 90 for five before Sharath and Mongia added 102. Batting a second time with a lead of 194, Mumbai were skittled out by Kumble, who became the first bowler to take ten or more wickets in two Irani Trophy matches. His match figures were 11 for 173, and he had taken 13 for 138 against Delhi in 1992–93. He was overshadowed on the last day by Sairaj Bahutule, the Mumbai leg-spinner, who returned the best bowling figures of his career and the third best in the 34 years of the Trophy matches.

Duleep Trophy

Quarter-Final

1, 2, 3, 4 and 5 December 1997
at Gymkhana Ground, Hyderabad
North Zone 295 (V. Rathore 94, A. Chopra 63) and 279 for 8 dec. (A. Chopra 69, U. Chatterjee 5 for 102)
East Zone 346 (N. Haldipur 103, R.S. Gavaskar 55) and 232 for 5 (S.S. Karim 80 not out)
East Zone won by 5 wickets

East Zone gained an invaluable first innings lead in the rain-affected and sometimes acrimonious quarter-final. North Zone wasted the advantage of winning the toss, and Nikhil Haldipur, a left-hander, made a century for East Zone. He offered chances that were not accepted.

Semi-Finals

7, 8, 9, 10 and 11 December 1997
at M. Chinnaswamy Stadium, Bangalore
East Zone 337 (D. Gandhi 158)

Central Zone 295 for 7 (J.P.Yadav 145 not out)
Match drawn

9, 10, 11, 12 and 13 December 1997
at Trishna Stadium, Ukkunagaram, Vishakhapatnam
West Zone 321 for 9 dec. (Wasim Jaffer 133, J.J. Martin 54) and 101 for 3
South Zone 262 (S. Sharath 111, S.V. Bahutule 4 for 79)
Match drawn

Rain played havoc with the semi-finals of the Duleep Trophy. No play was possible on the first day in Bangalore, and only 16 overs were bowled on the second, and 9.1 on the third. Deebang Gandhi's century was the highlight of East Zone's innings, but an unbeaten 145 from left-hander Jyothi Yadav took Central Zone into the final on a better run quotient.

No play was possible until the third day in Vishakhapatnam, where Wasim Jaffer and Jacob Martin gave substance to the West Zone innings with a fourth wicket partnership of 114. Sharath hit a fine century for South Zone, but Bahutule took four wickets, and West Zone reached the final by virtue of their first innings lead.

Final

17, 18, 19, 20 and 21 December 1997
at M.A. Chidambaram Stadium, Chepauk, Chennai (Madras)
West Zone 384 for 7 dec. (J.J. Martin 72, A.B. Agarkar 56 not out, J.V. Paranjpe 55)
Central Zone 36 for 5
Match drawn

With no play possible on the first three days and only 83 overs bowled before bad light ended play on the fourth, a draw was inevitable in the Duleep Trophy Final, and West Zone and Central Zone were declared joint winners.

Ranji Trophy

West Zone

6, 7, 8 and 9 November 1997
at Municipal Corporation Ground, Rajkot
Saurashtra 469 (J. Motivaras 99, P.J. Bhatt 85, S.H. Kotak 77, S.S. Tanna 52, R.A. Swaroop 4 for 90, D.G. Mulherkar 4 for 161)
Baroda 509 (R.A. Swaroop 165, J.J. Martin 104 not out, C.C. Williams 76, M. Kadri 68, H.J. Parsana 5 for 147)
Match drawn
Baroda 5 pts, Saurashtra 3 pts

at Sardar Patel Stadium, Bulsar
Gujarat 182 (M.H. Parmar 53, K.R. Patadiwala 50, P.L. Mhambrey 7 for 42) and 161 (P.L. Mhambrey 4 for 46)
Mumbai 411 for 8 dec. (S.R. Tendulkar 177, A.A. Muzumdar 68, B.N. Mehta 4 for 111)
Mumbai won by an innings and 68 runs
Mumbai 8 pts, Gujarat 0 pts

In Rajkot, Saurashtra's top order batting scored heavily, but their innings did not end until the third morning. Kadri and Swaroop scored 184 for Baroda's first wicket, and Swaroop and Williams 125 for the second. Rayapet Swaroop made the highest score of his career.

Not unexpectedly, Mumbai beat Gujarat in three days. There were outstanding individual performances from Tendulkar, playing his only match in the league, and from Mhambrey, the pace bowler who toured England in 1996 and was later discarded by the Test selectors.

16, 17, 18 and 19 November 1997
at Brabourne Stadium, Mumbai
Mumbai 426 (J.V. Paranjpe 91, A.A. Pagnis 56, M.S. Kulkarni 5 for 72) and 208 for 3 dec. (J.V. Paranjpe 81, S.V. Manjrekar 78 not out)

Anil Kumble – supreme among Indian bowlers. He excelled at every level. He took 29 wickets in the two Test series, and in first-class cricket he three times took ten or more wickets in a match. He finished the season with 85 from 13 matches, and he averaged just under 40 with the bat.
(David Munden / Sportsline)

Maharashtra 201 (S.S. Sugwekar 70, S. Saxena 4 for 61) and 122 (R. Pawar 4 for 33, A.B. Agarkar 4 for 38)
Mumbai won by 311 runs
Mumbai 8 pts, Maharashtra 0 pts

at Municipal Corporation Ground, Rajkot
Gujarat 147 (N.D. Modi 56, H.J. Parsana 5 for 50) and 259 (U.S. Belsare 56, Y. Bambhania 4 for 70)
Saurashtra 290 (S.H. Kotak 77, P. Khakkar 60, B.N. Mehta 5 for 119, H.D. Patel 4 for 56) and 119 for 4
Saurashtra won by 6 wickets
Saurashtra 8 pts, Gujarat 0 pts

Mumbai gained their second victory inside three days, and the reigning Ranji champions looked already certain to take the West Zone title. Their strength in depth seems ever to increase.

Gujarat suffered their second defeat and looked destined for the wooden spoon. For Saurashtra, left-hander Sitanshu Kotak and all-rounder Hitesh Parsana were again in fine form.

30 November, 1, 2 and 3 December 1997
at Sardar Patel Stadium, Ahmedabad
Maharashtra 367 (H.H. Kanitkar 125, A.V. Kale 76 not out, B.N. Mehta 5 for 110) and 51 for 3
Gujarat 214 (M. Sane 6 for 58) and 242 (N.A. Patel 62, M. Sane 5 for 68)
Match drawn
Maharashtra 5 pts, Gujarat 3 pts

at IPCL Sports Complex, Baroda
Baroda 382 (T.B. Arothe 123, J.J. Martin 101, C.C. Williams 55, S.V. Bahutule 6 for 122) and 282 for 5 (A.C. Bedade 103 not out, R.A. Swaroop 54)
Mumbai 380 (J.V. Paranjpe 135)
Match drawn
Baroda 5 pts, Mumbai 3 pts

Mandar Sane produced the best bowling performances of his career for innings and match, but the leg-spinner could not bring Maharashtra victory over Gujarat. Following on, Gujarat batted with such determination for more than 127 overs that Maharashtra were left only eight overs in which to score 90 to win, a task that was beyond them.

Jacob Martin scored his second century in successive matches and shared a fourth wicket stand of 185 with Arothe. In spite of another impressive innings from Paranjpe, Mumbai failed to take first innings points.

30, 31 December 1997, 1 and 2 January 1998
at Nehru Stadium, Pune
Saurashtra 327 (S.H. Kotak 131, B.M. Jadeja 123, M.S. Kulkarni 5 for 66) and 259 for 8 (B.M. Jadeja 112 not out, S.S. Tanna 53, I.R. Siddiqui 4 for 66)
Maharashtra 439 (S.S. Bhave 156, A.V. Kale 126, S.S. Sugwekar 76, R.R. Garsondia 4 for 101)
Match drawn
Maharashtra 5 pts, Saurashtra 3 pts

at IPCL Sports Complex, Baroda
Gujarat 248 (T.N. Varsani 93, B.N. Mehta 58 not out, T.B. Arothe 4 for 56) and 213 (M.H. Parmar 77, B.N. Mehta 72, T.B. Arothe 6 for 57)
Baroda 462 for 8 dec. (J.J. Martin 107, N.R. Mongia 76 not out)
Baroda won by an innings and 1 run
Baroda 8 pts, Gujarat 0 pts

Kotak and Bimal Jadeja put on 220 for Saurashtra's third wicket against Maharashtra, but, incredibly, the next highest scorers to these centurions made 12. With Bhave and Kale scoring 261 for the fourth wicket, Maharashtra swept into a big first innings lead, and Saurashtra's only consolation was that Bimal Jadeja made a century in each innings.

Gujarat suffered a third defeat, and Jacob Martin scored his third hundred in as many matches. Tushar Arothe's off-breaks brought him match figures of 10 for 111.

6, 7 and 8 January 1998
at Nehru Stadium, Pune
Maharashtra 171 (S.S. Sugwekar 63, D.G. Multherkar 4 for 9) and 238 (A.V. Kale 61, M. Kadri 4 for 34)
Baroda 151 (I.R. Siddiqui 7 for 49) and 78 (I.R. Siddiqui 5 for 30, M.S. Kulkarni 5 for 47)
Maharashtra won by 180 runs
Maharashtra 8 pts, Baroda 0 pts

7, 8, 9 and 10 January 1998
at Wankhede Stadium, Mumbai
Mumbai 538 for 5 dec. (V.G. Kambli 232 not out, J.V. Paranjpe 174, A.B. Agarkar 54 not out, S.K. Kulkarni 51) and 290 for 5 dec. (A.A. Muzumdar 113, S.V. Manjrekar 74)
Saurashtra 386 (H.J. Parsana 102, P.J. Bhatt 81, P.L. Mhambrey 5 for 78) and 9 for 2
Match drawn
Mumbai 5 pts, Saurashtra 3 pts

Baroda's collapse against the medium pace of Iqbal Siddiqui, who returned the best figures of his career for innings and match, gave Maharashtra an unexpected victory and a place in the final stages of the competition ahead of Saurashtra. In their second innings, Baroda lost their last six wickets for 17 runs.

Paranjpe and Kambli added 219 for Mumbai's fourth wicket against Saurashtra, and Kambli made the only double century in the West Zone league. The visitors died bravely, with Bhatt and Parsana putting on 153 after five wickets had fallen for 180, but a draw was not enough to

take them into the final stages of the Ranji Trophy. Mhambrey finished as the zone's leading wicket-taker with 22 victims. Paranjpe, 481 runs, average 120.25, was the leading batsman.

West Zone Final Table

	P	W	L	D	Pts
Mumbai	4	2	–	2	24
Baroda (Vadodara)	4	1	1	2	18
Maharashtra	4	1	1	2	18
Saurashtra	4	1	–	3	17
Gujarat	4	–	3	1	3

(Top three teams qualify for Ranji Trophy Super League.)

South Zone

21, 22, 23 and 24 October 1997

at M. Chinnaswamy Stadium, Bangalore
Kerala 181 (S.B. Joshi 4 for 33) and 141 (S. Shankar 60, A.R. Kumble 6 for 32)
Karnataka 345 (J. Arun Kumar 111, A.R. Kumble 58, B. Ramprakash 4 for 78)
Karnataka won by an innings and 23 runs
Karnataka 8 pts, Kerala 0 pts

at UKKU Stadium, Visakhapatnam
Andhra 202 (R.V.C. Prasad 54) and 389 for 5 (M.S.K. Prasad 123 not out, N. Veerabrahamam 78, A. Pathak 56)
Tamil Nadu 485 for 4 dec. (S. Sriram 213 not out, S. Ramesh 123, S. Sharath 80)
Match drawn
Tamil Nadu 5 pts, Andhra 3 pts

Karnatka, Ranji Trophy champions in 1996, had failed to qualify for the second stage of the competition in 1997, but they began the 1998 campaign in fine style. They overwhelmed Kerala, South Zone champions the previous year, and won early on the fourth day. Skipper Anil Kumble had a fine all-round match, and opener Jagdish Kumar made an accomplished century, dominating a first wicket partnership of 101 with Sujith Somasunder.

Tamil Nadu were thwarted by Andhra, whom they led by 283 on the first innings. The left-handed Sridharan Sriram, 21 years old, made the second century of his brief career and went on to reach 213 before Robin Singh declared. Ramesh and Sriram shared a second wicket stand of 213, but Andhra batted for more than four sessions to save the game. Their hero was wicket-keeper opening batsman Mannava Prasad, who batted throughout more than 155 overs for his unbeaten 123.

29, 30, 31 October and 1 November 1997

at Gymkhana Ground, Secunderabad
Hyderabad 284 (M. Azharuddin 82, V. Pratap 56, N. Madhukar 4 for 79)
Andhra 278 for 9 (M.S.K. Prasad 81, K.B.S. Naik 57)
Match drawn
Hyderabad 2 pts, Andhra 2 pts

at M. Chinnaswamy Stadium, Bangalore
Goa 152 (D.J. Johnson 4 for 57) and 127 (S.B. Joshi 5 for 25)
Karnataka 211 (S. Khalid 4 for 46) and 70 for 0 (S. Somasunder 55 not out)
Karnataka won by 10 wickets
Karnataka 8 pts, Goa 0 pts

There was no play on the first day in Secunderabad and very little on the second. There was a tense finish when Hyderabad captured the ninth Andhra wicket at 276, but neither side could claim first innings points and they had to settle for two each.

Karnataka beat Goa in three days on a pitch that was always helpful to the bowlers. The best batting came when Karnataka raced to victory in 13.2 overs, Sujith Somasunder making 55 out of 70.

6, 7, 8 and 9 November 1997

at Gymkhana Ground, Secunderabad
Hyderabad 433 (D. Manohar 144, A. Shetty 70, V.V.S. Laxman 67, M. Azharuddin 63, A.R. Kumble 6 for 73)
Karnataka 446 for 9 dec. (A.R. Kumble 113, R.S. Dravid 99, R. Vijay Bharadwaj 68)
Match drawn
Karnataka 5 pts, Hyderabad 3 pts

at Jawaharial Nehru Stadium, Kochi
Andhra 180 (R.V.C. Prasad 50, B. Ramprakash 4 for 47) and 33 (K. Chandrasekhara 4 for 1)
Kerala 163 and 41 for 8 (H. Ramkishen 5 for 21)
Match drawn
Andhra 5 pts, Kerala 3 pts

Manohar scored a century on his debut, shared an opening partnership of 155 with Arvind Shetty and a second wicket partnership of 134 with Laxman, but still saw his side surrender first innings points. Hyderabad lost their last six wickets to Kumble for 22 runs. Kumble's part in the match was not done, for, coming in at 238 for five, he hit 113 and steered his side into the lead and into the next stage of the competition.

There was an astonishing game in Kochi where batting was never easy. Andhra batted into the second day and scored at less than two an over after a rain-delayed start. Kerala were equally tardy and needed nearly 102 overs in which to score 163. Then the match turned on its head. Andhra were bowled out in 38.5 overs for just 33.

Left-arm spinner Koragappa Chandrasekhara took four for 1 in seven overs, while Ramprakash's off-spin brought him two for 6 in 10.5 overs. Kerala had 13 overs in which to score 51 to win, but, with three batsmen run out, they lost eight wickets and fell short of their target.

14, 15, 16 and 17 November 1997
at Jawaharial Nehru Stadium, Kochi
Hyderabad 272 (A. Shetty 141, C.T.K. Masood 5 for 78) and 56 for 5 (B. Ramprakash 4 for 24)
Kerala 163 (Venkatapathy Raju 5 for 60, Kanwaljit Singh 4 for 36)
Match drawn
Hyderabad 5 pts, Kerala 3 pts

at Sersa Stadium, Visakhapatnam
Andhra 201 (A. Pathak 50, P. Srihari Rao 50) and 157 (A. Pathak 67, S. Suresh 4 for 35)
Goa 237 (R.R. Naik 74, V.V. Kolambkar 69, N. Madhukar 4 for 50) and 125 for 3 (S. Suresh 85 not out)
Goa won by 7 wickets
Goa 8 pts, Andhra 0 pts

15, 16, 17 and 18 November 1997
at M. Chinnaswamy Stadium, Bangalore
Tamil Nadu 281 (H. Badani 85, W.V. Raman 56, D. Ganesh 4 for 63) and 233 for 5 (R.C.V. Kumar 103 not out)
Karnataka 146 (D. Vasu 5 for 26)
Match drawn
Tamil Nadu 5 pts, Karnataka 3 pts

Rain prevented any play on the last day at Kochi, when the match was in a fascinating position. However, Goa played convincingly to beat Andhra and to emphasise the advance they have made and continue to make under the stewardship of former Tamil Nadu opener Vakkadai Chandrasekhar. There was no play possible on the last day in Bangalore where Tamil Nadu held the upper hand in the battle of the South Zone giants.

22, 23, 24 and 25 November 1997
at M.A. Chidambaram Stadium, Chepauk, Chennai
Hyderabad 30 for 2 dec.
Tamil Nadu 33 for 1
Match drawn
Tamil Nadu 5 pts, Hyderabad 3 pts

at Panjim Gymkhana, Goa
Goa 339 (R.R. Naik 133, V. Jaisimha 100) and 176 for 5 (V.B. Chandrasekhar 87)
Kerala 291 (K.N.A. Padmanabhan 96, S.C. Oasis 57, J. Gokulkrishnan 6 for 79)
Match drawn
Goa 5 pts, Kerala 3 pts

at Indira Gandhi Municipal Ground, Vijayawada
Karnataka 381 for 4 dec. (R. Vijay Bharadwaj 101 not out, J. Arun Kumar 101, S. Somasunder 97) and 51 for 2
Andhra 247 (A. Pathak 138, D.J. Johnson 5 for 65)
Match drawn
Karnataka 5 pts, Andhra 3 pts

No play was possible on the second and fourth days at Chennai; the match lasted only 42 overs in all and the teams agreed to salvage some points from the deluge. Goa lost three wickets for 29 before Rajesh Naik and Jaisimha added 168. Medium-pacer Gokulkrishnan then bowled Goa to first innings points. Surith Somasunder and Arun Kumar scored 175 for Karnataka's first wicket against Andhra, and Vijay Bharadwaj put his side in an impregnable position on a truncated second day. Skipper Amit Pathak played a lone hand for Andhra, who lost their first three wickets for 41. Pathak and Srihari Rao, 49, put on 147, but nobody else reached double figures.

30, 31 December 1997, 1 and 2 January 1998
at Panjim Gymkhana, Goa
Goa 55 (N.P. Singh 7 for 24) and 166 (S. Suresh 62)
Hyderabad 297 (V.V.S. Laxman 145, M. Azharuddin 87, J. Gokulkrishnan 4 for 49, P.M. Kakade 4 for 68)
Hyderabad won by an innings and 76 runs
Hyderabad 8 pts, Goa 0 pts

31 December 1997, 1, 2 and 3 January 1998
at M.A. Chidambaram, Chepauk, Chennai
Kerala 323 (S.C. Oasis 134, K.N.A. Padmanabhan 74, M. Venkatarama 4 for 70) and 256 (A.S. Kudva 124 not out)
Tamil Nadu 466 (S. Ramesh 187, S. Sharath 129, R.R. Singh 51, B. Ramprakash 5 for 113, C.T.K. Masood 4 for 142) and 8 for 1
Match drawn
Tamil Nadu 5 pts, Kerala 3 pts

Hyderabad beat Goa in three days, but their batting showed how much it relied on the Test players Laxman and Azharuddin, who shared a stand of 165 after three wickets had fallen for 29. Sunil Oasis just failed to make the highest score of his career as, belatedly, Kerala showed something of the previous season's form. It was not enough to stop Tamil Nadu taking first innings points as Ramesh and Sharath shared a second wicket stand of 267. The failure by Kerala to take more than three points from the fixture meant that they had fallen from top to bottom in the South Zone in one season, an astonishing occurrence in the Ranji Trophy.

7, 8, 9 and 10 January 1998
at M. Chidambaram Stadium, Chepauk, Chennai
Goa 260 (V.B. Chandrasekhar 98, S. Suresh 55, T. Kumaran 5

for 61) and 225 (S. Suresh 123 not out, M.Venkatarama 4 for 92)
Tamil Nadu 602 for 4 dec. (S. Ramesh 182, R.C.V. Kumar 151, S. Sriram 129, S. Sharath 58 not out, W.V. Raman 54)
Tamil Nadu won by an innings and 116 runs
Tamil Nadu 8 pts, Goa 0 pts

A century stand for the first wicket and a second wicket stand of 255 between Ramesh and Vasanth Kumar brought Tamil Nadu a massive lead over Goa and ensured them of a place in the Super League. Goa died bravely on the last afternoon with Suresh carrying his bat through the 82.5 overs of their second innings.

The left-handed Sandagoppan Ramesh finished as the leading run-scorer in the South Zone. He hit three centuries in four matches and totalled 509 runs, average 127.25. The leading wicket-taker was Kerala's veteran off-spinner Bhaskaran Ramprakash, whose 28 wickets cost 17.39 runs each but could not prevent his side from finishing bottom.

South Zone Final Table

	P	W	L	D	Pts
Karnataka	5	2	–	3	29
Tamil Nadu	5	1	–	4	28
Hyderabad	5	1	–	4	21
Goa	5	1	3	1	13
Andhra	5	–	1	4	13
Kerala	5	–	1	4	12

East Zone

6, 7, 8 and 9 November 1997

at Railway Stadium, Mallgaon, Guwahati
Tripura 231 (V. Prajapati 62) and 107 (Iqbal Khan 5 for 34)
Assam 239 (Rajinder Singh 66, P. Dutta 52, S. Roy 5 for 83, H. Yadav 4 for 78) and 101 for 4
Assam won by 6 wickets
Assam 8 pts, Tripura 0 pts

at Permit Ground, Balasore
Orissa 165 (U. Chatterjee 7 for 59) and 158 (P. Mullick 55, Shivsagar Singh 4 for 47)
Bengal 176 and 151 for 2 (D. Gandhi 78 not out)
Bengal won by 8 wickets
Bengal 8 pts, Orissa 0 pts

The East Zone opened with a match between the two sides expected to be the weakest in the association, but Tripura showed considerable improvement on past seasons and Sujit Roy and Himulal Yadav nearly bowled them to a first innings lead. Assam's final pair added 11 for the last wicket to snatch a narrow lead, and from that point the home side dominated.

Veteran left-arm spinner Upal Chatterjee had match figures of 10 for 114 for Bengal against Orissa. His first innings figures were the best of his career, and he passed 250 wickets in first-class cricket. Bengal won easily after a tense first innings struggle.

14, 15, 16 and 17 November 1997

at Keenan Stadium, Jamshedpur
Bihar 242 (R. Kumar 126, G. Dutta 5 for 56) and 190 (Tariq-ur-Rehman 69, C.M. Jha 56, S.S. Sawant 4 for 32, Iqbal Khan 4 for 56)
Assam 224 (S.S. Sawant 66, K.V.P. Rao 4 for 59) and 89 (K.V.P. Rao 5 for 33, Avinash Kumar 4 for 27)
Bihar won by 119 runs
Bihar 8 pts, Assam 0 pts

17, 18, 19 and 20 November 1997

at Barabati Stadium, Cuttack
Orissa 521 for 8 dec. (P. Mullick 201, S. Raul 139, R.R. Parida 50, A. Shukla 4 for 136)
Tripura 235 (D.S. Mohanty 5 for 48) and 187 for 3 (R. Chowdhury 92, S. Lahiri 54)
Match drawn
Orissa 5 pts, Tripura 3 pts

Bihar gained an important victory in their opening match and were well served by Rajeev Kumar, who hit a century after four wickets had fallen for 23. Assam looked set to take first innings points, but lost four wickets for 22 runs towards the end of their innings. In their second innings, they collapsed against the two slow left-arm bowlers, Rao and Avinash Kumar.

In Cuttack, Orissa lost both openers for eight before Mullick and skipper Raul added 243.

Pravanjan Mullick, 21 years old, had made his debut the previous season and now reached a maiden first-class century. He went on to make 201 and was to be the leading run-scorer in the zone. Tripura lost two wickets at the end of the second day, but rain limited play on the third, and, on the last morning, they had to follow on after suffering the indignity of having number 11 batsman, Hemulal Yadav 'timed out', an extremely rare occurrence.

22, 23, 24 and 25 November 1997

at Barabati Stadium, Cuttack
Orissa 511 (B.B.C.C. Mohapatra 109, P. Mullick 96, R. Morris 90, P. Jayachandra 80, G. Gopal 62, Sukhvinder Singh 4 for 133)
Assam 119 (R.F. Morris 5 for 46) and 158 (R.F. Morris 5 for 35)
Orissa won by an innings and 234 runs
Orissa 8 pts, Assam 0 pts

at Keenan Stadium, Jamshedpur
Bengal 460 for 8 dec. (N. Haldipur 117, S.S. Karim 111, A. Verma 64, G. Shome jnr 54, Avinash Kumar 5 for 185)
Bihar 243 (Sunil Kumar 92, U. Chatterjee 7 for 88) and 187 for 5 (Tariq-ur-Rehman 59 not out)
Match drawn
Bengal 5 pts, Bihar 3 pts

A century on his debut from B.B.C.C. Mohaptra, who shared an opening stand of 182 with Jayachandra, provided the substance of Orissa's innings against Assam. Mullick also batted well, and Robin Morris, formerly of Mumbai, took five wickets in an innings and 10 wickets in a match for the first time. He also made his highest first-class score, 90. Another to excel was wicket-keeper Gautam Gopal, who made the second fifty of his career and took nine catches in the match. Orissa's victory gave them the advantage over Assam in the fight to qualify for the Super League.

Bengal were virtually assured of a place among the elite when they had the better of the draw with Bihar. Ajay Verma and Haldipur scored 140 for the first wicket, and, with Saba Karim making the 18th hundred of his career, Bengal reached a big total. Utpal Chatterjee was once more the master bowler, and Bihar, forced to follow on on the final day, did well to force a draw.

26, 27, 28 and 29 December 1997

at PTI Ground, Agartala
Bengal 263 (R.S. Gavaskar 80, G. Shome jnr 56, S. Roy 5 for 95) and 211 for 6 dec. (D. Gandhi 58)
Tripura 181 (S. Lahiri 88, R. Chowdhury 52, A. Verma 6 for 56) and 115 for 8 (R. Chowdhury 60, R.S. Gavaskar 5 for 3)
Match drawn
Bengal 5 pts, Tripura 3 pts

at Barabati Stadium, Cuttack
Orissa 534 for 5 dec. (S.S. Das 164, P. Mullick 141, S. Raul 100 not out)
Bihar 320 (R. Kumar 92, C.M. Jha 61, S. Khan 5 for 99) and 122 for 2 (D. Chakraborty 54 not out, C.M. Jha 51 not out)
Match drawn
Orissa 5 pts, Bihar 3 pts

Rain restricted play on the first two days in Agartala, and, on the third day, Tripura lost their nine wickets for 46 runs. They were set 294 to win, a task well beyond them, but they held out for a draw in spite of a remarkable spell of bowling by Rohan Gavaskar, whose left-arm spin is used very rarely. He had only two first-class wickets to his credit before this match, but, in eight overs, six of them maidens, he took five for 3.

Orissa moved a step nearer the Super League with the aid of another big score. Three of their first four batsmen scored hundreds, and Bihar were forced to follow on on the last day.

3, 4, 5 and 6 January 1998

at Eden Gardens, Calcutta
Assam 360 (Rajinder Singh 143, Iqbal Khan 74, U. Chatterjee 5 for 101) and 211 (Rajinder Singh 63, U. Chatterjee 4 for 81)
Bengal 255 (U. Chatterjee 56, G. Dutta 6 for 70) and 118 for 3 (D. Gandhi 54 not out)
Match drawn
Assam 5 pts, Bengal 3 pts

at PTI Ground, Agartala
Bihar 370 (Syed Arfi 101, C.M. Jha 77, Tariq-ur-Rehman 50, R. Deb Burman 5 for 134)
Tripura 166 (S. Lahiri 78, K.V.P. Rao 5 for 48) and 27 for 1
Match drawn
Bihar 5 pts, Tripura 3 pts

Assam played well against Bengal and took a substantial first innings lead thanks to Rajinder Singh hitting the highest score of his career, but they were ultimately thwarted by Bengal, who took the East Zone title and deprived Assam of a place in the Super League. Syed Arfi's hundred and solid middle order batting in the rain-affected match in Agartala was enough to give Bihar the points they needed to progress.

East Zone Final Table

	P	W	L	D	Pts
Bengal	4	1	–	3	21
Bihar	4	1	–	3	19
Orissa	4	1	1	2	18
Assam	4	1	2	1	13
Tripura	4	–	1	3	9

Central Zone

19, 20, 21 and 22 October 1997

at Mansarover Ground, Jaipur
Rajasthan 341 (V. Joshi 109, P.K. Krishnakumar 89, P.V. Gandhe 6 for 63) and 149 (P.V. Gandhe 6 for 50)
Vidarbha 212 (M.S. Dosi 52 not out, P. Yadav 4 for 54) and 157 for 4 (P. Sutane 72)
Match drawn
Rajasthan 5 pts, Vidarbha 3 pts

at Karnali Singh Stadium, Delhi
Railways 159 (S.B. Bangar 55, A.W. Zaidi 4 for 45) and 231 for 6 (S.B. Bangar 95)

Uttar Pradesh 346 for 6 dec. (R. Shamshad 134 not out, J.P. Yadav 100)
Match drawn
Uttar Pradesh 5 pts, Railways 3 pts

The first round of matches could not produce an outright result. Jyoti Prasad Yadav and Rizwan Shamshad put on 187 for Uttar Pradesh's third wicket, and Pritam Gandhe, who missed the 1996–97 season, took 12 for 113 for Vidarbha with his off-breaks.

27, 28, 29 and 30 October 1997

at Vidarbha CA Stadium, Nagpur
Railways 300 (S. Yadav 139, P.S. Rawat 68, P.V. Gandhe 5 for 88, P. Sadhu 4 for 104)
Vidarbha 200 (M. Kartik 4 for 28)
Match drawn
Railways 5 pts, Vidarbha 3 pts

at Digvijay Stadium, Rajnandagaon
Madhya Pradesh 206 for 5 (P.K. Dwevedi 102, Raja Ali 57 not out)
v. **Uttar Pradesh**
No result
Madhya Pradesh 2 pts, Uttar Pradesh 2 pts

The weather was so unkind that there could be no play after the first day in Rajnandagaon and there was limited play in Nagpur. Pritam Gandhe was again impressive, and Satyendra Yadav scored the second century of his career.

5, 6, 7 and 8 November 1997

at Vidarbha CA Stadium, Nagpur
Vidarbha 277 (L.S. Rajput 112, S. Pandey 5 for 67) and 267 (S. Pandey 4 for 74)
Madhya Pradesh 508 for 6 dec. (S. Abbas Ali 98, C.S. Pandit 83, R.K. Chauhan 78 not out, K.K. Patel 61, Raja Ali 56 not out) and 37 for 1
Madhya Pradesh won by 9 wickets
Madhya Pradesh 8 pts, Vidarbha 0 pts

at Karnali Singh Stadium, Delhi
Rajasthan 189 (G.K. Khoda 111, K.K. Parida 4 for 31, Javed Zaman 4 for 52) and 184 (M. Kartik 6 for 35)
Railways 374 for 9 dec. (P.S. Rawat 144, D.P. Singh 4 for 81)
Railways won by an innings and 1 run
Railways 8 pts, Rajasthan 0 pts

By becoming the first outright winners in the zone, Madhya Pradesh and Railways virtually assured themselves of places in the Super League. Madhya Pradesh were particularly impressive, scoring at nearly four runs an over in their victory over Vidarbha. Sanjay Pandey had the best bowling figures of his career for match and innings.

Gagan Khoda batted heroically for Rajasthan, making 111 out of his side's 189 with Anil Parmar, 23, the next highest scorer. Prahlad Singh Rawat responded with the highest score of his career, and Murali Kartik's left-arm spin proved decisive when Rajasthan batted a second time.

14, 15, 16 and 17 November 1997

at Green Park, Kanpur
Uttar Pradesh 577 for 5 dec. (R. Shamshad 224 not out, G.K. Pandey 68, R.V. Sapru 55, M.S. Mudgal 54, S.A. Shukla 53 not out)
Rajasthan 334 (P.K. Amre 99, Kuldip Singh 81, A.W. Zaidi 6 for 105) and 21 for 0
Match drawn
Uttar Pradesh 5 pts, Rajasthan 3 pts

at Usha Raja Trust Ground, Indore
Madhya Pradesh 571 for 8 dec. (S. Abbas Ali 251, P.K. Dwevedi 189)
Railways 282 (Y. Gowda 95, S. Pandey 4 for 72, N.D. Hirwani 4 for 106) and 165 for 3 (S.B. Bangar 74)
Match drawn
Madhya Pradesh 5 pts, Railways 3 pts

Rizwan Shamshad hit the first double century of his career, but Uttar Pradesh could not force victory over Rajasthan, who were led by Pravin Amre, once of Bengal and once a prospective jewel in India's crown. Syed Abbas Ali also hit a maiden double century, but Madhya Pradesh were thwarted in their attempts to beat Railways.

22, 23, 24 and 25 November 1997

at Mansarover Stadium, Jaipur
Madhya Pradesh 309 (C.S. Pandit 104, Samsher Singh 5 for 97)
Rajasthan 159 (S. Pandey 4 for 58, H.S. Sodhu 4 for 69) and 241 for 6 (G.K. Khoda 83)
Match drawn
Madhya Pradesh 5 pts, Rajasthan 3 pts

28, 29, 30 November and 1 December 1997

at Madan Mohan Malaviya Stadium, Allahabad
Uttar Pradesh 352 (R. Sharma 110, R. Shamshad 100, T.A. Gonsalves 5 for 128, Y.P. Chandurkar 4 for 98)
Vidarbha 130 for 4 (L.S. Rajput 57 not out)
No result
Uttar Pradesh 2 pts, Vidarbha 2 pts

Madhya Pradesh gained the five points necessary to make them champions of the Central Zone, but they had to be content with a draw against Rajasthan. Chandrakant Pandit, the Madhya Pradesh skipper, hit the 20th first-class hundred of his career. Pandit no longer keeps wicket, but he has proved to be an inspirational leader. He celebrated his 36th birthday in September, 1997.

For the second time, Uttar Pradesh had a match washed out, yet the game produced much of interest. Rakesh Sharma and Rizwan Shamshad put on 185 after the first two wickets had fallen for six. Shamshad reached his third century in as many innings and, in East Zone matches, reached a score of 458 runs for once out. The Vidarbha wicket-keeper Kartik Iyer established a Ranji Trophy record by taking seven catches in the innings. The only other Indian keeper to account for seven batsmen in an innings is Sunil Benjamin of Rajasthan, who had six catches and a stumping for Central Zone against North Zone in a Duleep Trophy match in Bombay, 1973–74. Iyer also holds the Indian wicket-keeping record in limited-over cricket, a catch and five stumpings for Vidarbha against Madhya Pradesh, 1994–95.

Central Zone Final Table

	P	W	L	D/NR	Pts
Madhya Pradesh	4	1	–	3	20
Railways	4	1	–	3	19
Uttar Pradesh	4	–	–	4	14
Rajasthan	4	–	1	3	11
Vidarbha	4	–	1	3	8

North Zone

19, 20, 21 and 22 October 1997
at Indira Gandhi Stadium, Una
Himachal Pradesh 383 (N. Gaur 97, C. Kumar 58, V. Sharma 5 for 70, A. Gupta 4 for 106)
Jammu & Kashmir 227 (Shakti Singh 5 for 70, Jaswant Rai 4 for 72) and 81 for 1 (R. Gill 58)
Match drawn
Himachal Pradesh 5 pts, Jammu & Kashmir 3 pts

at Punjab CA Stadium, Mohali
Punjab 339 for 9 dec. (N.S. Sidhu 83, Harvinder Singh 65 not out, M.V. Rao 5 for 68)
Services 78 (B. Vij 4 for 32) and 207 (B. Vij 5 for 67)
Punjab won by an innings and 54 runs
Punjab 8 pts, Services 0 pts

at Ferozesshah Kotla Ground, Delhi
Haryana 203 and 284 (Jitender Singh 111, Armajit Kaypee 62, Robin Singh 6 for 70)
Delhi 261 (M. Manhas 51, V.B. Jain 6 for 55) and 112 for 5
Match drawn
Delhi 5 pts, Haryana 3 pts

The North Zone opened with matches between the two minnows and the two Titans.

In the minnows match, Himachal Pradesh had far the better of the encounter and forced Jammu and Kashnmir to follow on, but the match was drawn, as was the match between Haryana and Delhi, runners up in last year's Ranji Trophy.

The only outright winners were Punjab, for whom Harvinder Singh, in good all-round form, hit the first fifty of his career. But the main bowling honours went to the left-arm spinner Bharati Vij, who had match figures of nine for 99.

26, 27, 28 and 29 October 1997
at Palam Air Force Ground, Delhi
Delhi 444 (A. Chopra 150, M. Manhas 115, A. Malhotra 56, P. Maitreya 5 for 117)
Services 210 (Robin Singh 6 for 85) and 204 (R.L. Sanghvi 5 for 96, F.K. Ghayas 4 for 56)
Delhi won by an innings and 30 runs
Delhi 8 pts, Services 0 pts

at Nahar Singh Stadium, Faridabad
Jammu & Kashmir 159 (P. Jain 4 for 22) and 309 (A. Gupta 112, Sanjay Sharma 56, Dhanraj Singh 4 for 36)
Haryana 445 for 5 dec. (Jitender Singh 175, N.R. Goel 143) and 26 for 1
Haryana won by 9 wickets
Haryana 8 pts, Jammu & Kashmir 0 pts

at Punjab CA Stadium, Mohali
Himachal Pradesh 119 (B. Bhushan 6 for 53) and 119 (Harvinder Singh 7 for 51)
Punjab 219 (A.R. Kapoor 65, P. Sharma 5 for 99, Shakti Singh 4 for 87) and 20 for 1
Punjab won by 9 wickets
Punjab 8 pts, Himachal Pradesh 0 pts

The second round of matches saw the three strongest sides confirm their authority with decisive victories. Jitender Singh made his second century of the season and shared an opening partnership of 319 with Nitin Goel, a record for Haryana. For Punjab, Harvinder Singh returned the best bowling figures of his career in the victory over Himachal Pradesh.

2, 3, 4 and 5 November 1997
at MLSN Ground, Sundernagar
Himachal Pradesh 163 (N. Gaur 53, Arun Sharma 4 for 32) and 100 (M.V. Rao 6 for 46)
Services 101 (Shakti Singh 7 for 37) and 154 for 4 (Sarabjit Singh 62 not out, Shakti Singh 4 for 59)
Services won by 6 wickets
Services 8 pts, Himachal Pradesh 0 pts

at Dhruv Pandove Stadium, Patiala
Delhi 311 (M. Manhas 65, A.K. Sharma 59, Harbhajan Singh

4 for 66, B. Vij 4 for 88) and 270 for 4 (A. Chopra 100 not out, A. Malhotra 87)
Punjab 488 for 8 dec. (R.S. Sodhi 200 not out, N.S. Sidhu 89, P. Dharmani 80)
Match drawn
Punjab 5 pts, Delhi 3 pts

Services overcame a first innings deficit of 62 to beat Himachal Pradesh, for whom medium pacer Shakti Singh returned the best bowling figures of his career. Reetinder Singh Sodhi made the first century of his career and carried on to reach an unbeaten 200 as Punjab had the better of the game against Delhi.

9, 10, 11 and 12 November 1997
at Burlton Park, Jalandhar
Punjab v. **Jammu & Kashmir**
Match abandoned
Punjab 2 pts, Jammu & Kashmir 2 pts

at Indira Gandhi Stadium, Una
Himachal Pradesh v. **Delhi**
Match abandoned
Himachal Pradesh 2 pts, Delhi 2 pts

at Nahar Singh Stadium, Faridabad
Haryana 413 (A.D. Jadeja 242 not out)
Services 234 (P. Maitrey 51, Dhanraj Singh 4 for 34) and 177 (Narinder Singh 58, P. Jain 4 for 59)
Haryana won by an innings and 2 runs
Haryana 8 pts, Services 0 pts

Two games were completely wiped out because of rain, but the third, in Faridabad, saw Adeja Jadeja make the highest North Zone score of the season and lead his side to an innings victory over Services.

16, 17, 18 and 19 November 1997
at Nehru Stadium, Gurgaon
Himachal Pradash 126 (N. Gaur 69) and 130 (N. Gaur 69)
Haryana 371 for 6 dec. (Jitender Singh 127, Armajit Kaypee 80, S. Dalal 56 not out)
Haryana won by an innings and 115 runs
Haryana 8 pts, Himachal Pradesh 0 pts

at Palam Air Force Ground, Delhi
Services 429 for 9 dec. (Narinder Singh 229 not out, Sarabjit Singh 58)
Jammu & Kashmir 137 (Harpreet Singh 6 for 36, Arun Sharma 4 for 27) and 107 (S.K. Kulkarni 5 for 19)
Services won by an innings and 185 runs
Services 8 pts, Jammu & Kashmir 0 pts

Both Haryana and Services won expected victories. Jitender Singh hit his third century of the season's competition in Haryana's crushing win in Gurgaon. In Delhi, Narinder Singh batted throughout Services' innings for the first double century of his career.

23, 24, 25 and 26 November 1997
at Ferozeshah Kotla Ground, Delhi
Jammu & Kashmir 183 (A. Nehra 4 for 45) and 151 for 4
Delhi 140 (V. Sharma 4 for 41)
Match drawn
Jammu & Kashmir 5 pts, Delhi 0 pts

at Nehru Stadium, Gurgaon
Punjab 286 (P. Dharmani 97, P. Thakur 7 for 107) and 89 for 2
Haryana 189 (V. Yadav 61, P. Thakur 50, B. Bhushan 4 for 29)
Match drawn
Punjab 5 pts, Haryana 3 pts

The North Zone kept its big surprise until the last when, in the rain-affected game in Delhi, Jammu and Kashmir took first innings points against Delhi. Punjab, too, caused something of a surprise in leading Haryana on the first innings in spite of the fact that off-break bowler Pankaj Thakur returned the best figures of his career.

Ajay Jadeja, 242 not for out for Haryana in the Ranji Trophy North Zone match against Services. Jadeja scored prolifically and was a vital part of India's side in one-day internationals, leading his country in the absence of Azharuddin.
(David Munden / Sportsline)

North Zone Final Table

	P	W	L	D/NR	Pts
Haryana	5	3	–	2	30
Punjab	5	2	–	3	28
Delhi	5	1	–	4	21
Services	5	2	3	–	16
Jammu & Kashmir	5	–	2	3	10
Himachal Pradash	5	–	3	2	7

Ranji Trophy Super League

Section A

5, 6, 7 and 8 February 1998
at Wankhede Stadium, Mumbai
Railways 124 (P.L. Mhambrey 4 for 43) and 197
Mumbai 497 for 4 dec. (V.G. Kambli 207 not out, S.R. Tendulkar 95, A.A. Muzumdar 63 not out)
Mumbai won by an innings and 176 runs
Mumbai 8 pts, Railways 0 pts

at M. Chinnaswamy Stadium, Bangalore
Karnataka 298 (S. Somasunder 58) and 254 for 9 dec. (R.V. Bharadwaj 57, R.S. Dravid 55)
Punjab 157 (A.R. Kumble 5 for 51) and 133
Karnataka won by 262 runs
Karnataka 8 pts, Punjab 0 pts

Railways and Mumbai met in the Ranji Trophy, and the Railways attack was put to the sword by Tendulkar and his legion, who scored at more than five runs an over. Tendulkar and Kambli put on 188 for the fourth wicket, and Kambli and Muzumdar shared an unbroken stand of 174 for the fifth wicket. The game was over in three days.

Karnataka had little trouble in disposing of Punjab, and, at full strength, looked a formidable side.

14, 15, 16 and 17 February 1998

at Wankhede Stadium, Mumbai
Orissa 150 (R.R. Parida 54, P.L. Mhambrey 6 for 45) and 297 (P.R. Mohapatra71, N.M. Kulkarni 5 for 74)
Mumbai 493 for 7 dec.(S.R. Tendulkar 135, S.V. Manjrekar 126, A.A. Pagnis 64 not out, S. Dahad 59)
Mumbai won by an innings and 46 runs
Mumbai 8 pts, Orissa 0 pts

at M. Chinnaswamy Stadium, Bangalore
Karnataka 462 for 8 dec. (R.V. Bharadwaj 164, R.S. Dravid 65, A.R. Kumble 59, K.K. Parida 5 for 116) and 22 for 4
Railways 269 (Z. Zuffri 99, S.B. Bangar 54, S.B. Joshi 4 for 57, A.R. Kumble 4 for 81) and 213 (Y. Gowda 54, A.R. Kumble 6 for 69)
Karnataka won by 6 wickets
Karnataka 8 pts, Railways 0 pts

Mumbai disposed of Orissa as easily as they had disposed of Railways and, with two wins in two matches, looked to have confirmed their place in the final stages of the competition. Manjrekar and Tendulkar put on 222 after two wickets had fallen for 28. Karnataka had slightly harder work in beating Railways, losing four wickets for 7 runs before reaching their target of 21.

23, 24, 25 and 26 February 1998
at Punjab CA Stadium, Mohali
Railways 300 (A.R. Kapoor 54)
Punjab 276 (V. Rathore 95)
Match drawn
Railways 5 pts, Punjab 3 pts

at Ispat Stadium, Rourkela
Orissa 183 (A.R. Kumble 5 for 34) and 92 (A.R. Kumble 5 for 9)
Karnataka 398 for 9 dec. (R.S. Dravid 138, S. Somasunder 67, P. Jayachandra 5 for 64)
Karnataka won by an innings and 123 runs
Karnataka 8 pts, Orissa 0 pts

No play was possible on the second and third days in Mohali, but Karnataka had ample time in which to beat Orissa. Kumble performed the hat-trick in the first innings and took five for 9 in six overs in the second innings. Out of favour with the Indian selectors, Dravid hit his first century of the season.

4, 5, 6 and 7 March 1998
at Punjab CA Stadium, Mohali
Punjab 272 (P. Dharmani 96, N.M. Kulkarni 4 for 77) and 73 for 8
Mumbai 280 (V.G. Kambli 86, A.A. Pagnis 56, A.R. Kapoor 5 for 98)
Match drawn
Mumbai 5 pts, Punjab 3 pts

at Barabati Stadium, Cuttack
Orissa 218 (P.M. Mullick 98 not out) and 265 for 5 dec. (S.S. Das 120, B.B.C.C. Mohapatra 57)
Railways 113 (S. Satpathy 5 for 25) and 254 (Jaswinder Singh 71, S. Satpathy 5 for 95)
Orissa won by 116 runs
Orissa 8 pts, Railways 0 pts

The penultimate round of matches confirmed that Mumbai and Karnataka would be the two sides from Group A to go forward to the final stages of the competition. Mumbai gained first innings points narrowly, overtaking Punjab with their last pair together, but the home side then collapsed and only the weather saved them from defeat.

Orissa gained consolation for two defeats with victory over Railways. Sanjay Satpathy, a month short of his 19th birthday, returned the best bowling figures of his career and took 10 wickets in a match for the first time with his off-breaks.

13, 14, 15 and 16 March 1998
at Wankhede Stadium, Mumbai
Mumbai 467 (V.G. Kambli 151, M. Phadke 114, A.A. Pagnis 72) and 196 for 1 dec. (S.S. More 82 not out, A.A. Muzumdar 53 not out)
Karnataka 313 (R.V. Bharadwaj 58, S.B. Joshi 55) and 177 for 6 (Fazal R. Khalil 83)
Match drawn
Mumbai 5 pts, Karnataka 3 pts

at Berhampur Stadium, Berhampur
Orissa 261 (S.S. Das 110, B. Vij 4 for 60) and 305 for 6 dec. (S.S. Das 131, R.R. Parida 99)
Punjab 145 and 88 for 9
Match drawn
Orissa 5 pts, Punjab 3 pts

The final round of matches in Group A saw the two strongest sides lock horns and Mumbai have decidedly the better of the encounter. Kambli, who was captaining Mumbai, and Phadke put on 170 for the sixth wicket.

Shiv Das, the Orissa skipper, scored a century in each innings for the first time and took his side to the brink of victory only to be thwarted by Punjab's last pair.

Section A Final Table

	P	W	L	D	Pts
Karnataka	4	3	–	1	27
Mumbai	4	2	–	2	26
Orissa	4	1	2	1	13
Punjab	4	–	1	3	9
Railways	4	–	3	1	5

Section B

5, 6, 7 and 8 February 1998
at Feroze Shah Kotla Ground, Delhi
Delhi 300 (A.K. Sharma 101, N. Chopra 84, S.C. Ganguly 6 for 87) and 194 for 6 (A. Chopra 65)
Bengal 527 for 6 dec. (D. Gandhi 176, S.S. Karim 97, A. Lahiri 87, A. Verma 75)
Match drawn
Bengal 5 pts, Delhi 3 pts

at M.A. Chidambaram Stadium, Madras
Uttar Pradesh 460 (S.A. Shukla 164, R.V. Sapru 99, G.K. Pandey 62, T. Kumaran 5 for 96)
Tamil Nadu 269 (H. Bedani 58, S. Chandramouli 51) and 215 for 3 (S. Sharath 108 not out, S. Sriram 65)
Match drawn
Uttar Pradesh 5 pts, Tamil Nadu 3 pts

The drawn match in Delhi saw Ajay Sharma and Devagang Gandhi make centuries, but it will be remembered mostly for the fact that it was the last first-class game in which Raman Lamba was to appear. Twelve days later, playing in a match in Bangladesh, he was hit on the head by a ball when fielding, and, in spite of great efforts on the part of a team of doctors, he died three days later, on 23 February. He was 38 years old. He played in four Test matches and 32 one-day internationals. His 312 against Himachal Pradesh, 1994–95, remains the record for a Delhi batsman in the Ranji Trophy. His tragic death was lamented throughout the cricketing world, for he truly loved the game.

14, 15, 16 and 17 February 1998
at M.A. Chidambaram Stadium, Madras
Tamil Nadu 473 (D. Vasu 148, S. Mahesh 77, W.V. Raman 67, H. Badani 57)
Delhi 183 for 4 (A.K. Sharma 55 not out)
Match abandoned

at OEF Stadium, Kanpur
Maharashtra 383 (H.H. Kanitkar 126, S.M. Kondhalkar 68, A.M. Zaidi 7 for 99)
Uttar Pradesh 498 for 9 (M.T. Saif 104 not out, R. Sharma 84, G.K. Pandey 67)
Match drawn
Uttar Pradesh 5 pts, Maharashtra 3 pts

A triple century for Laxman in the Ranji Trophy Super League, 301 not out for Hyderabad against Bihar at Jamshedpur, 5 February 1998.
(Craig Prentis / Allsport)

Delhi refused to continue the match in Madras after the third day, claiming that the Tamil Nadu players had dug up the pitch with their boots. Both sides were expelled from the competition.

The match in Kanpur was a tedious affair. Uttar Pradesh scored at little more than two runs an over, and Maharashtra used ten bowlers.

4, 5, 6 and 7 March 1998
at Calcutta C & FC Ground, Calcutta
Bengal 525 (A. Lahiri 94, S.S. Karim 93, D. Gandhi 91, S.J. Kalyani 76)
Maharashtra 301 (S.S. Bhave 140, U. Chatterjee 5 for 77, A. Das 4 for 67) and 127 for 4 (H.A. Kinikar 71 not out)
Match drawn
Bengal 5 pts, Maharashtra 3 pts

13, 14, 15 and 16 March 1998
at Calcutta C & FC Ground, Calcutta
Uttar Pradesh 293 (J. Yadav 82, R. Sharma 68, R.V. Sapru 50 not out, S. Banerjee 4 for 63)
Bengal 159 for 5 (A. Verma 73)
No result
Uttar Pradesh 2 pts, Bengal 2 pts

The expulsion of Delhi and Tamil Nadu turned Section B into a farce. Games that had involved those two sides were discounted, which meant that the teams left in the section played only two matches. As both Uttar Pradesh and Bengal both led Maharashtra on the first innings, they were the qualifiers for the final stages of the trophy.

Section B Final Table

	P	W	D	NR	Pts
Uttar Pradesh	2	–	1	1	7
Bengal	2	–	1	1	7
Maharashtra	2	–	2	–	6

Section C

5, 6, 7 and 8 February 1998
at Keenan Stadium, Jamshedpur
Hyderabad 529 for 8 dec. (V.V.S. Laxman 301 not out)
Bihar 248 (Tariq-ur-Rehman 70, Venkatapathy Raju 5 for 69) and 129 (K. Kumar 51, Venkatapathy Raju 4 for 51)
Hyderabad won by an innings and 152 runs
Hyderabad 8 pts, Bihar 0 pts

at IPCL Sports Complex, Baroda
Baroda 240 and 89 (M. Kumar 4 for 21, P. Jain 4 for 25)
Haryana 289 (R. Puri 143, Armajit Kaypee 58, A.R. Tandon 5 for 39) and 43 for 1
Haryana won by 9 wickets
Haryana 8 pts, Baroda 0 pts

Venkata Laxman hit the highest score of the season, a triple century in Hyderabad's innings of 529 in which the next highest score was 35. Venkatapathy Raju completed Hyderabad's victory over Bihar with match figures of nine for 120.

Haryana's victory in Baroda was founded on a third wicket stand of 139 between Rajesh Puri and Armajit Kaypee. There was consolation for the home side in some fine bowling by Ashish Tandon, the young medium-pacer, who brought about a collapse that saw Haryana lose their last seven wickets for 18 runs.

14, 15, 16 and 17 February 1998
at Digvijay Stadium, Rajnandagaon
Madhya Pradesh 596 for 8 dec. (A.R. Khurasiya 195, C.S. Pandit 104, Raja Ali 95, K.K. Patel 79, J.P. Yadav 63)
Baroda 305 (A.C. Bedade 81, N.R. Mongia 60, M. Kadri 56, R.K. Chauhan 4 for 103) and 176 for 6 (N.R. Mongia 88)
Match drawn
Madhya Pradesh 5 pts, Baroda 3 pts

at Nahar Singh Stadium, Faridabad
Haryana 308 (P. Thakur 85, V. Yadav 72, S. Panda 4 for 68) and 231 for 4 dec. (Jitender Singh 92, Armajit Kaypee 61 not out)
Bihar 323 (Rajeev Kumar 106, Sunil Kumar 76, P. Thakur 5 for 109, P. Jain 4 for 65) and 107 for 1 (Rajeev Kumar 53 not out)
Match drawn
Bihar 5 pts, Haryana 3 pts

Pandit hit his second century of the season and shared a fourth wicket stand of 167 with Khurasiya, who also shared a fifth wicket partnership of 219 with Raja Ali as Madhya Pradesh built a massive score. However the pitch was too placid for them to force a win. Haryana surprisingly conceded first innings points to Bihar, for whom Sunil Kumar and Rajeev Kumar added 108 for the second wicket.

22, 23, 24 and 25 February 1998
at Moin-ul-Haq Stadium, Patna
Baroda 389 (C.C. Willams 72, T.B. Arothe 72, A.C. Bedade 54, M. Kadri 53, Avinash Kumar 4 for 107)
Bihar 229 (Rajeev Kumar 73, A.R. Tandon 6 for 87) and 123 for 6 (A.R. Tandon 4 for 38)
Match drawn
Baroda 5 pts, Bihar 3 pts

at Jayanti Stadium, Bhilai
Hyderabad 536 for 6 dec. (A. Nand Kishore 136, M.V. Sridhar 108, V.V.S. Laxman 92, V. Pratap 51)
Madhya Pradesh 225 (N. Patwardhan 51, Venkatapathy Raju 5 for 49) and 226 for 4 (J.P. Yadav 106 not out)

Match drawn
Hyderabad 5 pts, Madhya Pradesh 3 pts

Baroda batted consistently against Bihar, who, in contrast, lost their last five wickets for 29 and were forced to follow on. The outstanding success for Baroda was the 23-year old medium pace bowler Ashish Tandon, who confirmed the advance shown against Haryana by claiming the best figures of his career for both innings and match.

Sridhar and Nand Kishore put on 209 for Hyderabad's fifth wicket, and the bowling of Venkatapthy Raju ensured that Madhya Pradesh would have to follow on, but Jai Prakash Yadav's century saved his side from defeat.

4, 5, 6 and 7 March 1998

at Roop Singh Stadium, Gwalior
Bihar 356 (Rajeev Kumar 108, N. Ranjan 78, S. Pandey 4 for 90) and 163 for 3 (Tariq-ur-Rehman 61 not out, Rajeev Kumar 55)
Madhya Pradesh 395 for 8 wickets dec. (N. Patwardhan 121 not out, D.S. Bundela 56, K.V.P. Rao 4 for 71)
Match drawn
Madhya Pradesh 5 pts, Bihar 3 pts

at Nahar Singh Stadium, Faridabad
Hyderabad 263 (S. Yadav 68, Yuvraj Singh 54)
Haryana 280 for 7 (Dhanraj Singh 83, V. Yadav 68)
Match drawn
Haryana 5 pts, Hyderabad 3 pts

A seventh wicket stand of 113 between Patwardhan and Harvinder Singh Sodhi gave Madhya Pradesh first innings points against Bihar, who were condemned to finish bottom of the table.

No play was possible on the first day in Faridabad, and Hyderabad and Haryana were only able to contest first innings points.

13, 14, 15 and 16 March 1998

at Gymkhana Ground, Secunderabad
Baroda 337 (C.C. Williams 94, T.B. Arothe 91, H.R. Jadhav 51) and 167 for 6 dec. (H.R. Jadhav 80 not out)
Hyderabad 222 (S. Yadav 58 not out, V. Pratap 50, T.B. Arothe 6 for 53) and 104 for 4
Match drawn
Hyderabad 5 pts, Baroda 3 pts

at Nahar Singh Stadium, Faridabad
Madhya Pradesh 298 (C.S. Pandit 82, P. Jain 4 for 75) and 242 for 9 dec. (J.P. Yadav 72, V.B. Jain 4 for 82)
Haryana 232 (Armajit Kaypee 84, P. Sharma 54, N.D. Hirwani 5 for 64) and 196 for 6 (P. Sharma 79 not out)
Match drawn
Madhya Pradesh 5 pts, Haryana 3 pts

Ironically, the two sides who were beaten on the first innings in the last round of matches were the two sides who topped the table and qualified for the final stages of the competition. Hyderabad lost their last four wickets for 15 runs against Baroda, for whom Tushar Arothe followed an innings of 91 with a fine display of off-break bowling which brought him the best figures of his career.

Haryana's last six wickets went down for 30 runs, the leg-spin of Hirwarni proving too much for the tail. He was also effective in the second innings, but Madhya Pradesh were thwarted. Haryana defended dourly for 93 overs to gain the draw that gave them a one-point advantage over their opponents.

Section C Final Table

	P	W	L	D	Pts
Hyderabad	4	1	–	3	19
Haryana	4	1	–	3	19
Madhya Pradesh	4	–	–	4	18
Baroda	4	–	1	3	13
Bihar	4	–	1	3	11

Quarter Finals

30, 31 March, 1, 2 and 3 April 1998

at OEF Sports Stadium, Kanpur
Haryana 156 and 423 (Jitender Singh 149, Dhanraj Singh 78, Shafiq Khan 61, A.W. Zaidi 4 for 111)
Uttar Pradesh 613 (S.A. Shukla 189, Mohammad Kaif 100, M.S. Mudgal 65, J.P. Yadav 51)
Uttar Pradesh won by an innings and 34 runs

at Gymkhana Ground, Secunderabad
Hyderabad 209 (A. Verma 4 for 31) and 244 (D. Manohar 66, N.A. David 59, S. Banerjee 5 for 58)
Bengal 243 (S.S. Karim 69, Charanjit Singh 51, N.P. Singh 7 for 103) and 166 (S.S. Karim 59 not out, D. Manohar 4 for 48)
Hyderabad won by 44 runs

Uttar Pradesh overwhelmed Haryana to qualify for the semi-final. Put in to bat, Haryana lost wickets regularly and were then savaged by Mohammad Kaif and Saurab Shukla, both of whom made the highest score of their careers. They added 183 for the second wicket, and the tail wagged strongly with the last three wickets realising 151 runs.

The match in Secunderabad was a much closer affair. Hyderabad chose to bat first, but they lost their last three wickets at the same score. Bengal were reduced to 39 for five by some inspired bowling from Narender Pal Singh, who returned the best bowling figures of his career. Karim and Kalyani effected a recovery, and Banerjee plundered well at the end of the innings so that Bengal surprisingly took a first innings lead. Hyderabad lost two wickets in clearing the deficit, but they showed great resolution in fighting back to set Bengal a target of 211. Five wickets went down for 64, Bengal made no true recovery, and Hyderabad gained an excellent victory.

Semi-Finals

9, 10, 11, 12 and 13 April 1998
at Wankedhe Stadium, Mumbai
Mumbai 94 (A.W. Zaidi 6 for 29) and 328 (A.A. Muzumdar 87, J.V. Paranjpe 83, M. Obaid Kamal 5 for 58)
Uttar Pradesh 293 (G.K. Pandey 109, R. Shamshad 64) and 135 for 7 (N.M. Kulkarni 4 for 46)
Uttar Pradesh won by 3 wickets

at Gymkhana Ground, Secunderabad
Hyderabad 283 (A. Shetty 58, V. Prathap 53, M.V. Sridhar 51, D. Ganesh 5 for 74) and 179 (D. Ganesh 4 for 74)
Karnataka 309 (J. Arun Kumar 85, R.S. Dravid 71, S. Somasunder 51, Kanwaljit Singh 7 for 62) and 157 for 9 (F. Khaleel 51, Kanwaljit Singh 7 for 38)
Karnataka won by 1 wicket

The two semi-finals were wonderfully exciting matches. Uttar Pradesh produced the surprise of the competition in beating Mumbai who, in fairness, were without some of their leading players. Muzumdar chose to bat when he won the toss. Two wickets went for nine before Paranjpe and Muzumdar himself added 75. Six wickets then fell for five runs and Mumbai were all out for 94. It was medium-pacer Ashish Zaidi who caused the collapse when he returned for a second spell. Uttar Pradesh lost four wickets for 67 before skipper Gyanendrakumar Pandey joined Rizwan Shamshad in a stand worth 174. Uttar Pradesh eventually took a first innings lead of 199. Once again it was Paranjpe and Muzumdar who gave Mumbai's innings some backbone with a third wicket partership of 122, and Uttar Pradesh were set a target of 130. They lost Rakesh Sharma for 0 and were 125 for seven when Mohammad Saif joined skipper Pandey, who, with the score on 129, hit Pawar for six to win the match.

The semi-final in Secunderabad was an even closer affair and was notable for some outstanding bowling by off-break bowler Kanwaljit Singh, who finished with 14 for 100, his best match figures, but still finished on the losing side. Hyderabad began well but lost their last seven wickets for 52 runs. Somasunder and Arun Kumar put on 105 for Karnataka's first wicket, and Dravid and Joshi brought substance to the middle order so that a first innings lead of 26 was gained. Ganesh bowled well for a second time, and Hyderabad were bowled out for 179 to leave Karnataka a target of 154 on a crumbling pitch. Somusander and Arun Kumar made 43 for the first wicket, but, at 177 for seven, the game was in the balance. When the ninth wicket went down Karnataka were still 16 short of victory. Mansoor Ali Khan stood firm, and Ganesh showed his batting skills were almost equal to his bowling ability as he made 18 and won the match with a boundary.

Ranji Trophy Final

19, 20, 21, 22 and 23 April 1998
at Chinnaswamy Stadium, Bangalore
Uttar Pradesh 134 (S.B. Joshi 4 for 37) and 416 for 7 (S.A. Shukla 91, J.P. Yadav 73, R. Sharma 65, Mohammad Kaif 62, G.K. Pandey 55)
Karnataka 617 for 9 dec. (R.S. Dravid 215, R.V. Bharadwaj 122, J. Arun Kumar 104, S. Somasunder 68, M. Obaid Kamal 4 for 95)
Match drawn
Karnataka won the Ranji Trophy by virtue of first innings lead

Choosing to bat, Uttar Pradesh lost Rakesh Sharma and Shukla to Srinath without a run scored, and from that point the Ranji Trophy drew further and further away from them. They were bowled out for 134, and Somasunder and Arun Kumar put on 135 for Karnataka's first wicket. The might of the innings, however, came from Dravid and Bharadwaj, who scored 257 for the fourth wicket. Rahul Dravid, leading the side in the absence of Kumble, was run out for 215, the highest score of his career and his second double century. He declared with a first innings lead of 483, knowing that Karnataka had won the Ranji Trophy for the fifth time.

Rahul Dravid made the highest score of his career, 215, when he captained Karnataka in the Ranji Trophy Final. He scored more first-class runs in the season, 1,264, than any other batsman in India. (David Munden / Sportsline)

Triangular Tournament

India's insatiable appetite for one-day cricket led to the arrangement of a triangular tournament in which the host nation entertained Bangladesh and Kenya, qualifiers for the 1999 World Cup.

India took the opportunity to look at some new players. Tendulkar was rested for the first two matches, and Gagan Khoda of Rajasthan was used as Ganguly's opening partner, while Mannava Prasad was introduced as wicket-keeper. Paranjpe and Karim also featured in the series, and Laxman, Sidhu and Dravid all earned recalls. All-rounder Nikhil Chopra of Delhi played in one match.

Bangladesh began promisingly. They gave India an unexpectedly hard game and broke their drought when they beat Kenya, who then batted well against India before beating Bangladesh in the return game. Bangladesh's hopes of reaching the final were dashed when India crushed them in the Wankhede Stadium, and Kenya pulled off the surprise of the tournament three days later when they beat India in Gwalior. They batted exceptionally well with Ravindu Shah, Maurice Odumbe and Hitesh Modi all scoring fifties. Maurice Odumbe completed a wonderful match by taking three of the last four Indian wickets and running out the fourth, Chopra, to take the individual award.

Kenya could not repeat this form in the final, where Tendulkar blasted them for a century off 103 balls to make him supreme among one-day international batsmen. He hit 13 fours and took India to victory with 15 overs to spare. The consolation for Kenya was that Steve Tikolo was named Man of the Series. All the games were day and night matches, and the weather was kind.

Steve Tikolo of Kenya was Man of the Series in the triangular one-day tournament that brought the Indian season to a close.
(Graham Chadwick / Allsport)

Qualifying Table

	P	W	L	Pts
India	4	3	1	6
Kenya	4	2	2	4
Bangladesh	4	1	3	2

Match One – India *v.* Bangladesh

14 May 1998 at Punjab CA Stadium, Mohali

Bangladesh

Athar Ali Khan	**c** Mohanty, **b** Agarkar	**15**
Sanwar Hussain	**b** Agarkar	**0**
Minhajul Abedin	**c** Dravid, **b** R.R. Singh	**14**
Aminul Islam *	**b** Agarkar	**70**
Mehrab Hussain	**b** Sanghvi	**6**
Naim-ur-Rehman	**c** Azharuddin, **b** Sanghvi	**25**
Khalid Mahmud	run out	**31**
Mohammad Rafique	**c** Mohanty, **b** Kanitkar	**1**
Hasibul Hussain	run out	**1**
Khalid Masud †	not out	**0**
Morshed Ali Kahn		
	lb **7**, w **9**, nb **5**	**21**
	50 overs (for 9 wickets)	**184**

	O	M	R	W
Agarkar	8	1	41	**3**
Mohanty	7	1	18	**–**
R.R. Singh	10	–	32	**1**
Sanghvi	10	–	35	**2**
Ganguly	6	–	21	**–**
Kanitkar	9	–	30	**1**

Fall of Wickets
1–**2**, 2–**33**, 3–**52**, 4–**61**, 5–**132**, 6–**163**, 7–**172**, 8–**182**, 9–**184**

India

S.C. Ganguly	**c** and **b** Morshed Ali Khan	**7**
G.K. Khoda	**c** Kahlid Masud, **b** Athar	**26**
M. Azharuddin *	**c** Khalid Masud, **b** Khalid Mahmud	**31**
A.D. Jadeja	**c** Khalid Masud, **b** Hasibul	**73**
R.S. Dravid	**c** and **b** Athar Ali Khan	**5**
R.R. Singh	not out	**27**
H.H. Kanitkar	not out	**1**
M.S.K. Prasad †		
A.B. Agarkar		
D.S. Mohanty		
R. Sanghvi		
	lb **7**, w **8**	**15**
	45.2 overs (for 5 wickets)	**185**

	O	M	R	W
Hasibul Hussain	9	–	44	**1**
Morshed Ali Khan	10	–	31	**1**
Kahlid Mahmud	9.2	1	35	**1**
Athar Ali Khan	10	–	33	**2**
Mohammad Rafique	7	–	35	**–**

Fall of Wickets
1–**12**, 2–**55**, 3–**85**, 4–**105**, 5–**183**

Umpires: I. Sivaram & K.N. Raghavan *Man of the Match:* A.D. Jadeja

India won by 5 wickets

Match Two – Bangladesh v. Kenya

17 May 1998 at Lal Bahadur Syadium, Hyderabad

Kenya

D. Chudasama	run out	37
K. Otieno †	c Hasibul Hussain, b Morshed Ali Khan	5
S.O. Tikolo	b Khalid Mahmud	13
M.O. Odumbe	c Hasibul Hussain, b Enam	20
H.S. Modi	lbw, b Enam-ul-Haq	40
Ravindu Shah	b Khalid Mahmud	52
T. Odoyo	b Mohammad Rafique	17
A. Suji	b Mohammad Rafique	21
Asif Karim *	st Khalid Masud, b Mohammad Rafique	6
M.A. Suji	not out	3
Mohammad Sheikh	run out	1
	lb 7, w 13	20
	49 overs	235

	O	M	R	W
Hasibul Hussain	4	–	16	–
Morshed Ali Khan	7	–	26	1
Kahild Mahmud	7	–	38	2
Enam–ul–Haq	10	–	46	2
Naim–ur–Rehman	10	1	42	–
Afthar Ali Khan	1	–	5	–
Mohammad Rafique	10	–	55	1

Fall of Wickets
1–**13**, 2–**29**, 3–**84**, 4–**89**, 5–**156**, 6–**193**, 7–**209**, 8–**220**, 9–**233**

Bangladesh

Athar Ali Khan	run out	47
Mohammad Rafique	c Otieno, b Mohammad Sheikh	77
Mimhajul Abedin	lbw, b Mohammad Sheikh	14
Animul Islam	not out	18
Akram Khan *	c Mohammad Sheikh, Odumbe	36
Naim–ur–Rehman	not out	5
Khalid Mahmud		
Enam–ul–Haq		
Hasibul Hussain		
Khalid Masud †		
Morshed Ali Khan		
	b 5, lb 4, w 24, nb 6	39
	47.5 overs (for 4 wickets)	236

	O	M	R	W
M.A. Suji	4	–	14	–
Tikolo	10	–	40	–
Odoyo	4	–	19	–
Odumbe	9	–	42	1
Asif Karim	9.5	–	54	–
Mohammad Sheikh	10	–	44	2
Modi	1	–	14	–

Fall of Wickets
1–**137**, 2–**157**, 3–**166**, 4–**228**

Umpires: S.K. Sharma & P.R. Mohile *Man of the Match*: Mohammad Rafique

Bangladesh won by 6 wickets

Match Three – India v. Kenya

20 May 1998 at Chinnaswamy Stadium, Bangalore

Kenya

D. Chudasama	b R.R. Singh	32
K. Otieno †	b Agarkar	0
S.O. Tikolo	c Laxman, b Sanghvi	77
M.O. Odumbe	c Prasad, b Agarkar	47
H.S. Modi	b Sanghvi	17
Ravindhu Shah	c and b Kanitkar	21
T. Odoyo	c Dravid, b Kanitkar	1
A. Suji	run out	8
Asif Karim *	b R.R. Singh	6
M.A. Suji	not out	1
Mohammad Sheikh	not out	2
	lb 6, w 2, nb 3	11
	50 overs (for 9 wickets)	223

	O	M	R	W
Agarkar	10	2	36	2
Mohanty	9	–	44	–
R.R. Singh	8	–	24	2
Sanghvi	10	–	52	2
Kanitkar	10	–	46	2
Ganguly	3	–	15	–

Fall of Wickets
1–**7**, 2–**70**, 3–**152**, 4–**175**, 5–**186**, 6–**199**, 7–**211**, 8–**215**, 9–**220**

India

G.K. Khoda	c and b Tikolo	89
S.C. Ganguly	b M.A. Suji	9
R.S. Dravid	b Asif Karim	49
A.D. Jadeja *	c Tikolo, b Mohammad Sheikh	50
H.H. Kanitkar	run out	1
V.V.S. Laxman	c and b Mohammas Sheikh	1
R.R. Singh	not out	2
M.V.S. Prasad †	not out	11
A.B. Agarkar		
R. Sanghvi		
D.S. Mohanty		
	b 2, lb 2, w 8	12
	47 overs (for 6 wickets)	224

	O	M	R	W
M.A. Suji	7	–	22	1
Tikolo	10	–	46	1
Odoyo	7	–	34	–
Asif Karim	10	–	39	1
Odumbe	6	–	38	–
Mohammad Sheikh	7	–	41	2

Fall of Wickets
1–**21**, 2–**119**, 3–**197**, 4–**200**, 5–**207**

Umpires: A. Bhattacharjee & Devendra Sharma *Man of the Match*: G.K. Khoda

India won by 4 wickets

Match Four – Bangladesh v. Kenya

23 May 1998 at M.A. Chidambaram Stadium, Chepauk, Chennai

Kenya

K. Otieno †	c Enam, b Naim-ur-Rehman	21
Ravindu Shah	c Aminul Islam, b Enam	62
S.O. Tikolo	c Enam-ul-Haq, b Hasibul	65
M.O. Odumbe	c Morshed, b Hasibul Hussain	40
H.S. Modi	c Enam, b Mohammad Rafique	0
T. Odoyo	b Mohammad Rafique	0
A. Vader	not out	11
L. Onyango	b Khalid Mahmud	2
Asif Karim *	b Khalid Mahmud	0
M.A. Suji	not out	3
Mohammad Sheikh		
	lb 11, w 10, nb 1	22
	50 overs (for 8 wickets)	226

	O	M	R	W
Hasibul Husain	10	–	44	2
Morshed Ali Khan	6	–	28	–
Khalid Mahmud	4	–	20	2
Enam-ul-Haq	10	–	35	1
Naim-ur-Rehman	10	1	43	1
Mohammad Rafique	10	–	45	2

Fall of Wickets
1–76, 2–99, 3–193, 4–203, 5–203, 6–203, 7–212, 8–212

Bangladesh

Athar Ali Khan	c Ravindhu Shah, b M.A. Suji	0
Mohammad Rafique	c Mohammad Sheikh, b Odoyo	23
Minhajul Abedin	c Tikolo, b Mohammad Sheikh	45
Aminul Islam	c and b Odoyo	6
Akram Khan *	run out	23
Naim-ur-Rehman	c Ravindhu Shah, b Asif Karim	41
Khalid Mahmud	b Tikolo	28
Khalid Masud †	c Odumbe, b Tikolo	5
Enam-ul-Haq	run out	4
Hasibul Hussain	b Asif Karim	2
Morshed Ali Khan	not out	2
	b 1, lb 3, w 10, n 5	19
	46.2 overs	198

	O	M	R	W
M.A. Suji	7	–	21	1
Onyango	2	–	20	–
Odoyo	7	1	31	2
Asif Karim	9	–	28	2
Tikolo	8.2	–	37	2
Mohammad Sheikh	7	–	27	1
Odumbe	6	–	30	–

Fall of Wickets
1–0, 2–57, 3–64, 4–102, 5–115, 6–171, 7–192, 8–194, 9–196

Umpires:Suresh Shastri & S. Asnani *Man of the Match*: S.O. Tikolo

Kenya won by 28 runs

Match Five – India v. Bangladesh

25 May 1998 at Wankhede Stadium, Mumbai

Bangladesh

Athar Ali Khan	b Mhambrey	0
Mohammad Rafique	c Karim, b Venkatesh Prasad	6
Minhajul Abedin	c Laxman, b Venkatesh Prasad	0
Animul Islam	c Jadeja, b Kumble	18
Akram Khan *	c and b R.R. Singh	8
Naim-ur-Rehman	c Laxman, b Kumble	6
Khalid Mahmud	c Karim, b Venkatesh Prasad	7
Khalid Masud †	not out	15
Enam-ul-Haq	c Karim, b Kumble	0
Hasibul Hussain	b Tendulkar	21
Anis-ur-Rehman	c Dravid, b Tendulkar	0
	lb 8, w 21, nb 5	34
	36.3 overs	115

	O	M	R	W
Venkatesh Prasad	9	2	26	3
Mhambrey	6	1	22	1
R.R. Singh	6	1	16	1
Kumble	10	4	17	3
Harbhajan Singh	4	–	18	–
Tendulkar	1.3	–	8	–

Fall of Wickets
1–17, 2–18, 3–21, 4–53, 5–55, 6–70, 7–71, 8–71, 9–115

India

N.S. Sidhu	lbw, b Khaild Mahmud	41
S.R. Tendulkar	c Animul, b Athar Ali Khan	33
R.S. Dravid	b Mohammad Rafique	1
A.D. Jadeja *	not out	16
V.V.S. Laxman	c Khalid Masud, b Khalid	4
S.S. Karim †	c Naim-ur-Rehman, b Mohammad Rafique	8
R.R. Singh	not out	1
A.R. Kumble		
Venkatesh Prasad		
P.L. Mhambrey		
Harbhajan Singh		
	lb 3, w 8, nb 1	12
	29.2 overs (for 5 wickets)	116

	O	M	R	W
Hasibul Hussain	5	–	30	–
Anis-ur-Rehman	3	–	26	–
Athar Ali Khan	4	–	24	1
Mohammad Rafique	10	5	21	2
Khalid Mahmud	7.2	2	12	2

Fall of Wickets
1–72, 2–84, 3–98, 4–107

Umpires: R.T. Ramachandran & B.K. Sadashiva *Man of the Match*:A.R. Kumble

India won by 5 wickets

Match Six – India v. Kenya
28 May 1998 at Roop Singh Stadium, Gwalior

Kenya

K. Otieno †	c Kumble, b Venkatesh Prasad	8
Ravindu Shah	c and b Kumble	70
S.O. Tikolo	run out	21
M.O. Odumbe	c Sidhu, b Kumble	83
H.S. Modi	c Dravid, b Chopra	51
A. Vader	not out	13
T. Odoyo	not out	11
M.A. Suji		
J. Angara		
Asif Karim *		
Mohammad Sheikh		
	lb 4, w 4	8
	50 overs (for 5 wickets)	265

	O	M	R	W
Venkatesh Prasad	6	1	28	1
R.R. Singh	5	1	18	–
Kulkarni	10	–	60	–
Tendulkar	5	–	34	–
Kumble	8	2	27	2
Chopra	10	1	65	1
Dravid	6	–	29	–

Fall of Wickets
1–**26**, 2–**93**, 3–**109**, 4–**209**, 5–**250**

India

N.S. Sidhu	run out	27
S.R. Tendulkar	c Asif Karim, b M.A. Suji	18
M. Azharuddin *	b Angara	9
R.S. Dravid	c Vader, b Tikolo	33
R.R. Singh	c Ravindu Shah, b Tikolo	11
J.V. Paranjpe	c and b Tikolo	27
N.R. Mongia †	c Tikolo, b Odumbe	21
N. Chopra	run out	3
A.R. Kumble	b Odumbe	20
Venkatesh Prasad	b Odumbe	19
N.M. Kulkarni	not out	1
	lb 3, w 3, nb 1	7
	47.1 overs	196

	O	M	R	W
M.A. Suji	9	–	50	1
Asif Karim	8	1	33	–
Angara	6	1	19	1
Tikolo	10	–	29	3
Mohammad Sheikh	6	–	24	–
Odoyo	4	–	24	–
Odumbe	4.1	–	14	3

Fall of Wickets
1–**34**, 2–**47**, 3–**62**, 4–**97**, 5–**106**, 6–**150**, 7–**155**, 8–**155**, 9–**189**

Umpires: R. Seth & S. Banerjee *Man of the Match*: M. Odumbe

Kenya won by 69 runs

Final – India v. Kenya
31 May 1998 at Eden Gardens, Calcutta

Kenya

D. Chudasama	c Azharuddin, b Agarkar	10
Ravindu Shah	c Kanitkar, b Venkatesh Prasad	8
S.O. Tikolo	c Mongia, b Agarkar	3
M.O. Odumbe	b Venkatesh Prasad	0
H.S. Modi	c Kanitkar, b R.R. Singh	71
K. Otieno †	lbw, b Kumble	28
T. Odoyo	b Kumble	21
Asif Karim *	c Mongia, b Venkatesh Prasad	13
M.A. Suji	c Mongia, b Venkatesh Prasad	4
Mohammad Sheikh	not out	6
J. Angara	c and b Agarkar	3
	b 2, lb 13, w 12, nb 2	29
	46.3 overs	196

	O	M	R	W
Venkatesh Prasad	10	2	23	4
Agarkar	9.3	–	31	3
R.R. Singh	6	–	41	1
Kumble	10	–	34	2
Sanghvi	7	–	26	–
Kanitkar	2	–	15	–
Ganguly	1	–	7	–
Tendulkar	1	–	4	–

Fall of Wickets
1–**13**, 2–**19**, 3–**21**, 4–**23**, 5–**105**, 6–**142**, 7–**164**, 8–**180**, 9–**185**

India

S.C. Ganguly	b Angara	36
S.R. Tendulkar	not out	100
A.D. Jadeja	not out	50
M. Azharuddin *		
H.H. Kanitkar		
R.R. Singh		
N.R. Mongia †		
A.R. Kumble		
A.B. Agarkar		
Venkatesh Prasad		
R. Sanghvi		
	lb 1, w 9, nb 1	11
	35 overs (for one wicket)	197

	O	M	R	W
M.A. Suji	5	–	30	–
Asif Karim	5	–	27	–
Angara	6	–	37	1
Odoyo	8	–	38	–
Tikolo	3	–	17	–
Odumbe	2	–	15	–
Mohammad Sheikh	5	–	27	–
Ravindu Shah	1	–	5	–

Fall of Wicket
1–**77**

Umpires: A.V. Jayaprakash & K. Parthasarathy *Man of the Match*: S.R. Tendulkar

India won by 9 wickets

First-Class Averages

Batting

	M	Inns	NOs	Runs	HS	Av	100s	50s
R.S. Sodhi	2	3	2	279	200*	279.00	1	
A.D. Jadeja	3	5	3	315	242*	157.50	1	
S.R. Tendulkar	10	13	2	1256	204*	114.00	6	2
V.G. Kambli	9	11	3	890	232*	111.25	3	1
S. Ramesh	6	6	–	614	167	102.33	3	1
V.V.S. Laxman	12	14	3	986	301*	89.62	3	4
S.S. Karim	8	9	2	602	111	86.00	1	5
J.V. Paranjpe	7	11	1	821	174	82.10	3	4
S. Abbas Ali	6	6	1	392	251	78.40	1	1
N. Patwardhan	3	5	2	333	121*	77.66	1	1
L.S. Rajput	4	6	2	301	112	75.25	1	1
S. Sharath	9	10	2	586	129	73.25	3	3
S. Sriram	7	10	3	505	213*	72.14	2	1
A. Raja Ali	6	7	3	283	95	70.75	3	
A. Chopra	6	9	1	554	150	69.25	2	3
H.H. Kanitkar	7	9	3	414	126	69.00	3	
Rajinder Singh	4	8	2	402	143	67.00	1	2
R. Shamshad	12	13	3	640	224*	64.00	3	1
R.S. Dravid	15	21	1	1264	215	63.20	2	10
R.C.V. Kumar	5	7	2	315	151	63.00	2	
S.S. Raul	6	8	2	370	139	61.66	2	
S.A. Shukla	10	11	1	615	189	61.50	2	2
D. Vasu	7	4	–	245	148	61.25	1	
A.R. Khurasiya	8	9	1	475	195	59.37	2	1
S.H. Kotak	5	9	2	415	131	59.28	1	2
C.S. Pandit	8	10	1	525	104	58.33	2	2
P.M. Mullick	8	13	1	698	201	58.16	2	3
Rajeev R. Kumar	8	15	1	805	126	57.50	3	5
D. Gandhi	10	15	2	740	176	56.92	2	4
J.J. Martin	9	14	3	623	107	56.63	3	3
N.S. Sidhu	11	15	–	842	131	56.13	1	7
B.M. Jadeja	4	7	2	277	123	55.40	2	
M. Azharuddin	10	13	1	664	163*	55.33	1	6
S.C. Ganguly	8	12	1	604	173	54.90	2	2
Jitender Singh	11	18	2	872	175	54.50	4	1
R. Vijay Bharadwaj	11	15	1	739	164	52.78	3	3
A. Gupta	2	3	–	158	112	52.66	1	
G.K. Pandey	10	11	2	471	109	52.33	1	4
J.P. Yadav	12	13	1	619	145*	51.58	2	3
Narinder Singh	5	9	1	409	229*	51.12	1	1
S.S. Das	8	13	–	662	164	50.92	4	
P.K. Dwevedi	8	10	2	401	189	50.12	2	
N. Gaur	4	7	–	337	97	48.14	4	
S.V. Manjrekar	8	11	1	478	126	47.80	1	2
A.B. Agarkar	5	7	2	236	56*	47.20	2	
A.A. Pagnis	8	13	3	469	72	46.90	5	
S.K. Yadav	3	5	2	140	68	46.66	2	
S. Lahiri	4	7	1	279	89*	46.50	3	
H.K. Badani	8	8	3	232	85*	46.40	3	
A.A. Muzumdar	13	19	2	788	113	46.35	1	5
S. Suresh	5	10	2	366	123*	45.75	1	3
Tariq-ur-Rehman	10	15	3	546	70*	45.50	5	
N.R. Mongia	13	18	5	585	88	45.00	6	
A.S. Pathak	6	9	–	398	138	44.22	1	3
A. Lahiri	4	5	–	215	94	43.00	2	
Jai P. Yadav	8	11	1	430	106*	43.00	1	3
A.V. Kale	6	10	1	382	126	42.44	1	2
Kuldip Singh	2	4	1	127	81	42.33	1	
R.S. Gavaskar	7	12	3	379	80	42.11	2	
S.S. Bhave	6	10	–	415	156	41.50	2	
S.J. Kalyani	3	4	1	123	76	41.00	1	
A. Nand Kishore	5	8	–	328	136	41.00	1	
C.C. Williams	8	13	–	526	94	40.46	4	
P.S. Rawat	8	12	1	440	144	40.00	1	1
M. Manhas	7	11	3	319	115	39.87	1	2
R. Puri	5	7	–	278	143	39.71	1	
A.R. Kumble	13	16	1	592	113	39.46	1	3
Armajit S. Kaypee	10	14	2	473	84	39.41	5	
S.B. Somasunder	12	18	2	629	97	39.31	6	
A.K. Sharma	7	11	1	386	101	38.60	1	2
Rakesh Sharma	9	10	–	384	110	38.40	1	3
P.J. Bhatt	4	6	–	230	85	38.33	2	
V.B. Chandrasekhar	5	9	–	344	98	38.22	2	
J. Arun Kumar	11	17	1	604	111	37.75	3	1
K.N.A. Padmanabhan	6	9	2	264	96	37.71	2	
R.V. Sapru	10	11	2	447	165	37.25	1	2
S.S. More	3	5	1	149	82*	37.25	1	
R.A. Swarup	8	13	1	447	165	37.25	1	2
P. Sharma	5	9	1	289	79*	36.12	2	
W. Jaffer	7	11	–	395	133	35.90	1	2
M.S.K. Prasad	6	8	1	251	123*	35.85	1	1
D. Manohar	10	14	–	501	144	35.78	1	1

Batting

	M	Inns	NOs	Runs	HS	Av	100s	50s
V. Yadav	10	12	2	357	72	35.70	3	
H.A. Kinikar	4	6	1	177	71*	35.40	1	
Mohammad Kaif	4	6	–	211	100	35.16	1	1
M. Phadke	3	4	–	140	114	35.00	1	
N.R. Goel	5	6	–	209	143	34.83	1	
R. Choudhury	4	8	–	275	92	34.37	3	
Mohammad Saif	9	10	4	205	104*	34.16	1	1
W.V. Raman	6	7	–	238	67	34.00	3	
Sri Hari Rao	2	3	–	101	50	33.66	1	
H.J. Parsana	4	6	1	168	102	33.60	1	
Sarabjit Singh	5	9	1	268	62*	33.50	2	
M. Kadri	7	11	–	368	76	33.45	4	
S.V. Bahutule	7	9	3	200	71	33.33	1	
G.K. Khoda	7	11	–	364	111	33.09	1	2
A.W. Zaidi	9	6	1	155	74*	33.00	1	
D.S. Bundela	7	9	2	296	56	32.28	1	
F.R. Khalil	8	13	1	387	83	32.25	2	
P. Sutane	4	6	–	193	72	32.16	1	
G. Shome jnr	7	7	–	225	56	32.14	2	
A.S. Kudva	5	8	1	225	124*	32.14	1	
R. Gill	3	6	–	190	58	31.66	1	
B.N. Mehta	5	8	1	220	72	31.42	2	
V. Rathore	9	14	–	440	95	31.42	2	
A.C. Bedade	8	13	3	312	103*	31.20	1	2
R.R. Parida	8	13	–	404	99	31.07	4	
U.V. Gandhe	4	6	2	124	48*	31.00		
S. Arfi	7	10	1	278	101	30.88	1	
V. Pratap	12	15	1	432	59*	30.85	5	
K.K. Patel	8	11	1	308	79	30.80	2	
A. Verma	8	10	–	307	75	30.70	3	
Y. Gowda	8	13	2	335	95*	30.45	2	
S. Yadav	7	12	–	363	139	30.25	1	
P. Dharmani	11	17	1	483	97	30.18	3	
P.K. Amre	4	7	–	211	99	30.14	1	
A. Shetty	11	15	–	452	141	30.13	1	2
T.B. Arothe	8	13	–	388	123	29.84	1	2
B.B.C.C. Mohapatra	5	9	–	266	109	29.55	1	1
T.N. Varsania	3	6	–	177	93	29.50	1	
A. Malhotra	6	9	–	262	87	29.11	2	
A.S. Bhatti	3	5	1	116	33	29.00		
C.M. Jha	7	12	1	316	77	28.72	4	
S.S. Sugwekar	6	10	–	287	76	28.70	3	
S.B. Bangar	9	14	–	400	95	28.57	4	
R. Sutar	4	4	–	114	49	28.50		
S. Kumar	8	15	1	395	92	28.21	2	
R.V.C. Prasad	5	8	–	223	54	27.87	2	
V. Joshi	4	7	–	195	109	27.85	1	
M.V. Sridhar	11	14	1	360	108	27.69	1	1
Sanjay Sharma	3	5	1	110	56	27.50	1	
N. Haldipur	7	12	–	329	117	27.41	2	
U.S. Belsare	2	4	–	108	56	27.00	1	
A. Nadkarni	4	7	–	189	58	27.00	1	
P. Jayachandra	8	12	–	323	80	26.91	1	
R.R. Singh	6	5	1	107	51	26.75	1	
N. Chopra	7	9	2	186	84	26.57	1	
I.R. Siddiqui	5	7	3	106	48	26.50		
M.H. Parma	4	8	–	210	77	26.25	2	
S.B. Joshi	12	15	2	338	55	26.00	1	
S. Panda	3	6	2	101	39	25.25		
D. Sharma	4	5	1	101	44	25.25		
H.D. Patel	3	6	–	151	47	25.16		
P.K. Hedaoo	3	5	1	100	41	25.00		
P. Thakur	10	11	1	250	85	25.00	2	
J.D. Motivaras	4	7	–	172	99	24.57	1	
Dhanraj Singh	9	12	1	269	83	24.45	2	
A. Kapoor	4	5	–	122	54	24.40	1	
P.K. Krishnakumar	4	7	1	146	89	24.33	1	
R.R. Naik	5	10	–	240	133	24.00	1	1
S.S. Tanna	4	7	–	168	53	24.00	2	
V. Projapati	4	6	–	141	62	23.50	1	
S.K. Dutta	3	5	–	117	48	23.40		
R.F. Morris	10	16	1	349	90	23.26	2	
M.V. Sane	6	8	1	160	49	22.85		
M.S. Mudgal	12	12	–	274	65	22.83	2	
U. Chatterjee	9	9	1	182	56	22.75	1	
N.D. Modi	4	8	–	181	56	22.62	1	
Yuvraj Singh	11	14	4	226	54	22.60	1	
G. Banik	4	6	1	110	43	22.00		
S.K. Kulkarni	11	15	2	286	51	22.00	1	
G. Gopal	8	10	–	219	62	21.90	1	
J. Gokulkrishnan	5	10	3	153	38*	21.85		
S.S. Bhatta	3	6	–	131	40	21.83		

First-Class Averages (continued)

Batting

	M	Inns	NOs	Runs	HS	Av	100s	50s
R. Jaswant	4	7	1	130	44	21.66		
R. Lamba	4	7	–	141	38	21.57		
A.R. Kapoor	9	13	–	279	65	21.46	2	
N. Veerabrahman	4	7	–	150	78	21.42	1	
K.V. Sharma	3	5	–	107	47	21.40		
A.S. Kotechra	4	8	–	171	47	21.37		
V.R. Samant	5	9	2	147	46*	21.00		
A.J. Parmar	3	5	–	105	42	21.00		
V. Sharma	4	6	–	125	48	20.83		
D.S. Chakraborty	5	6	1	104	54*	20.80	1	
Shafiq Khan	10	14	–	291	61	20.78	1	
D.G. Mulherkar	6	8	1	145	42	20.71		
V.M. Jaisimha	3	6	–	122	100	20.33	1	
K. Sriram	4	5	–	101	44	20.20		
R.K. Chauhan	9	8	1	141	78*	20.14	1	
K.B.S. Naik	3	5	–	100	67	20.00	1	
D. Mongia	7	11	1	194	35	19.40		
P.P. Maitrey	5	9	1	155	51	19.37	1	
Sukhvinder Singh	3	6	–	116	33	19.33		
R. Nayyar	4	7	–	135	45	19.28		
Iqbal Khan	4	7	–	132	74	18.85	1	
V.G.N. Kumar	4	6	–	111	35	18.50		
S.M. Manoj	5	7	–	129	42	18.42		
D. Vinay Kumar	4	7	–	126	41	18.00		
S.B. Saikia	5	10	–	176	35	17.60		
V.K. Kolkambar	5	10	–	176	69	17.60	1	
P.L. Mhambrey	13	12	2	169	30	16.90		
Harvinder Singh	9	11	2	152	65*	16.88	1	
S. Shankar	5	8	1	118	60	16.85	1	
S.M. Kondhalkar	6	8	–	130	68	16.25	1	
Sandeep Sharma	5	8	1	111	33	15.85		
B. Vij	8	11	1	156	33	15.60		
N.A. David	7	9	1	122	59	15.25	1	
S. Parab	5	8	1	106	48	15.14		
Z.S. Zuffri	8	13	1	178	99	14.83	1	
V. Saxena	6	8	–	118	37	14.75		
B. Ramprakash	5	8	–	117	37	14.62		
Shakti Singh	4	7	–	102	36	14.57		
P.R. Mohapatra	5	8	–	105	26	13.12		
N.P. Singh	9	10	1	116	34*	12.88		
Venkatapathy Raju	14	15	2	160	30	12.30		

Played in one match: H.R. Jadhav 80* & 51; N. Ranjan 78 & 22
(Qualification: 100 runs, average 10.00)

Bowling

	Overs	Mds	Runs	Wks	Best	Av	10/m	5/inn
S.K. Satpathy	115.3	35	221	17	5/25	13.00	1	2
Harpreet Singh	65.3	16	177	13	6/38	13.61	1	
V. Arun Sharma	65	14	155	11	4/27	14.09		
A.R. Kumble	611.2	186	1384	85	7/33	16.28	3	9
T. Kumaran	76	15	218	13	5/51	16.76	2	
D.V. Sharma	79.1	19	204	12	5/70	17.00	1	
P.L. Mhambrey	380.3	93	929	54	7/42	17.20	1	3
Dhanraj Singh	147.5	44	327	19	4/34	17.21		
B. Ramprakash	256.3	65	487	28	5/113	17.39	1	
J. Gokulkrishnan	136	38	280	16	6/79	17.50	1	
N.M. Kulkarni	367.1	127	811	45	5/23	18.02	2	
A.R. Tandon	111.4	29	315	17	6/87	18.52	1	2
Shakti Singh	151.5	35	415	22	7/37	18.86	1	2
A. Verma	159.5	53	340	18	6/56	18.88	1	
S.C. Ganguly	98.5	25	247	13	6/87	19.00	1	
S.V. Bahutule	228.3	49	601	29	8/71	20.72	1	3
P. Jain	455	136	918	44	4/22	20.86		
M.S. Kulkarni	208.5	46	454	26	5/47	20.96	3	
U. Chatterjee	561.2	189	1070	51	7/59	20.98	1	5
Kanwaljit Singh	351.1	116	739	35	7/38	21.11	1	2
P.V. Gandhe	180.3	42	427	20	6/50	21.35	1	3
B. Bhushan	104	19	305	14	5/53	21.78	1	
M. Obaid Kamal	250.5	87	551	25	5/58	22.04	1	
D Manohar	93.2	23	289	13	4/48	22.23		
A. Nehra	90.5	16	270	12	4/45	22.50		
A. Das	84	16	248	11	4/67	22.54		
G. Dutta	131.1	32	363	16	6/70	22.68	2	
R. Sridhar	120	38	298	13	3/43	22.92		
M.V. Rao	171.1	33	531	23	6/46	23.08	2	
S.B. Joshi	484	127	1092	46	5/25	23.73	1	
M. Kartik	183.1	60	384	16	6/35	24.00	1	

Bowling

	Overs	Mds	Runs	Wks	Best	Av	10/m	5/inn
I.R. Siddiqui	204.4	39	577	24	7/49	24.04	1	2
B. Vij	254.3	56	690	28	5/67	24.64	1	
S.T. Banerjee	132.4	33	323	13	5/58	24.84	1	
R.F. Morris	197	41	548	22	5/35	24.90	1	2
M.V. Sane	198.4	42	525	21	6/58	25.00	1	2
Iqbal Khan	139.5	28	325	13	5/34	25.00	1	
S. Pandey	230.5	38	730	29	5/67	25.17	1	
C.T.K. Masood	97.1	17	254	10	5/78	25.40	1	
D. Vasu	260.1	92	484	19	5/26	25.47	1	
Sukhvinder Singh	137.2	41	282	11	4/133	25.63		
J. Srinath	250.1	43	799	31	4/92	25.77		
T.B. Arothe	236.2	45	652	25	6/53	26.08	1	2
A.W. Zaidi	272.2	53	866	33	7/99	26.24	3	
N.P. Singh	230.2	60	609	23	7/24	26.47	1	2
P. Thakur	467.3	123	1157	43	7/107	26.90	2	
S.S. Raul	164.3	47	353	13	3/13	27.15		
M. Kadri	100.5	26	299	11	4/34	27.18		
A. Kuruvilla	239.1	50	818	30	4/88	27.26		
V.B. Jain	277.1	69	796	29	6/55	27.44	1	
A.R. Kapoor	271.2	58	788	28	5/98	28.14	1	
D.J. Johnson	136.2	8	621	22	5/65	28.22	1	
S.S. Lahore	269	76	480	17	3/42	28.23		
Harvinder Singh	178.1	42	565	20	7/51	28.25	1	
Venkatapathy Raju	559.2	172	1205	42	7/51	28.69	1	
M. Venkataramana	209.1	41	574	20	4/70	28.70		
H. Ramkishen	182	35	435	15	5/21	29.00	1	
N. Madhukar	185.2	50	438	15	4/50	29.20		
Sandeep Sharma	103	22	293	10	3/35	29.30		
Robin Singh	255.4	63	651	22	6/70	29.59	2	
B.N. Mehta	176	41	533	18	5/110	29.61	2	
H.S. Sodhi	133.1	27	386	13	4/69	29.69		
K.V.P. Rao	427.4	91	993	33	5/33	30.09	2	
Harbhajan Singh	303	78	799	26	4/66	30.73		
K.R. Powar	216	54	589	19	4/33	31.00		
N.D. Hirwani	335.2	82	854	27	5/64	31.62	1	
S. Sriram	126.2	34	318	10	3/51	31.80		
R. Deb Burman	138	26	351	11	5/134	31.90	1	
D. Ganesh	254.4	51	740	23	5/74	32.17	1	
K.S. Parida	296.4	73	783	24	5/116	32.62	1	
A.B. Agarkar	107	19	392	12	4/38	32.66		
D.G. Mulherkar	184	35	492	15	4/9	32.80		
Mohammad Saif	231.3	64	631	19	3/34	33.21		
Venkatesh Prasad	216.3	57	567	17	3/25	33.35		
T.A. Gonsalves	115	22	369	11	5/126	33.54	1	
Syed Khan	321.2	89	784	23	5/99	34.08	1	
A.B. Kumar	348.4	75	866	25	5/185	34.64	1	
S. Khalid	121.3	21	349	10	4/46	34.90		
H.D. Patel	116.1	27	353	10	4/56	35.30		
A. Barik	116.4	28	365	10	2/12	36.50		
R.A. Swarup	320.4	70	658	18	4/90	36.55		
S.A. Roy	194.1	46	479	13	5/83	36.84	2	
H.J. Parsana	192.5	34	584	15	5/50	38.93	2	
S. Saxena	150	40	471	12	4/61	39.25		
Y. Bambhania	165.3	32	485	12	4/70	40.41		
K.N.A. Padmanabhan	210	56	492	12	3/71	41.00		
A.P. Katti	157	33	410	10	2/15	41.00		
Hemulal Yadav	126.2	16	421	10	4/78	42.10		
R.L. Sanghvi	298.1	46	901	21	5/96	42.90	1	
S.P. Singh	227	83	472	11	4/47	42.90		
G.K. Pandey	273.3	94	516	12	2/24	43.00		
N. Chopra	272.3	47	694	16	3/104	43.37		
R.K. Chauhan	347.4	83	828	18	4/48	46.00		
Z. Hussain	209.5	29	753	15	3/15	50.20		

(Qualification: 10 wickets)

Leading Fielders

41 – S.K. Kulkarni (ct 31 / st 10); 38 – V. Yadav (ct 30 / st 8); 30 – G. Gopal (ct 27 / st 3); 29 – P. Dharmani (ct 24 / st 5); 25 – S.S. Karim (ct 18 / st 7); 22 – K.K. Patel; 20 – M.S. Mudgal (ct 18 / st 2) and R. Paul (ct 19 / st 1); 19 – Yuvraj Singh (ct 16 / st 3); 18 – S.N. Somasekhar (ct 14 / st 4); 17 – Shafiq Khan; 15 – K.S. More (ct 14 / st 1), V.R. Samant (ct 13 / st 2) and A.A. Muzumdar; 14 – S.B. Somasunder, U. Chatterjee, S.M. Kondhalkar (ct 12 / st 2), N.R. Mongia (ct 13 / st 1), D. Manohar and S.V. Manjrekar; 13 – N.M. Kulkarni, A.A. Pagnis and J. Srinath; 12 – S.S. Bhave, R.S. Dravid, J.J. Martin (ct 11 / st 1) and Saradjit Singh (ct 10 / st 2); 11 – M. Azharuddin, Armajit S. Kaypee, M.S.K. Prasad (ct 10 / st 1) and D. Sharma (ct 10 / st 1); 10 – D. Gandhi, K.S.K. Iyer (ct 8 / st 2), A.R. Kumble, V.V.S. Laxman, Venkatesh Prasaf, V. Rathore and Tariq-ur-Rehman

Pakistan

No cricketers in the world do more travelling nor play more international cricket than the cricketers of Pakistan.

All-rounder Shahid Afridi scored at a blistering pace in all forms of cricket, but at present, the Pakistan selectors regard him solely as a one-day specialist.
(Stephen Laffer / Sportsline)

The Sahara Cup competition in Canada engaged Pakistan and India during the third week in September, and the five one-day internationals played in Toronto were followed a week later in Pakistan by three more one-day matches between the same two nations.

Five days after the completion of this series, Pakistan entertained South Africa in the first of three Test matches. This series was scheduled to finish on 28 October, and three days later, the quadrangular one-day tournament between Pakistan, Sri Lanka, South Africa and West Indies for the Jinnah Cup began in Lahore. Pakistan then entertained West Indies in a three-Test series before journeying to Sharjah to participate in the Champions' Trophy. In early January, Pakistan joined India and Bangladesh in the Silver Jubilee Independence Cup in Dhaka, and then they travelled to South Africa for a three-Test series, which was followed by two Tests and two one-day internationals in Zimbabwe. A return to South Africa would see them in a triangular one-day tournament with Sri Lanka and the host country.

Wills Challenge

Pakistan *v.* India

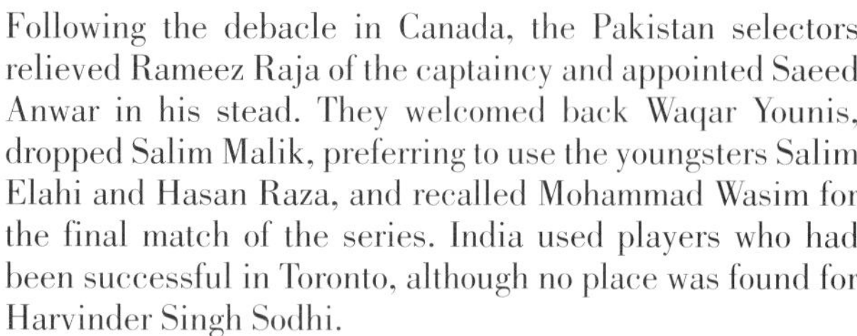

Following the debacle in Canada, the Pakistan selectors relieved Rameez Raja of the captaincy and appointed Saeed Anwar in his stead. They welcomed back Waqar Younis, dropped Salim Malik, preferring to use the youngsters Salim Elahi and Hasan Raza, and recalled Mohammad Wasim for the final match of the series. India used players who had been successful in Toronto, although no place was found for Harvinder Singh Sodhi.

Neither Saeed Anwar nor Sachin Tendulkar anticipated the variable bounce produced by the pitch at Hyderabad in the first match, and Tendulkar quickly regretted his decision to bat when he won the toss. Waqar Younis, his Glamorgan triumphs only days behind him, soon disposed of the Indian captain and of Ganguly, who had been so successful in the Sahara Cup. Robin Singh and Azharuddin tried to repair the damage, and Dravid and Jadeja appeared to have made the recovery totally effective, but they both fell to the aggressive Aqib Javed. Ably supported by Saqlain Mushtaq, Aqib brought about a dramatic collapse, and the last six wickets went down in 14 balls while four runs were scored.

Batting on a rapidly disintegrating pitch, Saeed Anwar and Shahid Afridi seemed completely uninhibited and went for their shots. They were particularly severe on the spinners Chauhan and Kulkarni, but the latter accounted for both openers with his intelligent left-arm leg-breaks. Ijaz Ahmed and Inzamam-ul-Haq batted responsibly in difficult circumstances, and Pakistan moved to a worthy and much needed victory with 5.3 overs to spare.

Winning the toss in Karachi, Saeed Anwar elected to bat first and although he fell to off-spinner Chauhan for 18, his partner, Shahid Afridi, was in electrifying form, racing to 72 off 56 balls. Ijaz Ahmed again batted responsibly, and Inzamam-ul-Haq gave further indication that he has matured and put the troubles of Toronto behind him. Moin Khan, too, acquitted himself creditably, but stone-throwing and crowd disturbance forced the Indians to leave the field and for Pakistan to be denied the last 16 balls of their innings from which they surely would have profited. They were on course to pass 300.

India faced a target of 266 at 5.6 runs an over, and Tendulkar and Ganguly gave them a merry start, being particularly severe on Waqar Younis. Kambli gave Ganguly fine support after Tendulkar had been caught behind, but Kambli and Azharuddin were run out, and Waqar returned to bowl Pakistan back into the game by dismissing Ganguly. Robin Singh and Saba Karim maintained India's challenge with a partnership worth 62, but Waqar struck again to leave the game delicately balanced. In the final over, Chauhan hit Saqlain Mushtaq for six to end Pakistan's hopes of snatching victory.

Once again Ganguly had played a decisive innings and had also bowled an economic spell when the batsmen were seeking quick runs. He was named Man of the Match, his sixth award in his last five one-day internationals. His four awards in succession in Toronto had established a world record.

With the series level at one game each, the final encounter, a day and night match in Lahore, took on an added lustre. Saeed Anwar asked India to bat when he won the toss, anticipating that the pitch would be at its most difficult early on. He was proved right, and Aqib Javed struck a vital blow when he accounted for Tendulkar, still searching for lost form. Ganguly did his best to push the score along, but he fell to Saqlain, and India were struggling at 77 for five. It was Jadeja who revived India's hopes with an innings that combined aggression with good sense. Karim and Chauhan again gave good support, but India failed to survive their full quota of overs, and although 216 was a better total than might have been expected earlier in the day, it never looked likely to be a winning score.

Saeed dropped himself down the order and promoted Ijaz Ahmed to open with Shahid Afridi, who once more gave his side an exhilarating start. He hit five fours and three sixes while making 47 off 23 balls. Ijaz Ahmed matched his partner stroke for stroke, and one over from Mohanty produced 24 runs. Shahid Afridi fell to Kulkarni, and Mohammad Wasim batted with a mature responsibility to give Ijaz the necessary support.

Ijaz Ahmed treated all the bowlers with contempt, hitting each of them for six as he led Pakistan to a storming victory with 23.4 overs to spare. Pakistan's 100 came off 11.1 overs, and Ijaz reached 50 off 36 balls. His hundred came 32 balls later, and his 139 occupied only 84 balls. His hitting was as clean as it was violent, and, in all, he claimed nine sixes. This was one of the truly great innings of limited-over international cricket. So Pakistan gained some revenge for the mauling that they had received in Toronto, but the brightest thing about the series was the spirit in which it was played, and, in general, the warm and appreciative reaction of the crowds to both teams. It was good for cricket and it was good to see the two nations being drawn closer together.

Match One – Pakistan v. India

28 September 1997 at Niaz Stadium, Hyderabad

India

Batsman	Dismissal	Runs
S.R. Tendulkar *	**b** Waqar Younis	**2**
S.C. Ganguly	**c** Hasan Raza, **b** Waqar Younis	**0**
R.R. Singh	**b** Saqlain Mushtaq	**20**
M. Azharuddin	**b** Shahid Afridi	**31**
R.S. Dravid	**b** Aqib Javed	**50**
A.D. Jadeja	**b** Aqib Javed	**41**
S.S. Karim †	**c** Ijaz Ahmed, **b** Saqlain	**0**
R.K. Chauhan	**c** Ijaz Ahmed, **b** Saqlain	**0**
A. Kuruvilla	**b** Aqib Javed	**0**
D.S. Mohanty	not out	**1**
N.M. Kulkarni	**b** Aqib Javed	**1**
	b **1**, lb **8**, w **13**, nb **2**	**24**
	49 overs	**170**

	O	M	R	W
Waqar Younis	7	1	21	**2**
Aqib Javed	8	1	29	**4**
Azhar Mahmood	9	–	35	**–**
Saqlain Mushtaq	9	3	13	**3**
Shahid Afridi	10	–	38	**1**
Ijaz Ahmed	6	–	25	**–**

Fall of Wickets
1–**2**, 2–**3**, 3–**61**, 4–**77**, 5–**166**, 6–**167**, 7–**167**, 8–**169**, 9–**169**

Pakistan

Batsman	Dismissal	Runs
Saeed Anwar *	lbw, **b** Kulkarni	**30**
Shahid Afridi	lbw, **b** Kulkarni	**45**
Ijaz Ahmed	**c** Tendulkar, **b** R.R. Singh	**22**
Salim Elahi	run out	**8**
Inzamam-ul-Haq	not out	**35**
Hasan Raza	**c** Tendulkar, **b** Kulkarni	**5**
Moin Khan †	not out	**12**
Saqlain Mushtaq		
Azhar Mahmood		
Waqar Younis		
Aqib Javed		
	b **2**, lb **6**, w **5**, nb **1**	**14**
	44.3 overs (for 5 wickets)	**171**

	O	M	R	W
Kuruvilla	8	1	23	**–**
Mohanty	4	–	23	**–**
Chauhan	10	2	40	**–**
Kulkarni	10	2	27	**3**
R.R. Singh	5	–	14	**1**
Ganguly	4	–	21	**–**
Tendulkar	3	1	11	**–**
Jadeja	0.3	–	4	**–**

Fall of Wickets
1–**70**, 2–**87**, 3–**106**, 4–**113**, 5–**138**

Umpires: Salim Badar & Said Shah *Man of the Match:* Aqib Javed

Pakistan won by 5 wickets

Match Two – Pakistan v. India

30 September 1997 at National Stadium, Karachi

Pakistan

Batsman	Dismissal	Runs
Saeed Anwar *	**c** and **b** Chauhan	**18**
Shahid Afridi	**c** Kuruvilla, **b** Kulkarni	**72**
Ijaz Ahmed	**c** Azharuddin, **b** Kulkarni	**31**
Inzamam-ul-Haq	not out	**74**
Salim Elahi	**c** Kulkarni, **b** Chauhan	**18**
Moin Khan †	not out	**31**
Hasan Raza		
Saqlain Mushtaq		
Azhar Mahmood		
Waqar Younis		
Aqib Javed		
	lb **7**, w **9**, nb **5**	**21**
	47.2 overs (for 4 wickets)	**265**

	O	M	R	W
Kuruvilla	7	2	50	**–**
Mohanty	3	–	25	**–**
Chauhan	10	–	48	**2**
Kulkarni	10	–	66	**2**
R.R. Singh	6	–	23	**–**
Ganguly	10	–	39	**–**
Tendulkar	1	–	7	**–**

Fall of Wickets
1–**55**, 2–**126**, 3–**148**, 5–**197**

India

Batsman	Dismissal	Runs
S.R. Tendulkar *	**c** Moin, **b** Azhar Mahmood	**21**
S.C. Ganguly	**c** Shahid Afridi, **b** Waqar	**89**
V.G. Kambli	run out	**53**
M. Azharuddin	run out	**6**
A.D. Jadeja	**c** Ijaz, **b** Shahid Afridi	**8**
R.R. Singh	not out	**31**
S.S. Karim †	**b** Waqar Younis	**26**
R.K. Chauhan	not out	**8**
A. Kuruvilla		
D.S. Mohanty		
N.M. Kulkarni		
	lb **7**, w **12**, nb **5**	**24**
	46.3 overs (for 6 wickets)	**266**

	O	M	R	W
Waqar Younis	9	–	36	**2**
Aqib Javed	10	–	73	**–**
Azhar Mahmood	9	–	56	**1**
Saqlain Mushtaq	9.3	1	46	**–**
Shahid Afridi	9	–	48	**1**

Fall of Wickets
1–**71**, 2–**169**, 3–**179**, 4–**185**, 5–**195**, 6–**257**

Umpires: Salim Badar & Mian Aslam *Man of the Match:* S.C. Ganguly

India won by 4 wickets

Match Three – Pakistan v. India

2 October 1997 at Gaddafi Stadium, Lahore

India

Batsman	Dismissal	Runs
S.R. Tendulkar*	c Inzamam, b Aqib Javed	7
S.C. Ganguly	c Mohammad Hussain, b Saqlain	26
R.R. Singh	b Azhar Mahmood	17
M. Azharuddin	c Moin, b Azhar Mahmood	6
V.G. Kambli	c Moin, b Azhar Mahmood	6
A.D. Jadeja	c Inzamam-ul-Haq, b Waqar	76
S.S. Karim †	b Mohammad Hussain	20
R.K. Chauhan	c Mohammad Hussain, b Waqar	32
A. Kuruvilla	run out	6
N.M. Kulkarni	c sub, b Aqib Javed	2
D.S. Mohanty	not out	0
	lb 5, w 11, nb 2	18
	(49.2 overs)	216

Bowler	O	M	R	W
Waqar Younis	8.3	–	33	2
Aqib Javed	7	–	35	2
Azhar Mahmood	9	–	34	3
Saqlain Mushtaq	10	–	46	1
Shahid Afridi	5	–	26	–
Mohammad Hussain	10	–	37	1

Fall of Wickets
1–12, 2–53, 3–56, 4–66, 5–77, 6–130, 7–206, 8–206, 9–215

Pakistan

Batsman	Dismissal	Runs
Ijaz Ahmed	not out	139
Shahid Afridi	c Tendulkar, b Kulkarni	47
Mohammad Wasim	not out	27
Inzamam-ul-Haq		
Saeed Anwar *		
Moin Khan †		
Saqlain Mushtaq		
Mohammad Hussain		
Azhar Mahmood		
Waqar Younis		
Aqib Javed		
	lb 2, w 4	6
	26.2 overs (for one wicket)	219

Bowler	O	M	R	W
Kuruvilla	6	1	42	–
Mohanty	3	–	38	–
Chauhan	5	–	30	–
Kulkarni	8	–	57	1
R.R. Singh	2	–	22	–
Ganguly	2.2	–	28	–

Fall of Wickets
1–80

Umpires: Javed Akhtar & Mohammad Nazir jnr *Man of the Match:* Ijaz Ahmed

Pakistan won by 9 wickets

South African Tour

The meetings between Pakistan and South Africa brought together the two sides who most had the right to challenge Australia for world supremacy. The two teams offered sharp contrasts, with South Africa, one of the most stable of cricketing nations, rarely disturbing their nucleus of thirteen or fourteen players, while Pakistan seemed ever mobile, constantly introducing, and discarding, young cricketers of precocious talent. The Test series in Pakistan in October, 1997, gave further evidence of these approaches to selection.

1, 2 and 3 October 1997

at National Stadium, Karachi

South Africans 305 for 7 dec. (S.M. Pollock 74 not out, J.H. Kallis 52, Ali Hussain Rizvi 5 for 89) and 254 for 8 dec. (G. Kirsten 61, Ali Hussain Rizvi 6 for 57)
Pakistan Cricket Board Combined XI 132 (Ali Naqvi 61, P.L. Symcox 4 for 24) and 237 for 4 (Ali Naqvi 113, Rana Qayyum-ul-Hasan 83 not out)
Match drawn

The South African tourists had one three-day warm-up match before the first Test and could have only been moderately satisfied with the outcome. The two outstanding performances were both from young Pakistani players. Ali Navqi, who had been in England with the Pakistan 'A' side and who had played club cricket for Southend in the second division of the Essex League, batted splendidly in both innings of what was his first first-class match in Pakistan. The 23-year old off-break bowler Ali Hussain Rizvi returned the best bowling figures of his career for innings and match. Ali Naqvi was to win a place in the Pakistan side for the first Test and to make a sensational debut.

First Test Match

Pakistan *v.* South Africa

While South Africa fielded a side of experienced Test cricketers, Pakistan awarded first Test caps to three young cricketers for the opening encounter of the series. Ali Naqvi's success against the tourists in Karachi earned him the place as Saeed Anwar's opening partner, while Mohammad Ramzan, a 27-year old right-handed batsman and medium-pace bowler from Faisalabad, who had been under scrutiny by the selectors for some time, came in at number three. All-rounder Azhar Mahmood from Rawalpindi had already shown impressive maturity in limited-over international cricket, and he was given his Test baptism in his home town. In the continued absence of Wasim Akram, Saeed Anwar again led Pakistan, who welcomed back leg-spinner Mushtaq Ahmed.

Saeed won the toss, and Pakistan batted with 20-year old Ali Naqvi as Saeed's opening partner, and it was to be a

A century on his Test debut for Ali Naqvi, 115 v. *South Africa in Rawalpindi.*
(Dave Pinegar / ASP)

memorable occasion for the debutant. While experienced cricketers like Saeed Anwar, Ijaz Ahmed and Inzamam-ul-Haq fell to irresponsible shots, Ali Naqvi batted with remarkable assurance and maturity. Particularly strong on the off side, he stood firm as his colleagues wilted. He and fellow debutant Mohammad Ramzan added 69 in 114 minutes for the second wicket, but, thereafter, he was left to fight a lone battle and he enjoyed an intriguing duel with off-spinner Pat Symcox, who bowled unchanged for 22 overs in sapping heat. Symcox might have dismissed Ali Naqvi when, on 96, the batsman went for a big hit and offered a return catch which should have been taken. Reprieved, Ali Naqvi hoisted Shaun Pollock over mid-wicket for the twelfth boundary of his innings to reach his century on his Test debut. He was the fifth Pakistani batsman to achieve this feat.

He was out when he tried to hit Allan Donald's fifth delivery with the second new ball over extra cover, only to see Gary Kirsten hold a fine catch. Ali Naqvi had batted splendidly and deserved all the praise that was heaped upon him. He began confidently, hitting 25 in as many minutes, and quickly adapted his batting to the needs of the moment. He was at the crease for 352 minutes, faced 270 balls and hit 14 fours. Bad light ended play some quarter of an hour early with Pakistan on 216 for six.

Overnight rain delayed the start of the second day by three hours as there were no adequate arrangements to cover the bowler's run-ups and the square itself. When play did begin Pakistan quickly lost two wickets. Subjected to a barrage of bouncers, Moin Khan was leg before to a ball of full length, and Saqlain Mushtaq was out fifth ball in the same manner. At 231 for eight, Pakistan were in crisis, although South Africa lost the services of Brett Schultz with a shoulder injury sustained while fielding. Debutant Azhar Mahmood was now joined by Waqar Younis, who immediately went onto the attack. The fast bowler hit two sixes and five fours in reaching the highest score of his Test career and helping to add 74 in 106 minutes for the ninth wicket. He was trapped leg before by an in-swinging yorker from Pollock, but Pakistan's resistance continued, and, by the close, the score was 345 for nine, with Azhar Mahmood unbeaten on 72, and Mushtaq Ahmed on six.

The third day witnessed the establishment of a world record, the equalling of a world record and a Royal visit. Azhar Mahmood emulated his colleague Ali Naqvi in scoring a century on his Test debut. It was the first time that two players had scored centuries in the same innings on their Test debuts, and it was the first first-class hundred of Azhar's career. He became the 27th batsman to make his first first-class century in a Test, but only the sixth to hit his maiden first-class century on his Test debut. He had hit 92 for Pakistan 'A' on the tour of England, and a century had escaped him in his matches for Islamabad.

He was given magnificent support by Mushtaq Ahmed, and, in three minutes over three hours, the pair added 151, equalling the last wicket record for Test cricket established by Hastings and Collinge for New Zealand against Pakistan in 1972–73. Mushtaq was bowled on the stroke of lunch after reaching his highest score in Test cricket, but he had failed by one run to register the best score by a Pakistan number eleven. Once Azhar had reached his century, Mushtaq opened his shoulders and hit Symcox for two sixes and a four in one over. In all, he hit four sixes and four fours in an innings that occupied 107 balls.

Azhar Mahmood reached his century when he steered a ball from McMillan to third man for two, and his innings was a model of calm and composure. He faced pace and spin with equal assurance and did not offer a chance during his 350 minutes at the wicket. He faced 287 balls and hit a six and eleven fours. His innings turned the match in favour of Pakistan, for the last two wickets realised 225 runs.

Her Majesty Queen Elizabeth II, the Duke of Edinburgh and the President of Pakistan, Farooq Ahmed Leghari, were introduced to the teams at the tea interval and watched the final session of play. Pakistan relied heavily on spin, and Saqlain Mushtaq captured the wicket of Bacher, but South Africa ended the day on 139 for one, Kirsten 62, Kallis 20, and a draw looked inevitable.

When Kirsten and Kallis took the score to 205 without further loss at lunch on the fourth day the draw became a certainty. Both batsmen were out in the early afternoon, falling in successive overs by Saqlain Mushtaq, who bowled quite splendidly in a mammoth spell. Mushtaq Ahmed also bowled well, without success, but the hero of the day was Gary Kirsten, who was masterly on a pitch that

Ten wickets for Pakistan in the first Test against West Indies and a decisive factor in his side's domination of the series – leg-spinner Mushtaq Ahmed.
(Nigel French / ASP)

was giving assistance to the spinners. He batted for 425 minutes, faced 342 balls, hit seven fours and took South Africa to a point where they were no longer in danger of defeat. He was out when a ball from Saqlain turned sharply, lifted and took the edge of his bat to have him caught at slip.

Azhar Mahmood claimed his first Test wicket when he trapped Cronje leg before, and South Africa ended the day at 359 for six. Saqlain had claimed his second five-wicket haul in Test cricket, and he deserved every success that came his way.

Overnight batsmen Richardson and Pollock were not separated until their stand was worth 106, and although the last four wickets fell quickly, three of them to Mushtaq Ahmed, South Africa came to within 53 of the Pakistan total. Briefly, there were hints of a sensational result as Pakistan began their second innings disastrously. By the 28th over, they were 80 for five, and it needed another fine innings from Azhar Mahmood to restore calm. He and Inzamam-ul-Haq put on 68 for the sixth wicket.

The last day was marred by an altercation between off-spinner Symcox and umpire Javed Akhtar. Symcox reacted angrily when the umpire rejected an appeal for a bat and pad catch by McMillan at silly point that would have got rid of Mohammad Wasim. Referee Madugalle imposed a heavy fine on Symcox, who lost half his match fee for two incidents of dissent.

On a brighter note, Azhar Mahmood, 178 runs in the match without being dismissed and two wickets, was named Man of the Match on his debut.

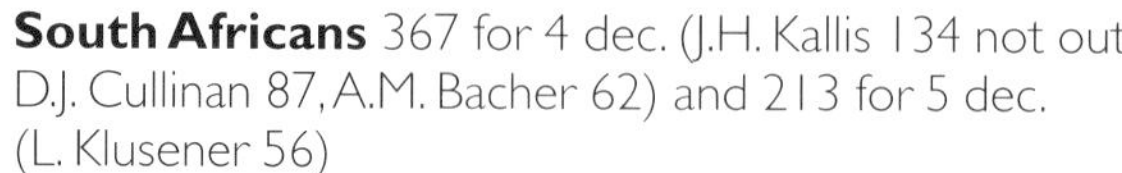

12, 13 and 14 October 1997
at Arbab Niaz Stadium, Peshawar
South Africans 367 for 4 dec. (J.H. Kallis 134 not out, D.J. Cullinan 87, A.M. Bacher 62) and 213 for 5 dec. (L. Klusener 56)
Allied Bank 275 for 3 dec. (Aamir Sohail 128, Mansoor Akhtar 117 not out) and 125 (P.R. Adams 4 for 19)
South Africans won by 180 runs

The South Africans had an encouraging victory between the first and second Test matches, when Adams and Klusener bowled them to victory on the last day, after batsmen had dominated. Bacher and Hudson had begun the match with a partnership of 78, and Kallis, who scored a sparkling century, shared a third wicket stand of 168 with Cullinan. The home side lost two wickets for 38 before Aamir Sohail and Mansoor Akhtar added 185.

Second Test Match

Pakistan *v.* South Africa

Brett Schultz had returned to South Africa for treatment on a ruptured shoulder muscle, and, on the eve of the second Test, Donald, Kallis and Richardson were all deemed unfit to play. In consequence, Richardson missed his first Test match since South Africa's return to international cricket in 1992. Klusener, Rhodes, Adams and Boucher came in as replacements. Wicket-keeper Mark Boucher from Border, six weeks short of his twenty-first birthday, was making his Test debut.

Pakistan made two changes from the side that drew the first Test. Ali Hussain Rizvi, who had bowled so well for the Combined XI in the first match of the South Africans' tour, won his first Test cap at the expense of Mohammad Ramzan, while Wasim Akram was declared fully fit again after his five-month lay-off. He replaced Waqar Younis, who was said to be not fully fit and in need of a rest. It came as something of a surprise then to see Waqar appear as a substitute fielder.

No play was possible on the first day, and a start could not be made until an hour after lunch on the second day. There were damp patches on the square, and the outfield was soggy. It was apparent that the ground staff had neither the equipment nor the knowledge that was necessary to prepare the ground as quickly as it should have been. Cronje won the toss, and South Africa batted first against an attack dominated by spin, a type of bowling against which the South Africans were judged to be vulnerable. It transpired that the pitch was a slow turner, and the batsmen had ample time in which to adjust their shots.

Kirsten and Bacher began comfortably, and the opening stand realised 135 in 159 minutes. McMillan went cheaply, caught behind cutting at Mushtaq Ahmed, and South Africa closed on 154 for two.

The first session of the third day brought 131 runs and four wickets. Cullinan was out without adding to his overnight score, and Bacher's purposeful innings came to an end when he was cruelly adjudged caught behind just four runs short of what would have been a maiden Test century. Cronje took the attack to the Pakistan bowlers, hitting three sixes and three fours before miscuing a lofted drive. Rhodes once again failed to do himself justice, but, in the afternoon session, Pollock and Klusener gave a batting display of considerable panache, adding 96 for the seventh wicket in under 73 minutes. Klusener made 58 off 54 balls with a six and nine fours before falling to a good delivery from Azhar Mahmood. Boucher went cheaply, and Symcox and Pollock then became Ali Hussain Rizvi's first victims in Test cricket. Both were taken in the slips. Pollock was last out, having faced 130 balls and hit a six and six fours in his 173-minute innings.

Ali Naqvi began in tearaway fashion, and his first seven scoring shots were boundaries. Saeed Anwar lost concentration and was bowled just before the close. That marked the end of the match. There was no play possible on the last two days.

Third Test Match

Pakistan *v.* South Africa

Because of the farce at Sheikhupura, a farce which threatened the future of Sheikhupura as a Test venue, the third match of the series took on an added significance as the game that would decide the rubber. South Africa welcomed back their walking wounded with the exception of Kallis so that Klusener and Adams were the only changes from the side that took the field in the first Test. Schultz, of course, had returned to South Africa. For Pakistan, Waqar Younis returned in place of Ali Hussain Rizvi, and Aamir Sohail was recalled at the expense of Mohammad Wasim. This was a surprise, as although he had scored a century for Allied Bank against the tourists, Aamir had expressed the view that he no longer wished to play for Pakistan. It appeared that he had now made his peace with the Board and the selectors. The same could not be said of Rameez Raja, who had refused to captain Allied Bank against the South Africans and, indignant at the way he had been treated by the selectors, indicated that he no longer had a desire to represent his country. Pakistan cricket has been consistently bedevilled by the fact that the national side rarely seems to consist of the best eleven players available.

Cronje won the toss, and South Africa batted, but the track was lively, and, at lunch, the visitors were in dire trouble at 99 for seven. Aamir Sohail injured a finger in the opening minutes of the match, and Mohammad Wasim came on as substitute. By the end of Wasim Akram's fourth over, Mohammad had held two stunning catches at third slip to get rid of Bacher and McMillan, and when Waqar Younis accounted for Cullinan and Cronje with in-swinging yorkers, South Africa were 30 for four. The introduction of Mushtaq Ahmed, the leg-spinner, brought three more quick wickets, and South Africa were in disarray.

In the post-lunch period, they were saved from humiliation by the determination of Gary Kirsten and by the bold aggression of Pat Symcox, a veteran with a Test career still in its infancy. The pair established a new eighth wicket Test record for any nation against Pakistan. They added 124 runs in as many minutes. Symcox's contribution was 81 off 94 balls, with two sixes and ten fours. It was his highest Test score, and it could not have come at a better time. He finally fell to Wasim Akram, who also accounted for Donald. Azhar Mahmood trapped Adams leg before, but by then Kirsten had completed a splendidly courageous hundred. In all, he batted for two minutes under five hours, faced 208 deliveries and hit 15 fours. He became the fifth South African to carry his bat through a Test innings, and never had such an innings been more welcome.

Ali Naqvi and Saeed Anwar were both out quickly, and Pakistan closed on 41 for two. South Africa had clawed their way back from the abyss. Ijaz Ahmed added only one to his overnight score on the second morning before falling to Adams, and Azhar Mahmood flattered to deceive. He hit a six and two fours and was then beaten by the pace of Klusener, who also accounted for Wasim Akram. Pakistan's

Wasim Akram led Pakistan to total triumph over West Indies and took 17 wickets in the three Tests, but only acrimony followed. He resigned the capitancy and was originally omitted from the party chosen to tour South Africa.
(Nigel French / ASP)

troubles were echoing those that South Africa had endured, but now they found their salvation in Inzamam-ul-Haq and Moin Khan. In the afternoon session, Cronje used seven bowlers in short spells in an effort to separate them, but they were resolute and aggressive. They put on 144 and were not separated until Inzamam, who batted quite magnificently for 225 minutes, tried to turn Cronje to leg and edged to slip. He had hit a six and 15 fours. The South African captain also bowled Moin, whose 80 came off 123 balls and included two sixes and 12 fours, but Pakistan had the luxury of Aamir Sohail at number eight, and he and Waqar added 58 for the ninth wicket at more than a run a minute. Pakistan led by 69 on the first innings, and they captured the wickets of both openers before the close of play, which came with South Africa at 21 for two, defeat looming.

By the end of the third day, defeat for South Africa seemed a certainty. Symcox had come in as night-watchman and gave another valiant, positive display. This time he batted two hours for his second fifty of the match and hit a six and seven fours. He was out when he misjudged Saqlain's turn and was leg before, but he was one of the very few South African batsmen to play the Pakistani spinners with any confidence. Waqar, too, posed many problems and, sensing victory, he lifted his pace and dismissed Cronje and Richardson with successive deliveries. Klusener hit two sixes and three fours as he made 38 off 36 balls, but he was out to the last ball before tea, and the South African innings ended early in the final session.

The umpires told Cronje that they would not be resuming because the light was bad, but they relented when the South African captain said that he would bowl his spinners. Even so, to the annoyance of the tourists, they called the game off after three overs. The South Africans believed that their only hope of victory was to capture two or three quick wickets on the third evening, and the early close to the day was not their only reason for anger. They had begun the match with a protest that the Pakistan side had been allowed some practice on the pitch on the day before the game was due to start. The matter was referred to the ICC Headquarters in England.

So Pakistan began the fourth day with their score at four without loss, needing just another 142 runs to complete the win, which would give them the series. The pitch was wearing, and Saeed was quoted as saying that he would not have relished chasing a target above two hundred, but the task seemed easy enough. Initially, there was no hint of trouble as Ali Naqvi and Aamir Sohail took 19 off the first 23 deliveries sent down by Pollock and Donald. Then Aamir mistimed a pull and Bacher, diving in front of gully, took a good catch. In the next over, Pollock's third of the day, Saeed Anwar was caught behind and Ijaz Ahmed leg before to successive deliveries. Inzamam survived the hat-trick, but he was taken at slip in Pollock's next over, which also saw the demise of Ali Naqvi. In seven balls, Pollock had broken the back of the Pakistan batting and had turned the match on its head.

First Test Match – Pakistan v. South Africa

6, 7, 8, 9 and 10 October 1997 at Rawalpindi Cricket Stadium, Rawalpindi

Pakistan

	First Innings		Second Innings	
Saeed Anwar*	c Richardson, b Donald	16	c sub (Rhodes), b Donald	4
Ali Navqi	c Kirsten, b Donald	115	c Richardson, b Kallis	19
Mohammad Ramzan	lbw, b Pollock	29	c Cronje, b Kallis	7
Ijaz Ahmed	b Symcox	11	b Symcox	16
Inzamam-ul-Haq	c Richardson, b Schultz	8	c Symcox, b Cronje	56
Mohammad Wasim	c Kirsten, b Symcox	11	c Pollock, b Symcox	10
Moin Khan †	lbw, b Donald	12	(8) not out	6
Azhar Mahmood	not out	128	(7) not out	50
Saqlain Mushtaq	lbw, b Pollock	0		
Waqar Younis	lbw, b Pollock	45		
Mushtaq Ahmed	b Cronje	59		
	b 2, lb 7, nb 13	22	b 2, lb 2, nb 10	14
		456	for 6 wickets	182

	O	M	R	W	O	M	R	W
Donald	33	3	108	3	11	4	25	1
Schultz	15	4	58	1				
Pollock	37	13	74	3	8	1	22	–
McMillan	17	5	36	–	8	1	24	–
Symcox	46	11	130	2	16	2	56	2
Kallis	7	3	15	–	7.4	1	21	2
Cronje	7.5	–	26	1	6	1	28	1
Cullinan					1	–	2	–

Fall of Wickets
1–**45**, 2–**114**, 3–**135**, 4–**152**, 5–**196**, 6–**206**, 7–**230**, 8–**231**, 9–**305**
1–**5**, 2–**33**, 3–**42**, 4–**66**, 5–**80**, 6–**148**

South Africa

	First Innings	
G. Kirsten	c Ijaz Ahmed, b Saqlain Mushtaq	98
A.M. Bacher	c Mohammad Ramzan, b Saqlain	50
J.H. Kallis	lbw, b Saqlain Mushtaq	61
D.J. Cullinan	lbw, b Saqlain Mushtaq	16
W.J. Cronje *	c Ijaz Ahmed, b Azhar Mahmood	24
B.M. McMillan	c Ijaz Ahmed, b Saqlain Mushtaq	7
S.M. Pollock	c Mohammad Wasim, b Azhar	48
D.J. Richardson †	not out	45
P.L. Symcox	st Mohammad Wasim, b Mushtaq	5
A.A. Donald	c Saeed Anwar, b Mushtaq Ahmed	0
B.N. Schultz	lbw, b Mushtaq Ahmed	1
	b 20, lb 9, w 4, nb 15	48
		403

	O	M	R	W
Waqar Younis	20	8	45	–
Azhar Mahmood	27	1	74	2
Mushtaq Ahmed	58.5	17	126	3
Saqlain Mushtaq	62	13	129	5

Fall of Wickets
1–**107**, 2–**221**, 3–**228**, 4–**249**, 5–**278**, 6–**282**, 7–**388**, 8–**393**, 9–**399**

Umpires: Javed Akhtar & S.Venkataraghavan

Match drawn

Second Test Match – Pakistan *v.* South Africa

17, 18, 19, 20 and 21 October 1997 at Municipal Stadium, Sheikhupura

South Africa

	First Innings	
G. Kirsten	**b** Wasim Akram	**56**
A.M. Bacher	**c** Moin Khan, **b** Mushtaq	**96**
B.M. McMillan	**c** Moin Khan, **b** Mushtaq	**7**
D.J. Cullinan	**c** Mohammad Wasim, **b** Saqlain	**1**
W.J. Cronje *	**c** sub (Waqar), **b** Mushtaq	**50**
J.N. Rhodes	**b** Mushtaq Ahmed	**11**
S.M. Pollock	**c** Ali Naqvi, **b** Ali Hussain Rizvi	**82**
L. Klusener	lbw, **b** Azhar Mahmood	**58**
M.V. Boucher †	**b** Azhar Mahmood	**6**
P.L. Symcox	**c** Mohammad Wasim, **b** Ali H. Rizvi	**17**
P.R. Adams	not out	**3**
	b **7**, lb **3**, nb **5**	**15**
		402

	O	M	R	W
Wasim Akram	13	3	26	**1**
Azhar Mahmood	14	3	52	**2**
Mushtaq Ahmed	38	12	122	**4**
Saqlain Mushtaq	32	7	120	**1**
Ali Hussain Rizvi	18.3	1	72	**2**

Fall of Wickets
1–**135**, 2–**152**, 3–**155**, 4–**179**, 5–**215**, 6–**252**, 7–**348**, 8–**356**, 9–**397**

Pakistan

	First Innings	
Ali Naqvi	not out	**30**
Saeed Anwar *	**b** Symcox	**17**
Saqlain Mushtaq	not out	**0**
Ijaz Ahmed		
Inzamam-ul-Haq		
Mohammad Wasim		
Moin Khan †		
Wasim Akram		
Azhar Mahmood		
Mushtaq Ahmed		
Ali Hussain Rizvi		
	b **4**, nb **2**	**6**
	for one wicket	**53**

	O	M	R	W
Pollock	7	1	35	–
Klusener	6	1	14	–
Adams	2	2	0	–
Symcox	2	2	0	**1**

Fall of Wickets
1–**53**

Umpires: K.T. Francis & Mohammad Nazir jnr

Match drawn

Third Test Match – Pakistan *v.* South Africa

24, 25, 26 and 27 October 1997 at Iqbal Stadium, Faisalabad

South Africa

	First Innings		Second Innings	
A.M. Bacher	**c** sub (Mohammad Wasim), **b** Wasim Akram	**1**	lbw, **b** Mushtaq Ahmed	**14**
G. Kirsten	not out	**100**	**c** Mushtaq Ahmed, **b** Wasim	**4**
B.M. McMillan	**c** sub (Mohammad Wasim), **b** Wasim Akram	**2**	**c** Moin, **b** Mushtaq Ahmed	**21**
D.J. Cullinan	lbw, **b** Waqar Younis	**0**	(5) lbw, **b** Mushtaq Ahmed	**15**
W.J. Cronje*	lbw, **b** Waqar	**9**	(6) **c** Azhar, **b** Waqar Younis	**21**
S.M. Pollock	**c** Aamir, **b** Mushtaq Ahmed	**5**	(7) not out	**21**
D.J. Richardson	**c** Saqlain, **b** Mushtaq Ahmed	**8**	(8) lbw, **b** Waqar Younis	**0**
L. Klusener	**c** Ijaz, **b** Mushtaq Ahmed	**18**	(9) lbw, **b** Saqlain Mushtaq	**38**
P.L. Symcox	**b** Wasim Akram	**81**	(4) lbw, **b** Saqlain Mushtaq	**55**
A.A. Donald	**c** Mushtaq Ahmed, **b** Wasim	**2**	**b** Saqlain Mushtaq	**8**
P.R. Adams	lbw, **b** Azhar Mahmood	**1**	**c** and **b** Mushtaq Ahmed	**0**
	b **4**, lb **3**, nb **5**	**12**	b **3**, lb **13**, nb **1**	**17**
		239		**214**

	O	M	R	W	O	M	R	W
Wasim Akram	16	6	42	**4**	11	–	46	**1**
Waqar Younis	10	1	36	**2**	14	2	43	**2**
Mushtaq Ahmed	22	3	81	**3**	22	5	57	**4**
Azhar Mahmood	10.4	2	36	**1**	7	2	16	–
Saqlain Mushtaq	10	2	37	–	15	6	36	**3**

Fall of Wickets
1–**2**, 2–**11**, 3–**12**, 4–**30**, 5–**40**, 6–**64**, 7–**98**, 8–**222**, 9–**230**
1–**16**, 2–**21**, 3–**63**, 4–**97**, 5–**140**, 6–**140**, 7–**140**, 8–**187**, 9–**201**

Pakistan

	First Innings		Second Innings	
Ali Naqvi	**b** Donald	**11**	**c** Cullinan, **b** Pollock	**6**
Saeed Anwar *	lbw, **b** Pollock	**3**	(3) **c** Richardson, **b** Pollock	**0**
Ijaz Ahmed	lbw, **b** Adams	**16**	(4) lbw, **b** Pollock	**0**
Inzamam-ul-Haq	**c** McMillan, **b** Cronje	**96**	(5) **c** McMillan, **b** Pollock	**5**
Azhar Mahmood	**b** Klusener	**19**	(6) **c** Richardson, **b** Klusener	**6**
Wasim Akram	**c** Richardson, **b** Klusener	**2**	(8) **c** Kirsten, **b** Symcox	**9**
Moin Khan †	**b** Cronje	**80**	**c** Donald, **b** Symcox	**32**
Aamir Sohail	**c** Donald, **b** Pollock	**38**	(2) **c** Bacher, **b** Donald	**14**
Saqlain Mushtaq	**c** Bacher, **b** Adams	**6**	**c** Bacher, **b** Symcox	**0**
Waqar Younis	**c** Cronje, **b** Donald	**34**	**b** Pollock	**0**
Mushtaq Ahmed	not out	**0**	not out	**4**
	lb **1**, w **1**, nb **1**	**3**	b **4**, lb **6**, w **1**, nb **5**	**16**
		308		**92**

	O	M	R	W	O	M	R	W
Donald	17.4	1	79	**2**	6	1	14	**1**
Pollock	20	5	64	**2**	11	1	37	**5**
Adams	23	5	69	**2**	5	2	10	–
Symcox	9	2	39	–	9.3	5	8	**3**
Klusener	8	1	30	**2**	6	1	13	**1**
McMillan	7	1	20	–				
Cronje	5	3	6	**2**				

Fall of Wickets
1–**10**, 2–**18**, 3–**42**, 4–**74**, 5–**80**, 6–**224**, 7–**229**, 8–**246**, 9–**304**
1–**23**, 2–**24**, 3–**24**, 4–**29**, 5–**31**, 6–**68**, 7–**85**, 8–**87**, 9–**88**

Umpires: R.S. Dunne & Mian Aslam

South Africa won by 53 runs

Test Match Averages – Pakistan v. South Africa

Pakistan Batting

	M	Inns	NOs	Runs	HS	Av	100s	50s
Azhar Mahmood	3	4	2	203	128*	101.50	1	1
Mushtaq Ahmed	3	3	2	63	59	63.00	1	
Ali Naqvi	3	5	1	181	115	45.25	1	
Moin Khan	3	4	1	130	80	43.33	1	
Inzamam-ul-Haq	3	4	–	165	96	41.25	2	
Waqar Younis	2	3	–	79	45	26.33		
Ijaz Ahmed	3	4	–	43	16	10.75		
Mohammad Wasim	2	2	–	21	11	10.50		
Saeed Anwar	3	5	–	40	17	8.00		
Wasim Akram	2	2	–	11	9	5.50		
Saqlain Mushtaq	3	4	–	6	6	2.00		

Played in one Test: Mohammad Ramzan 29 & 7; Ali Hussain Rizvi did not bat; Aamir Sohail 38 & 14

South Africa Batting

	M	Inns	NOs	Runs	HS	Av	100s	50s
G. Kirsten	3	4	1	258	100*	86.00	1	2
S.M. Pollock	3	4	1	156	82	52.00		1
A.M. Bacher	3	4	–	161	96	40.25	2	
P.L. Symcox	3	4	–	158	81	39.50		2
L. Klusener	2	3	–	114	58	38.00		1
D.J. Richardson	2	3	1	53	45*	26.50		
W.J. Cronje	3	4	–	104	50	26.00		1
B.M. McMillan	3	4	–	37	21	9.25		
D.J. Cullinan	3	4	–	32	16	8.00		
A.A. Donald	2	3	–	10	8	3.33		
P.R. Adams	2	3	1	4	3*	2.00		

Played in one Test: J.H. Kallis 61; B.N. Schultz 1; J.N. Rhodes 11; M.V. Boucher 6

Pakistan Bowling

	Overs	Mds	Runs	Wks	Av	Best	5/inn
Wasim Akram	40	9	114	6	19.00	4/42	
Mushtaq Ahmed	140.5	37	386	14	27.57	4/57	
Waqar Younis	44	10	124	4	31.00	2/36	
Azhar Mahmood	58.4	8	178	5	35.60	2/52	
Saqlain Mushtaq	119	28	322	9	35.77	5/129	1

Bowled in one innings: Ali Hussain Rizvi 18.3–1–72–2

South Africa Bowling

	Overs	Mds	Runs	Wks	Av	Best	5/inn
W.J. Cronje	18.5	9	60	4	15.00	2/6	
J.H. Kallis	14.4	4	36	2	18.00	2/21	
L. Klusener	20	3	57	3	19.00	2/30	
S.M. Pollock	83	21	232	10	23.20	5/37	1
P.L. Symcox	82.3	22	233	8	29.12	3/8	
A.A. Donald	67.4	9	226	7	32.28	3/108	
P.R. Adams	30	9	79	2	39.50	2/69	
B.M. McMillan	32	7	80	–	–		

Bowled in one innings: B.N. Schultz 15–4–58–1; D.J. Cullinan 1–0–2–0

Fielding Figures

6 – Mohmmad Wasim (ct 5/st 1) (inc. two catches as sub); 4 – Ijaz Ahmed; 3 – Moin Khan and Mushtaq Ahmed; 1 – Saeed Anwar, Ali Navqi, Mohammad Ramzan, Azhar Mahmood, Saqlain Mushtaq, Aamir Sohail and sub (Waqar Younis)

Fielding Figures

6 – D.J. Richardson; 3 – A.M. Bacher and G. Kirsten; 2 – W.J. Cronje, B.M. McMillan and A.A. Donald; 1 – D.J. Cullinan, S.M. Pollock, P.L. Symcox and sub (J.N. Rhodes)

There was some respite and even hope of recovery for the home side when Azhar Mahmood and Moin Khan put on 37 for the sixth wicket, but Klusener's fast medium proved too much for the patient Azhar just before lunch, which came with Pakistan 79 for six. Pollock claimed his fifth wicket when he bowled Waqar Younis, and Symcox, Man of the Match, took three wickets in two overs to give South Africa a sensational victory.

Moin Khan, 32 off 78 balls, was last man out, and while giving every credit to an inspired spell of pace bowling by Pollock, one must say that Moin's innings emphasised the mixture of panic and ineptitude that had seized his colleagues. South Africa had a mental strength which Pakistan supporters must have envied, for their side lacks nothing in ability. It is in composure and temperament where they are found wanting. This said, this was the tenth occasion this century that a side has lost a Test match after being set less than 150 to win, but it was the first time that Pakistan had failed in this respect. Only twice before in Pakistan had they been dismissed for lower totals.

Saeed Anwar had suffered a miserable series, and he was the first to pay the price. He was sacked as captain shortly after the match, and Wasim Akram, fully fit again, was reinstated for the one-day tournament.

Pakistan Golden Jubilee Tournament – The Jinnah Trophy

The Golden Jubilee tournament was, in many respects, a great success. It celebrated Pakistan's fifty years of independence and ended with a spectacular parade of those who had captained their country during that period, from Fazal Mahmood to the recently deposed Saeed Anwar. Sadly, Imran Khan was one who chose not to attend. The President of Pakistan did grace the occasion, and presentations were made to the array of captains.

All matches were played in Lahore and were day and night encounters. This proved to be rather unsatisfactory, for heavy evening dew prevalent in Lahore in early November gave all sides an uncomfortable time, particularly the team in the field. Before the final, Arjuna Ranatunga, the Sri Lankan captain, said that he believed whoever batted second would win, so difficult were the conditions for bowlers, who had problems gripping the damp ball.

This handicap was in evidence in the opening match. Ranatunga asked West Indies to bat first when he won the toss, and, in spite of the early loss of Stuart Williams, runs

Aamir Sohail hit 160 in the second Test against West Indies and followed with the same score in the third Test when he and Ijaz Ahmed established a new Pakistan first wicket record against West Indies of 298.
(Nigel French / ASP)

came freely from Lara, who hit his 40th fifty in one-day internationals, and from Chanderpaul and Hooper. A total of 237 seemed a challenging score, and when Atapattu was taken at slip off Walsh with only 17 on the board, West Indies looked to be set for victory. Such a view received further confirmation when Sri Lanka's two leading batsmen, Jayasuriya and Aravinda de Silva, fell in quick succession, but Roshan Mahanama played one of his finest innings in a limited-over international. He was joined by Ranatunga, who was in magnificent form, and Sri Lanka raced to victory with 58 balls to spare.

The second day saw the hosts' first appearance in the tournament. They were watched by a fervent crowd of 30,000, but once again they fell to the strength, calm and professional organisation of South Africa and once again it was Shaun Pollock who was their main tormentor. Wasim Akram chose to ask South Africa to bat first when he won the toss. Gary Kirsten continued the form he had shown in the Test series. Unaffected by the early loss of Hudson, he shared a stand of 90 in 56 minutes with Klusener, who hit 45 off 39 balls, and a stand of 98 in 67 minutes with Cullinan, who, having made 51 off 53 deliveries, was desperately unlucky to be out when Kirsten drove a ball from Azhar Mahmood which the bowler diverted onto the stumps with the batsman out of his ground. Kirsten was fourth out. He was leg before to Azhar after making 89 off 110 deliveries with a six and eight fours and giving the innings an excellent foundation. South Africa moved towards a formidable total, but the position could have been worse for Pakistan had Wasim Akram not clean bowled three batsmen, including the dangerous Symcox, in the last over.

Saeed Anwar's misery continued when he was caught at second slip off the first ball of the Pakistan innings, and Aamir Sohail and Ijaz Ahmed were leg before to the fourth and fifth deliveries. When Pollock bowled Shahid Afridi with the first ball of his third over it meant that the red-headed pace bowler had taken four wickets for one run in 13 balls and that Pakistan were nine for four. In the next 128 minutes, Inzamam-ul-Haq and Moin Khan, selected for his batting rather than his wicket-keeping, put on 133, but Moin and Wasim Akram were out in quick succession, and when Inzamam was bowled by Cronje at 180, Pakistan needed more than ten runs an over to pull off an improbable victory. In a spectacular innings, Azhar Mahmood almost achieved the impossible. With a six and five fours, he hit 59 off 43 balls, but Pakistan still fell ten short of their target.

A much smaller crowd saw South Africa gain a second victory and West Indies suffer a second defeat the following day. Put in to bat, West Indies lost Campbell in Pollock's opening over, but Stuart Williams and Brian Lara, aided by fielding which was well below South Africa's usual high standard, added 86 at more than a run a minute. Lara's 68 included a six and ten fours and came off 70 balls, but he was guilty of running out Stuart Williams before suffering the same fate himself when he was beaten by Rhodes's under-arm throw. Carl Hooper then took over with a majestic innings, his fourth century in limited-over internationals. He hit a six and eight fours and faced 101 balls. Chanderpaul showed unexpected hitting powers with 47 off 40 balls, and West Indies reached 293 against a below par South African attack.

With the bat, South Africa were a different proposition, even though they again lost Hudson, Klusener and Cullinan with only 81 scored. Cronje joined the ever dependable Kirsten, and the pair added 112. West Indies were now in trouble in the field. The ball was like a bar of soap, and Walsh sent down one over which included three no-balls and two wides. He also missed the stumps with an under-arm throw from a yard with Cronje well short of his ground. The South African captain was on 75 at the time and went on to make 94 before being run out by Lara. Cronje and Rhodes had added 66. Rhodes hit Ambrose over fine-leg for six and also made the winning runs with 11 balls to spare. His winning boundary brought him his fifty off 39 balls.

West Indies' exit from the tournament was confirmed in the fourth match when they were totally outplayed by Pakistan, who were very much in need of a victory themselves. Losing the toss for the third time in as many matches, West Indies had the heart torn out of their innings by the pace of Waqar Younis and the subtle off-breaks of Saqlain Mushtaq. Stuart Williams and Phil Simmons added 74, but West Indies' total of 215 was the lowest so far registered in the tournament and posed few problems for Pakistan. Shahid Afridi blazed away from the start, and, although Ijaz Ahmed fell to Bishop, Saeed Anwar ended his nightmare form with his 13th hundred in a one-day international. Aamir Sohail, too, was in fine form, and the pair shared an unbroken partnership of 164, which took Pakistan to victory with almost ten overs to spare.

If the victory gave Pakistan hope of reaching the final, that hope was shattered the following day when they were destroyed by a record stand between Jayasuriya and Aravinda de Silva. Put in to bat, Pakistan began well with Aamir Sohail passing 4,000 runs in limited-over internationals during his innings of 70, and Ijaz Ahmed joining him in a third wicket stand of 122. The rest of the Pakistan batting disappointed, and the side failed to last its full quota of overs to the disappointment of a capacity crowd. More disappointment followed, and the home crowd turned against their own side when they were battered by the Sri Lankans and handicapped by the wet ball. Atapattu was run out, and Mahanama was out for nought, but this only brought together Jayasuriya and de Silva. Jayasuriya began cautiously, scoring six off his first 16 balls, but he then moved into top gear by hooking Waqar for six. He added another six and ten fours as he raced to his century off 86 balls. In all, he faced 114 deliveries. Aravinda de Silva reached his hundred off 87 balls, and the partnership of 213, a record for any Sri Lankan wicket in a one-day international, occupied only 165 balls.

Having both qualified for the final, South Africa and Sri Lanka adopted a somewhat experimental approach to the last of the preliminary games. Lance Klusener hit 50 off 39 balls, and took his first four wickets in the space of 14 deliveries. His figures of six for 49 were his best in a one-day international. South Africa's victory ended a run of nine straight international wins by Sri Lanka.

Final Qualifying Table

	P	W	L	Pts
South Africa	3	3	–	6
Sri Lanka	3	2	1	4
Pakistan	3	1	2	2
West Indies	3	–	3	0

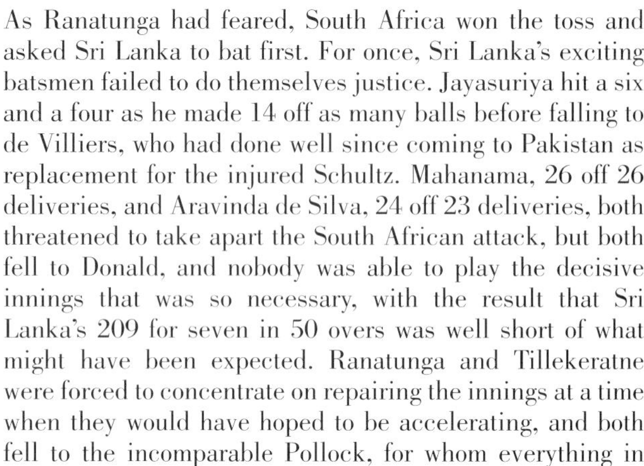

Final

South Africa *v.* Sri Lanka

As Ranatunga had feared, South Africa won the toss and asked Sri Lanka to bat first. For once, Sri Lanka's exciting batsmen failed to do themselves justice. Jayasuriya hit a six and a four as he made 14 off as many balls before falling to de Villiers, who had done well since coming to Pakistan as replacement for the injured Schultz. Mahanama, 26 off 26 deliveries, and Aravinda de Silva, 24 off 23 deliveries, both threatened to take apart the South African attack, but both fell to Donald, and nobody was able to play the decisive innings that was so necessary, with the result that Sri Lanka's 209 for seven in 50 overs was well short of what might have been expected. Ranatunga and Tillekeratne were forced to concentrate on repairing the innings at a time when they would have hoped to be accelerating, and both fell to the incomparable Pollock, for whom everything in Pakistan had turned to gold.

Sri Lanka's hopes were raised when Atapattu ran out the dangerous Kirsten and Vaas dismissed Hudson before the ball became too soggy. Symcox hit two sixes and departed after ten balls, but by now Lance Klusener had found the touch he had exhibited in the previous match. He hit two sixes and 11 fours in roaring to 99 off 96 balls, only to mishit the shot that would have taken him to his century. When he was out South Africa were just 13 short of victory. Pollock and Rhodes completed the win, which came with nearly ten overs to spare.

Unquestionably, South Africa were the best side in the tournament. They demonstrated the winning qualities that they had shown in claiming the Test series against Pakistan. Their organisation and professional approach to every aspect of the game could not be faulted. They were calm and diplomatic whenever confronted by controversy, and any complaints or criticisms were made through official channels without recourse to outbursts in the media. They were ambassadors of dignity, intelligence and charm. They were fit and ably led, and they could boast considerable talent in all departments. Pollock and, in the later stages, Klusener were outstanding, but the people's favourite, quite clearly, was Jonty Rhodes. If one is honest, Rhodes has failed to reach the necessary standard as a Test batsman, but, as a fielder, he has no superior in the world, and the Pakistan crowds thrilled to him.

Once again, the home side fell below the standard expected of them. Wasim Akram was their third captain in the space of two months, but there remained constant doubts as to the ability and temperament of some of the players, and the whims of the selectors are a perpetual cause for concern. There was criticism that Mushtaq Ahmed had withdrawn from the tournament because he was still recovering from a knee operation, but that operation had not prevented him from sending down more than 140 overs in four Test innings. The possibility is that Mushtaq, like several others, was beginning to believe that Pakistan cricketers were suffering from a surfeit of delights.

Match One – West Indies v. Sri Lanka
1 November 1997 at Gaddafi Stadium, Lahore

West Indies

S.C. Williams	c Ranatunga, b Vaas	5
S. Chanderpaul	lbw, b P.A. de Silva	42
B.C. Lara	b Jayasuriya	80
C.L. Hooper	c S.K.L. de Silva, b S.C. de Silva	68
P.V. Simmons	c Muralitharan, b Vaas	20
C.E.L. Ambrose	not out	4
F.A. Rose	run out	1
R.I.C. Holder	run out	2
D. Williams †	b S.C. de Silva	2
C.A. Walsh *		
R.N. Lewis		
	b 5, w 4, nb 4	13
	50 overs (for 8 wickets)	237

	O	M	R	W
Vaas	10	–	35	2
S.C. de Silva	10	2	31	2
Dharmasena	10	–	55	–
Muralitharan	6	–	46	–
Jayasuriya	8	–	33	1
P.A. de Silva	6	–	32	1

Fall of Wickets
1–**16**, 2–**98**, 3–**172**, 4–**221**, 5–**228**, 6–**229**, 7–**232**, 8–**237**

Sri Lanka

S.T. Jayasuriya	c Lewis, b Hooper	24
M.S. Atapattu	c Hooper, b Walsh	1
R.S. Mahanama	not out	94
P.A. de Silva	c Chanderpaul, b Rose	13
A. Ranatunga *	not out	87
H.P. Tillekeratne		
S.K.L. de Silva †		
H.D.P.K. Dharmasena		
W.P.U.J.C. Vaas		
M. Muralitharan		
S.C. de Silva		
	lb 4, w 9, nb 8	21
	39.2 overs (for 3 wickets)	240

	O	M	R	W
Ambrose	8	–	52	–
Walsh	9	1	41	1
Hooper	8	–	31	1
Lewis	5	–	24	–
Rose	7	–	64	1
Simmons	2.4	–	24	–

Fall of Wickets
1–**17**, 2–**56**, 3–**69**

Umpires: Javed Akhtar & Salim Badar *Man of the Match:* A. Ranatunga

Sri Lanka won by 7 wickets

Match Two – Pakistan v. South Africa
2 November 1997 at Gaddafi Stadium, Lahore

South Africa

A.C. Hudson	lbw, b Wasim Akram	2
G. Kirsten	lbw, b Azhar Mahmood	89
L. Klusener	b Saqlain Mushtaq	45
D.J. Cullinan	run out	51
W.J. Cronje*	run out	35
J.N. Rhodes	lbw, b Saqlain Mushtaq	5
S.M. Pollock	c Ijaz Ahmed, b Saqlain	15
D.J. Richardson †	not out	10
P.L. Symcox	b Wasim Akram	0
P.S. de Villiers	b Wasim Akram	1
A.A. Donald	b Wasim Akram	0
	lb 9, w 8, nb 1	18
	48 overs	271

	O	M	R	W
Wasim Akram	8	–	33	4
Waqar Younis	10	–	59	–
Saqlain Mushtaq	9	1	34	3
Azhar Mahmood	7	–	57	1
Aamir Sohail	4	–	23	–
Shahid Afridi	10	–	56	–

Fall of Wickets
1–**4**, 2–**94**, 3–**192**, 4–**221**, 5–**241**, 6–**254**, 7–**264**, 8–**269**, 9–**271**

Pakistan

Saeed Anwar	c Kirsten, b Pollock	0
Shahid Afridi	b Pollock	7
Aamir Sohail	lbw, b Pollock	0
Ijaz Ahmed	lbw, b Pollock	0
Inzamam-ul-Haq	b Cronje	85
Moin Khan	lbw, b de Villiers	59
Wasim Akram *	run out	9
Azhar Mahmood	not out	59
Rashid Latif †	c and b Klusener	14
Saqlain Mushtaq	c Rhodes, b Donald	11
Waqar Younis	not out	6
	lb 4, w 8	12
	50 overs (for 9 wickets)	262

	O	M	R	W
Pollock	10	2	49	4
de Villiers	10	1	49	1
Donald	10	1	44	1
Cronje	8	–	38	1
Klusener	8	–	50	1
Symcox	4	–	28	–

Fall of Wickets
1–**0**, 2–**0**, 3–**0**, 4–**9**, 5–**142**, 6–**152**, 7–**180**, 8–**206**, 9–**247**

Umpires: R.S. Dunne & I.D. Robinson *Man of the Match:* S.M. Pollock

South Africa won by 9 runs

Match Three – West Indies v. South Africa

3 November 1997 at Gaddafi Stadium, Lahore

West Indies

S.C. Williams	run out	26
S.L. Campbell	c Cullinan, b Pollock	0
B.C. Lara	run out	68
C.L. Hooper	c Cullinan, b Donald	105
S. Chanderpaul	c de Villiers, b Cronje	47
P.V. Simmons	not out	18
R.N. Lewis	c de Villiers, b Donald	7
C.E.L. Ambrose	b de Villiers	6
D. Williams †	b de Villiers	0
C.A. Walsh *		
M. Dillon		
	b 1, lb 10, w 4, nb 1	16
	50 overs (for 8 wickets)	293

	O	M	R	W
Pollock	8	–	52	1
de Villiers	10	1	40	2
Donald	10	–	58	2
Klusener	7	–	42	–
Symcox	10	–	52	–
Cronje	4	–	38	1

Fall of Wickets
1–1, 2–87, 3–131, 4–214, 5–270, 6–283, 7–293, 8–293

South Africa

A.C. Hudson	c Lewis, b Ambrose	6
G. Kirsten	run out	64
L. Klusener	b Hooper	17
D.J. Cullinan	b Lewis	23
W.J. Cronje *	run out	94
J.N. Rhodes	not out	53
S.M. Pollock	not out	11
D.J. Richardson †		
P.L. Symcox		
P.S. de Villiers		
A.A. Donald		
	b 1, lb 4, w 11, nb 13	29
	48.1 overs (for 5 wickets)	297

	O	M	R	W
Ambrose	10	–	52	1
Walsh	10	–	56	–
Hooper	10	1	49	1
Lewis	8.1	–	55	1
Dillon	9	–	68	–
Simmons	1	–	12	–

Fall of Wickets
1–10, 2–46, 3–81, 4–193, 5–259

Umpires: Javed Akhtar & Said Shah *Man of the Match:* W.J. Cronje

South Africa won by 5 wickets

Match Four – Pakistan v. West Indies

4 November 1997 at Gaddafi Stadium, Lahore

West Indies

S.C. Williams	b Azhar Mahmood	75
S.L. Campbell	c Rashid Latif, b Waqar Younis	6
B.C. Lara	b Waqar Younis	7
C.L. Hooper	c Shahid Afridi, b Saqlain	1
S. Chanderpaul	lbw, b Saqlain Mushtaq	0
P.V. Simmons	st Rashid Latif, b Saqlain	70
D. Williams †	c and b Azhar Mahmood	13
I.R. Bishop	not out	15
F.A. Rose	not out	7
M. Dillon		
C.A. Walsh *		
	b 5, lb 11, w 5	21
	50 overs (for 7 wickets)	215

	O	M	R	W
Wasim Akram	8	–	35	–
Waqar Younis	10	1	42	2
Saqlain Mushtaq	10	–	35	3
Shahid Afridi	8	–	41	–
Aamir Sohail	5	–	20	–
Azhar Mahmood	9	1	26	2

Fall of Wickets
1–24, 2–51, 3–54, 4–56, 5–130, 6–166, 7–204

Pakistan

Shahid Afridi	b Walsh	17
Saeed Anwar	not out	108
Ijaz Ahmed	lbw, b Bishop	5
Aamir Sohail	not out	71
Inzamam-ul-Haq		
Moin Khan		
Wasim Akram *		
Azhar Mahmood		
Rashid Latif †		
Saqlain Mushtaq		
Waqar Younis		
	lb 3, w 6, nb 9	18
	40.4 overs (for 2 wickets)	219

	O	M	R	W
Walsh	7.4	1	43	1
Rose	7	1	41	–
Dillon	8	1	37	–
Bishop	5	–	42	1
Hooper	9	1	29	–
Chanderpaul	1	–	5	–
Simmons	3	–	19	–

Fall of Wickets
1–34, 2–55

Umpires: R.S. Dunne & I.D. Robinson *Man of the Match:* Saeed Anwar

Pakistan won by 8 wickets

Match Five – Pakistan v. Sri Lanka
5 November 1997 at Gaddafi Stadium, Lahore

Pakistan

Shahid Afridi	**b** Vaas	**39**
Saeed Anwar	**c** Ranatunga, **b** Vaas	**26**
Aamir Sohail	**c** and **b** Muralitharan	**70**
Ijaz Ahmed	**c** sub (Chandana), **b** S.C. de Silva	**94**
Inzamam-ul-Haq	**c** P.A. de Silva, **b** Jayasuriya	**8**
Wasim Akram*	**c** S.K.L. de Silva, **b** Muralitharan	**6**
Moin Khan	run out	**10**
Azhar Mahmood	**c** S.K.L. de Silva, **b** S.C. de Silva	**15**
Rashid Latif †	**c** S.K.L. de Silva, **b** Vaas	**1**
Waqar Younis	**b** S.C. de Silva	**1**
Saqlain Mushtaq	not out	**1**
	lb **6**, w **3**	**9**
	49.4 overs	**280**

	O	M	R	W
Vaas	10	–	59	**3**
S.C. de Silva	9.4	1	58	**3**
Dharmasena	10	1	41	**–**
Muralitharan	10	–	37	**2**
Jayasuriya	6	–	54	**1**
P.A. de Silva	4	–	25	**–**

Fall of Wickets
1–**66**, 2–**73**, 3–**195**, 4–**205**, 5–**214**, 6–**234**, 7–**269**, 8–**278**, 9–**278**

Sri Lanka

S.T. Jayasuriya	not out	**134**
M.S. Atapattu	run out	**23**
R.S. Mahanama	**c** Aamir Sohail, **b** Azhar Mahmood	**0**
P.A. de Silva	not out	**102**
H.P. Tillekeratne		
A. Ranatunga *		
S.K.L. de Silva †		
W.P.U.J.C. Vaas		
H.D.P.K. Dharmasena		
M. Muralitharan		
S.C. de Silva		
	lb **6**, w **13**, nb **3**	**22**
	40 overs (for 2 wickets)	**281**

	O	M	R	W
Wasim Akram	8	–	44	**–**
Waqar Younis	6	–	49	**–**
Saqlain Mushtaq	8	–	55	**–**
Azhar Mahmood	8	–	53	**1**
Aamir Sohail	5	–	32	**–**
Shahid Afridi	5	–	42	**–**

Fall of Wickets
1–**65**, 2–**68**

Umpires: R.S. Dunne & I.D. Robinson *Man of the Match:* S.T. Jayasuriya

Sri Lanka won by 8 wickets

Match Six – Sri Lanka v. South Africa
6 November 1997 at Gaddafi Stadium, Lahore

South Africa

A.C. Hudson	**c** S.K.L. de Silva, **b** Liyanage	**10**
G. Kirsten	**c** Arnold, **b** P.A. de Silva	**50**
L. Klusener	**c** Atapattu, **b** Dharmasena	**54**
D.J. Cullinan	**c** Liyanage, **b** Chandana	**36**
W.J. Cronje *	**c** Chandana, **b** P.A. de Silva	**50**
J.N. Rhodes	**c** and **b** Dharmasena	**24**
S.M. Pollock	**c** Arnold, **b** Dharmasena	**37**
D.J. Richardson †	**c** Ranatunga, **b** S.C. de Silva	**5**
P.L. Symcox	not out	**22**
P.S. de Villiers	**b** S.C. de Silva	**6**
P.R. Adams	not out	**0**
	b **1**, lb **6**, w **7**, nb **3**	**17**
	50 overs (for 9 wickets)	**311**

	O	M	R	W
Liyanage	9	–	57	**1**
S.C. de Silva	9	1	51	**2**
Dharmasena	10	–	46	**3**
Chandana	10	–	65	**1**
P.A. de Silva	8	–	61	**2**
Arnold	4	–	24	**–**

Fall of Wickets
1–**12**, 2–**90**, 3–**154**, 4–**165**, 5–**200**, 6–**272**, 7–**274**, 8–**299**, 9–**308**

Sri Lanka

M.S. Atapattu	**c** Pollock, **b** Klusener	**25**
R.P. Arnold	**c** Richardson, **b** Pollock	**11**
R.S. Mahanama	lbw, **b** Klusener	**9**
P.A. de Silva	**c** Symcox, **b** Klusener	**6**
H.P. Tillekeratne	run out	**9**
A. Ranatunga *	lbw, **b** Klusener	**0**
S.K.L. de Silva †	lbw, **b** de Villiers	**57**
H.D.P.K. Dharmasena	not out	**69**
U.U. Chandana	**c** Rhodes, **b** Klusener	**2**
D.K. Liyanage	**c** and **b** Klusener	**22**
S.C. de Silva	not out	**5**
	lb **9**, w **17**, nb **4**	**30**
	50 overs (for 9 wickets)	**245**

	O	M	R	W
Pollock	10	–	37	**1**
de Villiers	9	2	38	**1**
Klusener	10	–	49	**6**
Adams	6	–	35	**–**
Symcox	4	–	25	**–**
Cronje	10	–	49	**–**
Hudson	1	–	3	**–**

Fall of Wickets
1–**35**, 2–**46**, 3–**55**, 4–**61**, 5–**62**, 6–**72**, 7–**165**, 8–**172**, 9–**227**

Umpires: Mian Aslam & Mohammad Nazir jnr *Man of the Match:* L. Klusener

South Africa won by 66 runs

Jinnah Cup Final – South Africa v. Sri Lanka

8 November 1997 at Gaddafi Stadium, Lahore

Sri Lanka

S.T. Jayasuriya	c Symcox, b de Villiers	14
M.S. Atapattu	c Cronje, b Klusener	22
R.S. Mahanama	c Hudson, b Donald	26
P.A. de Silva	c Klusener, b Donald	24
A. Ranatunga *	c Klusener, b Pollock	32
H.P. Tillekeratne	c Richardson, b Pollock	28
S.K.L. de Silva †	c Richardson, b Pollock	1
H.D.P.K. Dharmasena	not out	24
W.P.U.J.C. Vaas	not out	18
M. Muralitharan		
S.C. de Silva		
	lb 8, w 11, nb 1	20
	50 overs (for 7 wickets)	209

	O	M	R	W
Pollock	10	–	42	3
de Villiers	8	1	28	1
Donald	10	–	46	2
Klusener	7	–	29	1
Symcox	10	–	37	–
Cronje	5	–	19	–

Fall of Wickets
1–29, 2–66, 3–95, 4–101, 5–155, 6–157, 7–173

South Africa

A.C. Hudson	lbw, b Vaas	11
G. Kirsten	run out	7
L. Klusener	c and b S.C. de Silva	99
P.L. Symcox	b S.C. de Silva	15
D.J. Cullinan	st S.K.L. de Silva, b P.A. de Silva	20
W.J. Cronje *	c Tillekeratne, b Dharmasena	33
J.N. Rhodes	not out	5
S.M. Pollock	not out	10
D.J. Richardson †		
P.S. de Villiers		
A.A. Donald		
	w 3, nb 7	10
	40.4 overs (for 6 wickets)	210

	O	M	R	W
Vaas	6	1	34	1
S.C. de Silva	6	–	48	2
Muralitharan	10	–	34	–
Dharmasena	8.4	–	47	1
P.A. de Silva	5	–	25	1
Jayasuriya	5	–	22	–

Fall of Wickets
1–18, 2–40, 3–71, 4–109, 5–188, 6–197

Umpires: Javed Akhtar & Salim Badar *Man of the Match:* L. Klusener

South Africa won by 4 wickets

West Indies Tour

West Indies arrived in Pakistan to play a three-Test series, but before their tour had officially begun they suffered the humiliations of the Jinnah Cup, in which they failed to win a match and which revealed the uncertainty of their batting and the ageing limitations of their pace attack. Walsh was now 35, Ambrose 34 and Bishop 30. Rose had enjoyed a fruitful beginning to his Test career in the Caribbean with 31 wickets in seven matches, but he had been far from impressive in the quadrangular tournament in Lahore, while Dillon had yet to prove himself. The leg-spinner Rawl Lewis had no experience of Test cricket. Lara's form had been erratic for the best part of eighteen months, Holder had failed to establish himself at international level, Chanderpaul's development continued to be slow and Campbell and Stuart Williams remained an embryonic opening partnership. The West Indian selectors had shown their frustrations by turning once again to Phil Simmons, who had been found wanting at the highest level, and by recalling wicket-keeper David Williams more than four years after he had been discarded for one poor display. Had Pakistan been in better shape themselves, they could well have approached the series with supreme confidence.

29 October 1997
at Aitchison College, Lahore
West Indians 234 for 7 (S.C. Williams 67)
National Bank 212 for 8 (Saeed Azad 73 not out)
West Indians won by 22 runs

11, 12, 13 and 14 November 1997
at Pindi Cricket Stadium, Rawalpindi
West Indians 464 (C.L. Hooper 146, S.L. Campbell 76, P.V. Simmons 75)
Dr Abdul Qadir Khan's XI 267 (Babar Zaman 62) and 107 for 3
Match drawn

The West Indians played a 45-over game as a warm-up for the one-day tournament in Lahore and a four-day game as a prelude to the Test series. Another first-class match should have been played in Hyderabad in between the first and second Tests, but the West Indians refused to play because of sub-standard accommodation. A one-day game was arranged, but rain seeped through the covers, and the pitch was unfit.

Test Series

Pakistan *v.* West Indies

There were two Test debutants in the first match of the series, Arshad Khan, an off-spinner who had played in one-day internationals, and Rawl Lewis, the West Indian leg-spinner. Pakistan chose neither Saqlain Mushtaq nor Waqar Younis, bewildering decisions, and Walsh's decision to bat first when he won the toss seemed equally puzzling. Shortly after lunch, West Indies had descended to the pit of 58 for seven.

Play began half an hour late because of heavy dew on the outfield, but the pitch itself could not be blamed for the West Indian failings. Indeed, it is more correct to praise the skill of the Pakistan bowlers rather than to censure the batsmen, although Stuart Williams gifted the lively and impressive Shahid Nazir his wicket when he edged a wretched attempt at a drive. Two balls later, Chanderpaul was bowled by a delivery of full length. Wasim Akram had settled into a smooth and rhythmic action, generating pace and movement off twelve paces. In his fourth over, he tempted Lara with a wider delivery and Mushtaq Ahmed took a good catch falling to his left.

If Mushtaq had needed a fillip, this was it. When he was brought into the attack he had Campbell leg before almost immediately and completely deceived Simmons with a googly. Hooper hit him straight for six but was then caught at short-leg off an attempted sweep. Lewis swiped across the line and missed. Had Moin Khan held onto an inside edge offered by David Williams off Azhar Mahmood, it is most probable that West Indies would not have reached 100, but Williams survived, and he and Bishop added 48. Ambrose, too, hit lustily, but Mushtaq claimed five wickets in a Test innings for the eighth time, and West Indies were fortunate to make as many as 151. Walsh had Aamir Sohail taken at slip, and when the players came off for bad light in the fifth over Pakistan were 14 for one, and very much on top.

The second day saw them take total command. Saeed Anwar and Ijaz Ahmed put on 133 for the second wicket, and Walsh dropped the simplest of catches at mid-on to reprieve Inzamam-ul-Haq when the batsman was on five. Inzaman was forced to retire at 13. He had received a blow on the ankle when fielding at silly mid-off on the first day, and he was in some pain. His retirement brought no relief to West Indies. They were pelted with food in the outfield, and play was held up three times. Walsh was unwell and left the field for a time, while Lewis, on his debut, fell far short of Mushtaq in accuracy, control and potency. Ambrose had a barren day, was no-balled for bowling two short-pitched balls at Moin Khan, and conceded four runs when Walsh's attempt to run out Azhar Mahmood went to the boundary. Pakistan ended the day on 246 for five, and West Indies were relieved that play ended slightly early.

Inzamam returned on the third morning when Walsh dismissed Azhar Mahmood, and he settled to play a masterly innings that took the game out of West Indies' reach. He was merciless on Lewis, who was hit for two straight sixes, and he also hit nine fours as he was unbeaten on 92 off 191 balls. He nursed 77 runs from the last two wickets, both of which fell to Walsh, who thereby claimed five wickets in a Test innings for the 14th time.

Trailing by 230 runs on the first innings, West Indies lost Stuart Williams and Chanderpaul before the end of the third day. Lara sparkled, hitting eight fours as he moved to 36, so that West Indies, 99 for two, still had hope of saving the game. That hope evaporated early on the fourth morning. Dropped at gully, the miss giving him a single, Lara was leg before to Azhar Mahmood. Hooper drove Mushtaq for six and then spooned a catch to short extra cover in the next over. Campbell defended manfully for 231 minutes before falling leg before to a fine in-swinger from Wasim. David Williams made 20 in 66 minutes, and Bishop 21 in 58 minutes, but these were not even minor irritants to Pakistan, who won in three-and-a-half days by an innings and 19 runs. Mushtaq Ahmed finished with match figures of ten for 106 to claim the individual honours, but skipper Wasim Akram also bowled well and led his side admirably. West Indies were outplayed and humiliated.

West Indies made two changes for the second Test. Wallace replaced Simmons, who had had a miserable time in Peshawar, while Rose came in for Lewis, who had been wicketless and expensive on his Test debut. Pakistan had the luxury of recalling Waqar Younis and giving a first Test cap to Shoaib Akhtar, a lively pace bowler. Arshad Khan and Shahid Nazir were those to stand down, while the world's best off-spinner, Saqlain Mushtaq, remained on the sidelines. Wasim won the toss and asked West Indies to bat first on a greenish pitch. The start was delayed, and play finished early. There was enough time for West Indies to fall into another parlous state. Debutant Philo Wallace looked out of his depth as Waqar and Wasim swung and seamed the ball appreciably. Stuart Williams, too, failed, and Lara came to the crease at 37 for two. He flashed impatiently, took ten off three successive deliveries and was wrecked by a superb yorker from Waqar, which knocked him off his feet and his leg stump out of the ground. Hooper was caught behind for

In a struggling Customs side, Rana Qayyum showed his all-round ability and is considered to be a Test player of the near future.
(David Pinegar / ASP)

nought, but Chanderpaul batted with elegant composure, and he and Campbell took the score to 179 by the close.

Only five-and-a-half hours play was possible on the second day. Campbell and Chanderpaul added another 26 runs to make their fifth wicket partnership worth 147 before Campbell, who had batted nearly five-and-a-quarter hours and faced 254 deliveries, was caught when he attempted to hook a ball from Azhar Mahmood. Chanderpaul's confidence appeared to desert him as soon as he got into the nineties where he remained for over half an hour before being hit on the back pad as he moved across his stumps to Waqar, who was operating with the second new ball. David Williams batted doggedly for nearly two hours, and he had proved a valuable batsman in the late order since his return to Test cricket. West Indies, having been struggling at 58 for four, could be well content with a total of 303.

They would have been more content had Lara held onto a chance that Aamir Sohail offered off Bishop. By the close, Aamir was on 62, and Pakistan were 122 for two. On the third day, they battered West Indies into total submission. Although 30 overs were lost to heavy dew and bad light, Pakistan added 281 runs to their overnight score and lost only the wicket of Aamir Sohail. If Aamir had batted somewhat frenetically on the second evening, he settled to play with delightful ease on the third day. His timing was superb, and he was ever eager to attack. He hit a six and 17 fours and faced 297 balls for his 160, and he and Inzamam-ul-Haq scored at more than four runs an over as they added 323 for the third wicket, a record for Pakistan against West Indies.

Aamir's century was his third in Test cricket and confirmed his rehabilitation after a period of dissent, crisis and concern; Inzamam reached his sixth Test hundred, his first in Pakistan. He has always suggested power, but he seems now to have added the good sense that, hopefully, comes with maturity. His was a most impressive innings, sound in selection, brutal in execution. Aamir was well caught at backward point shortly before the close, and Inzamam ended the day on 169, so passing his previous Test best.

He added only eight on the fourth day, when more play was lost to damp and bad light, before being caught off Walsh. Inzamam's innings had lasted for 443 minutes, two minutes longer than Aamir's, and included two sixes and 19 fours. He faced 320 deliveries. The remaining Pakistan batsmen perished in the pursuit of quick runs, and Walsh finished with another five-wicket haul, but the West Indian bowling, fielding and general out-cricket was of an unacceptably low standard. Walsh and Ambrose each sent down 12 no-balls, while Bishop bowled six wides. This was awful stuff, but the batting that followed was even worse.

Wallace fell to a superb in-swinger from Waqar, and Stuart Williams was taken in the gully off Wasim. The Pakistan captain also accounted for Lara, whose misery continued. The left-hander had made one off 16 balls when Wasim caught and bowled him in his follow-through. Campbell offered solidity for a time before being completely bamboozled by Mushtaq Ahmed, and Chanderpaul became Wasim's third victim when the Pakistan captain brought himself back into the attack. Mushtaq ran out David Williams with a direct hit on the stumps from mid-off, and West Indies ended the day on 99 for six, staring into the abyss of a second humiliating defeat.

Hooper had offered defiance and hit Mushtaq for three sixes in one over as he moved to 44. He remained aggressively defiant on the last morning, but the last four wickets fell, as expected, inside 50 minutes. There were two more run outs, which were a clear definition of the paucity of West Indies' cricket, and Pakistan clinched a series against West Indies for the first time in 39 years. Hooper's 73 came off 94 balls and included four sixes and seven fours, but, in the context of the match, it meant little. Wasim Akram captured four wickets and led his side with vigour and intelligence. Inzamam-ul-Haq was named Man of the Match, but victory had come through a fine team effort.

The sole interest in the third and final Test was whether Pakistan could complete the total rout of West Indies, who could strive only to avoid further embarrassment. After the first day it was apparent that it would be Pakistan who would achieve their aim. West Indies brought in Holder for Wallace and Dillon for Ambrose. Pakistan at last turned to Saqlain Mushtaq in place of Shoaib Akhtar. Walsh won the toss, and West Indies batted first on a pitch that presented no eccentricities or problems.

The visitors began well enough. Stuart Williams hit 33 off as many balls before being run out by Mushtaq Ahmed. Even this carelessness failed to halt West Indies' positive approach, and Campbell and Lara took the score past a hundred. Lara had hit six fours when he drove expansively at Saqlain and was bowled. Mushtaq Ahmed trapped Hooper leg before fourth ball, and the decline had begun. Aamir Sohail had missed two chances, but he now caught the solidly determined Campbell when the ball rebounded off Wasim Akram's knee. Against the spinners, Chanderpaul's footwork was found wanting, but it was Wasim who trapped him leg before. The Pakistan captain also accounted for Rose and Dillon, but it was Saqlain who was the chief tormentor of the West Indians. He finished with five for 54 as the last nine wickets went down for 107 runs.

Ijaz Ahmed was pressed into opening with Aamir Sohail because Saeed Anwar had a stiff neck, and Pakistan began the second day with 34 on the board. By the end of the day, they had 327 to their credit and had lost only the wicket of Aamir Sohail, who fell to Chanderpaul's occasional leg-spin when he swatted at a long hop and missed. By that time, however, he had scored 160, his second century in successive Test innings after a barren run in which he had failed to reach three figures in 17 Tests. He played with characteristic fluent aggression, hitting 21 fours in his 255-ball innings. He and Ijaz put on 298 for the first wicket, a Pakistan record against West Indies.

Ijaz batted into the third day when the last nine wickets quickly crashed for 88 runs. West Indies' bowling and out-cricket were much improved, and Mervyn Dillon returned the best bowling figures of his young Test career. Ijaz was sixth out with the score on 388. He had batted five minutes over eight hours and faced 337 balls. He hit a six and 15 fours and showed remarkable restraint for one who has so often been criticised for his impetuosity. This was an innings of maturity, sensitive to the needs of the occasion and sensitive to the needs of his side.

So West Indies trailed by 201 on the first innings, and when Waqar Younis took two wickets in six balls at the start of their second innings they faced more humiliation. Hooper, aided by Lara, met the situation with bravado. He launched a violent attack on the leg-spin of Mushtaq Ahmed, who was hit for 67 runs in seven overs, Hooper claiming 47 of those runs. When Lara was caught at silly point off Saqlain the pair had added 121 in 111 minutes, but the breaking of the partnership gave Saqlain the opening he needed. It was Wasim, however, who struck the decisive blow. He cut a ball back at Hooper, who offered only a weary prod in defence. He had batted for 135 minutes and hit a superb 106 off 90 balls with three sixes and 19 fours. It was West Indies' last gesture of defiance. Saqlain sent back Chanderpaul, Holder and David Williams in quick succession, and West Indies ended the third day on 198 for seven.

The game was over within an hour on the fourth day. Wasim Akram took the last three wickets, but West Indies avoided an innings defeat for the first time in the series, scant consolation for a side that had been totally eclipsed and outclassed. Saqlain was named Man of the Match; Walsh and Aamir Men of the Series. Walsh had 14 wickets in the series and passed 350 wickets in Test cricket, but Ambrose and Bishop were shadows of their former selves. In spite of this, Walsh's hold on the captaincy was tenuous, and Lara now seemed about to take the crown, which his performances and attitude in the series had done nothing to deserve.

Pakistan should have been ecstatic, as they had made a positive challenge to be recognised as supreme in world cricket, but what followed was incomprehensible. Failure in the one-day tournament in Sharjah was followed by the announcement that Wasim Akram and Waqar Younis were to be rested from the side that was to represent Pakistan in the limited-over competition in Bangladesh. The team was to be led by Rashid Latif, reinstated as wicket-keeper in place of Moin Khan and elevated to the captaincy at the same time. Wasim Akram later announced that he was resigning the captaincy of Pakistan because of perpetual criticism and threats on his life. He had bowled outstandingly well against West Indies and had led his country to one of the greatest achievements in their cricketing history. In the process, he had also confirmed that he was now back to full fitness after a year of shoulder trouble and other niggles. When the party to tour South Africa was announced it was revealed that Wasim Akram had been omitted from the fifteen. The action was beyond comprehension. Cricket in Pakistan remains plagued by perennial political intrigue.

First Test Match – Pakistan *v.* West Indies

17, 18, 19 and 20 November 1997 at Arbab Niaz Stadium, Peshawar

West Indies

	First Innings		Second Innings	
S.C. Williams	c Moin Khan, b Shahid Nazir	4	lbw, b Wasim Akram	2
S.L. Campbell	lbw, b Mushtaq Ahmed	15	lbw, b Wasim Akram	66
S. Chanderpaul	b Shahid Nazir	0	c Ijaz Ahmed, b Mushtaq	14
B.C. Lara	c Mushtaq, b Wasim Akram	3	lbw, b Azhar Mahmood	37
C.L. Hooper	c Mohammad Wasim b Mushtaq Ahmed	26	c sub (Saqlain Mushtaq) b Mushtaq Ahmed	23
P.V. Simmons	b Mushtaq Ahmed	1	c Wasim Akram, b Mushtaq	1
D. Williams †	b Azhar Mahmood	31	c Ijaz Ahmed, b Mushtaq	20
R.N. Lewis	b Mushtaq	4	lbw, b Wasim Akram	0
I.R. Bishop	b Azhar Mahmood	20	lbw, b Wasim Akram	21
C.E.L. Ambrose	lbw, b Mushtaq Ahmed	30	st Mohammad Wasim, b Mushtaq Ahmed	1
C.A. Walsh *	not out	9	not out	6
	lb 6, nb 2	8	b 9, lb 4, nb 7	20
		151		**211**

	O	M	R	W	O	M	R	W
Wasim Akram	14	5	29	1	23.2	5	65	4
Shahid Nazir	10	1	32	2	7.5	1	27	–
Azhar Mahmood	14	3	35	2	10.1	3	17	1
Mushtaq Ahmed	18.2	7	35	5	23	5	71	5
Arshad Khan	4	1	14	–	6	2	18	–

Fall of Wickets
1–9, 2–9, 3–16, 4–29, 5–45, 6–50, 7–58, 8–106, 9–129
1–14, 2–56, 3–102, 4–145, 5–147, 6–163, 7–167, 8–195, 9–201

Pakistan

	First Innings	
Saeed Anwar	c D. WIlliams, b Hooper	65
Aamir Sohail	c Lara, b Walsh	4
Ijaz Ahmed	c Hooper, b Bishop	65
Mohammad Wasim	b Walsh	28
Inzamam-ul-Haq	not out	92
Moin Khan †	c Walsh, b Bishop	58
Wasim Akram *	st D. Williams, b Hooper	5
Azhar Mahmood	c Hooper, b Walsh	16
Arshad Khan	c Lara, b Bishop	4
Shahid Nazir	b Walsh	18
Mushtaq Ahmed	b Walsh	4
	b 2, lb 7, w 2, nb 11	22
		381

	O	M	R	W
Ambrose	25	4	76	–
Walsh	32	9	78	5
Bishop	29	7	76	3
Simmons	2	–	9	–
Lewis	24	6	93	–
Hooper	20	7	40	2

Fall of Wickets
1–10, 2–143, 3–145, 4–193, 5–207, 6–250, 7–294, 8–304, 9–347
Inzamam-ul-Haq (13) retired hurt at 184 for 3 and returned at 249 for 6

Umpires: Saeed Shah & D.R. Shepherd

Pakistan won by an innings and 19 runs

Second Test Match – Pakistan v. West Indies

29, 30 November, 1, 2 and 3 December 1997 at Pindi Cricket Stadium, Rawalpindi

West Indies

	First Innings		Second Innings	
S.L. Campbell	c Shoaib Akhtar, b Azhar	78	b Mushtaq Ahmed	34
P.A. Wallace	lbw, b Wasim Akram	5	lbw, b Waqar Younis	8
S.C. Williams	c Mushtaq, b Waqar	8	c Azhar, b Wasim Akram	1
B.C. Lara	b Waqar Younis	15	c and b Wasim Akram	1
C.L. Hooper	c Moin, b Azhar Mahmood	0	not out	73
S. Chanderpaul	lbw, b Waqar Younis	95	lbw, b Wasim Akram	7
D. Williams †	c Moin, b Shoaib Akhtar	48	run out	0
I.R. Bishop	b Shoaib Akhtar	10	run out	2
C.E.L. Ambrose	not out	10	(11) b Waqar Younis	0
F.A. Rose	b Azhar Mahmood	7	(9) c Mushtaq, b Wasim	6
C.A. Walsh *	lbw, b Azhar Mahmood	0	(10) run out	0
	b 1, lb 16, w 3, nb 7	27	nb 7	7
		303		139

	O	M	R	W	O	M	R	W
Wasim Akram	22	6	40	1	14	5	42	4
Waqar Younis	27	3	99	3	12	1	44	2
Shoaib Akhtar	15	2	47	2	7	2	21	–
Azhar Mahmood	20.5	7	53	4	2	1	4	–
Mushtaq Ahmed	17	3	47	–	6	2	28	1

Fall of Wickets
1–15, 2–37, 3–53, 4–58, 5–205, 6–249, 7–264, 8–291, 9–303
1–9, 2–10, 3–26, 4–67, 5–98, 6–98, 7–112, 8–126, 9–138

Pakistan

	First Innings	
Saeed Anwar	c D. Williams, b Ambrose	16
Aamir Sohail	c sub (Simmons), b Walsh	160
Ijaz Ahmed	c Wallace, b Rose	10
Inzamam-ul-Haq	c Campbell, b Walsh	177
Mohammad Wasim	c Hooper, b Walsh	26
Moin Khan †	c D. Williams, b Rose	1
Azhar Mahmood	c D. Williams, b Rose	14
Wasim Akram*	b Bishop	11
Waqar Younis	b Walsh	2
Shoaib Akhtar	c Hooper, b Walsh	1
Mushtaq Ahmed	not out	0
	b 13, lb 9, w 6, nb 25	53
		471

	O	M	R	W
Walsh	43.1	6	143	5
Ambrose	19	2	63	1
Bishop	24	3	80	1
Rose	33	7	92	3
Hooper	17	1	71	–

Fall of Wickets
1–41, 2–63, 3–387, 4–414, 5–415, 6–437, 7–459, 8–469, 9–469

Umpires: Javed Akhtar & D.R. Shepherd

Pakistan won by an innings and 29 runs

Third Test Match – Pakistan v. West Indies

6, 7, 8 and 9 December 1997 at National Stadium, Karachi

West Indies

	First Innings		Second Innings	
S.L. Campbell	c Wasim Akram, b Saqlain	50	c Inzamam-ul-Haq, b Waqar	5
S.C. Williams	run out	33	lbw, b Waqar Younis	12
B.C. Lara	b Saqlain Mushtaq	36	c Mohammad Wasim, b Saqlain Mushtaq	37
C.L. Hooper	lbw, b Mushtaq Ahmed	0	b Wasim Akram	106
S. Chanderpaul	lbw, b Wasim Akram	21	c Moin Khan, b Saqlain	16
R.I.C. Holder	b Saqlain Mushtaq	26	c Aamir Sohail, b Saqlain	5
D. Williams †	not out	22	b Saqlain Mushtaq	2
I.R. Bishop	st Moin Khan, b Saqlain	2	(9) not out	6
F.A. Rose	lbw, b Wasim Akram	13	(8) c Moin, b Wasim Akram	5
C.A. Walsh *	c Inzamam, b Saqlain	1	b Wasim Akram	0
M.V. Dillon	b Wasim Akram	0	lbw, b Wasim Akram	4
	b 4, lb 7, nb 1	12	b 7, lb 2, nb 5	14
		216		212

	O	M	R	W	O	M	R	W
Wasim Akram	17.1	2	76	3	16.4	7	42	4
Waqar Younis	9	3	21	–	6	–	31	2
Azhar Mahmood	10	3	14	–	3	–	32	–
Mushtaq Ahmed	13	2	40	1	8	–	72	–
Saqlain Mushtaq	24	6	54	5	19	9	26	4

Fall of Wickets
1–47, 2–109, 3–114, 4–126, 5–160, 6–188, 7–194, 8–209, 9–212
1–14, 2–19, 3–140, 4–182, 5–186, 6–191, 7–193, 8–207, 9–208

Pakistan

	First Innings		Second Innings	
Aamir Sohail	lbw, b Chanderpaul	160		
Ijaz Ahmed	c D. Williams, b Dillon	151		
Saeed Anwar	c D. Williams, b Dillon	15		
Inzamam-ul-Haq	lbw, b Dillon	4		
Mohammad Wasim	lbw, b Dillon	12	(1) not out	0
Moin Khan †	lbw, b Walsh	5		
Azhar Mahmood	not out	26	(2) not out	13
Wasim Akram *	lbw, b Walsh	0		
Saqlain Mushtaq	c Lara, b Walsh	0		
Mushtaq Ahmed	b Walsh	1		
Waqar Younis	c S.C. Williams, b Dillon	12		
	b 3, lb 9, w 2, nb 17	31	nb 2	2
		417	(for no wickets)	15

	O	M	R	W	O	M	R	W
Walsh	23	2	74	4	3	–	11	–
Rose	12	1	44	–	2	–	4	–
Dillon	29.4	4	111	5				
Bishop	15	–	68	–				
Hooper	32	10	74	–				
Chanderpaul	7	–	34	1				

Fall of Wickets
1–298, 2–239, 3–333, 4–359, 5–374, 6–388, 7–390, 8–390, 9–396

Umpires: Salim Badar & C.J. Mitchley

Pakistan won by 10 wickets

Test Match Averages – Pakistan *v.* West Indies

Pakistan Batting

	M	Inns	NOs	Runs	HS	Av	100s	50s
Inzamam-ul-Haq	3	3	1	273	177	136.50	1	1
Aamir Sohail	3	3	–	324	160	108.00	2	
Ijaz Ahmed	3	3	–	226	151	75.33	1	1
Azhar Mahmood	3	4	2	69	26*	34.50		
Saeed Anwar	3	3	–	96	65	32.00	1	
Mohammad Wasim	3	4	1	66	28	22.00		
Moin Khan	3	3	–	64	58	21.33	1	
Waqar Younis	2	2	–	14	12	7.00		
Wasim Akram	3	3	–	16	11	5.33		
Mushtaq Ahmed	3	3	1	5	4	2.50		

Played in one Test: Arshad Khan 4; Shahid Nazir 18; Shoaib Akhtar 1; Saqlain Muhstaq 0

West Indies Batting

	M	Inns	NOs	Runs	HS	Av	100s	50s
C.L. Hooper	3	6	1	228	106	45.60	1	1
S.L. Campbell	3	6	–	248	78	41.33		3
S. Chanderpaul	3	6	–	153	95	25.50		1
D. Willliams	3	6	1	123	48	24.60		
B.C. Lara	3	6	–	129	37	21.50		
C.E.L. Ambrose	2	4	1	41	30	13.66		
I.R. Bishop	3	6	1	61	21	12.20		
S.C. Williams	3	6	–	60	33	10.00		
F.A. Rose	2	4	–	31	13	7.75		
C.A. Walsh	3	6	2	16	9*	4.00		

Played in one Test: P.V. Simmons 1& 1;R.N. Lewis 4 & 0;P.A. Wallace 5 & 8; R.I.C. Holder 26 & 5; M.V. Dillon 0 & 4

Pakistan Bowling

	Overs	Mds	Runs	Wks	Av	Best	10/m	5/inn
Saqlain Mushtaq	43	15	80	9	8.88	5/54		1
Wasim Akram	107.1	30	294	17	17.29	4/42		
Azhar Mahmood	60	17	155	7	22.14	4/53		
Mushtaq Ahmed	85.2	19	293	12	24.41	5/35	1	2
Waqar Younis	54	7	195	7	27.85	3/99		
Shahid Nazir	17.5	2	59	2	29.50	2/32		
Shoaib Akhtar	22	4	68	2	34.00	2/47		
Arshad Khan	10	3	32	–	–			

West Indies Bowling

	Overs	Mds	Runs	Wks	Av	Best	10/m	5/inn
C.A. Walsh	101.1	17	306	14	21.85	5/78	2	
F.A. Rose	47	8	140	3	46.66	3/92		
I.R. Bishop	68	10	224	4	56.00	3/76		
C.L. Hooper	69	18	185	2	92.50	2/40		
C.E.L. Ambrose	44	6	139	1	139.00	1/63		

Bowled in one innings: R.N. Lewis 24–6–93–0; P.V. Simmons 2–0–9–0; M.V. Dillon 29.4–4–111–5; S. Chanderpaul 7–0–34–1

Fielding Figures

6 – Moin Khan (ct 5 / st 1); 3 – Mohammad Wasim (ct 2 / st 1), Wasim Akram and Mushtaq Ahmed; 2 – Ijaz Ahmed and Inzamam-ul-Haq; 1 – Aamir Sohail, Azhar Mahmood, Shoaib Akhtar and sub (Saqlain Mushtaq)

Fielding Figures

7 – D. Williams (ct 6 / st 1); 4 – C.L. Hooper; 3 – B.C. Lara; 1 – S.C. Williams, S.L. Campbell, C.A. Walsh, P.A. Wallace and sub (P.V. Simmons)

England Tour

As preparation for their participation in the Sharjah Champions Trophy, the England limited-over side, under the captaincy of Adam Hollioake, played two matches against Pakistan 'A' team in Lahore. Following a practice match against local cricketers, the England side moved to the Gaddafi Stadium for the first of the two matches.

5 December 1997
at Gaddafi Stadium, Lahore
England XI 264 for 9 (A.J. Hollioake 86, G.A. Hick 50, Fazi-i-Akbar 4 for 40)
Pakistan 'A' 229 (Akhtar Sarfraz 69, D.R. Brown 4 for 58)
England XI won by 35 runs

Adam Hollioake hit 86 off 99 balls as his side won the 50-over match with some ease. Headley bowled most economically, and Warwickshire's Dougie Brown took four wickets.

7 December 1997
at Gaddafi Stadium, Lahore
Pakistan 'A' 117
England XI 118 for 5
England XI won by 5 wickets

England completed their preparations with an emphatic victory, which came with 21.5 overs to spare. The home side were bowled out in 38.3 overs with Dougie Brown and Croft each taking three wickets.

India 'A' Tour

A strong Indian 'A' side toured Pakistan in February and March, playing four 'Tests' and three one-day internationals. The Pakistan selectors chose to field several experienced players such as Aqib Javed and Basit Ali in their sides, a move which did not meet with general approval.

3, 4 and 5 February 1998
at National Stadium, Karachi
Karachi City CA 338 (Basit Ali 133, Shahid Afridi 66)
India 'A' 382 for 5 (J.V. Paranjpe 115, G.K. Khoda 95, W. Jaffer 90)
Match drawn

The first match of the tour was abandoned after two days because the third day, 5 February, was the Kashmir

Solidarity Day Holiday. Basit Ali made 133 off 142 balls with a six and 14 fours. India 'A' replied with an opening stand of 180 in 185 minutes between Wasim Jaffer and skipper Gagan Khoda. Jatin Paranjpe made 115 off 131 balls with a six and 18 fours.

8, 9 and 10 February 1998

at Arbab Niaz Stadium, Peshawar
India 'A' 180 and 343 for 6 dec. (S. Raul 114 not out, A.B. Agarkar 109 not out)
Peshawar 203 (Taimur Ali Khan 58, A.B. Agarkar 6 for 75) and 89 for 3
Match drawn

The quicker bowlers dominated play on the first two days, and there was an outstanding all-round performance from Ajit Agarkar, soon to be recognised as an integral part of India's one-day international side.

13, 14, 15 and 16 February 1998

at Rawalpindi Cricket Stadium, Rawalpindi
Pakistan 'A' 112 (A.B. Agarkar 5 for 34)
India 'A' 43 for 3
Match drawn

No play was possible on the second and third days because of rain, and a wet outfield prevented any play on the fourth day. So the first 'Test' was drawn after Agarkar had again displayed his qualities as a bowler.

19, 20 and 21 February 1998

at Rawalpindi Cricket Stadium, Rawalpindi
India 'A' 234 for 6 dec. (R.S. Gavaskar 63, S. Abbas Ali 60)
Rawalpindi 216 for 7
Match drawn

With no play possible on the first day due to the damp conditions, the tourists settled for batting practice. They lost only two wickets, but four batsmen, including Gavaskar and Abbas Ali, retired after spending some time at the crease.

The second 'Test' was due to be played in Peshawar between 24 and 27 February, but rain caused it to be abandoned without a ball being bowled.

1, 2, 3 and 4 March 1998

at Gaddafi Stadium, Lahore
India 'A' 557 for 5 dec. (G.K. Khoda 189, R.S. Gavaskar 115 not out, S. Raul 115 not out, S. Abbas Ali 76)
Pakistan 'A' 69 for 3
Match drawn

Rain again plagued the India 'A' tour. Khoda won the toss and chose to bat. He was unbeaten on 181 at the end of the day, and India were 300 for two. He and Wasim Jaffer put on 108 for the first wicket, and Khoda shared a third wicket partnership of 194 with Abbas Ali. On the second day, Gavaskar and Raul put on 227 for the sixth wicket without being separated. Khoda declared at the overnight score, but only 19 overs were possible on the third day and none on the fourth.

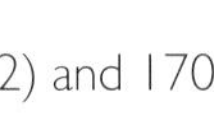

7, 8, 9 and 10 March 1998

at National Stadium, Karachi
India 'A' 260 (M.S.K. Prasad 64, Abdul Razzak 4 for 61, Aqib Javed 4 for 70) and 180 (M.S.K. Prasad 54, Murtaza Hussain 4 for 52)
Pakistan 'A' 212 (A.N. Agarkar 6 for 72) and 170 (Shahid Afridi 65, S.V. Bahutule 4 for 26)
India 'A' won by 58 runs

Put in to bat, India reached 230 for seven on the first day. Skipper Aqib Javed and Abdul Razzak had reduced them to 62 for five, but wicket-keeper Prasad and Raul added 81. Prasad was then joined by Bahutule in a stand worth 86, so that India were more than satisfied with their final total. Agarkar took six wickets on the second day, which ended with Pakistan 52 runs in arrears with the last pair together. Sairaj Bahutule took the final wicket on the third morning to give him figures of three for 33 from 29 overs, a remarkable performance and testimony to his accuracy.

Aqib Javed produced another fine burst to leave India on 42 for four in their second innings. Gavaskar and Prasad added 68 before both falling to off-break bowler Murtaza Hussain. There was another valuable contribution from Bahutule, but India were all out for 180, leaving Pakistan just over a day in which to score 229 to win. They lost Salim Elahi for 0 before the close, and night-watchman Murtaza went early next morning. Shahid Afridi and Bazid Khan took the score to 68 before both falling to Man of the Match Bahutule. Nobody else could play the innings of substance required. Aqib Javed hit lustily at the death, but India took the match and the series.

Ajit Agarkar had bowled outstandingly well, and Bahutule's second innings figures of four for 26 from 15.1 overs emphasised his immense potential.

One-Day Series

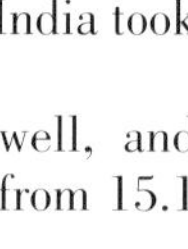

13 March 1998

at Sheikhupura Stadium, Sheikhupura
India 'A' 223 (R.S. Sodhi 51)
Pakistan 'A' 228 for 4 (Akhtar Sarfraz 90)
Pakistan 'A' won by 6 wickets

15 March 1998

at Gaddafi Stadium, Lahore
India 'A' 195
Pakistan 'A' 197 for 4 (Salim Elahi 89 not out,

Mohammad Hussain 54 not out)
Pakistan 'A' won by 6 wickets

17 March 1998
at National Stadium, Karachi
Pakistan 'A' 378 for 4 (Salim Elahi 142, Shahid Afridi 112, Akhtar Sarfraz 56)
India 'A' 208 (Mohammad Hussain 4 for 23)
Pakistan 'A' won by 170 runs

Pakistan 'A' gained consolation for their poor showing in the 'Tests' by making a clean sweep of the one-day series. They bowled out India in every game, and their narrowest margin of victory was in the first match when they won with 10.3 overs to spare. The series was a total triumph for Salim Elahi, who scored 276 runs, average 138, in the three matches.

Patron's Trophy

17, 18, 19 and 20 October 1997
at Gaddafi Stadium, Lahore
Water & Power DA 253 (Adil Nisar 61) and 124 for 2
PIA 153 (Asif Mujtaba 61 not out, Shabbir Ahmed 5 for 31)

Salim Elahi scored 276 runs in the three one-day matches against India 'A'.
(Ben Radford / Allsport)

Match drawn
Water & Power DA 2 pts, PIA 0 pts

at National Stadium, Karachi
National Bank 309 (Akhtar Sarfraz 63, Shahid Nazir 5 for 100) and 223 for 7 (Shahid Anwar 106 not out)
Habib Bank 446 (Shakeel Ahmed 132, Salim Malik 124, Asadullah Butt 58, Naeem Ashraf 4 for 97)
Match drawn
Habib Bank 2 pts, National Bank 0 pts

at KRL Ground, Rawalpindi
ADBP 181 (Manzoor Elahi 81 not out, Abdul Razzaq 5 for 73, Murtaza Hussain 4 for 17) and 276 for 2 (Atif Rauf 98 not out, Mujahid Hameed 71 not out)
KRL 299 (Abdul Razzaq 67, Murtaza Hussain 56, Mohammad Asif 4 for 86)
Match drawn
KRL 2 pts, ADBP 0 pts

18, 19, 20 and 21 October 1997
at United Bank Sports Complex, Karachi
Customs 323 (Azam Khan 92, Saeed Wasim 52, Aamir-ud-Din 50, Aqib Javed 5 for 77) and 80 (Aqib Javed 5 for 31, Ata-ur-Rehman 4 for 32)
Allied Bank 62 (Nadeem Iqbal 5 for 14, Azhar Shafiq 5 for 23) and 428 (Aamir Hanif 153, Manzoor Akhtar 64, Ali Raza 7 for 117)
Allied Bank won by 87 runs
Allied Bank 10 pts, Customs 0 pts

Put in to bat, WAPDA did well enough to take first innings points against PIA, who lost their first five wickets for 31 runs. Asif Mujtaba brought some respectability with a patient 61, but no play was possible on the final day because of rain.

Rejected by the Pakistan selectors, Salim Malik remains, in the opinion of many, the best batsman in the country, and he and Shakeel Ahmed displayed their class with excellent centuries in the match in the National Stadium. Habib Bank took a first innings lead of 137, but opening batsman Shahid Anwar saved National Bank from defeat with an undefeated 106 at a time when his side was in trouble.

Rain washed out the last day in Rawalpindi and ended any hope of a result. Atif Rauf and Mujahid Hameed had added 183 for ADBP's third wicket in the second innings when the game was abandoned.

There was a remarkable result at the United Bank Complex. Having put Customs in to bat, Allied Bank saw them amass 323. They themselves were then bowled out in 25.1 overs and forced to follow on. When their fifth wicket fell in the second innings, they were still three runs in arrears, but Aamir Hanif dominated the closing stages of the innings, hit the 11th century of his career and helped set Customs a target of 168. They had the last day in which to score the runs, but they were bowled out in 23 overs for 80. Aqib Javed had match figures of 10 for 108.

The Patron's Trophy, and all Pakistan cricket, had been shocked by United Bank's decision to withdraw their support from the game, and the season began in a state of uncertainty.

24, 25, 26 and 27 October 1997

at Jinnah Stadium, Gujranwala
KRL 472 for 8 dec. (Iftikhar Hussain 129, Nadeem Abbasi 82, Murtaza Hussain 67 not out, Nasir Ahmed 57)
Water & Power DA 265 (Tariq Aziz 76, Shahid Mansoor 52 not out. Jaffar Nazir 5 for 68) and 193 for 4 (Adil Nisar 51)
Match drawn
KRL 2 pts, Water & Power DA 0 pts

at Sheikupura Stadium, Sheikupura
PIA 407 (Sohail Jaffar 98, Gulam Ali 54, Shoaib Akhtar 6 for 136) and 151 for 5 dec. (Babar Zaman 54)
ADBP 325 (Javed Hayat 89, Zahoor Elahi 78, Mujahid Hameed 65, Nadeem Khan 5 for 132) and 76 for 1
Match drawn
PIA 2 pts, ADBP 0 pts

at National Stadium, Karachi
Customs 110 (Athar Laeeq 5 for 26, Mohammad Javed 4 for 11) and 271 (Aamir-ud-Din 73, Rana Qayyum 58, Saeed Wasim 50, Naeem Ashraf 4 for 37)
National Bank 146 (Tahir Shah 53, Nadeem Ashraf 7 for 59) and 238 for 4 (Mohammad Javed 54 not out)
National Bank won by 6 wickets
National Bank 12 pts, Customs 0 pts

at United Bank Sports Complex, Karachi
Habib Bank 152 (Aqib Javed 4 for 47) and 196 (Aqib Javed 6 for 59)
Allied Bank 377 (Manzoor Akhtar 113, Aamir Hanif 73, Shakeel Khan 8 for 74)
Allied Bank won by an innings and 29 runs
Allied Bank 12 pts, Habib Bank 0 pts

Rain limited play on the third day in Gujranwala and condemned the match to a draw. The same applied to the game in Sheikupura.

Nadeem Ashraf returned the best bowling figures of his career but ended on the losing side when National Bank showed positive application in their second innings. Allied Bank gained a resounding victory in three days over Habib Bank. Aqib Javed took ten wickets for the second match in succession, and Manzoor Akhtar hit 113 off 151 balls. He and Aamir Hanif added 142 for the fifth wicket.

14, 15, 16 and 16 November 1997

at Gaddafi Stadium, Lahore
Allied Bank 90 (Athar Laeeq 5 for 43) and 168 (Naeem Ashraf 7 for 41)
National Bank 227 (Aqib Javed 7 for 77) and 33 for 2
National Bank won by 3 wickets
National Bank 12 pts, Allied Bank 0 pts

at United Bank Sports Complex, Karachi
Habib Bank 336 (Salim Elahi 86, Naveed Anjum 69) and 252 for 8 dec. (Salim Malik 97, Mujahid Jamshed 58)
PIA 241 (Asif Mujtaba 64, Sajid Shah 4 for 65) and 270 for 4 (Asif Mujtaba 67 not out, Rizwan-uz-Zaman 50)
Match drawn
Habib Bank 2 pts, PIA 0 pts

at Sheikhupura Stadium, Sheikhupura
ADBP 368 (Mujahid Hameed 133 not out, Mansoor Rana 66, Zahoor Elahi 61, Anwar Ali 4 for 93) and 228 for 8 dec. (Zahoor Elahi 64, Shabir Ahmed 4 for 96)
Water & Power DA 277 (Yousuf Youhana 72, Shahid Aslam 50, Fazl-e-Akbar 9 for 116) and 298 for 9 (Adil Nisar 79, Yousuf Youhana 69)
Match drawn
ADBP 2 pts, Water & Power DA 0 pts

16, 17, 18 and 19 November 1997

at Iqbal Stadium, Faisalabad
KRL 404 (Abdur Razzaq 117, Mohammad Naved 61, Nadeem Ashraf 5 for 104) and 75 for 4
Customs 210 (Aamir Iqbal 64, Jaffar Nazir 5 for 88) and 268 (Rana Qayyum 78, Azam Khan 77, Murtaza Hussain 4 for 64)
KRL won by 6 wickets
KRL 12 pts, Customs 0 pts

Put in to bat at the Gaddafi Stadium, Allied Bank were bowled out in 30.1 overs, and, in spite of another magnificent effort from Aqib Javed, they made no effective

An emerging all-rounder talent who performed well against India 'A' and thrived in the one-day international series in South Africa, Abdur Razzaq.
(David Pinegar / ASP)

recovery. The experienced pace bowler took nine for 95 in the match, but National Bank won inside two days. The significant batting performances came from Shahid Anwar and Sajid Ali, who scored 105 for National Bank's first wicket. Naeem Ashraf took 10 for 70 in the match.

Habib Bank dominated the match in Karachi, but PIA batted throughout the last day to force a draw, and WAPDA drew with ADBP when their last pair held out for the final 30 minutes of the game in Sheikhupura. The match witnessed the best bowling performance of the season as the 17-year old pace bowler Fazl-e-Akbar took nine for 116 in 32 overs.

Another teenager, Abdur Razzaq, hit the first century of his career, 117 off 128 balls, for KRL in their victory over Customs.

19, 20, 21 and 22 November 1997

at Sheikhupura Stadium, Sheikhupura
Habib Bank 190 and 345 for 8 (Mujahid Jamshed 115, Shakeel Ahmed 75, Adil Nisar 4 for 57)
Water & Power DA 346 (Yousuf Youhana 163 not out, Akram Raza 4 for 72, Shahid Mahmood 4 for 96)
Match drawn
Water & Power DA 2 pts, Habib Bank 0 pts

22, 23, 24 and 25 November 1997

at Gaddafi Stadium, Lahore
PIA 287 (Rizwan-uz-Zaman 91, Naeem Ashraf 6 for 69) and 211 for 4 (Rizwan-uz-Zaman 65, Asif Mujtaba 50)
National Bank 306 (Akhtar Sarfraz 69, Hanif-ur-Rehman 61, Tahir Shah 53, Tariq Mohammad 51, Nadeem Afzal 4 for 107)
Match drawn
National Bank 2 pts, PIA 0 pts

at KRL Ground, Rawalpindi
Allied Bank 308 (Aamir Sohail 170, Shakeel Ahmed 7 for 91) and 24 for 3
KRL 158 (Naeem Akhtar 58, Bilal Rana 5 for 59, Mohammad Zahid 4 for 39) and 173 (Iftikhar Hussain 70, Bilal Rana 5 for 45)
Allied Bank won by 7 wickets
Allied Bank 12 pts, KRL 0 pts

at Iqbal Stadium, Faisalabad
ADBP 156 and 347 for 8 dec. (Mansoor Rana 107, Mujahid Hameed 51, Nadeem Ashraf 4 for 63)
Customs 168 (Fazl-e-Akbar 6 for 57) and 141 (Fazl-e-Akbar 4 for 40)
ADBP won by 194 runs
ADBP 10 pts, Customs 0 pts

No play was possible on the last day in Lahore, and, in Sheikhupura, WAPDA surprisingly took a big first innings lead over Habib Bank, who were asked to bat first. Another of Pakistan's proteges, Yousuf Youhana, 23 years old, hit the first century of his career. He was later to display his great talent at international level.

Aamir Sohail made 170 off 247 balls as Allied Bank beat KRL, and Fazl-e-Akbar gave another fine bowling performance to bring ADBP victory over Customs, who had taken a narrow lead on the first innings.

13, 14, 15 and 16 December 1997

at Gaddafi Stadium, Lahore
ADBP 135 (Mohammad Akram 6 for 49, Aamir Nazir 4 for 26) and 92 (Ata-ur-Rehman 7 for 20)
Allied Bank 132 (Fazl-e-Akbar 6 for 58) and 96 for 6
Allied Bank won by 4 wickets
Allied Bank 10 pts, ADBP 0 pts

at United Bank Sports Complex, Karachi
PIA 318 for 8 dec. (Sohail Jaffar 72, Asif Mujtaba 64 not out, Babar Zaman 60, Jaffar Nazir 4 for 113) and 107 for 9 dec. (Naeem Akhtar 5 for 38, Jaffar Nazir 4 for 50)
KRL 184 (Iftikhar Hussain 80 not out, Hasnain Kazim 6 for 73) and 122 for 7 (Ali Gauhar 4 for 63)
Match drawn
PIA 2 pts, KRL 0 pts

at Sheikhupura Stadium, Sheikhupura
Customs 109 (Nadeem Ghauri 5 for 39) and 138 (Sajid Shah 4 for 42)
Habib Bank 209 (Tahir Rasheed 57, Haaris A. Khan 5 for 59) and 44 for 3
Habib Bank won by 7 wickets
Habib Bank 12 pts, Customs 0 pts

at Jinnah Stadium, Gujranwala
Water & Power DA 329 for 7 dec. (Adil Nisar 98, Yousuf Youhana 56)
National Bank 173 for 8 (Irfan-ul-Haq 5 for 89)
No result
No points

Two pace bowlers anxious to reclaim Test places, Mohammad Akram and Ata-ur-Rehman, set up Allied Bank's victory over ADBP, but Fazl-e-Akbar again showed his quality with match figures of nine for 93. The highest score of the match was Taimur Khan's unbeaten 37 off 39 balls in Allied Bank's second innings, and the game was over early on the third day.

PIA were thwarted by KRL, although, arguably, Aamir Malik delayed his declaration too long. Rain spread WAPDA's first innings over three days in Gujranwala, and no decision could be reached on the first innings when rain returned on the last day. Habib Bank's hopes of a place in the final were boosted by victory over Customs, whose run of poor form continued.

20, 21, 22 and 23 December 1997

at Sheikhupura Stadium, Sheilkhupura

The most consistent of Pakistan batsmen in all forms of international cricket – Inzaman-ul-Haq.
(Nigel French / ASP)

Water & Power DA 134 (Mohammad Akram 5 for 33, Ata-ur-Rehman 4 for 44) and 86 for 5
Allied Bank 214 (Arshad Khan 50)
Match drawn
Allied Bank 2 pts, Water & Power DA 0 pts

at National Stadium, Karachi
PIA 334 (Zahid Fazal 132, Sohail Jaffar 61, Zahid Ahmed 57, Ali Raza 4 for 74) and 228 (Zahid Ahmed 65, Mohammad Zahid 5 for 73)
Customs 263 (Rana Qayyum 64, Ali Gauhar 6 for 76) and 300 for 3 (Aamir-ud-Din 84, Azhar Shafiq 82, Rana Qayyum 63 not out)
Customs won by 7 wickets
Customs 10 pts, PIA 0 pts

at Jinnah Stadium, Gujranwala
National Bank 376 (Shahid Anwar 103, Akhtar Sarfraz 71)
ADBP 24 for 2
No result
No points

at KRL Ground, Rawalpindi
KRL 276 (Maqsood Ahmed 64, Asif Mahmood 55, Shahid Afridi 6 for 101) and 128 for 5
Habib Bank 256 (Mujahid Jamshed 86 not out, Naeem Akhtar 4 for 49, Jaffar Nazir 4 for 96)
Match drawn
KRL 2 pts, Habib Bank 0 pts

Rain restricted play on the first and final days in Sheikhupura and made a draw inevitable. In Karachi, Customs surprised everyone with a sensational win over PIA. Zahid Fazal's century, 132 off 217 deliveries, and the medium pace bowling of Ali Gauhar gave PIA a first innings advantage of 71, and they then batted into the last day and set Customs a target of 300 at four runs an over. Aamir-ud-Din and Azhar Shafiq scored 131 for the first wicket, with Azhar hitting 82 off 73 balls. Aamir-ud-Din provided the solidity for just over four hours, and Rana Qayyum-ul-Hassan was then joined by Azam Khan. The pair scored the last 83 runs in 48 minutes.

No play was possible on the first day at the Jinnah Stadium, and there was very little on the last. Habib Bank failed to take first innings points against KRL, losing their last three wickets for one run.

10, 11, 12 and 13 January 1998
at Arbab Niaz Stadium, Peshawar
Customs 199 (Aamir Iqbal 62) and 356 (Mohammad Ramzan 91, Aamir-ud-Din 60, Anwar Ali 4 for 128)
Water & Power DA 277 (Adil Nisar 64, Tariq Aziz 57, Haaris A. Khan 5 for 78, Tauseef Ahmed 4 for 57) and 25 for 2
Match drawn
Water & Power DA 2 pts, Customs 0 pts

at National Stadium, Karachi
Allied Bank 266 (Ata-ur-Rehman jnr 80, Hasnain Kazim 4 for 101) and 227 (Ali Gauhar 4 for 63)
PIA 325 (Moin Khan 129, Wasim Akram 59, Aamir Nazir 5 for 104) and 170 for 6 (Zahid Fazal 78 not out)
PIA won by 4 wickets
PIA 12 pts, Allied Bank 0 pts

at Gaddafi Stadium, Lahore
ADBP 120 (Sajid Shah 6 for 56) and 242 (Sajid Shah 5 for 89)
Habib Bank 432 for 7 dec. (Salim Elahi 203 not out, Salim Malik 63, Shoaib Akhtar 5 for 166)
Habib Bank won by an innings and 70 runs
Habib Bank 12 pts, ADBP 0 pts

at KRL Ground, Rawalpindi
National Bank 169 (Akhtar Sarfraz 51, Shakeel Ahmed 5 for 52) and 98 for 9 (Shakeel Ahmed 4 for 33)
KRL 239 (Nadeem Abbasi 87 not out, Naseer A. Mughal 50, Salman Fazal 5 for 98, Naeem Tayyab 4 for 74)
Match drawn
KRL 2 pts, National Bank 0 pts

The last round of matches saw PIA, strengthened by the availablity of Moin Khan and Wasim Akram, beat league leaders Allied Bank. PIA were 78 for six before Moin and Wasim added 128 at a run a minute. Moin Khan's 129 came off 169 balls.

Habib Bank claimed a place in the final by beating ADBP by an innings. Sajid Shah took 10 wickets in a match for the second time in his career.

Patron's Trophy Final Table

	P	W	L	D	NR	Pts
Allied Bank	7	4	2	1	–	46
Habib Bank	7	2	1	4	–	28
National Bank	7	2	–	3	2	26
Khan Research Laboratories	7	1	1	5	–	20
Pakistan International Airlines	7	1	1	5	–	16
Agricultural Development Bank of Pakistan	7	1	2	3	1	12
Pakistan Customs	7	1	5	1	–	10
Water & Power Development Authority	7	–	–	6	1	6

Patron's Trophy Final

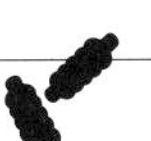

18, 19, 20, 21 and 22 February 1998
at Gaddafi Stadium, Lahore
Habib Bank 399 (Shakeel Ahmed 148, Naved Anjum 70, Arshad Khan 4 for 72) and 187 (Arshad Khan 4 for 25)
Allied Bank 175 and 251 (Wajahatullah Wasti 55, Sajid Ali 5 for 107)
Habib Bank won by 160 runs

Habib Bank blunted the pace attack of Aqib Javed and Ata-ur-Rehman to win the Patron's Trophy in convincing style. Aqib decided to field when he won the toss and relished the prospect of bowling on a green pitch, but his plan was thwarted when rain and bad light restricted play to 41 minutes on the opening day. The next day, the sun shone, and Habib Bank batted in good conditions. Former Test batsman Shakeel Ahmed hit 148 off 250 balls and was at the crease just under six hours. He hit 24 fours and shared a second wicket partnership of 111 with Salim Elahi after Shahid Afridi had been dismissed at six. Naveed Anjum and Kabir Khan put on 64 for the eighth wicket, and only off-spinner Arshad Khan gave the batsmen any trouble.

Facing a large total, Allied Bank collapsed on the third day when 15 wickets fell, but Salim Malik, for whom the match was a personal triumph, did not enforce the follow on. His side gave a rather cavalier display in their second innings, but Allied Bank were left 412 to win. They showed spirit, but the game was over before tea on the last day.

Allied Bank were disappointing. They were without Aamir Sohail and Rashid Latif, and it was believed that Rameez Raja would be called upon to boost the side, but he had not played since the Sahara Cup in Canada and he did not appear in any match during the season.

Quaid-e-Azam Trophy

3, 4, 5 and 6 October 1997
at Lahore CCA Ground, Lahore
Karachi Whites 149 (Mohammad Asif 4 for 22)
Lahore City 104 for 2
No result
No points

at Jinnah Stadium, Gujranwala
Gujranwala 240 for 7 dec. (Majid Saeed 68)
Multan 135 for 8 (Aamir Wasim 4 for 20)
No result
No points

at Bohranwali Ground, Faisalabad
Faisalabad 136 (Fazl-e-Akbar 4 for 28, Arshad Khan 4 for 37) and 167 (Fazl-e-Akbar 6 for 60)
Peshawar 246 (Wajatullah Wasti 72, Jahangir Khan snr 52, Akram Raza 7 for 102) and 58 for 2
Peshawar won by 8 wickets
Peshawar 12 pts, Faisalabad 0 pts

at Asghar Ali Shah Stadium, Karachi
Bahawalpur 401 (Aamir Bashir 94, Bilal M. Khelji 91, Sajid Ali 71, Lal Faraz 4 for 69) and 64 for 3
Karachi Blues 395 (Asif Mujtaba 119, Zafar Iqbal 110, Murtaza Hussain 5 for 114)
Match drawn
Bahawalpur 2 pts, Karachi Blues 0 pts

The matches in Lahore and Gujranwala were totally ruined by rain, and no play was possible on the second day in Faisalabad. In spite of this, Peshawar gained a fine victory and owed much to the inspired pace bowling of Fazl-e-Akbar. The youngster, who did so well in the Patron's Trophy, which was played on alternate weeks to the Quaid-e-Azam Trophy, had match figures of 10 for 88.

In the high-scoring game in Karachi, Asif Mujtaba and Zafar Iqbal put on 221 for the Blues' seventh wicket, but three wickets then fell for 13 runs and, with Nadim Khan ill and unable to bat, they conceded first innings points by six runs.

10, 11, 12 and 13 October 1997
at National Stadium, Karachi
Bahawalpur 402 (Aamir Bashir 122, Saifullah 80, Baqar Rivzi 5 for 86) and 202 (Murtaza Hussain 64, Shahid Mahboob 8 for 77)
Karachi Whites 521 for 3 dec. (Hasan Raza 204 not out, Shahid Afridi 118, Farhan Adil 100 not out, Iqbal Saleem 70) and 86 for 0 (Shahid Afridi 62 not out)
Karachi Whites won by 10 wickets
Karachi Whites 12 pts, Bahawalpur 0 pts

at Montgomery Biscuit Factory Ground, Sahiwal
Multan 152 (Abdul Razzaq 4 for 52)
Lahore City 76 for 8 (Azhar Abbas 4 for 29)
No result
No points

at Jinnah Stadium, Gujranwala
Gujranwala 211 (Zafar Iqbal 5 for 64, Ali Gauhar 4 for 65) and 151
Karachi Blues 239 (Basit Ali 55, Shoaib Malik 4 for 66, Ameem Abbas 4 for 101) and 127 for 2 (Shadab Kabir 55)
Karachi Blues won by 8 wickets
Karachi Blues 12 pts, Gujranwala 0 pts

at CRA Ground, Islamabad
Peshawar 168 (Hameed Gul 59 not out) and 238 for 5 (Abdul Salam 60, Taimur Khan 57 not out)
Islamabad 203 (Shahid Hussain 7 for 55)
Match drawn
Islamabad 2 pts, Peshawar 0 pts

at Bohranwali Ground, Faisalabad
Faisalabad 262 (Fida Hussain 99, Jaffar Nazir 4 for 57)
Rawalpindi 284 for 5 (Nasir Ahmed 152 not out)
Match drawn
Rawalpindi 2 pts, Faisalabad 0 pts

Lahore and Multan were again hit by the weather, but Karachi Whites had ample opportunity to display their prowess. Facing Bahawalpur's total of 402, they took first innings points for the loss of only three wickets as Pakistan's young batsmen gave indication of their prodigious talents. Shahid Afridi hit 118 off 72 balls and Hasan Raza, the youngest player to appear in Test cricket, hit a maiden first-class century, 204 not out off 315 balls. Farhan Adil, just 20 years old, also scored a maiden first-class century, 100 off 110 balls. Medium-pace bowler Shahid Mahboob took eight wickets as Bahawalpur were bowled out in 50.3 overs, and Shahid Afridi hit 62 off 46 balls as the Whites swept to victory.

Rain washed out play on the second day in Islamabad and made a draw inevitable, but Karachi Blues had time to spare, beating Gujranwala with less than an hour of the final day needed. Play could not begin until the afternoon of the second day in Faisalabad where Fida Hussain had the misfortune to be run out one run short of what would have been a maiden first-class century.

31 October, 1, 2 and 3 November 1997

at Asghar Ali Shah Stadium, Karachi
Karachi Whites 183 (Ali Hussain Rizvi 5 for 46) and 291 (Ali Raza 4 for 80)
Karachi Blues 247 (Asim Kamal 81, Rizwan Qureshi 57, Kashif Ibrahim 5 for 63) and 230 for 2 (Azam Khan 82 not out, Kashif Ahmed 73 not out, Shahdab Kabir 54)
Karachi Blues won by 8 wickets
Karachi Blues 12 pts, Karachi Whites 0 pts

at Jinnah Stadium, Gujranwala
Gujranwala 129 (Abdur Razzaq 4 for 40) and 431 (Majid Saeed 107, Shakeel Ahmed 89, Inam-ul-Haq 66, Abdur Razzaq 4 for 182)
Lahore City 502 for 8 dec. (Naeem Ashraf 139, Abdur Razzaq 103 not out, Salim Elahi 81, Tahir Mahmood 6 for 83) and 60 for 6 (Tahir Mahmmod 4 for 29)
Lahore City won by 4 wickets
Lahore City 12 pts, Gujranwala 0 pts

at Mahmood Stadium, Rahim Yar Khan
Multan 144 (Murtaza Hussain 6 for 44) and 177 (Murtaza Hussain 4 for 40, Mohammad Zahid 4 for 47)
Bahawalpur 183 (Shakir Qayyum 6 for 53) and 139 for 4 (Naved Latif 53 not out)
Bahawalpur won by 6 wickets
Bahawalpur 12 pts, Multan 0 pts

at CRA Ground, Islamabad
Islamabad 195 (Ghaffar Kazmi 103, Shahid Nazir 6 for 76) and 350 for 2 (Atif Rauf 155 not out, Ehsan Butt 102 not out)
Faisalabad 196 (Mohammad Nawaz snr 100, S. John 4 for 56, Fahad Khan 4 for 64)
Match drawn
Faisalabad 2 pts, Islamabad 0 pts

at Gymkhana Ground, Peshawar
Rawalpindi 104 (Sajid Shah 5 for 44) and 415 (Shahid

Hasan Raza made 204 not out for Karachi Whites against Bahawalpur at the National Stadium in early October. The youngest player to appear in a Test match, Hasan is a batsman of immense potential.
(David Munden / Sportsline)

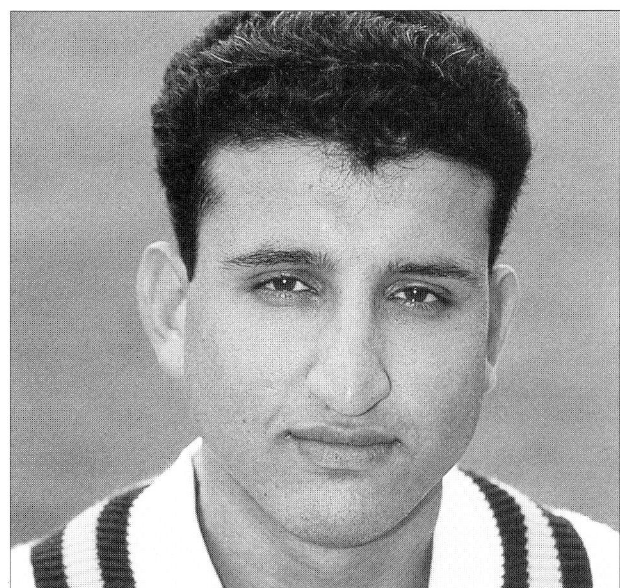

The bowler of the year, young pace man Fazl-e-Akbar, who finished the season with 86 wickets to his credit.
(Ben Radford / Allsport)

Javed 100, Nasir Ahmed 76, Fazl-e-Akbar 4 for 103)
Peshawar 321 (Akhtar Sarfraz 125, Wajahatullah Wasti 50, Shoaib Akhtar 5 for 127) and 116 for 4 (Wajahatullah Wasti 50 not out)
Match drawn
Peshawar 2 pts, Rawalpindi 0 pts

The Karachi rivalry game went very much in favour of the Blues, who gained their second win of the season and went top of the table. After two matches in which no decision was reached, Lahore won well against Gujranwala. Naaem Ashraf and Abdur Razzaq put on 229 for their seventh wicket at a lightning pace. Naeem hit 139 off 148 balls, while Abdur made an unbeaten 103 off 105 balls. The home side fought back splendidly, and Lahore made heavy weather of scoring the 59 they needed to win. The match was remarkable in that there were 99 extras in Lahore's first innings and 73 in Gujranwala's second. There were 138 runs from no-balls in the match, each no-ball costing two runs.

There was no such profligacy in the game between Multan and Bahawalpur, where off-spinner Murtaza Hussain enhanced his claims for a place in the national side with figures of 10 for 84. He was still a month short of his 22nd birthday.

In Islamabad's second innings, Ehsan Butt and Atif Rauf shared an unbroken third wicket partnership of 279.

7, 8, 9 and 10 November 1997

at National Stadium, Karachi
Islamabad 142 (Shahid Mahboob 5 for 40) and 261 (Bilal Asad 73, Azhar Mahmood 64)
Karachi Whites 293 (Farhan Adil 70) and 111 for 2
Karachi Whites won by 8 wickets
Karachi Whites 12 pts, Islamabad 0 pts

at Mahmood Stadium, Rahim Yar Khan
Lahore City 252 (Mansoor Rana 61, Abdur Razzaq 51, Mohammad Zahid 6 for 52) and 162 (Murtaza Hussain 5 for 62, Mohammad Zahid 4 for 30)
Bahawalpur 229 (Aamir Bashir 82) and 190 for 4 (Azhar Shafiq 61, Aamir Bashir 50 not out)
Bahawalpur won by 6 wickets
Bahawalpur 10 pts, Lahore City 0 pts

at Gymkhana Ground, Rawalpindi
Gujranwala 110 (Fazl-e-Akbar 5 for 44) and 231 (Shakeel Khan 56, Sajid Shah 6 for 85)
Peshawar 280 (Wasim Yousufi 103, Shahid Hussain 66) and 62 for 2
Peshawar won by 8 wickets
Peshawar 12 pts, Gujranwala 0 pts

at Montgomery Biscuit Factory, Sahiwal
Faisalabad 135 (Fida Hussain 55 not out, Imran Idrees 6 for 32) and 217 (Bilal Rana 5 for 46)
Multan 288 (Tariq Mahboob 55, Mohammad Wasim 4 for 51) and 65 for 2
Multan won by 8 wickets
Multan 12 pts, Faisalabad 0 pts

at Pindi Stadium, Rawalpindi
Rawalpindi 278 (Mohammad Wasim 111 not out)
Karachi Blues 195 (Jaffar Nazir 7 for 42)
Match drawn
Rawalpindi 2 pts, Karachi Blues 0 pts

Karachi Whites returned to winning ways, and there were first victories of the season for Peshawar and Multan. Mohammad Zahid took 10 for 82 to steer Bahawalpur to victory over Lahore, while rain ruined the game in Rawalpindi.

29, 30 November, 1 and 2 December 1997

at KRL Ground, Rawalpindi
Rawalpindi 337 (Nadeem Hussain 125, Asif Mahmood 101, Asim Zaidi 5 for 78) and 273 (Arif Butt 85)
Karachi Whites 286 (Shahid Afridi 123, Mohammad Akram 7 for 73) and 60 for 1
Match drawn
Rawalpindi 2 pts, Karachi Whites 0 pts

at Iqbal Stadium, Faisalabad
Faisalabad 299 (Fida Hussain 72 not out, Bilal Ahmed 52, Tahir Mahmood 5 for 69) and 61 for 1
Gujranwala 147 (Saadat Gul 5 for 36, Shahid Nazir 4 for 57) and 207 (Amim Abbas 50)
Faisalabad won by 9 wickets
Faisalabad 12 pts, Gujranwala 0 pts

at Gaddafi Stadium, Lahore
Lahore City 278 (Naeem Ashraf 74, Ali Gauhar 5 for 72) and 236 (Yousuf Youhana 60, Ali Gauhar 4 for 70)
Karachi Blues 194 (Naeem Ashraf 6 for 56) and 144 (Naeem Ashraf 4 for 33)
Lahore City won by 176 runs
Lahore City 12 pts, Karachi Blues 0 pts

at Arbab Niaz Stadium, Peshawar
Multan 92 (Sajid Shah 5 for 46) and 113 (Fazl-e-Akbar 5 for 61)
Peshawar 217 (Wajahatullah Wasti 81)
Peshawar won by an innings and 12 runs
Peshawar 12 pts, Multan 0 pts

at Mahmood Stadium, Rahim Yar Khan
Bahawalpur 183 (Rehan Rafiq 51, Azhar Shafiq 50, Khalid Zafar 5 for 43) and 215
Islamabad 250 (Qaiser Mahmood 64, Murtaza Hussain 7 for 110) and 109 (Mohammad Zahid 4 for 40)
Bahawalpur won by 39 runs
Bahawalpur 10 pts, Islamabad 0 pts

A restricted first day's play in Rawalpindi condemned the match against Karachi Whites to be drawn, but a fifth wicket partnership of 161 between Asif Mahmood and Nadeem Hussain gave Rawalpindi the upper hand and first innings points. Faisalabad gained their first win of the season, and Lahore caused a surprise with victory over Karachi Blues. The architect of their victory was left-arm medium-pacer Naeem Ashraf, who was well supported by Ata-ur-Rehman.

Peshawar's innings victory over Mulktan took them to the top of the table, while Bahawalpur's win over Islamabad took them into second place. Murtaza Hussain produced another fine performance, 10 for 127 in the match.

6, 7, 8 and 9 December 1997

at Lahore CA Ground, Lahore
Lahore City 332 (Javed Hayat 59, Shahid Nawaz 58, Zahoor Elahi 53)
Faisalabad 173 (Mohammad Asif 4 for 31) and 87 (Mohammad Asif 4 for 19)
Lahore City won by an innings and 72 runs
Lahore City 12 pts, Faisalabad 0 pts

at Arbab Niaz Stadium, Peshawar
Karachi Whites 295 (Shahid Afridi 88, Arshad Khan 4 for 97) and 110 (Fazl-e-Akbar 5 for 54)
Peshawar 342 (Taimur Khan 111, Shahid Hussain 55, Asim Zaidi 5 for 109, Kashif Ibrahim 5 for 119) and 67 for 3
Peshawar won by 7 wickets
Peshawar 12 pts, Karachi Whites 0 pts

at Montgomery Biscuit Factory, Sahiwal
Rawalpindi 158 (Asif Mahmood 68, Bilal Rana 6 for 29) and 209 (Azhar Abbas 4 for 44)

Ata-ur-Rehman enjoyed a successful season, but he failed to earn a recall to the national side.
(Nigel French / ASP)

Multan 151 (Naeem Akhtar 6 for 52) and 200 (Shakeel Ahmed 6 for 72)
Rawalpindi won by 16 runs
Rawalpindi 12 pts, Multan 0 pts

at Mahmood Stadium, Rahim Yar Khan
Gujranwala 275 (Hasan Adnan 64, Iqbal Zahoor 62 not out, Shehzad Malik 59, Murtaza Hussain 7 for 95) and 139 (Murtaza Hussain 5 for 66)
Bahawalpur 437 (Aamir Bashiq 173 not out, Rehan Rafiq 69, Murtaza Hussain 67)
Bahawalpur won by an innings and 23 runs
Bahawalpur 12 pts, Gujranwala 0 pts

at United Bank Sports Complex, Karachi
Karachi Blues 225 (Asif Mujtaba 86) and 270 (Zafar Aqbal 76, Azam Khan 51, S. John 6 for 99)
Islamabad 204 (Bilal Asad 78, Ali Gauhar 5 for 59) and 192 (Ali Raza 64, Lal Faraz 6 for 63)
Karachi Blues won by 99 runs
Karachi Blues 12 pts, Islamabad 0 pts

Lahore gained their second win in succession and moved into contention for a place in the final, being level on points with Karachi Blues, who beat Islamabad. Peshawar continued to set the pace. Their fourth win of the season took them clear of the pack. Shahid Afridi played another blistering innings for Karachi Whites, 88 off 75 balls, but Taimur Kahn's century took Peshawar to a first innings lead in spite of losing their first six wickets for 87 runs. Whites collapsed to 55 for seven in their second innings, and Peshawar never relaxed their grip on the game. Gujranwala lost their fifth match in succession as Bahawalpur moved into second place. Aamir Bashir made the highest score of his career, and he and Murtaza Hussain put on 131 for the eighth wicket. Rawalpindi gained their first win of the season.

27, 28, 29 and 30 December 1997

at Iqbal Stadium, Faisalabad
Faisalabad 298 (Ijaz Ahmed jnr 94, Kashif Ibrahim 4 for 52)
Karachi Whites 25 for 0
No result
No points

at Arbab Niaz Stadium, Peshawar
Lahore City 126 (Sajid Shah 5 for 41) and 120 for 3
Peshawar 204 for 6 dec. (Taimur Khan 52 not out, Naeem Ashraf 5 for 88)
Match drawn
Peshawar 2 pts, Lahore City 0 pts

at National Stadium, Karachi
Multan 190 (Mohammad Shafiq 71, Zafar Iqbal 4 for 42) and 230 (Majid Inayat 55, Ali Gauhar 4 for 43)
Karachi Blues 382 (Azam Khan 119, Asif Mujtaba 97, Kamal Merchant 67 not out, Nadeem Iqbal 4 for 98) and 39 for 0
Karachi Blues won by 10 wickets
Karachi Blues 12 pts, Multan 0 pts

at Pindi Stadium, Rawalpindi
Bahawalpur 244 (Rehan Rafiq 72 not out, Jaffar Nazir 6 for 94) and 26 for 1
Rawalpindi 342 (Asif Mahmood 63, Arif Butt 54)
Match drawn
Rawalpindi 2 pts, Bahawalpur 0 pts

The weather was most unkind. One game was abandoned completely, and no result was possible in Faisalabad. There was no play on the second day in Peshawar, and the only team to draw comfort was Karachi Blues, who overcame Multan easily to close the gap on Peshawar.

3, 4, 5 and 6 January 1998

at Mahmood Stadium, Rahim Yar Khan
Faisalabad 141 (Mohammad 6 for 50) and 303 (Mohammad Ramzan 94, Mohammad Nawaz jnr 61)
Bahawalpur 171 (Mohammad Wasim 4 for 58) and 275 for 9 (Azhar Shafiq 104 not out, Rehan Rafiq 54)
Bahawalpur won by 1 wicket
Bahawalpur 12 pts, Faisalabad 0 pts

at Asghar Ali Shah Stadium, Karachi
Peshawar 472 (Jahangir Khan 175, Asmatullah 63, Nadeem Khan 4 for 112) and 92 for 5
Karachi Blues 480 (Asif Mujtaba 191, Rashid Latif 91, Azam Khan 74, Sajid Shah 4 for 120)
Match drawn
Karachi Blues 2 pts, Peshawar 0 pts

at CRA Ground, Faisalabad
Islamabad 274 (Azhar Mahmood 52, Shahid Mahmood 4 for 58, Mohammad Asif 4 for 70) and 273 for 8 (Bilal Asad 105, Ghaffar Kazmi 58)
Lahore City 430 (Yousuf Youhana 120, Salim Elahi 113, Shahid Nawaz 72, Azhar Mahmood 5 for 115)
Match drawn
Lahore City 2 pts, Islamabad 0 pts

at National Stadium, Karachi
Multan 214 (Mohammad Shafiq 70, Arif Mahmood 4 for 54) and 241 (Shahid Afridi 5 for 53)
Karachi Whites 128 (Shabib Ahmed 4 for 33) and 328 for 5 (Aamir Hanif 113 not out, Frahan Adil 95, Iqbal Imam 55)
Karachi Whites won by 5 wickets
Karachi Whites 10 pts, Multan 0 pts

at Jinnah Stadium, Gujranwala
Rawalpindi 211 and 268 for 8 (Asif Mahmood 87)
Gujranwala 220 (Shahzad Malik 69, Hasan Adnan 64 not out)
Match drawn
Gujranwala 2 pts, Rawalpindi 0 pts

The results of the penultimate round of matches left three sides in contention for the two top spots that would earn them a place in the final. Bahawalpur gained a thrilling victory over Faisalabad. Needing 274 to win, they were 40 for three, but Azhar Shafiq batted with intelligence and sound technique to carry his side to victory. The ninth wicket fell at 270, but Mohammad Altaf, called upon to face one ball, hit a four.

Karachi Blues took first innings points against Peshawar, for whom Jahangir Khan hit a career best 175. The Blues owed a tremendous debt to Asif Mujtaba, who continues to display in domestic cricket the outstanding form that he has never been able to reproduce at Test level. His 191 came off 358 balls. Skipper Rashid Latif made 91 off 206 balls. The results meant that eight points separated Bahawalpur, Peshawar and Karachi Blues.

Salim Elahi and Yousuf Youhana shared an exhilarating third wicket stand of 191 as Lahore drew with Islamabad, and Karachi Whites overturned a first innings deficit of 86 to beat Multan by five wickets. Set a massive target of 328, they were 77 for three before Farhan Adil and Aamir Hanif took over. Iqbal Imam supplied the necessary verve with 55 off 79 balls.

17, 18, 19 and 20 January 1998
at PAF Faisal Sports Ground, Karachi
Karachi Whites 153 (Aamir Wasim 4 for 39, Abdul Rehmen 4 for 59) and 186 (Aamir Wasim 6 for 80)
Gujranwala 224 (Hasan Adnan 93, Tahir Andy 4 for 64) and 116 for 5
Gujranwala won by 5 wickets
Gujranwala 12 pts, Karachi Whites 0 pts

at KRL Ground, Rawalpindi
Rawalpindi 588 for 6 dec. (Asif Mahmood 250, Mohammad Wasim 165) and 127 for 5
Lahore City 264 (Salim Elahi 88, Shoaib Akhtar 5 for 95)
Match drawn
Rawalpindi 2 pts, Lahore City 0 pts

at Montgomery Biscuit Factory, Sahiwal
Islamabad 123 (Bilal Asad 51, Waqar Younis 6 for 16) and 307 (Bilal Asad 117, Khalid Zafar 54)
Multan 264 (Bilal Rana 78, Raja Arshad 59, Taimur Ali 4 for 84) and 67 (S. John 6 for 19)
Islamabad won by 99 runs
Islamabad 10 pts, Multan 0 pts

at Arbab Niaz Stadium, Peshawar
Peshawar 205 (Wajahatullah 87, Azhar Shafiq 5 for 25) and 211 (Akhtar Sarfraz 103 not out, Azhar Shafiq 4 for 78, Kamran Hussain 4 for 79)
Bahawalpur 190 (Bilal M. Khelji 72 not out, Waqar Ahmed 6 for 45) and 191 (Sajid Shah 4 for 51, Waqar Ahmed 4 for 64)
Peshawar won by 35 runs
Peshawar 12 pts, Bahawalpur 0 pts

at National Stadium, Karachi
Faisalabad 262 (Fida Hussain 57, Nadeem Khan 5 for 36) and 132 (Zafar Iqbal 6 for 18)
Karachi Blues 157 (Zafar Iqbal 57, Saeed Ajmal 5 for 4) and 238 for 4 (Munir-ul-Haq 60, Basit Ali 53 not out)
Karachi Blues won by 6 wickets
Karachi Blues 10 pts, Faisalabad 0 pts

Islamabad and Gujranwala claimed their first victories of the season in what was the last round of matches. Islamabad beat Multan in spite of being opposed by the pace of Waqar Younis, who routed them in the first innings. Islamabad had their own hero in left-arm fast medium pace bowler Stephen John, who took six for 19 in 9.3 overs to destroy Multan's second innings. The home side had led by 141 runs on the first innings, but Bilal Asad's fine hundred brought Islamabad back into contention.

A third wicket partnership of 328 between Asif Mahmood and Mahommad Wasim was the feature of the match in Rawalpindi. Both batsmen made the highest score of their careers. The main focus, however, was on the games in Peshawar and Karachi. In a closely fought contest, Peshawar beat Bahawalpur while Karachi Blues beat Faisalabad to move above Bahawalpur, and win a place in the final. Blues trailed by 105 runs on the first innings, and their hopes of victory had seemingly vanished, but medium-pacer Zafar Iqbal produced a splendid bowling performance, taking six for 18 in 11 overs, to revive the Blues' chances, and Basit Ali and Munir-ul-Haq did the rest.

Quaid-e-Azam Trophy Final Table

	P	W	L	D	NR	Pts
Peshawar	9	5	–	4	–	64
Karachi Blues	9	5	1	3	–	60
Bahawalpur	9	5	2	2	–	58
Lahore City	9	3	1	3	2	38
Karachi Whites	9	3	3	1	2	34
Rawalpindi	9	1	–	7	1	22
Gujranwala	9	1	5	1	2	14
Faisalabad	9	1	5	2	1	14
Islamabad	9	1	3	3	2	12
Multan	9	1	6	–	2	12

The matches between Islamabad and Rawalpindi, and Gujranwala and Islamabad were abandoned without a ball being bowled.

Captain of Karachi Blues when they won the Quaid-e-Azan Trophy and the scorer of most runs in first-class cricket in Pakistan, 1997–98, Asif Muhtaba.
(David Munden / Sportsline)

Quaid-e-Azam Trophy Final

1, 2, 3, 4 and 5 March 1998
at National Stadium, Karachi
Karachi Blues 394 (Azam Khan 136, Shoaib Mohammad 66, Kabir Khan 4 for 73) and 287 for 7 dec. (Sohail Jaffar 100, Manzoor Akhtar 58 not out)
Peshawar 211 (Wasim Yousufi 60, Nadeem Khan 4 for 41, Ali Gauhar 4 for 67) and 153 for 3 (Moin-ul-Atiq 55)
Match drawn
Karachi Blues won trophy on first innings lead

Put in to bat, Karachi Blues batted well in very difficult conditions. Shoaib Mohammad and Sohail Jaffar added 88 after two wickets had fallen for 15, but it was Azam Khan who played the outstanding innings. He batted just over six and a half hours and faced 277 balls for his 136 to take the Blues to a position of dominance. Peshawar lost three wickets before the close of the second day, and only a hard-hit 60 from Wasim Yousufi took them to respectability. There was limited play on the fourth day and then, in easier circumstances, Sohail Jaffar hit 100 off 131 balls so that Asif Mujtaba was able to declare on the last day with his side 470 runs ahead and the trophy won.

Azam Khan was named Man of the Match.

First-Class Averages

Batting

	M	Inns	NOs	Runs	HS	Av	100s	50s
Inzamam-ul-Haq	6	7	1	438	177	73.00	1	3
Asif Mujtaba	14	21	5	1084	191	67.75	2	7
Yousuf Youhana	9	15	4	727	163*	66.09	2	4
Aamir Sohail	8	11	–	720	170	65.45	4	
Iqbal Zahoor	2	4	2	117	62*	58.50		1
Hasan Adnan	5	9	3	324	93	54.00		3
Zahid Fazal	5	9	2	353	132	50.42	1	1
Shahid Afridi	10	15	1	685	123	48.92	2	4
Azhar Mahmood	8	12	4	391	128*	48.87	1	3
Bilal Asad	6	11	–	534	117	48.54	2	3
Basit Ali	8	10	2	379	133	47.37	1	2
Rehan Rafiq	7	12	4	367	72*	45.87		4
Salim Elahi	14	22	2	890	203*	44.80	2	3
Azam Khan	14	25	2	1014	136	44.08	2	5
Ali Naqvi	8	13	2	483	115	43.90	2	1
Nadeem Abbasi	10	11	4	303	87*	43.28		2
Fida Hussain	10	15	4	469	99	42.63	4	
Atif Rauf	8	14	3	463	155*	42.09	1	1
Moin Khan	8	11	2	376	129	41.77	1	2
Ghaffar Kazmi	3	5	–	201	103	40.20	1	1
Akhtar Sarfraz	16	25	6	750	125	39.47	2	4
Mohammad Shakeel	4	6	3	118	34	39.33		
Asif Mahmood	16	25	–	974	250	38.96	2	5
Mohammad Wasim	11	15	2	501	165	38.53	2	
Ijaz Ahmed	6	7	–	269	151	38.42	1	1
Shakeel Ahmed	13	21	–	794	148	37.80	2	3
Mujahid Hameed	12	18	3	556	133*	37.06	1	4
Abdur Razzaq	9	13	2	402	117	36.54	2	2
Wajatahullah	14	23	4	690	87	36.31		6
Wasim Yousufi	11	14	3	398	103	36.18	1	1
Kashif Ahmed	2	4	1	106	73*	35.33		1
Adil Nisar	8	13	–	459	98	35.30		5
Naved Anjum	5	8	–	280	70	35.00		2
Manzoor Akhtar	12	18	2	558	117*	34.87	2	2
Salim Malik	8	12	–	414	124	34.50	1	2
Aamir Hanif	13	21	2	650	153	34.21	2	1
Shahid Nawaz	7	9	1	273	72	34.12		2
Taimur Khan	14	23	5	612	111	34.00	1	3
Iftikhar Hussain	10	16	2	474	129	33.85	1	2
Aamir Bashir	14	24	2	744	173*	33.81	2	3
Mahmood Hamid	6	11	5	202	51*	33.66		1
Arif Butt	4	6	–	201	85	33.50		2
Nasir Ahmed Mughal	16	24	2	729	152*	33.13	1	4
Hasan Raza	11	15	2	430	204*	33.07	1	
Shehzad Malik	3	5	–	165	69	33.00		2
Shahid Hussain	7	7	2	165	66	33.00		2
S. Abbas Ali	6	8	1	225	76	32.14	2	
Farhan Adil	14	18	1	544	100*	32.00	1	2
Zafar Iqbal	13	18	2	511	110	31.93	1	2
Naeem Ashraf	13	16	1	477	139	31.80	1	1
Aamir Iqbal	5	9	–	278	64	30.88		2
Sajid Ali	4	6	–	185	71	30.83		1
Ata-ur-Rehman	2	4	–	119	80	29.75		1
Mohammad Javed	9	11	2	264	54*	29.33		1
Amir-ud-Din	6	12	–	352	84	29.33		4
Rana Qayyum	14	26	2	690*	83*	28.75		5

Batting

	M	Inns	NOs	Runs	HS	Av	100s	50s
Mujahid Jamshed	10	17	1	459	115	28.68	1	2
Maqsood Ahmed	5	9	3	172	64	28.66		1
Hameed Gul	4	7	2	140	59*	28.00		1
Murtaza Hussain	15	22	3	530	67*	27.89		4
Tariq Aziz	6	10	1	251	76	27.88		2
Rizwan-uz-Zaman	5	10	–	278	91	27.80		3
Sohail Jaffar	11	20	1	524	100	27.57	1	3
Shahid Javed	6	7	–	191	100	27.28	1	
Manzoor Elahi	5	6	1	136	81*	27.20		1
Javed Hayat	11	16	2	377	89	26.92		2
Shahid Anwar	12	19	2	456	106*	26.82	2	
Inam-ul-Haq	2	4	–	107	66	26.75		1
Mansoor Rana	9	13	–	346	107	26.61	1	2
Javed Sami Khan	7	13	1	319	50	26.58		1
Zahoor Elahi	13	21	1	529	78	26.45		4
Majid Saeed	6	10	–	263	107	26.30	1	1
Nadeem Hussain	12	19	2	436	125	25.64	1	
Babar Zaman	6	12	–	307	62	25.58		3
Ali Raza	2	4	–	100	64	25.00		1
Asmatullah	4	8	1	173	63	24.71		1
Jahangir Khan	11	20	–	293	175	24.65	1	2
Saifullah	3	6	–	144	80	24.00		1
Arshad Hayat	9	16	–	378	59	23.62		1
Bazid Khan	4	6	1	118	39	23.60		
Mohammad Shafiq	9	16	–	377	71	23.56		2
Mohammad Ali	3	6	1	117	36	23.40		
Naseer Shaukat	7	8	–	185	42	23.12		
Iqbal Salim	7	11	1	231	70	23.10		1
Bilal M. Khelji	7	13	1	272	91	22.66		2
Azhar Shafiq	17	31	1	671	104*	22.36	1	2
Shoaib Mohammad	5	7	–	156	66	22.28		1
Tahir Shah	6	9	–	198	53	22.00		2
Hanif-ur-Rehman	4	5	–	110	61	22.00		1
Shadab Kabir	8	13	1	262	55	21.83		2
Asim Kamal	4	6	–	131	81	21.83		1
Qaiser Mahmood	9	16	1	326	109*	21.73	1	1
Bilal Rana	8	13	1	255	78	21.25		1
Shahid Mansoor	5	8	1	148	52*	21.14		1
Tahir Rashid	8	13	2	232	57	21.09		1
Ehsan Butt	8	13	1	250	102*	20.83	1	
Mohammad Ramzan	12	21	–	435	94	20.71		2
Tariq Mohammad	5	7	1	121	51	20.16		1
Aamir Malik	7	12	1	214	47	19.45		
Ali Rafi	5	8	1	135	53*	19.28		1
Ameem Abbas	7	11	1	192	50	19.20		1
Khalid Zafar	5	9	2	131	54	18.71		1
Rashid Latif	9	12	–	223	91	18.58		1
Naved Ashraf	17	24	–	437	61	18.20		2
Mohammad Nawaz snr	10	16	–	291	100	18.18	1	
Zaheer Abbasi	6	9	–	163	46	18.11		
Jaffar Nazir	13	13	6	125	36	17.85		
Mohammad Nawaz jnr	4	7	–	124	61	17.71		1
Mohammad Zahid	9	13	3	177	45	17.70		
Javed Iqbal	6	10	–	177	46	17.70		
Abdul Basit	6	9	–	157	47	17.44		
Naeem Akhtar	16	20	1	331	58	17.42		1

First-Class Averages (continued)

Batting

	M	Inns	NOs	Runs	HS	Av	100s	50s
Zahid Umar	7	10	1	153	39	17.00		
Saeed Anwar	6	8	–	136	65	17.00		1
Abdus Salam	8	12	–	204	60	17.00		1
Mohammad Farukh	5	7	1	101	40	16.83		
Moin-ul-Atiq	4	7	–	116	55	16.57		1
Shakeel Ahmed	15	15	4	182	43	16.54		
Majid Inayat	6	10	–	162	55	16.20		1
Ijaz Ahmed jnr	13	20	–	322	94	16.20		1
Asadullah Butt	6	8	–	127	58	15.87	1	
Sabih Azhar	11	16	1	238	45	15.86		
Waqar Younis	5	7	–	111	45	15.85		
Saaed Wasim	4	8	–	126	52	15.75		1
Bilal Ahmed	5	8	–	125	52	15.62		1
Tariq Mahboob	6	12	1	171	55	15.54		1
Shahid Nazir	6	7	–	108	35	15.42		
Ijaz Mahmood	9	15	1	212	39	15.14		
Saeed Azad	7	12	1	165	48	15.00		
Mohammad Asif	11	13	5	120	45*	15.00		
Ghulam Ali	5	9	–	132	54	14.66		1
Kashif Ibrahim	7	10	2	112	48	14.00		
Ata-ur-Rehman	13	18	1	236	43	13.88		
Akram Raza	9	14	–	194	29	13.85		
Naved Latif	9	17	2	203	53*	13.53		1
Nadeem Younus	5	10	–	134	38	13.40		
Javed Qadir	8	11	3	103	21*	12.87		
Arshad Khan	18	22	1	264	50*	12.57		2
Aalay Haider	6	9	–	113	37	12.55		
Tauseef Ahmed	5	9	1	100	49	12.50		
Mohammad Siddiqi	5	9	–	112	28	12.44		
Masroor Hussain	7	11	–	135	38	12.27		
Imran Idrees	9	15	3	141	28	11.75		
Aqil Aziz	8	13	–	149	34	11.45		
Tahir Mahmood	7	12	–	135	29	11.25		
Nadeem Iqbal	7	13	3	108	39	10.80		
Asif Ali Saeed	8	14	1	139	47	10.69		
Ali Hussain Rizvi	14	17	1	168	27	10.50		
Sajid Shah	16	22	6	162	43	10.12		

Zahid Ahmed 67 & 57 (one match)
(Qualification – 100 runs, average 10.00)

Bowling

	Overs	Mds	Runs	Wks	Best	Av	10/m	5/inn
Bilal Rana	136.1	48	308	25	6/29	12.32	1	4
Aamir Wasim	106.5	33	199	15	6/60	13.26	1	1
Shahid Mahboob	83.3	20	252	18	8/77	14.00	1	2
Nadeem Ghauri	54	18	140	10	5/39	14.00		1
Adil Nisar	56.5	23	147	10	4/57	14.70		
Aqib Javed	222.2	43	661	42	7/77	15.73	2	4
Athar Laeeq	60.1	14	189	12	5/26	15.75		2
S. John	156.2	47	451	28	6/19	16.10		2
Wasim Akram	178.1	52	464	28	4/42	16.57		
Saadat Gul Khan	49.5	9	169	10	5/36	16.90		1
Fazl-e-Akbar	427.2	68	1518	86	9/116	17.65	2	7
Mohammad Akram	162.4	36	614	34	7/73	18.05		3
Azhar Abbas	81	15	257	14	4/29	18.25		
Mohamad Zahid	391	149	786	42	6/50	18.71	1	2
Naeem Ashraf	375	93	1016	54	7/41	18.81	2	4
Taimur Ali Khan	50	12	189	10	4/84	18.90		
Javed Hayat	184.1	47	458	24	3/4	19.08		
Waqar Younis	130	28	370	19	6/16	19.47		1
Sajid Shah	497.5	93	1607	82	6/56	19.59	1	7
Haaris A. Khan	99.2	20	256	13	5/59	19.69		2
Shahid Nazir	142.2	22	532	27	6/76	19.70		2
Murtaza Hussain	633	176	1570	76	7/95	20.65	3	7
Ali Gauhar	353	63	1164	56	6/76	20.78		3
Shakeel Khan	147.4	33	437	21	8/74	20.80		1
Mohammad Altaf	152.4	41	332	15	3/21	22.13		
Shakeel Ahmed	478	150	1113	50	7/91	22.26		4
Waqar Ahmed	86	14	291	13	6/45	22.38	1	1
Shakir Qayyum	122.4	30	359	16	6/53	22.43		1
Mohammad Asif	349.3	100	765	34	4/19	22.50		
Jaffar Nazir	368.3	86	1177	52	7/42	22.63		4
Azhar Shafiq	391.4	85	1162	51	5/23	22.78		2
Zafar Iqbal	252.5	43	908	39	6/18	23.28		2
Imran Idrees	211.3	60	516	22	6/32	23.45		1
Kashif Ibrahim	193.2	38	688	29	5/63	23.72		2
Tahir Mahmood	170.2	27	595	25	6/83	23.80	1	4
Shahid Hussain	141	47	310	13	7/55	23.84		1
Ali Raza	244.1	40	740	31	7/117	23.87		1
Alamgir Khan	92.2	20	288	12	3/50	24.00		
Akram Raza	272.3	58	697	29	7/102	24.03		1
Shahid Mahboob	86.4	22	241	10	4/58	24.10		
Nadeem Ashraf	172.5	30	675	27	7/59	24.33		2
Humayun Hussain	85	17	268	11	3/17	24.36		
Nadeem Khan	354.2	78	968	39	5/36	24.82		2
Lal Faraz	198.2	33	725	29	6/63	25.00		1
Shabbir Ahmed	287.3	79	780	31	5/31	25.16		1
Ata-ur-Rehman	306.4	67	1054	41	7/20	25.70		1
Anwar Ali	102.4	23	336	13	4/93	25.84		
Arshad Ali	551.1	136	1294	50	4/25	25.88		
Mushtaq Ahmed	226.2	58	679	26	5/35	26.11	1	2
Saqlain Mushtaq	210	55	556	21	5/54	26.47		2
Mohammad Wasim	116	19	379	14	4/51	27.07		
Azhar Mahmood	192.4	38	570	21	5/115	27.14		1
Naeem Akhtar	321.1	74	912	33	6/52	27.63		2
Shahid Afridi	184.1	28	665	24	6/101	27.70		2
Salman Fazal	151.5	37	361	13	5/98	27.76		1
Khalid Zafar	84.4	15	281	10	5/43	28.10		1
Asim Zaidi	98.3	14	394	14	5/78	28.14		2
Ali Hussain Rizvi	407.3	97	1117	39	6/57	28.64	1	3
Hasnain Kazim	98	19	404	14	6/73	28.85		1
Naved Nazir	99.4	20	302	10	3/61	30.20		
Shoaib Akhtar	298.3	38	1278	42	6/136	30.42		4
Mohammad Javed	149	31	470	15	4/11	31.33		
Nadeem Afzal	212	40	756	24	4/107	31.50		
Nasir Shaukat	167.3	53	444	14	3/22	31.71		
Fahad Khan	153.4	17	571	18	4/64	31.72		
Tariq Sheikh	194.4	56	415	13	3/55	31.92		
Abdur Razzaq	259	28	1214	38	5/73	31.94		1
Aamir Nazir	157.4	12	809	23	5/104	35.17		1
Aamir Hanif	111.2	18	360	10	3/55	36.00		
ShoaibMalik	132.3	24	396	11	4/66	36.00		
Nadeem Iqbal	204.4	41	659	17	5/14	38.76		1
Ameem Abbas	172.4	25	791	19	4/101	41.63		
Asadullah Butt	160.2	33	513	11	3/46	46.63		

(Qualification – 10 wickets)

Leading Fielders

31 – Wasim Yousufi (ct 30 / st 1); 28 – Nadeem Hussain (ct 26 / st 2); 27 – Wasim Arifi (ct 25 / st 2), Mohammad Shafiq (ct 22 / st 5) and Zahid Umar (ct 24 / st 3); 24 – Rashid Latif (ct 22 / st 2); 23 – Javed Qadir (ct 22 / st1); 22 – Iftikhar Ahmed (ct 14 / st 8); 21 – Qaiser Mahmood (ct 20 / st 1); 20 – Asif Mahmood; 19 – Tahir Rashid (ct 17 / st 2); 17 – Nadeem Abbasi; 16 – Bilal Ahmed, Moin Khan (ct 15 / st 1) and Wajatullah; 15 – Ahmed Zeeshan (ct 13 / st 2) and Murtaza Hussain; 14 – Taimur Khan; 13 – Aamir Iqbal (12 / st 1), Aqeel Aziz, Naved Ashraf, Ijaz Ahmed jnr, Mojammad Shakeel(ct 12 / st 1) and Rana Qayyum; 12 – Ali Hussain Rizvi, Iqbal Salim (ct 11 / st 1), Mahmood Hamid and Salim Elahi; 10 – Aalaay Haider, Aamir Bashir, Akhtar Sarfraz, Asif Mujtaba, Asim Kamal and Rehan Rafiq

Sri Lanka

Confident and proud as reigning world champions, Sri Lanka set out in August 1997 to prove themselves as efficient and successful in Test cricket as they are in the one-day game. They were to engage in home and away series with India, play in the Jinnah Cup tournament in Pakistan, entertain Zimbabwe, visit South Africa for Tests and one-day internationals and end their ambitious journey by playing England at The Oval in August 1998.

Sanath Jayasuriya established a permanent place in cricket history with his innings of 340 in the first Test match against India at the Premadasa Stadium. (Mike Hewitt / Allsport)

Sri Lanka's batting strength was renowned. Aravinda de Silva was at the height of his powers and had no superior in world cricket. Jayasuriya had matured from an exciting one-day cricketer into an exciting, dependable and top class Test player. The bowling was less reliable. Muralitharan, with an action still suspected by some, had become the first Sri Lankan to capture a hundred Test wickets and Vaas had performed well as a new-ball bowler, but there was a general lack of depth and consistency in attack which, hopefully, would be cured during the arduous international programme of 1997–98.

Indian Tour

India's visit to Sri Lanka to play two Test matches and three one-day internationals was to produce some astonishing cricket with the home side rewriting the record books. There was a preliminary first-class fixture before the first Test match when the tourists met the Board President's XI.

29, 30 and 31 July 1997
at P. Saravanamuttu Stadium, Colombo
Indians 308 (S.C. Ganguly 79, N.S. Sidhu 64, G.K. Khoda 59, U.U. Chandana 5 for 86) and 255 for 5 (N.S. Sidhu 100 not out, S.C. Ganguly 62)
Board President's XI 291 (R.P. Arnold 65, M.C. Mendis 55)
Match drawn

Test Series
Sri Lanka *v.* India

Winning the toss, Tendulkar chose to bat first on a pitch which was a batsman's paradise.

There were two Test debutants, Nilesh Kulkarni, the slow left-arm spinner who had played for India in the Asia Cup, and Mahela Jayawardena, a right-handed batsman and medium pace bowler who had played for Sri Lanka 'A' against the West Indians.

The early loss of Mongia caused Sidhu and Dravid to play with more caution than may have seemed necessary, but the pitch was slow and unresponsive to the efforts of the bowlers. Sidhu and Dravid added 147, and Sidhu hit 13 fours and two sixes before slashing wildly after a ball from Vaas just after tea and edging to the wicket-keeper. Dravid drove hard at Jayasuriya and the ball hit Atapattu at silly point and ballooned into the air for the bowler to take the catch. The rest of the day belonged to Tendulkar, who hammered his way to 65 before the close. The last two hours of play produced 106 runs, and India ended the day on 280 for three.

Tendulkar and Azharuddin were not separated until 45 minutes before tea on the second day, by which time they

Roshan Mahanama shared a second wicket stand of 576 with Jayasuriya in the first Test match against India. The partnership was a record for any wicket in Test cricket. Mahanama made 225. (Chris Cole / Allsport)

had added 221 and put India in a seemingly impregnable position. Tendulkar reached his 12th Test century, while Azharuddin, playing in his 84th Test, made his 18th. Both batsmen were particularly severe on pace bowler Pushpakumara, who conceded runs at the rate of nearly five an over. Azharuddin took 18 runs from one Pushpakumara over. Tendulkar's declaration left Sri Lanka ten overs to negotiate before the close of play. They had scored 39 when debutant Kulkarni was called up for the last over of the day. His first delivery was well flighted and deceived Atapattu, who edged to the keeper. Kulkarni had become the first Indian to take a wicket with his first ball in Test cricket.

The jubilation that India had felt at the end of the second day had disappeared completely by the close of play on the third day, a day on which they failed to capture a single wicket as Sri Lanka advanced to 322, with Jayasuriya reaching 175 and Mahanama 115.

There was no respite for India on the fourth day when, again, they were wicketless. Jayasuriya became the first Sri Lankan batsman to score a triple century in a Test match, and he and Mahanama, with 548 to their credit, had already established a world record partnership for Test cricket. Mahanama's 211 was his first double century, while Jayasuriya had 326 of Sri Lanka's 587 runs to his credit and stood within sight of Brian Lara's Test record. The stadium, which had been sparsely populated for the first four days of the Test, was packed to overflowing on the final day.

For the huge crowd, there was to be something of a disappointment. With the score on 615, Kumble trapped

Mahanama leg before, so ending a partnership that was finally worth 576, easily a record for any wicket in Test cricket. Jayasuriya had seemed in sublime form, cracking three fours in the first ten deliveries he had received in the morning, but, in the over following Mahanama's departure, he appeared to lose concentration and gave a simple catch to silly point. Deeply upset at missing the record, he wept openly on his return to the pavilion, believing that he had let down his friends and his fans. Disappointed he may have been, but he had secured his place in Test history. His 340 has been bettered only by Lara, Sobers and Hutton, and he had batted for 799 minutes, facing 578 balls and hitting two sixes and 36 fours. If the Sri Lankan supporters were saddened, they were soon to be uplifted. Aravinda de Silva hit his 12th Test century, and there were sparkling knocks from Ranatunga and Jayawardena as Sri Lanka ended the match on 952 for six, passing England's previous Test record score of 903 for seven against Australia at The Oval in 1938.

The Indian bowlers had suffered dreadfully for three days, and, as their captain commented, while nothing should detract from the achievements of Jayasuriya and Mahanama, 'this is not the type of wicket on which we should play Test cricket'.

Three days later, the two sides moved to another Colombo venue for the second Test. India made two changes, replacing Chauhan with medium-pacer Debasis Mohanty and recalling Jadeja in place of Kulkarni. Sri Lanka made one change, replacing Janantha Silva with Chanaka de Silva, the left-arm pace bowler. Mohanty was making his Test debut. Tendulkar again won the toss, but this time he asked Sri Lanka to bat first. There was some justification for his decision as his bowlers, particularly the lively debutant Mohanty, ate into the Sri Lankan batting. However, the visitors were thwarted by Aravinda de Silva, who was again in majestic form, hitting 20 fours on the first day when he finished unbeaten for 144 out of Sri Lanka's 316 for seven.

He was soon out on the second morning, but Sri Lanka responded quickly, getting rid of both Jadeja and Dravid before India had reached double figures. It was skipper Tendulkar who came to the rescue with his second century in successive innings. He hit 14 fours as he moved to 117 by the close. India had slipped to 126 for four, but Tendulkar and Ganguly had increased that score by exactly one hundred by the end of the second day.

If Tendulkar had been the hero of the second day, it was Ganguly who dominated the third. He scored 100 of the 149 runs that India added to their overnight score and was last out, half an hour after tea. He had batted for seven hours and had hit two sixes and 19 fours in his highest Test score. His innings was invaluable, for the Indian later order had collapsed, mostly against Muralitharan, the last five wickets going down for 47 runs. Sri Lanka ended the day on 77 for the loss of Atapattu.

The fourth day saw another mighty innings by Sanath Jayasuriya and Aravinda de Silva's second century of the

First Test Match – Sri Lanka v. India

2, 3, 4, 5 and 6 August 1997 at Premadasa Stadium, Colombo

India

N.R. Mongia †	**c** Jayawardena, **b** Pushpakumara	**7**
N.S. Sidhu	**c** Kaluwitharana, **b** Vaas	**111**
R.S. Dravid	**c** and **b** Jayasuriya	**69**
S.R. Tendulkar *	**c** Jayawardena, **b** Muralitharan	**143**
M. Azharuddin	**c** and **b** Muralitharan	**126**
S.C. Ganguly	**c** Mahanama, **b** Jayasuriya	**0**
A.R. Kumble	not out	**27**
R.K. Chauhan	**c** Vaas, **b** Jayasuriya	**23**
A. Kuruvilla	**c** Atapattu, **b** Pushpakumara	**9**
N.M. Kulkarni		
Venkatesh Prasad		
	b **10**, nb **12**	**22**
	(for 8 wickets, dec.)	**537**

	O	M	R	W
W. Vaas	23	5	80	**1**
Pushpakumara	19.3	2	97	**2**
Jayawardena	2	–	6	**–**
Muralitharan	65	9	174	**2**
Silva	39	3	122	**–**
Jayasuriya	18	3	45	**3**
Atapattu	1	–	3	**–**

Fall of Wickets
1–**36**, 2–**183**, 3–**230**, 4–**451**, 5–**451**, 6–**479**, 7–**516**, 8–**537**

Sri Lanka

S.T. Jayasuriya	**c** Ganguly, **b** Chauhan	**340**
M.S. Atapattu	**c** Mongia, **b** Kulkarni	**26**
R.S. Mahanama	lbw, **b** Kumble	**225**
P.A. de Silva	**c** Venkatesh Prasad, **b** Ganguly	**126**
A. Ranatunga *	run out	**86**
D.P.M. Jayawardena	**c** Kulkarni, **b** Ganguly	**66**
R.S. Kaluwitharana †	not out	**14**
W.P.U.J.C. Vaas	not out	**11**
K.J. Silva		
K.R. Pushpakumara		
M. Muralitharan		
	b **58**, lb **9**, w **7**, nb **14**	**58**
	(for 6 wickets, dec.)	**952**

	O	M	R	W
Venkatesh Prasad	24	1	88	**–**
Kuruvilla	14	2	74	**–**
Chauhan	78	2	276	**1**
Kumble	72	7	223	**1**
Kulkarni	70	12	195	**1**
Ganguly	9	–	53	**2**
Tendulkar	2	1	2	**–**
Dravid	2	–	4	**–**

Fall of Wickets
1–**39**, 2–**615**, 3–**615**, 4–**790**, 5–**921**, 6–**924**

Umpires: K.T. Francis & S.G. Randell

Match drawn

Second Test Match – Sri Lanka v. India

9, 10, 11, 12 and 13 August 1997 at Sinhalese Sports Club, Colombo

Sri Lanka

	First Innings		Second Innings	
S.T. Jayasuriya	c Tendulkar, b Mohanty	32	b Kuruvilla	199
M.S. Atapattu	c Azharuddin, b Venkatesh	19	c Azharuddin, b Kumble	29
R.S. Mahanama	c Azharuddin, b Mohanty	37	st Mongia, b Kumble	35
P.A. de Silva	c Mongia, b Mohanty	146	c sub (Kambli), b Kumble	120
A. Ranatunga *	c Mongia, b Ganguly	14	run out	1
D.P.M. Jayawardena	c Mongia, b Venkatesh Prasad	16	(7) c Mongia, b Kuruvilla	7
R.S. Kaluwitharana †	b Kuruvilla	7	(6) run out	2
W.P.U.J.C. Vaas	b Kuruvilla	10	not out	5
M. Muralitharan	c Azharuddin, b Kumble	39		
K.R. Pushpakumara	b Mohanty	0		
S.C. de Silva	not out	0		
	b 4, lb 4, nb 4	12	b 1, lb 4, w 1, nb 11	17
		332	(for 7 wickets, dec.)	415

	O	M	R	W	O	M	R	W
Venkatesh Prasad	26	5	104	2	16	1	72	–
Kuruvilla	20	5	68	2	24	2	90	2
Mohanty	20.4	5	78	4	15	–	72	–
Kumble	25	8	51	1	38.4	2	156	3
Ganguly	4	–	23	1	3	–	18	–
Dravid					1	–	2	–

Fall of Wickets
1–53, 2–59, 3–121, 4–192, 5–230, 6–249, 7–274, 8–332, 9–332
1–55, 2–145, 3–363, 4–369, 5–374, 6–394, 7–415

India

	First Innings		Second Innings	
A.D. Jadeja	c Kaluwitharana, b Vaas	1	c Atapattu, b S.C. de Silva	73
N.S. Sidhu	st Kaluwitharana, b Muralitharan	29	c Jayasuriya, b Vaas	16
R.S. Dravid	c Vaas, b S.C. de Silva	2	c Atapattu, b Muralitharan	6
S.R. Tendulkar *	c Muralitharan, b Pushpakumara	139	c S.C. de Silva, b Muralitharan	8
M. Azharuddin	c Mahanama, b Vaas	22	not out	108
S.C. Ganguly	c Vaas, b S.C. de Silva	147	c Kaluwitharana, b Muralitharan	45
N.R. Mongia †	b Muralitharan	15	not out	10
A.R. Kumble	c Jayawardena, b Muralitharan	0		
A. Kuruvilla	c Jayawardena, b Muralitharan	0		
Venkatesh Prasad	c Kaluwitharana, b S.C. de Silva	2		
D.B. Mohanty	not out	0		
	b 2, lb 3, nb 13	18	b 1, lb 7, nb 7	15
		375	(for 5 wickets)	281

	O	M	R	W	O	M	R	W
Vaas	27	5	69	2	17	3	42	1
Pushpakumara	19	3	79	1	14	1	50	–
S.C. de Silva	31.1	6	101	3	16	5	32	1
Muralitharan	48	17	99	4	35	5	96	3
Jayasuriya	10	6	15	–	10	4	24	–
Jayawardena	1	1	0	–	8	1	29	–
P.A. de Silva	5	2	7	–				

Fall of Wickets
1–2, 2–9, 3–81, 4–126, 5–276, 6–328, 7–334, 8–342, 9–359
1–55, 2–75, 3–100, 4–138, 5–248

Umpires: B.C. Cooray & R.E. Koertzen

Match drawn

match. It was his sixth century in his last six Test innings on home soil. The pair added 218 for the third wicket at a run a minute as Sri Lanka raced towards a declaration. No other nation in Test cricket can boast a more attractive pair of batsmen. Jayasuriya hit two sixes and 21 fours and became the first batsman to pass a thousand runs in Test cricket in 1997. Aravinda de Silva, who hit 13 fours, finished just seven short of a thousand Test runs in the year.

A brisk run-rate was maintained throughout the day. The first session produced 86 runs in 25 overs with Mahanama as the only casualty, while de Silva and Jayasuriya added 119 in 25 overs between lunch and tea. Three wickets fell for 11 runs in the final session as Sri Lanka pressed for quick runs, and Ranatunga's declaration left India a target of 373, which, in the 13 overs available to them, Jadeja and Sidhu reduced by 49 runs before the close.

The loss of two wickets before lunch on the final day ended any hope of an Indian victory, and had Sri Lanka held their catches, they could have claimed the match. Mohammad Azharuddin was missed three times on his way to his 19th Test century. He survived for 175 balls and hit 14 fours. Ganguly batted without his usual flair in a dour innings that helped Azharuddin to add 110 for the fifth wicket, a partnership which ensured a draw.

The Indians were fined heavily for their slow over-rate, and the Sri Lankans, too, were penalised, but they were also richly rewarded for their Test record score at the Premadasa Stadium.

Limited-Over International Series

The first of the three one-day internationals was a day/night game that produced a thrilling finish. Atapattu hit his first century in limited-over international cricket. He hit seven fours and shared an opening stand of 91 with Jayasuriya, who made 73 off 52 balls with two sixes and ten fours. Atapattu, who faced 153 balls, then added 108 for the second wicket with Mahanama and 80 for the third wicket with Aravinda de Silva. India sank to 64 for four before Azharuddin and Jadeja established a new record for one-day international cricket with a stand worth 223. Azharuddin hit five fours and faced 117 balls, while Jadeja hit a six and eight fours in his 121-ball innings. India needed nine from the last over, bowled by Jayasuriya, and five off the last ball, a task beyond them.

In spite of Saurav Ganguly's first century in a one-day international cricket, Sri Lanka gained a resounding victory in the second encounter and so clinched the series. Ganguly hit 11 fours, faced 126 balls and shared a second wicket stand of 99 with Robin Singh after Tendulkar had fallen in the first over. Facing a moderate target of 239, Sri Lanka raced to 79 in 12 overs before Atapattu fell to Kuruvilla. Mahanama and Aravinda de Silva added 89 for the third wicket before Mahanama was run out off a no-ball in the 38th over with only 20 runs required. Aravinda de Silva finished the match and reached his fifty when he lofted Robin Singh to the boundary. The match saw Muralitharan take his 100th wicket in limited-over internationals. Jayasuriya's 66 off 56 balls with a six and eight fours won him the individual award.

The third match was begun on 23 August when India made 291 for nine with Robin Singh hitting 100 off 102 balls. Sri Lanka made 80 for 0 in 7.3 overs before rain reduced their target to 195 in 25 overs, but only 19 were possible because of the weather, and the match was declared void. In the rescheduled game, Aravinda de Silva hit 104 off 117 balls, his ninth hundred in one-day internationals. Azharuddin hit 65 off 68 balls and became only the third batsman to pass 7,000 runs in limited-over international cricket, but Sri Lanka took the series three-nil, completing their seventh consecutive victory over India in one-day internationals.

Jayasuriya was named Man of the Series.

A master batsman in all forms of cricket – Aravinda de Silva. (Mike Hewitt / Allsport)

First One Day International – Sri Lanka v. India

17 August 1997 at Premadasa Stadium, Colombo

Sri Lanka

S.T. Jayasuriya	**b** Venkatesh Prasad	**73**
M.S. Atapattu	run out	**118**
R.S. Mahanama	**c** Jadeja, **b** R.R. Singh	**53**
P.A. de Silva	**c** Kumble, **b** Venkatesh Prasad	**34**
A. Ranatunga *	not out	**8**
H.P. Tillekeratne	not out	**0**
S.K.L. de Silva †		
W.P.U.J.C. Vaas		
H.D.P.K. Dharmasena		
M. Muralitharan		
S.C. de Silva		
	lb **7**, w **6**, nb **3**	**16**
	50 overs (for 4 wickets)	**302**

	O	M	R	W
Chauhan	10	–	64	**–**
Kuruvilla	9	–	59	**–**
Venkatesh Prasad	9	–	50	**2**
Kumble	8	–	50	**–**
Tendulkar	5	–	28	**–**
R.R. Singh	9	–	44	**1**

Fall of Wickets
1–**91**, 2–**199**, 3–**279**, 4–**300**

India

S.R. Tendulkar *	**c** Muralitharan, **b** Vaas	**27**
S.C. Ganguly	run out	**31**
R.R. Singh	**c** S.K.L. de Silva, **b** Vaas	**1**
R.S. Dravid	run out	**1**
M. Azharuddin	not out	**111**
A.D. Jadeja	**c** and **b** Vaas	**119**
N.R. Mongia †	run out	**1**
R.K. Chauhan	**c** Mahanama, **b** Jayasuriya	**1**
A.R. Kumble	not out	**0**
Venkatesh Prasad		
A. Kuruvilla		
	b **2**, lb **3**, w **2**, nb **1**	**8**
	50 overs (for 7 wickets)	**300**

	O	M	R	W
Vaas	10	–	63	**3**
S.C. de Silva	8	–	49	**–**
Dharmasena	10	–	40	**–**
Muralitharan	9	–	51	**–**
Jayasuriya	7	–	53	**1**
P.A. de Silva	2	–	14	**–**
Ranatunga	4	–	25	**–**

Fall of Wickets
1–**58**, 2–**59**, 3–**61**, 4–**64**, 5–**287**, 6–**296**

Umpires: K.T. Francis & P. Manuel *Man of the Match:* A.D. Jadeja

Sri Lanka won by 2 runs

Second One Day International – Sri Lanka v. India

20 August 1997 at Premadasa Stadium, Colombo

India

S.R. Tendulkar *	lbw, **b** Vaas	**6**
S.C. Ganguly	**c** Dharmasena, **b** Muralitharan	**113**
R.R. Singh	**c** and b Dharmasena	**42**
M. Azharuddin	**st** S.K.L. de Silva, **b** Muralitharan	**1**
R.S. Dravid	**c** S.K.L. de Silva, **b** Jayasuriya	**18**
A.D. Jadeja	**c** Mahanama, **b** Chandana	**28**
N.R. Mongia †	**c** P.A. de Silva, **b** Dharmasena	**16**
A.R. Kumble	**b** Chandana	**2**
R.K. Chauhan	**st** S.K.L. de Silva, **b** Chandana	**0**
A. Kuruvilla	not out	**2**
Venkatesh Prasad	lbw, **b** Jayasuriya	**0**
	b **2**, lb **3**, w **5**	**10**
	49.3 overs	**238**

	O	M	R	W
Vaas	6	1	38	**1**
S.C. de Silva	7	–	41	**–**
Dharmasena	10	–	48	**2**
Muralitharan	10	1	39	**2**
Jayasuriya	8.3	–	35	**2**
Chandana	8	–	32	**3**

Fall of Wickets
1–**6**, 2–**105**, 3–**106**, 4–**159**, 5–**212**, 6–**218**, 7–**229**, 8–**235**, 9–**237**

Sri Lanka

S.T. Jayasuriya	**c** Tendulkar, **b** Kumble	**66**
M.S. Atapattu	lbw, **b** Kuruvilla	**38**
R.S. Mahanama	run out	**66**
P.A. de Silva	not out	**52**
U.P.U. Chandana	not out	**4**
A. Ranatunga *		
S.K.L. de Silva †		
H.D.P.K. Dharmasena		
M. Muralitharan		
W.P.U.J.C. Vaas		
S.C. de Silva		
	b **8**, lb **2**, w **1**, nb **4**	15
	41.5 overs (for 3 wickets)	241

	O	M	R	W
W. Chauhan	9	–	45	**–**
Kuruvilla	7	1	35	**1**
Venkatesh Prasad	9	–	56	**–**
Kumble	6	–	44	**1**
R.R. Singh	6.5	–	34	**–**
Jadeja	4	–	17	**–**

Fall of Wickets
1–**79**, 2–**130**, 3–**219**

Umpires: B.C. Cooray & D.N. Panthirana *Man of the Match:* S.T. Jayasuriya

Sri Lanka won by 7 wickets

Third One Day International – Sri Lanka v. India

24 August 1997 at Sinhalese Sports Club, Colombo

Sri Lanka

S.T. Jayasuriya	**c** Jadeja, **b** Kuruvilla	**3**
M.S. Atapattu	**c** Azharuddin, **b** Kuruvilla	**3**
R.S. Mahanama	**b** Kulkarni	**50**
P.A. de Silva	**c** Azharuddin, **b** Kulkarni	**104**
A. Ranatunga *	**b** Kulkarni	**3**
S.K.L. de Silva	**c** Tendulkar, **b** Kuruvilla	**50**
U.P.U. Chandana	**b** Chauhan	**16**
D.K. Liyanage	**c** Jadeja, **b** Tendulkar	**20**
H.D.P.K. Dharmasena	run out	**1**
M. Muralitharan	**c** Tendulkar, **b** Kuruvilla	**7**
S.C. de Silva	not out	**0**
	lb **1**, w **1**, nb **5**	**7**
	49.4 overs	**264**

	O	M	R	W
Venkatesh Prasad	6	–	31	**–**
Kuruvilla	8.4	1	43	**4**
Kulkarni	10	–	73	**3**
Chauhan	10	–	43	**1**
R.R. Singh	7	–	32	**–**
Tendulkar	5	–	22	**1**
Ganguly	3	–	19	**–**

Fall of Wickets
1–**3**, 2–**22**, 3–**105**, 4–**113**, 5–**195**, 6–**226**, 7–**254**, 8–**256**, 9–**264**

India

S.R. Tendulkar *	**c** S.K.L. de Silva, **b** S.C. de Silva	**39**
S.C. Ganguly	**c** and **b** S.C. de Silva	**17**
R.R. Singh	**c** sub, **b** Muralitharan	**28**
R.S. Dravid	**c** Chandana, **b** Jayasuriya	**42**
M. Azharuddin	run out	**65**
A.D. Jadeja	run out	**22**
N.R. Mongia	not out	**14**
R.K. Chauhan	**c** Liyanage, **b** Chandana	**4**
A. Kuruvilla	**c** and **b** Jayasuriya	**7**
N.M. Kulkarni	not out	**3**
Venkatesh Prasad		
	b **1**, lb **9**, w **2**, nb **2**	**14**
	50 overs (for 8 wickets)	**255**

	O	M	R	W
S.C. de Silva	8	–	48	**2**
Liyanage	5	1	36	**–**
Dharmasena	9	–	33	**–**
Muralitharan	10	–	41	**1**
Jayasuriya	10	–	56	**2**
Chandana	8	–	31	**1**

Fall of Wickets
1–**50**, 2–**78**, 3–**107**, 4–**165**, 5–**221**, 6–**227**, 7–**235**, 8–**245**

Umpires: K.T. Francis & T.M. Samarasinghe *Man of the Match:* P.A. de Silva

Sri Lanka won by 9 runs

Zimbabwe Tour

Frustrated in their home Tests against New Zealand, but successful against lesser opposition in Kenya, Zimbabwe arrived in Sri Lanka at the beginning of 1998 for a brief tour, which would include two Tests and three one-day internationals. Like Sri Lanka, Zimbabwe had not suffered a Test defeat at the start of 1997–98 season, but, also like Sri Lanka, they had not tasted victory. There, really, the similarities ended, for the Sri Lankans were in a confident mood and started as firm favourites to beat Zimbabwe in both forms of international cricket.

2, 4 and 5 January 1998

at Tyronne Fernando Stadium, Moratuwa

Zimbabweans 314 for 6 dec. (A. Flower 101 not out, G.W. Flower 58, M.W. Goodwin 52, M. Samaraweera 4 for 90)

Sri Lankan Board XI 313 for 8 dec. (M.N. Nawaz 111, S.I. de Saram 56)

Match drawn

Andy Flower registered the highest score made by a Zimabwe batsman in Sri Lanka in his side's one warm-up match before the Test matches. The Sri Lankan side replied with a century from the young left-hander, Naveed Nawaz. There was little play possible on the last day because of rain.

Test Series

Sri Lanka *v.* Zimbabwe

Zimbabwe gave a first Test cap to Murray Goodwin, but he spent the first day fielding as Ranatunga won the toss and Sri Lanka reached 265 for four. There was early success for Zimbabwe as Streak dismissed the record-breaking pair Jayasuriya and Mahanama with only 33 on the board. Marvan Atapattu, who had played so well in India, and, inevitably, Aravainda de Silva came to Sri Lanka's rescue with a stand of 140. The stand was broken by leg-spinner Adam Huckle, who had de Silva caught at cover, and Andy Whittall claimed the wicket of Ranatunga, but Atapattu was unbeaten on 129 at the close, his second Test century.

On the second day, he turned his innings into his maiden double century. His start in Test cricket, one run in six innings, had been horrendous; now his restitution was complete. He faced 446 balls and hit a six and 29 fours. He could have been stumped off Paul Strang when he was on 217, but this was the only chance he offered. He showed remarkable discipline for one whose initial faults were diagnosed as impatience.

Sri Lanka took a firm grip on the game by accounting for Grant Flower and Murray Goodwin before the end of the second day, which saw them score 46 in 23 overs. Matters got worse for Zimbabwe on the third day. Andy Flower was leg before without addition to the overnight score, and a sixth wicket stand of 44 between Gavin Rennie and Paul Strang was the only gesture of defiance. Rennie batted for nearly four-and-three-quarter hours for his 58 in a painstaking attempt to rally his side, but Muralitharan mesmerised most batsmen, and he had good support from the other spinner, Silva. Although their innings lasted for just under 86 overs, Zimbabwe were routed for 140. Following on, they were given an encouraging start by Gavin Rennie and Grant Flower, but both were out before the close when the score was 71 for two.

A double century for Marvan Atapattu in Sri Lanka's victory in the first Test match against Zimbabwe.
(Clive Mason / Allsport)

Muralitharan again tantalised the Zimbabwean batsmen on the fourth day, but the visitors displayed commendable spirit with Goodwin hitting 70 in his first Test. Andy Flower and Alistair Campbell added 76 for the fifth wicket, but the stand was broken when Muralitharan was brought back and had Andy Flower taken at slip. Wishart went without scoring, and Campbell fell to Vaas before the close, which came with Zimbabwe on 289 for seven, still 40 runs short of avoiding an innings defeat.

Only eight runs had been scored on the final morning when Streak was caught behind, but the Strang brothers made certain that Sri Lanka would have to bat again when they added 37 before Muralitharan brought a hasty end to the innings. The off-spinner finished with match figures of 12 for 117, a record for a Sri Lankan bowler in Test cricket. The only surprise came when Sri Lanka lost the wickets of Jayasuriya and Mahanama in Heath Streak's opening over, but the game was over five balls into the next over.

Zimbabwe made two changes for the second Test. Leg-spinner Huckle was replaced by pace bowler Mbangwa, and Guy Whittall returned after injury and was preferred to Bryan Strang. Sri Lanka caused a surprise by recalling left-arm spinner Don Anurasiri to Test cricket after an absence of four years. He replaced Jayantha Silva. Campbell won the toss, and Zimbabwe batted.

Rennie and Grant Flower gave their side a good start, and, at lunch, the score was 101 for one. Murray Goodwin, who honed his skills in Western Australia, displayed an admirable blend of application and aggression to score his second seventy in consecutive Test innings, but Guy Whittall foolishly ran himself out, and the spinners began to take control as batsmen played injudicious shots. Campbell offered hope, but Zimbabwe closed on a bitterly disappointing 251 for nine.

Mbangwa was out with no addition to the score on the second morning, but suddenly Zimbabwe's score began to look better than anticipated. Jayasuriya drove ambitiously and skied to mid-on, and Mahanama played on to Mbangwa. Aravinda de Silva hit 27 off 28 balls before mis-hitting when he tried to pull. Atapattu was caught behind when he tried to cut, and Sri Lanka were 91 for four. Tillekeratne defended solidly for a time before lashing at a loose delivery and being caught at silly point. The only positive defiance came from Ranatunga and Kaluwitharana, who added 68. Kaluwitharana smashed his way to 51 off 47 balls before Paul Strang had him caught behind off a sharp leg-break, and the same bowler then had Ranatunga caught at square-leg. The last two wickets fell for one run, and, with Vaas out of the match with illness, to their surprise and elation, Zimbabwe had a first innings lead of 26. By the close, this was increased by 24 runs for the loss of Rennie.

Night-watchman Andy Whittall was soon out on the third morning, but Grant Flower and Murray Goodwin batted with great good sense to add 70. They both fell to Jayasuriya, whose left-arm spin looked more effective than that of Anurasiri, the specialist. With Ranatunga nursing a strained back, Aravinda de Silva led Sri Lanka and employed spin almost constantly throughout the 94 overs of the day. Muralitharan became the first Sri Lankan to capture 150 Test wickets when he had Guy Whittall caught at short-leg off an off-break that reared disconcertingly. This brought Campbell and Andy Flower together. They batted with care and intelligence in adding 75 in 34 overs. Campbell was caught behind, but Andy Flower stayed to the end of the day, unbeaten on 61 after nearly four hours at the crease. Wishart partnered him sensibly, and Zimbabwe were 241 for seven, a lead of 267 and hopes high.

Of the 58 runs Zimbabwe scored on the fourth morning before being all out shortly before lunch, Andy Flower made 44 to finish with 105 not out, a mighty knock that included a six and 10 fours. He faced 240 balls, and his innings gave Zimbabwe every chance of victory.

Sri Lanka made a dreadful start in their pursuit of a victory target of 326. They lost in-form Atapattu and prolific scoring Mahanama with only ten scored. Jayasuriya was joined by Aravinda de Silva in a stand worth 105, but Streak had Jayasuriya caught behind and two balls later trapped Tillekeratne leg before. Streak made it three wickets inside three overs when he had Kaluwitharana caught at first slip, and Sri Lanka were 137 for five. With Ranatunga, still troubled by a back injury, looking uncertain against Andy Whittall in particular, Zimbabwe scented victory, but tempers flared. The Sri Lankan captain survived a confident appeal for a catch behind off Andy Whittall, and moments later there was a strong altercation between Ranatunga and wicket-keeper Andy Flower. The trouble did not end there, for David Houghton, coach of Zimbabwe, openly criticised the umpiring, an action which brought him a ban from the one-day series. It should be noted that the admirable de Silva was not involved in the dissension, and he was unbeaten on 87 at the end of the day when Sri Lanka were 209 for five, 117 runs short of their target.

The umpiring continued to be a bone of contention on the final day when both batsmen survived appeals for leg before and the frustration of Zimbabwe's bowlers increased by the over. Ranatunga, batting with a runner, was particularly fortunate. Ranatunga and de Silva took their side to victory and success in the series with an unbroken partnership of 189 in 74 overs, a Sri Lankan sixth wicket record. Aravinda de Silva's 16th Test century was another masterly display of batting. He faced 313 balls for his 143 and hit two sixes and 16 fours. His shot selection had all the mark and quality of the great batsman that he is.

20 January 1998

at Sinhalese Sports Club, Colombo

Zimbabweans 244 for 6 (A. Flower 67)

Sri Lankan Board President's XI

245 for 6 (D.R.M. Jayawardene 87 not out, S.T. Jayasuriya 55)

Sri Lankan Board President's XI won by 4 wickets

First Test Match – Sri Lanka *v.* Zimbabwe

7, 8, 9, 10 and 11 January 1998 at Asgriya Stadium, Kandy

Sri Lanka

	First Innings		Second Innings	
S.T. Jayasuriya	lbw, b Streak	6	lbw, b Streak	0
M.S. Atapattu	c Campbell, b P.A. Strang	223	not out	6
R.S. Mahanama	c Campbell, b Streak	7	b Streak	0
P.A. de Silva	c A.R. Whittall, b Huckle	75	not out	4
A. Ranatunga *	b A.R. Whittall	27		
H.P. Tillekeratne	c and b A.R. Whittall	44		
R.S. Kaluwitharana †	c and b A.R. Whittall	29		
W.P.U.J.C. Vaas	c G.J. Rennie, b P.A. Strang	26		
M. Muralitharan	c B.C. Strang, b P.A. Strang	17		
K.R. Pushpakumara	not out	2		
K.J. Silva				
	b 2, lb 2, nb 9	13		0
	(for 9 wickets, dec.)	469	(for 2 wickets)	10

	O	M	R	W	O	M	R	W
Streak	34	11	96	2	1	–	4	2
B.C. Strang	30	7	78	–	0.5	–	6	–
P.A. Strang	35.3	10	123	3				
A.R. Whittall	30	4	73	3				
Huckle	21	3	88	1				
Goodwin	4	2	7	–				

Fall of Wickets
1–16, 2–33, 3–173, 4–226, 5–321, 6–383, 7–440, 8–461, 9–469
1–0, 2–0

Zimbabwe

	First Innings		Second Innings	
G.J. Rennie	c P.A. de Silva, b Silva	53	lbw, b Muralitharan	24
G.W. Flower	b Muralitharan	4	b P.A. de Silva	38
M.W. Goodwin	lbw, b Silva	2	b Muralitharan	70
A. Flower †	lbw, b Vaas	8	(5) c Mahanama, b Muralitharan	67
A.D.R. Campbell *	c Mahanama, b Pushpakumara	7	(6) lbw, b Vaas	40
C.B. Wishart	c Mahanama, b Muralitharan	3	(7) b Muralitharan	0
P.A. Strang	c P.A. de Silva, b Muralitharan	35	(8) c sub (Arnold), b Muralitharan	33
H.H. Streak	b Muralitharan	5	(9) c Kaluwitharana, b Pushpakumara	13
A.R. Whittall	not out	6	(4) b Muralitharan	14
B.C. Strang	b Muralitharan	2	not out	15
A.G. Huckle	lbw, b Silva	0	lbw, b Muralitharan	0
	b 6, lb 2, nb 7	15	b 5, lb 11, nb 8	24
		140		338

	O	M	R	W	O	M	R	W
Vaas	17	4	36	1	24	3	65	1
Pushpakumara	14	5	34	1	19	2	64	1
Muralitharan	29	18	23	5	42.5	13	94	7
Silva	19.4	9	27	3	11	2	35	–
P.A. de Silva	5	–	12	–	13	5	25	1
Jayasuriya	1	1	0	–	16	–	38	–
Atapattu					1	–	1	–

Fall of Wickets
1–29, 2–36, 3–46, 4–72, 5–75, 6–119, 7–127, 8–134, 9–136
1–68, 2–69, 3–103, 4–185, 5–261, 6–261, 7–271, 8–297, 9–334

Umpires: B.C. Coray & M.J. Kitchen

Sri Lanka won by 8 wickets

Second Test Match – Sri Lanka *v.* Zimbabwe

14, 15, 16, 17 and 18 January 1998 at Sinhalese Sports Club, Colombo

Zimbabwe

	First Innings		Second Innings	
G.J. Rennie	c Kaluwitharana, b Muralitharan	50	c Kaluwitharana, b P.A. de Silva	12
G.W. Flower	b Pushpakumara	41	b Jayasuriya	52
M.W. Goodwin	b Anurasiri	73	(4) b Jayasuriya	39
G.J. Whittall	run out	11	(5) c sub (D.P.M. Jayawardene), b Muralitharan	17
A. Flower †	c and b Anurasiri	8	(6) not out	105
A.D.R. Campbell *	c Kaluwitharana, b Vaas	44	(7) c Kaluwitharana, b Anurasiri	37
C.B. Wishart	lbw, b Muralitharan	2	(8) c Kaluwitharana, b Pushpakumara	18
P.A. Strang	c Pushpakumara, b Anurasiri	5	(9) b Muralitharan	3
H.H. Streak	b Vaas	3	(10) run out	1
A.R. Whittall	not out	1	(3) c Tillekeratne, b P.A. de Silva	2
M. Mbangwa	b Pushpakumara	0	c P.A. de Silva, b Muralitharan	4
	lb 3, w 1, nb 9	13	lb 6, w 1, nb 2	9
		251		299

	O	M	R	W	O	M	R	W
Vaas	12	1	35	2				
Pushpakumara	12.2	2	43	2	17	2	54	1
P.A. de Silva	7	1	33	–	23	4	61	2
Muralitharan	32	10	72	2	37.5	9	73	3
Anurasiri	27	7	65	3	19	7	41	1
Jayasuriya					29	9	64	2

Fall of Wickets
1–70, 2–110, 3–144, 4–174, 5–201, 6–206, 7–223, 8–240, 9–249
1–22, 2–34, 3–104, 4–117, 5–129, 6–204, 7–267, 8–284, 9–286

Sri Lanka

	First Innings		Second Innings	
S.T. Jayasuriya	c G.J. Whittall, b Streak	5	c A. Flower, b Streak	68
M.S. Atapattu	c A. Flower, b P.S. Strang	48	c A. Flower, b Streak	0
R.S. Mahanama	b Mbangwa	8	lbw, b Mbangwa	0
P.A. de Silva	c and b Streak	27	not out	143
A. Ranatunga *	c Streak, b P.A. Strang	52	(7) not out	87
H.P. Tillekeratne	c G.J. Rennie, b A.R. Whittall	7	(5) lbw, b Streak	0
R.S. Kaluwitharana †	c A. Flower, b P.A. Strang	51	(6) c Campbell, b Streak	4
S.D. Anurasiri	not out	3		
M. Muralitharan	c A. Flower, b Mbangwa	11		
K.R. Pushpakumara	b P.A. Strang	1		
W.P.U.J.C. Vaas	absent ill	–		
	lb 11, w 1	12	b 11, lb 13	24
		225	(for 5 wickets)	326

	O	M	R	W	O	M	R	W
Streak	15	5	28	2	24	6	84	4
Mbangwa	16	4	61	2	14	4	34	1
G.J. Whittall	3	–	18	–	7	1	12	–
P.A. Strang	19.5	2	77	4	24	4	75	–
A.R. Whittall	20	6	30	1	43	10	93	–
Goodwin					0.5	–	4	–

Fall of Wickets
1–12, 2–43, 3–91, 4–91, 5–130, 6–198, 7–213, 8–224, 9–225
1–1, 2–10, 3–115, 4–115, 5–137

Umpires: Salim Badar & K.T. Francis

Sri Lanka won by 5 wickets

One-Day International Series

Sri Lanka v. Zimbabwe

Zimbabwe played a fifty-over practice game before the start of the limited-over series and were well beaten by a strong Sri Lankan side for whom Mahela Jayawardene excelled. The young batsman was to force his way into the national side for the second match in the one-day series. The only debutant in the first game was Murray Goodwin who had already played Test cricket.

Put in to bat, Zimbabwe lost two vital wickets with only seven scored, but Grant Flower and Guy Whittall added 60. Campbell and Wishart also made fine contributions before the last six wickets fell for 34 runs. Disappointingly, Zimbabwe did not survive their 50 overs with leg-spinner Chandana providing major problems. Jayasuriya and Atappatu gave Sri Lanka a fine start, and Ranatunga, recovered from injury, batted with enough panache to claim the individual award. He took his side to victory with 28 balls to spare. He hit four fours and two sixes in his 79-ball innings.

Sri Lanka clinched the series by winning the second match, again in a convincing manner. Murray Goodwin showed how valuable an acquisition he was to the Zimbabwe side by hitting 111 off 134 balls in what was only his second international. His innings included seven fours, and he and Grant Flower put on 105 for the second wicket. Sadly, the later batsmen again failed, and Sri Lanka were faced with a moderate target. Jayasuriya and Atapattu gave them a rollicking start. They scored 82, and Jayasuriya hit 50 off 62 balls, an innings that included four fours, before he was brilliantly caught one-handed at long off by the diving Heath Streak. Mahanama and Ranatunga continued to plunder runs, and Sri Lanka won with ease.

Sri Lanka rested both Ranatunga and Aravinda de Silva for the final game, and Jayasuriya led his country for the first time. Gunawardena and Nawaz made their international debuts. Zimbabwe won the toss and batted and reached a commendable 281 in their 50 overs. They owed much to a splendid century from Grant Flower, his first in limited-over international cricket. He was outshone by Jayasuriya, whose 102 came off 100 balls with 13 fours and a six. He was named both Man of the Match and Man of the Series. Jayawardena, in his second match, was most impressive, making 74 off 78 balls with four fours. Chandana ended the game with a six, and Sri Lanka had made a clean sweep of both the Test and one-day series.

First One–Day International – Sri Lanka v. Zimbabwe

22 January 1998 at Sinhalese Sports Club, Colombo

Zimbabwe

G.W. Flower	c and b Dharmasena	40
A. Flower †	c Mahanama, b Pushpakumara	1
M.W. Goodwin	c P.A. de Silva, b Pushpakumara	1
G.J. Whittall	c Mahanama, b Jayasuriya	52
A.D.R. Campbell *	c and b Chandana	36
C.B. Wishart	b Chandana	41
P.A. Strang	c and b Muralitharan	3
G.J. Rennie	lbw, b Chandana	9
H.H. Streak	not out	7
J.A. Rennie	b Dharmasena	2
A.R. Whittall	lbw, b Chandana	5
	lb 6, w 3, nb 1	10
	48.4 overs	207

	O	M	R	W
Vaas	7	–	21	–
Pushpakumara	7	3	30	2
Dharmasena	10	–	29	2
Muralitharan	10	–	55	1
Chandana	7.4	–	31	4
Jayasuriya	7	–	35	1

Fall of Wickets
1–1, 2–7, 3–67, 4–118, 5–173, 6–180, 7–180, 8–193, 9–198

Sri Lanka

S.T. Jayasuriya	st A. Flower, b P.A. Strang	47
M.S. Atapattu	b J.A. Rennie	26
R.S. Mahanama	c Streak, b G.W. Flower	39
P.A. de Silva	c and b P.A. Strang	5
A. Ranatunga *	not out	58
R.S. Kaluwitharana †	c sub (H.R. Olonga), b G.W. Flower	15
U.D.U. Chandana	not out	16
H.D.P.K. Dharmasena		
M. Muralitharan		
W.P.U.J.C. Vaas		
K.R. Pushpakumara		
	lb 2, w 2	4
	45.2 overs (for 5 wickets)	210

	O	M	R	W
Streak	7	–	35	–
J.A. Rennie	7	–	25	1
A.R. Whittall	9	–	40	–
P.A. Strang	10	2	36	2
Goodwin	5	–	21	–
G.W. Flower	7.2	–	51	2

Fall of Wickets
1–66, 2–81, 3–91, 4–145, 5–183

Umpires: P. Manuel & D.N. Pathirana *Man of the Match:* A. Ranatunga

Sri Lanka won by 5 wickets

Second One–Day International – Sri Lanka v. Zimbabwe

24 January 1998 at R. Premadasa Stadium, Colombo

Zimbabwe

G.W. Flower	**b** Jayasuriya	**51**
A. Flower †	**b** Pushpakumara	**2**
M.W. Goodwin	**b** Chandana	**111**
G.J. Whittall	**b** Chandana	**13**
A.D.R. Campbell *	**c** Jayasuriya, **b** Muralitharan	**6**
C.B. Wishart	run out	**6**
P.A. Strang	**c** Mahanama, **b** Jayasuriya	**4**
H.H. Streak	run out	**4**
J.A. Rennie	not out	**4**
A.R. Whittall		
M. Mbangwa		
	lb **6**, w **3**, nb **2**	**11**
	50 overs (for 8 wickets)	**212**

	O	M	R	W
Pushpakumara	7	–	26	**1**
P.A. de Silva	4	–	14	**–**
Dharmasena	10	2	28	**–**
Muralitharan	10	–	43	**1**
Jayasuriya	10	–	53	**2**
Chandana	9	–	42	**2**

Fall of Wickets
1–**3**, 2–**108**, 3–**143**, 4–**165**, 5–**187**, 6–**203**, 7–**204**, 8–**212**

Sri Lanka

S.T. Jayasuriya	**c** Streak, **b** A.R. Whittall	**50**
M.S. Atapattu	**c** P.A. Strang, **b** G.W. Flower	**45**
R.S. Mahanama	run out	**52**
P.A. de Silva	**st** A. Flower, **b** P.A. Strang	**3**
A. Ranatunga *	**c** and **b** A.R. Whittall	**43**
R.S. Kaluwitharana †	not out	**8**
D.P.M. Jayawardena	not out	**1**
U.D.U. Chandana		
M. Muralitharan		
H.D.P.K. Dharmasena		
K.R. Pushpakumara		
	lb **6**, w **4**, nb **1**	**11**
	48.2 overs (for 5 wickets)	**213**

	O	M	R	W
Streak	8	–	37	**–**
J.A. Rennie	10	–	43	**–**
A.R. Whittall	8.2	–	33	**2**
Mbangwa	8	–	42	**–**
P.A. Strang	6	–	18	**1**
G.W. Flower	6	–	22	**1**
Campbell	2	–	12	**–**

Fall of Wickets
1–**76**, 2–**118**, 3–**127**, 4–**194**, 5–**212**

Umpires: Anandappa & U. Wickremasinghe *Man of the Match:* M.W. Goodwin

Sri Lanka won by 5 wickets

Third One–Day International – Sri Lanka v. Zimbabwe

26 January 1998 at Sinhalese Sports Club, Colombo

Zimbabwe

G.W. Flower	**c** Kalpage, **b** Chandana	**112**
C.B. Wishart	**c** Gunawardena, **b** Kalpage	**45**
M.W. Goodwin	**c** Chandana, **b** Jayasuriya	**18**
A. Flower †	**c** Kaluwitharana, **b** Dharmasena	**68**
G.J. Whittall	**c** S.C. de Silva, **b** Dharmasena	**3**
A.D.R. Campbell *	**st** Kaluwitharana, **b** Dharmasena	**9**
P.A. Strang	not out	**6**
H.H. Streak	not out	**2**
A.R. Whittall		
A.G. Huckle		
J.A. Rennie		
	b **2**, lb **8**, w **7**, nb **1**	**18**
	50 overs (for 6 wickets)	**281**

	O	M	R	W
Pushpakumara	6	–	34	**–**
S.C. de Silva	6	–	39	**–**
Dharmasena	10	–	47	**3**
Kalpage	10	1	34	**1**
Jayasuriya	10	–	66	**1**
Chandana	8	–	51	**1**

Fall of Wickets
1–**82**, 2–**114**, 3–**258**, 4–**264**, 5–**273**, 6–**274**

Sri Lanka

S.T. Jayasuriya *	**st** A. Flower, **b** G.J. Whittall	**102**
A.A.W. Gunawardena	**b** A.R. Whittall	**12**
M.N. Nawaz	**c** Goodwin, **b** P.A. Strang	**5**
D.P.M. Jayawardena	**c** Huckle, **b** G.W. Flower	**74**
R.S. Kalpage	run out	**37**
R.S. Kaluwitharana †	**c** Huckle, **b** G.W. Flower	**13**
H.D.P.K. Dharmasena	not out	**9**
U.D.U. Chandana	not out	**14**
R.P. Arnold		
S.C. de Silva		
K.R. Pushpakumara		
	b **1**, lb **4**, w **13**, nb **2**	**20**
	49 overs (for 6 wickets)	**286**

	O	M	R	W
Streak	2	–	21	**–**
J.A. Rennie	5	–	43	**–**
A.R. Whittall	10	–	46	**1**
P.A. Strang	10	–	54	**1**
G.W. Flower	7	–	36	**2**
Huckle	10	–	44	**–**
G.J. Whittall	4	–	23	**1**
Campbell	1	–	14	**–**

Fall of Wickets
1–**46**, 2–**87**, 3–**160**, 4–**233**, 5–**256**, 6–**266**

Umpires: P. Manuel & D.M. Samarasinghe *Man of the Match:* S.T. Jayasuriya

Sri Lanka won by 4 wickets

England 'A' Tour

Following their brief and soggy tour of Kenya, the England 'A' team arrived in Sri Lanka for what was to be the major part of their winter activities. Because of the continuance of terrorist activities, it was necessary to make adjustments to the itinerary and to shorten the tour slightly. The England side began its programme while the host country was engaged in the second Test match against Zimbabwe.

17 January 1998
at Police Park, Colombo
Sri Lankan Board President's XI 142
England 'A' 102
Sri Lankan Board President's XI won by 40 runs

19, 20 and 21 January 1998
at Nondescripts Ground, Colombo
England 'A' 384 (D.L. Maddy 101, S.P. James 66)
Sri Lanka Colts XI 213 (M.C. Mendis 67, S.I. Fernando 66) and 209 for 9 (M.C. Mendis 56, D.R. Brown 4 for 50)
Match drawn

England 'A' opened their tour with a fifty-over match in which they were surprisingly beaten. Ben Hollioake, Ashley Giles and Dean Cosker bowled out the home side in 46.2 overs, but the tourists were shot out in 39 overs by the Sri Lankan spinners. Only Mark Ealham, 43, showed sufficient aggression and resistance.

The opposition provided for the first first-class match of the tour was not as strong as had been expected, but this does not detract from the performance of Darren Maddy, who followed his double century in Nairobi with 101 in three-and-a-half hours. He and Steve James put on 95 after Knight had been caught for four. There were useful contributions from Ben Hollioake and Sales, while Ormond hit three sixes in his 49. A varied attack reduced the Sri Lankans to 208 for eight at the end of the second day, and they were forced to follow-on on the last morning. With Dougie Brown in fine form, the hosts lost seven wickets before avoiding an innings defeat, but the match was drawn. Inevitably, it seems, the tourists were far from happy about the umpiring in both matches.

24, 25, 26 and 27 January 1998
at P. Saravanamuttu Stadium, Colombo
England 'A' 353 (A. Flintoff 83, S.P. James 57, D.L. Maddy 51) and 244 for 3 dec. (D.L. Maddy 65, N.V. Knight 56, S.P. James 56)
Sri Lankan Board President's XI 249 (S. Ranatunga 120 not out) and 172 (N.R.G. Perera 51, A.F. Giles 4 for 54)
England 'A' won by 176 runs

England 'A' batted well on the opening day when they were put in on a damp pitch. James and Maddy continued their excellent form with a partnership of 100 for the second wicket, but the real hero was Andrew Flintoff. He exuded strength in a three-and-a-quarter hour innings, which ended abruptly on the second morning when England lost their last six wickets for 47 runs. Sanjeeva Ranatunga, leading the Sri Lankan side, stood firm as his colleagues struggled. He remained unbeaten after an innings that lasted nearly six hours, but his side trailed England by 104. James, Knight, Maddy and Ealham went for brisk runs, and the Sri Lankan side were left five overs and a day in which to score 349. It was a task that was beyond them as they fell to the combined left-arm spin of Giles and Cosker. The one problem for England was the loss of pace bowler Hutchison with back trouble.

30 January, 1, 2 and 3 February 1998
at Welagedera Stadium, Kurunegala
England 'A' 385 (M.A. Ealham 87, N.V. Knight 85, B.C. Hollioake 67, D.L. Maddy 50) and 154 for 3 (D.L. Maddy 56)
Sri Lanka 'A' 368 for 9 dec. (D.R.M. Jayawardena 110, M.S. Atapattu 52, M. Villavaryan 50 not out)
Match drawn

6, 7, 8 and 9 February, 1988
at Uyanwatta Stadium, Matara
Sri Lanka 'A' 171 (M.C. Mendis 58, A.A.W. Gunawardena 51, A.F. Giles 4 for 52) and 280 for 9 dec. (R.P. Arnold 79, P.B. Dassanayake 56)
England 'A' 260 (B.C. Hollioake 103, C.N. Bandaratilleke 4 for 57) and 192 for 9 (A. Junaid 4 for 28)
England 'A' won by 1 wicket

13, 14, 15 and 16 February 1998
at Tyronne Fernando Stadium, Moratuwa
Sri Lanka 'A' 371 (U.C. Hathurusinghe 90, G.P. Wickremasinghe 76 not out, C.N. Bandaratilleke 61, J. Ormond 4 for 76) and 168 (A.F. Giles 5 for 43)
England 'A' 466 (B.C. Hollioake 163, D.L. Maddy 99, C.N. Bandaratilleke 4 for 89, B. de Silva 4 for 131) and 76 for 3
England 'A' won by 7 wickets

The three-match international series went in favour of England 'A', and the matches were played over four days. There was no play on 31 January because of a state of national mourning for those killed in the terrorist attack in Kandy. The first day of this first match had been a dour affair, with Knight opting for caution, and only 202 runs for four wickets coming from 94 overs. Ealham and Ben Hollioake enlivened play with a fifth wicket stand of 132, and the beginning of Sri Lanka's innings contrasted sharply with England's. Mahela Jayawardena, a young batsman of immense promise, hit an accomplished century, but a draw was inevitable.

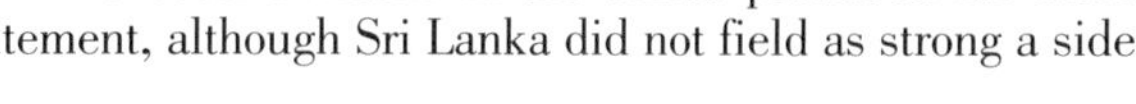

The second match in the series produced far more excitement, although Sri Lanka did not field as strong a side

Ben Hollioake had a highly successful tour of Sri Lanka for the England 'A' side and hit his maiden first-class centuries. (Graham Chadwick / Allsport)

as they had in the first match. An over-watered pitch delayed the start by 45 minutes, and Sri Lanka struggled when they batted, in spite of Gunawardena's 51 off 57 balls. Cosker and Giles, who had an outstanding tour, again bowled well in partnership, and, finishing the day on 47 for one, England had complete control. On the second day, Knight's men slipped to 122 for seven, but then came a brilliant innings from Ben Hollioake, who hit a maiden first-class century. Throwing off the casting as a mere slogger, he batted for three hours and hit nine fours before reaching his century with his second six. He displayed a growing maturity. On the third day, England lost their discipline and took only three wickets as Sri Lanka reached 196. The tourists became frustrated by umpiring decisions, although most observers thought that they had nothing at which to complain. Arnold eventually declared and set a generous target of 192 in 49 overs. The chase began badly, and England struggled against the off-spin of 17-year old Arshad Junaid. They were revived by Sales and Ben Hollioake, but when the ninth wicket fell England were nine short of victory. Giles had batted splendidly to bring England to this position, but Hutchison faced the remaining three balls with the scores level. He swept at Junaid and made enough contact to scamper the single that gave England victory.

Both sides made changes for the last game in the series, and Sri Lanka had their third captain in Tillekeratne, whose Test career seemed to be drawing to a close. On the first day, Sri Lanka scored 235 for eight. Ormond bowled well, and Hathurusinghe, a veteran of 24 Tests, made a delightful 90 in 275 minutes. The highlight of the Sri Lankan innings, however, came on the second morning when Bandaratilleke and Wickremasinghe extended their partnership until it was worth 134. England closed on 161 for two, but there was a disappointment on the third morning when Maddy, who had had an outstandingly successful tour, was run out for 99. There was ample compensation to follow as Ben Hollioake hit ten sixes and 17 fours in making his second century in successive matches, 163 off 189 balls. He and Giles added 154 for the sixth wicket to rally England after they had been 184 for five. Giles made 46, and he was again a hero when Sri Lanka batted a second time. He and Cosker proved decisive on a pitch giving them some help, and they set up the comfortable win that gave England the series.

Maddy, Giles, Ben Hollioake, Cosker were among those who had enhanced their reputations. The three one-day matches remained, but Messrs Gooch and Gatting deserved the highest praise for their coaching and management. England needs them.

18 February 1998
at Tyronne Fernando Stadium, Moratuwa
Sri Lanka 'A' 326 for 6 (R.P. Arnold 87, U.C. Hathurusinghe 56, D.R.M. Jayawardena 52)
England 'A' 184 (A. Flintoff 51, H. Boteju 4 for 33)
Sri Lanka 'A' won by 142 runs

20 February 1998
at Uyanwatta Stadium, Matara
England 'A' 186 (O.A. Shah 65)
Sri Lanka 'A' 190 for 7 (R.P. Arnold 88 not out)
Sri Lanka 'A' won by 3 wickets

21 February 1998
at Uyanwatta Stadium, Matara
Sri Lanka 'A' 236 for 9 (U.C. Hathurusinghe 51)
England 'A' 195 (D.L. Maddy 70, U.D.U. Chandana 5 for 46)
Sri Lanka 'A' won by 41 runs

Like their seniors, the Sri Lankan 'A' side excelled at the one-day game. England failed to last their full fifty overs in any of the three encounters, and only in the second match did they exert any real pressure on Sri Lanka. The home side scored at a fearsome pace in the first match. Hathurusinghe and Gunawardena put on 101 for the first wicket, and Arnold and Jayawardena 108 in 15 overs for the third wicket. Arnold's 87 came off 74 balls, while Chandana brought the innings to a dramatic close with three sixes in his 34 from 13 deliveries. England were all out in 35.2 overs.

England fared better in the second match, and when Darren Maddy took three wickets in 13 balls to reduce Sri Lanka to 140 for seven there were hopes of victory. Arnold and Dassanayake, both of whom have played Test cricket, ended speculation with an unbroken stand of 50, and victory came with seven balls to spare. Dassanayake's 30 came off 34 balls.

The tour ended with a third defeat for England. Sri Lanka chose to bat first and showed consistent authority in the sweltering heat. Giles was again the best of the England bowlers. Maddy, batting at number five, hit 70 off 94 balls to keep England's hopes alive, but the side was all out in 47 overs. Maddy worked hard for his runs, hitting only one four.

The fact that they were totally outplayed in the one-day series does not lessen the success of the tour from the England point of view. In difficult conditions, this side was well guided and performed with honour and commitment.

New Zealand Tour

New Zealand arrived in Sri Lanka for a three-match Test series in mid-May and played two warm up matches, both against the Board President's XI. Both were drawn.

18, 19 and 20 May 1998
at P. Saravanamuttu Stadium, Colombo
New Zealanders 274 (A.C. Parore 53, M.L.C.N. Bandaratilleke 4 for 80) and 178 for 5 dec.
Board President's XI 204 (P.J. Wiseman 5 for 65) and 157 for 5
Match drawn

22, 23 and 24 May 1998
at Asgiriya Stadium, Kandy
Board President's XI 300 for 9 dec. (S.T. Jayasuriya 83, D.P.M. Jayawardene 67, M.W. Priest 4 for 90) and 82 for 1
New Zealanders 344 for 9 dec. (M.J. Horne 92, C.D. McMillan 71, D.P.M. Jayawardene 4 for 29)
Match drawn

The New Zealanders had arrived in Sri Lanka fresh from their triumphs over Zimbabwe, and it was obvious from their performances in the two matches before the Test series that their confidence remained high. All of their batsmen played useful innings, and the bowlers were particularly impressive. The form of off-spinner Paul Wiseman was a great bonus to the New Zealand side. The only uncapped player in the party, he had seven wickets for 126 in the two matches and was selected ahead of Priest for the first Test.

Sri Lanka gave an indication of future planning by naming Sanath Jayasuriya and Denagamage Jayawardene as captains in the two games. Jayasuriya had been marked as the man to succeed Arjuna Ranatunga as captain of the Test side. Very impressive in the first match was Niroshan Bandaratilleke, the slow left-arm bowler, who, like Wiseman, was to make his international debut in the first Test. The third debutant at the Premadasa Stadium was 18-year old leg-spinner Malinga Bandara who was in his last year at school.

Test Series

Sri Lanka *v.* New Zealand

The first encounter, at the Premadasa Stadium in Colombo, went very much in favour of New Zealand, who won the toss and batted first. Young and Horne scored 25 for the first wicket, but there was early delight for Bandaratilleke, who took a wicket in his opening over in Test cricket, bowling Horne. Fleming quickly dispersed any ideas of a collapse, and when he fell to Kalpage, one of six spinners in the Sri Lankan side, Adam Parore took command. He finished the day unbeaten on 67, with New Zealand 282 for seven.

Parore was dismissed without addition the following morning as the last three wickets fell to Muralitharan for the addition of 23 runs. Sri Lanka were handicapped by the absence of the injured Vaas, but once again off-spinner Muralitharan had proved to be their most potent weapon, finishing with five for 90.

The Sri Lankan innings began disastrously. Cairns had Atapattu caught behind in his first over, and, in his next over, he dismissed the powerful Jayasuriya, who was caught down the leg side off his glove. Jayawardene and Aravinda de Silva added 80, but both fell in quick succession, Jayawardene becoming Wiseman's first Test victim. Arjuna Ranatunga and Romesh Kaluwitharana then added 101, but both were out before the close, which came with Sri Lanka on 251 for seven and the game evenly balanced.

On the third morning, the score moved on to 284 before left-arm spinner Daniel Vettori took two wickets in his opening over. Only one more run was scored before Bandaratilleke, who had added 47 for the eighth wicket with Wickremasinghe, was run out.

New Zealand led by 20 on the first innings, and left-arm spinner Niroshan Bandaratilleke soon trapped Bryan Young leg before. This gave Sri Lanka false hopes of success, for they took only one wicket in the afternoon session when Horne lobbed Muralitharan to short mid-wicket. In intense heat, Fleming and Astle added 92, and after Astle had fallen to Jayasuriya, McMillan launched a violent attack on the bowling, hitting 64 off 76 balls in the final session. He gave able support to Fleming, who batted magnificently to reach the second Test century of his career. He finished on 106, and New Zealand were in a commanding position at 260 for three.

The Fleming/McMillan fourth wicket partnership was worth 240 when McMillan was caught off Muralitharan, who finished the match with nine wickets to his credit. McMillan hit six sixes and 13 fours and faced 179 balls, while his captain faced 332 balls and hit a six and 16 fours in his unbeaten 174. Fleming's declaration left Sri Lanka a target of 465, and the home side went off at a blazing start, but both openers fell to Wiseman before the close, and they finished on 111 for two.

By lunch on the last day, Jayawardene and Aravinda de Silva had taken the score to 194, but Vettori trapped de Silva leg before with the first delivery of the afternoon, and, having broken through, the New Zealand spinners took control of the game. Victory came 44 minutes after tea, and Wiseman claimed five wickets in an innings on his debut. The individual award went to Fleming for his two splendid innings and inspiring leadership, but New Zealand suffered a blow in that Doull aggravated a groin injury and was forced to return home.

Doull's place in the side for the second Test was taken by O'Connor while Sri Lanka brought back the experienced Tillekeratne in place of Kalpage, and selected Dharmasena ahead of young Bandara, who had been used little in the first Test. The venue for the second Test was the International Stadium at Galle, which became the 79th ground at which Test cricket has been played. Fleming again won the toss and again chose to bat, but, on this occasion, little went right for New Zealand.

Rain restricted the first day's play to 55 overs, during which time New Zealand lost four wickets for 96 runs. Horne was out in the third over, caught behind off Bandaratilleke, and Fleming was soon leg before to Dharmasena, who bowled his off-breaks briskly. Astle and Young added 69, but Bandaratilleke dismissed both Young and night-watchman Vettori at the same score before bad light ended play early with Astle unbeaten on 30.

There was even less play on the second day than there had been on the first, and New Zealand lost McMillan while the score advanced to 122 from 73 overs. Astle remained steadfast on 42.

Sri Lanka took complete control of the match on the third day. Joining the attack some 20 minutes into the day, Kumara Dharmasena bowled unchanged for 11 overs and took the last five wickets at a personal cost of 33 runs. He finished with the best Test bowling figures of his career, six for 72.

Always positive in approach, the Sri Lankan batsmen began briskly, and, although de Silva went cheaply, they ended the day with a lead of four runs and seven wickets standing. Mahela Jayawardene was unbeaten on 88 and looked to be in excellent form.

Playing in only his fourth Test, Jayawardene duly completed his maiden Test century on the fourth morning. This was an outstanding innings. Jayawardene's 167 came off 273 balls and contained 18 fours. He was at the crease for just over five-and-a-half hours before falling to Chris Harris, who had a hand in capturing the last five Sri Lankan wickets, running out Kaluwitharana, Dharmasena and Bandaratilleke and catching Wickremasinghe. In spite of his efforts and some fine bowling by Vettori, Sri Lanka claimed a formidable first innings lead of 130.

On a pitch that was below Test standard and which gave considerable help to the spinners, New Zealand were soon in trouble. Muralitharan and Bandaratilleke reduced them to 41 for four, and when Aravinda de Silva bowled the redoubtable Astle off an inside edge Sri Lanka scented victory. Parore and Cairns took New Zealand to an uneasy 94 for five at the close.

With the third ball of the final morning, Niroshan Bandaratilleke had Cairns caught at silly point, and the last four wickets fell for 11 runs. In his second Test match, Bandaratilleke finished with nine wickets for 83, five of his wickets coming in the second innings. The individual award went to Mahela Jayawardene, whose magnificent century, studded with strokes of high quality, set up Sri Lanka's victory, which came less than three-quarters of an hour into the fifth day.

New Zealand made two changes for the third and final Test. Spearman replaced Harris and Horne dropped down the order to number five, while left-arm spinner Priest came

Mahela Jayawardene batted most impressively in the Test series against New Zealand and registered his first Test century in the match at Galle.
(Graham Chadwick / Allsport)

in for pace bowler O'Connor. Ranatunga won the toss, and Sri Lanka batted, but the first day was very much in favour of New Zealand. The opening session was curtailed by rain, but there was time for Chris Cairns to have Jayasuriya caught at slip. Cairns later sent back Jayawardene and when de Silva hooked into the hands of long leg, the New Zealand all-rounder had emulated his father Lance in taking 100 wickets in Test cricket. Ranatunga was run out when he backed up too far, and Craig McMillan accounted for both Tillekeratne and Kaluwitharana to leave Sri Lanka on a perilous 200 for eight at the close.

The innings was soon over on the second morning with Vettori trapping Bandaratilleke leg before and Cairns taking his fifth wicket of the innings when he had Muralitharan caught.

The New Zealand innings began disastrously when both openers were out with only seven scored, and matters could have been even worse, for Fleming was dropped on six when Dharmasena failed to hold on to a return catch. Fleming took advantage of this lapse to make the highest score of the innings, 78, before being last out, bowled off his pads by Wickremasinghe, who was operating with the second new ball. Fleming and Horne had seemed to be leading New Zealand out of danger in a fourth wicket stand worth 64 when Aravinda de Silva had Horne caught. He then dismissed McMillan and Parore to eat the heart out of the New Zealand innings and finish with three for 30, his best figures in Test cricket. He was pressed into service

A splendid Test debut for young slow left-arm spinner Niroshan Bandaratilleke. He took a wicket in the first over he bowled in Test cricket and captured 16 wickets in the series against New Zealand. (Mike Hewitt / Allsport)

because Muralitharan sustained a minor injury, but his efforts helped Sri Lanka to a first innings lead of 16.

This lead seemed totally insignificant when Vettori bowled his left-arm spin to such good effect that Sri Lanka lost their top four batsmen for 36 runs. Ranatunga and Tillekeratne stopped the rot with a stand of 102, and Kaluwitharana, dropped at slip before he had scored, made 88 off 140 balls with seven fours. When the ninth wicket went down Sri Lanka were 211, a lead of 227, and the game was in the balance, but Muralitharan now joined Kaluwitharana in a last wicket record partnership of 71. Crucially, this turned the match in favour of Sri Lanka. Vettori had bowled heroically to claim a career-best six for 64, but New Zealand faced a target of 296, a daunting task on a pitch that was a delight for spin bowlers. Young and Spearman scored 10 runs in the last six overs of the day.

The opening partnership was extended by another 34 runs on the fourth morning, but once Young and Spearman were separated the New Zealand innings fell apart against Muralitharan and Bandaratilleke, who captured 19 and 16 wickets respectively in the series. They shared nine wickets in this last innings as New Zealand were bowled out for 131 to give Sri Lanka victory by 164 runs inside four days. Arjuna Ranatunga became the first captain in the history of Test cricket to come from behind twice to win a three-Test series, and Muttiah Muralitharan was, not surprisingly, named Man of the Series.

From New Zealand, there were few complaints. They had had their chances, but their bowling had never maintained the consistency of their opponents.

First Test Match – Sri Lanka v. New Zealand

27, 28, 29, 30 and 31 May 1998 at R. Premadasa Stadium, Colombo

New Zealand

	First Innings		Second Innings	
B.A. Young	c Kaluwitharana, **b** Muralitharan	**30**	lbw, **b** Bandaratilleke	**11**
M.J. Horne	**b** Bandaratilleke	**15**	c Ranatunga, **b** Muralitharan	**35**
S.P. Fleming *	c Jayasuriya, **b** Kalpage	**78**	not out	**174**
N.J. Astle	c Jayawardene, **b** Kalpage	**30**	c Kaluwitharana, **b** Jayasuriya	**34**
C.D. McMillan	lbw, **b** Muralitharan	**0**	c Kalpage, **b** Muralitharan	**142**
A.C. Parore †	c Jayasuriya, **b** Wickremasinghe	**67**	c Kalpage, **b** Muralitharan	**1**
C.L. Cairns	c Bandaratilleke, **b** Muralitharan	**19**	c Jayasuriya, **b** Muralitharan	**6**
C.Z. Harris	lbw, **b** Wickremasinghe	**19**	not out	**14**
D.L. Vettori	c Kalpage, **b** Muralitharan	**20**		
P.J. Wiseman	c Atapattu, **b** Muralitharan	**6**		
S.B. Doull	not out	**1**		
	lb **10**, w **1**, nb **9**	**20**	b **5**, lb **10**, nb **12**	**27**
		305	(for 6 wickets, dec.)	**444**

	O	M	R	W	O	M	R	W
Wickremasinghe	14	2	55	**2**	7	–	21	**–**
Jayawardene	3	–	10	**–**				
Bandaratilleke	22	6	50	**1**	39	8	105	**1**
Muralitharan	38.2	9	90	**5**	36	5	137	**4**
Bandara	13	3	41	**–**	8	–	38	**–**
Kalpage	15	2	49	**2**	16	4	51	**–**
de Silva	2	–	14	**–**				
Jayasuriya	15	–	63	**1**				

Fall of Wickets
1–**25**, 2–**97**, 3–**141**, 4–**141**, 5–**188**, 6–**229**, 7–**269**, 8–**282**, 9–**296**
1–**11**, 2–**68**, 3–**160**, 4–**400**, 5–**404**, 6–**416**

Sri Lanka

	First Innings		Second Innings	
S.T. Jayasuriya	c Parore, **b** Cairns	**10**	c Young, **b** Wiseman	**59**
M.S. Atapattu	c Parore, **b** Cairns	**0**	c Horne, **b** Wiseman	**16**
D.P.M. Jayawardene	c Vettori, **b** Wiseman	**52**	c Horne, **b** Wiseman	**54**
P.A. de Silva	c Doull, **b** McMillan	**37**	lbw, **b** Vettori	**71**
A. Ranatunga *	**b** Cairns	**49**	c and **b** Vettori	**9**
R.S. Kaluwitharana †	**b** Vettori	**72**	c Parore, **b** McMillan	**39**
R.S. Kalpage	**b** Wiseman	**6**	c Young, **b** Vettori	**16**
G.P. Wickremasinghe	lbw, **b** Vettori	**27**	(9) c Young, **b** Cairns	**0**
M.L.C.N. Bandaratilleke	run out	**20**	(8) c Horne, **b** Wiseman	**16**
M. Muralitharan	**b** Vettori	**0**	not out	**9**
C.M. Bandara	not out	**0**	lbw, **b** Wiseman	**0**
	lb **8**, nb **4**	**12**	b **1**, lb **4**, nb **3**	**8**
		285		**297**

	O	M	R	W	O	M	R	W
Doull	12.2	2	43	**–**	3	–	15	**–**
Cairns	15	–	59	**3**	19	6	64	**1**
Harris	7	1	27	**–**	4	1	16	**–**
Vettori	24	8	56	**3**	51	23	101	**3**
Wiseman	20	4	61	**2**	46.5	17	82	**5**
McMillan	12	4	31	**1**	6	4	12	**1**
Astle					2	–	2	**–**

Fall of Wickets
1–**6**, 2–**21**, 3–**101**, 4–**105**, 5–**206**, 6–**221**, 7–**237**, 8–**284**, 9–**284**
1–**70**, 2–**89**, 3–**194**, 4–**216**, 5–**216**, 6–**239**, 7–**277**, 8–**279**, 9–**289**

Umpires: K.T. Francis & R.E. Koertzen *Man of the Match:* S.T. Jayasuriya

New Zealand won by 167 runs

Second Test Match – Sri Lanka v. New Zealand

3, 4, 5, 6 and 7 June 1998 at Galle International Stadium, Galle

New Zealand

	First Innings		Second Innings	
B.A. Young	**c** Jayasuriya, **b** Bandaratilleke	**46**	**c** Tillekeratne, **b** Bandaratilleke	**11**
M.J. Horne	**c** Kaluwitharana, **b** Bandaratilleke	**1**	lbw, **b** Bandaratilleke	**3**
S.P. Fleming *	lbw, **b** Dharmasena	**14**	lbw, **b** Muralitharan	**10**
N.J. Astle	**c** Tillekeratne, **b** Dharmasena	**53**	**b** de Silva	**13**
D.L. Vettori	**c** Tillekeratne, **b** Bandaratilleke	**0**	(9) run out	**0**
C.D. McMillan	**b** Bandaratilleke	**13**	(5) **c** Jayasuriya, **b** Bandaratilleke	**1**
A.C. Parore †	**c** Jayasuriya, **b** Dharmasena	**30**	(6) not out	**32**
C.L. Cairns	**c** Jayasuriya, **b** Dharmasena	**0**	(7) **c** Tillekeratne, **b** Bandaratilleke	**16**
C.Z. Harris	**c** Wickremasinghe, **b** Dharmesena	**4**	(8) **c** Jayawardene, **b** Muralitharan	**9**
P.J. Wiseman	**st** Kaluwitharana, **b** Dharmasena	**23**	**c** Tillekeratne, **b** Bandaratilleke	**2**
S.B. O'Connor	not out	**0**	**c** Jayasuriya, **b** Muralitharan	**0**
	lb **7**, nb **2**	**9**	b **5**, lb **9**, w **1**, nb **2**	**17**
		193		**114**

	O	M	R	**W**	O	M	R	**W**
Wickremasinghe	7	1	20	–	2	–	6	–
Dharmasena	24.1	4	72	6	6	–	16	–
Bandaratilleke	38	14	47	4	24	8	36	5
Muralitharan	23	9	33	–	16	7	24	3
Jayasuriya	4	1	8	–				
de Silva	5	2	6	–	7	1	18	1

Fall of Wickets
1–**5**, 2–**21**, 3–**90**, 4–**90**, 5–**110**, 6–**137**, 7–**137**, 8–**147**, 9–**190**
1–**18**, 2–**21**, 3–**40**, 4–**41**, 5–**69**, 6–**94**, 7–**103**, 8–**106**, 9–**109**

Sri Lanka

	First Innings	
S.T. Jayasuriya	**c** Harris, **b** Vettori	**21**
M.S. Atapattu	**c** Vettori, **b** Wiseman	**35**
D.P.M. Jayawardene	lbw, **b** Harris	**167**
P.A. de Silva	lbw, **b** Vettori	**10**
A. Ranatunga *	**c** O'Connor, **b** Vettori	**36**
H.P. Tillekeratne	**b** Wiseman	**10**
R.S. Kaluwitharana †	run out	**3**
H.D.P.K. Dharmasena	run out	**12**
G.P. Wickremasinghe	**c** Harris, **b** Vettori	**12**
M.L.C.N. Bandaratilleke	run out	**4**
M. Muralitharan	not out	**2**
	lb **9**, nb **2**	**11**
		323

	O	M	R	**W**
O'Connor	4	–	13	**–**
Cairns	5	–	20	**–**
Wiseman	30	3	95	**2**
Vettori	26	4	88	**4**
Harris	25.4	6	56	**1**
McMillan	11	3	30	**–**
Astle	5	3	12	**–**

Fall of Wickets
1–**44**, 2–**106**, 3–**135**, 4–**211**, 5–**262**, 6–**271**, 7–**301**, 8–**315**, 9–**319**

Umpires: B.C. Cooray & D.L. Orchard

Sri Lanka won by an innings and 16 runs

Third Test Match – Sri Lanka v. New Zealand

10, 11, 12 and 13 June 1998 at Sinhalese Sports Club, Colombo

Sri Lanka

	First Innings		Second Innings	
S.T. Jayasuriya	**c** Young, **b** Cairns	**13**	**c** Parore, **b** Cairns	**8**
M.S. Atapattu	**c** Vettori, **b** Wiseman	**48**	lbw, **b** Vettori	**5**
D.P.M. Jayawardene	**c** Parore, **b** Cairns	**16**	**c** Horne, **b** Vettori	**11**
P.A. de Silva	**c** Spearman, **b** Cairns	**4**	**c** Astle, **b** Vettori	**3**
A. Ranatunga *	run out	**4**	**c** Cairns, **b** Priest	**64**
H.P. Tillekeratne	**c** Young, **b** McMillan	**43**	**b** Vettori	**40**
R.S. Kaluwitharana †	**b** McMillan	**28**	lbw, **b** Priest	**88**
H.D.P.K. Dharmasena	**c** Parore, **b** Cairns	**11**	**b** McMillan	**11**
G.P. Wickremasinghe	not out	**24**	**c** Fleming, **b** Vettori	**0**
M.L.C.N. Bandaratilleke	lbw, **b** Vettori	**5**	**c** Fleming, **b** Vettori	**7**
M. Muralitharan	**c** Astle, **b** Cairns	**1**	not out	**26**
	b **1**, lb **8**	**9**	b **8**, lb **10**, nb **1**	**19**
		206		**282**

	O	M	R	**W**	O	M	R	**W**
Cairns	17.4	1	62	**5**	17	–	75	**1**
Vettori	25	7	52	**1**	33	10	64	**6**
Priest	24	11	35	**–**	11.5	–	42	**2**
Wiseman	10	4	21	**1**	6	2	29	**–**
McMillan	12	5	27	2	14	2	46	**1**
Astle	3	–	8	**–**				

Fall of Wickets
1–**23**, 2–**52**, 3–**56**, 4–**70**, 5–**102**, 6–**156**, 7–**163**, 8–**196**, 9–**201**
1–**12**, 2–**16**, 3–**24**, 4–**36**, 5–**138**, 6–**140**, 7–**188**, 8–**193**, 9–**211**

New Zealand

	First Innings		Second Innings	
B.A. Young	**c** Atapattu, **b** Bandaratilleke	**2**	**st** Kaluwitharana, **b** Muralitharan	**24**
C.M. Spearman	**c** de Silva, **b** Wickremasinghe	**4**	**c** and **b** Muralitharan	**22**
S.P. Fleming *	**b** Wickremasinghe	**78**	lbw, **b** Dharmasena	**3**
N.J. Astle	**c** Atapattu, **b** Dharmasena	**16**	**c** and **b** Muralitharan	**16**
M.J. Horne	**c** Tillekeratne, **b** de Silva	**35**	**c** Kaluwitharana, **b** Bandaratilleke	**12**
C.D. McMillan	**st** Kaluwitharana, **b** de Silva	**2**	**c** Jayawardene, **b** Muralitharan	**1**
A.C. Parore †	lbw, **b** de Silva	**19**	**b** Bandaratilleke	**2**
C.L. Cairns	run out	**6**	**b** Bandaratilleke	**26**
M.W. Priest	**c** sub (S.A. Perera), **b** Muralitharan	**12**	**b** Bandaratilleke	**2**
D.L. Vettori	**c** Jayasuriya, **b** Muralitharan	**0**	**b** Muralitharan	**3**
P.J. Wiseman	not out	**1**	not out	**0**
	b **9**, lb **4**, nb **5**	**18**	b **6**, lb **10**, nb **4**	**20**
		193		**131**

	O	M	R	**W**	O	M	R	**W**
Wickremasinghe	6.3	3	7	**2**	6	2	5	**–**
Bandaratilleke	20	6	48	**1**	17	3	52	**4**
Dharmasena	18	4	35	**1**	10	2	14	**1**
de Silva	18.5	7	30	**3**	3	–	14	**–**
Muralitharan	23.1	3	60	**2**	18.3	8	30	**5**

Fall of Wickets
1–**5**, 2–**7**, 3–**30**, 4–**94**, 5–**98**, 6–**128**, 7–**143**, 8–**181**, 9–**183**
1–**44**, 2–**57**, 3–**63**, 4–**82**, 5–**84**, 6–**93**, 7–**105**, 8–**128**, 9–**131**

Umpires: P. Manuel & V.K. Ramaswamy

Sri Lanka won by 164 runs

Test Match Averages – Sri Lanka v. New Zealand

Sri Lanka Batting

	M	Inns	NOs	Runs	HS	Av	100s	50s
D.P.M. Jayawardene	3	5	–	300	167	60.00	1	2
R.S. Kaluwitharana	3	5	–	230	88	46.00	2	
A. Ranatunga	3	5	–	162	64	32.40	1	
H.P. Tillekeratne	2	3	–	93	43	31.00		
P.A. de Silva	3	5	–	125	71	25.00	1	
S.T. Jayasuriya	3	5	–	111	59	22.20	1	
M.S. Atapattu	3	5	–	104	48	20.80		
M. Muralitharan	3	5	3	38	26*	19.00		
G.P. Wickremasinghe	3	5	1	63	27	15.75		
H.D.P.K. Dharmasena	2	3	–	34	12	11.33		
M.L.C.N. Bandaratilleke	3	5	–	52	20	10.40		

Played in one Test: R.S. Kalpage 6 & 16; C.M. Bandara 0* & 0

New Zealand Batting

	M	Inns	NOs	Runs	HS	Av	100s	50s
S.P. Fleming	3	6	1	357	174*	71.40	1	2
A.C. Parore	3	6	1	151	67	30.20	1	
N.J. Astle	3	6	–	162	53	27.00	1	
C.D. McMillan	3	6	–	159	142	26.50	1	
B.A. Young	3	6	–	124	46	20.66		
M.J. Horne	3	6	–	101	35	16.83		
C.Z. Harris	2	4	1	46	19	15.33		
C.L. Cairns	3	6	–	73	26	12.16		
P.J. Wiseman	3	5	2	32	23	10.66		
D.L. Vettori	3	5	–	23	20	4.60		

Played in one match: C.M. Spearman 4 & 22; M.W. Priest 12 & 2; S.B. O'Connor 0* & 0; S.B. Doull 1

Sri Lanka Bowling

	Overs	Mds	Runs	Wkts	Best	Av	10/m	5/inn
H.D.P.K. Dharmasena	58.1	10	141	8	6/76	17.62	1	
M. Muralitharan	155	41	334	19	5/30	17.57	2	
P.A. de Silva	35.5	10	82	4	3/30	20.50		
M.L.C.N. Bandaratilleke	160	45	338	16	5/36	21.12	1	
G.P. Wickremasinghe	42.3	8	114	4	2/7	28.50		
R.S. Kalpage	31	6	100	2	2/49	50.00		
S.T. Jayasuriya	19	1	71	1	1/63	71.00		
C.M. Bandara	21	3	79	–	–	–		

Bowled in one innings: D.P.M. Jayawardene 3–0–10–0

New Zealand Bowling

	Overs	Mds	Runs	Wkts	Best	Av	10/m	5/inn
D.L. Vettori	159	52	361	17	6/64	21.23	1	
C.L. Cairns	73.4	7	280	10	5/62	28.00	1	
P.J. Wiseman	112.5	30	288	10	5/82	28.80	1	
C.D. McMillan	55	18	146	5	2/27	29.20		
M.W. Priest	35.5	11	77	2	2/42	38.50		
C.Z. Harris	36.4	8	99	1	1/56	99.00		
N.J. Astle	10	3	22	–	–	–		
S.B. Doull	15.2	2	58	–	–	–		

Bowled in one innings: S.B. O'Connor 4–0–13–0

Sri Lanka Leading Fielders

8 – S.T. Jayasuriya; 7 – R.S. Kaluwitharana (ct 4 / st 3); 6 – H.P. Tillkeratne; 4 – D.P.M. Jayawardene; 3 – M.S. Atapattu and R.S. Kalpage; 2 – M. Muralitharan; 1 – P.A. de Silva, A. Ranatunga, G.P. Wickremasinghe, M.L.C.N. Bandaratilleke and sub (S.A. Perera)

New Zealand Leading Fielders

6 – A.C. Parore; 5 – B.A. Young; 4 – M.J. Horne and D.L. Vettori; 2 – S.P. Fleming, N.J. Astle and C.Z. Harris; 1 – C.M. Spearman, C.L. Cairns, S.B. O'Connor and S.B. Doull

16 June 1998
at Welagedera Stadium, Kurunegala
New Zealanders 240 for 8 (N.J. Astle 57, S.P. Fleming 52)
Board President's XI 208 for 9 (A.A.W. Gunawardena 96)
New Zealanders won by 32 runs

The New Zealanders had the better of a warm up match before the start of the Independence Cup, a triangular tournament in which India would compete with New Zealand and the host country.

Singer Akai Nidahas Trophy – The Independence Cup

The opening match of the competition saw Sri Lanka suffer their first home defeat in a one-day international for four years. Electing to bat first when they won the toss, Sri Lanka lost Jayasuriya in the fifth over and Kaluwitharana in the 13th, but Aravinda de Silva and Marvan Atapattu shared a third wicket record stand of 145 in 28 overs. Atapattu hit 70 off 97 balls, and de Silva batted with his usual mastery, making 97 off 119 balls with a six and five fours. Chasing a target of 244, India were given a blistering start by Tendulkar and Ganguly, who put on 116 off 106 balls. Tendulkar hit nine fours in his 50-ball innings, and Ganguly faced 114 deliveries and hit a six and seven fours in his 80. When the opening pair were dismissed, Azharuddin and Jadeja maintained the momentum, and India won with 38 balls to spare.

Sri Lanka returned to form two days later with a comfortable win over New Zealand, who chose to bat first when they won the toss. Young and Astle shared an opening stand of 71 in 14.4 overs. Young provided the impetus with 55 off 52 balls, but thereafter the pace slackened, and with six wickets falling for 31 runs, New Zealand reached a disappointing 200 in their 50 overs. Kaluwitharana was out in the first over, but Jayasuriya and Atapattu put on 82 in 17 overs. Atapattu was then joined by de Silva and 95 runs came in the next 18 overs to take Sri Lanka to the brink of a resounding victory.

The competition ran into problems in the third match when rain brought a halt to the game between India and New Zealand. New Zealand were put in to bat, and Astle gave the innings foundation by hitting 81 off 119 balls. Horne, 46 off 44 balls, and Cairns, 20 off as many deliveries without the help of a boundary, gave the score a boost in the last 10 overs, and New Zealand reached 219. They then captured the wicket of Ganguly in the fifth over before Tendulkar and Azharuddin scored 58 in the next five overs. Tendulkar hit three sixes and three fours as he made 53 off

36 balls. Azharuddin shared an unbroken stand of 53 with Jadeja, but rain ended the game after 24.2 overs. This was four balls short of the number of overs required to determine a result. India's target in 25 overs would have been 147.

Worse was to follow as the three games scheduled to be played in Galle were all abandoned without a ball being bowled: Sri Lanka *v.* India and New Zealand, and India *v.* New Zealand. Each side took one point from the matches.

The weather in Colombo was only marginally better, and Sri Lanka's match against India was restricted to 36 overs. The home side were much indebted to Aravinda de Silva, who hit 62 off 86 deliveries in difficult conditions and to Chandana, whose 26 came off 24 balls and included two sixes and a four. India's middle order fell apart with three wickets falling for one run. Robin Singh and Agarkar made 63 in 13 overs for the seventh wicket, but Robin Singh was ninth out when nine were needed from four balls and Harbhajan Singh was stumped first ball when he attempted a big hit.

There was a fourth abandoned match when rain intervened in the game between India and New Zealand at the start of the 32nd over, but, two days later, Sri Lanka overwhelmed New Zealand to confirm their place in the final against India. The visitors chose to field and saw Jayasuriya and Kaluwitharana score 69 in 12.2 overs, but the real might of the Sri Lankan innings came in a third wicket stand of 132 in 23 overs between Arjuna Ranatunga and Aravinda de Silva. The Sri Lankan skipper hit the first century of the tournament. His 102 came off 98 balls and included two sixes and six fours. His batting put Sri Lanka in a dominant position, and, although Nathan Astle batted valiantly in scoring 74 off 76 balls with three sixes and seven fours, New Zealand were never in contention. So, Sri Lanka finished with eight points, India with six and New Zealand with four. India and New Zealand had both suffered four abandoned matches while Sri Lanka had been more fortunate in losing just the two games in Galle.

If there had been disappointments, the final compensated for them in full measure. Azharuddin won the toss and India batted. Tendulkar and Ganguly were magnificent. They established a new first wicket record for one-day international cricket by scoring 251 in 44 overs. The partnership was broken when the third umpire (B.C. Cooray) ruled Tendulkar stumped off Jayasuriya off the last ball of the 44th over. Tendulkar had hit 128 off 132 balls with two sixes and eight fours. It was his 17th century in limited-over international cricket and it brought him level with Desmond Haynes, who hit 17 centuries in this form of international cricket during his career. Saurav Ganguly was out the ball after Tendulkar. His 109 came off 136 balls and included two sixes and six fours. It was the culmination of a year that had seen him outstanding in one-day international cricket.

Sri Lanka responded to India's 307 in brilliant fashion. Jayasuriya and Kaluwitharana scored 59 inside nine overs, and Aravinda de Silva launched a wonderfully exciting and ever delightful attack on the bowling. He made 105 off 94 balls and hit 10 fours. He could not quite bring victory to Sri Lanka, falling in the 44th over when 36 were still needed, but he was rightfully named Man of the Series. Sri Lanka required 14 from the last two overs, but the last three batsmen found the task beyond them and perished to suicidal run outs.

Match One – Sri Lanka *v.* India

19 June 1998 at R. Premadasa Stadium, Colombo

Sri Lanka

S.T. Jayasuriya	**b** Agarkar	**12**
R.S. Kaluwitharana †	**c** Agarkar, **b** Harbhajan Singh	**29**
M.S. Atapattu	**b** Kumble	**70**
P.A. de Silva	**c** Azharuddin, **b** Agarkar	**97**
A. Ranatunga *	**c** Azharuddin, **b** Kumble	**25**
R.S. Mahanama	run out	**0**
D.P.M. Jayawardene	not out	**1**
H.D.P.K. Dharmasena	not out	**2**
G.P. Wickremasinghe		
M. Muralitharan		
S.A. Perera		
	b **1**, lb **5**, w **1**	**7**
	50 overs (for 6 wickets)	**243**

	O	M	R	W
Agarkar	9	–	38	**2**
Venkatesh Prasad	7	–	32	**–**
Harbhajan Singh	10	–	45	**1**
R.R. Singh	8	–	30	**–**
Kumble	10	–	56	**2**
Kanitkar	4	1	19	**–**
Tendulkar	2	–	17	**–**

Fall of Wickets
1–**16**, 2–**50**, 3–**195**, 4–**236**, 5–**238**, 6–**238**

India

S.C. Ganguly	**c** Jayawardene, **b** Muralitharan	**80**
S.R. Tendulkar	**c** Atapattu, **b** Muralitharan	**65**
M. Azharuddin *	not out	**55**
A.D. Jadeja	not out	**22**
R.R. Singh		
H.H. Kanitkar		
N.R. Mongia †		
A. Kumble		
A.B. Agarkar		
Venkatesh Prasad		
Harbhajan Singh		
	lb **8**, w **14**, nb **2**	**24**
	43.4 overs (for 2 wickets)	**246**

	O	M	R	W
Wickremasinghe	5	–	36	**–**
Perera	10	–	58	**–**
Dharmasena	9.4	1	57	**–**
Muralitharan	10	–	48	**2**
Jayasuriya	9	–	39	**–**

Fall of Wickets
1–**115**, 2–**211**

Umpires: K.T. Francis & P. Manuel *Man of the Match:* S.C. Ganguly

India won by 8 wickets

Match Two – Sri Lanka v. New Zealand

21 June 1998 at R. Premadasa Stadium, Colombo

New Zealand

B.A. Young	**c** Chandana, **b** Dharmsena	**55**
N.J. Astle	**b** Muralitharan	**33**
S.P. Fleming *	run out	**47**
M.J. Horne	**st** Kaluwitharana, **b** Dharmasena	**1**
C.D. McMillan	**c** Muralitharan, **b** Chandana	**26**
C.L. Cairns	**c** Atapattu, **b** Chandana	**7**
A.C. Parore †	**c** Kaluwitharana, **b** Chandana	**1**
C.Z. Harris	**b** Dharmasena	**7**
D.J. Nash	run out	**1**
D.L. Vettori	not out	**4**
S.B. O'Connor	not out	**6**
	lb **9**, w **3**	**12**
	50 overs (for 9 wickets)	**200**

	O	M	R	W
Wickremasinghe	6	–	35	–
Bandaratilleke	10	–	41	–
Dharmasena	10	–	40	3
Muralitharan	10	1	24	1
Jayasuriya	7	–	27	–
Chandana	7	1	24	3

Fall of Wickets
1–**71**, 2–**107**, 3–**112**, 4–**169**, 5–**171**, 6–**176**, 7–**179**, 8–**186**, 9–**189**

Sri Lanka

S.T. Jayasuriya	**c** McMillan, **b** Vettori	**57**
R.S. Kaluwitharana †	hit wkt, **b** O'Connor	**2**
M.S. Atapattu	not out	**83**
P.A. de Silva	**b** Astle	**42**
A. Ranatunga *	not out	**4**
U.D.U. Chandana		
R.S. Mahanama		
H.D.P.K. Dharmasena		
G.P. Wickremasinghe		
M.L.C.N. Bandaratilleke		
M. Muralitharan		
	b **4**, lb **5**, w **4**	**13**
	40 overs (for 3 wickets)	**201**

	O	M	R	W
O'Connor	4	–	21	1
Nash	6	–	25	–
Cairns	5	–	24	–
Harris	10	–	50	–
Vettori	8	–	41	1
McMillan	4	–	29	–
Astle	3	2	2	1

Fall of Wickets
1–**3**, 2–**85**, 3–**180**

Umpires: B.C. Cooray & D.N. Pathirana *Man of the Match:* M.S. Atapattu

Sri Lanka won by 7 wickets

Match Three – India v. New Zealand

23 June 1998 at R. Premadasa Stadium, Colombo

New Zealand

B.A. Young	**b** Kumble	**23**
N.J. Astle	**c** Kanitkar, **b** Harbhajan Singh	**81**
S.P. Fleming *	**c** Venkatesh Prasad, **b** Harbhajan Singh	**5**
C.D. McMillan	**c** Jadeja, **b** Tendulkar	**23**
M.J. Horne	lbw, **b** Venkatesh Prasad	**44**
C.L. Cairns	**c** Mongia, **b** Agarkar	**20**
A.C. Parore †	lbw, **b** Agarkar	**1**
C.Z. Harris	**c** and **b** Agarkar	**3**
M.W. Priest	not out	**4**
D.L. Vettori	not out	**1**
P.J. Wiseman		
	lb **3**, w **10**, nb **1**	**14**
	50 overs (for 8 wickets)	**219**

	O	M	R	W
Agarkar	9	–	52	3
Venkatesh Prasad	7	1	21	1
Harbhajan Singh	9	–	30	2
R.R. Singh	2	1	8	–
Kumble	8	–	31	1
Kanitkar	9	–	42	–
Tendulkar	6	–	32	1

Fall of Wickets
1–**65**, 2–**73**, 3–**122**, 4–**185**, 5–**204**, 6–**209**, 7–**212**, 8–**215**

India

S.C. Ganguly	**c** Parore, **b** Cairns	**4**
S.R. Tendulkar	**c** and **b** Harris	**53**
M. Azharuddin *	not out	**53**
A.D. Jadeja	not out	**17**
R.R. Singh		
H.H. Kanitkar		
N.R. Mongia †		
A. Kumble		
A.B. Agarkar		
Venkatesh Prasad		
Harbhajan Singh		
	w **3**, nb **1**	**4**
	24.2 overs (for 2 wickets)	**131**

	O	M	R	W
Cairns	5	–	36	1
Vettori	6.2	–	32	–
Harris	6	–	40	1
Astle	4	–	12	–
Wiseman	3	–	11	–

Fall of Wickets
1–**20**, 2–**78**

Umpires: K.T. Francis & T.M. Samarasinghe *Man of the Match:* M.S. Atapattu

Match abandonned

Matches Four, Five and Six, scheduled to be played at Galle International Stadium, Galle, were all abandoned without a ball being bowled.

Match Seven – Sri Lanka *v.* India

1 July 1998 at Sinhalese Sports Club, Colombo

Sri Lanka

Batsman	Dismissal	Runs
S.T. Jayasuriya	**c** Kanitkar, **b** Venkatesh Prasad	**23**
A.A.W. Gunawardene	**c** Azharuddin, **b** Agarkar	**0**
M.S. Atapattu	**c** R.R. Singh, **b** Agarkar	**12**
P.A. de Silva	**c** Azharuddin, **b** Venkatesh Prasad	**62**
A. Ranatunga *	**c** Jadeja, **b** Harbhajan Singh	**11**
R.S. Kaluwitharana †	**st** Mongia, **b** Harbhajan Singh	**7**
U.D.U. Chandana	**b** Agarkar	**26**
H.D.P.K. Dharmasena	**c** Tendulkar, **b** Kumble	**11**
G.P. Wickremasinghe	not out	**5**
M. Muralitharan	not out	**3**
S.A. Perera		
	lb **4**, w **2**, nb **5**	**11**
	36 overs (for 8 wickets)	**171**

	O	M	R	W
Agarkar	7	–	38	**3**
Venkatesh Prasad	7	–	34	**2**
R.R. Singh	7	–	38	**–**
Harbhajan Singh	7	–	35	**2**
Kumble	8	–	22	**1**

Fall of Wickets
1–**1**, 2–**30**, 3–**38**, 4–**77**, 5–**90**, 6–**132**, 7–**160**, 8–**164**

India

Batsman	Dismissal	Runs
S.C. Ganguly	**c** de Silva, **b** Perera	**26**
S.R. Tendulkar	**c** and **b** Dharmasena	**17**
N.R. Mongia †	**c** Ranatunga, **b** Perera	**2**
M. Azharuddin *	**c** Ranatunga, **b** Dharmasena	**8**
A.D. Jadeja	run out	**0**
H.H. Kanitkar	**c** Ranatunga, **b** de Silva	**9**
R.R. Singh	**c** sub (D.P.M. Jayawardene), **b** Jayasuriya	**50**
A.B. Agarkar	**b** Jayasuriya	**30**
A. Kumble	**st** Kaluwitharana, **b** Jayasuriya	**4**
Venkatesh Prasad	not out	**1**
Harbhajan Singh	**st** Kaluwitharana, **b** Jayasuriya	**0**
	b **4**, lb **5**, w **6**, nb **1**	**16**
	35.4 overs	**163**

	O	M	R	W
Wickremasinghe	3	–	26	**–**
Perera	6	–	25	**2**
Dharmasena	7	–	29	**2**
Muralitharan	8	–	29	**–**
de Silva	6	–	27	**1**
Jayasuriya	5.4	–	18	**4**

Fall of Wickets
1–**41**, 2–**48**, 3–**57**, 4–**57**, 5–**58**, 6–**75**, 7–**138**, 8–**162**, 9–**163**

Umpires: B.C. Cooray & I. Anandappa *Man of the Match:* P.A. de Silva

Sri Lanka won by 8 runs

Match Eight – India *v.* New Zealand

3 July 1998 at Sinhalese Sports Club, Colombo

New Zealand

Batsman	Dismissal	Runs
B.A. Young	**st** Mongia, **b** Kumble	**26**
N.J. Astle	**c** Kumble, **b** Venkatesh Prasad	**15**
S.P. Fleming *	**c** Tendulkar, **b** Harbhajan Singh	**20**
C.D. McMillan	**c** Ganguly, **b** Kanitkar	**26**
M.J. Horne	**st** Mongia, **b** Harbhajan Singh	**0**
C.L. Cairns	not out	**19**
A.C. Parore †	not out	**9**
C.Z. Harris		
D.J. Nash		
D.L. Vettori		
P.J. Wiseman		
	lb **3**, w **10**	**13**
	31.1 overs (for 5 wickets)	**128**

	O	M	R	W
Agarkar	7	–	39	**–**
Venkatesh Prasad	5	1	23	**1**
Harbhajan Singh	8	–	26	**2**
Kumble	6	1	15	**1**
Kanitkar	5	–	21	**1**
R.R. Singh	0.1	–	1	**–**

Fall of Wickets
1–**28**, 2–**57**, 3–**85**, 4–**89**, 5–**111**

India

S.C. Ganguly
S.R. Tendulkar
M. Azharuddin *
A.D. Jadeja
H.H. Kanitkar
R.R. Singh
N.R. Mongia †
A.B. Agarkar
A. Kumble
Venkatesh Prasad
Harbhajan Singh

Umpires: K.B.C. Cooray & D.N. Pathirana

Match abandoned

Match Nine – Sri Lanka *v.* New Zealand

5 July 1998 at Sinhalese Sports Club, Colombo

Sri Lanka

S.T. Jayasuriya	c Cairns, b Vettori	24
R.S. Kaluwitharana †	c Astle, b Harris	54
P.A. de Silva	c Fleming, b Harris	62
A. Ranatunga *	c Fleming, b McMillan	102
U.D.U. Chandana	not out	27
M.S. Atapattu	not out	6
R.S. Mahanama		
H.D.P.K. Dharmasena		
M.C.L.N. Bandaratilleke		
M. Muralitharan		
S.A. Perera		
	lb 6, w 12	18
	50 overs (for 4 wickets)	293

	O	M	R	W
Cairns	7	–	52	–
Nash	5	–	30	–
Vettori	10	–	53	1
Harris	10	1	44	2
Wiseman	6	–	32	–
McMillan	7	–	38	1
Astle	5	–	38	–

Fall of Wickets
1–69, 2–92, 3–224, 4–282

New Zealand

B.A. Young	c Mahanama, b Perera	3
N.J. Astle	c de Silva, b Chandana	74
S.P. Fleming *	c Dharmasena, b Bandaratilleke	20
C.D. McMillan	c Muralitharan, b Bandaratilleke	5
M.J. Horne	c Kaluwitharana, b Muralitharan	4
C.L. Cairns	c Kaluwitharana, b Jayasuriya	28
A.C. Parore †	not out	28
C.Z. Harris	b Jayasuriya	2
D.J. Nash	c Chandana, b Muralitharan	3
D.L. Vettori	b Jayasuriya	0
P.J. Wiseman	b Dharmasena	16
	lb 10, w 12, nb 1	23
	39.1 overs	206

	O	M	R	W
Perera	4	–	34	1
Bandaratilleke	9	–	35	2
Dharmasena	2	–	24	–
Muralitharan	10	–	49	2
Jayasuriya	8	–	28	3
Chandana	6.1	–	26	2

Fall of Wickets
1–11, 2–78, 3–86, 4–106, 5–152, 6–154, 7–163, 8–172, 9–176

Umpires: P. Manuel & T.M. Samarasinghe *Man of the Match:* A. Ranatunga

Sri Lanka won by 87 runs

Final – Sri Lanka *v.* India

7 July 1998 at R. Premadasa Stadium, Colombo

India

S.C. Ganguly	c and b Muralitharan	109
S.R. Tendulkar	st Kaluwitharana, b Jayasuriya	128
A.D. Jadeja	b Jayasuriya	25
M. Azharuddin *	b Chandana	5
R.R. Singh	run out	15
H.H. Kanitkar	not out	5
A.B. Agarkar	run out	5
N.R. Mongia †		
A. Kumble		
Venkatesh Prasad		
Harbhajan Singh		
	lb 3, w 12	15
	50 overs (for 6 wickets)	307

	O	M	R	W
Wickremasinghe	7	–	43	–
Bandaratilleke	5	–	36	–
Dharmasena	10	–	67	–
Muralitharan	8	–	51	1
Jayasuriya	9	–	42	2
de Silva	6	–	32	–
Chandana	5	–	33	1

Fall of Wickets
1–251, 2–251, 3–261, 4–297, 5–297, 6–307

Sri Lanka

S.T. Jayasuriya	c Ganguly, b Agarkar	32
R.S. Kaluwitharana †	b Agarkar	24
P.A. de Silva	c Harbhajan Singh, b Agarkar	105
M.S. Atapattu	c Venkatesh Prasad, b Harbhajan Singh	39
A. Ranatunga *	c Mongia, b Agarkar	23
R.S. Mahanama	run out	44
U.DU. Chandana	b Kumble	4
H.D.P.K. Dharmasena	lbw, b Venkatesh Prasad	2
G.P. Wickremasinghe	run out	5
M.L.C.N. Bandaratilleke	run out	0
M. Muralitharan	not out	1
	b 1, lb 15, w 4, nb 2	22
	49.3 overs	301

	O	M	R	W
Agarkar	10	–	53	4
Venkatesh Prasad	10	–	56	1
Kumble	9.3	–	57	1
Harbhajan Singh	10	–	57	1
R.R. Singh	5	–	25	–
Kanitkar	4	–	24	–
Tendulkar	1	–	13	–

Fall of Wickets
1–59, 2–73, 3–160, 4–197, 5–272, 6–280, 7–287, 8–294, 9–297

Umpires: K.T. Francis & P. Manuel *Man of the Match:* S.R. Tendulkar

India won by 6 runs

Sara Trophy

Sri Lanka's domestic competition had a new format for the 1997–98 season. Sides were divided into two sections, with the two leading teams in each section meeting in the semi-finals.

Section A

2, 3 and 4 January 1998
at Nondescripts Ground
Nondescripts 217 (S. Warusamana 57, P.K. Serasinghe 5 for 46)
Police Sports 124 for 3 (R.C. Liyanage 51)
Match drawn

at Tyronne Fernando Stadium, Moratuwa
Sebastianites 281 (P. Salgado 78)
Panadura SC 254 (S.N. Liyanage 115, B.P. Perera 61)
Match drawn

at Reid Avenue, Colombo
Colombo Colts CC 203 (S.I. Fernando 93, S. Janaka 54, B. de Silva 6 for 63) and 176 (B. de Silva 6 for 40)
Bloomfield C & AC 165 (D. Hettiarachchi 4 for 44) and 14 for 2
Match drawn

The first round of matches was badly affected by the weather with late starts in all matches. Sham Liyanage of Panadura hit a maiden first-class century, and off-spinner Bathesha de Silva claimed ten wickets in a match for the third time in his career.

9, 10 and 11 January 1998
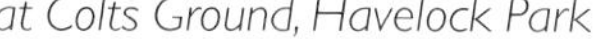
at Colts Ground, Havelock Park
Colombo Colts CC 279 (T.T. Samaraweera 85, M.C. Mendis 54) and 248 for 9 (D.P. Samaraweera 73, P.K. Serasinghe 5 for 62)
Police Sports 221 (S. Gunarathne 90, S. Alexander 5 for 62)
Match drawn

at Maitland Place, Colombo
Bloomfield C & AC 308 (M.N. Nawaz 61, A. Rideegammanagedera 4 for 65) and 86 for 2
Nondescripts 310 (G.R.P. Peiris 84)
Match drawn

Medium-pacer Suchitra Alexander had the second five-wicket haul of his career as Colts took first innings points against Police, while a last wicket stand of 23 gave Nondescripts the edge over Bloomfield in the clash of the giants at Maitland Place.

16, 17 and 18 January 1998
at Colts Ground, Havelock Park
Panadura SC 334 (S. Kumara 132, M. Jayasena 51) and 144 (T.T. Samaraweera 5 for 60, S.I. Fernando 4 for 32)
Colombo Colts CC 326 (S.I. Fernando 91, M.C. Mendis 64, M. Jayasena 7 for 109) and 48 for 1
Match drawn

at Uyanwatta Stadium, Matara
Matara SC 68 (K.S.C. de Silva 5 for 17, D. Samarasinghe 4 for 29) and 192
Nondescripts 274 (P.J. Rajapakse 61, C.D.U.S. Weerasinghe 58, A. Patharana 51)
Nondescripts won by an innings and 14 runs

at Maitland Place, Colombo
Colombo CC (402 for 4 dec.) (P.B. Ediriweera 154, N.S. Bopage 89)
Sebastianites 85 and 299 (N.R.G. Perera 102, M.S. Mendis 84, S.H. Alles 4 for 57)
Colombo CC won by an innings and 18 runs

at Reid Avenue, Colombo
Bloomfield C & AC 367 (R.S. Kalpage 189, R.J. Palliayage 59, T. Gunaratne 51, V.H.K. Ranaweera 8 for 95)
Police Sports 143 and 129 (H.D.P.K. Dharmasena 6 for 40)
Bloomfield C & AC won by an innings and 95 runs

Finer weather allowed for three outright results, all by an innings, in the third round of matches. Sunendra Kumara hit the third century of his career for Panadura against Colts, while Bradmon Ediriweera made the second and higher century of his career as Colombo overwhelmed Sebastianites. Ruwan Kalpage made the highest score of his

A valuable all-round cricketer, Kumata Dharmasena performed well for Sri Lanka in Tests and one-day internationals and scored heavily for Bloomfield in the Sara Trophy.
(Mike Hewitt / Allsport)

career for Bloomfield against Police, for whom medium-pacer Vajira Ranaweera returned the best bowling figures of his career and the best of the season.

23, 24 and 25 January 1998
at Reid Avenue, Colombo
Bloomfield C & AC 273 (R.J. Palliayage 51 not out) and 259 for 5 dec. (S.K. Perera 95, R.J. Palliayage 60 not out)
Sebastianites 182 (A. Cooray 95, P.P. Wickramasinghe 4 for 67) and 78 (R.J. Palliayage 4 for 31)
Bloomfield C & AC won by 272 runs

at Panadura Esplanade
Panadura SC 209 (S.N. Liyanage 55, S.D. Anurasiri 50, M.C. Waidiyarathne 6 for 60) and 97 for 5
Matara SC 112 (S.D. Anurasiri 4 for 11) and 97 for 5
Match drawn

at Police Park
Colombo CC 166 and 205 for 6 (C.P. Hadunettige 67 not out)
Police Sports 229 (S. Gunaratne 86, M.J.H. Rushdy 4 for 45)
Match drawn

at Nondescripts Ground
Nondescripts 298 (R.P. Arnold 149, S. Weerasinghe 63, D. Hettiarachchi 4 for 60, T.T. Samaweera 4 for 75) and 120 for 8 (D. Hettiarachchi 7 for 41)
Colombo Colts CC 374 (D.P. Samaraweera 104, MC. Mendis 66, S. Alexander 54 not out, S.I. Fernando 54, A. Rideegammanagedera 4 for 74)
Match drawn

Bloomfield again proved their all-round strength with a convincing victory over Sebastianites, but Nondescripts were thwarted by Colts. Left-hander Russel Arnold advanced his claims for a place in the party to tour England with a fine century in an opening partnership of 178 with Sanjeeva Weerasinghe, but Dulip Samaraweera and Chaminda Mendis responded with 122 for Colts first wicket. Slow left-arm bowler Dinuka Hettiarachchi had Nondescripts in all sorts of trouble and took 10 or more wickets in a match for the second time.

6, 7 and 8 February 1998
at Colts Ground, Havelock Park
Colombo Colts CC 349 (S. Alexander 72, D.P. Samaraweera 61, J. Kulatunga54, A. Perera 5 for 101) and 258 for 1 dec. (D.P. Samaraweera 140 not out, M.C. Mendis 60)
Sebastianites 264 (A. Perera 67) and 239 for 7 (A. Fernando 71 not out)
Match drawn

at Nondescripts Ground
Nondescripts 234 for 9 dec. (H.P. Tillekeratne 50, I.S. Gallage 4 for 45) and 189 for 4 (S. Warusamana 64, H.P. Tillekeratne 51 not out)
Colombo CC 398 (S.K.L. de Silva 154, D. Arnolda 77, G.R.P. Peiris 4 for 33)
Match drawn

9, 10 and 11 February 1998
at Panadura Esplanade
Panadura SC 217 (S.N. Liyanage 73, B.P. Perera 61, N.S. Rajan 6 for 38)
Colombo CC 262 (C.P. Handunettige 67, C. Perera 4 for 52)
Match drawn

Dulip Samaraweera and Chaminda Mendis scored 158 for Colts' first wicket in the second innings against Sebastianites, but Colts could not force victory. Lanka de Silva responded to losing his Test place with the tenth first-class hundred of his career.

13, 14 and 15 February 1998
at Reid Avenue, Colombo
Bloomfield C & AC 340 (R.S. Mahanama 104, H.D.P.K. Dharmasena 104, I.S. Gallage 5 for 80) and 251 for 6 (S.T. Jayasuriya 110, H.D.P.K. Dharmasena 58)
Colombo CC 263 (P.B. Ediriweera 110, P.P. Wickramasinghe 4 for 55)
Match drawn

Lanka de Silva hit 154 for Colombo against Nondescripts, 7 February, but could not regain his place in the Test side. (Graham Chadwick / Allsport)

at Colts Ground, Havelock Park
Matara CC 153 (D. Hettiarachchi 4 for 47) and 105
Colombo Colts CC 446 (S.I. Fernando 102, M.T. Sampath 78, T.T. Samaraweera 77, J. Kulatunga 76, D.P.M.C. Waidayarathne 5 for 79)
Colombo Colts CC won by an innings and 188 runs

at Panadura Esplanade
Panadura SC 217 (A.K.D.A.S. Kumara 102 not out, K.R. Pushpakumara 4 for 56) and 140 (K.R. Pushpakumara 5 for 40)
Nondescripts 263 (R.P. Arnold 112, S.D. Anurasiri 7 for 73) amd 95 for 2
Nondescripts won by 8 wickets

Test players were available for the sixth round of matches and immediately gave evidence of their class and experience. Mahanama and Dharmasena scored centuries and shared a fourth wicket stand of 111 for Bloomfield against Colombo. Jayasuriya made his mark with a century in 106 minutes in the second innings. Pushpakumara had match figures of nine for 96 for Nondescripts against Panadura, and Russel Arnold hit his second century of the season. Saman Kumara hit an unbeaten 102 off 196 balls, and Don Anurasiri's left-arm spin brought him seven for 73 in Nondescripts' first innings, but Pushpakumara wrecked Panadura's second innings with a hat-trick, all leg before, which left the home side reeling at 16 for four.

20, 21 and 22 February 1998

at Tyronne Fernando Stadium, Moratuwa
Sebastianites 173 and 177 (N.R.G. Perera 76)
Police Sports 233 (W.N.M. Soysa 75, R.C. Liyanage 70, N. Priyaratne 4 for 46) and 118 for 4
Police Sports won by 6 wickets

27, 28 February and 1 March 1998

at Panadura Esplanade
Panadura SC 287 (M. Jayasena 76 not out) and 202 for 6
Police Sports 208 (R.R. Wimalasiri 72 not out, W.N.M. Soysa 57)
Match drawn

at Moors Ground
Sebastianites 268 (M.S. Mendis 160) and 272 for 4 dec. (N.R.G. Perera 79 not out, M.S. Mendis 76, W.D.J. Abeywardene 72)
Matara SC 212 (T.D. Munasinghe 57, S.M. Faumi 57, N.R.G. Perera 4 for 75) and 152 (N.R.G. Perera 7 for 66)
Sebastianites won by 176 runs

A hundred from Shyam Mendis and some excellent all-round cricket from Nimesh Perera brought Sebastianites victory over Matara. Perera took 11 for 141 in the match, the first time he had claimed 10 or more wickets in a game.

6, 7 and 8 March 1998

at Colts Ground, Havelock Park
Colombo CC 352 (S.K.L. de Silva 75, D. Hettiarachchi 5 for 84, K.E.A. Upashantha 5 for 108) and 176 for 2 (N.S. Bopage 108 not out)
Colombo Colts CC 296 (D.P. Samaraweera 66, J. Kulatunga 55)
Match drawn

at Reid Avenue, Colombo
Bloomfield C & AC 517 for 7 dec. (M.T. Gunaratne 108, R.S. Kalpage 100 not out, S.K. Perera 73, R.J. Palliayage 62)
Panadura SC 191 (K.C. Silva 80 not out, P.W. Gunaratne 4 for 45) and 165 (D. Wickramanayake 60, P.W. Gunaratne 4 for 34)
Bloomfield C & AC won by an innings and 161 runs

at Tyronne Fernando Stadium, Moratuwa
Sebastianites 246 (S. Silva 60, N.R.G. Perera 53, A.T. Weerappuli 4 for 75) and 256 (M.S. Mendis 95, S. Silva 75, L.E. Hannibal 4 for 36)
Nondescripts 417 (A. Rideegammanagedera 121, C. Fernando 93, S. Warusamanna 69, C. Liyanage4 for 59) and 89 for 4
Nondescripts won by 6 wickets

Bloomfield consolidated their place at the top of the table with a massive victory over Panadura. Nondescripts were 280 for seven against Sebastianites, but the eighth and ninth wickets realised 135 runs with Fernando scoring 93 at number nine.

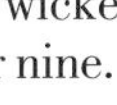

13, 14 and 15 March 1998

at Reid Avenue, Colombo
Matara SC 203 (S.M. Faumi 50) and 233 for 6 (T.D. Munasinghe 71, N.R.C.K. Guruge 59)
Bloomfield C & AC 566 for 7 dec. (P.P. Wickramasinghe 121 not out, M.N. Nawaz 109, P.B. Dassanayake 66, R.J. Palliayage 61, B. de Silva 54 not out, S.K. Perera 53)
Match drawn

20, 21 and 22 March 1998

at Maitland Place, Colombo
Colombo CC 241 (C. Waidayarathne 5 for 87) and 212 (N.S. Bopage 92, P.I.W. Jayasekera 7 for 48)
Matara SC 254 (LS. Suwadarathne 62, M.J.H. Rushby 5 for 74) and 114 (M.J.H. Rushby 5 for 40)
Colombo CC won by 95 runs

27, 28 and 29 March 1998

at Moors Ground
Matara SC 147 (I.D. Gunawardene 5 for 35) and 355 for 6 (S.M. Faumi 127, L.S. Suwadarathne 63 not out)
Police Sports 301 for 8 dec. (R.C. Liyanage 91, R.R. Wimalasiri 66 not out, M.N.C. Silva 54)
Match drawn

Three games involving Matara brought group A to an end. Bloomfield again scored heavily and finished top of the group, while Colombo's second victory helped them into second place.

Group A Final Table

	P	W	L	D	Pts
Bloomfield C & AC	7	3	–	4	104.00
Colombo CC	7	2	–	5	88.50
Colombo Colts CC	7	1	–	6	86.50
Nondescripts	7	3	–	4	86.00
Police Sports	7	1	1	5	58.50
Panadura SC	7	–	2	5	48.50
Sebastianites	7	1	4	2	43.00
Matara SC	7	–	4	3	27.50

Nondescripts, Police Sports, Sebastianites and Panadura SC were engaged in matches in which there was no result on the first innings, and these matches are recorded in the drawn column.

Section B

2, 3 and 4 January 1998

at Sinhalese Sports Club
Tamil Union 262 (U.D.U. Chandana 65, K.J. Silva 5 for 76) and 223 (S.H.S.M.K. Silva 4 for 50)
Sinhalese SC 246 (R.P.A.H. Wickramaratne 101)
Match drawn

at Colts Ground, Havelock Park
Moors SC 174 (S. Madanayake 5 for 19) and 185 (N. de Silva 70)
Burgher RC 154 (U.C. Hathurusinghe 4 for 25) and 199 (C.R. Perera 66, D. Rajapakse 52)
Moors SC won by 6 runs

Hemantha Wickramaratne hit a fine century for Sinhalese Sports Club, but his side failed to gain first innings points against Tamil Union while Moors gained a thrilling victory over Burgher Recreational Club, who, needing 12 to win with four wickets standing, lost those last four wickets for five runs.

9, 10 and 11 January 1998

at Colts Ground, Havelock Park
Singha SC 220 (S. Jayantha 77, W.C. Labrooy 4 for 57) and 172 (D.D. Madurapperuma 5 for 43)
Burgher RC 178 (D.D. Madurapperuma 52, M.M. de Silva 5 for 57) and 83 for 6
Match drawn

Fine all-round cricket from Hathurusinghe allied to intelligent leadership took Moors to the semi-final of the Sara Trophy and earned the 29-year old a place in the party to tour England. (Clive Mason / Allsport)

at Welagedera Stadium
Tamil Union 236 (D.N. Nadarajah 91, V.S.K. Warangoda 59, H.W. Kumara 5 for 48) and 146 for 7 dec. (E.M.I. Galagoda 59)
Kurunegala YCC 112 (M. Villavarayan 5 for 26) and 90 (U.D.U. Chandana 4 for 18, M. Villavarayan 4 for 18)
Tamil Union won by 80 runs

The medium pace bowling of Mario Villavarayan played a major part in Tamil Union's victory over Kurunegala and drew the attention of the selectors to the 28-year old.

16, 17 and 18 January 1998

at Burgher RC Ground
Tamil Union 95 (I. Amarasinghe 4 for 17) and 185 (S.I. de Saram 64, S. Madanayake 4 for 54)
Burgher RC 143 and 139 for 5 (D. Rajapakse 53 not out)
Burgher RC won by 5 wickets

at Moors Ground
Moors SC 315 (U.C. Hathurusinghe 125, S. Sampan 89, R.S. Priyadarshana 51, H.W. Kumara 5 for 104) and 183 for 5 dec. (A.S. Jayasinghe 58, U.C. Hathurusinghe 51 not out)
Kurunegala YCC 58 (U.C. Hathurusinghe 5 for 8) and 228 (M.A.W.R. Madurasinghe 61 not out, R.R. Jaymon 55)
Moors SC won by 212 runs

Some fine all-round cricket from skipper Chandika Hathurusinghe took Moors to their second win of the season. The 29-year old former Test player hit the 11th century of his career and produced some remarkable bowling figures, taking six for 8 in six overs with his medium pace.

23, 24 and 25 January 1998

at Burgher RC Ground
Sinhalese SC 208 (S. Kalawitigoda 77, A.A.W. Gunawardena 54, S. Madanayake 5 for 40) and 230 for 7 dec. (A.A.W. Gunawardena 102)
Burgher RC 207 (C.U. Jayasinghe 53, G.P. Wickremasinghe 4 for 44) and 101 for 4 (C.U. Jayasinghe 58 not out)
Match drawn

at Welagedera Stadium
Kurunegala YCC 248 (R. Kariyawasam 78, A.D.B. Ranjith 6 for 63) and 260 for 9 (R. Jaymon 58, M.A.W.R. Madurasinghe 51, M.M. de Silva 5 for 86)
Singha SC 402 (N.T. Thenuwara 107, A.S. Wewalwala 94, H. Premasiri 52)
Match drawn

Burgher's last pair scored 15, just two runs short of gaining a first innings lead over Sinhalese, while Nalin Thenuwara, 19 years old, hit a maiden century as Singha dominated the game against Kunrunegala Youth.

6, 7 and 8 February 1998

at Moors Ground
Tamil Union 216 (C.P.H. Ramanayake 57, U.C. Hathurusinghe 4 for 67) and 271 for 7 (N. Shiroman 69, U.D.U. Chandana 63)
Moors SC 440 (A.S. Jayasinghe 92, A. Hettiarachchi 64, U.C. Hathurusinghe 60, M. Villavarayan 4 for 90)
Match drawn

at Sinhalese Sports Club
Sinhalese SC 314 (S. Sanjeewa 4 for 78) and 272 for 4 dec. (U.N.K. Fernando 101 not out, R.P.A.H. Wickramaratne 62 not out, A.A.W. Gunawardene 51)
Singha SC 132 (S.H.S.M.K. Silva 4 for 30) and 218 (N.T. Thenuwara 64, A.S. Wewalwala 63)
Sinhalese SC won by 236 runs

at Welegedera Stadium
Antonians SC 350 for 8 dec. (W.A.M.P. Perera 106, P.N. Wanasinghe 79, S.K. Silva 65) and 165
Kurunegala YCC 214 (R. Jaymon 55, N.S. Samarawickrema 5 for 43)
Match drawn

Sinhalese crushed Singha and emerged as favourites to win section B with Moors their most likely challengers. Hathurusinghe continued his outstanding all-round form and made a strong case for inclusion in the party to tour England.

13, 14 and 15 February 1998

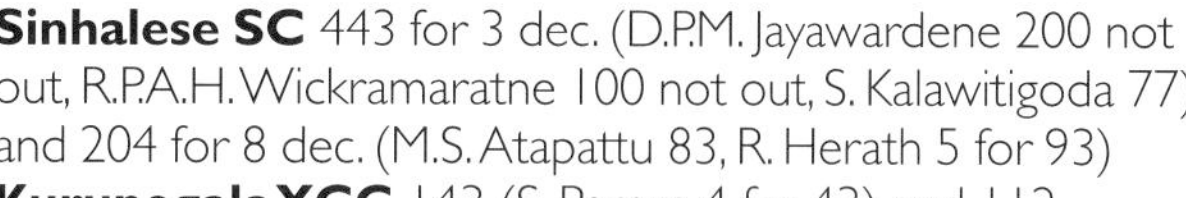

at Sinhalese Sports Club
Sinhalese SC 443 for 3 dec. (D.P.M. Jayawardene 200 not out, R.P.A.H. Wickramaratne 100 not out, S. Kalawitigoda 77) and 204 for 8 dec. (M.S. Atapattu 83, R. Herath 5 for 93)
Kurunegala YCC 143 (S. Perera 4 for 43) and 112 (K.J. Silva 4 for 17, S. Perera 2 for 18)
Sinhalese SC won by 392 runs

at Moors Ground
Singha SC 278 (A.D.N. Ranjith 55, S. Jayantha 53, R.S. Priyadarshana 4 for 70) and 290 for 8 dec. (T.M. Dilshan 124, S. Sanjeewa 57 not out)
Moors SC 216 (K. Jayasinghe 54) and 210 for 5 (A.S. Jayasinghe 127 not out)
Match drawn

at Colts Ground, Havelock Park
Burgher RC 231 (M. Rajapakse 78, S. Madanayake 52 not out, K.G. Perera 4 for 86) and 155 (T. Dhammika 6 for 40)
Antonians SC 173 (M. Fernando 51, S. Madanayake 4 for 52) and 214 for 9
Match drawn

Sinhalese were further strengthened by the availability of their Test players. Jayawardene, who had established himself at international level, hit the first double century of the domestic season and shared an unbroken fourth wicket stand of 274 with Wickramaratne who, with Atapattu, holds the Sri Lanka record for this wicket, 278. With Moors and Singha drawing, Sinhalese looked certain to win the section.

20, 21 and 22 February 1998

at Sinhalese Sports Club
Sinhalese SC 439 for 5 dec. (M.S. Atapattu 200, A. Ranatunga 103, R.P.A.H. Wickramaratne 55) and 251 for 7 dec. (A. Ranatunga 83, S. Ranatunga 52, R.S. Priyadarshana 5 for 88)
Moors SC 215 (S.H.S.M.K. Silva 4 for 57, G.P. Wickremasinghe 4 for 65) and 193 (S.H.S.M.K. Silva 5 for 74)
Sinhalese SC won by 282 runs

at P. Saravanamattu Stadium, Colombo
Antonians SC 236 (Y.N. Tillekeratne 76, M. Muralitharan 4 for 82) and 99 (C.P.H. Ramanayake 5 for 30)
Tamil Union 443 for 8 dec. (N. Shiroman 97, S.I. de Saram 97, V. Wijegunawardene 65, V.S.K. Warangoda 54, M. Fernando 4 for 82)
Tamil Union won by an innings and 108 runs

Marvan Atapattu followed Jayawardene as a double century maker for Sinhalese Sports Club, who, with Arjuna Rana-

tunga hitting a century, confirmed themselves as winners of Section B. Strengthened by the inclusion of off-spinner Muttiah Muralitharan and by the resurgence of former Test bowler Champaka Ramanayake, Tamil Union overwhelmed Antonians.

27, 28 and 29 February 1998
at P. Saravanamattu Stadium, Colombo
Tamil Union 233 (V.S.K. Warangoda 59, N. Shiroman 55, S. Sanjeewa 4 for 94) and 258 (M.M. de Silva 4 for 40)
Singha SC 147 and 178 (H. Premasiri 65, M.L.C.N. Bandaratilleke 5 for 48, M. Villavarayan 4 for 58)
Tamil Union won by 166 runs

Bandaratilleke had match figures of eight for 85 as Tamil Union won a low scoring match.

6, 7 and 8 March 1998
at Moors Ground
Antonians SC 118 and 252 (P.N. Wanasinghe 57, S.K. Silva 57, E.F.M.U. Fernando 56, U.C. Hathurusinghe 7 for 55)
Moors SC 262 (U.C. Hathurusinghe 83, R.S. Priyadarshana 80) and 109 for 3
Moors SC won by 7 wickets

at Welegedera Stadium
Burgher RC 219 (R. Herath 4 for 41) and 254 for 9 dec. (C.R. Perera 71)
Kurunegala YCC 157 (I. Amerasinghe 4 for 46) and 245 (R. Jaymon 63)
Burgher RC won by 71 runs

The astonishing success of Upul Hathurusinghe continued when he captured ten wickets in a match for the second time. He had match figures of 10 for 77 against Antonians and hit 83 and 44. Burgher finished the season in style, gaining their second victory.

12, 13 and 14 March 1998
at St Thomas's Ground
Sinhalese SC 257 (K.G. Perera 5 for 65, K. Dharmasena 4 for 75) and 111 (K.G. Perera 6 for 46)
Antonians 201 (P.N. Wanasinghe 88, H. Jayasuriya 4 for 25) and 86 (S. Perera 4 for 15)
Sinhalese SC won by 81 runs

Slow left-arm bowler Gamini Perera finished the season by taking 10 or more wickets in a match for the third time but still finished on the losing side. The game between Antonians and Singha was abandoned without a ball being bowled.

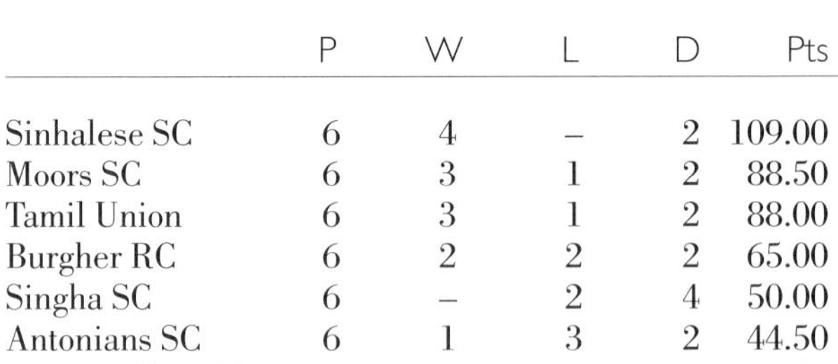

Group B Final Table

	P	W	L	D	Pts
Sinhalese SC	6	4	–	2	109.00
Moors SC	6	3	1	2	88.50
Tamil Union	6	3	1	2	88.00
Burgher RC	6	2	2	2	65.00
Singha SC	6	–	2	4	50.00
Antonians SC	6	1	3	2	44.50
Kurunegala YCC	6	–	4	2	16.50

Semi-Finals

27, 28 and 29 March 1998
at Reid Avenue, Colombo
Sinhalese SC 321 (S. Ranatunga 151, H. Jayasuriya 61, S.H. Alles 5 for 72)
Colombo CC 271 (S.K.L. de Silva 119, G.R.K. Wijekoon 5 for 79)
Match drawn
Sinhalese SC qualified for the final on first innings lead

17, 18 and 19 April 1998
at Reid Avenue, Colombo
Bloomfield C & AC 351 (S.K. Perera 75, M.T. Gunaratne 66, R.S. Kalpage 58) and 262 for 5 (M.N. Nawaz 93, M.T. Gunaratne 66)
Moors SC 298 (U.C. Hathurusinghe 74, P.W. Gunaratne 5 for 53)
Match drawn
Bloomfield C & AC qualified for the final on first innings lead

Final

30 April, 1, 2 and 3 May 1998
at Sinhalese SC, Colombo
Bloomfield C & AC 313 (H.D.P.K. Dharmasena 109) and 295 for 4 (R.S. Kalpage 120 not out, M.N. Nawaz 70, S.K. Perera 53)
Sinhalese SC 582 (A. Ranatunga 192, M.S. Atapattu 179, R.P.A.H. Wickramaratne 60)
Match drawn

Sinhalese SC won Sara Trophy on first innings lead

England

Success in a one-day tournament in Sharjah in October had convinced some that all was for the best in the best of all possible worlds of English cricket. Defeat in the Caribbean restored a sense of reality. The 1998 season began with a variety of contenders forwarding their claims to succeed Atherton as England captain, and with the counties, inevitably, being blamed for the state of English cricket.

The new Grand Stand at Lord's. (Adrian Murrell / Allsport)

Oxford and Cambridge Universities
Benson and Hedges Cup
South African Tour
Emirates Triangular Tournament
Sri Lanka Tour
NatWest Trophy
AXA Life League
The Britannic Assurance County Championship
First-Class Averages
Form Charts

This was unjust to the counties, who had seen the four-day game forced upon them as the panacea for the ills of the Test side and had witnessed only the undermining and erosion of the County Championship – the very competition that had been the life-blood of the game and that had produced our finest cricketers.

Several counties had found the close season a period of turmoil with the now ever increasing 'transfer' market most active. Derbyshire suffered many traumas. Adams and Malcolm departed for pastures new, Cork became captain, and even their first choice overseas player, Saeed Anwar, withdrew and was replaced by Slater, the Australian opener. Adams had several offers and eventually chose to become captain of Sussex, who continued to rebuild and gained Michael Bevan as their overseas player. The Australian left-hander had been a hero with Yorkshire before being supplanted by Darren Lehmann. Northamptonshire had wanted Shane Warne but settled for Paul Reiffel, who was then forced to withdraw because of injury, so that the West Indian pace bowler Rose was imported to partner the other new recruit, Devon Malcolm.

Coach David Gilbert left Surrey and took up a managerial position with Sussex. Surrey also lost Chris Lewis: he continued his eternal wanderings with a second coming to Leicestershire, who surprised their admirers by signing him and releasing Pierson, who joined Somerset. There was some discontent at Warwickshire when Munton was relieved of the captaincy, which was offered as bait to lure Lara back to the fold. The chorus of disapproval subsided as the start of the season neared and Munton still seemed unlikely to be fully fit. Another captain to be replaced was Lancashire's Mike Watkinson, who was succeeded by Wasim Akram, who had been at the centre of controversy in Pakistan.

Nottinghamshire made four signings: Read from Gloucestershire; Wharf from Yorkshire; Gallian from Lancashire; and Paul Strang, the leg-spinner from Zimbabwe who had played for Kent in 1997. Justin Langer joined Middlesex, and Hampshire got the services of McLean, the West Indian pace bowler, having ultimately been rejected by Kasprowicz. Reigning County Champions Glamorgan were content with what they had, although the loss of Morris and of coach Duncan Fletcher would inevitably leave them weaker.

Oxford and Cambridge Universities

14, 15 and 16 April
at Cambridge
Northamptonshire 122 for 3
v. **Cambridge University**
Match drawn

at Oxford
Sussex 182 for 6 (N.R. Taylor 74 not out, K. Newell 52 not out)
v. **Oxford University**
Match drawn

The cricket began with England gripped by cold, rain, snow and floods. Not surprisingly then, there was little play on the first day at Oxford and Cambridge, and none thereafter. New skipper Curran and Montgomerie had added 63 for Northamptosnhire's fourth wicket, and Taylor and Keith Newell had added 133 for Sussex's fifth when play was ended. Sussex had started by losing four wickets, including new captain Adams, for 49.

17, 18 and 19 April
at Cambridge
Leicestershire 24 for 1
v. **Cambridge University**
Match drawn

17, 18 and 20 April
at Oxford
Hampshire 394 for 5 dec. (G.W. White 150, J.S. Laney 101, M. Keech 70)
Oxford University 101 for 8
Match drawn

Cambridge University endured another hardship. Only 15.3 overs were possible in the match against Leicestershire, and after six days cricket no Cambridge batsman had yet been to the crease. No play was possible on the last day at Oxford, where Giles White, who made the highest score of his career, and Jason Laney enlightened the first day for Hampshire with an opening stand of 195. New captain Robin Smith used six bowlers when the University batted. Peter Hartley, the former Yorkshire medium pace bowler, was economic and effective, two for 7 in five overs. Only extras, 26, reached 20 in the Oxford innings.

11, 12 and 13 May
at Oxford
Worcestershire 310 for 3 dec. (D.A. Leatherdale 134 not out, G.A. Hick 124) and 93 for 0 dec. (V.S. Solanki 59 not out)
Oxford University 162 for 8 dec. (B.W. Byrne 69 not out, M.J. Rawnsley 5 for 72) and 126 (M.J. Rawnsley 6 for 44)
Worcestershire won by 115 runs

After a gap of nearly three weeks, Oxford were pleased to return to action, but the honours in The Parks went to Worcestershire. Mather bowled Weston for 0 and then broke his finger fielding, and Solanki was out for two so that Worcestershire were 6 for two. Hick and Leatherdale ended the Oxford jubilation with a partnership worth 210. Hick's century was the 97th of his career. The University declared at the end of the second day to compensate for time lost to rain, but they fell to left-arm spinner Rawnsley, who had career best figures for innings (twice) and match.

13, 14 and 15 May
at Cambridge
Glamorgan 342 for 4 dec. (A.W. Evans 125, A.D. Shaw 71, A. Dale 59) and 220 for 4 dec. (G.P. Butcher 82, P.A. Cottey 71)
Cambridge University 270 for 5 dec. (Q. Hughes 84, J.P. Pyemont 54, W.J. House 50) and 121 (G.P. Butcher 4 for 14)
Glamorgan won by 171 runs

Alun Evans made the highest score of his career as he and Adrian Shaw put on 158 for Glamorgan's first wicket. Cambridge responded well, but they collapsed in their second innings after Cottey had scored some much needed runs and shared a second wicket stand of 104 with Butcher.

16 May
at Cambridge
Cambridge University 257 for 8 (W.J. House 59, G.R. Loveridge 51)
Oxford University 123 (W.J. House 4 for 21)
Cambridge University won by 134 runs

Cambridge won the Johnson Fry Trophy, the Oxford and Cambridge 50-over competition, for the third year in sucession. They were 68 for three before Loveridge and House added 103 in 17 overs, and the last 10 overs of the innings realised 60 runs to give Oxford a demanding run-rate. They quickly succumbed with Will House's gentle medium pace again proving effective. Oxford were bowled out in 37.3 overs. House was named Man of the Match.

18, 19 and 20 May
at Cambridge
Durham 270 for 3 dec. (M.A. Gough 123, S. Hutton 100) and 186 for 1 dec. (J.E. Morris 110 not out)
Cambridge University 119 (S.J.E. Brown 6 for 17) and 242 (W.J. House 65, N.C. Phillips 4 for 58)
Durham won by 95 runs

at Oxford
Warwickshire 307 for 7 dec. (T. Frost 111 not out) and 226 for 1 dec. (D.P. Ostler 133 not out, D.L. Hemp 59 not out)
Oxford University 269 for 9 dec. (J.A.M. Mollins 73, R. Garland 54 not out) and 124 for 4
Match drawn

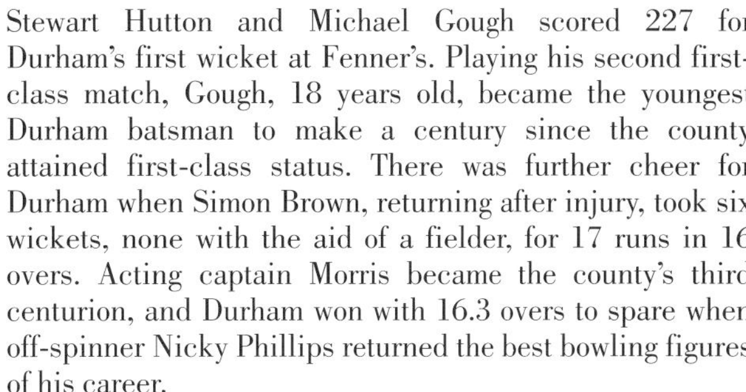

Stewart Hutton and Michael Gough scored 227 for Durham's first wicket at Fenner's. Playing his second first-class match, Gough, 18 years old, became the youngest Durham batsman to make a century since the county attained first-class status. There was further cheer for Durham when Simon Brown, returning after injury, took six wickets, none with the aid of a fielder, for 17 runs in 16 overs. Acting captain Morris became the county's third centurion, and Durham won with 16.3 overs to spare when off-spinner Nicky Phillips returned the best bowling figures of his career.

In The Parks, Warwickshire lost five wickets for 34 runs in 21 overs to slip to 105 for five before Tony Frost, contending with Piper for the job of first team wicket-keeper, hit his maiden first-class century. He played a faultless innings and his unbeaten 111 included a six and 15 fours. The Oxford first innings was enriched by maiden half-centuries from Mollins and Garland. Dominic Ostler, who had begun the season disastrously, reached his first first-class hundred for three years on the final day. He and Hemp added 150 in 36 overs for the second wicket.

29, 30 May and 1 June
at Oxford
Oxford University 260 for 7 dec. (J.A.M. Mollins 51) and 233 for 8 dec. (J.A.G. Fulton 78)
Yorkshire 203 for 4 dec. (C. White 80, M.P. Vaughan 69) and 209 for 7 (M.P. Vaughan 59)
Match drawn

The fixture list for the two universities was a fractured affair, but Oxford returned to the fray with a good performance against a Yorkshire side that rested Gough and Silverwood but had only Lehmann missing from its regular batting line-up. The most encouraging aspect of the game for Oxford was the return to form of skipper Fulton, who dropped down to number eight in the second innings and hit a powerful 78 off 109 balls. He and Barnes added 118 for the eighth wicket. Fulton set Yorkshire a target of 291 in over three hours, and, after early losses, the county side were happy to settle for a draw.

10, 11 and 12 June
at Cambridge
Cambridge University
v. **Derbyshire**
Match abandoned

13, 15 and 16 June
at Oxford
Middlesex 255 for 1 dec. (R.A. Kettleborough 92 not out, O.A. Shah 79 not out, M.W. Gatting 62)
Oxford University 100 for 6 (C.J. Batt 4 for 31)
Match drawn

The Universities' unhappy season continued unabated. Cambridge suffered the greatest of misfortunes. They had lost their leading batsman Edward Smith through injury. He was unlikely to be fit before August, by which time the university season would have finished. They had been frustrated by rain in their efforts to get to the crease, and their match against Derbyshire was abandoned without a ball being bowled.

Oxford fared little better. The pitch in The Parks was vandalised, and a new strip was prepared, but the bowlers' run ups were too damp to allow any play before the scheduled final day. There was a bright side to the game – for Middlesex. Chris Batt took a wicket with his first ball in first-class cricket for them and finished with four for 31 from nine overs. He was to fare well in the Championship in the following weeks.

27, 28 and 29 June
at Canterbury
Kent 291 for 8 dec. (S.C. Willis 58) and 57 for 2 dec.
Oxford University 108 for 4 dec. and 241 for 7 (M.A. Wagh 126, M.M. Patel 4 for 81)
Oxford University won by 3 wickets

Michael Gough, the youngest Durham batsman to score a century since the county attained first-class status.
(David Munden / Sportsline)

at Leeds
Cambridge University 366 (Imran Mohammad 136, W.J. House 51) and 0 for 0 dec.
Yorkshire 94 for 1 dec. (A. McGrath 51 not out) and 131 for 6 (G.R. Loveridge 4 for 47)
Match drawn

In their final matches before their meeting at Lord's, both universities acquitted themselves most favourably. In spite of losing two hours to rain on the last day, Oxford beat Kent off the last ball of the match. Mark Wagh scored a fine hundred to make the victory possible. He hit 17 fours and a six, and he reached three figures off 128 balls. Even so, 20 runs were needed from the last two overs. Garland hit Patel for six, and Pirihi hit the first ball of the last over, bowled by Thompson, for four. A leg-bye off the last ball won the game. Fleming's declaration had left the students 50 overs in which to score 241.

With a little more adventure, Cambridge might well have beaten Yorkshire, who, having been set a target of 273 in two-and-a-quarter hours plus 20 overs, declined to 73 for five against the leg-spin of New Zealand Test player Greg Loveridge. Earlier there had been encouragement when Imran Mohammad hit a century after a blank first day.

Varsity Match

1, 2 and 3 July
at Lord's
Cambridge University 294 for 9 dec. (A. Singh 117, D.P. Mather 4 for 65) and 176 (D.P. Mather 6 for 74)
Oxford University 180 for 3 dec. (M.A. Wagh 78 not out, J.A.M. Mollins 51) and 199 (G.R. Loveridge 5 for 59)
Cambridge University won by 91 runs

The positive attitude of both captains helped bring a result to the 152nd Varsity match and made it one of the most entertaining encounters of recent years. Jim Fulton won the toss and asked Cambridge to bat. Anurag Singh batted with great flair to make 117, while Oxford bowled and fielded well. Singh declared with half an hour of the first day remaining and opened his attack with leg-spinner Loveridge, but Oxford closed on 29 for 0. Mid-afternoon on the second day, Fulton declared 114 runs in arrears. It seemed that an agreement had been reached that Singh would set a target close to 300 on the last day. Cambridge plundered runs eagerly, but Mather returned career-best bowling figures and captured 10 wickets in a match for the first time so that the Oxford target came down to 291. They began slowly, but, inevitably, Wagh lifted the tempo. He was caught off Janisch, who bowled most economically, and the remaining batsmen fought a losing battle against Loveridge. The last wicket fell with nine overs of extra time unused. Credit is due to both sides for a fine game played in an excellent spirit.

Benson and Hedges Cup

28 April
at Derby
Durham 186 for 6
Derbyshire 179 for 6
Durham (2 pts) won by 6 runs
(Gold Award: P.D. Collingwood)

at Southampton
Surrey 267 for 8 (M.A. Butcher 67, A.D. Mascarenhas 4 for 28)
Hampshire 219 (M.P. Bicknell 4 for 38)
Surrey (2 pts) won by 48 runs
(Gold Award: MA. Butcher)

at Taunton
Match abandoned
Somerset 1 pt, Kent 1 pt

at Leeds
Worcestershire 128 (G.M. Hamilton 4 for 33)
Yorkshire 119 for 5
Yorkshire (2 pts) won on faster scoring rate
(Gold Award: G.M. Hamilton)

The 27th and last Benson and Hedges Cup began in weather that seemed to be in mourning for the demise of this popular competition. A delayed start at Derby meant that each innings was reduced to 36 overs. Boon won the toss and decided to bat, but run-getting was not easy. Jon Lewis made 47, but, at 140 for five, the visitors looked well short of a winning score. Paul Collingwood then clouted 30 off 18 balls and raised his side's hopes. There was more encouragement for Durham when Betts and Wood bowled economical spells, but Derbyshire reached 141 for five with Clarke going well. Much depended on him and DeFreitas, but, having hit 48 off 46 balls, Clarke was run out, and the task of scoring 23 from the last two overs proved to be beyond the capabilities of DeFreitas and Blackwell.

The match at Southampton was uninterrupted by rain, and the holders Surrey, put in to bat, began well with Brown and Stewart making 69 from 12 overs for the first wicket. There was a faltering when three wickets fell for 17 runs, but Mark Butcher, who had enjoyed a good start to the season, played with good sense to restore order. Hampshire were well served in attack by Hartley and Mascarenhas, whose inswing bowling brought him four wickets. However, McLean, newly arrived from the Caribbean and adjudged the fastest of the West Indian pace attack, and Renshaw both conceded more than six runs an over. Surrey's 267 always looked a winning score, and so it proved. Martin Bicknell removed the top order, and Ian Salisbury again bowled his leg-breaks to good effect. Smith and White scored 78 for the third wicket, but once they were separated the outcome was inevitable.

There was no play at Taunton, nor in the Parks where British Universities and Northamptonshire should have played a warm-up match, and at Headingley the Duckworth-Lewis method had to be employed. The contest was first reduced to 39 overs, and then to 35. Yorkshire won with 15 balls to spare. Their hero was Gavin Hamilton, who had played for his native Scotland in the competition but who was making his first appearance for Yorkshire in the Benson and Hedges Cup. His seam bowling brought him four wickets for six runs in 10 balls and broke the back of the Worcestershire innings.

29 April
at Cardiff
Glamorgan 254 for 5 (R.D.B. Croft 77, S.P. James 71, M.P. Maynard 55)
v. **Essex**
Match abandoned
Glamorgan 1 pt, Essex 1 pt

at Old Trafford
Warwickshire 234 for 8 (D.L. Hemp 55)
Lancashire 185 (J.P. Crawley 54)
Warwickshire (2 pts) won by 49 runs
(Gold Award: A.F. Giles)

Keith Brown scored prolifically for Middlesex in the early stages of the Benson and Hedges Cup. He hit centuries against both Sussex and Glamorgan.
(Nigel French / ASP)

at Lord's
Middlesex 283 for 5 (K.R. Brown 114, P.N. Weekes 66 not out)
Sussex 277 (K. Newell 62 not out, C.J. Adams 54)
Middlesex (2 pts) won by 6 runs
(Gold Award: K.R. Brown)

at Luton (Wandown Park)
Minor Counties 103 (F.A. Rose 5 for 14)
Northamptonshire 104 for 5
Northamptonshire (2 pts) won by 5 wickets
(Gold Award: F.A. Rose)

Essex were more than fortunate to escape with a point at Cardiff, where James and Croft hit 116 in 20 overs for the first wicket. Croft's 77 came off 64 balls, and Glamorgan looked set for a winning score when rain brought an end to the match with 22 balls of their innings remaining. The Essex spinners bowled tidily, but the seam attack looked well below par. Waqar Younis was back in the Glamorgan side after duty with Pakistan.

Wasim Akram had returned to lead Lancashire, but the greatest impact on the match at Old Trafford was made by Ashley Giles, who was returning to the Warwickshire side after injury. The visitors did not bat with conviction. Hemp did his best to hold the innings together, but the middle order wilted, and it was Giles, 37 off 38 balls, who lifted Warwickshire to a total that at least presented a challenge. That challenge seemed slight when Lancashire, aided by missed chances, reached 108 for one. Lara juggled with his bowlers. Giddins bowled Watkinson, who had looked in good form, and Small was brought back and immediately accounted for Flintoff and Lloyd. Crawley had raced to 54, but he was leg before to Smith, and Giles took three for 22 in 7.1 overs to leave Lancashire dazed and beaten.

The early loss of Langer did not upset Middlesex at Lord's. Keith Brown batted throughout the 50 overs, being last out to the last ball after hitting 114 from 145 balls. His innings included a six and nine fours. Adams has brought positivity to Sussex cricket, and he began with 54 off 49 balls. Sussex went from 74 for 0 to 79 for three before Bevan and Carpenter added 66 in 14 overs. They were both dismissed by Ramprakash, and it was left to Keith Newell to carry the hopes of Sussex. He was given able support by the tail, but 10 runs an over for the last 10 overs was a very difficult task. He hit the third ball of the final over for six, but he then lost the strike, and Weekes bowled Lewry and Robinson with the last two balls to give Middlesex victory by six runs. Keith Newell was unbeaten for 62, which came off 61 balls and included two sixes and five fours.

Franklyn Rose enjoyed bowling on an encouraging pitch at Luton, and his figures of five for 14 in 9.1 overs were Northamptonshire's best in the competition. Top scorer for the Minor Counties was former Nottinghamshire bowler Pennett, who made 26 not out batting at number 10. Paul Newman, once of Derbyshire, gave the first-class county problems, and they slipped to 39 for four before Curran and Penberthy steadied the innings.

30 April

at Taunton
British Universities 127 for 6
Somerset 130 for 8 (M. Burns 55)
British Universities (2 pts) won by 2 wickets
(Gold award: M. Burns)

at The Oval
Gloucestershire 266 for 7 (R.C. Russell 83, R.J. Cunliffe 58)
Surrey 270 for 3 (G.P. Thorpe 85, A.D. Brown 74)
Surrey (2 pts) won by 7 wickets
(Gold Award: A.D. Brown)

British Universities were narrowly beaten at Taunton in a match reduced to 20 overs. Mark Chilton's unbeaten 46 held their innings together, and a score of 127 was commendable. Somerset lost Ecclestone run out without a run scored, but Burns and Rose took the score to 98 by the 11th over. The batting then threatened to fall apart against some excellent spin bowling from Loveridge, the New Zealand Test player now up at Cambridge, and Davies of Loughborough and Northamptonshire. Seven wickets fell for 21 runs, and it took the experience of Pierson and Reeve to win the game with an over to spare.

Totally dominant in every phase of the Benson and Hedges Cup save the final – Darren Maddy of Leicestershire.
(Chris Georg / ASP)

Surrey's determination to hold on to the trophy was evident as they gained their second victory in three days. Put in to bat, Gloucestershire were well served by Cunliffe and Russell, who put on 96 for the second wicket. Cunliffe's 58 came off 59 balls, and Russell began to push the score along after a cautious start. The real impetus to the innings came from Dawson, who hit 29 off 17 balls, but Gloucestershire's 266 was never more than a reasonable score. It was put in to perspective when Alistair Brown thumped 74 off 68 deliveries. His opening stand of 88 with Stewart came at a rate close to eight an over. Thorpe maintained his impressive start to the English season with a fluent 85, Butcher continued Surrey's dominance and victory came with 15 balls to spare.

1 May
at Oxford
British Universities 209 for 8
Hampshire 212 for 7 (M. Keech 74, A.D. Mascarenhas 52 not out)
Hampshire (2 pts) won by 3 wickets
(Gold Award: R.S.C. Martin-Jenkins)

at Dublin (Castle Avenue)
Glamorgan 230 for 9 (R.D.B. Croft 67, P.A. Cottey 54)
Ireland 115
Glamorgan (2 pts) won by 115 runs
(Gold Award: R.D.B. Croft)

at Leicester
Leicestershire 283 for 2 (D.L. Maddy 136 not out, B.F. Smith 90)
Lancashire 287 for 8 (J.P. Crawley 88, N.H. Fairbrother 68)
Lancashire (2 pts) won by 2 wickets
(Gold Award: D.L. Maddy)

at Trent Bridge
Minor Counties 161 for 7
Nottinghamshire 162 for 1 (J.E.R. Gallian 74 not out, U. Afzaal 54 not out)
Nottinghamshire (2 pts) won by 9 wickets
(Gold Award: J.E.R. Gallian)

at Edgbaston
Warwickshire 260 for 9 (B.C. Lara 101, D.R. Brown 52)
Northamptonshire 189
Warwickshire (2 pts) won by 71 runs
(Gold Award: B.C. Lara)

at Worcester
Derbyshire 229 for 7 (A.S. Rollins 70 not out, P.A.J. DeFreitas 51 not out)
Worcestershire 231 for 9 (G.A. Hick 57)
Worcestershire (2 pts) won by 1 wicket
(Gold Award: S.J. Rhodes)

Darren Robinson, the Essex opening batsman, began the season in fine style with two centuries in the early rounds of the Benson and Hedges Cup, but injury and loss of form followed.
(Nigel French / ASP)

The British Universities gave Hampshire the hardest of struggles at Oxford. Put in to bat, the students were 96 for five when Martin-Jenkins came in and lost their sixth wicket at 100. Batting with the maturity he had shown in helping Sussex to victory in their opening championship match of the season, Martin-Jenkins made 39 off 53 balls before being run out. He and Leather added 48 for the eighth wicket to take the Universities to a respectable score. Leather batted admirably to finish unbeaten on 42. Martin-Jenkins then dismissed both openers, and Leather sent back White to leave Hampshire bewildered at 31 for three. They had more worries when skipper Smith was run out, but Keech hit 74 off 91 balls, and Mascarenhas provided the necessary flourish with an unbeaten 52 off 48 balls to win the game with seven balls remaining.

In spite of their innings creaking badly in the middle, Glamorgan had little difficulty in beating Ireland. Croft again enjoyed his role as pinch hitter and began with a flurry of boundaries. Cottey and Waqar Younis put on a very necessary 48 for the eighth wicket, and Waqar was quickly instrumental in reducing Ireland to 32 for four.

One of the most gripping encounters was at Leicester, where Lancashire won with three balls to spare. Leicestershire were again without skipper Whitaker, who was injured, and were led by Lewis. He lost the toss, but his side thrived because of an outstanding innings from Darren

Maddy. The opener batted throughout the 50 overs and scored 136 off 154 balls to emphasise his claim for a place in the England squad. He and Ben Smith put on 206 in 37 overs for the second wicket. Facing a target of 284, Lancashire soon lost Atherton, caught behind off Mullally, and the aggressive Flintoff was out at 47. Crawley and Fairbrother added 156 in 25 overs before the latter became Mullally's second victim, and Crawley and Wasim Akram fell to Lewis within the space of three balls. Dakin, too, struck with three wickets in two overs, but Hegg took charge and blasted Lancashire to victory, although the bowlers were now hampered by a wet ball and the fielders by gathering darkness.

Once more it was the late order batsmen who lifted Minor Counties. Newman and Pennett shared an unbroken eighth wicket stand of 66, but they caused only a temporary delay to Nottinghamshire, who won with 15.5 overs to spare.

Brian Lara scored his first limited-over hundred for Warwickshire, his 101 coming off 89 balls and including a six and nine fours. He and Dougie Brown shared a fifth wickets stand of 93, and with Giddins and Smith, in particular, bowling well, Northamptonshire were overwhelmed. Giddins is showing commitment, pace and discipline in his new life at Warwickshire. In the minds of the public, he still has something to expiate, but, at 26, he has the ability to become an England bowler.

The most exciting finish was at Worcester. Derbyshire were in considerable trouble at 134 for seven and were lifted when Rollins and DeFreitas hit 95 off the last 12 overs of the innings. To this stand, DeFreitas contributed 51. He then removed both Worcestershire openers with just 15 scored. Hick and Moody added 60, and Hick and Haynes put on 69. Three wickets fell for six runs to throw the home county into confusion. Lampitt and Rhodes provided a steadying influence, but when the final over arrived nine runs were needed with three wickets standing. Aldred had Illingworth leg before with the first ball and Newport was run out on the fifth after six runs had been added. Sheriyar drove the last ball square to the boundary to give his side victory.

2 May

at Canterbury
Gloucestershire 195 for 9 (T.H.C. Hancock 56)
Kent 196 for 7 (M.J. Walker 57)
Kent (2 pts) won by 3 wickets
(Gold Award: M.A. Ealham)

at Trent Bridge
Nottinghamshire 196 for 8 (U. Afzaal 78, P.R. Pollard 50)
Leicestershire 198 for 2 (I.J. Sutcliffe 105 not out)
Leicestershire (2 pts) won by 8 wickets
(Gold Award: I.J. Sutcliffe)

at Linlithgow
Scotland 168 for 7
Yorkshire 172 for 7
Yorkshire (2 pts) won by 3 wickets
(Gold Award: Asim Butt)

at Hove
Sussex 281 for 3 (K. Greenfield 93 not out, M.G. Bevan 87)
Essex 285 for 3 (D.D.J. Robinson 137 not out, N. Hussain 62)
Essex (2 pts) won by 7 wickets
(Gold Award: D.D.J. Robinson)

The match at Canterbury began late and was reduced to 43 overs. Put in to bat, Gloucestershire got off to a flying start. They were 81 in 15 overs before a wicket fell, but they squandered this advantage by losing four wickets in five overs for 17 runs. It was the combination of Fleming and Ealham, supported by Hooper's slip catching, that balanced the match in favour of Kent. In spite of the early loss of Ward, the home side looked to be moving comfortably to their target with Walker batting sensibly. Then runs dried up as Walsh bowled a demanding spell, and when Fleming joined Ealham 33 were needed at a run a ball. They added 20, and Ealham drove Alleyne for six so that 13 from the last three overs should have presented few problems. As it was, the game went to the final ball of the 43 overs. Phillips pushed to point and scampered through for the winning single.

At Trent Bridge, Nottinghamshire, asked to bat first, were given foundation by Pollard and Afzaal, who scored 104 for the first wicket. The liability was that the stand occupied 30 overs. Pollard was stumped by the admirable Nixon, and Johnson, in demonstrating that the run-rate must be lifted, was run out. Eight wickets fell for 90 runs. Leicestershire lost Maddy and Smith for 55, but left-hander Iain Sutcliffe, the former Oxford Blue, batted delightfully for his first century in the competition. He faced 147 balls, and he and Simmons took Leicestershire to victory with 29 balls to spare.

A decisive blow for Essex in the match against Sussex at Hove, 2 May. Michael Bevan is bowled by Paul Grayson for 87. Robert Rollins is the wicket-keeper.
(Craig Prentis / Allsport)

On a sluggish pitch, Scotland did quite well to reach 168, and their achievement looked even more impressive when they reduced Yorkshire to 79 for five. The bowler mainly responsible for this situation was Asim Butt, a left-arm medium-pacer who had qualified for Scotland by four years residency. He trapped McGrath leg before for 0 and then had Lehmann caught at the wicket and White lbw in the space of three balls. The match was turned by Blakey and Gough, who came together at 111 for six and added 49. Gough fell to Thomson, but Blakey, 43 not out, completed the job as Yorkshire won with 19 balls to spare.

Essex followed the conventional pattern by asking Sussex to bat when they won the toss. Hussain was leading the side in the absence of the injured Prichard, but it was his opposite number, Adams, who was capturing headlines with his dynamic approach as Sussex's new captain. On this occasion, he was not quite his usual electric self with the bat, but he and Edwards put on 70 for the first wicket only to fall within nine runs of each other. It was Bevan, 87 off 71 balls, and Greenfield who took the battle to Essex, adding 160 in 23 overs. Bevan was bowled by Grayson in the 45th over, but Greenfield, a most underrated cricketer, continued to hit the ball firmly and struck the only six of the innings. A target of 282 looked far from easy, especially when Stuart Law was caught at slip for 0, but Robinson and Hussain settled into a fluent partnership worth 154. Hussain hit 62 off 69 balls before falling to the generally wayward Jarvis, but Irani maintained the brisk scoring rate, hitting 41 before he, too, fell to Jarvis. Darren Robinson remained. Six days earlier, with Sussex again the opponents, he had hit a Sunday league century, his first in one-day cricket; now he completed a second and higher score, 137 off 168 balls, a beautifully judged innings that took his side to victory with seven balls to spare.

Asim Butt won the Gold Award for a splendid bowling performance for Scotland against Yorkshire, at Linlithgow, 2 May.
(Mark Thompson/Allsport)

4 May

at Derby
Yorkshire 271 for 7 (D.S. Lehmann 102 not out, A. McGrath 55)
Derbyshire 235 for 9 (K.J. Barnett 56, C. White 4 for 29)
Yorkshire (2 pts) won by 36 runs
(Gold Award: D.S. Lehmann)

at Chelmsford
Essex 359 for 6 (D.D.J. Robinson 114, N. Hussain 71, R.C. Irani 69)
Ireland 188 for 7 (N.C. Johnson 53)
Essex (2 pts) won by 171 runs
(Gold Award: D.D.J. Robinson)

at Bristol
Gloucestershire 234 for 7
Somerset 208
Gloucestershire (2 pts) won by 26 runs
(Gold Award: J. Lewis)

at Leicester
Warwickshire 263 for 6 (D.R. Brown 60, T.L. Penney 57 not out)
Leicestershire 269 for 7 (P.V. Simmons 89, I.J. Sutcliffe 50)
Leicestershire (2 pts) won by 3 wickets
(Gold Award: P.V. Simmons)

at Northampton
Nottinghamshire 272 for 7 (G.F. Archer 70, P. Johnson 69)
Northamptonshire 237 (K.M. Curran 71, P.A. Strang 4 for 49)
Nottinghamshire (2 pts) won by 35 runs
(Gold Award: G.F. Archer)

at The Oval
Surrey 263 (G.P. Thorpe 58, A.J. Hollioake 55, M.J. Chilton 4 for 28)
British Universities 158
Surrey (2 pts) won by 105 runs
(Gold Award: M.J. Chilton)

at Worcester
Scotland 140 (T.M. Moody 4 for 24)
Worcestershire 141 for 4 (G.A. Hick 61 not out, T.M. Moody 51)

Worcestershire (2 pts) won by 6 wickets
(Gold Award: T.M. Moody)

Yorkshire's success continued. Darren Lehmann reached his 92-ball century with a six and took the county to a score that would always challenge Derbyshire, whose position did not improve when they slipped to 58 for four. Following his successful season in Australia and his recall to the national side, Lehmann appears to be fulfilling the promise he showed as a youth. His development was cruelly halted by injury, but the confidence, the technical assurance and the positive approach are returning. Encouraging for both Yorkshire and England was again the form of Chris Silverwood. The pace bowler showed hostility and control to dismiss both Cork and Rollins for single figures and so undermine the Derbyshire innings.

Another young man to restate his credentials was the Essex opener Darren Robinson, who hit his third century in limited-over cricket in the space of eight days. His ability had not been doubted, but he has now shown the confidence he previously lacked. He hit a six and 13 fours against Ireland and faced 129 balls for his 114. Stuart Law, Hussain and Irani all plundered runs in a one-sided affair.

Having lost Hancock at 16, Gloucestershire offered gritty determination rather than flourish and excitement against Somerset. They were lifted when Wright and Dawson added 62 in 14 overs for the fourth wicket. Alleyne batted fluently towards the end, but the real impetus came from Lewis, who hit 33 off 13 balls. Somerset had lost the plot with their bowlers, and, although Gloucestershire had been reduced to 183 for six in 46 overs, their main strike force had all exhausted their quotas, and they had to turn to makeshift bowlers with the result that the last four overs produced 51 runs and changed the balance of the game. Gloucestershire's seamers bowled well, and Somerset slipped to 110 for seven in the 34th over. Reeve and Trescothick added 61, but Lewis bowled Reeve, and the end came soon after.

Leicestershire conceded a record 53 extras, 34 of them wides, against Warwickshire, but still managed to win with three balls to spare. Penney and Brown put on 116 for Warwickshire's fifth wicket, but the outstanding batting of the match came from Phil Simmons, who hit 89 off 75 balls with four sixes and five fours. He was out in the 48th over, but Nixon took command and finished the match by hitting Neil Smith for six.

As ever, Paul Johnson led Nottinghamshire from the front. He hit 69 off 83 balls after his side had suffered early setbacks, and he and Archer put on 72 in 12 overs for the fifth wicket. Archer was out in the last over, having hit 70 off 71 balls. He then pulled off a spectacular catch to dismiss Capel, and Northamptonshire were never really in contention.

British Universities bowled and fielded creditably to dismiss Surrey in 49.1 overs. Their hero was the Lancashire medium-pacer Mark Chilton, whose four for 28 in 10 overs rightly earned him the Gold Award. Loveridge batted with energy, but nobody played the decisive innings that might have embarrassed Surrey.

The same could be said of Scotland at Worcester. They crumbled before the medium pace of Tom Moody, who then combined with Graeme Hick to add 81 after openers Weston and Solanki had fallen for two.

---

5 May
at Lord's
Ireland 196 for 7 (A.R. Dunlop 59 not out)
Middlesex 199 for 4 (M.R. Ramprakash 55 not out)
Middlesex (2 pts) won by 6 wickets
(Gold Award: A.R. Dunlop)

at Lakenham
Minor Counties 52 (G. Chapple 5 for 7)
Lancashire 53 for 3
Lancashire (2 pts) won by 7 wickets
(Gold Award: G. Chapple)

at Taunton
Hampshire 169 for 9
Somerset 170 for 5
Somerset (2 pts) won by 5 wickets
(Gold Award: G.D. Rose)

at Hove
Sussex 302 for 9 (M.G. Bevan 95 not out, C.J. Adams 81, Waqar Younis 4 for 43)
Glamorgan 299 (P.A. Cottey 96, R.D.B. Croft 59, M.A. Robinson 4 for 53)
Sussex (2 pts) won by 3 runs
(Gold Award: M.G. Bevan)

Middlesex prevented a repeat of the 1997 surprise when they beat Ireland with two overs and six wickets to spare. An interesting selection for the Middlesex side was Alistair Fraser, the younger brother of the England bowler. He left Middlesex in 1989 and spent three years with Essex, but is to be used by his original county on a match to match basis when required. He took two wickets. The Gold Award went to Ireland's Angus Dunlop, who hit 59 off 66 balls.

Rain reduced the match at Lakenham to 43 overs, but Minor Counties lasted only 26.5 overs as Glen Chapple took five for 7 in five overs. Lancashire laboured somewhat in return, but this was a miserable display by the Minor Counties side.

Hampshire never truly recovered from an opening burst, headed by Rose, which left them on 39 for three. The only positivity in their innings came from James, Hartley and McLean who lifted them from 95 for eight to 169. Burns was out for 0, but Somerset had few problems thereafter and reached their target with 6.3 overs to spare.

The excitement came at Hove where Sussex won a rare limited-over victory, which came too late to win them a place in the later stages of the competition. Chris Adams was once more in belligerent mood, and his second wicket partnership of 118 with Wasim Khan took just 21 overs. His 81 came off 82 balls, and when he became one of Waqar's four victims Bevan took over. Waqar continued to bowl with venom and economy, but Bevan and Lewry added 50 in four overs towards the close of the innings. Waqar also shone with the bat, hitting 45 in an eighth wicket stand of 81 with Cottey which brought Glamorgan close to victory. Acting captain Cottey appeared to be winning the game, but he and Watkin were out to successive balls in the final over. It was some consolation for the bowler Edwards, who had been severely punished. Cottey was run out, but Edwards bowled Watkin and ended with figures of one for 77 in 7.3 overs.

6 May

at Riverside
Scotland 210 for 5 (D.R. Lockhart 75, B.G. Lockie 54)
Durham 213 for 8 (M.P. Speight 55)
Durham (2 pts) won by 2 wickets
(Gold Award: D.R. Lockhart)

at Bristol
British Universities 279 for 5 (W.J. House 64, A. Singh 56, M.J. Chilton 54)
Gloucestershire 272 for 9 (R.C. Russell 119 not out, A.J. Wright 93, W.J. House 5 for 58)
British Universities (2 pts) won by 7 runs
(Gold Award: W.J. House)

at Canterbury
Kent 260 for 9 (C.L. Hooper 69, M.A. Ealham 56, T.R. Ward 51)
Surrey 261 for 6 (G.P. Thorpe 85 not out)
Surrey (2 pts) won by 4 wickets
(Gold Award: G.P. Thorpe)

at Lakenham
Minor Counties 111 (D.L. Hemp 4 for 32)
Warwickshire 112 for 4
Warwickshire (2 pts) won by 6 wickets
(Gold Award: D.L. Hemp)

at Northampton
Northamptonshire 196 for 9 (A.L. Penberthy 62)
Leicestershire 199 for 2 (D.L. Maddy 89, I.J. Sutcliffe 56)
Leicestershire (2 pts) won by 8 wickets
(Gold Award: D.L. Maddy)

Scotland followed a familiar pattern – win the Gold Award, lose the match – but they pressed Durham hard at Chester-le-Street. Lockhart and Lockie put on 109 for Scotland's second wicket, and Lockhart batted splendidly to make 75 off 119 balls. He was out in the penultimate over of the innings after he and Parsons had added 60 in eight overs. Scotland's innings was boosted by 49 extras, 19 of them wides, and Durham profited in the same manner when they began to bat. Even so, they slipped to 120 for five, and it needed a sixth wicket stand of 83 in 11 overs between Speight and Foster to put them back on course.

British Universities won an outstanding victory at Bristol. They had given both Hampshire and Somerset difficult matches, bowled out Surrey and now they overcame Gloucestershire in a tense climax. Asked to bat first when losing the toss, Anurag Singh gave his side a firm foundation, adding 96 for the second wicket with Mark Chilton. The momentum of the innings increased with the arrival of Will House of Kent and Cambridge. He hit two sixes and seven fours in his 64, which came off 44 balls. The last 10 overs of the innings produced 86 runs, and 54 of these came from the final five overs. Ball and Lewis were treated ruthlessly, but the Gloucestershire fielding was dreadful. The undergraduates were as adept with the ball as they had been with the bat. Martin-Jenkins again impressed with the new ball, taking two wickets as the county side slipped to 29 for three. Russell and Wright then added 207, and, with six overs remaining and seven wickets standing, Gloucestershire were just 44 runs short of victory. House added bowling laurels to what he had achieved with the bat. He had Wright caught, and Lewis, having hit his first ball for four, was well caught by Pyemont off the second. Dawson and Windows followed in quick succession, and although Russell nudged and ran, the asking rate increased over by the over. Martin-Jenkins was relentlessly accurate and had Ball caught in the deep so that Walsh joined Russell with 16 needed. It proved too great a task, and Walsh was caught on the boundary off the last ball of the innings. Russell was unbeaten on 119, which had come off 137 balls and included eight fours, but the honours went to House, who took five wickets in the final seven overs of the innings.

Surrey moved relentlessly into the quarter-finals with their fourth win in as many matches. They asked Kent to bat first, and the home county always promised more than they achieved. Walker was run out early, and Ward and Hooper added 78 for the second wicket. Hooper and Ealham put on 91 for the fourth, but the innings was a stop/start affair and had no real impetus until Marsh hit two sixes in the final over, bowled by Saqlain, which realised 24 runs. This was soon put into perspective when Brown and Stewart began Surrey's innings with 93 in 12 overs. Stewart and Adam Hollioake were both out to debatable decisions, but Thorpe remained unflustered, and Surrey won with three overs to spare.

Fielding and Sharp put on 41 for Minor Counties' last wicket against Warwickshire, a record, but it only delayed the inevitable. David Hemp, bowling for the first time in a one-day game, took four wickets. He followed this with 34, and Lara entertained a long-suffering crowd with an unbeaten 30 as the county side won with 26 overs to spare.

Leicestershire kept alive their hopes of qualifying for the later stages of the competition, and, at the same time, ended Northamptonshire's hopes. The home county never truly recovered from the depths of 55 for four, and an opening stand of 123 between Sutcliffe and the mightily impressive Maddy soon confirmed who would win the match.

7 May
at Riverside
Worcestershire 161
Durham 162 for 8 (M.J. Foster 54, P.J. Newport 4 for 36)
Durham (2 pts) won by 2 wickets
(Gold Award: M.J. Foster)

at Chelmsford
Essex 233 for 9 (N. Hussain 101, A.G.J. Fraser 4 for 45)
Middlesex 234 for 6
Middlesex (2 pts) won by 4 wickets
(Gold Award: A.G.J. Fraser)

at Southampton
Kent 246 for 6 (A.P. Wells 111 not out, T.R. Ward 60)
Hampshire 121
Kent (2 pts) won by 125 runs
(Gold Award: A.P. Wells)

at Trent Bridge
Lancashire 298 for 5 (Wasim Akram 89 not out, J.P. Crawley 81)
Nottinghamshire 240 (M.P. Dowman 82)
Lancashire (2 pts) won by 58 runs
(Gold Award: Wasim Akram)

Durham qualified for the quarter-finals of the Benson and Hedges Cup for the first time. Worcestershire had won the toss, batted first and subsided to 113 for nine with Foster taking three wickets. Illingworth and Sheriyar put on 48 for the last wicket, and when Durham sank to 50 for five this partnership looked, in context, to have match-winning proportions. Foster, sent in first as pinch hitter, had to adjust his game somewhat, but his 54 off 77 balls was invaluable in a top eight in which the other seven mustered 35 between them. In spite of his efforts, his side seemed beaten when the eighth wicket fell at 112, but Betts and Killeen believed otherwise and shared an unbroken stand of 50, which took Durham into the last eight. Middlesex confirmed themselves as winners of Group D with victory over Essex, whose place in the quarter-finals remained in question. The Essex innings was held together by Nasser Hussain, the acting captain, who made his first century in the competition for the county. He had scored 118 for Combined Universities against Somerset in 1989. His 101 off 121 balls was not to earn him the Gold Award, however. That honour went to Alastair Fraser, who, in the second match of his cricketing renaissance, took four wickets and restricted Essex to a moderate total. Such limped off with a side injury. Cowan had another of his back spasms, and the Essex attack looked generally deflated. With left-handers Pooley and Weekes to the fore, Middlesex batted efficiently and won with seven balls to spare.

Not surprisingly, Kent brushed aside Hampshire. Ward and Wells scored 112 for the third wicket to give the Kent innings its backbone. Alan Wells batted impeccably to reach his first century in the competition, 111 off 106 balls, and earn his first Gold Award. He was particularly severe of McLean, who was finding it hard to adjust to English conditions. On a pitch that aided the seamers, Hampshire were soon in trouble, descending to 33 for five. Aymes and James provided some restoration.

In the keenly contested Group A, Lancashire beat Nottinghamshire, who had held their own for much of the game. Put in to bat, Lancashire were 246 for five after 48 overs, but Wasim Akram and Warren Hegg took 26 from each of the last two overs, bowled by Wharf and Oram, and what had been a moderate target suddenly became daunting. Pollard, Dowman and Gallian began the Nottinghamshire challenge well, and the score was 147 for one in the 28th over when Gallian was caught off Yates. Thereafter, the home county was in decline, and the run rate necessary increased by the over.

8 May
at Leicester
Leicestershire 382 for 6 (D.L. Maddy 151, C.C. Lewis 55 not out)
Minor Counties 126 (V.J. Wells 6 for 25)
Leicestershire (2 pts) won by 256 runs
(Gold Award: D.L. Maddy)

at Forfar
Scotland 174 (B.G. Lockie 51)
Derbyshire 177 for 7
Derbyshire (2 pts) won by 3 wickets
(Gold Award: T.A. Tweats)

at The Oval
Surrey 296 for 6 (A.J. Stewart 108, B.C. Hollioake 91)
Somerset 287 (M. Burns 95, D.A. Reeve 60)
Surrey (2 pts) won by 9 runs
(Gold Award: B.C. Hollioake)

Needing to increase their run-rate to have any chance of qualifying for the last eight, Leicestershire did all that could be expected of them against Minor Counties. Their 382 was the second highest score made in the 27 years of the competition. Darren Maddy was again the hero, hitting his second century of the season and winning his third Gold Award in four matches. For Minor Counties, who had endured a wretched tournament, Oakes and Pennett both considered more than nine runs an over, but Sharp bowled admirably for his one for 29 in 10 overs, three of them maidens. David Ward, formerly of Surrey and much missed on the county circuit, and skipper Dean began with a flourish, but the Minor Counties quickly faded away.

Scotland gave Derbyshire a hard game on a difficult pitch at Forfar. Needing 175 to win, Derbyshire were 116 for seven before Krikken, 22, joined Tweats, 42, in an unbroken stand of 61, which won the match with an over to spare.

Surrey made it five wins in five matches, but Somerset challenged them to the end. The Surrey innings was built around a second wicket partnership of 185 between Stewart and Ben Hollioake, whose 91 off 98 balls and three wickets were to earn him the Gold Award. Somerset responded splendidly to Surrey's 296 with Reeve and Burns scoring 158 for the first wicket. Late in the innings, Mushtaq Ahmed hit a brisk 26 and 21 were needed from the last three overs, but the demise of Mushtaq with seven balls remaining dashed Somerset's hopes.

---

9 May

at Oxford
British Universities 204 (L.D. Sutton 60, M.J. Chilton 56)
Kent 205 for 4 (M.V. Fleming 105 not out, M.A. Ealham 50 not out)
Kent (2 pts) won by 6 wickets
(Gold Award: M.V. Fleming)

at Cardiff
Middlesex 253 for 6 (K.R. Brown 109)
Glamorgan 234 (R.D.B. Croft 50)
Middlesex (2 pts) won by 19 runs
(Gold Award: K.R. Brown)

at Bristol
Hampshire 173 for 9 (J.P. Stephenson 53, A.D. Mascarenhas 53, M.J. Cawdron 4 for 28)
Gloucestershire 174 for 4 (M.J. Church 64 not out, A.J. Wright 59 not out)
Gloucestershire (2 pts) won by 6 wickets
(Gold Award: M.J. Church)

at Eglinton
Match abandoned
Ireland 1 pt, Sussex 1 pt

at Old Trafford
Lancashire 258 for 8 (A. Flintoff 92)
Northamptonshire 187 (A.L. Penberthy 56 not out)
Lancashire (2 pts) won by 71 runs
(Gold Award: A. Flintoff)

at Edgbaston
Warwickshire 228 for 9 (D.L. Hemp 50, K.P. Evans 4 for 27)
Nottinghamshire 223 for 8 (N.A. Gie 70)
Warwickshire (2 pts) won by 5 runs
(Gold Award: N.A. Gie)

at Leeds
Durham 172 (J.J.B. Lewis 67)
Yorkshire 175 for 2 (D.S. Lehmann 65 not out, D. Byas 52 not out)
Yorkshire (2 pts) won by 8 wickets
(Gold Award: J.J.B. Lewis)

The Benson and Hedges zonal rounds were crammed into a period of 12 days so that on 9 May final issues were decided. Matthew Fleming hit an unbeaten 105 off 104 balls, his first century in the competition, as Kent defeated British Universities. The students could not find the excellent form that they had shown in their previous matches, but Kent still had some jitters when they lost Ward for 0 and went from 91 for one to 102 for four. Ealham then joined Fleming in an unbroken partnership worth 103, and Kent won with 11 overs in hand to confirm their place in the quarter-finals.

Glamorgan, too, could have had a place in the last eight but for a rather bizarre performance against Middlesex whom they put in to bat. Brown and Langer began with a partnership of 117, and Brown went on to hit 109 off 115 balls, his second hundred of the campaign. His innings gave Glamorgan a bigger target than they would have wanted, for, in order to overtake Essex on run-rate, they had to score the 254 they needed inside 39 overs. Croft gave them a good start with another pugnacious 50, which took them to 83 in 12 overs, but Cottey, still leading the side in the absence of the injured Maynard, juggled his batting order, and Glamorgan lost their way. They went from 142 for four in 21 overs to 179 for eight in 30 overs, and hopes died.

Hampshire ended bottom of Group C after losing to a Gloucestershire side that was without Russell and Walsh. Medium-pacer Michael Cawdron returned his best bowling figures in the competition, and Matt Church, making his Benson and Hedges debut, shared a winning stand of 127 with Tony Wright after Gloucestershire had been 47 for four.

Lancashire qualified for the last eight with a resounding victory over Northamptonshire. Atherton's season of woe continued when he was out to the second ball of the day, but Flintoff, a very powerful batsman, hit 92 off 93 balls. Hegg offered violence towards the close of the innings, and a target of 259 always looked beyond Northamptonshire's reach. They had fared badly in the competition, and the decision to replace Bailey by Curran as captain had brought no recognisable dividends. Once again it was only Penberthy who offered any real resistance. Warwickshire's fourth victory in five matches could not earn them a place in the quarter-finals. Their batting never truly came to life on a seamer's pitch at Edgbaston, but they had every chance of overhauling Lancashire on run-rate when they reduced Nottinghamshire to 66 for five in 20 overs. Noel Gie and Wayne Noon added 121 in 24 overs as Lara perversely bowled spinners Smith and Gilles, and Nottinghamshire lost by just five runs.

At Headingley, Yorkshire beat Durham, but both sides had already qualified for the final stages of the competition. Byas and Lehmann took Yorkshire to victory with a century partnership, but the most impressive part of the home county's cricket was the pace bowling of Gough, Silverwood and Hutchison, each of whom took three wickets.

Final Group Tables

Group A	P	W	L	AB	Pts	R/R
Leicestershire	5	4	1		8	23.32
Lancashire	5	4	1		8	17.31
Warwickshire	5	4	1		8	16.35
Nottinghamshire	5	2	3		4	1.51
Northamptonshire	5	1	4		2	–10.40
Minor Counties	5	–	5		0	–50.57

Group B	P	W	L	AB	Pts	R/R
Yorkshire	4	4	–		8	13.13
Durham	4	3	1		6	–1.42
Worcestershire	4	2	2		4	3.66
Derbyshire	4	1	3		2	–3.27
Scotland	4	–	4		0	–10.51

Group C	P	W	L	AB	Pts	R/R
Surrey	5	5	–		10	13.16
Kent	5	3	1	1	7	14.17
Somerset	5	2	2	1	5	–0.43
Gloucestershire	5	2	3		4	2.89
British Universities	5	1	4		2	–13.26
Hampshire	5	1	4		2	–15.56

Group D	P	W	L	AB	Pts	R/R
Middlesex	4	4	–		8	3.71
Essex	4	2	1	1	5	19.48
Glamorgan	4	1	2	1	3	10.33
Sussex	4	1	2	1	3	–1.53
Ireland	4	–	3	1	1	–33.29

Top two sides in each group qualify for the quarter-finals.

Quarter-Finals

27 May
at Leicester
Kent 158 (C.L. Hooper 60, P.V. Simmons 5 for 33)
Leicestershire 159 for 2 (D.L. Maddy 93 not out)
Leicestershire won by 8 wickets
(Gold Award: D.L. Maddy)

at Leeds
Yorkshire 269 for 5 (D.S. Lehmann 119, M.P. Vaughan 70)
Durham 167
Yorkshire won by 102 runs
(Gold Award: D.S. Lehmann)

27 and 28 May
at The Oval
Lancashire 203 (M.A. Atherton 93, Saqlain Mushtaq 4 for 46)
Surrey 206 for 5
Surrey won by 5 wickets
(Gold Award: M.A. Atherton)

at Lord's
Essex 232 for 9 (S.D. Peters 58 not out)
Middlesex 224 for 7 (J.L. Langer 71, A.P. Cowan 5 for 28)
Essex won by 8 runs
(Gold Award: A.P. Cowan)

Leicestershire were once more profligate to an astonishing degree. Having put Kent in to bat, they conceded 55 runs in extras, 24 of these were wides and 20 were no-balls. The visitors had been reduced to 32 for four, but Ealham joined Hooper in a stand worth 76 that threatened to turn the course of the game. Ormond, returning after recovering from an abscess on the spine, took three of the first four wickets and bowled at a lively pace, but it was the gentle medium of

Ashley Cowan took the Gold Award for his outstanding bowling in the Benson and Hedges Cup quarter-final match, Essex v. Middlesex, at Lord's, 27 May.
(Nigel French / ASP)

Phil Simmons that cut down the Kent innings. He had Ealham caught off a skier and then dismissed Cowdrey and Marsh with successive deliveries. Hooper played well forward to everything and made 60 off 102 balls before being last out, caught in the deep by Maddy off Simmons, who finished with five for 33 from 9.1 overs, by far his best bowling performance in the competition. Kent committed the ultimate sin of being bowled out with 4.5 of their overs unused. Maddy and Sutcliffe scored 88 for Leicestershire's first wicket before Ealham claimed two wickets in four balls. This brought in Simmons to partner Maddy, and the pair hit off the 71 runs required in 12 overs. Maddy's gloriously golden run continued.

For one brief moment, Durham had hope of an upset at Headingley as McGrath and Byas were back in the pavilion with only two scored. The euphoria was soon over as Lehmann and Vaughan added 184 in 39 overs. Lehmann made his highest score for Yorkshire, 119 off 133 balls, while Vaughan, after an uneasy start, hit 70 off 124 balls before being bowled by an off-break from Phillips that turned prodigiously. Facing a target of 270, Durham were never in contention.

The two matches in London were delayed by rain and went into a second day. At The Oval, Lancashire were put in to bat and began well. The first wicket was worth 26 in seven overs when Flintoff fell to Martin Bicknell, but Crawley and Atherton put on 142 before Crawley charged at Saqlain Mushtaq and was stumped. It was the Pakistani off-spinner who turned the course of the match when he performed the hat-trick in the final over just as Lancashire needed runs. It was the second collapse of the innings, for, with a series of misjudgements and rash shots, they had gone from 164 for two to 168 for six. Atherton alone had batted with the necessary sense and composure and was unlucky not to complete the century he deserved. Brown and Stewart scored 35 from eight overs on the Wednesday, and their opening partnership was finally worth 78. There was an uncertain period when four wickets fell for 32 runs, but Butcher played positively, and the Hollioake brothers brought victory with 26 balls to spare. Surrey did not bat at their best, nor did they need to, and there was the suggestion that this Lancashire side, once a power in limited-over cricket, was in decline.

Put in to bat at Lord's, Essex lost Darren Robinson in the first over, and they limped their way to 137 for six. Stuart Law was caught off Johnson just as he threatened to take control, and Johnson also accounted for Robert Rollins, who hit 28 off 22 balls. Essex's salvation came from Stephen Peters, the 19-year old, who was deputising for the injured Prichard. He made an excellent unbeaten 58 off 57 balls as the last four Essex wickets realised 95 runs and provided Middlesex with an unexpected challenge. If Peters had been the hero of the first day, Cowan was the hero of the second. He had been missing for three weeks with a back injury, and his return brought great dividends and ended Middlesex's eight-match winning streak in one-day games. He sent back Johnson, Brown and Ramprakash as the home side slipped to 51 for three. Langer and Shah then added 108, and, with 13 overs left and only 74 runs needed, Essex faced defeat. Hussain took the gamble of bringing back Cowan, who responded by trapping both Langer and Shah leg before in his first over. Thereafter, Middlesex were struggling as the run-rate became more demanding and Pooley and Weekes were caught as they resorted to desperation. A requirement of 26 from the last two overs was beyond the capabilities of the remaining batsmen, and Angus Fraser's six off the final was a belated gesture of defiance.

Semi-Finals

9 June
at Leicester
Leicestershire 311 for 9 (D.L. Maddy 120 not out, B.F. Smith 89)
Surrey 291 for 8 (A.J. Hollioake 85, B.C. Hollioake 63, C.C. Lewis 4 for 40)
Leicestershire won by 20 runs
(Gold Award: D.L. Maddy)

at Leeds
Essex 258 for 7 (N. Hussain 78)
Yorkshire 163
Essex won by 95 runs
(Gold Award: N. Hussain)

Darren Maddy won his fifth Gold Award in seven Benson and Hedges Cup matches and set up Leicestershire's fine victory over Surrey, the cup holders. Put in to bat, the home side soon lost Sutcliffe, but Ben Smith joined Maddy in a partnership worth 172. Smith's 89 came off 102 balls, while Maddy carried his bat through the 50 overs for 120, which came off 138 balls. Smith and Maddy ran between the wickets with great zest and intelligence, and Surrey began to wilt. They were handicapped when Salisbury slipped as

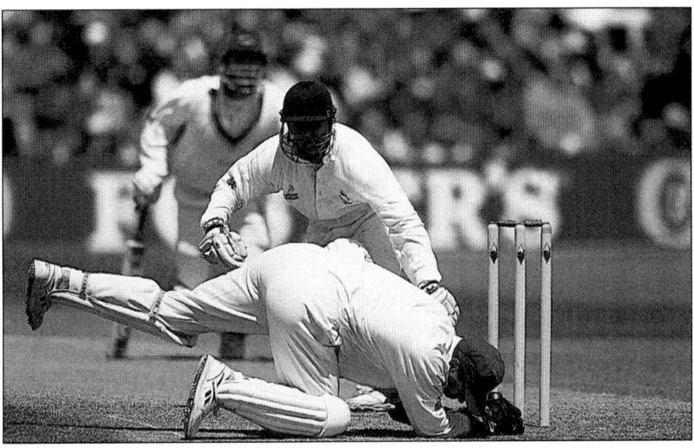

Alec Stewart fails to stump Ben Smith off the bowling of Saqlain Mushtaq in the Benson and Hedges Cup semi-final at Grace Road. Smith went on to make 89.
(David Munden / Sportsline)

Adam Hollioake, the Surrey captain, is bowled by Chris Lewis, the Leicestershire captain, for 85, and Leicestershire move closer to a place in the Benson and Hedges Cup Final.
(Graham Chadwick / Allsport)

he bowled his first (and only) delivery. It was hit for three, and he retired with a torn muscle, an injury that was to keep him out of the game for some weeks.

The Leicestershire innings was beautifully paced, and 100 runs came from the last 10 overs. Simmons made 40 off 35 balls, and the Hollioake brothers, in particular, received terrible punishment. Adam conceded 76 runs in eight overs, and Ben, who bowled Simmons, was hit for 60 in his 10 overs.

When Surrey batted, their hopes suffered an early blow when Alistair Brown was run out for three. Worse followed when Lewis brought himself into the attack. He removed Stewart, Thorpe and Butcher inside his first four overs, and Surrey were 72 for four. Revival came through Ben Hollioake, who hit 63 off 74 balls, and elder brother Adam made 85 off 97 balls as he and Martin Bicknell put on 81 in nine overs for the seventh wicket. Lewis returned to bowl Adam Hollioake, and Surrey's last glimmer of hope disappeared.

At Headingley, Yorkshire began in the best possible way and then totally lost their bearings. They won the toss and asked Essex to bat. Silverwood had Robinson leg before to the first ball of the match and had danger man Stuart Law caught at square-leg at 17. When Rollins, the promoted hitter, was caught at long leg, Essex were 33 for three and sinking fast. Hussain found a sensible partner in Irani, and the pair added 83. Hussain was the rock of the innings and was at the crease for 44 overs for his 78. It was an invaluable innings, and Danny Law provided the late panache with 36 off 33 balls so that Essex made 258, far more than they could have expected at the start of the day.

With confidence increased, Essex bowled with passion. Cowan had Vaughan leg before with the second ball of the innings, and Ilott quickly disposed of White and Byas to leave Yorkshire on 29 for three. As long as Lehmann remained, Yorkshire had sight of victory, and he and McGrath added 70. It was Such who captured the vital wicket. Lehmann tried to push the ball behind square, and Rollins took a simple catch. Three wickets went down for 19 runs. The Essex spinners took a grip on the game, and Yorkshire had lost their fourth semi-final in as many seasons.

Ashley Cowan leaps in triumph as he takes the wicket of Michael Vaughan with the second ball of the innings, and Essex go on to beat Yorkshire.
(Craig Prentis / Allsport)

Benson and Hedges Cup Final

Essex *v.* Leicestershire

Sadly and wrongly, this was the last final of a fine competition that has given pleasure to many thousands of people. It will be much missed by those who follow the county game. The weather was not kind to this grand finale, and days of rain had made even the start in doubt.

As it was, Lewis, a winner with Surrey the previous season, won the toss and asked Essex to bat. The conditions were difficult, and the ball moved appreciably, but the Leicestershire bowlers, Mullaly and Lewis himself, were wasteful. Wides were sprayed in all directions, and Law and Prichard were allowed some time to settle.

Stuart Law was never at ease on the pitch, but he showed grit and by the time he hit Wells to mid-wicket, Essex had 40 on the board. Prichard and Hussain took

Paul Prichard, the Essex skipper, in masterly form in the Benson and Hedges Cup Final. He hit 92 off 113 balls.
(Laurence Griffiths / Allsport)

Nasser Hussain reverse sweeps during his innings of 88. He and Prichard added 134 for Essex's second wicket, a match-winning partnership. Paul Nixon is the wicket-keeper.
(David Munden / Sportsline)

charge. This was the best of British batting, and, for an hour at least, the sun shone. They put on 134 for 152 balls and wrenched the game away from Leicestershire, who had started firm favourites. Prichard drove high to the Mound Stand where Maddy took a fine catch only to run over the boundary rope. Prichard celebrated by pulling another six into the Grand Stand. He also hit 11 fours. He was particularly strong square of the wicket on either side, and one has never seen him bat better for Essex. As a youngster, he looked certain to be an England player, but fortune has not always been kind to him. On this great ground, he was able to show his true worth for the second year in succession. His 92 came off 113 balls, and he was out when he steered Williamson into the hands of Simmons, whom Lewis relied on and recalled too often as a bowler. Both Prichard and Hussain feasted on gentle medium pace deliveries that drifted down the leg side.

Hussain began slowly, but once in his stride he was devastating. His 88 came off 102 balls with a six and eight fours. Irani did just what was required, 32 off 37 balls, and the rest fell in the late, mad dash for runs as Leicestershire began to hold the catches they had scorned when it really mattered. Nixon's wicket-keeping apart, Leicestershire did not impress in the field, and Lewis's captaincy was as enigmatic as his extrovert character. The Essex innings ended, and it rained.

So bad was the weather on the Sunday that it did not seem possible that there could be any play, but, to the surprise of all, a start was made at 3.25pm. Leicestershire faced a daunting target in normal conditions. With the ball still seaming dramatically, they faced mission impossible.

Sutcliffe was first out, slashing to slip, and Smith was out first ball, Stuart Law taking a brilliant catch low to his left at slip. In the next over, Simmons heaved at Ilott and was bowled. Wells was out to an in-swinger of full length, and Habib, having hit the first four of the innings, was out in the same manner. Maddy had battled bravely for 41 balls before he edged to slip, and Lewis lofted gently to square-leg. Leicestershire were 36 for seven.

Nixon used his feet intelligently, but the match had long since been lost. Essex won by 192 runs, a record for the final, and Prichard, most deservedly, was the Gold Award winner. For Essex, at least, the fine competition had ended on the highest possible note.

Mark Ilott bowls Phil Simmons as Essex sweep to victory.
(Laurence Griffiths / Allsport)

The last salute. Paul Prichard raises the Benson and Hedges Cup. The competition will be sadly missed.
(Laurence Griffiths / Sportsline)

MARYLEBONE CRICKET CLUB

50p **50p**

FINAL

ESSEX v. LEICESTERSHIRE

at Lord's Ground, Saturday & Sunday, 11 & 12 July, 1998

Any alterations to teams will be announced over the public address system

ESSEX

	Batsman	How out	Runs
†1	P. J. Prichard	c Simmons b Williamson	92
2	S. G. Law	c Mullally b Wells	6
3	N. Hussain	c Smith b Lewis	88
4	R. C. Irani	c Maddy b Mullally	32
5	D. R. Law	c Lewis b Williamson	1
6	A. P. Grayson	not out	9
*7	R. J. Rollins	c Brimson b Mullally	0
8	S. D. Peters	b Mullally	9
9	A. P. Cowan	not out	3
10	M. C. Ilott		
11	P. M. Such		
	B 2, l-b 8, w 18, n-b ,		28
		Total.........(7 wkts, 50 overs)	268

FALL OF THE WICKETS

1...40 2...174 3...234 4...244 5...245 6...250 7...265 8... 9... 10...

Bowling Analysis	O.	M.	R.	W.	Wd.	N-b.
Mullally	10	1	36	3	7	...
Lewis	9	0	59	1	2	...
Wells	10	0	34	1	4	...
Simmons	9	0	67	0	2	...
Brimson	2	0	13	0	2	...
Williamson	10	0	49	2	1	...
	...	...	...	...	...	...

LEICESTERSHIRE

	Batsman	How out	Runs
1	D. L. Maddy	c S. Law b Cowan	5
2	I. J. Sutcliffe	c S. Law b Cowan	1
3	B. F. Smith	c S. Law b Cowan	0
4	P. V. Simmons	b Ilott	2
5	V. J. Wells	lbw b Ilott	1
6	A. Habib	lbw b Ilott	5
*7	P. A. Nixon	not out	21
†8	C. C. Lewis	c Peters b Irani	0
9	D. Williamson	c Hussain b S. Law	11
10	A. D. Mullally	lbw b Irani	1
11	M. T. Brimson	b S. Law	0
	B , l-b 8, w 17, n-b 4,		29
		Total...................(27.4 overs)	76

FALL OF THE WICKETS

1...6 2...6 3...10 4...17 5...31 6...31 7...36 8...67 9...73 10...76

Bowling Analysis	O.	M.	R.	W.	Wd.	N-b.
Ilott	8	2	10	3	6	...
Cowan	10	2	24	3	6	2
Irani	6	2	21	2	1	...
S. Law	3.4	0	13	2	4	...
	...	...	...	...	...	...
	...	...	...	...	...	...
	...	...	...	...	...	...

†Captain *Wicket-keeper

Umpires—R. Julian, M. J. Kitchen & J. C. Balderstone

Scorers—C. F. Driver & G. A. York

Toss won by—Leicestershire who elected to field

RESULT—Essex won by 192 runs

The playing conditions for the Benson and Hedges Cup Competition are printed on the back of this score card.

Total runs scored at end of each over :—

Essex	1	2	3	4	5	6	7	8	9	10	11	12	13	14	15	16	17	18	19	20
	21	22	23	24	25	26	27	28	29	30	31	32	33	34	35	36	37	38	39	40
	41	42	43	44	45	46	47	48	49	50										
Leicestershire	1	2	3	4	5	6	7	8	9	10	11	12	13	14	15	16	17	18	19	20
	21	22	23	24	25	26	27	28	29	30	31	32	33	34	35	36	37	38	39	40
	41	42	43	44	45	46	47	48	49	50										

South African Tour

The South Africans arrived in England in mid-May for their first full tour of England since 1960. They were to play five Test matches, three Texaco Trophy matches against England and compete in the triangular one-day tournament with England and Sri Lanka. Richardson and Schultz had retired from Test cricket, and others, like Hudson, had faded from the scene, but the South African selectors still tended to be conservative in their choice, turning their backs on players of talent such as Gibbs and recalling McMillan, a veteran whose best days were thought to be behind him. The most interesting selection was that of Mornantau Hayward, the 21-year old fast bowler, who had done well against West Indies 'A' team. Tradition was re-established when the tour opened at Worcester. Thereafter, there was to be scant first-class practice before the first Test.

14, 15 and 16 May

at Worcester

South Africans 287 for 4 dec. (G.F.J. Liebenberg 98, J.H. Kallis 75, D.J. Cullinan 67 not out) and 219 for 6 dec. (J.H. Kallis 74, G. Kirsten 51)
Worcestershire 228 for 6 dec. (D.A. Leatherdale 69, L. Klusener 4 for 66) and 189 (G.A. Hick 58, A.A. Donald 6 for 56)
South Africans won by 89 runs

The South Africans gained a fine victory in their opening match and gave early indication that the power of their pace attack was in no way diminished. They chose to bat first in conditions that favoured swing bowling, but their batsmen coped admirably after the early loss of Gary Kirsten. Kallis, looking a batsman of the highest quality, and Liebenberg, not expected to play a major part in the tour, added 162 runs for the second wicket and showed great character and determination. They were followed by Cullinan, often enigmatic, undermined by Warne, but looking superbly at ease and in total control against the Worcestershire attack. When the county side batted, Klusener took four of the first five wickets to fall and bristled with aggression, but any South African joy was tempered by an injury to Telemachus, who dislocated his shoulder in pre-match team practice. Hick kept the game alive with his declaration, and Kallis gave further indication of his class when the South Africans batted a second time. Cronje left Worcestershire the challenge of making 279 off 62 overs, and the county began well. Solanki showed fluency, and Hick suggested that he might prosper, but Adams slowed the scoring, and then came Donald. He returned to take six wickets in eight overs, and when this mighty spell was at an end Klusener immediately bowled Rawnsley. This left last pair Newport and Sheriyar just under eight overs to survive. A catch was dropped off Klusener, and the last over arrived with Adams the bowler. He turned the second ball sharply, took the edge of Newport's bat and Cullinan dived to take the catch at slip.

The social start to the South Africa tour. Arundel. (Ben Radford/Allsport)

17 May

at Arundel

South Africans 295 for 7 (G. Kirsten 71)
Duke of Norfolk's XI 234 (H. Morris 54)
South Africans won by 61 runs

The South Africans dutifully won their social 50-over match in the beautiful grounds of Arundel Castle. Desmond Haynes and Allan Lamb were among the opposition.

19 May

at Canterbury

South Africans 290 for 7 (G.F.J. Liebenberg 72, W.J. Cronje 64, J.H. Kallis 61, A.P. Igglesden 4 for 40)
Kent 192 (R.W.T. Key 54)
South Africans won by 98 runs

The tourists made it three wins in three matches with a resounding victory over a below strength Kent side. South Africa fielded the eleven that were to face England in the first Texaco match, at The Oval, and they performed in a totally professional manner. Put in to bat, they responded with typical verve. Liebenberg was in dashing mood yet again, and Cronje and Kallis were fluently aggressive. Key, who was graduating confidently into the Kent side, hit 54 off 57 balls, but once he and Fulton had been separated there was no doubt as to who would win the match.

Texaco Trophy

England *v.* South Africa

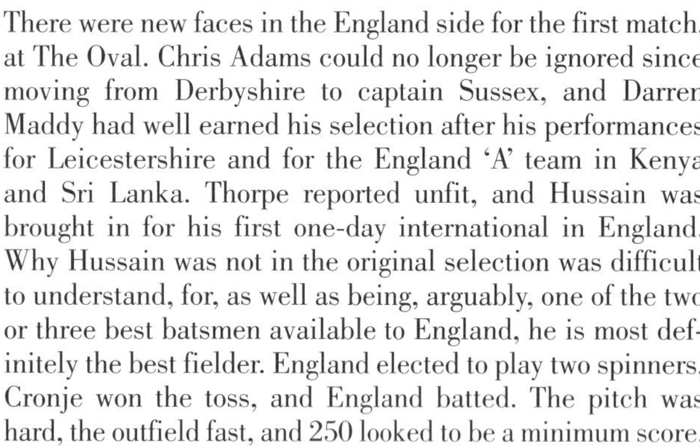

There were new faces in the England side for the first match, at The Oval. Chris Adams could no longer be ignored since moving from Derbyshire to captain Sussex, and Darren Maddy had well earned his selection after his performances for Leicestershire and for the England 'A' team in Kenya and Sri Lanka. Thorpe reported unfit, and Hussain was brought in for his first one-day international in England. Why Hussain was not in the original selection was difficult to understand, for, as well as being, arguably, one of the two or three best batsmen available to England, he is most definitely the best fielder. England elected to play two spinners, Cronje won the toss, and England batted. The pitch was hard, the outfield fast, and 250 looked to be a minimum score.

Stewart and Knight gave England a brisk start, scoring 58 in 13 overs before Stewart diverted a ball from Donald into his stumps via his arm. Knight had frequently played and missed, but he clouted the ball hard. His technique is too fallible for him to inspire confidence, but, for the present, he is a survivor. Adams had a testing time with the ball moving appreciably, and his attacking game was thwarted, but he is a gutsy player, and he came through the ordeal well, sharing in a stand of 51 in 13 overs before edging to the keeper. Hussain and Knight strove to get the score moving, but their partnership ended in disaster when Knight was sent back and beaten by Rhodes's throw to Symcox, the bowler. Maddy was deceived by the same bowler's quicker ball, and Hussain fell to a spectacular diving catch by Boucher. Ealham was run out when he attempted an unwise second run to Pollock, and although Hollioake and Lewis added 40 in just under eight overs, they did not indicate batting of international standard, and England's 223 looked well short of a winning total. It must be said that it was more the brilliance of the South African fielding and the accuracy and intelligence of their bowling that restricted the score rather than great deficiencies in England's batting.

There was a bright start for England when South Africa batted. Kirsten hit Gough's first ball for four; the second was edged to Adams at slip. Liebenberg and Kallis batted with assurance to add 72 in 16 overs. They were severe on Giles, but he gained revenge when he bowled Liebenberg as he attempted to sweep. Cullinan was run out by Maddy, and South Africa began to find it harder to force the pace, although they were never far from the required rate. Cronje was beginning to accelerate dangerously when, with the score on 175 in the 42nd over, he drove at Croft and was miraculously caught by Hussain at mid-wicket. This catch could have won the match for England, who cannot afford to omit such a fielder, for Croft bowled Pollock next ball, and South Africa were suddenly 175 for six. At this point, their strength became apparent. Klusener came in and hit 22 off 20 balls. With Rhodes making 39 off 43 balls,

Pat Symcox runs out England top-scorer Nick Knight in the first Texaco Trophy match, at the Oval.
(Graham Chadwick / Allsport)

all pressure was off, and South Africa had the luxury of Boucher and Symcox at numbers nine and ten. Lewis essayed a leg-break, which Rhodes accepted as a long hop and pulled for four to give South Africa victory with eight balls to spare.

South Africa duly won the Texaco Trophy when they skilfully outmanoeuvred and outwitted England at Old Trafford. Hollioake won the toss, asked South Africa to bat and was immediately rewarded with the wickets of Kirsten and Kallis, both of whom fell victims to Gough. The Yorkshireman bowled with pace and aggression, attacking the line of the off stump and moving the ball away from the batsman. Unfortunately, Lewis did not match Gough in control or fire, and Hollioake all too soon resorted to defensive fields that lacked perception and intelligence. Ealham had Cullinan leg before playing across the line, and South Africa were 42 for three in the 12th over. Liebenberg, not at ease, and Cronje, fluent and thoughtful, added 61 in 13 overs, but Lewis returned to account for the South African captain, and Liebenberg paid the price for playing across the line. Pollock again went cheaply, but the South African order has depth and belief, and Rhodes, aided by some ill-judged field settings, lit the torch that was taken up by Klusener, who hit 55 off 49 balls. He hit Fleming, chosen ahead of Giles, for three consecutive fours, and the over yielded 15 runs in all. In the context of the match, this was inflation, and South Africa's 226, while not looking unbeatable, exceeded expectation.

Alistair Brown had replaced Maddy in the England line-up, and he opened with Knight, but the pairing of two technically flawed dashers is perhaps not the best of blends. They went off at a rush, and Klusener's third over realised 15 runs, but it also saw the end of Brown, who chopped the ball to Rhodes at point. Stewart was in commanding mood, and 47 runs came in nine overs, but there is a resilience in the South African side that is to be envied. Donald joined the attack and, in his second over, was too quick for Knight, who was very well caught by the diving Boucher. Hussain

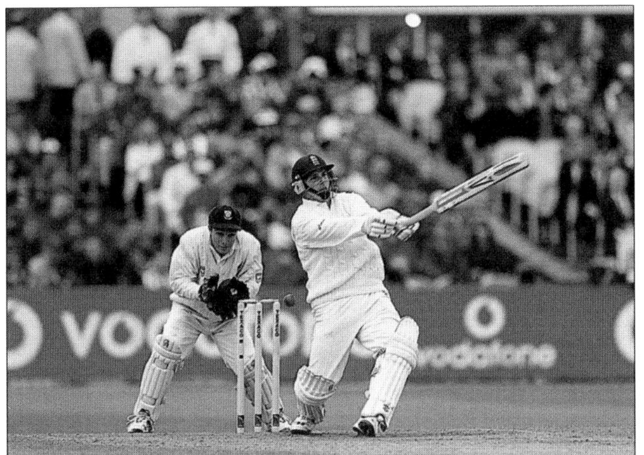

The second Texaco Trophy match, at Old Trafford. Mark Ealham takes a heave at Cullinan and is bowled for 12.
(Graham Chadwick / Allsport)

was out in Donald's next over, getting a faint touch to the keeper, and Adams struggled unhappily before fatally playing across the line to Symcox, who bowled admirably. He spun the ball more than Croft had done and maintained immaculate control. Momentarily, at least, Hollioake and Stewart lifted spirits in a stand of 53, which was ended when Hollioake called his partner for a suicidal single to the dynamic Rhodes. Stewart was well short of his ground when the ball reached Boucher, but whether the keeper had the ball in his gloves or lodged between his elbows was something of a mystery. Hollioake still fails to convince, and he became Pollock's solitary victim as England were hurried to defeat. Cronje had produced a surprise by bringing Cullinan into the attack to bowl gentle but effective off-breaks. The ploy bamboozled the host country, and Ealham missed a straight, short ball, while Fleming was brilliantly caught by Kallis. Had the game been decided solely on the out-cricket, South Africa's margin of victory would have been far greater than 32 runs.

South Africa remained unchanged for the third match, and England brought in Fraser for Lewis and Maddy for Adams. One hopes that the two matches in which he did not distinguish himself will not be the limit of Adams's international career, and one is also bewildered as to why, having been given a second game when nothing but pride was at stake, Maddy was left padded and waiting at number six. Cronje won the toss, and South Africa batted first, a great surprise. The sky was overcast, and the pitch was tinged with green. It was not surprising that South Africa struggled, and when Liebenberg was leg before to Ealham he had batted 24 overs for 13, and his side was 68 for four. Rhodes chased a wide ball and was caught behind 10 runs later, and the visitors needed all the resources of their lower order to save them from drowning without trace. Cronje, as ever, led from the front with 35 off 41 balls, and Pollock made his first real contribution to the series with 60 off 64 balls. Boucher, too, did well, but 205 did not look a formidable total.

With the sky lightened, Knight and Brown went off at a rush. The first 15 overs produced 113 runs, and when Brown was run out by Kallis in the 16th the game was as good as over. The Surrey man had hit 59 off 40 balls with 11 fours. Knight's 51 occupied 79 balls, and Fleming, promoted above Maddy for no apparent reason, was third out, having hit a six and two fours. Stewart and Hussain took England to victory with 58 in 12.2 unhurried overs. Hussain hit two sixes and two fours his 39-ball innings.

England had drawn some consolation, and there was even the superstition that the side that wins the Texaco Trophy usually loses the Test series. The problem was that at least half the England side were unlikely to figure in the Tests while South Africa seemed to be moving smoothly into top gear.

Rhodes and Gough were named as the Men of the Texaco series.

27 May
at Stone
South Africans 283 for 7 (B.M. McMillan 79, W.J. Cronje 58, J.H. Kallis 55)
Minor Counties 189 (M. Hayward 5 for 36)
South Africans won by 94 runs

The tourists lost four wickets for 114 runs in 27 overs before McMillan and Kallis revived them.

Cronje hit 58 off 38 balls with four sixes and four fours. The young fast bowler Mornantau Hayward tore the heart out of the Minor Counties innings, and the only cheer came in a last wicket stand of 40 between Humphries and Richardson.

29, 30, 31 May and 1 June
at Bristol
South Africans 416 for 8 dec. (G. Kirsten 125, L. Klusener 73 not out, J.N. Rhodes 59, M.W. Alleyne 4 for 63) and 288 for 4 dec. (G. Kirsten 131 not out, J.N. Rhodes 123)
Gloucestershire 403 for 9 dec. (M.W. Alleyne 109, M.G.N. Windows 68, R.C.J. Williams 67, G.I. Macmillan 52) and 134
South Africans won by 167 runs

The South Africans gained a heartening victory on the eve of the first Test, although the eleven they fielded gave little indication as to what their Test team would be. Kirsten won the toss and led from the front with a century in each innings. There was some fierce hitting from Klusener and Hayward in an eighth wicket stand of 112, but Gloucestershire responded most positively with Alleyne reaching a fine century and sharing a fourth wicket stand of 127 with Windows. There was also a late flourish from wicket-keeper Williams and the boost of 58 extras, 34 of them no-balls. When South Africa batted a second time, Kirsten was dominant in the early stages, making 77 out of 105 for three,

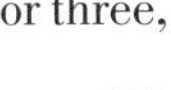

England regain some pride at Headingley in the third Texaco Trophy game – Man of the Match Ally Brown clouts a ball to the boundary.
(Graham Chadwick / Allsport)

but the advent of Rhodes saw him become the junior partner. There was conjecture that Rhodes was vying with McMillan for the number six spot in the Test side, and he put his case most emphatically, making 123 in a 176-run stand with Kirsten and reaching his century off 78 balls. Gloucestershire needed 302 to win, but they were shot out by the pace of Hayward and Ntini, neither of whom was likely to play in the Test. The county side were 86 for nine, and only a late hitting spree by Mike Smith helped to save them from total embarrassment.

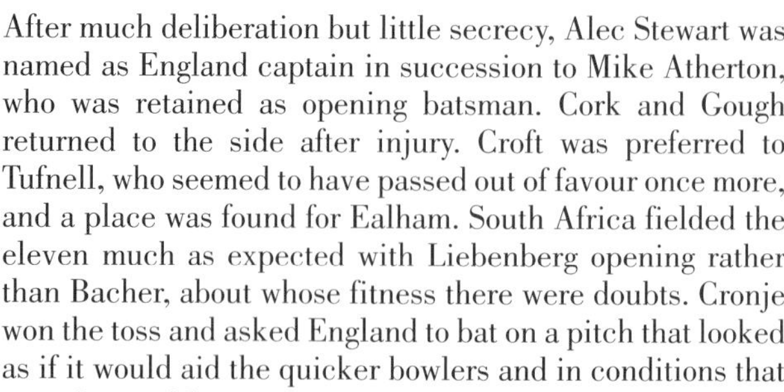

First Test Match
England *v.* South Africa

After much deliberation but little secrecy, Alec Stewart was named as England captain in succession to Mike Atherton, who was retained as opening batsman. Cork and Gough returned to the side after injury. Croft was preferred to Tufnell, who seemed to have passed out of favour once more, and a place was found for Ealham. South Africa fielded the eleven much as expected with Liebenberg opening rather than Bacher, about whose fitness there were doubts. Cronje won the toss and asked England to bat on a pitch that looked as if it would aid the quicker bowlers and in conditions that were favourable to swing.

Pitch and conditions might have been helpful to Pollock, Donald and Klusener, but the bowlers have to plant the ball in the right place and exploit what they have been offered if they are to succeed. This, most emphatically, they failed to do. Reprieved, the England batsmen seized the initiative in spectacular fashion. Atherton began with an inside edge, but was assured thereafter, while Butcher was very fortunate not to be adjudged leg before to Pollock in the tenth over, but batted with assurance from then on. Neither batsman took risks. Their task was to lay a foundation. At lunch, the score was 67 from 30 overs; at tea, it was 151 for 62 overs with both men on 65.

Eight overs into the final session, Butcher swept at Adams and was caught at backward square-leg. He had

First One-Day International – England *v.* South Africa
21 May 1998 at The Oval

England

N.V. Knight	run out	**64**
A.J. Stewart †	**b** Donald	**27**
C.J. Adams	**c** Boucher, **b** Kallis	**25**
N. Hussain	**c** Boucher, **b** Donald	**27**
D.L. Maddy	lbw, **b** Symcox	**1**
A.J. Hollioake *	**c** Symcox, **b** Klusener	**32**
M.A. Ealham	run out	**1**
C.C. Lewis	run out	**16**
A.F. Giles	**c** Boucher, **b** Cronje	**2**
R.D.B. Croft	not out	**7**
D. Gough	not out	**0**
	lb **7**, w **12**, nb **2**	**21**
	50 overs (for 9 wickets)	**223**

	O	M	R	W
Pollock	10	1	45	**–**
Klusener	8	1	33	**1**
Donald	10	2	45	**2**
Cronje	8	1	26	**1**
Kallis	4	–	24	**1**
Symcox	10	–	43	**1**

Fall of Wickets
1–**58**, 2–**109**, 3–**155**, 4–**158**, 5–**160**, 6–**161**, 7–**201**, 8–**209**, 9–**220**

South Africa

G. Kirsten	**c** Adams, **b** Gough	**4**
G.F.J. Liebenberg	**b** Giles	**30**
J.H. Kallis	**c** Hollioake, **b** Croft	**62**
D.J. Cullinan	run out	**16**
W.J. Cronje *	**c** Hussain, **b** Croft	**40**
J.N. Rhodes	not out	**39**
S.M. Pollock	**b** Croft	**0**
L. Klusener	lbw, **b** Giles	**22**
M.V. Boucher †	not out	**2**
P.L. Symcox		
A.A. Donald		
	b **4**, lb **2**, w **2**, nb **1**	**9**
	48.4 overs (for 7 wickets)	**224**

	O	M	R	W
Gough	10	1	38	**1**
Lewis	8.4	1	46	**–**
Ealham	10	–	38	**–**
Giles	9	–	37	**2**
Croft	10	–	51	**3**
Hollioake	1	–	8	**–**

Fall of Wickets
1–**4**, 2–**76**, 3–**105**, 4–**134**, 5–**175**, 6–**175**, 7–**214**

Umpires: J.C. Balderstone & P. Willey *Man of the Match:* J.H. Kallis

South Africa won by 3 wickets

Second One-Day International – England v. South Africa

23 May 1998 at Old Trafford, Manchester

South Africa

G.F.J. Liebenberg	lbw, **b** Ealham	**39**
G. Kirsten	**c** Adams, **b** Gough	**2**
J.H. Kallis	**c** Stewart, **b** Gough	**9**
D.J. Cullinan	lbw, **b** Ealham	**14**
W.J. Cronje *	**c** Stewart, **b** Lewis	**35**
J.N. Rhodes	lbw, **b** Croft	**41**
S.M. Pollock	lbw, **b** Croft	**3**
L. Klusener	not out	**55**
M.V. Boucher †	**b** Gough	**6**
P.L. Symcox	**b** Gough	**2**
A.A. Donald	not out	**6**
	b **2**, lb **6**, w **3**, nb **3**	**14**
	50 overs (for 9 wickets)	**226**

	O	M	R	W
Gough	10	–	35	**4**
Lewis	10	1	42	**1**
Ealham	10	–	34	**2**
Fleming	8	–	51	**–**
Croft	10	–	43	**2**
Hollioake	2	–	13	**–**

Fall of Wickets
1–**6**, 2–**24**, 3–**42**, 4–**103**, 5–**130**, 6–**143**, 7–**166**, 8–**189**, 9–**200**

England

N.V. Knight	**c** Boucher, **b** Donald	**34**
A.D. Brown	**c** Rhodes, **b** Klusener	**13**
A.J. Stewart †	run out	**52**
N. Hussain	**c** Boucher, **b** Donald	**1**
C.J. Adams	lbw, **b** Symcox	**3**
A.J. Hollioake *	lbw, **b** Pollock	**46**
M.A. Ealham	**b** Cullinan	**12**
M.V. Fleming	**c** Kallis, **b** Cullinan	**5**
C.C. Lewis	not out	**10**
R.D.B. Croft	run out	**7**
D. Gough	**c** Rhodes, **b** Donald	**2**
	lb **2**, w **7**	**9**
	46.4 overs	**194**

	O	M	R	W
Pollock	8	–	28	**1**
Klusener	9	–	58	**1**
Symcox	10	–	34	**1**
Donald	8.4	–	32	**3**
Cullinan	9	–	30	**2**
Kallis	2	–	10	**–**

Fall of Wickets
1–**30**, 2–**77**, 3–**83**, 4–**90**, 5–**143**, 6–**169**, 7–**169**, 8–**182**, 9–**190**

Umpires: R. Julian & D.R. Shepherd *Man of the Match*: L. Klusener

South Africa won by 32 runs

Third One-Day International – England v. South Africa

24 May 1998 at Headingley, Leeds

South Africa

G. Kirsten	**b** Fraser	**19**
G.F.J. Liebenberg	lbw, **b** Ealham	**13**
J.H. Kallis	run out	**1**
D.J. Cullinan	run out	**13**
W.J. Cronje *	**c** Stewart, **b** Ealham	**35**
J.N. Rhodes	**c** Stewart, **b** Ealham	**6**
S.M. Pollock	**b** Fleming	**60**
L. Klusener	**c** Stewart, **b** Fraser	**14**
M.V. Boucher †	not out	**26**
P.L. Symcox	not out	**1**
A.A. Donald		
	lb **9**, w **5**, nb **3**	**17**
	50 overs (for 8 wickets)	**205**

	O	M	R	W
Gough	10	2	57	**–**
Fraser	10	1	23	**2**
Fleming	10	1	41	**1**
Ealham	10	–	44	**3**
Croft	10	–	31	**–**

Fall of Wickets
1–**26**, 2–**29**, 3–**57**, 4–**68**, 5–**78**, 6–**118**, 7–**146**, 8–**198**

England

N.V. Knight	**c** Rhodes, **b** Donald	**51**
A.D. Brown	run out	**59**
M.V. Fleming	**b** Donald	**18**
A.J. Stewart †	not out	**26**
N. Hussain	not out	**33**
D.L. Maddy		
A.J. Hollioake *		
R.D.B. Croft		
M.A. Ealham		
D. Gough		
A.R.C. Fraser		
	b **4**, lb **2**, w **3**, nb **10**	**19**
	35 overs (for 3 wickets)	**206**

	O	M	R	W
Pollock	7	1	34	**–**
Klusener	6	–	45	**–**
Donald	7	–	35	**2**
Symcox	9	1	51	**–**
Cronje	6	–	35	**–**

Fall of Wickets
1–**114**, 2–**139**, 3–**148**

Umpires: J.H. Hampshire & G. Sharp *Man of the Match*: A.D. Brown

England won by 7 wickets

Nasser Hussain is leg before to a ball from Adams that keeps low. (Graham Chadwick / Allsport)

batted with such good judgement that his dismissal, victim of an unwise and ill-chosen shot, was much out of character. Stewart came in, and there was no drop in the tempo, with 79 runs coming from the last 22 overs of the day. Atherton 103, Stewart 28, England 249 for one – after one day, it seemed, the game was already out of South Africa's reach.

The uncertainty of the weather on the second day, when rain interrupted play for an hour, and the inability to force the pace when required, brought doubts that England would be able to force victory. They lost Atherton in the second over of the day when he sliced to the wicket-keeper without addition to the score. Stewart and Hussain were fluent and positive as they put on 60 in 23 overs, but both were out before lunch. Stewart edged Klusener to slip, and, four balls later, Hussain fell to a rogue delivery, leg before to a ball from Adams that shot along the ground. Thorpe was bowled by a fast in-swinging yorker, and Ealham batted painfully until deceived by Adams when he attempted an on-drive. Ramprakash batted with good sense and sound technique, but Donald and Pollock were far more in control of length and direction than they had been on the opening day, and there were few easy pickings. There were some good clouts from Cork, Gough, Croft and Fraser as the innings moved to its close, but the price for these quick runs was high. Gough sustained a broken index finger and could take no further part in the game. England were all out for 462.

Early rain delayed start on the third day until 1.20pm, and bad light cut nearly five overs off the end of the day, but, in the 75.2 overs possible, England took five South African wickets for 192 runs. Four of the wickets went to Dominic Cork, who returned from exile to bowl with pace and aggression. Liebenberg, looking short of Test class, was caught at short-leg, but Kirsten and Kallis looked settled until Kirsten went to cut Cork and steered the ball to third slip instead. Cullinan should have been stumped off Croft, but Stewart failed to gather the ball, and Cullinan went on to add 81 with Kallis, who fell to a Cork out-swinger. Cronje was taken bat and pad, and Fraser got just reward for his endeavours when he bowled Cullinan off an inside edge.

England's main hope lay in being able to force South Africa to follow on, but that hope was denied them, although two wickets in the first half hour of the fourth day made the dream seem possible. Pollock hit Fraser for four and was caught at long leg when he tried to repeat the shot, and Boucher was caught behind without scoring. South Africa were 224 for seven, and 39 runs were still needed to save the follow-on, but Klusener coming in at number nine was an awesome sight. A shower interrupted play for 40 minutes, and, on the resumption, a vital spark appeared to have deserted England's cricket. Croft lost direction and concentration, and there were errors in the field. In 28.3 overs, Rhodes and Klusener added 104. Rhodes is ever joyful and enterprising, and he had batted with confidence, authority and charm at a difficult time. He deserved a century, but, in a rather wayward over, Fraser took his inside edge and had him caught behind. Rhodes faced 156 balls and hit a six and eight fours. Five balls later, with no addition to the score, Stewart took a tumbling catch to dismiss Klusener, who had hit 11 fours in his 90-ball knock. Cork wrapped up the innings to finish with five for 93, and England led by 119, a fine performance considering that they had had to operate without the bowling of Gough.

The one hope of victory now rested in England scoring quick runs and bowling out South Africa on the last day. There were 46 overs remaining of the fourth day, and England managed 170 before the eighth wicket fell in the last over of the day. Mike Atherton followed his first innings century with seven fours, and he and Thorpe hit 68 in 16 overs for the fourth wicket. Stewart had set the tone with 28 off 34 balls, and Ramprakash's 11 included a six and a four. The last day promised excitement with England having established a lead of 289 runs, but the last day never came. The Monday brought nothing but rain, and the match was drawn. Mike Procter declared Atherton Man of the Match, a worthy reward for one who had relinquished the captaincy after buffets of criticism and loss of form and who had reasserted himself with a splendid century when it it was most needed, 103 off 279 balls with 12 fours.

The end of a good innings. Mark Butcher sweeps at Adams but is caught by Kallis. (David Munden / Sportsline)

The end result may have been a disappointment for England, but they had shown from the start that they could face the rest of the series with confidence.

10 June
at Trent Bridge
South Africans 284 for 6 (S.M. Pollock 87, B.M. McMillan 62, J.H. Kallis 52)
Nottinghamshire 262 for 8 (U. Afzaal 74, P.R. Pollard 56, R.T. Robinson 50, P.L. Symcox 4 for 43)
South Africans won by 22 runs

Pollock and McMillan scored 109 in 15 overs for the fifth wicket as the tourists beat Nottinghamshire in a spirited 50-over game.

12, 13 and 14 June
at Arundel
Sussex 277 (W.G. Khan 50, S. Elworthy 4 for 71)
South Africans 96 for 0 (G. Kirsten 51 not out)
Match drawn

The second day of the match at Arundel was completely washed out, and only 43.3 overs were possible on the last day. Kirsten and Bacher scored 96 in 36 overs, but the South Africans were denied valuable practice by the inclement weather.

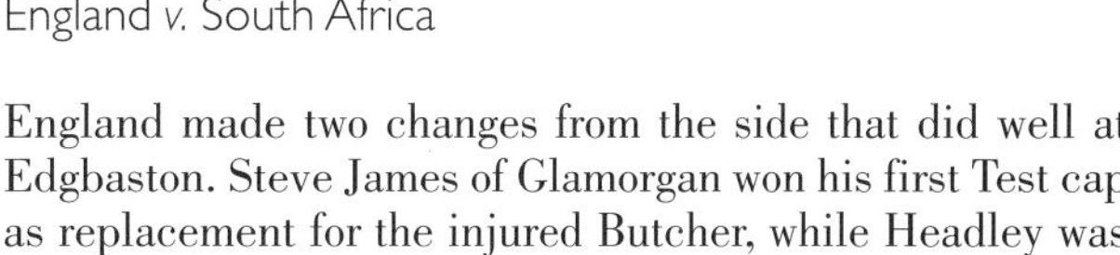

Second Test Match
England *v.* South Africa

England made two changes from the side that did well at Edgbaston. Steve James of Glamorgan won his first Test cap as replacement for the injured Butcher, while Headley was brought back in place of Gough, who was still troubled by his broken finger. South Africa brought in Bacher for Liebenberg.

Prince Philip opened the new Grand Stand, but play itself did not begin until 1.30pm and, a half an hour later, rain returned to bring a hold up for another hour-and-a-quarter, although one was tempted to feel that it could have restarted earlier. Players and umpires never seem in a hurry to restart. Stewart won the toss and was probably justified in the conditions to ask South Africa to bat first. Certainly, initial results vindicated his decision. In his second over, Cork dismissed Kirsten, who attempted to withdraw his bat when the ball lifted unexpectedly but succeeded only in diverting it into his stumps.

Operating from the Nursery End, Cork moved the ball appreciably and worked up a good pace. He twice beat Kallis before hitting his off stump to leave South Africa at 16 for two in the sixth over. Bacher was impressive. He drove sweetly through the covers and had hit four fours when he edged a ball of full length to Stewart, who took a good catch. Cullinan was also caught behind when he

First Cornhill Test Match – England v. South Africa
4, 5, 6, 7 and 8 June 1998 at Edgbaston, Birmingham

England

	First innings		Second innings	
M.A. Butcher	c Kallis, **b** Adams	**77**	lbw, **b** Pollock	**11**
M.A. Atherton	**c** Boucher, **b** Donald	**103**	**b** Klusener	**43**
A.J. Stewart * †	**c** Cullinan, **b** Klusener	**49**	(4) **b** Donald	**28**
N. Hussain	lbw, **b** Adams	**35**	(3) lbw, **b** Donald	**0**
G.P. Thorpe	**b** Pollock	**10**	**b** Klusener	**43**
M.R. Ramprakash	**b** Donald	**49**	**c** Kallis, **b** Adams	**11**
M.A. Ealham	**b** Adams	**5**	**c** Pollock, **b** Klusener	**7**
D.G. Cork	**c** Pollock, **b** Donald	**36**	**st** Boucher, **b** Adams	**2**
R.D.B. Croft	**c** Boucher, **b** Donald	**19**	not out	**1**
D. Gough	not out	**16**		
A.R.C. Fraser	**c** Cronje, **b** Pollock	**9**		
	b **18**, lb **26**, w **8**, nb **2**	**54**	b **10**, lb **6**, w **8**	**24**
		462	(for 8 wickets)	**170**

	O	M	R	W	O	M	R	W
Donald	35	9	95	**4**	10	1	48	**2**
Pollock	42	12	92	**2**	12	2	43	**1**
Klusener	31	7	74	**1**	11	4	27	**3**
Cronje	11	3	28	**–**				
Adams	42	10	83	**3**	12.1	3	36	**2**
Kallis	20	7	46	**–**				

Fall of Wickets
1–**179**, 2–**249**, 3–**309**, 4–**309**, 5–**329**, 6–**356**, 7–**411**, 8–**430**, 9–**437**
1–**24**, 2–**31**, 3–**80**, 4–**148**, 5–**153**, 6–**167**, 7–**167**, 8–**170**

South Africa

	First Innings	
G. Kirsten	**c** Butcher, **b** Cork	**12**
G.F.J. Liebenberg	**c** sub (Spendlove), **b** Cork	**3**
J.H. Kallis	**c** Stewart, **b** Cork	**61**
D.J. Cullinan	**b** Fraser	**78**
W.J. Cronje *	**c** sub (Spendlove), **b** Cork	**1**
J.N. Rhodes	**c** Stewart, **b** Fraser	**95**
S.M. Pollock	**c** Croft, **b** Fraser	**16**
M.V. Boucher †	**c** Stewart, **b** Fraser	**0**
L. Klusener	**c** Stewart, **b** Ealham	**57**
A.A. Donald	**c** and **b** Cork	**7**
P.R. Adams	not out	**6**
	lb **5**, nb **2**	**7**
		343

	O	M	R	W
Fraser	34	6	103	**4**
Cork	32.3	7	93	**5**
Ealham	23	8	55	**1**
Croft	27	3	85	**–**
Butcher	1	–	2	**–**

Fall of Wickets
1–**6**, 2–**38**, 3–**119**, 4–**125**, 5–**191**, 6–**211**, 7–**224**, 8–**328**, 9–**328**

Umpires: D.R. Shepherd & R.B. Tiffin

Match drawn

chased an out-swinger, and South Africa were 46 for four in 16 overs, all four wickets to Cork at a personal cost of 25 runs. It was a superb performance by the Derbyshire skipper. The conditions were in his favour, but he exploited them eagerly and sensibly.

Cronje and Rhodes took the score to 52 from 19 overs at tea. In the final session of the day, punctuated by a break for bad light, the pair launched a counter attack that brought their side right back into the game. In 15 overs, they scored 83 runs. Rhodes raced to 47 off 54 balls with a six and seven fours, and Cronje, who ended the day on 38, was equally aggressive. Headley and Ealham bowled badly, and the pressure was relaxed, but Rhodes and Cronje never profaned the art of batting. They played a series of glorious strokes and set the game alight.

For South Africa, the game burned even more brightly on the second day. In 29 overs before lunch, Cronje and Rhodes scored 89 runs. Rhodes moved to his fifty early in the day when he hit Cork to long-on for three; a magnificent drive off the same bowler through extra cover to the Mound Stand boundary gave Cronje his fifty. Headley was brought on at the Nursery End, and Rhodes immediately drove him straight for four. The running between the wickets was exemplary, and the partnership was shot with eagerness.

Rhodes has matured into a stronger, more discretionary batsman. At the crease he is balanced where once he paced and pounded fretfully, and his bat comes down straighter than of yore. Above all, he remains a joyful cricketer. At lunch, he was on 91; Cronje had 77.

Six runs into the afternoon, Cronje drove Ealham into the hands of extra cover. He had faced 169 balls and hit 11 fours, and his partnership with Rhodes was worth 184, a South African fifth wicket record against any country. Rhodes reached his century off 166 balls when he drove Ealham through mid-on for three, but the cricket moved into a somnolent period.

It brightened when England took a second new ball and Cork had Pollock well caught at slip off a delivery that rose sharply. Three overs later, Rhodes's wonderful innings came to an end when the persevering Fraser found an inside edge and had him caught behind. He had faced 200 balls, hit a six and 14 fours and been at the crease for 233 minutes. When he came in South Africa were 46 for four; when he was out they were 283 for seven.

The problem that confronted England was that South Africa had no tail. To have a batsman of the quality of Klusener at number nine is riches indeed, and he showed his worth in a stand of 57 in 15 overs with Boucher. Klusener was positive, aggressive and controlled. He hit seven fours in making 34 off 45 balls before playing over the top of a ball from Headley, who then had Boucher caught behind. Cork ended the innings with his sixth wicket.

The England innings began with as many traumas as South Africa had suffered at the start. The last ball of the fourth over saw Pollock have Atherton caught in the gully, and two balls later James was spectacularly caught down the leg side by the diving Boucher. Donald bowled a very

Mark Ealham is run out.
(Adrian Murrell / Allsport)

fast delivery, and the ball brushed James's glove. The Glamorgan opener was unlucky, for he had clipped Pollock for two fours off his legs and looked sound. Stewart hit two fours before being adjudged leg before to Pollock, and England closed on 40 for three. Twenty-four hours can be a long time in cricket.

Saturday was disaster day for England. Hussain had added five to his overnight score when Donald speared a ball at him that took the edge of his bat on its way to Boucher. Two overs later, Donald accounted for night-watchman Headley in the same manner. Thorpe and Ramprakash were faced by Pollock and Donald at their fastest, and both moved the ball menacingly. Thorpe was twice fortunate to escape the lifting of the umpire's finger. Most umpires would have adjudged him leg before first ball to Pollock, and he later clearly gloved a bouncer to the wicket-keeper. Paradoxically, he fell to Kallis rather than Donald or Pollock, being stunningly caught at short-leg by Bacher, who, sadly, was to disappear from the match and the tour with injury. South Africa were to miss him badly.

Ramprakash was becalmed, offering one scoring stroke in his first 80 minutes at the crease, and Ealham was insanely run out. The England fielding had not been bad, but the South African fielding was in a different class for its commitment and verve. England lunched at 94 for seven.

Eight balls after the interval, Ramprakash was given out, caught behind off a ball that seemed to brush his elbow. His obvious disagreement with the umpire's decision was to bring a fine from the match referee, but Stewart, who was to show equal disenchantment in the second innings, was to escape unpunished. Pollock and Donald quickly claimed the last two wickets. England were all out at six minutes past two and were asked to follow on. They lost James in the fourth over when he edged an outswinger to second slip, but Atherton and Hussain took the score to 47 at tea without further mishap. With the close just over four overs away, Atherton lost concentration and swung a ball from outside off stump to mid-wicket where Kallis took the catch.

Headley found himself batting for the second time in the day, and three runs later came the end of play.

Two overs and one run into the fourth day, Headley was caught bat and pad, but Hussain and Stewart batted through to lunch with sound technique and assurance to take the score to 200. They survived the second new ball and plundered runs from it greedily. The pace and fire of Donald and Pollock, it seemed, had been defied. It was the gentler, but equally subtle pace of Kallis and Klusener that was to be England's undoing as six wickets went down for six runs.

As we have indicated, Stewart showed that he did not think he had touched the ball when he drove at Kallis's away swinger. The bowler, the fielders and, significantly, umpire Sharp thought he had. Thorpe was leg before to the last ball of Kallis's next over, and Hussain was out the first ball of the next over, bowled by Klusener. Hussain hit 17 fours and faced 294 balls in an innings of great character, but once again a century by this determined batsman failed to save England from defeat. Ramprakash was yorked fourth ball, and Cork gave Boucher his seventh catch of the game. Ealham, totally out of his depth at this level, was bowled between bat and pad, but Fraser and Croft had a spirited last wicket stand of 31 in 46 minutes, which at least saved England from the indignity of an innings defeat.

It took South Africa seven balls in which to win the match, which ended shortly after 4.30pm. Kirsten and Cullinan managed three fours on the way to victory. Jonty Rhodes was rightly named Man of the Match, but the South Africans had produced a superb team effort.

24, 25 and 26 June
at Cambridge
South Africans 394 for 1 dec. (G. Kirsten 205 not out, J.H. Kallis 106 not out, G.F.J. Liebenberg 52) and 141 for 0 dec. (D.J. Cullinan 75 not out, G.F.J. Liebenberg 64 not out)

Ramprakash is bowled by Donald and defeat for England is close. (David Munden / Sportsline)

Second Cornhill Test Match – England v. South Africa

18, 19, 20 and 21 June 1998 at Lord's

South Africa

	First Innings		Second Innings	
A.M. Bacher	c Stewart, b Cork	22		
G. Kirsten	b Cork	4	(1) not out	9
J.H. Kallis	b Cork	0		
D.J. Cullinan	c Stewart, b Cork	16	(2) not out	5
W.J. Cronje *	c Ramprakash, b Ealham	81		
J.N. Rhodes	c Stewart, b Fraser	117		
S.M. Pollock	c Hussain, b Cork	14		
M.V. Boucher †	c Stewart, b Headley	35		
L. Klusener	b Headley	34		
A.A. Donald	not out	7		
P.R. Adams	c Stewart, b Cork	3		
	b 1, lb 20, nb 6	27	nb 1	1
		360	(for no wicket)	15

	O	M	R	W	O	M	R	W
Fraser	31	8	78	1	1	–	10	–
Cork	31.1	5	119	6	0.1	–	5	–
Headley	22	2	69	2				
Ealham	15	2	50	1				
Croft	9	3	23	–				

Fall of Wickets
1–**8**, 2–**16**, 3–**43**, 4–**46**, 5–**230**, 6–**273**, 7–**283**, 8–**340**, 9–**353**

England

	First Innings		Second Innings	
S.P. James	c Boucher, b Donald	10	(2) c Kallis, b Pollock	0
M.A. Atherton	c Kirsten, b Pollock	0	(1) c Kallis, b Adams	44
N. Hussain	c Boucher, b Donald	15	lbw, b Klusener	105
A.J. Stewart * †	lbw, b Pollock	14	(5) c Boucher, b Kallis	56
D.W. Headley	c Boucher, b Donald	2	(4) c Cronje, b Adams	1
G.P. Thorpe	c Bacher, b Kallis	10	lbw, b Kallis	0
M.R. Ramprakash	c Boucher, b Donald	12	b Klusener	0
M.A. Ealham	run out	8	b Kallis	4
D.G. Cork	c Klusener, b Pollock	12	c Boucher, b Kallis	2
R.D.B. Croft	not out	6	not out	16
A.R.C. Fraser	c Boucher, b Donald	1	c Pollock, b Adams	17
	b 8, lb 10, nb 2	20	b 1, lb 6, w 5, nb 7	19
		110		264

	O	M	R	W	O	M	R	W
Donald	15.3	5	32	5	24	6	82	–
Pollock	18	5	42	3	27	16	29	1
Klusener	8	5	10	–	23	5	54	2
Kallis	5	3	8	1	19	9	24	4
Adams					23	7	62	3
Cronje					4	2	6	–

Fall of Wickets
1–**15**, 2–**15**, 3–**40**, 4–**48**, 5–**49**, 6–**64**, 7–**74**, 8–**97**, 9–**109**
1–**8**, 2–**102**, 3–**106**, 4–**222**, 5–**224**, 6–**224**, 7–**225**, 8–**228**, 9–**233**

Umpires: G. Sharp & D.B. Hair

South Africa won by 10 wickets

British Universities 199 (A. Singh 64, P.L. Symcox 4 for 28) and 109 for 3
Match drawn

The opening day saw the South Africans score at just under four runs an over with Kirsten and Liebenberg putting on 137 for the first wicket, and Kirsten and Kallis sharing an unbroken stand of 257 for the second wicket. The tourists did not enforce the follow-on after bowling out the students for 199, and the last day was interrupted by rain. Sadly, Ed Smith broke the index finger of his right hand and the injury was to keep him out of the Varsity match.

28 June
at Northampton
South Africans 275 for 3 (L. Klusener 142 not out, W.J. Cronje 77 not out)
Northamptonshire 189 for 8 (R.J. Warren 81)
South Africans won on faster scoring rate

Lance Klusener hit 142 off 132 balls and shared a partnership of 185 in 26 overs with Hansie Cronje in a match that was reduced to 45 overs.

Third Test Match

England v. South Africa

South Africa were forced to make a significant change on the eve of the Old Trafford Test when Pollock reported unfit and was replaced by Ntini. With Butcher still injured, England decided to call upon Knight rather than James, while Giles made his Test debut in place of Ealham. His finger mended, Gough returned in place of Headley, and, with Bacher out of the tour with injury, Liebenberg returned to the South African side to open with Kirsten. Cronje won the toss and chose to bat first on a pitch that was as grassless as it was to prove blameless. It was slow, but perhaps not as slow as the South African scoring on the opening day, when 237 runs came from 97 overs for the loss of Liebenberg, who was beaten by a ball of full length in the ninth over. He seemed to play inside the line, and the ball hit his off stump.

For the remaining 88 overs, South Africa were in complete command. They ground their way to 59 from 31 overs by lunch, but the afternoon brought 93 runs, and the final session 85. Jacques Kallis gave more evidence that he is a batsman of real quality. He combines a compact defence with an eagerness to score. He has a wide range of shots at his command, and his temperament cannot be faulted. He is but 22 years old, and here is a player who will be among the rulers of world cricket in the decade ahead. He finished the day with 117 graceful runs to his credit, with Gary Kirsten having played the anchor role to reach 98 in six hours at the crease.

In the ninth over of the second day, Gough knocked back Kallis's off stump with an outswinger of perfect length. Kallis had faced 266 balls and hit 16 fours, and his 238-run partnership with Kirsten was a second wicket record for South Africa against England. There was no respite for England as Cullinan, a fluent stroke-maker, now joined Kirsten, who was not at his best but already had a century to his credit and was moving relentlessly onward. By lunch, he had 127, Cullinan had 16, and South Africa had posted 300. Between lunch and tea, 93 runs were scored, and there was no hint of another wicket.

Kirsten reached his highest Test score and his second double century in successive first-class matches before, in the 170th over of the innings, attempting to cut at Fraser, he was caught behind. He had faced 525 balls and hit a six and 24 fours. His innings had lasted 10 hours 53 minutes and was the longest in Test matches between England and South Africa. It had put South Africa in an impregnable position.

Cullinan chopped a ball onto his stumps to give Giles his first Test wicket, but Cronje and Rhodes raised the tempo of the innings late in the day, and South Africa closed on 487 for four, Cronje 27, Rhodes 12.

Rhodes mistimed a drive and was caught at mid-off without adding to his overnight score. Klkusener made 17 off 21 balls, and, with 65 runs coming in the hour, Cronje declared at midday.

The technical frailties of Knight were soon exposed. He hit a boundary before gloving a ball to the wicket-keeper in the seventh over. England were 34 for one at lunch, and, two overs after the interval, they were 34 for two when

Gary Kirsten sweeps a ball to the boundary during his double century. Alec Stewart and Nasser Hussain, England captain and vice-captain, look on.
(David Munden / Sportsline)

Hussain received a ferocious lifting delivery from which he attempted to withdraw his bat only for the ball to flick his glove on its way to the keeper. These disasters had seemed predictable, but Stewart and Atherton offered hope in a stand that lasted 26 overs. Then, with tea some quarter of an hour away, Atherton squirted a ball from Ntini to Boucher who took a splendid diving catch.

Five overs after the break, Stewart offered no shot to a ball from Kallis that clipped his off stump. This was the start of one of those inevitable declines that haunt English cricket. Cork appeared instead of Thorpe, who had a back problem. The Derbyshire captain blocked solidly for 45 minutes before prodding forward to Adams and edging the ball to silly point. Croft looked more purposeful than he was, being grotesquely bowled when he hoiked across the line at Ntini. Thorpe was in some discomfort, and, lacking mobility, he was struck on the back foot and most palpably leg before. Ramprakash's two-and-a-quarter-hour innings ended when, in the penultimate over of the day, he swept rashly at Adams and was adjudged caught behind. The close came with England on 162 for eight, and a sparse crowd booing in displeasure.

The last two wickets fell within 35 minutes on the fourth morning, and England were soon batting again. In the fifth over, Knight played a dreadful shot at a lifting outswinger from Donald and was caught behind. Hussain followed seven overs later, comprehensively beaten by a fine ball from Kallis that straightened and hit the off stump. Few believed that the game would go into a fifth day, but Atherton and Stewart fought a magnificent rearguard action. At lunch, the score was a grim 31 for two from 21 overs; by tea, it was 152 from 52 overs. The second new ball was taken shortly before the close, but it brought South Africa no immediate success, and England closed on 211 for two, Atherton 81, Stewart 114.

Surrendering the captaincy had brought Atherton a new lease of cricketing life. His application and concentration had been sharpened. His body language no longer hinted at frustration and resignation to the inevitable. None would say that Stewart is a great tactician. His constant praise of mediocre bowling from behind the stumps is as tedious as it is annoying, but his fighting spirit and determination are undeniable, and England are never beaten as long as he is at the crease. He believes that the best form of defence is attack, and the opposition are never able to relax. By the end of the fourth day, he had already hammered 16 fours, and he and Atherton had brought England more than a ray of hope.

In fairness, South Africa were greatly handicapped. Not only were they without Pollock, but Kluesner sustained a foot injury, which allowed him to bowl only three overs in the innings (none of them on the last day) and which ended his participation in the series. This was a grievous loss to the tourists.

Atherton had batted for six-and-a-quarter hours and faced 280 balls when he hooked Kallis to long leg where, on his 21st birthday, Ntini took a good catch. He also bowled with pace and enthusiasm, and he looks to be an excellent prospect for the future. Ramprakash's batting approach differs greatly between Test and county cricket, and he settled solidly to give stout support to Stewart. They were together at lunch with the score on 278, and it was nine overs into the afternoon before they were separated. Stewart, having batted for seven hours, hooked a ball that pitched outside the off stump into the hands of deep square-leg. He had faced 317 balls and hit 24 fours. Stewart's was a mighty innings, but England still trailed by 76 runs, and there was much left to be done.

Thorpe hobbled to the wicket with a runner, but his stumps were shattered third ball by an inswinging yorker. Cork prodded forward to Adams and played on. In three overs, England had lost three wickets and, at 296 for six, were still 73 runs away from an innings defeat.

Ramprakash and Croft took the score to 323 at tea, but two balls after the break Ramprakash was leg before to Donald. Four overs later, Giles steered Donald low to slip. The South African fast bowler, not fully fit, was putting in a magnificent effort, but Croft and Gough dealt with him sturdily. Croft had not inspired confidence as a Test batsman, and he began uncertainly here, but he survived. Gough has inevitable moments of rashness as a batsmen, but he stayed for a vital 78 minutes, and there were just 20 minutes remaining when he was taken at short-leg off Donald. All the pressure was now on Croft and the redoubtable Fraser. They had to negotiate 31 balls. Fraser had 13 to contend with, including the final over, bowled by Donald. The last ball brought a loud appeal for leg before, but umpire Cowie's finger stayed down, and England had saved the game. Wicketless in the series, Croft had batted for more than three hours to be the last bastion upon which England's resistance was founded. Kallis was named Man of the Match, but this was a game of many heroes.

8 July

at Amsterdam

South Africans 248 for 6 (G. Kirsten 123 not out, M.V. Boucher 52)

Holland 165

South Africans won by 83 runs

10 July

at Downpatrick

South Africans 333 for 9 (S.M. Pollock 116 not out, M.V. Boucher 79, G. Cooke 4 for 60)

Ireland 72 for 2

Match abandoned

at Dublin (Castle Avenue)

South Africans 289 for 5 (D.J. Cullinan 117 not out, W.J. Cronje 74)

Ireland 226 for 9 (A.R. Dunlop 101 not out)

South Africans won by 63 runs

The South Africans broke their tour of England with visits to Amsterdam and Ireland. In Holland, the home side were bowled out in the last over, while the first game in Ireland was ruined by rain. In Dublin, Cullinan hit 117 off 92 balls. His innings included four sixes and nine fours. Ireland were 44 for five in reply, but skipper Dunlop made a spirited century off 102 balls.

14, 15 and 16 July
at Riverside
South Africans 362 for 3 dec. (D.J. Cullinan 200 not out, G.F.J. Liebenberg 85) and 210 for 6 dec. (G.F.J. Liebenberg 104 not out)
Durham 286 (P.L. Symcox 5 for 60) and 107 for 4
Match drawn

18, 19 and 20 July
at Derby
Derbyshire 337 (M.J. Slater 185) and 337 for 4 (M.R. May 101, M.E. Cassar 91 not out, M.J. Slater 63)
South Africans 453 for 9 dec. (W.J. Cronje 195, D.J. Cullinan 80, T.M. Smith 5 for 88)
Match drawn

A return to England saw the South Africans play two three-day Vodaphone Challenge Matches before the fourth Test match at Trent Bridge. In the first game, Daryll Cullinan made an unbeaten 200 off 274 balls. It was the first double century hit on the Riverside ground, and it was Cullinan's first first-class three-figured innings of the tour. Pat Symcox bowled his off-spinners well enough to suggest he should earn a place in the Test side, and Liebenberg hit his first century of the tour when the tourists batted a second time. The match, inevitably, was drawn. Klusener flew back to South Africa for medical treatment. His part in the tour was over.

A hero of the last day. Robert Croft drives a ball past substitute fielder Brian McMillan. Mark Boucher is the wicket-keeper. Croft remained undefeated on 37 and played a major part in England escaping from a defeat that had looked certain.
(David Munden / Sportsline)

At Derby, Michael Slater, the Australian opening batsman, hit his first first-class century for the county. There was also cheer for Derbyshire in the continuing excellent form of the young seamer Trevor Smith, who captured five wickets, but the second day, on which 421 runs were scored, was dominated by Hansie Cronje, who made his highest score for the South African touring side. He and Cullinan added 138 in 19 overs for the fourth wicket. The match ended in a draw when Michael May earned a rugged century off 200 balls. Matt Cassar provided further frustration for the tourists.

Fourth Test Match

England v. South Africa

The Trent Bridge Test match was preceded by the opening of the new Grand Stand at the Radcliffe Road end of the ground. This magnificent building is the most imaginative and flexible to be seen on a cricket ground in England. It offers seating, hospitality facilities, a splendid press box that can be converted into a lecture theatre, a gymnasium, a sports injury clinic, dining areas, a high quality indoor cricket school and much else. Hospitality facilities can be easily and quickly converted into self-contained flats to be used as residential accommodation for those on coaching courses. All ages are catered for. While others dream of the millenium, Nottinghamshire County Cricket Club have moved well into the next century with this all purpose building. One can only hope that others will follow their lead.

The opening of the new centre provided an excellent prelude to the fourth Test. Butcher returned for England, and Hick came in for Thorpe, whose back problem made it unlikely that he would play again during the season. Croft had fought a wonderful rearguard action with the bat at Old Trafford, but he failed to take wickets, his principal job, and he was replaced by Salisbury. There was an interesting and surprising selection in Andy Flintoff, the burly young Lancashire player, who had become noted for some very hard hitting in recent weeks. Mullally, the Leicestershire left-arm pace bowler, was in the squad, and it was believed that he would replace Fraser, but the Middlesex man retained his place.

South Africa welcomed the return of Pollock, but, with Klusener now facing an operation back in the Republic and Ntini injured, a first Test cap was given to Elworthy, who had joined the party as a replacement following the injuries to Telemachus, Bacher and Klusener. Alec Stewart won the toss and surprised all by asking South Africa to bat first on a pitch which had a hint of green. There was some low cloud, and, after 13 balls, play was interrupted for 20 minutes by a shower.

Scoring was not brisk, but Kirsten straight drove Cork for four and the tempo was increasing when Liebenberg was caught behind in the ninth over. He had struck one impressive four, but he drove inside a straight ball of full

Third Cornhill Test Match – England v. South Africa

2, 3, 4, 5 and 6 July 1998 at Old Trafford, Manchester

South Africa

	First Innings	
G. Kirsten	**c** Stewart, **b** Fraser	**210**
G.F.J. Liebenberg	**b** Gough	**16**
J.H. Kallis	**b** Gough	**132**
D.J. Cullinan	**b** Giles	**75**
W.J. Cronje *	not out	**69**
J.N. Rhodes	**c** Cork, **b** Gough	**12**
L. Klusener	not out	**17**
M.V. Boucher †		
A.A. Donald		
P.R. Adams		
M. Ntini		
	b **4**, lb **10**, w **1**, nb **6**	**21**
	(for 5 wickets, dec.)	**552**

	O	M	R	W
Gough	37	5	116	**3**
Cork	35.5	7	109	**–**
Fraser	35	11	87	**1**
Croft	51	14	103	**–**
Giles	36	7	106	**1**
Ramprakash	5	–	17	**–**

Fall of Wickets
1–**25**, 2–**263**, 3–**439**, 4–**457**, 5–**490**

England

	First Innings		Second Innings	
N.V. Knight	**c** Boucher, **b** Donald	**11**	**c** Boucher, **b** Donald	**1**
M.A. Atherton	**c** Boucher, **b** Ntini	**41**	**c** Ntini, **b** Kallis	**89**
N. Hussain	**c** Boucher, **b** Donald	**4**	**b** Kallis	**5**
A.J. Stewart * †	**b** Kallis	**40**	**c** Klusener, **b** Donald	**164**
M.R. Ramprakash	**c** Boucher, **b** Adams	**30**	lbw, **b** Donald	**34**
D.G. Cork	**c** Cronje, **b** Adams	**6**	(7) **b** Adams	**1**
R.D.B. Croft	**b** Ntini	**11**	(8) not out	**37**
G.P. Thorpe	lbw, **b** Adams	**0**	(6) **b** Donald	**0**
A.F. Giles	not out	**16**	**c** sub (McMillan), **b** Donald	**1**
D. Gough	**c** Donald, **b** Adams	**6**	**c** Kirsten, **b** Donald	**12**
A.R.C. Fraser	lbw, **b** Kallis	**0**	not out	**0**
	b **5**, lb **12**, nb **1**	**18**	b **20**, lb **2**, w **1**, nb **2**	**25**
		183	(for 9 wickets)	**369**

	O	M	R	W	O	M	R	W
Donald	13	3	28	**2**	40	14	88	**6**
Klusener	14	4	37	**–**	3	–	15	**–**
Ntini	16	7	28	**2**	29	11	67	**–**
Adams	31	10	63	**4**	51	22	90	**1**
Kallis	8.1	3	10	**2**	41	19	71	**2**
Cronje					6	3	15	**–**
Cullinan					1	–	1	**–**

Fall of Wickets
1–**26**, 2–**34**, 3–**94**, 4–**108**, 5–**136**, 6–**155**, 7–**156**, 8–**161**, 9–**179**
1–**4**, 2–**11**, 3–**237**, 4–**293**, 5–**293**, 6–**296**, 7–**323**, 8–**329**, 9–**367**

Umpires: P. Willey & D.B. Cowie

Match drawn

length and was again out cheaply. Two overs later, Kirsten played on yet again, and, with South Africa on 26 for two, Stewart's gamble looked justified.

Flintoff was rather surprisingly brought into the attack for a spell of five overs of medium pace, and, in all, he was to be asked to bowl more for England than he had done for Lancashire all season. Cullinan looked in fine form, and, at lunch, South Africa were 67 for two from 25 overs. Immediately after lunch, Cullinan flicked a ball from Fraser into the hands of square-leg. It was a careless shot

Sir Garfield Sobers open the magnificent new stand at Trent Bridge.
(Clive Mason / Allsport)

and typical of the momentary lapses in concentration that prevent Cullinan from becoming a great batsman.

The English fielding was moderate rather than inspiring, but ten of the side were wearing their England caps, and there was an air of commitment. Kallis played two shots of exceptional quality through mid-wicket, but he became Flintoff's first victim in Test cricket, and only the seventh of the season, when he got an inside edge onto his pad and through to the keeper. Flintoff has a wonderful physique and has come up through the ranks of representative cricket to the Test side, but he is essentially an attacking batsman rather than an all-rounder.

When Kallis was out Cronje was on 42. He had come to the wicket bristling with purpose and he blasted the hapless Salisbury from the attack. He advanced down the pitch and drove the leg-spinner straight, and he pulled him over mid-wicket for six. This was vintage batting from the South African captain. At tea, Cronje had 51 to his credit, and South Africa had seemingly put uncertainties behind them and were 179 for four from 53 overs. The outfield was not quick, and this represented a very good rate of scoring.

The flow of runs dried up a little in the period just after tea, and they were set back by a dreadful decision that accounted for Rhodes. He had made 24 off 44 balls when Fraser cut the ball back at him and hit the top of his pad as he moved forward. Umpire Kitchen gave him out leg before. If Rhodes was aggrieved, he had worse to come. Pollock was quickly in full flow, driving stylishly off front and back foot. In 23 overs, he and Cronje put on 96 runs, and one

Hansie Cronje pulls Ian Salisbury over mid-wicket for six during his innings of 126.
(Clive Mason / Allsport)

shuddered to think what the score would have been had the outfield been quicker.

In the 79th over, Cronje drove Butcher through extra cover for his 13th four to reach his sixth hundred in his 50th Test. His century came off 169 balls and included a six as well as the 13 fours. It was a delightful innings, aggressive innings, full of elegant strokes and positive in every aspect. Pollock, who hit six fours, fell to the second new ball when a delivery from Fraser bounced surprisingly and took his glove. Boucher offered no shot to a ball from Fraser which hit his back leg, and South Africa closed on 302 for seven; Cronje 113.

South Africa were all out an hour-and-a-quarter into the second day, but they scored at a run a minute. Cronje never quite found the fluency of the previous day and, having added 13 to his overnight score, he steered Fraser to Hick at second slip. Cronje was at the crease for 13 minutes under five hours and hit a six and 16 fours. He showed that it is capable to play a highly responsible innings and to offer glorious entertainment at the same time.

In seven overs following Cronje's dismissal, Elworthy and Donald plundered 49 runs. Steve Elworthy's batting was a revelation. He might have been caught by Fraser off Cork, but he played a dynamic innings, hitting seven fours in making 48 off 52 balls before pulling Gough into the hands of square-leg. Adams flashed at Gough and was taken at second slip, and South Africa were out for 374.

England might well have lost a wicket in the opening over when Butcher started for a wild run, but they reached lunch unscathed, though not without some scares, with 28 from nine overs, Atherton having survived a united appeal for a catch behind off Pollock. The post-lunch period was a somnolent affair as England attempted to consolidate, and by tea England were 105 without loss. It was nine overs into the evening session before South Africa made the break-through. Atherton cut at a ball from Donald and Boucher took another spectacular catch in front of first slip. Eight balls later, Donald, bowling round the wicket, straightened a ball sufficiently to have Butcher leg before. Both Stewart and Hussain looked assured, but both fell before the close. They had batted positively before Stewart was caught high at second slip. Elworthy captured his first Test wicket when he trapped Hussain, who pushed forward and played outside the line. In an almost identical situation in the second innings, the Essex batsman was to be given 'not out'. England closed on 202 for four.

Night-watchman Salisbury did well. He negotiated the new ball and outscored his partner Ramprakash before being bowled between bat and pad for 23. Six overs, ten runs later, Hick joined him back in the pavilion. He edged a four, survived a close appeal for leg before and then, pulling at Donald, he bottom edged the ball into his stumps. Flintoff had a testing time before lunch, but he played positively after the interval, driving Kallis through the covers, hitting Donald straight and slashing a boundary over gully. He was out when he chased a wide ball and edged to Boucher. Cork and Gough suffered similar fates, and while Boucher is not, as yet, a tidy wicket-keeper, he is remarkably adept and seems capable of catching anything within reach of his dive. Ramprakash had looked unable to take command of the situation, but in the closing stages of the innings he at last began to play his shots before Fraser was leg before to Pollock.

Liebenberg failed once more to show that he is of Test standard, missing a straight ball in the first over of South Africa's second innings. Kallis was next to leave when umpire Kitchen believed him to have edged Cork's away swinger to Stewart, and, next over, Kirsten was given out leg before to Fraser after umpire Dunne had deliberated at considerable length. South Africa were 21 for three, but Cullinan and Cronje met the crisis with a fine array of strokes as Gough and Cork, in particularly, erred in direction. Salisbury had the luxury of bowling three overs at the end of the day and claimed two maidens as South Africa settled for 92 for three.

The partnership between Cullinan and Cronje was extended by only another 27 runs on the fourth morning before Cullinan fell in exactly the same lazy manner that

Mark Butcher, aggressive and determined in his fine innings of 75.
(Adrian Murrell / Allsport)

had brought his downfall in the first innings. Two overs later came one of the decisions which, arguably, turned the game in England's favour. A ball from Cork passed down the leg side and brushed Rhodes's back pad. Although the bat was nowhere near the ball, there was an appeal and umpire Kitchen gave Rhodes out. It was a most unfortunate occurrence. Mr Kitchen had entered the match in some tension, upset by excessive appealing and by the lack of sportsmanship he was witnessing. His gesture and body language when he indicated that Rhodes should leave the crease suggested that he was angered by the batsman's reluctance to walk. Rhodes himself exchanged words with Stewart. Pollock was soon out, and although Cronje and Boucher added 53, the heart appeared to have gone from the South African innings, and they were all out for 208. Angus Fraser took five wickets for the second time in the match to earn figures of 10 for 122, a just reward for bowling of consistent accuracy and wisdom.

England had a day and a half in which to make 247 to win. Disaster almost struck in the first over when Atherton played Donald into the covers and suddenly saw Butcher approaching fast. He ran and dived for the line, but had Rhodes's throw hit the stumps, he would have been out. The opening partnership lasted until the 18th over when Butcher edged a fine delivery from Pollock to Boucher, and then came the next unfortunate event. Atherton had reached 27 when a ball from Donald took his glove on its way to Boucher. The whole of the South African side appealed in triumph, but Atherton stood his ground, and umpire Dunne did not raise his finger. Unlike the umpire, we have the advantage of television replays, but even to the naked eye this looked a very bad decision. The South Africans were incensed, and Donald launched a ferocious attack on Atherton with the ball which was punctuated by some verbal

The moment that changed the game. Donald eagerly claims the wicket of Mike Atherton caught behind, but empire Dunne rules not out.
(Laurence Griffiths / Allsport)

Fourth Cornhill Test Match – England v. South Africa

23, 24, 25, 26 and 27 July 1998 at Trent Bridge, Nottingham

South Africa

	First Innings		Second Innings	
G. Kirsten	**b** Gough	**7**	lbw, **b** Fraser	**6**
G.F.J. Liebenberg	**c** Stewart, **b** Gough	**13**	lbw, **b** Gough	**0**
J.H. Kallis	**c** Stewart, **b** Flintoff	**47**	**c** Stewart, **b** Cork	**11**
D.J. Cullinan	**c** Ramprakash, **b** Fraser	**30**	**c** Ramprakash, **b** Fraser	**56**
W.J. Cronje *	**c** Hick, **b** Fraser	**126**	**c** Stewart, **b** Cork	**67**
J.N. Rhodes	lbw, **b** Fraser	**24**	**c** Stewart, **b** Cork	**2**
S.M. Pollock	**c** Stewart, **b** Fraser	**50**	**c** Stewart, **b** Cork	**7**
M.V. Boucher †	lbw, **b** Fraser	**4**	**c** Hussain, **b** Fraser	**35**
S. Elworthy	**c** Ramprakash, **b** Gough	**48**	lbw, **b** Fraser	**10**
A.A. Donald	not out	**4**	not out	**7**
P.R. Adams	**c** Hick, **b** Gough	**0**	**c** Stewart, **b** Fraser	**1**
	b **9**, lb **3**, nb **9**	**21**	b **1**, lb **4**, w **1**	**6**
		374		**208**

	O	M	R	W	O	M	R	W
Gough	30.2	4	116	**4**	16	4	56	**1**
Cork	17	2	65	**–**	20	4	60	**4**
Fraser	26	7	60	**5**	28.3	6	62	**5**
Flintoff	17	2	52	**1**	6	1	16	**–**
Salisbury	9	1	57	**–**	5	2	9	**–**
Butcher	4	1	12	**–**				

Fall of Wickets
1–**21**, 2–**26**, 3–**68**, 4–**147**, 5–**196**, 6–**292**, 7–**302**, 8–**325**, 9–**374**
1–**3**, 2–**17**, 3–**21**, 4–**119**, 5–**122**, 6–**136**, 7–**189**, 8–**193**, 9–**200**

England

	First Innings		Second Innings	
M.A. Butcher	lbw, **b** Donald	**75**	**c** Boucher, **b** Pollock	**22**
M.A. Atherton	**c** Boucher, **b** Donald	**58**	not out	**98**
N. Hussain	lbw, **b** Elworthy	**22**	**c** Kallis, **b** Donald	**58**
A.J. Stewart * †	**c** Kirsten, **b** Kallis	**19**	not out	**45**
M.R. Ramprakash	not out	**67**		
I.D.K. Salisbury	**b** Donald	**23**		
G.A. Hick	**b** Donald	**6**		
A. Flintoff	**c** Boucher, **b** Kallis	**17**		
D.G. Cork	**c** Boucher, **b** Pollock	**6**		
D. Gough	**c** Boucher, **b** Donald	**2**		
A.R.C. Fraser	lbw, **b** Pollock	**7**		
	b **7**, lb **13**, w **1**, nb **13**	**34**	b **2**, lb **11**, w **2**, nb **9**	**24**
		336	(for 2 wickets)	**247**

	O	M	R	W	O	M	R	W
Donald	33	8	109	**5**	23	8	56	**1**
Pollock	35.5	12	75	**2**	26	3	79	**1**
Elworthy	22	8	41	**1**	9	1	38	**–**
Kallis	28	9	60	**2**	13	5	26	**–**
Adams	9	2	31	**–**	12	4	23	**–**
Cronje					4	1	12	**–**

Fall of Wickets
1–**145**, 2–**150**, 3–**191**, 4–**199**, 5–**244**, 6–**254**, 7–**285**, 8–**302**, 9–**307**
1–**40**, 2–**192**

Umpires: M.J. Kitchen & R.S. Dunne

England won by 8 wickets

comments. Confidence in the umpiring was lost and appeals abounded. Hussain touched a fierce outswinger from Donald, and Boucher dived and dropped a catch for the first and only time in the series. Donald glared in disbelief, but before the start of the next over he ran from fine leg to console the wicket-keeper. This was a wonderful gesture from a great bowler. By then, South Africa must have known it was not their day. England closed on 108 for one.

By lunch on the last day, England were 190 and Atherton and Hussain were still together. Hussain was out shortly after the interval having added one run to his score, but Stewart came in and blasted away, hitting nine fours in making 45 off 34 balls before, after 356 minutes at the wicket, Atherton struck the 277th ball he received for the winning runs. He is technically proficient, temperamentally unflappable and a fighter without equal. It was sad that such a great victory was tarnished by some debatable umpiring.

Fraser was named Man of the Match.

29 July
at Chelmsford
South Africans 310 for 5 (G. Kirsten 141 not out, J.N. Rhodes 69, M.J.R. Rindel 50)
Essex 133 (P.L. Symcox 5 for 40)
South Africans won by 177 runs

31 July, 1 and 2 August
at Chelmsford
South Africans 406 for 5 dec. (D.J. Cullinan 157, G.F.J. Liebenberg 96) and 27 for 0
Essex 215
Match drawn

Much publicity was given to the fact that the South Africans were to play Essex at Chelmsford, but, in the event, the teams that Essex fielded for the two matches reduced the contests to farce. The tourists were far from happy, but, as ever under Cronje's leadership, they maintained their dignity and their good manners. Rindel, having arrived from the South Cheshire League to reinforce the side for the triangular tournament, made 50 off 53 balls in the 50-over game. Kirsten made 141 off 132 balls.

In the three-day game, Cullinan and Liebenberg scored 217 for the South Africans' second wicket in 200 minutes. It all mattered little. Essex fielded only four regular first team players, and one wonders if the Vodaphone Challenge has any meaning when it is treated in this way. The tourists had consistently been faced by weak sides as counties seemingly scorned the idea of winning £11,000 and entertaining the thousands who hire tents and make these festive occasions. The England selectors obviously have no liking for the Vodaphone Challenge, for David Graveney asked that Nasser Hussain should be rested even though he had appeared in only five first-class games for the county of which he is vice-captain.

Fifth Test Match

England *v.* South Africa

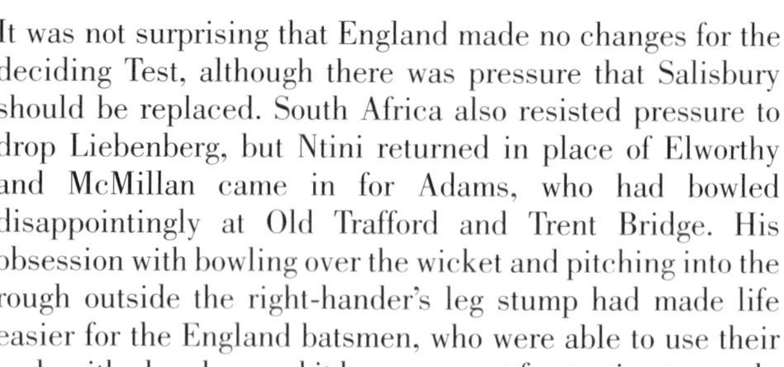

It was not surprising that England made no changes for the deciding Test, although there was pressure that Salisbury should be replaced. South Africa also resisted pressure to drop Liebenberg, but Ntini returned in place of Elworthy and McMillan came in for Adams, who had bowled disappointingly at Old Trafford and Trent Bridge. His obsession with bowling over the wicket and pitching into the rough outside the right-hander's leg stump had made life easier for the England batsmen, who were able to use their pads with abandon, and it became most frustrating to watch. Stewart won the toss and, rightly, elected to bat.

England began as well as could have been expected. The initial bursts of Pollock and Donald were repulsed, and it was Ntini who drew first blood. Atherton had looked settled, but Ntini found the outside edge of his bat in the 18th over and had him caught at second slip. At lunch, taken seven minutes early because of a shower, the score was 63 of which Butcher had made 37.

Play restarted at 2.10pm, and the afternoon session was dominated by Mark Butcher, who advanced his score by 56 runs out of the 84 registered during the period. He lost Hussain seven overs into the afternoon when Pollock gained extra bounce for the ball to touch the glove on its way to Boucher. Stewart hit Ntini for three fours in one over, but he was then forced onto the defensive. He attempted to drive at Donald, but the ball caught the edge and flew at throat height to second slip where Kallis took a splendid catch. Butcher remained confident and untroubled, and by tea, he was just seven runs short of his maiden Test century.

The century came shortly after tea and was thoroughly deserved. Butcher's approach had been mature and forceful, and he had provided the foundation for a big score by England. Ramprakash had joined Butcher in a useful partnership which was worth 81 when the Middlesex skipper got a bottom edge to a ball from Donald which went low to Boucher. There was a fraction of doubt that the ball may have gone to ground just before the keeper scooped it up, but this was not to be the last doubtful umpiring decision of the match. There was no doubt about Butcher's dismissal after 318 minutes at the crease. He edged a ball from Pollock into his stumps. He had faced 252 balls and hit 18 fours. In composure and application, in particular, it was a masterly innings, and England should have been ashamed at what followed. Flintoff appeared to be leg before wicket third ball, but the ball rebounded to short-leg, and it appears that he was adjudged caught. Hick floundered for nearly 40 minutes before slashing Ntini to cover, and when Salisbury fell to the same bowler four wickets had fallen for four runs, and most of Butcher's outstanding work had been undone. Gough and Fraser were both taken at slip, and England were all out for 230. Seven wickets had fallen in the evening session, and the last six had gone down for 34 runs. Ntini had taken four for 72, the best bowling performance of his brief Test career. Kirsten and Liebenberg scored nine runs in the last four overs of the day.

In the fourth over of the second day, Kirsten was given out leg before by umpire Javed Akhtar, although the ball appeared to pitch outside leg stump and to be going over the top of the stumps. Eight overs later there was no doubt when Liebenberg was caught at second slip to give Fraser his second wicket. Cullinan was in a hurry. He hit four fours as he raced to 27 off 28 balls, but the 29th he slashed at wildly and was caught behind. He has the habit of perpetually hinting at an impetuosity that wastes his talent. Four overs later it was lunch, and South Africa were 88 for three.

There seemed every likelihood of South Africa taking charge of the game in the early afternoon. Cronje was driving through the off side in majestic manner, and Kallis looked the very fine young player he is. They had added 37 when Kallis pulled hard to mid-wicket, where Ramprakash, diving to his right, took an astonishing one-handed catch. It should have lifted England, but quite the contrary happened as Hussain dropped a catch at slip, Ramprakash failed to hold on to a chance at square-leg immeasurably easier than the catch he had held and Hick put down a simple catch at slip. Cork was the bowler who suffered, but it was Fraser and Gough who righted the balance. Rhodes had batted with panache, scoring 32 off 39 balls before getting a thick edge to a ball from Gough. At tea, South Africa were 168 for five.

McMillan worked hard to re-establish himself at Test level, but he was surrounded by fielders and fell to the pressure when he lofted Cork to mid-on. Pollock batted with sense and purpose, and he and Cronje took South Africa into the lead. The new ball was taken with the conditions most suitable for seam bowling and the pitch increasingly causing doubts in batsmen's minds. Cronje's excellent innings was brought to an end when Fraser trapped him leg before half forward. Pollock fell in Fraser's next over, and Donald was leg before second ball, although all but umpire Javed Akhtar must have believed that the batsman got a considerable amount of bat on the ball. Fraser had taken three wickets in 11 balls. Gough finished off the innings, and South Africa's lead was restricted to 22, which was reduced by two runs before the close of play.

Lieberg is caught by Hick off Fraser in South Africa's first innings. (Adrian Murrell / Allsport)

Atherton fell to the first ball of the third day, trapped on the back foot by Donald, but Hussain entered to play one of the finest innings he has played for England. His concentration and application were exemplary, and the same could be said of Butcher, who, in truth, batted better than he had done when making a century in the first innings. When he first arrived on the Test scene one had doubts as to his technique at the highest level. He enjoyed considerable fortune because he was far too prone to hit the ball in the air, a weakness he has eradicated. He and Hussain gave a solid base to the England innings with a partnership of 79 in 35 overs. It was broken when Butcher received an excellent delivery from Pollock which he had to play, but the ball moved late, found the edge of the bat and was swallowed by McMillan at first slip.

Stewart began in his customary aggressive manner, but he could have fallen early to Pollock. He slashed at an away-swinger, and the ball, flew to Kallis at second slip. Kallis only succeeded in parrying the ball and it went to the boundary. This was a rare error by the South Africans, who made England earn every run.

When Donald returned, Hussain and Stewart launched an attack that temporarily unsettled the great fast bowler, and it was Pollock, at his best in this match, who broke the partnership shortly after tea. He produced another excellent delivery that found the edge of Stewart's bat on the way to Boucher. Ramprakash survived a unanimous appeal for leg before first ball, and he settled to play with the caution that has become his way at Test level and that was most necessary in the situation. There was an interruption for bad light, after which Pollock had Ramprakash unquestionably leg before to the second new ball. Salisbury survived an uncomfortable 20 minutes as night-watchman and hit a four so that England closed on 206 for four, a lead of 184, with Hussain unbeaten on 83, which had come from 294 balls.

On the Sunday morning, we witnessed one of Test cricket's great displays of fast bowling as Donald and Pollock, armed with a ball that was still new, tore into the England batting. The second ball of the day accounted for Salisbury, who touched a rearing delivery to the keeper. Three overs later, Hick was completely deceived by Donald's slower delivery and lofted the ball to extra cover. On the last ball of the same over, Flintoff was caught behind, and England were 207 for seven.

Momentarily, the South African advance was halted as Hussain and Cork added 22 valuable runs in ten overs. Having been at the crease for 428 minutes and hit 13 fours, Hussain played too early at the 341st ball he received and lifted a catch to mid-off. It was a sad end to a truly great innings, and the batsman was inconsolable, not simply for the fact that he had been denied the century he so richly deserved but because England desperately needed more runs. Only 11 more were to be scored after Hussain's departure, but if one man had given England a glimpse of a possible victory that man was Nasser Hussain.

So, South Africa began their second innings some half an hour before lunch needing 219 to win. Liebenberg hit an elegant four, and then, astonishingly, was given out leg before by umpire Javed Akhtar, although he was well forward and quite clearly edged the ball into his pad. Two overs after lunch, Kirsten drove Gough low to gully. With no addition to the score, Kallis played across the line to Fraser and was leg before. Two overs later, Cronje was adjudged caught behind although it seemed that the bat had only brushed the pad. The South African captain left the wicket smiling ruefully, which is the closest this man of dignity would ever get to dissent. Whatever the rights and wrongs, the indisputable fact was that South Africa were 12 for four, and England were winning. Cullinan was at the crease for nearly half an hour, but this was not an occasion to suit him, and he was leg before without scoring. Gough and Fraser had given all that could have been expected of them.

Now came the South African fight back. Rhodes denied the existence of crisis with a brilliant array of strokes, and McMillan was the ideal partner. They took the game to the enemy. Salisbury was blasted out of the attack, mainly by Rhodes, who pulled him over mid-wicket for six, but also by the crowd, who let Stewart know their feelings every time he handed the ball to the leg-spinner. Rhodes and McMillan shared the highest stand of the match, 117 in 151 minutes, and they looked confident enough to take South Africa to victory. They had forced England onto the defensive.

The partnership ended when McMillan lapsed in concentration. He essayed a hook at a bouncer from Cork and skied the ball for Stewart to take the catch. McMillan's departure seemed to slow the momentum of the innings, and the great breakthrough for England came when Rhodes chipped rather tamely to mid-wicket. He had hit a six and 10 fours and faced 147 balls for his 85. It was a glorious knock, but South Africa had needed a few more runs. Rhodes was Gough's 100th Test victim, and the local hero won another leg before decision to make Boucher his 101st.

There was confusion at the end of the day, with the South Africans, sensing the England bowlers were tired, wanted to claim the extra half-hour. Perhaps Cronje was late in sending twelfth man Adams with the request, but the umpires ruled otherwise, and the day ended with South Africa 185 for eight, 34 runs short of their target.

A large crowd, admitted free of charge, remained silent as Fraser and Gough ran into bowl on the final morning. They cheered every ball that did not produce a run and groaned when one over saw Pollock hit a four and another delivery produce four leg-byes. Six overs into the day, Donald was adjudged caught behind off Fraser, another decision not welcomed in the South African camp. Pollock was secure and positive, but too much now rested on his shoulders. Ntini is a batsman of limited capabilities and experience, and it was hard to believe that he could stay at the crease while 25 runs were scored. Pollock tried to shield him, but, having taken a single, he watched as Ntini lunged well forward to Gough, was struck on the pad and given out by umpire Javed Akhtar.

Fifth Cornhill Test Match – England v. South Africa

6, 7, 8, 9 and 10 August 1998 at Headingley, Leeds

England

	First Innings		Second Innings	
M.A. Butcher	**b** Pollock	**116**	**c** McMillan, **b** Pollock	**37**
M.A. Atherton	**c** Kallis, **b** Ntini	**16**	lbw, **b** Donald	**1**
N. Hussain	**c** Boucher, **b** Pollock	**9**	**c** Cronje, **b** Pollock	**94**
A.J. Stewart * †	**c** Kallis, **b** Donald	**15**	**c** Boucher, **b** Pollock	**35**
M.R. Ramprakash	**c** Boucher, **b** Donald	**21**	lbw, **b** Pollock	**25**
G.A. Hick	**c** Rhodes, **b** Ntini	**2**	(7) **c** Kirsten, **b** Donald	**1**
A. Flintoff	**c** Liebenberg, **b** Pollock	**0**	(8) **c** Boucher, **b** Donald	**0**
D.G. Cork	not out	**24**	(9) **c** Boucher, **b** Donald	**10**
I.D.K. Salisbury	**b** Ntini	**0**	(6) **c** Boucher, **b** Pollock	**4**
D. Gough	**c** McMillan, **b** Ntini	**2**	**c** Cullinan, **b** Donald	**5**
A.R.C. Fraser	**c** Cullinan, **b** Donald	**4**	not out	**1**
	b **4**, lb **5**, w **2**, nb **10**	**21**	b **14**, lb **1**, w **2**, nb **10**	**27**
		230		**240**

	O	M	R	W	O	M	R	W
Donald	20.3	6	44	**3**	29.2	9	71	**5**
Pollock	24	8	51	**3**	35	14	53	**5**
Ntini	21	5	72	**4**	15	4	43	**–**
Kallis	9	4	30	**–**	15	6	31	**–**
McMillan	9	–	24	**–**	11	–	22	**–**
Cullinan					1	–	1	**–**
Cronje					4	1	4	**–**

Fall of Wickets
1–**45**, 2–**83**, 3–**110**, 4–**181**, 5–**196**, 6–**196**, 7–**198**, 8–**200**, 9–**213**
1–**2**, 2–**81**, 3–**143**, 4–**200**, 5–**206**, 6–**207**, 7–**207**, 8–**229**, 9–**235**

South Africa

	First Innings		Second Innings	
G. Kirsten	lbw, **b** Fraser	**6**	**c** Atherton, **b** Gough	**3**
G.F.J. Liebenberg	**c** Hick, **b** Fraser	**21**	lbw, **b** Gough	**6**
J.H. Kallis	**c** Ramprakash, **b** Cork	**40**	lbw, **b** Fraser	**3**
D.J. Cullinan	**c** Stewart, **b** Gough	**27**	lbw, **b** Gough	**0**
W.J. Cronje *	lbw, **b** Fraser	**57**	**c** Stewart, **b** Fraser	**0**
J.N. Rhodes	**c** Stewart, **b** Gough	**32**	**c** Flintoff, **b** Gough	**85**
B.M. McMillan	**c** Salisbury, **b** Cork	**7**	**c** Stewart, **b** Cork	**54**
S.M. Pollock	**c** Salisbury, **b** Fraser	**31**	not out	**28**
M.V. Boucher †	**c** Atherton, **b** Gough	**6**	lbw, **b** Gough	**4**
A.A. Donald	lbw, **b** Fraser	**0**	**c** Stewart, **b** Fraser	**4**
M. Ntini	not out	**4**	lbw, **b** Gough	**0**
	lb **20**, nb **1**	**21**	lb **6**, nb **2**	**8**
		252		**195**

	O	M	R	W	O	M	R	W
Gough	24.3	7	58	**3**	23	6	42	**6**
Fraser	25	9	42	**5**	23	8	50	**3**
Cork	21	3	72	**2**	17	1	50	**1**
Flintoff	8	1	31	**–**	4	1	13	**–**
Salisbury	3	–	6	**–**	8	–	34	**–**
Butcher	9	4	23	**–**				

Fall of Wickets
1–**17**, 2–**36**, 3–**83**, 4–**120**, 5–**163**, 6–**184**, 7–**237**, 8–**242**, 9–**242**
1–**9**, 2–**12**, 3–**12**, 4–**12**, 5–**27**, 6–**144**, 7–**167**, 8–**175**, 9–**194**

Umpires: P. Willey & Javed Akhtar

England won by 23 runs

Jonty Rhodes hits out at Salisbury. Rhodes had enjoyed a fine series, but he just failed to bring South Africa victory in the final Test.
(Stu Foster / Allsport)

England deserved their victory for the tremendous resolve they had shown. They had won their first five-match series for 12 years. Butcher was named Man of the Match, although Hussain, Fraser, Gough, Donald and Pollock could have been chosen without causing argument. Gough and Fraser bowled with a passion and shrewdness that was refreshing to watch. Atherton and Donald were named Men of the Series. As they were the leading run-scorer and the leading wicket-taker, this seemed a logical decision.

The victory lifted English cricket at a time when it was desperately in need of a boost, but one should, perhaps, reflect on what the reaction would have been had England been on the Indian sub-continent and suffered the umpiring injustices that the South Africans had suffered, particularly in the fourth Test. The South Africans kept their thoughts to themselves, and the graciousness and dignity of Cronje in defeat should be taken as an example for all to follow.

12 August
at Leeds
First Class Counties XI 279 for 3 (A.D. Brown 79, B.C. Hollioake 70 not out)
South Africans 279 (J.N. Rhodes 90, S.M. Pollock 59)
First Class Counties XI won on faster scoring rate

The South Africans were engaged in one match after the final Test and before the start of the triangular tournament. They met a select team of England hopefuls and fell foul of the Duckworth-Lewis method. The Counties XI were deprived of seven overs by rain, and the revised target meant that the tourists must score 284 in their 43 overs. Rhodes hit 90 off 72 balls and added 127 in 15 overs for the sixth wicket with Pollock, but the South Africans were bowled out in 42.5 overs five short of their target.

Test Match Averages – England v. South Africa

England Batting

	M	Inns	NOs	Runs	HS	Av	100s	50s
M.A. Butcher	3	6	–	338	116	56.33	1	2
M.A. Atherton	5	10	1	493	103	54.77	1	3
A.J. Stewart	5	10	1	465	164	51.66	1	1
R.D.B. Croft	3	6	4	90	37*	45.00		
N. Hussain	5	10	–	347	105	34.70	1	2
M.R. Ramprakash	5	9	1	249	67*	31.12		1
D.G. Cork	5	9	1	99	36	13.27		
G.P. Thorpe	3	6	–	63	43	10.50		
I.D.K. Salisbury	2	3	–	27	23	9.00		
D. Gough	4	6	1	43	16*	8.60		
A.R.C. Fraser	5	8	2	39	17	6.50		
M.A. Ealham	2	4	–	24	8	6.00		
A. Flintoff	2	3	–	17	17	5.66		
G.A. Hick	2	3	–	9	6	3.00		

Played in one Test: D.W. Headley 2 & 1; S.P. James 10 & 0; A.F. Giles 16* & 1; N.V. Knight 11 & 1

England Bowling

	Overs	Mds	Runs	Wks	Best	Av	10/m	5/in
A.R.C. Fraser	203.3	55	492	24	5/42	20.50	1	3
D. Gough	130.5	26	388	17	6/42	22.82		1
D.G. Cork	174.4	29	573	18	6/119	31.83		1
M.A. Ealham	38	10	105	2	1/50	52.50		
A. Flintoff	35	4	112	1	1/52	112.00		
M.A. Butcher	14	3	37	–	–	–		
I.D.K. Salisbury	25	3	106	–	–	–		
R.D.B. Croft	87	20	211	–	–	–		

Bowled in one innings: D.W. Headley 22–2–69–2; A.F. Giles 36–7–106–1; M.R. Ramprakash 5–0–17–0

Fielding Figures

23 – A.J. Stewart; 5 – M.R. Ramprakash; 3 – G.A. Hick; 2 – N. Hussain, M.A. Atherton, D.G. Cork, I.D.K. Salisbury and sub (B.L. Spendlove); 1 – M.A. Butcher, R.D.B. Croft and A. Flintoff

South Africa Batting

	M	Inns	NOs	Runs	HS	Av	100s	50s
W.J. Cronje	5	7	1	401	126	66.83	1	4
L. Klusener	3	3	1	108	57	54.00		1
J.N. Rhodes	5	7	–	367	117	52.42	1	2
J.H. Kallis	5	7	–	294	132	42.00	1	1
D.J. Cullinan	5	8	1	287	78	41.00		3
G. Kirsten	5	8	1	257	210	36.71	1	
S.M. Pollock	4	6	1	146	50	29.20		2
M.V. Boucher	5	6	–	84	35	14.00		
G.F.J. Liebenberg	4	6	–	59	21	9.83		
A.A. Donald	5	6	3	29	7*	9.66		
M. Ntini	2	2	1	4	4*	4.00		
P.R. Adams	4	4	1	10	6*	3.33		

Played in one Test: B.M. McMillan 7 & 54; S. Elworthy 48 & 7; A.M. Bacher 22

South Africa Bowling

	Overs	Mds	Runs	Wks	Best	Average	10/m	5/in
A.A. Donald	243.2	69	653	33	6/88	19.78		4
S.M. Pollock	219.5	72	464	18	5/33	25.77		1
J.H. Kallis	158.1	65	306	11	4/24	27.81		
P.R. Adams	180.1	58	388	13	4/63	29.84		
M. Ntini	81	27	210	6	4/72	35.00		
L. Klusener	90	25	217	6	3/27	36.16		
S. Elworthy	31	9	79	1	1/41	79.00		
D.J. Cullinan	2	–	2	–	–	–		
B.M. McMillan	20	–	46	–	–	–		
W.J. Cronje	25	10	65	–	–	–		

Fielding Figures

26 – M.V. Boucher (ct 25 / st 1); 7 – J.H. Kallis; 4 – W.J. Cronje and G. Kirsten; 3 – D.J. Cullinan and S.M.Pollock; 2 – B.M. McMillan (plus one as sub) and L. Klusener; 1 – J.N. Rhodes, A.M. Bacher, A.A. Donald, M. Ntini and G.F.J. Liebenberg

Emirates Triangular Tournament

and Diana Princess of Wales Memorial Match

Diana, Princess of Wales Memorial Match

18 July 1998 at Lord's
at Lord's
MCC 261 for 4 (S. Chanderpaul 127 not out, M. Azharuddin 61)
Rest of the World XI 262 for 4 (S.R. Tendulkar 125, P.A. de Silva 82)
Rest of the World XI won by 6 wickets

MCC gathered together a wonderful array of talent for the memorial match, which was played in an atmosphere that was as relaxed as the game was entertaining. Chanderpaul made an unbeaten 127 off 144 balls, and the wristy shots of Azharuddin delighted a large crowd. Atherton led the MCC side, and he had an attack that included Srinath, Donald and McGrath at his disposal. They sent back Jayasuriya and Saeed Anwar, but this brought together the two most exciting batsmen in world cricket, Sachin Tendulkar, who was captaining the Rest, and Aravinda de Silva. They added 177 with Tendulkar racing to his hundred off 93 balls, and de Silva hitting 82 off 79 deliveries. They were both dismissed, but the Rest of the World reached their target with 39 balls to spare.

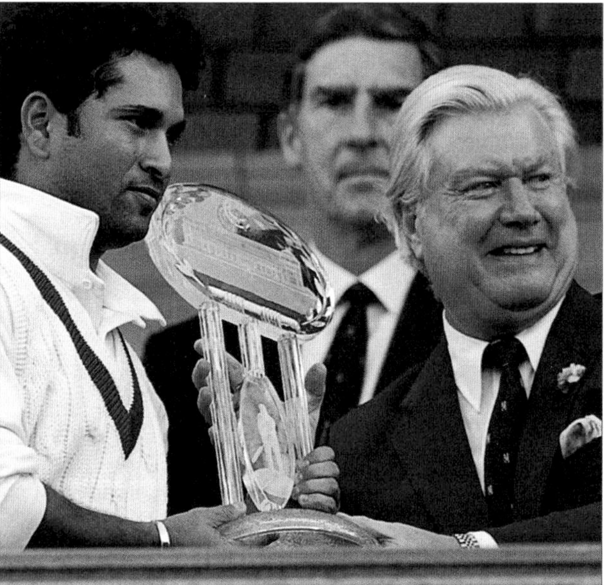

Diana, Princess of Wales Memorial Match, at Lord's. Captain of the Rest of the World XI Sachin Tendulkar receives the trophy from Colin Ingleby-Mackenzie, President of MMC.
(Laurence Griffiths / Allsport)

Teams

MCC M.A. Atherton (England)*, Aamir Sohail (Pakistan), S. Chanderpaul (West Indies), M. Azharuddin (India), S.C. Ganguly (India), B.M. McMillan (South Africa), I.A. Healy (Australia)†, A.R. Kumble (India), J. Srinath (India), A.A. Donald (South Africa) and G.D. McGrath (Australia)
Rest of the World S.T. Jayasuriya (Sri Lanka), S.R. Tendulkar (India)*, Saeed Anwar (Pakistan), P.A. de Silva (Sri Lanka), G.A. Hick (England), T.M. Moody (Australia), A. Flower (Zimbabwe)†, Wasim Akram (Pakistan), C.L. Cairns (New Zealand), I.R. Bishop (West Indies) and Mushtaq Ahmed (Pakistan)

Emirates Triangular Tournament

England, South Africa and Sri Lanka

In 1998, England staged a triangular one-day tournament for the first time. It separated the Test series against South Africa from the Test against Sri Lanka and was sponsored by Emirates, the airline.

The first match was played at Trent Bridge and featured the two visiting countries. Cronje won the toss and asked Sri Lanka to bat. The World Champions accepted the challenge with that zestful approach which has brought success and a legion of admirers. Jayasuriya might have been caught by Pat Symcox low at extra cover off the first ball of the match, but it was an extremely difficult chance. The ball swung massively, but this was more a problem for the bowlers than the batsmen. The South Africans conceded 16 wides. One over from Elworthy was to cost 15 runs, of which 11 were extras. The South Africans looked both tired and rattled. Four overthrows brought up the fifty in the sixth over, and it took Kallis and Donald to put some restraint on the scoring. It was Kallis who deceived Kaluwitharana with his pace. The batsman attempted a pull but skied over cover where Cronje took a fine running catch. The wicket fell on the first ball of the 12th over, and Sri Lanka already had 85 runs on the board. Jayasuriya was out in the next over, caught behind off Donald when he tried to run the ball down to third man. Two overs later and de Silva was gone. He had hit two fours, made 12 off nine balls and was out when he sliced to cover. At 102 for three in the 15th over, the Sri Lankan innings was tottering slightly. The glorious quality of Sri Lankan cricketers is that they never desert their philosophy of the game. In the next 16 overs, the impressive Atapattu and his skipper Ranatunga, playing in his 242nd one-day international, maintained the momentum of the innings and added 80. The partnership was broken when Atapattu was drawn wide by a ball from Symcox and, after much deliberation by the third umpire, adjudged stumped. Wickets tumbled in the late rush for runs, and when Ranatunga was last out, 13 balls of the Sri Lankans' quota remained unused.

Ranatunga had been struck on the knee when batting and did not take the field, and de Silva, equal in experience, led the side. The contest was virtually decided by the 12th over. Pramodya Wickremasinghe produced a fine spell of accurate medium pace bowling, and South Africa were reduced to 32 for four. Kirsten was out in an all too familiar pattern, edging an attempted drive into his stumps. Kallis was caught at extra cover, and Rindel pulled into the hands of square-leg. Perera bowled Cullinan, and the first hint of resistance came from Cronje and Symcox, who was, perhaps unwisely considering the situation, promoted in the order. They added 34 in nine overs, but it was Rhodes and Symcox who provided the real spark by adding 100 off 97 balls. They fell within two overs of each other, and the rest followed quickly.

Two days later, Sri Lanka met England, buoyant from their Test triumph against South Africa, at Lord's. Mark Ealham withdrew from the England side, and Ian Austin of Lancashire was called in as replacement and made his international debut. Ranatunga won the toss and asked England to bat. Brown and Knight were both caught at cover as they tried to hit over the top of the infield, but Stewart, missed twice, got off to a roaring start. He hit 51 off 67 balls before Jayasuriya beat him through the air as he moved down the pitch. Hick was assured and aggressive and looked a totally different batsman from the one seen at Headingley. He made 86 in 97 balls, and he and Hussain put on 91 in 19 overs before leaving in quick succession, after which wickets tumbled – the last seven, in fact, went for 24 runs.

The Sri Lankan challenge was over almost before it had begun. The England pace attack was very impressive, controlled and constantly searching. Kaluwitharana was out third ball. Jayasuriya hit two boundaries before being deceived by Gough's extra bounce, and Atapattu was leg before to the Yorkshireman. Arnold was bowled by Mullally, and when Austin claimed de Silva as a precious first victim in international cricket the game was decided. The later order did edge closer to the target without ever threatening it, but they did keep up a run rate, which was to prove crucial in the mathematics of the competition.

At Edgbaston, South Africa chose to bat first and, after losing two wickets cheaply, they scored consistently. Cullinan had made 70 off 73 balls when Gough bowled him, and when South Africa slipped to 172 for six, England seemed to have taken control of the game. Had Hollioake held on to a catch at long-on offered by Symcox that would certainly have been the case, but the Surrey captain, relieved of the England one-day captaincy and with doubts about his claims to be an international cricketer growing rapidly, spurned the chance. Symcox celebrated his escape by hitting four sixes and dominating a stand of 69 with Pollock which took South Africa to a much healthier position.

The catch of the season. Jonty Rhodes leaps high to his left to catch Robert Croft off the bowling of Rindel.
(Adrian Murrell / Allsport)

When England batted, Brown was run out by Rhodes in the third over, and Stewart was caught at backward point in the 12th. Hick and Knight added 113 in 22 overs with confident and positive batting, and, with 84 required from 16 overs and seven wickets in hand, an England victory looked most probable. However, the seemingly inevitable collapse followed. Hussain got a leading edge to be caught and bowled by Cronje, and Symcox added to his laurels with the wickets of Knight and Hollioake. It was one of the most memorable moments of the summer, however, that defined the game. Croft drove fiercely to extra cover at Rindel's left-arm spin. Rhodes flung himself upwards and to his left and, at full stretch, held a catch two-handed. It was an amazing piece of fielding and epitomised the exuberance, commitment and ability that this man brings to the game.

South Africa won by 14 runs, but it was not enough to earn them a place in the final. England had claimed that spot when they reached 198 in the 42nd over.

Final Positions

	P	W	L	Pts	RR
England	2	1	1	2	3.67
Sri Lanka	2	1	1	2	3.49
South Africa	2	1	1	2	-7.16

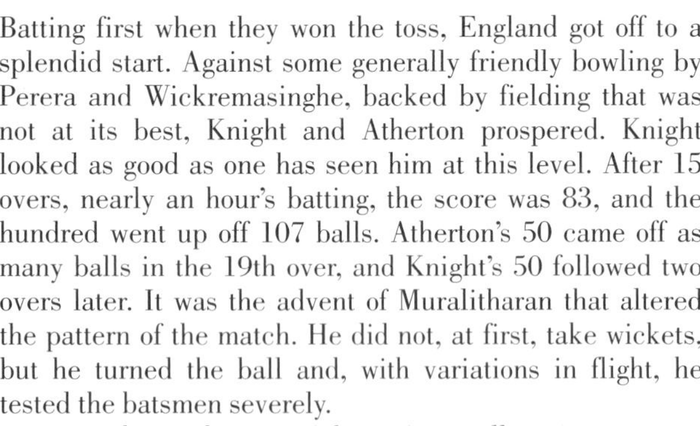

Final

England *v.* Sri Lanka

Batting first when they won the toss, England got off to a splendid start. Against some generally friendly bowling by Perera and Wickremasinghe, backed by fielding that was not at its best, Knight and Atherton prospered. Knight looked as good as one has seen him at this level. After 15 overs, nearly an hour's batting, the score was 83, and the hundred went up off 107 balls. Atherton's 50 came off as many balls in the 19th over, and Knight's 50 followed two overs later. It was the advent of Muralitharan that altered the pattern of the match. He did not, at first, take wickets, but he turned the ball and, with variations in flight, he tested the batsmen severely.

In the 26th over, Atherton's excellent innings was brought to an end when he pulled Muralitharan to mid-wicket. His 64 had come off 73 balls and included seven fours. Stewart had a most fortunate escape when he had scored eight. He drove a ball from Chandana onto his boot, and Kaluwitharana caught the rebound, but umpire Shepherd ruled not out. He had scored only another 10 runs, however, when he swept at Muralitharan and was caught off his glove. Five overs later, Chandana hit Hick's off stump with a leg-break. Hick had on-driven Muralitharan for four to register England's first boundary for half an hour.

The two hundred was posted in the 42nd over, and the 44th saw the end of Knight, who gave Muralitharan a return catch. Knight made 94 off 136 balls with four fours. He had begun well, but, just when he needed to be assertive, he appeared to bat for survival. More than any batsman in the England side, he lost the plot.

Nick Knight plays a ball to leg during his innings of 94 for England in the final against Sri Lanka. Knight began well but lost momentum, and England were beaten. Kaluwitharana is the wicket-keeper.
(David Munden / Sportsline)

Victorious captain Arjuna Ranatunga displays the trophy after his side had beaten England in the final by five wickets.
(David Munden / Sportsline)

The position worsened when Hussain was leg before second ball, and Muralitharan then confounded Brown with an off-break, so that he had taken three wickets in five balls without conceding a run. He finished with five for 34 in his 10 overs. It was the second time in 40 one-day internationals that he had taken five wickets and the fifth time he had taken four wickets. He had repelled England's charge towards 300.

In the final over of the innings, Perera had Croft caught behind and bowled Gough first ball. So excited at the prospect of a hat-trick, the young fast bowler sent the next ball down the leg side for four wides.

Gough imitated Perera by beginning with two wides when Sri Lanka went in search of 257, but he quickly corrected his line and bowled Jayasuriya between bat and pad second ball. The Sri Lankan opener played a really dreadful shot, but Atapattu and Kaluwitharana were totally unruffled by the setback. Atapattu looked a most stylish batsman while Kaluwitharana was more violent. At times, he would slash impetuously, but the Sri Lankans are wonderfully uninhibited cricketers, and their stroke play has moments of unparalleled beauty which hint at the golden age. The fifty was reached in the 10th over, and the hundred in the 19th. When Kaluwitharana finally sliced Croft at backward point the partnership had raised 138 in 26 overs.

The departure of Kaluwitharana offered no respite to England, for, in the next 14 overs, Atapattu and de Silva put on 70. De Silva pulled a ball from outside off stump to square-leg, and Ranatunga was very well caught at slip by Knight, who then took a brilliant catch in the deep. There was a suggestion that Sri Lanka might lose their nerve at the vital moment, but Tillekeratne immediately hit two boundaries, and Atapattu, Man of the Series, finished with a majestic 132 off 151 balls, an innings that included 14 fours and sealed the victory that Muralitharan's bowling had made possible.

Match One – South Africa v. Sri Lanka

14 August 1998 at Trent Bridge, Nottingham

Sri Lanka

S.T. Jayasuriya	c Boucher, b Donald	36
R.S. Kaluwitharana †	c Cronje, b Kallis	33
M.S. Atapattu	st Boucher, b Symcox	40
P.A. de Silva	c Kirsten, b Donald	12
A. Ranatunga *	run out	58
D.P.M. Jayawardene	c Boucher, b Cronje	5
U.C. Hathurusinghe	lbw, b Cronje	14
G.P. Wickremasinghe	b Pollock	8
H.D.P.K. Dharmasena	c Boucher, b Pollock	9
S.A. Perera	not out	0
M. Muralitharan	c Elworthy, b Pollock	4
	b 4, lb 12, w 16, nb 7	39
	47.5 overs	258

	O	M	R	W
Pollock	8.5	–	54	3
Elworthy	5	–	43	–
Donald	8	–	40	2
Kallis	7	–	22	1
Rindel	2	–	12	–
Symcox	9	1	42	1
Cronje	8	–	29	2

Fall of Wickets
1–**85**, 2–**88**, 3–**102**, 4–**182**, 5–**192**, 6–**224**, 7–**235**, 8–**253**, 9–**253**

South Africa

G. Kirsten	b Wickremasinghe	0
M.J.R. Rindel	c sub (Chandana), b Wickremasinghe	18
J.H. Kallis	c Atapattu, b Wickremasinghe	6
D.J. Cullinan	b Perera	2
P.L. Symcox	c sub (Chandana), b Dharmasena	58
W.J. Cronje *	lbw, b Muralitharan	21
J.N. Rhodes	c Hathurusinghe, b Dharmasena	54
S.M. Pollock	not out	11
M.V. Boucher †	run out	2
S. Elworthy	b Jayasuriya	0
A.A. Donald	b Dharmasena	12
	lb 7, w 10	17
	49 overs	201

	O	M	R	W
Wickremasinghe	7	2	20	3
Perera	7	–	22	1
Hathurusinghe	6	1	33	–
Muralitharan	10	1	42	1
Dharmasena	10	–	41	3
Jayasuriya	9	–	36	1

Fall of Wickets
1–**0**, 2–**8**, 3–**30**, 4–**32**, 5–**66**, 6–**166**, 7–**175**, 8–**178**, 9–**178**

Umpires: B. Dudleston & P. Willey *Man of the Match:* G.P. Wickremasinghe

Sri Lanka won by 57 runs

Match Two – England v. Sri Lanka

16 August 1998 at Lord's

England

N.V. Knight	c Atapattu, b Wickremasinghe	17
A.D. Brown	c Atapattu, b Wickremasinghe	12
A.J. Stewart * †	b Jayasuriya	51
G.A. Hick	run out	86
N. Hussain	b Dharmasena	39
A.J. Hollioake	b Jayasuriya	3
R.D.B. Croft	c Kaluwitharana, b Perera	3
I.D. Austin	b Jayasuriya	8
P.J. Martin	run out	3
D. Gough	not out	1
A.D. Mullally	b Perera	1
	lb 11, w 12	23
	49.3 overs	247

	O	M	R	W
Wickremasinghe	7	–	33	2
Perera	9.3	–	48	2
Hathurusinghe	3	–	23	–
Dharmasena	10	–	54	1
Muralitharan	10	–	42	–
Jayasuriya	10	–	36	3

Fall of Wickets
1–**14**, 2–**56**, 3–**132**, 4–**223**, 5–**224**, 6–**228**, 7–**233**, 8–**241**, 9–**244**

Sri Lanka

S.T. Jayasuriya	c Knight, b Gough	11
R.S. Kaluwitharana †	c Stewart, b Martin	2
M.S. Atapattu	lbw, b Gough	6
P.A. de Silva	lbw, b Austin	33
R.P. Arnold	b Mullally	3
A. Ranatunga *	b Croft	33
U.C. Hathurusinghe	c Stewart, b Mullally	7
H.D.P.K. Dharmasena	not out	33
S.A. Perera	c Brown, b Hollioake	17
G.P. Wickremasinghe	b Gough	18
M. Muralitharan	b Austin	18
	b 1, lb 13, w 10, nb 6	30
	49.3 overs	211

	O	M	R	W
Gough	10	–	51	3
Martin	8	–	34	1
Mullally	8	1	20	2
Austin	8.3	–	37	2
Croft	10	–	37	1
Hollioake	5	–	18	1

Fall of Wickets
1–**13**, 2–**17**, 3–**28**, 4–**49**, 5–**83**, 6–**97**, 7–**126**, 8–**159**, 9–**189**

Umpires: M.J. Kitchen & K.E. Palmer *Man of the Match:* G.A. Hick

England won by 36 runs

Match Three – England v. South Africa

18 August 1998 at Edgbaston, Birmingham

South Africa

G. Kirsten	c Stewart, b Gough	7
M.J.R. Rindel	lbw, b Gough	10
D.J. Cullinan	b Gough	70
J.N. Rhodes	c Stewart, b Mullally	15
W.J. Cronje *	lbw, b Croft	31
J.H. Kallis	b Austin	19
S.M. Pollock	not out	22
P.L. Symcox	b Mullally	51
M.V. Boucher †	not out	3
A.A. Donald		
M. Hayward		
	lb 9, w 5, nb 2	16
	50 overs (for 7 wickets)	244

	O	M	R	W
Gough	10	1	43	3
Martin	9	–	47	–
Austin	10	–	41	1
Mullaly	9	–	33	2
Hollioake	2	–	22	–
Croft	10	–	49	1

Fall of Wickets
1–20, 2–25, 3–73, 4–140, 5–160, 6–172, 7–241

England

N.V. Knight	b Symcox	74
A.D. Brown	run out	0
A.J. Stewart * †	c Rhodes, b Pollock	27
G.A. Hick	c Symcox, b Cronje	64
N. Hussain	c and b Cronje	1
A.J. Hollioake	b Symcox	10
R.D.B. Croft	c Rhodes, b Rindel	8
I.D. Austin	b Donald	10
D. Gough	lbw, b Pollock	15
P.J. Martin	c Cronje, b Donald	1
A.D. Mullally	not out	1
	lb 9, w 11, nb 1	21
	48.5 overs	232

	O	M	R	W
Donald	9	1	41	2
Pollock	8.5	–	36	2
Kallis	4	–	24	–
Hayward	4	–	35	–
Symcox	10	–	36	2
Cronje	10	–	43	2
Rindel	3	–	8	1

Fall of Wickets
1–7, 2–48, 3–161, 4–170, 5–186, 6–193, 7–208, 8–213, 9–217

Umpires: G. Sharp & J.W. Holder *Man of the Match:* P.L. Symcox

South Africa won by 14 runs

Emirates Triangular Tournament Final – England v. Sri Lanka

20 August 1998 at Lord's

England

N.V. Knight	c and b Muralitharan	94
M.A. Atherton	c Ranatunga, b Muralitharan	64
A.J. Stewart * †	c Kaluwitharana, b Muralitharan	18
G.A. Hick	b Chandana	14
A.D. Brown	b Muralitharan	18
N. Hussain	lbw, b Muralitharan	0
R.D.B. Croft	c Kaluwitharana, b Perera	17
I.D. Austin	not out	11
D. Gough	b Perera	0
P.J. Martin	not out	1
A.D. Mullally		
	b 4, lb 5, w 10	19
	50 overs (for 8 wickets)	256

	O	M	R	W
Wickremasinghe	5	–	29	–
Perera	9	–	44	2
Dharmasena	9	–	47	–
Muralitharan	10	–	34	5
de Silva	2	–	10	–
Jayasuriya	8	–	45	–
Chandana	7	–	38	1

Fall of Wickets
1–132, 2–170, 3–191, 4–218, 5–218, 6–223, 7–246, 8–246

Sri Lanka

S.T. Jayasuriya	b Gough	0
R.S. Kaluwitharana †	c Hick, b Croft	68
M.S. Atapattu	not out	132
P.A. de Silva	c Brown, b Gough	34
A. Ranatunga *	c Knight, b Martin	1
U.D.U. Chandana	c Knight, b Croft	2
H.P. Tillekeratne	not out	10
H.D.P.K. Dharmasena		
G.P. Wickremasinghe		
S.A. Perera		
M. Muralitharan		
	lb 7, w 6	13
	47.1 overs (for 5 wickets)	260

	O	M	R	W
Gough	10	–	50	2
Martin	10	1	60	1
Mullally	10	–	37	–
Austin	10	1	48	–
Croft	7	–	54	2
Hick	1	–	4	–

Fall of Wickets
1–2, 2–140, 3–210, 4–224, 5–233

Umpires: D.J. Constant & D.R. Shepherd *Man of the Match:* M. Muralitharan

Sri Lanka won by 5 wickets

Sri Lanka Tour

12 July
at Southampton
Hampshire *v.* **Sri Lankans**
Match abandoned

14, 15 and 16 July
at Taunton
Somerset 366 for 6 dec. (K.A. Parsons 101 not out, M.E. Trescothick 95, M.N. Lathwell 56) and 177 for 7 (P.D. Bowler 66)
Sri Lankans 190 and 483 for 6 dec. (R.P. Arnold 209, H.P. Tillekeratne 82, M.S. Atapattu 53)
Match drawn

The Sri Lankans arrived in England to play one Test match and to participate in the Emirates Triangular Tournament with England and South Africa. They were handicapped before their arrival in that neither of their leading pace bowlers, Zoysa and Vaas, was fit for the tour, although it was hoped that Vaas would join the party in time for the Test match. There was further misfortune when the opening fixture, a 50-over game with Hampshire, was abandoned without a ball being bowled.

At Taunton, Somerset scored freely on a fast, true pitch with Keith Parsons hitting the second century of his career. The Sri Lankans lost two wickets for eight runs before the close and were forced to follow on on the second day. Batting a second time, they scored at nearly five runs an over. Arnold, the young left-hander, hit a double century off 270 balls and was at the crease for 200 minutes. He struck 37 elegant fours in an innings of great charm. Somerset were asked to make 248 in 37 overs, but they got into considerable trouble and were nearly beaten.

18, 19 and 20 July
at Cardiff
Sri Lankans 54 (S.D. Thomas 4 for 10, A. Dale 4 for 20) and 222 (M.S. Atapattu 99, A. Dale 5 for 25)
Glamorgan 224 (M.P. Maynard 99, M. Muralitharan 5 for 77, U.D.U. Chandana 4 for 45) and 53 for 5 (M. Muralitharan 5 for 17)
Glamorgan won by 5 wickets

A slow, low pitch at Cardiff was anathema to the Sri Lankans, who were bowled out for the lowest score of the season 45 minutes before lunch on the first day. Maynard dominated an opening stand of 110 with Law, but Glamorgan did not find life easy against the spin combination of Chandana and Muralitharan and lost their last five wickets for 26 runs. In all, 22 wickets fell on the first day. Sri Lanka, too, collapsed 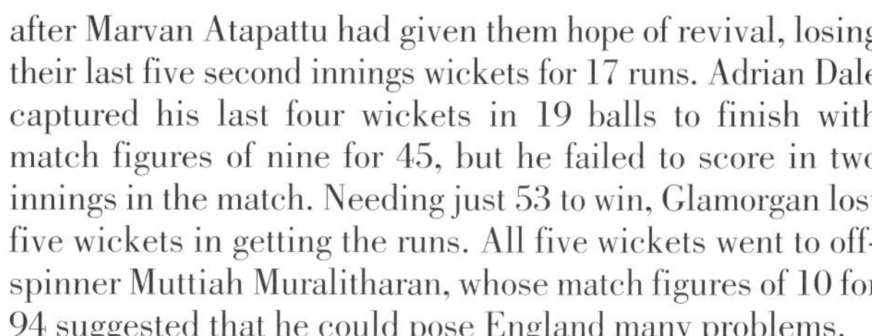after Marvan Atapattu had given them hope of revival, losing their last five second innings wickets for 17 runs. Adrian Dale captured his last four wickets in 19 balls to finish with match figures of nine for 45, but he failed to score in two innings in the match. Needing just 53 to win, Glamorgan lost five wickets in getting the runs. All five wickets went to off-spinner Muttiah Muralitharan, whose match figures of 10 for 94 suggested that he could pose England many problems.

24, 25, 26 and 27 July
at Leicester
Leicestershire 245 (J.M. Dakin 79) and 362 (B.F. Smith 75, M. Muralitharan 5 for 108)
Sri Lankans 509 (H.P. Tillekeratne 120, A. Ranatunga 110, U.C. Hathurusinghe 60, J.M. Dakin 4 for 110) and 99 for 1
Sri Lankans won by 9 wickets

The Sri Lankans gained their first victory of the tour and inflicted upon a weakened Leicestershire side their first defeat of the season. A spirited innings by Dakin, given too few chances in the county side, was the feature of Leicestershire's first innings, and he also bowled commendably – especially as his side were handicapped when Millns injured an ankle and retired from the attack after bowling one over in the Sri Lankans' first innings. Arjuna Ranatunga and Mahela Jayawardene added 137 in 32 overs for the 3rd wicket, and Ranatunga made 110 off 148 balls with 19 fours. Tillekeratne reached a more patient hundred, and he and Hathurusinghe put on 119 for the sixth wicket. The tourists conceded 65 extras when Leicestershire batted a second time, and the hosts offered dogged resistance, but the Sri Lankans won with 15 overs to spare.

28 July
at Worcester
Worcestershire 279 for 6 (G.A. Hick 111, E. Wilson 61)
Sri Lankans 281 for 3 (P.A. de Silva 73 not out, M.S. Atapattu 68, S.T. Jayasuriya 60)
Sri Lankans won by 7 wickets

The Sri Lankans displayed their great power in the one-day game by beating Worcestershire with 2.4 of their 50 overs not required. Hick made a century off 98 balls, but this was banished by the brilliance of Jayasuriya, 60 off 55 balls, and the exciting stroke-play of Atapattu and Aravinda de Silva.

31 July, 1, 2 and 3 August
at Lord's
Middlesex 313 (D.J. Goodchild 105, M. Vilavarayan 4 for 36) and 231 for 7

Sri Lankans 424 (M.S. Atapattu 114, D.P.M. Jayawardene 78, R.S. Kaluwitharana 74, C.J. Batt 4 for 103)
Match drawn

A weak Middlesex side and poor weather did this match no service, but David Goodchild made a patient maiden century, and the Sri Lankans showed some sparkling stroke-play in an unwelcoming climate. Atapattu hit 114 off 161 balls on the Saturday, while Kaluwitharana and Mahela Jayawardene were mainly responsible for 138 runs being scored before lunch on the Sunday.

5 August
at Lakenham
ECB XI 141 for 9
Sri Lankans 144 for 2 (P.A. de Silva 53 not out)
Sri Lankans won by 8 wickets

7 August
at Northampton
Northamptonshire 227 for 5 (D.J.G. Sales 91 not out)
Sri Lankans 231 for 9 (A. Ranatunga 69)
Sri Lankans won by 1 wicket

9 August
at Northampton
Sri Lankans 308 for 6 (S.T. Jayasuriya 119, P.A. de Silva 60)
Northamptonshire 292 (A.L. Penberthy 71, M.B. Loye 59)
Sri Lankans won by 16 runs

11 August
at Canterbury
Kent 176 for 8
Sri Lankans 179 for 2 (P.A. de Silva 66 not out, M.S. Atapattu 53 not out)
Sri Lankans won by 8 wickets

In preparation for the triangular tournament, the Sri Lankans played three limited-over matches. Having struggled to win the first, they won the remaining two with ease. In the second match against Northamptonshire, Jayasuriya played a scintillating innings of 119 off 116 balls. He and Kaluwitharana brought back memories of the World Cup with an opening stand of 100 in 15 overs, and de Silva joined Jayasuriya in a second wicket stand of 135.

The match at Canterbury brought memories of Sabina Park, for the original 50-over game had to be abandoned after four overs because of a dangerous pitch. The match was rescheduled for the pitch used for the previous Sunday's AXA League game and reduced to 45 overs. The visitors won this game with 11.2 overs to spare.

22, 23 and 24 August
at Southampton
Hampshire 347 for 8 dec. (G.W. White 156, W.S. Kendall 59) and 0 for 0 dec.
Sri Lankans 39 for 4 dec. and 309 for 5 (U.C. Hathurusinghe 108 not out, D.P.M. Jayawardene 90)
Sri Lankans won by 5 wickets

The Sri Lankans won their final game before the Test match, but they were indebted to Hampshire, who had a positive attitude towards the match. The county side scored 347 on the first day when the tourists used 10 bowlers. White continued his excellent run of form with an innings of 156. There was no play on the second day, and a bizarre 39 for four off 12 overs by the Sri Lankans on the last morning, followed by Robin Smith's forfeiture of Hampshire's second innings allowed the visitors a target of 309 in 82 overs. They lost Arnold, who 'bagged a pair', at nine, but Jayasuriya and Jayawardene added 61 for the second wicket, and Mahela Jayawardene was then joined by Hathurusinghe in a partnership worth 108. Hathurusinghe went on to reach a century and make the winning hit with 17 balls when 17 balls remained, but the Man of the Match award went to Giles White.

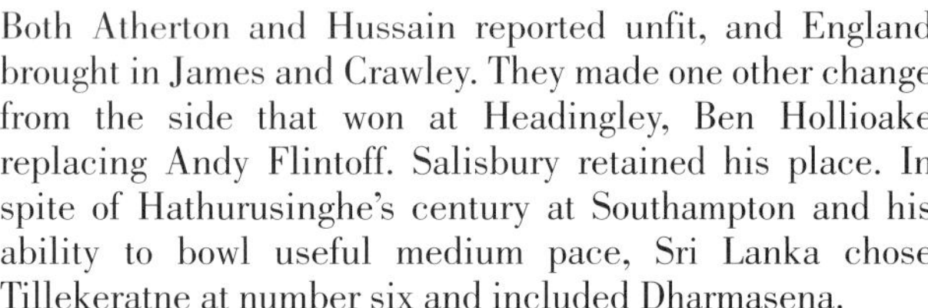

Test Match
England v. Sri Lanka

Both Atherton and Hussain reported unfit, and England brought in James and Crawley. They made one other change from the side that won at Headingley, Ben Hollioake replacing Andy Flintoff. Salisbury retained his place. In spite of Hathurusinghe's century at Southampton and his ability to bowl useful medium pace, Sri Lanka chose Tillekeratne at number six and included Dharmasena.

Ranatunga won the toss and surprised everyone by asking England to bat, but he had arrived at a campaign plan that he believed was best suited to his side's abilities, and he was determined to be patient and keep to the formula. He reasoned that the pitch would offer much help to the spinners on the fourth day and that the Sri Lankan spinners were superior to the England spinners and would use the conditions well. He also knew that Muralitharan was the focus of his attack and would be called upon to bowl a lot of overs and that it would be unwise to seek victory by hoping to make England follow on, for that would mean that the off-spinner would be asked to bowl some 80 plus overs without a rest.

There was unexpected early success for Sri Lanka when Butcher edged Wickremasinghe to Jayasuriya at second slip at the end of the seventh over. James hooked a bouncer from Wickremasinghe superbly for four, and the following over Hick square cut Perera, making his Test debut, to the boundary and repeated the shot of Wickremasinghe when the bowler gave him too much width.

Mutiah Muralithran leads Sri Lanka from the field after taking nine wickets in the second innings of the Test match, at The Oval. He had 16 wickets for 220 runs in the match, the best figures ever recorded at a Test match on the famous old ground.
(Laurence Griffths / Allsport)

Perera changed ends, and Dharmasena bowled a tight spell. When Muralitharan joined the attack from the Pavilion End Hick should have been run out in his first over. James was restrained but at last broke free to straight drive Muralitharan for four. He played and missed at Perera several times, and the bowling looked better than the batting, which was far from certain. At lunch, from 30 overs, the score was 74 for one.

Shortly after the break, James gave Muralitharan a simple return catch, and, 10 balls later, Stewart gave Perera his first Test wicket when he pushed tentatively and was caught at first slip. Hick and Ramprakash shared a record fourth wicket partnership for England against Sri Lanka which spanned 46 overs either side of tea. Hick improved as the day progressed, although he never looked happy against Muralitharan. He reached his century off 198 balls with 13 fours, and, two balls later, he lost Ramprakash, who was out when he swept to square-leg. Crawley was caught and bowled second ball, but the umpire's arm was extended wide in indication of a no-ball. A placid day ended with England 228 for four from 91 overs, Hick on 107, Crawley on 10. The rate of scoring was not one to put England in a commanding position, and there was too much thought, perhaps, on the party to tour Australia and not enough on contending with the Sri Lankans.

Hick left without addition to his overnight score in the fourth over of the second day, and what followed was an epic battle between Muralitharan and Crawley. Muralitharan never wavered in length or direction whether bowling from the Vauxhall End or the Pavilion End. He pitched the ball a foot outside off stump but turned it sufficiently to hit the stumps. He varied his flight and produced the occasional leg-break. Crawley played him wonderfully well, consistently getting onto the front foot with the left pad thrust well forward. In his field placings, Ranatunga aimed to frustrate, and, eventually, this tactic accounted for Ben Hollioake, who drove into the hands of mid-on two overs before lunch, which came with England 286 for six. Crawley had 51 to his credit.

Cork, never comfortable, stayed with Crawley while 56 were added and was finally bowled between bat and pad. Muralitharan's turn was too much for Salisbury, but Crawley's technique and application never wavered. He reached his century with Gough as his partner, and when the Yorkshireman spooned a catch to the wicket-keeper Crawley and Fraser enjoyed a rollicking last wicket stand. They put on a record 89 in 16 overs. Fraser clouted two sixes and three fours before becoming Muralitharan's seventh victim of the innings while Crawley ended unbeaten on 156, which came from 249 balls with a six and 19 fours. This was his golden summer and surely he has now confirmed himself as a Test player. He and Fraser had taken England to 445, a score from which defeat did not look possible.

Jayasuriya began in awesome fashion. He cut and drove with tremendous power, and his wrist work was a delight in itself. When Cork brought a ball back to trap Atapattu leg before with the first ball of the 13th over Sri Lanka already had 53 on the board. By the end of the day, from 20 overs, they had 79, of which Jayasuriya claimed 59.

It transpired that the Friday evening had just been an apéritif; the Saturday provided the main course. Mahela Jayawardene was caught in the gully with six added to the overnight score. This brought together Sanath Jayasuriya and Aravinda de Silva. Sri Lanka have been denied Test cricket in this country because they were considered unfashionable, a commercial risk. The followers of the game have pleaded otherwise, and The Oval was packed full for the first four days. On the Saturday, the faithful were rewarded with what they had paid to see. In 27 overs before lunch, Sri Lanka scored 113 runs for the loss of Jayawardene. In 29 overs in the afternoon session, 125 were scored; and 129 came from 34 overs in the last session when Jayasuriya was at last dismissed.

We can only read of the ancients, of Spooner and MacLaren and Ranjitsinhji, but surely they could have offered no more glory than this, however golden the age. This was joyful batting, supreme artists delighting in their craft. Jayasuriya's hundred came off 124 balls, and when he was out, caught off a long hop that he touched down the leg side, in only the 80th over, the score was 328, and he had made 213 from 278 deliveries. He had hit a six and 33 fours, and he and de Silva had added a record 243 in 54 overs. The England attack was shredded, and the paucity of the spin attack available to England was cruelly exposed. That Aravinda de Silva would reach his 17th Test century seemed apparent from the moment he walked to the crease. He announced himself with a glorious off-drive and flicked good length balls to the boundary as the mood took him. He was content to play a supporting role to the wonderful Jayasuriya for some of the day on which he became the first Sri Lankan to score 5,000 runs in Test cricket.

Aravinda de Silva strikes another boundary on his way to his 17th Test hundred.
(Laurence Griffiths / Allsport)

There was no relief for the England bowlers after Jayasuriya departed. Ranatunga and de Silva scored 118 in the 30 overs of the day that remained. England could not match Sri Lanka's over-rate, but then much time was spent retrieving the ball from beyond the boundary. By the close, Sri Lanka had a one-run lead, de Silva had 125 and Ranatunga 50. We yearned for Sunday.

In fact, the day began well for England with the quick dismissal of Ranatunga and Tillekeratne off successive balls. Kaluwitharana batted with his usual panache and was well caught at extra cover off a fierce drive. De Silva's innings ended shortly before lunch when he drove at Hollioake and was caught behind. His 152 had come off 292 balls and included 17 fours. At lunch, Sri Lanka were 518 for seven, a lead of 73.

If England had expected little more resistance, they were mistaken. Dharmsena was leg before to Fraser soon after the interval, and Wickremasinghe lasted only seven balls, but Perera, in his first Test, and Muralitharan made England suffer as much as Fraser and Crawley had frustrated Sri Lanka. Muralitharan, in particular, was not always orthodox, but he and Perera gathered 59 runs in 13 overs for the last wicket. England trailed by 146 runs and now faced a fight for survival.

The Sri Lankan plan of campaign had worked admirably to this point, and they retained their patience and discipline. Muralitharan had a stranglehold on the England batting. The last ball of the 15th over, with just 25 scored, saw Butcher attempt to break free. He charged down the pitch at Muralitharan, and when Kaluwitharana took the bails off there was no need to consult the third attempt. On the second ball of Muralitharan's next over, Hick went back on his stumps to an off-break and was unquestionably leg before. Stewart and James battled grimly to the end of the day, 54 for two from 42 overs. Muralitharan had two for 16 from 18 overs. Psychologically, Sri Lanka were already victorious.

James was being asked to play in a way that was against his natural instincts, and he had done well for over three hours when a lapse in technique led to him being caught bat and pad at silly point. Stewart had begun to look comfortable, and Ramprakash was defending in the manner that has become his Test match trade mark when the Middlesex skipper suddenly called Stewart for an unnecessarily quick single after turning the ball to leg. Chandana, fielding substitute for de Silva, who had hurt an ankle, swooped and threw in one movement to hit the only stump visible to him. Stewart was run out by more than a foot. It was a brilliant piece of fielding, but, in the context of the match, it was criminal folly by England. Crawley stayed with Ramprakash for 18 overs, and, then, in the last over before lunch, he was drawn into the drive by Muralitharan and bowled. It looked a spectacularly dreadful shot in the circumstances. The first ball after lunch saw Hollioake go back on his stumps, bat crooked and fall leg before to Muralitharan. England were 116 for six, and the alarm bells were ringing loudly.

Eight overs later, Cork swept and popped up a catch which Kaluwitharana took well. In the same over, Salisbury moved back fatally and became Muralitharan's 200th Test victim in 42 matches. Salisbury had had another unhappy match. Called into the attack belatedly, he had ended Sri Lanka's last wicket partnership, but it seemed very much that his captain had no confidence in him.

Ramprakash and Gough became the first English batsmen to trouble the Sri Lankans with the solidity of their defiance, and there were signs of frustration. They were

Sanath Jayasuriaya pulls a ball to the leg side boundary during his innings of 213.
(Adrian Murrell / Allsport)

together at tea with England 162 for eight, a new ball negotiated, and the innings defeat saved. It was an hour after tea that Muralitharan broke the partnership when he had Ramprakash taken at short-leg. In his next over he bowled Gough with a ball that went straight on and hit leg stump. Sri Lanka needed 36 to win.

They raced to their target at seven runs an over, a glorious epilogue to a wonderful victory. Jayasuriya celebrated in style. The England bowlers attempted to bowl down the leg side to reduce scoring opportunities. Jayasuriya stepped outside leg stump and pulled Fraser into the crowd. Hollioake replaced Fraser, and Jayasuriya cut him over point for six. His 24 came off 17 balls.

A memorably brilliant double century did not bring Jayasuriya the individual award, nor did de Silva win the accolade. Hick and Crawley, who was a delight, also received no more than a mention. The Man of the Match unquestionably was Muttiah Muralitharan. His rotating wrists, his marvellous command of length and flight, his manipulative fingers which can turn the ball more than any other spinner in the game – all these brought him 16 wickets for 220 runs in the match, figures bettered only four times in the history of Test cricket, and never at The Oval. Only Laker has taken more wickets in a Test innings. Only five others, including Laker, have taken nine wickets in a Test innings.

This was a joyful win for a happily committed side. How sad it was that Mr Lloyd, the England coach, chose to make innuendoes regarding Muralitharan's action in the hour of Sri Lanka's greatest victory. Muralitharan has been tried, tested and passed by the ICC as a legitimate bowler. The matter is closed. Mr Lloyd should learn from Hansie Cronje how to be gracious in defeat. To his credit, Alec Stewart, who does not relish losing, was fulsome in his praise for Muralitharan and the rest of Ranatunga's exciting side.

The moment of truth. Alec Stewart is run out by Chandana's direct hit on the stumps.
(Adrian Murrell / Allsport)

Cornhill Test Match – England *v.* Sri Lanka

27, 28, 29, 30 and 31 August 1998 at The Oval, Kennington

England

	First Innings		Second Innings	
M.A. Butcher	**c** Jayasuriya, **b** Wickremasinghe	**10**	**st** Kaluwitharana, **b** Muralitharan	**15**
S.P. James	**c** and **b** Muralitharan	**36**	**c** Jayasuriya, **b** Muralitharan	**25**
G.A. Hick	**c** Kaluwitharana, **b** Wickremasinghe	**107**	lbw, **b** Muralitharan	**0**
A.J. Stewart * †	**c** Tillekeratne, **b** Perera	**2**	run out	**32**
M.R. Ramprakash	**c** Jayasuriya, **b** Muralitharan	**53**	**c** Tillekeratne, **b** Muralitharan	**42**
J.P. Crawley	not out	**156**	**b** Muralitharan	**14**
B.C. Hollioake	**c** Atapattu, **b** Muralitharan	**14**	lbw, **b** Muralitharan	**0**
D.G. Cork	**b** Muralitharan	**6**	**c** Kaluwitharana, **b** Muralitharan	**8**
I.D.K. Salisbury	**b** Muralitharan	**2**	lbw, **b** Muralitharan	**0**
D. Gough	**c** Kaluwitharana, **b** Muralitharan	**4**	**b** Muralitharan	**15**
A.R.C. Fraser	**b** Muralitharan	**32**	not out	**0**
	b **1**, lb **11**, w **2**, nb **9**	**23**	b **7**, lb **8**, w **1**, nb **14**	**30**
		445		**181**

	O	M	R	W	O	M	R	W
Wickremasinghe	30	4	81	**2**	4	1	16	**–**
Perera	40	10	104	**1**	11	2	22	**–**
Dharmasena	18	3	55	**–**	19.3	13	12	**–**
Muralitharan	59.3	14	155	**7**	54.2	27	65	**9**
Jayasuriya	11	–	38	**–**	28	14	30	**–**
de Silva	10.3	3	16	**–**				
Jayawardene	2	–	5	**–**				

Fall of Wickets
1–**16**, 2–**78**, 3–**81**, 4–**209**, 5–**230**, 6–**277**, 7–**333**, 8–**343**, 9–**356**
1–**25**, 2–**25**, 3–**78**, 4–**93**, 5–**116**, 6–**116**, 7–**127**, 8–**127**, 9–**180**

Sri Lanka

	First Innings		Second Innings	
S.T. Jayasuriya	**c** Stewart, **b** Hollioake	**213**	not out	**24**
M.S. Atapattu	lbw, **b** Cork	**15**	not out	**9**
D.P.M. Jayawardene	**c** Hollioake, **b** Fraser	**9**		
P.A. de Silva	**c** Stewart, **b** Hollioake	**152**		
A. Ranatunga *	lbw, **b** Gough	**51**		
H.P. Tillekeratne	lbw, **b** Gough	**0**		
R.S. Kaluwitharana †	**c** Crawley, **b** Cork	**25**		
H.D.P.K. Dharmasena	lbw, **b** Fraser	**13**		
S.A. Perera	not out	**43**		
G.P. Wickremasinghe	**b** Fraser	**0**		
M. Muralitharan	**c** Stewart, **b** Salisbury	**30**		
	b **15**, lb **20**, w **1**, nb **4**	**40**	lb **4**	**4**
		591	(for no wicket)	**37**

	O	M	R	W	O	M	R	W
Gough	30	5	102	**2**				
Fraser	23	3	95	**3**	2	–	19	**–**
Cork	36	5	128	**2**	2	–	3	**–**
Hollioake	26	2	105	**2**	1	–	11	**–**
Salisbury	29.5	7	86	**1**				
Ramprakash	5	–	24	**–**				
Butcher	11	2	16	**–**				

Fall of Wickets
1–**53**, 2–**85**, 3–**328**, 4–**450**, 5–**450**, 6–**488**, 7–**504**, 8–**526**, 9–**532**

Umpires: D.R. Shepherd & E.A. Nicholls

Sri Lanka won by 10 wickets

NatWest Trophy

First Round

24 June
at Chester
Cheshire 92
Essex 96 for 0 (P.J. Prichard 55 not out)
Essex won by 10 wickets
(Man of the Match: R.C. Irani)

at Exmouth
Devon 80
Yorkshire 81 for 1
Yorkshire won by 9 wickets
(Man of the Match: P.M. Hutchison)

at Derby
Derbyshire 266 for 5 (M.E. Cassar 90 not out, A.S. Rollins 58)
Cumberland 202 (S.M. Dutton 68 not out, D.G. Cork 4 for 46)
Derbyshire won by 64 runs
(Man of the Match: M.E. Cassar)

at Canterbury
Cambridgeshire 153 for 9
Kent 154 for 2 (T.R. Ward 61 not out, A.P. Wells 53 not out)
Kent won by 8 wickets
(Man of the Match: B.J. Phillips)

at Leicester
Staffordshire 189 (C.C. Lewis 5 for 19)
Leicestershire 192 for 4 (P.V. Simmons 107 not out)
Leicestershire won by 6 wickets
(Man of the Match: P.V. Simmons)

Cricket at Lakenham. Norfolk v. Durham, First round of the NatWest Trophy.
(David Munden / Sportsline)

at Lord's
Herefordshire 213 for 8 (J.P.J. Sylvester 53, R.H. Hall 53)
Middlesex 215 for 3 (J.L. Langer 114 not out)
Middlesex won by 7 wickets
(Man of the Match: J.L. Langer)

at Lakenham
Norfolk 196 for 8 (D.R. Thomas 59)
Durham 199 for 2 (D.C. Boon 80 not out, N.J. Speak 57 not out)
Durham won by 8 wickets
(Man of the Match: N.C. Phillips)

at Edinburgh
Scotland 244 for 6 (B.M.W. Patterson 71, M.J.D. Allingham 54)
Worcestershire 240 for 9 (G.R. Haynes 74, S.R. Lampitt 54, C.M. Wright 5 for 23)
Scotland won by 4 runs
(Man of the Match: C.M. Wright)

at Taunton
Holland 117 (Mushtaq Ahmed 5 for 26)
Somerset 120 for 0 (M. Burns 84 not out)
Somerset won by 10 wickets
(Man of the Match: Mushtaq Ahmed)

at The Oval
Surrey 315 for 9 (A.J. Stewart 97, J.D. Ratcliffe 71)
Buckinghamshire 183 (A.J. Tudor 4 for 39)
Surrey won by 132 runs
(Man of the Match: A.J. Stewart)

24 and 25 June
at Bournemouth
Hampshire 315 for 5 (R.A. Smith 144 not out, A.N. Aymes 73)
Dorset 154 (S.D. Udal 4 for 20)
Hampshire won by 161 runs
(Man of the Match: R.A. Smith)

at Cardiff
Glamorgan 373 for 7 (A. Dale 89, P.A. Cottey 68, S.P. James 65)
Bedfordshire 225 (Waqar Younis 4 for 46)
Glamorgan won by 148 runs
(Man of the Match: A. Dale)

at Bristol
Gloucestershire 266 for 8 (T.H.C. Hancock 60)
Northamptonshire 246 (K.M. Curran 53)

Gloucestershire won by 20 runs
(Man of the Match: T.H.C. Hancock)

at Old Trafford
Lancashire 210 (M.A. Atherton 53, J.D. Lewry 4 for 42)
Sussex 162 (M. Newell 63 not out, P.J. Martin 5 for 30)
Lancashire won by 48 runs
(Man of the Match: P.J. Martin)

at Colwyn Bay
Nottinghamshire 258 for 7 (J.E.R. Gallian 63)
Minor Counties Wales 169 for 9
Nottinghamshire won by 89 runs
(Man of the Match: J.E.R. Gallian)

at Edgbaston
Warwickshire 302 for 5 (N.V. Knight 143 not out, N.M.K. Smith 52)
Ireland 261 for 8 (E.C. Joyce 73, A.F. Giles 4 for 29)
Warwickshire won by 41 runs
(Man of the Match: N.V. Knight)

The first round of the 60-over competition brought one great surprise, the defeat of Worcestershire by Scotland. Moody won the toss and asked Scotland to bat. Their innings was given a good foundation by Patterson and Allingham. The pair added 118 for the second wicket, with Patterson hitting a six and seven fours in his 71, which came off 136 balls. There was to be no respite for the Midland county as Salmond, Parsons and Stanger made valuable contributions to take Scotland to 244 for six – a sound but not formidable score. Worcestershire, however, were soon in trouble. After 12 overs, the score was 32 for one, and Craig Wright then produced a magnificent spell of seam bowling, taking five wickets for 23 runs to reduce the county side to 98 for six. Lampitt and Haynes arrested the slide with a partnership of 131, before Allingham bowled Haynes with 16 runs still needed for victory. Lampitt remained, but with five runs required from the last ball of the game he was bowled by Williamson.

The holders, Essex, had no difficulty in beating Cheshire, who had Grant Flower of Zimbabwe in their side. Cheshire were bowled out in 36.5 overs, and Essex reached their target in 24.5 overs without loss. Cumberland put up a brave fight against Derbyshire, but Devon and Cambridgeshire were comprehensively beaten by Yorkshire and Kent respectively. Chris Lewis took four wickets for 11 runs in 16 balls and finished with a competition best of five for 19 as Leicestershire beat Staffordshire. Phil Simmons opened and made 107 off 124 balls, including a six and 15 fours. Holland were most disappointing and were totally bemused by Mushtaq Ahmed. Somerset reached their target in 17.4 overs. Justin Langer scored an unbeaten 117 off 137 balls as Middlesex beat Herefordshire with 14.2 overs to spare, and England skipper Alec Stewart hit 97 off 106 balls and took four catches as Surrey crushed Buckinghamshire. Speak and Boon shared an unbroken third wicket stand of 145 and took Durham to victory over Norfolk with 35 overs to spare.

Both games involving two first-class counties went into a second day. Lancashire had looked to be well short of a winning total when, with Lewry again showing excellent form, they were bowled out for 210 in 51.3 overs. The Lancashire seam attack, lacking Wasim Akram, soon displayed their worth, reducing Sussex to 33 for six. Mark Newell battled bravely and put on 66 for the seventh wicket with Paul Jarvis, but, by then, the game had already been lost.

The match at Bristol was an all-round triumph for Tim Hancock. He hit 60 on the first day to help take Gloucestershire to 266 and took three wickets in 10 balls on the second day to break the back of the Northamptonshire innings. He dismissed Curran and Penberthy with successive deliveries and had the menacing Mal Loye caught at fine leg.

Bedfordshire's last three wickets realised 119 runs at Cardiff, but Glamorgan still won comfortably, as did Hampshire against Dorset. Hampshire had made a disastrous start, losing their first three wickets without a run on the board. Their saviour was skipper Robin Smith, who hit four sixes and 15 fours. Ireland dismissed Brian Lara for 0 but were well beaten by Warwickshire, while Nottinghamshire had no problem in beating Minor Counties Wales.

Second Round

8 July
at Cardiff
Glamorgan 188 (M.P. Maynard 66, D. Williamson 5 for 37)
Leicestershire 189 for 5 (A. Habib 67, V.J. Wells 51 not out)

Craig Wright who took five wicketsfor 23 runs and won the Man of the Match award at Scotland. He provided a surprise in the NatWest Trophy by beating Worcestershire in Edinburgh.
(Mark Thompson / Allsport)

Leicestershire won by 5 wickets
(Man of the Match: V.J. Wells)

at Bristol
Surrey 215 (A.J. Stewart 89, A.J. Hollioake 88, A.M. Smith 4 for 46)
Gloucestershire 163
Surrey won by 52 runs
(Man of the Match: A.J. Hollioake)

at Southampton
Essex 129 (C.A. Connor 4 for 13)
Hampshire 132 for 7 (R.C. Irani 4 for 41)
Hampshire won by 3 wickets
(Man of the Match: C.A. Connor)

at Old Trafford
Yorkshire 178
Lancashire 179 for 7 (N.H. Fairbrother 76 not out, D. Gough 4 for 50)
Lancashire won by 3 wickets
(Man of the Match: N.H. Fairbrother)

at Southgate
Durham 240 for 8 (N.J. Speak 73)
Middlesex 244 for 8
Middlesex won by 2 wickets
(Man of the Match: R.L. Johnson)

at Trent Bridge
Somerset 255 for 9 (R.J. Harden 61)
Nottinghamshire 256 for 9 (C.M. Tolley 77, J.E.R. Gallian 50, A.R. Caddick 4 for 63)
Nottinghamshire won by 1 wicket
(Man of the Match: C.M. Tolley)

at Edinburgh
Scotland 113
Derbyshire 114 for 3
Derbyshire won by 7 wickets
(Man of the Match: K.J. Dean)

at Edgbaston
Warwickshire 303 for 6 (B.C. Lara 133, D.L. Hemp 59)
Kent 136 (G. Welch 4 for 31)
Warwickshire won by 167 runs
(Man of the Match: B.C. Lara)

An innings of 66 from 122 balls by Matthew Maynard, who shared a stand of 55 with Adrian Dale for the third wicket, was the only substance in Glamorgan's 188 against Leicestershire. The last four Glamorgan wickets produced just eight runs, and Dominic Williamson, the sixth bowler used by the visitors, finished with his best bowling figures in any competition. At 42 for four, Leicestershire were in trouble, but Vince Wells and Aftab Habib put on 132, and victory came with 28 balls to spare.

A devastating opening spell by Cardigan Connor wrecked the Essex innings in the second round match at Southampton and was primarily responsible for taking Hampshire into the quarter-finals.
(Alex Livesey / Allsport)

Surrey won an incredible victory against Gloucestershire. They chose to bat first and lost four wickets for 20 runs. Stewart and Adam Hollioake then added 156. Adam Hollioake made 88 off 105 balls with eight fours, while Stewart, fresh from his match-saving innings in the Test at Old Trafford, hit 89 from 159 balls, being last out. No other Surrey batsman reached double figures. The Surrey new-ball bowling was impressive, with Martin Bicknell on top form. The home county never really mounted a serious challenge, although Russell and Walsh scored 33 for the last wicket. Russell was left unbeaten on 49.

Holders Essex were put in to bat at Southampton and were 2 for three after Cardigan Connor's first over. The three men out were Prichard, Hussain and Stuart Law. Essex plummeted lower, losing their sixth wicket with the score on 32. Danny Law hit a spirited 47, but a target of 130 was never likely to cause Hampshire many problems. In fact, they made rather hard work of their task, and it was the experience of James and Udal, and the significant improvement in the batting of Mascarenhas which brought victory with just under 19 overs to spare.

The Roses encounter provided a keen contest even though it was played on the same slow pitch on which England had drawn with South Africa. Yorkshire chose to bat first, Byas deciding, no doubt, that this was not a pitch on which to chase runs, but his side soon slipped to 42 for four. They had only themselves to blame. Vaughan chopped a ball into his own stumps, and, crucially, Lehmann ran himself out. Austin, in particular, brought run-scoring to a virtual standstill. McGrath offered patient resistance, and Hamilton and Gough breathed life into the final stages of the innings, but 178 did not look to be a winning score. Aggressive bowling and good catching sent back Atherton, Flintoff and Crawley with 32 on the board before Fairbrother and Lloyd turned the game decisively in favour of Lancashire with a stand worth 100. Three wickets fell for one run, but Hegg gave Fairbrother necessary support, and Lancashire won with three overs to spare. They owed much to Neil Fairbrother, whose unbeaten 76 came off 165 balls.

Durham were put in to bat on a sluggish pitch at Southgate, and, with Speak scoring 73 off 145 balls and all the top order batsmen making some contribution, they reached 240 for eight in their 60 overs. Middlesex began badly and were 62 for four, and when Pooley was run out on the last ball of the 44th over their position looked hopeless, for they were 129 for seven. They required another 112 runs in 16 overs, an asking rate of seven an over, with only the tail remaining. Dutch and Alastair Fraser hit 49 off 44 balls, and Johnson and Dutch then clouted 76 from 44 balls to win the match with eight balls to spare.

There was an equally dramatic finish at Trent Bridge, where Nottinghamshire beat Somerset by one wicket with three balls to spare. A fourth wicket partnership of 69 between Harden and Bowler and useful contributions from Parsons and Trescothick gave heart to the Somerset innings. When Nottinghamshire descended to 103 for five in 33 overs with all their main batsmen gone, victory for the visitors looked assured. Tolley and Strang added 68 in 16 overs, and Franks joined Tolley in a violent, bustling stand of 63 in eight overs. Both were out, as was Read, but Evans and Bates managed the last two runs.

Scotland could not reproduce their first round form and were bowled out by Derbyshire in 52.4 overs. They began dreadfully and lost their first four wicket for three runs. They were 19 for six before Stanger, 44, offered a hint of revival. When Derbyshire batted, Barnett and Weston put on 85 for the second wicket. The match was won after 39.2 overs.

At Edgbaston, Kent won the toss, sent back Knight and Smith with 28 scored and thereafter played some awful cricket to lose by 167 runs. Lara was circumspect in the early stages of his innings but gathered momentum. He and Hemp put on 169 for the third wicket. Lara, still without a first-class century to his credit in the season, reached his second hundred in one-day matches.

Quarter-Finals

28 July

at Leicester
Warwickshire 98 (A.D. Mullally 5 for 18)
Leicestershire 101 for 2
Leicestershire won by 8 wickets
(Man of the Match: A.D. Mullally)

at Lord's
Hampshire 295 for 5 (A.N. Aymes 73 not out, G.W. White 69)
Middlesex 151 (J.L. Langer 57)
Hampshire won by 144 runs
(Man of the Match: A.N. Aymes)

at Trent Bridge
Nottinghamshire 249 for 9 (J.E.R. Gallian 83, G. Chapple 5 for 57)
Lancashire 255 for 4 (M.A. Atherton 76)
Lancashire won by 6 wickets
(Man of the Match: M.A. Atherton)

at The Oval
Surrey 217 for 7
Derbyshire 218 for 5 (M.J. Slater 82, K.J. Barnett 60)
Derbyshire won by 5 wickets
(Man of the Match: K.J. Barnett)

Warwickshire suffered a terrible indignity at Leicester, where they were put in to bat. Mullally had Knight caught at slip in the opening over, and Neil Smith played a rash shot

Adrian Aymes enjoyed an outstanding season for Hampshire in all forms of cricket. He made an unbeaten 73 in the quarter-final match against Middlesex at Lord's, kept wicket most efficiently and took the individual award as his side won a place in the semi-finals. (Nigel French / ASP)

Dmitri Mascarenhas took three wickets for Hampshire in the semi-final against Lancashire. He followed his fine bowling performance with an innings of 72 but still finished on the losing side.
(Julian Herbert / Allsport)

and dragged the ball into his stumps in the fifth. Hemp and Penney both fell to excellent slip catches as the ball moved about on a greenish wicket that Mullally and Lewis exploited to the full. When they rested Vince Wells maintained a relentlessly taxing accuracy with his medium pace. Lara showed great discipline, but when he touched a ball down the leg side for Nixon to take a fine catch Warwickshire faced defeat. A stand of 52 for the eighth wicket between Welch and Piper gave a glimmer of respectability, but, although Maddy was bowled by Giddins for one, there was never any doubt about a Leicestershire victory. Disgruntled Warwickshire supporters demonstrated their displeasure to Brian Lara after this latest debacle.

Hampshire confounded the critics with a workmanlike win at Lord's by a large margin. They were put in to bat and were given a good start by Laney and Stephenson, who put on 70. Their dismissals and the quick departure of Robin Smith hinted at crisis, but Aymes and White came together in a stand worth 141. Aymes made an unbeaten 73 off 95 balls, and Dmitri Mascarenhas clouted 29 off 12 balls as the last 10 overs of the innings realised a cascade of 112 runs. Connor, McLean and Hartley soon struck, and Middlesex were reduced to 65 for five. Langer alone offered a challenge, but he fell to Mascarenhas, an increasingly valuable all-rounder, and Middlesex expired in the 43rd over.

Nottinghamshire began well enough against Lancashire with Gallian and Dowman taking the score to 145 before the second wicket fell. Although eight wickets were in hand at the start of the final 20 overs, only 100 runs were managed, and the home county's final total disappointed.

Chilton and Atherton scored 96 in 26 overs for Lancashire's first wicket, and the momentum was never lost. Their slow over-rate cost them two overs of their innings, but they still won with 13 balls to spare.

Surrey chose to bat first when they won the toss at The Oval, but the Derbyshire seam attack soon had them in trouble. Barnett, the fifth bowler, took the wickets of Brown and Adam Hollioake to reduce the home side to 139 for seven. Martin Bicknell and Ian Salisbury at last offered some positive stroke-play, and they added 78, of which 50 came from the last five overs. The inadequacy of the Surrey total was soon apparent as Slater and Barnett established a Derbyshire competition record in putting on 162 for the first wicket. Four wickets fell for 16 runs to hint at nerves, but Cork and Spendlove relieved pressure by adding 22 before Spendlove edged Salisbury to Stewart. Krikken settled matters by hitting successive deliveries through mid-wicket for four.

Semi-Finals

11 August
at Southampton
Lancashire 252 (J.P. Crawley 79, N.H. Fairbrother 58)
Hampshire 209 for 9 (A.D. Mascarenhas 72, K.D. James 52)
Lancashire won by 43 runs
(Man of the Match: A.D. Mascarenhas)

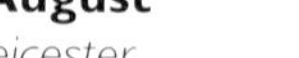

12 August
at Leicester
Derbyshire 298 for 7 (D.G. Cork 61 not out, B.L. Spendlove 58, R.M.S. Weston 56)
Leicestershire 295 for 6 (P.V. Simmons 90, B.F. Smith 60, A. Habib 56)
Derbyshire won by 3 runs
(Man of the Match: D.G. Cork)

There was much excitement on the South Coast at Hampshire's success in the NatWest Trophy. They had ousted Essex, the holders, and Middlesex and now entertained Lancashire, the most formidable of one-day sides. Smith won the toss and asked the visitors to bat, but there was to be no repeat of the manner in which Essex were destroyed. It was 17 overs before Hampshire captured their first wicket, Atherton edging James to the keeper with the score on 48. The arrival of Fairbrother lifted the scoring rate, and he and Crawley added 116 in 23 overs. Stephenson took a fine catch to dismiss Fairbrother, and the breaking of the partnership brought Hampshire back into the game. Six wickets fell for 45 runs. Mascarenhas, the young all-rounder, took three crucial wickets, and Connor, having had pain killing injections to enable him to play, also bowled well. Lancashire's final total of 252 was below expectations, and it was a target within Hampshire's reach, but the dreams were soon shattered. The powerful seam attack of Martin, Austin and Chapple, supported by Flintoff, reduced the home county to 28 for five. The collapse was halted by Mascarenhas and James, who put on 104, a Hampshire record for the tournament, but the asking rate grew ever higher. Austin was brought back and lured James into giving a return catch. McLean made some healthy swipes, but the task of scoring 112 from the last 10 overs proved too much, especially when Mascarenhas, who had batted splendidly for his 73 off 124 balls, became Austin's third victim.

The match at Leicester confounded the critics. Lewis, who had a back injury, returned to the Leicestershire side but was unable to bowl, and one wondered whether it would not have been better to have played the fully fit Dakin. Barnett was soon out, but Slater savaged Ormond, the wicket-taker, to such an extent that he had to be withdrawn from the attack. Having hit 30 off 42 balls, Slater was adjudged caught behind, and with Cassar going for 0, Derbyshire were suddenly 58 for three. Weston, looking a different player from the batsman who had struggled and withered at Durham, and Spendlove now brought an unexpected bonus when they added 120 in 26 overs. Spendlove was the more aggressive, reaching his fifty off 69 balls, but Weston's innings had equal value. They had prepared the way for Cork and DeFreitas, who attacked the bowling in spectacular fashion. They put on 75 in 11 overs, and Derbyshire climbed to a very respectable 298.

Leicestershire began the chase disastrously. Wells slipped as he backed up and was run out by DeFreitas's direct throw in the second over. Maddy had made 30 when he was caught at slip off DeFreitas, but Smith and Simmons raised the morale of the home supporters by adding 93 in 21 overs. Smith was caught and bowled by Dean, but Simmons, badly dropped by Cassar off a skier when 41, continued to batter the bowling. He and Habib scored 97 in 15 overs. Simmons hit a six and nine fours and made 90 in 99 balls before being bowled when he attempted a big hit off Cork. Leicestershire needed 56 off 11 overs when he was fourth out, but they batted poorly in the closing overs of the game. The veteran Barnett was pressed into service as a bowler and used all his experience in an economic spell that frustrated the home county. The last over arrived with 10 runs required, but that proved too much for Nixon and Williamson, and the favourites were beaten.

Final

Lancashire *v.* Derbyshire

The final of this excellent competition, generously supported and very well organised by NatWest, was cruelly treated by the weather and was most disappointing for a lot of people. It was a wonder that any play was possible on the Saturday, so harsh was the rain, but the new coverings at Lord's and the hard work of the groundstaff allowed a start to be made shortly before 4.30pm. Wasim Akram won the toss and, not surprisingly, asked Derbyshire to bat. What was surprising is how poorly Lancashire bowled at the ouset. Wasim and Martin sprayed the ball wide, and the Lancashire captain frequently overstepped and conceded no-balls. Barnett and Slater were in command, severely punishing the loose ball. Slater hit Chapple over extra cover for four and then hit him for six. In 18 overs, Derbyshire were 70 without loss.

Peter Martin celebrates as he has Adrian Rollins caught at slip, and Lancashire's demolition of the Derbyshire batting continues. (Clive Mason / Allsport)

Austin put a break on the scoring and had Slater leg before when he played across the line, although the batsman was well forward. In the next over, Barnett was bowled by Martin, who had returned to find length, direction and a deadly away-swinger. Austin bowled Weston off an inside edge, and Rollins was spectacularly caught at second slip by Flintoff, who dived to his right. Rollins had not played a first team game for two months, and it was hard to see why he was preferred to Blackwell, who had performed well enough in the earlier rounds and offered variety in attack. Derbyshire had lost four wickets for one run. Spendlove was trapped on his crease, as was DeFreitas, second ball. Cassar, attempting to hit his way out of trouble in the Australian manner, was caught at mid-off from an

Mike Atherton is bowled by a magnificent delivery from Dominic Cork, but this proved to be Derbyshire's solitary success. (Adrian Murrell / Allsport)

Wasim Akram, the Lancashire skipper, displays the trophy. (Adrian Murrell / Allsport)

unwise and inelegant shot. When bad light finally brought play to an end, Derbyshire were 92 for seven from 32.1 overs. Austin had three for 14 from 10 overs, and four of the runs against his name had come from overthrows.

Martin had four for 19 from nine overs. All four wickets had come in his second spell of six overs when he had conceded just seven runs.

Play began on time on the Sunday, but the crowd was meagre and the game, to most minds, was already decided. Two runs into the second day, Cork was given out caught behind, but he, like the majority of onlookers, was confident that he had not touched the ball. Krikken was caught behind off a magnificent delivery from Flintoff that moved late to take the edge of the bat. Clarke clouted Wasim for three fours before being bowled, and Derbyshire were out for 108, the second lowest total in a final in the history of the competition.

Lancashire had no need to hurry. Atherton and Crawley took the score to 28, before Atherton, who had hit one glorious cover drive, was bowled by Cork with what was arguably the best ball of the match. It mattered little. Crawley was sublime, violent on anything that was not of an exact length and constantly looking for runs. He collected 11 fours on his way to 53, and he and the evergreen Fairbrother, playing in a record 10th Lord's final, took Lancashire to victory before 1.00pm.

NatWest Trophy Final – Derbyshire v. Lancashire

5 and 6 September 1998 at Lord's

Derbyshire

M.J. Slater	lbw, **b** Austin	**34**
K.J. Barnett	**b** Martin	**23**
A.S. Rollins	**c** Flintoff, **b** Martin	**1**
R.M.S. Weston	**b** Austin	**0**
M.E. Cassar	**c** Chapple, **b** Austin	**6**
B.J. Spendlove	lbw, **b** Martin	**4**
D.G. Cork *	**c** Hegg, **b** Wasim Akram	**5**
P.A.J. DeFreitas	lbw, **b** Martin	**0**
K.M. Krikken †	**c** Hegg, **b** Flintoff	**2**
V.P. Clarke	**b** Wasim Akram	**13**
K.J. Dean	not out	**0**
	lb **5**, w **7**, nb **8**	**20**
	36.4 overs	**108**

	O	M	R	W
Wasim Akram	8.4	1	39	**2**
Martin	9	2	19	**4**
Chapple	6	–	27	**–**
Austin	10	5	14	**3**
Flintoff	3	1	4	**1**

Fall of Wickets
1–**70**, 2–**70**, 3–**71**, 4–**71**, 5–**81**, 6–**81**, 7–**81**, 8–**94**, 9–**102**

Lancashire

M.A. Artherton	**b** Cork	**10**
J.P. Crawley	not out	**53**
N.H. Fairbrother	not out	**38**
G.D. Lloyd		
A. Flintoff		
W.K. Hegg †		
Wasim Akram *		
G. Yates		
I.D. Austin		
G. Chapple		
P.J. Martin		
	lb **2**, w **4**, nb **2**	**8**
	30.2 overs (for one wicket)	**109**

	O	M	R	W
Cork	10.2	4	24	**1**
Dean	5	–	38	**–**
DeFreitas	9	3	13	**–**
Cassar	6	–	32	**–**

Fall of Wickets
1–**28**

Umpires: K.E. Palmer & G. Sharp *Man of the Match:* D. Austin

Lancashire won by 9 wickets

AXA Life League
and Minor Limited-Over Competitions

19 April
at Bristol
Match abandoned
Gloucestershire 2 pts, Glamorgan 2 pts

at Canterbury
Middlesex 206 for 7 (J.C. Pooley 94)
Kent 115 for 3
Kent (4 pts) won on faster scoring rate

at The Oval
Northamptonshire 162 for 5 (M.B. Loye 79)
v. **Surrey**
Match abandoned
Surrey 2 pts, Northamptonshire 2 pts

at Edgbaston
Match abandoned
Warwickshire 2 pts, Durham 2 pts

at Worcester
Match abandoned
Worcerstershire 2 pts, Essex 2 pts

at Leeds
Yorkshire 185 for 4 (M.P. Vaughan 52)
Somerset 79 for 6
Yorkshire (4 pts) won on faster scoring rate

Rain destroyed the first Sunday programme in the AXA Life League. A result was achieved in only two matches, and both had to employ the Duckworth-Lewis method. At Canterbury, Jason Pooley hammered 94 off 79 balls, but Kent's innings was reduced to 26 overs, and a single by Alan Wells off the penultimate ball gave the home side a winning margin of 0.71 of a run. There was no tight finish at Headingley, where Somerset reached 79 in 20 overs, 39 runs short of an adjusted target, when drizzle ended play. The match saw the reappearance of Dermot Reeve. Somerset's Director of Cricket had decided to play in one-day games, but, having bowled 4.4 overs for 12 runs, he limped off with a groin strain.

Lancashire begins with a flourish. Andy Flintoff in action against Sussex in the first match of the season, under floodlights at Hove. Flintoff hit 62 off 69 balls as the champions-to-be won by 10 runs. (Laurence Griffiths / Allsport)

21 April
at Derby
Derbyshire 176 for 8 (I.D. Blackwell 89, M.N. Bowen 4 for 35)
Nottinghamshire 179 for 8 (K.J. Barnett 4 for 25)
Nottinghamshire (4 pts) won by 2 wickets

at Hove
Lancashire 201 for 6 (A. Flintoff 62)
Sussex 191 for 9 (J.R. Carpenter 53, P.J. Martin 4 for 22)
Lancashire (4 pts) won by 10 runs

Derbyshire and Sussex chose to play their 40-over league games on the Tuesday, and both results were a reverse of what they had been in the championship matches. Put in to bat, Derbyshire floundered initially and lost four wickets for 42 runs before Ian Blackwell hit 89 off 80 deliveries, his highest score in the league. Nottinghamshire began well and were 108 for two, but six wickets fell for 26 runs, with Kim Barnett's gentle medium doing the damage and bringing him his best bowling figures in the 'Sunday' league. The visitors were steadied by Paul Strang, making his first appearance for Nottinghamshire, but it was Richard Bates who seized the initiative with a best league score of 28 not out. The pair shared an unbroken partnership of 45 and won the game with two balls to spare.

The match at Hove was played under floodlights and attracted a crowd of 3,000. Lancashire struggled at 84 for four before Flintoff hit 62 off 69 balls. Sussex began badly, but Greenfield and Carpenter added 79 for the fourth wicket in 15 overs. Carpenter and Martin-Jenkins put on 57 in 10 overs for the sixth wicket, but they were out to successive deliveries, and thereafter the game belonged to Lancashire.

26 April
at Riverside
Durham 146 for 6 (J.E. Morris 66)
Gloucestershire 144 for 8 (R.I Dawson 56)
Durham (4 pts) won by 2 runs

Ian Blackwell began the season with 89 off 80 balls for Derbyshire against Nottinghamshire. It was the highest score in the 40-over competition.
(Nigel French / ASP)

at Chelmsford
Essex 231 for 2 (D.D.J. Robinson 129 not out, R.C. Irani 68 not out)
Sussex 104
Essex (4 pts) won by 127 runs

at Cardiff
Glamorgan 132 for 8
Kent 134 for 2 (M.J. Walker 62 not out)
Kent (4 pts) won by 8 wickets

at Southampton
Northamptonshire 199 (M.B. Loye 65, S.J. Renshaw 4 for 44)
Hampshire 203 for 7 (A.D. Mascarenhas 55 not out)
Hampshire (4 pts) won by 3 wickets

at Old Trafford
Match abandoned
Lancashire 2 pts, Middlesex 2 pts

at Leicester
Leicestershire 218 for 7 (P.V. Simmons 60)
Worcestershire 169 for 9
Leicestershire (4 pts) won by 49 runs

at Taunton
Nottinghamshire 181
Somerset 181 for 9 (R.J. Turner 60)
Match tied
Nottinghamshire 2 pts, Somerset 2 pts

at The Oval
Surrey 81 for 5
Warwickshire 82 for 2
Warwickshire (4 pts) won by 8 wickets

at Leeds
Yorkshire 125 for 8 (A. McGrath 50)
Derbyshire 123 for 5 (K.J. Barnett 51 not out)
Derbyshire (4 pts) won on faster scoring rate

The weather was unkind for the second Sunday in succession, but only at Manchester was there total abandonment. At Riverside, John Morris hit 66 off 44 balls to set up Durham's win in the 19-over match with Gloucestershire. Roseberry retired hurt with a back strain, but Morris and Boon added 73 in nine overs. Gloucestershire were well served by Dawson, who had not had a good start to the season. He and Trainor scored 72 in 11 overs, but failure followed, and 14 from the last over proved to be too tough a demand. Essex completely overwhelmed Sussex in the 32-over game at Chelmsford. Darren Robinson and Ronnie Irani hammered 174 in 21 overs for the home county's third wicket, with Robinson, 129 not out off 103 balls, hitting his first limited-over century. His innings included two sixes and 14 fours. Sussex subsided quietly and were all out in 28.1 overs. Napier, Cowan and Such each took three wickets. James and Dale scored 58 for Glamorgan's first wicket, but there was little substance in the rest of the batting, and Kent, with 27 overs in which to make 133, won with 20 balls to spare.

The West Indian pace bowlers, Rose and McLean, were on opposite sides at Southampton. They each took two wickets, but McLean's Hampshire side came out on top in a match that had its full quota of 40 overs. Mascarenhas and Keech scored 90 in 11 overs, and Hampshire won with three balls to spare. Leicestershire had a full day's cricket and beat Worcestershire with ease. Phil Simmons returned in triumph and hit 60 off 54 balls. Chris Lewis also did well on his return to his first county, but he remains a more controversial figure upon whom judgement should be suspended until September.

Having put Nottinghamshire in to bat, Somerset, chasing a target of 182 in 38 overs, slipped to 74 for five. They were rescued by Turner and Parsons, who put on 67, but 12 were needed from the last over, and although Pierson hit a four, Trescothick could manage only two off the last ball when three were wanted, and the match was tied. Surrey and Warwickshire engaged in a 10-over thrash at The Oval, which, with Neil Smith making 48 off 31 balls, the visitors won with three balls to spare. The Duckworth-Lewis system gave Derbyshire a five-wicket win with 11 balls to spare at Headingley.

3 May
at Lord's
Glamorgan 218 for 8 (P.A. Cottey 56, R.D.B. Croft 50)

Middlesex 219 for 7 (O.A. Shah 87 not out)
Middlesex (4 pts) won by 7 wickets

at Arundel
Hampshire 183 for 9
Sussex 107
Hampshire (4 pts) won by 76 runs

at Worcester
Worcestershire 235 for 7 (T.M. Moody 80)
Durham 211 (J.J.B. Lewis 62, P.D. Collingwood)
Worcestershire (4 pts) won by 24 runs

Robert Croft again did well in his opening role, and he and Cottey put on 69 for the third wicket. Glamorgan were handicapped by the absence of Maynard, who strained a groin muscle in pre-match practice. Evans and Thomas gave the innings late impetus, and when Middlesex were 89 for five Glamorgan looked likely winners. Owais Shah batted with maturity and confidence to see them through the this difficult period, and Johnson hit 22 off 14 deliveries to bring victory with three balls to spare.

Sussex continued to labour in one-day cricket. Their bowlers, Kirtley in particular, did well to restrict Hampshire to 183, but the batting had no substance. Greenfield was the only batsman to reach 20, and Hampshire were again well served by Mascarenhas, who took three for 12 in 4.4 overs.

An opening stand of 110 between Moody and Solanki set Worcestershire on their way to a winning score against Durham. Moody hit 80 off 89 balls. Durham battled hard, with Lewis and Collingwood putting on 104 in 14 overs for the fifth wicket. The early season form of Collingwood was an encouraging aspect of Durham's cricket.

10 May
at Cardiff
Glamorgan 183 for 9
Somerset 188 for 2 (M. Burns 84 not out)
Somerset (4 pts) won by 8 wickets

at Bristol
Gloucestershire 182 for 7
Kent 186 for 4 (C.L. Hooper 68 not out, T.R. Ward 52)
Kent (4 pts) won by 6 wickets

at Southampton
Hampshire 193 for 8 (A.N. Aymes 59)
Essex 194 for 8 (N. Hussain 73, R.C. Irani 55)
Essex (4 pts) won by 2 wickets

at Old Trafford
Lancashire 219 for 5 (M.A. Atherton 98, N.H. Fairbrother 70)
Derbyshire 78 for 4
Lancashire (4 pts) won on faster scoring rate

at Trent Bridge
Nottinghamshire 134 (J. Boiling 5 for 23)
Durham 135 for 4 (M.J. Foster 53)
Durham (4 pts) won by 6 wickets

at Edgbaston
Warwickshire 163 for 5
Leicestershire 151
Warwickshire (4 pts) won on faster scoring rate

at Leeds
Yorkshire 162 for 9
Surrey 67 for 7 (D. Gough 5 for 25)
Yorkshire (4 pts) won on faster scoring rate

Glamorgan's disappointment at failing to qualify for the later stages of the Benson and Hedges Cup were compounded when they suffered a crushing Sunday League defeat at the hands of Somerset, who won with 40 balls to spare. Michael Burns hit an unbeaten 84 off 87 balls. Ward and Walker scored 72 for Kent's first wicket against Gloucestershire. Hooper followed this with an unbeaten 68 off 79 balls, and Kent went top of the league with their third win in three matches. Essex, two points behind them, beat Hampshire but made rather hard work of it. They restricted the home side to 193 on a slow pitch and reached 133 for two with Irani having made 55 off 56 balls. Hussain batted intelligently and the game seemed won, but collapse followed, and the last over arrived with eight needed and two wickets standing. Danny Law hit Peter Hartley for six, and a wide and a single gave the match to Essex. The Duckworth-Lewis system was in operation at Old Trafford, where Lancashire's winning margin was decreed to be 31 runs. Atherton came out of his valley of despair with an innings of 98 off 117 balls.

Warwickshire's 'pinch hitter' Neil Smith hits Phil Simmons to leg during his opening stand of 74 with Nick Knight against Leicestershire, 10 May.
(Philip Wilcox)

The match at Trent Bridge was reduced to 20 overs, and Durham beat Nottinghamshire with three balls to spare. Boiling bowled five lethal overs, and Foster, a man in form, and Speight added 101 in 15 overs for the second wicket. At Edgbaston, the Duckworth-Lewis method was employed after a shower curtailed Warwickshire's innings after 36 overs. Knight, struggling somewhat, and Neil Smith scored 74 for the home county's first wicket, and once Ben Smith, Simmons and, in particular, Nixon had been removed, Leicestershire's hopes vanished.

Duckworth-Lewis was also the order of the day at Headingley, where Yorkshire were restricted to 162 in their 40 overs. Surrey were soon swept away as Darren Gough took five wickets for two runs in the space of 11 balls. Having carried all before them in the Benson and Hedges Cup, Surrey had suffered two defeats and one abandonment in the first three AXA League games.

17 May

at Derby
Warwickshire 201 for 7 (D.R. Brown 63, D.P. Ostler 62)
Derbyshire 154 (A.F. Giles 4 for 17)
Warwickshire (4 pts) won by 47 runs

at Riverside
Essex 194 (A.P. Grayson 59)
Durham 194 for 9 (J.A. Daley 69)
Match tied
Durham 2 pts, Essex 2 pts

at Bristol
Leicestershire 206 (B.F. Smith 74, C.A. Walsh 5 for 23)
Gloucestershire 207 for 6 (M.W. Alleyne 63)
Gloucestershire (4 pts) won by 4 wickets

at Southampton
Hampshire 239 for 8 (R.A. Smith 62, G.W. White 58)
Surrey 164 (S.D. Udal 5 for 43)
Hampshire (4 pts) won by 75 runs

at Canterbury
Lancashire 240 for 6 (J.P. Crawley 100)
Kent 224 for 8 (T.R. Ward 101)
Lancashire (4 pts) won by 16 runs

at Lord's
Middlesex 160 for 9
Somerset 159 (R.J. Harden 52)
Middlesex (4 pts) won by 1 run

at Northampton
Yorkshire 198 for 6 (D.S. Lehmann 70, A. McGrath 52)
Northamptonshire 187 for 9 (M.B. loye 65)
Yorkshire (4 pts) won by 11 runs

at Trent Bridge
Sussex 236 for 7 (C.J. Adams 100)
Nottinghamshire 208
Sussex (4 pts) won by 28 runs

Warwickshire moved to equal first place in the table with a comfortable win over Derbyshire. Put in to bat, Warwickshire were 74 for four before Brown and Ostler added 109 in 18 overs. The home side were never in contention. A weakened Durham side managed an exciting tie against an Essex side also perplexed by injuries. Durham bowled well, and reserve wicket-keeper Pratt caught the first three Essex batsmen. Grayson hit 59 off 63 balls to give the Essex innings some substance, but Durham looked clear winners when Daley and Hutton shared a second wicket stand of 93 in 19 overs. Seven wickets fell for 25 runs, and Pratt and Foster were left needing to make seven to win. Pratt scrambled five off the two balls he faced, and the match was tied.

Courtney Walsh produced his best Sunday League figures and took five wickets for two runs in his last 14 deliveries to set up Gloucestershire's win over Leicestershire. The home side lost Cunliffe injured and laboured somewhat, but victory came with two balls to spare. Surrey were rooted to the bottom of the table after suffering a surprisingly large defeat at Southampton. White and Smith put on 124 in 23 overs for Hampshire's second wicket while Udal took five for 43, his best performance in the 40-over competition.

Lancashire became joint top of the table by beating Kent. John Crawley, in danger of becoming the forgotten man of English cricket, hit his first century in the league. His 100 came off 98 balls and included two sixes and seven fours. Trevor Ward responded with his fourth century in the competition, but Kent fell short of their target.

There was an exciting finish at Lord's where Somerset needed 10 off the last over to beat Middlesex. Mushtaq Ahmed hit Weekes's first ball for six, but two run outs followed, and Caddick could manage only one off the last delivery to leave the hosts winners by the narrowest of margins.

Trounced in the championship match, Yorkshire gained some revenge by narrowly defeating Northamptonshire. Lehmann and McGrath scored 110 in 20 overs for the fourth wicket. Loye made his third consecutive Sunday fifty, and Bailey became Northamptonshire's most prolific scorer in the league, but the home side were still beaten. Chris Adams made 100 off 113 balls to celebrate his selection for the England side in the Texaco Trophy. It was his third hundred since arriving at Sussex, who continued their revitalisation with victory over Nottinghamshire.

19 May

at Derby
Derbyshire 190 for 6 (M.J. Slater 68)
Leicestershire 183 for 7 (P.A. Nixon 50 not out)
Derbyshire (4 pts) won by 7 runs

at Cardiff
Yorkshire 225 for 5 (D. Byas 71, A. McGrath 55 not out)
Glamorgan 188 (P.A. Cottey 78, R.J. Sidebottom 6 for 40)
Yorkshire (4 pts) won by 37 runs

at Uxbridge
Middlesex 200 for 8 (M.R. Ramprakash 57)
Essex 198 for 7 (D.D.J. Robinson 83, S.D. Peters 54)
Middlesex (4 pts) won by 2 runs

at Trent Bridge
Gloucestershire 185 for 8 (T.H.C. Hancock 73)
Nottinghamshire 184 for 9 (N.A. Gie 57)
Gloucestershire (4 pts) won by 1 run

at Taunton
Somerset 246 for 7 (P.C.L. Holloway 77)
Northamptonshire 249 for 3 (A.L. Penberthy 79 not out, K.M. Curran 59)
Northamptonshire (4 pts) won by 7 wickets

Ryan Sidebottom took six for 40, his best figures in the competition, as Yorkshire beat Glamorgan at Cardiff, 19 May. Four of his wickets came in his final over.
(Nigel French / ASP)

at Worcester
Sussex 258 for 7 (K. Newell 97, M. Newell 77, G.A. Hick 4 for 46)
Worcestershire 155 (K. Newell 5 for 33)
Sussex (4 pts) won by 103 runs

The Sunday League moved to Tuesday as the most bizarre English fixture list in the game's history began to unfold. Michael Slater, playing only his second innings since joining Derbyshire, hit 68 off 81 balls to provide the foundation for his side's victory over Leicestershire.

Yorkshire beat Glamorgan in dramatic fashion. David Byas made 71 off 82 balls, sharing partnerships of 94 with Lehmann and 79 in nine overs with McGrath, to take his side to 225. In reply, Glamorgan were 181 for four in the 35th over, but Ryan Sidebottom took four wickets in his final over to finish with his best figures in the competition, six for 40, and win the match for Yorkshire, who moved two points clear at the top of the table.

The depleted Essex side went down to Middlesex at Uxbridge. They conceded 32 extras, 18 of them wides, as the hosts prospered late in their innings. Cousins bowled an excellent opening spell of three for 29 after Hussain had asked Middlesex to bat. Essex, too, benefited from wides, 16 of them, and they looked likely to win when Peters hit 54 off 57 balls, but, with five needed from the last two deliveries, Robinson, who had batted so well, was run out by Blanchett's well judged throw from long-on.

There was an even tighter finish at Trent Bridge where Gloucestershire's Hancock made his highest score in one-day cricket, and Walsh gave another star bowling performance. Nottinghamshire needed 11 from the last over. Gie was run out off the third ball, and, with four wanted off the last ball, Franks could manage only two before being run out by Hancock. Greg Macmillan, formerly of Leicestershire, made his debut for Gloucestershire.

Penberthy hit 79 off 67 balls and shared a third wicket stand of 124 with Curran as Northamptonshire beat Somerset with two deliveries to spare, while the Newell brothers dominated in another sparkling Sussex success. This time Worcestershire were their victims. With skipper Adams away on international duty, Keith and Mark Newell scored 181 in 25 overs for the second wicket, and Keith followed his innings of 97, a 'Sunday' league best, with his best bowling performance in the competition, five for 33. These were heady days for Sussex after the despair of recent seasons.

25 May
at Chelmsford
Lancashire 188 for 8 (M.A. Atherton 70, R.C. Irani 4 for 32)
Essex 190 for 7 (R.C. Irani 95 not out)
Essex (4 pts) won by 3 wickets

at Gloucester
Yorkshire 215 for 9 (A.M. Smith 4 for 29)

Gloucestershire 206 (M.W. Alleyne 88, P.M. Hutchison 4 for 34)
Yorkshire (4 pts) won by 9 runs

at Canterbury
Kent 319 for 4 (A.P. Wells 118, C.L. Hooper 100, M.A. Ealham 54 not out)
Durham 219 (P.D. Collingwood 62, D.W. Headley 4 for 36)
Kent (4 pts) won by 100 runs

at Leicester
Leicestershire 205 for 8 (P.A. Nixon 60 not out)
Hampshire 88 (J.M. Dakin 4 for 14, V.J. Wells 4 for 24)
Leicestershire (4 pts) won by 117 runs

at Uxbridge
Worcestershire 138 for 9 (J.P. Hewitt 4 for 24)
Middlesex 120 for 3 (O.A. Shah 61 not out)
Middlesex (4 pts) won on faster scoring rate

at Northampton
Northamptonshire 239 for 7 (J.N. Snape 77 not out)
Glamorgan 177 for 5 (P.A. Cottey 77 not out)
Glamorgan (4 pts) won on faster scoring rate

at Taunton
Surrey 127
Somerset 130 for 3 (M.N. Lathwell 64 not out)
Somerset (4 pts) won by 7 wickets

at Horsham
Sussex 148 (K.J. Dean 4 for 26)
Derbyshire 150 for 4 (M.J. Slater 66)
Derbyshire (4 pts) won by 6 wickets

at Edgbaston
Warwickshire 102 for 9 (P.A. Strang 6 for 32)
Nottinghamshire 122 for 3
Nottinghamshire (4 pts) won by 7 wickets

An outstanding all-round performance by Ronnie Irani gave Essex victory over Lancashire. He took four wickets and hit an unbeaten 95 off 100 balls with a six and seven fours. Lancashire were without Wasim Akram, who had a shoulder injury, and they were indebted to Atherton, who batted well and shared a third wicket stand of 60 in 10 overs with Fairbrother. Essex welcomed back Grayson from their injured list but were without Hussain. They were led by Stuart Law, who set a magnificent example in a fine fielding display as Essex won with 23 balls to spare.

Yorkshire edged out Gloucestershire to remain top of the table. Mike Smith performed the hat-trick at the end of the Yorkshire innings, and Alleyne hit 88 off 94 balls, but the asking rate became too demanding. From Hutchison's last over, 16 were needed. Six were scored, and the last two wickets fell.

Kent massacred Durham. Hooper and Alan Wells scored 208 off 24 overs for the third wicket, and Ealham made 54 off 30 balls to take Kent to their highest score in the competition. Wells hit six sixes in succession. He straight drove the last ball of a Phillips over for six, and after Hooper had taken a single off the first ball of the next over, bowled by Lewis, not usually a member of the Durham attack, Wells hit the next five for six. Hooper faced 90 balls and hit three sixes and nine fours while Wells reached three figures off 75 balls. In all, he hit eight sixes and eight fours. Foster yorked Wells, but his seven overs cost 74 runs. Lewis's one over cost 31. The rest was silence.

At Leicester, Nixon hit 60 off 52 balls and held four catches while Dakin had career best figures of four for 14. Hampshire were bowled out in 30.3 overs for 88, of which Kevan James made 30 not out. Duckworth-Lewis were in operation at Uxbridge, where James Hewitt produced his best bowling performance in the league as Middlesex beat Worcestershire. The Duckworth-Lewis system also came into use at Northampton, where Snape made his best score in any competition, Cottey hit 77 off 41 balls and Glamorgan gained their first league win of the season.

Surrey welcomed back their England players, but they were totally outplayed by Somerset, who won with 61 balls to spare to leave the London side bottom of the league without a win in five matches. Kevin Dean took three wickets in his first two overs to set Derbyshire on their way to a comfortable win over Sussex, and Paul Strang captured six wickets in 15 balls in the rain-affected match at Edgbaston, where Nottinghamshire beat Warwickshire for the second time in two days.

31 May (Bank Holiday Monday)
at Ilford
Northamptonshire 239 for 6 (T.C. Walton 51 not out)
Essex 240 for 2 (S.G. Law 83, D.D.J. Robinson 66, N. Hussain 62 not out)
Essex (4 pts) won by 8 wickets

at Taunton
Warwickshire 96 (P.S. Jones 5 for 23)
Somerset 97 for 6
Somerset (4 pts) won by 4 wickets

Only a late flourish from Tim Walton, inexplicably batting at number eight, took Northamptonshire to an even challenging score on a good Ilford pitch in bright sunshine. Walton and Bailey added 87 after the vistors had stumbled to 152 for six against some fine spin bowling from Such, which was aided by some excellent fielding. Chasing a target of 240, Essex were rampant. Stuart Law and Darren Robinson shared an opening partnership of 131, of which Law made 83 off 59 balls before being caught on the cover boundary. Somewhat overshadowed by Law's brilliant innings, Robinson was impressive in a quieter way and hit 66 off 78 balls before being stumped off Snape. Hussain continued the slaughter, and victory came with 22 balls to spare.

There was a complete contrast at Taunton, where Brian Lara arrived too late to play and had to watch his side being bowled out for 96 on a pitch that aided seam bowling. Philip Jones returned his best bowling figures for Somerset, taking five wickets in 19 balls. Warwickshire bowled better than they had batted, but the home side won with 45 balls to spare.

7 June
at Chesterfield
Match abandoned
Derbyshire 2 pts, Gloucestershire 2 pts

at Southampton
Hampshire 249 for 5 (R.A. Smith 103, G.W. White 76)
Glamorgan 119
Hampshire (4 pts) won by 130 runs

at Tunbridge Wells
Sussex 50 for 4
v. **Kent**
Match abandoned
Kent 2 pts, Sussex 2 pts

at Lord's
Durham 160 for 9 (M.J. Foster 70, A.G.J. Fraser 4 for 19)
Middlesex 163 for 7
Middlesex (4 pts) won by 3 wickets

at Northampton
Northamptonshire 125 for 7 (T.C. Walton 51 not out)
Lancashire 127 for 3 (N.H. Fairbrother 58 not out)
Lancashire (4 pts) won by 7 wickets

at Leeds
Yorkshire 93
Leicestershire 96 for 2
Leicestershire (4 pts) won by 8 wickets

With rain causing reductions and abandonments, Yorkshire lost the chance of drawing ahead of Essex, who had no game. Middlesex went two points clear at the top with Alastair Fraser giving further evidence of his renaissance. He took four for 19, his best figures in any competition for either Middlesex or Essex, in a match reduced to 38 overs. Foster hit a massive six high into the pavilion, but Middlesex won with 26 balls to spare. Hampshire completed the double with their second victory of the weekend over Glamorgan. The game was reduced to 33 overs, but Robin Smith hit two sixes and 14 fours, and his 103 came off 77 balls. He and White added 171 for the second wicket, White making 76 off 69 balls. Lancashire won a 22-over game at Northampton to move within two points of Essex and Yorkshire with a game in hand.

14 June
at Derby
Match abandoned
Derbyshire 2 pts, Middlesex 2 pts

at Riverside
Match abandoned
Durham 2 pts, Northamptonshire 2 pts

at Chelmsford
Essex 136 for 3
Surrey 49 for 7
Essex (4 pts) won on faster scoring rate

at Cardiff
Glamorgan 129 for 7
Worcestershire 131 for 3 (G.A. Hick 65)
Worcestershire (4 pts) won by 7 wickets

at Bristol
Gloucestershire 49 for 3
v. **Warwickshire**
Match abandoned
Gloucestershire 2 pts, Warwickshire 2 pts

at Old Trafford
Somerset 163 for 9
Lancashire 166 for 4
Lancashire (4 pts) won by 6 wickets

at Leicester
Leicestershire 25 for 5
v. **Kent**
Match abandoned
Leicestershire 2 pts, Kent 2 pts

at Leeds
Hampshire 78 for 8 (G.M. Hamilton 5 for 16)
v. **Yorkshire**
Match abandoned
Yorkshire 2 pts, Hampshire 2 pts

Only in Manchester was a full 40-over game possible, and Lancashire beat Somerset with 11.3 overs to spare to keep up the pressure on Essex, who had played one game more than the Red Rose county. The game at Chelmsford was reduced to 27 overs and, when Surrey batted, to 11, but the championship leaders, bottom of the Axa League, lost their way completely. Worcestershire won a 19-over contest with two balls to spare, and Gavin Hamilton produced the best Axa League bowling figures of his career for Yorkshire against Hampshire only to see the 30-over game abandoned before the home county could bat.

18 June
at Old Trafford
Surrey 182 for 6 (A.J. Hollioake 70, I.J. Ward 55)
Lancashire 135 for 6
Lancashire (4 pts) won on faster run rate

Bad weather hampered Lancashire's floodlit match with Surrey, but the home side, much indebted to Austin and Yates, won after the Duckworth-Lewis method decreed that they needed to score 132 in 22 overs in contrast to Surrey's 182 from 39 overs. The win took Lancashire to the top of the league.

21 June
at Riverside
Durham 180 (J.J.B. Lewis 61)
Yorkshire 182 for 4 (D. Byas 79 not out, D.S. Lehmann 52)
Yorkshire (4 pts) won by 6 wickets

at Pontypridd
Leicestershire 202 for 8 (C.C. Lewis 56 not out, P.A. Nixon 50)
Glamorgan 182 (M.P. Maynard 66)
Leicestershire (4 pts) won by 20 runs

at Basingstoke
Derbyshire 160 for 9 (K.J. Barnett 52 not out)
Hampshire 164 for 3 (R.A. Smith 88 not out)
Hampshire (4 pts) won by 7 wickets

at Canterbury
Kent 177 (R.W.T. Key 50)

AXA League at Basingstoke, 21 June. Cardigan Connor in action for Hampshire against Derbyshire. The batsman is Derbyshire's overseas player, the Australian opener Michael Slater.
(Julian Herbert / Allsport)

Nottinghamshire 178 for 1 (P. Johnson 78 not out, J.E.R Gallian 62 not out)
Nottinghamshire (4 pts) won by 9 wickets

at Northampton
Middlesex 205 for 8 (J.L. Langer 87 not out)
Northamptonshire 206 for 1 (M.B. Loye 108 not out, K.M. Curran 54 not out)
Northamptonshire (4 pts) won by 9 wickets

at Bath
Essex 209 for 9 (P.R. Prichard 60)
Somerset 126 for 3 (M. Burns 53)
Somerset (4 pts) won on faster scoring rate

at Hove
Warwickshire 236 for 8 (N.M.K. Smith 80, B.C. Lara 59)
Sussex 229 for 6 (M.G. Bevan 56)
Warwickshire (4 pts) won by 7 runs

at Worcester
Worcestershire 207 for 7 (G.A. Hick 116)
Gloucestershire 194 for 8
Worcestershire (4 pts) won by 13 runs

Yorkshire moved level with Lancashire at the top of the table when they beat Durham with five balls to spare. Byas, who batted throughout the innings, and Lehmann scored 94 for the second wicket. The batsman Robin Smith and Malachy Loye continued their outstanding recent form and were instrumental in taking Hampshire and Northamptonshire to comfortable victories. Loye and Curran shared an unbroken stand of 124 as Northamptonshire beat Middlesex with 23 balls to spare. Leicestershire completed a double over Glamorgan, while Nottinghamshire had a resounding revenge for a championship defeat when they beat Kent with 35 balls to spare. Gallian and Johnson took them to victory with an unbroken stand of 118. Having won their first championship match of the season, Essex suffered their first Axa League defeat. They made 209 in 40 overs against Somerset, whose target was reduced to 123 in 25 overs by a downpour. They won with seven balls to spare. Worcestershire and Warwickshire claimed narrow victories in matches that went the full 40 overs. Graeme Hick hit his 20th one-day century for Worcestershire.

28 June
at The Oval
Worcestershire 180
Surrey 179
Worcestershire (4 pts) won by 1 run

30 June
at Edgbaston
Warwickshire 181 for 4 (B.C. Lara 60)

Lancashire 154
Warwickshire (4 pts) won by 27 runs

Surrey's miserable form in the AXA league continued with the narrowest of defeats, while Lancashire flopped under the floodlights at Edgbaston and so undermined their position at the top of the league.

Darren Thomas enjoyed an exellent season for Glamorgan with bat and ball. In the AXA League game against Surrey at Swansea, 5 July, he took seven for 16, the third best bowling figures in the history of the competition.
(Chris Georg / ASP)

5 July
at Derby
Derbyshire 152 (K.J. Barnett 50, A.P. Grayson 4 for 28)
Essex 154 for 2 (S.G. Law 78 not out)
Essex (4 pts) won by 8 wickets

at Darlington
Leicestershire 174
Durham 169 (V.J. Wells 4 for 18)
Leicestershire (4 pts) won by 5 runs

at Swansea
Glamorgan 184 (A. Dale 65)
Surrey 77 (S.D. Thomas 7 for 16)
Glamorgan (4 pts) won by 107 runs

at Southampton
Hampshire 135
Gloucestershire 139 for 4
Gloucestershire (4 pts) won by 6 wickets

at Maidstone
Yorkshire 263 for 3 (D.S. Lehmann 99, D. Byas 86)
Kent 266 for 5 (T.R. Ward 85, C.L. Hooper 68, R.W.T. Key 55)
Kent (4 pts) won by 5 wickets

at Trent Bridge
Middlesex 173 for 4
Nottinghamshire 149 (M.P. Dowman 55)
Middlesex won by 24 runs

at Hove
Sussex 165 for 9 (M.G. Bevan 60)
Somerset 166 for 8
Somerset (4 pts) won by 2 wickets

at Worcester
Worcestershire 169 for 8 (T.M. Moody 68)
Northamptonshire 169 for 7 (K.M. Curran 51)
Match tied
Worcestershire 2 pts, Northamptonshire 2 pts

With Lancashire having no match, Essex climbed back to the top of the Axa League table. Stuart Law guided them to a comfortable win at Derby with 7.3 overs to spare. Having started the season well, Durham appeared to be reverting to old habits when they failed to reach a target of 175 against Leicestershire after looking to be well in command of the situation at the halfway stage. Glamorgan gained their second win of the season in the competition, and, in the process, inflicted upon Surrey their eighth defeat in nine matches. The match was a total triumph for Darren Thomas, the 23-year old fast medium pace bowler, who took seven for 16 in 6.5 overs, the best figures recorded by a Glamorgan bowler and the third best in the history of the competition.

Gloucestershire beat Hampshire with ease, but Kent had only three balls to spare in beating Yorkshire at Maidstone. Byas and Lehmann scored 172 in 28 overs for Yorkshire's second wicket, and Blakey and Parker took the visitors to 263, a challenging score. Key and Ward responded with 125 for Kent's first wicket, and Hooper raced to his fifty off 34 balls so that the later batsmen had much of the pressure taken from them. Yorkshire's defeat left them two points adrift of Essex, while Middlesex, who won at Trent Bridge, were level with the leaders. Sussex lost for the sixth time in 10 matches and dropped to the penultimate place in the league on a par with Glamorgan.

Hick and Moody put on 90 in 19 overs for Worcestershire's second innings against Northamptonshire, but the New Road wicket was not conducive to enterprising batting. Facing a target of 170, the visitors' hopes were kept alive by Curran and by Bailey, who was unbeaten on 48 at the end. From the last ball, Franklyn Rose needed to hit a six to win, but his brave effort fell short of the boundary, and the four gave Northamptonshire a tie.

12 July
at Derby
Worcestershire 271 for 1 (V.S. Solanki 120 not out, G.A. Hick 88 not out)

Derbyshire 223 (M.J. Slater 110, D.A. Leatherdale 4 for 19, S.R. Lampitt 4 for 33)
Worcestershire (4 pts) won by 48 runs

at Trent Bridge
Glamorgan 177 for 9
Nottinghamshire 168 for 8 (J.E.R. Gallian 74)
Glamorgan (4 pts) won by 9 runs

at Edgbaston
Kent 159 for 7 (M.A. Ealham 55)
Warwickshire 161 for 5
Warwickshire (4 pts) won on faster scoring rate

13 July
at The Oval
Leicestershire 252 for 9 (P.V. Simmons 114, B.F. Smith 87, A.J. Hollioake 4 for 49)
Surrey 212 for 9 (I.J. Ward 68)
Leicestershire (4 pts) won by 44 runs

14 July
at Edgbaston
Warwickshire 128
Hampshire 132 for 9
Hampshire (4 pts) won by 1 wicket

With none of the leading sides involved, the Axa League had a tranquil period over the weekend, during which the Benson and Hedges Cup Final was played. Vikram Solanki made his first century in the competition as Worcestershire beat Derbyshire, who lost their last eight wickets for 44 runs. Leicestershire gained some consolation for their defeat in the Benson and Hedges Cup Final when Phil Simmons and Ben Smith added 195 in 30 for their second wicket as they trounced Surrey.

18 July
at Cheltenham
Gloucestershire 219 for 9 (R.I. Dawson 60)
Sussex 184 (M.G. Bevan 78)
Gloucestershire (4 pts) won by 35 runs

at Leicester
Leicestershire 140 for 9
Northamptonshire 144 for 5
Northamptonshire (4 pts) won by 5 wickets

19 July
at Southend
Essex 259 for 7 (S.G. Law 126, D.R. Law 50)
Kent 229 (R.W.T. Key 68)
Essex (4 pts) won by 30 runs

at Cheltenham
Northamptonshire 250 (M.B. Loye 92)
Gloucestershire 178 (R.I. Dawson 75)
Northamptonshire (4 pts) won by 72 runs

at Taunton
Hampshire 178 for 6 (J.P. Stephenson 77 not out)
Somerset 181 for 7 (K.A. Parsons 55, P.D. Bowler 50)
Somerset (4 pts) won by 3 wickets

at Guildford
Surrey 223 for 9 (I.J. Ward 91, N. Shahid 58)
Middlesex 222 (J.L. Langer 60)
Surrey (4 pts) won by 1 run

at Scarborough
Nottinghamshire 168 for 7 (P. Johnson 88 not out)
Yorkshire 120 for 9 (M.P. Vaughan 57, P.J. Franks 4 for 21)
Nottinghamshire (4 pts) won on faster scoring rate

20 July
at Old Trafford
Worcestershire 92 for 8
Lancashire 93 for 9
Lancashire (4 pts) won by 1 wicket

at Hove
Middlesex 125 (C.J. Adams 5 for 16)
Sussex 134 for 4 (C.J. Adams 58)
Sussex (4 pts) won on faster scoring rate

21 July
at Edgbaston
Essex 204 for 7 (R.C. Irani 68 not out)
Warwickshire 187 for 7 (T.L. Penney 64 not out)
Essex (4 pts) won by 17 runs

What was once referred to as the Sunday League now spreads to every day of the week. Gloucestershire staged games at Cheltenham on both days of the weekend while Lancashire, Sussex and Warwickshire settled for floodlit matches on the Monday and Tuesday. Essex and Northamptonshire were double winners, and Essex's victory at Edgbaston, where the lighting was below standard took them six points clear of Lancashire who had two games in hand. In the Essex win over Kent, Stuart Law hit 126 off 115 balls and was at his very best in a season in which he had generally failed to reach his own high standard. Lancashire, maintained their title challenge before a big crowd at Old Trafford. The weather was unfriendly, the pitch poor and the match was reduced to 25 overs. Martin hit the last ball of the contest for the winning single.

The Duckworth-Lewis system came into operation at Scarborough and Hove, where Chris Adams bowled his medium-pacers to such good effect that he captured five wickets for 16 runs in 32 balls. This represented his best bowling figures in any competition, and, in the AXA League, he had previously just three wickets to his credit. He followed his fine performance with the ball with an innings of 58 and led Sussex to the first home league victory for a year.

Middlesex's defeat was their second in successive matches and virtually ended their hopes of overhauling Essex and Lancashire. They provided Surrey with their first win of the season. Middlesex seemed to have lost their way, but Dutch made 40 off 24 balls with two sixes and three fours before being run out off the last ball of the match when he attempted to take the single to the wicket-keeper which would have tied the match.

26 July
at Colwyn Bay
Match abandoned
Glamorgan 2 pts, Lancashire 2 pts

at Cheltenham
Gloucestershire 261 for 8 (R.I. Dawson 68, M.G.N. Windows 59)
Surrey 239 (J.A. Knott 98, J.D. Ratcliffe 80)
Gloucestershire (4 pts) won by 22 runs

at Portsmouth
Nottinghamshire 167 for 6
Hampshire 137 (J.P. Stephenson 59)
Nottinghamshire (4 pts) won by 30 runs

at Lord's
Middlesex 177 for 4 (J.L. Langer 86)
Yorkshire 129 (K.P. Dutch 4 for 22)
Middlesex (4 pts) won by 48 runs

at Northampton
Derbyshire 286 (M.E. Cassar 134, P.A.J. DeFreitas 69)
Northamptonshire 254 (A.L. Penberthy 71)
Derbyshire (4 pts) won by 32 runs

at Taunton
Durham 218 for 5 (N.J. Speak 90 not out)
Somerset 212 (P.C.L. Holloway 52, N.C. Phillips 4 for 24)
Durham (4 pts) won by 6 runs

With Essex not playing and Lancashire rained off, Middlesex took the opportunity to move back into contention in a match reduced to 28 overs. The game at Portsmouth was restricted to 37 overs, but elsewhere the matches went the full 40 overs and produced some high scoring. At Taunton, Nicky Phillips brought about a collapse that saw three Somerset wickets fall in four balls. Durham won when, with seven runs needed and four balls remaining, Wood bowled Jones. In spite of Jason Knott's 98 off 95 balls, his highest score in any competition, Surrey lost for the 10th time in 12 matches, and Gloucestershire celebrated a highly successful Cheltenham Festival.

Keith Dutch returned his best bowling figures in the competition as Middlesex won, but the outstanding performance of the day came from Matthew Cassar, who helped Derbyshire to beat Northamptonshire with an innings of 134 off 108 balls. He hit two sixes and 16 fours in his first century in any competition.

2 August
at Derby
Kent 155 for 8
Derbyshire 156 for 2 (M.E. Cassar 67 not out)
Derbyshire (4 pts) won by 8 wickets

at Southampton
Durham 229 (J.J.B. Lewis 67 not out, P.D. Collingwood 53)
Hampshire 230 for 3 (A.N. Aymes 60 not out, G.W. White 56 not out, J.P. Stephenson 56, R.A. Smith 50)
Hampshire (4 pts) won by 7 wickets

at Old Trafford
Lancashire 183 for 7 (N.H. Fairbrother 82 not out)
Leicestershire 163
Lancashire (4 pts) won by 20 runs

at Trent Bridge
Nottinghamshire 154 for 8
Northamptonshire 155 for 5
Northamptonshire (4 pts) won by 5 wickets

at Worcester
Yorkshire 202 (M.J. Wood 64, D.S. Lehmann 59, R.J. Chapman 5 for 30)

Matthew Cassar hit 134 for Derbyshire against Northamptonshire at Northampton, 26 July. It was his first century in any competition. (David Munden / Sportsline)

Worcestershire 168 (D. Gough 4 for 30)
Yorkshire (4 pts) won by 34 runs

3 August
at The Oval
Surrey 143 for 8
Sussex 144 for 2 (C.J. Adams 64 not out)
Sussex (4 pts) won by 8 wickets

at Edgbaston
Glamorgan 172 for 5
Warwickshire 146
Glamorgan (4 pts) won by 38 runs

5 August
at The Oval
Derbyshire 245 for 7 (M.J. Slater 58, P.A.J. DeFreitas 56)
Surrey 217 (N. Shahid 58)
Derbyshire (4 pts) won by 28 runs

Lancashire closed the gap on Essex to two points, and the Red Rose county had the luxury of a game in hand. Their victory over Leicestershire was an astonishing affair. Having recovered from a sprained ankle, Neil Fairbrother was a Lancashire hero with 82 off 98 balls. The innings had considerable merit in that the pitch was dry, and when Wasim won the toss he believed that a total of between 160 and 170 would be a winning one. Even so, his calculations looked wrong when Leicestershire were 135 for two with some ten overs remaining. The turning point came when Martin took three wickets in one over, and, in all, four wickets fell for one run to destroy Leicestershire's challenge.

At Southampton, Adrian Aymes showed he was as adept at the one-day game as he was in the first-class game, and he and White shared an unbroken stand of 118 to take Hampshire to victory over Durham with 15 balls to spare. Cassar's good form continued as Derbyshire won twice in the space of four days, and Wood and Lehmann mirrored their performance in the championship match by adding 111 for Yorkshire's third wicket in the win over Worcestershire. Darren Gough had a spell of four for four in 11 balls, which destroyed the Worcestershire tail.

Nottinghamshire looked doomed for the second division in 1999 when they lost to Northamptonshire, and Warwickshire slipped again, beaten by Glamorgan. Surrey stayed rooted to the bottom after two defeats in three days, both at The Oval. The consolation was that the public showed an appetite for the floodlit game.

9 August
at Chelmsford
Glamorgan 172 for 9 (I. Dawood 57, R.C. Irani 4 for 26)
Essex 173 for 2 (P.J. Prichard 99 not out)
Essex (4 pts) won by 8 wickets

at Canterbury
Hampshire 187 (A.D. Mascarenhas 65)
Kent 138 for 3
Kent (4 pts) won by 7 wickets

at Old Trafford
Lancashire 222 for 6 (N.H. Fairbrother 76, Wasim Akram 75 not out)
Gloucestershire 151
Lancashire (4 pts) won by 71 runs

at Leicester
Leicestershire 165 for 7
Somerset 160 (J. Ormond 4 for 32)
Leicestershire (4 pts) won by 5 runs

at Lord's
Middlesex 102 (G.C. Small 5 for 18)
Warwickshire 105 for 4
Warwickshire (4 pts) won by 6 wickets

at Eastbourne
Durham 156 for 9
Sussex 157 for 3 (C.J. Adams 73)
Sussex (4 pts) won by 7 wickets

at Worcester
Nottinghamshire 154 (P. Johnson 53)
Worcestershire 155 for 3 (V.S. Solanki 88)
Worcestershire (4 pts) won by 7 wickets

Essex maintained their narrow lead at the top of the table with an emphatic win over Glamorgan. The visitors never really recovered from being 46 for five, and, with Prichard dominating, Essex won with 45 balls to spare. Lancashire kept pace with an equally convincing victory over Gloucestershire. After 30 overs, Lancashire were 108 for four; in the last 10 overs, they scored 114. The force behind this onslaught on the Lancashire bowling was Wasim Akram, who hit six sixes and five fours in making an unbeaten 75 off 42 balls. Gloucestershire lost their first four wickets for 45 runs and were never really in contention.

Hampshire were 19 for five against Kent, who won with 46 balls to spare. Only Keech and Mascarenhas reached double figures in the Hampshire innings. Leicestershire had a narrow win over Somerset and retained a slim chance of catching Essex and Lancashire, but Middlesex slipped again with only openers Brown and Langer and number 11 Bloomfield reaching double figures. The veteran Gladstone Small tore out the heart of the Middlesex batting and returned his best bowling figures in the competition. Warwickshire raced to victory in 23.3 overs.

Chris Adams emphasised once again how much he has done to transform Sussex cricket with a match-winning 73 against Durham, but Paul Johnson's continued rejuvenation prevented Nottinghamshire losing at Worcester.

23 August
at Riverside
Lancashire 43 for 4
v. **Durham**
Match abandoned
Durham 2 pts, Lancashire 2 pts

at Colchester
Gloucestershire 14 for 1
v. **Essex**
Match abandoned
Essex 2 pts, Gloucestershire 2 pts

at Canterbury
Worcestershire 16 for 2
v. **Kent**
Match abandoned
Kent 2 pts, Worcestershire 2 pts

at Leicester
Match abandoned
Leicestershire 2 pts, Sussex 2 pts

at Northampton
Match abandoned
Northamptonshire 2 pts, Warwickshire 2 pts

at Trent Bridge
Match abandoned
Nottinghamshire 2 pts, Surrey 2 pts

at Taunton
Match abandoned
Somerset 2 pts, Derbyshire 2 pts

24 August
at Leeds
Lancashire 182 for 8 (J.P. Crawley 73)
Yorkshire 81 (G. Chapple 6 for 25)
Lancashire (4 pts) won by 101 runs

25 August
at Bristol
Somerset 193 (G.D. Rose 59)
Gloucestershire 67 for 0
Gloucestershire (4 pts) won on faster scoring rate

Dreadful weather on the Sunday caused all matches to be abandoned, but, on the Monday, under floodlights at Headingley, Lancashire beat Yorkshire and went top of the table, four points ahead of Esssex, who had a game in hand. Lancashire batted first when they won the toss and were given substance by the in-form Crawley and by the master of one-day cricket, Fairbrother. The visitors were rocked by Gough's hat-trick. He had Wasim Akram and Hegg caught

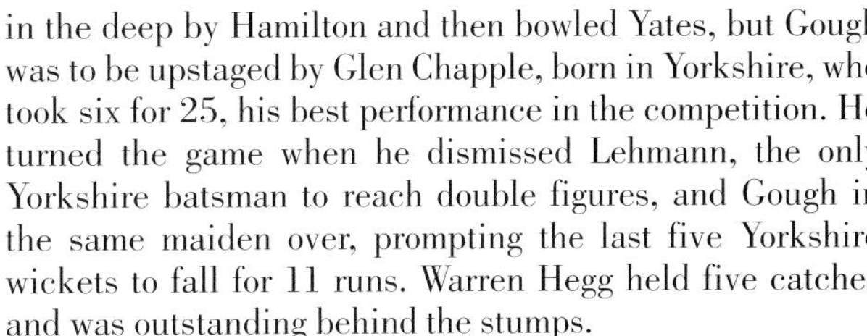

in the deep by Hamilton and then bowled Yates, but Gough was to be upstaged by Glen Chapple, born in Yorkshire, who took six for 25, his best performance in the competition. He turned the game when he dismissed Lehmann, the only Yorkshire batsman to reach double figures, and Gough in the same maiden over, prompting the last five Yorkshire wickets to fall for 11 runs. Warren Hegg held five catches and was outstanding behind the stumps.

The weather was less kind to the floodlit game at Bristol, but the venture was just as financially successful as the one at Headingley. Rain began as the Somerset innings was coming to a close, and the Duckworth-Lewis method came into operation. Gloucestershire's innings started, but after four overs there was more rain, and their target became 67 in 10 overs. They won with two balls to spare.

30 August
at Derby
Durham 217 for 9 (J.E. Morris 50)
Derbyshire 195
Durham (4 pts) won by 22 runs

at Southampton
Hampshire 210 for 5 (G.W. White 51)
Middlesex 198 for 7
Hampshire (4 pts) won by 12 runs

at Northampton
Northamptonshire 168 for 6
Kent 172 for 3 (C.L. Hooper 65 not out)
Kent (4 pts) won by 7 wickets

at Trent Bridge
Nottinghamshire 225 for 8 (P. Johnson 74)
Leicestershire 221 for 9 (A. Habib 71)
Nottinghamshire (4 pts) won by 4 runs

at Hove
Glamorgan 212 for 7 (P.A. Cottey 63)
Sussex 175 (A. Dale 4 for 36)
Glamorgan (4 pts) won by 37 runs

at Edgbaston
Worcestershire 127
Warwickshire 128 for 6
Warwickshire (4 pts) won by 4 wickets

at Scarborough
Essex 129
Yorkshire 131 for 2 (M.J. Wood 65 not out)
Yorkshire (4 pts) won by 8 wickets

Essex's hopes of winning the AXA League virtually disappeared when they received a crushing defeat at Scarborough. They chose to bat first but were torn apart by Yorkshire's young lions. The home side reached their target with 12.3 overs to spare. With two matches remaining, Lancashire led Essex by four points. Warwickshire moved into third place with victory in a low scoring match at Edgbaston, and Hampshire's most encouraging season was boosted further when they moved level with Kent and Yorkshire in fourth place. At the other end of the table, Durham gained their fourth win of the season as David Boon bowled a full quota of overs and took two wickets in the win over Derbyshire. Carl Hooper hit five sixes and two fours in his unbeaten 65, which took Kent to victory over Northamptonshire. He hit three sixes in an over off Bailey to win the match. Johnson's enjoyment of success since relinquishing the captaincy of Nottinghamshire was sustained in the close win over Leicestershire, while a good all-round team effort took Glamorgan to a convincing win at Hove.

6 September
at Riverside
Glamorgan 232 for 7 (M.P. Maynard 90, S.P. James 78)
Durham 206 for 8 (D.C. Boon 76)
Glamorgan (4 pts) won by 26 runs

at Chelmsford
Nottinghamshire 192 for 6 (G.F. Archer 50 not out)
Essex 141 for 9
Nottinghamshire (4 pts) won by 41 runs

at Leicester
Leicestershire 222 for 8 (V.J. Wells 77, R.L. Johnson 4 for 45)
Middlesex 62 (J. Ormond 4 for 12)
Leicestershire (4 pts) won by 160 runs

at Taunton
Somerset 77 for 4
v. **Worcestershire**
Match abandoned
Somerset 2 pts, Worcestershire 2 pts

at The Oval
Surrey 183 for 8
Kent 142 (A.J. Hollioake 4 for 18)
Surrey (4 pts) won by 41 runs

at Hove
Yorkshire 89 (R.J. Kirtley 4 for 21)
Sussex 90 for 4
Sussex (4 pts) won by 6 wickets

7 September
at Old Trafford
Lancashire 202 (A. Flintoff 69)
Hampshire 186 for 7
Lancashire (4 pts) won by 16 runs

While Lancashire were engaged in the NatWest Trophy Final, Essex were losing at home to Nottinghamshire and surrendering their challenge for the AXA League title. Lancashire confirmed themselves as champions by beating Hampshire at Old Trafford on the Monday. Essex's defeat was a shattering one. Facing a target of 193, they collapsed to 89 for nine, and only some clouts from Cowan and Such gave the score a tinge of respectability. Also humiliated were Middlesex, once in contention for the title, who were routed by Leicestershire's Ormond and Dakin and looked likely to be condemned to the second division in 1999. Ormond's figures were his best in the competition.

Maynard and James scored 170 for Glamorgan's first wicket against Durham, and Sussex beat Yorkshire with 16 overs to spare. Surrey claimed a rare victory in a low-scoring match at The Oval. Surrey included Carl Greenidge, son of the great West Indian opening batsman, in their side. He opened the bowling and sent down seven overs for 35 runs but did not take a wicket.

9 September
at Trent Bridge
Lancashire 221 for 2 (A. Flintoff 93 not out, M. Watkinson 56)
Nottinghamshire 169 for 4 (P. Johnson 51 not out)
Lancashire (4 pts) won by 52 runs

13 September
at Riverside
Surrey 237 for 6 (M.A. Butcher 85 not out, A.J. Stewart 58)
Durham 136
Surrey (4 pts) won by 101 runs

at Cardiff
Glamorgan 210 for 6 (A. Dale 82, M.J. Powell 55)
Derbyshire 154 for 9
Glamorgan (4 pts) won by 56 runs

at Canterbury
Somerset 164 for 7 (M.N. Lathwell 87)
Kent 174 for 4 (C.L. Hooper 62, M.J. Walker 50)
Kent (4 pts) won on faster scoring rate

at Leicester
Leicestershire 219 for 9 (P.V. Simmons 56, B.F. Smith 54)
Essex 91 (T.J. Mason 4 for 12)
Leicestershire (4 pts) won by 128 runs

at Lord's
Gloucestershire 196 for 6 (T.H.C. Hancock 61 not out)
Middlesex 174 for 8 (M.R. Ramprakash 56)
Gloucestershire (4 pts) won by 22 runs

at Northampton
Northamptonshire 181 for 6
Sussex 92
Northamptonshire (4 pts) won by 89 runs

at Worcester
Worcestershire 181 for 9
Hampshire 177
Worcestershire (4 pts) won by 4 runs

at Leeds
Yorkshire 191 for 7
Warwickshire 192 for 5 (N.V. Knight 92 not out)
Warwickshire (4 pts) won by 5 wickets

With the title already won, Lancashire played their final game under floodlights at Trent Bridge two days after their success against Hampshire at Old Trafford. They celebrated in style in a match reduced to 26 overs by a delayed start, and, in Nottinghamshire's case, reduced to 24. Flintoff, Young Cricketer of the Year, blasted 93 off 56 balls with three sixes and 11 fours, and Nottinghamshire were never in contention. The defeat meant that Nottinghamshire would play in the Second Division in 1999.

Surrey gained a rare win but still finished bottom while Glamorgan's win over Derbyshire still could not find them a place in the top nine. The Duckworth-Lewis method came into operation at Canterbury, where the match was reduced to 28 overs. Kent had a revised target of 172, and a third wicket stand of 105 in 14 overs between Hooper and Walker ensured that they would reach it. Hooper made 62 off 58 balls in what was his last innings for Kent and left the field to a standing ovation. Essex's season came to the most miserable of conclusions. Having invested all in the AXA League, they suffered their third defeat in succession and finished in third place. Against Leicestershire, they lost 10 wickets for 46 runs.

Gloucestershire confirmed their place in the First Division and condemned Middlesex to the Second, but neither Northamptonshire nor Sussex retained a real hope of finishing in the top nine. Worcestershire had a narrow win over Hampshire, whose tail, inspired by McLean and James, performed nobly. Warwickshire's win at Headingley gave them second place above Essex.

AXA League Final Table

	P	W	L	NR/T	Pts	RR
Lancashire (3)	17	12	2	3	54	12.18
Warwickshire (1)	17	9	5	3	42	4.23
Essex (7)	17	9	5	2/1	42	1.27
Leicestershire (4)	17	9	6	2	40	15.13
Kent (2)	17	8	6	3	38	1.19
Gloucestershire (11)	17	7	6	4	36	–1.65
Worcestershire (8)	17	7	6	3/1	36	–4.60
Hampshire (15)	17	8	8	1	34	0.95
Yorkshire (10)	17	8	8	1	34	–2.47
Glamorgan (13)	17	7	8	2	32	–0.25
Nottinghamshire (12)	17	7	8	1/1	32	–0.67
Middlesex (16)	17	7	8	2	32	–4.90
Northamptonshire (9)	17	6	7	3/1	32	2.80
Somerset (6)	17	6	8	2/1	30	–0.10
Derbyshire (14)	17	6	8	3	30	–5.10
Sussex (18)	17	6	9	2	28	–1.84
Durham (17)	17	4	9	3/1	24	–7.89
Surrey (5)	17	3	12	2	16	–8.17

(1997 positions are in brackets)
Top nine teams will compete in Division One in 1999; bottom nine will form Division Two.

Scarborough Festival

10 July
Yorkshiremen 254 for 7 (D. Byas 70, A. McGrath 60, S.J. Rhodes 50 not out, J.L. Langer 4 for 39)
Sir Tim Rice's International XI 257 for 5
Sir Tim Rice's International XI won by 5 wickets

Northern Electric Trophy

11 July
at Scarborough
Yorkshire 324 for 4 (M.P. Vaughan 130, D.S. Lehmann 93 not out)
Durham 271 (J.E. Morris 107, N.J. Speak 79)
Yorkshire won by 53 runs

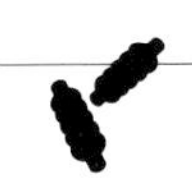

Tetley Bitter Festival Trophy

13 July
at Scarborough
Sir Tim Rice's XI 242 for 6 (R.J. Bailey 86)
Yorkshire 230 for 7 (M.J. Wood 66)
Yorkshire won on faster scoring rate

14 July
at Scarborough
Lord's Taverners 198 for 7 (J.E.R. Gallian 79, P.A. Strang 53 not out)
Heartaches XI 183 for 7 (G.R.J. Roope 83)
Lord's Taverners won by 15 runs

The Britannic Assurance County Championship

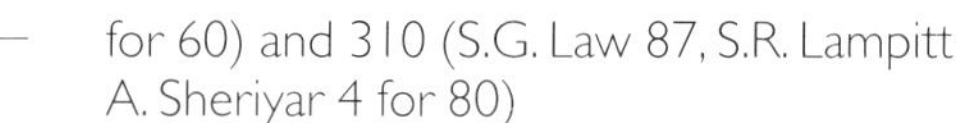

17, 18, 19 and 20 April

at Derby
Nottinghamshire 118 and 312 (U. Afzaal 109 not out, C.M. Tolley 51, P.A.J. DeFreitas 4 for 89)
Derbyshire 388 (T.A. Tweats 161, K.M. Krikken 83, I.D. Blackwell 53, K.P. Evans 5 for 92) and 43 for 4
Derbyshire won by 6 wickets
Derbyshire 24 pts, Nottinghamshire 2 pts

at Hove
Lancashire 266 (A. Flintoff 68, W.K. Hegg 59) and 68 for 0 dec.
Sussex 75 for 4 dec. and 260 for 8 (R.S.C. Martin-Jenkins 63, K. Newell 52, G. Keedy 4 for 58)
Sussex won by 2 wickets
Sussex 20 pts, Lancashire 3 pts

17, 18, 19 and 21 April

at Bristol
Glamorgan 236 (A. Dale 75) and 138 (S.P. James 76, J. Lewis 6 for 49)
Gloucestershire 144 (S.L. Watkin 4 for 53) and 89 (G.P. Butcher 4 for 22, S.D. Thomas 4 for 37)
Glamorgan won by 141 runs
Glamorgan 21 pts, Gloucestershire 4 pts

at Canterbury
Middlesex 228 and 23 for 0 dec.
Kent 0 for 0 dec. and 253 for 6 (A.P. Wells 77, M.J. Walker 68)
Kent won by 4 wickets
Kent 20 pts, Middlesex 1 pt

at The Oval
Surrey 351 for 5 dec. (A.D. Brown 100, G.P. Thorpe 63 not out, J.D. Ratcliffe 61, N. Shahid 58)
Northamptonshire 44 for 2 dec. and 46 for 1
Match drawn
Surrey 7 pts, Northamptonshire 5 pts

at Edgbaston
Warwickshire 336 (N.M.K. Smith 113, D.L. Hemp 52, M.M. Betts 5 for 66) and 187 (N.M.K. Smith 90)
Durham 305 (D.C. Boon 107, P.D. Collingwood 105, E.S.H. Giddins 6 for 89, D.R. Brown 4 for 89) and 90 for 5 (N.J. Speak 50 not out)
Match drawn
Warwickshire 10 pts, Durham 10 pts

at Worcester
Essex 257 (N. Hussain 66, A.P. Grayson 53, A. Sheriyar 4 for 60) and 310 (S.G. Law 87, S.R. Lampitt 4 for 61, A. Sheriyar 4 for 80)
Worcestershire 446 (W.P.C. Weston 95, G.R. Haynes 86, S.J. Rhodes 66, R.K. Illingworth 61) and 122 for 4 (V.S. Solanki 53, R.C. Irani 4 for 38)
Worcestershire won by 6 wickets
Worcestershire 23 pts, Essex 4 pts

at Leeds
Yorkshire 383 (D. Byas 101, D. Gough 89, M.J. Wood 52, M.E. Trescothick 4 for 82) and 204 for 9 dec. (D. Byas 52, A.R. Caddick 4 for 33)
Somerset 237 (G.D. Rose 62) and 135 (C. White 4 for 13)
Yorkshire won by 215 runs
Yorkshire 23 pts, Somerset 4pts

The County Championship began in damp and cold conditions but with a romantic overture as the two counties who beset by problems in 1997, Derbyshire and Sussex, started with victories. Led by Dominic Cork, the Derbyshire pace attack quickly disposed of Nottinghamshire, who fielded newcomers Wharf and Gallian. All did not go well for the home county, however, as their new overseas player Michael Slater broke a finger fielding, and it was thought he would be unable to play for a month. A cheering performance came from Tim Tweats who, on his 24th birthday, hit 161. He and Krikken added 142 in 41 overs for the sixth wicket and took Derbyshire to a commanding lead. They seemed to be in sight of a comfortable victory when Nottinghamshire were 173 for five in their second innings, but Afzaal and Tolley were defiant and put on 124. Afzaal finished unbeaten on 109, a maiden first-class century, and Derbyshire had six overs in which to score 43. They started frenetically and lost two

Crawley enjoyed an outstanding season in the successful Red Rose side and regained his place in the England team, winning a trip to Australia for the Ashes tour.
(Tony Edenden / ASP)

wickets in the first over. Blackwell was bowled in the second over, and it took a more measured approach from Barnett and DeFreitas to win the match with one ball to spare.

Sussex's win was equally dramatic, although it needed arranged declarations to bring about a result. Ultimately, Sussex were set the task of scoring 260 in 88 overs. At 121 for five, with the top batsmen having departed, their chances looked slim. Robin Martin-Jenkins, on the eve of returning to Durham University for his final year of study, joined Keith Newell, and the pair added 106 in 26 overs. Martin-Jenkins hit 63 off 91 balls before falling to Keedy, but when Keith Newell, who played an important anchor innings, was dismissed by the same bowler Sussex needed just 12 from as many overs. A shower reduced the number of overs to two. Lewry was bowled by Keedy, but Kirtley swept his first ball for four and Sussex won their first match at Hove for 22 months with two balls to spare. Reigning champions Glamorgan, awaiting the return of Waqar Younis, had an impressive three-day win over Gloucestershire, whose bowlers were poorly supported by their batsman. On the Monday, 19 wickets fell in 42.5 overs while 121 runs were scored, and Jon Lewis, the Gloucestershire medium-pacer had a career-best six for 49. Glamorgan lost their last nine wickets for 32 runs. Steve James continued the wonderful form he had shown in 1997, batting with a composure that no one else could manage as he hit 76 off 151 balls. Needing 231 to win, Gloucestershire were destroyed by the Glamorgan seam attack and were dismissed in under 30 overs.

As no play was possible on the first day at Canterbury and only two overs were bowled on the second, it needed connivance between the captains to bring a result. Middlesex, with their new opening pair of Langer, the Australian, and Kettleborough from Yorkshire, struggled against the Kent attack, and the home side were set the target of 252 off 60 overs. Walker and Wells provided an excellent foundation with a brisk third wicket stand of 91, and Fleming finished the job with an unbeaten 40 off 44 balls.

The captains could not agree to make up for lost time at The Oval. Alistair Brown hit 100 off 72 balls in 76 minutes, but Adam Hollioake and Kevan Curran found no common ground after discussion. The result was that Curran declared after Northamptonshire had lost two wickets to prevent Surrey taking a bowling bonus point. He was quite happy to accept that his side would be asked to follow on and bat out the last 13 overs of a meaningless contest.

Neither Surrey nor Northamptonshire had been able to call upon their overseas players, but Lara had arrived from the Caribbean in time to lead Warwickshire against Durham. In his last innings against this county, Lara had scored 501, but this time he was caught behind off Wood for 0 as Warwickshire, having been put in, were reduced to 115 for five. They were rallied by Neil Smith, who, batting at number seven, hit two sixes and 13 fours as he savaged an inexperienced attack for a 111-ball century. It was the third first-class hundred of his career. Although lacking six players through injury, Warwickshire still looked strong in attack, and Ed Giddins, returning to championship cricket

Ally Brown cracks a boundary as he begins the season with a 72-ball century for Surrey against Northamptonshire, but the match ended in stalemate.
(Craig Prentis / Allsport)

after a year's ban for drug abuse, took a wicket with the fifth ball he bowled for his new county. He was to finish with six for 89, but Durham found their own heroes. They rose from the depths of 45 for five through the efforts of skipper David Boon and of 21-year old Paul Collingwood who put on 193 for the sixth wicket. Collingwood scored his first championship century. Batting a second time, Warwickshire were again rescued by Neil Smith. Durham were left the final day in which to score 219 to win, but they batted with a lack of belief and were 90 for five when rain ended the match. What hopes they had remained with Speak, who batted with more positivity and confidence than he had shown in 1997.

Put in to bat at Worcester, Essex struggled against Sheriyar and only Hussain and the determined Grayson showed early season form. The home county applied themselves more assiduously, and a consistent batting performance took them to a first innings lead of 189. Thanks to Stuart Law, Essex lost only three wickets in wiping out the arrears, and, with gloom and damp around, it seemed they might force a draw. In the field, they had been handicapped by the loss of Ilott with an injured arm, but they showed fighting qualities with their second innings batting and Worcestershire were forced to chase 122 in 15 overs if they wanted victory on the last evening. There was another handicap for Essex when Cowan, having bowled one over and conceded 19 runs, retired hurt. Irani stuck to his task manfully, but others struggled with a greasy ball. Solanki hit five sixes and two fours in making 53 off 26 balls, and Worcestershire won with three balls to spare, a happy result for Hick, who was leading the county in the absence of Moody.

Yorkshire were missing some familiar faces. Hartley and Morris had departed for Hampshire, and Moxon had been forced to retire because of injury. Lehmann was still on duty with Australia. A century from skipper Byas gave substance to the Yorkshire innings after they had been put in to bat by Somerset, and Matthew Wood scored a pleasing fifty in his first championship match. Yorkshire's pace attack, led by fit again Gough, took the first seven Somerset wickets for 136 runs before Rose and Pierson, newly acquired from Leicestershire, offered the first real resistance. Byas handled his forces admirably, and his declaration at the end of the third day gave Somerset an unpleasant 18 overs batting in which they lost five wickets for 46 runs. The gentler medium paced seam bowling of Craig White brought Yorkshire victory before lunch on the Tuesday. Interestingly, Somerset batted Trescothick down the order and used him primarily for his medium pace bowling.

23, 24, 25 and 27 April

at Riverside
Gloucestershire 287 (R.C. Russell 60, M.W. Alleyne 51, S.J. Harmison 5 for 70) and 103 for 6 dec.
Durham 143 and 201 (N.J. Speak 74, C.A. Walsh 6 for 42)
Gloucestershire won by 46 runs
Gloucestershire 22 pts, Durham 4 pts

at Chelmsford
Sussex 369 (C.J. Adams 135) and 173 for 4 (C.J. Adams 105)
Essex 299 (D.D.J. Robinson 85, A.P. Cowan 66)
Match drawn
Sussex 11 pts, Essex 9 pts

at Cardiff
Kent 166 (D.P. Fulton 61) and 142 for 3 dec. (D.P. Fulton 71 not out)
Glamorgan 63 for 3 dec. and 212 for 8 (A. Dale 54)
Match drawn
Glamorgan 7 pts, Kent 4 pts

at Southampton
Northamptonshire 275 for 5 dec. (M.B. Loye 77, K.M. Curran 58 not out, J.P. Taylor 58, R.J. Bailey 53 not out) and 0 for 0 dec.
Hampshire 0 for 0 dec. and 193 for 8 (M. Keech 67, K.D. James 54, D.E. Malcolm 5 for 60)
Match drawn
Hampshire 5 pts, Northamptonshire 5 pts

at Old Trafford
Middlesex 205 for 4 (J.L. Langer 68, O.A. Shah 64 not out)
v. **Lancashire**
Match drawn
Lancashire 4 pts, Middlesex 4 pts

at Leicester
Worcestershire 268 for 7 (D.A. Leatherdale 99, W.P.C. Weston 77)
v. **Leicestershire**
Match drawn
Leicestershire 6 pts, Worcestershire 5 pts

at Taunton
Somerset 255 (A.R.K. Pierson 71, M.N. Bowen 7 for 73) and 0 for 0 dec.
Nottinghamshire 0 for 0 dec. and 16 for 2
Match drawn
Nottinghamshire 7 pts, Somerset 5 pts

at The Oval
Warwickshire 207 (D.R. Brown 60, I.D.K. Salisbury 4 for 7) and 149 (B.C. Lara 57, M.P. Bicknell 5 for 27)
Surrey 405 for 6 dec. (G.P. Thorpe 114, J.D. Ratcliffe 93, N. Shahid 90, M.A. Butcher 72, N.M.K. Smith 5 for 128)
Surrey won by an innings and 49 runs
Surrey 24 pts, Warwickshire 3 pts

at Leeds
Yorkshire 352 for 5 dec. (D. Byas 103, M.J. Wood 103) and 105 for 0 dec. (A. McGrath 63 not out)
Derbyshire 136 for 5 dec. (K.J. Barnett 55 not out, C.E.W. Silverwood 5 for 38) and 210 (K.J. Barnett 68, A.S. Rollins 63, C.E.W. Silverwood 4 for 42)
Yorkshire won by 111 runs
Yorkshire 22 pts, Derbyshire 2 pts

The rain and the cold were unrelenting. Middlesex had 79 overs batting on the third day at Old Trafford, and then there was no more. No play was possible until the last day at Leicester, where no agreement could be reached and the cricket became meaningless. At Southampton, Northamptonshire were put in and scored 35 for two in 16 overs on the Saturday. On the Monday, the captains debated and Aymes and Robin Smith bowled 18 overs from which 240 runs were scored, and Hampshire went in search of 276 in 76 overs.

The first hat-trick of the season was performed by Danny Law of Essex. It was also the first hat-trick of his career, but his achievement could not prevent Durham from winning the match at Riverside, 16 May.
(John Gichigi / Allsport)

Devon Malcolm destroyed the top order, and the home county were reeling at 54 for five. The indespensable Kevan James joined Keech in a partnership worth 96, and Aymes completed the task of surviving.

A career best bowling performance by Mark Bowen was nullified by the weather after the innings had been forfeited, and the determination of Croft saved Glamorgan against Kent. Maynard put the visitors in to bat, and Glamorgan were on top until the weather intervened.

Another to be thwarted by weather was Chris Adams, captain of Sussex. Essex won the toss and asked Sussex to bat. Adams responded with 135 off 196 balls. He hit two sixes and 18 fours and took his side to maximum batting points. His innings ended when he was brilliantly caught by Hussain off Irani. Night-watchman Cowan joined Robinson in a second wicket stand of 115, but Essex fell apart against a varied attack. Sussex led by 70 on the first innings, and Adams hit his second century of the match, 105 off 122 balls with four sixes and 10 fours, but just as he was contemplating a declaration the rain returned.

There was no play on the first day at Riverside, and when Gloucestershire chose to bat on the second day they fell foul of Durham's 19-year old pace bowler Stephen Harmison. He took the first four wickets, and Gloucestershire were reduced to 78 for five. Alleyne, Russell, Ball and Lewis brought about a revival, and although Harmison finished with the first five-wicket haul of his career, Gloucestershire had seized the initiative. They tightened their grip on the game on the Saturday afternoon when Durham were bowled out for 143. Harmison took three more wickets, and Gloucestershire, resuming on the last morning at 32 for 0, lost six wickets for 34 runs in 50 minutes. Alleyne's declaration generously left Durham 74 overs in which to score 248, but they soon descended to 42 for four, with Walsh taking three of the wickets. Speak again batted well, but when Ball bowled Wood Durham's last pair, Walker and Harmison, had 26 balls to negotiate if they were to save the game. Walsh was recalled, and Harmison edged him to Russell to give Gloucestershire victory with 19 balls to spare.

Warwickshire were totally outplayed by Surrey. Put in to bat, they lost four wickets for 82 runs. Ostler, a makeshift opener, registered his third 'duck' in as many innings. Lara, at the crease in the first over, for the third time, made 38, but Penney and Brown restored pride with a stand of 94. Salisbury wrapped up the tail with four for 7 in 11.3 overs. The last six wickets went down for 31 runs. By the end of the second day, Surrey were 162 for 0, and Butcher, who had bowled well, and Ratcliffe made their stand worth 172 on the Saturday. They were out in quick succession, but Shahid and Thorpe then added 190. Thorpe was at his best, and Shahid, who promised so much in his early days with Essex, suggested he might yet fulfil that potential rather than remain one of cricket's 'nearly men'. Neil Smith bowled with customary endeavour, but his performance emphasised how much the injured Giles was missed. Batting a second time, Warwickshire surrendered to the impressive Martin Bicknell. Their last seven wickets went down for 40.

Yorkshire made it two wins in two matches, but it needed a brave declaration by Dominic Cork to keep the game at Headingley. Yorkshire scored five runs off the 17 balls bowled on the first day, and by the end of the second they were 157 for two from 55 overs. Byas hit his second century of the season and Wood the first of his career in sharing a third wicket partnership of 230. Byas declared as soon as maximum points had been achieved. Cork's response was to declare 216 runs in arrears after Silverwood had taken all five wickets to fall. Byas was less generous in setting Derbyshire a target of 322 in 91 overs. A third wicket stand of 104 between Rollins and Barnett gave the visitors some hope, but Silverwood was again in fine form. He finished with match figures of nine for 80 as Yorkshire won by mid-afternoon on the fourth day.

13, 14, 15 and 16 May

at Derby
Derbyshire 98 (D.R. Brown 5 for 40) and 173 (E.S.H. Giddins 4 for 62)
Warwickshire 332 (N.V. Knight 109, D.L. Hemp 54, G. Welch 54)
Warwickshire won by an innings and 61 runs
Warwickshire 23 pts, Derbyshire 4 pts

at Riverside
Durham 276 (M.A. Gough 62, M.C. Ilott 4 for 49) and 247 (D.R. Law 5 for 46)
Essex 185 and 243 (N. Hussain 63, M.M. Betts 6 for 83)
Durham won by 95 runs
Durham 22 pts, Essex 4 pts

at Bristol
Gloucestershire 134 (C.C. Lewis 6 for 60, A.D. Mullally 4 for 33) and 259 (M.W. Alleyne 56, A.D. Mullally 4 for 54)
Leicestershire 351 (B.F. Smith 121 not out, V.J. Wells 120, A.M. Smith 5 for 66) and 44 for 1
Leicestershire won by 9 wickets
Leicestershire 24 pts, Gloucestershire 4 pts

at Southampton
Surrey 591 (A.D. Brown 155, M.A. Butcher 106, J.N. Batty 63, A.J. Stewart 59, N.A.M. McLean 4 for 107)
Hampshire 189 (A.D. Mascarenhas 60 not out, A.J. Tudor 4 for 32) and 218
Surrey won by an innings and 184 runs
Surrey 24 pts, Hampshire 2 pts

at Canterbury
Kent 186 (M.A. Ealham 73) and 517 (C.L. Hooper 203, D.P. Fulton 96, S.A. Marsh 50 not out, M. Watkinson 4 for 94)
Lancashire 445 (M.A. Atherton 152, M. Watkinson 87, W.K. Hegg 64) and 125 for 2 (N.H. Fairbrother 52 not out)
Match drawn
Lancashire 10 pts, Kent 5 pts

at Lord's
Middlesex 204 (A.R. Caddick 4 for 74) and 450 for 4 dec. (J.L. Langer 233 not out, D.C. Nash 114)
Somerset 253 (M.N. Lathwell 91, R.J. Harden 63, R.L. Johnson 7 for 86) and 190 (M.N. Lathwell 88, A.R.C. Fraser 4 for 39)
Middlesex won by 211 runs
Middlesex 21 pts, Somerset 6 pts

at Northampton
Yorkshire 148 (D.E. Malcolm 6 for 54) and 288 (D. Gough 58)
Northamptonshire 332 (D.J.G. Sales 60, C. White 5 for 46) and 105 for 2
Northamptonshire won by 8 wickets
Northamptonshire 23 pts, Yorkshire 4 pts

at Trent Bridge
Nottinghamshire 275 (P. Johnson 68, J.D. Lewry 4 for 57) and 122 (R.J. Kirtley 7 for 29)
Sussex 324 (M.T.E. Peirce 96, J.R. Carpenter 65) and 74 for 6
Sussex won by 4 wickets
Sussex 23 pts, Nottinghamshire 6 pts

Of the eight matches, only three lasted into the fourth day, the Saturday, and of those two ended before lunch. Having failed to qualify for the final stages of the Benson and Hedges Cup, Warwickshire were in desperate need of a victory. They achieved it at Deby in a most comprehensive manner. Lara won the toss, asked Derbyshire to bat and his seam bowlers dismissed them for 98 in 31.5 overs. Powell was out for 0, but Knight and Hemp scored 129 for the second wicket. Knight went on to reach his first hundred of the season on a day that saw 18 wickets fall. There was a sting in the Warwickshire tail with the eighth and ninth wickets producing 134 runs between them, thanks mostly to Welch and the improving Frost. Batting a second time, Derbyshire fared only marginally better than they had done in the first innings, and Warwickshire won inside two days.

Both Essex and Durham had qualified for the quarter-final of the Benson and Hedges Cup and both were weakened by injury, but Durham had more cause for optimism. They batted first at Riverside and debutant Michael Gough provided substance for their innings when it threatened to fall apart. He batted for four-and-three-quarter hours and faced 227 balls to display immense character and determination. On the second day, Essex failed to cope with the Durham seam attack. Wood ripped out the middle order, and, leading by 91 on the first innings, the home county reached 104 for three by the end of the second day. The third day threatened a transformation. Danny Law took a wicket his first ball of the day, and later in the morning performed the first hat-trick of the season. He had Foster and Phillips caught at second slip by Stuart Law and then trapped Betts leg before to put Essex back in the game, but the last two Durham wickets added 70 to the score. Needing 339 to win in the best part of five sessions, the visitors were soon struggling and finished the day on 196 for six. The end came quickly on the last morning, with Betts taking three of the last four wickets in another good bowling performance.

Leicestershire asked Gloucestershire to bat first when they won the toss at Bristol, and Mullally and acting captain Lewis dismissed the home county inside 42 overs. Vince Wells and Ben Smith then shared a third wicket partnership of 153 to put Leicestershire in total command. Wells batted at his best, and, on the second day, Ben Smith, whose career has had the best of fortune, completed a more patient but equally important hundred. Gloucestershire were 16 for three in their second innings, but they fought tenaciously, with their last two wickets realising 70 runs. It meant that Leicestershire would have to bat again, but the visitors still completed victory in mid-afternoon of the third day.

Surrey's outstanding form continued as they totally outplayed Hampshire. Winning the toss, Surrey amassed 434 for five in 104 overs on the first day. They were indebted to missed chances as Butcher and Stewart benefited in an opening stand of 118. Butcher went on to hit 19 fours in his 106, which occupied 282 minutes. Alistair Brown reached his second century of the season before the close, and when he was out to McLean on the second day he had made 155 off 147 balls. His batting is littered with technical imperfections, but few hit the ball as hard or as often. The late order plundered runs merrily, the ninth wicket adding 91, and Hampshire, without Stephenson, faced an immense task. Tudor took wickets at the beginning and end as they were dismissed for 189, and, following on 402 in arrears, they lost both openers for nine. They offered sterner resistance on the third day, but Surrey were never going to be denied.

Only at Canterbury was there no outright result. Kent, choosing to bat first on a good pitch, collapsed on the opening day. They were undone by the heavy, misty atmosphere, and although Hooper and Patel took three wickets for 28 runs at the end of the day, Lancashire dominated. That domination became absolute on the second day when Atherton came out of his nightmare spell with an innings of 152 in 466 minutes. There were positive later contributions from Watkinson and Hegg, and all that was left to Kent was to hope to save the game. This they did through a third wicket stand of 132 between Fulton and Hooper, who batted into the final day to reach 203 off 210 balls. He hit six sixes and 23 fours.

There was also a double century at Lord's in a game that saw fortunes change dramatically. The opening day belonged to Somerset, who bowled out Middlesex for 204 and reached 157 for five themselves. A fourth wicket stand of 97 between Harden and Lathwell had been the only occasion when bat had dominated ball on a hard pitch enjoyed by the quicker bowlers. Had Lathwell had better support, Somerset would have led by more than 49 on the first innings, but Richard Johnson, an England prospect of recent memory, bowled with accuracy and hostility to keep Middlesex in contention. Batting a second time, Middlesex lost three wickets for 108 runs before Nash joined Langer. They batted into the third day, adding 223. David Nash reached the second century of his career while Justin Langer revealed his great quality with an innings of 233 off 369 balls. He hit a six and 33 fours and demonstrated that he had command of all the shots in the repertoire. Brown's declaration left Somerset the task of scoring 402 to win. Angus Fraser took four wickets in 25 balls, and they ended the day on 50 for six. Lathwell again offered stout and purposeful resistance on the last morning, but the end was not long in coming.

At Northampton, Yorkshire were put into total disarray by Devon Malcolm. He bowled McGrath with the third ball of the match and maintained a lively pace in conditions that helped him swing the ball. His six wickets were no more than he deserved. Yorkshire's hitherto highly successful pace attack could not emulate him and by the end of the second day Northamptonshire, who batted consistently, had taken a first innings lead of 185 and had reduced Yorkshire to 147 for seven in their second innings. It was the young off-spinner Graeme Swann who was mainly responsible for their demise this time, taking three wickets, including that of Lehmann, for 20 runs in seven overs. There was brave rearguard action from Blakey, Gough and Silverwood on the third day when Yorkshire's eighth and ninth wickets realised 153 runs, but this only delayed the inevitable. Yorkshire's defeat meant that Surrey went a point clear at the top of the table.

Second to Surrey were Sussex. Adams won the toss at Trent Bridge and asked Nottinghamshire to bat first. Kirtley and Lewry exploited a grassy pitch and a heavy atmosphere, and, but for Paul Johnson's 68 off 75 balls and Paul Strang's positive 48, the home county would have come nowhere near 275. Strang and Bowen made 57 for the ninth wicket, and 51 extras, 22 of them wides and 22 no-balls, boosted the Nottinghamshire total. Sussex closed on 49 for three, but two left-handers, Toby Peirce and James Carpenter, added 147 for the fifth wicket on the second day. Carpenter made the highest score of his brief career, and Peirce was denied a deserved second century when he was leg before to Dowman for 96. Kirtley produced a late burst that left Nottinghamshire staggering at 11 for three. This soon became 23 for seven on the third morning as Kirtley extended his figures to six for 3 in 39 deliveries. Gallian, batting with a runner because of a groin injury, and Strang counterattacked with 83 in 19 overs. They both fell to Lewry, and Kirtley finished with seven for 29, the season's best analysis to date. Needing 74 to win, Sussex reached 52 without loss and then saw six wickets fall for 17 runs, a reminder of recent agonies. Keith Newell and Jarvis took root, and victory came with a wide, not entirely inappropriate in this match.

21, 22, 23 and 24 May

at Chelmsford
Essex 242 (S.G. Law 55, G. Chapple 5 for 49) and 244 (M. Watkinson 5 for 45)
Lancashire 314 (N.H. Fairbrother 126, D.R. Law 4 for 70) and 175 for 3 (J.P. Crawley 64 not out)
Lancashire won by 7 wickets
Lancashire 23 pts, Essex 5 pts

at Gloucester
Gloucestershire 329 (R.C. Russell 63 not out, A.M. Smith 61, G.I. Macmillan 53, C. White 8 for 55) and 328 for 8 dec. (M.G.N. Windows 100 not out, A.J. Wright 57, M.W. Alleyne 55)
Yorkshire 143 and 214 (D.S. Lehmann 69, M.C.J. Ball 4 for 72)
Gloucestershire won by 300 runs
Gloucestershire 23 pts, Yorkshire 4 pts

at Canterbury
Durham 229 (M.J. Foster 76, M.M. Patel 5 for 73) and 239 (J.J.B. Lewis 72, D.W. Headley 6 for 71)
Kent 495 (R.W.T. Key 101, A.P. Wells 95, S.A. Marsh 92, D.P. Fulton 65)
Kent won by an innings and 27 runs
Kent 24 pts, Durham 4 pts

at Leicester
Hampshire 361 (A.N. Aymes 133, A.D. Mullally 5 for 72) and 276 for 8 (A.D. Mascarenhas 63, S.D. Udal 62, K.D. James 55 not out)
Leicestershire 305 for 7 dec. (A. Habib 112, N.A.M. McLean 6 for 101)
Match drawn
Hampshire 9 pts, Leicestershire 8 pts

at Uxbridge
Worcestershire 627 for 6 dec. (G.A. Hick 166, D.A. Leatherdale 137, T.M. Moody 132, V.S. Solanki 78, S.J. Rhodes 67 not out)
Middlesex 389 (M.R. Ramprakash 122, J.L. Langer 97) and 373 for 5 dec. (J.L. Langer 118, M.R. Ramprakash 108, M.W. Gatting 83 not out)
Match drawn
Worcestershire 10 pts, Middlesex 9 pts

at Northampton
Northamptonshire 172 (D. Ripley 59, K.M. Curran 54) and 712 (M.B. Loye 322 not out, D. Ripley 209)
Glamorgan 563 (S.P. James 227, P.A. Cottey 113, M.J. Powell 106) and 44 for 0
Match drawn
Glamorgan 11 pts, Northamptonshire 6 pts

at Taunton
Somerset 176 (M.P. Bicknell 4 for 14) and 475 (P.C.L. Holloway 123, R.J. Turner 88, G.D. Rose 76, I.D.K. Salisbury 5 for 98)
Surrey 241 (I.D.K. Salisbury 51) and 245 (M.A. Butcher 109 not out)
Somerset won by 165 runs
Somerset 20 pts, Surrey 5 pts

at Horsham
Sussex 325 (M. Newell 135 not out, W.G. Khan 70, D.G. Cork 4 for 77) and 374 (M.G. Bevan 127, W.G. Khan 125)
Derbyshire 593 (K.J. Barnett 162, M.E. Cassar 121, D.G. Cork 102 not out, P.A.J. DeFreitas 87, A.S. Rollins 58,

J.D. Lewry 6 for 72) and 107 for 3
Derbyshire won by 7 wickets
Derbyshire 24 pts, Sussex 6 pts

at Edgbaston
Warwickshire 130 (M.J. Powell 70 not out, M.N. Bowen 4 for 22) and 280 (B.C. Lara 80, M.J. Powell 73)
Nottinghamshire 218 (E.S.H. Giddins 4 for 47) and 193 for 4 (U. Afzaal 78 not out, M.P. Dowman 63)
Nottinghamshire won by 6 wickets
Nottinghamshire 21 pts, Warwickshire 4 pts

Essex's misery continued. Weakened by injuries, they suffered their third defeat in four championship matches, losing to Lancashire before lunch on the Saturday. Put in to bat, they lost Flanagan and Peters without a run scored and struggled from that point onwards. Robinson and Stuart Law added 91 but three wickets then fell for eight runs, and the lower order did well to take them to 242. Chapple claimed five wickets, and later shone with the bat as he and Fairbrother put on 103 for the eighth wicket. Fairbrother hit 20 fours and Danny Law gave an impressive bowling performance, taking three wickets in quick succession as Lancashire slipped from 179 for four to 181 for seven. In spite of this, the visitors' first innings lead of 72 was decisive. The Essex middle order collapsed in the second innings, and Lancashire had few problems in gaining their first championship win of the season.

Mal Loye of Northamptonshire hit an unbeaten 322 against Glamorgan at Northampton. He and Ripley added 401 for the fifth wicket, a record for any Northamptonshire wicket. *(Michael Regan / Allsport)*

Having started the season in fine style, Yorkshire suffered defeat for the second championship match in succession in spite of the fact that Craig White took eight for 55, the best bowling figures of his career and the best of the season to date. Macmillan played his first championship match for Gloucestershire and made 53 off 39 balls before becoming White's first victim. The home county reached 196 for three before White took five wickets for one run in 10 balls. At 199 for eight, Gloucestershire staged a remarkable rally. Russell was solid, but Mike Smith threw his bat at everything in reaching the highest score of his career, 61 off 65 balls with 14 fours. He then dismissed McGrath before the close, and on the second day, Yorkshire capitulated to a varied attack. Gloucestershire had now taken a grip on the game, and Matt Windows hit a fluent century, the third of his career, on the third day to put the game out of Yorkshire's reach. They began the last day on 136 for five, and the game was over before lunch with Martyn Ball's off-spin doing most of the damage.

Kent overpowered Durham in three days. Put in to bat, the northern county were indebted to a last wicket stand of 102 in 20 overs between Foster and Harmison for saving them from total humiliation. Foster's 76 came off 84 balls, and Harmison's 36 was his highest score. The second day saw Kent put some wayward Durham bowling to the sword. Fulton and Key scored 168 for the first wicket, and 19-year old Robert Key, playing only his fourth championship innings, reached a maiden century. Given a firm basis, Kent launched a violent attack on the bowling, and 173 runs came in the 33 overs before tea with skipper Marsh lashing 92 off 95 balls. Gough was out before the end of the second day, and Headley and Patel completed Kent's maximum point victory in three days. Headley had match figures of nine for 120, and Patel had figures of eight for 140.

There was dour stuff at Leicester. Hampshire, electing to bat first, made 276 for six from 111 overs on the first day against an attack deprived of Millns, Lewis and Ormond. Aymes made the highest score of his career, and Habib made a century for the home county, who scored at a quicker rate than their opponents and declared in arrears to compensate for lost time. Hampshire slipped to 77 for six and batted out time in tedious fashion.

An outright result never looked to be possible on the pitch at Uxbridge – there was no balance between bat and ball. Worcestershire scored 435 for four in 104 overs on the first day. Hick and Solanki scored 133 for the second wicket; Hick and Moody 222 for the fourth. Leatherdale scored the third century of the innings on the second day, and Worcestershire's 627 for six was the highest score ever recorded against Middlesex. Not to be outdone, Langer and Ramprakash hit 175 for the home side's second wicket in the first innings, and, following on, 125 for the second wicket in the second innings. Ramprakash completed an elegant century in each innings, and Langer confirmed that he was much enjoying cricket in England.

There were extraordinary events at Northampton where the home county were put in to bat and bowled out by

Glamorgan's eager attack for 172. Glamorgan were already in the lead by the end of the first day as they scored at five an over with James powering to his century. The opener carried on where he ended the previous season and hit 36 fours in his 312-ball innings of 227. He and Powell added 186 in 33 overs for the third wicket, and Powell hit his first championship century. Cottey also plundered a century, and Glamorgan took a first innings lead of 391. At 142 for four, Northamptonshire looked doomed to defeat, but Ripley joined Loye, and the pair batted into the final day, adding 401 for the fifth wicket. This was not only a Northamptonshire record for any wicket; it was also a fifth wicket record for English cricket. The stand occupied just over 92 overs. Ripley's maiden double century included a seven, a six and 34 fours, while Mal Loye batted for 10 hours 48 minutes and hit 49 fours in what was the highest score ever recorded for Northamptonshire, whose 712 was the biggest total ever made against Glamorgan. Ripley, a popular man who has accepted an uneven career with grace and humour, deserved his triumph, as did young Loye who suffered setbacks after a most promising start. With such a mighty achievement to his credit, he should now have the confidence to fulfil the immense potential that, most assuredly, he possesses.

There was a surprise at Taunton where Surrey, without Stewart, Brown, Adam Hollioake, Thorpe and Saqlain Mushtaq, were humbled by Somerset. Put in to bat, Somerset were reduced to 65 for seven on the opening day. Their tail rallied bravely, and Surrey finished the day 20 runs in arrears with three wickets standing. Somerset gave a debut to left-arm seamer Matt Bulbeck, and he sent back Butcher and Knott. Salisbury's fifty gave Surrey a slender lead on the second day, and Somerset again started badly, losing four wickets for 72 runs. Holloway and Turner stopped the rot with a stand of 214, and the tail oozed runs. Holloway reached the second and higher century of his career, and Surrey were left to make 411 to win. Acting captain Mark Butcher carried his bat through the innings, and he and Ratcliffe scored 85 for the first wicket, but there was little else to halt Somerset's march to their first championship win of the season. Why, with so many players on international duty, Surrey relegated Saqlain to twelfth man remains a mystery.

In spite of this defeat, Surrey remained top of the table, but Sussex now joined them on 60 points although they were also beaten. They had begun well enough against Derbyshire. Wasim Khan and Mark Newell put on 110 for their second wicket, and Mark Newell, at number three, was unbeaten at the end of the innings on the second morning for his second and higher first-class hundred. Despite his efforts, Sussex were in trouble by the end of the second day when Barnett and Cassar savaged 254 in 74 overs for Derbyshire's fourth wicket. Matthew Cassar, a tall, strong all-rounder, made the first century of his career and kept pace with the more experienced Barnett. They both played innings of quality. Sussex's problems increased when Kirtley withdrew from the attack with an injured ankle, and, on the third day, DeFreitas hit five sixes and 11 fours in a 94-ball innings. Cork supported DeFreitas initially and then cut loose to hit a century of 187 balls as the last four wickets realised 208 runs. On a flat pitch, with the smoothest of outfields, Lewry's figures of six for 72 from 36 overs were outstanding. There still seemed no way that Sussex would lose the match as Wasim Khan and Bevan shared a third wicket stand of 192 in 57 overs. Both reached their first centuries for their new county, but once they were dismissed Sussex fell apart, and Derbyshire gained a surprisingly easy victory.

They same applied to Nottinghamshire against Warwickshire. Johnson asked the home county to bat first when he won the toss, and Bowen, Franks and Oram did all that was asked of them by bowling Warwickshire out for 130. But for Michael Powell carrying his bat throughout the innings, the 'Bears' would have fared much worse. Nottinghamshire took a first innings lead of 88, and their pace attack again did well in spite of Lara, hitting 80. Powell played his second patient and technically competent innings of the match and shared a third wicket stand of 116 with Lara, but Nottinghamshire were left needing 193 to win. A second wicket stand of 112 between Dowman and Afzaal brushed away any doubts that they might not accomplish their first championship win of the season.

29, 30, 31 May and 1 June

at Chesterfield
Leicestershire 246 (I.J. Sutcliffe 82, D.G. Cork 5 for 72) and 186 (V.J. Wells 64, P.A.J. DeFreitas 5 for 38, K.J. Dean 5 for 57)
Derbyshire 177 (J. Ormond 5 for 50) and 217 (K.J. Barnett 57, A.D. Mullally 4 for 57)
Leicestershire won by 38 runs
Leicestershire 21 pts, Derbyshire 4 pts

at Lord's
Glamorgan 308 (P.A. Cottey 81, S.P. James 79, J.P. Hewitt 5 for 69) and 260 (M.J. Powell 79 not out, A.D. Shaw 51)
Middlesex 256 (D.C. Nash 76, S.L. Watkin 5 for 30) and 314 for 1 (J.L. Langer 153 not out, M.R. Ramprakash 128 not out)
Middlesex won by 9 wickets
Middlesex 22 pts, Glamorgan 7 pts

at Trent Bridge
Nottinghamshire 211 (P.J. Franks 66, M.M. Betts 5 for 59) and 224 (R.T. Robinson 64, M.J. Foster 4 for 41)
Durham 269 (P.D. Collingwood 97 not out, M.J. Foster 68, C.M. Tolley 5 for 48) and 167 for 2 (N.J. Speak 77 not out, D.C. Boon 54 not out)
Durham won by 8 wickets
Durham 22 pts Nottinghamshire 5 pts

at The Oval
Surrey 342 (A.J. Stewart 86, I.D.K. Salisbury 56 not out, M.A. Butcher 51, C.L. Hooper 7 for 93)
Kent 86 and 226 (C.L. Hooper 94, Saqlain Mushtaq 4 for 100)
Surrey won by an innings and 30 runs
Surrey 23 pts, Kent 4 pts

On 31 May, Graeme Hick scored 132 for Worcestershire against Sussex. It was the 100th hundred of his career, and he became only the 24th batsman in the history of the game to have reached this landmark.
(Mike Hewitt / Allsport)

at Worcester
Worcestershire 353 for 9 dec. (G.A. Hick 104, J.D. Lewry 4 for 104) and 343 for 3 dec. (V.S. Solanki 155, G.A. Hick 132)
Sussex 278 (M.G. Bevan 96, S.R. Lampitt 5 for 56) and 123 for 0 (W.G. Khan 53 not out, M.T.E. Peirce 51 not out)
Match drawn
Worcestershire 11 pts, Sussex 9 pts

Of the five county matches, three were over in three days, but all produced a variety of fascinating cricket. Leicestershire, still without Whitaker and Millns, welcomed back Ormond after an abscess on the spine, and he made a vital contribution to their three-day win at Chesterfield. The pitch, as is traditional at Queen's Park, offered help to the seamers, and, having chosen to bat, Leicestershire did not find batting easy as the ball presented the added hazard of swinging under some heavy cloud. Wickets fell regularly with only Sutcliffe mastering the conditions. Cork gained just reward for some good bowling, and he was ably supported by DeFreitas. Even so, Leicestershire's 246 turned out to be the highest score of the match. Ormond returned in fine style, and he, Mullally and Lewis proved too much for the home county. With a first innings lead of 69, Leicestershire looked in total control as Wells and Maddy began their second innings with a stand of 76, but the combination of DeFreitas and the left-arm medium pace of Dean proved too much for the later batsmen, and Derbyshire were left to score 256 to win with more than two days in which to get the runs. The loss of Slater on the Saturday evening was a severe blow. Barnett and May hinted at permanence, and shortly before tea on the third day, Derbyshire were 182 for four against an attack deprived of Ormond and Simmons with minor injuries. On that score, however, three wickets fell, and from that point on, there was only one winner.

The match at Lord's went the full four days. Ramprakash chose to field when he won the toss, but his bowlers gained no tangible reward. Glamorgan batted into the second day, and, with James and Dale making 107 for the second wicket, they reached 293 for five before losing their last five wickets for 15 runs. Hewitt was the principal reason for the collapse, and the veteran Watkin proved the undoing of Middlesex, who trailed by 52 on the first innings. Their plight would have been worse but for a fighting innings from Nash, who, with Hewitt and Fraser, cajoled 129 from the last four wickets. Glamorgan had welcomed back skipper Maynard, but they suffered a dreadful blow when Waqar Younis withdrew from the attack with an injured elbow after bowling just three overs. James and Shaw began the Welsh county's second innings with a stand of 96, but the middle offered no substance, and it was left to the very promising Michael Powell to see that Middlesex faced a stiff challenge, a target of 313. They began the last day with six to their credit and lost Kettleborough at 38. That was the last of their troubles as Langer and Ramprakash shared an unbroken stand of 276. The pair gave another majestic display to take Middlesex to their second win of the season.

Durham also gained their second victory of the season and found themselves in the dizzy heights of third place in the championship. David Boon returned after injury and shared an unbroken stand of 120 with Nick Speak, which gave his side an eight-wicket win in three days. There was sad news that Simon Brown was in need of surgery on an injured knee and was likely to miss the rest of the season, but Betts, Wood, Harmison and Foster all performed nobly in attack. Michael Foster, once of Yorkshire and Northamptonshire, appears to have found his true worth at Durham and had a fine all-round match. Facing Nottinghamshire's 211, the visitors were 98 for six before Foster joined Collingwood in a stand worth 110 which turned the match. Chris Tolley's fine bowling effort was in vain, as Nottinghamshire again proved a model of inconsistency. One of the major reasons for Durham's success was Paul Collingwood's excellent form, which at last gave some substance to the middle order. 22 years old, he is a home-grown product rather than an import.

Surrey extended their lead at the top of the table when they beat Kent by an innings and 30 runs just 25 minutes into the third day. Stewart and Butcher had begun the match with a partnership of 142, and Saqlain Mushtaq and Ian Salisbury added 72 for the seventh wicket when the innings threatened to crumble. Spin dominated from the start, and Carl Hooper's off-breaks brought him the best bowling figures of his career. Kent collapsed against Saqlain and Salisbury, and it was the same two spinners who bowled them out for a second time when they were asked to follow on. Saqlain had match figures of seven for 118, and Salisbury returned six for 88. Hooper alone defied them, and the weakness of the Kent batting had begun to give cause for concern. Thorpe held seven catches in the match, six of them in the first innings.

The match at Worcester ended in a draw when rain arrived on the last afternoon, but it was a game of historic significance. Graeme Hick hit a century in each innings. His 132 on the Sunday was the 100th of his career, and he joined Hammond, Grace, Bradman, Hutton, Compton, Graveney, Gooch and others as the 24th member of the illustrious band who have 100 hundreds to their credit. If he has not achieved all that had once seemed inevitable, he has records that few have emulated and of which he has reason to be proud. In the second innings against Sussex, he and Solanki put on 243 for the second wicket. Poor Solanki – he chose the wrong day to make the second century of his career, and, in the shadow of Hick's achievement, got none of the praise that was his due.

3, 4, 5 and 6 June

at Chesterfield
Gloucestershire 459 for 8 dec. (M.G.N. Windows 143, T.H.C. Hancock 94, J. Lewis 54 not out, D.R. Hewson 52)
Derbyshire 295 (M.E. Cassar 78 not out, K.J. Barnett 74, K.M. Krikken 60, J. Lewis 6 for 48) and 300 for 5 (A.S. Rollins 107, M.R. May 54)
Match drawn
Gloucestershire 11 pts, Derbyshire 7 pts

at Ilford
Nottinghamshire 342 (P. Johnson 95, G.F. Archer 63, M.C. Ilott 4 for 62) and 279 for 9 dec. (G.F. Archer 69, R.T. Robinson 54, P.M. Such 5 for 73)
Essex 322 (S.G. Law 106, S.D. Peters 64, I.N. Flanagan 57) and 198 for 8 (S.D. Peters 53 not out)
Match drawn
Essex 10 pts, Nottinghamshire 9 pts

at Southampton
Glamorgan 269 (A. Dale 92, M.J. Powell 52, A.D. Mascarenhas 4 for 68) and 285 (A.W. Evans 87, G.P. Butcher 85, P.J. Hartley 4 for 77)
Hampshire 471 (A.N. Aymes 120, R.A. Smith 84, P.R. Whitaker 74, G.W. White 56)and 84 for 1
Hampshire won by 9 wickets
Hampshire 23 pts, Glamorgan 4 pts

at Tunbridge Wells
Sussex 189 (S. Humphries 66, M.V. Fleming 4 for 24) and 303 for 7 dec. (C.J. Adams 84, W.G. Khan 72)
Kent 211 (J.D. Lewry 4 for 55) and 206 (R.J. Kirtley 4 for 19)
Sussex won by 75 runs
Sussex 20 pts, Kent 5 pts

at Lord's
Middlesex 335 (P.N. Weekes 93 not out, J.P. Hewitt 53, M.M. Betts 4 for 83, S.J. Harmison 4 for 88) and 216 (M.W. Gatting 66, P.N. Weekes 51 not out, M.M. Betts 5 for 52)
Durham 312 (J.J.B. Lewis 68, D.C. Boon 68, P.D. Collingwood 66, T.F. Bloomfield 5 for 98) and 240 for 9 (M.A. Gough 56)
Durham won by 1 wicket
Durham 23 pts, Middlesex 7 pts

at Northampton
Lancashire 230 (I.D. Austin 64, F.A. Rose 5 for 89) and 438 for 8 dec. (A. Flintoff 124, J.P. Crawley 124, J.P. Crawley 109, W.K. Hegg 56 not out, D.E. Malcolm 4 for 145)
Northamptonshire 332 (M.B. Loye 149, D. Ripley 56, P.J. Martin 4 for 56) and 274 for 6 (K.M. Curran 90 not out, M.B. Loye 71)
Match drawn
Northamprtonshire 10 pts, Lancashire 8 pts

at Taunton
Somerset 364 (M.E. Trescothick 96, S.C. Ecclestone 94) and 70 for 2
Warwickshire 129 (N.V. Knight 67 not out, G.D. Rose 4 for 25) and 304 (N.M.K. Smith 147, A.R. Caddick 4 for 79)
Somerset won by 8 wickets
Somerset 24 pts, Warwickshire 4 pts

at The Oval
Surrey 502 for 7 dec. (N. Shahid 124, J.D. Ratcliffe 100, A.D. Brown 72, I.J. Ward 64, B.C. Hollioake 51) and 130 for 4 dec. (I.J. Ward 58)
Worcestershire 367 (G.A. Hick 119, Saqlain Mushtaq 4 for 116) and 186 (T.M. Moody 62, Saqlain Mushtaq 7 for 41)
Surrey won by 79 runs
Surrey 23 pts, Worcestershire 5 pts

at Leeds
Leicestershire 353 for 9 dec. (V.J. Wells 144, P.A. Nixon 63) and 78 for 2
Yorkshire 273 for 3 dec. (D. Byas 116, M.P. Vaughan 77, M.J. Wood 52 not out)
Match drawn
Yorkshire 9 pts, Leicestershire 8 pts

There was no play on the first day at either Chesterfield or Leeds, and the matches on these grounds ended in draws. Matthew Windows made his second century in successive innings for Gloucestershire, and Walsh sent back Slater and Tweats before Derbyshire scored a run, but Barnett scored freely before playing on to Alleyne. Later Cassar and Krikken added 112 for the sixth wicket. In spite of their efforts, Derbyshire were forced to follow on as Jon Lewis, having hit a maiden first-class fifty, compounded an excellent performance with career-best bowling figures, six for 48. Adrian Rollins's century saved the home side from defeat.

At Leeds, Vince Wells revived Leicestershire with an excellent century after four wickets had fallen before lunch for 116. On the third day, Vaughan and Byas made 114 for

The season most successful bowler, the first to 100 wickets, makes an early strike in June when he traps Michael Powell leg before, Somerset v. Warwickshire, at Taunton.
(Philip Wilcox)

Yorkshire's second wicket, and Byas and Wood 129 for the third, but rain washed out play on the Saturday.

Essex continued to struggle in the Championship, and, after five matches, they were the only side without a victory to their credit. At Ilford, Nottinghamshire scored 288 for seven on an abbreviated first day, with Johnson and Archer putting on 120 for the fourth wicket. The visitors were bowled out for 342 on the second morning, and when Franks dismissed both Robinson and Grayson in the second over of the Essex innings, they were very much in control of the game. Stuart Law came to the rescue of the home side as he hit 19 fours in his innings of 106, which dominated a third wicket stand of 152 with Ian Flanagan, who celebrated his 18th birthday by batting through 65 overs for a maiden first-class fifty. Law's century was the first championship hundred of the season for Essex, whose middle order offered little. Peters and Ilott earned a third batting point, and Such, like several of his team mates troubled by injury, claimed five wickets on a pitch that was now giving the bowler some help. Set a target of 300, Essex were 148 for six with 27 overs still remaining, but Peters and Danny Law showed welcome discipline in keeping Paul Strang at bay and earning a draw.

Essex's misery was compounded by the fact that Hampshire had an emphatic victory over Glamorgan and so left the Axa League leaders bottom of the championship. Robin Smith won the toss and asked Glamorgan, who were without the injured Waqar Younis, to bat first on a green pitch. The conditions were difficult, but Dale and Powell responded positively, and the day ended with Glamorgan bowled out for 269 in 86 overs and honours even. Robin Smith made 84 pugnacious runs on the second day, and Giles White offered stout defence as Hampshire batted with defiance to slip to 163 for five before Whitaker joined Aymes. They batted into the third day, adding 145, with Aymes hitting his second championship century in successive matches. The later order gave solid support, and Hampshire took a commanding lead. Hartley made early inroads into the Glamorgan second innings, and the last day began with the visitors on 127 for five. They resisted well until tea when Hartley had Butcher caught behind to end the innings and set up Hampshire's first win of the season.

Revitalised Sussex came from behind to gain an impressive victory over Kent at Tunbridge Wells. Put in to bat, Sussex were reduced to 84 for seven. Humphries, 66, and Kirtley, 24, made their highest first-class scores and added 102 in 60 overs, a stand that was to have a significant influence on the match. There was further satisfaction for Sussex on the second day. Lewry and Bevan helped restrict Kent's lead to 22, and Peirce and Khan scored 46 before the close. An hour was lost to rain on the third day before Adams and Khan scored 138 in 43 overs for Sussex's second wicket. On the last day, Adams declared and set Kent a target of 282 in 84 overs. Hooper batted with flourish, but wickets fell regularly to a keen attack backed by equally keen fielding, and Sussex claimed their third win of the season.

History was made at Lord's where Durham gained a memorable victory. After two days, the game was well balanced. Weekes and Hewitt had added 143 for Middlesex's seventh wicket after the hosts had been put in to bat and had lost six wickets for 163. Durham lost Gough and Speak for 58 before Boon and Lewis added 122. Collingwood also batted well, but a flurry of wickets at the close of the innings saw Durham trail by 23 runs. Betts produced a fiery spell and Harmison again impressed as Middlesex were reduced to 139 for six by the close on the third day. This quickly became 158 for eight as Harmison and Betts struck again, but concentration wavered, and Middlesex's ninth wicket realised 55 quick runs. Durham were left a target of 240 in 76 overs. At 191 for six, the odds were on Durham, but Foster was caught on the boundary and two more wickets fell so that when last man Harmison joined Betts 12 runs were still needed. When the penultimate over began, nine were needed, and Betts responded by hitting Tufnell into the Grand Stand for six and taking three off the next ball.

There was no such excitement at Northampton, where the bat ruled. Lancashire were put in to bat and were boosted by Austin and the late order after losing their first five wickets for 68. The Northamptonshire innings followed a similar pattern with Loye and Penberthy adding 100 after four wickets had gone for 78. Loye and Ripley then added 126, and the home county took a first innings lead of 102. Lancashire lost two wickets in clearing the arrears, but there were centuries from Crawley and Flintoff in a third wicket partnership of 166. Flintoff's 124 was a rousing affair, the highest score of his career, and included two sixes and 17 fours. Crawley's declaration set Northamptonshire a target of 337 in 66 overs. It never looked possible. Loye's fine form continued with three sixes and seven fours, and Curran gave brief hope, but a draw was inevitable.

The match at Taunton was over in three days. Warwickshire asked Somerset to bat first and took four wickets for 52 runs. Turner was forced to retire hurt before he had scored a run, and the Warwickshire joy ended. Ecclestone and Trescothick, two left-handers, added 190 exciting runs in 49 overs and completely transformed the game. On the second day, the Somerset innings ended at 364, Turner returning to make an unbeaten 33, and Warwickshire were bowled out by Caddick, Rose and Bulbeck for 129. Following-on, they were 53 for three in their second innings. The decline continued on the third morning, and seven wickets were down for 84 when Neil Smith came to the crease. He hit three sixes and 22 fours in a bravely vigorous knock of 147. He and Penney added 109 in 22 overs for the eighth wicket, and Giles helped him to add 90 for the ninth. Smith's heroics could not stave off defeat, but he made sure that Warwickshire would die with honour.

Surrey gained their fourth victory of the season and led the championship by 17 points from Sussex and 21 from Durham. Under 67 overs were possible on the first day at The Oval, and Surrey scored 193 for three, of which Ratcliffe made 100 off 193 balls. He and Ian Ward made 164 for the first wicket. Even without their leading batsmen, who were on Test duty, Surrey are a formidable side. Shahid, who looked such a good player when he first appeared for Essex nine years earlier, and Brown, more at home in the middle order, added 153 for the fourth wicket. Ben Hollioake hit a breezy fifty. The declaration came when 500 was passed, but Worcestershire showed no sign of limp capitulation. Hick hit his fourth consecutive championship century, and there was a positive contribution from the tail as well as 52 extras. Adam Hollioake was confronted by the dilemma of when to declare, but his decision was the right one, to go for victory. He asked Worcestershire to make 266 at under four runs an over on a pitch that had seen 999 runs scored for the loss of 21 wickets in over three days. Tudor soon bowled Solanki, and Saqlain Mushtaq then took over, claiming a career best seven for 41 and bringing victory with a quarter of an hour to spare.

11, 12, 13 and 15 June

at Riverside
Northamptonshire 163 (J. Wood 5 for 52)
Durham 249 for 4 (M.P. Speight 66 not out, P.D. Collingwood 50 not out)
Match drawn
Durham 8 pts, Northamptonshire 4 pts

at Chelmsford
Surrey 373 (A.D. Brown 79, A.J. Hollioake 59, J.N. Batty 52, M.C. Ilott 4 for 64)
Essex 203 and 75 for 4
Match drawn
Surrey 11 pts, Essex 8 pts

at Cardiff
Worcestershire 273 (S.J. Rhodes 104 not out, P.J. Newport 56, S.D. Thomas 5 for 92) and 296 for 7 dec. (T.M. Moody 104 not out, G.A. Hick 66, D.A. Leatherdale 54)
Glamorgan 288 for 9 dec. (S.D. Thomas 69 not out, G.R. Haynes 5 for 59) and 268 for 8 (S.P. James 152, D.A. Leatherdale 4 for 16)
Match drawn
Glamorgan 9 pts, Worcestershire 9 pts

at Bristol
Gloucestershire 181 (T.H.C. Hancock 62, E.S.H. Giddins 6 for 79) and 307 (M.W. Alleyne 137, E.S.H. Giddins 5 for 85, A.F. Giles 4 for 60)
Warwickshire 187 (C.A. Walsh 6 for 88) and 131 (C.A. Walsh 6 for 65, A.M. Smith 4 for 54)
Gloucestershire won by 170 runs
Gloucestershire 20 pts, Warwickshire 4 pts

at Old Trafford
Lancashire 267 (J.P. Crawley 72, W.K. Hegg 54 not out, A.R. Caddick 4 for 67) and 236 (A.R. Caddick 5 for 80)
Somerset 233 (P.D. Bowler 63, P.J. Martin 4 for 66) and 261 (M.E. Trescothick 73 not out, G.D. Rose 56, Wasim Akram 4 for 105)
Lancashire won by 9 runs
Lancashire 22 pts, Somerset 5 pts

at Leicester
Leicestershire 103 (M.A. Ealham 5 for 23)
Kent 120 for 7 (A.D. Mullally 4 for 45)
Match drawn
Kent 7 pts, Leicestershire 6 pts

at Leeds
Yorkshire 327 for 9 dec. (M.J. Wood 108, M.P. Vaughan 86, A.D. Mascarenhas 4 for 31)
Hampshire 104 (C.E.W. Silverwood 5 for 13) and 272 for 9 (A.N. Aymes 73, G.W. White 67)
Match drawn
Yorkshire 10 pts, Hampshire 7 pts

Another success for Andy Caddick as he sends Neil Smith's off stump cartwheeling. Caddick took seven wickets in the match, which Somerset won by eight wickets.
(Philip Wilcox)

There was little play after the second day at Riverside, none on the first day at Leicester and only five overs after the second. Surrey's bid to strengthen their position at the top of the table was thwarted by the weather. Essex put Surrey in to bat, took four wickets for 66 and then resorted to negative tactics. Brown and Adam Hollioake added 131, and the only consolation for Essex was the bowling of debutant pace bowler Jamie Grove, 18 years old, who captured three wickets. He also scored 33 at number 10 to help gain a batting point. He could not save Essex from having to follow on, but the rain saved them from defeat.

Glamorgan and Worcestershire contrived a thrilling finish in spite of the weather. Worcestershire were 155 for eight before Rhodes and Newport added 114 with Rhodes reaching the fourth century of his career. Darren Thomas had been the bowler to cause most damage, and he now became the saviour batsman. Glamorgan were 169 for seven, but he and Croft put on 100, and Maynard declared with a lead of 15. Rival skipper Moody hit an unbeaten century and set Glamorgan a target of 282 from 58 overs. Steve James gave them a magnificent platform with 152 off 192 balls, and 26 were needed from the last three overs with six wickets standing. Leatherdale dismissed Cottey and Powell with successive deliveries, and then accounted for Croft and James in his next over, four wickets for three runs in nine balls, and Glamorgan's challenge was at an end. Honours were even.

Sixteen wickets fell on the first day at Bristol as Giddins prompted the selectors yet again with six for 79, his best bowling performance for Warwickshire. Walsh restricted the visitors' lead to six runs with a fine display of fast bowling, and Alleyne gained the advantage for Gloucestershire with a defiant century. Even so, the home side were 190 with eight wickets down, but, at this point, Mike Smith joined his captain in a stand worth 105 to which he contributed 41. Giddins finished with match figures of 11 for 164, but Walsh was to outshine him. He dismissed Powell and Hemp on the Saturday evening to set Gloucestershire on the road to victory. Smith played a vital role on the Monday morning when he took four wickets in quick succession, including that of Lara, who was leg before third ball. There was no recovery. Walsh finished with match figures of 12 for 153, and Gloucestershire moved into fourth place in the table.

Lancashire gained their second win of the season in spite of some excellent bowling by Caddick. It was he who kept Somerset in the match, but a target of 271 proved to be just beyond them. They seemed without hope when they were 123 for seven, but Rose and Trescothick shared a stand of 102 in 75 minutes. Rose's valiant effort was ended by Wasim, and, 11 runs later, Mushtaq was caught at mid-on off Martin. Trescothick continued to dominate, but, with 10 runs needed, Caddick got a thin edge to a delivery from Wasim and was caught behind.

A depleted Yorkshire side were denied victory by the weather and by Hampshire's determined rearguard action. Matthew Wood and Michael Vaughan put on 122 for the home county's second wicket, with Wood reaching his second championship century of the season. The last seven Yorkshire wickets fell for 58 runs, but Hampshire fared even worse, losing their first seven wickets for 29 runs. The Yorkshire hero was Chris Silverwood, who took five for 13 in 10 overs and was the main reason for Hampshire being forced to follow on. No play was possible on the Saturday, and a start was not made until 12.25pm on the Monday. Adrian Aymes had consistently displayed excellent batting form throughout the season, and he did not let Hampshire down now. He offered stout defence, and when he was sixth out, for 73, his side led by 12 runs and 20 overs of the match remained. Three wickets fell, but the wisdom of James and Hartley, long in experience, ended any doubts as to the outcome of the match.

Dougie Brown catches Humphries, and Warwickshire are close to victory over Sussex. Humphries became Sussex's regular wicket-keeper early in the season when Moores announced his retirement to concentrate on his job as a coach.
(Philip Wilcox)

17, 18, 19 and 20 June

at Riverside
Durham 337 (D.C. Boon 139 not out, N.J. Speak 57) and 74 (R.D. Stemp 4 for 13)
Yorkshire 319 (M.P. Vaughan 177, N.C. Phillips 4 for 89) and 93 for 1
Yorskhire won by 9 wickets
Yorkshire 23 pts, Durham 7 pts

at Cardiff
Leicestershire 292 (P.A. Nixon 101 not out, C.C. Lewis 50) and 66 for 2 dec.
Glamorgan 74 for 3 dec. and 144 (M.T. Brimson 4 for 4)
Leicestershire won by 140 runs
Leicestershire 19 pts, Glamorgan 4 pts

at Basingstoke
Derbyshire 350 (A.S. Rollins 89) and 140 for 3 dec.
Hampshire 210 for 4 dec. (R.A. Smith 104 not out) and 281 for 5 (J.P. Stephenson 75, A.N. Aymes 61 not out, A.D. Mascarenhas 51)

Hampshire won by 5 wickets
Hampshire 21 pts, Derbyshire 5 pts

at Canterbury
Nottinghamshire 309 (J.E.R. Gallian 92, R.T. Robinson 58, M.V. Fleming 4 for 49) and 307 for 5 dec. (J.E.R. Gallian 80, R.T. Robinson 76, P.J. Franks 66 not out, G.F. Archer 51)
Kent 283 (R.W.T. Key 115, P.J. Franks 4 for 104) and 334 for 7 (C.L. Hooper 122, A.P. Wells 78 not out, P.A. Strang 5 for 166)
Kent won by 3 wickets
Kent 22 pts, Nottinghamshire 7 pts

at Northampton
Northamptonshire 366 (A.L. Penberthy 102 not out, M.B. Loye 78, K.M. Curran 61, D. Ripley 51, T.F. Bloomfield 5 for 67) and 0 for 0 dec.
Middlesex 81 for 0 dec. (J.L. Langer 55 not out) and 147 for 5
Match drawn
Northamptonshire 7 pts, Middlesex 7 pts

at Bath
Somerset 231 and 68 for 6 dec.
Essex 0 for 0 dec. and 300 for 9 (R.C. Irani 127 not out, G.D. Rose 5 for 48)
Essex won by 1 wicket
Essex 20 pts, Somerset 1 pt

at Hove
Warwickshire 490 for 9 dec. (N.V. Knight 159, M.J. Powell 132, T.L. Penney 53 not out, J.D. Lewry 4 for 89)
Sussex 172 (M.T.E. Peirce 64) and 286 (C.J. Adams 79, M.G. Bevan 71, N.M.K. Smith 4 for 72)
Warwickshire won by an innings and 32 runs
Warwickshire 23 pts, Sussex 1 pt

at Worcester
Gloucestershire 188 (D.A. Leatherdale 5 for 20) and 141 for 5 dec.
Worcestershire 122 for 8 dec. (C.A. Walsh 5 for 44) and 211 for 5 (A. Hafeez 55)
Worcestershire won by 5 wickets
Worcestershire 20 pts, Gloucestershire 3 pts

18, 19, 20 and 21 June

at Old Trafford
Surrey 146 (Wasim Akram 4 for 42) and 254 for 1 dec. (N. Shahid 126 not out, I.J. Ward 81 not out)
Lancashire 151 for 7 dec. (A.J. Tudor 5 for 43) and 250 for 4 (N.T. Wood 80 not out, J.P. Crawley 78, A. Flintoff 61)
Lancashire won by 6 wickets
Lancashire 20 pts, Surrey 3 pts

The match to be least affected by the weather was the one at Riverside, where Yorkshire beat Durham inside three days. Put in to bat, Durham were inconsistent, but Boon held the innings together with an accomplished display. Vaughan carried the Yorkshire reply single-handed. McGrath, 31, shared an opening stand of 62, but no other batsman reached 20, and Vaughan was last out for 177, a masterly innings that spanned 437 minutes. Durham led by 18 on the first innings, but they gave an abject display in their second. They surrendered without a fight, and Yorkshire claimed an astonishingly easy and surprise win on a blameless pitch.

A restricted first day at Cardiff was followed by a blank second. On the third day, Nixon and Lewis added 107 in 29 overs for Leicestershire's seventh wicket. With so much time lost to rain, declarations and agreements were inevitable if a result was to be achieved. Ultimately, Glamorgan were set a target of 285 in 84 overs. They were never in contention. Law and Dale opened with a stand of 30, and three wickets then fell for two runs. Maynard and Cottey added 68, after which four wickets went down for 19 runs. Left-arm spinner Matthew Brimson finished with four wickets for four runs from eight overs as Leicestershire won with 30 overs to spare.

Hampshire gained their second win after a blank second day at Basingstoke. With Rollins and Slater scoring 92 for the first wicket, Derbyshire batted consistently to take maximum points, but Robin Smith made the visitors pay for dropped catches by scoring his first first-class century of the summer. He and Aymes added 133 in 40 overs for the fourth wicket. Smith declared 140 runs in arrears and offered 'joke' bowling so that his side could be set a target of 281 in 64 overs. Stephenson ended a miserable run of form with 75 off 67 balls, and Aymes and Mascarenhas scored 114 in 24 overs for the fifth wicket to bring victory with 15 balls to spare.

Kent gained a glorious win over Nottinghamshire after looking to be second best for most of the match. The one bright spot of the Kent first innings was Robert Key's splendid knock, the highest of his first-class career. He opened the innings and stood firm while wickets tumbled and Kent descended to 152 for seven, but Phillips and McCague gave him admirable support in stands of 76 and 55, and his century took Kent to within 26 of the visitors' score. Paul Strang took one for 30 in 25 overs. Nottinghamshire batted with spirit in their second innings, but Johnson set a demanding target of 334 in 58 overs. Events were to prove his judgement almost correct. When Hooper came to the wicket Kent were 74 for two after 10.3 overs, and they lost Key at 113. Hooper and Wells now added 134, with the West Indian playing an amazing innings. He hit 122 off 97 balls, and when he was out Kent needed 87 off as many balls. McCague and Wells maintained the momentum, and Kent won with 15 deliveries to spare. Strang, so economic in the first innings, took five wickets but conceded 166 runs in 23 overs.

Northamptonshire and Middlesex could not overcome two blank days, although Tony Penberthy did have time for a maiden first-class century. Only 35.3 overs were possible in the first two days at Bath, but Somerset and Essex did contrive a result. The visitors were left the last day in which to score 300 runs to win. The conditions were not favourable for batsmen, and, at 84 for five, with Irani at the crease and a tail that had conspicuously failed to wag all season, Essex looked doomed. Robert Rollins cannot be relied upon, but he hits hard and is capable of producing a burst of scoring that can turn a game. He made 42 in a stand of 76 and raised the momentum. Irani had now settled and was driving with authority. Danny Law bludgeoned ferociously so that 113 runs came in 13 overs, and when Law was caught off Caddick for 42 only 27 runs were required. The game now swung in favour of Somerset as Rose dismissed Cowan and Ilott for ducks with successive deliveries. Irani struck two fours, and Such survived an over from Rose, and, in all, faced 14 balls for his one run before Irani hit two fours and a two off Caddick to give Essex their first win of the season.

Sussex's run of success was brought to an end by Warwickshire, whose innings victory was founded on an opening partnership of 272 between Michael Powell and Nick Knight. Powell reached a maiden first-class hundred while Knight batted patiently into the second day. In fact, Lara did not declare Warwickshire's innings closed until the third morning, but Sussex were bowled out in 76.5 overs and forced to follow on. Adams, who had asked Warwickshire to bat when he won the toss, and Bevan shared a fourth wicket stand of 118 in Sussex's second innings, but once they were separated there was little resistance.

Leatherdale's career best bowling figures were a ray of light among the drizzle at Worcester, where a determined Gloucestershire looked the better side for most of the match only to lose at the end. In an effort to force victory and to compensate for lost play, Alleyne offered the home side a target of 208 in 40 overs. Abdul Hafeez hit his first championship fifty, all made contributions and Worcestershire won with an over to spare, but Gloucestershire could not have been expected to bowl out their opponents in 40 overs.

Wasim Akram won the toss, asked Surrey to bat and he and the Lancashire pace attack bowled out the championship leaders in 53.1 overs. Rain intervened, and contrivances were the order of the last day. Shahid scored a century off 74 balls against some friendly bowling, and he and Ward shared an unbroken stand of 185 for the second wicket with runs coming at more than six an over. Adam Hollioake's declaration gave Lancashire 53 overs in which to make 250, which was charitable. The home side lost their second wicket in the 34th over with the score on 151. Crawley had been stumped off Amin for a fine 78, and Flintoff joined Nathan Wood. The burly 20-year old launched a violent attack on the Surrey bowling, reaching the fastest fifty of the season. Flintoff hit 38 off one over from Alex Tudor, 10 of the runs coming off the two no-balls that were bowled in the over, and his fifty came off 20 balls. He was eventually caught at long-on, but by then Lancashire were home and dry, and victory came with 52 balls to spare. In spite of this defeat, Surrey remained 20 points clear at the top of the table.

26, 27, 28 and 29 June

at Leicester

Leicestershire 289 (C.C. Lewis 63, R.J. Kirtley 5 for 83) and 6 for 1

Sussex 302 (M.G. Bevan 149 not out, N.R. Taylor 51, D.J. Millns 4 for 68)

Match drawn

Sussex 10 pts, Leicestershire 9 pts

at Southgate

Middlesex 488 for 2 dec. (M.W. Gatting 241, J.L. Langer 166) and 0 for 0 dec.

Essex 151 for 3 dec. (A.P. Grayson 54) and 315 for 9 (R.C. Irani 104, D.R. Law 62, S.G. Law 62, S.D. Peters 59)

Match drawn

Middlesex 8 pts, Essex 3 pts

at Trent Bridge

Glamorgan 351 for 8 dec. (S.P. James 121, R.D.B. Croft 63 not out) and 0 for 0 dec.

Nottinghamshire 31 for 2 dec. and 274 (G.F. Archer 107, U. Afzaal 51, S.D. Thomas 4 for 78)

Glamorgan won by 46 runs

Glamorgan 20 pts, Nottinghamshire 3 pts

at Taunton

Somerset 378 (P.D. Bowler 104, M.N. Lathwell 76, K.A. Parsons 58, A.D. Mascarenhas 4 for 55)

Hampshire 350 for 5 (G.W. White 101, P.R. Whitaker 72, J.P. Stephenson 67)

Match drawn

Hampshire 11 pts, Somerset 9 pts

at Edgbaston

Warwickshire 374 for 5 dec. (N.V. Knight 192, M.J. Powell 53, D.R. Brown 51 not out) and 0 for 0 dec.

Lancashire 39 for 0 dec. and 338 for 6 (N.T. Wood 79, A. Flintoff 70, N.H. Fairbrother 54, D.R. Brown 5 for 125)

Lancashire won by 4 wickets

Lancashire 18 pts, Warwickshire 4 pts

Wretched weather dogged the last round of championship matches in June. Returning to the scene of glories many years past, Middlesex entertained Essex at Southgate, and Gatting and Langer celebrated the occasion by establishing a new first wicket record partnership of 372. The pitch was a paradise for batsmen, and Essex were eventually set a target of 338 in 104 overs. At 31 for three, all hope seemed to have gone, but Essex had been in a similar position against Somerset. Stuart Law gave the innings a boost with 62 off 82 balls, and Irani again batted splendidly. He and the most promising Peters added 84 for the fifth wicket, and Danny Law hit five sixes in his emphatic innings of 62. At 314 for seven, with 24 needed from 27 balls, Cowan unwisely hit high to Weekes on the mid-wicket boundary, and Irani, equally unwisely, was bowled when he attempted a reverse sweep next ball. Such and Ilott played out for a draw.

The sides were unable to come to any agreement at Leicester, and a tedious game saw Bevan's second hundred of the summer help Sussex to three batting points after

Mike Gatting scored 241 for Middlesex against Essex at Southgate. Gatting announced his retirement at the end of the season and will concentrate on coaching and on his job as an England selector.
(Graham Chadwick / Allsport)

losing their first four wickets for 43 runs. Millns showed an encouraging return to fitness for Leicestershire.

Omitted from the England squad after his appearance at Lord's, James hit a century for Glamorgan, who forfeited their second innings and left Nottinghamshire 96 overs in which to score 321. Graeme Archer put recent failures behind him with a positive innings of 107 in 178 balls. He had little support, reaching three figures when last man Oram partnering him. Glamorgan well deserved their victory for controlled bowling supported by keen fielding.

Rain on the last day at Taunton destroyed any hope of captains coming to an understanding as play could not begin until 3pm. Hampshire added 91 to their overnight score, losing three wickets in the process, and claimed a fourth batting point.

Nick Knight celebrated his recall to the England squad with the highest score of his career, but the ultimate honours went to Lancashire. Play at Edgbaston was limited to two days, and Warwickshire's declaration left Lancashire 96 overs in which to make 336. Once again, Lancashire responded to the challenge, and once again Flintoff was at the heart of a victory, which came with nine balls to spare. Flintoff hit two sixes and eight fours in making 70 off 95 balls.

1, 2, 3 and 4 July

at Derby
Derbyshire 70 (M.C. Ilott 6 for 20) and 319 (M.E. Cassar 58)
Essex 65 (P.A.J. DeFreitas 4 for 19, K.J. Dean 4 for 39) and 143 (T.M. Smith 6 for 32, K.J. Dean 4 for 27)
Derbyshire won by 181 runs
Derbyshire 20 pts, Essex 4 pts

at Darlington
Leicestershire 414 (D.L. Maddy 162, A. Habib 96, J. Wood 5 for 104)
Durham 134 (P.V. Simmons 7 for 49) and 177
Leicestershire won by an innings and 103 runs
Leicestershire 24 pts, Durham 3 pts

at Swansea
Glamorgan 197 (M.P. Maynard 65, A.J. Hollioake 5 for 62) and 212 (M.P. Maynard 71, I.D.K. Salisbury 7 for 65)
Surrey 199 (I.J. Ward 50) and 214 for 4 (A.D. Brown 100, I.J. Ward 79 not out)
Surrey won by 6 wickets
Surrey 20 pts, Glamorgan 4 pts

at Southampton
Hampshire 184 (K.D. James 57) and 322 (J.P. Stephenson 114, C.A. Walsh 4 for 90)
Gloucestershire 176 (T.H.C. Hancock 65, N.A.M. McLean 4 for 39) and 333 for 8 (D.R. Hewson 78 not out, M.C.J. Ball 54, N.J. Trainor 52, N.A.M. McLean 4 for 71)
Gloucestershire won by 2 wickets
Gloucestershire 20 pts, Hampshire 4 pts

at Maidstone
Yorkshire 423 for 7 dec. (D.S. Lehmann 136, G.M. Hamilton 73, C.E.W. Silverwood 57 not out)
Kent 165 and 580 for 9 dec. (D.P. Fulton 207, M.A. Ealham 121, T.R. Ward 94, S.A. Marsh 56 not out, R.D. Stemp 5 for 191, D.S. Lehmann 4 for 42)
Match drawn
Yorkshire 11 pts, Kent 6 pts

at Trent Bridge
Middlesex 198 (J.L. Langer 74, C.M. Tolley 4 for 51) and 123 (P.J. Franks 5 for 58)
Nottinghamshire 413 (C.M.W. Read 76, U. Afzaal 73, J.E.R. Gallian 52, G.F. Archer 51, C.J. Batt 6 for 101)
Nottinghamshire won by an innings and 92 runs
Nottinghamshire 23 pts, Middlesex 3 pts

at Hove
Somerset 303 (R.J. Turner 105, M.N. Lathwell 87, M.E. Trescothick 67 not out, J.D. Lewry 5 for 89) and 307 for 2 dec. (A.R.K. Pierson 108 not out, P.D. Bowler 101, R.J. Hraden 56 not out)
Sussex 493 (M.G. Bevan 146 not out, M. Newell 118, C.J. Adams 102)
Match drawn
Sussex 11 pts, Somerset 7 pts

at Worcester
Worcestershire 136 (F.A. Rose 7 for 39) and 212 (W.P.C. Weston 91 not out, F.A. Rose 4 for 51)

Northamptonshire 114 (T.M. Moody 4 for 20, D.A. Leatherdale 4 for 24) and 77 (R.J. Chapman 4 for 9)
Worcestershire won by 157 runs
Worcestershire 20 pts, Northamptonshire 4 pts

Twenty-three wickets fell on the first day at Derby. Electing to bat, the home county were shot out in 33.3 overs for 70, but their own pace attack dismissed Essex for five runs less in one over less. In their second innings, Derbyshire applied themselves well and batted consistently. By the end of the second day, they had grafted their way to 319, and Essex, needing 325 to win, were 92 for four. All four wickets had gone to seamer Trevor Smith, who was to finish with career best figures of six for 32 in 21 overs. He had match figures of eight for 38, Dean had match figures for 66, and Derbyshire won before lunch on the third day.

The match in Darlington was also over in three days. Darren Maddy's success in the one-day game had been paralleled by a miserable run in the championship, but, after a truncated first day, he and Habib put on 209 for the fifth wicket. Maddy's 162 was his highest first-class score in England. This was followed by a devastating bowling performance from Phil Simmons, who took seven for 49 with his medium pace seamers, a career best. Following on, Durham surrendered meekly for a second time.

Surrey strengthened their position at the top of the table with a good win over Glamorgan – another match to finish in three days. Fifteen wickets fell on the first day with Adam Hollioake getting the first five-wicket haul of his career. Only two runs separated the sides after one innings, but Salisbury bowled Surrey into a strong position with his best figures for his adopted county. Needing 211 to win, Surrey slipped to 52 for three before Brown and Ward added 156 and sealed the victory. Brown reached his hundred with his fifth six shortly before being leg before to Cottey.

Another Derbyshire seam bowler of great promise, Trevor Smith had match figures of eight for 38 against Essex, 1–4 July, in what was only his second championship match. He enjoyed an exellent season. (Ben Radford / Allsport)

The game at Southampton did last into the fourth day, and Gloucestershire beat Hampshire in dramatic style. Alleyne had won the toss and asked Hampshire to bat. His decision proved right as his pace attack reduced the home county to 47 for six. Keech, James and Morris offered late resistance as the eight and ninth wickets added 106 runs. Gloucestershire succumbed to McLean on the second day, and Hampshire, leading by eight runs on the first innings, reached 156 before losing their second wicket. Gloucestershire were left to make 331 to win, and when they were 112 for five all hope seemed to have gone. Dominic Hewson stayed firm at one end while Martyn Ball reached 50 off 39 balls. He was bowled by Stephenson, but Lewis joined Hewson in a partnership worth 74, which took Gloucestershire to within eight runs of their target. Finally Hewson straight drove McLean for four to bring victory.

There were no such fireworks at Maidstone, where Yorkshire batted into the second day. Lehmann and Hamilton added 174 for the sixth wicket, and Silverwood and Stemp shared an unbroken eighth wicket partnership of 109. Kent collapsed before Yorkshire's talented young pace attack and followed on 258 runs in arrears. On the third day, Fulton and Ward put on 172 for the second wicket. David Fulton, who had not enjoyed a good season, went on to reach the first double century of his career, and Mark Ealham made the game safe for Kent with a century on the last afternoon.

The game at Trent Bridge also finished in three days. Middlesex chose to bat first and began well only to lose their last five wickets for 10 runs. Making his championship debut, Chris Batt took three wickets for 11 runs on the first evening and was to finish with six wickets, but Nottinghamshire took control on the second day. Read, deputising as wicket-keeper for the injured Noon, batted impressively, and he and Strang added 96 for the ninth wicket. Middlesex offered limp resistance in their second innings when another young player of talent, Paul Franks, took five wickets and helped bowl Nottinghamshire to an innings victory.

A placid pitch at Hove produced six centurions but no result. Jason Lewry's left-arm fast medium pace had Somerset in trouble on the first day, and they were 46 for four before Turner and Lathwell came together in a stand worth 181. Sussex were 30 for two, but the next three batsmen all scored centuries, with Mark Newell making the highest score of his career. Sussex led by 163 on the first innings, but the last day belonged to Somerset. Bowler and night-watchman Pierson scored 105 for the second wicket, and Harden then joined Pierson in an unbroken stand of 127. Pierson, formerly of Warwickshire and Leicestershire, reached the first hundred of his career.

Worcestershire beat Northamptonshire in two days. On the first day, the ball swung dramatically, and Rose routed the home county and returned the best bowling figures of his career. Leatherdale and Moody routed the visitors to give Worcestershire a first innings lead of 22 on a day on which 21 wickets fell. The outstanding batting performance came on the second day as Philip Weston carried his bat through the 63.5 overs of the Worcestershire second innings to score 93 out of 212. Seamers continued to dominate, and Northamptonshire were shot out in just over 39 overs for 77. Newport took three for 3 in nine overs, and Chapman had four for 9 in 37 balls.

14, 15, 16 and 17 July

at Cheltenham
Sussex 191 (W.G. Khan 59) and 162 (M.T.E. Peirce 59, A.M. Smith 4 for 31)
Gloucestershire 238 (T.H.C. Hancock 76) and 118 for 3 (M.G.N. Windows 60 not out)
Gloucestershire won by 7 wickets
Gloucestershire 21 pts, Sussex 4 pts

at Lytham
Worcestershire 350 (V.S. Solanki 87, R.K. Illingworth 50) and 237 for 6 dec. (T.M. Moody 107 not out)
Lancashire 307 (I.D. Austin 59 not out, M. Watkinson 55, W.K. Hegg 54) and 281 for 8 (J.P. Crawley 108)
Lancashire won by 2 wickets
Lancashire 23 pts, Worcestershire 8 pts

at Leicester
Northamptonshire 322 (G.P. Swann 92, M.B. Loye 76, A.D. Mullally 5 for 62) and 365 (G.P. Swann 111, J.P. Taylor 56, A.D. Mullally 4 for 48)
Leicestershire 484 (A. Habib 198, B.F. Smith 153, F.A. Rose 5 for 123) and 204 for 6 (C.C. Lewis 71 not out, V.J. Wells 58)
Leicestershire won by 7 wickets
Leicestershire 24 pts, Northamptonshire 7 pts

15, 16, 17 and 18 July

at Southend
Essex 295 and 223 (D.R. Law 52, M.A. Ealham 5 for 45)
Kent 364 (C.L. Hooper 100, D.P. Fulton 50, M.C. Ilott 4 for 91) and 155 for 8 (D.P. Fulton 56)
Kent won by 2 wickets
Kent 23 pts, Essex 5 pts

at Guildford
Surrey 150 (A.D. Brown 51, C.J. Batt 5 for 51, A.R.C. Fraser 4 for 34) and 420 (A.D. Brown 79, I.D.K. Salisbury 61, A.J. Hollioake 59)
Middlesex 115 (A.J. Tudor 4 for 47) and 175 (K.R. Brown 59 not out, I.D.K. Salisbury 4 for 43)
Surrey won by 280 runs
Surrey 20 pts, Middlesex 4 pts

at Edgbaston
Warwickshire 367 (A.F. Giles 75, D.R. Brown 51, N.M.K. Smith 51, A.C. Morris 4 for 75) and 187

Hampshire 249 (G.W. White 79, A.F. Giles 5 for 48) and 80 (A.F. Giles 4 for 9)
Warwickshire won by 225 runs
Warwickshire 24 pts, Hampshire 5 pts

at Scarborough
Nottinghamshire 234 (R.T. Robinson 114, U. Afzaal 71, G.M. Hamilton 4 for 59, D. Gough 4 for 72) and 160 for 6
Yorkshire 406 (D.S. Lehmann 131, D. Byas 54, P. Franks 5 for 107, K.P. Evans 5 for 120)
Match drawn
Yorkshire 11 pts, Nottinghamshire 7 pts

Batting first at Cheltenham, Sussex were soon in trouble against Lewis and Smith. Khan offered some stability, and there were later flourishes from Bevan and Martin-Jenkins. These two were among the wicket-takers when Gloucestershire lost three for 94 before the close. Hancock played well, but there was promise rather than performance from the rest, and the home county's lead was restricted to 47. It proved ample as the Gloucestershire seam attack wrecked the Sussex middle order. Batsmen had shown a reluctance to play their shots, but Windows threw off all inhibitions on the last afternoon, reaching 50 off as many balls and hitting 13 fours in his 60, which brought his side an early victory.

Twenty-four overs were lost to rain on the first day at Lytham where Solanki gave further evidence of his class and Warren Hegg held six catches in Worcestershire's first innings. Lancashire struggled to avoid the follow-on on the second day, but their tail wagged vigorously with Hegg, enjoying sublime form, and Austin particularly effective. Worcestershire's second innings revolved around Moody who made a century and asked Lancashire to score 279 at just over four runs an over. Crawley set up the victory with a stylish 108, and Hegg and Austin again played crucial innings. They added 62 for the seventh wicket when the game was in the balance and made possible Lancashire's victory.

More sensational was Leicestershire's win over Northamptonshire. The first day at Grace Road belonged to the visitors, who were rescued from 124 for six by Loye and Graeme Swann, who added 111 in 28 overs. Swann's 92 came off 118 balls, and when he departed Taylor continued the revival. Leicestershire were 41 for three at the close, but the next day, Habib and Smith took their fourth wicket stand to 249, and the home county eventually gained a first innings lead of 162. They were thwarted by Graeme Swann, who followed his first innings 92 with his maiden first-class century. His resistance meant that Leicestershire were left with only 20 overs in which to score 204 to win. Few counties would have attempted such a target; Leicestershire had title aspirations. They had 60 on the board in under six overs when Maddy was run out. Wells, who reached his half-century off 25 balls, and Simmons were out in quick succession just before the hundred was posted, and two more wickets fell, but Chris Lewis blazed 71 off 33 balls and, although Sutcliffe was bowled behind his legs, Leicestershire won with five deliveries to spare, an astonishing achievement.

Essex's championship misery continued. They won the toss against Kent and were bowled out on the first day. Such and Hyam added 47 for the last wicket. Rollins, who had started the season as a contender for the wicket-keeping spot in the England side, had lost form and was replaced by Hyam. For Kent, Hooper hit a majestic hundred and the late order scored freely. Trailing by 69 on the first innings, Essex lost four wickets in clearing the arrears, and it was only the determination of Danny Law, Hyam and Neil Williams that allowed the home to set Kent a target of 155 on the last day. The Essex bowlers showed more belief than the batsmen had done, and five Kent men were out for 88 runs, but Wells steadied the innings and victory came by two wickets.

At Guildford, 20 wickets fell on the first day. The seamers captured the majority of the wickets, but, with Surrey having snatched a lead of 35, the whole complexion of the game changed on the second day when Surrey made 335 for eight. The runs came from consistent application throughout the order, but the bonus came on the third morning when Salisbury and Tudor added 83 for the ninth wicket. Middlesex batted as poorly in their second innings as they had done in the first, and they succumbed to Saqlain and Salisbury. Surrey won in three days by a margin of 280 runs, which, considering that they had been bowled out for 150 on the first day was remarkable.

For Warwickshire, Smith, Giles and Giddins boosted the total as the last three wickets realised 183 runs. Giles also bowled with success, but Hampshire avoided the follow-on. They were left a target of 306, but they were bowled out for 80 in 33.2 overs. Giles had four for 9 in 6.2 overs.

Robinson and Afzaal put on 161 for Nottinghamshire's third wicket, but only one other batsman reached double figures. The Yorkshire innings was built around Lehmann's century, but they tended to labour. The White Rose county continued to be dogged by bad luck as rain thwarted their attempt to bowl out Nottinghamshire, and the match was drawn.

22, 23, 24 and 25 July

at Colwyn Bay
Lancashire 366 (J.P. Crawley 124, G.D. Lloyd 50, R.D.B. Croft 4 for 76) and 334 (J.P. Crawley 136, G.D. Lloyd 73, D.A. Cosker 6 for 140)
Glamorgan 383 for 8 dec. (W.L. Law 131, M.J. Powell 88, A. Dale 73, I.D. Austin 4 for 33) and 100 for 3
Match drawn
Glamorgan 11 pts, Lancashire 10 pts

at Cheltenham
Surrey 297 (A.J. Hollioake 112, A.M. Smith 6 for 66) and 135 (C.A. Walsh 6 for 47)
Gloucestershire 167 (D.R. Hewson 52, M.P. Bicknell 5 for 34, Saqlain Mushtaq 4 for 84) and 266 for 8 (M.G.N. Windows 60, R.J. Cunliffe 53)
Gloucestershire won by 2 wickets
Gloucestershire 20 pts, Surrey 6 pts

at Portsmouth
Nottinghamshire 128 (N.A.M. McLean 4 for 45) and 243 (J.E.R. Gallian 113 not out, P. Johnson 66, A.C. Morris 4 for 35)
Hampshire 301 (A.D. Mascarenhas 89, J.S. Laney 67) and 73 for 3
Hampshire won by 7 wickets
Hampshire 23 pts, Nottinghamshire 4 pts

at Lord's
Middlesex 448 (O.A. Shah 140, P.N. Weekes 67, J.L. Langer 63) and 207 for 1 dec. (M.W. Gatting 103 not out, D.J. Goodchild 83 not out)
Yorkshire 335 (M.P. Vaughan 107, G.M. Hamilton 72, R.J. Blakey 65, P.C.R. Tufnell 4 for 65, R.L. Johnson 4 for 72) and 285 for 8 (D.S. Lehmann 93, P.C.R. Tufnell 4 for 77)
Match drawn
Middlesex 10 pts, Yorkshire 7 pts

at Northampton
Northamptonshire 608 for 6 dec. (R.J. Bailey 188, M.B. Loye 157, G.P. Swann 91, A.L. Penberthy 68 not out, K.M. Curran 59)
Derbyshire 225 (R.M.S. Weston 51) and 289 (K.J. Barnett 68, M.E. Cassar 60, J.F. Brown 4 for 62, G.P. Swann 4 for 91)
Northamptonshire won by an innings and 94 runs
Northamptonshire 24 pts, Derbyshire 2 pts

at Taunton
Durham 259 (D.C. Boon 73, N.J. Speak 51, A.R. Caddick 5 for 116) and 128 (A.R. Caddick 5 for 49)
Somerset 318 (M.J. Foster 4 for 48, S.J. Harmison 4 for 98) and 72 for 0
Somerset won by 10 wickets
Somerset 23 pts, Durham 6 pts

23, 24, 25 and 26 July

at Edgbaston
Warwickshire 190 and 280 (A.F. Giles 63)
Essex 139 (E.S.H. Giddins 4 for 37) and 332 for 8 (R.C. Irani 69, D.R. Law 65, I.N. Flanagan 61)
Essex won by 2 wickets
Essex 20 pts, Warwickshire 4 pts

Only two matches went into a fourth day, and both of those were drawn. Rain restricted play on the first and second days at Colwyn Bay, where Crawley and Wasim Akram gave impetus to a sluggish Lancashire innings by adding 87 in 17 overs for the seventh wicket. John Crawley made the 35th century of his career, maintaining his excellent run of form. The Glamorgan innings was lively from the outset, and Wayne Law, 19 years old, reached an excellent maiden first-class century in what was only his second championship match. He and Dale scored 161 for the second wicket, and Powell refound his form with a sound and attractive 88.

Maynard declared with a lead of 17, and Watkin dismissed Wood before the close, but the last day saw Crawley make his second century of the match. Sadly, rain made a draw inevitable, and the match meandered to a slow death.

Cheltenham provided livelier fare. Adam Hollioake won the toss, and Surrey batted. Hollioake himself led by example, holding the innings together with a disciplined century. On the second morning, Mike Smith took three wickets, including that of Hollioake, for five runs in 22 balls as Surrey lost their four outstanding wickets for 31 runs. His effort seemed to be in vain, for Gloucestershire, having reached 145 for three, were bowled out for 167. The combination of Martin Bicknell and Saqlain Mushtaq proved lethal. Bicknell had been in top form all season, and one could only speculate that had he not been so injury prone in his early years, he might have become England's main strike bowler. Inevitably, Walsh struck back for Gloucestershire. Well supported by Smith and Lewis, he was instrumental in Surrey losing their last five wickets for 20 runs to be all out for 135. When Gloucestershire went in search of 266 for victory they were given a useful start by Cunliffe and Hancock, but Surrey captured three wickets in quick succession. Cunliffe was out at 100 having hit a six and six fours in his 140-ball innings, and Alleyne and Windows then put on 61. Alleyne fell to Bicknell who soon accounted for Church to leave Gloucestershire on 163 for six, and Surrey seemingly poised for victory. Ball adopted the positive approach, and he and Windows added 79 in 16 overs before Windows's excellent innings came to an end, caught behind sweeping at Saqlain. Surrey missed vital catches and, although Lewis was quickly dismissed, Ball, unbeaten on 48, and Smith took Gloucestershire to a victory that put them second in the table.

Hampshire's new found confidence gave them a three-day win over Nottinghamshire, who were put in to bat and bowled out in under in 42 overs. McLean and Morris bowled well, but the batting was poor. It was the late order that turned the game decisively in favour of the home county. Laney, having watched five colleagues disappear for 54, added 103 with Mascarenhas, who then added 67 with Udal. Gallian carried his bat through Nottinghamshire's second innings, but the last six wickets fell for 20 runs, and Hampshire moved to a comfortable victory.

Owais Shah's century put Middlesex in a strong position against Yorkshire, but runs did not come quickly. Shah's fifth wicket stand of 161 with Weekes provided the backbone of the Middlesex innings. Yorkshire had substance from Vaughan, but Blakey and Hamilton gave the innings a late flourish by adding 108 for the eighth wicket. Newcomer Goodchild and Gatting shared an unbroken second wicket stand of 197 when Middlesex batted a second time. Yorkshire were left 70 overs in which to score 321. Lehmann and McGrath put on 104 in 28 overs, and Blakey then helped Lehmann to add 56 in 12, but once Lehmann was caught behind off Weekes, who had Hamilton leg before three balls later, the chase was off and survival was paramount.

Northamptonshire savaged Derbyshire mercilessly. Loye and Bailey put on 296 for the second wicket, and the massacre continued into the second day when Derbyshire were further handicapped by the loss of Trevor Smith with a groin strain. Runs came effortlessly, and Graeme Swann continued to confirm that he was an all-rounder with 91 off 75 balls. The pitch remained good, but Derbyshire, faced by a massive total, were bowled out twice in a day and a half.

Discarded by the England selectors, Andy Caddick continued to take wickets, and, with a consistent batting display that saw the last three wickets add 144 runs, Somerset beat Durham in three days. The early season confidence of the northerners had evaporated, and it was hard to believe that they had been with the leaders at the start of the season.

There was a remarkable first day at Edgbaston where 21 wickets fell. Essex sent back Powell, Wagh and Lara for 'ducks', but Warwickshire, in spite of Brown suffering a broken finger, had a sting in the tail. Essex, too, found most of their runs at the end of their innings after Giddins and Welch had reduced them to 86 for seven. Warwickshire's late order again brought substance to their second innings score, and Essex were left a target of 332 and more than two days in which to get the runs. The task seemed well beyond them when, after an excellent innings from left-hander Ian Flanagan, Irani, Grayson and Stuart Law were dismissed as 20 runs were scored to take Essex to 246 for seven. Danny Law found an able partner in Barry Hyam, and the pair added 74 in 27 overs. With 12 needed, Law was caught on the boundary off Wagh, but Hyam stayed calm and he and the veteran Williams took Essex to their second win of the season. Ironically, they were bottom of the table as Northamptonshire's maximum point win had lifted them to 15th in the championship.

30, 31 July, 1 and 2 August

at The Oval

Sussex 125 (M.T.E. Peirce 54, Saqlain Mushtaq 7 for 30) and 170 (C.J. Adams 99 not out, M.P. Bicknell for 45, Saqlain Mushtaq 4 for 74)

Surrey 364 (A.J. Stewart 96, A.D. Brown 94, J.J. Bates 5 for 100)

Surrey won by an innings and 69 runs

Surrey 24 pts, Sussex 4 pts

at Edgbaston

Glamorgan 315 (P.A. Cottey 74, S.D. Thomas 64, S.P. James 53, G. Welch 4 for 94) and 109 for 1 dec. (S.P. James 52)

Warwickshire 135 for 4 dec. (N.V. Knight 52) and 253 for 8 (N.M.K. Smith 72 not out, S.D. Thomas 5 for 84)

Match drawn

Warwickshire 7 pts, Glamorgan 7 pts

30, 31 July, 1 and 3 August

at Derby

Kent 165 (P.A.J. DeFreitas 5 for 55, K.J. Dean 4 for 52) and 129 for 5 (M.A. Ealham 61 not out)

Derbyshire 260 (R.M.S. Weston 97, D.W. Headley 5 for 64)

Match drawn

Derbyshire 9 pts, Kent 7pts

Ally Brown catches Chris Adams for 0 as Surrey trounce Sussex by an innings at The Oval, 30–2 August. Adams was left stranded, unbeaten on 99 in the second innings.
(Stu Foster / Allsport)

at Southampton
Durham 203 (A.C. Morris 4 for 30) and 332 for 9 (M.P. Speight 97 not out, D.C. Boon 54, J.E. Morris 50)
Hampshire 396 (R.A. Smith 134, A.N. Aymes 54)
Match drawn
Hampshire 11 pts, Durham 8 pts

at Old Trafford
Leicestershire 218 for 7 (A. Habib 56)
v. **Lancashire**
Match drawn
Lancashire 6 pts, Leicestershire 4 pts

at Trent Bridge
Northamptonshire 346 (M.B. Loye 103, R.R. Montgomerie 54, P.A. Strang 4 for 92)
Nottinghamshire 380 for 5 (P. Johnson 105, U. Afzaal 103 not out, G.E. Welton 55, J.P. Taylor 4 for 62)
Match drawn
Nottinghamshire 11 pts, Northamptonshire 8 pts

at Worcester
Yorkshire 455 for 9 dec. (D.S. Lehmann 200, M.J. Wood 94, A. McGrath 50)
Worcestershire 201 and 94 (D. Gough 5 for 36, G.M. Hamilton 4 for 17)
Yorkshire won by an innings and 160 runs
Yorkshire 24 pts, Worcestershire 4 pts

Surrey's pursuit of the title became more intense when they overcame Sussex in three days while challengers Leicestershire and Lancashire had to sit and watch the rain after a limited first day at Old Trafford. Sussex chose to bat first, and Peirce and Khan gave them a good start with a stand of 93, but Mark Newell and Adams were dismissed without scoring, and ten wickets fell for 32 runs. The arch-destroyer was the Pakistan off-spinner Saqlain Mushtaq, whose seven for 30 surpassed a recently established career-best. He also contributed 40 runs at the end of the Surrey innings after Stewart and Brown had played forceful knocks to take their side to a strong position. Anticipating that the pitch would take spin, Sussex had included off-spinner Justin Bates for the first time in the season, and he captured five wickets, but he is a young man still learning his trade. Sussex batted again, trailing by 239 runs and were soon in trouble, but Chris Adams played an heroic innings only to see last man Robinson caught at slip when he was one short of a most deserved century.

Glamorgan and Warwickshire strove to overcome inclement weather at Cardiff. Maynard eventually offered Warwickshire a target of 290 in 75 overs. Andrew Davies gave Glamorgan a good start when he knocked back Nick Knight's off stump in the first over, and Darren Thomas trapped both Wagh and Powell leg before in the space of three overs. Thomas bowled exceptionally well, and, with Warwickshire 190 for seven, the home county were in charge. Smith and Giles added 43, and Neil Smith's positive batting – he reached fifty off 65 balls – kept Warwickshire's hopes alive. When Thomas bowled Giles, however, Smith and Munton had to turn their attention to defence for the last eight overs.

The match at Derby was ruined by the weather, but the home county had much with which to be pleased. Robin Weston, discarded by Durham, played an innings of discipline and character, which was ended three short of a century by Llong's fine catch at cover while Kevin Dean performed the hat-trick. In his fourth over of the second innings, Dean had Ed Smith caught in the gully and brought the ball back to have Hooper palpably leg before. The hat-trick ball saw Llong tickle a catch to Krikken down the leg side. Ealham and Fleming took Kent to a narrow lead, but Kent would have been hard pressed to save the game but for the rain.

Robin Smith and Adrian Aymes scored 159 for the fifth wicket to put Hampshire in a strong position against Durham, who began their second innings 193 runs in arrears. Aymes continued an outstanding season with four catches and a stumping as Durham lost five wickets before clearing their deficit. Speight batted with great determination, but Durham began the last day on 288 for nine. Only ten overs were possible on the final day, and those were dominated by Speight, whose unbroken last wicket stand with Lugsden was worth 61.

Following Nottinghamshire's defeat in the NatWest Trophy, Paul Johnson resigned the captaincy and handed Jason Gallian his county cap and the leadership at the same time. Loye's summer of success for Northamptonshire continued with another fine century, but the honours went to Johnson. He had been an unselfish captain for Nottinghamshire, and he celebrated his resignation with his first century of the season. He reached his hundred off 98 balls and shared a third wicket stand of 170 with Afzaal. There was no play on the fourth day.

Darren Lehmann and Matthew Wood put on 236 in 53 overs for Yorkshire's third wicket against Worcestershire. Wood gave further indication of immense promise with 17 fours in his innings of 94. Lehmann made his highest score for Yorkshire, a magnificent double century that came off

269 balls and included two sixes and 28 fours. Worcestershire batted limply in reply and surrendered with little fight.

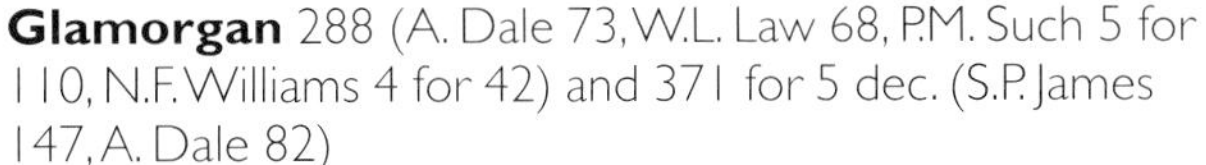

5, 6, 7 and 8 August
at Chelmsford
Glamorgan 288 (A. Dale 73, W.L. Law 68, P.M. Such 5 for 110, N.F. Williams 4 for 42) and 371 for 5 dec. (S.P. James 147, A. Dale 82)
Essex 260 (A.P. Grayson 59, R.C. Irani 51) and 183
Glamorgan won by 216 runs
Glamorgan 22 pts, Essex 6 pts

at Canterbury
Kent 391 (D.W. Headley 81, M.M. Patel 58 not out, D.P. Fulton 54, M.V. Fleming 51, A.C. Morris 4 for 72) and 227 (S.D. Udal 4 for 37)
Hampshire 173 (R.A. Smith 72, C.L. Hooper 4 for 14) and 153 (C.L. Hooper 4 for 29, M.J. McCague 4 for 40)
Kent won by 292 runs
Kent 24 pts, Hampshire 4 pts

at Old Trafford
Lancashire 386 (G. Chapple 69, G. Yates 55)
Gloucestershire 158 (C.P. Schofield 4 for 56, G. Yates 4 for 64) and 193 (C.P. Schofield 4 for 60, G. Yates 4 for 91)
Lancashire won by an innings and 35 runs

at Leicester
Somerset 74 (J. Ormond 6 for 33) and 112
Leicestershire 271 (D.L. Maddy 107, B.F. Smith 67, A.R. Caddick 7 for 96)
Leicestershire won by an innings and 85 runs
Leicestershire 22 pts, Somerset 4 pts

at Lord's
Warwickshire 466 (B.C. Lara 226, N.M.K. Smith 61, R.L. Johnson 4 for 60) and 150 for 8 (B.C. Lara 51, P.C.R. Tufnell 4 for 24)
Middlesex 297 (P.N. Weekes 89, O.A. Shah 52, T.A. Munton 7 for 66) and 373 (M.W. Gatting 91, D.J. Goodchild 73, J.L. Langer 55, O.A. Shah 52, M.A. Wagh 4 for 11)
Match drawn
Warwickshire 11 pts, Middlesex 8 pts

at Eastbourne
Sussex 460 (M.G. Bevan 95, W.G. Khan 91, C.J. Adams 56, S.J. Harmison 4 for 94, J. Wood 4 for 107)
Durham 198 (M.P. Speight 60 not out, J.D. Lewry 4 for 63) and 181 (P.D. Collingwood 56 not out, R.J. Kirtley 4 for 41)
Sussex won by an innings and 81 runs
Sussex 24 pts, Durham 3 pts

at Kidderminster
Nottinghamshire 164 and 401 (P. Johnson 139, R.J. Chapman 6 for 105)
Worcestershire 289 (T.M. Moody 112, P.J. Franks 6 for 63) and 186 (C.M. Tolley 7 for 45)
Nottinghamshire won by 90 runs
Nottinghamshire 20 pts, Worcestershire 6 pts

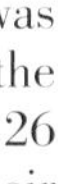

6, 7, 8 and 9 August
at The Oval
Surrey 333 (A.D. Brown 132, I.D. Blackwell 5 for 115) and 238 for 9 dec. (I.D. Blackwell 4 for 94)
Derbyshire 139 (B.C. Hollioake 4 for 36) and 206 (M.J. Slater 99, Saqlain Mushtaq 8 for 65)
Surrey won by 226 runs
Surrey 23 pts, Derbyshire 4 pts

The probability that Essex would finish bottom began to look ever more certain when they crashed to a Glamorgan side that had been badly hit by a long term injury to Waqar Younis and the loss of Watkin, their main strike bowlers. Glamorgan won the toss and batted first. They survived a mid-order collapse when seven wickets went down for 58 runs, mainly through Parkin, 24 not out, and Davies, 34, who made the highest scores of their careers and added 58 for the last wicket. Essex lost wickets regularly on the second day but got to within 28 of the Glamorgan total. By the end of the third day, however, the visitors were in total command. Steve James may have been rejected by England, but he continues to be among the very best of county batsmen. He hit a chanceless 147 and shared a third wicket stand of 169 in 39 overs with Adrian Dale. Maynard's declaration left Essex more than a day in which to score 400, but Flanagan and Hodgson were out before the close. They offered some resistance on the last day, but Glamorgan's mainly youthful attack proved themselves equal to the task of winning the match.

For Kent, the sting was in the tail. Hampshire reduced them to 172 for seven at Canterbury, at which point Headley joined Fleming in a stand worth 85, but there was greater despair for the visitors when Patel, who made the highest score of his career, and Headley put on 123 in 26 overs for the last wicket. In contrast, Hampshire lost their last seven wickets for 30 runs. There was to be no recovery from this collapse, and Kent won in three days.

Lancashire also won in three days, and their resounding victory over Gloucestershire not only enhanced their own chances of winning the championship, it also virtually brought an end to Gloucestershire's. With Yates and Chapple to the fore, Lancashire's eighth and ninth wickets increased the score by 124 runs, and when Gloucestershire batted the pitch was offering the spinners massive aid. Yates and Schofield took their chance avidly. They took 16 wickets between them and were held up only by Ball and Lewis, who scored 83 for Gloucestershire's last wicket in the second innings.

Leicestershire maintained their title challenge with a two-day victory over Somerset, who won the toss and chose to bat. They were routed by James Ormond, who, having been troubled by illness and injury, was playing in only his third championship match of the season. His six for 33 represented the best bowling figures of his career. By the end of the day, with Maddy and Smith having put on 96 for the third wicket, Leicestershire already had a lead of 164. Maddy, who had thrived in the one-day game but struggled in the championship, duly reached his second first-class century of the summer on the second morning. His innings was ended by a spectacular catch on the boundary by Caddick, who took seven for 96 and proved to be Somerset's highest scorer of the match. Batting at number ten, he made 31 as his side were bowled out by Ormond, Wells and Millns for 112.

Lara's return to Warwickshire in 1998 had been far from successful, and debate raged within the county. His own form had been well below par, but, at Lord's, going to the crease after two wickets had fallen for 38 runs, he reached 226. He was given sensible and able support by Anurag Singh in a third wicket stand worth 156. Lara had faced 281 balls and hit a six and 33 fours in an innings that lasted almost six hours. Tim Munton, playing in only his second match since his long lay-off, took seven for 66 in 28 overs. There was some encouragement for Middlesex in the impressive batting of Goodchild, who had seized the opportunity given him since being brought into the side to open the innings. He made 73 when the home county were asked to follow on and shared a first wicket partnership of 130 with Langer. Gatting, Batt and Shah all played resolutely only to see their side collapse after tea on the last day, losing their last five wickets for 17 runs. Warwickshire were left with 24 overs in which to score 205 if they wished to win. They went at the task with a will, but batsmen perished in the attempt, and Munton and Piper had to play out the last six overs to earn a draw.

A stand of 117 for the third wicket between Adams and Khan gave initial substance to the Sussex innings against Durham. Bevan was again a tower of strength as he hit 95 off 107 balls with a six and 13 fours, and the last three Sussex wickets brought 138 runs. James Kirtley made the highest score of his career. Durham were five wickets down by the end of the second day and surrendered the remaining 15 on the third, with Kirtley, Lewry and Robinson all enjoying a festival occasion.

Paul Johnson scored his second century in two matches since giving up the Nottinghamshire captaincy and brought his side an unexpected victory. Gallian won the toss at Kidderminster, but his side batted poorly and were all out for 164. Worcestershire were 51 for four before Moody and Leatherdale halted the slide with a stand of 77, and Moody and Rhodes then added 112. Paul Franks returned the best bowling figures of his career. He is a young all-rounder who will do well at the highest level. At the close of play on the second day, Nottinghamshire had lost two second innings wickets and still trailed by 25 runs. Johnson at last found a capable partner in Tolley, and the pair added 122 for the fifth wicket. Kevin Evans master-minded 68 from the last two wickets, and Nottinghamshire were back in the game, setting Worcestershire a target of 277. Chapman, a former Nottinghamshire player, took a career best six for 105. Tolley dismissed the two newcomers to the Worcestershire side, Wilson and Batson, before the close of play on Friday, and, by lunch on the Saturday, the home county were 87 for seven. Newport hit an unbeaten 45 off 50 balls, but just after 3pm the game was over. Having trailed by 125 on the first innings, Nottinghamshire so reversed fortune as to win by 90 runs. Chris Tolley celebrated his return to his home town with the best bowling performance of his career, seven for 45.

Surrey moved on with relentless speed. They won the toss, batted and were 57 for three. There had been a sensation before the start when Ratcliffe was omitted from the Surrey side for undisclosed reasons and was replaced by the second XI coach Alan Butcher, 44 years old and father of the England opening batsman. Alan Butcher had last played for Surrey in 1986 and for Glamorgan in 1992. He had also coached and captained Essex second XI until 1997. He was not to be the hero of the hour; that honour went to Alistair Brown, who hit a six and 16 fours in another blistering century that took Surrey to 333 in 86 overs. Derbyshire were soon in trouble and were bowled out for 139, but Adam Hollioake did not enforce the follow-on on a pitch that was showing signs of rapid wear. Surrey themselves were 123 for seven in their second innings before Martin Bicknell launched a violent attack on the bowling, and Derbyshire were left the unenviable task of scoring 433 to win. Slater batted splendidly, dancing down the pitch to Saqlain, but it was the off-spinner who won the day. The last eight Derbyshire wickets fell for 46 runs, and Saqlain finished with eight for 65, bettering the career-best figures he had achieved a week earlier.

14, 15, 16 and 17 August

at Derby

Derbyshire 280 (R.M.S. Weston 84, S.R. Lampitt 5 for 33) and 168 (T.M. Moody 5 for 64, P.J. Newport 4 for 44)
Worcestershire 104 (K.J. Dean 4 for 52) and 316 (V.S. Solanki 170, K.J. Dean 5 for 90, P.A.J. DeFreitas 5 for 95)
Derbyshire won by 28 runs
Derbyshire 22 pts, Worcestershire 4 pts

at Riverside

Durham 396 (D.C. Boon 106, N.J. Speak 59, S.D. Thomas 5 for 107) and 385 for 7 dec. (J.E. Morris 163, D.C. Boon 62 not out, J.J.B. Lewis 54)
Glamorgan 486 (P.A. Cottey 123, M.P. Maynard 79, S.D. Thomas 74, M.J. Powell 67)
Match drawn
Durham 11 pts, Glamorgan 9 pts

at Bristol

Gloucestershire 142 (M.W. Alleyne 55, M.J. McCague 4 for 41, J.B.D. Thompson 4 for 52) and 456 (M.G.N. Windows 103, M.W. Alleyne 83, T.H.C. Hancock 63, J.B.D. Thompson 4 for 82)
Kent 163 (S.A. Marsh 60, C.A. Walsh 4 for 77) and 297 (C.L. Hooper 111)
Gloucestershire won by 138 runs
Gloucestershire 20 pts, Kent 4 pts

at Portsmouth

Essex 141 (N.A.M. McLean 5 for 37, P.J. Hartley 4 for 42)

and 238 (A.C. Morris 4 for 39)
Hampshire 490 (R.A. Smith 138, M. Keech 61, G.W. White 58, A.D. Mascarenhas 53, A.C. Morris 51)
Hampshire won by an innings and 111 runs
Hampshire 24 pts, Essex 3 pts

at Taunton
Northamptonshire 187 (G.D. Rose 5 for 57, A.R. Caddick 5 for 70) and 205 (D. Ripley 54 not out, A.L. Penberthy 53, A.R. Caddick 4 for 45)
Somerset 179 (P.D. Bowler 78, J.F. Brown 5 for 49) and 214 for 8 (J.F. Brown 6 for 53)
Somerset won by 2 wickets
Somerset 20 pts, Northamptonshire 4 pts

at Hove
Sussex 392 (C.J. Adams 170, R.K. Rao 54, J.P. Hewitt 6 for 71)
Middlesex 142 (J.D. Lewry 5 for 43) and 90 (R.J. Kirtley 4 for 29)
Sussex won by an innings and 160 runs
Sussex 24 pts, Middlesex 4 pts

at Leeds
Lancashire 484 (J.P. Crawley 180, G.D. Lloyd 56) and 215 (W.K. Hegg 85, J.P. Crawley 56, P.M. Hutchison 5 for 39)
Yorkshire 457 for 8 dec. (D. Byas 101, D.S. Lehmann 71, R.J. Blakey 67 not out, G.M. Hamilton 56) and 183 (G. Keedy 5 for 35, G. Yates 4 for 69)
Lancashire won by 59 runs
Lancashire 22 pts, Yorkshire 7 pts

Derbyshire beat Worcestershire in three days. Put in to bat, the home county were held together by Robin Weston, whose confidence increased with every match. The Derbyshire seam attack proved far too strong for some limp Worcestershire batting. The first five wickets went down for 30, and only Rhodes reached 20. Derbyshire fared almost as badly and were rescued by Spendlove, who hit 45. Batting at number nine, he was mainly responsible for the last three wickets realising 81 runs. Needing 345 to win, Worcestershire lost three wickets for 29 runs, but their hopes were lifted by a quite splendid innings from Vikram Solanki, who reached the second and higher century of his career. He began batting on the Saturday evening, and he hit 108 before lunch on the Sunday as Worcestershire made 165 in that session. He and Leatherdale added 100 in 20 overs for the fourth wicket, and he and Newport 79 for the eighth. Solanki and Newport both fell to DeFreitas, and Dean trapped Rawnsley leg before to win the match. Derbyshire were somewhat fortunate, as they had fielded poorly, putting down several chances, and had not bowled particularly well.

Durham scored 269 for four from 99 overs on the first day at Riverside, and Boon completed his century on the Saturday. Glamorgan demonstrated much more enterprise in making 486 at more than four runs an over. They lost three wickets for 85 before Cottey and Maynard added 132. Cottey, who hit his second century of the season, then added 121 with Powell. Darren Thomas emphasised his all-round abilities with a six and 11 fours in his 64-ball innings. Durham soon cleared the first innings deficit of 90 and batted throughout the last day to draw the match. John Morris hit an entertaining 163 on an otherwise dull day.

Gloucestershire's great problem in their challenge for the title was their inability to score runs in the first innings and so gain valuable batting points. They beat Kent to go fourth in the table, but, after 12 matches, had only 10 batting points. They were bowled out for 142 on the first day at Bristol when 17 wickets fell. Marsh rallied Kent on the second day to claim a first innings lead of 21, but this was soon wiped out by Cunliffe and Hancock, who began the home county's second innings with a stand of 84, Gloucestershire's highest first wicket stand of the season. Windows and Lewis were both capped during the match, and Windows celebrated with his third championship century of the season. He and Alleyne added 185 for the fourth wicket. The tail wagged strongly, and Kent were set a target of 436. In spite of Hooper's effortless 111 off 131 balls and a brief intervention by rain, Kent could not deny Gloucestershire.

An ageing but improving Hampshire crushed Essex in three days. Essex appeared both rudderless and spiritless. They were put in to bat and quickly disposed of by the Hampshire pace attack. Robin Smith then led his side to a massive total, and Morris and Hartley, the exiled Yorkshiremen, again proved too much for an Essex side that surrendered meekly. The game was over well inside three days.

Somerset beat Northamptonshire in three days, but it was a close contest. Caddick and Rose bowled out Northamptonshire on the first day after the visitors had chosen to bat first. The pitch was lively, and Somerset fared no better than their opponents had done, although it was off-spinner Brown who did most of the damage with bowling figures of five for 49. Penberthy and Ripley gave Northamptonshire's second innings middle order substance before four wickets fell for 12 runs. Somerset were left to make 214 to win on a pitch that was increasingly helping the bowlers. Jason Brown, the 23-year old off-spinner, again excelled. He bowled a good line, turned the ball appreciably and finished with 11 for 102 in the match. Somerset lost their seventh wicket at 164, but Rose joined Bowler, who batted with great application in both innings, to add 40. It was skipper Bowler who took his side to victory. He faced 165 deliveries and hit just two boundaries in his unbeaten 41.

A green pitch at Hove did not prevent Sussex from deciding to bat first when Chris Adams won the toss. Adams justified his decision by hitting his fourth century of the season, which was also his highest score for the county he has reinvigorated. He shared a fourth wicket stand of 96 with Bevan and a fifth wicket stand of 152 with Rao as Sussex raced towards maximum batting points. James Hewitt took six wickets, but Middlesex batted deplorably. They were bowled out twice on the Saturday so that Sussex won in two days, and they looked the most likely contenders to deprive Essex of the wooden spoon.

The Roses match was a typically tense battle. Lancashire won the toss, and with John Crawley again playing wonderfully well, they made 455 for eight in 107.2 overs on the opening day. Crawley passed a thousand runs for the season and batted with a majesty that has been latent for some time. His footwork and his supple wrists have the flavour of the Orient, and he is ever looking for runs. His 180 came in five-and-a-half hours. He struck fours and a slice off a no-ball went over the slips and the boundary to bring eight runs in all. Yorkshire could not match Lancashire's run-getting, but they fought their way back into the match with gritty application. Byas led the way with a century, and he and Lehmann put on 117 for the third wicket, but it was the strength of the late middle order, Blakey, Hamilton and Middlebrook that enabled Byas to declare just 27 short of Lancashire's total. The visitors were 22 for four in their second innings, but they were rallied by Crawley and Hegg, and Yorkshire were left 63 overs in which to score 243. They began well, but where the Lancashire seamers had enjoyed no fortune, the spinners revelled. The last six wickets went down for 38 runs, with off-spinner Yates and left-arm spinner Keedy rampant, and Lancashire won with 32 balls to spare to go second in the table, 21 points behind Surrey with four games remaining.

19, 20, 21 and 22 August
at Riverside
Lancashire 196 (Wasim Akram 68, N. Killeen 5 for 49) and 434 (N.H. Fairbrother 138, G.D. Lloyd 104, Wasim Akram 63)
Durham 158 (J.J.B. Lewis 70 not out) and 122 (G. Chapple 4 for 26, Wasim Akram 4 for 40)
Lancashire won by 350 runs
Lancashire 20 pts, Durham 4 pts

at Colchester
Gloucestershire 564 (M.G.N. Windows 151, T.H.C. Hancock 135)
Essex 176 and 107 (C.A. Walsh 4 for 18, M.C.J. Ball 4 for 26)
Gloucestershire won by an innings and 281 runs
Gloucestershire 24 pts, Essex 2 pts

at Canterbury
Worcestershire 360 (W.P.C. Weston 60, M.M. Patel 4 for 55) and 333 for 8 dec. (S.J. Rhodes 95, D.A. Leatherdale 79, T.M. Moody 59)
Kent 344 (C.L. Hooper 154, R.J. Chapman 4 for 79) and 270 for 9 (M.M. Patel 55 not out, B.J. Phillips 54, T.M. Moody 4 for 63)
Match drawn
Worcestershire 10 pts, Kent 9 pts

at Leicester
Middlesex 307 (P.N. Weekes 139, M.R. Ramprakash 110, D.J. Millns 4 for 65) and 245 (M.W. Gatting 73)
Leicestershire 452 (I.J. Sutcliffe 167, A. Habib 84, V.J. Wells 67, J.P. Hewitt 4 for 85, R.L. Johnson 4 for 129) and 101 for 2
Leicestershire won by 8 wickets
Leicestershire 24 pts, Middlesex 6 pts

at Northampton
Northamptonshire 319 (A.L. Penberthy 128, D. Ripley 98, D.R. Brown 4 for 68) and 214 (T.A. Munton 5 for 41, E.S.H. Giddins 4 for 52)
Warwickshire 412 (B.C. Lara 158, A. Singh 56, N.M.K. Smith 56, J.F. Brown 5 for 114) and 122 for 6 (J.P. Taylor 4 for 58)
Warwickshire won by 4 wickets
Warwickshire 24 pts, Northamptonshire 7 pts

at Trent Bridge
Nottinghamshire 213 (C.M.W. Read 66 not out) and 125 (B.C. Hollioake 4 for 28)
Surrey 270 (M.A. Butcher 77, N. Shahid 64, A.R. Oram 4 for 37) and 72 for 3
Surrey won by 7 wickets
Surrey 22 pts, Nottinghamshire 5 pts

at Taunton
Derbyshire 290 (R.M.S. Weston 73, G.D. Rose 4 for 75) and 139 (A.R. Caddick 5 for 49, M. Bulbeck 4 for 40)
Somerset 181 (K.J. Dean 6 for 70) and 176 (M.E. Trescothick 60, K.J. Dean 6 for 63)
Derbyshire won by 72 runs
Derbyshire 22 pts, Somerset 4 pts

20, 21, 22 and 23 August
at Cardiff
Yorkshire 306 (G.M. Hamilton 79, R.J. Sidebottom 54) and 296 (G.M. Hamilton 70, M.J. Wood 62, O.T. Parkin 5 for 67, S.D. Thomas 4 for 72)
Glamorgan 266 (W.L. Law 57, G.M. Hamilton 5 for 69) and 222 (A. Dale 67, M.J. Powell 54, G.M. Hamilton 5 for 53)
Yorkshire won by 114 runs
Yorkshire 23 pts, Glamorgan 6 pts

Lancashire maintained their title challenge with a three-day victory over Glamorgan. The first day at Riverside saw 21 wickets fall. Lancashire chose to bat and found themselves 80 for seven. The boost came in a 68-run stand for the ninth wicket between Wasim and Ridgway. Killeen, playing his first game since May, had the best bowling figures of his career, while Ridgway registered his first runs in first-class cricket, 35 of them, and followed with career best bowling figures of three for 51. Jon Lewis carried his bat through the 40 overs of the Durham innings. Lancashire relished the chance to reassert themselves after their poor first innings batting performance. Fairbrother ended a lean spell with a century and a third wicket stand of 172 with Nathan Wood. Fairbrother's 138 came from 153 balls. Lloyd made his first hundred of the season, and the game was beyond Durham, who subsided quietly to Wasim and Chapple in their second innings.

Essex gave another abject display against a vital Gloucestershire side and, for the second match running were

Matt Windows was Gloucestershire's leading batsman as they made a strong bid for the title. He hit 151 in the destruction of Essex at Colchester, 19–21 August.
(George Herringshaw / ASP)

beaten by an innings shortly after lunch on the third day. Winning the toss, Gloucestershire reached 401 for five on the first day. Tim Hancock hit a six and 21 fours in a career best 135. His innings took Gloucestershire to maximum batting points for only the second time in the season. Having enjoyed a fifth wicket stand of 124 with Dawson, Windows ended the first day unbeaten on 69, and he reached his second successive century the following morning. Even though Walsh did not take a wicket, Essex succumbed quickly enough and were following on in the late evening. Hancock brought about a middle order collapse with three wickets in eight balls. Hyam, showing more determination than his more experienced colleagues, added 51 for the eight wicket, but the home county offered little else. In their second innings, Essex lost their last seven wickets for 28 runs.

In contrast, Kent put up a stubborn rearguard action to hold Worcestershire at bay at the St Lawrence ground. The visitors batted solidly down the order to reach 360 while Kent's reply revolved around a sparkling century from Carl Hooper. He equalled the fastest century of the season, racing to three figures off 72 balls with 15 fours and three sixes. He finished with 154 off 157 balls. Kent came to within 16 runs of the Worcestershire total, and they seemed to have taken a grip on the game when they captured four of the visitors' second innings wickets for 51 runs. Moody, Leatherdale and Rhodes transformed the situation, and Moody was able to set Kent a target of 350. Hooper completed a thousand runs for the season in a cameo that produced 33 brisk runs, but Kent were 127 for seven when Headley joined Phillips. They added 51, and Patel then joined Phillips in a stand worth 66. Phillips was bowled by Moody, but Thompson and Patel held out and scored 26 to gain the draw.

The fact that Middlesex scored 307 in their first innings at Leicester suggests an improvement after the debacle at Hove, but they were 20 for four before Weekes joined Ramprakash in adding 229. Both batsmen made centuries, but no one else reached 20. Iain Sutcliffe made the highest score of his career. He and Wells scored 156 for the second wicket, and he and Habib added 115 for the fifth. When Middlesex batted a second time they lost Goodchild and Ramprakash in Millns's opening over before a run had been scored. Langer and Gatting added 96, but the innings fell way, and Leicestershire moved to a comfortable win which took them to within 39 points of Surrey with a game in hand.

Brian Lara hit his second century in successive championship matches and took Warwickshire to victory over Northamptonshire in three days. Northamptonshire decided to bat when they won the toss and soon found themselves at 52 for four. Opening the innings for the first time, Tony Penberthy stopped the rot with his second century of the season, a career best 128. He and Ripley, enjoying a fine season with the bat, restored order with a fifth wicket stand worth 195. Graeme Swann also showed enterprise, and the home side passed 300 and captured the wicket of Wagh before the close. Northamptonshire's joy ended there. Lara hit fives sixes and 18 fours the following day as Warwickshire took a lead of 93. They then captured the wickets of two nightwatchmen to leave Northamptonshire 0 for two. They rallied on the third day with Sales and the reliable Ripley putting on 69 for the seventh wicket, but, in spite of being in too much of a hurry to finish the game, Warwickshire triumphed.

Surrey's winning ways continued with an emphatic win at Trent Bridge. They put Nottinghamshire in to bat and reduced them to 112 for seven, but Read, an outstanding young wicket-keeper, made an unbeaten 66 and helped his side to 213. Surrey did not find batting easy themselves, and they relied heavily on partnerships between Mark Butcher, captaining the side, and Ben Hollioake, and between Shahid and Batty. Nevertheless, a first innings lead of 57 proved decisive when Nottinghamshire colllapsed to 79 for seven by the end of the second day. Read and Evans offered minor late resistance, but Surrey moved to a three-day victory with ease.

At Taunton, 15 wickets fell on the first day. Weston, Blackwell and Spendlove led an assault on the Somerset bowling, which took Derbyshire to 290 at well over four runs an over, and then Dean and Cork reduced the home county to 96 for five. Useful contributions from most of the later batsmen revived Somerset on the second morning, but Kevin Dean, the left-arm pace bowler still finished with career best bowling figures. It was then the turn of Caddick and the left-arm medium pacer Bulbeck to dominate, bowling out Derbyshire for 139. Somerset, needing 249, were right back in the game, but their batsmen again floundered against Cork and Dean. Trescothick gave hope, ending the second innings unbeaten on 43 out of 93 for five. He and Turner extended their stand until it was worth 50 on the second morning, but four wickets then fell for 22 runs, and Derbyshire were comfortable winners in three days. Dean improved on his figures of the first innings, and his match figures of 12 for 133 were also

An all-rounder who improved with every game – Yorkshire's Gavin Hamilton.
(Nigel French / ASP)

the best of his career and further encouragement to Derbyshire in the continuing improvement of their young players.

Put in to bat at Cardiff, Yorkshire were very brisk scorers, and they effected a remarkable recovery from the depths of 88 for six. Gavin Hamilton hit 13 fours in the highest score of his career, and Ryan Sidebottom reached a maiden first-class fifty. Hamilton continued an excellent personal all-round performance with the first five-wicket haul of his career, which helped Yorkshire to a 40-run first innings lead. This was followed by another fifty and a career best five for 43, which took Yorkshire to a resounding three-day win. For Glamorgan, the only consolation was a career best return from Owen Parkin, deputising for the injured Watkin.

26, 27, 28 and 29 August
at Derby
Derbyshire 205 (I.D. Blackwell 57, M.J. Slater 54) and 269 for 9 (K.J. Barnett 98, N.C. Phillips 5 for 56)
Durham 434 for 6 dec. (J.A. Daley 157, M.A. Roseberry 97, M.P. Speight 52 not out, G.M. Roberts 4 for 105)
Match drawn
Durham 10 pts, Derbyshire 9 pts

at Northampton
Kent 218 (A.P. Wells 79, J.P. Taylor 4 for 71, F.A. Rose 4 for 75) and 377 for 7 dec. (C.L. Hooper 157 not out, A.P. Wells 77)
Northamptonshire 391 (A.J. Swann 85, R.J. Bailey 79, A.L. Penberthy 61, D.W. Headley 5 for 79)
Match drawn
Northamptonshire 11 pts, Kent 4 pts

at Worksop
Nottinghamshire 61 (V.J. Wells 5 for 18, A.D. Mullally 4 for 34) and 221 (P.R. Pollard 69, M.P. Dowman 52, A.D. Mullally 7 for 55)
Leicestershire 505 for 6 dec. (P.V. Simmons 194, B.F. Smith 159, I.J. Sutcliffe 60)
Leicestershire won by an innings and 223 runs
Leicestershire 24 pts, Nottinghamshire 1 pt

at Hove
Sussex 187 (M.G. Bevan 58) and 245 (N.A.M. McLean 4 for 46)
Hampshire 224 (J.P. Stephenson 84) and 209 for 1 (G.W. White 95 not out, J.P. Stephenson 50)
Hampshire won by 9 wickets
Hampshire 21 pts Sussex 4 pts

at Worcester
Warwickshire 544 (B.C. Lara 144, M.A. Wagh 119, N.V. Knight 63, S.R. Lampitt 5 for 120)
Worcestershire 236 (S.J. Rhodes 54) and 192 (S.J. Rhodes 79, T.A. Munton 5 for 43, E.S.H. Giddins 5 for 87)
Warwickshire won by an innings and 116 runs
Warwickshire 24 pts, Worcestershire 4 pts

at Scarborough
Essex 200 (G.M. Hamilton 6 for 50) and 261 (A.P. Grayson 57, T.P. Hodgson 54, M.J. Hoggard 5 for 57)
Yorkshire 314 (D.S. Lehmann 99, M.P. Vaughan 71, R.J. Blakey 51, R.C. Irani 5 for 47) and 150 for 9 (M.C. Ilott 5 for 54)
Yorkshire won by 1 wicket
Yorkshire 23 pts, Essex 5 pts

27, 28, 29 and 30 August
at Bristol
Gloucestershire 355 (M.W. Alleyne 116, T.H.C. Hancock 65, M.C.J. Ball 58, A.R. Caddick 5 for 97) and 204 (T.H.C. Hancock 73, A.R. Caddick 4 for 66)
Somerset 396 (M. Burns 96, M.E. Trescothick 92, C.A. Walsh 4 for 80) and 164 for 5 (P.C.L. Holloway 58 not out)
Somerset won by 5 wickets
Somerset 24 pts, Gloucestershire 7 pts

31 August, 1, 2 and 3 September
at Hove
Sussex 332 (K. Newell 84, R.S.C. Martin-Jenkins 78, R.K. Rao 76, S.D. Thomas 4 for 63) and 166
Glamorgan 353 for 8 dec. (M.P. Maynard 94, P.A. Cottey 91) and 127 (R.S.C. Martin-Jenkins 7 for 54)
Sussex won by 18 runs
Sussex 22 pts, Glamorgan 8 pts

at Southampton
Middlesex 437 (A.J. Strauss 83, M.W. Gatting 77, R.A. Kettleborough 60, K.R. Brown 53) and 173 for 2 dec. (R.A. Kettleborough 62 not out)
Hampshire 311 (G.W. White 106, A.D. Mascarenhas 63,

R.L. Johnson 4 for 75) and 301 for 3 (J.P. Stephenson 105, W.S. Kendall 78 not out)
Hampshire won by 7 wickets
Hampshire 21 pts, Middlesex 8 pts

As the season drew to its close, the focus centred on the Britannic Assurance County Championship and the struggle for the title. Matches tumbled over each other, and the weather was not always kind. There was no play on the first day at Derby, and Boon asked the home side to bat when he won the toss. On the third day, Durham built a big lead through Roseberry and Daley who put on 204 for the third wicket. Roseberry, once captain and now something of a forgotten soul, was yorked by Dean three runs short of his century while Daley, of whom so much was expected, hit the second century of his career. He made 157 off 289 balls before charging at left-arm spinner Glenn Roberts and being stumped. Derbyshire had no trouble in claiming a draw.

Only 23 overs were possible on the first day at Northampton where the game was also drawn. Kent chose to bat first but were quickly undermined by Rose and Taylor. Northamptonshire at last had a substantial opening partnership, Rob Bailey and Alec Swann scoring 166 for the first wicket, and the home county led by 173 on the first innings. Kent lost five second innings wickets for 114 before Carl Hooper scored his third century in as many matches. He made 157 from 224 balls with four sixes and 16 fours and saved the game. He and Wells out on 176 for the sixth wicket.

It is generally accepted that it is a great advantage to win the toss at Worksop. Leicestershire proved this when their seam attack bowled out Nottinghamshire for 61 in 29.3 overs. They themselves lost their first four wickets for 127, but Smith and Simmons then shared a county record fifth wicket stand of 322. Lewis and Millns had been suspended from the match for arriving late at training, and Simmons led the side and hit 30 fours and a six. He and Smith set up their side's victory, which was duly completed by Mullally on the third day.

Sussex surrendered rather meekly to Hampshire and were beaten in three days. It was Hampshire's first away win of the season. Giles White's excellent season reached a climax when he passed a thousand runs, and he and John Stephenson began Hampshire's second innings with a fierce onslaught on the bowling that seemed to unsettle the Sussex attack.

Lara's third century in successive matches and a most cultured hundred from Wagh took Warwickshire to 476 from 104 overs on the first day at Worcester, whose misery was compounded by the fact that they had asked the visitors to bat first. Worcestershire's position grew worse and worse. They were bowled out on the second day and, following on, lost five second innings wickets for 29 runs. They descended to 43 for seven on the third morning. Rhodes and Lampitt added 134 but defeat was inevitable.

Essex at least showed some fight before falling to their ninth defeat of the season. They were put in to bat and were bowled out for 200, the last six wickets going down for 38 runs. Vaughan and Lehmann put on 158 for Yorkshire's third wicket, and although the last four wickets fell for 25 runs, the home county took a first innings lead of 114 runs. Wicket-keeper Barry Hyam held six catches. Essex began badly in their second innings, but there was some dogged resistance from the lower order. Hoggard returned the best bowling figures of his career in what was his fifth championship match, and Yorkshire needed 148 to win, a seemingly simple task. Irani and Ilott bowled with tremendous spirit, and, with Yorkshire on 81 for eight, a great Essex victory looked probable. Hamilton's all-round prowess was the barrier to their success. He found an able partner in Hutchison and the pair added 61. Hutchison was leg before to Danny Law, but Hoggard saw that Hamilton's effort was not in vain and contributed six runs as Hamilton finished undefeated on 41.

Gloucestershire's title hopes were ended by Somerset who took a first innings lead through sheer determination and the strength of their tail. Caddick had another outstanding match. The last four Gloucestershire second innings wickets went down for 17 on the last morning, and Somerset needed 164 to win. Walsh dismissed Bowler and Trescothick, a first innings hero, with successive balls, and Smith claimed Kennis for 0 to leave Somerset on 21 for three. Five men were out for 112, but Holloway stayed calm throughout the innings and, aided by Turner, saw Somerset to their fifth win of the season.

Sussex achieved a wonderful victory over Glamorgan in a match which was a personal triumph for the young all-rounder Robin Martin-Jenkins. Choosing to bat first, Sussex were in considerable trouble at 23 for three. Chris Adams's customary positive approach helped restore some order before he was run out for 43. Rao and Keith Newell added 97. Keith Newell was the solid backbone to the innings, and Robin Martin-Jenkins provided the dash with a brisk 78, the highest score of his brief career. Sussex missed a fourth batting point on the second morning, and Glamorgan romped along at four-and-a-half runs an over with Maynard and Cottey putting on 102 and both getting into the nineties. Maynard hit a six and 16 fours before being run out, and he declared at the end of the day when Glamorgan claimed their fourth batting point. The Welshmen took charge on the third day, reducing Sussex 163 for nine before rain ended play. They soon captured the final wicket on the fourth morning and set out on the simple task of scoring 146 to win. At 40 for one, victory seemed axiomatic, but three wickets went down for two runs. Martin-Jenkins, given the new ball because Lewry was injured, produced a magnificent spell of seam bowling. His seven for 54 in 16 overs was a career best bowling performance and took Sussex to a remarkable victory as Glamorgan were bowled out for 127 in 34.3 overs. Mention should also be made of some fine slip catching by Adams.

Hampshire gained an equally surprising and impressive victory over Middlesex, who, put in to bat, reached 357 for five on the opening day. Kettleborough, back in the side because Langer had returned to Australia, and Strauss, making his debut, put on 99 for the second wicket, and Gatting and Strauss added 85 for the third. Strauss hit 14 fours in an impressive first first-class innings. On the second day, Hampshire just avoided the follow-on. They owed much to Giles White, who added 119 in 20 overs for the sixth wicket with Dmitri Mascarenhas, nearly double the rate of scoring earlier in the innings. Rain on the third day prevented Middlesex from making substantial additions to their lead, and, eventually, Hampshire were left a target of 300 in 67 overs. The South Coast side had started the season dreadfully, but by August they were full of confidence. White and Stephenson scored 141 for the first wicket, and Kendall joined Stephenson, who hit his second century of the season, to add 90 for the second. Victory came with ease. Kendall made his highest score of the season and won the match when he hit Weekes for six with 19 balls to spare.

1, 2, 3 and 4 September

at Bristol
Northamptonshire 123 (C.A. Walsh 6 for 36) and 95 (A.M. Smith 6 for 32, C.A. Walsh 4 for 63)
Gloucestershire 210 (R.J. Cunliffe 53, F.A. Rose 4 for 63) and 9 for 0
Gloucestershire won by 10 wickets
Gloucestershire 21 pts, Northamptonshire 4 pts

at Old Trafford
Derbyshire 281 (M.E. Cassar 70, P.A.J. DeFreitas 69) and 198 (D.G. Cork 50, P.J. Martin 4 for 45, Wasim Akram 4 for 66)
Lancashire 487 (G.D. Lloyd 212 not out, J.P. Crawley 100)
Lancashire won by an innings and 8 runs
Lancashire 24 pts, Derbyshire 6 pts

at Taunton
Worcestershire 224 (G.R. Haynes 56, A.R. Caddick 8 for 64) and 254 for 6 (G.A. Hick 110)
Somerset 283 (M. Burns 53, G.D. Rose 52, G.R. Haynes 4 for 74)
Match drawn
Somerset 9 pts, Worcestershire 8 pts

at Edgbaston
Leicestershire 389 (D.J. Millns 99, B.F. Smith 86, T.M. Brimosn 54 not out, T.A. Munton 4 for 90) and 291 for 6 dec. (B.F. Smith 87, P.V. Simmons 68)
Warwickshire 276 (D.R. Brown 75, C.C. Lewis 5 for 76, P.V. Simmons 4 for 54) and 331 (D.L. Hemp 102, M.A. Wagh 60, D.J. Millns 4 for 60)
Leicestershire won by 73 runs
Leicestershire 24 pts, Warwickshire 6 pts

at Leeds
Yorkshire 250 for 9 dec. (C. White 55, D. Byas 52, M.A. Butcher 4 for 41) and 196 for 4 dec. (C. White 104 not out)
Surrey 147 (G.M. Hamilton 7 for 50) and 135 (B.C. Hollioake 60, C.E.W. Silverwood 5 for 30, G.M. Hamilton 4 for 22)
Yorkshire won by 164 runs
Yorkshire 22 pts, Surrey 4 pts

Gloucestershire beat Northamptonshire in two days. Put in to bat, Northamptonshire were routed by Walsh and Smith, and Gloucestershire had a 27-run lead by the end of the first day. They eventually led by 87, and Walsh and Smith then destroyed the visitors. There was a pause for rain, but they bowled unchanged and shot out Northamptonshire in 24.4 overs. They bowled well and exploited favourable conditions, but the Northamptonshire batting lacked application and leadership. The win revived Gloucestershire's hopes of taking the title, but, for a day, Lancashire led the table.

There was no play on the first day at Old Trafford. Lancashire made up for lost time on the second. They put Derbyshire in to bat, and they dismissed the visitors in 71.2 overs for 281 runs. By the end of the day, they had replied with 214 for two at four runs an over. Crawley completed his seventh first-class hundred of the season on the second morning, and Graham Lloyd reached the third double century of his career. It was an exciting affair. He and Crawley put on 143 for the third wicket, and he and Chapple scored 140 in 24 overs for the eighth. Lloyd hit a six and 21 fours and faced 227 balls for his 212 as Lancashire maintained a scoring rate of more than five runs an over. Wasim Akram and Peter Martin bowled Lancashire to an innings victory in what was two days play, and the sides prepared to meet at Lord's in the NatWest Final in two days time.

Omitted from the England parties for the winter tours, Andrew Caddick gave his answer to the selectors with match figures of 11 for 111 in the rain-ruined game at Taunton where only a few minutes play was possible on the final day.

Millns and Lewis returned to the Leicestershire side, but Simmons retained the captaincy. Winning the toss at Edgbaston, Leicestershire did not enjoy a good first day, closing on 190 for six from 48 overs. The second day saw a transformation and showed the spirit and determination that made Leicestershire strong title challengers. They slipped to 203 for eight, but Mullally and Millns then added 77. This was followed by a last wicket partnership of 109 between Millns and Brimson, which was ended when Millns was caught behind off Giddins one short of a century. Brimson hit a maiden first-class fifty, and Leicestershire took maximum batting points. Lewis then took four wickets, and Warwickshire ended the day on 157 for six. They, too, showed some zest in the late order, and a ninth wicket stand of 51 between Brown and Giles saved the follow-on. Leicestershire needed quick runs, and they were provided by Ben Smith, 87 off 113 balls, and Phil Simmons, 68 off 62 balls. The declaration left Warwickshire a target of 405. They negotiated 10 overs at the end of the third day without problems, but Knight was out early on the last morning. Wagh had hit a 10 fours when he was bowled by Millns, who had Singh caught at slip next ball. Crucially, Millns trapped Lara leg before six runs later. Hemp reached his first century of what had been a troublesome summer for him, and Brown, Neil Smith and Piper all resisted firmly, but Leicestershire were not to be denied and went top of the table.

Surrey were beaten at Headingley after a blank first day. It was their fourth defeat of the season, and it cost them

Robin Martin-Jenkins achieved the best batting and bowling performances of his young career and took Sussex to a totally unexpected victory over Glamorgan at Hove at the beginning of September. A hard-hitting batsman and fast medium pace bowler, Martin-Jenkins has tremendous potential allied to a refreshing zest for the game.
(Craig Prentis /Allsport)

dearly. They asked Yorkshire to bat when they won the toss, and Craig White, returning after his long absence through injury, Byas and Parker saw that the home county reached 250 in difficult conditions. Surrey realised how difficult on the third day when they lost 10 wickets for 67 runs. Their destroyer was Gavin Hamilton, who continued to improve his career best performance match after match. Leading by 103 on the first innings, Yorkshire moved smoothly to 151 for four in their second innings, and, on the last morning, White completed a 'welcome back' century, and Byas set Surrey a target of 300. They never had the slightest chance of attaining it. They lost both openers to Silverwood for 11 and were soon 63 for six. Ben Hollioake hit a lusty 60, but Yorkshire's excellent medium pace bowling won the game with ease.

Having led the table from the second week of the season, Surrey were now in second place with two matches remaining. Leicestershire had 244 points, Surrey 239, Lancashire 236, and Gloucestershire and Yorkshire 223.

9, 10, 11 and 12 September

at Riverside
Surrey 323 (A.J. Hollioake 67, A.D. Brown 51, J. Wood 4 for 87) and 142 for 1 dec. (A.J. Stewart 63 not out, M.A. Butcher 60)
Durham 253 for 3 dec. (J.E. Morris 140 not out) and 91 (J.E. Benjamin 6 for 35)
Surrey won by 121 runs
Surrey 20 pts, Durham 6 pts

at Cardiff
Glamorgan 114
Derbyshire 199 for 5 (K.J. Barnett 75 not out, D.G. Cork 64 not out)
Match drawn
Derbyshire 7 pts, Glamorgan 5 pts

at Canterbury
Somerset 342 (M.N. Lathwell 106, M. Burns 69, R.J. Turner 51, D.W. Headley 6 for 97)
Kent 86 (A.R. Caddick 5 for 40, A.P. van Troost 4 for 18) and 210 (R.W.T. Key 56, A.R. Caddick 5 for 61)
Somerset won by an innings and 46 runs
Somerset 23 pts, Kent 4 pts

at Leicester
Leicestershire 395 (V.J. Wells 171, P.V. Simmons 61)
Essex 95 and 201 (A.P. Cowan 94, C.C. Lewis 4 for 72)
Leicestershire won by an innings and 99 runs
Leicestershire 24 pts, Essex 4 pts

at Lord's
Gloucestershire 238 (M.C.J. Ball 67 not out, R.L. Johnson 4 for 56) and 88 (A.R.C. Fraser 6 for 23)
Middlesex 158 (A.M. Smith 5 for 40, C.A. Walsh 4 for 41) and 72 (C.A. Walsh 4 for 22)
Gloucestershire won by 96 runs
Gloucestershire 21 pts, Middlesex 4 pts

at Northampton
Northamptonshire 178 (K.M. Curran 60, J.J. Bates 4 for 69) and 165 (J.J. Bates 5 for 67)
Sussex 72 (M.K. Davies 5 for 19, J.F. Brown 5 for 23) and 135 (G.P. Swann 5 for 29)
Northamptonshire won by 136 runs
Northamptonshire 20 pts, Sussex 4 pts

at Worcester
Worcestershire 212 (J.P. Stephenson 4 for 29, N.A.M. McLean 4 for 82) and 144 for (W.P.C. Weston 57 not out)
Hampshire 178 (G.R. Haynes 6 for 50)
Match drawn
Worcestershire 8 pts, Hampshire 7 pts

at Leeds
Yorkshire 408 for 6 dec. (M.J. Wood 200 not out, G.M. Hamilton 78)
Warwickshire 84 (P.M. Hutchison 6 for 25) and 297 (N.V. Knight 130 not out, A.F. Giles 83, G.M. Hamilton 4 for 79)
Yorkshire won by an innings and 27 runs
Yorkshire 24 pts, Warwickshire 2 pts

11, 12, 13 and 14 September

at Trent Bridge
Lancashire 218 (N.H. Fairbrother 88, C.M. Tolley 6 for 74) and 357 (Wasim Akram 155, J.P. Crawley 58, P.J. Franks 6 for 99)

Jason Lewry, the Sussex left-arm pace bowler whose feats captured the attention of the England selectors.
(Nigel French / ASP)

Nottinghamshire 115 (P.J. Martin 4 for 21, I.D. Austin 4 for 21) and 171 (P. Johnson 90, Wasim Akram 5 for 56)
Lancashire won by 289 runs
Lancashire 21 pts, Nottinghamshire 4 pts

The penultimate round of championship matches was plagued by the weather, and the games at Cardiff and Worcester were abandoned on the last day. At Worcester, Gavin Haynes returned the best bowling figures of his career.

There was rain at Riverside, but good fortune and the ineptitude of Durham smiled on Surrey, who gained an unexpected victory on the Saturday afternoon to maintain their challenge for the title. Adam Hollioake had won the toss and batted, but the Surrey innings had failed to sparkle. Martin Bicknell helped his skipper add 95 for the seventh wicket, and, boosted by 54 extras, the visitors reached 323. Durham batted with supreme confidence, but rain meant that they reached the last day on 231 for three. The captains consulted. The Surrey wicket-keeper bowled an over on the final day that cost 22 runs and allowed Morris to reach 140, and Durham to claim a second batting point. Surrey, who had conceded 63 extras in the Durham innings, made 142 off the 15.4 overs bowled by Lewis and Boon and set the home side a target of 213 from 61 overs. This seemed foolhardy, but Adam Hollioake had to gamble for a win. It did not even seem a gamble as Durham crashed to Benjamin and the rest of the Surrey seam attack in 37.5 overs. Wood, who scored 33 at number nine, was the only one to give a hint of resistance.

Surrey's win left them nine points adrift of Leicestershire, who had an emphatic win over Essex. Leicestershire were put in to bat by Essex, who then bowled rather poorly. Vince Wells, one of the very best of county cricketers, held the innings together with a splendid 171. He and Simmons added 118 for the fourth wicket, and there were some useful contributions from the lower order. The Leicestershire seam attack, backed by some magnificent close catching, routed Essex in under 36 overs and, following on, Essex plummeted to 99 for nine in their second innings. Ashley Cowan then put his team mates to shame by hitting 94, the highest score of his career, off 81 balls. He was ably supported by Such in a last wicket stand of 102. This was a lively response, but it could not hide what, for the most part, had been another spiritless display. The bowling of Grove alone gave some hope for the future. In contrast, Leicestershire's success was testimony to their work as a unit and their dynamic approach to the game.

Somerset also won in three days. They beat Kent by an innings and had reason to be pleased with two individual triumphs. Mark Lathwell ended an unhappy batting spell with a century that recalled the year of '93, and Andy Caddick had match figures of 10 for 101 to become the first bowler in the country to reach 100 wickets, an outstanding performance.

His nearest rival, Courtney Walsh, reached 97 wickets when he took eight for 63 in Gloucestershire's win over Middlesex. It was their 10th win of a fine season and had their batting been able to match the bowling of Walsh, Smith and Lewis, they would have made an even greater challenge for the title.

The match at Lord's was a very low-scoring affair and cast doubts upon the pitch, but not as grave as those cast upon the pitch at Northampton. Left-arm spinner Michael Davies, playing his first game of the season, returned the best bowling figures of his career in Sussex's first innings and finished with match figures of seven for 51. His colleagues Jason Brown and Graeme Swann also enjoyed themselves as Northamptonshire had a crushing victory, while Justin Bates, the Sussex off-spinner, had the best bowling figures of his career for innings and match. However much these spinners enjoyed themselves, the pitch inspectors from the ECB took a different view and Northamptonshire were deducted 25 points.

Matthew Wood reached a wonderful climax to his first full season in first-class cricket with an innings of 200 not out for Yorkshire against Warwickshire. Wood's performance was complemented by the bowling of Hutchison, Hamilton and Hoggard as Warwickshire were beaten by an innings. With such talented youth in their side, one would not bet against Yorkshire taking the title in the next two or three years. They must start favourites for 1999. Warwickshire's only resistance was a second innings eighth wicket stand of 122 between Giles and Knight, who carried his bat through the innings.

Lancashire's three-day win over Nottinghamshire took them to within 11 points of Leicestershire and two points behind Surrey. They did not bat well in their first innings, falling to the left-arm swing bowling of Tolley and the slip catching of Archer, but Nottinghamshire's batting is ever vulnerable. Leading by 103 on the first innings, Lancashire put the game out of the home side's reach when they batted a second time. Franks took six wickets, and

Lancashire were 144 for seven. The last three wickets realised 113 runs, due almost entirely to a wonderful innings from Wasim Akram. The Lancashire skipper, batting at number eight and soon to depart the county, hit 155 off 181 balls with five sixes and 14 fours. He followed this by taking five wickets for 56 runs. Johnson and Franks held Lancashire at bay in a sixth wicket stand of 90, but no other Nottinghamshire batsman reached double figures.

17, 18, 19 and 20 September

at The Oval
Leicestershire 585 for 6 dec. (B.F. Smith 204, Aftab Habib 114, P.A. Nixon 101 not out, C.C. Lewis 54 not out)
Surrey 146 and 228 (A.J. Hollioake 54 not out)
Leicestershire won by an innings and 211 runs
Leicestershire 24 pts, Surrey 2 pts

at Derby
Middlesex 195 (T. M. Smith 4 for 60) and 354 (O. A. Shah 116, M.W. Gatting 62, P.N. Weekes 96, D.G. Cork 4 for 97, K.J. Dean 6 for 97)
Derbyshire 383 (A.S. Rollins 91, K.M. Krikken 58) and 167 for 6
Derbyshire won by 4 wickets
Derbyshire 24 pts, Middlesex 4 pts

at Chelmsford
Essex 283 (S.G. Law 165, G.P. Swann 4 for 47) and 95 (D.E. Malcolm 4 For 48, J.P. Taylor 4 for 31)
Northamptonshire 262 (J.P. Taylor 58, D.J.G. Sales 53, A.L. Penberthy 50) and 120 for 3
Northamptonshire won by 7 wickets
Northamptonshire 22 pts, Essex 6 pts

at Old Trafford
Lancashire 185 (K.D. James 4 for 22, A.C. Morris 4 for 57) and 449 for 4 dec. (J.P. Crawley 239, N.H. Fairbrother 103)
Hampshire 172 (Wasim Akram 4 for 37, I.D. Austin 4 for 50) and 301 (D.A. Kenway 57)
Lancashire won by 161 runs
Lancashire 20 pts, Hampshire 4 pts

at Trent Bridge
Gloucestershire 319 (M.W. Alleyne 72, M.G.N. Windows 63) and 411 for 7 dec. (T.H.C. Hancock 220 not out, A.M.S. Smith 55, M.G.N. Windows 52, U. Afzaal 4 for 101)
Nottinghamshire 249 (N.A. Gie 50, C.A. Walsh 4 for 72) and 292 (G.F. Archer 52, C.M. Tolley 78, C.A. Walsh 5 for 82)
Gloucestershire won by 189 runs
Gloucestershire 23 pts, Nottinghamshire 5 pts

at Hove
Sussex 129 (P.M. Hutchinson 7 for 31) and 170 (M.J. Hoggard 4 for 50)
Yorkshire 252 (M.J. Wood 118 not out, R.J. Kirthey 5 for 80, M.A. Robinson 4 for 72) and 51 for 0
Yorkshire won by 10 wickets
Yorkshire 22 pts, Sussex 4 pts

at Cardiff
Glamorgan 246 (P.A. Cottey 64, A. Dale 60, A.R.K. Pierson 4 for 94) and 278 for 9 dec. (S.P. James 54, A.R.K. Pierson 5 for 117)
Somerset 133 (S.D. Thomas 4 for 56) and 93 (O.T. Parkin 5 for 24)
Glamorgan won by 298 runs
Glamorgan 21 pts, Somerset 4 pts

at Worcester
Worcestershire 310 (S.J. Rhodes 72, G.R. Haynes 72, S. J. Harmison 4 for 88) and 312 for 9 dec.(G.R. Haynes 52, R.K. Illingworth 84)
Durham 342 (J.A. Daley 60, M.A. Roseberry 87, P.D. Collingwood 56, A. Sheriyar 5 for 85) and 125 (S.R. Lampitt 5 for 39)
Worcestershire won by 155 runs
Worcestershire 23 pts, Durham 7 pts

at Edgbaston
Warwickshire 323 (N.V. Knight 68, M.A. Wagh 65, N.M.K. Smith 59, M.A. Ealham 5 for 49) and 262 for 5 dec. (D.L. Hemp 74, T. Frost 50, D.R. Brown 81 not out)
Kent 197 (M.J. Walker 57, S.A. Marsh 57, E.S.H. Giddins 5 for 61) and 202 (E.T. Smith 58, N.M.K. Smith 4 for 92)
Warwickshire won by 186 runs
Warwickshire 23 pts, Kent 4 pts

As the final series of matches began it was theoretically possible for any one of four counties to win the Championship: Leicestershire, Surrey, Lancashire or Yorkshire. Nine points ahead, Leicestershire were the favourites and were at The Oval to face their nearest rivals, Surrey, who had led the championship for most of the summer.

At the end of the first day's play, the result of this match was beyond doubt in one sense; Leicestershire were unlikely to lose and Surrey were unlikely to win. Not that the Midlanders reached their place of greater safety without travail; after 25 overs they were in disorder at 102 for four. But Ben Smith and Aftab Habib rescued the innings with a partnership of 252, a record for any Leicestershire wicket against Surrey. These two players took advantage of a dry and easy pitch, which nevertheless took spin. It was unfortunate for Surrey that spinner Saqlain Mushtaq was absent. Runs mounted on the second day as Smith made his first double century and Paul Nixon raced to 101 not out. Faced with a total of 585 for six declared, a Surrey collapse seemed inevitable. At close of play they were 13 for four, with bowling honours shared by Mullally and Millns. Hustled out for 146, Surrey followed on, and in the waning light of an autumn evening, the last Surrey wicket fell to give Leicestershire their second championship win in three years. In that time they have lost just two matches and in the final phase of the championship they won six in a row. One newspaper called Leicestershire 'a team of no stars'. Perhaps – but they had the consistency, founded on a deep-seated collective spirit, that distinguishes true champions from also-rans. As their cricket manager, Jack Birkenshaw, put it: 'They like playing and don't need motivating'.

Just when they needed maximum bonus points to put pressure on Leicestershire, Lancashire managed to record their lowest score of the season. Only Atherton showed any form, but the bowlers pulled some chestnuts out of the fire by dismissing Hampshire for 172 to give Lancashire a lead of 13 runs. Crawley then played a formidably fluent and aggressive innings of 239, to emphasize what might have been achieved in the first knock. In due course, Hampshire were soundly beaten, Lancashire came second in the championship, and Crawley was named captain for the following season. Defeated, Hampshire took consolation in finishing in sixth position in the table, their best effort for eight years. It gave them a place in the 1999 Super Cup.

A curious match unfolded at Hove, where Yorkshire's ambitions seemed focused only on finishing in the top three in the championship. One wonders what the players imbibed for lunch, since 11 wickets fell afterwards for 64 runs. Yorkshire attained maximum bowling points and Paul Hutchinson had a career-best return of seven for 31. James Kirtley struck back for Sussex by taking the first four Yorkshire wickets, but Matthew Wood stood firm with an unbeaten 118. Yorkshire won by 10 wickets and achieved their target of finishing in the top three.

Yorkshire's gain was at the expense of Surrey, and also of Gloucestershire, who made a strong start at Trent Bridge with an innings of 319. Having bowled out Nottinghamshire for 249 they had a lead of 144 at the end of the second day. Tim Hancock then made 220 not out, and Gloucestershire earned 23 points and fourth position in the table.

Glamorgan, the defending champions, managed a belated home win, their fourth of the season, over Somerset by 298 runs. But the Welsh side finished in 13th place.

The former powerhouses of county cricket, Middlesex and Essex, propped up the table. Essex cricket is in a trough. The last and only other time the country has held the wooden spoon was in 1950. They maintained their pitiable form by losing to Northamptonshire. Middlesex were beaten by Derbyshire, who just failed to qualify for the Super Cup. The match was Mike Gatting's final first-class match for his county and he scored 62 in his second innings. He has been the dominant figure at Middlesex for over two decades, a trenchant destroyer of anything but the best bowling and a spirited leader. To mention his record of more than 36,000 runs at an average of nearly 50 merely skims the surface of his splendid achievements.

Warwickshire also scraped into the Super Cup by dint of a comprehensive defeat of Kent by 186 runs. Worcestershire and Durham had little at which to tilt at Worcester; the home team won the battle of the stragglers with some ease.

Matthew Wood of Yorkshire had an outstanding first season in the county championship, which culminated in an unbeaten double century against Warwickshire at Headingley.
(Mark Thompson / Allsport)

Britannic Assurance County Championship – Final Table

	P	W	L	D	Bt	Bl	Pts
Leicestershire (10)	17	11	0	6	47	51	292
Lancashire (11)	17	11	1	5	30	56	277
Yorkshire (6)	17	9	3	5	47	63	269
Gloucestershire (7)	17	11	5	1	23	65	267
Surrey (8)	17	10	5	2	38	57	261
Hampshire (14)	17	6	5	6	27	61	202
Sussex (18)	17	6	7	4	30	63	201
Warwickshire (4)	17	6	8	3	35	60	200
Somerset (12)	17	6	7	4	30	54	192
Derbyshire (16)	17	6	7	4	28	55	191
Kent (2)	17	5	5	7	18	59	178
Worcestershire (3)	17	4	6	7	32	59	176
Glamorgan (1)	17	4	6	7	36	55	176
Durham (17)	17	3	9	5	30	65	158
Northants (15)	17	4	5	8	31	52	146
Nottinghamshire (13)	17	3	10	4	20	60	140
Middlesex (4)	17	2	9	6	28	52	130
Essex (8)	17	2	11	4	16	58	118

Northants deducted 25 pts for unsuitable pitch.
1997 positions in brackets.

First-Class Averages

Batting

	M	Inns	NO	Runs	HS	Av	100s	50s
S. Hutton	1	1	0	100	100	100.00	1	0
P.A. de Silva	2	2	0	153	152	76.50	1	0
J.P. Crawley	18	28	3	1851	239	74.04	8	5
W.J. Cronje	11	12	2	704	195	70.40	2	4
D.J. Cullinan	12	17	4	900	200*	69.23	2	6
L. Klusener	5	5	2	207	73*	69.00	0	2
G. Kirsten	12	19	5	892	210	63.71	4	2
J.L. Langer	15	28	5	1448	233*	62.95	4	6
B.F. Smith	19	24	4	1240	204	62.00	4	4
D.S. Lehmann	10	16	0	969	200	60.56	3	4
M.B. Loye	15	22	2	1198	322*	59.90	4	4
A. Habib	19	22	5	952	198	56.00	3	3
J.H. Kallis	10	14	3	612	132	55.63	2	3
M.G. Bevan	12	19	2	935	149*	55.00	3	4
M.S. Atapattu	4	7	1	316	114	52.66	1	2
V.C. Hathurusingha	5	8	3	255	108*	51.00	1	1
N.H. Fairbrother	12	17	2	759	138	50.60	3	3
S.P. James	15	28	1	1339	227	49.59	4	5
A.D. Brown	15	22	1	1036	155	49.33	4	6
D.J. Millns	11	10	4	289	99	48.16	0	1
S.T. Jayasuriya	5	9	1	382	213	47.75	1	0
K.J. Barnett	17	32	6	1229	162	47.26	1	7
M.J. Wood	19	29	6	1080	200*	46.95	4	4
G.F.J. Liebenberg	10	17	3	642	104*	45.85	1	5
A. Ranatunga	3	4	0	181	110	45.25	1	1
C.L. Hooper	15	28	1	1218	203	45.11	6	1
N.V. Knight	15	26	2	1069	192	44.54	4	4
M.W. Gatting	17	29	3	1139	241	43.80	2	7
A.J. Stewart	14	24	2	963	164	43.77	1	5
G.A. Hick	17	30	0	1304	166	43.46	7	2
M.G.N. Windows	16	29	2	1173	151	43.44	4	5
J.N. Rhodes	11	14	1	562	123	43.23	2	3
P.N. Weekes	16	26	5	903	139	43.00	1	5
M.R. Ramprakash	15	26	3	979	128*	42.56	4	2
W.S. Kendall	8	11	3	340	78*	42.50	0	2
T.M. Moddy	13	23	2	886	132	42.19	4	2
C.J. Adams	18	29	1	1174	170	41.92	4	4
N.M.K. Smith	18	29	5	1002	147	41.75	2	6
G.W. White	19	31	2	1211	156	41.75	4	5
M.P. Vaughan	19	31	3	1161	177	41.46	2	5
M.A. Butcher	16	26	1	1024	116	40.96	3	6
D.C. Boon	16	29	4	1024	139*	40.96	3	5
S.G. Law	14	26	2	982	165	40.91	2	3
D. Ripley	17	22	2	805	209	40.25	1	5
B.C. Lara	15	26	0	1033	226	39.73	3	3
A.L. Penberthy	14	21	2	755	128	39.73	2	4
M.A. Atherton	13	24	2	874	152	39.72	2	3
H.P. Tillakaratne	6	9	1	317	120	39.62	1	1
C. White	10	15	3	475	104*	39.58	1	2
G.D. Lloyd	15	22	1	831	212*	39.57	2	3
I. Mohammad	6	7	1	237	136	39.50	1	0
O.A. Shah	15	23	3	786	140	39.30	2	4
P. Johnson	15	26	1	976	139	39.04	2	4
R.P. Arnold	5	9	1	312	209	39.00	1	0
M.W. Alleyne	18	33	2	1189	137	38.35	3	6
T.H.C. Hancock	18	34	2	1227	220*	38.34	2	7
R.S. Kaluwitharana	3	4	0	153	74	38.25	0	1
P.A. Nixon	19	21	4	638	101*	37.52	2	1
R.A. Smith	17	25	2	853	138	37.08	3	2
W.L. Law	9	14	2	444	131	37.00	1	2
W.K. Hegg	15	21	4	628	85	36.94	0	6
V.J. Wells	17	25	2	836	171	36.34	3	3
A. Singh	10	12	0	434	117	36.16	1	2
N. Shahid	12	22	3	683	126*	35.94	2	3
A.N. Aymes	18	27	6	754	133	35.90	2	3
S.J. Rhodes	18	33	5	1000	104*	35.71	1	6
S.L. Watkin	13	16	13	107	25*	35.66	0	0
M.J. Slater	14	24	0	848	185	35.33	1	3
M.J. Powell (Glam)	16	27	3	840	106	35.00	1	5
P.A. Cottey	19	32	3	1012	123	34.89	2	5
J.E. Morris	13	24	2	767	163	34.86	3	1
G. Yates	4	6	1	174	55	34.80	0	1
R.T. Robinson	11	18	2	553	114	34.56	1	4
R.J. Bailey	16	24	2	759	188	34.50	1	2
G.P. Swann	14	18	2	548	111	34.25	1	2
A.J. Hollioake	15	22	2	684	112	34.20	1	4
K.D. James	18	26	9	570	57	33.52	0	3
D.A. Leatherdale	18	32	2	1001	137	33.36	2	4
C.C. Lewis	13	14	3	367	71*	33.36	0	4
G.R. Haynes	12	21	5	532	86	33.25	0	4

Batting

	M	Inns	NO	Runs	HS	Av	100s	50s
M.A. Wagh	14	23	2	686	126	32.66	2	3
A.S. Rollins	10	19	0	618	107	32.52	1	4
N.R. Taylor	6	8	1	227	74*	32.42	0	2
T. Frost	8	14	2	389	111*	32.41	1	1
R.C. Irani	18	33	2	1001	127*	32.29	2	2
K.M. Curran	18	26	4	709	90*	32.22	0	6
A. Dale	19	33	1	1028	92	32.12	0	9
G.M. Hamilton	15	19	1	578	79	32.11	0	6
J.D. Ratcliffe	9	15	1	449	100	32.07	1	2
B.W. Byrne	8	12	5	256	69*	32.00	0	1
K. Newell	11	19	6	414	84	31.84	0	3
I.J. Sutcliffe	19	26	4	698	167	31.72	1	2
J.A. Daley	12	22	2	634	157	31.70	1	1
D.P. Fulton	17	31	1	951	207	31.70	1	7
R. Garland	8	9	4	158	56*	31.60	0	1
R.M.S. Weston	9	17	0	537	97	31.58	0	4
R.K. Illingworth	15	21	6	473	84	31.53	0	3
M.E. Trescothick	18	29	2	847	98	31.37	0	6
Wasim Akram	13	18	1	531	155	31.23	1	2
D. Byas	18	28	1	842	116	31.18	4	3
S.M. Pollock	6	8	2	187	50	31.16	0	1
I.J. Ward	10	19	2	529	81*	31.11	0	5
N. Hussain	10	19	0	591	105	31.10	1	4
S.D. Udal	14	18	5	404	62	31.07	0	1
Q.J. Hughes	6	7	0	217	84	31.00	0	1
P.R. Whitaker	7	11	1	309	74	30.90	0	2
P.D. Collinwood	19	32	5	833	105	30.85	1	5
K.R. Brown	17	25	6	576	59*	30.31	0	2
M.N. Lathwell	12	19	0	574	106	30.21	1	5
D.R. Brown	16	27	4	691	81*	30.04	0	5
A.W. Evans	8	14	1	386	125	29.69	1	1
M. Newell	10	14	1	386	135*	29.69	2	0
W.P.C. Weston	17	31	3	829	95	29.60	0	5
J.P. Stephenson	16	24	1	681	114	29.60	2	4
D.P.M. Jayawardene	6	10	1	265	90	29.44	0	2
R.S.C. Martin-Jenkins	8	13	1	353	78	29.41	0	2
W.J. House	8	11	0	322	65	29.27	0	3
M. Watkinson	10	12	1	318	87	28.90	0	2
W.G. Khan	18	30	1	837	125	28.86	1	6
M.P. Maynard	17	29	2	776	99	28.74	0	5
N.T. Wood	12	19	3	457	80*	28.56	0	2
V.S. Solanki	19	36	1	999	170	28.54	2	4
A.F. Giles	14	21	4	485	83	28.52	0	3
R.A. Kettleborough	12	22	4	512	92*	28.44	0	3
M.A. Gough	10	18	0	508	123	28.22	1	2
M.P.L. Bulbeck	8	11	6	141	35	28.20	0	0
G.F. Archer	13	23	0	647	107	28.13	1	5
A.D. Mascarenhas	17	25	2	645	89	28.04	0	6
R.J. Turner	14	22	2	558	105	27.90	1	2
A.P. Wells	15	26	1	684	95	27.36	0	5
M.E. Cassar	17	31	5	708	121	27.23	1	5
J.E.R. Gallian	14	25	3	592	113*	26.90	1	3
M.A. Roseberry	6	11	0	295	97	26.81	0	2
J.A.M. Mollins	7	10	0	268	73	26.80	0	3
M.J. Foster	8	13	1	321	76*	26.75	0	2
R.W.T. Key	13	23	0	612	115	26.60	2	1
P.C. McKeown	5	7	0	186	42	26.57	0	0
S.C. Ecclestone	5	7	0	186	94	26.57	0	1
M. Burns	10	17	0	450	96	26.47	0	3
M.J. Chilton	3	6	0	158	47	26.33	0	0
N.J. Speak	15	27	2	658	77*	26.32	0	6
P.D. Bowler	18	32	2	789	104	26.30	2	3
M.J. Walker	8	14	1	341	68	26.23	0	2
G.P. Thorpe	9	13	1	314	114	26.16	1	1
G.P. Butcher	9	14	2	311	85	25.91	0	2
D.L. Hemp	15	26	1	646	102	25.84	1	4
S.A. Marsh	16	28	4	620	92	25.83	0	5
A.R.K. Pierson	13	20	3	438	108*	25.76	1	1
U. Afzaal	17	30	3	686	109*	25.40	2	4
G.D. Rose	17	26	2	606	76	25.25	0	4
C.M.W. Read	13	22	6	401	76	25.06	0	2
P.C.L. Holloway	16	28	3	624	123	24.96	1	1
D.J. Goodchild	7	14	1	324	105	24.92	1	2
E.T. Smith	11	18	1	422	58	24.82	0	1
M.P. Speight	17	29	4	614	97*	24.56	0	4
A. McGrath	17	28	3	612	63*	24.48	0	3
P.V. Simmons	17	19	0	464	194	24.42	1	2
A.J. Strauss	3	6	0	146	83	24.33	0	1
M.J. Powell (Warw)	13	22	1	511	132	24.33	1	3
A. Flintoff	17	25	0	608	124	24.32	1	3

First-Class Averages (continued)

Batting

	M	Inns	NO	Runs	HS	Av	100s	50s
M.A. Ealham	12	22	3	461	121	24.26	1	2
M.T.E. Peirce	19	32	1	744	96	24.00	0	5
M. Keech	12	14	0	335	70	23.92	0	3
C.E.W. Silverwood	13	13	3	239	57*	23.90	0	1
G.M. Roberts	8	13	3	237	44	23.70	0	0
D.L. Maddy	18	26	2	569	162	23.70	2	0
M.C.J. Ball	18	30	5	592	67*	23.68	0	3
D.A. Kenway	3	5	0	118	57	23.60	0	1
M.V. Fleming	17	30	4	612	51	23.53	0	1
D.R. Hewson	12	22	3	447	78*	23.52	0	3
T.L. Penney	9	16	2	329	53*	23.50	0	1
M.V. Boucher	11	10	1	211	46	23.44	0	0
I.D. Austin	13	17	4	304	64	23.38	0	2
I.N. Flanagan	6	11	0	254	61	23.09	0	2
S.D. Peters	13	23	2	484	64	23.04	0	3
J.J.B. Lewis	15	28	1	622	72	23.03	0	4
S.R. Lampitt	18	28	7	481	48	22.90	0	0
R.D.B. Croft	13	22	7	343	63*	22.86	0	1
A.M. Smith	18	30	13	384	61	22.58	0	2
B. Parker	8	10	2	180	41	22.50	0	0
S.D. Thomas	18	26	3	507	74	22.04	0	3
D.G. Cork	16	27	4	506	102*	22.00	1	3
C.M. Tolley	11	19	2	374	78	22.00	0	2
A.C. Morris	12	15	5	219	51	21.90	0	1
J.P. Taylor	15	20	3	371	58	21.82	0	3
P.A.J. DeFreitas	14	23	3	435	87	21.75	0	2
P.J. Franks	12	20	2	390	66*	21.66	0	2
M.P. Bicknell	17	21	1	433	81	21.65	0	1
J.M. Dakin	6	6	0	128	79	21.33	0	1
R.J. Blakey	17	23	2	448	67*	21.33	0	3
D.C. Nash	14	19	0	404	114	21.26	1	1
P.J. Newport	13	16	3	270	56	20.76	0	1
M.J. McCague	10	15	7	166	38	20.75	0	0
J.N. Batty	16	19	2	351	63	20.64	0	2
R.R. Montgomerie	10	16	3	268	54	20.61	0	1
B.C. Hollioake	17	26	3	469	60	20.39	0	2
R.K. Rao	10	17	1	325	76	20.31	0	2
R.C. Russell	16	28	2	527	63*	20.26	0	2
M.M. Patel	14	20	5	303	58*	20.20	0	2
J.A. Claughton	5	8	1	140	45	20.00	0	0
P.A. Strang	13	18	3	300	48	20.00	0	0
R.J. Kirtley	18	26	10	320	59	20.00	0	1
K.M. Krikken	17	27	5	439	83	19.95	0	3
B.M. McMillan	6	6	0	119	54	19.83	0	1
M.R. May	13	24	0	473	101	19.70	1	1
I.D.K. Salisbury	15	18	2	314	61	19.62	0	3
M.P. Dowman	13	24	1	451	63	19.60	0	2
G.I. MacMillan	5	9	0	176	53	19.55	0	2
G. Welch	12	18	1	332	54	19.52	0	1
B.J. Spendlove	10	19	1	350	49	19.44	0	0
K.J. Dean	15	21	13	154	27*	19.25	0	0
D.P. Ostler	6	10	1	173	133*	19.22	1	0
D. Gough	11	15	1	269	89	19.21	0	2
B.J. Hyam	10	19	3	307	47*	19.18	0	0
P.M. Such	16	25	18	133	25	19.00	0	0
R.D. Stemp	12	16	9	133	43*	19.00	0	0
A.R. Caddick	17	25	8	322	37	18.94	0	0
T.R. Ward	12	22	0	416	94	18.90	0	1
G. Chapple	14	18	3	282	69	18.80	0	1
D.R. Law	14	25	0	466	65	18.64	0	3
T.A. Tweats	9	18	0	332	161	18.44	1	0
P.W. Jarvis	5	7	1	110	39	18.33	0	0
T.P. Hodgson	7	13	0	236	54	18.15	0	1
D.D.J. Robinson	14	25	0	446	85	17.84	0	1
A. Hafeez	10	18	1	303	55	17.82	0	1
M.N. Bowen	10	13	5	142	32	17.75	0	0
I. Dawood	7	12	1	194	40	17.63	0	0
Saqlain Mushtaq	12	15	5	176	45*	17.60	0	0
A.P. Cowan	8	13	0	228	94	17.53	0	2
D.J.G. Sales	14	21	1	346	60	17.30	0	2
P.R. Pollard	4	7	0	121	69	17.28	0	1
A.J. Wright	11	20	0	345	57	17.25	0	1
J.S. Laney	8	13	0	224	101	17.23	1	1
J.A. Knott	5	9	3	103	41*	17.16	0	0
N.F. Williams	9	16	6	171	36	17.10	0	0
G.E. Welton	5	9	0	152	55	16.88	0	1
A.J. Tudor	10	13	3	167	48	16.70	0	0
K.A. Parsons	14	23	4	367	101*	16.68	1	1
D.W. Headley	14	21	5	265	81	16.56	0	1
A.D. Shaw	11	16	1	248	71	16.53	0	2

Batting

	M	Inns	NO	Runs	HS	Av	100s	50s
A.P. Grayson	17	31	0	509	59	16.41	0	4
J.A.G. Fulton	8	12	1	180	78	16.36	0	1
N.A. Gie	4	8	0	128	50	16.00	0	1
P.M. Hutchison	17	16	8	127	30	15.87	0	0
R.J. Harden	12	21	2	301	63	15.84	0	2
J.P. Hewitt	15	19	2	268	53	15.76	0	1
K.J. Piper	13	23	5	283	44*	15.72	0	0
D.R. Lockhart	7	11	0	173	35	15.72	0	0
P.J. Martin	14	15	5	154	26	15.40	0	0
R.J. Cunliffe	12	22	0	339	53	15.40	0	2
Mushtaq Ahmed	6	9	1	121	37	15.12	0	0
J.P. Pyemont	6	7	0	105	54	15.00	0	1
G.R. Loveridge	7	9	1	118	41	14.75	0	0
A.J. Swann	11	17	0	250	85	14.70	0	1
A.D. Mullally	15	11	2	132	38*	14.66	0	0
N.A.M. McLean	16	22	2	288	43	14.40	0	0
M.T. Brimson	18	14	6	115	54*	14.37	0	1
R.J. Rollins	8	12	0	171	42	14.25	0	0
I.D. Blackwell	11	18	0	254	57	14.11	0	2
J.D. Middlebrook	8	12	2	139	41	13.90	0	0
J.R. Carpenter	9	16	0	222	65	13.87	0	1
N.J. Trainor	4	8	0	109	52	13.62	0	1
S. Humphries	14	22	1	286	66	13.61	0	1
R.I. Dawson	8	15	2	177	46	13.61	0	0
R.L. Johnson	14	21	3	242	43	13.44	0	0
J. Lewis	18	31	2	390	54*	13.44	0	1
P.J. Prichard	10	18	0	237	24	13.16	0	0
R.J. Chapman	11	16	8	102	43*	12.75	0	0
C.J. Batt	9	14	2	150	43	12.50	0	0
S.J. Harmison	14	22	4	223	36	12.38	0	0
P.J. Hartley	13	16	3	160	29	12.30	0	0
M.M. Betts	12	18	7	135	29*	12.27	0	0
B.J. Phillips	11	17	0	203	54	11.94	0	1
M.C. Ilott	17	30	4	307	38	11.80	0	0
J. Wood	17	26	4	236	37	10.72	0	0
D.E. Malcolm	14	16	5	114	42	10.36	0	0
E.J. Wilson	5	10	0	101	27	10.10	0	0
K.P. Evans	9	13	0	129	36	9.92	0	0
N.C. Phillips	17	25	2	227	35	9.86	0	0
P.C.R. Tufnell	17	22	6	155	24	9.68	0	0
A.R.C. Fraser	14	19	5	134	32	9.57	0	0
F.A. Rose	14	17	2	133	21	8.86	0	0
C.A. Walsh	17	23	10	111	25	8.53	0	0
D.A. Cosker	15	21	3	123	37	6.83	0	0
J.D. Lewry	17	23	0	132	24	5.73	0	0

(Qualification: 100 runs; average 10.00)

Bowling

	Overs	Mds	Runs	Wks	Av	Best	5/inn	10/m
M. Muralitharan	226.3	77	463	34	13.61	9/65	5	2
V.J. Wells	199.1	66	514	36	14.27	5/18	1	0
C. White	147.1	37	391	25	15.64	8/55	2	0
J. Ormond	133.3	51	311	19	16.36	6/33	2	0
T.H.C. Hancock	68.0	16	214	13	16.46	3/5	0	0
P.L. Symcox	92.3	26	207	12	17.25	5/60	1	0
C.A. Walsh	633.0	164	1835	106	17.31	6/36	7	2
Saqlain Mushtaq	475.0	135	1119	63	17.76	8/65	3	3
A.D. Mullally	449.4	156	1133	60	18.88	7/55	3	1
M.P.L. Bulbeck	154.4	28	609	32	19.03	4/40	0	0
T.A. Munton	278.5	72	708	37	19.13	7/66	3	0
J.J. Bates	102.5	24	273	14	19.50	5/67	2	0
D.A. Leatherdale	111.4	22	416	21	19.80	5/20	1	0
A.R. Caddick	687.1	156	2082	105	19.82	8/64	10	3
R.S.C. Martin-Jenkins	141.5	45	437	22	19.86	7/54	1	0
A.R.C. Fraser	476.3	122	1224	61	20.06	6/23	4	1
A.A. Donald	302.2	89	785	39	20.12	6/56	5	0
A.C. Morris	314.0	64	1012	50	20.24	4/30	0	0
G.M. Hamilton	415.0	100	1212	59	20.54	7/50	4	2
M.P. Bicknell	493.1	141	1340	65	20.61	5/27	2	0
M.J. Foster	113.0	23	351	17	20.64	4/41	0	0
A.M. Smith	522.3	139	1440	68	21.17	6/32	4	0
K.J. Dean	465.3	96	1572	74	21.24	6/63	5	1
P.V. Simmons	170.5	44	491	23	21.34	7/49	1	0
Wasim Akram	335.5	75	1025	48	21.35	5/56	1	0
G. Chapple	313.0	57	942	44	21.40	5/49	1	0

Bowling

	Overs	Mds	Runs	Wks	Av	Best	5/inn	10/m
D.W. Headley	410.2	88	1175	54	21.75	6/71	4	0
M.J. Hoggard	258.0	51	895	41	21.82	5/57	1	0
S.L. Watkin	370.4	107	917	42	21.83	5/30	1	0
J.F. Brown	280.2	68	726	33	22.00	6/53	4	1
M.M. Betts	363.0	81	1061	48	22.10	6/83	4	0
P.J. Martin	388.0	94	1062	48	22.12	4/21	0	0
O.T. Parkin	300.3	99	757	34	22.26	5/24	2	0
J.D. Lewry	461.3	112	1409	62	22.72	6/72	3	0
T.M. Smith	150.3	42	484	21	23.04	6/32	2	0
M.C. Ilott	506.5	138	1345	58	23.18	6/20	2	0
C.E.W. Silverwood	391.1	100	1123	48	23.39	5/13	3	0
E.S.H. Giddins	668.2	162	2006	84	23.88	6/79	5	1
G. Yates	131.3	26	432	18	24.00	4/64	0	0
D.J. Millns	243.3	55	817	34	24.02	4/60	0	0
P.M. Hutchison	474.3	119	1432	29	24.27	7/31	3	0
J. Lewis	462.1	108	1447	59	24.52	6/48	3	0
S.D. Thomas	544.1	94	1749	71	24.63	5/84	3	0
S.M. Pollock	266.5	87	594	24	24.75	5/53	1	0
J.P. Taylor	436.5	105	1337	54	24.75	4/31	0	0
P.J. Newport	335.1	115	893	36	24.80	4/44	0	0
C.C. Lewis	266.4	53	972	39	24.92	6/60	2	0
B.C. Hollioake	274.4	51	903	36	25.08	4/28	0	0
D. Gough	339.3	65	1067	42	25.40	6/42	2	0
N.A.M. McLean	518.5	105	1575	62	25.40	6/101	2	0
A.J. Tudor	184.5	34	737	29	25.41	5/43	1	0
A. Dale	249.3	46	794	31	25.61	5/25	1	0
M.A. Ealham	242.4	83	593	23	25.78	5/23	3	0
I.D.K. Salisbury	387.5	109	958	37	25.89	7/65	2	0
S. Elworthy	127.0	31	415	16	25.93	4/71	0	0
P.A.J. DeFreitas	482.4	114	1363	52	26.21	5/38	3	0
P.J. Franks	404.2	87	1375	52	26.44	6/63	4	0
M.V. Fleming	404.4	115	1008	38	26.52	4/24	0	0
S.R. Lampitt	416.0	97	1330	50	26.60	5/33	4	0
M.A. Robinson	416.1	107	1126	42	26.80	4/72	0	0
G.D. Rose	480.3	132	1399	52	26.90	5/48	2	0
G.R. Haynes	227.5	61	705	26	27.11	6/50	2	0
I.D. Austin	345.4	80	978	36	27.16	4/21	0	0
K.P. Evans	273.0	73	735	27	27.22	5/92	2	0
M.T. Brimson	369.5	129	901	33	27.30	4/4	0	0
F.A. Rose	373.2	59	1367	50	27.34	7/39	3	1
R.L. Johnson	377.2	77	1369	50	27.38	7/86	1	0
A.P. Van Troost	118.0	24	415	15	27.66	4/18	0	0
A.P. Davies	135.5	41	390	14	27.85	2/22	0	0
M.J. McCague	235.1	48	758	27	28.07	4/40	0	0
M.N. Bowen	309.1	76	875	31	28.22	7/73	1	0
C.M. Tolley	324.3	76	960	34	28.23	7/45	3	0
R.J. Kirtley	490.4	116	1532	54	28.37	7/29	3	1
A.F. Giles	429.3	154	1025	36	28.47	5/48	1	0
R.J. Chapman	246.1	46	943	33	28.57	6/105	1	0
J.E. Benjamin	190.1	42	631	22	28.68	6/35	1	0
D.G. Cork	545.0	111	1618	56	28.89	6/119	3	0
G.P. Butcher	152.4	24	551	19	29.00	4/14	0	0
N. Killeen	101.2	25	349	12	29.08	5/49	1	0
M.J. Rawnsley	172.3	46	497	17	29.23	6/44	2	1
T.M. Moody	251.1	73	790	27	29.25	5/64	1	0
Mushtaq Ahmed	136.0	40	411	14	29.35	3/26	0	0
D.R. Brown	438.2	92	1489	50	29.78	5/40	2	0
C.P. Schofield	79.4	9	299	10	29.90	4/56	0	0
T.F. Bloomfield	168.5	34	660	22	30.00	5/67	2	0
G.P. Swann	199.4	41	666	22	30.27	5/29	1	0
L. Klusener	156.0	38	424	14	30.28	4/66	0	0
S.J. Harmison	455.5	93	1545	51	30.29	5/70	1	0
M. Ntini	184.3	48	578	19	30.42	4/72	0	0
J.B.D. Thompson	95.4	21	335	11	30.45	4/52	0	0
G.P. Wickramasingh	135.1	27	397	13	30.53	4/69	0	0
J. Wood	571.5	113	1910	62	30.80	5/52	2	0
C.L. Hooper	386.2	104	957	31	30.87	7/93	1	0

Bowling

	Overs	Mds	Runs	Wks	Av	Best	5/inn	10/m
M.A. Butcher	119.4	29	340	11	30.90	4/41	0	0
A.R. Oram	305.5	75	969	31	31.25	4/37	0	0
G. Keedy	182.3	38	563	18	31.27	5/35	1	0
C.J. Batt	201.5	23	846	27	31.33	6/101	2	0
J.P. Stephenson	286.4	71	770	24	32.08	4/29	0	0
J.D. Middlebrook	164.1	45	422	13	32.46	3/20	0	0
D. Follett	103.0	17	325	10	32.50	3/48	0	0
N.F. Williams	246.5	47	849	26	32.65	4/42	0	0
P.A. Strang	353.3	105	983	30	32.76	5/166	1	0
M.M. Patel	418.3	102	1123	34	33.02	5/73	1	0
J.H. Kallis	226.1	79	529	16	33.06	4/24	0	0
M.P. Dowman	139.0	31	397	12	33.08	2/10	0	0
Waqar Younis	100.1	13	397	12	33.08	3/147	0	0
D.E. Malcom	334.0	48	1331	40	33.27	6/54	2	0
A.D. Mascarenhas	280.5	59	1000	30	33.33	4/31	0	0
D.J. Eadie	113.5	19	434	13	33.38	2/34	0	0
J.P. Hewitt	377.3	64	1378	41	33.60	6/71	2	0
P.J. Hartley	353.5	66	1109	33	33.60	4/42	0	0
M. Watkinson	175.4	22	607	18	33.72	5/45	1	0
D.P. Mather	168.5	32	574	17	33.76	6/74	1	1
K.D. James	340.0	70	1083	32	33.84	4/22	0	0
R.C. Irani	444.3	105	1392	41	33.95	5/47	1	0
M.W. Alleyne	284.1	84	818	24	34.08	4/63	0	0
S.D. Udal	191.2	44	549	16	34.31	4/37	0	0
M.G. Bevan	175.4	27	653	19	34.36	3/36	0	0
M.C.J. Ball	433.0	108	1173	34	34.50	4/26	0	0
D.A. Cosker	483.5	127	1265	36	35.13	6/140	1	0
D.R. Law	247.5	34	1045	29	36.03	5/46	1	0
R.D. Stemp	409.0	144	1001	27	37.07	5/191	1	0
I.D. Blackwell	156.2	32	524	14	37.42	5/115	1	0
M.E. Trescothick	193.3	45	654	17	38.47	4/82	0	0
A.P. Grayson	248.2	62	734	19	38.63	3/13	0	0
P.M. Such	525.0	128	1475	38	38.81	5/73	2	0
P.R. Adams	281.2	79	666	17	39.17	4/63	0	0
G. Welch	314.3	71	996	25	39.84	4/94	0	0
N.M.K. Smith	329.3	84	957	24	39.87	5/128	1	0
A. Sheriyar	286.1	70	962	24	40.08	5/85	1	0
A.R.K. Pierson	258.1	53	842	21	40.09	5/117	1	0
P.C.R. Tufnell	632.0	162	1602	39	41.07	4/24	0	0
M. Hayward	121.0	21	518	12	43.16	3/34	0	0
N.C. Phillips	425.4	101	1216	28	43.42	5/56	1	0
P.D. Collingwood	200.1	53	582	13	44.76	3/89	0	0
A.P. Cowan	238.3	54	859	19	45.21	3/18	0	0
P. Aldred	181.4	38	556	12	46.33	3/30	0	0
G.R. Loveridge	204.0	33	655	13	50.38	5/59	1	0
B.W. Byrne	174.1	31	583	11	53.00	3/103	0	0
P.N. Weekes	237.0	37	702	13	54.00	3/113	0	0
B.J. Phillips	294.0	55	928	17	54.58	3/66	0	0
R.D.B. Croft	453.5	117	1144	20	57.20	4/76	0	0
M.E. Cassar	157.0	29	614	10	61.40	3/26	0	0
R.K. Illingworth	304.0	80	853	13	65.61	3/28	0	0

(Qualification: 10 wickets)

Leading Fielders

71 – R.J. Blakey (ct 69 / st 2); 60 – M.P. Speight (ct 57 / st 3); 57 – R.C. Russell; 54 – A.N. Aymes (ct 52 / st 2); 47 – P.A. Nixon (ct 42 / st 5); 45 – S.J. Rhodes (ct 43 / st 2), K.R. Brown (ct 40 / st 5), S.A. Marsh (ct 41 / st 4), M.V. Boucher (ct 44 / st 1) and J.N. Batty (ct 39 / st 6); 43 – R.J. Turner; 41 – A.J. Stewart and C.M.W. Read (ct 38 / st 3); 39 – K.M. Krikken (ct 37 / st 2); 38 – W.K. Hegg (ct 35 / st 3); 34 – B.J. Hyam (ct 32 / st 2); 32 – D. Ripley (ct 31 / st 1); 31 – K.J. Piper (ct 28 / st 3); 30 – C.J. Adams; 28 – V.S. Solanki; 26 – A.D. Shaw and S. Humphries; 24 – G.A. Hick; 23 – M.W. Allyene, K.M. Curran, G.F. Archer, P.V. Simmons, A. Flintoff and M.C.J. Ball; 21 – T. Frost, D.P. Fulton and M.P. Maynard; 20 – A.D. Brown, P.N. Weekes, P.A. Cottey, M.E. Trescothick, D. Byas and I. Dawood (ct 19 / st 1)

Derbyshire CCC First-Class Matches Batting

	v. Nottinghamshire (Derby) 17–20 April		v. Yorkshire (Leeds) 23–27 April		v. Warwickshire (Derby) 13–16 May		v. Sussex (Horsham) 21–24 May		v. Leicestershire (Chesterfield) 29 May–1 June		v. Gloucestershire (Chesterfield) 3–6 June		v. Hampshire (Basingstoke) 17–20 June		v. Essex (Derby) 1–4 July		v. South Africans (Derby) 18–20 July		v. Northamptonshire (Northampton) 22–25 July		M	Inns	NO	Runs	HS	Av
A.S. Rollins	44	0	3	63	4	0	58	37	0	44	34	107	89	9	1	12					10	19	–	618	107	32.52
T.A. Tweats	161	2	3	5	2	14	11	0	26	13	0	0	9	44	0	5	10	27			9	18	–	332	161	18.44
I.D. Blackwell	53	0	14	3	0	3	1	–													11	18	–	254	57	14.11
K.J. Barnett	0	8*	55*	68	20	39	162	12*	30	57	74	28	43	44*	16	48			24	68	17	32	6	1229	162	47.26
M.E. Cassar	5	–	3	0			121	13*	0	9	78*	22*	10	24*	0	58	1	91*	38	60	17	31	5	708	121	27.23
D.G. Cork	6	1	–	21	8	32*	102*	–	8	8											10	16	3	393	102*	30.23
K.M. Krikken	83	–	14*	0	5	2	12	–	5	0	60	12*	29	–			7	–	7	9	17	27	5	439	83	19.95
P.A.J. DeFreitas	13	22*	–	12	30*	9	87	–	19	6	0	–	2	–	4	2			19	27	14	23	3	435	87	21.75
P. Aldred	14	–	–	3*	0	6			7	10*	3	–	37*	–			15	–			7	9	3	95	37*	15.83
K.J. Dean	1*	–					8	–	0*	12	1	–	5	–	1*	25*	27*	–	8	0*	15	21	13	154	27*	19.25
M.J. Slater	–	–					0	39	24	13	0	31	47	14	0	24	185	63	27	46	14	24	–	848	185	35.33
M.R. May			22	0					16	22	11	54					0	101	32	0	13	24	–	473	101	19.70
A.J. Harris			–	4	0	5															2	3	–	9	5	3.00
B.J. Spendlove					16	6									0	45	0	32*	1	28	10	19	1	350	49	19.44
V.P. Clarke					2	26															4	7	–	67	26	9.57
S.J. Lacey							11	–			0	–	17	–							3	3	–	28	17	9.33
G.M. Roberts													35	–	30	44	40	–	6*	5	8	13	3	237	44	23.70
S.P. Griffiths															12	3					1	2	–	15	12	7.50
T.M. Smith															1	29	13	–	1	0	7	10	1	94	29	10.44
R.M.S. Weston																	10	3	51	33	9	17	–	537	97	31.58
Byes				4		13	2	4	12	1		3					9	3	1	4						
Leg-byes	6		1	7	1	10	16	2	8	7	4	15	9	1	5	6	3	9	6	5						
Wides					2	2			6	3	2		4			8	1									
No-balls	2		21	20	8	6	2		16	12	28	28	14	4		10	16	8	4	4						
Total	388	43	136	210	98	173	593	107	177	217	295	300	350	140	70	319	337	337	225	289						
Wickets	9	4	5	10	10	10	10	3	10	10	10	5	10	3	10	10	10	4	10	10						
Result	W		L		L		W		L		D		L		W		D		L							
Points	24		2		4		24		4		7		5		20		–		2							

Derbyshire CCC First-Class Matches Batting

	v. Kent (Derby) 30 July–3 August		v. Surrey (The Oval) 6–9 August		v. Worcestershire (Derby) 14–17 August		v. Somerset (Taunton) 19–22 August		v. Durham (Derby) 26–29 June		v. Lancashire (Old Trafford) 1–4 September		v. Glamorgan (Cardiff) 9–12 September		v. Middlesex (Derby) 17–20 September		M	Inns	NO	Runs	HS	Av
A.S. Rollins													9	–	91	13	10	19	–	618	107	32.52
T.A. Tweats																	9	18	–	332	161	18.44
I.D. Blackwell			10	2	0	23	44	4	57	5	6	0	–	–	29	–	11	18	–	254	57	14.11
K.J. Barnett	21	–	13	18	21	0	30	0	11	98	28	25	75*	–	44	49*	17	32	6	1229	162	47.26
M.E. Cassar	4	–	4	9	11	0	4	10	14	9	70	4	4	–	7	25	17	31	5	708	121	27.23
D.G. Cork	11	–					0	8			23	50	64*	–	51	0	10	16	3	393	102*	30.23
K.M. Krikken	2	–	11	0	27	19	10*	1	5	5	22	7*	–	–	58	27*	17	27	5	439	83	19.95
P.A.J. DeFreitas	9	–	4	6	21	8	32	12*			69	12					14	23	3	435	87	21.75
P. Aldred																	7	9	3	95	37*	15.83
K.J. Dean	4*	–	0*	2	10*	10*	1	1	12*	5*			–	–	21*	–	15	21	13	154	27*	19.25
M.J. Slater	34	–	7	99	23	32	15	48	54	9			14	–			14	24	–	848	185	35.33
M.R. May	19	–	1	43	24	21	14	4	24	24	4	11	3	–	10	3	13	24	–	473	101	19.70
A.J. Harris																	2	3	–	9	5	3.00
B.J. Spendlove					16	45	49	27	1	15	0	9	19	–	30	11	10	19	1	350	49	19.44
V.P. Clarke	4	–	16	1							7	11					4	7	–	67	26	9.57
S.J. Lacey																	3	3	–	28	17	9.33
G.M. Roberts	38	–	8	2*					1	28	0*	0					8	13	3	237	44	23.70
S.P. Griffiths																	1	2	–	15	12	7.50
T.M. Smith					23	5			22	0*			–	–	0	–	7	10	1	94	29	10.44
R.M.S. Weston	97	–	37	16	84	0	73	6	2	45	18	40			0	22	9	17	–	537	97	31.58
Byes	4		1	2	1					8	4		4		12	2						
Leg-byes	9		8	6	7	5	8	6	2	14	6	5	7		14	7						
Wides											8				6							
No-balls	4		19		12		10	2		4	16	24			10	8						
Total	260		139	206	280	168	290	139	205	269	281	198	199		383	167						
Wickets	10		10	10	10	10	10	10	10	9	10	10		5	10	6						
Result	D		L		W		W		D		L		D		W							
Points	9		4		22		22		5		6		7		24							

Fielding Figures

39 – K.M. Krikken (ct 37 / st 2)
10 – M.J. Slater and A.S. Rollins
9 – D.G. Cork
8 – K.J. Barnett and T.A. Tweats
6 – P.A.J. DeFreitas, P. Aldred, S.P. Griffiths and I.D. Blackwell
5 – G.M. Roberts and R.M.S. Weston
4 – M.E. Cassar, M.R. May, B.J. Spendlove and V.P. Clarke
3 – sub.
1 – S.J. Lacey and K.J. Dean

Derbyshire CCC First-Class Matches

Bowling

	P.A.J. DeFreitas	D.G. Cork	K.J. Dean	P. Aldred	M.E. Cassar	I.D. Blackwell	A.J. Harris	G.M. Roberts	T.M. Smith	V.P. Clarke	K.J. Barnett	S.J. Lacey	Byes	Leg-byes	Wides	No-balls	Total	Wkts	
v. Nottinghamshire	10–4–12–1	12.4–4–45–3	11–4–29–3	14–2–30–3										2	2	16	118	10	
(Derby) 17–20 April	35.2–8–89–4	26–3–93–3	22–8–70–2	22–8–41–1	3–2–4–0	5–1–11–0							1	3		20	312	10	
v. Yorkshire	34–6–102–2	19–1–60–0		30.4–9–77–1		8–1–23–0	18–3–73–2				3–0–6–0		1	10	8	40	352	5	
(Leeds) 23–27 April		3.4–0–15–0					2–0–10–0								2	4	105	0	A
v. Warwickshire	29.2–7–91–3	24–3–81–1		27–4–69–3		3–1–11–1	12–0–53–2			4–0–10–0			8	9		32	332	10	
(Derby) 13–16 May																			
v. Sussex	23–1–74–3	28–9–77–4	26.1–8–90–2		19–6–35–0	4–2–5–0						12–3–33–0	1	10	2	8	235	10	
(Horsham) 21–24 May	32–4–101–2	14–5–30–1	17–4–63–1		4–0–12–0	11.4–2–38–3					7–0–24–1	35–9–89–2		17	4	16	374	10	
v. Leicestershire	25.1–3–81–3	28–7–72–5	12–0–44–1	17–4–42–1										7	2	24	246	10	
(Chesterfield) 29 May–1 June	24–10–38–5	22–5–60–0	16.2–3–57–5	7–2–25–0										6		2	186	10	
v. Gloucestershire	33–7–74–1		32–4–123–3	31–3–117–1	10.3–1–58–0						20–7–30–2	10–0–51–0		6		16	459	8	
(Chesterfield) 3–6 June																			
v. Hampshire	22–8–54–1		11–5–17–1	10–1–25–1				14–0–48–0				18–5–53–1	11	2	4	8	210	4	
(Basingstoke) 17–20 June	13–2–50–1		10.3–1–51–1	6–1–44–1				17–2–65–1			2–0–8–0	13–2–48–1	6	9		8	281	5	
v. Essex	16.2–6–19–4		10–2–39–4						6–3–6–2					1			65	10	
(Derby) 1–4 July	27–12–60–0		9.3–1–27–4					7–2–20–0	21–10–32–6					4		6	143	10	
v. South Africans			24.1–4–86–3	17–4–86–0	20–3–90–1			16–0–100–0	26–6–88–5					3	1	6	453	9	
(Derby) 18–20 July																			
v. Northamptonshire	36–3–117–3		29–3–121–1		17–2–97–0			43–4–161–1	8–0–43–0		13–0–59–1		1	9	2	2	608	6	
(Northampton) 22–25 July																			
v. Kent	18.2–3–55–5	10–2–39–0	12–2–52–4					3–0–14–0						5		20	165	9	
(Derby) 30 July–3 August	5–2–18–0	13–2–27–2	13.2–1–47–3					4–2–2–0		9–1–32–0				3		6	129	5	
v. Surrey	13–2–50–1		10–1–34–3		5–0–28–0	33–6–115–5		14–1–51–0		11–2–50–1				5		2	333	10	
(The Oval) 6–9 August	13–5–26–1		20–2–70–2			38–9–94–4		15–4–39–2		2–0–4–0				5	4		238	9	
v. Worcestershire	13–8–10–3		15.5–2–52–4		6–2–14–1				9–3–27–2				1				104	10	
(Derby) 14–17 August	21.1–4–95–5		25–5–90–5		5–0–40–0	6–1–21–0			13–3–58–0				2	10	2	14	316	10	
v. Somerset	11–2–46–2	16–5–32–2	22.1–6–70–6		4–1–14–0	4–1–14–0							4	1		10	181	10	
(Taunton) 19–22 August	12–4–33–0	24–6–68–3	21–6–63–6			2.4–0–5–1								7		4	176	10	
v. Durham			29–9–76–1		19–7–46–0	30–7–98–0		31–9–105–4	23–6–90–1				6	13	16	2	434	6	
(Derby) 26–29 June																			
v. Lancashire	17–3–68–2	19–3–57–2			13.1–0–65–3	10–1–87–0		21–3–124–1		15–1–77–1			5	4	8	6	487	10	
(Old Trafford) 1–4 September																			
v. Glamorgan		17–6–29–3	14–1–37–2		8.2–2–26–3				8–3–17–1					5		6	114	10	
(Cardiff) 9–12 September																			
v. Middlesex		18–6–32–3	19–6–67–1		9–1–27–2				16.3–4–60–4				1	8	2	18	195	10	
(Derby) 17–20 September		38–10–97–4	33.3–8–97–6		14–2–58–0	1–0–2–0			20–4–63–0		9–3–21–0		4	12	4	4	354	10	
	482.4–114– 1363–52	332.2–77– 914–36	465.3–96– 1572–74	181.4–38– 556–12	157–29– 614–10	156.2–32– 524–14	32–3– 136–4	185–27– 729–9	150.3–42– 484–21	41–4– 173–2	54–10– 148–4	88–19– 274–4							
Bowler's average	26.21	25.38	21.24	46.33	61.40	37.42	34.00	81.00	23.04	86.50	37.00	68.50							

A M.R. May 3–0–51–0; T.W. Tweats 3–0–29–0

Durham CCC First-Class Matches Batting

Batting	v. Warwickshire (Edgbaston) 17–21 April		v. Gloucestershire (Riverside) 23–27 April		v. Essex (Riverside) 13–16 May		v. Cambridge University (Cambridge) 18–20 May		v. Kent (Canterbury) 21–24 May		v. Nottinghamshire (Trent Bridge) 29 May–1 June		v. Middlesex (Lord's) 3–6 June		v. Northamptonshire (Riverside) 11–14 June		v. Yorkshire (Riverside) 17–20 June		v. Leicestershire (Darlington) 1–4 July		M	Inns	NO	Runs	HS	Av
J.J.B. Lewis	0	19	7	0					7	72	15	8	68	8	39	–	22	8	0	16	15	128	1	622	72	23.03
M.A. Roseberry	10	2	23	9	26	20															6	11	–	295	97	26.81
J.E. Morris	17	5	3	12			–	110*	28	32									9	0	13	24	2	767	163	34.86
N.J. Speak	8	50*	16	74	41	41			0	0	16	77*	0	0	31	–	57	0	30	25	15	27	2	658	77*	26.32
D.C. Boon	107	2	37	5							4	54*	68	21	36	–	139*	8	9	22	16	29	4	1024	139*	40.96
M.P. Speight	0	3	3	29	30	10			7	18	0	–	2	17	66*	–	41	4	16	11	17	29	4	614	97*	24.56
P.D. Collingwood	105	–	3	10	26	42	–	24*	18	0	97*	–	66	33	50*	–	0	13	10	8	19	32	5	833	105	30.85
N.C. Phillips	23	–	0	35	12	0	–	–	1	5	4	–	16	28	–	–	4	5	4*	0	17	25	2	227	35	9.86
M.M. Betts	2*	–			3	0			0	12*	0	–	0	29*	–	–	18	6*	0	0	12	18	7	135	29*	12.27
J. Wood	2	–	1	7	4	37			0	0	16	–	26*	4	–	–	2	4	0	36	17	26	4	236	37	10.72
S.J. Harmison	7	–	12	1	4*	28*			36	30	3	–	3	0*	–	–	0	10	4	4	14	22	4	223	36	12.38
A. Walker			3*	2*																	1	2	2	5	3*	–
M.A. Gough					62	16	123	–	31	2	23	21	38	56	9	–	0	9			10	18	–	508	123	28.22
J.A. Daley					8	26	–	47											30	42*	12	22	2	634	157	31.70
M.J. Foster					21	11			76*	39	68	–	6	27	–	–	35	2			8	13	1	321	76*	26.75
S. Hutton							100	–													1	1	–	100	100	100.00
A. Pratt							6	–													2	3	–	40	34	13.33
N. Killeen							15*	–													3	3	1	27	15*	13.50
M.J. Symington							8*	–													2	1	1	8	8*	–
S.J.E. Brown							–	–													1	–	–	–	–	–
J.P. Searle							–	–													2	2	–	0	0	0.00
S. Lugsden																					3	5	2	15	8*	5.00
S. Chapman																					1	2	–	13	11	6.50
M.J. Saggers																					2	4	2	25	10	12.50
Byes	3	1				2	12	4	4	7	1			2	2			2								
Leg-byes	9	6	9	3	11	8	2	1	7	6	12	7	5	11	8		15	1	6	5						
Wides	4		2		2	2	4		6		10		4	2				2		2						
No-balls	8	2	24	14	26	4			8	16			10	2	8		4		16	6						
Total	305	90	143	201	276	247	270	186	229	239	269	167	312	240	249		337	74	134	177						
Wickets	10	5	10	10	10	10	3	1	10	10	10	2	10	9	4		10	10	10	10						
Result	D		L		W		W		L		W		W		D		L		L							
Points	10		4		22		–		4		22		23		8		7		3							

Batting

Batting	v. South Africans (Riverside) 14–16 July		v. Somerset (Taunton) 22–25 July		v. Hampshire (Southampton) 30 July–3 August		v. Sussex (Eastbourne) 5–8 August		v. Glamorgan (Riverside) 14–17 August		v. Lancashire (Riverside) 19–22 August		v. Derbyshire (Derby) 26–29 August		v. Surrey (Riverside) 9–12 September		v. Worcestershire (Worcester) 17–20 September		M	Inns	NO	Runs	HS	Av
J.J.B. Lewis	26	15	19	0					34	54	70*	0	26	–	13	10	38	25	15	128	1	622	72	23.03
M.A. Roseberry													97	–	8	9	87	4	6	11	–	295	97	26.81
J.E. Morris			30	9	48	50	15	8	27	163	12	4	4	–	140*	7	21	13	13	24	2	767	163	34.86
N.J. Speak	16	4	51	10	11	2	7	7	59	25	–	–							15	27	2	658	77*	26.32
D.C. Boon	31	40*	73	0	12	54	20	5	106	62*	3	20	40	–	–	10	35	1	16	29	4	1024	139*	40.96
M.P. Speight	33	–	10	9	18	97*	60*	19	40	0			52*	–	–	1	18	0	17	29	4	614	97*	24.56
P.D. Collingwood	12	4*	16	1	14	39	29	56*	20	11	36	25	0	–	–	1	56	8	19	32	5	833	105	30.85
N.C. Phillips	2	–	6	5			9	9	8	21			21*	–	–	3	1	5	17	25	2	227	35	9.86
M.M. Betts	10	–	2*	20*	20	2			11*	–									12	18	7	135	29*	12.27
J. Wood	11*	–			5	0	12	1	6	6*	10	8*	–	–	–	33	4	1	17	26	4	236	37	10.72
S.J. Harmison	9	–	0	18			12	0							–	6*	0	36	14	22	4	223	36	12.38
A. Walker																			1	2	2	5	3*	–
M.A. Gough	39	17			11	20	5	26											10	18	–	508	123	28.22
J.A. Daley	25	8	2	36	36	33	16	18	20	22	0	13	157	–	19*	0	60	16	12	22	2	634	157	31.70
M.J. Foster			15	5	2	14													8	13	1	321	76*	26.75
S. Hutton																			1	1	–	100	100	100.00
A. Pratt											0	34							2	3	–	40	34	13.33
N. Killeen											12	0	–	–					3	3	1	27	15*	13.50
M.J. Symington													–	–					2	1	1	8	8*	–
S.J.E. Brown																			1	–	–	–	–	–
J.P. Searle											0	0							2	2	–	0	0	0.00
S. Lugsden					8*	3*			4	–	0	0							3	5	2	15	8*	5.00
S. Chapman							2	11											1	2	–	13	11	6.50
M.J. Saggers															10	0	6*	9*	2	4	2	25	10	12.50
Byes	3		13	4	1	5		5	15	4			6		12			1						
Leg-byes	8	3	8	3	9	11	3	4	13	9	3	6	13		8	7	6	2						
Wides								2	15		8	2	16		2									
No-balls	58	16	14	8	8	2	8	10	18	8	4	10	2		41	4	10	4						
Total	286	107	259	128	203	332	198	181	396	385	158	122	434		253	91	342	125						
Wickets	10	4	10	10	10	9	10	10	10	7	9	9	6		3	10	10	10						
Result	D		L		D		L		D		L		D		L		L							
Points	–		6		8		3		11		4		10		6		7							

Fielding Figures

60 – M.P. Speight (ct 57 / st 3)
16 – P.D. Collingwood
12 – D.C. Boon and M.A Gough
10 – J.J.B. Lewis
9 – N.J. Speak
8 – N.C. Phillips
5 – J.A. Daley and J.E. Morris
4 – P.A. Pratt
3 – N. Killeen, S.J. Harmison, M.M. Betts and J. Wood
2 – M.A. Roseberry, M.J. Foster and J.P. Searle
1 – S. Lugsden, M.J. Saggers, M.J. Symington and sub

Durham CCC First-Class Matches

Bowling

	M.M. Betts	J. Wood	S.J. Harmison	P.D. Collingwood	N.C. Phillips	A. Walker	D.C. Boon	M.J. Foster	S.J.E. Brown	N. Killeen	M.A. Gough	S. Lugsden	Byes	Leg-byes	Wides	No-balls	Total	Wkts	
v. Warwickshire	17.2–2–66–5	17–2–65–2	19–4–76–2	8–1–33–0	15–2–76–1								7	13	8	8	336	10	
(Edgbaston) 17–21 April	2–0–15–1	21–3–74–3	17–3–74–3	4–1–13–2	1–0–5–1								2	4	8	4	187	10	
v. Gloucestershire		34–5–101–1	36–13–70–5	8–3–23–1	13–1–34–0	23.5–5–51–1							3	5	2	22	287	10	
(Riverside) 23–27 April		15–2–48–3	14–3–32–3		2–0–7–0		2–0–10–0												
v. Essex	17–8–30–2	16–4–53–3	17.4–3–47–2		6–2–16–1			10–1–29–1					3	6	12	10	185	10	
(Riverside) 13–16 May	28–6–83–6	16–6–31–2	22–4–71–1		9.4–1–23–1			10–4–18–0					9	8	10	4	243	10	
v. Cambridge University					15–10–8–0				16–8–17–6	11–1–47–1				5	2	4	119	10	A
(Cambridge) 18–20 May					24–11–58–4				15–4–37–1	14–5–27–1	6–4–4–1		7	12	4		242	10	
v. Kent	27–7–86–1	22–2–87–1	22–3–91–3		26–3–97–2			20–2–75–2			7.2–0–39–1		4	16	16	17	495	10	
(Canterbury) 21–24 May																			
v. Nottinghamshire	21–7–59–5	16.3–5–50–2	16–5–57–1		4–0–7–0			9–4–26–2					9	3	20	14	211	10	
(Trent Bridge) 29 May–1 June	22–5–71–2	21–5–62–3	9.1–3–29–1		5–1–16–0			15–3–41–4			1–0–3–0		1	1	13	4	224	10	
v. Middlesex	29–6–83–4	23–5–89–1	26–3–88–4	8–2–26–0	13–5–17–0			8–2–18–1					5	9	2	18	335	10	
(Lord's) 3–6 June	19–4–52–5	9–3–20–1	20–4–57–3		12–1–52–0			7–2–22–1					8	5		17	216	10	
v. Northamptonshire	22–7–33–3	19.2–3–52–5	16–2–49–1		2–1–5–0			4–0–17–1					1	6	10	10	163	10	
(Riverside) 11–14 June																			
v. Yorkshire	27–4–79–2	13–2–46–0	22–4–76–3		52–13–89–4			5.2–1–15–1					2	8		24	319	10	B
(Riverside) 17–20 June	4–0–23–0	3–1–14–0	6–0–42–0		5.4–0–14–1											6	93	1	
v. Leicestershire	41–11–98–3	33–11–104–5	28.2–4–107–2	16–5–40–0	13–2–48–0								8	9	2	12	414	10	
(Darlington) 1–4 July																			
v. South Africans	18–4–77–2	21–4–86–0	20–5–82–0	20.1–6–54–1	12–2–48–0						2–0–6–0		4	5	2	20	362	3	
(Riverside) 14–16 July	14–1–40–2	8–1–30–1	20–3–63–2	10–5–9–0	12–0–65–1									3		2	210	6	
v. Somerset	25–6–80–2		28–6–98–4	7–1–22–0	12–2–56–0			17.4–3–48–4					12	2	8	10	318	10	
(Taunton) 22–25 July	2–0–11–0		4–0–29–0		2.1–0–11–0			4–1–20–0						1		2	72	0	
v. Hampshire	27–3–74–3	26.2–2–106–3		18–8–47–1				3–0–22–0			16–4–67–0	22–5–67–3		13	9	4	396	10	
(Southampton) 30 July–3 August																			
v. Sussex		37–12–107–4	39.4–13–94–4	25–5–80–1	23–7–81–0								10	9	8	14	460	10	C
(Eastbourne) 5–8 August																			
v. Glamorgan	0.4–0–1–0	30.4–1–143–3		29–8–89–3	21–0–78–1							29.2–1–151–2	5	10	6	8	486	10	D
(Riverside) 14–17 August																			
v. Lancashire		20–4–70–3		4–0–13–0						15.2–4–49–5		8–1–45–2	10	9		2	196	10	E
(Riverside) 19–22 August		28–3–81–2		24–1–78–2						25–6–109–2		13–0–62–1	1	11			434	10	
v. Derbyshire		24–4–58–3			12–3–37–2					18–6–53–2				2			205	10	F
(Derby) 26–29 August		25–5–74–2		9–4–19–1	38–19–56–5		5–3–2–0			18–3–64–1			8	14		4	269	9	
v. Surrey		25–5–87–4	15–2–89–2	10–3–36–1	12.1–1–41–2								4	12	8	30	323	10	G
(Riverside) 9–12 September							7.4–0–68–0							1		2	142	1	
v. Worcestershire		23–8–74–2	23–2–88–4		32–8–95–1									6	6	6	310	10	H
(Worcester) 17–20 September		25–5–97–3	15–4–36–1		29–6–76–1		14–5–33–1						4	18	2	6	312	9	
Bowler's average	363–81– 1061–48 22.10	571.5–113– 1910–62 30.80	455.5–93– 1545–51 30.29	200.1–53– 582–13 44.76	423.4–101– 1216–28 43.42	23.5–5– 51–1 51.00	28.4–8– 113–1 113.00	113–23– 351–17 20.64	31–12– 54–7 7.71	101.2–25– 349–12 29.08	32.2–8– 119–2 59.50	72.2–7– 325–8 40.62							

A M.J. Symington 6–1–34–2, 7–1–27–1; J.P. Searle 7.4–4–8–1, 14.3–1–58–1; J.A. Daley1–0–12–1
B N.J. Speak 1–0–4–0
C S. Chapman 29–6–79–0
D N.J. Speak 1–0–9–0
E J.P. Searle 20.4–4–92–3
F M.J. Symington 15.2–3–55–3, 8–2–32–0
G M.J. Saggers 19–5–54–1; J.J.B. Lewis 8–0–73–1
H M.J. Saggers 25–7–47–3, 14.2–2–48–3

Essex CCC First-Class Matches

Batting

Batting	v. Worcestershire (Worcester) 17–21 April		v. Sussex (Chelmsford) 23–27 April		v. Durham (Riverside) 13–16 May		v. Lancashire (Chelmsford) 21–24 May		v. Nottinghamshire (Ilford) 3–6 June		v. Surrey (Chelmsford) 11–14 June		v. Somerset (Bath) 17–20 June		v. Middlesex (Southgate) 26–29 June		v. Derbyshire (Derby) 1–4 July		v. Kent (Southend) 15–18 July		M	Inns	NO	Runs	HS	Av
P.J. Prichard	14	24	15	–									–	3	23	2	9	21	15	7	10	18	–	237	24	13.16
D.D.J. Robinson	0	35	85	–	11	15	32	26	3	0	23	5	–	7	5	3	0	7			14	25	–	446	85	17.84
N. Hussain	68	15	1	–	12	63					25	0							48	12	5	9	–	244	68	27.11
S.G. Law	45	87	43	–	18	12	55	49	106	22	31	29*	–	33	48*	62	4	8	47	38	14	26	2	982	165	40.91
R.C. Irani	41	37	47	–	29	3	4	2	7	27	0	13	–	127*	8*	104	26	18	47	2	18	33	2	1001	127*	32.29
A.P. Grayson	53	0	17	–	8	10			0	3	8	1	–	23	54	3	6	33	6	6	17	31	–	509	59	16.41
R.J. Rollins	8	23	1	–	1	41	23	4	12	13	1	–	–	42	–	2					8	12	–	171	42	14.25
D.R. Law	1	0			25	7	13	17	19	22	9	–	–	46	–	62	3	0	18	52	14	25	–	466	65	18.64
M.C. Ilott	4	11			8	1	24	14	38	0*	5	–	–	0	–	0*	4*	0	15	3	17	30	4	307	38	11.80
A.P. Cowan	2	37	66	–					1	1			–	0	–	5	0	14			8	13	–	228	94	17.53
P.M. Such	0*	2*	6*	–					3*	–	1*	–	–	1*	–	1*	2	19*	25	9*	16	25	18	133	25	19.00
G.R. Napier			4	–																	2	3	–	15	7	5.00
N.F. Williams			0	–	12*	11	11*	5*											2	36	9	16	6	171	36	17.10
S.D. Peters					16	35	0	45	64	53*	33	17*	–	1	–	59	5	2	9	19 †	13	23	2	484	64	23.04
D.G. Wilson					14	14*															2	3	1	31	14*	15.50
I.N. Flanagan							0	44	57	33											6	11	–	254	61	23.09
A.J.E. Hibbert							47	6													3	5	–	85	47	17.00
D.M. Cousins							8	6													1	2	–	14	8	7.00
J.O. Grove											33	–									4	7	1	88	33	14.66
B.J. Hyam																	5	11	47*	25	10	19	3	307	47*	19.18
T.P. Hodgson																					7	13	–	236	54	18.15
Byes		1	1		3	9	2	9		9	4			3		1			6	4						
Leg-byes	9	12	7		6	8	15	9	10	15	6	2		4	1	7	1	4	4	10						
Wides					12	10		8			2	2				2										
No-balls	12	26	6		10	4	8		2		22	6		10	12	2		6	6							
Total	257	310	299		185	243	242	244	322	198	203	75	0	300	151	315	65	143	295	223						
Wickets	10	10	10		10	10	10	10	10	8	10	4	0	9	3	9	10	10	10	10						
Result	L		D		L		L		D		D		W		D		L		L							
Points	4		9		4		5		10		8		20		3		4		5							

Batting	v. Warwickshire (Edgbaston) 23–26 July		v. South Africans (Chelmsford) 31 July–2 August		v. Glamorgan (Chelmsford) 5–8 August		v. Hampshire (Portsmouth) 14–17 August		v. Gloucestershire (Colchester) 19–22 August		v. Yorkshire (Scarborough) 26–29 August		v. Leicestershire (Leicester) 9–12 September		v. Northamptonshire (Chelmsford) 17–20 September		M	Inns	NO	Runs	HS	Av
P.J. Prichard	7	18									20	24	18	1	5	11	10	18	–	237	24	13.16
D.D.J. Robinson			17	–	14	24	0	36	16	40	42	0					14	25	–	446	85	17.84
N. Hussain																	5	9	–	244	68	27.11
S.G. Law	8	14									47	2	7	0	165	2	14	26	2	982	165	40.91
R.C. Irani	39	69	33	–	51	31	34	35	36	1	22	43	11	27	11	16	18	33	2	1001	127*	32.29
A.P. Grayson	1	33	2	–	59	3	16	5	0	28	11	57	11	6	46	0	17	31	–	509	59	16.41
R.J. Rollins																	8	12	–	171	42	14.25
D.R. Law	10	65			0	0	11	48	3	0	6	29					14	25	–	466	65	18.64
M.C. Ilott	17	8	26	–	22	13	14	23	35*	3	3	3	0	2	3	8	17	30	4	307	38	11.80
A.P. Cowan													4	94	1	3	8	13	–	228	94	17.53
P.M. Such	12	–	0*	–	2*	3*	2*	10	8	0*	0	1*	0*	24*	2*	0	16	25	18	133	25	19.00
G.R. Napier							7	4									2	3	–	15	7	5.00
N.F. Williams	0	4*	10	–	13	25	8	27*			7*	0					9	16	6	171	36	17.10
S.D. Peters	0	26			20	47			1	3			2	8	19	–	13	23	2	484	64	23.04
D.G. Wilson			3	–													2	3	1	31	14*	15.50
I.N. Flanagan	13	61	6	–	5	0			29	6							6	11	–	254	61	23.09
A.J.E. Hibbert			13	–			17	2									3	5	–	85	47	17.00
D.M. Cousins																	1	2	–	14	8	7.00
J.O. Grove									3	1			12	0	14	25*	4	7	1	88	33	14.66
B.J. Hyam	20*	19*	38	–	15	11	0	31	33	3	14	22	1	0	0	12	10	19	3	307	47*	19.18
T.P. Hodgson			46	–	35	17	16	2	5	4	13	54	20	14	1	9	7	13	–	236	54	18.15
Byes	1	1	5		11	2	4			5	1		1	2	4	5						
Leg-byes	5	4	2		7	3	6	7	3	1	4	14	6	11	2	2						
Wides			2		4	2	2	4	2		6											
No-balls	6	10	12		2	2	4	4	2	12	4	12	2	12	10	2						
Total	139	332	215		260	183	141	238	176	107	200	261	95	201	283	95						
Wickets	10	8	10		10	10	10	10	10	10	10	10	10	10	10	9						
Result	W		D		L		L		L		L		L		L							
Points	20		–		6		3		2		5		4		6							

† S.D. Peters absent hurt

Fielding Figures

34 – B.J. Hyam (ct 32 / st 2)
19 – S.G. Law
13 – R.J. Rollins
11 – D.D.J. Robinson
10 – D.R. Law
9 – A.P. Grayson and I.N. Flanagan
7 – P.J. Prichard, N. Hussain and S.D. Peters
6 – R.C. Irani
5 – P.M. Such
4 – T.P. Hodgson and A.P. Cowan
3 – M.C. Ilott and sub
2 – N.F. Williams and A.J.E. Hibbert

Essex CCC First-Class Matches

Bowling

	M.C. Ilott	A.P. Cowan	R.C. Irani	P.M. Such	A.P. Grayson	D.R. Law	N.F. Williams	G.R. Napier	D.G. Wilson	D.M. Cousins	J.O. Grove	A.J.E. Hibbert	Byes	Leg-byes	Wides	No-balls	Total	Wkts	
v. Worcestershire	20.4–7–50–2	30.2–4–118–3	29.4–10–64–1	36–12–63–0	31.2–12–54–3	14–2–78–1							1	18	2	28	446	10	
(Worcester) 17–21 April		1–0–19–0	6.3–0–38–4	3–0–24–0	3–0–30–0	1–0–11–0									2	4	122	4	
v. Sussex		21.4–6–67–1	23–7–66–2	23–6–81–2	9–4–14–1		22–7–71–2	14–3–59–2					4	7		14	369	10	
(Chelmsford) 23–27 April		6–2–32–1	11–2–24–3	4–0–29–0	10–2–26–0		10–1–38–0	4–1–17–0					4	3		6	173	4	
v. Durham	23.1–8–49–4		22–8–50–2		11–3–21–0	16–2–51–1	21–4–72–2		7–2–22–1					11	2	26	276	10	
(Riverside) 13–16 May	17–2–61–0		11.1–1–44–2		8–2–24–0	17–6–46–5	20–5–46–3		3–0–16–0				2	8	2	4	247	10	
v. Lancashire	23.4–8–49–3		22–6–64–1			22–6–70–4	20–5–58–1			15–5–52–1		5–1–13–0		8	12	6	314	10	
(Chelmsford) 21–24 May	14–7–37–1		6.1–1–29–0			9–2–56–0	10–2–50–2						1	1		4	175	3	A
v. Nottinghamshire	21.1–5–62–4	28–9–73–1	22–8–66–3	23–5–70–2	6–3–15–0	10–2–42–0							4	10	12	2	342	10	
(Ilford) 3–6 June	18–6–33–1	15–5–70–1	10–1–50–2	32–11–73–5	9.2–1–44–0								1	8		12	279	9	
v. Surrey	21.5–3–64–4		15–2–72–0	9–0–18–0	11–3–30–1	17–1–91–2					14–1–74–3		4	20	6	16	373	10	
(Chelmsford) 11–14 June																			
v. Somerset	22–10–27–3	17–5–67–1	19–4–35–0	26.5–10–38–3	7–2–23–2	6–1–29–1							5	7	2	32	231	10	
(Bath) 17–20 June	6–1–14–1	5–0–22–0		10–5–8–1	14–8–13–3	4.1–1–7–1							1	3		14	68	6	
v. Middlesex	24–3–85–0	28–3–93–0	21–3–74–1	26–6–78–0	22–1–78–0	18–2–63–1							6	11	7	13	488	2	
(Southgate) 26–29 June																	0	0	
v. Derbyshire	13–5–20–6	9.3–4–18–3	7–2–19–1	4–1–8–0										5			70	10	
(Derby) 1–4 July	25–8–68–2	25–4–107–3	8–2–30–0	11.5–4–28–2	10–4–22–1	16–2–58–2								6	8	10	319	10	
v. Kent	35–9–91–4		15–6–30–0	29.1–10–101–3	14–6–24–1	7–0–38–0	27–4–67–2						4	9		12	364	10	
(Southend) 15–18 July	13–4–28–2		7–0–24–2	26–8–67–3	8.4–2–24–1		2–0–6–0						2	4		2	155	8	
v. Warwickshire	13–2–36–3		13.4–2–49–3			11–0–45–1	15–3–57–3						1	2		8	190	10	
(Edgbaston) 23–26 July	18.2–4–64–2		11–3–30–0	23–6–62–3		9–2–36–2	19–5–68–3						4	16		12	280	10	
v. South Africans	16–4–48–2		12–2–44–1	23–0–76–0	14–1–60–1		15–2–79–0		13–2–68–1			5–1–19–0	3	9		16	406	5	
(Chelmsford) 31 July–2 August	4–3–4–0			1–0–5–0			4–0–7–0		2–0–8–0				2	1			27	0	
v. Glamorgan	10–2–30–0		15–2–59–0	39.2–12–110–5		14–3–36–1	13–3–42–4						2	9	4	8	288	10	
(Chelmsford) 5–8 August	9–2–28–0		19–1–74–0	25–1–90–0	16–0–69–3	5–0–29–0	17–0–77–2						1	3	8	9	371	5	
v. Hampshire	32–13–70–2		24–3–92–2	21–3–75–0	13–2–53–0	17–1–92–1	23–5–85–2					6.3–2–16–3	2	5	2	32	490	10	
(Portsmouth) 14–17 August																			
v. Gloucestershire	22–1–81–1		16–5–39–0	48.4–7–168–2	15–4–47–2	17–0–77–3					27–4–119–2		15	18	2	22	564	10	
(Colchester) 19–22 August																			
v. Yorkshire	20–4–64–3		21.2–9–47–5	17.1–4–58–0	7–1–27–0	16–1–75–2	8.5–1–26–0						8	9	2	17	314	10	
(Scarborough) 26–29 August	18–3–54–5		18–4–55–3		4–1–14–0	3.4–0–15–1							10	2		4	150	9	
v. Leicestershire	25–7–68–1	19–4–79–2	23–6–80–3	19–4–63–1	4–0–20–0						17.3–1–76–3		3	6		16	395	10	
(Leicester) 9–12 September																			
v. Northamptonshire	17–6–41–2	22–7–57–3	13–4–34–0	34–13–53–3	1–0–2–0						10–2–59–1		12	4	2	18	262	10	
(Chelmsford) 17–20 September	5–1–19–0	11–1–37–0	3–1–10–0	10–0–29–3							5.4–0–19–0		2	4		4	120	3	
	506.5–138–	238.3–54–	444.3–105–	525–128–	248.2–62–	249.5–34–	246.5–47–	18–4–	25–4–	15–5–	74.1–8–	16.3–4–							
	1345–58	859–19	1392–41	1475–38	734–19	1045–29	849–26	76–2	114–2	52–1	347–9	48–3							
Bowler's average	23.18	45.21	33.95	38.81	38.63	36.03	32.65	38.00	57.00	52.00	38.55	16.00							

A I.N. Flanagan 1–0–1–0

Glamorgan CCC First-Class Matches Batting

Batting	v. Gloucestershire (Bristol) 17–21 April		v. Kent (Cardiff) 23–27 April		v. Cambridge University (Cambridge) 13–15 May		v. Northamptonshire (Northampton) 21–24 May		v. Middlesex (Lord's) 29 May–1 June		v. Hampshire (Southampton) 3–6 June		v. Worcestershire (Cardiff) 11–14 June		v. Leicestershire (Cardiff) 17–20 June		v. Nottinghamshire (Trent Bridge) 26–29 June		v. Surrey (Swansea) 1–4 July		M	Inns	NO	Runs	HS	Av
S.P. James	27	76	2	18			227	10*	79	45	34	20	43	152			121	–	9	7	13	24	1	1268	227	55.13
A.W. Evans	27	1	20	17	125	–	10	25*			10	87									8	14	1	386	125	29.69
A. Dale	75	31	0	54	59	–	45	–	38	1	92	0	8	35	11	5	22	–	1	29	19	33	1	1028	92	32.12
M.P. Maynard	9	0	34*	9					25	10	7	5	8	20	0	32	2	–	65	71	17	29	2	776	99	28.74
P.A. Cottey	15	0	–	27	4	71	113	–	81	7	14	17	0	29	9*	41	37	–	3	4	19	32	3	1012	123	34.89
G.P. Butcher	23	4	–	16	43*	82	1	–			5	85	9	0*	–	4	31	–	4	4	9	14	2	311	85	25.91
R.D.B. Croft	4	0	–	42*					18	1			35	3			63*	–			10	16	3	253	63*	19.46
A.D. Shaw	4	0	–	15	71	–	0	–	0	51	7	3	34	2	–	4	6	–	27	21	11	16	1	248	71	16.53
S.D. Thomas	19	11	–	1			17	–	3	25	11	18	69*	0*	–	9	41	–	22	18	18	26	3	507	74	22.04
D.A. Cosker	0	0	0*	0*	–	–	3	–	0	12					–	1*			2	12	15	21	3	123	37	6.83
S.L. Watkin	5*	0*	–	–			1*	–	0*	6	12*	2*	–	–			2*	–	10*	13	13	16	13	107	25*	35.66
M.J. Powell					21*	27	106	–	43	79*	52	20	40	0	23	0	7	–	0	4	16	27	3	840	106	35.00
W.L. Law					–	1									21*	25					9	14	2	444	131	37.00
I.J. Thomas					–	9*															1	1	1	9	9*	–
S.P. Jones					–	–															3	3	3	2	2*	–
O.T. Parkin					–	–					13	3			–	0	–	–	3	6*	11	13	4	85	24*	9.44
Waqar Younis							2	–	1	9			4	15	–	8					4	6	–	39	15	6.50
I. Dawood																					7	12	1	194	40	17.63
A.P. Davies																					5	6	1	55	34	11.00
D.D. Cherry																					1	1	–	11	11	11.00
Byes			1	5	4	4	6	4	1		4		8	1	1	4	5		5	8						
Leg-byes	6	11		4	5	8	16	1	7	6	2	7	15	3	1	7	8		14	7						
Wides	4				2	2	2			6									6							
No-balls	18	4	6	4	8	16	14	4	12	2	6	18	15	8	8	4	6		26	8						
Total	236	138	63	212	342	220	536	44	308	260	269	285	288	268	74	144	351	0	197	212						
Wickets	10	10	3	8	4	4	10	0	10	10	10	10	9	8	3	10	8	0	10	10						
Result	W		D		W		D		L		L		D		L		W		L							
Points	21		7		–		11		7		4		9		4		20		4							

Batting	v. Sri Lankans (Cardiff) 18–20 July		v. Lancashire (Colwyn Bay) 22–25 July		v. Warwickshire (Edgbarton) 30 July–2 August		v. Essex (Chelmsford) 5–8 August		v. Durham (Riverside) 14–17 August		v. Yorkshire (Cardiff) 20–23 August		v. Sussex (Hove) 30 August–3 September		v. Derbyshire (Cardiff) 9–12 September		v. Somerset (Cardiff) 17–20 September		M	Inns	NO	Runs	HS	Av
S.P. James					53	52	11	147	42	–	31	7					1	54	13	24	1	1268	227	55.13
A.W. Evans													26	9	14	–	2	13	8	14	1	386	125	29.69
A. Dale	0	0	73	23	3	8*	73	82	34	–	31	67	18	37	1	–	60	12	19	33	1	1028	92	32.12
M.P. Maynard	99	5	–	–	20	47*	30	29	79	–	5	29	94	0	8	–	11	23	17	29	2	776	99	28.74
P.A. Cottey	27	9*	0	28	74	–	2	38*	123	–	42	0	91	1	4	–	64	37	19	32	3	1012	123	34.89
G.P. Butcher																			9	14	2	311	85	25.91
R.D.B. Croft	24	7	18	1*	18	–	4	–					15	0					10	16	3	253	63*	19.46
A.D. Shaw													–	3*					11	16	1	248	71	16.53
S.D. Thomas	15	–	12	–	64	–	6	–	74	–	9	3	0	23	8	–	28*	1	18	26	3	507	74	22.04
D.A. Cosker	0	–	24	–	11	–	7	37	1	–	1	0			9	–	0	3	15	21	3	123	37	6.83
S.L. Watkin	0*	–	4*	–	12*	–									8*	–	7	25*	13	16	13	107	25*	35.66
M.J. Powell	2	7	88	25*	18	–			67	–	43	54	23	5	0	–	49	37	16	27	3	840	106	35.00
W.L. Law	28	1*	131	–			68	8	0	–	57	9	45	25	25	–			9	14	2	444	131	37.00
I.J. Thomas																			1	1	1	9	9*	–
S.P. Jones									0*	–	0*	2*							3	3	3	2	2*	–
O.T. Parkin			–	–			24*	–			9	0	0*	1	15	–	0	11*	11	13	4	85	24*	9.44
Waqar Younis																			4	6	–	39	15	6.50
I. Dawood	4	22	14	19	7	–	6	9*	32	–	0	29					12	40	7	12	1	194	40	17.63
A.P. Davies	1	–			11	–	34	–	5	–			0*	4					5	6	1	55	34	11.00
D.D. Cherry															11	–			1	1	–	11	11	11.00
Byes			1		4		2	1	5		4	5	4				3	4						
Leg-byes	10		10	2	10		9	3	10		8	7	3	5	5		7	6						
Wides					8		4	8	6		4	2	2	2				4						
No-balls	14	2	8	2	2	2	8	9	8		22	8	32	12	6		2	8						
Total	224	53	383	100	315	109	288	371	486		266	222	353	127	114		246	278						
Wickets	10	5	8	3	10	1	10	5	10		10	10	8	10	10		10	9						
Result	W		D		D		W		D		L		L		D		W							
Points	–		11		7		22		9		6		8		5		21							

Fielding Figures

26 – A.D. Shaw
21 – M.P. Maynard
20 – P.A. Cottey and I. Dawood (ct 19 / st 1)
11 – D.A. Cosker
10 – S.D. Thomas and M.J. Powell
9 – S.P. James
8 – R.D.B. Croft
7 – A. Dale and A.W. Evans
5 – G.P. Butcher
4 – S.L. Watkin, W.L. Law and sub.
2 – O.T. Parkins and I.J. Thomas
1 – S.P. Jones, A.P. Davies and Waqar Younis

Glamorgan CCC First-Class Matches

Bowling

	S.L. Watkin	S.D. Thomas	G.P. Butcher	R.D.B. Croft	D.A. Cosker	A. Dale	O.T. Parkin	A.P. Davies	P.A. Cottey	S.P. Jones	W.L. Law	Waqar Younis	Byes	Leg-byes	Wides	No-balls	Total	Wkts	
v. Gloucestershire	17–5–53–4	16–5–30–2	9–2–17–1	13.3–2–36–3									2	6	2	4	144	10	
(Bristol) 17–21 April	12–2–28–2	9–2–37–4	8.3–3–22–4											2	2		89	10	
v. Kent	17–7–31–2	21–8–46–3	14–4–35–3	24–8–33–1	7.5–1–17–1									4	2	2	166	10	
(Cardiff) 23–27 April	7–2–21–0	6–1–20–1	3–0–14–0	5–0–12–0	8–0–39–0	5–2–13–2										4	142	3	A
v. Cambridge University			12–2–43–0		21–4–57–1	12–3–38–1	16–6–39–0			13–1–56–1	8–1–29–2		4	4		13	270	5	
(Cambridge) 13–15 May			8.4–4–14–4		17–4–31–2	4–2–15–0	8–1–19–3			10–2–28–1	1–0–6–0		5	3			121	10	
v. Northamptonshire	15–5–30–3	7–0–27–2	7.2–2–22–2		1–0–9–0	9–2–25–1						12–1–54–2		5	4	2	172	10	
(Northampton) 21–24 May	34–5–131–2	31.5–3–154–3	17–1–79–0		39–12–107–0	11–0–63–1			6–2–14–1			35–2–147–3	12	5	6	10	712	10	
v. Middlesex	21.5–10–30–5	19–1–56–3		38–6–91–1	18–2–36–1	2–0–3–0			1–1–0–0			3–0–26–0	5	9	2	2	256	10	
(Lord's) 29 May–1 June	18–5–49–1	16–3–69–0		26–7–65–0	16–1–73–0	12–3–36–0								14	2		314	1	B
v. Hampshire	37–9–106–3	34–7–106–0	26–3–86–2			17–1–72–2	34–16–47–2		16–2–38–0				1	15	4	6	471	10	
(Southampton) 3–6 June	8–0–28–1	4–0–14–0	3.1–0–14–0				8–2–21–0						5	2		4	84	1	
v. Worcestershire	25.4–9–48–2	27–4–92–5	8–1–37–1	15–3–43–0		3.5–0–9–0						15.1–5–36–2		8	2	2	273	10	
(Cardiff) 11–14 June	10–4–27–1		9–0–49–1	35.2–7–119–3		6–0–27–0						15–3–68–2		6	2	4	296	7	
v. Leicestershire		22–5–71–2	14–2–58–1		20.3–3–53–2		17–7–27–1				8–1–31–1	14–2–36–2	4	12		4	292	10	
(Cardiff) 17–20 June			2–0–12–0		4–1–5–0		5–1–15–1		2–0–3–0			6–0–30–1		1		2	66	2	
v. Nottinghamshire	3–1–8–1					2–0–11–1	3–3–0–0		2–1–7–0								31	2	C
(Trent Bridge) 26–29 June	18–4–43–1	20–4–78–4	8–0–37–0	13–4–25–0		8–1–22–1	21–8–60–3						8	1	4	8	274	10	
v. Surrey	13–2–40–2	19–3–47–3	3–0–12–0		19–4–47–1		17.4–4–50–3						1	2	2	6	199	10	
(Swansea) 1–4 July	11–4–20–0	15–3–28–1			30–7–101–2	6.2–0–32–0	7–1–16–0		6–1–15–1				2			2	214	4	
v. Sri Lankans	7–2–13–1	4–1–10–4				5.5–1–20–4		5–2–9–1					1	1			54	10	
(Cardiff) 18–20 July	17–6–38–2	15–1–52–1		14–6–38–1	16–5–51–1	10.3–2–25–5		6–2–12–0					1	5		8	222	10	
v. Lancashire	22–11–49–2	26–7–76–1		27–7–76–4	13–3–48–0	9–2–30–1	20.2–9–76–2						1	10		10	366	10	
(Colwyn Bay) 22–25 July	7–1–20–1	6–1–23–0		44–14–139–3	34–8–140–6		2–0–8–0		1–1–0–0				2	2		2	334	10	
v. Warwickshire	12–4–17–1	9.5–0–38–2		3–1–5–0	1–0–1–0	6–1–21–0		13–5–47–1					1	5	2	2	135	4	
(Edgbaston) 30 July–2 August		20–1–84–5		23–7–48–0	14–1–52–1	3–0–14–0		14.5–1–46–2						9	8	8	253	8	
v. Essex		13.5–2–44–2		34–8–84–1	37–13–60–3		15–4–29–2	12–6–25–2					11	7	4	2	260	10	
(Chelmsford) 5–8 August		18–9–38–2		23–7–37–1	19.4–9–31–2	9–3–17–2	10–4–27–1	12–4–28–2					2	3	2	2	183	10	
v. Durham		30.1–2–107–5			43–15–69–2	24–5–52–1		23–9–61–2		21–3–74–0	1–0–5–0		15	13	15	18	396	10	
(Riverside) 14–17 August		18–4–41–1			49–16–124–3	12–2–33–1		18–4–72–0	5–0–15–1	18–2–61–1	5–0–14–0		4	9		8	385	7	D
v. Yorkshire		18–1–70–1			13–5–14–2	12–4–48–2	16.5–3–59–1			14–0–94–3			4	17	2	27	306	10	
(Cardiff) 20–23 August		25–4–72–4			11–4–24–0	13–1–49–0	25.4–7–67–5			10–3–32–1			12	27	10	8	296	10	E
v. Sussex		28.3–5–63–4		16–6–48–0		20–5–51–1	28–9–88–2	21–5–68–2					8	6	2	4	332	10	
(Hove) 30 August–3 September		14–2–48–2		13–4–34–2		10–3–23–3	14–7–26–1	11–3–22–2					2	11			166	10	
v. Derbyshire	18.1–3–43–2	17–1–48–0			5–1–13–0	13–2–40–1	17–5–44–2						4	7			199	5	
(Cardiff) 9–12 September																			
v. Somerset	8–1–15–1	16–3–56–4			20.4–8–38–3	2–1–4–1	5–1–15–0						2	3			133	10	
(Cardiff) 17–20 September	12–5–29–2	3–1–4–0			6.1–0–25–3	1–0–1–0	10–1–24–5		1–1–0–0					10			93	10	
	370.4–107–917–42	549.1–94–1749–71	152.4–24–551–19	366.5–97–933–20	483.5–127–1265–36	249.3–46–794–31	300.3–99–757–34	135.5–41–390–14	40–9–92–3	86–11–345–7	23–2–85–3	100.1–13–397–12							
Bowler's average	21.83	24.63	29.00	46.65	35.13	25.61	22.26	27.85	30.66	49.28	28.33	33.08							

A A.D. Shaw 1–0–7–0; M.P. Maynard 1–0–16–0
B M.J. Powell 0.2–0–8–0
C M.P. Maynard 0.4–0–5–0
D M.P. Maynard 2–0–12–0
E M.P. Maynard 2–0–13–0

Gloucestershire CCC First-Class Matches Batting

Batting	v. Glamorgan (Bristol) 17–21 April		v. Durham (Riverside) 23–27 April		v. Leicestershire (Bristol) 13–16 May		v. Yorkshire (Gloucester) 21–24 May		v. South Africans (Bristol) 29 May–1 June		v. Derbyshire (Chesterfield) 3–6 June		v. Warwickshire (Bristol) 11–14 June		v. Worcestershire (Worcester) 17–20 June		v. Hampshire (Southampton) 1–4 July		v. Sussex (Cheltenham) 14–17 July		M	Inns	NO	Runs	HS	Av
N.J. Trainor	11	7	20	17													0	52	2	0	4	8	–	109	52	13.62
R.J. Cunliffe	19	3	17	24	0	8			0	3											12	22	–	339	53	15.40
T.H.C. Hancock	13	6	5	7	19	4	49	4	11	35	94	–	62	9	29	25	65	41	76	16	18	34	2	1227	220*	38.34
A.J. Wright	24	3	9	0	3	2	44	57			17	–	30	2	36	13	13	7			11	20	–	345	57	17.25
R.I. Dawson	5	4	1	23*																	8	15	2	177	46	13.61
M.W. Alleyne	0	32	51	0	27	56	19	55	109	4	43	–	33	137	0	43*	1	2	17	27*	18	33	2	1189	137	38.35
R.C. Russell	31	11	60	2	15	14	63*	37			8	–	1	11			1	0	25	–	16	28	2	527	63*	20.26
M.C.J. Ball	0	15	42	22*	0	44	0	6	2	1	7	–	6	6	9	–	25	54	33	–	18	30	5	592	67*	23.68
J. Lewis	25	0	44*	–	2	22	0	5	11	23	54*	–	0	10	14	3	18	27	22	–	18	31	2	390	54*	13.44
A.M. Smith	2*	0	6	–	6	14	61	24*	0*	31*	17*	–	0	41	0	–	0	4*	4	–	18	30	13	384	61	22.58
C.A. Walsh	0	4*	0	–	4*	11	9	–			–	–	1	0*	4*	–	0*	–	6*	–	17	23	10	111	25	8.53
M.G.N. Windows					9	38	20	100*	68	22	143	–	0	38	43	0	1	38	14	60*	16	29	2	1173	151	43.44
M.J. Church					30	5	0	23											22	–	4	7	–	85	30	12.14
G.I. Macmillan							53	0	52	3	2	–	0	11	25	30					5	9	–	176	53	19.55
D.R. Hewson									19	0	52	–	27*	0	0	5*	38	78*	13	0	12	22	3	447	78*	23.52
R.C.J. Williams									67	0					5	–					2	3	–	72	67	24.00
J.M.M. Averis									6*	0											1	2	1	6	6*	6.00
Byes	2		3	2	9	2	4	13	12									6	1	4						
Leg-byes	6	2	5	4	2	11	3	2	8	4	6		7	20	3	14	14	12	1	7						
Wides	2	2	2			6		2	4				2	12				6		2						
No-balls	4		22	2	8	22	4		34	8	16		12	10	20	8		6	2	2						
Total	144	89	287	103	134	259	329	328	403	134	459		181	307	188	141	176	333	238	118						
Wickets	10	10	10	6	10	10	10	8	9	10	8		10	10	10	5	10	8	10	3						
Result	L		W		L		W		L		D		W		L		W		W							
Points	4		22		4		23		–		11		20		3		20		21							

Batting

Batting	v. Surrey (Cheltenham) 22–25 July		v. Lancashire (Old Trafford) 5–8 August		v. Kent (Bristol) 14–17 August		v. Essex (Colchester) 19–22 August		v. Somerset (Bristol) 27–30 August		v. Northamptonshire (Bristol) 1–4 September		v. Middlesex (Lord's) 9–12 September		v. Nottinghamshire (Trent Bridge) 17–20 September		M	Inns	NO	Runs	HS	Av
N.J. Trainor																	4	8	–	109	52	13.62
R.J. Cunliffe	16	53	20	6	32	40	7	–	0	3	53	–	26	4	5	0	12	22	–	339	53	15.40
T.H.C. Hancock	37	13	0	2	0	63	135	–	65	73	7	3*	23	15	1	220*	18	34	2	1227	220*	38.34
A.J. Wright									14	36	25	–			10	0	11	20	–	345	57	17.25
R.I. Dawson			0	10	5	12	46	–	27	5	2	4*	31	2			8	15	2	177	46	13.61
M.W. Alleyne	1	27	30	14	55	83	47	–	116	15	18	–	6	27	72	22	18	33	2	1189	137	38.35
R.C. Russell	0	9	11	8	14	41	28	–	12	3	26	–	40	3	38	15*	16	28	2	527	63*	20.26
M.C.J. Ball	0*	48*	9	40*	0	6	32	–	58	45	0	–	67*	0	15		18	30	5	592	67*	23.68
J. Lewis	0	1	0	35	2	13	4	–	2	1	5	–	0	4	40	3	18	31	2	390	54*	13.44
A.M. Smith	1	9*	2*	31	1*	28*	6*	–	0	1*	5	–	0	29	6*	55	18	30	13	384	61	22.58
C.A. Walsh	0	–	6	0	2	25	7	–	1*	1	6*	–	20	0*	4		17	23	10	111	25	8.53
M.G.N. Windows	23	60	21	12	11	103	151	–	39	6	35	–	0	3	63	52	16	29	2	1173	151	43.44
M.J. Church	5	0															4	7	–	85	30	12.14
G.I. Macmillan																	5	9	–	176	53	19.55
D.R. Hewson	52	0	37	1	0	9	44	–					5	0	39	28	12	22	3	447	78*	23.52
R.C.J. Williams																	2	3	–	72	67	24.00
J.M.M. Averis																	1	2	1	6	6*	6.00
Byes		14	8	10	8	10	15		1	4	4											
Leg-byes	14	10	6	10	2	7	18		8	5	6		8	1	4	2						
Wides					2	2	2		2	2												
No-balls	18	22	8	14	8	14	22		10	4	18	2	12		22	14						
Total	167	266	158	193	142	456	564		355	204	210	9	238	88	319	411						
Wickets	10	8	10	10	10	10	10		10	10	10	0	10	10	10	7						
Result	W		L		W		W		L		W		W		W							
Points	20		3		20		24		7		21		21		23							

Fielding Figures

57 – R.C. Russell
23 – M.W. Alleyne and M.C.J. Ball
16 – T.H.C. Hancock
13 – M.G.N. Windows and R.J. Cunliffe
5 – M.J. Church, J. Lewis, A.J. Wright and A.M. Smith
4 – R.C.J. Williams (ct 3 / st 1), D.R. Hewson, G.I. Macmillan, N.J. Trainor and C.A. Walsh
3 – R.I. Dawson

Gloucestershire CCC First-Class Matches Bowling

	C.A. Walsh	A.M. Smith	J. Lewis	M.W. Alleyne	M.C.J. Ball	R.I. Dawson	J.M.M. Averis	T.H.C. Hancock	M.G.N. Windows	G.I. Macmillan	D.R. Hewson	Byes	Leg-byes	Wides	No-balls	Total	Wkts
v. Glamorgan	20–3–58–2	22.2–3–79–2	19–5–52–3	14–6–35–2	2–0–6–0								6	4	18	236	10
(Bristol) 17–21 April	17–6–42–3	7–2–16–1	14.2–4–49–6	5–0–14–0	5–2–6–0								11		4	138	10
v. Durham	19–5–50–2	12–3–33–2	10–2–24–2	4–1–13–1	9.2–6–14–3								9	2	24	143	10
(Riverside) 23–27 April	18.5–6–42–6	15–2–52–0	14–2–46–1		20–5–53–3	1–0–5–0							3		14	201	10
v. Leicestershire	26–1–131–1	24.1–7–66–5	22–4–67–3	15–5–51–1	16–5–25–0							1	10	6	14	351	10
(Bristol) 13–16 May	6–1–24–1	4–1–8–0			2.1–0–10–0								2		2	44	1
v. Yorkshire	19–10–30–3	13–8–15–2	10–0–58–2	7–0–19–1	13.4–9–13–2							2	6	2	6	143	10
(Gloucester) 21–24 May	16–3–55–2	16–2–55–3	5–1–22–0	5–1–9–0	26.4–6–72–4								1		12	214	10
v. South Africans		22–3–75–1	21–2–91–0	26–9–62–4	28–10–65–3		17–3–87–0	8–1–24–0	1–0–7–0				4	2	12	416	8
(Bristol) 29 May–1 June		11–4–29–0	16–1–79–1	10–3–37–0	15–3–66–0		18–7–40–2	7–1–35–1					2		4	288	4
v. Derbyshire	20–3–76–2	17–2–59–1	21.3–7–48–6	13–2–63–1	7–2–45–0								4	2	28	295	10
(Chesterfield) 3–6 June	12–0–87–1	6–1–31–0	17–2–61–2	11–2–39–2	20–2–50–0					5–2–14–0		3	15		28	300	5
v. Warwickshire	24.2–6–88–6	20–4–46–2	11–5–22–1	10–5–18–1								1	12		12	187	10
(Bristol) 11–14 June	18.3–3–65–6	14–4–54–4	7–0–11–0										1		2	131	10
v. Worcestershire	17–4–44–5	11–3–33–0	15–5–27–1	11–4–16–2									2		4	122	8
(Worcester) 17–20 June	12–0–63–1	10–0–57–2	6–1–39–1	9–2–39–1	2–0–13–0										2	211	5
v. Hampshire	16.2–5–39–3	20–9–38–1	12–4–29–3	10–3–27–1	8–1–36–1			2–0–9–0					6		10	184	10
(Southampton) 1–4 July	33–8–90–4	21.3–4–59–3	25–14–27–0	16–8–20–1	40–10–108–2			6–2–5–0				4	9	2	8	322	10
v. Sussex	21.1–3–52–3	18–10–30–3	15–3–42–3	12–2–46–0	6–1–19–1								2		10	191	10
(Cheltenham) 14–17 July	22–8–46–1	19–9–31–4	15.1–6–39–3	9–6–3–0	12–4–34–2								9	4	2	162	10
v. Surrey	21–6–57–3	19.5–2–66–6	15–2–69–0	9–1–53–0	11–1–37–0			2–1–4–1				4	7	2	23	297	10
(Cheltenham) 22–25 July	14–1–47–6	14.4–3–43–2	6–1–16–1	5–0–24–1									5		10	135	10
v. Lancashire	24–10–33–1	14–3–44–0	18–7–35–1	17–3–59–1	52–10–153–3	4.5–0–15–3		10–2–28–1				8	11			386	10
(Old Trafford) 5–8 August																	
v. Kent	23–5–77–4	19–5–47–1	12.4–7–21–1	9–4–16–3								2		2	12	163	10
(Bristol) 14–17 August	25–13–62–2	21–5–60–2	15–3–38–2		28–6–92–1	1–0–6–0		7–1–25–2			3–1–7–1	2	5		14	297	10
v. Essex	11–2–40–0	9–2–14–0	11–1–51–3		13–4–29–2	5.4–0–34–2		3–1–5–3					3	2	2	176	10
(Colchester) 19–22 August	12–4–18–4	7–5–9–0	5–0–17–0		11.1–4–26–4	2–0–7–0		9–4–24–2				5	1		12	107	10
v. Somerset	33.1–12–80–4	25–5–79–2	26–4–110–3	22–11–41–1	19–4–59–0			3–1–8–0				8	11		16	396	10
(Bristol) 27–30 August	22–6–36–3	8–0–34–1	14–3–28–0	5.1–1–13–0	23–3–47–1								6		2	164	5
v. Northamptonshire	17.4–8–36–6	10–6–9–2	12–3–40–1	6–1–19–0				3–1–7–1				10	2		24	123	10
(Bristol) 1–4 September	12.4–2–50–4	12–3–32–6										8	5		10	95	10
v. Middlesex	19.2–5–41–4	15–5–40–5	11–2–35–1	9–0–31–0	3–1–6–0								5		8	158	10
(Lord's) 9–12 September	10–3–22–4	10–2–17–3	9.2–2–32–3										1	2	10	72	10
v. Nottinghamshire	25–8–72–4	18–7–34–2	12–1–56–0	7–2–16–0	29–7–54–2			4–0–15–2				2		2	12	249	10
(Trent Bridge) 17–20 September	25–4–82–5	17–5–46–0	19.1–4–66–5	8–2–34–0	11–2–35–0			4–1–25–0				2	2		6	292	10
	633–164–	522.3–139–	462.1–108–	284.1–84–	433–108–	14.3–0–	35–10–	68–16–	1–0–	5–2–	3–1–						
	1835–106	1440–68	1447–59	818–24	1173–34	67–5	127–2	214–13	7–0	14–0	7–1						
Bowler's average	17.31	21.17	24.52	34.08	34.50	13.40	63.50	16.46	–	–	7.00						

Hampshire CCC First-Class Matches Batting

	v. Oxford University (Oxford) 17–20 April		v. Northamptonshire (Southampton) 23–27 April		v. Surrey (Southampton) 13–16 May		v. Leicestershire (Leicester) 21–24 May		v. Glamorgan (Southampton) 3–6 June		v. Yorkshire (Leeds) 11–14 June		v. Derbyshire (Basingstoke) 17–20 June		v. Somerset (Taunton) 26–29 June		v. Gloucestershire (Southampton) 1–4 July		v. Warwickshire (Edgbaston) 15–17 July		M	Inns	NO	Runs	HS	Av
G.W. White	150	–	–	0	23	1	14	21	56	27*	0	67	16	7	101	–	10	22	79	22	19	31	2	1211	156	41.75
J.S. Laney	101	–	–	9	2	0	8	0											1	0	8	13	–	224	101	17.23
R.A. Smith	1	–	–	7	29	42	40	3	84	–	0	13	104*	17	21	–	8	4			17	25	2	853	138	37.08
M. Keech	70	–	–	67	1	31	4	33	4	–					–	–	25	2			12	14	–	335	70	23.92
W.S. Kendall	36*	–	–	1																	8	11	3	340	78*	42.50
J.P. Stephenson	0	–	–	11	–	–			0	21	2	0	1	75	67	–	4	114	4	12*	16	24	1	681	114	29.60
A.N. Aymes	13*	–	–	15*	1	30*	133	4	120	–	17	73	40	61*	41*	–	3	22	28	5	18	27	6	754	133	35.90
S.D. Udal	–	–	–	0	20	30	44	62	42*	–	18	4	–	2*	–	–			17*	4	14	18	5	404	62	31.07
S.J. Renshaw	–	–	–	10*																	2	1	1	10	10*	–
P.J. Hartley	–	–			6	18	21	5	18	–	8*	5*	–	–					29	3*	13	16	3	160	29	12.30
C.A. Connor	–	–	–	–			0*	–					–	–							4	1	1	0	0*	–
K.D. James			–	54	18	1	20	55*	36	–	4	7*	24	–	22*	–	57	29*	0	12	18	26	9	570	57	33.52
A.D. Mascarenhas					60*	13	46	63	0	–	0	34	0*	51	3	–	10	3	14	0	17	25	2	645	89	28.04
N.A.M. McLean					0	15	6	17*	11	–	33	8	–	–	–	–	18	43	4	20	16	22	2	288	43	14.40
P.R. Whitaker									74	25*	6	32	–	45	72	–	0	40	15	0	7	11	1	309	74	30.90
D.A. Kenway											0	19									3	5	–	118	57	23.60
A.C. Morris															–	–	33*	10	46	0	12	15	5	219	51	21.90
Z.C. Morris																	0	10			1	2	–	10	10	5.00
M. Garaway																					1	1	–	19	19	19.00
R.J. Maru																					2	3	1	27	14	13.50
S.R.G. Francis																					1	–	–	–	–	–
Byes	2				1	8	4	5	1	5		1	11	6				4								
Leg-byes	11			4	6	7	9	4	15	2	8	5	2	9	8		6	9	8	2						
Wides	10				4	4	6	2	4		6		4					2								
No-balls				15	18	18	6	2	6	4	2	4	8	8	15		10	8	4							
Total	394		0	193	189	218	361	276	471	84	104	272	210	281	350		184	322	249	80						
Wickets	5		0	8	9	9	10	8	10	1	10	9	4	5	5		10	10	10	9						
Result	D		D		L		D		W		D		W		D		L		L							
Points	–		5		2		9		23		7		21		11		4		5							

Hampshire CCC First-Class Matches Batting

	v. Nottinghamshire (Portsmouth) 22–25 July		v. Durham (Southampton) 30 July–3 August		v. Kent (Canterbury) 5–8 August		v. Essex (Portsmouth) 14–17 August		v. Sri Lankans (Southampton) 22–24 August		v. Sussex (Hove) 26–29 August		v. Middlesex (Southampton) 31 August–3 September		v. Worcestershire (Worcester) 9–12 September		v. Lancashire (Old Trafford) 17–20 September		M	Inns	NO	Runs	HS	Av
G.W. White	11	16	18	–	13	19	58	–	156	–	13	95*	106	47	30	–	1	12	19	31	2	1211	156	41.75
J.S. Laney	67	0	20	–	4	12													8	13	–	224	101	17.23
R.A. Smith			134	–	72	1	138	–	11	–	14	–	7	21*	33	–	2	47	17	25	2	853	138	37.08
M. Keech							61	–	3	–	18	–	11	–	5	–			12	14	–	335	70	23.92
W.S. Kendall							20	–	59	–	4	49*	29	78*	0	–	33	31	8	11	3	340	78*	42.50
J.P. Stephenson	11	6	40	–	21	4	2	–			84	50	0	105	47	–			16	24	1	681	114	29.60
A.N. Aymes	0	19*	54	–	29	8	11	–			1	–	16	–	0	–	2	8	18	27	6	754	133	35.90
S.D. Udal	35	–	8	–	2	25*									15	–	33*	43	14	18	5	404	62	31.07
S.J. Renshaw																			2	1	1	10	10*	–
P.J. Hartley	16	–	6	–	0	0	0	–			17	–	8	–					13	16	3	160	29	12.30
C.A. Connor																			4	1	1	0	0*	–
K.D. James	0	29*	40*	–	8	12	49*	–	11	–	14*	–	17*	–	9	–	39	3	18	26	9	570	57	33.52
A.D. Mascarenhas	89	–	47	–	4	16	53	–	0	–	15	–	63	–	14	–	21	26	17	25	2	645	89	28.04
N.A.M. McLean	36	–	0	–	4	10	6	–			10	–	0	10	11	–	2	24*	16	22	2	288	43	14.40
P.R. Whitaker	0	–																	7	11	1	309	74	30.90
D.A. Kenway									38	–							4	57	3	5	–	118	57	23.60
A.C. Morris	15*	–	3	–	2*	22	51	–	35*	–	2	–	0	–	0*	–	0	0	12	15	5	219	51	21.90
Z.C. Morris																			1	2	–	10	10	5.00
M. Garaway									19	–									1	1	–	19	19	19.00
R.J. Maru									0*	–							13	14	2	3	1	27	14	13.50
S.R.G. Francis									–	–									1	–	–	–	–	–
Byes					3	10	2		2		2	1	8	6	4		9	4						
Leg-byes	11	3	13		3	8	5		3		6	2	7	4	2		3	8						
Wides			9				2				6		9	18				2						
No-balls	10		4		8	6	32		10		18	12	30	12	8		10	22						
Total	301	73	396		173	153	490		347	0	224	209	311	301	178		172	301						
Wickets	10	3	10		10	10	10		8	0	10	1	10	3	10		10	10						
Result	W		D		L		W		L		W		W		D		L							
Points	23		11		4		24		–		21		21		7		4							

Fielding Figures

54 – A.N. Aymes (ct 52 / st 2)
14 – J.P. Stephenson
12 – G.W. White, M. Keech and A.D. Mascarenhas
10 – J.S. Laney and R.A. Smith
9 – S.D. Udal
8 – W.S. Kendall and P.R. Whitaker
6 – A.C. Morris
5 – N.A.M. McLean and K.D. James
3 – R.J. Maru and P.J. Hartley
1 – sub

Hampshire CCC First-Class Matches

Bowling

	C.A. Connor	P.J. Hartley	J.P. Stephenson	S.D. Udal	S.J. Renshaw	J.S. Laney	K.D. James	N.A.M. McLean	P.R. Whitaker	A.C. Morris	A.D. Mascarenhas	G.W. White	Byes	Leg-byes	Wides	No-balls	Total	Wkts	
v. Oxford University (Oxford) 17–20 April	16–6–32–0	5–1–7–2	15–5–35–2	15–10–7–3	11–4–15–1	1–0–1–0								4	10	12	101	8	
v. Northamptonshire (Southampton) 23–27 April	5–0–15–0		2–1–2–1		6–1–9–1		3–1–8–0							1		2	275	5	A
																	0	0	
v. Surrey (Southampton) 13–16 May		28–0–107–1	5–1–23–0	27.2–3–94–1		2–0–14–0	27–8–104–1	29–4–107–4			25–4–119–6	1–0–5–0	5	13	14	8	591	10	
v. Leicestershire (Leicester) 21–24 May	16–4–43–0	17–4–45–0		2–0–9–0			15–1–50–0	28–6–101–6			11–1–31–1		15	11	6	16	305	7	
v. Glamorgan (Southampton) 3–6 June		18–3–65–1		7–2–13–0			21–2–75–2	19–5–42–3			21–6–68–4		4	2		6	269	10	
		21.1–2–77–4	15–7–22–2	4–0–8–0			19–5–51–1	22–2–87–1	2–0–2–1		9–2–31–1			7		18	285	10	
v. Yorkshire (Leeds) 11–14 June		23–3–74–1	15–4–37–1	20.3–7–40–1			16–4–47–2	19–3–81–0			12.3–5–31–4			17	4	6	327	9	
v. Derbyshire (Basingstoke) 17–20 June	8–0–41–0	25–4–85–1	28–6–75–3	11.3–3–25–3			7–2–31–2	18–3–56–1			12–5–28–0			9	4	14	350	10	
	6–1–23–2							6–1–15–0				8–1–38–0		1		4	140	3	B
v. Somerset (Taunton) 26–29 June			17–2–48–0	13–3–43–0			11–1–43–2	20–2–92–2	1–0–5–0	20–1–90–2	19.2–3–55–4			2	18	4	378	10	
v. Gloucestershire (Southampton) 1–4 July			17–2–46–2				10–2–28–1	20.5–5–39–4		12–4–25–1	5–1–19–2			14			176	10	C
			24–7–58–1				16–3–65–0	28.3–11–71–4	3–1–8–0	22–3–78–2	11–1–35–0		6	12	6	6	333	8	
v. Warwickshire (Edgbaston) 15–17 July		23–5–94–2	12–5–23–2	10–3–30–0			4–0–22–0	21–4–71–2		16.5–2–75–4	12–3–31–0		5	16	2	2	367	10	
		15.4–4–41–2	8–1–20–2				10–2–23–1	15–5–53–2		14–5–27–3	2–0–10–0		5	8	4	2	187	10	
v. Nottinghamshire (Portsmouth) 22–25 July		10–2–41–1	2–1–4–1	1–1–0–0				14–4–45–4		8.2–1–26–3	6–1–11–0			1	8		128	9	
		16–2–38–2	7–1–18–0	7–1–15–0			12–2–34–0	15.5–1–65–2		12–1–35–4	7–1–36–1			2	4	2	243	9	
v. Durham (Southampton) 30 July–3 August		10–3–20–0	10–3–17–1				12–2–35–2	22–3–62–0		13.4–4–30–4	13–3–29–2		1	9		8	203	10	
		22–7–56–2	14.4–4–36–0	19–1–80–3			9–3–17–2	27–4–61–2		19–4–49–0	6–1–17–0		5	11		12	332	9	
v. Kent (Canterbury) 5–8 August		17–1–54–1	16–4–56–1	11–2–39–0			16.2–2–66–3	19–5–65–1		18–2–72–4	6–0–23–0		6	10	14	24	391	10	
		13–3–21–3	17–3–58–1	11–3–37–4			3–2–2–0	11–1–29–1		10–2–36–0	10–4–30–1		4	10		2	227	10	
v. Essex (Portsmouth) 14–17 August		16–3–42–4	5–2–18–0				3–0–17–0	15.4–3–37–5		6–2–17–1			4	6	2	6	141	10	
		25–6–90–3	9–1–30–0					19–3–69–2		13–1–39–4	1–0–3–0			7	4	4	238	10	
v. Sri Lankans (Southampton) 22–24 August										6–1–15–2				3			39	4	D
							20–3–78–1			12–2–53–1	14–0–66–0	1.1–1–4–1	4	2		8	309	5	
v. Sussex (Hove) 26–29 August		10–2–23–0	8–1–28–0				11.3–3–24–2	14–3–41–3		12–4–33–3	8–2–24–2		4	10	10	10	187	10	
		11–3–43–1	7–2–20–0				8–2–28–1	23–9–46–4		18–7–46–2	9–2–45–2		2	15	21	22	245	10	
v. Middlesex (Southampton) 31 August–3 September		21–6–67–1	13–3–47–0				24–7–64–3	30–6–67–2		24.1–2–106–3	19–5–53–1		15	18	2	34	437	10	
		7–2–19–1	1–0–3–0				5–1–21–0	9–3–19–0		6–1–31–1			16	4	8	4	173	2	E
v. Worcestershire (Worcester) 9–12 September			12–3–29–4	1–0–1–0			11–2–25–0	21–1–82–4		16–4–47–2	3–0–14–0			14	4	2	212	10	
			7–2–17–0	3–1–3–0			10–3–15–1	11–3–37–3		14–4–25–0	9–3–40–0		1	6	2	4	144	4	
v. Lancashire (Old Trafford) 17–20 September							13.1–5–22–4	17–4–27–0		21–7–57–4	14–3–56–2			12		2	185	10	F
				28–4–105–1			23–5–88–1	4–1–8–0			16–3–95–0	2–0–4–0	7	8	2	2	449	4	
	51–11–	353.5–66–	286.4–71–	191.2–44–	17–5–	3–0–	340–70–	518.5–105–	6–1–	314–64–	280.5–59–	12.1–2–							
	154–2	1109–33	770–24	549–16	24–2	15–0	1083–32	1575–62	15–1	1012–50	1000–30	51–1							
Bowler's average	77.00	33.60	32.08	34.31	12.00	–	33.84	25.40	15.00	20.24	33.33	51.00							

A A.N. Aymes 9–0–135–2; R.A. Smith 9–0–105–1
B R.A. Smith 9–1–63–1
C Z.C. Morris 1–0–5–0
D S.R.G. Francis 6–2–21–2, 15–1–47–2; R.J. Maru 17–4–55–0
E R.A. Smith 3–0–29–0; A.N. Aymes 2–0–31–0
F R.J. Maru 3–0–11–0, 28–5–101–2; D.A. Kenway 2–0–17–0; W.S. Kendall 40–0–16–0

Kent C.C.C. First-Class Matches Batting

	v. Middlesex (Canterbury) 17–21 April		v. Glamorgan (Cardiff) 23–27 April		v. Lancashire (Canterbury) 13–16 May		v. Durham (Canterbury) 21–24 May		v. Surrey (The Oval) 29 May–1 June		v. Sussex (Tunbridge Wells) 3–6 June		v. Leicestershire (Leicester) 11–14 June		v. Nottinghamshire (Canterbury) 17–20 June		v. Oxford University (Canterbury) 26–29 June		v. Yorkshire (Maidstone) 1–4 June		M	Inns	NO	Runs	HS	Av
R.W.T. Key	–	15			7	41	101	–	10	0	45	17	19	–	115	45			6	23	13	23	–	612	115	26.60
D.P. Fulton	–	4	61	71*	25	96	65	–	3	0	4	37	44	–	14	20			21	207	17	31	1	951	207	31.70
A.P. Wells	–	77	46	–	20	35	95	–	24	24	0	4	14	–	2	78*			1	8	15	26	1	684	95	27.36
M.J. Walker	–	68	0	8			13	–			45	21			0	1	31	34*			8	14	1	341	68	26.23
M.A. Ealham	–	15	0	45*	73	22			5	7			17*	–					0	121	10	18	3	437	121	29.13
M.V. Fleming	–	40*	12	–	7	2			10	22	19	41*	6	–	6	16	41	–	49	2	17	30	4	612	51	23.53
S.A. Marsh	–	7	10	–	12	50*	92	–	1	3	1	6			21	1			2	56*	16	28	4	620	92	25.83
B.J. Phillips	–	–	9	–	7	4					2	2			23	–	10	–	28	3	11	17	–	203	54	11.94
D.W. Headley	–	–	5	–	10	0	31	–	3*	5			1	–							13	19	5	262	81	18.71
M.M. Patel	–	–			6*	5	24	–	0	24	17	8	–	–			0	–	36*	1	14	20	5	303	58*	20.20
M.J. McCague	–	6*					0	–	0	13*			–	–	38	25*			0	18*	10	15	7	166	38	20.75
T.R. Ward			11	10	6	19	19	–	9	21	27	8	2	–	40	3			9	94	12	22	–	416	94	18.90
C.L. Hooper			1	4	4	203	1	–	4	94	7	49	0	–	7	122			0	24	15	28	1	1218	203	45.11
A.P. Igglesden			3*	–			1*	–			4*	0									3	4	3	8	4*	8.00
S.C. Willis													0*	–			58	–			2	2	1	58	58	58.00
J.M. de la Pena															0*	–	–	–			2	1	1	0	0*	–
C.D. Walsh																	4	0			3	6	–	42	20	7.00
J.B. Hockley																	21	9			1	2	–	30	21	15.00
N.J. Llong																	16	12*			2	4	1	32	16	10.66
J.B.D. Thompson																	65*	–			4	6	4	89	65*	44.50
D.A. Scott																	17*	–			2	3	3	22	17*	–
E.T. Smith																					7	14	–	321	58	22.92
W.J. House																					1	2	–	5	5	2.50
Byes					1	11	4		9	2	8		1			10	2		11	4						
Leg-byes		9	4		4	19	16		2	1	8	4	4		1	9	10		2	5						
Wides		6	2			6	16			2	2	5	2		2		6	2		6						
No-balls		6	2	4	4	4	17		6	8	22	4	10		14	4	10			8						
Total	0	253	166	142	186	517	495		86	226	211	206	120		283	334	291	57	165	580						
Wickets	0	6	10	3	10	10	10		10	10	10	10	7		10	7	8	2	10	9						
Result	W		D		D		W		L		L		D		W		L		D							
Points	20		4		5		24		4		5		7		22		–		6							

Batting

	v. Essex (Southend) 15–18 July		v. Derbyshire (Derby) 30 July–3 August		v. Hampshire (Canterbury) 5–8 August		v. Gloucestershire (Bristol) 14–17 August		v. Worcestershire (Canterbury) 19–22 August		v. Northamptonshire (Northampton) 26–29 August		v. Somerset (Canterbury) 9–12 September		v. Warwickshire (Edgbaston) 17–20 September		M	Inns	NO	Runs	HS	Av
R.W.T. Key	6	5			34	33			9	4			5	56	11	5	13	23	–	612	115	26.60
D.P. Fulton	50	56	28	0	54	2	18	9	17	15	0	20	5	0	0	5	17	31	1	951	207	31.70
A.P. Wells	30	20					12	7	9	8	79	77	0	3	11	0	15	26	1	684	95	27.36
M.J. Walker													11	39	57	13	8	14	1	341	68	26.23
M.A. Ealham	28	8	1	61*	11	10									8	5	10	18	3	437	121	29.13
M.V. Fleming	44	15	26	15*	51	21	3	22	42	33	2	8	25*	1	10	21	17	30	4	612	51	23.53
S.A. Marsh	9	16	4	–	0	47	60	15*	48	10	33	15*	0	27	57	17	16	28	4	620	92	25.83
B.J. Phillips							34	14	0	54	2	5	4	2			11	17	–	203	54	11.94
D.W. Headley	24	2*	3*	–	81	10*			17	20	12*	–	0	7	5	26	13	19	5	262	81	18.71
M.M. Patel	0	–			58*	6			0	55*	0	–	8	6*	1	48	14	20	5	303	58*	20.20
M.J. McCague	16*	6*	6	–	7	26	0*	5									10	15	7	166	38	20.75
T.R. Ward	32	7	0	34			0	29			13	23					12	22	–	416	94	18.90
C.L. Hooper	100	12	26	0	36	12	13	111	154	33	22	157*	8	14			15	28	1	1218	203	45.11
A.P. Igglesden																	3	4	3	8	4*	8.00
S.C. Willis																	2	2	1	58	58	58.00
J.M. de la Pena																	2	1	1	0	0*	–
C.D. Walsh							0	10			20	8					3	6	–	42	20	7.00
J.B. Hockley																	1	2	–	30	21	15.00
N.J. Llong			4	0													2	4	1	32	16	10.66
J.B.D. Thompson			8*	–			4	5	2*	5*							4	6	4	89	65*	44.50
D.A. Scott															3*	2*	2	3	3	22	17*	–
E.T. Smith			34	10	0	44	3	49	21	10	1	33	0	34	24	58	7	14	–	321	58	22.92
W.J. House					5	0											1	2	–	5	5	2.50
Byes	4	2			6	4	2	2	1	3	4	12			2							
Leg-byes	9	4	5	3	10	10		5	10	2	8	7	8	11	8	2						
Wides					14		2		6	4	4			2								
No-balls	12	2	20	6	24	2	12	14	8	14	18	12	12	8								
Total	364	155	165	129	391	227	163	297	344	270	218	377	86	210	197	202						
Wickets	10	8	9	5	10	10	10	10	10	9	10	7	10	10	10	10						
Result	W		D		W		L		D		D		L		L							
Points	23		7		24		4		9		6		4		4							

Fielding Figures

45 – S.A. Marsh (ct 41 / st 2)
21 – D.P. Fulton
15 – C.L Hooper
11 – R.W.T. Key
9 – M.V. Fleming
8 – M.J. McCague and T.R. Ward
7 – M.M. Patel
6 – M.J. Walker
5 – D.W. Headley and S.C. Willis (ct 3 / st 1)
3 – A.P. Wells
2 – M.A. Ealham, B.J. Phillips, N.J Llong and A.P. Igglesden
1 – C.D. Walsh, W.J. House and E.T. Smith

Kent CCC First-Class Matches

Bowling

	M.J. McCague	D.W. Headley	M.M. Patel	B.J. Phillips	M.A. Ealham	M.V. Fleming	M.W. Walker	A.P. Igglesden	C.L. Hooper	D. Scott	J. de la Pena	J.B. Thompson	Byes	Leg-byes	Wides	No-balls	Total	Wkts	
v. Middlesex	12–3–42–0	22–6–50–2	10.1–2–12–2	21–8–66–3	11–4–16–0	13–5–32–3								10	8	24	228	10	
(Canterbury) 17–21 April			2–0–7–0				3–0–16–0										23	0	
v. Glamorgan		6–3–7–2		4–0–21–0	6–3–8–0	4–1–7–1		5–0–18–0	5–4–1–0				1			6	63	3	
(Cardiff) 23–27 April		16.5–1–56–3		10–0–37–1	9–2–30–0	8–2–24–2		5–0–27–0	11–4–29–2				5	4		4	212	8	
v. Lancashire		33.3–4–105–2	30–8–80–2	19–6–59–1	18–9–36–0	19–3–51–2			38–9–92–3				13	9	2	4	445	10	
(Canterbury) 13–16 May		8–6–63–2	17–4–40–0	5–0–16–0	3–0–22–0	2–0–9–0			14–6–26–0				7	1	2	4	125	2	A
v. Durham	10–1–44–0	18–5–49–3	22.2–5–73–5					12–3–31–0	11–4–21–2				4	7	6	8	229	10	
(Canterbury) 21–24 May	12–1–58–1	19–4–71–6	15.2–1–67–3					7–0–30–0	1–1–0–0				7	6		16	239	10	
v. Surrey	9–1–35–0	17–5–40–2	43–10–129–1		11–5–16–0	4–2–8–0			39.1–7–93–7				11	10		4	342	10	
(The Oval) 29 May–1 June																			
v. Sussex			8–3–9–0	25–4–72–2		23.3–14–24–4	2–0–4–0	24–9–36–2	26–12–30–1					14	16		189	10	
(Tunbridge Wells) 3–6 June			28–9–57–3	15–1–38–1		33–10–76–3		17–1–60–0	23–7–48–0				5	19	10		303	7	
v. Leicestershire	14–4–34–2	13–4–29–1			18.4–10–23–5	6–2–9–1							6	2	2	2	103	10	
(Leicester) 11–14 June																			
v. Nottinghamshire	29–7–69–1			22–3–73–1		19–4–49–4			18–4–51–0		21–2–54–2			13	10	8	309	10	
(Canterbury) 17–20 June	19–4–70–1			20–3–56–2		18.4–6–46–1	4–0–21–0		15–2–37–0		12–0–72–1			1	4	4	307	5	B
v. Oxford University			14–3–27–1	8–1–36–2						3–1–5–0	2–2–0–0	8–1–33–0		7	2	8	108	4	
(Canterbury) 26–29 June			17–3–81–4	11–1–53–2						4–0–16–0	7–4–28–0	11–2–51–0	2	10		6	241	7	
v. Yorkshire	21–2–77–3		10–1–34–0	19–6–58–0	27–6–86–1	31–10–76–2			23–4–80–1				10	2	6	8	423	7	
(Maidstone) 1–4 June																			
v. Essex	18.2–5–78–3	17–2–53–0	20–5–42–2		15–4–42–2	14–5–30–2			10–2–40–1				6	4		6	295	10	
(Southend) 15–18 June	13–1–33–2	16–3–36–0	17–4–56–0		24–9–45–5	10.3–2–28–3			4–0–11–0				4	10			223	10	
v. Derbyshire	13–2–35–0	28.2–6–64–5			16–3–36–2	17–4–56–1			6–2–14–0			21–7–42–2	4	9		4	260	10	
(Derby) 30 July–5 August																			
v. Hampshire	13–4–33–3	12–4–42–3	4–1–14–0		7–2–23–0	8–1–41–0			14.4–9–14–4				3	3		8	173	10	
(Canterbury) 5–8 August	13–2–40–4	9–4–9–1	22–7–54–1			7–4–3–0			21–12–29–4				10	8		6	153	10	
v. Gloucestershire	16.5–3–41–4			7–1–18–1		9–3–21–1						14–5–52–4	8	2	2	8	142	10	
(Bristol) 14–17 August	22–5–69–3			23–3–89–0		31–6–81–2			44–8–118–1			23.4–5–82–4	10	7	2	14	456	10	
v. Worcestershire		30–7–84–3	40–16–55–4	20–1–65–0		15–4–36–0			4–0–25–1			18–1–75–1	15	5	2	26	360	10	
(Canterbury) 19–22 August		16–2–56–3	38.4–9–92–1	16–5–46–0		9–1–32–2			23–4–87–1				10	10	2	26	333	8	
v. Northamptonshire		31–5–79–5	15–1–73–1	27–9–56–0		37–11–87–1			24.3–1–80–3				2	14	8	12	391	10	
(Northampton) 26–29 August																			
v. Somerset		33.4–7–97–6	10–1–33–0	22–3–69–1		33–10–83–3	3–0–10–0		11–2–31–0				6	13	4	10	342	10	
(Canterbury) 9–12 September																			
v. Warwickshire		22–6–98–1	26–9–49–3		23–12–49–5	18–3–61–0				23–8–55–0			8	3	2	2	323	10	
(Edgbaston) 17–20 September		20–2–78–2	9–0–39–1		16–4–56–1	15–2–38–0				18–5–48–1				3			262	5	
Bowler's average	235.1–45– 758–27 28.07	388.2–86– 1106–52 21.26	418.3–102– 1123–34 33.02	294–55– 928–17 54.58	204.4–73– 488–21 23.23	404.4–115– 1008–38 26.52	12–0– 51–0 –	70–13– 202–2 101.00	386.2–104– 957–31 30.87	48–14– 124–1 124.00	42–6– 154–3 51.33	95.4–21– 335–11 30.45							

A R.W.T. Key 1–0–1–0
B T.R. Ward 2–0–4–0

Lancashire CCC First-Class Matches Batting

Batting	v. Sussex (Hove) 17–20 April		v. Middlesex (Old Trafford) 23–27 April		v. Kent (Canterbury) 13–16 May		v. Essex (Chelmsford) 21–24 May		v. Northamptonshire (Northampton) 3–6 June		v. Somerset (Old Trafford) 11–14 June		v. Surrey (Old Trafford) 18–21 June		v. Warwickshire (Edgbaston) 26–29 June		v. Worcestershire (Lytham) 14–17 July		v. Glamorgan (Colwyn Bay) 22–25 July		M	Inns	NO	Runs	HS	Av
N.T. Wood	11	32*	–	–	27	12	14	32	3	5			5	80*	14*	79			37	13	12	19	3	457	80*	28.56
M.A. Atherton	0	33*			152	2	20	13			0	28			–	31	3	22			8	14	1	381	152	29.30
J.P. Crawley	49	–	–	–	0	45*	1	64*	22	109	72	44	3	78	–	34	39	108	124	136	17	26	2	1681	239	70.04
N.H. Fairbrother	8	–			16	52*	126	–	7	37					–	54	–	–			12	17	2	759	138	50.60
G.D. Lloyd	20	–	–	–					8	49	0	47	21	1	–	30	27	18	50	73	15	22	1	831	212*	39.57
A. Flintoff	68	–	–	–	42	–	29	37	46	142	18	1	0	61	–	70	15	8			15	22	–	591	124	26.86
W.K. Hegg	59	–	–	–	64	–	0	–	22	56*	54*	23*					54	37	25	10	15	21	4	628	85	36.94
I.D. Austin	1	–	–	–	7	–			64	0	0	0			23*	12*	59*	44*	3	2	12	17	4	304	64	23.38
P.J. Martin	14*	–	–	–	11	–			17	7*	18	3	–	–	–	–	3	2*	26	4	14	15	5	154	26	15.40
G. Chapple	7	–	–	–			31	23*	4	7	0	26	0*	–	–	–	0	10			14	31	3	282	69	18.80
G. Keedy	4	–			4*	–															7	10	5	44	13	8.80
S.P. Titchard			–	–																	1	–	–	–	–	–
M. Watkinson			–	–	87	–	40	–	0	20	19	17	42	–	–	5*	55	22	3	8	10	12	1	318	87	28.90
R.J. Green			–	–			14	–	0*	–			–	–	–	–					6	3	1	14	14	7.00
Wasim Akram					7	–	0	–			32	4	23*	–			38	0	43	0	13	18	1	531	155	31.23
D.J. Shadford							13*	–													1	1	1	13	13*	–
P.C. McKeown											39	23	42	10					20	31	5	7	–	186	42	26.57
M.E. Harvey													0	0*							1	2	1	0	0*	0.00
M. Chilton																			13	47	2	4	–	125	47	31.25
C.P. Schofield																			1*	4*	2	3	2	5	4*	5.00
G. Yates																					4	6	1	174	55	34.80
P.M. Ridgway																					1	2	–	39	35	19.50
Byes	1				13	7		1	4	2						4		2	1	2						
Leg-byes	6	1			9	1	8	1	2	20	7	14	9	6		7	12		10	2						
Wides	2				2	2	12		9			2		6		2		2								
No-balls	16	2			4	4	6	4	22	2	8	4	6	8	2	10	2	6	10	2						
Total	266	68			445	125	314	175	230	438	267	236	151	250	39	338	307	281	366	334						
Wickets	10	0			10	2	10	3	10	8	10	10	7	4	0	6	9	8	10	10						
Result	L		D		D		W		D		W		W		W		W		D							
Points	3		4		10		23		8		22		20		18		23		10							

Batting	v. Leicestershire (Old Trafford) 30 July–3 August		v. Gloucestershire (Old Trafford) 5–8 August		v. Yorkshire (Leeds) 14–17 August		v. Durham (Riverside) 19–22 August		v. Derbyshire (Old Trafford) 1–4 September		v. Nottinghamshire (Trent Bridge) 11–14 September		v. Hampshire (Old Trafford) 17–20 September		M	Inns	NO	Runs	HS	Av
N.T. Wood	–	–	24	–	7	0	14	48							12	19	3	457	80*	28.56
M.A. Atherton									4	–			45	28	8	14	1	381	152	29.30
J.P. Crawley	–	–	43	–	180	56	4	14	100	–	44	58	15	239	17	26	2	1681	239	70.04
N.H. Fairbrother			35	–	27	0	0	138	48	–	88	4	16	103*	12	17	2	759	138	50.60
G.D. Lloyd	–	–	38	–	56	2	15	104	212*	–	13	2	0	45	15	22	1	831	212*	39.57
A. Flintoff	–	–			16	3	2	0	14	–	9	23	1	4	15	22	–	591	124	26.86
W.K. Hegg	–	–	26	–	39	85	12	21	19	–	7	0	4	11*	15	21	4	628	85	36.94
I.D. Austin	–	–			49	x			3	–	1	9	27	–	12	17	4	304	64	23.38
P.J. Martin	–	–	19*	–					2	–	4*	11	13	–	14	15	5	154	26	15.40
G. Chapple	–	–	69	–	4	1*	15	12	42	–	2	29			14	31	3	282	69	18.80
G. Keedy					13	1	5*	4*	7	–	2	4*	0*	–	7	10	5	44	13	8.80
S.P. Titchard															1	–	–	–	–	–
M. Watkinson	–	–													10	12	1	318	87	28.90
R.J. Green					x	0									6	3	1	14	14	7.00
Wasim Akram	–	–	37	–	14	21	68	63	13	–	0	155	13	–	13	18	1	531	155	31.23
D.J. Shadford															1	1	1	13	13*	–
P.C. McKeown	–	–	21	–											5	7	–	186	42	26.57
M.E. Harvey															1	2	1	0	0*	0.00
M. Chilton											28	37			2	4	–	125	47	31.25
C.P. Schofield			0	–											2	3	2	5	4*	5.00
G. Yates			55	–	37*	26	5	14					37	–	4	6	1	174	55	34.80
P.M. Ridgway							35	4							1	2	–	39	35	19.50
Byes			8		8	6	10	1	5					7						
Leg-byes			11		8	2	9	11	4		6	9	12	8						
Wides									8		4	2		2						
No-balls					26	12	2		6		10	14	2	2						
Total			386		484	215	196	434	487		218	357	185	449						
Wickets			10		10	10	10	10	10		10	10	10	4						
Result	D		W		W		W		W		W		W							
Points	6		23		22		20		24		21		20							

Fielding Figures

38 – W.K. Hegg
22 – A. Flintoff
12 – N.H. Fairbrother
11 – G.D. Lloyd
8 – Wasim Akram
7 – M.A. Atherton, I.D. Austin and G. Chapple
6 – M. Watkinson, J.P. Crawley and P.C. McKeown
5 – sub
3 – P.J. Martin
2 – G. Keedy and G. Yates
1 – R.J. Green and C.P. Schofield

In the match *v.* Yorkshire, 14–17 August, R.J. Green replaced I.D. Austin when Austin was called up for international duty.

Lancashire CCC First-Class Matches

Bowling

	P.J. Martin	G. Chapple	I.D. Austin	G. Keedy	A. Flintoff	R.J. Green	M. Watkinson	Wasim Akram	D.J. Shadford	G. Yates	M.J. Chilton	C.P. Schofield	Byes	Leg-byes	Wides	No-balls	Total	Wkts	
v. Sussex (Hove) 17–20 April	9–5–18–1	10–2–33–1	9.3–3–19–2											5	2		75	4	
	25–9–61–2	15–1–65–1	18–2–57–1	15.4–2–58–4	4–1–12–0									7		10	260	8	
v. Middlesex (Old Trafford) 23–27 April	13–2–42–1	20–7–43–0	17–3–41–1		6–5–6–0	13–4–37–1	10–0–30–1						2	4		4	205	4	
v. Kent (Canterbury) 13–16 May	16–4–37–3		15–1–56–2	10–6–13–2	7–4–13–1		6–1–17–1	19–5–45–1					1	4		4	186	10	
	31–5–74–3		26–104–0	36–2–134–2	7–0–30–0		23.5–1–94–4	14–1–51–0					11	19	6	4	517	10	
v. Essex (Chelmsford) 21–24 May		18–2–49–5			8–3–18–1	14–4–41–0	7–3–12–2	16.5–2–49–1	18–1–56–1				2	15		8	242	10	
		20–4–59–3			4–1–10–1	21–7–57–1	24.5–6–45–5	7.1–2–21–0	12.5–4–34–0				9	9	8		244	10	
v. Northamptonshire (Northampton) 3–6 June	28–7–56–4	22.1–1–92–3	22–6–58–3		12–3–27–0	18–6–52–0	7–1–25–0						5	17		2	332	10	
	16–2–72–1	5–0–12–1	16–5–38–2			10–0–41–1	16–0–103–1						4	4		6	274	6	
v. Somerset (Old Trafford) 11–14 June	20–3–66–4	15–5–42–3	20–5–53–0		5–0–19–0			20.2–7–42–3					5	6		14	233	10	
	25–4–63–2	16–4–47–3	11–4–25–1				2–0–11–0	30.1–6–105–4					5	5	8	28	261	10	
v. Surrey (Old Trafford) 18–21 June	17–5–35–3	8.1–1–32–1				9–1–32–1		19–6–42–4					1	4	6	6	146	10	
	7–1–24–0	4–2–8–1				6–0–23–0	6–0–23–0	5–1–11–0					2	6	2	4	254	1	A
v. Warwickshire (Edgbaston) 26–29 June	21–4–59–0	21–3–74–3	21–2–62–0		2–0–12–0	14–3–53–0	25–1–100–1						4	10		4	374	5	
																	0	0	
v. Worcestershire (Lytham) 14–17 July	20–6–58–2	15–2–45–0	31–9–82–3		14–2–51–3		3–1–15–0	26–5–77–2					10	12	22	4	350	10	
	18–2–44–1	12–2–39–3	14–2–39–2		6–2–16–0		6–2–15–0	13–4–35–0					5	3	2	18	237	6	B
v. Glamorgan (Colwyn Bay) 22–25 July	17–2–71–1		16.5–6–33–4				26–4–74–2	12–1–39–1			3–1–16–0	29–0–139–0	1	10		8	383	8	
			4–0–19–0				9–2–27–1				5–1–8–0	11–3–44–2		2		2	100	3	
v. Leicestershire (Old Trafford) 30 July–3 August	15–3–41–3	11–2–28–1	14–3–35–0		6–2–27–0		4–0–16–0	16–4–58–3					2	11	4	8	218	7	
v. Gloucestershire (Old Trafford) 5–8 August	5–3–3–0	4–3–1–0						10–3–20–2		26–5–64–4		16.4–3–56–4	8	6		8	158	10	
	5–3–5–2							4–0–17–0		21.3–3–91–4		23–3–60–4	10	10		14	193	10	
v. Yorkshire (Leeds) 14–17 August		32–9–59–3	10–3–28–0	50–12–161–2	5–2–8–0	20–3–83–0				41–12–107–3				11		10	457	8	
		8–0–23–0		22.4–7–35–5		1–0–5–0		5–0–30–1		18–2–69–4			17	4	7		183	10	
v. Durham (Riverside) 19–22 August		10–0–37–3		4–0–11–0	4–0–17–0			12–3–39–3						3	8	4	158	9	C
		12.4–3–26–4		2–1–2–0	4–1–12–0			16–5–40–4		1–0–4–0				6	2	10	122	9	
v. Derbyshire (Old Trafford) 1–4 September	15–1–70–3	12–0–37–2	13.2–5–50–2	9–2–35–0	4–0–19–0			18–7–60–3					4	6	8	16	281	10	
	16–4–45–4	5–0–18–1	10–2–26–1	8–1–38–0				16–2–66–4						5		24	198	10	
v. Nottinghamshire (Trent Bridge) 11–14 September	10–1–21–4	10–3–40–1	11.2–3–21–4					9–2–23–1					8	2		2	115	10	
	9–6–11–1	7–1–33–1	16–4–54–3		3–0–7–0			13.2–1–56–5					2	8		10	171	10	
v. Hampshire (Old Trafford) 17–20 September	16–8–30–1		17.4–3–50–4	7–2–19–1	3–0–13–0			18–5–37–4		4–1–11–0			9	3		10	172	10	
	14–4–56–2		12–3–28–1	18.1–3–57–2				16–3–62–2		20–3–86–3			4	8	2	22	301	10	
	388–94–	313–57–	345.4–80–	182.3–38–	104–26–	126–28–	175.4–22–	335.5–75–	30.5–5–	131.3–26–	8–2–	79.4–9–							
	1062–48	942–44	978–36	563–18	317–6	424–4	607–18	1025–48	90–1	432–18	24–0	299–10							
Bowler's average	22.12	21.40	27.16	31.27	52.83	106.00	33.72	21.35	90.00	24.00	–	29.90							

A G.D. Lloyd 6–1–29–0; N.T. Wood 5.1–0–80–0; M.E. Harvey 5–0–48–0
B J.P. Crawley 1–0–21–0; G.D. Lloyd 1.3–0–20–0
C P.M. Ridgway 10–1–51–3, 8–1–32–1

Leicestershire CCC First-Class Matches Batting

Batting	v. Cambridge University (Cambridge) 17–19 April		v. Worcestershire (Leicester) 23–27 April		v. Gloucestershire (Bristol) 13–16 May		v. Hampshire (Leicester) 21–24 May		v. Derbyshire (Chesterfield) 29 May–1 June		v. Yorkshire (Leeds) 3–6 June		v. Kent (Leicester) 11–14 June		v. Glamorgan (Cardiff) 17–20 June		v. Sussex (Leicester) 26–29 June		v. Durham (Darlington) 1–4 July		M	Inns	NO	Runs	HS	Av
V.J. Wells	10*	–			120	12	15	–	27	64	144	24	6	–	6	11	26	6*	11	–	17	25	2	286	171	36.34
D.L. Maddy	2	–	–	–	0	24*			7	40	0	3	2	–	40	31*	15	0	162	–	18	26	2	569	162	23.70
I.J. Sutcliffe	7*	–	–	–	2	4*	17	–	82	6	30	–	20	–	0	1	38	0*	13	–	19	26	4	698	167	31.72
J.J. Whitaker	–	–																			1	–	–	–	–	–
B.F. Smith	–	–	–	–	121*	–	40	–	25	11	4	35*	6	–	24	20*	2	–	47	–	18	24	4	1240	204	62.00
A. Habib	–	–	–	–	5	–	112	–	39*	33	10	11*	23	–	27	–	20	–	96	–	18	22	5	952	198	56.00
C.C. Lewis	–	–	–	–	22	–			0	0	35	–	8	–	50	–	63	–	9	–	13	14	3	367	71*	33.36
P.A. Nixon	–	–	–	–	24	–	31	–	20	0	63	–	8	–	101*	–	45	–	1	–	19	21	4	638	101*	37.52
J. Ormond	–	–							0	9			0	–							6	5	–	15	9	3.00
T.J. Mason	–	–					–	–													2	–	–	–	–	–
M.T. Brimson	–	–	–	–	2	–	–	–	3	0*	–	–	1*	–	5	–	14	–	4	–	18	14	6	115	54*	14.37
J.M. Dakin			–	–			0	–			0	–			3	–					6	6	–	128	79	21.33
P.Y. Simmons			–	–	0	–	1	–	10	1	21	–	17	–	16	–	0	–	0	–	17	19	–	464	194	24.42
D.J. Millns			–	–	14	–											26*	–			11	10	4	289	99	48.16
A.D. Mullally			–	–	10	–	–	–	0	14	28*	–	0	–	0	–	16	–	38*	–	15	11	2	132	38*	14.66
D. Williamson							41*	–													2	3	1	95	41*	47.50
D.I. Stevens																					1	2	–	3	2	1.50
C.D. Crowe																			2	–	6	6	1	88	29*	17.60
Byes	2				1		15					4	6		4		6		8							
Leg-byes	3				10	2	11		7	6	4	1	2		12	1	12		9							
Wides					6		6		2		6		2				2		2							
No-balls					14	2	16		24	2	8		2		4	2	4		12							
Total	24				351	44	305		246	186	353	78	103		292	66	289	6	414							
Wickets	1				10	1	7		10	10	9	2	10		10	2	10	1	10							
Result	D		D		W		D		W		D		D		W		D		W							
Points	–		3		24		8		21		8		6		19		9		24							

Batting

Batting	v. Northamptonshire (Leicester) 14–17 July		v. Sri Lankans (Leicester) 24–27 July		v. Lancashire (Old Trafford) 30 July–3 August		v. Somerset (Leicester) 5–8 August		v. Middlesex (Leicester) 19–22 August		v. Nottinghamshire (Worksop) 26–29 August		v. Warwickshire (Edgbaston) 1–4 September		v. Essex (Leicester) 9–12 September		v. Surrey (The Oval) 17–20 September		M	Inns	NO	Runs	HS	Av
V.J. Wells	1	58			0	–	5	–	67	8	3	–	2	15	171	–	24		17	25	2	286	171	36.34
D.L. Maddy	3	15	26	29	0	–	107	–	1	9	11	–	9	19	7	–	7		18	26	2	569	162	23.70
I.J. Sutcliffe	1	12	17	15	32	–	17	–	167	40*	60	–	24	36	39	–	18		19	26	4	698	167	31.72
J.J. Whitaker																			1	–	–	–	–	–
B.F. Smith	153	6	0	75	19	–	67	–	9	39	159	–	86	87	1	–	204		18	24	4	1240	204	62.00
A. Habib	198	7*	0	23	56	–	8	–	84	–	33*	–	29	16*	8	–	114		18	22	5	952	198	56.00
C.C. Lewis	8	71*											13	20*	14	–	54*		13	14	3	367	71*	33.36
P.A. Nixon	27	2	20	38	42*	–	0	–	34	–	19*	–	24	12	26	–	101*		19	21	4	638	101*	37.52
J. Ormond							5	–	1	–	–	–							6	5	–	15	9	3.00
T.J. Mason																			2	–	–	–	–	–
M.T. Brimson	18*	–	1	2*	–	–	0*	–	7	–	4	–	54*	–			–		18	14	6	115	54*	14.37
J.M. Dakin			79	42					4	–									6	6	–	128	79	21.33
P.Y. Simmons	7	25			6	–	16	–	0	–	194	–	0	68	61	–	21		17	19	–	464	194	24.42
D.J. Millns	20	–	46*	14	9	–	0	–	24*	–			99	–	37*	–	–		11	10	4	289	99	48.16
A.D. Mullally	0	–			–	–					–	–	26	–	0	–	–		15	11	2	132	38*	14.66
D. Williamson			20	34															2	3	1	95	41*	47.50
D.I. Stevens			1	2															1	2	–	3	2	1.50
C.D. Crowe			2	23	29*	–	26	–			–	–			6	–			6	6	1	88	29*	17.60
Byes	12	4		4	2				3				1	8	3									
Leg-byes	12		8	22	11		8		25	3	9		4	8	6		14							
Wides	2		9	5	4						4		2	2			14							
No-balls	22	4	16	34	8		12		26	2	9		16		16		14							
Total	484	204	245	362	218		271		452	101	505		389	291	395		585							
Wickets	10	6	10	10	7		10		10	2	6		10	6	10		6							
Result	W		L		D		W		W		W		W		W		W							
Points	24		–		4		22		24		24		24		24		24							

Fielding Figures

47 – P.A. Nixon (ct 42 / st 5)
23 – P.V. Simmons
17 – D.L. Maddy
13 – B.F. Smith
12 – I.J. Sutcliffe
11 – V.J. Wells and A. Habib
9 – C.C. Lewis
4 – D.J. Millns
3 – D. Williamson, C.D. Crowe, A.D. Mullally and M.T. Brimson
2 – J.M. Dakin
1 – sub

Leicestershire CCC First-Class Matches

Bowling

Match	A.D. Mullally	D.J. Millns	C.C. Lewis	M.T. Brimson	J.M. Dakin	D.L. Maddy	C.D. Crowe	J. Ormond	D. Williamson	V.J. Wells	P.Y. Simmons	T.J. Mason	Byes	Leg-byes	Wides	No-balls	Total	Wkts	
v. Cambridge University (Cambridge) 17–19 April																		Ab	
	18–8–48–0	17–6–72–2	5–1–23–2	20–10–21–3	14–5–37–0	1–1–0–0							2	11	9	29	268	7	A
v. Worcestershire (Leicester) 23–27 April	14–7–33–4	7–1–25–0	16.3–3–60–6							4–2–5–0			9	2		8	134	10	
	24–10–54–4	15–3–44–2	22.2–5–85–2	7–2–15–0		5–2–9–1				6–2–13–0	7–1–26–1		2	11	6	22	259	10	
v. Gloucestershire (Bristol) 13–16 May	36.5–15–72–5			22.4–9–36–0	14–4–58–1				20–4–59–1	16–8–34–3	7–0–22–0	20.2–5–67–0	4	9	6	6	361	10	
	20–8–45–3			28–9–68–1	25–8–38–3				3–0–14–0	5–2–7–0		25–4–72–0	5	4	2	2	276	8	B
v. Hampshire (Leicester) 21–24 May	14–3–51–2		12–2–56–3					14.1–6–50–5					12	8	6	16	177	10	
	23.4–9–57–4		19–4–76–0	12–7–24–2		2–1–11–0		5–0–22–1		13–7–19–3			1	7	3	12	217	10	
v. Derbyshire (Chesterfield) 29 May–1 June	21–10–53–0		14–2–41–1	24.2–8–60–2	6–1–33–0	6–1–18–0				3–0–10–0	17–5–52–0			6		14	273	3	
v. Yorkshire (Leeds) 3–6 June	18–5–45–4		14–1–40–2	5–3–8–1				15–9–18–0		3–1–4–0			1	4	2	10	120	7	
v. Kent (Leicester) 11–14 June	6–3–12–1		5–2–17–0	1–1–0–0	8–3–14–0					6–0–18–2	3–2–11–0		1	1		8	74	3	
v. Glamorgan (Cardiff) 17–20 June	18–7–47–2		15–5–47–3	8–6–4–4	5–1–12–0					8–3–23–0			4	7		4	144	10	
	28–11–56–1	25–6–68–4	12–4–49–2	20–5–72–2						11–1–48–1			4	5		22	302	10	
v. Sussex (Leicester) 26–29 June	22–10–33–1		9–2–29–1	2–2–0–0			1–0–2–0			10–3–15–1	19.2–4–49–7			6		16	134	10	
v. Durham (Darlington) 1–4 July	11–3–28–1		9–1–24–0	6.4–2–21–2			13–2–49–3			12–5–30–3	6–1–20–1			5	2	6	177	10	
v. Northamptonshire (Leicester) 14–17 July	18–3–62–5	19–4–61–1	14.5–1–73–1	16–5–55–1		3–0–19–1				11–2–45–1			4	3		30	322	10	
	27.1–9–48–4	28–4–83–2	23–3–82–1	51–23–88–3		3–0–15–0				4–1–8–0	6–1–17–0		1	23	4	34	365	10	
v. Sri Lankans (Leicester) 24–27 July		1–0–14–0		22–3–84–2	38–6–110–4	10–2–47–0	33.4–3–120–1		28–6–110–3				5	19	1	12	509	10	
		10–2–49–0		2.5–0–7–0	5–0–21–0		7–2–20–1							2		2	99	1	
v. Lancashire (Old Trafford) 30 July–3 August																		Ab	
v. Somerset (Leicester) 5–8 August		6–3–8–0						11.4–2–33–6		9–1–30–3	2–0–3–1				2	2	74	10	
		12–0–46–2		8–3–17–1			1–0–2–0	16.4–8–29–3		8–3–12–3	5–3–6–1					10	112	10	
v. Middlesex (Leicester) 19–22 August		25.3–7–65–4		12–5–38–0	15–2–46–0	4–2–11–0		26–11–56–2		19–6–27–3	22–6–56–1		5	3		6	307	10	
		16.3–3–49–3		24–5–52–1	1–1–0–0			21–5–46–1		14–3–42–3	24–6–42–1		2	12		4	245	10	
v. Nottinghamshire (Worksop) 26–29 August	12–2–34–4							9–5–9–1		8.3–4–18–5					2		61	10	
	26–10–55–7			22.4–5–63–2			1–0–3–0	15–5–48–0		8–3–31–0	8–6–9–0		8	4		12	221	10	
v. Warwickshire (Edgbaston) 1–4 September	17–1–77–0	8–1–35–0	18–2–76–5	10–4–19–1						3–1–10–0	10.3–2–54–4		1	4	8	35	276	10	
	19–3–75–1	14–1–60–4	17–5–51–2	17–5–54–1						6–1–36–0	10–0–50–2		1	4	4	14	331	10	
v. Essex (Leicester) 9–12 September	11–4–23–2	7–5–8–3	11–4–40–2							6.4–2–17–3			1	6		2	95	10	
	15–2–45–2	10.3–1–62–3	20–5–72–4				5–3–5–1			4–3–1–0	4–3–3–0		2	11		12	201	10	
v. Surrey (The Oval) 17–20 September	10–4–26–2	9–3–36–2	6–1–12–2	6–1–33–1						6–2–11–0	6–1–21–1		4	3		4	146	10	
	20–9–54–1	13–5–32–2	4–0–19–0	21.4–6–62–3							14–3–50–3			11	4	10	228	10	
	449.4–156–113–60	243.3–55–817–34	266.4–53–972–39	369.5–129–901–33	131–31–369–8	34–9–130–2	61.4–10–201–6	133.3–51–311–19	51–10–183–4	199.1–66–514–36	170.5–44–491–23	45.2–9–139–0							
Bowler's average	18.88	24.02	24.92	27.30	46.12	65.00	33.50	16.36	45.75	14.27	21.34	–							

A I.J. Sutcliffe 6–0–34–0, A. Habib and B.F. Smith 2–0–5–0
B I.J. Sutcliffe 3–0–17–1 and B.F. Smith 3–0–6–0

Fielding Figures

45 – K.R. Brown (ct 40 / st 5)
20 – P.N. Weekes
19 – M.W. Gatting
12 – J.L. Langer
10 – O.A. Shah
9 – D.C. Nash (ct 8 / st 1)
7 – R.A. Kettleborough
5 – R.L. Johnson, J.R. Hewitt and M.R. Ramprakash
3 – K.P. Dutch and A.J. Strauss
2 – P.C.R. Tufnell and sub
1 – C.J. Batt, D.J. Goodchild, A.R.C. Fraser and I.N. Blanchett

Middlesex CCC First-Class Matches Batting

Batting	v. Kent (Canterbury) 17–21 April		v. Lancashire (Old Trafford) 23–27 April		v. Somerset (Lord's) 13–16 May		v. Worcestershire (Uxbridge) 21–24 May		v. Glamorgan (Lord's) 29 May–1 June		v. Durham (Lord's) 3–6 June		v. Oxford University (Oxford) 13–16 June		v. Northamptonshire (Northampton) 17–20 June		v. Essex (Southgate) 26–29 June		v. Nottinghamshire (Trent Bridge) 1–4 July		M	Inns	NO	Runs	HS	Av
R.A. Kettleborough	27	11*	20	–	31	19	5	24	19	17	18	0	92*	–	18*	0					12	22	4	512	92*	28.44
J.L. Langer	44	12*	68	–	5	233*	97	118	35	153*	35	1			55*	3*	166	–	74	29	15	28	5	1448	233*	62.95
M.R. Ramprakash	25	–	10	–			122	108*	3	128*							43*	–			9	15	2	635	128*	48.84
M.W. Gatting	5	–			22	20	39	83*	12	–	13	66	62	–	–	17	241	–	32	4	17	29	3	1139	241	43.80
O.A. Shah	40	–	64*	–	0	0	17	20	15	–	47	14	79*	–	–	48	1*	–	0	0	15	23	3	786	140	39.30
D.C. Nash	10	–	12	–	0	114	15	0	76	–	26	10	–	–	–	0	–	–	15	10	14	19	–	404	114	21.26
K.R. Brown	17	–	–	–	1	45*			17	–	3	5			–	27*	–	–	22	9	17	25	6	576	59*	30.31
R.L. Johnson	1	–	–	–	27	–	2	–											0	0	14	21	3	242	43	13.44
J.P. Hewitt	3	–	–	–	47	–	25	–	24	–	53	19			–	30*	–	–	22	19	15	19	2	268	53	15.76
A.R.C. Fraser	6	–	–	–	6	–			30	–							–	–			8	9	2	63	30	9.00
T.F. Bloomfield	8*	–									0	0			–	–	–	–	0	3*	8	10	5	37	20*	7.40
P.N. Weekes			21*	–	42	–	11	0*			93*	51*			–	10	–	–	0	25	16	26	5	903	139	43.00
P.C.R. Tufnell			–	–	0*	–	10*	–	7*	–	7	19			–	–	–	–	0*	8	17	22	6	155	24	9.68
I.N. Blanchett							18	–	0	–	6	1	–	–							4	4	–	25	18	6.25
J.C. Pooley													–	–							1	–	–	–	–	–
K.P. Dutch													–	–							4	5	–	41	16	8.20
A. Laraman													–	–							1	–	–	–	–	–
N.D. Martin													–	–	–	–					2	–	–	–	–	–
C.J. Batt													–	–					6	7	9	14	2	150	43	12.50
U.B.A. Rashid													–	–							1	–	–	–	–	–
D.J. Goodchild																					7	14	1	324	105	24.92
A.J. Strauss																					3	6	–	146	83	24.33
Byes			2			1	6	2	5		5	8	3				6		3							
Leg-byes	10		4		5	10	16	6	9	14	9	5	7			8	11		8	1						
Wides	8				4			2	2	2	2		10		2		7		2							
No-balls	24		4		14	8	6	10	2		18	17	2		6	4	13		14	8						
Total	228	23	205		204	450	389	373	256	314	335	216	255		81	147	488	0	198	123						
Wickets	10	0	4		10	4	10	5	10	1	10	10	1		0	5	2	0	10	10						
Result	L		D		W		D		W		L		D		D		D		L							
Points	1		4		21		9		22		7		–		7		8		3							

Batting	v. Surrey (Guildford) 15–18 July		v. Yorkshire (Lord's) 22–25 July		v. Sri Lankans (Lord's) 31 July–3 August		v. Warwickshire (Lord's) 5–8 August		v. Sussex (Hove) 14–17 August		v. Leicestershire (Leicester) 19–22 August		v. Hampshire (Southampton) 31 August–3 September		v. Gloucestershire (Lord's) 9–12 September		v. Derbyshire (Derby) 17–20 September		M	Inns	NO	Runs	HS	Av
R.A. Kettleborough					9	38							60	62*	0	11	30	1	12	22	4	512	92*	28.44
J.L. Langer	14	20	63	9	43	12	33	55	13	4	10	44							15	28	5	1448	233*	62.95
M.R. Ramprakash	13	16							3	36	110	0			10	8			9	15	2	635	128*	48.84
M.W. Gatting	0	0	22	103*			11	91	0	6	0	73	77	33*	35	2	8	62	17	29	3	1139	241	43.80
O.A. Shah			140	–			52	52			2	11			36	4	28	116	15	23	3	786	140	39.30
D.C. Nash	0	25	23	–	1	42	23	2											14	19	–	404	114	21.26
K.R. Brown	30	59*	40	–	25	40*	26	37*	18	21	19	20	53	–	9	0	27*	6	17	25	6	576	59*	30.31
R.L. Johnson	11	8	17	–	8	4	17	2	30	0*	4	23*	23	–	9*	4	43	9	14	21	3	242	43	13.44
J.P. Hewitt			5	–					0	6	0	1	1	–	0	3*	1	9	15	19	2	268	53	15.76
A.R.C. Fraser	11*	10													0	0	0	0*	8	9	2	63	30	9.00
T.F. Bloomfield					2*	–	3*	0	20*	1									8	10	5	37	20*	7.40
P.N. Weekes	5	7	67	–	43	49	89	0	31	3	139	49	17	29*	21	5	0	96	16	26	5	903	139	43.00
P.C.R. Tufnell	2	8	14	–	24	–	0	0	1	0	4*	6	7*	–	1	16	11	10	17	22	6	155	24	9.68
I.N. Blanchett																			4	4	–	25	18	6.25
J.C. Pooley																			1	–	–	–	–	–
K.P. Dutch	11	6			0	8							16	–					4	5	–	41	16	8.20
A. Laraman																			1	–	–	–	–	–
N.D. Martin																			2	–	–	–	–	–
C.J. Batt	0	5	23*	–	11	18*	6	43	11	0	5	0	15	–					9	14	2	150	43	12.50
U.B.A. Rashid																			1	–	–	–	–	–
D.J. Goodchild			0	83*	105	6	14	73	0	4	0	0	16	5			10	8	7	14	1	324	105	24.92
A.J. Strauss													83	12	24	6	8	13	3	6	–	146	83	24.33
Byes	4	2	9	6		2		7	1		5	2	15	16			1	4						
Leg-byes	4	5	13	4	7	4	12	9	2	1	3	12	18	4	5	1	8	12						
Wides	4	2	2		4					4			2	8		2	2	4						
No-balls	6	2	10	2	31	8	11	2	12	4	6	4	34	4	8	10	18	4						
Total	115	175	448	207	313	231	297	373	142	90	307	245	437	173	158	72	195	354						
Wickets	10	10	10	1	10	7	10	10	10	10	10	10	10	2	10	10	10	10						
Result	L		D		D		D		L		L		L		L		L							
Points	4		10		–		8		4		6		8		4		4							

Middlesex CCC First-Class Matches

Bowling

	A.R.C. Fraser	J.P. Hewitt	T.F. Bloomfield	R.L. Johnson	M.R. Ramprakash	O.A. Shah	P.C.R. Tufnell	P.N. Weekes	I.N. Blanchett	J.L. Langer	C.J. Batt	K.P. Dutch	Byes	Leg-byes	Wides	No-balls	Total	Wkts	
v. Kent (Canterbury) 17–21 April																	0	0	
	19.4–1–79–1	14–3–49–2	6–1–29–1	14–2–71–2	5–1–16–0									9	6	6	253	6	
v. Lancashire (Old Trafford) 23–27 April																		Ab	
v. Somerset (Lord's) 13–16 May	21–5–51–3	20–4–74–0		23–4–86–7		2–0–12–0	11–2–18–0	2–0–5–0					5	2	8	10	253	10	
	17–3–39–4	9–0–41–2		17–4–48–2			13–3–34–2	6–2–14–0					4	10		4	190	10	
v. Worcestershire (Uxbridge) 21–24 May		27–5–105–2		29–7–105–1		8.5–0–46–1	40–4–136–1	25–0–86–0	28–1–125–1				1	7	2	16	627	6	A
v. Glamorgan (Lord's) 29 May–1 June	26.1–7–66–3	24–5–69–5			14–2–33–2		31–6–76–0		15–1–56–0				1	7		12	308	10	
	19–5–47–3	11–1–49–0			12.2–3–32–3		36–13–88–2		12–1–38–2					6	6	2	260	10	
v. Durham (Lord's) 3–6 June		26–7–82–3	22.5–0–98–5			1–0–3–0	25–11–29–0	10–0–43–0	20–6–52–2					5	4	10	312	10	
		18–0–59–2	16–3–43–3				30.2–11–89–3	7–0–22–1	3–0–14–0				2	11	2	2	240	9	
v. Oxford University (Oxford) 13–16 June									6–0–22–0		9–1–31–4	9–0–25–1				2	100	6	B
v. Northamptonshire (Northampton) 17–20 June		27–6–109–3	21–12–67–5			4–1–9–0	23–4–72–0	11.3–3–31–1		5–3–10–1			1	6	6	18	366	10	C
																	0	0	
v. Essex (Southgate) 26–29 June	11–5–19–1	6–2–8–1	12–0–56–0		1–1–0–0		14–1–43–0	9–0–24–1						1		12	151	3	
	20–5–45–2	7–2–9–0	8–3–20–1		5–0–18–0		34–9–102–3	30–3–113–3					1	7	2	2	315	9	D
v. Nottinghamshire (Trent Bridge) 1–4 July		18–6–60–0	23–6–74–1	27–5–89–2			21–9–43–0	16–6–17–1		1–1–0–0	29–6–101–6		3	26	4	10	413	10	
v. Surrey (Guildford) 15–18 July	16.1–6–34–4			6–0–24–0			18–10–24–1				15–3–51–5	2–0–3–0		14	4	2	150	10	
	25–5–76–2			21–1–85–3			27–5–59–2	4–1–10–0		2–0–6–0	27–1–109–2	22–7–47–1	9	19	6	8	420	10	
v. Yorkshire (Lord's) 22–25 July		17–1–80–0		24–8–72–4			35.3–10–65–4	16–4–47–1		1–0–1–0	18–5–60–0		4	6		32	335	10	
		10–1–49–0		15.5–3–58–2			36–13–77–4	12–1–45–2			5–0–27–0		11	18	6	24	285	8	
v. Sri Lankans (Lord's) 31 July–3 August			22–2–74–2	22–5–72–1			24–4–90–3				22.5–1–103–4	13–4–43–0	8	14	2	10	424	10	E
v. Warwickshire (Lord's) 5–8 August			22–6–101–2	26.2–7–60–4		2–0–9–0	35–6–93–2	12–1–53–0		4–1–17–0	21–2–88–2		4	21		6	466	10	F
			4–0–53–1	8.5–2–32–3			7–1–24–4	1–0–4–0			3–0–24–0		8	5	6	8	150	8	
v. Sussex (Hove) 14–17 August		17.3–3–71–6	12–1–45–1	21–7–63–0			22–6–58–1	20–1–43–0			20–2–85–1			14		38	392	10	G
v. Leicestershire (Leicester) 19–22 August		26–2–85–4		31.2–6–129–4	4–1–4–0		37–8–76–1	16–2–49–0			11–1–72–0		3	25		26	452	10	H
		5–1–16–1		6–1–33–1	1–0–9–0		10–3–16–0	11–3–24–0						3		2	101	2	
v. Hampshire (Southampton) 31 August–3 September		18–2–82–1		17–4–75–4			24–4–79–2				16–1–60–3		8	7	9	30	311	10	
		13–0–79–0		11–2–42–0			21–2–80–2	10.5–3–42–1			5–0–35–0	3–0–13–0	6	4	18	12	301	3	
v. Gloucestershire (Lord's) 9–12 September	25.4–7–48–3	22–5–61–3		23–6–56–4			12–3–42–0	1–0–4–0						8	12		238	10	
	13.2–4–23–6	7–3–14–2		8–0–50–2										1			88	10	I
v. Derbyshire (Derby) 17–20 September	26–7–7–78–1	28–4–95–3		14–0–82–2			19.1–4–34–2	4–1–5–0					12	14	6	10	383	10	
	12–4–13–1	7–1–32–1		12–3–37–2			26–11–55–0	12.4–3–21–2					2	7		8	167	6	J
Bowler's average	252–64– 618–34 18.17	377.3–64– 1378–41 33.60	168.5–34– 660–22 30.00	377.2–77– 1369–50 27.38	42.2–8– 112–5 22.40	17.5–1– 79–1 79.00	632–163– 1602–39 41.07	237–37– 702–13 54.00	84–9– 307–5 61.40	13–5– 34–1 34.00	210.5–23– 846–27 31.33	49–11– 131–2 65.50							

A R.A. Kettleborough 4–0–16–0
B N.D. Martin 6–1–22–1
C N.D. Martin 12–1–6–0
D D.C. Nash 0.1–0–0–0
E D.J. Goodchild 6–0–20–0
F D.J. Goodchild 7–1–20–0
G D.J. Goodchild 3–0–13–0
H D.J. Goodchild 1–0–9–0
I R.A. Kettleborough 5–0–19–0
J R.A. Kettleborough 14–1–54–0
J M.W. Satting 5–1–9–1

Northamptonshire CCC First-Class Matches Batting

Batting	v. Cambridge University (Cambridge) 14–16 April		v. Surrey (The Oval) 17–21 April		v. Hampshire (Southampton) 23–27 April		v. Yorkshire (Northampton) 13–15 May		v. Glamorgan (Northampton) 21–24 May		v. Lancashire (Northampton) 3–6 June		v. Durham (Riverside) 11–14 June		v. Middlesex (Northampton) 17–20 June		v. Worcestershire (Worcester) 1–4 July		v. Leicestershire (Leicester) 14–17 July		M	Inns	NO	Runs	HS	Av
R.R. Montgomerie	46*	–	13	29*	3	–	22	49*	1	2	6	21									10	16	3	268	54	20.61
A.J. Swann	1	–	29	1	19	–	5	1	5	2			30	–	1	–					11	17	–	250	85	14.70
M.B. Loye	14	–	0*	–	77	–	28	4	29	322*	149	71	6	–	78	–			76	19	15	22	2	1198	322*	59.90
D.J.G. Sales	9	–	–	–	4	–	60	–	0	22							4	5	5	10	14	21	1	346	60	17.30
K.M. Curran	41*	–	–	–	58*	–	2	–	54	21	4	90*	8	–	61	–	4	12	18	18	18	26	4	709	90*	32.22
D. Ripley	–	–	–	–	–	–	35	–	59	209	56	24	9	–	51	–	18	5	10	32	17	22	2	805	209	40.25
A.L. Penberthy	–	–									47	15	20	–	102*	–	6	2	18	17	14	21	2	755	128	39.73
D.J. Capel	–	–	–	–																	2	–	–	–	–	–
G.P. Swann	–	–	–	14*	–	–	49	–	4	17	12	4*	31	–	3	–	5	12	92	111	14	18	2	548	111	34.25
S.A.J. Boswell	–	–																			1	–	–	–	–	–
J.A.R. Blain	–	–																			1	–	–	–	–	–
R.J. Bailey			–	–	53*	–	35	46*	4	32	19	31	10	–	10	–	21	24	5	29	16	24	2	759	188	34.50
J.P. Taylor			–	–	58	–	32*	–	0	0	4	–					4	7*	41	56	15	20	3	371	58	21.82
D.E. Malcom			–	–	–	–	0	–	2	42	0*	–	2*	–	14	–	1*	0	14*	4*	14	16	5	114	42	10.36
F.A. Rose					–	–	10	–	3*	10	0	–	12	–	12	–	0	0	1	5	14	17	2	133	21	8.86
R.J. Warren											11	4	1	–	3	–	3	1	5	2	5	8	–	30	11	3.75
D. Follett													7	–	0	–					5	7	1	13	7	2.16
D.J. Roberts																	39	0			1	2	–	39	39	19.50
J.F. Brown																					8	11	5	18	6*	3.00
K.J. Innes																					1	2	0	37	31	18.50
M.K. Davies																					1	2	1	7	4	7.00
T.M.B. Bailey																					1	1	0	12	12	12.00
Byes	4						6	2		12	5	4	1		1				4	1						
Leg-byes	3				1		12	1	5	5	17	4	6		6		1	3	3	23						
Wides	2						6		4	6			10		10		6	4		4						
No-balls	2		2	2	2		30	2	2	10	2	6	10		18		2	2	30	34						
Total	122		44	46	275	0	332	105	172	712	332	274	163		366	0	114	77	322	365						
Wickets	3		2	1	5	0	10	2	10	10	10	6	10		10	0	10	10	10	10						
Result	D		D		D		W		D		D		D		D		L		L							
Points	–		5		5		23		6		10		4		7		4		7							

Batting

Batting	v. Derbyshire (Northampton) 22–25 July		v. Nottinghamshire (Trent Bridge) 30 July–2 August		v. Somerset (Taunton) 14–17 August		v. Warwickshire (Northampton) 19–22 August		v. Kent (Northampton) 26–29 August		v. Gloucestershire (Bristol) 1–4 September		v. Sussex (Northampton) 9–12 September		v. Essex (Chelmsford) 17–20 September		M	Inns	NO	Runs	HS	Av
R.R. Montgomerie	2	–	54	–	15	3					0	2					10	16	3	268	54	20.61
A.J. Swann									85	–	0	10	9	12	0	40	11	17	–	250	85	14.70
M.B. Loye	157	–	103	–	13	0	1	1	38	–	0	12					15	22	2	1198	322*	59.90
D.J.G. Sales			20	–	41	9	4	40	22	–	25	0	13	0	53	0*	14	21	1	346	60	17.30
K.M. Curran	59	–	15	–	41	44	17	17	3	–	7	0	60	46	0	9*	18	26	4	709	90*	32.22
D. Ripley	29	–	11*	–	6	54*	98	48	20	–	4	17	5	5			17	22	2	805	209	40.25
A.L. Penberthy	68*	–	49	–	0	53	128	45	61	–	30	6	12	11	50	15	14	21	2	755	128	39.73
D.J. Capel																	2	–	–	–	–	–
G.P. Swann	91	–					32	13					26	12	20	–	14	18	2	548	111	34.25
S.A.J. Boswell																	1	–	–	–	–	–
J.A.R. Blain																	1	–	–	–	–	–
R.J. Bailey	188	–	42	–	1	17	0	35	79	–			9	4	19	46	16	24	2	759	188	34.50
J.P. Taylor	–	–	20	–	22	5	4*	0	21	–	6	4	7	22	58	–	15	20	3	371	58	21.82
D.E. Malcom	–	–	0	–	12	7	8	0							8	–	14	16	5	114	42	10.36
F.A. Rose	–	–	7	–	21	0			19	–	13*	18			2	–	14	17	2	133	21	8.86
R.J. Warren																	5	8	–	30	11	3.75
D. Follett							0	0	6*	–	0	0					5	7	1	13	7	2.16
D.J. Roberts																	1	2	–	39	39	19.50
J.F. Brown	–	–	0	–	6*	0	0	0*	1	–	2	3*	2	0*	4*	–	8	11	5	18	6*	3.00
K.J. Innes													6	31			1	2	0	37	31	18.50
M.K. Davies													3*	4			1	2	1	7	4	7.00
T.M.B. Bailey															12	–	1	1	0	12	12	12.00
Byes	1				4	4	13	2	2		10	8	4	4	12	2						
Leg-byes	9		3		3	7	8	5	14		2	5	4	10	4	4						
Wides	2							2	8						2							
No-balls	2		22		2	2	6	6	12		24	10	18	4	18	4						
Total	608		346		187	205	319	214	391		123	95	178	165	262	120						
Wickets	6		10		10	10	10	10	10		10	10	10	10	10	3						
Result	W		D		L		L		D		L		W		W							
Points	24		8		4		7		11		4		20		22							

Fielding Figures

32 – D. Ripley (ct 31 / st 1)
23 – K.M. Curran
14 – A.L. Penberthy
10 – D.J.G. Sales and R.J. Bailey
7 – R.J. Warren and M.B. Loye
6 – G.P. Swann and A.J. Swann
5 – J.P. Taylor
4 – R.R. Montgomerie and sub
3 – D.J. Roberts and D.E. Malcolm
2 – K.J. Innes, T.M.B. Bailey and D. Follet
1 – J.F. Brown

Northamptonshire CCC First-Class Matches Bowling

	D.E. Malcom	J.P. Taylor	K.M. Curran	D.J. Capel	G.P. Swann	F.A. Rose	R.J. Bailey	D.J.G. Sales	A.J. Swann	A.L. Penberthy	D. Follett	J.F. Brown	Byes	Leg-byes	Wides	No-balls	Total	Wkts	
v. Cambridge University																			
(Cambridge) 14–16 April	23–5–72–1	27–4–90–2	8–3–17–0	13–1–66–1	13–1–91–1								4	11	8		351	Ab. 5	
v. Surrey																			
(The Oval) 17–21 April																	0	0	
v. Hampshire	21–4–60–5	15–5–38–0	6–1–18–0		13–5–12–0	18.5–4–57–2	2–1–4–1							4		15	193	8	
(Southampton) 23–27 April	18–4–54–6	16–5–50–3				10–1–36–1								8	2	4	148	10	
v. Yorkshire	22.3–2–87–3	14–4–37–3	1–0–1–0		22–4–69–3	26–7–73–1	1–0–6–0						1	14		14	288	10	
(Northampton) 13–16 May	28–3–144–3	25.5–1–105–3	5–3–24–0		24–3–98–1	28–3–130–2	1–1–0–0	9–2–28–1	3–0–12–0				6	16	2	14	563	10	
v. Glamorgan		2–0–20–0				4–1–15–0			1–0–4–0				4	1		4	44	0	
(Northampton) 21–24 May	15.1–2–52–3	13–2–49–2	7–2–22–0			24–4–89–5				4–0–12–0			4	2	9	22	230	10	
v. Lancashire	25–0–145–4	18–3–61–2	5–2–17–0		21–2–80–1	16–0–66–1	1–0–6–0			8–1–41–0			2	20		2	438	8	
(Northampton) 3–6 June	22–8–66–2		5–0–19–0		11–2–38–0	14.3–2–55–1				7–1–10–0	17–3–51–1		2	8		8	249	4	
v. Durham																			
(Riverside) 11–14 June									1.3–0–39–0						2	6	81	0	A
v. Middlesex	19–4–42–2				11–5–27–1	14–3–35–0					8–1–35–2			8		4	147	5	
(Northampton) 17–20 June	6–0–33–0	15.5–3–33–1	6–0–25–1			16–5–39–7							1	5		4	136	10	
v. Worcestershire	12–1–67–3	18–9–43–2	10–3–35–1			17.5–5–51–4				6–2–10–0				6	2	6	212	10	
(Worcester) 1–4 July	25–2–113–2	34–9–75–2	10–3–22–0		13–2–56–0	28.2–1–123–5	11–2–21–0			15–2–50–0			12	12	2	22	484	10	
v. Leicestershire	1–0–16–0	9–0–91–1				9.1–0–93–3							4			4	204	6	
(Leicester) 14–17 July	8–2–26–0	21–5–54–2	2–1–1–0		7.3–4–6–2	17–2–53–3						28–5–78–3	1	6		4	225	10	
v. Derbyshire	11–2–38–1	10–1–42–0			23–4–91–4	8–0–47–1						21.4–4–62–4	4	5		4	289	10	
(Northampton) 22–25 July	21–2–93–0	30.1–13–62–4	4–1–13–0			24–5–105–0	5–1–12–1	2–0–8–0		7–2–21–0		14–2–48–0	5	13		22	380	5	
v. Nottinghamshire																			
(Trent Bridge) 30 July–3 August	9–1–37–0	19–6–32–3	4–1–13–0			20–3–45–2						20–4–49–5	1	2		2	179	10	
v. Somerset	7–3–20–0	15–3–48–1				2–0–9–0	27–8–57–1					41.1–18–53–6	10	17			214	8	
(Taunton) 14–17 August	13–2–55–0	18–3–74–3	3–0–25–0		8–2–17–0		7–0–20–2				18–1–83–0	37–7–114–5	8	16		4	412	10	
v. Warwickshire		12–2–58–4									9–0–40–2	2.4–0–14–0		10		6	122	6	
(Northampton) 19–22 August		25–4–71–4				20.3–2–75–4					10–5–19–1	15–3–41–1	4	8	4	18	218	10	
v. Kent		13–5–30–2				15–2–51–1	11–1–52–1		1–0–4–0	6–0–26–0	23–4–47–1	43–8–148–2	12	7		12	377	7	
(Northampton) 26–29 August		23–7–55–3	2–0–13–0			23.5–8–63–4					17–3–48–3	5–1–21–0	4	6		18	210	10	
v. Gloucestershire						1.5–0–7–0					1–0–2–0					2	9	0	
(Bristol) 1–4 September		7–2–20–0								2–1–2–0		15.5–3–23–5	1	7	2		72	10	B
v. Sussex		6–2–10–2			13.1–5–29–5					3–1–17–0		13–5–27–0	5	12			135	10	
(Northampton) 9–12 September	12–0–63–1	14–2–58–1			16–1–47–4	14.3–1–50–3				7–3–15–0		19–6–44–1	4	2		10	283	10	
v. Essex	15.2–1–48–4	16–5–31–4			4–1–5–0							5–2–4–1	5	2		2	95	9	
(Chelmsford) 17–20 September																			
	334–48–	436.5–105–	78–20–	13–1–	199.4–41–	373.2–59–	66–14–	11–2–	6.3–0–	65–13–	103–17–	280.2–68–							
	1331–40	1337–54	265–2	66–1	666–22	1367–50	178–6	36–1	59–0	204–0	325–10	726–33							
Bowler's average	33.27	24.75	132.50	66.00	30.27	27.34	29.66	36.00	–	–	32.50	22.00							

A M.D. Loye 2–0–42–0
B M.K. Davies 19–10–19–5, 20–7–35–2

Nottinghamshire CCC First-Class Matches Batting

	v. Derbyshire (Derby) 17–20 April		v. Somerset (Taunton) 23–27 April		v. Sussex (Trent Bridge) 13–16 May		v. Warwickshire (Edgbaston) 21–24 May		v. Durham (Trent Bridge) 29 May–1 June		v. Essex (Ilford) 3–6 June		v. Kent (Canterbury) 17–20 June		v. Glamorgan (Trent Bridge) 26–29 June		v. Middlesex (Trent Bridge) 1–4 July		v. Yorkshire (Scarborough) 15–18 July		M	Inns	NO	Runs	HS	Av
M.P. Dowman	19	4	–	4	1	7	44	63	13	8	48	12	12	1*	4	10			4	36	13	24	1	451	63	19.60
P.R. Pollard	12	0	–	10	24	0															4	7	–	121	69	17.28
J.E.R. Gallian	2	26	–	0*	3	33							92	80	13*	3	52	–	0	4	14	25	3	592	113*	26.90
P. Johnson	13	49	–	0*	68	7	45	17			95	17	46	16	–	40	0	–	5	23	15	26	1	976	139	39.04
R.T. Robinson	5	41	–	–	31	0	11	8	0	64	3	54	58	76	13*	12	35	–	114	28	11	18	2	553	114	34.56
U. Afzaal	0	109*	–	–	22	0	0	73*	25	0	31	4	18	4	1	51	73	–	71	4	17	30	3	686	109*	25.40
C.M. Tolley	9	51					12	3*	7	6					–	1	15	–			11	19	2	374	78	22.00
A.G. Wharf	2	3	–	–	0	0											1*	–	2	–	5	6	1	8	3	1.60
W.M. Noon	6	0	–	–	0	0	16*	–													4	5	1	22	16*	5.50
K.P. Evans	28	0													–	1	22	–	3	–	9	13	–	129	36	9.92
M.N. Bowen	2*	5	–	–	25	8*	18	–	9*	32	0	8*	16	–	–	14					10	13	5	142	32	17.75
P.A. Strang			–	–	48	48	18*	–	13	10	30	14	23*	–			40	–	2*	–	13	18	3	300	48	20.00
P.J. Franks			–	–			33	–	66	4	3	34	3	66*			5	–	0	29*	12	20	2	390	66*	21.66
A.R. Oram					2*	4	0	–	1	1	2*	0*	1	–	–	0*					11	19	8	39	13	3.54
N.A. Gie							1	5	20	20	12	18									4	8	–	128	50	16.00
G.F. Archer									11	44	63	69	1	51	–	107	51	–	10	12	13	23	–	647	107	28.13
C.M.W. Read									0	16*	27	28	8	4*	–	14	76	–	5	1*	13	22	6	401	76	25.06
G.E. Welton																					5	9	–	152	55	16.88
R.T. Bates																					2	4	2	17	7	8.50
M.J.A. Whiley																					1	2	1	0	0*	–
Byes		1					2	2	9	1	4	1				8	3		2	4						
Leg-byes	2	3			7	9	4	6	3	1	10	8	13	1		1	26		10	5						
Wides	2				22				20	13	12		10	4		4	4		2							
No-balls	16	20		2	22	6	14	16	14	4	2	12	8	4		8	10		4	14						
Total	118	312	0	16	275	122	218	193	211	224	342	279	309	307	31	274	413		234	160						
Wickets	10	10	0	2	10	10	9	4	10	10	10	9	10	5	2	10	10		10	6						
Result	L		D		L		W		L		D		L		L		W		D							
Points	2		7		6		21		5		9		7		3		23		7							

Batting

	v. Hampshire (Portsmouth) 22–25 July		v. Northamptonshire (Trent Bridge) 30 July–3 August		v. Worcestershire (Kidderminster) 5–8 August		v. Surrey (Trent Bridge) 19–22 August		v. Leicestershire (Worksop) 26–29 August		v. Lancashire (Trent Bridge) 11–14 September		v. Gloucestershire (Trent Bridge) 17–20 September		M	Inns	NO	Runs	HS	Av
M.P. Dowman	16	1	20	–					0	52			23	49	13	24	1	451	63	19.60
P.R. Pollard									6	69					4	7	–	121	69	17.28
J.E.R. Gallian	15	113*	25	–	14	6	23	17	4	14	3	0	33	17	14	25	3	592	113*	26.90
P. Johnson	18	66	105	–	43	139	8	14			19	90	0	33	15	26	1	976	139	39.04
R.T. Robinson	0*	–													11	18	2	553	114	34.56
U. Afzaal	15	18	103*	–	10	34	8	0	0	0	1	4	0	7	17	30	3	686	109*	25.40
C.M. Tolley			20*	–	1	48	4	17	12	25	27	8	30	78	11	19	2	374	78	22.00
A.G. Wharf															5	6	1	8	3	1.60
W.M. Noon															4	5	1	22	16*	5.50
K.P. Evans	4	0	–	–	6	36	6	19			4	0			9	13	–	129	36	9.92
M.N. Bowen	3*	2	–	–											10	13	5	142	32	17.75
P.A. Strang	4	0	–	–	11	0	18	5	8	8					13	18	3	300	48	20.00
P.J. Franks	23	22			0	19	8	0			13	30	32	0	12	20	2	390	66*	21.66
A.R. Oram					0*	4*	13	0	2*	1	1	0*	4	3	11	19	8	39	13	3.54
N.A. Gie													50	2	4	8	–	128	50	16.00
G.F. Archer	16	7	12	–	27	1	37	0	10	23	20	8	15	52	13	23	–	647	107	28.13
C.M.W. Read	5	6	–	–	13	17	66*	10*	10	0	4	4	46*	41	13	22	6	401	76	25.06
G.E. Welton			55	–	18	44	7	15	0	0	7	6			5	9	–	152	55	16.88
R.T. Bates									7	5*	4*	1			2	4	2	17	7	8.50
M.J.A. Whiley													0	0*	1	2	1	0	0*	–
Byes			5					8		8	8	2	2	2						
Leg-byes	1	2	13		1	12	3	12		4	2	10		2						
Wides	8	4				4	2		2				2							
No-balls		2	22		20	37	10	8		12	2	10	12	6						
Total	128	243	380		164	401	213	125	61	221	115	171	249	292						
Wickets	9	9	5		10	10	10	10	10	10	10	10	10	10						
Result	L		D		W		L		L		L		L							
Points	4		11		20		5		1		4		5							

Fielding Figures

41 – C.M.W. Read (ct 38 / st 3)
23 – G.F. Archer
19 – P.A. Strang
14 – P. Johnson
9 – W.M. Noon
8 – J.E.R. Gallian
7 – U. Afzaal and M.P. Dowman
6 – P.J. Francis, R.T. Robinson and A.G. Wharf
5 – C.M. Tolley
4 – sub
3 – P.R. Pollard, G.E. Welton, N.A. Gie and K.P. Evans
2 – M.N. Bowen
1 – A.R. Oram

Nottinghamshire CCC First-Class Matches Bowling	M.N. Bowen	A.G. Wharf	K.P. Evans	C.M. Tolley	J.E.R. Gallian	M.P. Dowman	P.J. Franks	P.A. Strang	A.R. Oram	U. Afzaal	R.T. Bates	M.J.A. Whiley	Byes	Leg-byes	Wides	No-balls	Total	Wkts
v. Derbyshire (Derby) 17–20 April	39–10–109–2	20–3–71–1	32.1–8–92–5	22–5–72–1	15–5–37–0	1–0–1–0								6		2	388	9
	3–0–13–1		2.5–0–30–1														43	4
v. Somerset (Taunton) 23–27 April	27.4–8–73–7	16–1–93–3			5–2–4–0		17–4–63–0	8–3–20–0						2	2	20	255	10
																	0	0
v. Sussex (Trent Bridge) 13–16 May	30.5–7–79–3	18–3–61–0			1.1–1–0–0	18–5–33–2		29.3–10–74–2	23–6–61–1				3	13	10	18	324	10
	6–1–11–0	8–3–25–3						10–2–26–3	4–0–11–0					1	4	2	74	6
v. Warwickshire (Edgbaston) 21–24 May	16–6–22–4			3–0–17–0			19–6–39–3	2–1–1–0	17.2–6–36–3				6	9	2		130	10
	28.3–8–59–3			8–1–46–1		14–5–45–2	19–2–64–1	3–1–11–0	24–11–35–3				7	13	2	2	280	10
v. Durham (Trent Bridge) 29 May–1 June	21–8–45–0			25–10–48–5		6–1–21–0	19–4–73–2	7.3–3–17–2	18–8–52–1				1	12	10		269	10
	7–1–20–0			5–0–17–0		4–0–19–0	11–1–32–0	13.2–4–37–1	10–2–35–1					7			167	2
v. Essex (Ilford) 3–6 June	27–9–71–1					1–1–0–1	26–10–57–3	36–13–84–1	29–8–89–3	5–2–11–1				10		2	322	10
	11–3–28–2					2–0–6–0	14–3–61–1	28–14–41–3	13–5–27–2	5.5–1–11–0			9	15			198	8
v. Kent (Canterbury) 17–20 June	24.1–5–66–2					7–4–10–2	27.5–4–104–4	25–13–30–1	17.1–2–67–1	2–0–5–0				1	2	14	283	10
	8–0–63–0					1–0–5–0	9–2–40–1	23–1–166–5		14.3–1–41–1			10	9		4	334	7
v. Glamorgan (Trent Bridge) 26–29 June	17–2–66–0		21–2–84–2	25–5–77–1		19–7–42–2			13–5–40–2	6–1–29–1			5	8		6	351	8
																	0	0
v. Middlesex (Trent Bridge) 1–4 July		9–2–40–0	20–8–43–0	18–7–51–4			15–5–38–3	7.2–3–15–2					3	8	2	14	198	10
		8.1–1–27–2	10–6–8–2	8–0–23–1			14–3–58–5	1–0–6–0						1		8	123	10
v. Yorkshire (Scarborough) 15–18 July		4–1–16–0	39–5–120–5			21–2–63–0	38.3–9–107–5	32–6–84–0						16	2	20	406	10
v. Hampshire (Portsmouth) 22–25 July	19–2–64–3		27–9–74–2			3–0–12–0	24–4–99–2	16.2–6–41–2		1.2–0–9–0				11		10	301	10
	9–4–32–2		8–1–23–1					3–1–6–0		3–1–17–0				3			73	3
v. Northamptonshire (Trent Bridge) 30 July–3 August	15–2–54–1		31–6–88–3	26–7–61–1		14–1–31–1		30.5–4–92–4						3		22	346	10
v. Worcestershire (Kidderminster) 5–8 August			28–8–52–1	25.4–4–66–2			30–13–63–6	16–4–56–1	9–0–45–0					7		20	289	10
			9–2–27–2	21.2–7–45–7			21–2–69–1	8–3–19–0	2–0–17–0				4	5	2	24	186	10
v. Surrey (Trent Bridge) 19–22 August			21–7–53–2	21–8–55–1			24–6–81–2	17–7–38–0	21–6–37–4				1	5		14	270	10
							4–0–12–2	3.4–0–15–1	5–0–22–0	4–0–19–0				4			72	3
v. Leicestershire (Worksop) 26–29 August				34–7–110–1	3–1–7–0	11–2–48–1		33–6–104–2	30–4–114–2	10–0–49–0	14–1–64–0			9	4	9	505	6
v. Lancashire (Trent Bridge) 11–14 September			20–8–40–1	22.5–5–74–6			13–4–35–1		16–2–63–2					6	4	10	218	10
			4–3–1–0	31–4–88–2	11–3–19–1		24–4–99–6		19.2–1–107–1		7–1–34–0			9	2	14	357	10
v. Gloucestershire (Trent Bridge) 17–20 September				15.4–4–57–1	7–1–14–1	8–2–34–1	20–1–89–3		14–4–55–3			15–1–66–1		4		22	319	10
				13–2–53–0	5–0–22–0	9–1–27–0	15–0–92–1		21–5–56–2	24–3–10–4		14–3–58–0		2		14	411	7
Bowler's average	309.1–76– 875–31 28.22	83.1–14– 333–9 37.00	273–73– 735–27 27.22	324.3–76– 960–34 28.33	47.1–13– 103–2 51.50	139–31– 397–12 33.08	404.2–87– 1375–52 26.44	353.3–105– 983–30 32.76	305.5–75– 969–31 31.25	75.4–9– 292–7 41.71	21–3– 98–0 –	29–4– 124–1 124.00						

Somerset CCC First-Class Matches Batting

	v. Yorkshire (Leeds) 17–21 April		v. Nottinghamshire (Taunton) 23–27 April		v. Middlesex (Lord's) 13–16 May		v. Surrey (Taunton) 21–24 May		v. Warwickshire (Taunton) 3–6 June		v. Lancashire (Old Trafford) 11–14 June		v. Essex (Bath) 17–20 June		v. Hampshire (Taunton) 26–29 June		v. Sussex (Hove) 1–4 July		v. Sri Lankans (Taunton) 14–16 July		M	Inns	NO	Runs	HS	Av
P.D. Bowler	13	3	0	–	19	21	9	9	9	10	63	7	35	1	104	–	18	101	27	66	18	32	2	789	104	26.30
P.C.L. Holloway	0	6	22	–			5	123	2	22*	36	47	35	25	0	–	10	27			16	28	3	624	123	24.96
K.A. Parsons	4	1	0	–	3	4	9	28							58	–	1	–	101*	25	14	23	1	367	101*	16.68
R.J. Harden	39	4	36	–	63	2			13	4*	0	6	2	9	4	–	0	56*	8	0	12	21	2	301	63	15.84
S.C. Ecclestone	21	23	0	–					94	–	23	11	14	–							5	7	–	186	94	26.57
R.J. Turner	3	16	45	–	0	1	7	88	33*	–	0	7	22	4	40	–	105	–			14	22	2	558	105	27.90
M.E. Trescothick	27	26	6	–	1	3	9	4	98	–	13	73*	32	11	9	–	67*	–	95	26	18	29	2	847	98	31.37
G.D. Rose	62	19	7	–	16	16	15	76	11	–	47	56	15	0*	32	–	7	–			17	26	2	606	76	25.25
A.R.K. Pierson	47	0	71	–											20	–	4	108*	39	3	13	20	3	438	108*	25.76
A.R. Caddick	7	0	26*	–	0	15*	30	37	7	–	21	2	2*	–	8*	–	0	–			17	25	8	322	37	18.94
K.J. Shine	0*	15*	18	–	9	2															3	5	2	44	18	14.66
M. Burns					4	8	5	40											13	13	10	17	–	450	96	26.47
M.N. Lathwell					91	88	2	0	18	–	4	5	16	0	76	–	87	–	56	5	12	19	–	574	106	30.21
Mushtaq Ahmed					22*	12			14	21	0	1	11	–	3	–					6	9	1	121	37	15.12
M.P.L. Bulbeck							27*	18*	35	–	1*	0	1	0*					–	–	8	11	6	141	35	28.20
A.P. Van Troost							23	0									16	–			5	7	1	61	23	10.16
L.D. Sutton																			3*	16*	2	4	2	24	16*	12.00
P.S. Jones																			–	8*	4	5	3	31	22*	15.50
B.J. Trott																			–	–	1	–	–	–	–	–
G.J. Kennis																					3	6	–	71	49	11.83
Byes	1	1			5	4		12	6	8	5	5	5	1			1		2							
Leg-byes	5	11	2		2	10	7	7	8	1	6	5	7	3	2		6	3	10	13						
Wides			2		8			11				8	2		18		2		2							
No-balls	8	10	20		10	4	28	22	16	4	14	28	32	14	4		6	8	10	2						
Total	237	135	255	0	253	190	176	475	364	70	233	261	231	68	378		330	307	366	177						
Wickets	10	10	10	0	10	10	10	10	10	2	10	10	10	6	10		10	2	6	7						
Result	L		D		L		W		W		L		L		D		D		D							
Points	4		5		6		20		24		5		1		9		7		–							

Somerset CCC First-Class Matches Batting

	v. Durham (Taunton) 22–25 July		v. Leicestershire (Leicester) 5–8 August		v. Northamptonshire (Taunton) 14–17 August		v. Derbyshire (Taunton) 19–22 August		v. Gloucestershire (Bristol) 27–30 August		v. Worcestershire (Taunton) 1–4 September		v. Kent (Canterbury) 9–12 September		v. Glamorgan (Cardiff) 17–20 September		M	Inns	NO	Runs	HS	Av
P.D. Bowler	12	44*	17	5	78	41*	5	21	7	6	4	–	17	–	15	2	18	32	2	789	104	26.30
P.C.L. Holloway	42	25*	7	8	8	27	6	8	36	58*	8	–	5	–	10	16	16	28	3	624	123	24.96
K.A. Parsons	4	–	5	2	10	22	30	8	2	25	21	–			4	0	14	23	1	367	101*	16.68
R.J. Harden			0	25	5	3					22	–					12	21	2	301	63	15.84
S.C. Ecclestone																	5	7	–	186	94	26.57
R.J. Turner							21	27	36	36*	4	–	51	–	2	10	14	22	2	558	105	27.90
M.E. Trescothick	25	–	16	14	22	30	0	60	92	0	38	–	7	–	26	17	18	29	2	847	98	31.37
G.D. Rose	22	–	8	4	18	15	29	23	28	–	52	–	0	–	28*	0	17	26	2	606	76	25.25
A.R.K. Pierson	43	–	7	3*	3	9	15	7	25	–	6	–	17	–	0	11*	13	20	3	438	108*	25.76
A.R. Caddick	31*	–	2	31	7*	7*	0	2	27*	–	24	–	4	–	25	7	17	25	8	322	37	18.94
K.J. Shine																	3	5	2	44	18	14.66
M. Burns	43	–	7	5	20	18			96	31	53	–	69	–	16	9	10	17	–	450	96	26.47
M.N. Lathwell	4	–					11	2					106	–	2	1	12	19	–	574	106	30.21
Mushtaq Ahmed	37	–															6	9	1	121	37	15.12
M.P.L. Bulbeck	23	–					0*	7*					29	–			8	11	6	141	35	28.20
A.P. Van Troost									8	–			4*	–	0	10	5	7	1	61	23	10.16
L.D. Sutton			0	5													2	4	2	24	16*	12.00
P.S. Jones			1*	0	0	–					22*	–					4	5	3	31	22*	15.50
B.J. Trott																	1	–	–	–	–	–
G.J. Kennis					3	15	49	0	4	0							3	6	–	71	49	11.83
Byes	12				1	10	4		8				6		2							
Leg-byes	2	1			2	17	1	7	11	6	7		13		3	10						
Wides	8		2								16		4									
No-balls	10	2	2	10	2		10	4	16	2	6		10									
Total	318	72	74	112	179	214	181	176	396	164	283		342		133	93						
Wickets	10	0	10	10	10	8	10	10	10	5	10		10		10	10						
Result	W		L		W		L		W		D		W		L							
Points	23		4		20		4		24		9		23		4							

Fielding Figures

43 – R.J. Turner
20 – M.E. Trescothick
18 – P.D. Bowler
17 – K.A. Parsons
16 – M. Burns (ct 15 / st 1)
15 – R.J. Harden
7 – P.C.L. Holloway and M.N. Lathwell
6 – A.R.K. Pierson
5 – G.J. Kennis, L.A. Sutton and A.R. Caddick
4 – S.C. Ecclestone
3 – G.A. Rose
2 – M.P.L. Bulbeck and sub
1 – Mushtaq Ahmed

Somerset CCC First-Class Matches

Bowling

	A.R. Caddick	G.D. Rose	A.R.K. Pierson	K.A. Parsons	K.J. Shine	M.E. Trescothick	Mushtaq Ahmed	A.P. Van Troost	M.P.L. Bulbeck	P.D. Bowler	P.S. Jones	B.J. Trott	Byes	Leg-byes	Wides	No-balls	Total	Wkts	
v. Yorkshire (Leeds) 17–21 April	32-6-97-0	29.2-11-71-2	15-3-33-0	20.4-9-43-2	16.4-6-40-2	22-7-82-4							4	13	6	12	383	10	
	11-2-33-4	7-1-35-0	12-3-34-1	4-0-14-0	11-1-53-1	10.3-3-24-3							1	10	6	10	204	9	
v. Nottinghamshire (Taunton) 23–27 April																	0	0	
	5-3-7-1	4-2-9-1														2	16	2	
v. Middlesex (Lord's) 13–16 May	20.5-3-74-4	15-4-43-3			10-1-37-1	2-0-19-0	6-1-26-2							5	4	14	204	10	
	33-6-118-3	25.5-5-94-0		6-0-29-0	20-2-86-0	16-2-36-1	30-8-76-0						1	10		8	450	4	
v. Surrey (Taunton) 21–24 May	28.4-8-73-2	25-11-51-3				12-2-34-2		8-1-22-0	11-0-52-3					9		20	241	10	
	31.4-5-91-3	12-5-18-2				13-3-52-1		4-0-30-1	22-7-48-3					6	2	10	245	10	
v. Warwickshire (Taunton) 3–6 June	14-2-58-3	9.4-3-25-4				7-4-15-0	11-6-20-0		8-2-10-3					1		2	129	10	
	29-10-79-4	18-5-68-0				3-1-13-0	15.2-3-63-3		16-4-70-3				2	9	2	8	304	10	
v. Lancashire (Old Trafford) 11–14 June	22.2-8-67-4	22-7-60-3				19-5-65-2	12-8-29-1		8-2-39-0					7		8	267	10	
	29-5-80-5	26-6-68-2				3-0-11-0	9-0-38-1		6-1-25-2					14	2	4	236	10	
v. Essex (Bath) 17–20 June																	0	0	
	26.4-5-126-2	20-4-48-5				5-1-15-0	9-2-48-1		11-0-56-1				3	4		10	300	9	
v. Hampshire (Taunton) 26–29 June	24-4-91-1	16.3-6-56-0	31-9-80-2	7-0-26-1		8-3-28-0	20-6-57-1			2-1-4-0				8		15	350	5	
v. Sussex (Hove) 1–4 July	39.4-11-107-2	35-11-75-3	25-8-88-2	10-2-41-0		21-2-76-1		30-6-93-0		3-2-4-1			1	8	2	27	493	10	
v. Sri Lankans (Taunton) 14–16 July				10.4-3-26-2		11-4-25-1			11-4-20-3		12-3-32-2	8-2-16-2		11			130	10	
			15-3-54-0	11-4-29-1		20-3-83-2			19-1-104-3	9-3-25-0	20-2-84-0	9-2-40-0	4	4	6		483	6	A
v. Durham (Taunton) 22–25 July	31-3-116-5	19-6-51-0	1-0-4-0	9-6-4-1		2-1-5-0	14-4-28-2		11-2-30-2				13	8		14	259	10	
	17-4-49-5	11-4-35-2	1-0-11-0				9.4-2-26-3						4	3		8	128	10	
v. Leicestershire (Leicester) 5–8 August	32-5-96-7	25.5-6-62-3	4-1-11-0	6-1-31-0		7-2-29-0				1-0-10-0	8-2-24-0			8		12	271	10	
v. Northamptonshire (Taunton) 14–17 August	21.2-5-70-5	18-4-57-5	7-2-26-0	6-2-16-0							4-2-11-0		4	3		2	187	10	
	17-5-45-4	10-2-30-0	22-5-64-3							7.5-0-25-3	8-2-30-0		4	7		2	205	10	
v. Derbyshire (Taunton) 19–22 August	21-6-72-2	16.5-1-75-4	3-1-8-1	13-0-60-0					12-2-67-3					8		10	290	10	
	16.2-3-49-5	7-1-44-1							11-3-40-4					6		2	139	10	
v. Gloucestershire (Bristol) 27–30 August	36.2-9-97-5	22-4-63-0	26-5-87-2	5-2-18-0				24-5-73-3					1	8	2	10	355	10	B
	25-4-66-4	14.3-3-34-3	16-2-52-1					13-3-41-2		1-0-2-0			4	5	2	4	204	10	
v. Worcestershire (Taunton) 1–4 September	31-13-64-8	22-10-62-0	10-1-32-0	2-0-8-0		9-2-28-0					12.5-2-25-2			5		6	224	10	
	19-6-47-3	11-2-48-2	13.1-4-47-0	15-4-46-1		3-0-14-0				1-0-8-0	10-3-39-0			5		4	254	6	
v. Kent (Canterbury) 9–12 September	14-3-40-5							11-5-18-4	2.4-0-20-1					8		12	86	10	
	23.5-4-61-5	13-4-36-2						16-3-74-2	6-0-28-1					11	2	8	210	10	
v. Glamorgan (Cardiff) 17–20 September	21.1-5-56-3	5-1-36-2	29-2-94-4					9-1-49-3		7-1-18-0			3	7		2	246	10	
	15-3-53-1	20-3-62-2	28-4-117-5	4-1-21-0				3-0-15-0					4	6	4	8	278	9	
	687.2-156- 2082-105	480.3-132- 1399-52	258.1-53- 842-21	129.2-34- 412-8	57.4-10- 216-4	193.3-45- 654-17	136-40- 411-14	118-24- 415-15	154.4-28- 609-32	31.5-7- 96-4	74.5-16- 245-4	17-4- 56-2							
Bowler's average	19.82	26.90	40.09	51.50	54.00	38.47	29.35	27.66	19.03	24.00	61.25	28.00							

A M. Burns 6-1-44-0; R.J. Harden 4-1-12-0
B M. Burns 2-0-8-0

Surrey CCC First-Class Matches

Batting

Batting	v. Northamptonshire (The Oval) 17–21 April		v. Warwickshire (The Oval) 23–27 April		v. Hampshire (Southampton) 13–16 May		v. Somerset (Taunton) 21–24 May		v. Kent (The Oval) 29 May–1 June		v. Worcestershire (The Oval) 3–6 June		v. Essex (Chelmsford) 11–14 June		v. Lancashire (Old Trafford) 18–21 June		v. Glamorgan (Swansea) 1–4 July		v. Middlesex (Guildford) 15–18 July		M	Inns	NO	Runs	HS	Av
M.A. Butcher	29	–	72	–	106	–	28	109*	51	–			1	–					0	10	12	18	1	661	109*	38.88
J.D. Ratcliffe	61	–	93	–			0	33			100	9	25	–	11	33	0	14			9	15	1	449	100	32.07
N. Shahid	58	–	90	–			6	0			124	9			0	126*	14	17			12	22	3	683	126*	35.94
G.P. Thorpe	63*	–	114	–	32	–			26	–			14	–							6	7	1	251	114	41.83
A.J. Hollioake	7	–	9*	–	30	–			32	–	0	47	59	–	22	–	7	0	0	59	15	22	2	684	112	34.20
A.D. Brown	100	–	6	–	155	–			0	–	72	0*	79	–	26	–	24	100	51	79	15	22	1	1036	155	49.33
B.C. Hollioake	10*	–	0	–	13	–	37	28	4	–	51	1*	2	–	7	–			6	12	16	24	3	455	60	21.66
J.N. Batty	–	–	6*	–	63	–	39	5	33	–	–	–	52	–	5	–	30	–	0	5	16	19	2	351	63	20.64
I.D.K. Salisbury	–	–	–	–	7	–	51	10	56*	–	28*	–					11	–	31	61	12	13	2	285	61	25.90
M.P. Bicknell	–	–	–	–	38	–	6	23	14	–	7*	–	13	–	41	–	13	–	6	26	17	21	1	433	81	21.65
J.E. Benjamin	–	–	–	–			18*	1							15	–					8	9	3	57	18*	9.50
A.J. Stewart					59	–			86	–			20	–					0	46	8	12	1	464	96	42.18
A.J. Tudor					48	–	1	9	6	–	26	–	17	–	1	–	9*	–	1*	41	10	13	3	167	48	16.70
Saqlain Mushtaq					0*	–			9	–	–	–	45*	–			25	–	0	0*	12	15	5	176	45*	17.60
I.J. Ward							14	5			64	58			1	81*	50	79*	35	39	10	19	2	529	81*	31.11
J.A. Knott							12	4									5	0*			5	9	3	103	41*	17.16
R.M. Amin															0*	–		–			3	4	2	14	12	7.00
A.R. Butcher																					1	2	–	34	22	17.00
Byes	4		9		5				11		3	2	4		1	2	1	2		9						
Leg-byes	11		2		13		9	6	10		13	2	20		4	6	2		14	19						
Wides	8				14			2				2	6		6	2	2		4	6						
No-balls			4		8		20	10	4		14		16		6	4	6	2	2	8						
Total	351		405		591		241	245	342		502	130	373		146	254	199	214	150	420						
Wickets	5		6		10		10	10	10		7	4	10		10	1	10	4	10	10						
Result	D		W		W		L		W		W		D		L		W		W							
Points	7		24		24		5		23		23		11		3		20		20							

Batting

Batting	v. Gloucestershire (Cheltenham) 22–25 July		v. Sussex (The Oval) 30 July–2 August		v. Derbyshire (The Oval) 6–9 August		v. Nottinghamshire (Trent Bridge) 19–22 August		v. Yorkshire (Leeds) 1–4 September		v. Durham (Riverside) 9–12 September		v. Leicestershire (The Oval) 17–20 September		M	Inns	NO	Runs	HS	Av
M.A. Butcher			34	–			77	8	40	0	12	60	0	24	12	18	1	661	109*	38.88
J.D. Ratcliffe	38	8					1	23*							9	15	1	449	100	32.07
N. Shahid	12	14			6	27	64	9*	7	30	20	16*	0	34	12	22	3	683	126*	35.94
G.P. Thorpe													0	2	6	7	1	251	114	41.83
A.J. Hollioake	112	30	28	–	36	25			16	4	67	–	40	54*	15	22	2	684	112	34.20
A.D. Brown	22	13	94	–	132	11			6	0	51	–	3	12	15	22	1	1036	155	49.33
B.C. Hollioake	19	27	1	–	16	4	34	26	0	60	34	–	46*	17	16	24	3	455	60	21.66
J.N. Batty	14	6	1	–	21	21	31	–	8*	9	2	–			16	19	2	351	63	20.64
I.D.K. Salisbury			8	–			0	–			20	–	1	1	12	13	2	285	61	25.90
M.P. Bicknell	5	0	35	–	32	81	9	–	6	8	39	–	0	31	17	21	1	433	81	21.65
J.E. Benjamin							1*	–	3	1*	6	–	12	0	8	9	3	57	18*	9.50
A.J. Stewart			96	–					13	15	17	63*	33	16	8	12	1	464	96	42.18
A.J. Tudor	0	0	8*	–											10	13	3	167	48	16.70
Saqlain Mushtaq	4*	10	40	–	31	0	8	–	2	1	1*	–			12	15	5	176	45*	17.60
I.J. Ward	0	8	4	–	26	7	25	2	26	5					10	19	2	529	81*	31.11
J.A. Knott	35	4*			2	41*	0	–							5	9	3	103	41*	17.16
R.M. Amin					2*	–							0	12	3	4	2	14	12	7.00
A.R. Butcher					22	12									1	2	–	34	22	17.00
Byes	4		3				1		10	2	4		4							
Leg-byes	7	5	4		5	5	5	4	4		12	1	3	11						
Wides	2		4			4			2		8			4						
No-balls	23	10	4		2		14		4		30	2	4	10						
Total	297	135	364		333	238	270	72	147	135	323	142	146	228						
Wickets	10	10	10		10	9	10	3	10	10	10	1	10	10						
Result	L		W		W		W		L		W		L							
Points	6		24		23		22		4		20		2							

Fielding Figures

45 – J.N. Batty (ct 39 / st 6)
20 – A.D. Brown
17 – A.J. Hollioake
15 – A.J. Stewart
13 – N. Shahid
9 – I.J. Ward, G.P. Thorpe and M.A. Butcher
7 – B.C. Hollioake and Saqlain Mushtaq
6 – I.D.K. Salisbury
5 – M.P. Bicknell
3 – A.J. Tudor
2 – J.D. Ratcliffe
1 – J.E. Benjamin and J.A. Knott

Surrey CCC First-Class Matches

Bowling

	M.P. Bicknell	J.E. Benjamin	I.D.K. Salisbury	B.C. Hollioake	N. Shahid	M.A. Butcher	A.J. Hollioake	A.J. Tudor	Saqlain Mushtaq	J.D. Ratcliffe	J.A. Knott	R.M. Amin	Byes	Leg-byes	Wides	No-balls	Total	Wkts	
v. Northamptonshire	5–3–7–0	6–0–17–0	5–2–14–0	3.2–1–6–2												2	44	2	
(The Oval) 17–21 April			6–1–13–0	4–0–17–1	3–0–16–0											2	46	1	
v. Warwickshire	21–5–55–2	15–5–53–0	11.3–7–7–4	13–1–47–1		13–4–39–3	1–1–0–0							6		4	207	10	
(The Oval) 23–27 April	20–6–27–5	12–4–36–1	21–12–30–2	5–0–18–0		6–0–30–1	1.3–0–3–1							5			149	10	
v. Hampshire	7–3–22–0		15–3–51–2	4–1–15–0				8–3–32–4	20–5–62–3				1	6	4	18	189	9	
(Southampton) 13–16 May	14–6–43–3		19–6–43–1	3–0–7–0				16–4–53–3	24.5–8–57–1				8	7	4	18	218	9	
v. Somerset	10.3–2–14–4	13–1–69–2		11–1–55–3				3–0–31–1						7		28	176	10	
(Taunton) 21–24 May	25–7–77–0	23–7–71–3	47.2–9–98–5	23–2–85–0	6–0–19–1	8–3–20–0		20–4–80–1		2–1–4–0	1–0–2–0		12	7	11	22	475	10	
v. Kent	10–5–26–2		11.4–4–13–3					6–1–18–1	14–6–18–3				9	2		6	86	10	
(The Oval) 29 May–1 June	7–1–15–2		24–6–75–3	2–0–7–0				3–0–26–1	24.5–6–100–4				2	1	2	8	226	10	
v. Worcestershire	24.4–7–61–3		50–19–100–1				1–0–4–0	11–0–61–2	60–17–116–4				3	22	2	26	367	10	
(The Oval) 3–6 June	6–3–19–0		24.5–6–81–2					8–0–39–1	28–11–41–7				4	2		10	186	10	
v. Essex	24–6–68–3			10–2–21–3		4–1–13–0		12.3–2–49–2	19–5–42–2				4	6	2	22	203	10	
(Chelmsford) 11–14 June	11–3–26–3							10–0–47–1						2	2	6	75	4	
v. Lancashire	14–6–39–0	12.5–1–37–2					6–2–17–0	16–6–43–5				3–1–6–0		9		6	151	7	
(Old Trafford) 18–21 June	14–3–65–2	11–2–35–1		2–0–13–0			0.2–0–4–0	11–1–82–0				6–0–45–1		6	6	8	250	4	
v. Glamorgan	22–7–53–3						22–5–62–5	4–1–25–0	18.1–5–38–2				5	14	6	26	197	10	
(Swansea) 1–4 July	9–3–16–1		30.2–7–65–7				8–3–17–0	4–0–14–0	36–9–85–2				8	7		8	212	10	
v. Middlesex	12–2–25–3			7–2–12–1			3–1–8–0	14–2–47–4	6–1–15–2				4	4	4	6	115	10	
(Guildford) 15–18 July	14–5–33–2		18–4–43–4	5–3–8–0			1–0–1–0	10–3–31–2	15.5–1–52–2				2	5	2	2	175	10	
v. Gloucestershire	14–5–34–5			8–3–12–1				11–3–23–0	24–5–84–4					14		18	167	10	
(Cheltenham) 22–25 July	21–2–81–3			12–1–35–1			2–1–5–0	13.5–4–27–1	38–12–94–3				14	10		22	266	8	
v. Sussex	14–4–35–2			15–3–43–1				3–0–9–0	19.2–9–30–7				5	3		6	125	10	
(The Oval) 30 July–2 August	15–4–45–4		17.2–7–22–2	3–1–11–0			6–3–12–0		35–10–74–4					6	2	6	170	10	
v. Derbyshire	17–3–48–3			11–4–36–4			1–1–0–0		24.3–9–42–3			1–0–4–0	1	8		19	139	10	
(The Oval) 6–9 August	12–2–47–0			11–0–41–0			2–0–13–0		27.3–4–65–8			10–0–32–2	2	6			206	10	
v. Nottinghamshire	25–8–64–2	16–2–59–3		15.3–5–45–3		4–1–12–0			10–3–30–1					3	2	10	213	10	
(Trent Bridge) 19–22 August	17–6–51–3	10.2–4–21–2		13–7–28–4					4–1–5–1				8	12		8	125	10	
v. Yorkshire	26–7–59–1	13–4–43–0		14–5–31–2		14.4–4–41–4	8–5–19–2		20–7–39–0				6	12	8	20	250	9	
(Leeds) 1–4 September	17–4–52–1	4–1–14–0		14–2–35–2		10–2–26–1	10–2–35–0		2–0–18–0				1	15		4	196	4	
v. Durham	20–6–54–0	10–1–46–1		10–2–45–1		12–3–36–1	7–3–18–0		4–1–12–0				12	8	2	41	253	3	
(Riverside) 9–12 September	12–3–30–2	17–5–35–6		1.5–0–8–1		7–1–11–1								7		4	91	10	A
v. Leicestershire	13–4–49–1	27–5–95–1	36–6–111–0	27–3–106–3	7–1–31–1	16–3–59–0	13–2–29–0					39–8–89–0		14	14	14	585	6	B
(The Oval) 17–20 September																			
	494.1–141– 1340–65	190.1–42– 631–22	337–99– 766–36	247.4–49– 787–34	16–1– 66–2	94.4–22– 287–11	92.5–29– 247–8	184.2–34– 737–29	475–135– 1119–63	2–1– 4–0	1–0– 2–0	59–9– 176–3							
Bowler's average	20.61	28.68	21.27	23.14	33.00	26.09	30.87	25.41	17.76	–	–	58.66							

A J.N. Batty 1–0–22–0
B A.D. Brown 2–1–2–0

Fielding Figures

30 – C.J. Adams
26 – S. Humphries
10 – M.G. Bevan
7 – K. Newell and M.T.E. Pierce
6 – M. Newell
5 – W.G. Khan and N.J. Wilton
4 – N.R. Taylor, A.A. Khan and J.J. Bates
3 – R.S.C. Martin–Jenkins, P.W. Jarvis, J.R. Carpenter and A.D. Edwards
2 – P. Moores, R.J. Kirtley and M.A. Robinson
1 – J.D. Lewry

Sussex CCC First-Class Matches

Batting

Batting	v. Oxford University (Oxford) 14–16 April		v. Lancashire (Hove) 17–20 April		v. Essex (Chelmsford) 23–27 April		v. Nottinghamshire (Trent Bridge) 13–16 May		v. Derbyshire (Horsham) 21–24 May		v. Worcestershire (Worcester) 29 May–1 June		v. Kent (Tunbridge Wells) 3–6 June		v. South Africans (Arundel) 12–14 June		v. Warwickshire (Hove) 17–20 June		v. Leicestershire (Leicester) 26–29 June		M	Inns	NO	Runs	HS	Av
M.T.E. Peirce	14	–	30	1	20	45	96	21	18	12	2	51*	11	23	5	–	64	46	0	–	19	32	1	744	96	24.00
W.G. Khan	12	–	10	40			0	27	70	125	9	53*	12	72	50	–	8	5	0	–	18	30	1	837	125	28.86
C.J. Adams	17	–	5	39	135	105	0	4			9	–	12	84	41	–	22	79	10	–	18	29	1	1174	170	41.92
M. Newell	0	–							135*	7					48	–	24	11	18	–	10	14	1	386	135*	29.69
N.R. Taylor	74*	–	21	16	35	–													51	–	6	8	1	227	74*	32.42
K. Newell	52*	–	0*	52	13	1*	48	4*	13	16	8	–	16	40*	37*	–					11	19	6	414	84	31.84
P. Moores	–	–	–	20	36	0*															3	3	2	56	36	56.00
A.A. Khan	–	–			5	–			23	4	9	–									4	4	–	41	23	10.25
J.D. Lewry	–	–	–	2	18	–	0	–	0	2	5	–	1	–			0	11	4	–	17	23	–	132	24	5.73
R.J. Kirtley	–	–	–	4*	12*	–	6	–	17	1*	22*	–	24	18*			7*	15*	27	–	18	26	10	320	59	20.00
M.A. Robinson	–	–	–	–			3*	–			0	–	0*	–			1	7	0	–	16	21	8	40	7	3.07
R.K. Rao			2*	6	12	0									5	–					10	17	1	325	76	20.31
R.S.C. Martin–Jenkins			–	63																	8	13	1	353	78	29.41
J.R. Carpenter					19	9	65	1	1	19	33	–	1	0	29	–	9	1			9	16	–	222	65	13.87
P.W. Jarvis					39	–	25	1*	22	8					3	–			12	–	5	7	1	110	39	18.33
M.G. Bevan							18	7	5	127	96	–	6	25			2	71	149*	–	12	19	2	935	149*	55.00
S. Humphries							19	2	0	16	43	–	66	3	14	–	17	17	0	–	14	22	1	286	65	13.61
A.D. Edwards													10	4	4	–	0	2			4	7	–	30	10	4.28
M.R. Strong															2*	–					1	1	1	2	2*	–
J.J. Bates																					4	7	–	54	38	7.71
N.J. Wilton																					2	4	2	46	19*	23.00
Byes	1				4	4	3		1			1		5	4			1	4							
Leg–byes	4		5	7	7	3	13	1	10	17	2	8	14	19	7		6	4	5							
Wides	8		2				10	4	2	4			16	10			6									
No–balls				10	14	6	18	2	8	16	40	10			28		6	16	22							
Total	182		75	260	369	173	324	74	325	374	278	123	189	303	277		172	286	302							
Wickets	4		4	8	10	4	10	6	10	10	10	0	10	7	9		10	10	10							
Result	D		W		D		W		L		D		W		D		L		D							
Points	–		20		11		23		6		9		20		–		1		10							

Batting

Batting	v. Somerset (Hove) 1–4 July		v. Gloucestershire (Cheltenham) 14–17 July		v. Surrey (The Oval) 30 July–2 August		v. Durham (Eastbourne) 5–8 August		v. Middlesex (Hove) 14–17 August		v. Hampshire (Hove) 26–29 August		v. Glamorgan (Hove) 30 August–2 September		v. Northamptonshire (Northampton) 9–12 September		v. Yorkshire (Hove) 17–20 September		M	Inns	NO	Runs	HS	Av
M.T.E. Peirce	3	–	5	59	54	29	16	–	20	–	10	24	0	11	9	1	44	0	19	32	1	744	96	24.00
W.G. Khan	19	–	59	9	41	0	91	–	13	–	2	11	3	9	0	28	10	49	18	30	1	837	125	28.86
C.J. Adams	102	–	0	7	0	99*	56	–	170	–	8	8	43	47	13	14	18	27	18	29	1	1174	170	41.92
M. Newell	118	–	0	12	0	0	7	–	6	–									10	14	1	386	135*	29.69
N.R. Taylor	14	–	6	10															6	8	1	227	74*	32.42
K. Newell													84	11	3	14	0	2	11	19	6	414	84	31.84
P. Moores																			3	3	2	56	36	56.00
A.A. Khan																			4	4	–	41	23	10.25
J.D. Lewry	9	–	0	16	0	0	24	–	5	–	20	0	4	2			0	9	17	23	–	132	24	5.73
R.J. Kirtley	11	–	16	17*	1	5	59	–	12*	–	1	12	6	11*	2*	12	0	2	18	26	10	320	59	20.00
M.A. Robinson	0	–	6*	1	2*	4	3*	–	0	–	0	2	2*	4*	0	4*	0	1	16	21	8	40	7	3.07
R.K. Rao					1	6	18	–	54	–	31	40	76	8	15	0	42	9	10	17	1	325	76	20.31
R.S.C. Martin–Jenkins	28	–	40	4					5	–	2	22	78	30	10	20	7	44*	8	13	1	353	78	29.41
J.R. Carpenter											2	13	0	20					9	16	–	222	65	13.87
P.W. Jarvis																			5	7	1	110	39	18.33
M.G. Bevan	146*	–	47	0	5	1	95	–	35	–	58	42							12	19	2	935	149*	55.00
S. Humphries	5	–	0	12	7	5	12	–	20	–					0	17	2*	9	14	22	1	286	65	13.61
A.D. Edwards															6	4			4	7	–	30	10	4.28
M.R. Strong																			1	1	1	2	2*	–
J.J. Bates					0	7	38	–							4	4	1	0	4	7	–	54	38	7.71
N.J. Wilton											19*	11*	16	0					2	4	2	46	19*	23.00
Byes	1				5		10				4	2	8	2	1	5		1						
Leg–byes	8		2	9	3	6	9		14		10	15	6	11	7	12	1	7						
Wides	2			4		2	8				10	21	2		2									
No–balls	27		10	2	6	6	14		38		10	22	4				4	10						
Total	493		191	162	125	170	460		392		187	245	332	166	72	135	129	170						
Wickets	10		10	10	10	10	10		10		10	10	10	10	10	10	10	10						
Result	D		L		L		W		W		L		W		L		L							
Points	11		4		4		24		24		4		22		4		4							

Sussex CCC First-Class Matches

Bowling

Match	J.D. Lewry	R.J. Kirtley	M.A. Robinson	R.S.C. Martin-Jenkins	P.W. Jarvis	A.A. Khan	K. Newell	C.J. Adams	J.J. Bates	M.G. Bevan	M.T.E. Peirce	A.D. Edwards	Byes	Leg-byes	Wides	No-balls	Total	Wkts	
v. Oxford University (Oxford) 14–16 April																		Ab.	
	25–5–78–3	23–7–66–1	24.2–6–73–3	19–9–42–3									1	6	2	16	266	10	
v. Lancashire (Hove) 17–20 April								4–0–36–0						1		2	68	0	A
v. Essex (Chelmsford) 23–27 April	9–2–42–0	25–5–90–2			20–1–67–3	20–5–69–2	8.4–1–23–3						1	7		6	299	10	
v. Nottinghamshire (Trent Bridge) 13–16 May	18.3–3–57–4	19–5–59–3	14–0–60–1		18–3–59–0					6–1–28–2	1–0–5–0			7	22	22	275	10	
	13–6–32–3	14.3–6–29–7	4–0–17–0		6–0–35–0									9		6	122	10	
v. Derbyshire (Horsham) 21–24 May	36–12–72–6	20–3–98–0			34–5–118–2	59–12–185–2	10–3–23–0			12–0–66–0	1–0–13–0		2	16		2	593	10	
	7–2–21–0				3–0–16–0	8–1–24–2				7.4–0–40–1			4	2			107	3	
v. Worcestershire (Worcester) 29 May–1 June	24–5–104–4	20–5–47–2	24–6–68–1			10–4–43–0	13–4–35–0			13–4–48–2			4	4	6	14	353	9	
	15–1–51–0	17–2–61–0	19.2–4–77–2			19–4–68–0	10–4–33–1			1–0–7–0	8–2–32–0		5	9	2	11	343	3	
v. Kent (Tunbridge Wells) 3–6 June	23–8–55–4	13–5–32–0	19–5–47–2				12–8–5–1			13–3–36–3		5–0–20–0	8	8	2	22	211	10	
	9–1–32–0	10.3–4–19–4	16–5–34–2							11–1–57–1		15–3–60–2		4	5	4	206	10	
v. South Africans (Arundel) 12–14 June					12–2–21–0							6–0–15–0		2			96	0	B
v. Warwickshire (Hove) 17–20 June	35.1–7–89–4	38–8–81–0	33–5–85–1					3–0–8–0		27–3–83–3	9–2–16–1	25–6–91–0	10	27	2	10	490	9	
v. Leicestershire (Leicester) 26–29 June	19–7–59–0	27–5–83–5	20–7–33–0		15–2–52–2					15–4–44–3			6	12	2	4	289	10	
	1–1–0–1	2–0–6–0															6	1	
v. Somerset (Hove) 1–4 July	21.4–2–89–5	20–2–81–3	16–4–46–2	17–4–56–0						11–1–51–0			1	6	2	6	330	10	
	20–5–32–0	22–7–59–0	19–8–37–2	19–11–30–0				11–2–26–0		23–2–72–0	24–14–33–0			3	4	8	307	2	C
v. Gloucestershire (Cheltenham) 14–17 July	19.5–3–73–3	17–4–53–1	14–6–27–2	19–9–56–2						8–0–27–2			1	1		2	238	10	
	10–4–18–3	7–0–25–0	3.1–1–20–0	2–0–20–0						4–0–24–0			4	7	2	2	118	3	
v. Surrey (The Oval) 30 July–2 August	14.2–3–65–3	24–3–105–1	22–3–57–1						33–7–100–5	9–2–30–0			3	4	4	4	364	10	
v. Durham (Eastbourne) 5–8 August	30–12–63–4	22–7–54–2	21–9–47–3						11–4–28–0	3–2–3–1				3		8	198	10	
	16–5–44–2	17.2–6–41–4	15–5–21–3					7–2–21–0	5–1–8–0	12–4–37–1			5	4	2	10	181	10	
v. Middlesex (Hove) 14–17 August	15–4–43–5	14–4–49–2	9–2–21–1	10–2–26–2									1	2		12	142	10	
	7–2–20–3	7–0–29–4	7–1–18–0	6.1–0–22–3										1	4	4	90	10	
v. Hampshire (Hove) 26–29 August	16–4–64–3	16.2–4–63–3	14–3–58–2	11–4–31–2									2	6	6	18	224	10	
	9–1–36–0	8–0–49–0	10–2–40–0	8–1–35–1				2.5–0–13–0					1	2		12	209	1	D
v. Glamorgan (Hove) 30 August–2 September	22–2–86–2	21–2–71–0	16–2–69–3	14.4–3–65–2			6–0–36–0						4	3	2	32	353	8	E
		6–2–35–0	12.3–2–33–3	16–2–54–7										5	2	12	127	10	
v. Northamptonshire (Northampton) 9–12 September		15–2–48–3	19–9–34–2						28–4–4–69–4			5–0–19–1	4	4		18	178	10	
		7–4–9–2	14–6–32–2						23.5–7–67–5			3–0–8–0	4	10		4	165	10	F
v. Yorkshire (Hove) 17–20 September	24–5–73–0	35–13–80–5	30.5–6–72–4				3–1–12–0	3–1–5–0	2–1–1–0				4	4	2	8	252	10	
	2–0–11–0	3–1–10–0					3–1–23–0								4		51	0	G
Bowler's average	461.3–112–1409–62 22.72	490.4–116–1532–54 28.37	416.1–107–1126–42 26.80	141.5–45–437–22 19.86	108–13–368–7 52.57	116–26–389–6 64.83	65.4–22–190–5 38.00	30.5–5–109–0 –	102.5–24–273–14 19.50	175.4–27–653–19 34.36	43–18–99–1 99.00	59–9–213–3 71.00							

A R.K. Rao 3–0–31–0
B R.K. Rao 7–1–17–0; M.R. Strong 11–2–41–0
C M. Newell 2–0–15–0
D R.K. Rao 8–0–33–0
E R.K. Rao 3–0–19–0
F R.K. Rao 12–2–35–0
G R.K. Rao 1–0–1–1; W.G. Khan 1.5–2–7–0

Warwickshire CCC First-Class Matches Batting

	v. Durham (Edgbaston) 17–21 April		v. Surrey (The Oval) 23–27 April		v. Derbyshire (Derby) 13–16 May		v. Oxford University (Oxford) 18–20 May		v. Nottinghamshire (Edgbaston) 21–24 May		v. Somerset (Taunton) 3–6 June		v. Gloucestershire (Bristol) 11–14 June		v. Sussex (Hove) 17–20 June		v. Lancashire (Edgbaston) 26–29 June		v. Hampshire (Edgbaston) 15–17 July		M	Inns	NO	Runs	HS	Av
D.P. Ostler	0	0	0	9	1	–	2	133*	6	18											6	10	1	173	133*	19.32
N.V. Knight	6	12	27	6	109	–					67*	5	8	15	159	–	192	–			14	24	2	1057	192	48.04
B.C. Lara	0	13	38	57	23	–			2	80	21	21	16	0	0	–	25	–	35	22	15	26	–	1033	226	39.73
D.L. Hemp	52	6	2	37	59	–	9	59*	0	4	11	25	9	12	19	–	7	–	4	8	15	26	1	646	102	25.84
T.L. Penney	35	3	46	2							0	36	19	9	53*	–	23	–	20	14	9	16	2	329	53*	23.50
D.R. Brown	32	27	60	4	0	–	33	–	6	1	0	0	23	39	8	–	51*	–	51	25	16	27	4	691	81*	30.04
N.M.K. Smith	113	90	10	0	3	–	43*	–	0	0	4	147	30	0	14	–	–	–	51	27*	18	29	5	1002	127	41.75
T. Frost	21	5			33	–	111*	–	13	40									13	22	8	14	2	389	111*	32.41
M.D. Edmond	32	13					16	–	0	3*											3	5	1	64	32	16.00
E.S.H. Giddins	7	0*	0*	4*	0*	–	–	–	1	0	0	0*	0	4*	–	–	–	–	11*	0	18	23	9	47	11*	3.35
D.A. Altree	2*	0																			1	2	1	2	2*	2.00
K.J. Piper			0	4							1	19	14	6	7	–	5*	–	44	7	13	23	5	283	44*	15.72
G. Welch			12	16	54	–	9	–	14	12	19	0	40*	12	27	–	–	–	38	8	12	18	1	332	54	19.52
T.A. Munton			2	5			–	–													9	12	2	72	20	7.20
M.J. Powell					0	–	30	26	70*	73	2	2	3	4	132	–	53	–	0	27	13	22	1	511	132	24.33
A.F. Giles					1	–					1	28	0	27	22	–	–	–	75	8	13	19	3	468	83	29.25
M.A. Sheikh							30	–	1	25											2	3	–	56	30	18.66
M.A. Wagh																					8	15	–	391	119	26.06
A. Singh																					5	7	–	185	56	26.42
Byes	7	2			8		2		6	7		2	1		10		4		5	5						
Leg-byes	13	4	6	5	9		8	2	9	13	1	9	12	1	27		10		16	8						
Wides	8	8					6	6	2	2		2			2				2	4						
No-balls	8	4	4		32		8			2	2	8	12	2	10		4		2	2						
Total	336	187	207	149	332		307	226	130	280	129	304	187	131	490		374	0	367	187						
Wickets	10	10	10	10	10		7	1	10	10	10	10	10	10	9		5	0	10	10						
Result	D		L		W		D		L		L		L		W		L		W							
Points	10		3		23		–		4		4		4		23		4		24							

Batting

	v. Essex (Edgbaston) 23–26 July		v. Glamorgan (Edgbaston) 30 July–2 August		v. Middlesex (Lord's) 5–8 August		v. Northamptonshire (Northampton) 19–22 August		v. Worcestershire (Worcester) 26–29 August		v. Leicestershire (Edgbaston) 1–4 September		v. Yorkshire (Leeds) 9–12 September		v. Kent (Edgbaston) 17–20 September		M	Inns	NO	Runs	HS	Av
D.P. Ostler															4		6	10	1	173	133*	19.32
N.V. Knight	34	29	52	0	36	28			63	–	5	6	0	130*	68	0	14	24	2	1057	192	48.04
B.C. Lara	0	26	15	22	226	51	158	7	144	–	26	5					15	26	–	1033	226	39.73
D.L. Hemp							31	31	28	–	0	102	16	29	12	74	15	26	1	646	102	25.84
T.L. Penney							26*	13					17	13			9	16	2	329	53*	23.50
D.R. Brown	26	1*					6	28*	3	–	75	39	18	19	35	81*	16	27	4	691	81*	30.04
N.M.K. Smith	43*	47	–	72*	61	4	56	11	47	–	13	41	4	2	59	10*	18	29	5	1002	127	41.75
T. Frost	5	23	7*	22											24	50	8	14	2	389	111*	32.41
M.D. Edmond																	3	5	1	64	32	16.00
E.S.H. Giddins	1	1	–	–	6*	–	3	–	5	–	0	0	4*	0	0		18	23	9	47	11*	3.35
D.A. Altree																	1	2	1	2	2*	2.00
K.J. Piper	37	20	3*	21	0	7*	34	7*	3	–	0	44*	0	0			13	23	5	283	44*	15.72
G. Welch	29	26	–	9	6	1											12	18	1	332	54	19.52
T.A. Munton			–	4*	20	4*	0	–	12	–	5	11	1	8	0		9	12	2	72	20	7.20
M.J. Powell	0	5	9	21	8	0	11	–							13	22	13	22	1	511	132	24.33
A.F. Giles	4	63	–	23	29	13			29*	–	34*	0	0	83	28*		13	19	3	468	83	29.25
M.A. Sheikh																	2	3	–	56	30	18.66
M.A. Wagh	0	7	39	34	2	1	3	5	119	–	33	60	1	0	65	22	8	15	–	391	119	26.06
A. Singh					41	14	56	4	33	–	37	0	–	–			5	7	–	185	56	26.42
Byes	1	4	1		4	8	8		2		1	1	4	9	8							
Leg-byes	2	16	5	9	21	5	16	10	22		4	4	15	4	3	3						
Wides			2	8		6			4		8	4	2		2							
No-balls	8	12	2	8	6	8	4	6	30		35	14	2		2							
Total	190	280	135	253	466	150	412	122	544		276	331	84	297	323	262						
Wickets	10	10	4	8	10	8	10	6	10		10	10	9	9	10	5						
Result	L		D		D		W		W		L		L		W							
Points	4		7		11		24		24		6		2		23							

Fielding Figures

31 – K.J. Piper (ct 28 / st 3)
21 – T. Frost
18 – N.V. Knight
15 – D.L. Hemp and B.C. Lara
14 – M.J. Powell
9 – D.R. Brown
7 – D.P. Ostler, G. Welch, A.F. Giles and sub
5 – T.L. Penney
4 – M.A. Wagh and E.S.H. Giddins
2 – A. Singh and N.M.K. Smith
1 – M.D. Edmond

Warwickshire CCC First-Class Matches

Bowling

	E.S.H. Giddins	D.R. Brown	D.A. Altree	M.D. Edmond	N.M.K. Smith	T.A. Munton	G. Welch	D.L. Hemp	A.F. Giles	M.A. Sheikh	M.A. Wagh	M.J. Powell	Byes	Leg-byes	Wides	No-balls	Total	Wkts	
v. Durham	31.2–5–89–6	28–7–89–4	11–2–34–0	10–1–32–0	16–2–49–0								3	9	4	8	305	10	
(Edgbaston) 17–21 April	14–5–47–1	12.1–7–23–3	2–2–0–0	7–3–13–1									1	6		2	90	5	
v. Surrey	21–2–72–0	18–3–67–1			26.4–2–128–5	16–2–46–0	14–2–51–0	6–0–30–0					9	2		4	405	6	
(The Oval) 23–27 April																			
v. Derbyshire	11.5–3–35–3	14–2–40–5					6–0–22–2							1	2	8	98	10	
(Derby) 13–16 May	20.1–6–62–4	12–3–45–2					8–4–17–2		16–7–26–2				13	10	2	6	173	10	
v. Oxford University	17–8–31–0			13–3–42–1	15–4–26–2	13.4–6–17–1	14–2–24–3	14–2–68–2		4.2–0–18–0			8	27	4	22	269	9	A
(Oxford) 18–20 May	7–2–23–1	8–1–31–0			15–8–17–1		5–1–11–0	4–1–21–0				9–5–16–2				6	124	4	
v. Nottinghamshire	22.4–9–47–4	23–6–77–3		3–1–7–0			20–3–63–0			10–2–18–2			2	4		14	218	9	
(Edgbaston) 21–24 May	25.4–5–74–3	13–4–19–0			8–2–16–0		10–3–26–0	3–0–12–0		17–5–38–1			2	6		16	193	4	
v. Somerset	25–4–79–3	22.5–5–79–3			25–6–71–1		15–6–48–0	2–0–5–1	19–3–68–2				6	8		16	364	10	
(Taunton) 3–6 June	3–0–9–0	8–2–21–0			1.5–1–1–0				7–2–30–2				8	1		4	70	2	
v. Gloucestershire	23–3–79–6	17–4–50–1					15.3–5–45–3							7	2	12	181	10	
(Bristol) 11–14 June	27.4–3–85–5	18–3–83–1			4–1–17–0		10–0–39–0	1–0–3–0	24–6–60–4					20	12	10	307	10	
v. Sussex	14–5–34–3	14.5–3–40–3			19–6–32–0		12–6–26–2		17–6–34–2					6	6	6	172	10	
(Hove) 17–20 June	21.5–3–64–2	17–5–35–0			35–9–72–4		15–4–63–1		41–25–47–2				1	4		16	286	10	
v. Lancashire																2	39	0	B
(Edgbaston) 26–29 June	13–2–53–0	27.3–5–125–5			13–3–31–0		11–2–50–0		30–8–68–1				4	7	2	10	338	6	
v. Hampshire	25–7–45–1	23–5–74–2			10–3–29–0		15–3–44–1	1–0–1–1	22–8–48–5					8		4	249	10	
(Edgbaston) 15–17 July	9–5–24–2	8–2–18–1			2–0–16–2		8–3–11–0		6.2–4–9–4					2			80	9	
v. Essex	12–1–37–4						18–3–69–3		7.1–1–27–3				1	5		6	139	10	
(Edgbaston) 23–26 July	34–8–102–3				10–3–46–1		36–5–121–1		40–23–42–1		9–1–16–2		1	4		10	332	8	
v. Glamorgan	33.3–3–110–2				10–3–25–1	21–8–41–3	32–8–94–4		15–3–31–0				4	10	8	2	315	10	
(Edgbaston) 30 July–2 August	4–0–42–0					4–0–11–1	5–1–29–0					5–0–21–0				2	109	1	C
v. Middlesex	26–10–55–1				16–3–37–0	28–9–66–7	19–5–52–1		28–7–56–0		3–0–19–0			12		11	297	10	
(Lord's) 5–8 August	16–4–46–1				16–5–44–0	20–3–46–1	26–5–91–2		40–14–94–2		6–3–11–4	2–0–9–0	7	9		2	373	10	D
v. Northamptonshire	23–8–56–3	17–2–68–4			28–9–86–2	18–4–48–1					10–4–36–0		13	8		6	319	10	E
(Northampton) 19–22 August	21–6–52–4	19–2–65–0			16–5–41–0	16.1–3–41–5					2–0–8–1		2	5	2	6	214	10	
v. Worcestershire	14–2–55–3	23.5–3–73–3			5–1–34–0	9–0–26–2			13–3–37–2		3–1–5–0		4	2	2	4	236	10	
(Worcester) 26–29 August	27.2–6–87–5	13–1–51–0				19–7–43–5			5–2–8–0					3		4	192	10	
v. Leicestershire	30.4–6–124–3	26–1–129–3			6–2–16–0	29–4–90–4			15–5–25–0				1	4	2	16	389	10	
(Edgbaston) 1–4 September	12–3–50–2	7–1–35–0			4–0–24–1	20–2–74–2			20–0–92–1				8	8	2		291	6	
v. Yorkshire	39–10–133–1	31.1–8–110–3			2–0–7–0	33–10–94–2			17–6–34–0				15	15		2	408	6	
(Leeds) 9–12 September																			
v. Kent	30.2–14–61–5	14–6–33–3				25–11–46–2			18–5–47–0				2	8			197	10	
(Edgbaston) 17–20 September	13.2–4–44–3	3–1–9–0			26–6–92–4	7–3–19–1			23–9–36–2					2			202	10	
	668.2–162–	438.2–92–	13–4–	33–8–	329.3–84–	278.5–72–	314.3–71–	31–3–	423.3–147–	31.2–7–	33–9–	16–5–							
	2006–84	1489–50	34–0	94–2	957–24	708–37	996–25	140–4	919–35	74–3	95–7	46–2							
Bowler's average	23.88	29.78	–	47.00	39.87	19.13	39.84	35.00	26.25	24.66	13.57	23.00							

A D.P. Ostler 2–0–8–0, 1–0–5–0
B B.C. Lara 2–0–24–0; N.V. Knight 1.5–0–15–0
C T. Frost 1–0–6–0
D B.C. Lara 2–0–16–0
E B.C. Lara 1–0–4–0

Fielding Figures

45 – S.J. Rhodes (ct 43 / st 2)
28 – V.S. Solanki
21 – G.A. Hick
10 – T.M. Moody
9 – D.A. Leatherdale
8 – W.P.C. Weston and S.R. Lampitt
7 – M.J. Rawnsley and sub
6 – A. Hafeez
5 – R.K. Illingworth
4 – P.J. Newport
3 – E.J. Wilson and B.J. Pipe (ct 2 / st 1)
2 – R.J. Chapman and G.R. Haynes
1 – A. Sheriyar, N.E. Batson and S.W.K. Ellis

Worcestershire CCC First-Class Matches Batting

	v. Essex (Worcester) 17–21 April		v. Leicestershire (Leicester) 23–27 April		v. Oxford University (Oxford) 11–13 May		v. South Africans (Worcester) 14–16 May		v. Middlesex (Uxbridge) 21–24 May		v. Sussex (Worcester) 29 May–1 June		v. Surrey (The Oval) 3–6 June		v. Glamorgan (Cardiff) 11–14 June		v. Gloucestershire (Worcester) 17–20 June		v. Northamptonshire (Worcester) 1–4 July		M	Inns	NO	Runs	HS	Av
W.P.C. Weston	95	–	77	–	0	32*	18	48	21	–	14	21					6	25	12	91*	17	31	3	829	95	29.60
V.S. Solanki	6	53	0	–	2	59*	0	34	78	–	28	155	0	4	1	32	24	40	8	3	19	36	1	999	170	28.54
G.A. Hick	15	25	10	–	124	–	33	58	166	–	104	132	119	22	13	66			38	0	14	25	–	1188	166	47.52
G.R. Haynes	86	26*	16	–			25	1	0	–	20	8*	14	9	3	8	21	20*			12	21	5	532	86	33.25
D.A. Leatherdale	21	7	99	–	134*	–	69	3	137	–	39	–	9	9	30	54	30*	14	12	1	18	32	2	1001	137	33.36
A. Hafeez	15	–			33*	–							33	30	42	1	0	55	4	23	10	18	1	303	55	17.82
S.R. Lampitt	16	0	0*	–	–	–	20*	11	–	–	31*	–	43	7	6	2	1	–			18	28	7	481	48	22.90
S.J. Rhodes	66	5*	13	–			45	3	67*	–	28	–	0	1	104*	4	14	10*	12	5	18	33	5	1000	104*	35.71
R.K. Illingworth	61	–	2*	–					–	–	0	–	45*	7	6	13*	0	–	23*	28	15	21	6	473	84	31.53
A. Sheriyar	2*	–	–	–	–	–	–	5*	–	–	0*	–	11	0*	0	–	–	–	6	8	12	10	4	66	20	11.00
P.J. Newport	14	–	–	–			–	9	–	–	13	–	18	19	56	–	19*	–	3	6	13	16	3	270	56	20.76
T.M. Moody			0	–					132	–	48	–	22	62	0	104*	1	45	8	33	13	23	2	886	132	42.19
S.W.K. Ellis					–	–	0*	0													2	2	1	0	0*	0.00
D.J. Piper					–	–															1	–	–	–	–	–
M.J. Rawnsley					–	–	–	0													6	8	–	55	21	6.87
R.J. Chapman					–	–													0	0	11	16	8	102	43*	12.75
E. Wilson																					5	10	–	101	27	10.10
N.E. Batson																					3	6	–	50	18	8.33
D. Catterall																					1	1	–	0	0	0.00
R.C. Driver																					1	2	0	5	5	2.50
Byes	1		2		1		4	5	1		4	5	3	4					1							
Leg-byes	18		11		6		6	9	7		4	9	22	2	8	6	2		5	6						
Wides	2	2	9		6	2	2	1	2		6	2	2		2	2				2						
No-balls	28	4	29		4		6	2	16		14	11	26	10	2	4	4	2	4	6						
Total	446	122	268		310	93	228	189	627		353	343	367	186	273	296	122	211	136	212						
Wickets		4	7		3	0	6	10	6		9	3	10	10	10	7	8	5	10	10						
Result	W		D		W		L		D		D		L		D		W		W							
Points	23		3		–		–		10		11		5		9		20		20							

Batting

	v. Lancashire (Lytham) 14–17 July		v. Yorkshire (Worcester) 30 July–2 August		v. Nottinghamshire (Kidderminster) 5–8 August		v. Derbyshire (Derby) 14–17 August		v. Kent (Canterbury) 19–22 August		v. Warwickshire (Worcester) 26–29 August		v. Somerset (Taunton) 1–4 September		v. Hampshire (Worcester) 9–12 September		v. Durham (Worcester) 17–20 September		M	Inns	NO	Runs	HS	Av
W.P.C. Weston	21	36	23	4	4	29	3	7	60	23	19	0	8	3	22	57*	15	35	17	31	3	829	95	29.60
V.S. Solanki	87	2	9	0	0	0	9	170	15	0	1	3	47	38	17	6	46	22	19	36	1	999	170	28.54
G.A. Hick	34	8	8	12									44	110	6	5	23	13	14	25	–	1188	166	47.52
G.R. Haynes											31	14*	56	36*	14	–	72	52	12	21	5	532	86	33.25
D.A. Leatherdale	0	0	4	30	36	19	16	26	24	79	0	11	27	16	21	24			18	32	2	1001	137	33.36
A. Hafeez	14	5							31	1			4	1	6	5			10	18	1	303	55	17.82
S.R. Lampitt	36	38*	8	24	20	24	10*	2	22	9*	9	48	11	41*	6	–	17	19	18	28	7	481	48	22.90
S.J. Rhodes	44	13	45	0	44	19	34	0	42	95	54	79	0	0	34	34*	72	14	18	33	5	1000	104*	35.71
R.K. Illingworth	50	–	25	0					42	6	31*	3	16*	–	27	–	4	84	15	21	6	473	84	31.53
A. Sheriyar															20	–	14	–	12	10	4	66	20	11.00
P.J. Newport	4	–	2*	4	26	45*	1	31											13	16	3	270	56	20.76
T.M. Moody	11	107*	9	8	112	0	12	31	41	59	22	19							13	23	2	886	132	42.19
S.W.K. Ellis																			2	2	1	0	0*	0.00
D.J. Piper																			1	–	–	–	–	–
M.J. Rawnsley					1	5	7	6	21	–							15	0	6	8	–	55	21	6.87
R.J. Chapman	1*	–	1	5*	0*	5	6	0*	0*	–	12	1	0	–	19*	–	9*	43*	11	16	8	102	43*	12.75
E. Wilson			25	3	4	1	0	12	14	13	27	2							5	10	–	101	27	10.10
N.E. Batson					15	4	5	3			18	5							3	6	–	50	18	8.33
D. Catterall													0	–					1	1	–	0	0	0.00
R.C. Driver																	5	0	1	2	0	5	5	2.50
Byes	10	5	19			4	1	2	15	10	4					1		4						
Leg-byes	12	3	11	4	7	5		10	5	10	2	3	5	5	14	6	6	18						
Wides	22	2	2			2		2	2	2	2				4	2	6	2						
No-balls	4	18	10		20	24		14	26	26	4	4	6	4	2	4	6	6						
Total	350	237	201	94	289	186	104	316	360	333	236	192	224	254	212	144	310	312						
Wickets	10	6	10	10	10	10	10	10	10	8	10	10	10	6	10	4	10	9						
Result	L		L		L		L		D		L		D		D		W							
Points	8		4		6		4		10		4		8		8		23							

Worcestershire CCC First-Class Matches Bowling

	P.J. Newport	A. Sheriyar	S.R. Lampitt	G.R. Haynes	D.A. Leatherdale	R.K. Illingworth	G.A. Hick	R.J. Chapman	S.W.K. Ellis	M.J. Rawnsley	V.S. Solanki	T.M. Moody	Byes	Leg-byes	Wides	No-balls	Total	Wkts	
v. Essex (Worcester) 17–21 April	19–6–52–2	18.2–3–60–4	15–1–66–1	5–0–26–0	3–1–16–0	16–7–28–3								9		12	257	10	
	22–8–45–1	24–6–80–4	23–5–61–4	17–3–69–0	3–0–14–0	10–5–13–1	8–3–15–0						1	12		26	310	10	
v. Leicestershire (Leicester) 23–27 April																		Ab	
v. Oxford University (Oxford) 11–13 May		8–4–7–0	11–5–13–0				7–3–10–1	7–1–11–0	12–5–15–1	29.3–7–72–5	10–4–25–1		1	8		2	162	8	
		5–2–14–0	6–2–16–1				15–8–25–3	6–2–18–0	3–1–7–0	23–9–44–6			1	1		8	126	10	
v. South Africans (Worcester) 14–16 May	15.1–6–43–1	20–6–47–1	15–6–26–0	12–2–24–0	4–2–12–0		11–1–43–1			15–0–85–0			2	5		10	287	4	
	16–9–30–3	16–3–57–0	9–3–22–1	6–2–13–0			4–0–12–1		6–1–26–0	16–2–55–1			2	2		6	219	6	
v. Middlesex (Uxbridge) 21–24 May	25–10–54–2	23.3–7–75–3	6–0–34–0	13–4–29–2		28–4–75–0	5–0–20–0				21–7–55–2	7–2–25–1	6	16		6	389	10	
	11–3–32–1	5–0–26–0	11–0–56–0	13–6–31–1		28–7–69–1	14–0–62–0				23–6–77–1	4–1–12–0	2	6	2	10	373	5	
v. Sussex (Worcester) 29 May–1 June	20–5–65–2	18–6–66–0	18.2–4–56–5	9–5–24–0		9–3–17–1						20–9–48–1		2		40	278	10	
	10–4–32–0	13–6–22–0	9–3–16–0	4–2–9–0		13–2–25–0						6–3–10–0	1	8		10	123	0	
v. Surrey (The Oval) 3–6 June	21–9–42–0	22–2–118–1	19–5–68–0	12.4–4–46–3	1–0–8–0	30–8–90–3	3–0–10–0				10–1–44–0	13–4–60–0	3	13		14	502	7	
	5–1–15–1	6–1–31–1	4–0–25–0		3–0–12–2	8–1–43–0							2	2	2		130	4	
v. Glamorgan (Cardiff) 11–14 June	11–2–39–1	15–4–52–0		25.3–9–59–5	4–0–22–0	14–8–27–1						21–6–66–2	8	15		15	288	9	
	7–2–19–0	12–0–72–1	6–0–17–0	3–0–20–0	3–0–16–4	18–2–84–0					9–0–36–2		1	3		8	268	8	
v. Gloucestershire (Worcester) 17–20 June	12–1–46–0	4–0–18–0	11–2–36–2	6–2–16–0	9.5–4–20–5	3–0–7–0						16–6–42–3		3		20	188	10	
	5–2–37–0		8–0–31–2	8–1–38–1	5–0–21–1									14		8	141	5	
v. Northamptonshire (Worcester) 1–4 July	10–0–29–1	7–1–17–1			8–3–24–4			4–1–23–0				15–8–20–4		1	6	2	114	10	
	9–7–3–3	13–1–38–0						6.1–4–9–4				11–3–24–3		3	4	2	77	10	
v. Lancashire (Lytham) 14–17 July	18–6–53–3		19–5–55–2		14–1–56–1	18–7–42–1		12.5–6–31–2			2–1–4–0	24–10–54–0		12		2	307	9	
	17–4–61–3		11–1–56–3		6.5–0–36–2	14–2–39–0		11–3–56–0			2–1–4–0	6–2–27–0	2		2	6	281	8	
v. Yorkshire (Worcester) 30 July–2 August	22–8–58–3		23–3–73–3		5–0–31–0	25–5–83–0	15–3–45–1	23–3–81–2			10–1–46–0	6–0–24–0	5	9	2	16	455	9	
v. Nottinghamshire (Kidderminster) 5–8 August	14–6–25–2		15–7–35–2		3–1–14–0			13.5–4–52–2		7–2–14–2		5–0–23–1		1		20	164	10	
	15–7–34–2		21–2–84–1		19–7–48–1			31.5–6–105–6		29–11–50–0	3–0–28–0	12–3–40–0		12	4	37	401	10	
v. Derbyshire (Derby) 14–17 August	14–5–35–1		16–7–33–5					13.4–1–63–2		22–7–53–0		13–0–68–2	1	7		12	280	10	A
	17–6–44–4		5–1–15–0					5–0–40–0				11.1–2–64–5		5			168	10	
v. Kent (Canterbury) 19–22 August			17–4–55–3		6–0–38–0	9–2–21–0		20.1–3–79–4		13–0–74–2		19–4–66–1	1	10	6	8	344	10	
			15–4–63–0		8–2–9–0	12–3–41–1		17–3–67–3		11–7–22–1		24–8–63–4	3	2	4	14	270	9	
v. Warwickshire (Worcester) 26–29 August			27.3–2–120–5	19–2–106–1		23–4–98–1		33–2–138–3			2–0–4–0	18–2–54–0	2	22	4	30	544	10	
v. Somerset (Taunton) 1–4 September			20–5–54–2	24–7–74–4	6–1–19–1	5–2–17–0		20.4–4–81–2						7	16	6	283	10	B
v. Hampshire (Worcester) 9–12 September		20–8–48–3	21–7–45–1	22.4–6–50–6				8–1–29–0					4	2		8	178	10	
v. Durham (Worcester) 17–20 September		30.2–10–85–5	23–9–60–2	25–6–65–3		21–8–34–0		4–0–34–0		7–1–28–0	8–1–30–0			6		10	342	10	
		6–0–29–0	11.1–4–39–5	3–0–6–0				9–2–26–3			5–0–22–2		1	2		4	125	10	
Bowler's average	335.1–115– 893–36 24.80	286.1–70– 962–24 40.08	416–97– 1330–50 26.60	227.5–61– 705–26 27.11	111.4–22– 416–21 19.80	304–80– 853–13 65.61	82–18– 242–7 34.57	246.1–46– 943–33 28.57	21–7– 48–1 48.00	172.3–46– 497–17 29.23	105–22– 375–8 46.87	251.1–73– 790–27 29.25							

A W.P.C. Weston 2–0–20–0

B D. Catterall 13–2–31–0

Yorkshire CCC First-Class Matches Batting

Batting	v. Somerset (Leeds) 17–21 April		v. Derbyshire (Leeds) 23–27 April		v. Northamptonshire (Northampton) 13–16 May		v. Gloucestershire (Gloucester) 21–24 May		v. Oxford University (Oxford) 29 May–1 June		v. Leicestershire (Leeds) 3–6 June		v. Hampshire (Leeds) 11–14 June		v. Durham (Riverside) 17–20 June		v. Cambridge University (Leeds) 27–29 June		v. Kent (Maidstone) 1–4 July		M	Inns	NO	Runs	HS	Av
A. McGrath	0	3	42	63*	0	26	6	16	2	13*	8	–	14	–	31	33	51*	28	28	–	17	28	3	612	63*	24.48
M.P. Vaughan	46	37	33	36*	17	13	10	4	69	59	77	–	86	–	177	36*	11	–	33	–	19	31	3	1161	177	41.46
D. Byas	101	52	103	–	5	34	2	15	4	28	116	–	11	–	3	18			7	–	18	28	1	842	116	31.18
M.J. Wood	52	22	103	–	0	3	0	25	28*	6	52*	–	108	–	1	–	25*	30*	17	–	19	29	6	1080	200*	46.95
C. White	23	8	9*	–	42	10	24	19	80	37	–	–					–	2			10	15	3	475	104*	39.58
B. Parker	12	41	0	–					5*	3	–	–	41	–			–	18			8	10	2	180	41	22.50
R.D. Stemp	0	1*			14	1*	6	9	–	26*	–	–	0	–	8	–			43*	–	12	16	9	133	43*	19.00
R.J. Blakey	20	13	3*	–	0	49	14	34			–	–	4	–	14	–			3	–	17	23	2	448	67*	21.33
D. Gough	89	0	–	–	3	58											–	21			6	7	–	207	89	29.57
C.E.W. Silverwood	5	0	–	–	40	34					–	–	10	–			–	–	57*	–	13	13	3	239	57*	23.90
P.M. Hutchison	0*	–	–	–	8*	4	23*	1*			–	–	13*	–	5	–	–	–	–	–	17	16	8	127	30	15.87
I.D. Fisher			–	–																	1	–	–	–	–	–
D.S. Lehmann					5	27	41	69							6	–			136	–	10	16	–	969	200	60.56
G.M. Hamilton							0	9	–	6	–	–	0	–	19	–			73	–	15	19	1	578	79	32.11
M.J. Hoggard							1	0	–	–					13*	–					9	10	3	35	13*	5.00
R.J. Sidebottom									–	–			13*	–	8	–			–	–	5	4	2	84	54	42.00
C.A. Chapman									–	20							–	7*			2	2	1	27	20	27.00
J.D. Middlebrook																	–	7			8	12	2	139	41	13.90
R. Wilkinson																	–	9			1	1	–	9	9	9.00
G.D. Clough																					1	2	–	34	33	17.00
G.M. Fellows																					1	2	–	21	18	10.50
Byes	4	1	1			1	2								2		2		10							
Leg-byes	13	10	10		8	14	6	1	3	1	6		17		8		3	9	2							
Wides	6	6	8	2	2		2		10	2			4				2		6							
No-balls	12	10	40	4	4	14	6	12	2	8	14		6		24	6			8							
Total	383	204	352	105	148	288	143	214	203	209	273		327		319	93	94	131	423							
Wickets	10	9	5	0	10	10	10	10	4	7	3		9		10	1	1	6	7							
Result	W		W		L		L		D		D		D		W		D		D							
Points	23		22		4		4		–		9		10		23		–		11							

Batting

Batting	v. Nottinghamshire (Scarborough) 15–18 July		v. Middlesex (Lord's) 22–25 July		v. Worcestershire (Worcester) 30 July–3 August		v. Lancashire (Leeds) 14–17 August		v. Glamorgan (Cardiff) 20–23 August		v. Essex (Scarborough) 26–29 August		v. Surrey (Leeds) 1–4 September		v. Warwickshire (Leeds) 9–12 September		v. Sussex (Hove) 17–20 September		M	Inns	NO	Runs	HS	Av
A. McGrath	14	–	15	37	50	–	40	24	10	9	0	7					42	–	17	28	3	612	63*	24.48
M.P. Vaughan	41	–	107	29	23	–	45	15	0	12	71	8	23	8	23	–	11	1*	19	31	3	1161	177	41.46
D. Byas	54	–	9	12	13	–	101	27	25	2	12	0	52	6	28	–	2	–	18	28	1	842	116	31.18
M.J. Wood	26	–	14	8	94	–	5	44	0	62	1	1	15	20	200*	–	118*	–	19	29	6	1080	200*	46.95
C. White													55	104*	9	–	7	46*	10	15	3	475	104*	39.58
B. Parker													32	20*	8	–			8	10	2	180	41	22.50
R.D. Stemp	0*	–	0*	0*	6*	–	5*	14											12	16	9	133	43*	19.00
R.J. Blakey	16	–	65	25	0	–	67*	2	0	18	51	6	10	–	29	–	5	–	17	23	2	448	67*	21.33
D. Gough	30	–			6	–													6	7	–	207	89	29.57
C.E.W. Silverwood	22	–	4	18*							0	5	7*	–	–	–	37	–	13	13	3	239	57*	23.90
P.M. Hutchison	11	–	1	–	4	–	5	10*			6*	30	0*	–	–	–	6	–	17	16	8	127	30	15.87
I.D. Fisher																			1	–	–	–	–	–
D.S. Lehmann	131	–	6	93	200	–	71	7	29	24	99	25							10	16	–	969	200	60.56
G.M. Hamilton	23	–	72	4	24	–	56	11	79	70	13	41*	0	–	78	–	0	–	15	19	1	578	79	32.11
M.J. Hoggard							–	0	0*	2	5	6*	7	–	–	–	1	–	9	10	3	35	13*	5.00
R.J. Sidebottom									54	9*									5	4	2	84	54	42.00
C.A. Chapman																			2	2	1	27	20	27.00
J.D. Middlebrook			0	0	3*	–	41	1	26	30	20	5			1*	–	5	–	8	12	2	139	41	13.90
R. Wilkinson																			1	1	–	9	9	9.00
G.D. Clough									33	1									1	2	–	34	33	17.00
G.M. Fellows													3	18					1	2	–	21	18	10.50
Byes			4	11	5			17	4	12	8	10	6	1	15		4							
Leg-byes	16		6	18	9		11	4	17	27	9	2	12	15	15		4							
Wides	2			6	2			7	2	10	2		8				2	4						
No-balls	20		32	24	16		10		27	8	17	4	20	4	2		8							
Total	406		335	285	455		457	183	306	296	314	150	250	196	408		252	51						
Wickets	10		10	8	9		8	10	10	10	10	9	9	4	6		10	0						
Result	D		D		W		L		W		W		W		W		W							
Points	11		7		24		7		23		23		22		24		22							

Fielding Figures

71 – R.J. Blakey (ct 69 / st 2)
20 – D. Byas
17 – M.J. Ward and C. White
9 – M.P. Vaughan
7 – J.D. Middlebrook
6 – R.D. Stemp
5 – A. McGrath and C.A. Chapman
4 – D.S. Lehmann and P.M. Hutchison
3 – M.J. Hoggard, G.M. Hamilton and R.J. Sidebottom
2 – B. Parker, C.E.W. Silverwood and sub.
1 – G.D. Clough and D. Gough

Yorkshire CCC First-Class Matches

Bowling

	D. Gough	C.E.W. Silverwood	P.M. Hutchison	C. White	R.D. Stemp	M.P. Vaughan	A. McGrath	J.D. Middlebrook	D.S. Lehmann	C.M. Hamilton	M.J. Hoggard	R.J. Sidebottom	Byes	Leg-byes	Wides	No-balls	Total	Wkts	
v. Somerset	18.4–5–48–3	21–5–52–3	15–5–35–2	12–3–28–1	21–8–42–1	7–2–13–0	3–0–13–0						1	5		8	237	10	
(Leeds) 17–21 April	14–4–61–2	10–4–34–2	10–5–15–2	12.2–5–13–4									1	11		10	135	10	
v. Derbyshire	9–2–49–0	11–1–38–5	8–1–31–0	3–0–14–0										1		21	136	5	A
(Leeds) 23–27 April	9–0–46–2	13–5–42–4	10–2–44–1	13–1–49–3		7–3–18–0							4	7		20	210	10	
v. Northamptonshire	28–5–82–2	27–6–84–1	25–6–68–2	20.3–5–46–5	8–1–34–0								6	12	6	30	332	10	
(Northampton) 13–16 May	5–1–16–0	4–0–9–0	4–0–16–0	4–2–10–1	4–0–27–1	4–1–24–0			0.2–0–0–0				2	1		2	105	2	
v. Gloucestershire			24–5–102–1	22–9–55–8	18.1–6–49–1	2–0–10–0				11–0–37–0	15–2–69–0		4	3		4	329	10	
(Gloucester) 21–24 May			15–2–43–1	16.2–3–50–1	17–5–41–1	15–1–80–1				14–2–56–1	13–2–43–3		13	2	2		328	8	
v. Oxford University					24–8–54–0	22–5–89–3				16–6–25–2	20–5–58–2	12–4–27–0		7		4	260	7	
(Oxford) 29 May–1 June				8–3–11–0	25–12–25–1	20.1–4–73–3	1–0–1–0			12–3–44–1	11–0–32–3	14–4–41–0		6		10	233	8	
v. Leicestershire		17.3–3–83–1	16–5–52–1	18–3–61–1	18–6–64–2	6–1–22–1				19–2–67–3				4	6	8	353	9	
(Leeds) 3–6 June		5–0–30–0	7–4–17–1	3–0–11–1	3–2–8–0					4–2–7–0			4	1			78	2	
v. Hampshire		10–3–13–5	9.1–2–49–3							6–1–21–2		6–3–13–0		8	6	2	104	10	
(Leeds) 11–14 June		28–8–87–3	20.3–11–22–3		34–13–64–2					21–3–63–1		10–1–30–0	1	5		4	272	9	
v. Durham			24.1–5–55–3		25–6–60–1				5–0–12–0	20.3–4–58–2	22–5–79–2	17–4–58–1		15		4	337	10	
(Riverside) 17–20 June			10–4–22–3		21–17–13–4					3–0–13–0	1–0–10–0	9–3–13–3	2	1	2		74	10	
v. Cambridge University	23–7–54–2	14–2–38–2	14–4–35–2	15–3–43–0		9–2–34–1	5–2–23–0	27.5–4–84–2					12	8	6	6	366	10	B
(Leeds) 27–29 June																	0	0	
v. Kent		15–4–39–2	11–1–41–3		13.3–3–29–2					11–4–26–1		6–1–17–2	11	2			165	10	
(Maidstone) 1–4 July		32–7–92–0	21–2–73–0		71–27–191–5	26–11–49–0			26–10–42–4	26–6–63–0		15–2–61–0	4	5	6	8	580	9	
v. Nottinghamshire	20.1–3–72–4	17–7–28–1	16–1–58–1		3–2–1–0		3–2–4–0			20–3–59–4			2	10	2	4	234	10	
(Scarborough) 15–18 July	18–1–53–2	20–4–55–2	9–2–21–1		3.5–2–2–1					8–4–20–0			4	5		14	160	6	
v. Middlesex		34–13–62–3	24.3–3–93–1		43–7–117–3		3–1–12–0	33–15–64–2	4–2–7–0	28–9–71–1			9	13	2	10	448	10	
(Lord's) 22–25 July		6–1–16–0	10–1–37–1		10.3–0–57–0		3–0–18–0	4–0–18–0	1–0–11–0	8–2–40–0			6	4		2	207	1	
v. Worcestershire	22–4–60–1		21–7–54–3		7–2–17–0			12.2–4–20–3		12–4–20–3			19	11	2	10	201	10	
(Worcester) 30 July–3 August	11.5–2–36–5		5–1–19–0		9–6–3–1			4–0–15–0		14–5–17–4				4			94	10	
v. Lancashire			23–4–88–3		13–2–60–0		6–1–33–2	24–5–74–2	8–3–20–0	18–4–71–0	23–0–122–3		8	8		26	484	10	
(Leeds) 14–17 August			13–2–39–5		17–6–43–1			13–2–27–0	8–1–21–1	8–1–36–0	10–1–41–3		6	2		12	215	10	
v. Glamorgan								3–0–7–0		15.5–1–69–5	20–1–92–3	17–0–75–2	4	8	4	22	266	10	C
(Cardiff) 20–23 August							4–0–26–0	8–3–31–2	0.4–0–0–1	15–5–43–5	18–4–55–1	13–3–55–1	5	7	2	8	212	10	
v. Essex		14–4–37–0	15–3–51–0				8–3–13–1	3–1–10–1	1–0–2–0	18.4–4–50–6	15–7–32–2		1	4	6	4	200	10	
(Scarborough) 26–29 August		23–5–70–3	10–2–36–1				4–0–13–0	7–0–29–0	3–0–9–0	10–2–33–1	20–5–57–5			14		12	261	10	
v. Surrey		9–2–41–0	11–3–24–0							17.1–4–50–7	15–6–18–3		10	4	2	4	147	10	
(Leeds) 1–4 September		14.4–6–30–5	8–1–34–0							14–7–22–4	11–3–26–1		2				135	10	D
v. Warwickshire		12–1–40–3	11.3–6–25–6										4	15	2	2	84	9	
(Leeds) 9–12 September		13–3–47–0	23–10–47–1					18–8–27–1		24.4–8–79–4	18–4–84–3		9	4			297	9	
v. Sussex		8–2–25–0	13.4–4–31–7				1–0–3–0	2–0–6–0		9–0–36–0	10–2–27–3			1		4	129	10	
(Hove) 17–20 September		13–4–31–3	17–5–55–1				1–1–0–0	5–3–10–0		11.1–4–16–2	16–4–50–4		1	7		10	170	10	
Bowler's average	178.4–34– 577–23 25.08	391.1–100– 1123–48 23.39	474.3–119– 1432–59 24.27	147.1–37– 391–25 15.64	409–141– 1001–27 37.07	118.1–30– 412–9 45.77	42–10– 159–3 53.00	164.1–45– 422–13 32.46	57–16– 124–6 20.66	415–100– 1212–59 20.54	258–51– 895–41 21.82	119–25– 390–9 43.33							

A I.D Fisher 3–1–3–0
B R. Wilkinson 15–3–35–1
C G.D. Clough 2–0–11–0
D G.M. Fellows 3–0–21–0